Big Book of Colleges

Compiled by
The College Prowler Team

ISBN: 978-1-4274-0326-1

© Copyright 2011 College Prowler

All Rights Reserved
Printed in the U.S.A.
www.collegeprowler.com

College Prowler®

5001 Baum Blvd., Suite 750
Pittsburgh, PA 15213

Phone: (800) 290-2682
Fax: (800) 772-4972
E-mail: info@collegeprowler.com
Web: www.collegeprowler.com

Welcome to College Prowler

When we created College Prowler, we felt it was critical that our content was unbiased and unaffiliated with any college or university. We think it's important that our readers get honest information and a realistic impression of the student opinions on any campus—that's why if any aspect of a particular school is terrible, we (unlike a campus brochure) intend to publish it. While we do keep an eye out for the occasional extremist—the cheerleader or the cynic—we take pride in letting the students tell it like it is. We strive to create a guide that's as representative as possible of each particular campus. Our guides cover both the good and the bad, and whether the survey responses point to recurring trends or a variation in opinion, these sentiments are directly and proportionally expressed through our guides.

College Prowler guidebooks are in the hands of students throughout the entire process of their creation. Because you can't make student-written guides without the students, we have students at each campus who help write, randomly survey their peers, edit, layout, and perform accuracy checks on every guide that we publish. From the very beginning, student writers gather the most up-to-date stats, facts, and inside information on their colleges. They fill each section with student quotes and summarize the findings in editorial reviews. In addition, each school receives a collection of letter grades (A through F) that reflect student opinion and help to represent contentment or satisfaction for each of our 20 specific categories. Just as in grade school, the higher the mark the more content or more satisfied the students are with the particular category.

Each guide is the result of endless student contributions, hundreds of pages of research and writing, and countless hours of hard work. All of this has led to the creation of a student information network that stretches across the nation to every school that we cover. It's no easy accomplishment, but it's the reason that our guides are such a great resource.

When reading our guides and looking at our grades, keep in mind that every college is different and that the students who make up each school are not uniform—as a result, it is important to assess schools on a case-by-case basis. Because it's impossible to summarize an entire school with a single number or description, each guide provides a dialogue, not a decision, that's made up of 20 different topics and hundreds of student quotes.

In the end, we hope that College Prowler will serve as a valuable tool in your college selection process. Enjoy!

What's in This Book?

Welcome to College Prowle

Rankings & Grades

Picking a college is hard, but we're here to help. The lists at the beginning of this book group 410 schools in a variety of categories. Interested in location, size, or selectivity? Check the lists. Curious about which schools have the best dining, dorms, or local atmosphere? We rank those, too. Crosscompare between the different lists to find the schools that match all of your needs.

TIP: First, decide what's important to you. Are you a party animal or straight-laced? A sports nut or a bookworm? A city kid or a nature-lover? Numbers and rankings can never provide the final answer; this is why we cover everything from academics to dining. It might be helpful to make some notes that detail what each category means to you. It's your four years—make the most of it.

Individual School Profiles

Dive into our school-specific sections and find out why those colleges you have your eye on scored well in one category and poor in another. Just like the original College Prowler guidebooks, each school's overview is student-written and provides its own unique dialogue to help you discover if the college is right for you.

Each in-depth section dedicates two pages to a specific school and provides stats and reviews on a sampling of our categories. There's also a report card for each school that lists student satisfaction grades for all of the 20 areas we cover.

Verbal Outtakes

We come across a lot of crazy student quotes, so we figured we'd share. Flip through these pages if you need a good laugh. Choosing a college doesn't have to be so stressful.

Words to Know

Learn a few new words to stay in the know.

About the Authors

Each college's section was written by its own student author. Read this for more information about each writer. Good luck with your college search—maybe *you'll* be the next student to write a College Prowler guidebook!

Need More?

Once you've narrowed down your choices, check out CollegeProwler.com for expanded online guides with more student quotes, more admissions statistics, and more categories.

We also have print and eBook versions of our most popular school guides so you can take them on the go!

Great for campus visits, making your final decision, and preparing for your first year, College Prowler guides are your last stop in the college search process.

BIG BOOK OF COLLEGES
Table of Contents

Rankings & Grades 1

    Region 1

    Setting 4

    Size 7

    Selectivity 10

    Academics 13

    Athletics 16

    Campus Dining 19

    Campus Housing 22

    Campus Strictness 25

    Computers 28

    Diversity 31

    Drug Safety 34

    Facilities 37

    Girls 40

    Greek Life 43

    Guys 46

    Health & Safety 49

    Local Atmosphere 52

    Nightlife 55

    Off-Campus Dining 58

    Off-Campus Housing 61

    Parking 64

    Transportation 67

    Weather 70

Individual School Profiles 73

    Albion College 73

    Alfred University 75

    Allegheny College 77

    Alverno College 79

    American University 81

    Amherst College 83

    Arcadia University 85

    Arizona State University 87

    Auburn University 89

    Austin College 91

Ave Maria University 93

Babson College 95

Ball State University 97

Bard College. 99

Barnard College 101

Barry University. 103

Baruch College. 105

Bates College 107

Bay Path College 109

Baylor University. 111

Belmont University 113

Beloit College. 115

Bentley University. 117

Berea College. 119

Binghamton University 121

Birmingham-Southern College. 123

Bob Jones University 125

Boston College. 127

Boston University 129

Bowdoin College 131

Bradley University. 133

Brandeis University. 135

Brigham Young University 137

Brigham Young University - Idaho 139

Brown University. 141

Bryant University. 143

Bryn Mawr College. 145

Bucknell University 147

Cal Poly. 149

Cal Poly Pomona 151

Cal State Long Beach. 153

Cal State Monterey Bay 155

Cal State Northridge 157

Cal State San Marcos 159

California College of the Arts. 161

California University of Pennsylvania 163

Caltech 165

Carleton College 167

Carnegie Mellon University 169

Case Western Reserve University. 171

Catawba College 173

Catholic University of America 175

Centenary College of Louisiana 177

Centre College 179

Chapman University 181

Chatham University 183

City College of New York 185

Claflin University 187

Claremont McKenna College 189

Clark Atlanta University 191

Clark University 193

Clemson University 195

Cleveland State University 197

Coe College 199

Colby College 201

Colgate University 203

College for Creative Studies 205

College of Charleston 207

College of Mount Saint Vincent 209

College of Notre Dame of Maryland 211

College of the Holy Cross 213

College of William & Mary 215

College of Wooster 217

Colorado College 219

Colorado State University - Pueblo 221

Columbia College Chicago 223

Columbia University 225

Concordia College at Moorhead 227

Connecticut College 229

Converse College 231

Cornell College 233

Cornell University 235

Creighton University 237

CUNY Lehman College 239

CUNY Queens College 241

Dartmouth College 243

Davidson College 245

Denison University 247

DePaul University 249

DePauw University 251

Dickinson College 253

Dordt College 255

Drexel University 257

Duke University 259

Duquesne University 261

Earlham College 263

East Carolina University 265

Eastern Kentucky University 267

Eckerd College.. 269

Elizabethtown College 271

Elmhurst College 273

Elmira College 275

Elon University 277

Emerson College 279

Emory University... 281

Fashion Institute of Technology 283

Ferris State University.. 285

Florida A&M University.. 287

Florida Atlantic University....................................... 289

Florida Southern College 291

Florida State University... 293

Fordham University... 295

Franklin & Marshall College 297

Freed-Hardeman University 299

Furman University.. 301

Gannon University 303

Geneva College 305

George Mason University.. 307

George Washington University................................... 309

Georgetown University.. 311

Georgia State University.. 313

Georgia Tech 315

Gettysburg College 317

Gonzaga University... 319

Goucher College 321

Grambling State University...................................... 323

Grand Valley State University 325

Grinnell College.. 327

Grove City College... 329

Guilford College.. 331

Gustavus Adolphus College...................................... 333

Hamilton College 335

Hampshire College... 337

Hampton University 339

Hanover College 341

Harvard University 343

Harvey Mudd College 345

Hastings College 347

Haverford College 349

Hofstra University 351
Hollins University 353
Hood College 355
Howard University 357
Hunter College 359
Idaho State University 361
Illinois State University 363
Illinois Wesleyan University 365
Indiana University 367
Indiana University of Pennsylvania 369
Iowa State University 371
Ithaca College 373
IUPUI 375
Jackson State University 377
James Madison University 379
John Carroll University 381
Johns Hopkins University 383
Juniata College 385
Kansas State University 387
Kent State University 389
Kenyon College 391
La Roche College 393
Lafayette College 395
Lawrence University 397
Lehigh University 399
Lewis & Clark College 401
Linfield College 403
Louisiana College 405
Louisiana State University 407
Loyola Marymount University 409
Loyola University Chicago 411
Loyola University Maryland 413
Luther College 415
Macalester College 417
Manhattan College 419
Manhattanville College 421
Marlboro College 423
Marquette University 425
Maryville University 427
Massachusetts College of Art & Design 429
McGill University 431
Mercer University 433
Mercyhurst College 435

Messiah College 437

Miami University 439

Michigan State University 441

Middle Tennessee State University 443

Middlebury College 445

Millsaps College 447

Minnesota State University 449

Minnesota State University - Moorhead 451

Misericordia University 453

Missouri State University 455

MIT 457

Montana State University 459

Montclair State University 461

Mount Holyoke College 463

Muhlenberg College 465

New College of Florida 467

New York University 469

North Carolina A&T State University 471

North Carolina State University 473

North Central College 475

Northeastern University 477

Northern Arizona University 479

Northern Illinois University 481

Northwestern College - Saint Paul 483

Northwestern University 485

Oakwood University 487

Oberlin College 489

Occidental College 491

Oglethorpe University 493

Ohio State University 495

Ohio University 497

Ohio Wesleyan University 499

Old Dominion University 501

Oral Roberts University 503

Pace University 505

Penn State 507

Penn State Altoona 509

Pepperdine University 511

Pitzer College 513

Pomona College 515

Princeton University 517

Providence College 519

Purchase College 521

Purdue University 523

Radford University 525

Ramapo College of New Jersey 527

Reed College 529

Regis University 531

Rensselaer Polytechnic Institute 533

Rhode Island School of Design 535

Rhodes College 537

Rice University 539

Rider University 541

Robert Morris University 543

Rochester Institute of Technology 545

Rollins College 547

Rowan University 549

Russell Sage College 551

Rutgers University 553

Sacramento State 555

Saint Francis University 557

Saint Joseph's University 559

Saint Leo University 561

Saint Louis University 563

Salem College 565

Salisbury University 567

Sam Houston State University 569

Samford University 571

San Diego State University 573

San Francisco State University 575

Santa Clara University 577

Sarah Lawrence College 579

Scripps College 581

Seattle Pacific University 583

Seattle University 585

Seton Hall University 587

Simmons College 589

Skidmore College 591

Slippery Rock University 593

Smith College 595

Southern Methodist University 597

Southwestern University 599

Spelman College 601

St. Edward's University 603

St. John's University 605

St. Lawrence University 607

St. Mary's College of Maryland. 609

St. Mary's University 611

St. Olaf College 613

Stanford University 615

Stetson University. 617

Stevenson University 619

Stony Brook University 621

SUNY Fredonia. 623

SUNY New Paltz 625

SUNY Oswego 627

Susquehanna University 629

Swarthmore College. 631

Syracuse University. 633

Taylor University 635

Temple University 637

Tennessee State University. 639

Texas A&M International University 641

Texas A&M University. 643

Texas Christian University. 645

Texas Lutheran University 647

Texas State University - San Marcos 649

Texas Tech University 651

Thomas College 653

Towson University. 655

Trinity College 657

Trinity University 659

Troy University 661

Truman State University 663

Tufts University 665

Tulane University. 667

UC Berkeley 669

UC Davis. 671

UC Irvine. 673

UC Merced 675

UC Riverside. 677

UC San Diego. 679

UC Santa Barbara 681

UC Santa Cruz 683

UCLA 685

Union College. 687

University at Albany 689

University at Buffalo 691

University of Alabama. 693

University of Arizona. 695
University of Arkansas. 697
University of Arkansas at Little Rock. 699
University of Baltimore 701
University of Central Florida. 703
University of Central Oklahoma 705
University of Chicago 707
University of Cincinnati. 709
University of Colorado 711
University of Connecticut 713
University of Delaware 715
University of Denver. 717
University of Florida 719
University of Georgia 721
University of Hartford 723
University of Illinois. 725
University of Illinois at Chicago 727
University of Iowa 729
University of Kansas 731
University of Kentucky 733
University of Louisville 735
University of Maine. 737
University of Maryland 739
University of Maryland Baltimore County. 741
University of Maryland Eastern Shore. 743
University of Massachusetts 745
University of Miami. 747
University of Michigan 749
University of Minnesota 751
University of Mississippi 753
University of Missouri 755
University of Montana. 757
University of Mount Union 759
University of Nebraska 761
University of New Hampshire 763
University of North Carolina 765
University of North Carolina - Greensboro. 767
University of Notre Dame. 769
University of Oklahoma 771
University of Oregon 773
University of Pennsylvania 775
University of Pittsburgh 777
University of Puget Sound 779

University of Rhode Island 781

University of Richmond. 783

University of Rochester. 785

University of San Diego 787

University of San Francisco. 789

University of South Carolina 791

University of South Dakota. 793

University of South Florida 795

University of Southern California 797

University of St Thomas - Texas 799

University of Tampa 801

University of Tennessee 803

University of Tennessee at Chattanooga 805

University of Texas 807

University of Texas - El Paso 809

University of the District of Columbia. 811

University of the Incarnate Word 813

University of Utah 815

University of Vermont. 817

University of Virginia. 819

University of Washington 821

University of Western Ontario 823

University of Wisconsin. 825

University of Wisconsin - Stout. 827

UNLV. 829

Urbana University 831

Ursinus College 833

Valparaiso University. 835

Vanderbilt University. 837

Vassar College 839

Villanova University. 841

Virginia Commonwealth University. 843

Virginia Tech 845

Wagner College 847

Wake Forest University 849

Warren Wilson College. 851

Washington & Jefferson College 853

Washington & Lee University 855

Washington University in St. Louis 857

Wayne State University. 859

Wellesley College. 861

Wesleyan University 863

West Point Military Academy 865

West Virginia University 867

Western Illinois University. 869

Western Kentucky University 871

Wheaton College - Illinois 873

Wheaton College - Massachusetts 875

Whitman College 877

Wilkes University. 879

Willamette University 881

Williams College. 883

Worcester Polytechnic Institute 885

Xavier University. 887

Yale University. 889

Youngstown State University 891

Verbal Outtakes. 893

Words to Know 902

About the Authors. 904

Region

New England

Amherst College
Babson College
Bates College
Bay Path College
Bentley University
Boston College
Boston University
Bowdoin College
Brandeis University
Brown University
Bryant University
Clark University
Colby College
College of the Holy Cross
Connecticut College
Dartmouth College
Emerson College
Hampshire College
Harvard University
Jackson State University
Marlboro College
Massachusetts College of Art & Design
Middlebury College
Millsaps College
MIT
Mount Holyoke College
Northeastern University
Providence College
Rhode Island School of Design
Simmons College
Smith College
Thomas College
Trinity College
Tufts University
University of Connecticut
University of Hartford
University of Maine
University of Massachusetts
University of Mississippi
University of New Hampshire
University of Rhode Island
University of Vermont
Wellesley College
Wesleyan University
Wheaton College - Massachusetts
Williams College
Worcester Polytechnic Institute
Yale University

Mid-Atlantic

Alfred University
Allegheny College
Arcadia University
Bard College
Barnard College
Baruch College
Binghamton University
Bryn Mawr College
Bucknell University
California University of Pennsylvania
Carnegie Mellon University
Chatham University
City College of New York
Colgate University
College of Mount Saint Vincent
College of Notre Dame of Maryland
Columbia University
Cornell University
CUNY Lehman College
CUNY Queens College
Dickinson College
Drexel University
Duquesne University
Elizabethtown College
Elmira College
Fashion Institute of Technology
Fordham University
Franklin & Marshall College
Gannon University
Geneva College
Gettysburg College
Goucher College
Grove City College
Hamilton College
Haverford College
Hofstra University
Hood College
Hunter College
Indiana University of Pennsylvania
Ithaca College
Johns Hopkins University
Juniata College
La Roche College
Lafayette College
Lehigh University
Loyola University Maryland
Manhattan College
Manhattanville College
Mercyhurst College
Messiah College
Misericordia University
Montclair State University
Muhlenberg College
New York University
Pace University
Penn State
Penn State Altoona
Princeton University
Purchase College
Ramapo College of New Jersey
Rensselaer Polytechnic Institute
Rider University
Robert Morris University
Rochester Institute of Technology
Rowan University
Russell Sage College
Rutgers University
Saint Francis University
Saint Joseph's University
Salisbury University
Sarah Lawrence College
Seton Hall University
Skidmore College
Slippery Rock University
St. John's University
St. Lawrence University
St. Mary's College of Maryland
Stevenson University
Stony Brook University
SUNY Fredonia
SUNY New Paltz
SUNY Oswego
Susquehanna University
Swarthmore College
Syracuse University
Temple University
Towson University
Union College
University at Albany
University at Buffalo
University of Baltimore
University of Delaware
University of Maryland
University of Maryland Baltimore County
University of Maryland Eastern Shore
University of Pennsylvania
University of Pittsburgh
University of Rochester
Ursinus College
Vassar College
Villanova University
Wagner College
Washington & Jefferson College
West Point Military Academy
Wilkes University

Southeast

American University
Auburn University
Ave Maria University
Barry University
Belmont University
Berea College
Birmingham-Southern College
Bob Jones University
Catawba College
Catholic University of America
Centenary College of Louisiana
Centre College
Claflin University
Clark Atlanta University
Clemson University
College of Charleston
College of William & Mary
Converse College
Davidson College
Duke University
East Carolina University
Eastern Kentucky University
Eckerd College
Elon University
Emory University
Florida A&M University
Florida Atlantic University
Florida Southern College
Florida State University
Freed-Hardeman University
Furman University
George Mason University
George Washington University
Georgetown University
Georgia State University
Georgia Tech
Grambling State University
Guilford College
Hampton University
Hollins University
Howard University
James Madison University
Louisiana College
Louisiana State University

Mercer University
Middle Tennessee State University
New College of Florida
North Carolina A&T State University
North Carolina State University
Oakwood University
Oglethorpe University
Old Dominion University
Radford University
Rhodes College
Rollins College
Saint Leo University
Salem College
Samford University
Spelman College
Stetson University
Tennessee State University
Troy University
Tulane University
University of Alabama
University of Arkansas
University of Arkansas at Little Rock
University of Central Florida
University of Florida
University of Georgia
University of Kentucky
University of Louisville
University of Miami
University of North Carolina
University of North Carolina - Greensboro
University of Richmond
University of South Carolina
University of South Florida
University of Tampa
University of Tennessee
University of Tennessee at Chattanooga
University of the District of Columbia
University of Virginia
Vanderbilt University
Virginia Commonwealth University
Virginia Tech
Wake Forest University
Warren Wilson College
Washington & Lee University
West Virginia University
Western Kentucky University

Great Lakes

Albion College
Alverno College
Ball State University
Beloit College
Bradley University
Case Western Reserve University
Cleveland State University
College for Creative Studies
College of Wooster
Columbia College Chicago
Denison University
DePaul University
DePauw University
Earlham College
Elmhurst College
Ferris State University
Grand Valley State University
Hanover College
Illinois State University
Illinois Wesleyan University
Indiana University
IUPUI

John Carroll University
Kent State University
Kenyon College
Lawrence University
Loyola University Chicago
Marquette University
Miami University
Michigan State University
North Central College
Northern Illinois University
Northwestern University
Oberlin College
Ohio State University
Ohio University
Ohio Wesleyan University
Purdue University
Taylor University
University of Chicago
University of Cincinnati
University of Illinois
University of Illinois at Chicago
University of Michigan
University of Mount Union
University of Notre Dame
University of Wisconsin
University of Wisconsin - Stout
Urbana University
Valparaiso University
Wayne State University
Western Illinois University
Wheaton College - Illinois
Xavier University
Youngstown State University

Great Plains

Carleton College
Coe College
Concordia College at Moorhead
Cornell College
Creighton University
Dordt College
Grinnell College
Gustavus Adolphus College
Hastings College
Iowa State University
Kansas State University
Luther College
Macalester College
Maryville University
Minnesota State University
Minnesota State University - Moorhead
Missouri State University
Northwestern College - Saint Paul
Saint Louis University
St. Olaf College
Truman State University
University of Iowa
University of Kansas
University of Minnesota
University of Missouri
University of Nebraska
University of South Dakota
Washington University in St. Louis

Southwest

Arizona State University
Austin College
Baylor University
Northern Arizona University

Oral Roberts University
Rice University
Sam Houston State University
Southern Methodist University
Southwestern University
St. Edward's University
St. Mary's University
Texas A&M International University
Texas A&M University
Texas Christian University
Texas Lutheran University
Texas State University - San Marcos
Texas Tech University
Trinity University
University of Arizona
University of Central Oklahoma
University of Oklahoma
University of St Thomas - Texas
University of Texas
University of Texas - El Paso
University of the Incarnate Word

Rockies

Brigham Young University
Brigham Young University - Idaho
Colorado College
Colorado State University - Pueblo
Idaho State University
Montana State University
Regis University
University of Colorado
University of Denver
University of Montana
University of Utah

West Coast

Cal Poly
Cal Poly Pomona
Cal State Long Beach
Cal State Monterey Bay
Cal State Northridge
Cal State San Marcos
California College of the Arts
Caltech
Chapman University
Claremont McKenna College
Gonzaga University
Harvey Mudd College
Lewis & Clark College
Linfield College
Loyola Marymount University
Occidental College
Pepperdine University
Pitzer College
Pomona College
Reed College
Sacramento State
San Diego State University
San Francisco State University
Santa Clara University
Scripps College
Seattle Pacific University
Seattle University
Stanford University
UC Berkeley
UC Davis
UC Irvine
UC Merced
UC Riverside

UC San Diego
UC Santa Barbara
UC Santa Cruz
UCLA
University of Oregon
University of Puget Sound
University of San Diego
University of San Francisco
University of Southern California
University of Washington
UNLV
Whitman College
Willamette University

Outside US

McGill University
University of Western Ontario

New England: Connecticut, Maine, Massachusetts, New Hampshire, Rhode Island, and Vermont

Mid-Atlantic: Delaware, Maryland, New Jersey, New York, and Pennsylvania

Southeast: Alabama, Arkansas, Florida, Georgia, Kentucky, Louisiana, Mississippi, North Carolina, South Carolina, Tennessee, Virginia, Washington D.C., and West Virginia

Great Lakes: Illinois, Indiana, Michigan, Ohio, and Wisconsin

Great Plains: Iowa, Kansas, Minnesota, Missouri, Nebraska, North Dakota, and South Dakota

Southwest: Arizona, New Mexico, Oklahoma, and Texas

Rockies: Colorado, Idaho, Montana, Utah, and Wyoming

West Coast: Alaska, California, Hawaii, Nevada, Oregon, and Washington

Outside US: Canada, Europe, and U.S. Territories

Setting

Large City

Alverno College
American University
Barnard College
Baruch College
Belmont University
Boston University
Cal State Long Beach
Cal State Northridge
California College of the Arts
Carnegie Mellon University
Case Western Reserve University
Catholic University of America
Chatham University
City College of New York
Clark Atlanta University
Cleveland State University
College for Creative Studies
College of Mount Saint Vincent
College of Notre Dame of Maryland
Colorado College
Columbia College Chicago
Columbia University
Creighton University
CUNY Lehman College
CUNY Queens College
DePaul University
Drexel University
Duquesne University
Emerson College
Fashion Institute of Technology
Fordham University
George Washington University
Georgetown University
Georgia State University
Guilford College
Howard University
Hunter College
IUPUI
Johns Hopkins University
Lewis & Clark College
Loyola Marymount University
Loyola University Chicago
Loyola University Maryland
Macalester College
Manhattan College
Marquette University
Massachusetts College of Art & Design
McGill University
New York University
North Carolina A&T State University
North Carolina State University
Northeastern University
Occidental College
Ohio State University
Oral Roberts University
Pace University
Reed College
Regis University
Rhodes College
Rice University
Sacramento State
Saint Joseph's University
Saint Louis University
San Diego State University
San Francisco State University
Seattle Pacific University

Seattle University
Simmons College
Spelman College
St. Edward's University
St. John's University
St. Mary's University
Temple University
Tennessee State University
Texas Christian University
Trinity University
Tulane University
UC Riverside
UC San Diego
UCLA
University at Buffalo
University of Arizona
University of Baltimore
University of Chicago
University of Cincinnati
University of Denver
University of Illinois at Chicago
University of Kentucky
University of Louisville
University of Minnesota
University of Nebraska
University of North Carolina - Greensboro
University of Pennsylvania
University of Pittsburgh
University of San Diego
University of San Francisco
University of South Florida
University of Southern California
University of St Thomas - Texas
University of Tampa
University of Texas
University of Texas - El Paso
University of the District of Columbia
University of the Incarnate Word
University of Washington
Vanderbilt University
Wagner College
Wayne State University
Xavier University

Mid-Size City

Arizona State University
Baylor University
Birmingham-Southern College
Bradley University
Brigham Young University
Brown University
Caltech
Centenary College of Louisiana
Chapman University
Clark University
Coe College
College of Charleston
College of the Holy Cross
Colorado State University - Pueblo
Duke University
Eckerd College
Florida A&M University
Florida State University
Gannon University
Gonzaga University
Hampton University
Harvard University

Jackson State University
Louisiana State University
Mercyhurst College
Middle Tennessee State University
Millsaps College
Missouri State University
MIT
Muhlenberg College
North Central College
Oakwood University
Old Dominion University
Providence College
Rhode Island School of Design
Salem College
Santa Clara University
Syracuse University
Texas Tech University
Trinity College
UC Berkeley
UC Irvine
University of Arkansas at Little Rock
University of Florida
University of Georgia
University of Michigan
University of Missouri
University of Oregon
University of Puget Sound
University of Richmond
University of Rochester
University of South Carolina
University of Tennessee
University of Tennessee at Chattanooga
University of Utah
University of Wisconsin
UNLV
Virginia Commonwealth University
Wake Forest University
Willamette University
Worcester Polytechnic Institute
Yale University

Suburban

Arcadia University
Babson College
Barry University
Bay Path College
Beloit College
Bryn Mawr College
Cal Poly
Cal Poly Pomona
Claremont McKenna College
College of William & Mary
Concordia College at Moorhead
Davidson College
Denison University
Elmhurst College
Emory University
Franklin & Marshall College
Furman University
Geneva College
George Mason University
Georgia Tech
Grand Valley State University
Hamilton College
Harvey Mudd College
Haverford College
Hofstra University

Hollins University
Ithaca College
John Carroll University
Kent State University
La Roche College
Lafayette College
Louisiana College
Manhattanville College
Maryville University
Messiah College
Minnesota State University - Moorhead
Misericordia University
Montclair State University
Mount Holyoke College
Northern Illinois University
Northwestern College - Saint Paul
Oberlin College
Oglethorpe University
Pepperdine University
Pitzer College
Pomona College
Princeton University
Purchase College
Purdue University
Ramapo College of New Jersey
Rider University
Robert Morris University
Rochester Institute of Technology
Rollins College
Rowan University
Salisbury University
Samford University
Sarah Lawrence College
Scripps College
Seton Hall University
Skidmore College
Smith College
Southern Methodist University
Stanford University
Stetson University
Stevenson University
Stony Brook University
Swarthmore College
Tufts University
UC Davis
UC Santa Barbara
University of Central Florida
University of Central Oklahoma
University of Delaware
University of Maine
University of Maryland
University of Maryland Baltimore County
University of Miami
University of New Hampshire
University of Notre Dame
University of Oklahoma
University of Rhode Island
University of Virginia
University of Western Ontario
Ursinus College
Valparaiso University
Villanova University
Warren Wilson College
Washington & Jefferson College
Washington University in St. Louis
Wellesley College
West Point Military Academy
Wheaton College - Illinois
Wheaton College - Massachusetts

Small City

Auburn University
Austin College
Ball State University
Bates College
Bentley University
Binghamton University
Bob Jones University
Boston College
Brandeis University
Connecticut College
Converse College
Cornell University
East Carolina University
Elmira College
Florida Atlantic University
Florida Southern College
Goucher College
Grambling State University
Hood College
Idaho State University
Illinois State University
Illinois Wesleyan University
Indiana University
Iowa State University
James Madison University
Lehigh University
Mercer University
New College of Florida
Northern Arizona University
Northwestern University
Penn State
Penn State Altoona
Rensselaer Polytechnic Institute
Russell Sage College
Rutgers University
Texas A&M University
Texas Lutheran University
Towson University
UC Santa Cruz
Union College
University at Albany
University of Alabama
University of Arkansas
University of Colorado
University of Hartford
University of Illinois
University of Iowa
University of Kansas
University of North Carolina
University of Vermont
Vassar College
Virginia Tech
Wesleyan University
West Virginia University
Western Kentucky University
Wilkes University
Youngstown State University

College Town

Albion College
Alfred University
Allegheny College
Amherst College
Bard College
Berea College
Bowdoin College
Brigham Young University - Idaho
Bucknell University

California University of Pennsylvania
Carleton College
Catawba College
Centre College
Claflin University
Clemson University
Colby College
Colgate University
College of Wooster
Cornell College
Dartmouth College
DePauw University
Dickinson College
Dordt College
Earlham College
Eastern Kentucky University
Elizabethtown College
Ferris State University
Freed-Hardeman University
Gettysburg College
Grinnell College
Grove City College
Gustavus Adolphus College
Hampshire College
Hanover College
Hastings College
Indiana University of Pennsylvania
Juniata College
Kansas State University
Linfield College
Miami University
Minnesota State University
Montana State University
Ohio University
Ohio Wesleyan University
Radford University
Sam Houston State University
Slippery Rock University
Southwestern University
St. Lawrence University
St. Olaf College
SUNY Fredonia
SUNY New Paltz
SUNY Oswego
Susquehanna University
Taylor University
Texas State University - San Marcos
Truman State University
University of Connecticut
University of Maryland Eastern Shore
University of Massachusetts
University of Mount Union
University of South Dakota
University of Wisconsin - Stout
Urbana University
Washington & Lee University
Western Illinois University
Whitman College
Williams College

Rural

Ave Maria University
Bryant University
Cal State Monterey Bay
Cal State San Marcos
Elon University
Kenyon College
Lawrence University
Luther College
Marlboro College

Michigan State University
Middlebury College
Saint Francis University
Saint Leo University
St. Mary's College of Maryland
Texas A&M International University
Thomas College
Troy University
UC Merced
University of Mississippi
University of Montana

Large City: *Within city limits in an urban area with a population of 250,000 or more*

Mid-Size City: *Within city limits in an urban area with a population of 100,000-250,000*

Suburban: *Urban area outside of city limits*

Small City: *Within city limits in an urban area with population of less than 100,000*

College Town: *Within municipality located outside of a major urban area*

Rural: *Sparsely populated area or within a village with a population of less than 2,500*

Size

Super-Small

Albion College
Alfred University
Amherst College
Austin College
Ave Maria University
Babson College
Bard College
Bates College
Bay Path College
Beloit College
Berea College
Birmingham-Southern College
Bowdoin College
Bryn Mawr College
California College of the Arts
Caltech
Carleton College
Catawba College
Centenary College of Louisiana
Centre College
Chatham University
Claflin University
Claremont McKenna College
Coe College
Colby College
College for Creative Studies
College of Mount Saint Vincent
College of Notre Dame of Maryland
College of Wooster
Connecticut College
Converse College
Cornell College
Davidson College
Dordt College
Earlham College
Elmira College
Freed-Hardeman University
Geneva College
Goucher College
Grinnell College
Hamilton College
Hampshire College
Hanover College
Harvey Mudd College
Hastings College
Haverford College
Hollins University
Hood College
Juniata College
Kenyon College
La Roche College
Lawrence University
Lewis & Clark College
Linfield College
Louisiana College
Macalester College
Manhattanville College
Marlboro College
Millsaps College
New College of Florida
Oakwood University
Occidental College
Oglethorpe University
Ohio Wesleyan University
Pitzer College
Pomona College

Reed College
Rhode Island School of Design
Rhodes College
Russell Sage College
Saint Francis University
Saint Leo University
Salem College
Sarah Lawrence College
Scripps College
Simmons College
Southwestern University
Swarthmore College
Texas Lutheran University
Thomas College
University of St Thomas - Texas
Urbana University
Ursinus College
Wagner College
Warren Wilson College
Washington & Jefferson College
Washington & Lee University
Wheaton College - Massachusetts
Whitman College
Willamette University

Small

Allegheny College
Alverno College
Arcadia University
Barnard College
Bob Jones University
Brandeis University
Bryant University
Bucknell University
Catholic University of America
Clark Atlanta University
Clark University
Colgate University
College of the Holy Cross
Colorado College
Concordia College at Moorhead
Denison University
DePauw University
Dickinson College
Eckerd College
Elizabethtown College
Elmhurst College
Emerson College
Florida Southern College
Franklin & Marshall College
Furman University
Gannon University
Gettysburg College
Grove City College
Guilford College
Gustavus Adolphus College
Illinois Wesleyan University
John Carroll University
Lafayette College
Loyola University Maryland
Luther College
Manhattan College
Maryville University
Massachusetts College of Art & Design
Messiah College
Middlebury College
Misericordia University

Mount Holyoke College
Muhlenberg College
North Central College
Northwestern College - Saint Paul
Oberlin College
Oral Roberts University
Pepperdine University
Rice University
Robert Morris University
Rollins College
Samford University
Seattle Pacific University
Skidmore College
Smith College
Spelman College
St. Lawrence University
St. Mary's College of Maryland
St. Mary's University
St. Olaf College
Stetson University
Stevenson University
Susquehanna University
Taylor University
Trinity College
Trinity University
Union College
University of Baltimore
University of Maryland Eastern Shore
University of Mount Union
University of Puget Sound
University of Richmond
Valparaiso University
Vassar College
Wellesley College
Wesleyan University
Wheaton College - Illinois
Wilkes University
Williams College
Worcester Polytechnic Institute

Mid-Sized

American University
Barry University
Belmont University
Bentley University
Boston College
Bradley University
Brown University
Cal State Monterey Bay
Cal State San Marcos
California University of Pennsylvania
Carnegie Mellon University
Case Western Reserve University
Chapman University
Cleveland State University
College of William & Mary
Colorado State University - Pueblo
Columbia University
Creighton University
CUNY Lehman College
Dartmouth College
Duke University
Duquesne University
Elon University
Emory University
Fordham University
Georgetown University

Gonzaga University
Grambling State University
Hampton University
Hofstra University
Howard University
Ithaca College
Jackson State University
Johns Hopkins University
Lehigh University
Loyola Marymount University
Marquette University
Mercer University
Mercyhurst College
Minnesota State University - Moorhead
MIT
North Carolina A&T State University
Northwestern University
Pace University
Penn State Altoona
Princeton University
Providence College
Purchase College
Radford University
Ramapo College of New Jersey
Regis University
Rensselaer Polytechnic Institute
Rider University
Rowan University
Saint Joseph's University
Salisbury University
Santa Clara University
Seattle University
Seton Hall University
Slippery Rock University
Southern Methodist University
St. Edward's University
Stanford University
SUNY Fredonia
SUNY New Paltz
SUNY Oswego
Tennessee State University
Texas A&M International University
Texas Christian University
Truman State University
Tufts University
Tulane University
UC Merced
University of Arkansas at Little Rock
University of Chicago
University of Denver
University of Hartford
University of Maine
University of Notre Dame
University of Rochester
University of San Diego
University of San Francisco
University of South Dakota
University of Tampa
University of Tennessee at Chattanooga
University of the District of Columbia
University of the Incarnate Word
University of Wisconsin - Stout
Vanderbilt University
Villanova University
Wake Forest University
Washington University in St. Louis
West Point Military Academy
Xavier University
Yale University

Large

Auburn University
Ball State University
Baruch College
Baylor University
Binghamton University
Boston University
Brigham Young University - Idaho
Cal Poly
City College of New York
Clemson University
College of Charleston
Columbia College Chicago
Cornell University
CUNY Queens College
DePaul University
Drexel University
Eastern Kentucky University
Fashion Institute of Technology
Ferris State University
Florida A&M University
George Mason University
George Washington University
Georgia Tech
Harvard University
Hunter College
Idaho State University
Illinois State University
Indiana University of Pennsylvania
James Madison University
Kansas State University
Kent State University
Loyola University Chicago
Miami University
Minnesota State University
Missouri State University
Montana State University
Montclair State University
Northeastern University
Northern Arizona University
Northern Illinois University
Ohio University
Old Dominion University
Rochester Institute of Technology
Saint Louis University
Sam Houston State University
St. John's University
Stony Brook University
Syracuse University
Towson University
UC Riverside
UC Santa Barbara
UC Santa Cruz
University at Albany
University at Buffalo
University of Arkansas
University of Central Oklahoma
University of Connecticut
University of Delaware
University of Illinois at Chicago
University of Kentucky
University of Louisville
University of Maryland Baltimore County
University of Miami
University of Mississippi
University of Montana
University of Nebraska
University of New Hampshire
University of North Carolina
University of North Carolina - Greensboro

University of Oklahoma
University of Oregon
University of Pennsylvania
University of Pittsburgh
University of Rhode Island
University of Southern California
University of Texas - El Paso
University of Vermont
University of Virginia
Western Illinois University
Western Kentucky University
Youngstown State University

Huge

Arizona State University
Brigham Young University
Cal Poly Pomona
Cal State Long Beach
Cal State Northridge
East Carolina University
Florida Atlantic University
Florida State University
Georgia State University
Grand Valley State University
Indiana University
Iowa State University
IUPUI
Louisiana State University
McGill University
Michigan State University
Middle Tennessee State University
New York University
North Carolina State University
Ohio State University
Penn State
Purdue University
Rutgers University
Sacramento State
San Diego State University
San Francisco State University
Temple University
Texas A&M University
Texas State University - San Marcos
Texas Tech University
Troy University
UC Berkeley
UC Davis
UC Irvine
UC San Diego
UCLA
University of Alabama
University of Arizona
University of Central Florida
University of Cincinnati
University of Colorado
University of Florida
University of Georgia
University of Illinois
University of Iowa
University of Kansas
University of Maryland
University of Massachusetts
University of Michigan
University of Minnesota
University of Missouri
University of South Carolina
University of South Florida
University of Tennessee
University of Texas
University of Utah

University of Washington
University of Western Ontario
University of Wisconsin
UNLV
Virginia Commonwealth University
Virginia Tech
Wayne State University
West Virginia University

Super-small: *Fewer than 2,000 undergrads*
Small: *2,000–4,000 undergrads*
Mid-sized: *4,000–10,000 undergrads*
Large: *10,000–20,000 undergrads*
Huge: *More than 20,000 undergrads*

Selectivity

Albion College
Alfred University
Allegheny College
Alverno College
Arcadia University
Arizona State University
Auburn University
Austin College
Ball State University
Barry University
Bay Path College
Belmont University
Beloit College
Bob Jones University
Bradley University
Brigham Young University
Brigham Young University - Idaho
Cal State Monterey Bay
Cal State Northridge
Cal State San Marcos
California College of the Arts
California University of Pennsylvania
Case Western Reserve University
Catawba College
Catholic University of America
Centre College
Chatham University
Clark University
Cleveland State University
Coe College
College of Charleston
College of Mount Saint Vincent
College of Notre Dame of Maryland
Colorado State University - Pueblo
Columbia College Chicago
Concordia College at Moorhead
Converse College
Creighton University
DePaul University
DePauw University
Dordt College
Duquesne University
Earlham College
East Carolina University
Eastern Kentucky University
Eckerd College
Elizabethtown College
Elmhurst College
Elmira College
Florida A&M University
Florida Southern College
Florida State University
Freed-Hardeman University
Gannon University
Geneva College
George Mason University
Georgia Tech
Gonzaga University
Goucher College
Grand Valley State University
Grove City College
Guilford College
Gustavus Adolphus College
Hampshire College
Hampton University
Hanover College

Hastings College
Hollins University
Hood College
Idaho State University
Illinois State University
Indiana University
Indiana University of Pennsylvania
Iowa State University
Ithaca College
IUPUI
James Madison University
John Carroll University
Juniata College
Kansas State University
Kent State University
La Roche College
Lawrence University
Lewis & Clark College
Linfield College
Louisiana State University
Loyola University Chicago
Loyola University Maryland
Luther College
Manhattan College
Marlboro College
Marquette University
Maryville University
Mercer University
Mercyhurst College
Messiah College
Miami University
Michigan State University
Middle Tennessee State University
Millsaps College
Minnesota State University
Minnesota State University - Moorhead
Misericordia University
Montana State University
North Central College
Northern Arizona University
Northwestern College - Saint Paul
Ohio State University
Ohio University
Ohio Wesleyan University
Old Dominion University
Oral Roberts University
Pace University
Penn State Altoona
Purdue University
Radford University
Regis University
Rider University
Robert Morris University
Rochester Institute of Technology
Rollins College
Rowan University
Russell Sage College
Rutgers University
Sacramento State
Saint Francis University
Saint Joseph's University
Saint Leo University
Saint Louis University
Samford University
San Francisco State University
Sarah Lawrence College
Seattle Pacific University
Seattle University
Seton Hall University

Southwestern University
St. Edward's University
St. Mary's University
Susquehanna University
Syracuse University
Taylor University
Temple University
Tennessee State University
Texas A&M University
Texas Lutheran University
Texas State University - San Marcos
Texas Tech University
Thomas College
Towson University
Troy University
Truman State University
UC Merced
UC Riverside
UC Santa Cruz
University of Arizona
University of Arkansas at Little Rock
University of Baltimore
University of Central Oklahoma
University of Cincinnati
University of Colorado
University of Denver
University of Hartford
University of Illinois
University of Illinois at Chicago
University of Iowa
University of Kansas
University of Kentucky
University of Louisville
University of Maine
University of Maryland Baltimore County
University of Massachusetts
University of Mississippi
University of Missouri
University of Montana
University of Mount Union
University of Nebraska
University of New Hampshire
University of North Carolina - Greensboro
University of Oklahoma
University of Oregon
University of Puget Sound
University of Rhode Island
University of San Francisco
University of South Dakota
University of St Thomas - Texas
University of Tampa
University of Tennessee
University of Tennessee at Chattanooga
University of Texas - El Paso
University of the District of Columbia
University of the Incarnate Word
University of Utah
University of Vermont
University of Washington
University of Wisconsin - Stout
UNLV
Urbana University
Valparaiso University
Virginia Commonwealth University
Virginia Tech
Wagner College
Warren Wilson College
Wayne State University
West Virginia University

Western Illinois University
Western Kentucky University
Wheaton College - Illinois
Wilkes University
Worcester Polytechnic Institute
Xavier University
Youngstown State University

Mid-Range

American University
Babson College
Baylor University
Bentley University
Birmingham-Southern College
Boston University
Bryant University
Bryn Mawr College
Cal Poly Pomona
Cal State Long Beach
Centenary College of Louisiana
Chapman University
Clark Atlanta University
Clemson University
College of Wooster
Cornell College
Denison University
Dickinson College
Drexel University
Elon University
Emerson College
Fashion Institute of Technology
Ferris State University
Florida Atlantic University
Fordham University
Franklin & Marshall College
Furman University
Georgia State University
Gettysburg College
Hofstra University
Howard University
Illinois Wesleyan University
Jackson State University
Lafayette College
Louisiana College
Loyola Marymount University
Macalester College
Manhattanville College
Massachusetts College of Art & Design
McGill University
Missouri State University
Montclair State University
Mount Holyoke College
Muhlenberg College
New College of Florida
North Carolina A&T State University
North Carolina State University
Northeastern University
Northern Illinois University
Oakwood University
Occidental College
Oglethorpe University
Penn State
Providence College
Ramapo College of New Jersey
Reed College
Rensselaer Polytechnic Institute
Rhodes College
Salem College
Salisbury University
Sam Houston State University

Santa Clara University
Simmons College
Skidmore College
Slippery Rock University
Smith College
Southern Methodist University
St. John's University
St. Mary's College of Maryland
St. Olaf College
Stetson University
Stevenson University
SUNY Fredonia
SUNY Oswego
Texas A&M International University
Texas Christian University
Trinity College
Trinity University
UC Davis
UC Irvine
UC Santa Barbara
Union College
University at Albany
University at Buffalo
University of Alabama
University of Arkansas
University of Central Florida
University of Connecticut
University of Delaware
University of Florida
University of Georgia
University of Maryland
University of Maryland Eastern Shore
University of Miami
University of Michigan
University of Minnesota
University of Pittsburgh
University of San Diego
University of South Carolina
University of South Florida
University of Texas
University of Wisconsin
Ursinus College
Villanova University
Washington & Jefferson College
Wheaton College - Massachusetts
Whitman College
Willamette University

Selective

Ave Maria University
Bard College
Barnard College
Bates College
Binghamton University
Boston College
Brandeis University
Bucknell University
Cal Poly
Carleton College
Carnegie Mellon University
City College of New York
Claflin University
Colby College
Colgate University
College for Creative Studies
College of the Holy Cross
College of William & Mary
Colorado College
Connecticut College
CUNY Lehman College

CUNY Queens College
Davidson College
Emory University
George Washington University
Grambling State University
Grinnell College
Hamilton College
Harvey Mudd College
Haverford College
Hunter College
Johns Hopkins University
Kenyon College
Lehigh University
New York University
Northwestern University
Oberlin College
Pepperdine University
Purchase College
Rhode Island School of Design
San Diego State University
Scripps College
Spelman College
St. Lawrence University
Stony Brook University
SUNY New Paltz
Tufts University
Tulane University
UC San Diego
University of Chicago
University of North Carolina
University of Notre Dame
University of Richmond
University of Rochester
University of Virginia
University of Western Ontario
Wake Forest University
Wellesley College
Wesleyan University

Ultra Selective

Amherst College
Baruch College
Berea College
Bowdoin College
Brown University
Caltech
Claremont McKenna College
Columbia University
Cornell University
Dartmouth College
Duke University
Georgetown University
Harvard University
Middlebury College
MIT
Pitzer College
Pomona College
Princeton University
Rice University
Stanford University
Swarthmore College
UC Berkeley
UCLA
University of Pennsylvania
University of Southern California
Vanderbilt University
Vassar College
Washington & Lee University
Washington University in St. Louis
West Point Military Academy

Williams College
Yale University

Less Selective: *Acceptance rates of 60 percent and up*

Mid-Range: *Acceptance rates between 40–59 percent*

Selective: *Acceptance rates between 25–39 percent*

Ultra Selective: *Acceptance rates below 25 percent*

Academics

A high Academics grade generally indicates that professors are knowledgeable, accessible, and genuinely interested in their students' welfare. Other determining factors include class size, how well professors communicate, and whether or not classes are engaging.

A+

Caltech
Claremont McKenna College
Columbia University
Dartmouth College
Duke University
MIT
Princeton University
Stanford University
Swarthmore College
University of Chicago
Washington University in St. Louis
Yale University

A

Amherst College
Barnard College
Boston College
Bowdoin College
Brandeis University
Brown University
Carleton College
Carnegie Mellon University
Colby College
College of William & Mary
Cornell University
Davidson College
Emory University
Georgetown University
Hamilton College
Harvard University
Harvey Mudd College
Middlebury College
Mount Holyoke College
Northwestern University
Pitzer College
Pomona College
Rice University
Smith College
Tufts University
UC Berkeley
University of Notre Dame
University of Pennsylvania
University of Southern California
Vanderbilt University
Vassar College
Washington & Lee University
Wellesley College
Williams College

A-

American University
Austin College
Bard College
Bates College

Belmont University
Bryn Mawr College
Colgate University
Colorado College
Connecticut College
Elon University
George Washington University
Grinnell College
Hastings College
Haverford College
Johns Hopkins University
Kenyon College
Lehigh University
Loyola Marymount University
Macalester College
New York University
Oberlin College
Ohio State University
Reed College
Santa Clara University
Scripps College
Southern Methodist University
Trinity College
UCLA
University of Illinois
University of Michigan
University of North Carolina
University of Rochester
University of Virginia
Wake Forest University
Wesleyan University
Wheaton College - Illinois

B+

Allegheny College
Alverno College
Babson College
Baruch College
Baylor University
Bentley University
Binghamton University
Boston University
Brigham Young University
Bucknell University
Case Western Reserve University
Centre College
Clark University
Clemson University
College for Creative Studies
College of the Holy Cross
Dickinson College
Drexel University
Fordham University
Franklin & Marshall College
Georgia Tech
Gonzaga University
Grove City College
Hofstra University
Illinois Wesleyan University
Ithaca College
Lafayette College
Lawrence University
Lewis & Clark College

Linfield College
Marquette University
McGill University
Mercer University
Muhlenberg College
New College of Florida
North Carolina State University
Northeastern University
Occidental College
Penn State
Rensselaer Polytechnic Institute
Rhode Island School of Design
Rhodes College
Rochester Institute of Technology
Rutgers University
Sarah Lawrence College
St. Lawrence University
St. Olaf College
Syracuse University
Taylor University
Tulane University
UC Irvine
UC San Diego
UC Santa Barbara
UC Santa Cruz
University of Connecticut
University of Delaware
University of Denver
University of Florida
University of Georgia
University of Maryland
University of Miami
University of Minnesota
University of Missouri
University of Nebraska
University of New Hampshire
University of Richmond
University of San Diego
University of San Francisco
University of Texas
University of Vermont
Ursinus College
Villanova University
Virginia Tech
West Point Military Academy
Wheaton College - Massachusetts
Whitman College
Willamette University

B

Albion College
Alfred University
Auburn University
Beloit College
Berea College
Birmingham-Southern College
Bradley University
Brigham Young University - Idaho
Bryant University
Cal Poly
Cal State Long Beach
Catholic University of America
Centenary College of Louisiana

Chapman University
College of Charleston
College of Notre Dame of Maryland
College of Wooster
Concordia College at Moorhead
Cornell College
Creighton University
Denison University
DePaul University
DePauw University
Earlham College
Eckerd College
Elizabethtown College
Elmhurst College
Emerson College
Florida State University
Furman University
George Mason University
Gettysburg College
Goucher College
Hampshire College
Hanover College
Hollins University
Hunter College
Indiana University
Iowa State University
John Carroll University
Juniata College
Kansas State University
Loyola University Chicago
Loyola University Maryland
Luther College
Manhattan College
Manhattanville College
Marlboro College
Messiah College
Miami University
Michigan State University
Millsaps College
Misericordia University
Montclair State University
Ohio University
Ohio Wesleyan University
Pepperdine University
Providence College
Purdue University
Rider University
Rollins College
Saint Louis University
Salisbury University
San Diego State University
Seattle University
Seton Hall University
Simmons College
Skidmore College
Southwestern University
Spelman College
St. Edward's University
St. Mary's University
Stetson University
Stony Brook University
SUNY New Paltz
Susquehanna University
Texas A&M University
Texas Christian University
Trinity University
Truman State University
UC Davis
Union College
University at Buffalo
University of Alabama
University of Arizona

University of Arkansas
University of Central Florida
University of Iowa
University of Kansas
University of Maine
University of Maryland Baltimore County
University of Massachusetts
University of Mississippi
University of Oklahoma
University of Oregon
University of Pittsburgh
University of Puget Sound
University of Rhode Island
University of South Carolina
University of South Florida
University of Tampa
University of Tennessee
University of Utah
University of Washington
University of Western Ontario
University of Wisconsin
University of Wisconsin - Stout
Virginia Commonwealth University
Warren Wilson College
Washington & Jefferson College

B-

Arcadia University
Arizona State University
Barry University
Bay Path College
Bob Jones University
California University of Pennsylvania
Chatham University
City College of New York
Columbia College Chicago
Converse College
CUNY Lehman College
CUNY Queens College
East Carolina University
Fashion Institute of Technology
Florida Atlantic University
Freed-Hardeman University
Georgia State University
Grand Valley State University
Guilford College
Gustavus Adolphus College
Hood College
Howard University
Idaho State University
Illinois State University
Indiana University of Pennsylvania
James Madison University
La Roche College
Louisiana State University
Massachusetts College of Art & Design
Missouri State University
Montana State University
North Central College
Northern Arizona University
Northern Illinois University
Northwestern College - Saint Paul
Old Dominion University
Oral Roberts University
Pace University
Purchase College
Radford University

Robert Morris University
Saint Francis University
Saint Joseph's University
Saint Leo University
Samford University
Slippery Rock University
St. John's University
Stevenson University
SUNY Fredonia
Temple University
Tennessee State University
Texas State University - San Marcos
Texas Tech University
Towson University
UC Merced
UC Riverside
University at Albany
University of Cincinnati
University of Colorado
University of Hartford
University of Illinois at Chicago
University of Kentucky
University of Louisville
University of Montana
University of Mount Union
University of North Carolina - Greensboro
University of South Dakota
Valparaiso University
Wagner College
Wayne State University
West Virginia University
Western Illinois University
Wilkes University
Xavier University

C+

Ball State University
Cal Poly Pomona
Cal State Northridge
Cal State San Marcos
Claflin University
Cleveland State University
Dordt College
Duquesne University
Eastern Kentucky University
Elmira College
Florida A&M University
Florida Southern College
Gannon University
Geneva College
Hampton University
IUPUI
Jackson State University
Kent State University
Louisiana College
Mercyhurst College
Middle Tennessee State University
Minnesota State University - Moorhead
North Carolina A&T State University
Rowan University
Russell Sage College
Sacramento State
Sam Houston State University
San Francisco State University
SUNY Oswego
Troy University
University of Central Oklahoma

University of the Incarnate Word
UNLV
Western Kentucky University

Athletics

A high grade in Athletics indicates that students have school spirit, that sports programs are respected, that games are well-attended, and that intramurals are a prominent part of student life.

A+

Louisiana State University
Ohio State University
Syracuse University
University of Alabama
University of Florida
University of Georgia
University of Kentucky
University of Mississippi
University of Missouri

A

Arizona State University
Auburn University
Baylor University
Clemson University
Davidson College
Duke University
Florida State University
Georgia Tech
Kansas State University
Michigan State University
Penn State
Purdue University
Rutgers University
Stanford University
Texas A&M University
Texas Tech University
UC Berkeley
UCLA
University of Arizona
University of Arkansas
University of Connecticut
University of Iowa
University of Kansas
University of Louisville
University of Maryland
University of Miami
University of Michigan
University of Minnesota
University of Nebraska
University of North Carolina
University of Oklahoma
University of Oregon
University of South Carolina
University of South Florida
University of Southern California
University of Tennessee
University of Texas
University of Virginia
University of Washington
University of Wisconsin
Villanova University
Virginia Tech
West Virginia University

A-

Colgate University
Gonzaga University
Hastings College
Indiana University
Iowa State University
Lehigh University
North Carolina State University
Providence College
University of Cincinnati
University of Illinois
University of Notre Dame
University of Pittsburgh
Vanderbilt University
Xavier University

B+

Babson College
Boston College
College of the Holy Cross
Dartmouth College
Harvard University
MIT
Northwestern University
Princeton University
Rowan University
Seton Hall University
University of Colorado
University of Pennsylvania
University of Richmond
Wake Forest University
Washington & Jefferson College
West Point Military Academy

B

Albion College
Bradley University
Bucknell University
Carleton College
College of Wooster
Georgetown University
Gustavus Adolphus College
Lafayette College
Loyola University Maryland
Manhattan College
Marquette University
Messiah College
Middlebury College
Rice University
Rollins College
St. John's University
Stetson University
Texas Christian University
Union College
University of Denver

University of Montana
University of South Dakota
University of Utah
University of Western Ontario
Wheaton College - Massachusetts
Wilkes University

B-

Amherst College
Bates College
Belmont University
Birmingham-Southern College
Bowdoin College
Brigham Young University
Brown University
Cal Poly
California University of Pennsylvania
Centenary College of Louisiana
Chatham University
Clark Atlanta University
Cleveland State University
Colby College
Colorado College
Connecticut College
Creighton University
DePaul University
DePauw University
Dickinson College
Dordt College
Drexel University
East Carolina University
Elon University
Florida A&M University
Florida Southern College
Furman University
George Mason University
Gettysburg College
Grand Valley State University
Hamilton College
Idaho State University
Illinois Wesleyan University
Jackson State University
James Madison University
Juniata College
Kent State University
Linfield College
Macalester College
Manhattanville College
Miami University
Middle Tennessee State University
Missouri State University
Montana State University
North Carolina A&T State University
North Central College
Northern Illinois University
Northwestern College - Saint Paul
Ohio University
Old Dominion University
Oral Roberts University
Pepperdine University
Rensselaer Polytechnic Institute
Rider University
Sacramento State

Saint Joseph's University
Salisbury University
Sam Houston State University
San Diego State University
Santa Clara University
Skidmore College
Southern Methodist University
St. Lawrence University
SUNY Oswego
Taylor University
Temple University
Tennessee State University
Texas State University - San Marcos
Trinity College
Troy University
UC Davis
UC Irvine
UC Santa Barbara
University of Central Florida
University of Central Oklahoma
University of Delaware
University of Maine
University of Massachusetts
University of Mount Union
University of New Hampshire
University of Rochester
University of Tampa
University of Vermont
University of Wisconsin - Stout
Ursinus College
Virginia Commonwealth University
Warren Wilson College
Wheaton College - Illinois
Williams College
Yale University

C+

Ball State University
Barry University
Baruch College
Beloit College
Bentley University
Berea College
Binghamton University
Bob Jones University
Boston University
Brandeis University
Brigham Young University - Idaho
Bryant University
Cal State Long Beach
Cal State Northridge
Carnegie Mellon University
Case Western Reserve University
Centre College
City College of New York
Claremont McKenna College
Cornell University
CUNY Lehman College
CUNY Queens College
Denison University
Duquesne University
Earlham College
Eckerd College
Elmhurst College
Elmira College
Ferris State University
Florida Atlantic University

Freed-Hardeman University
Gannon University
Geneva College
Georgia State University
Grinnell College
Grove City College
Harvey Mudd College
Haverford College
Hunter College
IUPUI
Johns Hopkins University
Kenyon College
Lawrence University
Louisiana College
Loyola Marymount University
Luther College
Mercer University
Millsaps College
Montclair State University
Northeastern University
Oakwood University
Occidental College
Ohio Wesleyan University
Pomona College
Robert Morris University
Rochester Institute of Technology
Saint Leo University
Saint Louis University
Seattle University
Smith College
St. Mary's University
St. Olaf College
Stevenson University
Stony Brook University
SUNY Fredonia
Susquehanna University
Texas A&M International University
Trinity University
Truman State University
Tulane University
UC Merced
University of Chicago
University of Puget Sound
University of Rhode Island
University of Tennessee at Chattanooga
UNLV
Valparaiso University
Vassar College
Wagner College
Washington & Lee University
Wellesley College
Western Kentucky University
Whitman College
Willamette University
Youngstown State University

C

Alfred University
Allegheny College
American University
Austin College
Cal Poly Pomona
Cal State San Marcos
Claflin University
College of Charleston
College of William & Mary
Columbia University

Concordia College at Moorhead
Cornell College
Eastern Kentucky University
Elizabethtown College
Emory University
Franklin & Marshall College
Hampton University
Hanover College
Hollins University
Hood College
Illinois State University
Indiana University of Pennsylvania
Ithaca College
John Carroll University
Loyola University Chicago
Mercyhurst College
Minnesota State University - Moorhead
Muhlenberg College
Northern Arizona University
Oberlin College
Pitzer College
Purchase College
Radford University
Russell Sage College
San Francisco State University
Slippery Rock University
Southwestern University
St. Edward's University
SUNY New Paltz
Swarthmore College
Towson University
Tufts University
UC Riverside
UC San Diego
University at Albany
University at Buffalo
University of Hartford
University of Illinois at Chicago
University of Maryland Eastern Shore
University of North Carolina - Greensboro
University of San Diego
University of San Francisco
University of the Incarnate Word
Washington University in St. Louis
Wayne State University
Wesleyan University
Western Illinois University

C-

Arcadia University
Bard College
Bay Path College
Cal State Monterey Bay
Caltech
Catholic University of America
Chapman University
College of Mount Saint Vincent
College of Notre Dame of Maryland
Converse College
Fordham University
George Washington University
Goucher College
Guilford College
Hofstra University
Howard University
La Roche College
Lewis & Clark College

Massachusetts College of Art & Design
Misericordia University
Mount Holyoke College
Rhodes College
Saint Francis University
Samford University
Scripps College
Simmons College
University of Maryland Baltimore County

Barnard College
Bryn Mawr College
Clark University
College for Creative Studies
Columbia College Chicago
Fashion Institute of Technology
McGill University
New York University
Pace University
Sarah Lawrence College
UC Santa Cruz

Alverno College
Emerson College

Reed College
Rhode Island School of Design
Spelman College

Hampshire College
Marlboro College
New College of Florida

Campus Dining

Our grade on Campus Dining addresses the quality of both school-owned dining halls and independent on-campus restaurants as well as the price, availability, and variety of food.

A+

Bowdoin College
Claremont McKenna College
Colby College
Dartmouth College
Pitzer College
Stanford University
UCLA
University of Georgia
Virginia Tech
Washington University in St. Louis

A

Bryn Mawr College
Columbia University
Concordia College at Moorhead
Cornell University
Georgetown University
Hamilton College
Harvey Mudd College
James Madison University
Lewis & Clark College
Macalester College
Middlebury College
Mount Holyoke College
Muhlenberg College
Oberlin College
Pomona College
Purdue University
Scripps College
St. Olaf College
UC Davis
UC Santa Cruz
University of Massachusetts
University of Notre Dame
Wheaton College - Illinois
Yale University

A-

Babson College
Bates College
Boston College
Boston University
Colorado College
Dickinson College
Duke University
Gustavus Adolphus College
Iowa State University
Ithaca College
Louisiana State University
Miami University
New York University
Ohio State University

Penn State
Princeton University
Salisbury University
Seton Hall University
Smith College
St. Lawrence University
Texas Tech University
Tufts University
University of Alabama
University of Florida
University of Illinois
University of Iowa
University of Kentucky
University of New Hampshire
University of Oklahoma
University of Oregon
University of Puget Sound
University of San Diego
University of Texas
University of Wisconsin
Virginia Commonwealth University
Wheaton College - Massachusetts

B+

Albion College
Alverno College
American University
Arizona State University
Auburn University
Baruch College
Baylor University
Brigham Young University
Bucknell University
Cal State Long Beach
Cal State Northridge
Cleveland State University
Colgate University
College of the Holy Cross
College of Wooster
Davidson College
DePauw University
East Carolina University
Elon University
Emerson College
Franklin & Marshall College
Furman University
Gettysburg College
Grand Valley State University
Harvard University
Illinois Wesleyan University
Indiana University
Kansas State University
Kent State University
Lehigh University
Loyola University Maryland
Michigan State University
Northeastern University
Ohio Wesleyan University
Old Dominion University
Rensselaer Polytechnic Institute
Rollins College

Sacramento State
San Diego State University
Santa Clara University
Southern Methodist University
SUNY Oswego
Texas A&M University
Trinity University
UC Berkeley
UC Irvine
UC San Diego
University of Arizona
University of Central Florida
University of Chicago
University of Colorado
University of Connecticut
University of Delaware
University of Kansas
University of Miami
University of Mississippi
University of Missouri
University of Nebraska
University of San Francisco
University of South Carolina
University of South Florida
University of Southern California
University of Tampa
University of Western Ontario
University of Wisconsin - Stout
Villanova University
West Virginia University
Western Kentucky University
Whitman College
Wilkes University
Willamette University
Williams College

B

Amherst College
Ball State University
Beloit College
Binghamton University
Birmingham-Southern College
Brandeis University
Brigham Young University - Idaho
Cal Poly Pomona
Case Western Reserve University
Catholic University of America
Connecticut College
Creighton University
DePaul University
Earlham College
Elizabethtown College
Emory University
Florida A&M University
Florida Atlantic University
Florida State University
Freed-Hardeman University
George Mason University
George Washington University
Goucher College
Grinnell College

Haverford College
Hollins University
Idaho State University
Illinois State University
Indiana University of Pennsylvania
Jackson State University
Johns Hopkins University
Kenyon College
Loyola University Chicago
Manhattanville College
McGill University
Messiah College
Missouri State University
MIT
Northern Arizona University
Northwestern University
Occidental College
Ohio University
Providence College
Purchase College
Rhode Island School of Design
Rice University
Rider University
Rochester Institute of Technology
Rutgers University
Saint Francis University
Seattle University
Skidmore College
St. John's University
SUNY New Paltz
Susquehanna University
Swarthmore College
Temple University
Texas Christian University
Texas State University - San Marcos
Towson University
UC Santa Barbara
Union College
University at Albany
University of Arkansas
University of Cincinnati
University of Illinois at Chicago
University of Maryland Baltimore County
University of Michigan
University of Minnesota
University of Montana
University of North Carolina
University of Pittsburgh
University of Tennessee at Chattanooga
University of Utah
University of Vermont
University of Washington
UNLV
Valparaiso University
Vanderbilt University
Washington & Lee University
Wellesley College
Wesleyan University

B-

Brown University
Cal State Monterey Bay
Carleton College
Chapman University
Clark Atlanta University
Clemson University
College of Charleston

Columbia College Chicago
Denison University
Drexel University
Florida Southern College
Georgia State University
Hampshire College
Hofstra University
Lafayette College
Loyola Marymount University
Luther College
Mercyhurst College
Middle Tennessee State University
Minnesota State University - Moorhead
North Carolina A&T State University
North Carolina State University
Northern Illinois University
Northwestern College - Saint Paul
Oral Roberts University
Pace University
Pepperdine University
Radford University
Saint Louis University
San Francisco State University
Simmons College
Slippery Rock University
Southwestern University
St. Edward's University
Stony Brook University
Troy University
Truman State University
Tulane University
UC Merced
UC Riverside
University at Buffalo
University of Central Oklahoma
University of Denver
University of Maryland
University of Maryland Eastern Shore
University of Mount Union
University of Rhode Island
University of Richmond
University of the Incarnate Word
Wayne State University

C+

Alfred University
Allegheny College
Barnard College
Barry University
Bentley University
Bryant University
Cal Poly
California University of Pennsylvania
Chatham University
City College of New York
College of William & Mary
Converse College
Duquesne University
Eckerd College
Elmhurst College
Elmira College
Ferris State University
Georgia Tech
Gonzaga University
Hunter College
John Carroll University
Juniata College

Lawrence University
Linfield College
Manhattan College
Marlboro College
Marquette University
Massachusetts College of Art & Design
Millsaps College
Montana State University
Montclair State University
New College of Florida
North Central College
Oakwood University
Reed College
Sam Houston State University
Samford University
Sarah Lawrence College
Spelman College
St. Mary's University
SUNY Fredonia
Syracuse University
Taylor University
Texas A&M International University
Trinity College
University of Hartford
University of Maine
University of North Carolina - Greensboro
University of Pennsylvania
University of Rochester
University of South Dakota
University of Tennessee
University of Virginia
Ursinus College
Vassar College
Warren Wilson College
Washington & Jefferson College
Western Illinois University
Xavier University
Youngstown State University

C

Austin College
Bay Path College
Berea College
Bob Jones University
Cal State San Marcos
Caltech
Carnegie Mellon University
Centre College
Claflin University
Clark University
College for Creative Studies
CUNY Lehman College
CUNY Queens College
Dordt College
Eastern Kentucky University
Fashion Institute of Technology
Gannon University
Geneva College
Grove City College
Hanover College
Hastings College
Hood College
Howard University
IUPUI
Mercer University
Rhodes College
Robert Morris University

Rowan University
Saint Joseph's University
Saint Leo University
Stevenson University
Tennessee State University
University of Louisville
Wake Forest University

Belmont University
Bradley University
Centenary College of Louisiana
College of Mount Saint Vincent
College of Notre Dame of Maryland
Cornell College
Fordham University
Guilford College
Louisiana College
Misericordia University
Stetson University
West Point Military Academy

Arcadia University
Bard College
Hampton University
Russell Sage College
Wagner College

La Roche College

—

—

Campus Housing

A high Campus Housing grade indicates that dorms are clean, well-maintained, and spacious. Other determining factors include variety of dorms, proximity to classes, and social atmosphere.

Bowdoin College
Bryn Mawr College
Claremont McKenna College
Harvard University
Loyola University Maryland
Washington University in St. Louis
Wheaton College - Illinois
Yale University

Chatham University
Colby College
Elon University
Harvey Mudd College
Hollins University
Pitzer College
Reed College
Rice University
Santa Clara University
Scripps College
Smith College
Southern Methodist University
St. Edward's University
Stanford University
Trinity University
UC Merced
University of San Diego
University of Tampa
Wilkes University

Alverno College
Auburn University
Bentley University
Brigham Young University
Brown University
Cal State San Marcos
California University of Pennsylvania
College for Creative Studies
Concordia College at Moorhead
Dartmouth College
Davidson College
DePaul University
Duke University
Emory University
Freed-Hardeman University
Gonzaga University
Grand Valley State University
Hastings College
Haverford College
Johns Hopkins University
La Roche College
Lawrence University
Linfield College

Middlebury College
Mount Holyoke College
New College of Florida
Northwestern College - Saint Paul
Occidental College
Oral Roberts University
Russell Sage College
Skidmore College
Slippery Rock University
Swarthmore College
Taylor University
Texas Christian University
UC Davis
University of Alabama
University of Notre Dame
University of Puget Sound
University of Virginia
Vassar College

Amherst College
Austin College
Ball State University
Binghamton University
Bob Jones University
Brigham Young University - Idaho
Bryant University
Caltech
Cleveland State University
Colgate University
College of Wooster
Colorado College
Columbia College Chicago
Connecticut College
Converse College
DePauw University
Elmhurst College
Florida Southern College
George Washington University
Georgetown University
Georgia State University
Grinnell College
Hampshire College
Indiana University
Jackson State University
James Madison University
Lafayette College
Loyola Marymount University
Michigan State University
Muhlenberg College
Oberlin College
Pepperdine University
Providence College
Purdue University
Rhodes College
Seton Hall University
Southwestern University
St. John's University
St. Mary's University
St. Olaf College
Stevenson University
SUNY New Paltz
Texas A&M International University

Texas Tech University
Union College
University of Central Florida
University of Colorado
University of Kansas
University of Maryland Baltimore County
University of Miami
University of Richmond
University of San Francisco
University of South Carolina
University of Southern California
University of Texas
University of the Incarnate Word
University of Western Ontario
Villanova University
Wake Forest University
Washington & Jefferson College
Willamette University
Xavier University

Albion College
American University
Arizona State University
Babson College
Belmont University
Beloit College
Boston College
Bucknell University
Cal Poly
Carleton College
Catholic University of America
Centenary College of Louisiana
Centre College
Chapman University
Clark University
Clemson University
College of Charleston
College of the Holy Cross
College of William & Mary
Cornell College
Cornell University
Creighton University
CUNY Queens College
Duquesne University
Earlham College
East Carolina University
Elizabethtown College
Elmira College
Emerson College
Furman University
Gannon University
Geneva College
Gettysburg College
Hamilton College
Illinois Wesleyan University
Indiana University of Pennsylvania
Iowa State University
John Carroll University
Juniata College
Kansas State University
Kenyon College
Lehigh University

Lewis & Clark College
Louisiana State University
Macalester College
Manhattan College
Manhattanville College
Marlboro College
Massachusetts College of Art & Design
McGill University
Messiah College
Miami University
Minnesota State University - Moorhead
Misericordia University
Northeastern University
Northern Arizona University
Northwestern University
Ohio Wesleyan University
Old Dominion University
Penn State
Radford University
Rensselaer Polytechnic Institute
Rhode Island School of Design
Rider University
Saint Joseph's University
Saint Leo University
Salisbury University
Samford University
Sarah Lawrence College
Seattle University
Spelman College
St. Lawrence University
Susquehanna University
UC Irvine
UC Santa Barbara
UC Santa Cruz
UCLA
University of Arkansas
University of Chicago
University of Connecticut
University of Delaware
University of Denver
University of Florida
University of Georgia
University of Kentucky
University of Michigan
University of Minnesota
University of Mississippi
University of Missouri
University of Montana
University of Mount Union
University of New Hampshire
University of Oklahoma
University of Pittsburgh
University of Rochester
University of Tennessee at Chattanooga
University of Vermont
University of Wisconsin - Stout
Ursinus College
Vanderbilt University
Virginia Tech
Washington & Lee University
Wellesley College
Wesleyan University
West Virginia University
Wheaton College - Massachusetts
Whitman College

B-

Alfred University
Allegheny College
Barnard College
Bay Path College
Baylor University
Bradley University
Cal State Long Beach
Clark Atlanta University
Denison University
Dordt College
Drexel University
Eckerd College
Fordham University
George Mason University
Grove City College
Guilford College
Hanover College
Hood College
Illinois State University
Kent State University
Loyola University Chicago
Luther College
Mercyhurst College
Middle Tennessee State University
Missouri State University
MIT
Montana State University
North Carolina State University
North Central College
Northern Illinois University
Ohio State University
Ohio University
Pace University
Pomona College
Princeton University
Rochester Institute of Technology
Saint Louis University
San Diego State University
San Francisco State University
Simmons College
Stetson University
Stony Brook University
SUNY Fredonia
Temple University
Texas A&M University
Texas State University - San Marcos
Towson University
Trinity College
Troy University
Truman State University
Tufts University
Tulane University
UC Berkeley
University at Albany
University at Buffalo
University of Arizona
University of Illinois
University of Iowa
University of Nebraska
University of North Carolina
University of Oregon
University of Pennsylvania
University of Rhode Island
University of South Florida
University of Tennessee
University of Utah

University of Washington
University of Wisconsin
UNLV
Wayne State University
Williams College

C+

Arcadia University
Bates College
Birmingham-Southern College
Boston University
Brandeis University
Cal State Monterey Bay
Cal State Northridge
Carnegie Mellon University
Case Western Reserve University
City College of New York
Claflin University
College of Notre Dame of Maryland
Columbia University
Dickinson College
Fashion Institute of Technology
Florida A&M University
Florida Atlantic University
Florida State University
Goucher College
Gustavus Adolphus College
Howard University
Idaho State University
Marquette University
Mercer University
New York University
North Carolina A&T State University
Rollins College
Rowan University
Rutgers University
Sacramento State
Syracuse University
UC Riverside
University of Cincinnati
University of Illinois at Chicago
University of Louisville
University of Maine
University of Maryland
University of Maryland Eastern Shore
University of Massachusetts
University of North Carolina - Greensboro
Valparaiso University
Warren Wilson College
Western Kentucky University
Youngstown State University

C

Bard College
Barry University
Berea College
Cal Poly Pomona
Eastern Kentucky University
Ferris State University
Georgia Tech
Hofstra University
Hunter College
Ithaca College

Louisiana College
Millsaps College
Montclair State University
Oakwood University
Purchase College
Saint Francis University
Sam Houston State University
Tennessee State University
UC San Diego
University of Central Oklahoma
University of Hartford
University of South Dakota
Virginia Commonwealth University
Wagner College
Western Illinois University

Baruch College
College of Mount Saint Vincent
Franklin & Marshall College
IUPUI
Robert Morris University
SUNY Oswego

CUNY Lehman College
Hampton University

West Point Military Academy

—

—

Campus Strictness

A high Campus Strictness grade implies an overall lenient atmosphere, RAs are fairly tolerant, campus police are kind and helpful, and the administration's rules are flexible.

A+

Bard College
Beloit College
Claremont McKenna College
Marlboro College
McGill University
Oberlin College
Pitzer College
Swarthmore College
University of Chicago
Yale University

A

Barnard College
Bryn Mawr College
Carleton College
Colorado College
Elmhurst College
Grinnell College
Harvey Mudd College
Haverford College
La Roche College
Lawrence University
Macalester College
Pomona College
Reed College
Stanford University
University of Pennsylvania
Washington & Jefferson College
Washington University in St. Louis

A-

Binghamton University
Bowdoin College
Brown University
Caltech
Colby College
Columbia University
Cornell College
Duke University
Emerson College
George Washington University
Hamilton College
Hampshire College
Harvard University
Juniata College
Lewis & Clark College
Rice University
St. Lawrence University
Trinity College
University of Virginia
Vanderbilt University
Vassar College
Whitman College

B+

Alfred University
American University
Amherst College
Belmont University
Birmingham-Southern College
Brandeis University
Bryant University
Carnegie Mellon University
Case Western Reserve University
Centre College
College of William & Mary
Connecticut College
Cornell University
Creighton University
Eckerd College
Emory University
Hollins University
Hunter College
Illinois Wesleyan University
Johns Hopkins University
Louisiana State University
Luther College
Massachusetts College of Art & Design
Middlebury College
Mount Holyoke College
Ohio State University
Princeton University
Rhode Island School of Design
Rhodes College
Scripps College
Simmons College
Smith College
SUNY New Paltz
SUNY Oswego
Texas Christian University
Trinity University
Tufts University
UC Berkeley
UC Santa Cruz
UCLA
University at Buffalo
University of Delaware
University of Oregon
University of Puget Sound
University of Southern California
University of Texas
University of Wisconsin
UNLV
Ursinus College
Wagner College
Warren Wilson College
Williams College

B

Alverno College
Bentley University
Clark University
Clemson University

Cleveland State University
College of Mount Saint Vincent
CUNY Queens College
Dartmouth College
Davidson College
DePauw University
Drexel University
Elizabethtown College
Georgetown University
Georgia Tech
Gettysburg College
Gonzaga University
Goucher College
Hofstra University
Indiana University
Ithaca College
IUPUI
Linfield College
Loyola Marymount University
Manhattanville College
Millsaps College
Montana State University
Muhlenberg College
New York University
Northern Arizona University
Occidental College
Ohio University
Old Dominion University
Penn State
Purchase College
Rensselaer Polytechnic Institute
Rochester Institute of Technology
Rollins College
Rutgers University
San Francisco State University
Sarah Lawrence College
Southern Methodist University
Stevenson University
SUNY Fredonia
Syracuse University
Texas A&M International University
Texas State University - San Marcos
Truman State University
UC Merced
UC Santa Barbara
Union College
University at Albany
University of Cincinnati
University of Connecticut
University of Denver
University of Hartford
University of Illinois
University of Kansas
University of Maine
University of Maryland
University of Massachusetts
University of Miami
University of Michigan
University of Minnesota
University of Mississippi
University of Montana
University of North Carolina
University of North Carolina - Greensboro
University of Pittsburgh
University of Rhode Island
University of Rochester
University of San Francisco
University of South Dakota

University of Utah
University of Vermont
University of Washington
University of Western Ontario
Virginia Tech
Wesleyan University
West Virginia University
Western Illinois University
Xavier University

B-

Albion College
Allegheny College
Arcadia University
Arizona State University
Austin College
Baruch College
Cal Poly Pomona
Cal State Northridge
Chatham University
Colgate University
College of Charleston
Columbia College Chicago
DePaul University
Eastern Kentucky University
Elmira College
Elon University
Ferris State University
Florida Atlantic University
Florida State University
Franklin & Marshall College
George Mason University
Grand Valley State University
Gustavus Adolphus College
Hanover College
Howard University
Iowa State University
James Madison University
John Carroll University
Kent State University
Kenyon College
Lafayette College
Loyola University Maryland
Middle Tennessee State University
MIT
New College of Florida
North Central College
Northeastern University
Northern Illinois University
Northwestern University
Providence College
Purdue University
Rowan University
Sacramento State
Saint Joseph's University
Saint Leo University
Saint Louis University
Sam Houston State University
San Diego State University
Santa Clara University
Skidmore College
St. Mary's University
Stony Brook University
Temple University
Tennessee State University
Texas A&M University
Texas Tech University

Tulane University
UC Riverside
UC San Diego
University of Alabama
University of Arizona
University of Central Florida
University of Colorado
University of Florida
University of Georgia
University of Maryland Baltimore County
University of Notre Dame
University of South Florida
University of Wisconsin - Stout
Virginia Commonwealth University
Wake Forest University
Wayne State University

C+

Ball State University
Bates College
Bay Path College
Bradley University
Cal Poly
Cal State Long Beach
Cal State San Marcos
California University of Pennsylvania
Catholic University of America
Centenary College of Louisiana
Chapman University
College for Creative Studies
College of the Holy Cross
Converse College
CUNY Lehman College
Denison University
Duquesne University
Earlham College
East Carolina University
Fordham University
Georgia State University
Guilford College
Hood College
Indiana University of Pennsylvania
Kansas State University
Lehigh University
Loyola University Chicago
Marquette University
Michigan State University
Minnesota State University - Moorhead
Misericordia University
Montclair State University
Ohio Wesleyan University
Pace University
Russell Sage College
Salisbury University
Seattle University
Seton Hall University
Southwestern University
St. John's University
St. Olaf College
Stetson University
Taylor University
Towson University
Troy University
UC Davis
UC Irvine
University of Arkansas
University of Illinois at Chicago

University of Louisville
University of Missouri
University of Mount Union
University of New Hampshire
University of Oklahoma
University of Richmond
University of South Carolina
University of Tampa
University of Tennessee
Wilkes University
Youngstown State University

C

Auburn University
Babson College
Barry University
Boston College
Boston University
Brigham Young University
Brigham Young University - Idaho
Bucknell University
Cal State Monterey Bay
City College of New York
Clark Atlanta University
College of Notre Dame of Maryland
College of Wooster
Concordia College at Moorhead
Dordt College
Florida A&M University
Florida Southern College
Furman University
Hastings College
Idaho State University
Illinois State University
Jackson State University
Louisiana College
Mercer University
Mercyhurst College
Miami University
Missouri State University
North Carolina A&T State University
North Carolina State University
Northwestern College - Saint Paul
Oral Roberts University
Rider University
Robert Morris University
Saint Francis University
Samford University
Slippery Rock University
St. Edward's University
Susquehanna University
University of Central Oklahoma
University of Iowa
University of Kentucky
University of Nebraska
University of San Diego
University of Tennessee at Chattanooga
Washington & Lee University
Wheaton College - Illinois
Willamette University

C-

Baylor University
Dickinson College
Fashion Institute of Technology
Freed-Hardeman University
Gannon University
Geneva College
Manhattan College
Messiah College
Oakwood University
Radford University
University of the Incarnate Word
Valparaiso University
Villanova University
Western Kentucky University

D+

Berea College
Bob Jones University
Claflin University
Hampton University
University of Maryland Eastern Shore

D

Pepperdine University
Spelman College
Wheaton College - Massachusetts

D-

Grove City College
Wellesley College

F

West Point Military Academy

Computers

A high grade in Computers designates that computer labs are available, the computer network is easily accessible, and the campus's computing technology is up-to-date.

A+

Albion College
Bentley University
Bowdoin College
Bryant University
Caltech
Carnegie Mellon University
MIT
Rensselaer Polytechnic Institute
Rochester Institute of Technology
Stanford University
Wake Forest University

A

Amherst College
Babson College
Case Western Reserve University
Dartmouth College
Duke University
Elmhurst College
Elon University
Georgia Tech
Mount Holyoke College
Saint Leo University
Seton Hall University
Stetson University
Texas State University - San Marcos
University at Buffalo
University of Wisconsin - Stout
Vanderbilt University
Yale University

A-

Bay Path College
Baylor University
Beloit College
Brigham Young University - Idaho
Claremont McKenna College
Colby College
College of William & Mary
Davidson College
Earlham College
Emory University
Grand Valley State University
Harvard University
Harvey Mudd College
IUPUI
Lewis & Clark College
Louisiana State University
Manhattanville College
Middle Tennessee State University
North Carolina State University
Princeton University
Reed College
Rice University

Samford University
Scripps College
St. Lawrence University
St. Olaf College
Swarthmore College
Temple University
Texas A&M University
Texas Tech University
University of Chicago
University of Kentucky
University of Nebraska
University of Notre Dame
University of Pennsylvania
University of San Francisco
University of Texas
University of Utah
Ursinus College
Vassar College
Washington & Lee University
West Virginia University
Western Kentucky University
Whitman College

B+

Alfred University
Alverno College
Arizona State University
Ball State University
Binghamton University
Birmingham-Southern College
Boston College
Brigham Young University
Brown University
Bryn Mawr College
Bucknell University
Cal State Northridge
Cal State San Marcos
Carleton College
Centre College
Chapman University
Clark University
Clemson University
Colgate University
Cornell University
Creighton University
East Carolina University
Florida Atlantic University
Furman University
Goucher College
Grinnell College
Hamilton College
Hastings College
Indiana University
Iowa State University
Johns Hopkins University
Lehigh University
Loyola University Chicago
Loyola University Maryland
Macalester College
Middlebury College
Minnesota State University - Moorhead
Missouri State University
New College of Florida

Northern Illinois University
Penn State
Pepperdine University
Pitzer College
Pomona College
Purdue University
Radford University
Rhode Island School of Design
Rider University
Rutgers University
Sacramento State
Saint Francis University
Sam Houston State University
Simmons College
St. John's University
Stony Brook University
SUNY New Paltz
Susquehanna University
Syracuse University
Truman State University
UCLA
University of Alabama
University of Arkansas
University of Cincinnati
University of Florida
University of Georgia
University of Illinois
University of Iowa
University of Kansas
University of Miami
University of Michigan
University of Minnesota
University of Missouri
University of North Carolina
University of Oklahoma
University of Pittsburgh
University of Puget Sound
University of South Carolina
University of South Dakota
University of South Florida
University of Southern California
University of Tennessee
University of Wisconsin
UNLV
Villanova University
Virginia Tech
Wesleyan University
West Point Military Academy
Willamette University
Xavier University

B

Auburn University
Barnard College
Barry University
Baruch College
Bates College
Berea College
Bradley University
Brandeis University
Cal Poly
Cal State Long Beach
California University of Pennsylvania

Catholic University of America
Centenary College of Louisiana
Chatham University
Clark Atlanta University
Cleveland State University
College for Creative Studies
College of the Holy Cross
Colorado College
Columbia College Chicago
Columbia University
Concordia College at Moorhead
Converse College
Denison University
DePaul University
Dickinson College
Drexel University
Eckerd College
Florida State University
Fordham University
Franklin & Marshall College
Georgia State University
Gettysburg College
Gonzaga University
Guilford College
Gustavus Adolphus College
Haverford College
Idaho State University
Illinois State University
Illinois Wesleyan University
Jackson State University
James Madison University
John Carroll University
Juniata College
Kansas State University
Kent State University
Lafayette College
Lawrence University
Linfield College
Loyola Marymount University
Luther College
Messiah College
Miami University
Northeastern University
Northwestern University
Oberlin College
Ohio State University
Ohio University
Ohio Wesleyan University
Pace University
Rhodes College
Robert Morris University
Rollins College
Rowan University
San Diego State University
Santa Clara University
Skidmore College
Southwestern University
Spelman College
St. Edward's University
SUNY Fredonia
Texas A&M International University
Texas Christian University
Trinity University
Troy University
Tufts University
Tulane University
UC Berkeley
UC Davis
UC Irvine
UC Merced
UC Riverside
UC San Diego

Union College
University of Arizona
University of Central Florida
University of Colorado
University of Denver
University of Hartford
University of Illinois at Chicago
University of Maine
University of Maryland
University of Massachusetts
University of Mississippi
University of Mount Union
University of New Hampshire
University of North Carolina - Greensboro
University of Richmond
University of San Diego
University of Tampa
University of Vermont
University of Virginia
University of Washington
University of Western Ontario
Valparaiso University
Virginia Commonwealth University
Washington & Jefferson College
Washington University in St. Louis
Wayne State University
Wellesley College
Wheaton College - Massachusetts

American University
Belmont University
Boston University
Cal Poly Pomona
Cal State Monterey Bay
College of Wooster
CUNY Lehman College
DePauw University
Dordt College
Emerson College
Freed-Hardeman University
Gannon University
George Mason University
George Washington University
Grove City College
Hampshire College
Hofstra University
Hollins University
Hunter College
Indiana University of Pennsylvania
Ithaca College
Kenyon College
Manhattan College
Marquette University
Massachusetts College of Art & Design
Mercyhurst College
Michigan State University
Millsaps College
Montana State University
Montclair State University
Muhlenberg College
New York University
North Central College
Northern Arizona University
Northwestern College - Saint Paul
Occidental College
Oral Roberts University

Salisbury University
Sarah Lawrence College
Seattle University
Slippery Rock University
SUNY Oswego
Taylor University
Trinity College
University at Albany
University of Central Oklahoma
University of Connecticut
University of Delaware
University of Maryland Baltimore County
University of Rochester
University of Tennessee at Chattanooga
Wilkes University
Williams College

Arcadia University
Austin College
Bob Jones University
City College of New York
College of Charleston
College of Notre Dame of Maryland
Cornell College
Eastern Kentucky University
Elizabethtown College
Ferris State University
Florida A&M University
Hanover College
Marlboro College
Mercer University
Misericordia University
North Carolina A&T State University
Oakwood University
Old Dominion University
Providence College
Saint Joseph's University
Saint Louis University
Smith College
Southern Methodist University
Stevenson University
Towson University
UC Santa Barbara
UC Santa Cruz
University of Louisville
University of Montana
University of Oregon
University of Rhode Island
University of the Incarnate Word
Wheaton College - Illinois
Youngstown State University

Allegheny College
Connecticut College
CUNY Queens College
Elmira College
Georgetown University
Hampton University
La Roche College
McGill University
Purchase College

San Francisco State University
St. Mary's University
Tennessee State University
University of Maryland Eastern Shore
Wagner College
Warren Wilson College
Western Illinois University

Bard College
Duquesne University
Fashion Institute of Technology
Geneva College
Hood College
Russell Sage College

Claflin University
College of Mount Saint Vincent
Florida Southern College
Howard University
Louisiana College

—

—

—

Diversity

A high grade in Diversity indicates that ethnic minorities and international students have a notable presence on campus and that students of different economic backgrounds, religious beliefs, and sexual preferences are well-represented and accepted by other students.

Barry University
Baruch College
Carnegie Mellon University
City College of New York
MIT
Mount Holyoke College
Princeton University
Stanford University
Swarthmore College

Boston University
Cal State Long Beach
Caltech
Columbia University
Fashion Institute of Technology
George Mason University
Georgia State University
Harvard University
Hunter College
Occidental College
San Francisco State University
Stony Brook University
UC Riverside
University of Maryland Baltimore County
University of Miami
University of Texas
Virginia Commonwealth University
Wellesley College
Yale University

Amherst College
Babson College
Binghamton University
Brown University
Cal Poly Pomona
Cal State Northridge
CUNY Lehman College
Dartmouth College
Duke University
Johns Hopkins University
Manhattanville College
Montclair State University
New York University
Rice University
St. Edward's University
St. John's University
SUNY New Paltz
UC Berkeley
UC Merced
UCLA
University of Chicago
University of Illinois at Chicago

University of Pennsylvania
University of San Francisco
University of Southern California
Wayne State University
Wesleyan University

American University
Brandeis University
Case Western Reserve University
Claremont McKenna College
College for Creative Studies
Columbia College Chicago
Cornell University
CUNY Queens College
DePaul University
Drexel University
Emory University
George Washington University
Georgetown University
Macalester College
Massachusetts College of Art & Design
Northeastern University
Oberlin College
Oral Roberts University
Pace University
Pepperdine University
Pitzer College
Pomona College
Rhode Island School of Design
Rutgers University
Sacramento State
San Diego State University
Seattle University
Seton Hall University
Smith College
Temple University
Troy University
Tufts University
University at Buffalo
University of Rochester
University of South Florida
University of Tampa
University of Washington
UNLV
Williams College

Arizona State University
Austin College
Bard College
Barnard College
Bay Path College
Berea College
Bowdoin College
Bryn Mawr College
Chatham University
College of Mount Saint Vincent
College of William & Mary

Florida Atlantic University
Florida State University
Georgia Tech
Grinnell College
Harvey Mudd College
Haverford College
Indiana University
IUPUI
Loyola Marymount University
Loyola University Chicago
McGill University
Mercer University
Michigan State University
Middlebury College
Northwestern University
Purdue University
Rider University
Saint Leo University
Syracuse University
Texas State University - San Marcos
Tulane University
UC Davis
UC Santa Cruz
University of Arizona
University of Central Florida
University of Central Oklahoma
University of Florida
University of Hartford
University of Illinois
University of Maryland
University of Michigan
University of North Carolina - Greensboro
University of the Incarnate Word

Arcadia University
Cal State San Marcos
Carleton College
Chapman University
Cleveland State University
Colby College
College of Notre Dame of Maryland
Converse College
East Carolina University
Florida Southern College
Fordham University
Guilford College
Hamilton College
Hofstra University
Howard University
Iowa State University
Ithaca College
Lewis & Clark College
Linfield College
Middle Tennessee State University
North Carolina State University
Northern Arizona University
Northern Illinois University
Ohio State University
Old Dominion University
Purchase College
Rochester Institute of Technology
Sam Houston State University

Santa Clara University
St. Mary's University
Stevenson University
Towson University
UC Irvine
UC San Diego
UC Santa Barbara
University of Cincinnati
University of Connecticut
University of Denver
University of Kansas
University of Louisville
University of Maryland Eastern Shore
University of Massachusetts
University of Minnesota
University of North Carolina
University of Oklahoma
University of Oregon
University of South Carolina
University of Tennessee at Chattanooga
University of Utah
University of Virginia
University of Wisconsin
Vanderbilt University
Vassar College
Washington University in St. Louis
Western Kentucky University

Southern Methodist University
St. Lawrence University
Stetson University
SUNY Fredonia
Taylor University
Texas A&M University
Texas Christian University
Trinity College
University of Alabama
University of Arkansas
University of Colorado
University of Delaware
University of Georgia
University of Kentucky
University of Missouri
University of Nebraska
University of Pittsburgh
University of Rhode Island
University of San Diego
University of Western Ontario
Virginia Tech
West Point Military Academy
West Virginia University
Western Illinois University
Whitman College
Willamette University
Youngstown State University

Skidmore College
Slippery Rock University
SUNY Oswego
Tennessee State University
Texas A&M International University
Texas Tech University
Trinity University
University at Albany
University of Iowa
University of Maine
University of Montana
University of Mount Union
University of New Hampshire
University of Notre Dame
University of Richmond
University of Tennessee
University of Vermont
Ursinus College
Valparaiso University
Villanova University
Wagner College
Wake Forest University
Wheaton College - Massachusetts

Bates College
Baylor University
Bentley University
Bryant University
Cal Poly
Cal State Monterey Bay
Catholic University of America
Claflin University
Clark Atlanta University
Concordia College at Moorhead
Cornell College
Eckerd College
Elmhurst College
Elmira College
Grand Valley State University
Hood College
Illinois State University
Indiana University of Pennsylvania
James Madison University
Kansas State University
Kent State University
Lawrence University
Louisiana State University
Mercyhurst College
Minnesota State University - Moorhead
Missouri State University
Montana State University
Oakwood University
Ohio University
Penn State
Reed College
Rensselaer Polytechnic Institute
Rhodes College
Robert Morris University
Rowan University
Russell Sage College
Salisbury University
Scripps College

Alverno College
Ball State University
Boston College
Brigham Young University
Brigham Young University - Idaho
California University of Pennsylvania
Clark University
Colgate University
Colorado College
Connecticut College
Davidson College
Dickinson College
Dordt College
Duquesne University
Earlham College
Eastern Kentucky University
Elizabethtown College
Elon University
Emerson College
Ferris State University
Franklin & Marshall College
Freed-Hardeman University
Gannon University
Geneva College
Hampshire College
Hanover College
Jackson State University
La Roche College
Lehigh University
Louisiana College
Manhattan College
Millsaps College
Muhlenberg College
North Carolina A&T State University
North Central College
Rollins College
Saint Louis University
Simmons College

Allegheny College
Auburn University
Beloit College
Bob Jones University
Bucknell University
Centenary College of Louisiana
Clemson University
Creighton University
Denison University
Florida A&M University
Gonzaga University
Hampton University
Hollins University
John Carroll University
Kenyon College
Lafayette College
Messiah College
Misericordia University
New College of Florida
Ohio Wesleyan University
Saint Francis University
Sarah Lawrence College
Southwestern University
Union College
University of Puget Sound
Wheaton College - Illinois
Xavier University

Alfred University
Bradley University
College of Charleston
College of the Holy Cross
College of Wooster
DePauw University
Furman University
Gettysburg College
Idaho State University

Loyola University Maryland
Luther College
Marlboro College
Marquette University
Miami University
Northwestern College - Saint Paul
Providence College
Saint Joseph's University
Samford University
Spelman College
Truman State University
University of Mississippi
Warren Wilson College

Albion College
Belmont University
Birmingham-Southern College
Centre College
Goucher College
Illinois Wesleyan University
Juniata College
Radford University
St. Olaf College
Susquehanna University
Washington & Lee University

Grove City College
Gustavus Adolphus College
Hastings College
University of South Dakota
University of Wisconsin - Stout
Washington & Jefferson College
Wilkes University

—

Drug Safety

A high grade in Drug Safety indicates that drugs are not a noticeable part of campus life; drug use is not visible, and no pressure to use them seems to exist.

A+

Alverno College
Brigham Young University
Brigham Young University - Idaho
Freed-Hardeman University
Northwestern College - Saint Paul
Oral Roberts University
Taylor University
West Point Military Academy
Wheaton College - Illinois

A

Bob Jones University
Caltech
Grove City College
Spelman College
Wellesley College

A-

CUNY Lehman College
CUNY Queens College
Furman University
Geneva College
Harvey Mudd College
Idaho State University
Juniata College
MIT
Rensselaer Polytechnic Institute
University of Chicago
Williams College

B+

Barnard College
Bay Path College
Bryn Mawr College
Catholic University of America
Centre College
Converse College
Davidson College
Harvard University
Haverford College
Hollins University
La Roche College
McGill University
Messiah College
Millsaps College
Pepperdine University
Rice University
Scripps College
Southwestern University

Tennessee State University
University of the Incarnate Word
Whitman College
Xavier University

B

Amherst College
Babson College
Baruch College
Baylor University
Belmont University
Birmingham-Southern College
Brown University
Centenary College of Louisiana
Clark Atlanta University
Colgate University
College of Wooster
Creighton University
Earlham College
Emerson College
Florida A&M University
Florida Atlantic University
Gonzaga University
Hastings College
Illinois Wesleyan University
Lawrence University
Luther College
Manhattanville College
Middlebury College
New College of Florida
Samford University
Seattle University
Simmons College
St. Edward's University
St. Olaf College
Stetson University
Trinity University
Truman State University
Tufts University
University of Central Oklahoma
University of Pennsylvania
University of Puget Sound
Ursinus College
Washington & Lee University
Wheaton College - Massachusetts

B-

Alfred University
Beloit College
Berea College
Bradley University
Cal State Long Beach
Carnegie Mellon University
Chatham University
City College of New York
Claflin University
Clark University
College of the Holy Cross
Columbia University

Concordia College at Moorhead
Connecticut College
Dartmouth College
Dordt College
Florida Southern College
Franklin & Marshall College
Gannon University
Georgia State University
Goucher College
Grand Valley State University
Hunter College
Louisiana College
Manhattan College
Middle Tennessee State University
Misericordia University
Missouri State University
Occidental College
Pomona College
Princeton University
Providence College
Radford University
Robert Morris University
Rowan University
Sacramento State
St. Mary's University
Stanford University
Susquehanna University
Swarthmore College
Texas A&M University
Tulane University
University of Arkansas
University of Maryland Baltimore County
University of North Carolina - Greensboro
University of Oklahoma
University of Utah
University of Wisconsin - Stout
UNLV
Villanova University
Wayne State University
Willamette University

C+

Albion College
Allegheny College
Auburn University
Barry University
Brandeis University
Bucknell University
Cal State Northridge
Cal State San Marcos
California University of Pennsylvania
Carleton College
Chapman University
Cleveland State University
College for Creative Studies
College of Notre Dame of Maryland
College of William & Mary
Columbia College Chicago
Cornell University
Denison University
DePauw University
Dickinson College
Duquesne University

East Carolina University
Elizabethtown College
Elmhurst College
Elon University
George Mason University
Gettysburg College
Gustavus Adolphus College
Hood College
Howard University
IUPUI
Jackson State University
John Carroll University
Kenyon College
Lafayette College
Lehigh University
Loyola Marymount University
Loyola University Maryland
Marlboro College
Marquette University
Mercer University
Mercyhurst College
Minnesota State University - Moorhead
Montclair State University
Mount Holyoke College
New York University
North Carolina A&T State University
North Carolina State University
North Central College
Northern Illinois University
Oakwood University
Ohio Wesleyan University
Old Dominion University
Rhode Island School of Design
Russell Sage College
Saint Francis University
Sam Houston State University
San Diego State University
San Francisco State University
Seton Hall University
Slippery Rock University
Stevenson University
Towson University
Troy University
UC Davis
UC Irvine
UC Merced
UC San Diego
Union College
University of Delaware
University of Hartford
University of Illinois at Chicago
University of Kansas
University of Louisville
University of Miami
University of Michigan
University of Missouri
University of Nebraska
University of New Hampshire
University of North Carolina
University of Notre Dame
University of Richmond
University of Rochester
University of South Dakota
University of South Florida
University of Western Ontario
Valparaiso University
Warren Wilson College
Washington & Jefferson College
Wesleyan University
Wilkes University

Arizona State University
Austin College
Ball State University
Bentley University
Binghamton University
Cal Poly
Cal Poly Pomona
Case Western Reserve University
Claremont McKenna College
Colby College
Cornell College
DePaul University
Drexel University
Eastern Kentucky University
Elmira College
Emory University
Georgia Tech
Grinnell College
Guilford College
Hampshire College
Hampton University
Hanover College
Iowa State University
Kansas State University
Lewis & Clark College
Louisiana State University
Macalester College
Michigan State University
Montana State University
Muhlenberg College
Northern Arizona University
Northwestern University
Oberlin College
Purdue University
Reed College
Rider University
Salisbury University
Skidmore College
Southern Methodist University
St. John's University
Stony Brook University
Texas A&M International University
Texas State University - San Marcos
Texas Tech University
UC Riverside
University of Central Florida
University of Florida
University of Kentucky
University of Maine
University of Maryland
University of Maryland Eastern Shore
University of Minnesota
University of Mount Union
University of Oregon
University of San Diego
University of Southern California
University of Tennessee
University of Tennessee at Chattanooga
University of Texas
University of Virginia
University of Washington
Virginia Commonwealth University
Virginia Tech
Wake Forest University
Washington University in St. Louis

West Virginia University
Western Kentucky University

American University
Arcadia University
Bard College
Bates College
Boston College
Boston University
Bowdoin College
Bryant University
Cal State Monterey Bay
Clemson University
College of Mount Saint Vincent
Colorado College
Fashion Institute of Technology
Ferris State University
Florida State University
Fordham University
George Washington University
Hamilton College
Hofstra University
Illinois State University
Indiana University
Ithaca College
James Madison University
Kent State University
Linfield College
Loyola University Chicago
Massachusetts College of Art & Design
Northeastern University
Ohio University
Pace University
Penn State
Pitzer College
Rhodes College
Rochester Institute of Technology
Rollins College
Rutgers University
Saint Leo University
Sarah Lawrence College
Smith College
St. Lawrence University
SUNY Fredonia
SUNY New Paltz
SUNY Oswego
Syracuse University
Temple University
Texas Christian University
UC Berkeley
UC Santa Barbara
UCLA
University at Albany
University at Buffalo
University of Arizona
University of Cincinnati
University of Connecticut
University of Denver
University of Georgia
University of Illinois
University of Iowa
University of Pittsburgh
University of San Francisco
University of South Carolina
University of Tampa
University of Vermont

University of Wisconsin
Vanderbilt University
Vassar College
Wagner College
Western Illinois University
Youngstown State University

College of Charleston
Duke University
Eckerd College
Georgetown University
Indiana University of Pennsylvania
Johns Hopkins University
Miami University
Ohio State University
Purchase College
Saint Joseph's University
Saint Louis University
Santa Clara University
Trinity College
UC Santa Cruz
University of Alabama
University of Colorado
University of Massachusetts
University of Mississippi
University of Montana
University of Rhode Island
Yale University

—

—

—

Facilities

A high Facilities grade indicates that the campus is aesthetically pleasing and well-maintained; facilities are state-of-the-art, and libraries are exceptional. Other determining factors include the quality of both athletic and student centers and an abundance of things to do on campus.

Amherst College
Auburn University
Belmont University
Bowdoin College
Hamilton College
Mount Holyoke College
Ohio State University
Smith College
St. Lawrence University
Stanford University
University of Georgia
University of Notre Dame
Yale University

Brigham Young University
Colby College
Duke University
Elmhurst College
Emory University
Grand Valley State University
Louisiana State University
Loyola Marymount University
Middlebury College
Muhlenberg College
Southern Methodist University
St. Olaf College
Susquehanna University
Swarthmore College
Texas Christian University
Texas Tech University
University of Alabama
University of North Carolina
University of Oklahoma
University of Southern California
Washington University in St. Louis

Arizona State University
Babson College
Baylor University
Birmingham-Southern College
Brigham Young University - Idaho
Bucknell University
Centre College
Colgate University
Columbia University
Cornell University
Davidson College
East Carolina University
Elon University
Florida State University
Franklin & Marshall College
Gustavus Adolphus College

Harvard University
Harvey Mudd College
Hollins University
Idaho State University
Indiana University
Iowa State University
James Madison University
Juniata College
Kansas State University
Lafayette College
Linfield College
Loyola University Maryland
Manhattanville College
Messiah College
Missouri State University
Oberlin College
Ohio University
Penn State
Pepperdine University
Pitzer College
Rollins College
Salisbury University
Santa Clara University
Scripps College
Seton Hall University
Slippery Rock University
Texas A&M University
Texas State University - San Marcos
UC Berkeley
UCLA
University of Arizona
University of Central Florida
University of Denver
University of Kentucky
University of Maryland
University of Miami
University of Michigan
University of Missouri
University of New Hampshire
University of South Carolina
University of Texas
Vassar College
Virginia Tech
Wellesley College
Wheaton College - Illinois
Williams College

Albion College
Alfred University
Alverno College
Ball State University
Bryn Mawr College
Cal State Long Beach
Caltech
Carleton College
College of William & Mary
Columbia College Chicago
Concordia College at Moorhead
Connecticut College
Converse College
DePaul University
DePauw University

Dickinson College
Dordt College
Earlham College
Florida Atlantic University
Freed-Hardeman University
Furman University
Georgetown University
Gettysburg College
Grinnell College
Hanover College
Hastings College
Haverford College
Illinois Wesleyan University
Ithaca College
Johns Hopkins University
Kent State University
La Roche College
Lehigh University
Lewis & Clark College
MIT
Northeastern University
Northern Arizona University
Northwestern University
Ohio Wesleyan University
Old Dominion University
Pomona College
Princeton University
Reed College
Rensselaer Polytechnic Institute
Rhodes College
Rice University
Robert Morris University
Rowan University
Saint Louis University
Skidmore College
St. John's University
Temple University
Truman State University
Tulane University
UC Davis
UC Irvine
UC Merced
UC San Diego
University of Central Oklahoma
University of Chicago
University of Colorado
University of Connecticut
University of Florida
University of Illinois
University of Iowa
University of Kansas
University of Minnesota
University of Mount Union
University of Nebraska
University of Oregon
University of Pennsylvania
University of Rochester
University of San Diego
University of San Francisco
University of South Florida
University of Tennessee at Chattanooga
University of Utah
University of Virginia
University of Washington
University of Wisconsin
UNLV
Ursinus College
Wake Forest University

Washington & Lee University
Wesleyan University
West Point Military Academy
West Virginia University
Western Kentucky University
Wheaton College - Massachusetts
Xavier University

Allegheny College
Bates College
Bentley University
Bob Jones University
Boston College
Boston University
Brown University
Cal Poly
Cal State Northridge
California University of Pennsylvania
Carnegie Mellon University
Centenary College of Louisiana
Chapman University
Clark Atlanta University
Clemson University
Cleveland State University
College of the Holy Cross
College of Wooster
Creighton University
Dartmouth College
Denison University
Duquesne University
Emerson College
Florida Southern College
George Mason University
George Washington University
Georgia State University
Georgia Tech
Gonzaga University
Guilford College
Illinois State University
IUPUI
Kenyon College
Lawrence University
Luther College
Macalester College
Marlboro College
Miami University
Michigan State University
Middle Tennessee State University
Minnesota State University - Moorhead
Misericordia University
Montana State University
New York University
North Carolina A&T State University
Providence College
Purdue University
Radford University
Rider University
Rochester Institute of Technology
Rutgers University
Sam Houston State University
Samford University
San Diego State University
Seattle University
Simmons College
Southwestern University
St. Edward's University

Stetson University
SUNY New Paltz
Syracuse University
Tennessee State University
Trinity College
Trinity University
Troy University
Tufts University
UC Riverside
UC Santa Barbara
UC Santa Cruz
Union College
University at Buffalo
University of Arkansas
University of Cincinnati
University of Maine
University of Maryland Baltimore County
University of Mississippi
University of Montana
University of Pittsburgh
University of Puget Sound
University of Rhode Island
University of Richmond
University of Tennessee
University of the Incarnate Word
University of Vermont
University of Western Ontario
University of Wisconsin - Stout
Valparaiso University
Vanderbilt University
Villanova University
Washington & Jefferson College
Wayne State University
Whitman College
Wilkes University
Willamette University

American University
Austin College
Barnard College
Bay Path College
Beloit College
Binghamton University
Cal Poly Pomona
Cal State San Marcos
Case Western Reserve University
Claremont McKenna College
College of Charleston
Colorado College
CUNY Lehman College
Eckerd College
Florida A&M University
Fordham University
Grove City College
Hofstra University
Indiana University of Pennsylvania
Jackson State University
Loyola University Chicago
Manhattan College
Marquette University
Mercer University
Mercyhurst College
Montclair State University
North Carolina State University
North Central College
Northwestern College - Saint Paul

Oral Roberts University
Rhode Island School of Design
Sacramento State
Saint Francis University
Sarah Lawrence College
Spelman College
SUNY Fredonia
Taylor University
Towson University
University of Delaware
University of Hartford
University of Illinois at Chicago
University of Louisville
University of Maryland Eastern Shore
University of Massachusetts
University of North Carolina - Greensboro
University of South Dakota
University of Tampa
Virginia Commonwealth University
Warren Wilson College
Western Illinois University

Bard College
Baruch College
Berea College
Bryant University
Catholic University of America
Chatham University
Clark University
College for Creative Studies
Cornell College
Drexel University
Eastern Kentucky University
Elizabethtown College
Ferris State University
Goucher College
Hampshire College
John Carroll University
McGill University
Millsaps College
New College of Florida
Northern Illinois University
Occidental College
Purchase College
Saint Leo University
Stevenson University
Stony Brook University
SUNY Oswego
Texas A&M International University
University at Albany
Youngstown State University

Bradley University
Brandeis University
Cal State Monterey Bay
City College of New York
Elmira College
Gannon University
Hood College
Saint Joseph's University
San Francisco State University

St. Mary's University
Wagner College

Barry University
Claflin University
College of Notre Dame of Maryland
CUNY Queens College
Fashion Institute of Technology
Geneva College
Howard University
Hunter College
Massachusetts College of Art & Design
Pace University
Russell Sage College

Arcadia University
College of Mount Saint Vincent
Hampton University
Louisiana College
Oakwood University

—

—

—

Girls

A high grade for Girls not only implies that the women on campus are attractive, smart, friendly, and engaging, but also that there is a fair ratio of girls to guys.

A+

Clemson University
Duke University
Florida State University
Freed-Hardeman University
Loyola University Maryland
Ohio University
Oral Roberts University
Pepperdine University
St. Olaf College
Stanford University
Texas A&M University
University of Alabama
University of Kansas
University of Mississippi
University of Tampa
Vanderbilt University

A

Boston College
Brigham Young University
Brigham Young University - Idaho
Colby College
Colgate University
Concordia College at Moorhead
DePauw University
Elmhurst College
Emory University
Florida A&M University
Florida Southern College
Georgetown University
Georgia State University
Gonzaga University
Hamilton College
Howard University
Illinois State University
James Madison University
Michigan State University
Muhlenberg College
Northern Illinois University
Penn State
Pitzer College
Rollins College
Southern Methodist University
St. Edward's University
Taylor University
Texas State University - San Marcos
UC Davis
UC Santa Barbara
University of Florida
University of Illinois
University of Missouri
University of Texas
University of Vermont
University of Virginia
University of Western Ontario
Villanova University
Virginia Tech
West Virginia University

Wheaton College - Illinois
Yale University

A-

Alverno College
Auburn University
Belmont University
Birmingham-Southern College
Bowdoin College
Bucknell University
Cal Poly
Cal State Long Beach
Claremont McKenna College
Cleveland State University
College for Creative Studies
Colorado College
Dickinson College
Dordt College
Elon University
Emerson College
Gustavus Adolphus College
Indiana University
Ithaca College
Kent State University
Lewis & Clark College
Linfield College
McGill University
Miami University
Middlebury College
Mount Holyoke College
New York University
Oberlin College
Providence College
Saint Francis University
Saint Louis University
San Diego State University
Scripps College
Seattle University
Seton Hall University
Smith College
St. Lawrence University
Susquehanna University
Tennessee State University
Trinity College
Trinity University
UC Santa Cruz
UCLA
University of Kentucky
University of Miami
University of Minnesota
University of Nebraska
University of North Carolina
University of Oklahoma
University of Rhode Island
University of Richmond
University of Rochester
University of South Carolina
University of Southern California
Wake Forest University

B+

Albion College
Arizona State University
Barnard College
Bates College
Cal Poly Pomona
Cal State San Marcos
Catholic University of America
City College of New York
Clark Atlanta University
College of Charleston
College of the Holy Cross
College of William & Mary
Connecticut College
Converse College
CUNY Lehman College
Denison University
Duquesne University
East Carolina University
Fordham University
Furman University
Guilford College
Hampton University
Hastings College
Hollins University
Idaho State University
John Carroll University
La Roche College
Lafayette College
Louisiana College
Louisiana State University
Macalester College
Manhattan College
Manhattanville College
Messiah College
Montana State University
Northwestern College - Saint Paul
Northwestern University
Occidental College
Ohio State University
Ohio Wesleyan University
Radford University
Rhode Island School of Design
Rhodes College
Rowan University
Rutgers University
Santa Clara University
Sarah Lawrence College
Simmons College
Skidmore College
Southwestern University
Spelman College
Stetson University
SUNY Fredonia
Texas Tech University
Tulane University
UC Merced
Union College
University of Arizona
University of Central Florida
University of Cincinnati
University of Delaware
University of Georgia

University of Maine
University of Maryland Baltimore County
University of Michigan
University of New Hampshire
University of Oregon
University of San Diego
University of Wisconsin
Ursinus College
Vassar College
Virginia Commonwealth University
Wagner College
Warren Wilson College
Washington & Lee University
Wheaton College - Massachusetts
Whitman College
Willamette University

B

Amherst College
Austin College
Bard College
Baruch College
Bentley University
Boston University
Bradley University
Brown University
Bryant University
Centenary College of Louisiana
Centre College
Chapman University
Chatham University
College of Wooster
Columbia College Chicago
Cornell University
Creighton University
Davidson College
Drexel University
Earlham College
Eastern Kentucky University
Eckerd College
Fashion Institute of Technology
Florida Atlantic University
Franklin & Marshall College
Gettysburg College
Grand Valley State University
Hanover College
Hood College
Hunter College
Illinois Wesleyan University
Jackson State University
Juniata College
Kansas State University
Lehigh University
Loyola Marymount University
Luther College
Marlboro College
Massachusetts College of Art & Design
Middle Tennessee State University
Millsaps College
Minnesota State University - Moorhead
Misericordia University
Montclair State University
New College of Florida
North Carolina A&T State University
Northeastern University
Oakwood University
Old Dominion University

Princeton University
Purdue University
Reed College
Russell Sage College
Sacramento State
Slippery Rock University
St. John's University
St. Mary's University
SUNY New Paltz
Swarthmore College
Temple University
Texas Christian University
Towson University
Troy University
UC Berkeley
UC Irvine
University at Albany
University of Arkansas
University of Connecticut
University of Denver
University of Hartford
University of Iowa
University of Louisville
University of Maryland
University of Massachusetts
University of Montana
University of Notre Dame
University of Pittsburgh
University of San Francisco
University of South Florida
University of Tennessee
University of the Incarnate Word
University of Utah
University of Wisconsin - Stout
Wellesley College
Western Kentucky University
Wilkes University

B-

Alfred University
Bay Path College
Baylor University
Binghamton University
Bob Jones University
Brandeis University
Bryn Mawr College
Cal State Northridge
Case Western Reserve University
Clark University
College of Notre Dame of Maryland
Columbia University
Dartmouth College
DePaul University
Elizabethtown College
Elmira College
Geneva College
George Mason University
Goucher College
Hampshire College
Harvard University
Haverford College
Hofstra University
Indiana University of Pennsylvania
Iowa State University
Johns Hopkins University
Kenyon College
Loyola University Chicago

Marquette University
Mercer University
Missouri State University
North Carolina State University
North Central College
Northern Arizona University
Pomona College
Rice University
Robert Morris University
Rochester Institute of Technology
Saint Joseph's University
Salisbury University
Samford University
San Francisco State University
Stevenson University
Syracuse University
Texas A&M International University
University at Buffalo
University of Central Oklahoma
University of Colorado
University of Illinois at Chicago
University of Maryland Eastern Shore
University of Mount Union
University of North Carolina - Greensboro
University of Pennsylvania
University of Puget Sound
University of South Dakota
University of Tennessee at Chattanooga
University of Washington
UNLV
Wayne State University
Western Illinois University
Xavier University

C+

Allegheny College
American University
Arcadia University
Babson College
Ball State University
Barry University
Berea College
Carnegie Mellon University
Claflin University
Cornell College
CUNY Queens College
Ferris State University
Gannon University
Grinnell College
Grove City College
IUPUI
Lawrence University
Mercyhurst College
MIT
Pace University
Rensselaer Polytechnic Institute
Rider University
Saint Leo University
Sam Houston State University
Stony Brook University
SUNY Oswego
Truman State University
Tufts University
UC Riverside
University of Chicago
Valparaiso University
Washington University in St. Louis

Wesleyan University
Williams College

College of Mount Saint Vincent
Harvey Mudd College
Purchase College
Washington & Jefferson College

Beloit College
Cal State Monterey Bay
California University of Pennsylvania
Caltech
Carleton College
George Washington University
Georgia Tech
UC San Diego
West Point Military Academy
Youngstown State University

—

—

—

—

—

Greek Life

A high grade in Greek Life indicates that sororities and fraternities are not only present but active on campus. Other determining factors include the variety of houses available and the respect the Greek community receives from the rest of the campus.

A+

Austin College
Birmingham-Southern College
Bucknell University
Centre College
Cornell University
DePauw University
Duke University
Emory University
Gannon University
Kansas State University
Lehigh University
Millsaps College
MIT
University of Illinois
University of Richmond
Vanderbilt University
Washington & Lee University
Washington University in St. Louis

Clark Atlanta University
Colgate University
Davidson College
Denison University
East Carolina University
Elon University
Franklin & Marshall College
Hanover College
Rensselaer Polytechnic Institute
Rhodes College
Stetson University
Syracuse University
Truman State University
Tulane University
UC Berkeley
UCLA
University of Alabama
University of Kentucky
University of Missouri
University of Oklahoma
University of Rochester
University of Southern California
Wake Forest University
Washington & Jefferson College

Clemson University
College of William & Mary
George Washington University
Georgia Tech
Hastings College
Illinois State University
James Madison University
Kenyon College
Lawrence University
Linfield College
Louisiana State University
Loyola Marymount University
Michigan State University
Middle Tennessee State University
Muhlenberg College
North Carolina A&T State University
Northern Illinois University
Pace University
Purdue University
Rider University
Rochester Institute of Technology
Sam Houston State University
Seton Hall University
Spelman College
Stanford University
SUNY Fredonia
Tennessee State University
Texas A&M University
Texas Tech University
Troy University
University of Central Oklahoma
University of Denver
University of Georgia
University of Louisville
University of Maryland Eastern Shore
University of Nebraska
University of New Hampshire
University of North Carolina
University of Oregon
University of Puget Sound
University of San Diego
University of South Florida
University of Tennessee
University of Texas
University of the Incarnate Word
University of Utah
University of Vermont
University of Wisconsin
Valparaiso University
Villanova University
Wagner College
West Virginia University
Whitman College

A

Belmont University
Centenary College of Louisiana
Chapman University
Dartmouth College
Furman University
Gettysburg College
Illinois Wesleyan University
Iowa State University
Jackson State University
Johns Hopkins University
Lafayette College
Mercer University
Northwestern University
Ohio Wesleyan University
Radford University
Rollins College
Southern Methodist University
Southwestern University
Texas Christian University
Trinity College
Union College
University of Arkansas
University of Cincinnati
University of Florida
University of Michigan
University of Pennsylvania
Ursinus College

B+

Allegheny College
Creighton University
Dickinson College
Florida A&M University
Florida Southern College
Florida State University
Grand Valley State University
Howard University
Miami University
Missouri State University
Montclair State University
Pepperdine University
Rowan University
Saint Francis University
Samford University
San Diego State University
Slippery Rock University
Trinity University
University of Arizona
University of Connecticut
University of Maine
University of Mississippi
University of Mount Union
University of South Carolina
University of South Dakota
University of Virginia
Virginia Tech
Willamette University

B-

American University
Babson College
Ball State University
Baylor University
Beloit College
Bob Jones University
Cal Poly Pomona
College of Charleston

A-

Albion College
Auburn University
Bradley University
Case Western Reserve University
Claflin University

B

Binghamton University
Cal Poly
Carnegie Mellon University

College of Notre Dame of Maryland
Cornell College
CUNY Queens College
Drexel University
Duquesne University
Georgia State University
Gustavus Adolphus College
Hamilton College
Hofstra University
Indiana University
Indiana University of Pennsylvania
Northern Arizona University
Ohio State University
Ohio University
Old Dominion University
Penn State
Rutgers University
Sacramento State
Saint Leo University
Saint Louis University
St. John's University
St. Mary's University
Stony Brook University
SUNY New Paltz
Susquehanna University
Texas State University - San Marcos
UC Davis
UC Irvine
UC Merced
UC Riverside
UC Santa Barbara
University of Central Florida
University of Colorado
University of Delaware
University of Hartford
University of Kansas
University of Maryland
University of Massachusetts
University of Miami
University of Minnesota
University of Pittsburgh
University of Tampa
University of Washington
University of Western Ontario
UNLV
Virginia Commonwealth University
Western Illinois University
Western Kentucky University

Arizona State University
Barry University
Baruch College
Bentley University
Boston University
Bryant University
Cal State Long Beach
Cal State San Marcos
California University of Pennsylvania
Cleveland State University
Eastern Kentucky University
Elmhurst College
Ferris State University
Florida Atlantic University
Hampton University
John Carroll University
Kent State University

Loyola University Chicago
Marquette University
North Carolina State University
Northeastern University
Robert Morris University
Saint Joseph's University
Salisbury University
SUNY Oswego
Temple University
Texas A&M International University
UC San Diego
University of Iowa
University of Montana
University of Tennessee at Chattanooga
Yale University
Youngstown State University

Cal State Northridge
College of Wooster
Colorado College
Columbia University
George Mason University
Grove City College
IUPUI
Minnesota State University - Moorhead
Montana State University
San Francisco State University
St. Lawrence University
Swarthmore College
Towson University
Tufts University
UC Santa Cruz
University at Buffalo
University of Chicago
University of Illinois at Chicago
University of Maryland Baltimore County
University of North Carolina - Greensboro
Wayne State University

Brown University
City College of New York
DePaul University
Idaho State University
Luther College
New York University
University at Albany
University of San Francisco
University of Wisconsin - Stout
Wesleyan University

Cal State Monterey Bay
Ithaca College
Louisiana College

Alverno College
Amherst College
Barnard College
Emerson College
Harvard University
Manhattan College
McGill University
Occidental College
Pomona College
Wellesley College

—

—

Alfred University
Arcadia University
Bard College
Bates College
Bay Path College
Berea College
Boston College
Bowdoin College
Brandeis University
Brigham Young University
Brigham Young University - Idaho
Bryn Mawr College
Caltech
Carleton College
Catholic University of America
Chatham University
Claremont McKenna College
Clark University
Colby College
College for Creative Studies
College of Mount Saint Vincent
College of the Holy Cross
Columbia College Chicago
Concordia College at Moorhead
Connecticut College
Converse College
CUNY Lehman College
Dordt College
Earlham College
Eckerd College
Elizabethtown College
Elmira College
Fashion Institute of Technology
Fordham University
Freed-Hardeman University

Geneva College
Georgetown University
Gonzaga University
Goucher College
Grinnell College
Guilford College
Hampshire College
Harvey Mudd College
Haverford College
Hollins University
Hood College
Hunter College
Juniata College
La Roche College
Lewis & Clark College
Loyola University Maryland
Macalester College
Manhattanville College
Marlboro College
Massachusetts College of Art & Design
Mercyhurst College
Messiah College
Middlebury College
Misericordia University
Mount Holyoke College
New College of Florida
North Central College
Northwestern College - Saint Paul
Oakwood University
Oberlin College
Oral Roberts University
Pitzer College
Princeton University
Providence College
Purchase College
Reed College
Rhode Island School of Design
Rice University
Russell Sage College
Santa Clara University
Sarah Lawrence College
Scripps College
Seattle University
Simmons College
Skidmore College
Smith College
St. Edward's University
St. Olaf College
Stevenson University
Taylor University
University of Notre Dame
University of Rhode Island
Vassar College
Warren Wilson College
West Point Military Academy
Wheaton College - Illinois
Wheaton College - Massachusetts
Wilkes University
Williams College
Xavier University

Guys

A high grade for Guys indicates that the male population on campus is attractive, smart, friendly, and engaging, and that the school has a decent ratio of guys to girls.

A+

Auburn University
Bowdoin College
Brigham Young University
Claremont McKenna College
Clark Atlanta University
Clemson University
Colby College
Concordia College at Moorhead
Duke University
Florida A&M University
Florida State University
Freed-Hardeman University
Georgetown University
Gonzaga University
Howard University
Northern Illinois University
Ohio University
Oral Roberts University
Penn State
Texas A&M University
Texas State University - San Marcos
University of Alabama
University of Florida
University of Illinois
University of Kentucky
University of Mississippi
University of Notre Dame
University of Southern California
University of Texas
University of Western Ontario
Virginia Commonwealth University
Virginia Tech
Wake Forest University
West Virginia University
Yale University

A

Brigham Young University - Idaho
Cal State San Marcos
Colorado College
CUNY Lehman College
Duquesne University
Elon University
Florida Southern College
Hamilton College
Illinois State University
Indiana University
Jackson State University
Lewis & Clark College
Miami University
Michigan State University
Muhlenberg College
New York University
Oberlin College
Pepperdine University
Pitzer College
Saint Louis University
St. Edward's University

St. John's University
Stanford University
SUNY New Paltz
Taylor University
Trinity College
UC Santa Barbara
UC Santa Cruz
University of Delaware
University of Kansas
University of Miami
University of North Carolina
University of Oklahoma
University of Tampa
University of Virginia
University of Wisconsin
Vanderbilt University

A-

Arizona State University
Austin College
Ball State University
Belmont University
Bentley University
Boston College
Bucknell University
Cal Poly
Cal State Long Beach
Catholic University of America
Chapman University
City College of New York
Colgate University
College for Creative Studies
College of William & Mary
DePauw University
Dordt College
East Carolina University
Eckerd College
Emory University
Georgia State University
Hampton University
Iowa State University
Ithaca College
James Madison University
John Carroll University
Kent State University
Lehigh University
Linfield College
Louisiana State University
Loyola Marymount University
Loyola University Maryland
Macalester College
Massachusetts College of Art & Design
Messiah College
Middlebury College
Montana State University
Oakwood University
Ohio State University
Old Dominion University
Purdue University
Rhodes College
Rutgers University
Samford University
San Diego State University

Santa Clara University
Seton Hall University
Slippery Rock University
St. Lawrence University
SUNY Fredonia
Susquehanna University
Swarthmore College
Texas Tech University
Troy University
UC Berkeley
UC Davis
UCLA
Union College
University of Central Florida
University of Central Oklahoma
University of Cincinnati
University of Georgia
University of Hartford
University of Iowa
University of Maine
University of Maryland Baltimore County
University of Michigan
University of Minnesota
University of Missouri
University of Montana
University of New Hampshire
University of Rhode Island
University of Richmond
University of Rochester
University of San Diego
University of South Carolina
University of South Florida
University of Tennessee
University of Vermont
Villanova University
Wheaton College - Illinois

B+

Babson College
Baruch College
Baylor University
Berea College
Birmingham-Southern College
Bob Jones University
Boston University
Bryant University
Cal Poly Pomona
Cal State Northridge
Carnegie Mellon University
Cleveland State University
College of Charleston
Columbia College Chicago
Davidson College
DePaul University
Drexel University
Elmhurst College
Florida Atlantic University
Geneva College
George Mason University
Grand Valley State University
Gustavus Adolphus College
Hanover College
Hastings College

Johns Hopkins University
Kansas State University
Lafayette College
Louisiana College
Loyola University Chicago
Manhattan College
Mercer University
Millsaps College
Montclair State University
North Carolina A&T State University
North Carolina State University
Northeastern University
Northern Arizona University
Northwestern College - Saint Paul
Northwestern University
Ohio Wesleyan University
Pace University
Providence College
Robert Morris University
Rollins College
Sacramento State
Saint Joseph's University
San Francisco State University
Southern Methodist University
St. Olaf College
Stetson University
Syracuse University
Temple University
Texas Christian University
Towson University
Trinity University
Tulane University
UC Merced
University at Buffalo
University of Arkansas
University of Connecticut
University of Denver
University of Illinois at Chicago
University of Louisville
University of Maryland
University of Maryland Eastern Shore
University of Massachusetts
University of Mount Union
University of Nebraska
University of North Carolina - Greensboro
University of Pittsburgh
University of the Incarnate Word
University of Utah
Ursinus College
Wagner College
Washington University in St. Louis
Wayne State University
West Point Military Academy
Western Kentucky University

B

Albion College
Allegheny College
Amherst College
Arcadia University
Barry University
Bates College
Binghamton University
Brandeis University
Brown University
Cal State Monterey Bay
Case Western Reserve University

Centre College
Claflin University
College of the Holy Cross
College of Wooster
Columbia University
Cornell University
Dartmouth College
Denison University
Eastern Kentucky University
Elmira College
Fashion Institute of Technology
Franklin & Marshall College
Furman University
Gannon University
Georgia Tech
Gettysburg College
Grove City College
Harvard University
Hofstra University
Hood College
Hunter College
La Roche College
Manhattanville College
Marquette University
Mercyhurst College
Middle Tennessee State University
Minnesota State University - Moorhead
Misericordia University
Missouri State University
North Central College
Occidental College
Princeton University
Purchase College
Radford University
Rensselaer Polytechnic Institute
Rice University
Rider University
Rochester Institute of Technology
Saint Francis University
Saint Leo University
Salisbury University
Sam Houston State University
St. Mary's University
Stevenson University
Tennessee State University
Texas A&M International University
UC Irvine
UC Riverside
UC San Diego
University at Albany
University of Arizona
University of Colorado
University of Oregon
University of Pennsylvania
University of San Francisco
University of South Dakota
University of Tennessee at Chattanooga
University of Washington
University of Wisconsin - Stout
Valparaiso University
Vassar College
Warren Wilson College
Washington & Lee University
Western Illinois University
Whitman College
Wilkes University
Willamette University

B-

Alfred University
American University
Bard College
Bradley University
Chatham University
Connecticut College
Converse College
Cornell College
CUNY Queens College
Dickinson College
Earlham College
Elizabethtown College
Emerson College
Ferris State University
Fordham University
Guilford College
Hampshire College
Harvey Mudd College
Haverford College
Idaho State University
Illinois Wesleyan University
Indiana University of Pennsylvania
IUPUI
Juniata College
Kenyon College
Marlboro College
McGill University
MIT
New College of Florida
Pomona College
Russell Sage College
Seattle University
Skidmore College
Southwestern University
Stony Brook University
SUNY Oswego
Truman State University
University of Chicago
UNLV
Washington & Jefferson College
Xavier University

C+

Beloit College
Caltech
Centenary College of Louisiana
College of Mount Saint Vincent
Creighton University
George Washington University
Grinnell College
Lawrence University
Luther College
Reed College
Rhode Island School of Design
Sarah Lawrence College
Tufts University
University of Puget Sound
Wesleyan University
Wheaton College - Massachusetts
Youngstown State University

C

California University of Pennsylvania
Goucher College
Rowan University
Smith College
Williams College

C-

Bay Path College
Carleton College
Clark University
College of Notre Dame of Maryland
Mount Holyoke College

D+

—

D

—

D-

—

F

—

N/A

Alverno College
Barnard College
Bryn Mawr College
Hollins University
Mount Holyoke College
Scripps College
Simmons College
Spelman College
Wellesley College

Health & Safety

A high grade in Health & Safety means that students generally feel safe, campus police are visible, blue-light phones and escort services are readily available, and safety precautions are not overly necessary.

A+

Bob Jones University
Bucknell University
Colgate University
Concordia College at Moorhead
Dartmouth College
Elmhurst College
Grove City College
Hollins University
Idaho State University
Juniata College
Lawrence University
Luther College
Middlebury College
Oral Roberts University
Swarthmore College
Truman State University
Wheaton College - Illinois

A

Alfred University
Alverno College
Beloit College
Boston College
Carleton College
Davidson College
DePauw University
Dickinson College
Earlham College
Elizabethtown College
Emory University
Furman University
Hamilton College
Manhattanville College
Radford University
Robert Morris University
Southwestern University
St. Olaf College
SUNY New Paltz
Susquehanna University
University of Mississippi
University of South Dakota
Washington & Lee University
West Point Military Academy
Whitman College

A-

Albion College
Brigham Young University
Brigham Young University - Idaho
Centre College
Colby College
College of the Holy Cross
College of William & Mary
George Mason University

Grinnell College
Illinois Wesleyan University
Ithaca College
Kenyon College
Lewis & Clark College
Marlboro College
Misericordia University
New College of Florida
Oberlin College
Rhodes College
Simmons College
St. Lawrence University
SUNY Fredonia
Taylor University
UC Davis
University of Puget Sound
University of Richmond
University of the Incarnate Word
Villanova University
Warren Wilson College
Washington & Jefferson College
Willamette University

B+

American University
Amherst College
Babson College
Bay Path College
Bentley University
Boston University
Bowdoin College
Bryant University
Bryn Mawr College
Cal State Long Beach
Carnegie Mellon University
Claremont McKenna College
Connecticut College
Denison University
Elon University
Franklin & Marshall College
Freed-Hardeman University
Gettysburg College
Goucher College
Guilford College
Hampshire College
Hastings College
Haverford College
Iowa State University
Johns Hopkins University
Lafayette College
Manhattan College
Mercer University
Messiah College
Montana State University
Mount Holyoke College
North Central College
Occidental College
Penn State
Pepperdine University
Pitzer College
Princeton University
Purdue University
Reed College

Rice University
Saint Leo University
Santa Clara University
Scripps College
Skidmore College
Southern Methodist University
Spelman College
St. John's University
St. Mary's University
Stetson University
Texas State University - San Marcos
Trinity University
Tufts University
UC Irvine
Union College
University at Albany
University of Alabama
University of Maine
University of Montana
University of Nebraska
University of Notre Dame
University of San Diego
University of Vermont
University of Wisconsin
University of Wisconsin - Stout
Vanderbilt University
Vassar College
Wagner College
Wake Forest University
Wellesley College
Williams College

B

Arcadia University
Austin College
Barnard College
Baruch College
Bates College
Belmont University
Birmingham-Southern College
Bradley University
Cal Poly
Clemson University
College of Wooster
Columbia University
CUNY Lehman College
Duquesne University
Emerson College
Florida Southern College
Gonzaga University
Gustavus Adolphus College
Harvey Mudd College
Kansas State University
Lehigh University
Louisiana State University
Loyola Marymount University
Loyola University Maryland
Macalester College
Northern Illinois University
Ohio State University
Pomona College
Providence College
Rensselaer Polytechnic Institute

Rhode Island School of Design
Rider University
Rochester Institute of Technology
Sam Houston State University
Seattle University
Smith College
Stanford University
Stevenson University
Texas A&M International University
Texas Christian University
Texas Tech University
UCLA
University of Arizona
University of Central Florida
University of Colorado
University of Denver
University of Georgia
University of Kansas
University of Missouri
University of North Carolina - Greensboro
University of Oklahoma
University of South Florida
University of Utah
University of Western Ontario
Ursinus College
Valparaiso University
Wayne State University
Wheaton College - Massachusetts
Wilkes University
Xavier University

B-

Allegheny College
Auburn University
Baylor University
Brandeis University
Centenary College of Louisiana
Chapman University
Chatham University
Clark University
College of Notre Dame of Maryland
Colorado College
Converse College
Dordt College
Eastern Kentucky University
Eckerd College
Florida Atlantic University
Fordham University
Geneva College
Georgia State University
Grand Valley State University
Hood College
Hunter College
Indiana University
IUPUI
La Roche College
Linfield College
Louisiana College
Marquette University
McGill University
Miami University
Middle Tennessee State University
New York University
North Carolina State University
Northern Arizona University
Northwestern College - Saint Paul
Northwestern University

Oakwood University
Ohio University
Ohio Wesleyan University
Rollins College
Sacramento State
Saint Francis University
San Diego State University
San Francisco State University
Slippery Rock University
St. Edward's University
Stony Brook University
Texas A&M University
Troy University
UC Merced
UC Santa Cruz
University of Arkansas
University of Central Oklahoma
University of Chicago
University of Delaware
University of Florida
University of Illinois at Chicago
University of Iowa
University of Kentucky
University of Maryland Baltimore County
University of Miami
University of Michigan
University of Minnesota
University of New Hampshire
University of North Carolina
University of Pennsylvania
University of Rhode Island
University of Rochester
University of South Carolina
University of Southern California
University of Texas
UNLV
Virginia Commonwealth University
Virginia Tech
Western Kentucky University

C+

Arizona State University
Bard College
Barry University
Binghamton University
Brown University
Cal Poly Pomona
Cal State Monterey Bay
Cal State Northridge
Cal State San Marcos
Case Western Reserve University
City College of New York
Cleveland State University
Cornell College
Cornell University
CUNY Queens College
Drexel University
Duke University
Elmira College
Fashion Institute of Technology
Ferris State University
Florida State University
Harvard University
Hofstra University
Jackson State University
James Madison University
John Carroll University

Kent State University
Michigan State University
Minnesota State University - Moorhead
MIT
Montclair State University
Muhlenberg College
Northeastern University
Old Dominion University
Pace University
Purchase College
Saint Joseph's University
Sarah Lawrence College
SUNY Oswego
Syracuse University
Temple University
Tennessee State University
Towson University
UC Berkeley
UC San Diego
UC Santa Barbara
University of Connecticut
University of Hartford
University of Maryland Eastern Shore
University of Massachusetts
University of Mount Union
University of Oregon
University of San Francisco
University of Tennessee at Chattanooga
University of Virginia
Washington University in St. Louis
Wesleyan University
Western Illinois University
Youngstown State University

C

Ball State University
California University of Pennsylvania
Caltech
Catholic University of America
Claflin University
College for Creative Studies
College of Mount Saint Vincent
Columbia College Chicago
East Carolina University
Gannon University
George Washington University
Georgetown University
Georgia Tech
Hanover College
Indiana University of Pennsylvania
Loyola University Chicago
Mercyhurst College
Millsaps College
Missouri State University
Rowan University
Rutgers University
Saint Louis University
Samford University
Seton Hall University
Trinity College
Tulane University
UC Riverside
University of Cincinnati
University of Pittsburgh
University of Tennessee
University of Washington

West Virginia University
Yale University

C-

Clark Atlanta University
College of Charleston
Creighton University
DePaul University
Florida A&M University
Hampton University
Howard University
Illinois State University
North Carolina A&T State University
Russell Sage College
University at Buffalo
University of Illinois
University of Louisville
University of Maryland
University of Tampa

D+

Berea College
Massachusetts College of Art & Design
Salisbury University

D

—

D-

—

F

—

Local Atmosphere

A high Local Atmosphere grade indicates that the area surrounding campus is safe and scenic. Other factors include nearby attractions, proximity to other schools, and the town's attitude toward students.

A+

American University
Barnard College
Boston University
Columbia University
DePaul University
Emerson College
Harvard University
McGill University
MIT
Occidental College
Simmons College
Southern Methodist University
St. Edward's University
University of San Francisco
University of Texas

A

Baruch College
Belmont University
Boston College
College of Charleston
Columbia College Chicago
Drexel University
Elmhurst College
Emory University
Fashion Institute of Technology
Fordham University
George Washington University
Georgetown University
Loyola Marymount University
Loyola University Chicago
Manhattan College
New York University
Northeastern University
San Diego State University
Spelman College
Texas Christian University
University of Chicago
University of Denver
University of Minnesota
University of Pennsylvania
University of San Diego
University of Washington
University of Wisconsin

A-

Alverno College
Bowdoin College
Brigham Young University
Brown University
Cal State Long Beach
Chatham University
Clark Atlanta University
Eckerd College

Georgia State University
Hunter College
Ithaca College
Loyola University Maryland
Macalester College
Ohio State University
Pace University
Reed College
Rhode Island School of Design
Rice University
Rollins College
Saint Louis University
San Francisco State University
Seattle University
St. John's University
Trinity University
Tufts University
Tulane University
UC Irvine
UC San Diego
UCLA
University of Alabama
University of Central Florida
University of Cincinnati
University of Georgia
University of Kansas
University of Miami
University of Missouri
University of Pittsburgh
University of South Florida
University of the Incarnate Word
University of Utah
Vanderbilt University

B+

Arizona State University
Birmingham-Southern College
Cal Poly
Caltech
Cleveland State University
Duquesne University
Florida State University
Georgia Tech
Goucher College
Howard University
Indiana University
IUPUI
La Roche College
Lewis & Clark College
Louisiana State University
Manhattanville College
Marquette University
Middle Tennessee State University
Montana State University
North Carolina State University
North Central College
Northern Arizona University
Northwestern College - Saint Paul
Ohio University
Pitzer College
Providence College
Purdue University
Rider University

Robert Morris University
Sacramento State
Smith College
SUNY New Paltz
Temple University
Tennessee State University
Texas A&M University
Texas State University - San Marcos
Texas Tech University
Towson University
University of Colorado
University of Florida
University of Illinois at Chicago
University of Iowa
University of Kentucky
University of Louisville
University of Michigan
University of Montana
University of North Carolina
University of North Carolina - Greensboro
University of Oregon
University of South Carolina
University of Tampa
University of Tennessee at Chattanooga
University of Vermont
University of Western Ontario
UNLV
Virginia Commonwealth University
Virginia Tech
Washington University in St. Louis
West Virginia University
Wheaton College - Illinois

B

Auburn University
Babson College
Bentley University
Bradley University
Bryn Mawr College
Carnegie Mellon University
Case Western Reserve University
Catholic University of America
Centenary College of Louisiana
Chapman University
City College of New York
Clemson University
Concordia College at Moorhead
Cornell University
Creighton University
CUNY Lehman College
East Carolina University
Eastern Kentucky University
Florida A&M University
Florida Atlantic University
Furman University
Gonzaga University
Grand Valley State University
Guilford College
Haverford College
Hood College
Idaho State University
Illinois State University
Illinois Wesleyan University

Iowa State University
James Madison University
Johns Hopkins University
Kansas State University
Kent State University
Massachusetts College of Art & Design
Michigan State University
Missouri State University
North Carolina A&T State University
Old Dominion University
Oral Roberts University
Penn State
Pepperdine University
Rhodes College
Rochester Institute of Technology
Saint Joseph's University
Samford University
Santa Clara University
Southwestern University
St. Mary's University
Stanford University
Stetson University
SUNY Fredonia
Swarthmore College
UC Berkeley
UC Davis
UC Santa Barbara
UC Santa Cruz
University at Albany
University at Buffalo
University of Arizona
University of Arkansas
University of Central Oklahoma
University of Delaware
University of Illinois
University of Massachusetts
University of Mississippi
University of Nebraska
University of New Hampshire
University of Oklahoma
University of Richmond
University of South Dakota
University of Southern California
University of Tennessee
University of Virginia
Villanova University
Wagner College
Wellesley College

B-

Bay Path College
Beloit College
Bob Jones University
Brigham Young University - Idaho
Cal State Northridge
Claremont McKenna College
College for Creative Studies
College of Mount Saint Vincent
College of Notre Dame of Maryland
College of Wooster
Colorado College
Davidson College
Duke University
Elizabethtown College
Florida Southern College
Gannon University
George Mason University

Hamilton College
Harvey Mudd College
Hastings College
Hollins University
John Carroll University
Juniata College
Lawrence University
Linfield College
Marlboro College
Mercer University
Mercyhurst College
Messiah College
Miami University
Middlebury College
Millsaps College
Minnesota State University - Moorhead
Mount Holyoke College
Muhlenberg College
New College of Florida
Northwestern University
Oakwood University
Oberlin College
Ohio Wesleyan University
Pomona College
Princeton University
Radford University
Sarah Lawrence College
Scripps College
St. Olaf College
Stevenson University
SUNY Oswego
Syracuse University
Taylor University
Troy University
University of Puget Sound
University of Rhode Island
University of Rochester
University of Wisconsin - Stout
Ursinus College
Vassar College
Wayne State University
Western Kentucky University

C+

Albion College
Amherst College
Barry University
Baylor University
Berea College
Binghamton University
Brandeis University
Bryant University
Bucknell University
Cal State Monterey Bay
Cal State San Marcos
Carleton College
Clark University
Colby College
Colgate University
College of the Holy Cross
College of William & Mary
Connecticut College
Converse College
Denison University
Dickinson College
Elon University
Franklin & Marshall College

Freed-Hardeman University
Gettysburg College
Hampshire College
Hampton University
Kenyon College
Montclair State University
Northern Illinois University
Purchase College
Rutgers University
Sam Houston State University
Skidmore College
Stony Brook University
Susquehanna University
Truman State University
UC Riverside
Union College
University of Connecticut
University of Hartford
University of Maine
University of Maryland
University of Maryland Baltimore County
Warren Wilson College
Washington & Jefferson College
West Point Military Academy
Wheaton College - Massachusetts
Whitman College
Xavier University
Yale University

C

Alfred University
Allegheny College
Arcadia University
Ball State University
Bard College
Bates College
Cal Poly Pomona
Centre College
Cornell College
CUNY Queens College
Dartmouth College
DePauw University
Geneva College
Grinnell College
Grove City College
Gustavus Adolphus College
Hofstra University
Lafayette College
Lehigh University
Louisiana College
Luther College
Misericordia University
Rensselaer Polytechnic Institute
Rowan University
Russell Sage College
Saint Leo University
Salisbury University
Seton Hall University
Slippery Rock University
University of Maryland Eastern Shore
University of Notre Dame
Valparaiso University
Wake Forest University
Willamette University
Williams College
Youngstown State University

C-

Dordt College
Earlham College
Ferris State University
Hanover College
Indiana University of Pennsylvania
Jackson State University
Saint Francis University
St. Lawrence University
Texas A&M International University
UC Merced
University of Mount Union
Washington & Lee University
Wesleyan University
Wilkes University

D+

Austin College
California University of Pennsylvania
Claflin University
Elmira College
Trinity College
Western Illinois University

D

D-

—

F

—

Nightlife

A high grade in Nightlife indicates that there are many bars and clubs in the area that are easily accessible and affordable. Other determining factors include the number of options for the under-21 crowd and the prevalence of house parties.

Belmont University
Manhattan College
New York University
Ohio University
University of Alabama
University of South Carolina
University of Texas
West Virginia University

Alverno College
Auburn University
Barnard College
Catholic University of America
Clark Atlanta University
College of Charleston
Drexel University
Duquesne University
Florida State University
George Washington University
Howard University
Indiana University
Louisiana State University
MIT
Occidental College
Ohio State University
Penn State
Southern Methodist University
SUNY New Paltz
Texas Tech University
Tulane University
University of Arkansas
University of Denver
University of Florida
University of Georgia
University of Illinois
University of Iowa
University of Kansas
University of Kentucky
University of Michigan
University of Pennsylvania
University of Tampa
University of Washington
University of Western Ontario
University of Wisconsin
UNLV
Virginia Commonwealth University

American University
Arizona State University
Birmingham-Southern College
Clemson University
Columbia College Chicago

Columbia University
Cornell University
DePaul University
Duke University
East Carolina University
Fashion Institute of Technology
Florida A&M University
Fordham University
Gannon University
Georgetown University
Gonzaga University
Illinois State University
Loyola University Chicago
Manhattanville College
Marquette University
McGill University
Miami University
Middle Tennessee State University
North Carolina A&T State University
Northeastern University
Pace University
Purdue University
Rhodes College
Rice University
Rollins College
Rutgers University
Spelman College
SUNY Fredonia
Syracuse University
Temple University
Tennessee State University
Texas A&M University
Texas Christian University
Texas State University - San Marcos
Trinity University
UC Santa Barbara
UCLA
University of Arizona
University of Central Florida
University of Delaware
University of Minnesota
University of Mississippi
University of Missouri
University of New Hampshire
University of Oklahoma
University of Pittsburgh
University of Richmond
University of Southern California
University of Tennessee
University of Virginia
Vanderbilt University
Virginia Tech
Western Illinois University
Yale University

Ball State University
Binghamton University
Boston University
Brown University
Bryant University
Cal Poly
Cal State Long Beach

Carnegie Mellon University
City College of New York
Colby College
College for Creative Studies
Colorado College
Eastern Kentucky University
Eckerd College
Elmira College
Emerson College
Emory University
Georgia State University
Georgia Tech
Goucher College
Hamilton College
Harvard University
Hofstra University
Hunter College
Indiana University of Pennsylvania
Iowa State University
Ithaca College
Jackson State University
James Madison University
Johns Hopkins University
Kansas State University
Kent State University
Lewis & Clark College
Loyola Marymount University
Macalester College
Massachusetts College of Art & Design
Mercer University
Michigan State University
Missouri State University
North Carolina State University
North Central College
Northern Illinois University
Northwestern University
Old Dominion University
Pitzer College
Providence College
Purchase College
Sacramento State
Saint Joseph's University
Saint Louis University
San Diego State University
San Francisco State University
Santa Clara University
Seattle University
Simmons College
Southwestern University
St. Edward's University
St. John's University
SUNY Oswego
Towson University
Trinity College
Tufts University
University at Albany
University at Buffalo
University of Chicago
University of Cincinnati
University of Colorado
University of Connecticut
University of Hartford
University of Louisville
University of Maryland
University of Massachusetts
University of Miami
University of Montana
University of Nebraska

University of North Carolina
University of North Carolina - Greensboro
University of Notre Dame
University of Oregon
University of Rochester
University of San Diego
University of San Francisco
University of South Florida
University of Tennessee at Chattanooga
University of Vermont
Wake Forest University
Wayne State University

B

Allegheny College
Austin College
Babson College
Barry University
Baruch College
Bentley University
Bowdoin College
Cal Poly Pomona
Cal State Northridge
Case Western Reserve University
Centenary College of Louisiana
Cleveland State University
Colgate University
College of the Holy Cross
College of William & Mary
College of Wooster
Cornell College
CUNY Lehman College
Elmhurst College
Elon University
Ferris State University
Florida Southern College
George Mason University
Grand Valley State University
Guilford College
Hood College
Illinois Wesleyan University
IUPUI
John Carroll University
Linfield College
Loyola University Maryland
Minnesota State University - Moorhead
Misericordia University
New College of Florida
Northern Arizona University
Oberlin College
Ohio Wesleyan University
Oral Roberts University
Pepperdine University
Pomona College
Reed College
Rhode Island School of Design
Rider University
Rochester Institute of Technology
Salisbury University
Sam Houston State University
Samford University
Seton Hall University
Slippery Rock University
Smith College
St. Lawrence University
Stanford University
Stetson University

UC Berkeley
UC Davis
UC Riverside
UC San Diego
UC Santa Cruz
Union College
University of Illinois at Chicago
University of Maine
University of South Dakota
University of the Incarnate Word
University of Utah
University of Wisconsin - Stout
Ursinus College
Valparaiso University
Villanova University
Wagner College
Washington University in St. Louis
Wellesley College
Western Kentucky University
Youngstown State University

B-

Amherst College
Bard College
Baylor University
Boston College
Bradley University
Bucknell University
Cal State San Marcos
Chapman University
Chatham University
Claremont McKenna College
College of Mount Saint Vincent
College of Notre Dame of Maryland
Concordia College at Moorhead
Creighton University
CUNY Queens College
Denison University
Elizabethtown College
Florida Atlantic University
Gettysburg College
Hampton University
Hanover College
Harvey Mudd College
La Roche College
Lehigh University
Mercyhurst College
Millsaps College
Montana State University
Montclair State University
Muhlenberg College
Rensselaer Polytechnic Institute
Robert Morris University
Russell Sage College
Saint Leo University
Scripps College
St. Mary's University
Stevenson University
Stony Brook University
UC Irvine
University of Central Oklahoma
University of Maryland Baltimore County
University of Rhode Island

C+

Arcadia University
Bay Path College
Brandeis University
Bryn Mawr College
California University of Pennsylvania
Clark University
Converse College
Davidson College
DePauw University
Dordt College
Furman University
Grinnell College
Gustavus Adolphus College
Hampshire College
Hastings College
Idaho State University
Lawrence University
Marlboro College
Mount Holyoke College
Northwestern College - Saint Paul
Oakwood University
Radford University
Rowan University
Saint Francis University
Sarah Lawrence College
Skidmore College
Swarthmore College
Texas A&M International University
Troy University
Truman State University
University of Mount Union
Washington & Jefferson College
Wheaton College - Massachusetts
Wilkes University
Xavier University

C

Albion College
Bates College
Berea College
Brigham Young University
Cal State Monterey Bay
Caltech
Carleton College
Centre College
Claflin University
Connecticut College
Dickinson College
Franklin & Marshall College
Geneva College
Haverford College
Hollins University
Lafayette College
Luther College
Messiah College
Princeton University
Susquehanna University
UC Merced
University of Maryland Eastern Shore
University of Puget Sound
Warren Wilson College
Wheaton College - Illinois

Whitman College
Willamette University

C-

Alfred University
Earlham College
Freed-Hardeman University
Juniata College
Vassar College
Washington & Lee University
Wesleyan University
West Point Military Academy

D+

Beloit College
Bob Jones University
Brigham Young University - Idaho
Dartmouth College
Grove City College
Kenyon College
Louisiana College
St. Olaf College
Taylor University

D

Middlebury College

D-

Williams College

F

—

Off-Campus Dining

A high Off-Campus Dining grade implies that off-campus restaurants are affordable, accessible, and worth visiting. Other factors include the variety of cuisine and the availability of alternative options (vegetarian, vegan, Kosher).

A+

Barnard College
Elmhurst College
Ithaca College
McGill University
Occidental College
Rice University
Smith College
Tulane University
University of Chicago
University of Kansas
University of San Francisco

A

Alverno College
Catholic University of America
Centenary College of Louisiana
College of Charleston
Columbia University
DePaul University
Emerson College
Fordham University
Georgetown University
Harvard University
Lewis & Clark College
Loyola University Maryland
MIT
New York University
Northwestern University
Ohio State University
Ohio University
Oral Roberts University
Pitzer College
Rhodes College
Seattle University
Simmons College
Spelman College
St. Edward's University
SUNY New Paltz
Tufts University
UC Davis
UC Santa Cruz
UCLA
University of Florida
University of Massachusetts
University of Michigan
University of Pennsylvania
University of Texas
University of Vermont
University of Virginia
University of Western Ontario
University of Wisconsin
Washington University in St. Louis
Yale University

A-

American University
Belmont University
Birmingham-Southern College
Bob Jones University
Boston College
Bowdoin College
Bradley University
Brown University
Chatham University
Clemson University
Columbia College Chicago
Cornell University
Creighton University
East Carolina University
Fashion Institute of Technology
George Washington University
Goucher College
Guilford College
Illinois State University
Indiana University
Lawrence University
Missouri State University
Montana State University
North Central College
Northwestern College - Saint Paul
Oberlin College
Providence College
Radford University
Reed College
Rhode Island School of Design
Southern Methodist University
Trinity University
UC Berkeley
University of Arkansas
University of Central Florida
University of Colorado
University of Delaware
University of Denver
University of Illinois at Chicago
University of Missouri
University of Nebraska
University of Oregon
University of Rochester
University of San Diego
University of South Florida
University of Washington
Vanderbilt University
Villanova University
Virginia Commonwealth University
West Virginia University

B+

Arizona State University
Babson College
Baruch College
Cal Poly
Caltech
Clark University

College of the Holy Cross
College of Wooster
Drexel University
Elon University
Emory University
Florida State University
Georgia Tech
Gonzaga University
Haverford College
Hood College
Iowa State University
IUPUI
Kansas State University
La Roche College
Louisiana State University
Macalester College
Manhattan College
Manhattanville College
Miami University
Michigan State University
Middle Tennessee State University
Northeastern University
Ohio Wesleyan University
Pace University
Penn State
Rollins College
Rutgers University
Samford University
St. John's University
St. Olaf College
Tennessee State University
Texas A&M University
Texas Christian University
Texas Tech University
Towson University
UC San Diego
University of Cincinnati
University of Georgia
University of Iowa
University of Kentucky
University of Maine
University of Miami
University of Minnesota
University of New Hampshire
University of North Carolina
University of Notre Dame
University of Oklahoma
University of Pittsburgh
University of South Carolina
University of Tennessee at Chattanooga
University of Wisconsin - Stout
UNLV
Virginia Tech
Warren Wilson College
Washington & Lee University
Wellesley College
Wheaton College - Illinois
Xavier University

B

Amherst College
Auburn University
Ball State University

Bentley University
Boston University
Brigham Young University
Bryn Mawr College
Cal State Long Beach
Cal State Monterey Bay
Cal State Northridge
Carleton College
Carnegie Mellon University
Case Western Reserve University
Claremont McKenna College
Cleveland State University
Colby College
College for Creative Studies
College of Notre Dame of Maryland
College of William & Mary
Colorado College
Concordia College at Moorhead
Connecticut College
Duke University
Eastern Kentucky University
Furman University
George Mason University
Georgia State University
Gettysburg College
Hampshire College
Howard University
Idaho State University
James Madison University
John Carroll University
Johns Hopkins University
Kent State University
Lehigh University
Linfield College
Marlboro College
Mercer University
Millsaps College
Minnesota State University - Moorhead
Montclair State University
North Carolina A&T State University
North Carolina State University
Northern Arizona University
Northern Illinois University
Pepperdine University
Princeton University
Purdue University
Rider University
Rochester Institute of Technology
Sacramento State
Saint Joseph's University
Saint Louis University
San Diego State University
Santa Clara University
Sarah Lawrence College
Seton Hall University
Southwestern University
Stanford University
Stevenson University
Syracuse University
Texas State University - San Marcos
UC Riverside
UC Santa Barbara
University at Albany
University at Buffalo
University of Alabama
University of Arizona
University of Illinois
University of Mississippi
University of Montana
University of Rhode Island
University of Richmond
University of Tennessee

University of the Incarnate Word
Ursinus College
Wake Forest University
Washington & Jefferson College
Wayne State University
Wheaton College - Massachusetts

B-

Alfred University
Bates College
Baylor University
Brandeis University
Clark Atlanta University
Converse College
CUNY Lehman College
Davidson College
Denison University
Duquesne University
Florida Southern College
Franklin & Marshall College
Gannon University
Geneva College
Hamilton College
Hofstra University
Hollins University
Hunter College
Illinois Wesleyan University
Indiana University of Pennsylvania
Juniata College
Lafayette College
Loyola University Chicago
Luther College
Messiah College
Misericordia University
Muhlenberg College
New College of Florida
Old Dominion University
Russell Sage College
Salisbury University
Skidmore College
Stetson University
SUNY Fredonia
UC Irvine
Union College
University of Central Oklahoma
University of Connecticut
University of Hartford
University of Louisville
University of Maryland
University of North Carolina - Greensboro
University of South Dakota
University of Utah
Valparaiso University
Vassar College
Wesleyan University
Western Kentucky University
Wilkes University
Willamette University

C+

Albion College
Beloit College
Binghamton University

Brigham Young University - Idaho
Bucknell University
Cal Poly Pomona
Cal State San Marcos
Centre College
Chapman University
Colgate University
CUNY Queens College
DePauw University
Dickinson College
Eckerd College
Ferris State University
Florida A&M University
Florida Atlantic University
Freed-Hardeman University
Grand Valley State University
Grinnell College
Grove City College
Hastings College
Jackson State University
Loyola Marymount University
Middlebury College
Mount Holyoke College
Oakwood University
Purchase College
Rensselaer Polytechnic Institute
Rowan University
Stony Brook University
Susquehanna University
Swarthmore College
Temple University
Trinity College
Truman State University
UC Merced
University of Mount Union
University of Puget Sound
University of Southern California
University of Tampa
Whitman College
Williams College

C

Allegheny College
Arcadia University
Austin College
Bard College
Bay Path College
Berea College
Bryant University
City College of New York
College of Mount Saint Vincent
Cornell College
Elizabethtown College
Hanover College
Harvey Mudd College
Marquette University
Mercyhurst College
Pomona College
Robert Morris University
Saint Leo University
San Francisco State University
Scripps College
St. Lawrence University
SUNY Oswego
Texas A&M International University
Troy University

Western Illinois University
Youngstown State University

Claflin University
Dartmouth College
Dordt College
Elmira College
Gustavus Adolphus College
Hampton University
Kenyon College
Louisiana College
Massachusetts College of Art & Design
Saint Francis University
Sam Houston State University
Slippery Rock University
Taylor University
University of Maryland Baltimore County
University of Maryland Eastern Shore
Wagner College
West Point Military Academy

Barry University
California University of Pennsylvania
Earlham College
St. Mary's University

—

—

—

Off-Campus Housing

A high grade in Off-Campus Housing indicates that apartments are of high quality, close to campus, and affordable. Other factors include the schools services to help students move off campus and how easy it is to secure housing.

A+

Auburn University
Brigham Young University - Idaho
Clemson University
Idaho State University
James Madison University
University of Western Ontario

A

Alverno College
East Carolina University
Florida A&M University
Lewis & Clark College
McGill University
Oberlin College
Radford University
Slippery Rock University
Texas A&M University
Texas Christian University
Truman State University
University of Alabama
University of Arkansas
University of Georgia
University of Kansas
University of Missouri
University of Notre Dame
University of South Carolina
University of South Dakota
University of South Florida
University of Tampa

A-

Belmont University
Brigham Young University
Duquesne University
Elmhurst College
Elon University
Emory University
Grand Valley State University
Indiana University
Johns Hopkins University
Macalester College
Missouri State University
Muhlenberg College
North Carolina A&T State University
Pitzer College
Southern Methodist University
Tennessee State University
Texas State University - San Marcos
Texas Tech University
Towson University
Tulane University
UC Irvine
UC Merced
University at Buffalo

University of Florida
University of Iowa
University of Michigan
University of Nebraska
University of Tennessee
University of Virginia
University of Wisconsin - Stout
Virginia Tech
Washington & Lee University
Washington University in St. Louis
Wheaton College - Illinois

B+

American University
Bard College
Baylor University
Boston College
Cal State Northridge
Carnegie Mellon University
Case Western Reserve University
Cleveland State University
Colorado College
Columbia College Chicago
Concordia College at Moorhead
Cornell University
DePaul University
Florida State University
Hastings College
Iowa State University
Ithaca College
La Roche College
Loyola Marymount University
Marquette University
Middle Tennessee State University
Minnesota State University - Moorhead
Montana State University
North Carolina State University
Northern Illinois University
Purdue University
Rhodes College
Rochester Institute of Technology
Saint Joseph's University
Saint Louis University
Salisbury University
Sam Houston State University
Seattle University
SUNY New Paltz
Swarthmore College
Taylor University
UC Davis
UC San Diego
University of Central Florida
University of Delaware
University of Denver
University of Illinois
University of Illinois at Chicago
University of Maine
University of Miami
University of Mississippi
University of New Hampshire
University of Oklahoma
University of Rochester
University of San Diego

University of Texas
University of Vermont
University of Wisconsin
Virginia Commonwealth University
Wake Forest University
Western Kentucky University
Wilkes University
Willamette University

B

Arcadia University
Arizona State University
Austin College
Ball State University
Binghamton University
Bradley University
Cal Poly Pomona
Cal State Long Beach
Cal State San Marcos
Catholic University of America
Clark Atlanta University
Colby College
College of Charleston
CUNY Lehman College
CUNY Queens College
Drexel University
Eastern Kentucky University
Eckerd College
Florida Atlantic University
Freed-Hardeman University
Gannon University
Hampton University
Hood College
Howard University
Illinois Wesleyan University
IUPUI
John Carroll University
Kansas State University
Kent State University
Lehigh University
Louisiana State University
Loyola University Chicago
Miami University
Michigan State University
North Central College
Northern Arizona University
Northwestern College - Saint Paul
Oakwood University
Ohio State University
Ohio University
Oral Roberts University
Pace University
Penn State
Rensselaer Polytechnic Institute
Sacramento State
Samford University
Santa Clara University
St. Edward's University
Syracuse University
Troy University
UC Riverside
UC Santa Cruz
UCLA

University of Colorado
University of Connecticut
University of Kentucky
University of Louisville
University of Maryland Baltimore County
University of Maryland Eastern Shore
University of Massachusetts
University of Montana
University of Oregon
University of Rhode Island
University of Southern California
University of Tennessee at Chattanooga
University of Utah
University of Washington
Valparaiso University
Vanderbilt University
West Virginia University
Western Illinois University
Xavier University

B-

Barry University
Bentley University
Berea College
Bob Jones University
Bowdoin College
Brandeis University
Cal Poly
Cal State Monterey Bay
Chapman University
Chatham University
City College of New York
Claflin University
Claremont McKenna College
College for Creative Studies
College of William & Mary
Creighton University
Duke University
Emerson College
Ferris State University
Florida Southern College
Fordham University
Geneva College
George Mason University
George Washington University
Georgetown University
Georgia State University
Georgia Tech
Gonzaga University
Hofstra University
Illinois State University
Indiana University of Pennsylvania
Linfield College
Manhattan College
Mercer University
Northeastern University
Northwestern University
Old Dominion University
Reed College
Rider University
Rutgers University
San Diego State University
San Francisco State University
Seton Hall University
Simmons College
Spelman College
St. John's University

St. Mary's University
Stevenson University
Stony Brook University
SUNY Fredonia
Susquehanna University
Temple University
University at Albany
University of Arizona
University of Central Oklahoma
University of Chicago
University of Cincinnati
University of Hartford
University of Minnesota
University of Mount Union
University of North Carolina
University of North Carolina - Greensboro
University of Pittsburgh
University of San Francisco
UNLV
Wayne State University
Whitman College
Yale University

C+

Alfred University
Baruch College
Boston University
Centenary College of Louisiana
Earlham College
Elizabethtown College
Fashion Institute of Technology
Grinnell College
Hamilton College
Jackson State University
Juniata College
Massachusetts College of Art & Design
Mercyhurst College
Misericordia University
New College of Florida
New York University
Robert Morris University
Russell Sage College
Saint Leo University
SUNY Oswego
Texas A&M International University
Trinity College
Trinity University
UC Berkeley
UC Santa Barbara
University of Maryland
University of Pennsylvania
University of Puget Sound
University of the Incarnate Word
Villanova University
Youngstown State University

C

Allegheny College
Bay Path College
Clark University
College of Notre Dame of Maryland
Columbia University
Dordt College

Guilford College
Gustavus Adolphus College
Hunter College
Loyola University Maryland
Marlboro College
Montclair State University
Purchase College
Rhode Island School of Design
Rice University
Rollins College
Stanford University
Stetson University
Tufts University
University of Richmond

C-

Albion College
Beloit College
Birmingham-Southern College
Brown University
Bryant University
Bucknell University
California University of Pennsylvania
Carleton College
Colgate University
Converse College
Dartmouth College
Davidson College
Dickinson College
Louisiana College
Luther College
Millsaps College
Mount Holyoke College
Occidental College
Pepperdine University
Providence College
Rowan University
Smith College
Southwestern University
St. Lawrence University
Union College
Wagner College
Washington & Jefferson College

D+

Babson College
Bates College
College of Mount Saint Vincent
College of Wooster
Cornell College
Elmira College
Furman University
Hampshire College
Hanover College
Hollins University
Messiah College
Ohio Wesleyan University
Saint Francis University
Skidmore College
St. Olaf College
Warren Wilson College
Wesleyan University
Williams College

D

Amherst College
Caltech
Centre College
College of the Holy Cross
Denison University
DePauw University
Gettysburg College
Goucher College
Kenyon College
Lafayette College
Middlebury College
Sarah Lawrence College
Vassar College
Wheaton College - Massachusetts

D-

Barnard College
Bryn Mawr College
Connecticut College
Franklin & Marshall College
Harvard University
Harvey Mudd College
Haverford College
Lawrence University
Manhattanville College
MIT
Pomona College
Princeton University
Scripps College
Ursinus College
Wellesley College

F

—

Parking

A high grade in the Parking section indicates that parking is available, affordable, and convenient and that parking enforcement isn't overly severe.

Austin College
Colby College
College for Creative Studies
Converse College
Louisiana College
Millsaps College
Oakwood University
Oral Roberts University
Pitzer College
Stevenson University
Taylor University

Alverno College
Bard College
Birmingham-Southern College
Bowdoin College
Centenary College of Louisiana
Centre College
Colorado College
Gonzaga University
Hanover College
Illinois Wesleyan University
Macalester College
Reed College
Rhodes College
Susquehanna University
Wheaton College - Illinois

Albion College
Beloit College
Bob Jones University
Bryant University
Chapman University
Creighton University
Davidson College
DePauw University
Earlham College
Elmira College
Geneva College
Grinnell College
Hamilton College
Hampshire College
Harvey Mudd College
Hollins University
Lewis & Clark College
Linfield College
Loyola Marymount University
Marlboro College
Muhlenberg College
New College of Florida
Occidental College
Rider University

Santa Clara University
University at Buffalo
University of Notre Dame
University of Wisconsin - Stout
Wagner College
Warren Wilson College
Washington & Jefferson College
Whitman College

Amherst College
Babson College
Bates College
Bay Path College
Bentley University
Brigham Young University
Brigham Young University - Idaho
Bucknell University
Cal State Monterey Bay
Claremont McKenna College
Colgate University
Concordia College at Moorhead
Connecticut College
Cornell College
Duke University
Eckerd College
Elizabethtown College
Elon University
Fordham University
Freed-Hardeman University
Furman University
Gettysburg College
Guilford College
Gustavus Adolphus College
Hastings College
Haverford College
Hofstra University
Juniata College
Loyola University Chicago
Manhattanville College
Mercyhurst College
Messiah College
Middlebury College
Minnesota State University - Moorhead
Mount Holyoke College
Northwestern College - Saint Paul
Oberlin College
Ohio Wesleyan University
Pepperdine University
Samford University
Southwestern University
St. John's University
St. Lawrence University
St. Mary's University
Texas Tech University
Trinity University
Truman State University
UC Merced
University of Maryland Baltimore County
University of Mount Union
University of Puget Sound
University of San Francisco
Valparaiso University

Washington University in St. Louis
Western Illinois University
Xavier University
Yale University

Alfred University
Allegheny College
Arcadia University
Binghamton University
Cal Poly
Cal State Long Beach
Cal State Northridge
Caltech
Chatham University
Clark University
Clemson University
Cleveland State University
College of Mount Saint Vincent
College of Notre Dame of Maryland
CUNY Lehman College
Denison University
Dordt College
Emory University
Florida A&M University
Florida State University
Grand Valley State University
Grove City College
Hood College
Iowa State University
John Carroll University
Kansas State University
Kenyon College
Luther College
Mercer University
Northern Arizona University
Northern Illinois University
Old Dominion University
Pomona College
Purchase College
Rice University
Rollins College
Saint Francis University
Seton Hall University
Skidmore College
Slippery Rock University
St. Edward's University
Stanford University
Stony Brook University
SUNY New Paltz
Trinity College
Troy University
UC Davis
UC Santa Barbara
University of Alabama
University of Colorado
University of Delaware
University of Georgia
University of Hartford
University of Kansas
University of Nebraska
University of San Diego
University of Tampa

Ursinus College
Virginia Commonwealth University
Wesleyan University
Western Kentucky University
Wheaton College - Massachusetts
Williams College

B-

Auburn University
Barry University
Baylor University
Berea College
Boston University
Brandeis University
Bryn Mawr College
Cal Poly Pomona
Carleton College
Case Western Reserve University
Claflin University
Clark Atlanta University
College of Wooster
Columbia College Chicago
CUNY Queens College
DePaul University
Duquesne University
East Carolina University
Eastern Kentucky University
Florida Atlantic University
Franklin & Marshall College
Gannon University
Howard University
Idaho State University
Illinois State University
Ithaca College
Kent State University
La Roche College
Lawrence University
Louisiana State University
Marquette University
Miami University
Middle Tennessee State University
Misericordia University
Missouri State University
Montana State University
Ohio State University
Ohio University
Pace University
Princeton University
Providence College
Purdue University
Robert Morris University
Rochester Institute of Technology
Russell Sage College
Sacramento State
Saint Joseph's University
Saint Louis University
San Diego State University
Scripps College
Smith College
Southern Methodist University
St. Olaf College
SUNY Fredonia
SUNY Oswego
Swarthmore College
Syracuse University
Temple University
Texas A&M International University

Texas A&M University
Tufts University
UC Riverside
UC Santa Cruz
University of Arizona
University of Central Florida
University of Cincinnati
University of Connecticut
University of Denver
University of Illinois at Chicago
University of Maine
University of Maryland Eastern Shore
University of Miami
University of Mississippi
University of Richmond
University of South Carolina
University of South Florida
University of Southern California
University of Tennessee at Chattanooga
University of the Incarnate Word
University of Vermont
University of Western Ontario
UNLV
Vassar College
Wayne State University
Willamette University
Youngstown State University

C+

American University
Belmont University
Boston College
Brown University
Cal State San Marcos
Carnegie Mellon University
City College of New York
College of the Holy Cross
Columbia University
Cornell University
Dartmouth College
Dickinson College
Elmhurst College
Ferris State University
Florida Southern College
Georgia State University
Georgia Tech
Indiana University
Johns Hopkins University
Lehigh University
Michigan State University
MIT
North Carolina A&T State University
North Carolina State University
North Central College
Northeastern University
Penn State
Rutgers University
Saint Leo University
Salisbury University
Sam Houston State University
San Francisco State University
Sarah Lawrence College
Seattle University
Stetson University
Tennessee State University
Texas Christian University
Texas State University - San Marcos

Towson University
Tulane University
UC Berkeley
UC Irvine
University of Central Oklahoma
University of Florida
University of Illinois
University of Iowa
University of Louisville
University of Maryland
University of Massachusetts
University of Michigan
University of Minnesota
University of Missouri
University of Montana
University of New Hampshire
University of Oregon
University of South Dakota
University of Utah
University of Virginia
University of Washington
University of Wisconsin
Vanderbilt University
Virginia Tech
Wake Forest University
Wellesley College
Wilkes University

C

Arizona State University
Ball State University
Catholic University of America
College of William & Mary
Drexel University
Georgetown University
Goucher College
Harvard University
Indiana University of Pennsylvania
IUPUI
Jackson State University
James Madison University
Lafayette College
Manhattan College
Massachusetts College of Art & Design
Northwestern University
Rensselaer Polytechnic Institute
UC San Diego
UCLA
Union College
University at Albany
University of Arkansas
University of Kentucky
University of North Carolina - Greensboro
University of Oklahoma
University of Pittsburgh
University of Rochester
University of Tennessee
University of Texas
Villanova University
Washington & Lee University
West Point Military Academy
West Virginia University

C-

Baruch College
California University of Pennsylvania
College of Charleston
George Mason University
George Washington University
Hampton University
Loyola University Maryland
McGill University
Montclair State University
Rhode Island School of Design
Rowan University
Spelman College
University of North Carolina
University of Pennsylvania
University of Rhode Island

D+

Fashion Institute of Technology
Hunter College
New York University
Radford University
Simmons College

D

Bradley University
Emerson College
University of Chicago

D-

Barnard College

F

—

Transportation

A high grade for Transportation indicates that campus buses, public buses, cabs, and rental cars are readily available and affordable. Other determining factors include proximity to an airport and the necessity of transportation.

American University
Barnard College
Columbia College Chicago
Elmhurst College
Iowa State University
Manhattan College
Penn State
Texas Tech University
UC Davis
University of Colorado
University of Pittsburgh
University of San Francisco
University of Utah
University of Vermont

Auburn University
Bowdoin College
Cal State Long Beach
Catholic University of America
Clemson University
College of Charleston
DePaul University
Florida State University
Fordham University
George Washington University
Harvard University
Howard University
Johns Hopkins University
Loyola University Chicago
Manhattanville College
Marquette University
Miami University
Michigan State University
MIT
Ohio State University
Reed College
San Francisco State University
Seattle University
SUNY Fredonia
UC San Diego
University of Arkansas
University of Chicago
University of Massachusetts
University of Michigan
University of Minnesota
University of New Hampshire
University of Texas
Western Illinois University

Alverno College
Ball State University
Bentley University

Boston College
Brown University
Case Western Reserve University
Clark Atlanta University
Cornell University
Drexel University
East Carolina University
Emerson College
Emory University
George Mason University
Georgetown University
Georgia Tech
Grand Valley State University
Lewis & Clark College
Loyola University Maryland
McGill University
Missouri State University
Montana State University
North Carolina A&T State University
North Carolina State University
Providence College
Purdue University
Rhode Island School of Design
Rochester Institute of Technology
Rutgers University
Simmons College
Smith College
St. John's University
SUNY New Paltz
Swarthmore College
Temple University
Texas A&M University
Texas State University - San Marcos
Towson University
UC Irvine
UC Riverside
UC Santa Barbara
UC Santa Cruz
University at Buffalo
University of Central Florida
University of Cincinnati
University of Denver
University of Florida
University of Georgia
University of Illinois
University of Illinois at Chicago
University of Kansas
University of Louisville
University of Maine
University of Montana
University of Oregon
University of Pennsylvania
University of Rochester
University of South Florida
University of Southern California
University of Tennessee at Chattanooga
University of Virginia
University of Western Ontario
University of Wisconsin
Virginia Commonwealth University
Virginia Tech
West Virginia University

Arizona State University
Binghamton University
Boston University
Brandeis University
Cal Poly
Carnegie Mellon University
Chatham University
Cleveland State University
Columbia University
CUNY Lehman College
Fashion Institute of Technology
Florida A&M University
Hunter College
Illinois State University
Indiana University
Indiana University of Pennsylvania
James Madison University
Kansas State University
Louisiana State University
Massachusetts College of Art & Design
Middle Tennessee State University
New York University
Northeastern University
Northern Illinois University
Northwestern University
Ohio University
Oral Roberts University
Pace University
Purchase College
Robert Morris University
Russell Sage College
Saint Louis University
Salisbury University
San Diego State University
Seton Hall University
Slippery Rock University
Southern Methodist University
Spelman College
St. Edward's University
Stanford University
Stony Brook University
Syracuse University
Tennessee State University
Troy University
Tulane University
UC Berkeley
UCLA
University of Connecticut
University of Delaware
University of Hartford
University of Iowa
University of Kentucky
University of Maryland
University of Miami
University of Mississippi
University of Nebraska
University of North Carolina
University of North Carolina - Greensboro
University of Notre Dame
University of Puget Sound
University of South Carolina
University of Tennessee

University of the Incarnate Word
Wagner College
Washington University in St. Louis
Western Kentucky University
Wheaton College - Illinois
Yale University

Austin College
Baylor University
Brigham Young University
Brigham Young University - Idaho
Cal State Monterey Bay
California University of Pennsylvania
Centenary College of Louisiana
City College of New York
Colby College
College for Creative Studies
College of Mount Saint Vincent
Concordia College at Moorhead
CUNY Queens College
Duke University
Eastern Kentucky University
Gannon University
Georgia State University
Guilford College
IUPUI
John Carroll University
Kent State University
Louisiana College
Minnesota State University - Moorhead
Mount Holyoke College
Northern Arizona University
Northwestern College - Saint Paul
Oberlin College
Old Dominion University
Sacramento State
Saint Joseph's University
Santa Clara University
Stevenson University
SUNY Oswego
Texas Christian University
Tufts University
University of Alabama
University of Arizona
University of Missouri
University of Oklahoma
University of Rhode Island
University of Washington
Vanderbilt University
Villanova University
Xavier University

Arcadia University
Bard College
Baruch College
Bay Path College
Birmingham-Southern College
Bob Jones University
Bradley University
Bryant University
Cal Poly Pomona

Cal State Northridge
Claremont McKenna College
Clark University
College of William & Mary
Creighton University
Davidson College
Dordt College
Elon University
Ferris State University
Gonzaga University
Idaho State University
Ithaca College
Jackson State University
Macalester College
Montclair State University
Muhlenberg College
New College of Florida
North Central College
Occidental College
Pitzer College
Princeton University
Rollins College
Sam Houston State University
Sarah Lawrence College
Skidmore College
Stetson University
Texas A&M International University
Trinity College
Trinity University
University at Albany
University of Maryland Baltimore County
University of Richmond
University of San Diego
UNLV
Ursinus College
Valparaiso University
West Point Military Academy
Wheaton College - Massachusetts
Willamette University

Allegheny College
Amherst College
Barry University
Berea College
Caltech
Colorado College
Converse College
Duquesne University
Elmira College
Hamilton College
Hampshire College
Haverford College
Hofstra University
Hood College
Illinois Wesleyan University
Linfield College
Loyola Marymount University
Mercer University
Mercyhurst College
Messiah College
Millsaps College
Misericordia University
Rensselaer Polytechnic Institute
Rider University
St. Lawrence University
Taylor University

UC Merced
Union College
Warren Wilson College
Washington & Lee University
Wayne State University
Wellesley College
Wilkes University
Youngstown State University

Babson College
Bates College
Bryn Mawr College
Cal State San Marcos
Chapman University
College of Notre Dame of Maryland
College of the Holy Cross
Connecticut College
Cornell College
Denison University
Eckerd College
Elizabethtown College
Freed-Hardeman University
Geneva College
Hanover College
Hastings College
Hollins University
La Roche College
Oakwood University
Rhodes College
Rice University
Saint Leo University
Samford University
University of Central Oklahoma
University of Mount Union
University of Tampa
University of Wisconsin - Stout
Wake Forest University
Washington & Jefferson College

Carleton College
Colgate University
College of Wooster
Dickinson College
Earlham College
Florida Atlantic University
Furman University
Goucher College
Harvey Mudd College
Kenyon College
Lawrence University
Lehigh University
Marlboro College
Middlebury College
Ohio Wesleyan University
Pepperdine University
Pomona College
Rowan University
Saint Francis University
Scripps College
Southwestern University
St. Olaf College

University of Maryland Eastern Shore
Vassar College
Wesleyan University
Whitman College

D+

Albion College
Beloit College
Bucknell University
Claflin University
Dartmouth College
Florida Southern College
Franklin & Marshall College
Grove City College
Gustavus Adolphus College
Hampton University
Luther College
St. Mary's University
Susquehanna University
Truman State University
University of South Dakota
Williams College

D

Belmont University
Centre College
Radford University

D-

Alfred University
DePauw University
Gettysburg College
Grinnell College
Juniata College
Lafayette College

F

—

Weather

A high Weather grade designates that temperatures are mild and rarely reach extremes, that the campus tends to be sunny rather than rainy, and that weather is fairly consistent rather than unpredictable.

A+

Cal State Long Beach
Chapman University
Eckerd College
Pepperdine University
San Diego State University
Santa Clara University
UC Santa Barbara
University of Miami
University of San Diego

A

Barry University
Cal Poly
Cal State San Marcos
Caltech
Claremont McKenna College
Colorado College
Florida Atlantic University
Florida Southern College
Harvey Mudd College
Loyola Marymount University
New College of Florida
Occidental College
Pitzer College
Pomona College
Rollins College
Saint Leo University
Scripps College
St. Mary's University
Stanford University
Stetson University
UC Irvine
UC San Diego
UCLA
University of Southern California
University of Tampa
University of Texas

A-

Arizona State University
Birmingham-Southern College
Cal Poly Pomona
Cal State Northridge
Louisiana College
Louisiana State University
Millsaps College
Montana State University
Southwestern University
St. Edward's University
Texas State University - San Marcos
Texas Tech University
UC Santa Cruz
University of Arizona

University of Central Florida
University of South Florida

B+

Boston College
Centenary College of Louisiana
City College of New York
CUNY Lehman College
CUNY Queens College
Davidson College
Fordham University
Freed-Hardeman University
Furman University
Guilford College
Hunter College
Northern Arizona University
Sacramento State
Sam Houston State University
San Francisco State University
Southern Methodist University
Spelman College
Texas A&M University
Texas Christian University
UC Berkeley
University of Colorado
University of Denver
University of Mississippi
University of San Francisco
University of the Incarnate Word
University of Virginia
UNLV
Wagner College
Wake Forest University
Warren Wilson College

B

Arcadia University
Auburn University
Baylor University
Belmont University
Cal State Monterey Bay
Clemson University
Colby College
College of Charleston
College of Mount Saint Vincent
Concordia College at Moorhead
Converse College
Duke University
Elizabethtown College
Elmhurst College
Elon University
Emory University
Florida State University
Georgetown University
Gonzaga University
Hanover College
Hollins University
Jackson State University
Lewis & Clark College

Loyola University Chicago
Old Dominion University
Oral Roberts University
Radford University
Rhodes College
Rice University
Saint Joseph's University
Samford University
Seton Hall University
Swarthmore College
Taylor University
Tennessee State University
Trinity University
Tulane University
UC Merced
UC Riverside
University of Alabama
University of Florida
University of Georgia
University of North Carolina - Greensboro
University of Oklahoma
University of Richmond
University of Tennessee at Chattanooga
Vanderbilt University

B-

Austin College
Barnard College
Baruch College
Bay Path College
Boston University
Bowdoin College
Bryn Mawr College
California University of Pennsylvania
Catholic University of America
Centre College
Cleveland State University
Columbia College Chicago
Columbia University
Drexel University
East Carolina University
Elmira College
Fashion Institute of Technology
Florida A&M University
George Mason University
George Washington University
Georgia State University
Goucher College
Hampton University
Hastings College
Haverford College
Hofstra University
Howard University
Idaho State University
James Madison University
John Carroll University
Kansas State University
Linfield College
Loyola University Maryland
Manhattan College
Manhattanville College
Messiah College
Miami University

Montclair State University
Muhlenberg College
New York University
North Carolina State University
Northwestern College - Saint Paul
Princeton University
Purchase College
Purdue University
Reed College
Rider University
Robert Morris University
Rowan University
Sarah Lawrence College
St. John's University
Stevenson University
SUNY New Paltz
Temple University
Texas A&M International University
Towson University
Troy University
UC Davis
University at Buffalo
University of Arkansas
University of Delaware
University of Iowa
University of Kansas
University of Kentucky
University of Louisville
University of Maryland
University of Maryland Baltimore County
University of Maryland Eastern Shore
University of Montana
University of Nebraska
University of North Carolina
University of Pennsylvania
University of South Carolina
University of South Dakota
University of Tennessee
University of Utah
University of Washington
University of Western Ontario
Ursinus College
Villanova University
Virginia Commonwealth University
West Virginia University
Western Kentucky University
Willamette University

American University
Amherst College
Ball State University
Berea College
Bob Jones University
Brigham Young University
Bryant University
Bucknell University
Carnegie Mellon University
Claflin University
Clark Atlanta University
College of Notre Dame of Maryland
College of William & Mary
College of Wooster
Cornell College
Creighton University
Denison University
DePaul University

Dickinson College
Dordt College
Duquesne University
Earlham College
Ferris State University
Franklin & Marshall College
Gannon University
Geneva College
Georgia Tech
Gettysburg College
Grinnell College
Hamilton College
Hampshire College
Hood College
Illinois State University
Illinois Wesleyan University
Indiana University
Iowa State University
Ithaca College
IUPUI
Johns Hopkins University
Kenyon College
La Roche College
Lafayette College
Lehigh University
Mercer University
Mercyhurst College
Michigan State University
Middle Tennessee State University
North Carolina A&T State University
North Central College
Northeastern University
Ohio State University
Ohio University
Ohio Wesleyan University
Pace University
Russell Sage College
Rutgers University
Saint Louis University
St. Lawrence University
Stony Brook University
SUNY Fredonia
SUNY Oswego
Susquehanna University
Trinity College
Truman State University
University of Central Oklahoma
University of Illinois
University of Maine
University of Michigan
University of Minnesota
University of Missouri
University of Notre Dame
University of Oregon
University of Rhode Island
University of Rochester
Washington & Jefferson College
Washington & Lee University
Washington University in St. Louis
Wayne State University
Wesleyan University
West Point Military Academy
Wheaton College - Illinois
Xavier University
Yale University

Alverno College
Bentley University
Brigham Young University - Idaho
Brown University
Chatham University
College for Creative Studies
Dartmouth College
Grove City College
Juniata College
Lawrence University
Luther College
Macalester College
Massachusetts College of Art & Design
Minnesota State University - Moorhead
Northern Illinois University
Penn State
Providence College
Rhode Island School of Design
Saint Francis University
Salisbury University
Slippery Rock University
Smith College
University of Cincinnati
University of Illinois at Chicago
University of Massachusetts
University of Pittsburgh
University of Wisconsin
University of Wisconsin - Stout
Valparaiso University
Virginia Tech
Western Illinois University
Whitman College
Wilkes University

Albion College
Babson College
Bates College
Beloit College
Binghamton University
Carleton College
Case Western Reserve University
Clark University
College of the Holy Cross
Connecticut College
Eastern Kentucky University
Emerson College
Grand Valley State University
Harvard University
Indiana University of Pennsylvania
Kent State University
Marquette University
McGill University
Middlebury College
Misericordia University
MIT
Mount Holyoke College
Seattle University
Simmons College
St. Olaf College
Tufts University
University of Connecticut

University of Hartford
University of Mount Union
University of Puget Sound
University of Vermont
Vassar College
Wellesley College
Wheaton College - Massachusetts
Williams College
Youngstown State University

D+

Allegheny College
Bard College
Bradley University
Brandeis University
Colgate University
Cornell University
Missouri State University
Northwestern University
Oakwood University
Oberlin College
Rochester Institute of Technology
Syracuse University
University of New Hampshire

D

Alfred University
DePauw University
Gustavus Adolphus College
Marlboro College
Rensselaer Polytechnic Institute
Skidmore College
Union College
University at Albany
University of Chicago

D-

—

F

—

Albion College

611 E. Porter St.; Albion, MI 49224
(517) 629-1000; www.albion.edu

THE BASICS:

Acceptance Rate: 79%	Student-Faculty Ratio: 13:1
Yield: 31%	Retention Rate: 85%
Setting: Town	Graduation Rate: 73%
Control: Private Non-Profit	Tuition: $30,006
Total Undergrads: 1,738	Room & Board: $8,510
SAT Range: 1590–1960*	Avg. Aid Package: $21,044
ACT Range: 22–28	Students With Aid: 99%

* of 2400

Academics	B	Greek Life	A-
Athletics	B	Guys	B
Campus Dining	B+	Health & Safety	A-
Campus Housing	B	Local Atmosphere	C+
Campus Strictness	B-	Nightlife	C
Computers	A+	Off-Campus Dining	C+
Diversity	D	Off-Campus Housing	C-
Drug Safety	C+	Parking	A-
Facilities	B+	Transportation	D+
Girls	B+	Weather	C-

CP's Student Author On...
OVERALL EXPERIENCE

Overall, Albion College is great for a number of reasons. The small campus makes it easy to make friends immediately and meet new people. While living in Albion can be boring at times, making the most of it is sometimes what will leave you with the most memories. There is a sense of community on Albion's campus that is hard to duplicate anywhere else. This isn't to say that everyone gets along, but there is a certain bond between all Albion students.

Albion's liberal arts education is something that also seems to be unique to the College. The professors are approachable, and their excitement for their courses is infectious. Even when you're taking a class that is not related to your major, you appreciate what you learn and are proud of what you've learned in looking back. Beneath the exterior sometimes, Albion is just a down-home friendly kind of place, and a lot of students seek comfort in that and learn to love where they are.

Students Speak Out On...
OVERALL EXPERIENCE

Q The Briton Experience

"Albion is a top-notch school. The campus is small, but you're not on top of other students. There are beautiful places to study outside in the summer and quiet places to study on cooler days. The academics are chanllenging, but the professors there know their stuff and are willing to help you whenever you need it. This is my favorite place to be."

Q "Despite all the negatives, I have come to really enjoy Albion. It's true that there isn't a lot to do on campus or in town, but relying on yourself and your friends to make the fun is a good skill to have. Overall, I've been satisfied."

Q "Overall, I like Albion. I love my professors, classes, and extracurricular groups. I appreciate the opportunities Albion gives me, such as a chance to study abroad or get involved in research. I love the very small pocket of unique and liberal friends I have found. However, I am frustrated about how narrow-minded and backwards Albion can be. Albion College still has a long way to go."

BEST OF ALBION

1. The education
2. Professors
3. Unlimited meal plan
4. Small campus size
5. Free movies at the Bohm Theatre
6. Painting the Rock
7. $25 Eat Shop cards

Happy Students
85% of students return after their first year.

Proven Success
73% of students will complete their education and graduate with a degree.

WORST OF ALBION

1. The library closes at 2 a.m.
2. Food at Baldwin
3. Impossible process to live off campus
4. Small-town size
5. Alcohol policies

Expensive
Tuition is a steep $30,006, one of the most expensive rates in the country.

Want a Job? On Your Own
There aren't any placement services for graduates.

Student Body

African American:	3%	Male Undergrads:	47%
Asian American:	2%	Female Undergrads:	53%
Hispanic:	1%	Living On Campus:	90%
International:	1%	Living Off Campus:	9%
Native American:	0%	Male Athletes:	36%
White:	87%	Female Athletes:	20%
Unknown:	4%	Fraternity Members:	44%
From Out-of-State:	13%	Sorority Members:	43%

Frequently Compared Schools:

Allegheny College
Case Western Reserve University
Michigan State University
University of Michigan

Students Speak Out On...
EVERYTHING!

ACADEMICS

"I have been very pleased overall with the professors at Albion. They seem to really care about the students and are eager to help everyone understand. They are very knowledgeable and find ways to make the material interesting."

"The benefit of Albion professors is that the enthusiasm that comes from your professor will be infectious, and you can't help but enjoy yourself. However, if you find yourself wavering on a subject or show some form of disdain towards what you're learning, it's usually best to get out of that class. If not, it'll soon become the longest semester of your life."

"I have loved almost all of the teachers I have had at Albion. They're fun, interesting, and really love the subjects they're teaching. They really want to help students and go well beyond basic office hours to do this."

ATHLETICS

"Varsity sports are fairly big on campus. Lots of students participate, but there are also a great deal of students who do not. IM sports are huge, and they tend to draw in a variety of different people, which is pretty cool."

"Basketball, football, and sometimes baseball are big on campus, and IM sports are huge. Tons of people play IM sports and really like it. I would say only about half of people actually go to the football game, but a lot of people tailgate."

CAMPUS DINING

"At first, I hated Baldwin, but now I don't mind it too much. The Eat Shop is super expensive, but because Albion is so small, it's sometimes your only choice. I like New China, and you can always order pizza."

"The food is one of the best parts about Albion. There's so much variety and so much food at Baldwin. Even if you don't like the 'meal of the day,' you can make a sandwich, stir-fry, Belgian waffle, pasta creation, pizza, or anything else you can come up with. Plus, the cafeteria has really good desserts."

CAMPUS HOUSING

Average

"The campus is beautiful and one of the things that drew a lot of people here. The dorms are in decent condition and of a decent size-- the biggest problem is lack of cellphone reception and occasional problems with internet connection. I personally think the cost of living here is too high, for what you get."

"Even though Wesley is a total dump, it's a great experience for all freshmen. Mitchell is probably the nicest dorm on campus because they just redid it, but Whitehouse is the more social upperclassmen dorm."

GUYS & GIRLS

Strange

"Albion, to me, feels strangely cliquey. I feel like people latch onto others either in their program, or in fraternities/sororities, and don't really break out of that. Most students dress casually-- there are a few stand-out characters."

"Like any place, some are hot, some are not, and some are in-between. Most that are hot, nice, and intelligent are already taken."

HEALTH & SAFETY

"The security is good on campus. Campus Safety will provide escorts to students who feel unsafe walking from place to place late at night. However, as a woman, I've never used the service and have always felt safe on my own."

"Campus Safety is always around, which can be a good or bad thing depending on your perspective. The campus is pretty safe overall, though. Sure, there have been a few incidents, but none of them were serious, and they all could have been prevented if the students had requested rides from Campus Safety."

LOOKING FOR MORE?

Check out our full-length guide to this school at collegeprowler.com/albion-college/.

74 | Albion College

www.collegeprowler.com

Alfred University

One Saxon Drive; Alfred, NY 14802
(607) 871-2115; www.alfred.edu

THE BASICS:

Acceptance Rate: 70%	Student-Faculty Ratio: 12:1
Yield: 26%	Retention Rate: 71%
Setting: Town	Graduation Rate: 67%
Control: Private Non-Profit	Tuition: $25,096
Total Undergrads: 1,909	Room & Board: $11,532
SAT Range: 1470–1783*	Avg. Aid Package: $21,552
ACT Range: 22–27	Students With Aid: 95%

* of 2400

Academics	B	Greek Life	N/A
Athletics	C	Guys	B-
Campus Dining	C+	Health & Safety	A
Campus Housing	B-	Local Atmosphere	C
Campus Strictness	B+	Nightlife	C-
Computers	B+	Off-Campus Dining	B-
Diversity	D+	Off-Campus Housing	C+
Drug Safety	B-	Parking	B
Facilities	B+	Transportation	D-
Girls	B-	Weather	D

CP's Student Author On...
OVERALL EXPERIENCE

Throughout your Alfred experience, you or someone close to you will utter the phrase, "I've got to get out of here." Students at AU make threats to transfer at least twice daily. Still very few actually do. Many of us stay for an extra year. Some of us stay for grad school, and a good portion of our staff are also AU alum. Why?

We're spoiled! It's comfortable here, the financial aid is great, and many of our professors are also great mentors. Who would want to leave all that personal attention and a close-knit group of friends to just be a number at another university with a better football team?

AU students will disparage their time at AU with venom. When asked to appraise their experience honestly, however, they'll shrug their shoulders and admit that Alfred has helped them to learn and grow as an individual. While some individuals transfer, the majority of students who chose Alfred know deep down that they couldn't be anywhere else.

Students Speak Out On...
OVERALL EXPERIENCE

Q "Alfred has given me everything it could since I was a sophomore. By the end of my second year, I was seriously thinking about transferring, but never did. Entering my senior year, I deeply regret my decision. Despite what people tell you, school name recognition is important, and no one in Rochester even knows about Alfred. Going to school in a bigger city will allow easier networking and internship opportunities."

Q "Knowing how much you can actually get from the close-knit community at Alfred, I would never change the choice I made. My experience is something that I would not have gotten anywhere else."

Q "I like the small-town feeling; it helps you to concentrate on what you have to do. It was meant to be that I ended up there."

Q "AU is wonderful, and I wouldn't have wanted to be anywhere else. In fact, I transferred to Alfred, so I was somewhere else and came here!"

BEST OF ALFRED

1. Your friends
2. Financial aid
3. Cool teachers
4. Nature
5. Senior shows
6. Networking
7. Hot Dog Day
8. Visiting artists/lecturers

Genders Equally Represented
A male-to-female ratio of 50/50 means there's a pretty even balance of students on campus.

WORST OF ALFRED

1. Sporadic weather
2. Isolation
3. Boredom
4. Finding a parking spot
5. Ade Dining Hall
6. Bars close at 2 a.m.
7. Fighting with the registrar's office

Lowest Grades
Transportation: D-
Weather: D
Diversity: D+

Student Body

African American:	4%	Male Undergrads:	51%
Asian American:	2%	Female Undergrads:	49%
Hispanic:	2%	Living On Campus:	67%
International:	3%	Living Off Campus:	33%
Native American:	1%	Male Athletes:	31%
White:	66%	Female Athletes:	22%
Unknown:	23%	Fraternity Members:	0%
From Out-of-State:	32%	Sorority Members:	0%

Frequently Compared Schools:

Allegheny College
Ithaca College
Rochester Institute of Technology
University of Rochester

Students Speak Out On...
EVERYTHING!

ACADEMICS

Q "The teachers at Alfred all seem to know their stuff. They have worked in their fields and bring in real world experience."

Q "The teachers are kind of a toss-up. There are a lot of really cool, interesting professors, but then a lot of average or below average professors, too. But you can usually figure out pretty quickly which professors to take classes from by asking the upperclassmen and trial and error."

Q "I find my classes very interesting. The teachers are great! Some of them are like your best friends, and others are like parents away from home."

ATHLETICS

Q **Athletic Facilities Are Very Poor**
"the available athletics facilities are not up to modern standard."

Q "I don't know actually. I never went to a game. From what I heard, some of them can get pretty big, but there's more alternative sports stuff rather than the football/baseball type stuff, like ultimate Frisbee"

Q "Sports are not big on campus, though most people play them. The teams are bad to mediocre."

CAMPUS DINING

Q "The dining hall food is bad. You know, poor quality, presentation, and taste. Li'l Alf is okay."

Q "People will complain about dining hall food just like every other college. However, the staff really does try very hard to expand their menu and bring in restaurants and cafés for special meals."

CAMPUS HOUSING

Q **AU Housing Options**
"The pine hill suites are nice and comfortable, but you have to walk up a big hill. The upper class apartments are bigger and more conveniently located. Isolated living at on campus houses is also an option. Many students move off campus after two years."

Q THE DORMS

"I really hate the dorm at Alfred university. They have RA'S that want to treat you like children, and dirty people who can't clean u after themselves on the weekends the restrooms are horrible. On the weekends there is nothing to do but the the same things over and over again. Since so many people are local they go home dont he weekends making the school feel lonely."

GUYS & GIRLS

Q **Eh.**
"There are a few good looking girls and a few good looking guys but overall, I'd give the campus a 6/10. The dress is interesting and it varies as there are many art students and many engineers. Boys are sex crazy as usual but so are the girls. You'll find mostly country types, city types, and a few crazies."

Q "Can't help you on the guys. I was busy checking out the women, then after the first five minutes was over . . . The women and men are varied. It seems that every year it gets better. I think because you get so tired of seeing the same people, you want the next bunch to be prettier!"

HEALTH & SAFETY

Q **Alfred**
"Alfred is so small I feel safe no matter what. I am out and about two three even four in the morning without any worry. Crime in Alfred?? Never even really hear about any of that stuff."

Q **Safety**
"The campus is small and very safe. You can go out alone at night without worrying about your safety. The local Police work closely with the schools public safety and rescue squad. However it is a university and things will happen once in a while."

LOOKING FOR MORE?
Check out our full-length guide to this school at collegeprowler.com/alfred-university/.

Allegheny College

520 N. Main St.; Meadville, PA 16335
(814) 332-3100; www.allegheny.edu

THE BASICS:

Acceptance Rate: 66%
Yield: 22%
Setting: Town
Control: Private Non-Profit
Total Undergrads: 2,132
SAT Range: 1650–1950*
ACT Range: 23–29

Student-Faculty Ratio: 12:1
Retention Rate: 88%
Graduation Rate: 74%
Tuition: $33,560
Room & Board: $8,440
Avg. Aid Package: $25,134
Students With Aid: 98%

of 2400

Academics	B+	Greek Life	B+
Athletics	C	Guys	B
Campus Dining	C+	Health & Safety	B-
Campus Housing	B-	Local Atmosphere	C
Campus Strictness	B-	Nightlife	B
Computers	C	Off-Campus Dining	C
Diversity	C-	Off-Campus Housing	C
Drug Safety	C+	Parking	B
Facilities	B	Transportation	C+
Girls	C+	Weather	D+

CP's Student Author On...
OVERALL EXPERIENCE

Something commonly heard from recent graduates is how much easier graduate programs were after the rigorous Allegheny courseload. Whether at grad school or at their first job out of college, Allegheny graduates have the skills to succeed in their fields. When considering their time at Allegheny, most students are very thankful for the education they received and all of the great people they got to know. There are so many different kinds of people and points of view that students are encouraged to do anything they truly want to do. Most people feel that they have really grown and changed as a result of the Allegheny experience—and in a good way.

There are students who have regrets or who feel they were in some way disappointed with their Allegheny education or experience. For one thing, Meadville does not provide the kinds of opportunities or the nightlife that a big-city university would. Succeeding at Allegheny is a lot of work and students looking for a party school will not find it here. It takes a lot of time and effort, and for some, it might not be worth it. But all that time and effort is meant to pay off, and for hard-working students, it does.

Students Speak Out On...
OVERALL EXPERIENCE

Q Allegheny - the Steping Stone to Real Life

"Allegheny is a great chance for college students to become a part of the college community and community. In both cases you get that next step of independence and as the years go one you have the choice to experiance more through classes and housing. Allegheny has made my life enjoyable while helping to teach me how to adjust to the world to come!"

Q I've Never Looked Back

"I find that sometimes the amount of work that Professors expect us to do is overwhelming. That being said, I think the work that they have us doing really teaches you not only to learn, but to think. We know how to have fun and a good time here, but during the week don't expect to party. You can, but that will not do well for you."

Q I'm Lovin' It!

"My overall experience at Allegheny College has been a positive one; I really enjoyed the personal interaction with professors, and although you have to work really hard, there are plenty of resources to help you succeed. I really broke the bank coming here, but I feel it'll be worth it."

BEST OF ALLEGHENY

1. The academic atmosphere
2. Being able to have a car
3. Being able to walk everywhere
4. Being close to so many cities
5. Fall

Happy Students
88% of students return after their first year.

Proven Success
74% of students will complete their education and graduate with a degree.

WORST OF ALLEGHENY

1. Administrative red tape
2. Broken computer labs
3. Common showers
4. Construction
5. Meal plan/dining
6. Network/Internet connection
7. The nightlife

Expensive
Tuition is a steep $33,560, one of the most expensive rates in the country.

Not Much Diversity
One of the least racially diverse campuses—only 10% of students are minorities.

Student Body

African American:	3%	Male Undergrads:	44%
Asian American:	3%	Female Undergrads:	56%
Hispanic:	2%	Living On Campus:	78%
International:	2%	Living Off Campus:	22%
Native American:	0%	Male Athletes:	39%
White:	90%	Female Athletes:	20%
Unknown:	0%	Fraternity Members:	22%
From Out-of-State:	48%	Sorority Members:	33%

Frequently Compared Schools:

College of Wooster
Denison University
Dickinson College
Oberlin College

Students Speak Out On...
EVERYTHING!

ACADEMICS

Great Academics, Big Workload

"I have been intellectually challenged at Allegheny. However, whenever I am having a hard time, my professors happily meet with me to make sure that I fully understand the material. Overall, it's a great learning environment."

Professors Have Office Hours

"Professors are required to have a certain amount of office hours outside of class so they are most always available to help you with homework or projects outside of class. My professors have put their home and cell numbers on their syllabi if we ever need to get in contact with them when office hours are closed."

ATHLETICS

We Have a Good Sports Program.

"The sports at our school are well supported. I know people that go to all the games, but there is no pressure to feel obligated to go if one does not want to. The athletic facilities at Allegheny are awesome."

Athletics

"I am not an athlete nor an I interested so I cannot comment other than that the fitness center is very nice and provides a variety of classes."

CAMPUS DINING

Two Choices: Parkhurst Dining, or Parkhurst Dining

"Granted, the food isn't that bad. I've had worse. But there are only two places to eat, and they are both college-sponsored, and therefore have the same supplier. Though one looks like Hogwarts dining hall... anyway, learn to switch it up or befriend someone who likes to cook (which isn't hard here)."

This Is Why...

"I think that the dinning halls are very good but because there are only two it gets really boring. The food is very good but the items vary awhile."

CAMPUS HOUSING

Good on-Campus Housing

"You are required to live on-campus for three years at Allegheny so the dorms are pretty good generally speaking. The all freshman dorm (Baldwin) is for those who like a crazy atmosphere. The mixed under/uperclassman dorms are all pretty average--the rooms aren't huge but there pretty nice. Everything is close except Ravine-its kind of a hike. For upperclassman theres also North Village I & II which are brand new, really nice apartment style dorms."

Upperclassmen Dorms Best, Avoid" Baldwin Juice"

"I've heard that the all-freshman dorm(Baldwin)is kind of gross(one kid referred to stickiness on a hall floor as "Baldwin juice"). Brooks/Walker are pretty much standard dorm fare(though they recently carpeted the entire building, which is an improvement). North Village is amazing(but pricey), but North Village II and College Court are also popular options for upperclassmen."

GUYS & GIRLS

Guys and Girls

"normal social relations you would expect at a college. If you sought popular and beautiful in High School, you will find it here. If you kept to the side tables and sneered at the beautiful, or were just frankly disintersted in them, you'll still find company."

HEALTH & SAFETY

Great Safety and Security

"The campus security is on duty 24/7 and they respond to calls promptly and politely. They are willing to help you with big and small problems. If there is an event that poses a threat, the entire campus is notified via email within hours. Things do get stolen and pranks happen quite often but as long as you lock up and are aware of your surroundings you should be fine"

LOOKING FOR MORE?

Check out our full-length guide to this school at collegeprowler.com/allegheny-college/.

Alverno College

3400 S. 43rd St.; Milwaukee, WI 53234
(414) 382-6000; www.alverno.edu

THE BASICS:

Acceptance Rate: 85%
Yield: 53%
Setting: Large city
Control: Private Non-Profit
Total Undergrads: 2,387
SAT Range: —
ACT Range: 17–22

Student-Faculty Ratio: 13:1
Retention Rate: 73%
Graduation Rate: 40%
Tuition: $19,074
Room & Board: $6,486
Avg. Aid Package: $14,191
Students With Aid: 100%

Academics	B+	Greek Life	D
Athletics	D	Guys	N/A
Campus Dining	B+	Health & Safety	A
Campus Housing	A-	Local Atmosphere	A-
Campus Strictness	B	Nightlife	A
Computers	B+	Off-Campus Dining	A
Diversity	C	Off-Campus Housing	A
Drug Safety	A+	Parking	A
Facilities	B+	Transportation	A-
Girls	A-	Weather	C

CP's Student Author On...
OVERALL EXPERIENCE

Most students who have made it through the majority of their years at Alverno say that they cannot imagine being anywhere else. In fact, many students who leave Alverno to go to other schools because of finances or because they didn't think Alverno was a good fit, often come back. Alverno is not just a school—it's a place that teaches women to think outside of the box and to understand themselves. It becomes a home for many people. Alverno graduates go on to become important women in their workplaces, communities, churches, and homes. The College offers students a unique opportunity to take a really good look at themselves and say, "Who am I?" and "Is this who I really want to be?"

Most people say that going to college is an investment in your future, but coming to Alverno is an investment in not only your future, but also your community's future. Almost all students who graduate from Alverno get a job within six months of graduation. Its graduates are competent, well-rounded, and have made a name both locally and internationally.... For the rest of this editorial, visit collegeprowler.com.

Students Speak Out On...
OVERALL EXPERIENCE

Q **I have really enjoyed my years at Alverno**

"I have really enjoyed my years at Alverno. Now that graduation is approaching, I am reflecting more on where I started and where I am today. Alverno has really helped me understand who I am and what's important to me. I feel that if I would have attended a bigger university I would not have had the opportunity to explore some of my interests to the extent that I have here at Alverno."

Q **Choosing Alverno was one of the best choices I've made**

"Choosing Alverno College was one of the best choices I've made. I know that when I graduate in May, 2009, I will be prepared to interview for jobs and make a strong first impression on employers. Alverno has helped me to grow into a strong, independent woman."

Q **Small College**

"very easy to focus here and alot help and support."

BEST OF ALVERNO

1. You are pushed to be the best you can be
2. No letter grading scale
3. Professors give feedback and a chance for revision
4. Less distractions within the classroom

Learn from the Best
90% of faculty have earned the highest degree in their field.

Personal Attention
You can expect personal attention with 55% of classes having less than 20 students.

WORST OF ALVERNO

1. Transferring credits from other schools is tricky.
2. Not enough socialization with guys
3. Living on campus means living with all women, all the time.
4. Students are not very involved on campus.

Want a Job? On Your Own
There aren't any placement services for graduates.

Student Body

African American:	17%	Male Undergrads:	0%
Asian American:	5%	Female Undergrads:	100%
Hispanic:	12%	Living On Campus:	10%
International:	1%	Living Off Campus:	90%
Native American:	1%	Male Athletes:	0%
White:	63%	Female Athletes:	3%
Unknown:	1%	Fraternity Members:	0%
From Out-of-State:	7%	Sorority Members:	2%

Frequently Compared Schools:

Barnard College
Beloit College
Boston College
Marquette University

Students Speak Out On... EVERYTHING!

ACADEMICS

Teachers are basically amazing

"The teachers are basically amazing. I know when I walk into each and every class that the only agenda my teachers have is to benefit my development as a student. I know so many of my teachers and they know me, there are relationships and connections being made, we are like an awesome super functioning community of learners."

The professors are kind, understanding, and helpful

"The professors at Alverno College happen to be some of the most kind, understanding and helpful individuals I have ever had the pleasure to meet. I have never had a question that couldn't be answered or an issue with an assignment that they weren't happy to help me figure out. I love that I can call my professors by their first names and they call me the same. I'm not just a number – I am an individual and I find that to be very beneficial towards my education."

ATHLETICS

Benefits of athletics

"I think the Athletics are a great way to promote a positive body image in women and they can accompany strong academic achievement. And can also assist your time management skills."

All sporting events at Alverno are free!

"One of the great things about sports on campus is that all the sporting events at Alverno are free! Being able to go to sporting events makes me feel more involved and like a part of the community here. And as a student going to a private college, free events on campus rock!"

CAMPUS DINING

The Mug is the best coffee house in the world

"The Mug is the best coffee house in the world!! It's a student-run coffee house that provides tons of delicious drinks and a great study environment. It's an awesome place to meet friends, hang out, or see a cool band."

The Mug is the best coffee house in the world

"The Mug is the best coffee house in the world!! It's a student-run coffee house that provides tons of delicious drinks and a great study environment. It's an awesome place to meet friends, hang out, or see a cool band."

CAMPUS HOUSING

Dorms are great

"The dorms are great. The rooms are fairly large compared to other campuses in the area, and all rooms are provided with a sink. There are only two dorms; Clare is for the more studious, quiet types, and Austin houses all incoming students (unless not coming from high school) and the general population. Alverno is mostly a commuter college, so less than half of the students live on campus. The residence hall has a lot of fun programs that the RAs put on and it is very social and active."

Both Austin Hall and Clare Hall are nice

"Both Austin Hall and Clare Hall are nice. The dorm rooms are large and include a sink. The halls are clean and quiet (for the most part!)"

GUYS & GIRLS

Girls Only

"There are only girls on this campus which make it easier to focus in class. It is also better for us to voice our opinions without the male point of view being around all the time."

No guys, but the girls are great

"No guys, sorry girls. However, I've made some friends that I will have for the rest of my life. It is amazing. You will meet so many friends and have so much fun."

HEALTH & SAFETY

Alverno does a lot to ensure safety

"There has not been a single day or night where I did not feel safe here at Alverno. There are security guards walking around campus 24/7. There are also Community Advisors (CAs) that are on duty every night with a walkie talkie to have one on one access to the security guards if there was anything wrong."

LOOKING FOR MORE?

Check out our full-length guide to this school at collegeprowler.com/alverno-college/.

American University

4400 Massachusetts Ave. NW; Washington, DC 20016
(202) 885-1000; www.american.edu

THE BASICS:

Acceptance Rate: 53%
Yield: 19%
Setting: Large city
Control: Private Non-Profit
Total Undergrads: 6,648
SAT Range: 1750–2060*
ACT Range: 26–30

Student-Faculty Ratio: 13:1
Retention Rate: 90%
Graduation Rate: 76%
Tuition: $34,973
Room & Board: $12,930
Avg. Aid Package: $24,294
Students With Aid: 80%

of 2400

Academics	A-	Greek Life	B-
Athletics	C	Guys	B-
Campus Dining	B+	Health & Safety	B+
Campus Housing	B	Local Atmosphere	A+
Campus Strictness	B+	Nightlife	A-
Computers	B-	Off-Campus Dining	A-
Diversity	B+	Off-Campus Housing	B+
Drug Safety	C-	Parking	C+
Facilities	B-	Transportation	A+
Girls	C+	Weather	C+

CP's Student Author On...
OVERALL EXPERIENCE

Many AU students agree that there is something for everyone at their school, and they are rarely ever bored. Though the school's population is relatively small and has fewer parties compared to state schools, many claim that it is worth it for the culture present in DC and the surrounding area.

Upon arrival at AU, the adjustment period can be tough for people not accustomed to an urban setting. However, making friends is quite easy here for even the shyest of students because of the small, tight-knit AU community. Students here, for the most part, have no problems expressing themselves socially or academically. It seems that a "work hard, play hard" philosophy best suits the students at American University.

Students Speak Out On...
OVERALL EXPERIENCE

Q Everyone Fits in

"I can't be happier with my decision to attend American. There's a place for everyone here. Everyone seems to find their own niche, and the student body is overall pretty friendly."

Q My AU

"I've really come to enjoy my school and its openness. Going into college I didn't place much emphasis on where I went but I count myself lucky that Au was such a good match more me. Being able to jump into any class I want or join groups or even audition for school plays without being a major is really a plus for me. In all honesty the only real draw back for me is how expensive the school is."

Q Advice

"AU first semester is often very quiet and shy. This turns off many new students who are outgoing and vibrant like myself. Spring semester gets 100000000 times better I PROMISED. I also joined Greek like which at a state school I would never have done but at AU it is a great way to meet more people and make lots of friends and party connections."

BEST OF AMERICAN

1. Small classes
2. Politically passionate students and faculty
3. Great food off campus
4. Internship opportunities in the city
5. Comfortable, clean, and friendly dorms

Happy Students
90% of students return after their first year.

Proven Success
76% of students will complete their education and graduate with a degree.

WORST OF AMERICAN

1. Administrative bureaucracy
2. Expensive tuition
3. Very limited math program
4. Cost of living
5. Overwhelming political focus of the campus

Expensive
Tuition is a steep $34,973, one of the most expensive rates in the country.

Expensive to Just Get By
77% of students surveyed felt that the amount it costs to live while at school was worse than average.

Student Body

African American:	4%	Male Undergrads:	39%
Asian American:	5%	Female Undergrads:	61%
Hispanic:	4%	Living On Campus:	75%
International:	7%	Living Off Campus:	25%
Native American:	0%	Male Athletes:	5%
White:	56%	Female Athletes:	4%
Unknown:	23%	Fraternity Members:	14%
From Out-of-State:	99%	Sorority Members:	16%

Frequently Compared Schools:

Boston College
Boston University
George Washington University
Northeastern University

Students Speak Out On... EVERYTHING!

ACADEMICS

Q Elementary Education

"The classes needed for the major are very enjoyable, the professors are extremely approachable, and because it is a very small major the advisors really have the oppurtunity to focus on and get to know the students."

Q Great Professors

"Where AU really shines is the quality of professors. Active in their fields, AU professors are generally ble to give students a view from both the practical and academic sides of an issue. Every school has its bad professors, but the good ones go far beyond expectation."

ATHLETICS

Q Fan Support & School Spirit

"Woosh Go AU!!!! The fans aka AU's "Blue Crew" really make the sport games on campus exciting. Everyone comes out to cheer on our teams and the entire arena is filled with screaming fans!"

Q Athletics

"The athletic scene is not huge at American. The school spirit is there if you want it but not overwhelming, its no penn state or maryland when it comes to that. The athletic facilities are nice."

CAMPUS DINING

Q Food

"Excellent food and consideration for vegetarians/vegans"

Q Limited Variety, but Pretty Good.

"While many students hate on TDR (Terrance Dining Room), but I think that its good for college food. Tons of vegetarian options for sure, which I like even as a meat eater. Cons: Tavern is greasy besides the pizza and only two places on campus take meal swipes."

CAMPUS HOUSING

Q Good but Not Great.

"Most student move off campus after two years. This is generally because it is very easy to get caught breaking the rules (ex. drinking) in the dorms, because living off campus is cheaper, and because it is very tough to get the room you want as a sophomore."

Q North Side Vs South Side

"On-campus housing for AU is split into North Side and South Side, with each having its own benefits and draw backs. North Side is much quieter, no fire alarms, and you might actually get some studying done in your dorm. South Side is where the social center is on campus, and you don't miss a thing, but it's the part of campus that never sleeps."

GUYS & GIRLS

Q AU Girls Are Absolutely Beautiful

"American University girls are absolutely beautiful. Not only are they generally in (at least) good shape and are otherwise physically attractive, they are intellectually stimulating, fashionable, sophisticated chicks. Not your run-of-the-mill college fare. Sometimes they're kind of stuck up, but where are they not? And anywhere you go you're going to have some undesirables, but for a school that's 60+%% female, there are surprisingly few of them."

Q People Are Average

"Most students at American are average in every arena with the exception of politics, where they really shine, in terms of both knowledge and involvement."

HEALTH & SAFETY

Q Very Safe

"You won't be targeted unless you make yourself a target. Also I'm a big dude who is probably intimidating to many"

LOOKING FOR MORE?

Check out our full-length guide to this school at collegeprowler.com/american-university/.

Amherst College

Boltwood Avenue; Amherst, MA 01002
(413) 542-2000; www.amherst.edu

THE BASICS:

Acceptance Rate: 16%	Student-Faculty Ratio: 8:1
Yield: 38%	Retention Rate: 96%
Setting: Town	Graduation Rate: 95%
Control: Private Non-Profit	Tuition: $38,928
Total Undergrads: 1,750	Room & Board: $10,150
SAT Range: 1970–2310*	Avg. Aid Package: $35,055
ACT Range: 30–34	Students With Aid: 70%

of 2400

Academics	A	Greek Life	D
Athletics	B-	Guys	B
Campus Dining	B	Health & Safety	B+
Campus Housing	B+	Local Atmosphere	C+
Campus Strictness	B+	Nightlife	B-
Computers	A	Off-Campus Dining	B
Diversity	A-	Off-Campus Housing	D
Drug Safety	B	Parking	B+
Facilities	A+	Transportation	C+
Girls	B	Weather	C+

CP's Student Author On...
OVERALL EXPERIENCE

Students usually don't choose Amherst because of its academic reputation, although a sound reputation is a must when the competing schools are Harvard and Williams. Rather, students come here because of the promise of experiencing an eclectic array of stimulating peers, professors, classes, and activities. Some become disillusioned, not finding their niche within the abundance of opportunities and freedom. Some succeed in familiarizing themselves with the ways of this place, find that they're having the time of their life midway through college and become depressed that this whole thing is going to end soon. Chronologically speaking and with clear generalization, freshman year can go by in a rush, with everyone immersed in the whole college experience with their freshmen friends and classmates. Sophomore year can be the most challenging, since a lot of people go through "sophomore slump"—a state of mild or not-so-mild depression caused by the sad fact that all their freshman friends suddenly are not living in the same dorm but are now in far corners of campus.... For the rest of this editorial, visit collegeprowler.com.

Students Speak Out On...
OVERALL EXPERIENCE

Q "It is the greatest liberal arts college in the states! Really!"

Q "I learned a lot, not only from classes, but from the people around me as well. You just have to be willing to engage in conversations. I know this is corny, but I really love this place. I led a very stimulating life here, and I grew up a lot."

Q "Although I was somewhat disappointed with the academics, the interesting people more than made up for it, and in the end, I am happy to have gone to Amherst. It's not perfect. There are plenty of things that I would have liked to see improved. Ultimately though, I know that I'm having a great college experience and if I could turn back time, I probably wouldn't go anywhere else."

Q "I love Amherst, and I am glad that I am here. This place offers a perfect environment to learn and find out who I am and what I like to do. The open curriculum is incredible because I take only the classes that I think are interesting and not the classes some random person who doesn't even know me thought were important to take."

BEST OF AMHERST

1. Awesome people
2. Cream-of-the-crop academics
3. Great parties
4. Free alcohol everywhere
5. Highly generous financial aid program and school funding for student projects

Happy Students
96% of students return after their first year.

Commitment to Teaching
There are 8 students for every member of faculty on campus.

WORST OF AMHERST

1. The town of Amherst
2. The weather, oh the weather
3. Valentine Dining Hall and the gastronomical aspect of central dining
4. Students who don't make an effort and hurt class discussion

Expensive
Tuition is a steep $38,928, one of the most expensive rates in the country.

AP Credit Wasted
Any AP credits earned in high school aren't eligible for college credit.

Student Body

African American:	10%	Male Undergrads:	49%
Asian American:	10%	Female Undergrads:	51%
Hispanic:	10%	Living On Campus:	98%
International:	7%	Living Off Campus:	2%
Native American:	0%	Male Athletes:	45%
White:	42%	Female Athletes:	33%
Unknown:	15%	Fraternity Members:	0%
From Out-of-State:	87%	Sorority Members:	0%

Frequently Compared Schools:

Bowdoin College
Brown University
Middlebury College
Williams College

Students Speak Out On... EVERYTHING!

ACADEMICS

Q Professor Willing to Reach Out

"The major advantage of Amherst College is that the population is so small; this leaves more than enough resources for students to get extra help from professors and other tutoring services. I found that my professors were always excited to engage in conversation outside of the classroom setting, and it really enriched my college experience."

Q "The teachers are very friendly and ready to help you out with any problem. The classes are bound to be interesting if you choose topics you like."

Q "Professors are really accessible here. Some have even abandoned set office hours and will make themselves free for any students who wish to come and see them almost at any time. It's great to be able to be lectured formally and then to come talk about the class with the professor one-on-one. I feel more connected to the course material, since I know what the professor is trying to get at and what he or she wants to emphasize."

ATHLETICS

Q Lacking on Fan Support

"Sports are a major part of the Amherst community, but because of the small number of students in the community, fan-support at games is low. Those who care about sports are often engaged in their own team obligations, and the non-athletes go out to support the athletes on campus less than regularly."

Q "Varsity sports are quite a big thing here, since Amherst offers athletic scholarships."

Q "The majority of people play some sport: club, varsity, whatever. The culture is more athletic than some comparable schools."

CAMPUS DINING

Q Valentine Dining Hall

"You can always find good food to eat at val but the food does get repetitive. Dining services does make an effort however to cater to all needs. This includes vegetarians and vegans."

Q "The food is nutritional, and there is a pretty good variety, particularly among the salad bar and cereals (if that's a big deal). But the entrées are generally bland."

CAMPUS HOUSING

Q Oldish, but Nice

"Relatively nice, and although some of it's old, it's all very accessible and generally pretty."

Q "Housing on campus is generally good. Dorms to avoid: Appleton and Williston, James and Stearns, and Waldorf-Astoria and Plaza (the last two are modular units/trailer parks). Upperclassman housing is usually better than freshmen housing, though some dorms are more far away. Nice dorms are Pratt, Moore, Morrow, and Valentine, which is the dorm above the dining hall."

GUYS & GIRLS

Q Decent

"Everyone is decent-looking, and dresses similarly."

Q "Some guys are really cool. There are datable people on both sides. The girls, in my opinion, are simply gorgeous. Some guys are good-looking."

HEALTH & SAFETY

Q Very Safe

"There are almost no problems on campus; everyone knows each other to a certain extent, and although there is some theft, it is minor."

Q "It seems very safe at Amherst, but I am still afraid to walk alone at night since the school is off of Route 9, which is a busy street."

LOOKING FOR MORE?

Check out our full-length guide to this school at collegeprowler.com/amherst-college/.

Arcadia University

450 S. Easton Road; Glenside, PA 19038
(215) 572-2900; www.arcadia.edu

THE BASICS:

Acceptance Rate: 61%	Student-Faculty Ratio: 13:1
Yield: 17%	Retention Rate: 77%
Setting: Suburban	Graduation Rate: 68%
Control: Private Non-Profit	Tuition: $31,260
Total Undergrads: 2,253	Room & Board: $10,680
SAT Range: 1510–1810*	Avg. Aid Package: $21,411
ACT Range: 21–27	Students With Aid: 100%

of 2400

Academics	B-	Greek Life	N/A
Athletics	C-	Guys	B
Campus Dining	D+	Health & Safety	B
Campus Housing	C+	Local Atmosphere	C
Campus Strictness	B-	Nightlife	C+
Computers	C+	Off-Campus Dining	C
Diversity	B-	Off-Campus Housing	B
Drug Safety	C-	Parking	B
Facilities	D+	Transportation	B-
Girls	C+	Weather	B

CP's Student Author On...
OVERALL EXPERIENCE

Arcadia has a great close-knit community of students that makes everyone feel very welcome. It is a great University for personalized attention, with professors who are all very helpful and knowledgeable in their areas and work well with students. In addition to their dedication, most professors have the highest level of recognized achievement in their fields, so they know what they are talking about. Outside of classroom activities and involvement, there are also many study abroad opportunities, where students can meet people from all over the world.

The best way to have an amazing experience is to get involved right away. While some feel that Arcadia does not offer much in the way of partying or crazy nightlife, it has other perks, including its small community of people passionate about what they are doing. Get involved, talk to people, and you'll have a great college experience.

Students Speak Out On...
OVERALL EXPERIENCE

Q It's Pretty Great :)
"Arcadia is actually a great place to go to school. If you come here to party, you'll probably be disappointed; but if you want to actually make friends and remember your time in college, it's amazing. The academics are decent, and events are actually fun if you give them a chance."

Q I Love It.
"I couldn't picture myself anywhere else but here. This university wasn't on the top of my list but I am so glad I reconsidered. The programs and teachers are wonderful. The campus is beautiful and clean. I am glad I chose this university."

Q Arcadia Has Grown on Me.
"With good friends and campus involvement, I've learned to love this school. You have to give in what you want to get out of it and make the most of it."

BEST OF ARCADIA

1. The study abroad opportunities available to every student, beginning the first year
2. Small class sizes
3. Awesome mix of all kinds of people from every background

Knowledgeable Professors
100% of students surveyed rated the general knowledge of professors as above average.

Low-Stress Course Load
63% of students surveyed rated the manageability of work as above average.

WORST OF ARCADIA

1. High tuition
2. Relatively small campus
3. Sometimes, it gets boring seeing the same people and not having much to do on campus.
4. Getting housing for the next semester is a difficult and confusing process.

Expensive
Tuition is a steep $31,260, one of the most expensive rates in the country.

Expensive Dorms
Living on campus doesn't come cheap, with an average housing price tag of $7,620.

Student Body

African American:	8%	Male Undergrads:	28%
Asian American:	3%	Female Undergrads:	72%
Hispanic:	4%	Living On Campus:	72%
International:	2%	Living Off Campus:	28%
Native American:	0%	Male Athletes:	18%
White:	69%	Female Athletes:	11%
Unknown:	15%	Fraternity Members:	0%
From Out-of-State:	44%	Sorority Members:	0%

Frequently Compared Schools:

Drexel University
Saint Joseph's University
Temple University
Ursinus College

Students Speak Out On...
EVERYTHING!

ACADEMICS

Q Good

"I really like Arcadia but there are some problems as with any school."

Q Small Campus Great Academics

"Physical Therapy is number seven in the nation. Arcadia has wonderful advisors and the curriculum is easy to finish in four years. Freshman get to study abroad for under 1,000 dollars."

ATHLETICS

Q No Football Team at Arcadia?

"There's no football team! Some say it's due to the fact that Arcadia has a pretty decent rate of boys who are homosexual. This is unfortunate, since other sports at Arcadia seem to have a lot of intensity and fan support, and a football team would only increase that."

Q AU!

"Arcadia has a bunch of really good sports teams that put on a pretty good show. The fact of the matter is we are lacking fan support. We need a way to get the school active and out there supporting our teams! For example the womens soccer team is a very good team but they lack fans."

CAMPUS DINING

Q Lots of Food

"The Chat and the Dining Hall offers a lot of options from a deli, to grill, to homestyle cooked foods. The salad bar and breakfast bar are always stocked fresh. The food downstairs is cooked to order and is quick to go through if you are first in line."

Q Arcadia Dining

"The Chat is a good place to go but the dining hall is generally perceived as awful. The Cafe is a popular choice as well."

CAMPUS HOUSING

Q Its Okay

"I really enjoyed living on campus in a dorm. I 've done it for two years and I enjoy how close we all are. I find everything else I've ever had a problem with all condusive to who is living there at the time."

Q Freshman Dorms.

"I lived on the third floor of Dilworth hall for my freshman term--the stairs are a great way to get rid of the "freshman fifteen." The rooms are nice if you know how to decorate, and the walls are thick enough to eliminate outside noise. The upperclassmen dorms in Knight are nicer, and you can also live in apartments through Arcadia."

GUYS & GIRLS

Q There Are a Wide Variety of Guys and Girls

"There are many different guys and girls at Arcadia. There used to be more girls than guys, but a lot of the guys who go here are gay. There is a wide diversity of looks and interests. There are also many international students."

Q Ok I Guess

"The people here are generally attractive, there are some stragglers here and there, but the students are usually either preppy or sporty-sweat pants wearers. The guys who play in sports look like they belong in the modeling world, but they tend to be really stuck up. You don't find a lot of people who are in serious relationships, it's mostly short hookups or flings."

HEALTH & SAFETY

Q Safety at Arcadia Is Excellent!

"Arcadia university is extremely safe. I would be able to walk around campus by myself if I wanted to. There are call boxes everywhere around campus if necessary."

Q Health & Safety

"I have never felt unsafe at Arcadia University. The Campus Security is friendly and helpful and is always willing to help students out."

LOOKING FOR MORE?

Check out our full-length guide to this school at collegeprowler.com/arcadia-university/.

Arizona State University

University Drive & Mill Avenue; Tempe, AZ 85287
(480) 965-9011; www.asu.edu

THE BASICS:

Acceptance Rate: 90%
Yield: 40%
Setting: Mid-sized city
Control: Public
Total Undergrads: 54,277
SAT Range: 950–1210*
ACT Range: 20–26

Student-Faculty Ratio: 23:1
Retention Rate: 81%
Graduation Rate: 56%
Tuition: $19,629
Room & Board: $9,210
Avg. Aid Package: $8,792
Students With Aid: 81%

* of 1600

Academics	B-	Greek Life	C+
Athletics	A	Guys	A-
Campus Dining	B+	Health & Safety	C+
Campus Housing	B	Local Atmosphere	B+
Campus Strictness	B-	Nightlife	A-
Computers	B+	Off-Campus Dining	B+
Diversity	B	Off-Campus Housing	B
Drug Safety	C	Parking	C
Facilities	A-	Transportation	B+
Girls	B+	Weather	A-

CP's Student Author On...
OVERALL EXPERIENCE

Though some students are occasionally discouraged by the school's sub-par academic reputation, the lure of all manner of social temptations, or the University's confounding and convoluted bureaucracy, most discover those feelings to be only temporary. Any student with a capacity for commitment and initiative, as well as a certain social aptitude, can tell you that Arizona State is a terrific environment in which to achieve the sort of growth, both personal and academic, that is expected of a college education. ASU is a large school with a diverse culture and a lot of great people. Students feel that they have met people that have all changed their lives in some way. It's agreed that there are endless things to do here, and there are never-ending possibilities and opportunities as well.

For many, college is all about breaking away and living your own life; that can be hard if ASU is around the corner from your parent's house. Still, there is amazing opportunity for growth and learning here, and even if you are from the local area, it's possible to break away and get caught up in the separate world that lives within ASU.... For the rest of this editorial, visit collegeprowler.com.

Students Speak Out On...
OVERALL EXPERIENCE

Q Amazing

"It's nice to finally choose a path on your own. I know that I was given more opportunities at ASU than I ever would have been offered anywhere else. It's such a large school, but that only means more variety, and I'm finding that variety is a very positive thing."

Q Great Education Program, Art Program, Secured, Nice Environment, Have Fun

"I really like the art and education program at ASU. I also like the fact that walking around campus at any time is really secured"

Q It's One of a Kind

"Every where you turn on the Arizona State campus you will see yellow and maroon. The school is so school spirited. I couldn't imagine anyone diliking this school. Everyone joins together for sporting events and shows their pride for their school, the whole ASU experience will be one I will never forget."

BEST OF ARIZONA STATE

1. Atmosphere
2. Location
3. Nightlife
4. Beautiful people
5. Seeing palm trees and sunshine in December
6. ASU sporting events
7. Dining

Happy Students
81% of students return after their first year.

Knowledgeable Professors
86% of students surveyed rated the general knowledge of professors as above average.

WORST OF ARIZONA STATE

1. Distractions
2. Sushi in Arizona
3. Cab fares
4. Police
5. High costs
6. Summer heat
7. Parking
8. Bouncers

Lowest Grades
Drug Safety: C
Parking: C
Health & Safety: C+

Student Body

African American:	5%	Male Undergrads:	48%
Asian American:	6%	Female Undergrads:	52%
Hispanic:	15%	Living On Campus:	17%
International:	2%	Living Off Campus:	84%
Native American:	2%	Male Athletes:	2%
White:	65%	Female Athletes:	1%
Unknown:	5%	Fraternity Members:	7%
From Out-of-State:	30%	Sorority Members:	8%

Students Speak Out On...
EVERYTHING!

ACADEMICS

Q Can't Wait!

"At this very moment I am still attending Glendale Community College receiving my associates by the end of the fall semester. I am majoring in Broadcast Journalism and am very excited. I am looking forward to being on camera, meeting new people, gossiping about the problems and what is going on in the world, and much more.Right now, I am all about keeping a good GPA and getting all my core requirements out of the way. Although I might get nervous at times, I am very excited for my future!"

Q ASU Football

"Arizona State is known for having one of the best football teams in the state. They work hard during practice and their games and it makes us proud to be a ASU SunDevil!"

Q Fashion

"I feel the fashion class was not all it should have been."

ATHLETICS

Q ASU

"There is a lot of team spirit and most of our teams do exceptionally well."

Q Go Sundevils!

"I can't say this school excels in every activity, but there will always be a crowd of screaming fans. ASU is known for it's post-game partying and wild spirit."

Q Football

"Extremely popular, it seems like everyone is involved in every game"

CAMPUS DINING

Q Plenty of Choice

"Finding a place to eat on campus is fairly easy, as there are several fast food restaurants in the MU, but it's typically packed. There are also plenty of places near the school that are sit down restaurants, mostly on Mill Ave."

Q GREAT Food Town

"The MU has great food options from healthy to fast-food. It is usually packed but there is a TON of great dining just around the edge of campus - lots of ethnic options, cheap eats, plus chain staples so everyone will feel at home."

CAMPUS HOUSING

Q All Dorms Offer Equality

"The dorms are stupendous, they offer great rooms and usually room mates are excellent. The rooms are comfy and makes it great for studying. The students are friendly and easy to get along with."

Q Barrett

"While I can not say much about the housing for the rest of ASU Barrett housing is amazing! It is a great community with plenty of space and many perks!"

GUYS & GIRLS

Q THE HOTTEST

"bleach blonde scottsdale girls and just about any other kind of girl you could want. freshman girls aren't looking for relationships."

Q Diverse

"diverse population, friendly, social although lax in attire"

HEALTH & SAFETY

Q Corona Del Sol

"Corona's campus is generally pretty well-known to be the one of the safest campuses around. Around the school, fights are rare and mild, and security is almost everywhere. As ir relates to safety after school and at dances and the like, it all depends on what crowds one moves in. Overall, I would have to say safety is one of the least of my worries."

Q Safe

"Safety escort is always available and very friendly!"

LOOKING FOR MORE?

Check out our full-length guide to this school at collegeprowler.com/arizona-state-university/.

Auburn University

Auburn, AL 36849
(334) 844-4000; www.auburn.edu

THE BASICS:

Acceptance Rate: 80%
Yield: 33%
Setting: Small city
Control: Public
Total Undergrads: 19,926
SAT Range: 1570–1920*
ACT Range: 23–29

Student-Faculty Ratio: 18:1
Retention Rate: 86%
Graduation Rate: 64%
Tuition: $19,452
Room & Board: $8,972
Avg. Aid Package: $7,917
Students With Aid: 75%

* of 2400

Academics	B	Greek Life	A-
Athletics	A	Guys	A+
Campus Dining	B+	Health & Safety	B-
Campus Housing	A-	Local Atmosphere	B
Campus Strictness	C	Nightlife	A
Computers	B	Off-Campus Dining	B
Diversity	C-	Off-Campus Housing	A+
Drug Safety	C+	Parking	B-
Facilities	A+	Transportation	A
Girls	A-	Weather	B

CP's Student Author On...
OVERALL EXPERIENCE

Overall, students are very happy to be in Auburn. They love the people around them and the experiences that they get to have.

College is what you make of it. If you sit at home and don't do anything, then you won't enjoy yourself no matter where you go. With all the options you have offered to you at Auburn, you have to try to not have a good time. And with a student body that is so happy to be here, it's also hard not to get swept up in the excitement. As always, it's a good idea to visit a college or university before making a final decision. Make sure you're as happy and comfortable as you can possibly be.

Students Speak Out On...
OVERALL EXPERIENCE

Q Amazing

"I was wavering between schools and finally picked auburn. it was the best decision i have ever made. I never want to leave!"

Q Best School Ever

"I love it here. Fall semesters are always tough with football season distracting from the studying, but always a great time. There is a lot of traditions unique to the school that makes coming here and being a part of it the best experience ever. (the warm weather compared to my N. Il. hometown is great)"

Q College Life Is Making Me Into an Adult

"So far college life has been an experience that I will never forget. I have had a lot of growing pains because my mom is not here to do my thinking for me. I'm learning that my education is very important for my future and there is no one to make me get it, I have to get it for myself."

BEST OF AUBURN

1. School Spirit
2. The "Auburn Family" and friendly atmosphere
3. Football games
4. Nice campus and college town
5. The weather
6. Helpful faculty

Happy Students
86% of students return after their first year.

Low-Stress Course Load
70% of students surveyed rated the manageability of work as above average.

WORST OF AUBURN

1. Parking
2. Construction
3. Hard to get on-campus housing
4. Hard to get off-campus housing
5. Traffic on game days

Not Much Diversity
One of the least racially diverse campuses—only 14% of students are minorities.

Student Body

African American:	9%	Male Undergrads:	52%
Asian American:	2%	Female Undergrads:	48%
Hispanic:	2%	Living On Campus:	14%
International:	1%	Living Off Campus:	86%
Native American:	1%	Male Athletes:	3%
White:	86%	Female Athletes:	3%
Unknown:	1%	Fraternity Members:	22%
From Out-of-State:	43%	Sorority Members:	31%

Frequently Compared Schools:

Clemson University
University of Alabama
University of Florida
University of Georgia

Students Speak Out On...
EVERYTHING!

ACADEMICS

Very Down to Earth Atmosphere.

"I love Auburn and how all of the students have such pride in the school! The professors are nice and willing to help as long as you put forth the effort in coming to talk to them. They would much rather help you succeed than see you fail."

College of Education Is Very Close Knit and Helpful

"I am in the College of Education at Auburn University and it is a great college. All of my advisers and teachers have been exceptional and helpful. Any question I have had has been answered before I've had to ask it. I feel like I belong in this college."

ATHLETICS

Sports

"Football season is an obvious plus. Tailgating is fun and friendly. There are several options for athletic involement."

We Believe in Auburn!!

"Sports are a big deal at Auburn. The students love to get involved with pep rallies, Tiger Walk, and we always have a huge crowd at every sporting event. Through Auburn's Ignited program students are encouraged to come support their school at sporting events. We have great facilities, great staff, and Auburn sports are amazing!"

CAMPUS DINING

Variety in Food and Places to Eat

"There are many places to eat on campus. There is a great variety from fast food to sit down. If I get bored at the Student Center, I just walk to Foy or to the Village dining hall. It's amazing to have a Starbucks on campus."

Good =)

"Auburn University has a wide variety of food on campus. From the normal places like Chic-Fil-A, Papa Johns and Au Bon Pain to the food dining halls like Terrell and Foy that provide a wide variety of food. The meal plan is also very generous."

CAMPUS HOUSING

Campus Housing

"I live off campus in a nice apartment. I love it it has all the amenities that a college student needs. There is also a pool, exercise room and even a game room. It is moderately priced ane in a good location."

Pick the Quad or the Hill If You Can

"Auburn has three on campus dorm areas: The Hill, The Quad, and The Village. The Quad is great, due to its location in the heart of campus. The Village sacrifices location for the best quality dorms on campus. My experience with The Hill would leave me not recommending it."

GUYS & GIRLS

A wide range of student types

"There are a wide range of student types."

Auburn Men and Women

"We all love Auburn and so we all love each other like a big family!! Everyone on this campus is beautiful inside and out!! :)"

HEALTH & SAFETY

Auburn's Campus Is a Safe Place to Be.

"I always feel safe when I'm on campus, day or night. If you stay into the late hours of the night at the library, you can opt to be escorted to your car by a security guard. I've never felt that this was necessary, but it's good that it's offered to the students."

Auburn Is Always Going to Great Lengths to Improve Safety.

"Just recently auburn addded more pedestrian signs, helpful pedestrian hints, there are signs everyone on safety for individuals walking at night, they have a transit system that will get you at night, as well as an alarm/emergency system that you can push if you are being chased/stalked/etc."

LOOKING FOR MORE?

Check out our full-length guide to this school at collegeprowler.com/auburn-university/.

Austin College

900 N. Grand Ave.; Sherman, TX 75090
(903) 813-2000; www.austincollege.edu

THE BASICS:

Acceptance Rate: 80%
Yield: 30%
Setting: Small city
Control: Private Non-Profit
Total Undergrads: 1,335
SAT Range: 1670–2000*
ACT Range: 24–28

Student-Faculty Ratio: 13:1
Retention Rate: 86%
Graduation Rate: 78%
Tuition: $27,850
Room & Board: $9,090
Avg. Aid Package: $26,331
Students With Aid: 99%

* of 2400

Academics	A-	Greek Life	A+
Athletics	C	Guys	A-
Campus Dining	C	Health & Safety	B
Campus Housing	B+	Local Atmosphere	D+
Campus Strictness	B-	Nightlife	B
Computers	C+	Off-Campus Dining	C
Diversity	B	Off-Campus Housing	B
Drug Safety	C	Parking	A+
Facilities	B-	Transportation	B
Girls	B	Weather	B-

CP's Student Author On...
OVERALL EXPERIENCE

Austin College has a statue nicknamed "Roo Poo," it isn't situated in the city of Austin like some people sorely realize after being accepted, and it may have just as much gossip and drama as high school; however, because of these things, there is an overwhelming sense of community. After four years of constant interaction, you would think AC students would want to get away from one another, but there's a reason why AC students who end up going to the same law or medical school after graduation pair up as roommates—there's a feeling of "home" people feel when surrounded by others who shared the AC experience. And this sense of community is incurable. While in school, there are endless opportunities to take part as global citizens through studying abroad and service fellowships, and AC students only continue this tradition after getting their diplomas through things like AmeriCorps, the Fulbright Scholar Program, and the Peace Corps. Graduates are known for gallivanting off into the world after graduation and serving the global community. AC students embrace the world as their community after leaving Sherman, but they never forget where they came from.... For the rest of this editorial, visit collegeprowler.com.

Students Speak Out On...
OVERALL EXPERIENCE

Q What Makes Austin College Unique

"AC has many things that make it unique such as Jan Term. It gives us the opportunity to travel or stay on campus and enjoy a stress free couple of weeks with just one class."

Q Great School

"It's small, and I like that. My largest class has either people. There's plenty of one-on-one time with professors if you want it."

Q Life Changing

"It has its problems, but I love Austin College. Jan Terms are great, and the professors are approachable and friendly. I enjoy the small class sizes, but also the availability to meet such a diverse group of people that I now call my best friends."

Q Great for Me, but Not for Everyone

"I love it here, but it's not for everyone. You should definitely visit before you come."

BEST OF AUSTIN COLLEGE

1. Close-knit campus community
2. Great professor-student relationships
3. Small classes
4. Abundance of study abroad opportunities
5. Liberal arts education

Happy Students
86% of students return after their first year.

Proven Success
78% of students will complete their education and graduate with a degree.

WORST OF AUSTIN COLLEGE

1. Sherman nightlife
2. Dorm visitation rules
3. The food could be better
4. Everybody is always in everybody else's business
5. Inconvenience of getting around town
6. The distance from Dallas

Expensive
Tuition is a steep $27,850, one of the most expensive rates in the country.

Student Body

African American:	2%	Male Undergrads:	45%
Asian American:	15%	Female Undergrads:	55%
Hispanic:	9%	Living On Campus:	70%
International:	2%	Living Off Campus:	30%
Native American:	1%	Male Athletes:	30%
White:	70%	Female Athletes:	15%
Unknown:	0%	Fraternity Members:	27%
From Out-of-State:	9%	Sorority Members:	28%

Frequently Compared Schools:

Southern Methodist University
Southwestern University
Texas Christian University
Trinity University

Students Speak Out On... EVERYTHING!

ACADEMICS

Q Great

"Academics are the reason I am here, and they are phenomenal. A liberal arts education is an invaluable one, and the pre-med program is rigorous and prepares you for medical school."

Q Professors Are Open and Easily Available.

"The professors are easily contacted and very willing to answer any questions. The class options are great, and the registration process works well."

ATHLETICS

Q School Spirit Does It Exist?

"Though a lot of students and alumni go to the homecoming football game, there really aren't that many fans at every game, especially away games. Only friends of players on teams really go to home games."

Q Fan Support

"Most sports have a devout following, but of a limited number. Homecoming always brings out a lot of fans because all of our alums are back in town."

CAMPUS DINING

Q General Dining

"My only complaint in this department would be the lack of options as far as location is concerned ... but I think that since I graduated, they have added more options. I think there's a Starbucks on campus now? That's great!"

Q Food Is Average

"I can usually find stuff that I like, whether it be in the cafeteria or the Pub. I usually check to see what's in the caf on that day, and if I don't like it, the pub is my fall back. The meal plan is pretty expensive though, although I enjoy the selection of foods available in the cafeteria combined with the consistency of food in the pub."

CAMPUS HOUSING

Q Roo Suites Are Nice

"The dorms for freshmen and sophomores are okay for a college dorm. Pretty average compared to other schools, sometimes a bit more spacious. Roo Suites are nice because you get your own room but still have three other people to converse with."

Q They're Normal

"The campus is small, so nothing is actually that far. Caruth (girls dorm) has the most central location and is newer, but Clyce rooms are generally bigger. I would have preferred Caruth if I'd have known. The best place I've lived on campus was the Jordan Family Language House, but it requires applying and extra classwork as it is for language majors or people who want to study abroad. If you're one of those people, definitely apply, it is a great place to live."

GUYS & GIRLS

Q You Could Consider AC a Nerd School in a Sense

"You could say that AC is a "nerd school" since the acceptance rate is limited. It is almost in the country, so there are many guys who have country accents or wear cowboy boots. The girls don't give away their hometown normally by how they dress—they are usually wearing comfy and easy clothes."

Q Social Life

"The students here are very diverse. Everyone is very accepting, and the different sexes are treated equally on campus. The guys are usually Southern gentlemen and are very sweet to the girls, and the girls show the guys the same amount of respect."

HEALTH & SAFETY

Q Austin College

"It's very friendly and helpful here."

LOOKING FOR MORE?

Check out our full-length guide to this school at collegeprowler.com/austin-college/.

Ave Maria University

5050 Ave Maria Blvd.; Ave Maria, FL 34142
(239) 280-2500; www.avemaria.edu

THE BASICS:

Acceptance Rate: 37%
Yield: 38%
Setting: Rural
Control: Private Non-Profit
Total Undergrads: 669
SAT Range: 1500–1860*
ACT Range: 21–26

Student-Faculty Ratio: 11:1
Retention Rate: 69%
Graduation Rate: 52%
Tuition: $18,025
Room & Board: $8,350
Avg. Aid Package: $14,900
Students With Aid: 96%

* of 2400

This School Isn't Graded Yet!

College Prowler grades are calculated using tons of criteria, including survey responses that come from students at this school.

Unfortunately, we haven't gathered enough student surveys yet for this school to be able to calculate the grades for each section. Stay tuned to *CollegeProwler.com* for grade updates and more!

CP's Student Author On...
OVERALL EXPERIENCE

Ave Maria offers a unique and fulfilling experience to its students by providing an excellent and well-rounded education, a Catholic foundation and community, and an opportunity for growth and spiritual development. Overall, it's an experience that cannot be found anywhere else! Although Ave Maria is a new university, it has grown despite the hardships of the recession, demonstrating the determination of the school and student body. While this may not be the school for everyone, Ave Maria will definitely help you grow intellectually, emotionally, physically, and spiritually. The combination of a liberal arts education and love for God helps to drive the University and its students. The University may not have the best sports teams and isn't located in the most exciting town, but the knowledge and wisdom gained here is incomparable.

While the academics and modernity of the school are certainly impressive, it's the community and faith of the school that ultimately attract its students.... For the rest of this editorial, visit collegeprowler.com.

Students Speak Out On...
OVERALL EXPERIENCE

Q It's a Happy Place
"Campus is safe, fun, and friendly. Students are open and greet each other with smiles. Academics are top priority, but there is plenty of room to have a good time."

Q Hell
"this place sucks. you get fined for every little thing. you can't have tvs in your dorms and no girls allowed in your dorms."

BEST OF AVE MARIA

1. University potential and newness
2. Student community
3. Spirituality and growth
4. Friendly atmosphere
5. Financial aid
6. Elite faculty
7. Availability of professors

Big Dorms
75% of students surveyed felt that dorms were more spacious than average.

WORST OF AVE MARIA

1. Lack of shopping variety
2. Small town/not enough to do
3. Some policy strictness
4. Lack of variety in majors
5. Mosquito problem
6. Lack of variety in campus dining

Life is NOT a Party
50% of students surveyed said it's almost impossible to find a good party.

Want a Job? On Your Own
There aren't any placement services for graduates.

Student Body

African American:	3%	Male Undergrads:	46%
Asian American:	3%	Female Undergrads:	54%
Hispanic:	18%	Living On Campus:	95%
International:	4%	Living Off Campus:	5%
Native American:	1%	Male Athletes:	19%
White:	69%	Female Athletes:	13%
Unknown:	2%	Fraternity Members:	0%
From Out-of-State:	63%	Sorority Members:	0%

Students Speak Out On...
EVERYTHING!

ACADEMICS

ℚ Some of the Best

"The academics are for sure one of the best things about Ave. The professors are all learned in their respective fields, and most of them demand respect. The academics are challenging but good and definitely worth the effort."

ℚ Tough Courses, Smart Professors

"The professors at Ave Maria University are, without a doubt, extremely knowledgeable and intelligent. Because of this, in addition to other factors, the academics at Ave Maria are often extremely difficult. The downside of this, of course, is that it can be hard to meet the expectations of professors. The upside is that provided you are willing to learn, you will learn, and the majority of professors are very willing to help you do that, both in and outside of class."

ATHLETICS

ℚ Oh, we're involved!

"Our school spirit is off the charts. The athletic facilities are awesome. Go Gyrenes!"

ℚ Expanding

"Hands down, the girls basketball program is soaring, and the soccer teams are greatly improving. This year, we've gained an amazing coach for cross county and track and field. Scholarships for the sports are very available, and the teams themselves are a huge strength to the campus as far as leadership and academics. I'm looking forward to what will become of the school athletically."

CAMPUS DINING

ℚ The Dining Hall

"It's great. I love the windows. And the food is swell."

ℚ Limited

"Quality has improved each semester I have been here, though there is only one option for students and that is for a full meal plan. 50 flex dollars are given for the adjacent cafe."

Frequently Compared Schools:

Brenau University
Carlos Albizu University
Clayton State University
Coastal Carolina University

CAMPUS HOUSING

ℚ Pretty Good

"It's nice, for the most part."

GUYS & GIRLS

ℚ Not Too Shabby

"Most of the students are decently attractive people and lots of them dress well to class. Not like super fancy or anything, but they usually dress nicely. Most of the people are looking for long-term relationships, and a lot of the couples end up getting married after senior year."

ℚ Athletic People All Over

"The average student tends to dress either fairly casual. Since the school attracts so many differenbt states (49) and nationalities, you are apt to meet people you wouldn't have otherwise. Many of the guys and girls are very athletic (something like one-third of the student body participates in sports). The ones who aren't athletic seem to dress very nicely."

HEALTH & SAFETY

ℚ It's All Good!

"Seriously. It's wonderful."

ℚ Safe.

"Hands down, one of the safest places I've ever been. We have security and all that, but it's the students and the university town that really make up the community life. I've left my laptop in public for hours and other personal belongings for days, and have never worried nor lost anything save a Pop-Tart, and that surprised me considering the campus. I would never do anything of the sort anywhere else in the world."

LOOKING FOR MORE?

Check out our full-length guide to this school at collegeprowler.com/ave-maria-university/.

Babson College

231 Forest St.; Wellesley, MA 02457
(781) 235-1200; www.babson.edu

THE BASICS:

Acceptance Rate: 40%	**Student-Faculty Ratio:** 13:1
Yield: 28%	**Retention Rate:** 92%
Setting: Suburban	**Graduation Rate:** 88%
Control: Private Non-Profit	**Tuition:** $37,824
Total Undergrads: 1,901	**Room & Board:** $12,500
SAT Range: 1730–2020*	**Avg. Aid Package:** $30,666
ACT Range: 25–29	**Students With Aid:** 57%

* of 2400

Academics	B+	Greek Life	B-
Athletics	B+	Guys	B+
Campus Dining	A-	Health & Safety	B+
Campus Housing	B	Local Atmosphere	B
Campus Strictness	C	Nightlife	B
Computers	A	Off-Campus Dining	B+
Diversity	A-	Off-Campus Housing	D+
Drug Safety	B	Parking	B+
Facilities	A-	Transportation	C
Girls	C+	Weather	C-

CP's Student Author On...
OVERALL EXPERIENCE

The best way to describe Babson is at first you'll feel like a fish out of water, but as time goes on you somehow survive and become a lizard with tougher skin. No matter how hard you think your high school was, nothing can prepare you for the incredible and challenging academic life of a Babson freshman. Most students agree that the workload is by far larger than they initially expected. And although it takes some time to get used to the curriculum, students feel that the impeccable education is worth it.

Those who are unhappy with their education here are usually just not used to it yet. Many say that the school is too small and they get bored walking around campus and seeing the same people all the time. Voicing the fact that this college is smaller than many high schools is not uncommon here. Some students also complain that too many of their peers come from the same economic backgrounds, even though the campus is diverse in other aspects. The social scene, however, is better than expected for a business-oriented school, although it's not a party school by far.... For the rest of this editorial, visit collegeprowler.com.

Students Speak Out On...
OVERALL EXPERIENCE

Q Come Here Only If You're Into Entrepreneurship
"Amazing business curriculum, but otherwise may be disappointed."

Q "There are a lot of things I would change about Babson—workload, GPA deflation, and some social aspects of Babson. At times, I enjoy it, and at other times, I am totally ready to leave. Right now, I'm having a good time."

Q "Excellent. I wouldn't want to be anywhere else. Too bad I am already halfway done. It is a unique college, but it lacks something socially. All-in-all, for some reason, I like it a lot, though."

Q "I love Babson. It is not a college for those who wish to do no work, not attend class, or just party. It is a school for people who want to do well in life. Babson trains people for the rigorous business world. I would not rather be at any other college. The education here is priceless, especially because much of it is 'hands-on,' and I feel it's good practice for my future career."

BEST OF BABSON

1. The academic program
2. Good alumni connections
3. Movie nights in Sorenson rock
4. Technology is constantly being updated
5. Internet in classrooms and wireless in dorms

Happy Students
92% of students return after their first year.

Proven Success
88% of students will complete their education and graduate with a degree.

WORST OF BABSON

1. The business classes are top-notch, but the liberal arts programs suck
2. Some foreign professors are hard to understand
3. Too many fire alarms on the weekends

Expensive
Tuition is a steep $37,824, one of the most expensive rates in the country.

Expensive Dorms
Living on campus doesn't come cheap, with an average housing price tag of $8,066.

Student Body

African American:	4%	Male Undergrads:	59%
Asian American:	13%	Female Undergrads:	41%
Hispanic:	9%	Living On Campus:	83%
International:	20%	Living Off Campus:	17%
Native American:	0%	Male Athletes:	21%
White:	42%	Female Athletes:	21%
Unknown:	12%	Fraternity Members:	10%
From Out-of-State:	76%	Sorority Members:	10%

Frequently Compared Schools:

Bentley University
Boston College
Boston University
Northeastern University

Students Speak Out On...
EVERYTHING!

ACADEMICS

Q "In general, classes that are revolved around solid concepts like economics, marketing, accounting, and more are very well taught and interesting. Things like organizational behavior (OB) and literature are quite dry and not inspiring. Faculty are very available to students and, in general, are passionate about the subjects they teach, which rubs off on the students."

Q "Faculty and teachers, for the most part, are very enthusiastic and truly want their students to do well. At times, it seems like they do not communicate with each other and all decide to assign the most work at the same time. This is being looked into by Babson, however. Most of my classes are interesting, and I intentionally picked two of my professors from last semester for this semester because I enjoyed their classes."

ATHLETICS

Q **More Than You Would Think**
"Babson may be only a Division III school, but the sports here at Babson are amazing. Varsity games always have a huge crowd of people there to cheer them. This has especially increased in the last year or two. Surprisingly club sports also develop quite a following with people always at our rugby games. I didn't expect much of a sports following on campus, but I sure found one."

Q "Sports are huge on campus; they are almost like fraternities. They foster good attitudes, competitiveness, and teamwork."

CAMPUS DINING

Q **Trim Food**
"Good at first, DULL after the first semester. Eat at Olin."

Q **Dining Hall Is Terrible, Other Options Are Good**
"The main dining hall, Trim, has gotten progressively worse over the last three years. Gets very boring, plates and utensils are often dirty. The other options on campus are pretty good, but are more expensive. New Dunkin Donuts is a nice addition."

CAMPUS HOUSING

Q **Awesome - Guarenteed All 4 Years**
"My freshman room was a quad with only two of us, our own kitchen, bathroom shared with another double on the other side of it, and a balcony overlooking the quad... Upperclassman get suites with their own single, a kitchen, bathroom with two showers, two stalls, two sinks, a common room, and all the freedom you could ask for."

Q "All the dorms are nice, but I tried to avoid substance-free housing. All four years, I have lived on upper campus in Coleman, Van Winkle, Canfield, and McCullough, and it was a lot of fun. I almost prefer living there to the Park Manors."

GUYS & GIRLS

Q **Guys and Girls**
"I think there are some great guys and girls here at Babson. Everyone here wants to succeed and do well in life so it is nice to be among people who are similar. As an athlete, I surround myself with other athletes who are funny, smart, genuinely nice people. It is a community unto itself and I love being a part of it."

Q "There is a lack of ideal men on the campus. Most guys do not dress as well as they should in such a business school. The ones that got their fashion down are usually from a foreign country and clump with others alike. However, there are many guys that are very caring and make good friends."

HEALTH & SAFETY

Q **Completely Safe**
"When I went on a tour of campus, the girl who was a junior at the time said that she would feel completely safe walking naked across the campus at 1 o'clock in the morning. How much safer could the campus be??"

LOOKING FOR MORE?

Check out our full-length guide to this school at collegeprowler.com/babson-college/.

Ball State University

2000 University Ave.; Muncie, IN 47306
(765) 289-1241; www.bsu.edu

THE BASICS:

Acceptance Rate: 74%	Student-Faculty Ratio: 18:1
Yield: 44%	Retention Rate: 78%
Setting: Small city	Graduation Rate: 60%
Control: Public	Tuition: $20,398
Total Undergrads: 17,415	Room & Board: $8,052
SAT Range: 1400–1710*	Avg. Aid Package: $5,552
ACT Range: 19–24	Students With Aid: 84%

of 2400

Academics	C+	Greek Life	B-
Athletics	C+	Guys	A-
Campus Dining	B	Health & Safety	C
Campus Housing	B+	Local Atmosphere	C
Campus Strictness	C+	Nightlife	B+
Computers	B+	Off-Campus Dining	B
Diversity	C	Off-Campus Housing	B
Drug Safety	C	Parking	C
Facilities	B+	Transportation	A-
Girls	C+	Weather	C+

CP's Student Author On...
OVERALL EXPERIENCE

Ask a Ball State student, and they'll tell you they're happy to be where they are. Sure, there's Parking Services to deal with, UPD crack-downs, and a ban on kegs, but these drawbacks pale when compared to the friends and memories students say they've acquired at BSU. Although recent policies threaten to end the party-school reputation, Ball State still has a strong social scene that continues to build friendships most students would be unwilling to give up.

Depending on your major, courses can be extremely trying. Be prepared for some late nights—especially if you're interested in architecture, nursing, or journalism as a major. Whatever your field of study, it is important to focus and remember what you're here for.

Students Speak Out On...
OVERALL EXPERIENCE

Q School Experience
"My school is great. They offer so many different clubs that one can be active in and make lots of new friends. Also helping the community is big, and people can get involved with that easily. I would pick this school again."

Q Experience
"I love Ball State University and I am so glad I go there. I love the school spirit and how nice everyone is. I wouldn't want to be at any other school."

Q Ball State Is My Kind of School!
"Ball State is one of the best schools I know of. We have so much to offer and there is never a boring day. Keeping up with your school work is difficult but worth while."

Q I Love It.
"I love Ball State. All of the experiences I have had on and off campus have been awesome. In general, my classes have gone well and have been fairly successful. I will miss Ball State when I leave."

BEST OF BALL STATE

1. The friends you meet
2. The parties and bars
3. Some great restaurants
4. Great computer network
5. Good workout facilities
6. The student publications
7. The Atrium

Knowledgeable Professors
82% of students surveyed rated the general knowledge of professors as above average.

Low-Stress Course Load
82% of students surveyed rated the manageability of work as above average.

WORST OF BALL STATE

1. University Parking Services
2. You can't buy kegs in Muncie
3. University Police Department crackdowns
4. Limited diversity
5. Dorm food

Students Can't Wait to Get Out of Town
60% of students surveyed said that there's no way they would live here after graduation.

Student Body

African American:	7%	Male Undergrads:	48%
Asian American:	1%	Female Undergrads:	52%
Hispanic:	2%	Living On Campus:	43%
International:	1%	Living Off Campus:	57%
Native American:	0%	Male Athletes:	3%
White:	85%	Female Athletes:	3%
Unknown:	4%	Fraternity Members:	7%
From Out-of-State:	13%	Sorority Members:	10%

Frequently Compared Schools:

Indiana University
Indiana University-Purdue University Indianapolis
(IUPUI)
Ohio University

Students Speak Out On...
EVERYTHING!

ACADEMICS

We Love TCOM

"Ball State's Telecommunications program is the best in the area, if not the state. It is the most popular major at the university and also the most competitive in nature. The program encourages students to take a hands on approach to the processes of film making, news broadcasting, and web designing. The facilities are all state-of-the art with the most up to date software and internships are available to students who meet the criteria."

Professor Availability

"The Classes at Ball State are small compared to some Universities. Since the classes are relatively small the professors are available to students most of the time. By emailing them and asking for a meeting. Or a student can go to the professors office when they hold office hours."

ATHLETICS

I Love Ball State Sports

"They are very competitive and show great sportsmanship! The student body is also very supportive! Go Ball State!"

Fan Fare

"the students around campus all wear there colors and come out to games and support the teams. and the athletes all seem to be just average people"

CAMPUS DINING

Ball State Dining Facilities

"The university has many different dining facilities on campus. The student center is a hub of student snacking, however, there are many other places to eat and hang out. The menus and variety change every couple of days, which is nice. The best places to eat are in Woodworth Dorm. It has a great mix of choices."

Menus

"The food choices picked out by the college are excellent choices. There are always variety of food choices from American to Asian, Spanish, and etc. The quality and the test of the food are pretty good too. There are nothing to complain about towards the menus set by Ball State University."

CAMPUS HOUSING

Lots of Places to Live.

"Here at Ball State, there are several places you can live, none of which are that bad. To my knowledge there are 9 different buildings to live in, with a 10th being built right now. They are all very nice, and most have air conditioning. Food is available in alot, but not all of the halls. The Freshman dorms, I think, are the best place to meet tons of people."

Dorms

"The majority of the dorms are located in one area. Students have close access to their friends since the campus is small and the dorms are close to each other. Every dorm has a computer lab and living space with a TV and couches in it for students to use. Every dorm has a fitness room and each hall has a study lounge ."

GUYS & GIRLS

Girls and Guys-Chill:)

"I am happy with Ball State's atmosphere. Everyone is layed back and relaxed. No one dresses up to go to class. The guys dress casual along with the girls. The girls and the guys are not stuck up. We all realize that we are at school to get a degree but to enjoy our young,college years!"

HEALTH & SAFETY

Special Security Measures

"At Ball State the crime rate is mediocre. To ensure that each student is safe they have Blue Emergency buttons that sound off an alarm if the button is pressed. If you get even the slightest bit frightened, just push the button and the campus police will be there in less than a minute (about 30 seconds). There are Blue Emergency buttons all over campus, you walk lets say 10 15 meters and theres another one. So Ball State goes the extra step to ensure students are safe."

LOOKING FOR MORE?

Check out our full-length guide to this school at collegeprowler.com/ball-state-university/.

Bard College

Annandale-On-Hudson, NY 12504
(845) 758-6822; www.bard.edu

THE BASICS:

Acceptance Rate: 33%	**Student-Faculty Ratio:** 10:1
Yield: 28%	**Retention Rate:** 87%
Setting: Town	**Graduation Rate:** 75%
Control: Private Non-Profit	**Tuition:** $39,880
Total Undergrads: 1,939	**Room & Board:** $11,300
SAT Range: 1320–1430*	**Avg. Aid Package:** $28,352
ACT Range: —	**Students With Aid:** 63%

* of 1600

Academics	A-	Greek Life	N/A
Athletics	C-	Guys	B-
Campus Dining	D+	Health & Safety	C+
Campus Housing	C	Local Atmosphere	C
Campus Strictness	A+	Nightlife	B-
Computers	C-	Off-Campus Dining	C
Diversity	B	Off-Campus Housing	B+
Drug Safety	C-	Parking	A
Facilities	C+	Transportation	B-
Girls	B	Weather	D+

CP's Student Author On...
OVERALL EXPERIENCE

What Bard students esteem most about in their overall experience is that they've had the chance to develop what so many other college students haven't—a personal connection with their school. This is deceivingly rare, as many students at big universities miss out on the things Bard students take for granted, like small, intimate classes, personal relationships with professors, and a tightly-knit community in which people share similar interests and commitments. For all of its cliquishness, Bard's student body ultimately possesses a unique understanding of itself. On the whole, Bardians seem to own the idea that, although not every person at Bard shares a friendship, each is still connected in some way by a willingness to accept what is different from him- or herself. And, while Bard students admittedly have a hard time showing compassion for conservatism or ignorance, they do welcome people of any gender, sexuality, and race.

Some suggest that Bard is like a bubble—an isolated, introverted space closed off from the rest of the world. In some ways, this is true.... For the rest of this editorial, visit collegeprowler.com.

Students Speak Out On...
OVERALL EXPERIENCE

Q Oh, Bard!

"Bard has given me ups and downs, twisted me sideways, and smacked me around. But I wouldn't trade it for the world. From the old falling apart dorms to the rigorous classroom discussion. Bard is where I rest my head."

Q It's been the best of times...

"Seriously. I'm getting a wonderful education. I;m surrounded by transplendent beings. Its a shame it only lasts 4 years."

Q Academically Great, Socially and Everything Else Weird

"bard is a top notch school academically, however, in most other ways it can be hard to deal with. kids here are weird so if you consider yourself normal, you might have a hard time connecting with people. plus you're in the middle of nowhere which makes many people go a little crazy after awhile. it definitely takes some adjusting to. if you can get over all these things, bard can give you an amazing education."

BEST OF BARD

1. The eclectic student body
2. Eminent professors
3. Small classes
4. Beautiful Campus
5. Lots of freedom
6. Great parties
7. Blithewood Estate
8. Some amazing dorms

Happy Students
87% of students return after their first year.

Commitment to Teaching
There are 10 students for every member of faculty on campus.

WORST OF BARD

1. Isolated location
2. Cliquey social scene
3. Kline food
4. Winter weather
5. Repetitive party scene
6. Sharing bathrooms
7. Printer problems
8. Workload

Expensive
Tuition is a steep $39,880, one of the most expensive rates in the country.

Student Body

African American:	3%	Male Undergrads:	44%
Asian American:	2%	Female Undergrads:	56%
Hispanic:	3%	Living On Campus:	77%
International:	9%	Living Off Campus:	23%
Native American:	0%	Male Athletes:	12%
White:	60%	Female Athletes:	7%
Unknown:	23%	Fraternity Members:	0%
From Out-of-State:	69%	Sorority Members:	0%

Frequently Compared Schools:

New York University
Oberlin College
Skidmore College
Vassar College

Students Speak Out On... EVERYTHING!

ACADEMICS

Q Incredible Professors

"I would say that most Bard professors are absolutely incredible. We get the best of the best. They are intelligent, talented, several are famous, they all still work in the field, and most are also good at teaching, not just knowing their subject. We also have our fair share of crazies, but that can be fun too. ALWAYS ask your professors for help if you need it. They will be there. They care."

Q Amazing Classes and Professors.

"You can learn a lot here at Bard. They offer an amazing range of classes, and the professors will blow your mind. If you're picking a school based on strong academics, Bard is the way to go."

ATHLETICS

Q Event Staff

"The Bard Raptors are pretty good, I believe that effort is what counts, no matter what the sport."

Q More people are interested in discussing literature

"the athletic department at bard is still building. basically this is not by any means a big sports school. more people are interested in discussing literature than playing catch. the good news is that we are joining the liberty league in 2012 which means that sports will be taken a lot more seriously here. the gym is super old and the weight room is so small. its really only the athletes that use it."

CAMPUS DINING

Q Not bad

"Campus dining has improved drastically. The dining facilities make an effort to provide locally produced food items."

Q Better Eat Off-Campus...

"Kline, the main dining hall, is sort of hit or miss... you can get more variety there than anywhere else, but it often leaves me unfulfilled. The vegetarian 'meat substitutes' are also usually pretty bad. Food is better at DTR and Manor, but there's often not too many fresh options there and it can get tiring pretty quickly."

CAMPUS HOUSING

Q Iffy, but Fun at Times

"some are really old. some are new. the process for selecting them is totally random and often complicated. but when i lived on campus i had some of the best experiences ever."

Q It Varies...

"It really depends - you could be living in a converted mansion or in a trailer. But a word about the trailers: although you might look at them in total shock and disgust, they are great places (aside from the fluorescent lighting)."

GUYS & GIRLS

Q Guys and Girls are great

"friendly, attractive, and Unpretentious. 'Tis a very good situation."

Q Boys, Boys, Boys

"Ladies (and gay men) put on your high-heeled shoes, cause there are some sexy mancakes at Bard. True, the pickings for the ladies can at times be a bit slim (be sure to check out the rugby or lacross practices) but for the gays, it's an all you can eat buffet. The gay crowd tends to be a bit queeny, but there are some good, level-headed ones in the mix as well. Lots of hippers, so if that's your thing, go for it. Also, lots of foreigners withs sexy accents."

HEALTH & SAFETY

Q Eazzzzy Life

"Lots of birds singing, insects jumping, no gangs or prostitutes. The waters close, people cool, and the active feel eazzzy.See the stars, familiar for you, your safeties fine."

LOOKING FOR MORE?

Check out our full-length guide to this school at collegeprowler.com/bard-college/.

Barnard College

3009 Broadway; New York, NY 10027
(212) 854-2014; www.barnard.edu

THE BASICS:

Acceptance Rate: 28%	Student-Faculty Ratio: 9:1
Yield: 45%	Retention Rate: 93%
Setting: Large city	Graduation Rate: 89%
Control: Private Non-Profit	Tuition: $30,868
Total Undergrads: 2,400	Room & Board: $12,950
SAT Range: 1910–2180*	Avg. Aid Package: $32,153
ACT Range: 28–32	Students With Aid: 54%

of 2400

Academics	A	Greek Life	D
Athletics	D+	Guys	N/A
Campus Dining	C+	Health & Safety	B
Campus Housing	B-	Local Atmosphere	A+
Campus Strictness	A	Nightlife	A
Computers	B	Off-Campus Dining	A+
Diversity	B	Off-Campus Housing	D-
Drug Safety	B+	Parking	D-
Facilities	B-	Transportation	A+
Girls	B+	Weather	B-

CP's Student Author On...
OVERALL EXPERIENCE

Barnard College provides a great experience for aspiring young women who want it all. There is a nice, small college feel from small discussion classes and one-on-one advising while being able to take part in a large Ivy League University. There are large libraries, well-equipped athletic facilities, and well-known faculty at a school where the president of the college might serve you breakfast at midnight before finals. Most students find that Barnard is a place to feel at home in one of the busiest cities in the world. On the flip-side, many students also feel the pressure of tough academic work, as well. With so much to do in New York City and on campus, it can be very frustrating for students when they have to spend hours on homework and studying.

Barnard appears to work very diligently at making sure that it is both academically very rigorous, and that students have many opportunities to enrich their lives socially and financially. This is both a blessing and a curse because classwork takes up such a great deal of time.... For the rest of this editorial, visit collegeprowler.com.

Students Speak Out On...
OVERALL EXPERIENCE

Q "I've enjoyed every second at Barnard so far, but my first year was really tough. I don't know if I can do three more."

Q "I wasn't sure if Barnard was the right choice for me when I came here, but now I am much more confident of my decision. I've thought about transferring before, but I guess since I haven't made time to do it, I don't really want to."

Q "Barnard is alright, although if I had it to do over I would like a college with a more 'college-y' atmosphere. The girls at Barnard sometimes act like they're already grown professionals."

Q "I love Barnard, and I am really happy to be here. I would definitely come here if I had to do the whole process over. If you are female, interested in living in New York City, and considering Columbia, you should definitely come to Barnard. It has all that Columbia has to offer, and more."

Q "Barnard has really opened my eyes to what being a modern woman really is. This school has taught me that I can want it all and have it all."

BEST OF BARNARD

1. Columbia University affiliation
2. The lawn
3. Midnight Breakfast
4. Doris in the College Activities Office
5. Street vendors
6. Subways

Happy Students
93% of students return after their first year.

Commitment to Teaching
There are 9 students for every member of faculty on campus.

WORST OF BARNARD

1. No air-conditioning in most dorms
2. No retaking classes you've done poorly in
3. The cold, cold winters
4. Only one dining hall open for dinner
5. Loud fraternity guys that live behind the dorms

Expensive
Tuition is a steep $30,868, one of the most expensive rates in the country.

Expensive Dorms
Living on campus doesn't come cheap, with an average housing price tag of $7,577.

Student Body

African American:	5%	Male Undergrads:	0%
Asian American:	16%	Female Undergrads:	100%
Hispanic:	9%	Living On Campus:	90%
International:	4%	Living Off Campus:	10%
Native American:	0%	Male Athletes:	0%
White:	66%	Female Athletes:	2%
Unknown:	0%	Fraternity Members:	0%
From Out-of-State:	69%	Sorority Members:	0%

Frequently Compared Schools:

Brown University
Columbia University
New York University
Wellesley College

Students Speak Out On... EVERYTHING!

ACADEMICS

Professor

"As a first year student I did not know what to expect from my Professors, but I surprisingly found them to be very eager to help. The teachers (at least the ones I have) are excited about what they teach and will meet with you whenever to discuss the class or assignments you might have. My English teacher sat with me for over an hour discussing how to make my essay stronger which I found very helpful. The school also offers a free writing and speaking programs that are very informative."

"Amazing" Is All I Can Say...

"Every time I sit in a classroom, I am amazed at how lucky I am. I'm being taught by professors who are the best in their field (Look up Janna Levin. Yep, she was in Morgan Freeman's Through the Wormhole with Stephen Hawking. The best part: as famous and awesome as she is, she still teaches Intro to Physics!). I have had the most fascinating discussions in my class (all have been less than 20 students) and I always come out excited for the next class."

ATHLETICS

Not a Huge Prescence

"I am in the horseback riding club, which I love, but that is a joint club with both Barnard and Columbia. I think that's how most of the sports are here. Its nice because its a great way to meet people, but Barnard's main attraction and focus is definitely not athletics (Unless the Greek Games count...)."

"There are lots of fun classes like aerobics and kickboxing that you can take at Dodge, but other than that, things aren't very physically-oriented here."

CAMPUS DINING

Pretty Good

"The food quality is decent relative to college dining services, however I can hardly call the food a luxury. The dining hall facilitates student socialization and the food options vary, but are not countless."

"Barnard's main dining areas, Hewitt and McIntosh, offer a good variety of food, especially in comparison to Columbia's main dining area, John Jay Dining Hall. Java City is also until midnight, which can be convenient at times. The only inconvenience is that Barnard and Columbia have different dining services, so we can't use our 'points' in the other campus dining areas."

CAMPUS HOUSING

New York City

"I think the fact that the college is located in such an expensive and desirable city says it all. New York is such a great place place to be (despite the cost of living) other than that if you enjoy the idea of living in such a diverse, exciting place Barnard is right for you."

"Dorms are nice for the city. Avoid Elliott and most Quad singles and go for the 600s or 110th Street instead."

GUYS & GIRLS

Variety

"Since the college is located in the city there are all types of people walking around. There is not stereotypical Barnard student (except that they are all girls, but you will see guys on campus)."

"The good-looking guys are few and far between, especially the available, nice ones, but the girls are awesome! Of course we're hot."

HEALTH & SAFETY

Safety and Security in Barnard

"I have never felt unsafe on Barnard's campus. The presence of security officers obvious and ubiquitous. However, do be careful when stepping off campus late at night... Barnard/Columbia is right next to Harlem, after all. However, there are multiple call boxes and security will walk you to your dorm/wherever if you just give them a call. The most common incidences are theft/robbery, usually when a person is walking alone and late at night. Just use common sense."

LOOKING FOR MORE?

Check out our full-length guide to this school at collegeprowler.com/barnard-college/.

Barry University

11300 NE Second Ave.; Miami, FL 33161
(800) 756-6000; www.barry.edu

THE BASICS:

Acceptance Rate: 62%	**Student-Faculty Ratio:** 18:1
Yield: 24%	**Retention Rate:** 66%
Setting: Suburban	**Graduation Rate:** 41%
Control: Private Non-Profit	**Tuition:** $26,400
Total Undergrads: 4,978	**Room & Board:** $9,152
SAT Range: 1250–1510*	**Avg. Aid Package:** $15,599
ACT Range: 17–21	**Students With Aid:** 99%

* of 2400

Academics	B-	Greek Life	C+
Athletics	C+	Guys	B
Campus Dining	C+	Health & Safety	C+
Campus Housing	C	Local Atmosphere	C+
Campus Strictness	C	Nightlife	B
Computers	B	Off-Campus Dining	D+
Diversity	A+	Off-Campus Housing	B-
Drug Safety	C+	Parking	B-
Facilities	C-	Transportation	C+
Girls	C+	Weather	A

CP's Student Author On...
OVERALL EXPERIENCE

Barry is a great university because it feels like its own community, yet everyone is so diverse and different. The class sizes here are small, and the professors are welcoming, warm, and give students personal attention, allowing for close-knit relationships to form between faculty and students. This makes each student feel like an individual who actually matters to the University. And it's not just the professors who are welcoming—the other students here are very friendly, as well. From late-night snack runs to eating at the local restaurants with friends, students will create enough memories here to last a lifetime. Another perk is that Barry is very generous with financial aid, so if you think you can't afford the tuition at this private school, think again.

And the fact that Barry is in Miami makes it even better. With its amazing beaches, clubs, restaurants, and entertainment, this city truly has it all! So if you're looking for a unique college experience, give Barry a try, because as the motto says, "Barry is where you belong."

Students Speak Out On...
OVERALL EXPERIENCE

Q Barry
"I made the best choice for my future because at Barry University, the teachers care about your education."

Q Excellent Accreditation
"Barry offers top notch accreditation for a number of fields. Excellent in the Mental Health Counseling for being CAECREP accredited."

Q My Money's Worth
"Barry is a good school. It's a private school, so the class sizes are pretty small, and students get the extra attention they need from the professors. I believe that I'm getting my money's worth and will be a proud graduate of this fine institution."

Q Great School
"besides the building looking old and a lack of resources the teachers are very super knowledgeable."

BEST OF BARRY

1. School's location
2. On-campus non-cafeteria dining spots
3. Campus Activities Board events
4. Wireless Internet
5. Free laundry on campus
6. The Barry Bookstore

Knowledgeable Professors
90% of students surveyed rated the general knowledge of professors as above average.

Big Dorms
50% of students surveyed felt that dorms were more spacious than average.

WORST OF BARRY

1. Roussell Dining Hall
2. Slow Internet speed in the library
3. Dunspaugh community bathrooms/hallway noise
4. Required courses (theology, biology, mathematics)
5. Campus Security

Expensive
Tuition is a steep $26,400, one of the most expensive rates in the country.

Expensive to Just Get By
57% of students surveyed felt that the amount it costs to live while at school was worse than average.

Student Body

African American:	20%	Male Undergrads:	32%
Asian American:	1%	Female Undergrads:	68%
Hispanic:	27%	Living On Campus:	35%
International:	5%	Living Off Campus:	65%
Native American:	0%	Male Athletes:	7%
White:	18%	Female Athletes:	4%
Unknown:	29%	Fraternity Members:	15%
From Out-of-State:	43%	Sorority Members:	6%

Frequently Compared Schools:

Florida Gulf Coast University
Florida International University
University of Miami
University of South Florida

Students Speak Out On... EVERYTHING!

ACADEMICS

Barry's Business School

"The classes are really small, which can be an extreme asset if you need individual attention."

Curriculum

"The curriculum at Barry University is great there is a great amount of different courses you can choose from and the required classes are clearly stated. The curriculum in class is pretty laid out in the syllabus, all the dates are there so there is no confusion."

Professors Actually Care That You Learn Something

"Barry is not a easy school academically. The professors give their best effort to see that you graduate with the knowledge you are paying to receive. It's a good academic institution."

ATHLETICS

Sports

"Sports are not really my interest, so I don't know about Barry's."

Good Basketball Team

"Barry has a great Basketball team for both sexes. Basketball is really good for the girls, and men tend to be better in baseball."

Varsity Sports Are Pretty Good

"Both of our basketball teams finished second at the conference championships and made it to nationals. Our men's soccer team won its conference championship."

CAMPUS DINING

very content with dining hall...

"i don't know why people hate the dining hall so much. to me, they do have varieties..they serve different food each day and some are the same kind. they also serve vegetarian food...what more do these people want?? i don't really care to go to other food places on campus. i like eating at the dining hall because i can get any kind of food i want, it's convenient, and cheaper.

i am looking forward to go back there tomorrow! i wouldn't want it any other way."

Good but Repetitive

"Nice to environment to socialize with students. The food there is good both sometimes has its days. and sometimes you get tired of eating the same thing every week."

CAMPUS HOUSING

Location Is Everything

"Here at Barry University the dorms surround the heart of the campus. The underclassman halls are closest to the classrooms and next to the Buc Stop, which has Starbucks and Einstein Bagels inside. The upperclassman halls are closer to the dining hall and Landon Student Union."

Laundry

"Laundry is free!!!!!!!"

GUYS & GIRLS

Girls Girls Girls

"Barry used to be an all-girls school, so most of the student body is girls."

Nothing Extra

"some sloppy, some good looking, I have seen better group."

HEALTH & SAFETY

Very safe!

"I have no reason to feel that i am in danger. The campus has gates and there are security guards upfront and in the parking area. There is also a crossing section for students who have to get to the Landon Student Union or to their classes. I think that's wonderful."

Health and Saftey

"There is security everywhere so i feel completely safe on campus and the buildings are cleaned vigorously so i dont have to worry about getting sick."

LOOKING FOR MORE?

Check out our full-length guide to this school at collegeprowler.com/barry-university/.

Baruch College

One Bernard Baruch Way (55 Lexington at 24th Street); New York, NY 10010
(646) 312-1000; www.baruch.cuny.edu

THE BASICS:

Acceptance Rate: 23%
Yield: 34%
Setting: Large city
Control: Public
Total Undergrads: 12,401
SAT Range: 1040–1260*
ACT Range: —

Student-Faculty Ratio: 17:1
Retention Rate: 88%
Graduation Rate: 58%
Tuition: $10,330
Room & Board: —
Avg. Aid Package: $6,598
Students With Aid: 83%

* of 1600

Academics	B+	Greek Life	C+
Athletics	C+	Guys	B+
Campus Dining	B+	Health & Safety	B
Campus Housing	C-	Local Atmosphere	A
Campus Strictness	B-	Nightlife	B
Computers	B	Off-Campus Dining	B+
Diversity	A+	Off-Campus Housing	C+
Drug Safety	B	Parking	C-
Facilities	C+	Transportation	B-
Girls	B	Weather	B-

CP's Student Author On...
OVERALL EXPERIENCE

Baruch is a strong choice for students who want a quality education at a low price. But, some say the overall experience can be quite lonely unless you make friends quickly. Most Baruchians seem too busy studying, building their resumes, and hanging out at their apartment to stick around on campus, so unless you join a club or organization, it may be difficult to actively socialize. A high workload and other demands can also make this hard, particularly if you plan to work. In fact, many Baruchians work part time, while some are employed full time, in addition to taking classes. It's a true business-oriented, urban environment, which can make some students feel left out. Luckily, if you're longing for human connection, there are plenty of organizations and clubs to join.

Baruch can be as stressful as any demanding school, but overall, the College is capable of shaping students into well-rounded, tough-skinned leaders. It may not be Ivy League, but out of all the public schools in the area, Baruch has a serious reputation. However, if you don't like to be in the minority, think twice about your major.... For the rest of this editorial, visit collegeprowler.com.

Students Speak Out On...
OVERALL EXPERIENCE

Q **Excellent School, Great Reputation!**
"We have great profs and a great curriculum."

Q **Location, Programs**
"The programs are among the best in the country, and the location is great. I can easily get there by train."

Q **Baruch Experience**
"I love the diversity at Baruch. The facilities are very modern, and the networking at this school is great. I feel like Baruch can open many doors for my future. I do wish the administration was a little better. It's difficult for advisers to really pay personal attention to every individual because there's a large student body at Baruch. However, I am self sufficient and do not mind it that much."

BEST OF BARUCH

1. Location—heart of Manhattan!
2. The academics
3. Student population is extremely diverse
4. Student Life events
5. The facilities
6. Affordable tuition

Affordable
Tuition is only $10,330, one of the most affordable rates in the country.

Happy Students
88% of students return after their first year.

WORST OF BARUCH

1. Lack of student housing
2. Parking
3. Traffic in the area
4. Urban coldness
5. Narrow academic choices in the not-so-popular majors

Don't Move Off Campus
Average off-campus housing is a steep $10,382.

Student Body

African American:	11%	Male Undergrads:	47%
Asian American:	30%	Female Undergrads:	53%
Hispanic:	16%	Living On Campus:	1%
International:	11%	Living Off Campus:	99%
Native American:	0%	Male Athletes:	2%
White:	32%	Female Athletes:	2%
Unknown:	0%	Fraternity Members:	10%
From Out-of-State:	3%	Sorority Members:	10%

Students Speak Out On...
EVERYTHING!

ACADEMICS

It can be hard
"It can get hard, but the truth is the harder you try, the better you will do."

Haven't Declared Major Yet
"I am a freshman and have not been required to declare a major. But, in my other classes, I have a 3.6 GPA."

Academics are strong here
"The academics are VERY strong at Baruch. That was the reason why I transferred here."

ATHLETICS

Good way to get involved
"I'm not that into athletics at Baruch College, but they do offer a variety of sports. It is good to get involved in sports since Baruch does not have dorms."

Teams are very successful
"Sports at Baruch College are very successful. Every year, a sports team from Baruch wins a title. At basketball games during the winter, the stands get filled up, and the fans are really supportive."

Athletic Facilities
"I'm not much of an athlete myself, but I know that Baruch is known for its great athletic facilities. Our school has a huge gym, lockers, swimming pool, and other things for all types of sports."

CAMPUS DINING

Campus Dining
"The college cafeteria is decent, but the campus is also surrounded by all kinds of different foods. Only in New York can you have so many types of food on a single block."

Great Menu
"I like the variety of food."

Frequently Compared Schools:
Binghamton University
Hunter College
New York University
St. John's University

Best Dining Area is in Fine Arts Section
"The dining halls are decent, but I especially like the dining area in the fine arts section. It's very well presented."

CAMPUS HOUSING

Campus Life
"The students at Baruch college truly enjoying being there. Becoming active in a club is the best way to love your Baruch experience and make the best of it!"

Living Conditions Are Okay
"The dorms are a little bit overpriced compared to other options off campus."

GUYS & GIRLS

There Are Differernt Kinds of Girls and Guys at Baruch
"Baruch is the most diverse university in the U.S., so you can see different faces from every corner of the world at Baruch. Every guy and girl is nice and willing to help you if you have any problem."

Guys and Girls are Friendly
"Everyone is really friendly and respectful. People dress very casual but nice. There is a lot of diversity from all over the city and different interests floating around campus."

HEALTH & SAFETY

Security Guards
"The campus is very safe. Even though the security guards know you are a student, they make sure you swipe your Baruch card on the turnstiles, or else they don't let you in."

Safety is Excellent
"I have never felt unsafe on the Baruch campus."

LOOKING FOR MORE?
Check out our full-length guide to this school at collegeprowler.com/baruch-college/.

Bates College

2 Andrews Road; Lewiston, ME 04240
(207) 786-6000; www.bates.edu

THE BASICS:

Acceptance Rate: 27%
Yield: 37%
Setting: Small city
Control: Private Non-Profit
Total Undergrads: 1,738
SAT Range: 1890–2150*
ACT Range: —

Student-Faculty Ratio: 10:1
Retention Rate: 94%
Graduation Rate: 89%
Tuition: $49,350
Room & Board: $0
Avg. Aid Package: $30,093
Students With Aid: 48%

of 2400

Academics	A-	Greek Life	N/A
Athletics	B-	Guys	B
Campus Dining	A-	Health & Safety	B
Campus Housing	C+	Local Atmosphere	C
Campus Strictness	C+	Nightlife	C
Computers	B	Off-Campus Dining	B-
Diversity	C+	Off-Campus Housing	D+
Drug Safety	C-	Parking	B+
Facilities	B	Transportation	C
Girls	B+	Weather	C-

CP's Student Author On...
OVERALL EXPERIENCE

Bates students vary greatly in their opinions of their school. Some feel that Bates is a great school and wouldn't dream of having gone to another. Others spend their four years at Bates wishing they were someplace else. Bates is a very unique school, and for the people it suits, it's amazing. People who were looking for a different college experience are less happy. Bates does provide its students with a number of opportunities, and considering its size and resources, tries hard to accommodate every student. However, it is a small school in a small city and obviously can't have all the same resources that are available at larger universities. The student body isn't characterized by diversity, so if people who go to Bates aren't your type, it's easy to feel frustrated and out of place.

But whether you love Bates or hate it, when you graduate, you'll have a degree from one of the most selective liberal arts schools in the country, which definitely counts for something. Before you decide which school you want to go to, you need to be very sure what you want from a college.... For the rest of this editorial, visit collegeprowler. com.

Students Speak Out On...
OVERALL EXPERIENCE

Q Some Surprises
"When I entered Bates, I was hoping for a little bit of a less cliquey high school atmosphere, people settle in quickly, other than that, people are very friendly and I love it here."

Q "I do wish I was somewhere other than Bates. In high school, my big complaint in life was that I learned nothing from school and more from my peers. Now, I feel the reverse. Academically, I feel challenged by my classes and professors now that I know how to pick good classes. However, I do not feel challenged by my peers. I think I would have done better in a more intellectually-driven school."

Q "Bates is the greatest place I could ever end up. I love it here. It is important to remember that Bates is academically rigorous-it's just as important to study as it is to make great friends. I was sure I had to come to Bates the first time I saw it, even though it was in April and it had snowed 10 inches the night before. Campus was beautiful, and all the students were so excited to be here. I went early decision, and I couldn't be happier with where I am."

BEST OF BATES

1. Strong academic programs
2. Lick-It and Gala
3. The Strange Bedfellows improv comedy group
4. Dollar chai nights at the Ronj
5. The Bates computer network

Happy Students
94% of students return after their first year.

Commitment to Teaching
There are 10 students for every member of faculty on campus.

WORST OF BATES

1. Finding a parking spot
2. Six months of winter
3. Lewiston
4. People playing beer pong outside your room at 4 a.m.
5. No cable in dorm rooms

Expensive
Tuition is a steep $49,350, one of the most expensive rates in the country.

Student Body

African American:	4%	Male Undergrads:	46%
Asian American:	6%	Female Undergrads:	54%
Hispanic:	3%	Living On Campus:	92%
International:	6%	Living Off Campus:	8%
Native American:	0%	Male Athletes:	56%
White:	79%	Female Athletes:	39%
Unknown:	3%	Fraternity Members:	0%
From Out-of-State:	89%	Sorority Members:	0%

Frequently Compared Schools:
Bowdoin College
Colby College
Hamilton College
Middlebury College

Students Speak Out On... EVERYTHING!

ACADEMICS

ℚ Resources and Extra Help
"Bates has numerous programs and workshops for students who need extra assistance in their major, primarily the sciences. Professors go out of their way to help students and giv them any extra assistance that they may need."

ℚ "Professors, for the most part, are very serious about their fields. They have studied their subjects in depth and continue to do so. Some of my classes are interesting, and some aren't."

ℚ "For me, it often depends on the personality of the professor and what they choose to focus on."

ATHLETICS

ℚ Student Involvement
"students at bates college really get involved in athletics. The support of students at games is really good and a high percent of students play a varsity sport which keeps our campus really active"

ℚ "At Bates, it completely depends on the sport. Men's basketball is huge—they get a huge turnout for games, and people get pretty into it. Football, however, not so much. The team isn't great, so people don't pay much attention. IMs are pretty big, though, because anybody can participate."

CAMPUS DINING

ℚ "I have visited many colleges and other large universities, and it is always a pleasure to come back to food at Bates. Apart from the food being absolutely amazing, the one thing that sets Bates dining aside is the enthusiasm and kindness of the dining staff. They are motivated, eager to keep us happy, and proud to serve the food that they make every day."

ℚ "Food at Bates is probably the best food you will find at college. What I like best about Bates dining is the variety. In addition to the hot-food line, which changes every meal, there is always pizza, bagels, bread, peanut butter and jelly, a huge salad bar, a huge cereal selection, and a pasta bar to choose from."

CAMPUS HOUSING

ℚ Compact, Yet Quaint!
"First year dorms are fairly good; large closet space and good locations throughout the campus. There are places for all types of people: if you want a party scene, live in Smith, Page or Parker. If not, there are many other chem-free or low-chem housing options."

ℚ "Each dorm has a pretty different feel to it. The New Dorm—which still doesn't really have a name—is really nice, but doesn't have the character that some of the old ones do. Rand—or Old Rand, as people call it—is also a great place to be. The houses on Frye Street are also a lot of fun, but living there can mean a 10-minute walk to class."

GUYS & GIRLS

ℚ "The guys and girls here are all drunks! I found a great group of guys, and the girls, well, they're alright. But I heard a rumor that 60 percent of Batesies marry Batesies, so who knows."

ℚ "The guys and girls are often hippies who don't shower, so I'd have to say they're not that hot."

HEALTH & SAFETY

ℚ "It seems odd to say that I feel safe on a campus that experienced a murder and a rape within two months of one another. But I have always felt reasonably safe here; certainly I'm in no more danger here than at any other at-risk environment. I also think most colleges are inherently at-risk environments. I've locked my doors, not traveled downtown at night, and have been lucky, so I feel fairly safe."

ℚ "Security on campus is pretty good. There are Saferide shuttles at night if you need them. However, I feel perfectly safe walking around campus alone at night."

LOOKING FOR MORE?
Check out our full-length guide to this school at collegeprowler.com/bates-college/.

Bay Path College

588 Longmeadow St.; Longmeadow, MA 01106
(413) 565-1000; www.baypath.edu

THE BASICS:

Acceptance Rate: 66%
Yield: 33%
Setting: Suburban
Control: Private Non-Profit
Total Undergrads: 1,423
SAT Range: 1120–1780*
ACT Range: 16–26

Student-Faculty Ratio: 20:1
Retention Rate: 69%
Graduation Rate: 55%
Tuition: $24,530
Room & Board: $10,035
Avg. Aid Package: $11,453
Students With Aid: 99%

of 2400

Academics	B-	Greek Life	N/A
Athletics	C-	Guys	C-
Campus Dining	C	Health & Safety	B+
Campus Housing	B-	Local Atmosphere	B-
Campus Strictness	C+	Nightlife	C+
Computers	A-	Off-Campus Dining	C
Diversity	B	Off-Campus Housing	C
Drug Safety	B+	Parking	B+
Facilities	B-	Transportation	B-
Girls	B-	Weather	B-

CP's Student Author On...
OVERALL EXPERIENCE

At Bay Path College you get a unique college experience. It is a small, private college for girls where you can really explore your options and find your individual major and degree. The academics here are extensive, and the professors are fair and just. They enjoy teaching and challenge their students on every aspect of their learning. The professors also try their hardest to get to know their students so they can assist them to their fullest extent. The staff are fun and friendly, eager to help, and do what they can to keep the students enthusiastic about their education. The other students are nice and cordial, and the class sizes are small enough that no one really feels forgotten in a discussion because everyone gets a chance to speak their mind. The campus is well kept and absolutely beautiful, situated in a quiet and safe neighborhood.

Overall, Bay Path has a comfortable and wonderful atmosphere. Being here is good for those students who wish to devote themselves to academics.... For the rest of this editorial, visit collegeprowler.com.

Students Speak Out On...
OVERALL EXPERIENCE

Q **Perfect Fit**

"Leaving highschool i believed that I would always have those friendships, I have kept very few and all my old BFF's are now aquitances. I have made amazing friendships and good relationships with all the staff."

Q **I LOVE BAY PATH!!**

"I love Bay Path and would recommend it to anyone. Not many schools have the president of the college out on Campus Day doing the Booty Drop. She brought the electric slide into the lives of all the girls here and it is now a staple to our school. We have great events, like Miss Bay Path, a mock beauty pageant where one of the students ends up winning. If I had to do this all over again I would definitely choose Bay Path and be way more confident about it than I was when I enrolled."

Q **I Love School**

"I love that BPC is a small school, with small personal classes. I am happy I have talked with the President, and she knows many by name."

BEST OF BAY PATH

1. Beautiful campus
2. Nurturing, outgoing enviroment
3. The hardworking professors
4. Helpful faculty and staff
5. Close-knit community
6. Small campus

Easy Financial Aid Process
53% of students surveyed told us that the financial aid process went smoothly and they received the financial aid they needed.

WORST OF BAY PATH

1. Expensive
2. The food service
3. Most students travel off campus for entertainment.
4. Not enough events with neighboring colleges
5. There is not much to participate in on the weekends.

Life is NOT a Party
88% of students surveyed said it's almost impossible to find a good party.

Student Body

African American:	11%	Male Undergrads:	0%
Asian American:	2%	Female Undergrads:	100%
Hispanic:	12%	Living On Campus:	62%
International:	1%	Living Off Campus:	38%
Native American:	0%	Male Athletes:	0%
White:	71%	Female Athletes:	5%
Unknown:	4%	Fraternity Members:	0%
From Out-of-State:	45%	Sorority Members:	0%

Students Speak Out On...
EVERYTHING!

ACADEMICS

Q Academics are awesome!

"The academics offered are varied and good for their specific majors. The job opportunities are low, but the work-study jobs are nice. The workload from the teacher is average but the courses do challenge you intellectually."

Q Excellent Place for Help

"I have never had more one on one help in my life. Every single person who works at Bay Path helps you and is so wonderful .They simply go above their job. I had help every step of the way and encouragement. Everyone continues to do this. The professors are excellent and really there for every student. The workload is alot but helpful and enjoyable with all the help received."

ATHLETICS

Q Varisty Sports Are Good

"Varsity sports are Bay Path are not hard to get into but are a good experience. Very few sports have tryouts allowing experienced players to play with non experienced players. They are lots of sports ranging from tennis to soft ball to woman's ice hockey"

Q Athletics at Bay Path Are Enthusiastic.

"I have been to a few college games and I enjoyed them. I haven't participated as an athlete though."

CAMPUS DINING

Q Luch Room

"There is a lunch room. Great place to relax. Vending machine has good choices."

Q DINING HALL

"Food is not always fresh, time spent standing in line to pay for our meal can take up half our lunch period.I like the variety of food offered, jsut wish there were better dessert options. Would appreciated fresh fruit. Staff members are always polite and very helpful."

Frequently Compared Schools:

Amherst College
Bates College
Brandeis University
Chatham University

CAMPUS HOUSING

Q Convenience

"All the dorms are less than five minutes from the class buildings."

Q Bollum Hall

"The dorms are great. You know everyone on your floor, and each floor has its own personality. Sometimes there is drama but nothing to break the floor bond."

GUYS & GIRLS

Q People at My College

"People come from different parts of the world to attend college and to become a successful individual. My school is all girls and some dress high fashion while others dress in slacks and a t-shirt. People are comfortable in what they wear. My college demonstrates true leadership among women who want to become someone in life and lead the today's world."

Q What Are Guys?

"This is an all women's college so there are no male students here."

HEALTH & SAFETY

Q Safe and Sound

"the campus public safety officers can always be seen around campus. If anyone ever has a problem they are only a phone call away. They really care about our safety and make sure to notify us when ever anything is going on in our community."

Q Crime?

"There is no crime at Bay Path, at worst you might get a parking ticket. Even if someone steals something, you will be able to tell based on the small population and CamPo is always willing to help."

LOOKING FOR MORE?

Check out our full-length guide to this school at collegeprowler.com/bay-path-college/.

Baylor University

500 Speight Ave.; Waco, TX 76798
(254) 710-1011; www.baylor.edu

THE BASICS:

Acceptance Rate: 50%
Yield: 20%
Setting: Mid-sized city
Control: Private Non-Profit
Total Undergrads: 12,149
SAT Range: 1610–1930*
ACT Range: 23–29

Student-Faculty Ratio: 15:1
Retention Rate: 84%
Graduation Rate: 73%
Tuition: $28,070
Room & Board: $7,971
Avg. Aid Package: $17,250
Students With Aid: 95%

* of 2400

Academics	B+	Greek Life	B-
Athletics	A	Guys	B+
Campus Dining	B+	Health & Safety	B-
Campus Housing	B-	Local Atmosphere	C+
Campus Strictness	C-	Nightlife	B-
Computers	A-	Off-Campus Dining	B-
Diversity	C+	Off-Campus Housing	B+
Drug Safety	B	Parking	B-
Facilities	A-	Transportation	B
Girls	B-	Weather	B

CP's Student Author On...
OVERALL EXPERIENCE

When polling immediate post-graduation opinions, it's pretty common to hear "Happiness is seeing Waco in the rearview mirror." However, most students are relatively satisfied with their time at Baylor after nostalgia has set in. That nostalgia seems to be proportionate to the amount of time they've spent out of school, but before long, the newly-made alumni have nothing but rosy stories and donations to share. Their bad experiences fall under the omerta code of silence. For four years, at least, count on being frustrated with the social scene, overloaded with classes, poor, and running on no sleep and caffeine. The friends you make by going through that become your family and are there for life. It's all part of the college experience.

The odd thing is, an unusual amount of graduates, despite their protests, never leave Waco. Baylor family feels kin to the mob because just when you thought you were out, they suck you back in. It's blood in, blood out, and if you hate it enough, you'll leave before you're in too deep. The family environment really does seep through.... For the rest of this editorial, visit collegeprowler.com.

Students Speak Out On...
OVERALL EXPERIENCE

Q Couldn't Be Happier
"I love Baylor and everything about it. It's the best school for me and I have a lot of school pride. The campus is small and has such a friendly atmosphere. Professors are great and the whole Baptist idea is never shoved down your throat."

Q I Like Baylor...
"The education possibilities in the English or Great Text Departments are great. I enjoy Waco, have gotten into gardening, and have made incredible friends."

Q No Place Like the Bear's House
"Baylor is the greatest place. We have all you can think of sports, hunting game, and great social life."

Q I Love the Small Community Feel of It.
"Baylor is wonderful. I love how the school is a little big but it feels so small. Baylor does an excellent job at gettting students involved and integrated into school as well as possible. I immediately felt at home from my first visit and after starting school, I adapted to the college life quickly with all the events that were planned for us. I could not see myself happy at any other college."

BEST OF BAYLOR

1. Great place for networking
2. The professors are down to earth and genuinely care
3. You can get the most of your education through smaller class sizes

Happy Students
84% of students return after their first year.

Proven Success
73% of students will complete their education and graduate with a degree.

WORST OF BAYLOR

1. Dealing with financial aid can be disastrous. Don't get stuck in the Tower!
2. The social scene can be a little too tight knit
3. Lack of political and ideological diversity

Expensive
Tuition is a steep $28,070, one of the most expensive rates in the country.

Student Body

African American:	8%	Male Undergrads:	42%
Asian American:	7%	Female Undergrads:	58%
Hispanic:	11%	Living On Campus:	36%
International:	2%	Living Off Campus:	70%
Native American:	1%	Male Athletes:	5%
White:	70%	Female Athletes:	4%
Unknown:	2%	Fraternity Members:	13%
From Out-of-State:	19%	Sorority Members:	17%

Students Speak Out On... EVERYTHING!

ACADEMICS

Q University Scholars

"I'm in a very selective program called University Scholars. It basically lets me design my own degree. I enjoy it, but it's a lot of work. I have to maintain a 3.5 GPA, do an independent reading list, and write a thesis, on top of all my regular course work. But this program is perfect for me. I love it!"

Q Lots of Opportunities

"As a journalism major, I am receiving constant updates about available internship opportunities. I feel that when I am prepared to move from a purely classroom environment to an internship, I will have plenty of opportunity to do so. I feel my classes are preparing me for a future career in journalism very well."

Q Psychology Rules!

"Most students at my university take medical majors and the other majors are considered the minority. However, this doesn't take away from the teaching skills of the other professors. I really like my major, psychology, and the classes I've taken and have to take in the future."

ATHLETICS

Q Athletics

"from what i have seen and learned from college visits, the athletics at baylor is up there with all the other colleges"

Q Baylor Performs Well in All Sports

"Students at Baylor have a lot of team spirit and participate in a lot of sports. Our football team is not the strongest which is a big deal in the Big 12 conferance but there is still a lot of fan support."

Q Go Baylor Bears!!!

"Baylor Athletics is so much fun! The students are SO supportive of our teams. Football and basketball get the most recognition and the games are so exciting to be apart of!"

CAMPUS DINING

Q Great Food

"there are a variety of dining halls and they have great food!"

Q Great Food

"The food in the baylor cafeterias are so good!! You are required to have a meal plan freshman year, but I ate there the next three years also. There are lots of options and healthy choices."

CAMPUS HOUSING

Q Brooks College Is Awesome

"I have lived in Brooks College, and plan to continue to do so until I graduate. I love it! The building is very nice, but what I really love is the community. Living there is like being part of a family. It's definitely the best place to live on campus!"

Q Atmosphere

"The Social atmosphere of the campus appears to be great"

GUYS & GIRLS

Q Great

"Everyone is very accessible an non judgmental. There is a diverse student body but all are very accepting. Great place to be."

Q Friendliness of Campus

"You can talk to anyone here at Baylor. Almost anyone is willing to stop and help another person out."

HEALTH & SAFETY

Q Baylor Safety

"Feel very safe, campus police and emergency phones are seen almost everywhere."

Q Baylor Life

"Baylor university is probably the safest place I have ever lived in. I have lived in areas of high crime all of my life and it was extremely refreshing to arrive at a place where I could finally let my guard down a little for once."

LOOKING FOR MORE?

Check out our full-length guide to this school at collegeprowler.com/baylor-university/.

Belmont University

1900 Belmont Blvd.; Nashville, TN 37212
(615) 460-6000; www.belmont.edu

THE BASICS:

Acceptance Rate: 77%	**Student-Faculty Ratio:** 13:1
Yield: 40%	**Retention Rate:** 82%
Setting: Large city	**Graduation Rate:** 66%
Control: Private Non-Profit	**Tuition:** $22,360
Total Undergrads: 4,360	**Room & Board:** $8,590
SAT Range: 1070–1280*	**Avg. Aid Package:** $19,486
ACT Range: 23–29	**Students With Aid:** 84%

* of 1600

Academics	A-	Greek Life	A
Athletics	B-	Guys	A-
Campus Dining	C-	Health & Safety	B
Campus Housing	B	Local Atmosphere	A
Campus Strictness	B+	Nightlife	A+
Computers	B-	Off-Campus Dining	A-
Diversity	D	Off-Campus Housing	A-
Drug Safety	B	Parking	C+
Facilities	A+	Transportation	D
Girls	A-	Weather	B

CP's Student Author On...
OVERALL EXPERIENCE

People aren't sucking up to any University officials when they say Belmont is unique. Because of its music business program, Belmont draws a lot of musically-inclined people, and the general population is pretty artsy and a little beatnik-esque. Belmont, despite its pesky little hangups on alcohol and alcohol paraphernalia on campus, is a sweet little school. Its size defines its nature—the classes are more intimate and allow the students to get a great deal more attention than that of a huge lecture hall setting. The teachers want to engage the students and learn from them, as well. They teach the students to think beyond the "now" and into the future and outside world. The students' relationships with each other are also affected by the size of the school. After a few months at Belmont, faces become familiar, and campus begins to feel like home. The people are pleasant, and, in true Southern fashion, people will smile and say, "Hi," even if they don't know you.... For the rest of this editorial, visit collegeprowler.com.

Students Speak Out On...
OVERALL EXPERIENCE

Q Dream Come True
"Belmont is my dream school. It is everything I wanted so much more. I work so hard on my classes but have learned so much. Every day I am provided with amazing opportunities and I couldn't ask for a better place to be."

Q The 'Mont
"Belmont is a very unique campus. The is barely any social opportunities but you do receive a good education in a safe and small environment. I love my school and I'm glad I chose to be here."

Q Why Belmont
"Belmont is an okay school, the people there are very nice for the most part; however one would have to look hard to find friends that are not music types.I love being in the Beaman or the University Ministries hanging out with friends and meeting tons of new people at the same time."

Q This school sucks
"Don't go. NO nightlife. Too religious."

BEST OF BELMONT

1. Creative environment
2. Helpful teachers
3. Internships and networking opportunities
4. Location—close to a lot of good restaurants, bars, clubs, and music venues
5. On-campus jobs

Happy Students
82% of students return after their first year.

Big Dorms
60% of students surveyed felt that dorms were more spacious than average.

WORST OF BELMONT

1. Convocation
2. Most of the alternative eateries (aside from the caf) on campus serve subs. That gets old after a while.
3. The no-alcohol on-campus policy

Don't Move Off Campus
Average off-campus housing is a steep $11,520.

Not Much Diversity
One of the least racially diverse campuses—only 13% of students are minorities.

Student Body

African American:	4%	Male Undergrads:	42%
Asian American:	2%	Female Undergrads:	58%
Hispanic:	2%	Living On Campus:	52%
International:	1%	Living Off Campus:	48%
Native American:	0%	Male Athletes:	7%
White:	87%	Female Athletes:	5%
Unknown:	4%	Fraternity Members:	3%
From Out-of-State:	65%	Sorority Members:	5%

Frequently Compared Schools:

Clemson University
College of Charleston
Elon University
Vanderbilt University

Students Speak Out On...
EVERYTHING!

ACACEMICS

Q Not Easy, but Nothing Is Hard

"Well, I am speaking from a different stand point. I have an intensive workload due to the fact that I am a triple major in International Business with my emphasis in Marketing snd my language in Arabic, Economics, Finance, and a minor in Political Science. But this gives me an advatage to speak on the academics. The faculty is great, the programs are intense and beneficial, offer more than fifteen study abroad trips per year, and even offer an honors program."

Q FNP Program

"The program is small with adequate face to face time with instructions. If something is difficult to grasp or if there are any problems, an instructor is readily available to help. It is a wonderful program!"

Q Academics

"I cam to Belmont University because it has one of the best, if not the best Music Business program in the nation. All of the professors know what they are talking about and have had years of experience in the music industry. Some of the professors are adjuncts who are still playing an active role in the music world."

ATHLETICS

Q Student Support

"The students at Belmont really support their athletics! They really come out to watch and encourage the basketball team. The facility is beautiful and is the same one that was used for the Presidential Debates several years ago. I have also attended baseball games, track and cross country events and soccer games!"

CAMPUS DINING

Q Cafe

"The cafeteria on campus is great! The food choices are healthy and delicious. They have a different hot meal for lunch and dinner. They also have pizza, burgers, fries all the time. You can also use your Bruin Bucks at other locations on campus to grab a quick bite if you aren't near the cafeteria.

It is also light and pretty. The employees are friendly and helpful!"

CAMPUS HOUSING

Q Dorms Are Very Nice

"Belmont's campus housing is very nice. In my two years at belmont I have lived in two of the newer dorms, and these dorms have been spectacular. As I have visited older dorms, they seem to be more average, but the amenities and social atmosphere of all the dorms are great. The newer dorms are fantastic; they are all extremely clean, very roomy, and just nice all the way around. They are very convenient to campus and reasonably priced."

Q Freshman All Guys Dorm Isn't That Great

"Some of the dorms aren't that great. But a new dorm was just built and that one is really nice."

GUYS & GIRLS

Q Peeps at Belmont

"There are all kinds of individuals at Belmont University. All kinds of styles can be seen, also: skinny jeans, v-neck tops, skirts, dresses, unique styles, business type clothing, polos, etc. There are the people from all deptartments getting together and having a good time every day."

HEALTH & SAFETY

Q Very Safe

"The campus security is very good, especially considering a rough neighbor is nearby. Health Services are also good with top-notch facilities."

Q Health and Safety

"I have never felt unsafe, or heard of anyone feeling unsafe at Belmont. The Belmont Campus police do an excellent job of patrolling the campus all day long. Plus the fact that Belmont is a small campus and is very well lit helps out also."

LOOKING FOR MORE?

Check out our full-length guide to this school at collegeprowler.com/belmont-university/.

Beloit College

700 College St.; Beloit, WI 53511
(608) 363-2000; www.beloit.edu

THE BASICS:

Acceptance Rate: 73%	Student-Faculty Ratio: 11:1
Yield: 23%	Retention Rate: 90%
Setting: Suburban	Graduation Rate: 78%
Control: Private Non-Profit	Tuition: $33,418
Total Undergrads: 1,383	Room & Board: $6,830
SAT Range: 1135–1380*	Avg. Aid Package: $24,506
ACT Range: 25–30	Students With Aid: 92%

of 1600

Academics	B	Greek Life	B-
Athletics	C+	Guys	C+
Campus Dining	B	Health & Safety	A
Campus Housing	B	Local Atmosphere	B-
Campus Strictness	A+	Nightlife	D+
Computers	A-	Off-Campus Dining	C+
Diversity	C-	Off-Campus Housing	C-
Drug Safety	B-	Parking	A-
Facilities	B-	Transportation	D+
Girls	C-	Weather	C-

CP's Student Author On...
OVERALL EXPERIENCE

Let's get one thing straight: Beloit is not for everyone—and thank God, because we only have so much room here. There is a certain bond with people who have gone to Beloit, who have seen its idiosyncrasies first-hand, who know the weirdos personally and still keep nicknames for them. A four-year trudge through the thicket of Beloit education will put anyone in shape for a new challenge afterward. Some will say "if I survived Beloit College, I can survive this," while others will boast "Beloit College has prepared me well to face challenges head on, and it has made me confident that I can survive anything." Either way, they're right. Beloit is good at making a paradox out of itself.

People either love Beloit, hate Beloit, or both, but it is pretty much guaranteed that whatever you feel for Beloit, it will be strong. Beloit can definitely provide students with an amazing experience if you use your resources right. Study abroad options are spectacular, and an overwhelming amount of students end up in a different country or a different part of the U.S. at some point during their four years.... For the rest of this editorial, visit collegeprowler.com.

Students Speak Out On...
OVERALL EXPERIENCE

Q Love It.
"I love Beloit. The Winters are harsh but it helps you appreciate the people around you more for distracting you, and appreciate the good weather when it arrives. The people are odd, quirky, and individual in being individual. A great place to create who you want to be."

Q One of the Best Experiences I've Had
"Beloit College is one of the best places on Earth. No joke. The people here are lovely and it is easy to find and make friends. The professors are amazing and really dedicated to their students. The classes are tough, so people can't party all the time. But it is college, and that's why you go. To learn."

Q "I think Beloit is a great place to get an undergrad degree, but four years is more than enough time for me at Beloit."

Q "Sometimes, I wish I had gone to a bigger school for a different social scene, but since I'm planning on going to grad school, I feel I'll get that large school experience at some point. But in terms of small, liberal arts colleges, I'm glad I chose Beloit. I do love it."

BEST OF BELOIT

1. The sense of community
2. International programs
3. Diversity
4. Flexibility in studies
5. Enthusiasm of students
6. The general laid-back attitude

Happy Students
90% of students return after their first year.

Proven Success
78% of students will complete their education and graduate with a degree.

WORST OF BELOIT

1. The town
2. Isolation ("Beloit Bubble")
3. The speed of gossip
4. Parking
5. Lack of scheduling options due to the small size of the school

Expensive
Tuition is a steep $33,418, one of the most expensive rates in the country.

Student Body

African American:	4%	Male Undergrads:	43%
Asian American:	3%	Female Undergrads:	57%
Hispanic:	3%	Living On Campus:	96%
International:	7%	Living Off Campus:	7%
Native American:	0%	Male Athletes:	35%
White:	76%	Female Athletes:	19%
Unknown:	6%	Fraternity Members:	15%
From Out-of-State:	81%	Sorority Members:	5%

Frequently Compared Schools:

Earlham College
Lawrence University
Macalester College
Oberlin College

Students Speak Out On... EVERYTHING!

ACADEMICS

Amazing

"I love the academics at Beloit College. The professors are there to help you grasp and understand the material, and to help you grow beyond your own expectations. The liberal arts approach broadens the individuals mind in many ways."

"The professors, as a whole, are great. They're easy to talk to, and they really take the time to get to know you. The biggest problem I ever had was not having enough time in my four-year schedule to take all the classes that I wanted to."

ATHLETICS

Pretty Bad.

"Very few people come to this school for their athletics. If you did a sport in high school and want to keep doing it, but don't mind not being on a competitive team, then Beloit would be a good choice. A variety of sports are offered but the school spirit and competition aren't valued."

Eh...

"Most of the campus is pretty apathetic towards sports, but apparently this year the administration is putting more money into our varsity athletics so that might change. Ultimate Frisbee is definitely the most popular sport on campus, and it's pretty common to see lots of groups of people throwing a frisbee around during class."

CAMPUS DINING

Disgusting

"The food here is greasy and salty at best, and disgusting at worst."

"The food in Commons is pretty good. Some people like it, some don't. There are always many options, though, so you will always find something that suits your fancy. If nothing looks good, you can always resort to the sandwich deli or to the cereal bar. There is so much cereal selection; it's great. Also, there's DK's, which is the alternative to Commons. There's less selection, but it's quite good. We also have a coffee shop on campus which is open pretty late."

CAMPUS HOUSING

Good Housing Options

"Housing at Beloit is good, the rooms are clean and nice for the most part, and it isn't hard to get a single. The 64 Halls can feel slightly cavernous, but are fine apart from Peet, the worst dorm on campus. Aldrich is often considered the best because it is the newest dorm, but it can have a slightly hotel-like feel. Wood is a great option for upperclassmen."

Dorms

"The upperclassmen have the best dorms. Freshman dorms aren't that bad. Bushnell has split doubles and a lot of singles plus it has airconditioning. 609 and 840 are good for freshman bonding but they don't have airconditioning. Aldrich is like a hotel."

GUYS & GIRLS

People at Beloit

"It's difficult to rate how the people look phsically, since different people have differnt preferences and it's not something I don't pay attention to for the most part. There is an extremely wide range of interests that are held by this group of people."

"There are lots of insecure people with major weight issues. There are also lots of open gays, including faculty. It was hard as a straight guy with latent homophobia."

HEALTH & SAFETY

Pretty Lax

"You can often spot security guards walking around campus, but they don't bother anyone. You can drink openly on campus as long as you're not puking or passed out or something you're fine. They're a little bit strict about parties but that doesn't stop people from having them."

LOOKING FOR MORE?

Check out our full-length guide to this school at collegeprowler.com/beloit-college/.

Bentley University

175 Forest St.; Waltham, MA 02452
(800) 523-2354; www.bentley.edu

THE BASICS:

Acceptance Rate: 43%	Student-Faculty Ratio: 14:1
Yield: 33%	Retention Rate: 93%
Setting: Small city	Graduation Rate: 82%
Control: Private Non-Profit	Tuition: $35,828
Total Undergrads: 4,247	Room & Board: $11,740
SAT Range: 1690–1950*	Avg. Aid Package: $26,584
ACT Range: 25–28	Students With Aid: 65%

of 2400

Academics	B+	Greek Life	C+
Athletics	C+	Guys	A-
Campus Dining	C+	Health & Safety	B+
Campus Housing	A-	Local Atmosphere	B
Campus Strictness	B	Nightlife	B
Computers	A+	Off-Campus Dining	B
Diversity	C+	Off-Campus Housing	B-
Drug Safety	C	Parking	B+
Facilities	B	Transportation	A-
Girls	B	Weather	C

CP's Student Author On...
OVERALL EXPERIENCE

The Bentley experience is hardly a normal college experience. From day one, you will be set off on a track to receive a unique business education. Hard work and effort are mandatory, but the rewards are endless. Students who are unhappy with their Bentley experience can actually attribute some of their issues to their own introverted-ness that keeps them from exploring Waltham and Boston and the events, concerts, and meetings the school offers. Other factors, such as the disconnect in the concept of diversity and inability to form a relationship with local businesses, are out of students' control.

The opportunity to interact with professors who are leaders in the field, learn from renowned companies in the classroom, and have access to the latest technology is such a distinctive idea that Bentley is in a class of its own as a business university. If you want to have a college experience that you can reflect back on and say you received an excellent real-world business education, were exposed to state-of-the-art technology, and had a good time while doing it, then your four years at Bentley will have been a success.

Students Speak Out On...
OVERALL EXPERIENCE

Q **Come to Bentley!**

"Bentley is a great community to be a part of. While you do have to pay attention to your studies, it is also easy to have a great social life. There are plenty of events and activities going on, and if not, there's always someone willing to head into the city. It was definitely the right choice of schools for me."

Q **Bentley**

"Bentley's community is what attracted me to the school and what makes it unique. Also, the learning environment and classroom setup definitely makes it easier to learn. the resources Bentley has allows access to different tools to help get the subject matter across."

Q **Ups and Downs**

"Not a partying school until I joined Greek life. Now it's so legit."

BEST OF BENTLEY

1. State-of-the-art technology at your fingertips
2. Up-and-coming reputation as the recognized leader in business education

Happy Students
93% of students return after their first year.

Proven Success
82% of students will complete their education and graduate with a degree.

WORST OF BENTLEY

1. Intense business focus
2. Cliques
3. Walking up the hill to class
4. Requirement to take (and pass) economics and finance classes

Expensive
Tuition is a steep $35,828, one of the most expensive rates in the country.

Expensive to Just Get By
56% of students surveyed felt that the amount it costs to live while at school was worse than average.

Frequently Compared Schools:

Babson College
Boston College
Boston University
Northeastern University

Students Speak Out On... EVERYTHING!

ACADEMICS

Business
"The professors are very engaged and they care about their students, I feel as if I am getting an amazing education here"

Actuarial Sciences
"The Actuarial program at Bentley is superb. I passed an exam freshman year and sophomore year and then took a year away from exams to study abroad. Now in my senior year I am taking another prep course for my third exam in May."

Business
"Fantastic business school with excellent career services. Highly recommended to any business student."

ATHLETICS

Social and Fun
"Bentley Athletics are fun because they really try to incorporate fans into the game, especially basketball."

Need Spirit for Good Teams
"The athletics at Bentley are really good overall. The facilities are all brand new and well maintained (and a new hockey rink is being discussed). The teams perform very well, especially the basketball team. The only issue is a lack of school spirit. Most games have mediocre turnouts, and students have to be bribed with free giveaways to attend games. School spirit is something that CAB works on frequently."

Teams Are Great
"but no one really attends the games or meets unless free stuff is being handed out."

CAMPUS DINING

One the Edge
"The food here apparently used to be terrible but they make great strides every semester. Just this year the food has gotten 50% better. It's not A food but it should be within a few years."

Good but Boring
"Seasons does not serve bad or unsafe food, but it had very little variety when I had a meal plan. Eating there the first day was not a problem. Eating there every day was."

Food
"Not enough food options. Same food all of the time."

CAMPUS HOUSING

Housing Is Huge
"Some of the biggest and most modern dorms I've ever seen. When your siblings/friends come it, they will be envious."

Expensive but Worth It
"Although the housing costs at Bentley are high, after freshman year the housing options are much better in comparison to other schools. The selection process is fair and easy, and keeps the majority of students living on campus."

GUYS & GIRLS

Dress
"Very conservatively dressed, rarely any sweat pants or sweat shirts, men and women dress nicely for classes"

Attractive Campus
"There are a lot of attractive people on campus. Everyone is well dressed. There are a lot of foreign students as well."

HEALTH & SAFETY

Safety/Security
"I have never felt unsafe or in a dangerous situation. Bentley is a closed campus and is safe for the most part."

Safe and Sound
"I don't know one person, boy or girl, that has ever felt unsafe here. People walk alone at 4 a.m. in the morning and don't even think about it."

LOOKING FOR MORE?

Check out our full-length guide to this school at collegeprowler.com/bentley-university/.

Berea College

101 Chestnut St.; Berea, KY 40404
(859) 985-3000; www.berea.edu

THE BASICS:

Acceptance Rate: 19%
Yield: 76%
Setting: Town
Control: Private Non-Profit
Total Undergrads: 1,553
SAT Range: 1475–1795*
ACT Range: 21–26

Student-Faculty Ratio: 10:1
Retention Rate: 82%
Graduation Rate: 64%
Tuition: $876
Room & Board: $5,768
Avg. Aid Package: $32,141
Students With Aid: 100%

* of 2400

Academics	B	Greek Life	N/A
Athletics	C+	Guys	B+
Campus Dining	C	Health & Safety	D+
Campus Housing	C	Local Atmosphere	C+
Campus Strictness	D+	Nightlife	C
Computers	B	Off-Campus Dining	C
Diversity	B	Off-Campus Housing	B-
Drug Safety	B-	Parking	B-
Facilities	C+	Transportation	C+
Girls	C+	Weather	C+

CP's Student Author On...
OVERALL EXPERIENCE

The experience at Berea College is so indescribable, but the best way to describe it is "a transformative experience." For most students who come here, Berea College is far from home, so they have a feeling of being out on their own and doing things for themselves. The people at Berea definitely contribute to each student's overall experience because of the exposure to different backgrounds, races, religions, cultures, and perspectives. The diversity is a key component to a student's experience here because listening to others' unique ideologies forces everyone to challenge themselves and grow mentally. And, the courses are as mentally stimulating as the diversified student body. Most Berea students also take advantage of the study abroad program. Traveling to different continents and countries introduces students to a different way of thinking and living, expanding their horizons even more.

Berea is so different from typical colleges—if you're accepted, there is no reason to even consider not choosing this school as your future alma mater. The College prepares students for the real world.... For the rest of this editorial, visit collegeprowler.com.

Students Speak Out On...
OVERALL EXPERIENCE

Q I Can't Complain

"Even though I have my issues here I love it. I have not only learned things about myself, but I have grown as a person and maturely. I love my school and I can't complain about it because I have had some of the greatest experiences since I have come here. I am grateful for coming to Berea!"

Q I Love Berea College

"I really love Berea College. I believe it is a great college that has great community values with very friendly people, very nice and dedicated professors, and small convenient classes. The classes are very challenging, so if you are very worried about your GPA, understand that it may not be the way you want it because it is extremely challenging."

Q What About Berea?

"I had a great experience at Berea College. I had come to love the education offered here at Berea College, which enriched my experience here at this institution."

BEST OF BEREA

1. No tuition
2. Free laptop
3. Helpful professors
4. Quality education
5. Diversity
6. Guaranteed on-campus job
7. The people

Affordable
Tuition is only $876, one of the most affordable rates in the country.

Happy Students
82% of students return after their first year.

WORST OF BEREA

1. Lack of activities
2. Visitation hours
3. The food options
4. Campus can feel too small at times.
5. Everything closes early.
6. Parking

Students Can't Wait to Get Out of Town
64% of students surveyed said that there's no way they would live here after graduation.

Student Body

African American:	16%	Male Undergrads:	40%
Asian American:	2%	Female Undergrads:	60%
Hispanic:	2%	Living On Campus:	87%
International:	7%	Living Off Campus:	13%
Native American:	1%	Male Athletes:	24%
White:	69%	Female Athletes:	13%
Unknown:	3%	Fraternity Members:	0%
From Out-of-State:	57%	Sorority Members:	0%

Frequently Compared Schools:

Bob Jones University
Centre College
Clemson University
Davidson College

Students Speak Out On...
EVERYTHING!

ACADEMICS

The Scholarly Aspect

"My college's main focus is academics. It is a liberal arts college so the education is broad; therefore, students will learn so much. The professors here are strict and have high expectations of their students, so this is a no nonsense college."

Academically Driven

"I am a Sociology major, as well as an African and African American Studies major. The Sociology major is very challenging, and the professors are great. The capstone course for the Sociology major is the hardest course. The African and African American Studies major is not as difficult as the Sociology major but still challenging. The workload is hard because of class and labor."

ATHLETICS

Berea College sports

"The sports here at Berea College are great. The students at the school support every sport that is provided. School spirit is everywhere."

From what I can see, they suck.

"None of the people I know are big into the sports here. Athletics are not really all that popular and the school does not seem to be recruiting that much, and it is hard when everyone receives full tuition scholarships (there's nothing to offer the athletes that they wouldn't get anyway). Bottom line, sports are not that great because our athletes are not either, but there are always people at the games and everyone knows it is more fun when you're rooting for the home team."

CAMPUS DINING

Eateries

"Berea College has Mountaineer Dining Hall and the Crossroads Cafe. The food in the dining hall is not the best of foods, but it is enough to satisfy. The cafe is great. It has a nice aura and good food."

Food Service and cafe

"I love the idea of the cafe and that it gives students an alternative place to eat; however, if you are not careful with your Berea Bucks, you will run out too fast and that is not convenient. I do love the dining hall because of the variety of food it serves but I wish it was open late hours, so that we always had access to food."

CAMPUS HOUSING

Freshman Dorm

"The first-year female dorms are clean, and the RA's are very nice and helpful."

Great!

"It is great. The rooms are a bit small, but it works. Equipment and furnishings are good. Social atmosphere is great. It is cheap. It is also conveniently placed."

GUYS & GIRLS

Academically focused campus

"The reason I chose Berea College is because it is a academically focused campus and provides a great education. Most of the students of academically focused, as well."

Different, Cool, & Likeable.

"The guys and girls here usually do their own thing, and it's nice to see that not everyone looks forward to a group norm."

HEALTH & SAFETY

Public Safety

"I feel very safe on campus. Usually I leave the library at midnight and walk to my room on my own. I am naturally a paranoid person and I try to take care of myself, but after the past two years that I have been walking to my room alone at those times, I am not scared. A lot of measures are put in place, many places on campus are lit at night, and Public Safety is almost always watching us and making sure we are behaving right and are safe. They do a very great job."

LOOKING FOR MORE?

Check out our full-length guide to this school at collegeprowler.com/berea-college/.

Binghamton University

Vestal Parkway E; Binghamton, NY 13902
(607) 777-2000; www.binghamton.edu

THE BASICS:

Acceptance Rate: 40%
Yield: 24%
Setting: Small city
Control: Public
Total Undergrads: 11,677
SAT Range: 1190–1350*
ACT Range: 26–29

Student-Faculty Ratio: 20:1
Retention Rate: 90%
Graduation Rate: 78%
Tuition: $14,661
Room & Board: $10,614
Avg. Aid Package: $10,696
Students With Aid: 58%

* of 1600

Academics	B+	Greek Life	B
Athletics	C+	Guys	B
Campus Dining	B	Health & Safety	C+
Campus Housing	B+	Local Atmosphere	C+
Campus Strictness	A-	Nightlife	B+
Computers	B+	Off-Campus Dining	C+
Diversity	A-	Off-Campus Housing	B
Drug Safety	C	Parking	B
Facilities	B-	Transportation	B+
Girls	B-	Weather	C-

CP's Student Author On...
OVERALL EXPERIENCE

While some students show disappointment with the school's facilities, professors, climate, and social scene, most come away from Binghamton with an overall positive opinion. More importantly, many have found a home at Binghamton, raving about the people they have met and the opportunities the school has provided. And why not? As a large and highly competitive public institution, Binghamton attracts a wide variety of talented students and faculty. No matter what you are interested in, you will have an opportunity to explore it at Binghamton, as well as expand your experiences. The key is to get involved. Nobody is going to hold your hand and guide you through school, but if you search for even a short time, you are bound to find your place.

It is true that Binghamton is not a school for everyone. If you are looking for the atmosphere of a large party or athletics-oriented school or the hands-on attention of a small private school, you will not find what you are looking for at Binghamton.... For the rest of this editorial, visit collegeprowler.com.

Students Speak Out On...
OVERALL EXPERIENCE

Q Great Experience
"Binghamotn has been a great overall experience. The academics are top notch and the social life is great"

Q Its Real Nice
"While Binghamton might not be the nicest place at first sight everyone is awesome. Theres always something to do on the weekends and you can always have a great time."

Q Good School
"I had a good time there, met a lot of good people and learned a lot."

Q Good Place for Better Career
"Just like the title says, great place for bright future. If you are looking for fun, it is not not a good place though."

Q I Like It
"its great here, mostly because the people are awesome. there is always something to do (prom parties to movies to the nature preserve). the food is ok. workload depends on major. i would choose bing again"

BEST OF BINGHAMTON

1. Price
2. Safety
3. Academics
4. Off-campus housing
5. Nightlife
6. The guy/girl ratio
7. Spring, when it finally comes

Happy Students
90% of students return after their first year.

Proven Success
78% of students will complete their education and graduate with a degree.

WORST OF BINGHAMTON

1. Weather
2. Parking
3. Ugly campus
4. Campus dining
5. The city of Binghamton
6. No football team
7. Gen-ed classes
8. Greek life

Students Can't Wait to Get Out of Town
90% of students surveyed said that there's no way they would live here after graduation.

Student Body

African American:	5%	Male Undergrads:	53%
Asian American:	12%	Female Undergrads:	47%
Hispanic:	7%	Living On Campus:	65%
International:	9%	Living Off Campus:	35%
Native American:	0%	Male Athletes:	5%
White:	43%	Female Athletes:	5%
Unknown:	23%	Fraternity Members:	8%
From Out-of-State:	28%	Sorority Members:	9%

Frequently Compared Schools:

Boston University
Cornell University
Stony Brook University
University at Buffalo

Students Speak Out On... EVERYTHING!

ACADEMICS

Super Happy

"The school is great. It can be cloudy and gloomy sometimes, but it is so active here on campus, there is too much to do. I feel bad I haven't done more!"

Professors in Upper Level Class Good

"The professors in the upper-level classes are usually good. The more research-oriented can be pretty busy but usually can make time for the students. The professors in the intro classes can be inconsistent. Some of them aren't that great, but some of the best professors I've had taught big lecture classes to Freshman and Sophomores."

ATHLETICS

DON't Judge Based on Basketball

"lots of great sports, sports events, and opportunities for students. the basketball team had some problems and it's really ridiculous because athletics is suffering overall because of it."

Basketball Is Where It's at

"Most of our teams aren't as popular as our basketball team, which went as far as the east conference's if only for a short run."

CAMPUS DINING

Food Is Good but Can Get Repetitive

"The food is fairly good but can get repetitive, especially if want to eat healthy. The upside is the value is great; I pay significantly less than a lot of my friends at public schools."

Menus

"Good food choices, good food quality, plenty of areas to eat"

CAMPUS HOUSING

Mountainview

"I absolutely LOVE my dorming community. Mountainview has air conditioning and heat, and are mostly suite-style rooms. I lived in a 6-person suite that came with two bathrooms (with two showers/toilets) and a common room which was basically like a living room with couches and chairs. I love living in mountainview and i would not want to live everywhere else!"

Campus Life

"Mountainview dorms are by far the best, they are almost like living in a hotel because the rooms are huge and a cleaner takes care of the bathroom once a week. The suite style is great, you have a roommate but also four other people and a common room. A lot of people leave their doors open and frequently have floor functions from parties to movie nights"

GUYS & GIRLS

Lots of Smart Guys & Gals from Long Island, Jewish & Aisian

"I transfered here and found everyone pretty friendly and smart."

Decent amount of hot girls

"There's a range of hot girls. I think maybe every 4 out of every 10 girls are hot. I think sororities tend to have the hottest girls. Dress, interests, and relationships tend to vary between social groups"

HEALTH & SAFETY

Safety Is a First at BU

"BU's number one priority after education and it's students is safety. Our campus includes everything from 24 hour police patrol, walking and driving escorts for late night trips on campus, late night security entrance to ensure only students enter campus, blue lights safety phones, etc. I even live in corridor style buildings and leave my door open all the time and nothing has ever been stolen. There isn't a time when I have felt unsafe."

Very Safe

"I can walk around the Binghamton University campus at 3 or 4 in the morning and still feel ok."

LOOKING FOR MORE?
Check out our full-length guide to this school at collegeprowler.com/binghamton-university/.

Birmingham-Southern College

900 Arkadelphia Road; Birmingham, AL 35254
(205) 226-4600; www.bsc.edu

THE BASICS:

Acceptance Rate: 59%
Yield: 28%
Setting: Mid-sized city
Control: Private Non-Profit
Total Undergrads: 1,508
SAT Range: 1560–1900*
ACT Range: 23–28

Student-Faculty Ratio: 12:1
Retention Rate: 81%
Graduation Rate: 66%
Tuition: $26,746
Room & Board: $9,800
Avg. Aid Package: $15,595
Students With Aid: 96%

* of 2400

Academics	B	Greek Life	A+
Athletics	B-	Guys	B+
Campus Dining	B	Health & Safety	B
Campus Housing	C+	Local Atmosphere	B+
Campus Strictness	B+	Nightlife	A-
Computers	B+	Off-Campus Dining	A-
Diversity	D	Off-Campus Housing	C-
Drug Safety	B	Parking	A
Facilities	A-	Transportation	B-
Girls	A-	Weather	A-

CP's Student Author On...
OVERALL EXPERIENCE

When people reflect on their college experience at Birmingham-Southern, they usually talk about what great opportunities they have access to, and what an outstanding education they're receiving. For the price of the school, there's got to be some kind of long-term benefit. It's no secret that if you graduate from BSC, then you're pretty much guaranteed to get a job in the metro area right out of college. Students also talk about the lifelong friendships they formed, and all the different kinds of people they met while at Southern. It's the kind of place that alumni love to come back to and reminisce about, as well as encourage their kids to come.

The whole school feels like one big family. While there are struggles, it seems as though everyone at BSC is looking to improve upon their mistakes and make it a place that everyone can enjoy. The administration is always changing curriculum to fit the needs of the students, and the students are always challenging the faculty in order to improve upon the status quo.... For the rest of this editorial, visit collegeprowler.com.

Students Speak Out On...
OVERALL EXPERIENCE

Q I Love It Here!

"BSC is a great school! Students are truly interested in their academic work and professors are actively engaged in their students' educations. The general atmosphere on campus is one of respect for each other and the mission of the College. Most everyone is involved in some organization or sports team and this shared desire and respect makes for a close-knit community. If I were to design a liberal arts college from the ground up, it would look very similar to Birmingham Southern."

Q Overall Experience

"My overall experience at BSC is a very positive one. I left to attend a state school and returned. I enjoy the small size the most. I like having a close relationship with professors and students."

Q "I love BSC. It is everything I expected and more. The service-learning programs are great, and there are many opportunities to get involved in things, despite the size of the school."

BEST OF BIRMINGHAM-SOUTHERN

1. Teachers that actually speak English
2. SoCo
3. E-fest
4. Starbucks coffee
5. Free laundry
6. New computers

Happy Students
81% of students return after their first year.

Genders Equally Represented
A male-to-female ratio of 52/48 means there's a pretty even balance of students on campus.

WORST OF BIRMINGHAM-SOUTHERN

1. Finding a parking spot
2. Meal plans
3. Living in the ghetto
4. Cultural events
5. New Men's dorm
6. Walking uphill both ways
7. The bubble atmosphere
8. Alabama heat and rain

Expensive
Tuition is a steep $26,746, one of the most expensive rates in the country.

Want a Job? On Your Own
There aren't any placement services for graduates.

Student Body

African American:	8%	Male Undergrads:	49%
Asian American:	3%	Female Undergrads:	51%
Hispanic:	1%	Living On Campus:	76%
International:	0%	Living Off Campus:	24%
Native American:	0%	Male Athletes:	36%
White:	84%	Female Athletes:	18%
Unknown:	2%	Fraternity Members:	40%
From Out-of-State:	41%	Sorority Members:	50%

Frequently Compared Schools:

Clemson University
Furman University
Rhodes College
Wake Forest University

Students Speak Out On...
EVERYTHING!

ACADEMICS

Q English Major

"The English teachers are awesome, they really encourage you to use their office hours if you need help or even just to talk. You can bounce ideas off of them for your papers, whatever you need. I love that the professors are not all scary and non-relatable. I suppose because of the small class sizes, you feel like you can go to them with a problem and not face back lash."

Q

"Some professors excel at discussion-based classes, some with lecture style, and some with collaborative learning. You just have to figure out what kind of class you're signing up for, and pick the professor accordingly. Once you learn who to avoid, it's smooth sailing."

ATHLETICS

Q Division III

"Our athletics are Division III but we still remain very competitive in all sports. Soon we will be able to compete for the national tournament and we are expected to do very well."

Q

"Basketball is fairly big. I think sports aren't as big of a deal for us as for most other schools, since we don't have a football team."

CAMPUS DINING

Q Love the Caf

"The caf is the best ... from home-cooked specials to fast food, there is variety and it doesn't get boring or tiring. The staff is always helpful and it is always great."

Q Newly Renovated Dining Areas

"Birmingham-Southern's dining services feature a Subway, 2 convenience stores, and a cafeteria which is the center of campus. The cafeteria does not have any commercial brand food, though."

CAMPUS HOUSING

Q My Dorm Hall

"My dorm hall is the noisiest hall in the building. Most of the girls who reside there are sorority sisters, have late-night visitors, and are very loud. The cost of the dorm is covered by my financial aid, so it's no biggie. The RAs are very helpful with providing space and ease of the housing process. The showers are well provided, and it is right next door to our on-campus grocery store. So I give it a B-."

Q

"The dorms are generally pretty good. New Men's (the freshman male dorm) is absolutely terrible, with furniture that doesn't move and a smell that doesn't leave. If you can make it through your first year, though, you can move into Hanson (with its very large rooms) or one of the fraternity houses which were all built a few years ago (and have yet to be trashed, amazingly enough)."

GUYS & GIRLS

Q Average Southern People

"The Guys are alright, not alot to choose from if you're a minority. It really depends on what you're looking for in a guy, but for the most part you won't have any issues with finding a guy."

Q Social Life

"The guys and girls at Birmingham-SOuthern are almost all smilliar in economic status, ethnicity, and religious affiliation. The greek system definitely controls the social life at BSC."

HEALTH & SAFETY

Q Top Ranked

"Our safety is consistently ranked in the top 5 for colleges and universities. There is only one way in and out of the campus and you have to pass through a guarded gate. You always see police driving around everywhere monitoring camputs."

LOOKING FOR MORE?

Check out our full-length guide to this school at collegeprowler.com/birmingham--southern-college/.

Bob Jones University

1700 Wade Hampton Blvd.; Greenville, SC 29614
(864) 242-5100; www.bju.edu

THE BASICS:

Acceptance Rate: Open
Yield: —
Setting: Small city
Control: Private Non-Profit
Total Undergrads: 3,452
SAT Range: —
ACT Range: 19–25

Student-Faculty Ratio: 13:1
Retention Rate: 72%
Graduation Rate: 61%
Tuition: $12,130
Room & Board: $5,100
Avg. Aid Package: —
Students With Aid: 71%

Academics	B-	Greek Life	B-
Athletics	C+	Guys	B+
Campus Dining	C	Health & Safety	A+
Campus Housing	B+	Local Atmosphere	B-
Campus Strictness	D+	Nightlife	D+
Computers	C+	Off-Campus Dining	A-
Diversity	C-	Off-Campus Housing	B-
Drug Safety	A	Parking	A-
Facilities	B	Transportation	B-
Girls	B-	Weather	C+

CP's Student Author On...
OVERALL EXPERIENCE

BJU is known as the world's most unusual school, and it appeals to driven young Christian students from all over the place. BJU challenges students in many ways, fostering academic, spiritual, and personal growth. A student's first challenge starts on the first day of school. Enormous amounts of syllabi overwhelm the students, but semesters fly by because of all the hard work. Classes at BJU demand students' best efforts, and the motto of every class is "to become more like Christ." Students appreciate BJU's Christian atmosphere, and soon realize that the University's challenges will only help them grow as people.

Students love and respect the University for not only academic excellence, but also for its caring and loving faculty. The faculty helps students proceed and graduate from college successfully. Overall, BJU alumni tend to find a job right out of the nest and adjust to the real world quickly since BJU prepared them through tactics like a strict dress code. Attending school makes the students feel like they are a part of BJU history. When entering BJU as a student, the journey of life has begun.

Students Speak Out On...
OVERALL EXPERIENCE

Q Experience

"The experience is great they offer many different ways to interact with other students, but also allow you to make time to study. there are a lot of on campus things to do and places you can get to off campus just by walking. they also make a lot of off campus trip if you're interested (i.e. horseback riding, rafing, etc.)"

Q The Place to Be

"BJU is awesome: I learn so much about life outside of my major. I love the faculty and the people. The education is excellent and dorm life is crazy, but fun."

Q Oppotunity Place

"Bob Jones is very rightly named the "Opportunity Place." I have absolutely loved being here"

Q Nice Try

"Grateful for teachers and excellent academics. I wish the board of directors would give us more freedom."

BEST OF BOB JONES

1. Christian atmosphere
2. Clean facilities
3. Caring faculty/staff
4. Networking
5. Unity
6. Academic excellence

Affordable
Tuition is only $12,130, one of the most affordable rates in the country.

Knowledgeable Professors
85% of students surveyed rated the general knowledge of professors as above average.

WORST OF BOB JONES

1. Strictness of unusual rules
2. Dress code
3. 12 a.m. bedtime
4. Limited Internet access
5. Unpredictable weather
6. Required activities/events
7. Racial/religious/political/ social prejudice

Life is NOT a Party
100% of students surveyed said it's almost impossible to find a good party.

Not Much Diversity
One of the least racially diverse campuses—only 10% of students are minorities.

Student Body

African American:	1%	Male Undergrads:	45%
Asian American:	5%	Female Undergrads:	55%
Hispanic:	3%	Living On Campus:	76%
International:	0%	Living Off Campus:	24%
Native American:	0%	Male Athletes:	0%
White:	90%	Female Athletes:	0%
Unknown:	0%	Fraternity Members:	—
From Out-of-State:	75%	Sorority Members:	—

Students Speak Out On...
EVERYTHING!

ACADEMICS

Music Education
"I absolutely love my major, and I can see that the music education program at BJU is excellent! The way the program is set up, the offered classes, and the faculty are some very amazing aspects to this major offered."

The Curriculum
"They are very involved and you have to work for the grades you earn. In my opinion, BJU is one of the hardest Christian colleges academically."

ATHLETICS

Very Good
"Soccer is very big on campus. We play soccer between our Greek Literary societies."

Good Sportsmanship
"No matter how competitive intermiral athletics are at Bob Jones, the University always encourages good sportsmanship between athletes and competitive teams."

CAMPUS DINING

A New Dining Common
"I am an off-campus student so I rarely frequent BJU's imfamous Mckenzie Dining Common. I believe the food is decent, but I'll tell you this: They are renovating the whole dining common structure/ appearance (as well as the menu) beginning the summer of 2011 (or until funds permit). It should be more functional and capable of housing more than the number of students comfortably."

Variety
"The dining hall at Bob Jones University has a variety of foods to choose from at one meal. It contains a salad and sandwhich bar, hot food bar, fruit stand, and a drink wall on both ends of the cafeteria. For the size of the student body, BJU does an excellent job with the food that it prepares."

CAMPUS HOUSING

Social Atmosphere
"Normally in the dorm room, there are four girls or four guys living together in one room at BJU. It is a very socially interactive environment because each hall shares a bathroom and often eats meals together, and has parties together as well. Very often, one or more of the individuals on a hall actually end up being in the same class!"

Mixed Classes and Fair Space
"While there's always room for improvement, there are some perks and quirks when it comes to BJU dorms. The average room is home to three students, though I do know people stuck in a room with four or five people! When there's only three people, there is plenty of space for everyone. Freshmen, Sophomores, Juniors and Seniors are all pooled together. This is very good because the Freshmen get a chance to learn from the experienced upperclassmen."

GUYS & GIRLS

Quality Students
"Each student acts and dresses professionally. Most students are christians and have dedicated their lives to glorifying God. This focus has crated a uniquely pleasant and positive environment that many visitors have commented on."

Dress
"The typical dress on BJU campus is conservative. BJU holds its dress standard to be one of importance and modesty."

HEALTH & SAFETY

A
"WE HAVE PUBLIC SAFETY, AND PASSES are required all the time. very safe!"

Personal Safety
"I feel very safe on BJU's campus. It is a well protected area, especially with the help of our public safety crew who make it their goal to keep BJU safe."

LOOKING FOR MORE?
Check out our full-length guide to this school at collegeprowler.com/bob-jones-university/.

Boston College

140 Commonwealth Ave.; Chestnut Hill, MA 02467
(617) 552-8000; www.bc.edu

THE BASICS:

Acceptance Rate: 30%
Yield: 25%
Setting: Small city
Control: Private Non-Profit
Total Undergrads: 9,836
SAT Range: 1880–2150*
ACT Range: 29–32

Student-Faculty Ratio: 14:1
Retention Rate: 95%
Graduation Rate: 91%
Tuition: $39,130
Room & Board: $11,840
Avg. Aid Package: $26,101
Students With Aid: 55%

* of 2400

Academics	A	Greek Life	N/A
Athletics	B+	Guys	A-
Campus Dining	A-	Health & Safety	A
Campus Housing	B	Local Atmosphere	A
Campus Strictness	C	Nightlife	B-
Computers	B+	Off-Campus Dining	A-
Diversity	C	Off-Campus Housing	B+
Drug Safety	C-	Parking	C+
Facilities	B	Transportation	A-
Girls	A	Weather	B+

CP's Student Author On...
OVERALL EXPERIENCE

The general feeling seems to be that Boston College is a wonderful school and an incredible experience. However, the first few years can be tough, as you may not be prepared for the enormity of the college experience. If you're from a very diverse high school, you will certainly be shocked at the very different atmosphere that will surround you at BC. Furthermore, so many of your peers can appear like they're having the time of their lives, and you might feel like you're faking it, especially at first. Yet, staying the course is absolutely worth it, as Boston College is a wonderful institution with many dynamic people who will truly challenge and amaze you. If you give the school a little time to grow on you, it certainly will and you'll be really glad you gave it
a chance.

Also keep in mind that while parties and tailgates are enjoyable, they are not the only things college life is about. Yes, you want to have fun, and you will once you get to know people a little better, but there are other reasons you came here.... For the rest of this editorial, visit collegeprowler.com.

Students Speak Out On...
OVERALL EXPERIENCE

Q **Fun Place All Around**
"Even with all the work I had this year, I loved pretty much all of my classes and professors. My professors were great about being available outside the class through their office hours and email. You can have fun on campus or off. Also, because BC is right on the outskirts of Boston it was easy to head into town for dinner or whatever else you decide to do."

Q "I love BC. There are obvious downsides that may tip the scales a different way for you in making your decision, but I think that BC is the place I was meant to be. I'm so happy here. I would never think of transferring."

Q "Honestly, I am having a good time at school because I found a really nice group of friends freshman year."

Q "I love it here. It was the best choice I have ever made for myself."

Q "I had an incredible four years. I took some wonderful classes, made several amazing friends, worked hard, and had plenty of fun. I wish, though, that I had been more promiscuous."

BEST OF BOSTON COLLEGE

1. Gorgeous campus
2. Proximity to city
3. Excellent education
4. Awesome athletics
5. Major history and tradition
6. Knowledgeable professors

Happy Students
95% of students return after their first year.

Proven Success
91% of students will complete their education and graduate with a degree.

WORST OF BOSTON COLLEGE

1. Minimal diversity
2. Depressing weather
3. Not enough housing
4. No parking
5. The Plex is so crowded
6. Some dorms need a makeover

Expensive
Tuition is a steep $39,130, one of the most expensive rates in the country.

Expensive to Just Get By
60% of students surveyed felt that the amount it costs to live while at school was worse than average.

Student Body

African American:	6%	Male Undergrads:	48%
Asian American:	9%	Female Undergrads:	52%
Hispanic:	7%	Living On Campus:	82%
International:	4%	Living Off Campus:	18%
Native American:	0%	Male Athletes:	9%
White:	65%	Female Athletes:	10%
Unknown:	9%	Fraternity Members:	0%
From Out-of-State:	72%	Sorority Members:	0%

Frequently Compared Schools:

Boston University
Cornell University
New York University
Northeastern University

Students Speak Out On...
EVERYTHING!

ACADEMICS

Studying History at BC

"Being a history major at Boston College provides students with a diverse list of course offerings. Professors in the History Department are rivaled by few in terms of approachability, depth of knowledge, and interest in subject matter. The workload is challenging but fair. Also, the career services office frequently communicates available internship/job opportunities to students."

The Academics at Boston College

"it's a very difficult school and you must put in a lot of effort but the professors are always there to help."

It's All Good

"The professors in my field have been very helpful and knowledgeable so far. Some of the classes I have taken in my one year of college have become my all-time favorites. I feel like I'm learning from intelligent people who care about their subjects and students."

ATHLETICS

Everyone Loves the Eagles

"But no one loves the club sports. Athletic facilities for non-athletes and non-varsity athletes are sub-par for a d1 athletic school"

Not That Big of a Deal

"BC sports/the extent of the role of sports in students' lives is really exaggerated. About a quarter of the students body goes to the football games, and it isn't uncommon to see only 25-75 students at Basketball games. The facilities are among the worst in the country"

CAMPUS DINING

Good but Tiresome

"Campus dining as a whole is decent. Generally everything is made on site whether it be the chips or sandwiches. As it stands, dining halls have delicious sandwiches that grow repetitive. Meals are a la carte and tend to be very expensive. A dinner can easily run one student ~$25. One dining hall does have Starbucks drinks though."

Pretty Good, but Repetitive

"They're good at what they do, but the menu cycle starts to seem pretty short after a few weeks"

CAMPUS HOUSING

Special Interest Housing

"Excellent, allows students to pick housing before the lottery"

Better as You Become an Upper Classman

"almost all freshman get the standard double. They're nice, but its either on the outskirts of campus or a bus ride away. Once you get older however, the dorms are suit style and much nicer"

GUYS & GIRLS

Guys and Girls

"BC is a good-looking school. There's the occasional tool and annoying girl, but almost everyone is pretty agreeable/attractive. The main thing, though, is that there are just a lot of really nice people."

Both Girls & Guys Are Hot

"Girls at BC are almost all beautiful, thin, and well dressed. Many spend time in the rec center working out, or can be seen running around the streets around campus. Guys are also pretty good looking. Both guys and girls are very preppy."

HEALTH & SAFETY

Super Safe

"I have never once felt in any sort of danger here. The BCPD is not hard to contact either, what with the blue light stations all around campus."

Very Safe

"Very safe, blue light system, BC Police Department"

LOOKING FOR MORE?

Check out our full-length guide to this school at collegeprowler.com/boston-college/.

Boston University

One Silber Way; Boston, MA 02215
(617) 353-2000; www.bu.edu

THE BASICS:

Acceptance Rate: 54%
Yield: 20%
Setting: Large city
Control: Private Non-Profit
Total Undergrads: 18,187
SAT Range: 1770–2040*
ACT Range: 25–30

Student-Faculty Ratio: 13:1
Retention Rate: 90%
Graduation Rate: 80%
Tuition: $38,440
Room & Board: $11,848
Avg. Aid Package: $31,650
Students With Aid: 63%

* of 2400

Academics	B+	Greek Life	C+
Athletics	C+	Guys	B+
Campus Dining	A-	Health & Safety	B+
Campus Housing	C+	Local Atmosphere	A+
Campus Strictness	C	Nightlife	B+
Computers	B-	Off-Campus Dining	B
Diversity	A	Off-Campus Housing	C+
Drug Safety	C-	Parking	B-
Facilities	B	Transportation	B+
Girls	B	Weather	B-

CP's Student Author On...
OVERALL EXPERIENCE

While BU certainly has its downfalls, most of which are due to the sheer size of the University, there are plenty of opportunities to take full advantage of all that it has to offer. For the resourceful and motivated, a little effort will go a long way. The most important thing is to utilize your professors to your advantage. It is their job to be available to their students, and while some are certainly more attentive than others, students are not turned away by a professor when they have gone looking for opportunities or support.

Keeping busy, being well-organized, and choosing a course of study that truly stimulates your intellectual interests will all be really helpful in having a successful experience at BU. Many students dread graduation day, and therefore, leaving Boston is not something they look forward to. On the flip-side, countless others would argue the opposite perspective. Accept your environment and work with it, as well as against it. Do not stay inside for too long, and do not drink away your college years.... For the rest of this editorial, visit collegeprowler.com.

Students Speak Out On...
OVERALL EXPERIENCE

Q Excellent School.

"Fantastic school. Recommended to everyone of all majors. It is a bit more on the science research focus but it will really welcoming to everyone of all backgrounds. There are many foreign students with which bring with them a diverse culture which is great!"

Q Love it

"I absolutely love BU in every way possible, but definitely visit before committing because it's not the perfect school for everyone. A lot of people have trouble finding a group of friends because there is such a large population of students and it can be tough to find your nice. If I could go back in time, I would still choose to attend BU."

BEST OF BOSTON UNIVERSITY

1. The size of BU. The sheer size of the University allows for a huge selection of courses, from French Regional Wines to Nietzsche to Stalking the Wild Mind.
2. The professors.

Happy Students
90% of students return after their first year.

Proven Success
80% of students will complete their education and graduate with a degree.

WORST OF BOSTON UNIVERSITY

1. The conservative administration is an ever-present source of distress for students.

Expensive
Tuition is a steep $38,440, one of the most expensive rates in the country.

Expensive to Just Get By
50% of students surveyed felt that the amount it costs to live while at school was worse than average.

Student Body

African American:	3%	Male Undergrads:	41%
Asian American:	10%	Female Undergrads:	59%
Hispanic:	5%	Living On Campus:	65%
International:	16%	Living Off Campus:	35%
Native American:	0%	Male Athletes:	5%
White:	46%	Female Athletes:	3%
Unknown:	20%	Fraternity Members:	3%
From Out-of-State:	80%	Sorority Members:	7%

Students Speak Out On... EVERYTHING!

ACADEMICS

Athletic Training

"This program;s curriculum is very science concentrated. It is also very hand on. Statin spring semester of freshman year you are required to do clinical hours. THe number of hours you have to do increases each semester."

Amazingly Superior Academics

"The academics and School of Management at Boston University are amazing and nationally ranked. Not only does the School of Management immediately immerse students in business-related scenarios and education, but it allows for hands-on work and experience."

ATHLETICS

HOCKEY

"Hockey is huge at Boston University. Our dog pound is essential to winning the games and home support is great. Overall, it's a fun and loving atmosphere, great place to meet new people and get involved."

Best Hockey Team Ever

"BU is big on hockey. Other sports don't have such a large following, but students always stand behind their school. The hockey team, however, always has a large crowd and the students go crazy for the terriers. The hockey team is one of the best in the country, everyone wants to watch the action."

CAMPUS DINING

Tasty AND Healthy!

"Get a meal plan! There are a whole variety of different places to eat, and there are multiple options for kind of food at each! The best part is that the school of health has to do a senior project and create healthy meals which we then get to test!"

Great.

"We're so spoiled here with dining. We complain that the food is repetitive or bland, but compared to other schools we really have amazing food! Also it's "all-you-care-to-eat" style, which is great since you don't have to pay for individual items. I love BU's food and dining services!"

Frequently Compared Schools:

Boston College
Cornell University
New York University
Northeastern University

CAMPUS HOUSING

South Campus Is Ideal

"South campus is great for students who are looking to avoid the awkward, over populated mass that is the freshmen dorms. Look into specialty housing there for a community feel."

Apartment-Style Dorms

"The newest dorms at Boston University are beautiful! They have kitchens, private bathrooms, and an amazing study lounge. The view on the top floor is spectacular."

GUYS & GIRLS

Diversity at BU

"There are all different types of people at BU. Since the school is relatively big, you are bound to run into both attractive and cool guys and girls. The Greek Life at BU is pretty small which is good because there are those type of people if you are looking for, but at the same time, it doesnt run the school. Students are from all over the US and the world, so if you are looking for diversity BU has it."

Quantity and Quality

"The school is so large and there is no majority. There is a guy for every girl and there is a large variety of both as well as a good way to find people to your taste via clubs."

HEALTH & SAFETY

Excellent

"Despite living on a urban campus, the security here is surprisingly great."

A Good Environment With Good Flow of People

"I always feel safe around campus area because people are always walking around and I believe that a place with people is a place is less crime."

LOOKING FOR MORE?

Check out our full-length guide to this school at collegeprowler.com/boston-university/.

Bowdoin College

5700 College Station; Brunswick, ME 04011
(207) 725-3000; www.bowdoin.edu

THE BASICS:

Acceptance Rate: 19%
Yield: 43%
Setting: Town
Control: Private Non-Profit
Total Undergrads: 1,777
SAT Range: 1980–2250*
ACT Range: 30–33

Student-Faculty Ratio: 9:1
Retention Rate: 96%
Graduation Rate: 91%
Tuition: $40,020
Room & Board: $10,880
Avg. Aid Package: $29,641
Students With Aid: 45%

* of 2400

Academics	A	Greek Life	N/A
Athletics	B-	Guys	A+
Campus Dining	A+	Health & Safety	B+
Campus Housing	A+	Local Atmosphere	A-
Campus Strictness	A-	Nightlife	B
Computers	A+	Off-Campus Dining	A-
Diversity	B	Off-Campus Housing	B-
Drug Safety	C-	Parking	A
Facilities	A+	Transportation	A
Girls	A-	Weather	B-

CP's Student Author On...
OVERALL EXPERIENCE

College is a place where people from many different backgrounds come together, so it would be impossible to meet every desire of every student, and it's doubtful that any university or college could achieve a perfect environment with no area for improvement. However, at Bowdoin, a strong majority of the students say they are glad they made the decision to come here. Even those who initially didn't feel comfortable at Bowdoin admit to eventually developing a strong fondness for the school. And even when certain administrative procedures or requirements don't seem to make sense, the discourse that develops from these issues only adds to the vibrancy of Bowdoin's ongoing intellectual conversations. Bowdoin represents a place for students to experience a new way of seeing and interpreting life—students here come to realize that attending college is not just about going to classes, participating in sports, and partying on weekends, but it's about doing everything with passion, determination, and the ability to give back.... For the rest of this editorial, visit collegeprowler.com.

Students Speak Out On...
OVERALL EXPERIENCE

Q Lots of Fun but Academically Very Rigorous
"Know that you can have lots of good times but that you'll probably have an equal amount of work."

Q IT IS SICK
"This is an amazing school, and it has amazing food."

Q Really Great Close-Knit Community
"Bowdoin is a small school, but that is part of its charm. If you want a school with a small, caring, supportive environment, Bowdoin is the place to be. People here study hard but aren't competitive and know how to have a good time, as well."

Q Overall Bowdoin Is Fun
"Academically, Bowdoin is a great place to get an education and have a social life. There are great people and great professors."

Q "I'm very happy here. I think Bowdoin is a great school. It's a great place to spend four years."

BEST OF BOWDOIN

1. The close-knit community
2. The dining hall food and service people
3. The huge Outing Club program
4. The awesome housing available to students
5. Ivies Weekend

Happy Students
96% of students return after their first year.

Commitment to Teaching
There are 9 students for every member of faculty on campus.

WORST OF BOWDOIN

1. The administration seems very bureaucratic at times.
2. Being towed without warning
3. Brunswick doesn't stay up all night.
4. Twenty-five percent of the campus claims to be from Boston.

Expensive
Tuition is a steep $40,020, one of the most expensive rates in the country.

Student Body

African American:	6%	Male Undergrads:	48%
Asian American:	12%	Female Undergrads:	52%
Hispanic:	9%	Living On Campus:	94%
International:	3%	Living Off Campus:	6%
Native American:	1%	Male Athletes:	43%
White:	68%	Female Athletes:	35%
Unknown:	2%	Fraternity Members:	0%
From Out-of-State:	88%	Sorority Members:	0%

Frequently Compared Schools:

Brown University
Colby College
Middlebury College
Williams College

Students Speak Out On... EVERYTHING!

ACADEMICS

Q Classes Are So Hard

"I recently heard this quote in the library, "My idiot brother just graduated Summa Cum Laude from Wesleyan, but I'm struggling to get C's here". Academics is a huge part of going to Bowdoin. You can try to find an easy way through but it's really not possible. If you take lots of English or history classes, you'll be writing several ten page papers every week. If you take math or physics then you'll have 10-20 hour problem sets for each class."

Q The Bowdoin B

"There's a joke between students about "The Bowdoin B" because of how hard it is to get an A at Bowdoin. Of course, there are easy classes you can take to make your semester work load a little easier. However, the majority of classes are pretty tough. On the other hand, grad schools and such know how tough Bowdoin can be, so students don't really freak out too much when they can't seem to get better than a B- in a class."

ATHLETICS

Q Great Facilities

"It seems like everybody is really active. If you don't play a sport you still do other things to stay in shape."

Q Sports Are Big, but Not Too Big

"a lot of people play sports, but if you don't, you will still fit in."

CAMPUS DINING

Q Amazing Food

"Bowdoin food is amazing! There are two dining halls, and meals there are all-you-can-eat. The campus also has a pub/grill, a convenience store, and a café. Also available at one of the dining halls is Super Snacks, which is food offered from 10 p.m.-1 a.m. on Thursday, Friday, and Saturday nights."

Q We Revere Dinning

"Food at Bowdoin is legendary. Dining Services goes out of its way to provide options for everyone that are extremely tasty. They have response cards that allow you to write anything you want about dining. Some are requests, others are praise, and all are answered by the wonderful Patty and posted inside the cafeteria. We also have Super Snacks every Thursday, Friday, and Saturday night."

CAMPUS HOUSING

Q Great

"The lottery may be crazy but the housing is pretty great."

Q Bowdoin Trumps All Other

"The freshmen dorms are awesome, especially Osher and West. People seem to think that upperclassmen housing aren't as good but that's only because we're so spoiled as freshmen. If you compare our upperclassmen housing to any other college dorms, you would still be extremely impressed. Almost every dorm has its own common room. Upperclassmen often have kitchens too, and their own bathrooms. You probably won't find that in other places..."

GUYS & GIRLS

Q Nice.

"It's a well known fact our guys are gorgeous, considering most of them are athletes. However, the girls are starting to get prettier and prettier every year, probably because they realize that's where all the hot guys are. The guys and girls aren't your typical state school/west coast "hot," but that's because they're all very classy and New Englandy, especially when the sun comes out and the winter layers come off."

HEALTH & SAFETY

Q Randy

"Bowdoin Security is the best. We even have shirts with the face of our head of security on them, that's how much we love them. They're always watching out for the students, always polite, and some are really funny."

LOOKING FOR MORE?

Check out our full-length guide to this school at collegeprowler.com/bowdoin-college/.

Bradley University

1501 W. Bradley Ave.; Peoria, IL 61625
(309) 676-7611; www.bradley.edu

THE BASICS:

Acceptance Rate: 74%
Yield: 24%
Setting: Mid-sized city
Control: Private Non-Profit
Total Undergrads: 5,061
SAT Range: 990–1240*
ACT Range: 22–27

Student-Faculty Ratio: 13:1
Retention Rate: 87%
Graduation Rate: 78%
Tuition: $24,224
Room & Board: $7,650
Avg. Aid Package: $16,201
Students With Aid: 98%

* of 1600

Academics	B	Greek Life	A-
Athletics	B	Guys	B-
Campus Dining	C-	Health & Safety	B
Campus Housing	B-	Local Atmosphere	B
Campus Strictness	C+	Nightlife	B-
Computers	B	Off-Campus Dining	A-
Diversity	D+	Off-Campus Housing	B
Drug Safety	B-	Parking	D
Facilities	C	Transportation	B-
Girls	B	Weather	D+

CP's Student Author On...
OVERALL EXPERIENCE

Bradley is what students make of it. Some love it, and some hate it. A college experience is only as good as a student makes it. Some focus on the negatives—such as the shady neighborhood, mediocre food, frustrating registration process, and lack of parking—but those people don't get much out of their experience. Students who look past Bradley's flaws have a worthwile journey for the four years they're there. If you want a school where you'll get personal attention from professors, have a short walk to class, make lifelong relationships, and get a solid, reputable education, Bradley is worth looking into. But it's not for everybody. Peoria doesn't offer the big-town buzz of cabs and car horns, and Bradley doesn't have all the draws of a large state school, such as a campus bus system, a state-of-the-art library, or a football team. Students don't get gourmet meals or 500-person lectures where the professors don't take attendance. But each person must weigh what's most important to them, which makes the overall Bradley experience different through each person's eyes.... For the rest of this editorial, visit collegeprowler.com.

Students Speak Out On...
OVERALL EXPERIENCE

Q **I Love Bradley**

"Bradley is unique because of the diversity and the campus size. It is a small campus with a lot of different people and experiences. I have been able to join a sorority and have a great nursing experience as well. The amount of activities on Bradley campus helps me keep busy during the school year."

Q **My experience so far has been amazing**

"My experience so far has been amazing. I attended Illinois Central College for two years and then transferred to Bradley, and the transition could not have been any smoother. I love the campus and the sense of community here. As a marketing major, I have taken courses where teamwork and team development are key components of the classes. This not only gives me a taste of what to expect in a real-world setting, but it has also helped me get to know my classmates better."

BEST OF BRADLEY

1. Personal attention
2. Small campus means a quick walk to class
3. The sense of community
4. Cost compared to other Midwestern private schools
5. Quantity and quality of student organizations

Happy Students
87% of students return after their first year.

Proven Success
78% of students will complete their education and graduate with a degree.

WORST OF BRADLEY

1. Parking
2. Registering for classes
3. The food
4. Student apathy
5. The lack of landscaping
6. Bradley is in a bad neighborhood.

Lowest Grades
Parking: D
Diversity: D+
Weather: D+

Student Body

African American:	7%	Male Undergrads:	47%
Asian American:	4%	Female Undergrads:	53%
Hispanic:	3%	Living On Campus:	68%
International:	3%	Living Off Campus:	32%
Native American:	0%	Male Athletes:	4%
White:	80%	Female Athletes:	5%
Unknown:	2%	Fraternity Members:	33%
From Out-of-State:	14%	Sorority Members:	27%

Frequently Compared Schools:
DePaul University
Illinois State University
Marquette University
University of Illinois

Students Speak Out On...
EVERYTHING!

ACADEMICS

Q Amazing Array of Academics
"For such a small campus, Bradley offers a ton of academic programs. They have almost everything; art, science, business, engineering, communications, education, etc. It makes for a very diverse learning environment."

Q Professors at Bradley are very diverse
"The professors at Bradley are very diverse. They know what the right amount of work is to push a student to be at his or her best. At times the workload gets tough, but they are usually flexible to work around other classes."

ATHLETICS

Q The Markins
"The Markins is a new addition to bradley and is an excellent activities facility, with numerous courts, indoor soccer court, with a rock climing wall, pool, weight room, cardio room, yoga class, and dance hall. Including a health center and Medical Training rooms. It's awesome, and brand new!"

Q Varsity and intramural sports are pretty fun on campus
"The varsity sports are pretty fun on campus. The soccer games are really fun. I love the intramural program here because it gives everyone the opportunity to play any sport they want. I played volleyball with my friends last year, and it was a blast! It was so easy to sign up, and it's nice that you can pick from three skill levels."

CAMPUS DINING

Q Favorite place to eat on campus is Center Court
"The food on campus was never so great, but now that I've graduated and have moved on to graduate school, pinching pennies and seeing how far macaroni and cheese will last me, I sort of miss it. I miss the cafeteria ladies most of all, because they always remembered you and your regular orders. My favorite spots to dine on campus would probably be Center Court, though that's definitely the most expensive."

Q I've Had Better
"I'm not a big fan of the cafeteria food. The other eating options are far too expensive and are a sure way to run out of your meal plan dollars."

CAMPUS HOUSING

Q Singles
"The singles are great and the distance between the main building and dorms are like 5-6 min away from each other. The Markin Center is my favorite, so many machines to explore."

Q Dorms are actually pretty nice
"The dorms at Bradley are actually pretty nice. I was told to avoid Heitz Hall, but that's where I'm living, and it's honestly not that bad. Heitz is a little smaller than some of the other dorms, that being its only downfall. Harper-Wycoff and U-Hall would probably be my top picks because the beds are lofted, and you have much more closet space than in Heitz or Williams."

GUYS & GIRLS

Q Some hot girls
"There are some hot girls and also bigger girls, too."

HEALTH & SAFETY

Q Some vandalism to cars and underage drinking
"There's some vandalism to cars and underage drinking, but that's pretty much the extent of it, at least that's what I notice. As far as special safety measures, I know we have the security phones on campus that can call the police in the event of an emergency, but I've never heard of one being used. At least they are there for students' use. Also, the school just implemented safety patrol with lime green jackets, which may help students feel safer."

LOOKING FOR MORE?
Check out our full-length guide to this school at collegeprowler.com/bradley-university/.

Brandeis University

415 South St.; Waltham, MA 02454
(781) 736-2000; www.brandeis.edu

THE BASICS:

Acceptance Rate: 32%	**Student-Faculty Ratio:** 9:1
Yield: 30%	**Retention Rate:** 94%
Setting: Small city	**Graduation Rate:** 89%
Control: Private Non-Profit	**Tuition:** $38,762
Total Undergrads: 3,302	**Room & Board:** $10,792
SAT Range: 1930–2180*	**Avg. Aid Package:** $27,354
ACT Range: 29–32	**Students With Aid:** 66%

* of 2400

Academics	A	Greek Life	N/A
Athletics	C+	Guys	B
Campus Dining	B	Health & Safety	B-
Campus Housing	C+	Local Atmosphere	C+
Campus Strictness	B+	Nightlife	C+
Computers	B	Off-Campus Dining	B-
Diversity	B+	Off-Campus Housing	B-
Drug Safety	C+	Parking	B-
Facilities	C	Transportation	B+
Girls	B-	Weather	D+

CP's Student Author On...
OVERALL EXPERIENCE

It may seem like a lot of Brandeis students really hate their school, but deep down, most know they would not be happy anywhere else. Some students seem to be bitter when they first get to Brandeis because they are either here since it made financial sense or because Brandeis was not their first choice. After a little time to get adjusted, that bitterness soon subsides. You must work to have a positive experience at Brandeis, more so than at a lot of other colleges. There are many opportunities out there, but you need to be willing to put forth the effort to get the most out of them. If you sit in your room and do nothing, you will get nothing out of your experience. Students are very studious, but they are also very involved, so the best way to meet people and have fun is to join clubs and be active in them.

There is a stigma attached to Brandeis of not being a school that knows how to party, and certainly there are schools that do it better. The administration and faculty here sometimes seem to have the position that the cheapest way to do it is the best way.... For the rest of this editorial, visit collegeprowler.com.

Students Speak Out On...
OVERALL EXPERIENCE

Q It's Great Here

"Coming to Brandeis was one of the best decision I've ever made. I was not expecting to like it so much. But the moment I arrived, the orientation program helped us get comfortable and I met one of my best friends. To do well, you have to study, but the classes are interesting and engaging and most professors are great lecturers who want to help you do well."

Q A Great Education

"I'm loving Brandeis! It's not a party school, but I'm here for the superb Academics. All my Professors went to Harvard, Yale, Berkley, etc. I've met the most amazing friends!"

Q Not a Party School but a Good Education

"Many people complain that Brandeis is boring, but I believe that college is for the education. So if you are into partying every weekend like crazy this school is not for you. But the classes at Brandeis are the perfect size and the professors are amazing. The classes are a bit challenging but it keeps you on your toes."

BEST OF BRANDEIS

1. Academics
2. Being close to Boston
3. Free admission to the Museum of Fine Arts in Boston
4. If you keep kosher, the food is amazing.

Happy Students
94% of students return after their first year.

Commitment to Teaching
There are 9 students for every member of faculty on campus.

WORST OF BRANDEIS

1. "Brandeis Tuesdays"
2. It is really expensive.
3. It rains all the time, and the campus floods.
4. It sometimes gets bitterly cold.
5. Parking is a mess.

Expensive
Tuition is a steep $38,762, one of the most expensive rates in the country.

Expensive Dorms
Living on campus doesn't come cheap, with an average housing price tag of $6,070.

Student Body

African American:	4%	Male Undergrads:	44%
Asian American:	9%	Female Undergrads:	56%
Hispanic:	5%	Living On Campus:	83%
International:	8%	Living Off Campus:	17%
Native American:	0%	Male Athletes:	13%
White:	51%	Female Athletes:	8%
Unknown:	22%	Fraternity Members:	0%
From Out-of-State:	75%	Sorority Members:	0%

Frequently Compared Schools:

Boston College
Boston University
Brown University
Tufts University

Students Speak Out On...
EVERYTHING!

ACADEMICS

Sciences are outstanding

"Brandeis is a very competitive small liberal arts school with the research power of a large school. The sciences here are outstanding. The psychology classes here are pretty good too. As far as the rest go, I'm not too familiar with it."

Incredible

"Pretty much anything is at your disposal here. The facilities are incredible, professors are world-renowned, workload is a lot but manageable, and popular study areas include science (biological sciences) and inter-culutural studies"

ATHLETICS

Top Notch

"Brandeis has incredible athletic facilities. Pretty much everything (from weight rooms, tennis courts, tracks, fields, basketball courts, squash courts, dance studios) are included."

Not Your Average Athlete

"Surprisingly the athletes here are not your typical athletes. They range from gnomes to tall and awkward looking. They are, unfortunately, often very ugly too. Sometimes I am shocked at how some of these people even play sports. So this pretty much summarizes the skill of our sports teams. Except for basketball, we're pretty good at that, and fencing too I guess."

CAMPUS DINING

Yummy

"Brandeis has a great baguette/panini station, and the Japanese is sure to please. Overall, the food is good, though of course it's still campus food. Einstein's bagels provides a change of pace, but the Stein (the on-campus restaurant) could use some help."

Average

"There are some good meals. It's not terrible but also not great. It is also repetitive."

CAMPUS HOUSING

Dorms

"Freshman dorms are okay, they're kind of like a box. Sophomore housing is depressing. But once you're an upperclassman housing is nice."

Not So Happy With Dorms

"Freshman and sophomore dorms at Brandeis are not very nice. Upper classman dorms are much nicer, but farther away from everything on campus. Plus, the Village used to be for upperclassman housing and it has been taken away and given to some underclassmen because of larger class sizes coming in."

GUYS & GIRLS

Questionable at Times

"Looks are often questionable here on campus. It's not that we have ugly people, but rather the fact that most people here just don't care, and those that do seem a bit out of place. In general the ethnic population of brandeis tends to be way more attractive."

Typical Jewish Girls

"About half the school's girls fall into the range of stereotypes for Jewish girls: from JAP to hippy."

HEALTH & SAFETY

Campus Is Completely Fine

"You are perfectly safe at Brandeis and in Waltham. I walk around all the time late at night/early in the morning, there's absolutely nothing. There's actually too many police on campus, who are so bored at the lack of real crime that they hassle you for doing perfectly legal actions (i.e. entering Sachar Woods at night) just to provide some excitement."

Brigham Young University

Provo, UT 84602
(801) 422-4636; www.byu.edu

THE BASICS:

Acceptance Rate: 69%	**Student-Faculty Ratio:** 23:1
Yield: 77%	**Retention Rate:** 84%
Setting: Mid-sized city	**Graduation Rate:** 79%
Control: Private Non-Profit	**Tuition:** $4,290
Total Undergrads: 30,745	**Room & Board:** $6,840
SAT Range: 1130–1350*	**Avg. Aid Package:** $4,168
ACT Range: 25–30	**Students With Aid:** 65%

* of 1600

Academics	B+	Greek Life	N/A
Athletics	B-	Guys	A+
Campus Dining	B+	Health & Safety	A-
Campus Housing	A-	Local Atmosphere	A-
Campus Strictness	C	Nightlife	C
Computers	B+	Off-Campus Dining	B
Diversity	C	Off-Campus Housing	A-
Drug Safety	A+	Parking	B+
Facilities	A	Transportation	B
Girls	A	Weather	C+

CP's Student Author On...
OVERALL EXPERIENCE

A BYU experience is unlike anything else. The things that you will learn go far beyond what is taught in the classrooms, and the people that you will meet are exceptional. Researching the school, and being familiar with the rules and expectations of students, will make the transition smoother and help you get the most out of your BYU experience.

Talking with people who have attended, reading books such as this one, and looking at the BYU Web site (www.byu.edu) are all great ways to make sure that this is really the school for you. If you decide that BYU is what you want, then jump in and enjoy it! You are in for a great and character-building experience.

Students Speak Out On...
OVERALL EXPERIENCE

Q In Love With BYU

"I absolutely love BYU, everything about it is just right for me, the positive atmosphere, the strong commitment to achievement, the affordable price and beautiful campus. It all combines to be the best school possible for me."

Q Wonderful, Spiritual, Uplifting

"BYU makes me want to be a better person. Most people are just all trying to get better at school, work, spiritually, morally, and all other aspects of life. It is a wonderful place to be."

Q I Love BYU

"BYU has the greatest atmosphere ever. The students and professors are kind and respectful to eachother. Although the academic side hard I've learned alot and feel very prepared for the future. I love the social aspect too. There are many opportunities to get involved."

Q I Love It Here

"I love the people at BYU. They are so much fun and I've had a great time. The social life is great, the education is excellent and it provides great life experience."

BEST OF BRIGHAM YOUNG

1. The friendly, welcoming student body
2. The clean campus
3. People understand your "Mormon quirks"
4. Ice cream from the Creamery
5. Football season

Affordable
Tuition is only $4,290, one of the most affordable rates in the country.

Happy Students
84% of students return after their first year.

WORST OF BRIGHAM YOUNG

1. Parking
2. The housing monopoly
3. So many students that you can feel lost in the crowd
4. Walking up the stairs south of campus

Life is NOT a Party
53% of students surveyed said it's almost impossible to find a good party.

Not Much Diversity
One of the least racially diverse campuses—only 14% of students are minorities.

Student Body

African American:	0%	Male Undergrads:	51%
Asian American:	4%	Female Undergrads:	49%
Hispanic:	4%	Living On Campus:	20%
International:	3%	Living Off Campus:	80%
Native American:	1%	Male Athletes:	3%
White:	86%	Female Athletes:	2%
Unknown:	2%	Fraternity Members:	0%
From Out-of-State:	68%	Sorority Members:	0%

Frequently Compared Schools:

Harvard University
University of Colorado
University of Southern California
University of Utah

Students Speak Out On...
EVERYTHING!

ACADEMICS

BYU

"I really love the teachers and faculty. Everyone is nice and very knowledgeable about the subject area"

Amazing

"Every Professor is very helpful. Though the curriculum is difficult, there is always someone there to help you, whether it's a TA, tutor, or a study group. Classes are very enjoyable, especially the religion classes."

ATHLETICS

Way Fun to Watch!

"I've enjoyed watching BYU's sports teams play ever since I was little. I love the vibe I get when I go to the games. The Athletic Department has enjoyed quite a bit of success in the past year, and I appreciate the integirty of the players."

NA

"I am not athletic, but the teams here are great! Go Cougars!"

CAMPUS DINING

Food

"There is great food on campus. I never had a meal plan, but I sure eat on campus. From the vending machines, to hot affordable breakfast's its all amazing. Alot of the food options come from local vendors, and BYU has their own brand as well which makes it really nice knowing my milk came from local cows."

Accommodating

"As you find places to eat on campus you will not be disappointed. they have brought all the popular restaurants into campus, if you don't like something on campus, BYU is surrounded by places to eat so the only problem is trying to figure out where to eat out of all the good places there are."

CAMPUS HOUSING

Lovely.

"BYU is a fabulous place. I adore my dorm room, it's little, but lovable. It is such a fun excepting place. Everyone is so nice and there are so many chances to make friends."

Living on Campus

"The dorms are a great place to live your first year at BYU! You get a social, safe, fun, all-around fantastic atmosphere. The RA's are helpful and caring and even though space is limited it is set up SMART. If you figure out the system you have plenty of room for all your things."

GUYS & GIRLS

Girls Are Gorgeous

"Honestly the student body is awesome. The girls are beautiful and the guys are fun. Overall very good people attend."

Social Atmosphere

"The atmosphere at BYU is amazing. Everyone is so happy and friendly, its difficult NOT to enjoy yourself. Everyone dresses in a modest way that keeps the atmosphere clean. There is ALWAYS an activity to be found. From dances, to comedy shows, to sliding down hills in blue foam, there is always something fun to find at BYU!"

HEALTH & SAFETY

Definitely Safe

"Security on BYU's campus is almost unnecessary as the students are all under an Honor Code. A lot of the time the campus security officers look for work and end up busting students for cutting in the cafeteria lunch line. That might be an exaggeration, but that's how safe I see our campus."

Safest Campus Around

"I definitely feel safe on campus, and even off campus. Provo is a great city because there's little to no crime, and people even leave their doors unlocked when they're just stepping out for awhile because we have that much trust. Nothing happens on campus, and police and security are definitely well-staffed."

LOOKING FOR MORE?

Check out our full-length guide to this school at collegeprowler.com/brigham-young-university/.

Brigham Young University - Idaho

525 S. Center; Rexburg, ID 83460
(208) 496-2411; www.byui.edu

THE BASICS:

Acceptance Rate: 97%	Student-Faculty Ratio: 23:1
Yield: 59%	Retention Rate: 63%
Setting: Town	Graduation Rate: 65%
Control: Private Non-Profit	Tuition: $3,580
Total Undergrads: 13,879	Room & Board: $4,486
SAT Range: 950–1150*	Avg. Aid Package: —
ACT Range: 20–25	Students With Aid: 65%

* of 1600

Academics	B	Greek Life	N/A
Athletics	C+	Guys	A
Campus Dining	B	Health & Safety	A-
Campus Housing	B+	Local Atmosphere	B-
Campus Strictness	C	Nightlife	D+
Computers	A-	Off-Campus Dining	C+
Diversity	C	Off-Campus Housing	A+
Drug Safety	A+	Parking	B+
Facilities	A-	Transportation	B
Girls	A	Weather	C

CP's Student Author On...
OVERALL EXPERIENCE

BYU-Idaho professors and other students take a lot of interest in students personally, to help them achieve their academic goals and improve their overall well-being. They care about how you do in classes, what you have to contribute to the school, and what you're doing besides school to enhance your lifelong learning. The BYU-I experience really becomes what the students make it. Students who just study to get by learn to do the bare minimum with the least amount of effort, and students who want to make the most of their education and learn and grow from being a student work longer and harder in a variety of pursuits that span beyond academics.

It may be hard to believe that there are so many opportunities to develop skills in a given area from attending a little school in Rexburg, Idaho. But just as BYU-Idaho takes huge steps in innovating learning and maximizing resources, students learn to be innovative hard-workers who know how to problem-solve and communicate effectively.... For the rest of this editorial, visit collegeprowler.com.

Students Speak Out On...
OVERALL EXPERIENCE

Q Super Greatness

"The BYU-I experience is one that inflicts awe into all those who attend this incredible university."

Q Wonderful School

"I have loved the time that I have spent at BYU-Idaho. This is an incredible school and has a wonderful reputation for its students being great people. Some people that go to school here don't like the strictness of the honor code, but I have found that if you are willing to follow the things that you said you would, it can help you to become a much better person. I would hope that anyone who chooses to come here would have many wonderful experiences in there time here."

Q Spirit

"I love the Spirit and the love that is constantly exemplified here. I love this school, academics, policies, and everything that goes along with the atmosphere. It is a very good school and I love it here. It is a big school in a small town and I am so grateful to be going here."

BEST OF BYU IDAHO

1. BYU-Idaho is a clean campus. No drugs. No alcohol.
2. Students are outgoing and enjoy being social.
3. Your BYU-I experience is what you make it.

Affordable
Tuition is only $3,580, one of the most affordable rates in the country.

WORST OF BYU IDAHO

1. BYU-Idaho doesn't have a very large sports program to unify the school and increase school pride.
2. Finding parking can be very difficult for students who have to drive.
3. Class registration usually fills up quite quickly.

Not Much Diversity
One of the least racially diverse campuses—only 9% of students are minorities.

Student Body

African American:	0%	Male Undergrads:	44%
Asian American:	2%	Female Undergrads:	56%
Hispanic:	4%	Living On Campus:	6%
International:	3%	Living Off Campus:	94%
Native American:	1%	Male Athletes:	0%
White:	91%	Female Athletes:	0%
Unknown:	0%	Fraternity Members:	0%
From Out-of-State:	76%	Sorority Members:	0%

Students Speak Out On...
EVERYTHING!

ACADEMICS

Q School of Knowledge

"This school provides amazing teachers as well as a rigorous ciriculum, and a very tough major program for all the different majors. This school has a very unique teaching program which is integrated into every subject and class known as the Learning Model. This model consists of 3 elements that are heavily emphasized, preapre; teach one another; and ponder/prove."

Q Professional and Helpful

"The professors at Brigham Young University Idaho truly care about every single student enrolled. Each and every professor is willing to take the time to help the students understand and grasp difficult concepts with a one-on-one basis. I have had great opportunities to grow in my education at this school. Everyone is willing and ready to help with any concerns or questions any student has no matter what the situation is."

ATHLETICS

Q Athletic Facilities

"The Hart building is an awesome place for people to go and get physically fit. It includes two different weight rooms, and several different gyms where students can exercise. Although our sports are only intramural and not competitive, students still participate in them. There is always opportunities to go and watch sports or join a team."

Q Good Student Athletics

"Athletics are almost entirely student-based and mostly student-run. It is all intramural, with both recreational and competitive levels, but still there's a lot of good participation from students. In general, the school has pretty good school spirit, and decent facilities."

CAMPUS DINING

Q The Crossroads

"The food is very good, and they even have a dollar menu. It is easy to stop in and grab a bite to eat when you are in between classes. Great location too."

Q Food on the Campus

"You can get set on a food plan, and it is really tasty and healthy. You have main course meals with lots of delicious sides. There are many diners on campus."

CAMPUS HOUSING

Q Nauvoo House

"I love living at Nauvoo House. It's right off of campus, the apartments are great and there are some really awesome people living here. I wouldn't want to live anywhere else."

Q The Dorms Are a Wonderful Place to Live in While You Start Out Your College Life!

"The Dorms at BYU-I are a wonderful place for Freshmen to start out college life. They are nice, have all the updated appliances, can be either cooking or none cooking dorms, and are a safe environment. The dorms are located in a very good spot on campus and not far from the library or most of the buildings on campus. They are also very safe and are taken care of by a head resident."

GUYS & GIRLS

Q Girl to Guy Ratio.

"the girl to guy ratio is great here. there is 3 girls to every guy!"

HEALTH & SAFETY

Q Great

"This is an exceptionally safe campus and town. Emergency call buttons are placed all over campus. Theft happens, of course, but at far lower-than-average rates. I have never felt unsafe here at any time or place."

Brown University

1 Prospect St.; Providence, RI 02912
(401) 863-1000; www.brown.edu

THE BASICS:

Acceptance Rate: 11%
Yield: 54%
Setting: Mid-sized city
Control: Private Non-Profit
Total Undergrads: 6,232
SAT Range: 1990–2300*
ACT Range: 29–34

Student-Faculty Ratio: 9:1
Retention Rate: 97%
Graduation Rate: 94%
Tuition: $38,848
Room & Board: $10,280
Avg. Aid Package: $30,588
Students With Aid: 61%

* of 2400

Academics	A	Greek Life	C-
Athletics	B-	Guys	B
Campus Dining	B-	Health & Safety	C+
Campus Housing	A-	Local Atmosphere	A-
Campus Strictness	A-	Nightlife	B+
Computers	B+	Off-Campus Dining	A-
Diversity	A-	Off-Campus Housing	C-
Drug Safety	B	Parking	C+
Facilities	B	Transportation	A-
Girls	B	Weather	C

CP's Student Author On...
OVERALL EXPERIENCE

Brown has a reputation that precedes itself. As an Ivy League school, Brown carries a distinction that many students desire, while knowing little about what they need or want in a liberal arts education. In that sense, Brown's liberal nature and open curriculum exceed that of the average liberal arts school. Many students redefine and rediscover themselves in college, and Brown's biggest strength is that it promotes individual development and self-discovery over the course of the undergraduate career. Internally, you have a lot of chances to make mistakes, which the University calls "discoveries," in the course of your studies. It's easy to change your concentration in the fifth or even sixth semester.

Few people who choose Brown regret it. While it's not the school for everyone, almost anyone can find what they are looking for at Brown. Whether you are from New England or Siberia, there are clubs, organizations, classes, and fellow students who share your academic and personal interests. Most people choose Brown for its liberal nature and its strong academic resources, and few are disappointed.

Students Speak Out On...
OVERALL EXPERIENCE

What Makes My School Unique

"Brown has the open curriculum, which gives many students the opportunity to try out new things. As a freshman, I took a musical theatre class pass/fail, which was something new to me. It was a great class, and I learned many interesting things about musical theatre. The diversity on campus is also really unique. Compared to other campuses, I think Brown has a very different mix of students from different backgrounds."

Brown - The Best IVY

"I decided that I will go to Brown, after my sixth grade. Something fascinated me about Browm. Before email was everywhere, my dad, always the techie type, was connected to the net. Anyway, I wrote to Brown about what it will take to get there. They replied with a canned answer. needles to sya that I got in and was wait-listed at Harvard. After one semester at Brown, I couldn't have chosen a perfect school for myself. Brown is nuturing and a great school and to me, it is the best of the IVYs."

BEST OF BROWN

1. The New Curriculum
2. The student body
3. President Ruth Simmons
4. Thayer Street
5. The College Greens
6. The restaurants off campus
7. Cheap rent

Happy Students
97% of students return after their first year.

Commitment to Teaching
There are 9 students for every member of faculty on campus.

WORST OF BROWN

1. On-campus cable
2. The paltry endowment
3. Long winters
4. The meal plan
5. Providence parking laws
6. Bars close too early (2 a.m.)

Expensive
Tuition is a steep $38,848, one of the most expensive rates in the country.

AP Credit Wasted
Any AP credits earned in high school aren't eligible for college credit.

Student Body

African American:	6%	Male Undergrads:	47%
Asian American:	15%	Female Undergrads:	53%
Hispanic:	8%	Living On Campus:	80%
International:	8%	Living Off Campus:	20%
Native American:	1%	Male Athletes:	18%
White:	45%	Female Athletes:	16%
Unknown:	16%	Fraternity Members:	10%
From Out-of-State:	95%	Sorority Members:	7%

Frequently Compared Schools:
Cornell University
Harvard University
University of Pennsylvania
Yale University

Students Speak Out On...
EVERYTHING!

ACADEMICS

Amazing Freedom and Standards

"The curriculum was flexible, and students pushed each other without being competitive with one another. Professors were always available and are amazing mentors if you seek them out."

A Good Number of Premeds

"Many people who are in biology are, by extension, premed. Because of Brown's flexible curriculum, many biology majors double major-- usually in a humanities or arts. The academics are decently challenging, and most of the intro courses are curved."

ATHLETICS

Top-Notch Sailing Team - Bravo!

"Brown University has a fantastic sailing team - consistently among the top ten in the country for both coed and womens, despite it's 'club varsity' status"

School Spirit

"Many Brown students enjoy going to athletic events and games, but sports culture is not that big on campus. The athletes usually stick with other athletes. I personally haven't been to any sports related events yet at Brown."

CAMPUS DINING

I Like It.

"I am a big fan of the food on campus, however, my parents were not the best cooks. My favorite things are the fact that you can make your own panini if you're not diggin the meal of the night and the Blue Room, which has (pricey) food from a great local bakery and Indian restaurant."

Pretty Repetitive

"I'm only a freshman and I already feel like I have the Ratty's rotation memorized. The food is pretty good quality, but and if you're creative with the choices there's always something to eat."

CAMPUS HOUSING

Life at Brown

"Life at Brown Dorms is great. As many college dorms, there are big rooms, average rooms, and small rooms. The housing lottery for sophomores is a bit stressful, but everyone is guaranteed housing, and living on campus provides a great social atmosphere!"

Campus Housing Is Very Good

"all the dorms are very spacious. and everyone on campus is amazing"

GUYS & GIRLS

Brunonians Are Lovely!

"People at Brown seem to be either single or in a long-term relationship. I'm not entirely sure how that happens. People at Brown are fantastic in general!!"

A Beautiful Rainbow

"The typical student looks very comfortable. Everyone has their own distinct style, so there isn't an overwhelming need to fit in. The social life is always vibrant, there is always something going on. Interests vary, depending on lifestyles, gender, and where people are from. The relationships in the academic environment are respectful and always a learning experience."

HEALTH & SAFETY

Police and Safety Services at Brown

"I would have to say that Brown provides services to keep students safe but we are always encouraged to take personal safety measures (carry a whistle, walk in groups, etc.). We have SafeRide that travels all around campus to pick up students. We also have shuttle services students can call. In addition, there is SafeWalk (people walk students to necessary destinations) and emergency poles all around campus."

Safe

"I feel pretty safe walking around Brown. The only people who get mugged are people walking around by themselves after midnight. Brown does not care if you smoke pot or drink."

LOOKING FOR MORE?
Check out our full-length guide to this school at collegeprowler.com/brown-university/.

Bryant University

1150 Douglas Pike; Smithfield, RI 02917
(401) 232-6000; www.bryant.edu

THE BASICS:

Acceptance Rate: 45%	**Student-Faculty Ratio:** 18:1
Yield: 32%	**Retention Rate:** 87%
Setting: Rural	**Graduation Rate:** 68%
Control: Private Non-Profit	**Tuition:** $32,106
Total Undergrads: 3,386	**Room & Board:** $11,991
SAT Range: 1590–1830*	**Avg. Aid Package:** $20,116
ACT Range: 23–26	**Students With Aid:** 84%

* of 2400

Academics	B	Greek Life	C+
Athletics	C+	Guys	B+
Campus Dining	C+	Health & Safety	B+
Campus Housing	B+	Local Atmosphere	C+
Campus Strictness	B+	Nightlife	B+
Computers	A+	Off-Campus Dining	C
Diversity	C+	Off-Campus Housing	C-
Drug Safety	C-	Parking	A-
Facilities	C+	Transportation	B-
Girls	B	Weather	C+

CP's Student Author On...
OVERALL EXPERIENCE

Bryant has a lot to offer, especially to business students, and gives everyone the opportunity to thrive academically and socially. The University's academic programs help prepare students for the real world, and with all the different courses students are required to take, they learn a lot about numerous subjects and get a well-rounded education. Students also get the chance to interact with professors who have the highest degrees in their fields, as well as real world experience. Although there is a lot of hard work and effort involved, the experience Bryant gives students is well worth it. Plus, with more than 70 clubs and organizations on campus, students can get involved and meet new people. Whether it's a club meeting or a networking event, there is always something going on to keep students active at Bryant.

Although many students complain about the "bubble-like" atmosphere created by the isolated campus, Bryant's small size creates a sense of community that few schools can offer.... For the rest of this editorial, visit collegeprowler. com.

Students Speak Out On...
OVERALL EXPERIENCE

Q Wouldn't Change It for the World
"I love everything about Bryant University, and I wish everyone could have a college experience even half as great as the one I've had. I feel like I had a great time and I got a great education."

Q Incredible School I Love Bryant
"its a great school, good job placement and parties are huge and crazy fun. lots of drinking"

Q Great Atmosphere
"There is always something to do, either on campus or off. our school is unique because we have a great community like atmosphere and everyone is friendly. I would always choose Bryant."

Q Amazing
"Bryant is incredible. The campus is beautiful. The class size is small. The professors are so helpful. We focus on business classes but also know it's necessary to get a well-rounded education. Therefore, we study not only business but also liberal arts. The only downfall is the huge price tag."

BEST OF BRYANT

1. The parties.
2. A great sense of community.
3. The residence halls are in close proximity to classes.
4. Greek life.
5. The University president and his wife are very generous.

Happy Students
87% of students return after their first year.

Knowledgeable Professors
100% of students surveyed rated the general knowledge of professors as above average.

WORST OF BRYANT

1. 8 a.m. classes.
2. Curriculum requirements.
3. The workload can be demanding at times.
4. When it rains, campus is inundated with big puddles.

Expensive
Tuition is a steep $32,106, one of the most expensive rates in the country.

Expensive Dorms
Living on campus doesn't come cheap, with an average housing price tag of $7,038.

Frequently Compared Schools:

Bentley University
Northeastern University
Providence College
University of Connecticut

Students Speak Out On...
EVERYTHING!

ACADEMICS

Economics Professors

"The economics professors really know their stuff. The classes are pretty difficult, but the professors are genuinely passionate about their field and will be more than happy to talk to you for as long as you need to understand the material. My favorite part about the economics department is that since the classes are small, you get a chance to really know the professors. I stop by my former professors' offices all the time just to say hi and discuss current events."

Accounting

"I have not had any classes pertaining to my major thus far. However, I have heard that it is a very good program. I have had a business 101 course and it was great. The workload wasn't too difficult but it was difficult enough to be challenging. The professors that teach the business 101 courses are extremely helpful."

Teachers Understand That You Have Other Classes.

"I usually have just the right amount of homework. It is not so much that it is impossible, but it is challenging. Most professors know that we have other classes and other work to do, so they respect that."

ATHLETICS

Athletic Facilities

"Beautiful gym and lots of exercise classes, especially spinning."

Big Changes

"Sports are definitely coming around at this school. We recently went Division I so we've had the opportunity to play some really great competitors. And we are doing very well for moving up into such a competitive range!"

CAMPUS DINING

It's a Cafeteria

"There is only one dining hall that accepts meal swipes. The food there is actually pretty good, as far as school cafeterias go. There is also a Subway, Dunkin Donuts, "Scoop" (ice cream), and South Deli that accept dining dollars and bulldog bucks. South Deli is awesome - make your own grinders, wrap, or pick from the grill menu."

Improving

"The food at Bryant has been worse than what it is now. They are trying to improve and bring more options."

CAMPUS HOUSING

New, Clean, Comfortable

"The housing at Bryant is new, clean, and comfortable. Everything is pretty easy to get to if you're coming from any of the residence halls, and the suites and townhouses are great living arrangements."

Suites Are Sweet

"Only freshmen live in traditional-style dorm rooms, and some freshmen even live in suites. All sophomores and juniors live in six-person suites, and it's great because you get to know at least five people."

GUYS & GIRLS

NOT COOL

"Everyone is judging and too serious. I transferred to CO, and it's much much, much better. Everyone is friendly and there is not drama. All Bryant is is drama."

Guys & Girls.

"Preppy. Rich. Uggs. Northface. Globally aware. Clicky. Spoiled"

HEALTH & SAFETY

Second Safest Campus in the Country

"The campus is so secure because there's only one way to get in and one way to get out, which is highly monitored. I always feel safe walking anywhere by myself at any time."

I'd give an A++ if I could!

"I would walk across this campus alone any time of the day or night and not think a thing of it."

LOOKING FOR MORE?

Check out our full-length guide to this school at collegeprowler.com/bryant-university/.

Bryn Mawr College

101 N. Merion Ave.; Bryn Mawr, PA 19010
(610) 526-5000; www.brynmawr.edu

THE BASICS:

Acceptance Rate: 49%
Yield: 33%
Setting: Suburban
Control: Private Non-Profit
Total Undergrads: 1,307
SAT Range: 1790–2080*
ACT Range: 26–30

Student-Faculty Ratio: 8:1
Retention Rate: 93%
Graduation Rate: 86%
Tuition: $38,034
Room & Board: $12,000
Avg. Aid Package: $35,513
Students With Aid: 61%

* of 2400

Academics	A-	Greek Life	N/A
Athletics	D+	Guys	N/A
Campus Dining	A	Health & Safety	B+
Campus Housing	A+	Local Atmosphere	B
Campus Strictness	A	Nightlife	C+
Computers	B+	Off-Campus Dining	B
Diversity	B	Off-Campus Housing	D-
Drug Safety	B+	Parking	B-
Facilities	B+	Transportation	C
Girls	B-	Weather	B-

CP's Student Author On...
OVERALL EXPERIENCE

Like any highly-rated liberal arts college, Bryn Mawr provides a stellar education to a vibrant student body on a campus so beautiful that sometimes it looks surreal. During the school year, especially in the dead of winter, it is easy to overlook these tremendous offerings and instead focus on the massive amount of work, as it contrasts to what can seem like a dearth of social opportunities. These are the times where some freshmen consider transferring.

Traditions help lighten the mood on campus, and despite what seems to be stress oozing out of every pore, most students manage to do a lot more than just handle their school work—though everyone agrees that academics is a priority. In the end, students are most proud of their academic work, but also fond of the school and experiences that they had here. Mawrters come to Bryn Mawr to benefit from the faculty and coursework the school is known for. Some women find the lack of boys on campus difficult to adjust to, or they find the general smallness of the campus undesirable, but in the end, most stay for the same reason they came: academics. When it's over, few look back on the decision with regret.

Students Speak Out On...
OVERALL EXPERIENCE

Q Traditions

"The most unique thing about Bryn Mawr is the history of traditions. From Lantern Night to Hell Week, new students are the focus of a whole lot of lovin' from their upperclassmen! Most students end up really enjoying the experience, but like everything else at BMC, traditions are optional. There are plenty of other reasons - great professors, small class sizes, beautiful campus - to choose Bryn Mawr."

Q

"Bryn Mawr College offered me everything I wanted in one package: small-town life, big-city fun, efficient transportation, challenging professors and classes, travel opportunities, lots of learning and growing, skills for the future, friendships that will last a lifetime, and what might be the most stunning college setting with the most memorable traditions I've ever experienced."

Q

"I would never change my decision to attend Bryn Mawr. It was the best thing that ever happened to me, it opened doors for me, and it gave me beautiful women to spend time with for the four best years of my life so far."

BEST OF BRYN MAWR

1. Timeless traditions
2. The Honor Code & Self-Government Association (SGA)
3. Beautiful campus
4. Inspiring professors
5. Administration that works with students

Happy Students
93% of students return after their first year.

Commitment to Teaching
There are 8 students for every member of faculty on campus.

WORST OF BRYN MAWR

1. Students who only talk about work
2. (For some) no guys
3. The absence of real economic and political diversity
4. Lack of parking
5. Guild closes at 2 a.m.

Expensive
Tuition is a steep $38,034, one of the most expensive rates in the country.

Expensive Dorms
Living on campus doesn't come cheap, with an average housing price tag of $6,860.

Student Body

African American:	6%	Male Undergrads:	0%
Asian American:	11%	Female Undergrads:	100%
Hispanic:	4%	Living On Campus:	95%
International:	7%	Living Off Campus:	5%
Native American:	0%	Male Athletes:	0%
White:	46%	Female Athletes:	8%
Unknown:	26%	Fraternity Members:	0%
From Out-of-State:	90%	Sorority Members:	0%

Frequently Compared Schools:

Haverford College
Mount Holyoke College
Smith College
Wellesley College

Students Speak Out On...
EVERYTHING!

ACADEMICS

"Having worked at an international news agency abroad and a political think tank in New York, my employers were consistently impressed with the breadth of knowledge and understanding that I possessed as an undergraduate. The economics courses I have taken have also served to provide a strong financial and market-based way of looking at political issues, which is often foreign to people in that field."

"I would say that the professors and classes I have been privileged to have at Bryn Mawr are extremely intense, but they have provided me with an invaluable, multi-faceted base of knowledge."

ATHLETICS

Sports Are Low Key

"The athletic scene is low key but the athletes are very committed. They play because they want to play, not because of academic scholarships or crowds cheering them on - both are non-existent at Bryn Mawr. Bring a friend if you want someone to watch your match. Few students participate in intramural sports once they are done with their mandatory 8 quarters of physical education."

Sports at BMC

"We are a Division III school and our sports are horrible. it seems to stem from poor coaching and a disorganized program and student disinterest. Some of the students work hard, but there are also student prone to going to parties before games and they may claim to not drink, but will still stay out very late at night and then are upset when we lose our games."

CAMPUS DINING

"The food is excellent. It's on a six week rotation. You do not eat the same foods that often. It is highly, highly vegan and vegetarian friendly. There isn't really anywhere else to eat but the dining halls."

"The food is really pretty good. The dining hall staff is friendly, creative, and accommodating. We have special Dining Services events, like the International Dining Series and Midnight Breakfast during finals. Some are wonderful and some aren't. I still have dreams about the luau-themed dinner my freshman year, but I could have lived a complete life without Cambodian night. Either way, it keeps things interesting."

CAMPUS HOUSING

BRYN MAWR LIFE

"fun, unique, quirky, interesting, frustrating, comfortable"

Erdman

"Although this dorm is known as "the ugliest building on campus," it is my personal favorite. I lived there happily for three years enjoying its unusual architecture, cavernous hallways, and student dining hall on the first floor."

GUYS & GIRLS

BMC Peeps

"Bryn Mawr is a woman's college, but boys from Haverford and Swarthmore can take classes (and vice-versa at their schools) and the schools are close enough that we can indulge in their campus activities as well."

What Dating Scene?

"Half of the students don't care about their looks. Why should they, with no dating scene around?"

HEALTH & SAFETY

Public Safety at Brynmawr College

"I have never felt unsafe at Bryn Mawr, public safety takes their job seriously. Because it is a small all woman's college it is easy to recognize people and easy notice people who are out of place. Also public safety is here to help no matter what even if your drunk."

LOOKING FOR MORE?

Check out our full-length guide to this school at collegeprowler.com/bryn-mawr-college/.

Bucknell University

Dent Drive; Lewisburg, PA 17837
(570) 577-2000; www.bucknell.edu

THE BASICS:

Acceptance Rate: 30%	**Student-Faculty Ratio:** 10:1
Yield: 41%	**Retention Rate:** 93%
Setting: Town	**Graduation Rate:** 88%
Control: Private Non-Profit	**Tuition:** $40,816
Total Undergrads: 3,543	**Room & Board:** $9,504
SAT Range: 1840–2100*	**Avg. Aid Package:** $23,400
ACT Range: 27–31	**Students With Aid:** 51%

of 2400

Academics	B+	Greek Life	A+
Athletics	B	Guys	A-
Campus Dining	B+	Health & Safety	A+
Campus Housing	B	Local Atmosphere	C+
Campus Strictness	C	Nightlife	B-
Computers	B+	Off-Campus Dining	C+
Diversity	C-	Off-Campus Housing	C-
Drug Safety	C+	Parking	B+
Facilities	A-	Transportation	D+
Girls	A-	Weather	C+

CP's Student Author On... OVERALL EXPERIENCE

An overwhelming amount of students say that they cannot imagine being in college anywhere else and are extremely happy with their decision to attend Bucknell. Many students have gripes about the isolated location, lack of diversity, and emphasis on Greek life, but these issues all seem to dull in comparison to the overwhelming sense of community that many Bucknellians admit to feeling. Most think of the "Bucknell Bubble" as a bad aspect of their college experience, but it also appears to be the very thing that has made Bucknell the cohesive place that students say they love. Bucknell has gotten the reputation of being a private institution filled with rich kids that think too highly of themselves, but while some kids do fit that description here, it is not the norm—most of the people you will meet here are truly genuine.

Bucknell is a place where students can flourish academically and socially in a small, supportive environment. Professors are deeply committed to the students, and the students seem to be genuinely interested in learning.... For the rest of this editorial, visit collegeprowler.com.

Students Speak Out On... OVERALL EXPERIENCE

Q It's Not What I Thought but I Am Alive

"My experience at Bucknell is unique. I am a Posse scholar from Boston and I am a non-traditional student. I have been around diverse circles of people all my life and expected it to continue at Bucknell but that wasn't the case. There are very interesting people at Bucknell that can change and expand perspectives. Students are motivated and high achievers. Some of the people in my hall last year were upset because their GPAs' were below a 3.5"

Q Not for Me

"Bucknell is not for me. The Greek life dominates the social scene, and the people here seem to be cold. As a freshman guy here, who is on a full ride scholarship, I dont feel welcomed by the guys. It's all politics about the Greek system. The programs that I came here for are not what I expected. I have yet to have had a lot of fun here."

Q "There is nowhere else I could picture myself. I love the people I've met at Bucknell, and my academic experience has been irreplaceable thus far."

BEST OF BUCKNELL

1. The people
2. Lounging on the grass on the first warm day of spring
3. Houseparty Weekend
4. The gym
5. Quality professors

Happy Students
93% of students return after their first year.

Commitment to Teaching
There are 10 students for every member of faculty on campus.

WORST OF BUCKNELL

1. Location
2. The winter
3. Lack of diversity
4. Bucknell anthem that sounds at 5:30 p.m. everyday from Rooke Chapel
5. No 24-hour dining

Expensive
Tuition is a steep $40,816, one of the most expensive rates in the country.

Student Body

African American:	3%	Male Undergrads:	47%
Asian American:	5%	Female Undergrads:	53%
Hispanic:	3%	Living On Campus:	87%
International:	3%	Living Off Campus:	13%
Native American:	0%	Male Athletes:	26%
White:	82%	Female Athletes:	26%
Unknown:	3%	Fraternity Members:	39%
From Out-of-State:	80%	Sorority Members:	40%

Students Speak Out On...
EVERYTHING!

ACADEMICS

Profs Are Great

"The curriculum and workload is tough. The facilities and professors are great."

"Personal student-teacher relationships are often found at Bucknell due to the smaller class sizes. Teachers are always willing and available to help you whenever you need it."

ATHLETICS

Athletics at Bucknell

"There is a lot to do at Bucknell in the way of athletics. 70% of Bucknell students played at least one varsity sport in high school. Although not all students compete at a varsity level as students at Bucknell, many do continue to play their sport on a club or intramural level. 90% of Bucknell students play intramural sports, of which there are 22 with both men's and women's leagues with a variety of skill levels. 100% of varsity student athletes graduate from Bucknell."

Sports?

"Athletic teams have some support from the community but not enough. Many teams compete for the Patriot League championship each year."

CAMPUS DINING

Great Compared to Most!

"The food here on campus is wayyy better than most college campuses. The caf always has something you will like and if you want a treat you can head downstairs to the Bison. The Bison is the best because you can get things ordered just the way you like it, but as freshman the caf is your best bet because you have to get an unlimited meal plan."

Dining on Campus

"There is a central cafeteria at the LC. As a freshman, you are required to buy a meal plan that has unlimited caf entries. There is also a deli type food mart downstairs called THE BISON, with tables and seats outside of it. When you become a sophomore and beyond, you can choose different meal plans."

Frequently Compared Schools:
Colgate University
Lafayette College
Lehigh University
Villanova University

CAMPUS HOUSING

Best Options

"The great thing about Bucknell is that there are so many living options on campus. For a fairly small school, Bucknell offers a plethora of living options for every kind of student. There are the typical double rooms, as well as triples and quads. Then starting sophomore year, you can live in anything from a house to a loft to a single all on one campus. Personally, I am living in a loft next year and am so excited to have an upper living area and a hangout area underneath!"

Great Housing

"Dorms for every year are great. There aren't really any awful dorms on campus. I guess the least preferable would be Larison, but at least that has a nice lounge/computer lab. If you want some of the best dorms as a freshman, sign up for the Residential College system."

GUYS & GIRLS

Bucknell Beauties.

"Bucknell has a very attractive student body. Most girls are always dressed up (in and out of class) and most guys don the standard sperry's and hats. Also, calling Bucknell "JCREW U" technically wouldn't be an exaggeration. Relationships aren't unusual, but you don't see a lot of couples walking around on campus. There is however an old saying that most Bucknellians marry each other."

HEALTH & SAFETY

Quiet Town = Virtually No Crime

"Lewisburg is really small and rural which I think contributes to the extremely low-crime rate on campus. Last year I never locked my door (except around Houseparty weekend) and I never had anything taken or messed with."

LOOKING FOR MORE?
Check out our full-length guide to this school at collegeprowler.com/bucknell-university/.

Cal Poly

1 Grand Ave.; San Luis Obispo, CA 93407
(805) 756-1111; www.calpoly.edu

THE BASICS:

Acceptance Rate: 33%	**Student-Faculty Ratio:** 21:1
Yield: 31%	**Retention Rate:** 91%
Setting: Suburban	**Graduation Rate:** 69%
Control: Public	**Tuition:** $17,658
Total Undergrads: 18,316	**Room & Board:** $9,846
SAT Range: 1100–1310*	**Avg. Aid Package:** $7,724
ACT Range: 24–29	**Students With Aid:** 44%

* of 2400

Academics	B	Greek Life	B
Athletics	B-	Guys	A-
Campus Dining	C+	Health & Safety	B
Campus Housing	B	Local Atmosphere	B+
Campus Strictness	C+	Nightlife	B+
Computers	B	Off-Campus Dining	B+
Diversity	C+	Off-Campus Housing	B-
Drug Safety	C	Parking	B
Facilities	B	Transportation	B+
Girls	A-	Weather	A

CP's Student Author On...
OVERALL EXPERIENCE

Any visitor would be hard-pressed to find alumni who are unhappy with their stay at Cal Poly. In fact, graduates tend to be very sentimental about their college days and enjoy discussing time-tested sights and activities with current students whenever they run into them. While current students may be unhappy with one or two aspects of their college life, the overall experience is a positive one. The education is hands-on and prepares students well for professional life. The social scene helps to form lifelong friendships and contacts within the industry.

In fact, so many people enjoy their stay at Cal Poly that they decide to settle down either in San Luis, or one of the adjoining cities, so that they can continue to benefit from the ideal climate, the optimistic outlook that comes from people in their 20s, and the sense of community in the area. The overall student attitude is that the time at Cal Poly will definitely become some of the most memorable years of your life.

Students Speak Out On...
OVERALL EXPERIENCE

Q Experience
"I absolutely love it here. It is a BEAUTIFUL campus, and the surrounding areas always have something fun to do(shopping, kayaking, tanning at the beach, etc.) Professors are also great, but the classes are hard. I LOVE POLY!"

Q OUR S**T IS DOPE
"Cal poly is sick. If you want to have fun, learn with smart people and good professors, and make a ton of money when you're done, come here"

Q Cal Poly!
"I LOVE CAL POLY! Just the only thing is is that you HAVE to study study study. But there is always room for fun."

Q Best College Ever
"The town is beautiful, with the ocean so close it creates a wonderful environment. Everyone is friendly and nice. The campus is small that you can walk almost anywhere withing 10-15 minutes. There are tons of fun things to do on and off campus. I would never choose anywhere else to go to school."

BEST OF CAL POLY

1. The people
2. Educational quality
3. Hands-on training for industries
4. The weather
5. The ladies
6. The teachers
7. Coastal location

Happy Students
91% of students return after their first year.

Knowledgeable Professors
100% of students surveyed rated the general knowledge of professors as above average.

WORST OF CAL POLY

1. No parking--anywhere
2. The Cal Poly Foundation
3. Campus Police
4. The guys (compared to the ladies, at least)
5. Lack of any real divesity
6. Snubbing of arts and humanities majors

Lowest Grades
Drug Safety: C
Diversity: C+
Campus Dining: C+

Student Body

African American:	1%	Male Undergrads:	56%
Asian American:	11%	Female Undergrads:	44%
Hispanic:	11%	Living On Campus:	22%
International:	1%	Living Off Campus:	78%
Native American:	1%	Male Athletes:	3%
White:	65%	Female Athletes:	3%
Unknown:	9%	Fraternity Members:	11%
From Out-of-State:	7%	Sorority Members:	12%

Frequently Compared Schools:

San Diego State University
University of California - Berkeley
University of California - Davis
University of California - Santa Barbara

Students Speak Out On... EVERYTHING!

ACADEMICS

Quarter System

"I LOVE the quarter system. Its fast-pace keeps me focused and on track, because if I slack off, I will immediately fall behind. If I dislike certain courses or professors, I only have to deal with them for 10 weeks, which is better than 15."

Great Academics

"The faculty in my department (Earth and Soil science) are extremely amazing people. They are extremely passionate and well informed in their areas of expertise. The students are also great people, an amazing group to be around."

ATHLETICS

Sports Are Wonderful!

"I am a college athlete myself and Cal Poly's sports are very good! I love watching the soccer games because we have huge rivalries. Everything is good when it comes to Cal Poly athletics. It is also very school spirited."

YAY Basketball.

"Basketball team is stellar, they won the championship in their division."

CAMPUS DINING

Grat Choices but Not All the Time

"The food court is great because it allows me to choose fast food and fresh and some organic food. I love that it allows students to eat healthy when he or she desires. The small buffet that they have is ok since sometimes some of the food they tell us that they offered are close at times."

Great Variety

"Cal Poly has several places to eat on campus with a wide range of items and styles to choose from the menus. The locations of these dining halls, restaurants, and food carts are evenly distributed throughout campus so that students have a place to eat just about anywhere around campus. This is convenient for students with small breaks between classes, as well as students who spend most of their day on campus."

CAMPUS HOUSING

Living in Club Med

"When I lived on campus it was a lot like being on vacation with some busy work. You have a pool, a meal plan, gatherings, a big room, and the "Poly Dolly's"."

On-Campus Apartments

"I live in Cerro Vista and the apartments are very clean. The social atmosphere is great, and it never gets to noisy to distract me from homework. It is about average cost to live on campus. Living on campus is convenient because I don't have to drive to class, meaning I don't get stuck in the bad traffic."

GUYS & GIRLS

Everyone Is Beautiful

"Cal poly has a very attractive campus. Almost everyone there is average to highly above average in looks. It's rare to find an ugly or overweight person on campus."

Be Yourself.

"There is not really any "popular" groups, at Cal Poly everyone is themselves, I never hear gossip or judging. Every student chooses their own style. If you are a friendly person you can meet a lot of people as well as if you are more submissive then you can just be you and no one will bother you. You just be yourself nobody will criticize that's for sure."

HEALTH & SAFETY

Safety Is a Must

"Cal Poly Pomona is a very safe campus to be at. I have never heard of or seen any crimes committed on campus. We have many security officers, and danger does not seem as a concern. I feel very safe on campus."

Awesome Health

"Health is awesome here although it is only open during the weekdays there are hospitals within a mile of the school"

LOOKING FOR MORE?

Check out our full-length guide to this school at collegeprowler.com/california-polytechnic-state-university/.

Cal Poly Pomona

3801 W. Temple Ave.; Pomona, CA 91768
(909) 869-7659; www.csupomona.edu

THE BASICS:

Acceptance Rate: 53%	**Student-Faculty Ratio:** 27:1
Yield: 20%	**Retention Rate:** 85%
Setting: Suburban	**Graduation Rate:** 50%
Control: Public	**Tuition:** $15,711
Total Undergrads: 20,120	**Room & Board:** $9,570
SAT Range: 920–1170*	**Avg. Aid Package:** $7,329
ACT Range: 19–25	**Students With Aid:** 55%

* of 2400

Academics	C+	Greek Life	B-
Athletics	C	Guys	B+
Campus Dining	B	Health & Safety	C+
Campus Housing	C	Local Atmosphere	C
Campus Strictness	B-	Nightlife	B
Computers	B-	Off-Campus Dining	C+
Diversity	A-	Off-Campus Housing	B
Drug Safety	C	Parking	B-
Facilities	B-	Transportation	B-
Girls	B+	Weather	A-

CP's Student Author On...
OVERALL EXPERIENCE

At Cal Poly Pomona, the SoCal attitude slowly spreads to those that haven't been raised with it, creating a relaxed atmosphere on campus. Students aren't intensely competitive here as some would be at say, USC or Berkeley, but that doesn't mean that a large percentage of students don't constantly push for that high GPA.

Most people are commuters who work as well as attend classes. Many students don't expect to have a great college experience when they come to CPP because it is known as a commuter school. More often than not, people are surprised at how involved so many students are. You would be impressed to hear how many things an average Cal Poly student juggles, between work, classes, Greek life, and participating in other clubs on campus. When students take advantage of all the fun clubs and activities offered on campus, they always end up admitting how enjoyable their time in college was.

Cal Poly is a unique university, with its hands-on learning policy, widespread diversity, and large spread of majors.... For the rest of this editorial, visit collegeprowler.com.

Students Speak Out On...
OVERALL EXPERIENCE

Q AWESOME experience so far
"This is my first year at Cal Poly Pomona, but I can honestly say that I have had an awesome experience so far. I was so nervous when I started but then I realized that it did not even feel like school. There were no mean teachers and when I would walk outside it would feel like I was taking a walk in a park which would always make me feel relaxed. :)"

Q Mellow and relaxed
"CPP is a very kicked-back campus as far as students' ways of life go. We are in Southern California, and a lot of the students live up to the reputation of being mellow and relaxed"

Q Academics/Athletics
"i picked it because they have high academic standards and awesome athletes and dedicated coaches"

Q Cal Poly Is Great, If You Make It That Way
"Being a largely commuter school, it will take effort to have a good social life. Recommend joining clubs/Greek Life."

BEST OF CAL POLY POMONA

1. Diversity
2. Concerts put on by ASI
3. Hands-on classes
4. Residential suites
5. Painting the CPP on the hill
6. University Hour

Happy Students
85% of students return after their first year.

Knowledgeable Professors
72% of students surveyed rated the general knowledge of professors as above average.

WORST OF CAL POLY POMONA

1. Parking spots are very difficult to find.
2. Long lines for lunch at U-Hour
3. Smells of animals on campus (cows, sheep, pigs)
4. It's a commuter campus
5. No football team

Overextended Faculty
There are 27 students for every faculty member on campus.

Expensive Dorms
Living on campus doesn't come cheap, with an average housing price tag of $6,027.

Student Body

African American:	4%	Male Undergrads:	57%
Asian American:	28%	Female Undergrads:	43%
Hispanic:	30%	Living On Campus:	9%
International:	6%	Living Off Campus:	91%
Native American:	0%	Male Athletes:	1%
White:	24%	Female Athletes:	1%
Unknown:	9%	Fraternity Members:	2%
From Out-of-State:	2%	Sorority Members:	1%

Students Speak Out On... EVERYTHING!

ACADEMICS

Q Awesome Professors
"Best architecture professors with real life experience."

Q Awesome Architecture Program
"Great professors. My design instructors have also taught at USC, SciArc, and UCLA only, only I paid a lot less for them. Being close to LA is awesome for an architect."

Q Hotel, Tourism and Hospitality Mangement
"I believe the Collins college is an excellent program and is recognized as one of the top Hospitality collegea in the nation. Students are given the opportunity to take exciting classes providing the essential mechanics of what creates a great cook and gives you a true understanding of the business behind food."

ATHLETICS

Q Great for a Div 2 School
"Maybe not a Div 1 school, but at least we win championships."

Q Not Division 1
"But we won the Division 2 basketball title last year. Come out to the games. Maybe we'll make the jump to Div 1 if we keep it up!"

Q Inter-Mural Sports!
"Being in a fraternity, Tau Kappa Epsilon, it is very easy to get involved in sports, and i am pleased to say that we are the raining champs of the Iron Man trophy. this trophy is only give out to the organization that excels in sports above everyone else. last year we won this title, and we are going to take it again for going undefeated in all but one sport."

CAMPUS DINING

Q Option, Options, Options.....
"The commons are pretty good. I hear there will be a Denny's on campus at the suites this year. Coool!"

Frequently Compared Schools:

California Polytechnic State University
San Diego State University
University of California - Irvine
University of California - Santa Barbara

Q And on Dining...
"You will never get tired of the choices at Cal Poly. For one you have major chains such as Panda Express, Taco Bell, Carl's Jr., and Subway directly on campus. These places are great to go to in between classes but you can also have the choice of eating at the dinning hall. The Olivos Commons has really good food. For $6.25 you get an all you can eat buffet style. And the food is really good and will never get old."

CAMPUS HOUSING

Q Plenty of Options
"from the suites and dorms to the village. Awesome!"

Q Dorms Suites and Village
"although freshman must live their first year at school. there is a diversity of living spaces on campus and off. the dorms are pretty old and not too attractive. its close to the commons that is the only advantage. the suites are the newest buildings available. these are the desired living space but comes at a hefty price. and for those that like apartment the village has many rooms available."

GUYS & GIRLS

Q Cute Girls!
"Though there are slightly more guys than girls. Dorms are a great place to meet."

Q Student Life
"the guys and girls at cal poly are great, they are very friendly and outgoing. The guys and girls dress from a range of comfort casual to classy and sophisticated. Many of the students are willing to help each other out."

HEALTH & SAFETY

Q Personal Safety
"I feel really comfortable on campus, whatever time of day."

Q Very Safe Campus
"Not much crime and the police station is right on campus. very visible presence."

LOOKING FOR MORE?

Check out our full-length guide to this school at collegeprowler.com/cal-poly-pomona/.

Cal State Long Beach

1250 Bellflower Blvd.; Long Beach, CA 90840
(562) 985-4111; www.csulb.edu

THE BASICS:

Acceptance Rate: 42%
Yield: 23%
Setting: Large city
Control: Public
Total Undergrads: 29,348
SAT Range: 900–1130*
ACT Range: 18–24

Student-Faculty Ratio: 24:1
Retention Rate: 87%
Graduation Rate: 55%
Tuition: $15,530
Room & Board: $10,832
Avg. Aid Package: $12,627
Students With Aid: 61%

of 2400

Academics	B	Greek Life	C+
Athletics	C+	Guys	A-
Campus Dining	B+	Health & Safety	B+
Campus Housing	B-	Local Atmosphere	A-
Campus Strictness	C+	Nightlife	B+
Computers	B	Off-Campus Dining	B
Diversity	A	Off-Campus Housing	B
Drug Safety	B-	Parking	B
Facilities	B+	Transportation	A
Girls	A-	Weather	A+

CP's Student Author On...
OVERALL EXPERIENCE

Long Beach State is a very prestigious and well-known university, with alumni ranging from Steven Spielberg to Steve Martin. Having popular names attached to CSULB always helps draw in students because they realize that the University breeds leaders. CSULB is also known for being a large commuter campus. But around campus, there is a consensus that the more you are involved, the more likely you are going to enjoy yourself. Having great professors with adaptable teaching styles helps add to the experience. Academic programs and learning communities are noted as being extremely helpful towards student networking and connections with faculty as well as other students. For students who love to party, they also find a connection with friends on campus and in surrounding areas. However, CSULB is not the university for everyone.

For students who live in the surrounding area, the University is the number-one choice.... For the rest of this editorial, visit collegeprowler.com.

Students Speak Out On...
OVERALL EXPERIENCE

Q **GO BEACH!**

"I love going to CSULB because the teachers and the students are all laid back. How could you not be when you're near the beach? There is always something going on on campus and the weather is amazing. Classes are interesting and not too hard, and teachers aren't stuck up so they're always willing to help."

Q **Real-World Contact**

"If college is meant to prep us for a future in our respective fields, CSULB has done a great job. Among the music faculty are many of the areas (and beyond) top performers and educators, many of whom are active and connected with the music industry. If you want a gig, someone around campus will have one."

Q **Favorited Experinces**

"from the time i came as an unknowing freshmen, to a now new sorority girl, i am absolutly in love with this school"

BEST OF CAL STATE LONG BEACH

1. The campus is simply amazing and beautiful.
2. When you walk to class, you see Walter Pyramid in the sky, and it looks like a painting every day!
3. A lot of people wear CSULB gear.
4. Horn Center

Happy Students
87% of students return after their first year.

Knowledgeable Professors
94% of students surveyed rated the general knowledge of professors as above average.

WORST OF CAL STATE LONG BEACH

1. The campus is large, so the walk between classes can be tiring.
2. Parking is not the best.
3. There is currently no free fitness facility, though one is being constructed.
4. No football team

Overextended Faculty
There are 24 students for every faculty member on campus.

Don't Move Off Campus
Average off-campus housing is a steep $10,872.

Student Body

African American:	5%	Male Undergrads:	41%
Asian American:	24%	Female Undergrads:	59%
Hispanic:	28%	Living On Campus:	7%
International:	5%	Living Off Campus:	93%
Native American:	1%	Male Athletes:	2%
White:	30%	Female Athletes:	1%
Unknown:	8%	Fraternity Members:	4%
From Out-of-State:	3%	Sorority Members:	4%

Students Speak Out On... EVERYTHING!

ACADEMICS

Q Counselors Provide Good Information

"I am still undecided as to what I am going to major in, but I have spoken to guidance counselors and am strongly thinking about one major in particular. I am sure I will declare that major soon."

Q LBSU Academics

"Needs cheaper classes and more vocational programs"

ATHLETICS

Q Sports Are Great

"All the athletes at our school are very dedicated. And many students support our school teams."

Q The Althletic Scene

"Home games get pretty rowdy. Students get into the game for free. Our athletic teams are good."

CAMPUS DINING

Q Campus Restaurant

"The restaurants on campus are great! These include two Starbucks's, Quiznos, Subway, Carl's Junior, El Pollo Loco, Taco Bell and one of our luxury places--The Chart Room (they change the menu daily). In addition, for rapid pick-ups there are several convenience stores located throughout campus. Food, is not a problem--and the prices are very affordable."

Q YoGo frozen yogurt

"I'm so glad they added a froyo shop to the student union. I swing by between classes to try new flavors or get my fav - green apple tart! Employees are friendly and place is clean. It's nice not having to leave campus too."

CAMPUS HOUSING

Q Awesome Experience

"The dorms here are really awesome. They are that far away from campus. If you don't want to live near campus you can live on the off campus dorms. If you get a roomate that you don't like or suitemates you don't like then you can ask to

move to another room. Most of my housing was covered by financial aid so I really didn't have to worry about that."

Q Best Experience for College Students

"CSU Long Beach has many amenities on campus and convenience access to a wide variety of entertainments make this school great. The rec center provide me with a place to exercise and stay fit. The gym, field and pool are available for students to participate in all kind of sport activities. In addition, students are friendly and willing to lend a hand in need."

GUYS & GIRLS

Q Night Life at Beach

"Students dress in varieties ways. you might have your typical student come in sweats and PJ early morning or have Guys working out at the gym. Some people come dress to impress and are always on the run. Hot boys!"

Q Boys and Girls

"there are so many different people on campus. you see a big variety. i notice that many boys and girls have braces, which is kind of odd. everyone is really nice."

HEALTH & SAFETY

Q Extremely Safe

"The saftey at Cal State Long Beach is wonderful with our campus police here on campus also we have emergency call booths i never feel unsafe."

Q Campus Police

"Cal State Long Beach is one of the safest CSU campuses. It has numerous emergency stations and the CSULB campus police pride themselves with their amazing response time of 2 minutes or less."

LOOKING FOR MORE?

Check out our full-length guide to this school at collegeprowler.com/california-state-university----long-beach/.

Cal State Monterey Bay

100 Campus Center; Seaside, CA 93955
(831) 582-3330; www.csumb.edu

THE BASICS:

Acceptance Rate: 71%
Yield: 14%
Setting: Rural
Control: Public
Total Undergrads: 4,260
SAT Range: 880–1100*
ACT Range: 18–23

Student-Faculty Ratio: 24:1
Retention Rate: 71%
Graduation Rate: 39%
Tuition: $15,672
Room & Board: $9,152
Avg. Aid Package: $9,181
Students With Aid: 60%

* of 2400

Academics	C-	Greek Life	D+
Athletics	C-	Guys	B
Campus Dining	B-	Health & Safety	C+
Campus Housing	C+	Local Atmosphere	C+
Campus Strictness	C	Nightlife	C
Computers	B-	Off-Campus Dining	B
Diversity	C+	Off-Campus Housing	B-
Drug Safety	C-	Parking	B+
Facilities	C	Transportation	B
Girls	C-	Weather	B

CP's Student Author On...
OVERALL EXPERIENCE

Opened in 1994, CSUMB has since been a work in progress. Although the University has made great strides within the past 16 years, much of the school appears to not be fully developed and is still in the process of improvement. Most students' experiences at CSUMB appear to be both love and hate. On one side, students are happy to attend a small institution that is located in the beautiful Monterey Bay and is among the cheaper CSU campuses. Unfortunately, issues such a poor athletics and the lack of exciting campus activities are enough to give students an overall negative perspective toward the school. It is no secret, however, that CSUMB has a rather large transfer/drop out rate and many students would choose to transfer if given the chance. Despite this, many feel that they are being properly prepared for the future and look forward to their upcoming years at CSUMB. Like many things, it seems that the university will only get better with age.

Students Speak Out On...
OVERALL EXPERIENCE

Q Great Experience
"This school is a great place to be in which all the staff members are very helpful in every way. Its a peaceful campus where one can walk to the beach just to relax on your break or just to have fun with friends."

Q Having Fun!
"I am having lots of fun at csumb. I've met some cool homies and some fine cuties. My classes have been easy and the partys are funnn. I cant wait for next year"

Q Go Otters!
"I've had a good time so far at CSUMB. I've met some cool people and taken some cool classes. I love the independence of being on my own. CSUMB isn't like an average college, it lacks many things that most colleges have. I still am having a good time."

BEST OF CAL STATE MONTEREY BAY

1. The Monterey Bay
2. Small classes
3. Monterey Bay Aquarium
4. Distance from Santa Cruz, San Jose, and San Francisco
5. The beach
6. Science classes

Easy Financial Aid Process
54% of students surveyed told us that the financial aid process went smoothly and they received the financial aid they needed.

WORST OF CAL STATE MONTEREY BAY

1. Campus Police
2. RAs
3. Weather
4. Furlough days and budget cuts
5. Classes fill up quickly
6. Lack of school spirit and exciting sports events

Overextended Faculty
There are 24 students for every faculty member on campus.

Not Everyone Graduates
39% of students do not complete their education or graduate with a degree.

Student Body

African American:	4%	Male Undergrads:	42%
Asian American:	7%	Female Undergrads:	58%
Hispanic:	27%	Living On Campus:	54%
International:	1%	Living Off Campus:	46%
Native American:	1%	Male Athletes:	8%
White:	45%	Female Athletes:	7%
Unknown:	15%	Fraternity Members:	3%
From Out-of-State:	2%	Sorority Members:	3%

Frequently Compared Schools:

California State University - Long Beach
Sonoma State University
University of California - Santa Barbara
University of California - Santa Cruz

Students Speak Out On... EVERYTHING!

ACADEMICS

Q Much Individual Help

"The school only has 5000 or so students, so with classes averaging 20ish students each, it's very easy to get individual help and really get to know your professors."

Q MB Academics

"Since I am only a freshman at the college, and have only completed my first semester which consisted of all first year some-what easy classes, I think the academics is not too hard. The professors that I had my first semester were not the best, but I got through the semester. Some of my classes did not really have a set curriculum, which wasn't always the best. Other than that, the registration process is great, workload isnt too bad, and there are many study areas and help around campus."

ATHLETICS

Q Sports at CSUMB

"CSUMB's basketball team is really good, as well as soccer. I see many involvement in this school not only on the two sports mentioned above but the rest of the ones offered at school."

Q Otters

"Only sum of the studetns care about sports at csu monterey bay. we hav sum ok sports teams but i dunno ppl just dont rly care, lol"

CAMPUS DINING

Q Yummy in My Tummy

"We have three different food places on campus; each place is great for its purpose. The Dining Commons is great because it keeps some of the more traditional food items all year long but also adds variety to keep it from getting routine-like. The Otter Express is great for food on-the-go and those options change as well. The Otter Bay Restaurant is great for a real restaurant experience minus the costly paycheck! All great places if you ask me!"

Q Good Fast Food

"Campus dining options are usually mostly fast food or a buffet at Dinning commons where there is a variety of food ranging from pizza to vegetables. It is basically good fast food"

CAMPUS HOUSING

Q East Campus

"I really like east campus. There is alot of freedom and its pretty affordable.North quad is cool too, its a nice set up. The freshman dorms are okay. You get space and have ur own bathroom"

Q Dorms

"The freshman dorms are really spacious and it's an easier way to meet new people and make friends."

GUYS & GIRLS

Q Guys and Girls

"Everyone is really friendly, for the most part good looking, although a lot of girls have a big fat friend. The social life is what we make it. There are both extremely wild weekends, and extremely mellow. There are movies shown on campus on thursday nights and big parties once or twice a weekend."

Q Mixed Crowd

"Like any campus, CSUMB has its share of attractive people at the school. Because its a small school, there isn't a whole lot to choose from and that is why most people complain about the lack of interesting/good looking people. I feel that there are definitely some cool people here, but others who are not."

HEALTH & SAFETY

Q Safety

"This school has more police and military personnel than any of the schools that my friends go to. Within the first week of school at CSU Sonoma, a girl in my friend's building was raped. Here at CSU Monterey Bay, however, no one has been raped."

LOOKING FOR MORE?

Check out our full-length guide to this school at collegeprowler.com/california-state-university---monterey-bay/.

Cal State Northridge

18111 Nordhoff St.; Northridge, CA 91330
(818) 677-1200; www.csun.edu

THE BASICS:

Acceptance Rate: 75%	**Student-Faculty Ratio:** 25:1
Yield: 27%	**Retention Rate:** 71%
Setting: Large city	**Graduation Rate:** 41%
Control: Public	**Tuition:** $15,961
Total Undergrads: 29,275	**Room & Board:** $10,872
SAT Range: 800–1050*	**Avg. Aid Package:** $6,012
ACT Range: 16–21	**Students With Aid:** 66%

* of 2400

Academics	C+	Greek Life	C
Athletics	C+	Guys	B+
Campus Dining	B+	Health & Safety	C+
Campus Housing	C+	Local Atmosphere	B-
Campus Strictness	B-	Nightlife	B
Computers	B+	Off-Campus Dining	B
Diversity	A-	Off-Campus Housing	B+
Drug Safety	C+	Parking	B
Facilities	B	Transportation	B-
Girls	B-	Weather	A-

CP's Student Author On...
OVERALL EXPERIENCE

On the whole, students most satisfied with their experience are very involved in the heart of the school. Many students choose to become RAs, Ambassadors, work in the Matador Involvement Center, the Design Factory, join a sorority/fraternity, or get involved in intramurals or club sports. Coming to the school for the first time, you are bound to notice the construction that is taking place on campus. CSUN is definitely in a state of flux as it waits for the new University Student Union and the parking structure to be finished.

CSUN is a commuter school (as you have probably heard mentioned somewhere else in this book), meaning that most students live at home and commute to school. Because so many students are native to the area, they are not compelled to meet new people and participate in school activities. Years later, many of these commuter students say that the school lacks a social scene and they wish they had moved away from home to go to college.... For the rest of this editorial, visit collegeprowler.com.

Students Speak Out On...
OVERALL EXPERIENCE

Q It's a Great Program for the Deaf and Hard of Hearing Students

"CSUN is one of the programs that any Deaf and Hard of hearing students could get a good services quailty for their major and they have interpreters services that they can provide for thier classes. I really enjoyed going to school there and I am happy with how it turned out so far."

Q Social Is Unique Beaccuse Help Us Reality

"everyone need friends to help and support"

Q I Love It Here!

"I love it here! It's a fun place and theres so much to do around here...You just need to find it. It's a great atmospher!"

Q I'm Seeing Improvement

"I had a rough time getting acclimated at the beginning, however, getting involved helped me fix that. It's a commuter campus, so the campus life isn't as exciting as I would have liked, but our sports programs have been getting better and students are getting more and more involved. We've also had several recent renovations that are constantly improving the campus."

BEST OF CAL STATE NORTHRIDGE

1. Wireless Internet connection anywhere on campus.
2. The events: Film Festival, The Big Show, Free Concerts, Art Exhibits, Craft Corners
3. The weather: never too cold

Knowledgeable Professors
93% of students surveyed rated the general knowledge of professors as above average.

Low-Stress Course Load
75% of students surveyed rated the manageability of work as above average.

WORST OF CAL STATE NORTHRIDGE

1. Parking
2. Lack of school spirit
3. Printing costs--10 cents a page adds up.
4. Campus is very cliquey
5. It's a commuter campus
6. Confusing registration system

Overextended Faculty
There are 25 students for every faculty member on campus.

Expensive Dorms
Living on campus doesn't come cheap, with an average housing price tag of $6,142.

Student Body

African American:	9%	Male Undergrads:	43%
Asian American:	13%	Female Undergrads:	57%
Hispanic:	29%	Living On Campus:	8%
International:	6%	Living Off Campus:	92%
Native American:	0%	Male Athletes:	2%
White:	30%	Female Athletes:	2%
Unknown:	13%	Fraternity Members:	6%
From Out-of-State:	4%	Sorority Members:	4%

Students Speak Out On... EVERYTHING!

ACADEMICS

Q Kinesiology at CSUN

"The study of Kinesiology at CSUN offers a diversity of career choices to the students. There are six different option within the Kinesiology major. I truly believe that with these variety of options in Kinesiology, we can certainly promote healthy and active habits in our community."

Q Good Experience

"I love my major! The Professors are extremely dedicated to their students and they keep us involved in the latest internships, seminars, or volunteer work. As a transfer student, i noticed that the workload isn't too heavy and the work that we do do is related to what we need to know for our future."

ATHLETICS

Q Basketball Tickets...

"Cal State Northridge Matadors Basketball tickets are now available for admittance to the Matadome on the CSU-Northridge campus. Come see the Matadors run, jump, and shoot their way to victory. Now is the time to catch a live b-ball game and root for your beloved Matadors as they sink in another 3-pointer. These tickets are great for students, alumni or any fan of collegiate basketball. By getting these tickets, you'll be witnessing an exciting basketball game."

Q Solid teams

"No frills, just good solid teams that win championships."

CAMPUS DINING

Q Food and Dining on Campus

"The food and dining options on campus are good and varied. There is a Fruedian sip on every side of the campus so students always have a place to grab a snack. Our bookstore offers many great dining options like Panda Express, El Pollo Loco, and Burger King. The University Student Union has a Pub which is a nice place for sports fanatics to hang out between classes. The USU also offers a market, Subway, and occasional events where free food is distributed."

Frequently Compared Schools:

California State University - Fullerton
California State University - Long Beach
San Diego State University
University of California - Los Angeles

Q Meals

"The schools offers different varieties for the students to choose from. The food is enjoyable and everyone gets their food on time before it's time to go back to class."

CAMPUS HOUSING

Q Great Social Atmosphere!

"The residence life at CSUN is perfect for a campus newcomer to quickly make friends and great to make a new home-away-from-home"

Q Northridge Housing

"The housing at Northridge isn't cheap but its a better deal than paying for an apartment in the area. We have several Living Learning Communities like the "Lighthouse"- a deaf/deaf ally housing option. We also have dorms just for freshman that help build a great sense of community. The housing process is fairly easy and the housing staff are very helpful."

GUYS & GIRLS

Q About people going here.

"This is not a party school. You go to this college to develop friendships here. Long lasting friendships mostly. This is not a place to meet people."

Q Grad School Students from 21-70 Yrs Old

"The age range of the graduate students at CSUN spans from recent college youth to the inquisitive senior citizen! My peers are from all walks of life, and this brings a rich diversity to class discussions on topics from philosophy, religion, and psychology."

HEALTH & SAFETY

Q Safety and Security Is Good.

"The school police is very visible on campus. I always feel safe especially when it comes to having to leave my bicycle parked outside."

LOOKING FOR MORE?

Check out our full-length guide to this school at collegeprowler.com/california-state-university----northridge/.

Cal State San Marcos

333 S. Twin Oaks Valley Road; San Marcos, CA 92096
(760) 750-4000; www.csusm.edu

THE BASICS:

Acceptance Rate: 73%
Yield: 22%
Setting: Rural
Control: Public
Total Undergrads: 8,749
SAT Range: 870–1080*
ACT Range: 18–23

Student-Faculty Ratio: 23:1
Retention Rate: 76%
Graduation Rate: 45%
Tuition: $15,810
Room & Board: $10,035
Avg. Aid Package: $6,924
Students With Aid: 55%

* of 1600

Academics	C+	Greek Life	C+
Athletics	C	Guys	A
Campus Dining	C	Health & Safety	C+
Campus Housing	A-	Local Atmosphere	C+
Campus Strictness	C+	Nightlife	B-
Computers	B+	Off-Campus Dining	C+
Diversity	B-	Off-Campus Housing	B
Drug Safety	C+	Parking	C+
Facilities	B-	Transportation	C
Girls	B+	Weather	A

CP's Student Author On...
OVERALL EXPERIENCE

The CSUSM experience is generally a positive one for most students, despite a few minor issues now and again. The parking on campus is a huge deterrent for many students, who often grow easily frustrated with the process. Plus, the price of the parking pass alone is unfair and highly priced.

Another issue students often face is trying to get an academic advising appointment, a process which is often difficult and a hassle. Because of this, some students try to figure out for themselves what classes are needed and when to take them, when ultimately they need some guidance. Also, the food on campus is not that great. In order to have a good meal, most students have to drive off campus, which is a pain. Finally, another issue is the printing or copying on campus, which is too overpriced. On a positive note, once a week, vendors come on campus sometimes to give away free food or gear.

Students Speak Out On...
OVERALL EXPERIENCE

Q I Love This School!

"It's beautiful, and really clean. There are not even gum marks on the cement! It's easy to navigate around and the atmosphere nice."

Q Still Starting Out

"CSUSM Is now at least a 20 year old college with wonderful and helpful teachers. I feel safe on campus and I can learn a lot from the teachers and active students on campus. As an art major, I feel the campus lacks the general or advance art programs that I need."

Q Balance Makes Perfect.

"The school is gorgeous and the class sizes are very nice, and the teachers are very open to help during their office hours. The only trouble is if you cant seem to balance your school work and your socail life, balance makes the whole situation of school life easier."

BEST OF CAL STATE SAN MARCOS

1. "Green" initiatives
2. Beautiful beachy location
3. Diversity
4. Lots of transit options
5. Plenty of off-campus dining

Big Dorms
77% of students surveyed felt that dorms were more spacious than average.

WORST OF CAL STATE SAN MARCOS

1. Bad cafeteria food
2. Commuter campus
3. Dull nightlife
4. No football or basketball teams
5. Parking

Disappointed Students
30% of students surveyed would not choose to attend this school if they could do it all over again.

Student Body

African American:	3%	Male Undergrads:	39%
Asian American:	11%	Female Undergrads:	61%
Hispanic:	24%	Living On Campus:	6%
International:	2%	Living Off Campus:	94%
Native American:	1%	Male Athletes:	5%
White:	48%	Female Athletes:	4%
Unknown:	11%	Fraternity Members:	—
From Out-of-State:	2%	Sorority Members:	—

Frequently Compared Schools:

California State University - Fullerton
California State University - Long Beach
San Diego State University
University of California - San Diego

Students Speak Out On...
EVERYTHING!

ACADEMICS

ℚ Specific Major at My School

"I would have to say that at CSUSM professors are very challenging and very well prepared. I am a Psychologist major and my professors are the best of the best there could be. All my professors have at least their PHD and have traveled and worked for many years on their major. I would say the professors at CSUSM are great!!!"

ℚ Classes

"The professors at CSUSM are excellent. They are always willing to help and give great lectures. They are always extremely prepared and know their stuff. The workload is definately heavy because the university has a ridiculous writing requirement so no matter what class you're taking, you have to write an assigned amount of words/papers. (even in math!)"

ATHLETICS

ℚ Sports....

"The sports that we do have are amazing and the programs are excellent however we do not have every sport that most would think colleges have. We do not have a football team or a basketball team which is a downer but we do have an awesome baseball team."

ℚ Not Many

"There aren't too many sports at CSUSM... at least not yet. A basketball team will hopefully be added soon. We're working on it!"

CAMPUS DINING

ℚ Food

"Food at my school is not very good, most times it is expired are not very tasty."

ℚ Good Food

"The meal plans guen are excellent especially since they base it on your income. There are many options as well."

CAMPUS HOUSING

ℚ Community

"Even though the cost of living in the dorms is somewhat high, there is a great community and sense of family. If a student gets involved in activities, they will always feel like they have a sense of belonging. the staff have a huge sense of pride towards their community and want to share it."

ℚ The Dorms Have Fair Pricing

"You get three options to live in and all of the prices are exceptional. Everything is provided except food, but that makes for a healthy lifestyle."

GUYS & GIRLS

ℚ Modern Society

"The guys and girls are both dress trendy have a california type of personality. They love to surf and hang out at the beach, however they also love to drive downtown to have some fun at a hip club."

ℚ Sunny and Bright

"Everyone at San Marcos has a typical "San Diego look". Both guys and girls are very bright looking and always ready for the beach. Social life here is low key because we are not a big school but if you find the right people, it will be a good time. Bars and nightlife places around here are close and taxis always available. Everyone at school knows everyone which is great!"

HEALTH & SAFETY

ℚ School Safety

"The campus seems safe to me! There are multiple security cameras, school police willing to escort you, security buttons, and i never here of much crime! I feel safe in campus!"

LOOKING FOR MORE?

Check out our full-length guide to this school at collegeprowler.com/california-state-university----san-marcos/.

California College of the Arts

1111 Eighth St.; San Francisco, CA 94107
(800) 447-1278; www.cca.edu

THE BASICS:

Acceptance Rate: 76%
Yield: 24%
Setting: Large city
Control: Private Non-Profit
Total Undergrads: 1,389
SAT Range: 1400–1800*
ACT Range: 19–26

Student-Faculty Ratio: 9:1
Retention Rate: 72%
Graduation Rate: 60%
Tuition: $34,872
Room & Board: $9,850
Avg. Aid Package: $22,702
Students With Aid: 89%

* of 2400

This School Isn't Graded Yet!

College Prowler grades are calculated using tons of criteria, including survey responses that come from students at this school.

Unfortunately, we haven't gathered enough student surveys yet for this school to be able to calculate the grades for each section. Stay tuned to *CollegeProwler.com* for grade updates and more!

CP's Student Author On...
OVERALL EXPERIENCE

The education you get from CCA is far different than any other art college in California because you will not only learn skills for your major, but outside of your art form, as well. The College strongly encourages its students to take an elective class every semester or so in order to explore and try out things they might never have thought of doing, such as 3-D work, computer animation, drawing, fashion, illustration, painting, photography, printmaking, textiles, and more. This is important because art is always changing, and the development of an artist is a constant process that will change many times in a lifetime. So, even if you think you know exactly what you want to do now, you may discover a new passion at CCA and pursue that, as well.

Not only does the school provide a lot of diversity and opportunities to try out lots of things, almost every teacher at CCA is a working artist, as well. Therefore, the teachers here do not just teach from a book—they have real-world experience and have been in the very same position as the students.... For the rest of this editorial, visit collegeprowler. com.

Students Speak Out On...
OVERALL EXPERIENCE

CCA Is What All College Should Be...

"What makes CCA unique is the fact that the college is committed to the students by giving back $13 million in college-funded scholarships and more than $34 million in combined scholarships, grants, loans, and employment. These gestures really show where the students stand in the culture of the college."

Overall Experience

"I enjoy the classes and professors but the experience at the school is very uncommon for a college. There is no housing in San Francisco, there is no meal plan, it is not a practical college experience. It's a great and prestigious school, but for the amount the students pay for tuition, we should have more benefits and facilities."

BEST OF CCA

1. The CCA community is very collabortive.
2. Everyone is here because they have a passion for the arts, so it's easy to relate to the other students.

Commitment to Teaching
There are 9 students for every member of faculty on campus.

Personal Attention
You can expect personal attention with 93% of classes having less than 20 students.

WORST OF CCA

1. The Internet connection in Clifton and Irwin halls. So many share the same server that many have complained about not being able to use the Internet for days at a time.

Expensive
Tuition is a steep $34,872, one of the most expensive rates in the country.

Expensive Dorms
Living on campus doesn't come cheap, with an average housing price tag of $6,800.

Frequently Compared Schools:

Academy of Art University
Otis College of Art & Design
Pratt Institute
Rhode Island School of Design

Students Speak Out On... EVERYTHING!

ACADEMICS

ℚ Stellar Faculty

"But the most important thing here is the faculty, which is among the best in the industry. From the practicing professionals, to the academics, these people have a strong passion for design and deep expertise."

ℚ Academic Studies

"I decided to attend California College of the Arts because of its Architecture program. The professors are good and attentive to each student. They make time to answer questions after class time. The program is rigorous and difficult but is mostly successful."

ℚ Mostly Good

"I chose CCA because of the network it would provide when I graduated. All my professors are practicing professionals. I do think CCA does a very poor job of accommodating second degree students like myself by forcing them to do a number of pre-reqs that are unnecessary. Makes it feel like CCA is just trying to get more money out of us. Facilities seem adequate."

ATHLETICS

ℚ Athletics

"CalArts is an art school. I consider our dance majors our athletes. The campus does have a pool, basketball court, volleyball court, tennis court, weight room, soccer field, and small walking trail to encourage us to be physically active."

ℚ None That I Know of

"This is an art school, so we don't do sports."

ℚ No Sports

"There are no sports but plenty of walking or biking to different destinations."

CAMPUS DINING

ℚ Good but a little pricey

"It's always good with a big variety to choose from. It could be a bit cheaper, though."

ℚ Alright

"There is A2, the main cafe, and 2 other options within walking range of the campus. A2 is ridiculously and stupidly expensive, the 2 others are okay. It's better to just make a sammich at home."

ℚ No Meal Plans

"There are no meal plans. There is only a cafe on each campus. It's a little expensive, but at least the food is really good. There is a grocery store very close to the Oakland campus. Other than that, there are a bunch of restaurants near the Oakland campus ranging from fast food affordable to expensive, and really nothing near the San Francisco campus."

CAMPUS HOUSING

ℚ Campus Housing...

"there's on campus housing? which campus? never been."

GUYS & GIRLS

ℚ There's Great People Everywhere!

"I love this school! There are so many people to meet and get know. It's awesome—I would highly recommend making the effort to get to know these people!"

ℚ Guys and Girls...

"I feel like the people here are generally more laid-back than at most art colleges. Of course, there are a few stuck-ups here and there (my suitemate, for example) but the majority of the student population is a relief compared to the ones I dealt with in high school."

HEALTH & SAFETY

ℚ I Feel Safe

"I think that security does its job well."

ℚ Not in a Great Location

"The security inside the school is great but laptops have still been stolen from inside the school and students still get mugged walking to/from both campuses."

LOOKING FOR MORE?

Check out our full-length guide to this school at collegeprowler.com/california-college-of-the-arts/.

California University of Pennsylvania

250 University Ave.; California, PA 15419
(724) 938-4400; www.calu.edu

THE BASICS:

Acceptance Rate: 63%	Student-Faculty Ratio: 20:1
Yield: 46%	Retention Rate: 77%
Setting: Town	Graduation Rate: 48%
Control: Public	Tuition: $11,010
Total Undergrads: 7,206	Room & Board: $4,137
SAT Range: 870–1050*	Avg. Aid Package: $9,406
ACT Range: 17–20	Students With Aid: 83%

* of 1600

Academics	B-	Greek Life	C+
Athletics	B-	Guys	C
Campus Dining	C+	Health & Safety	C
Campus Housing	A-	Local Atmosphere	D+
Campus Strictness	C+	Nightlife	C+
Computers	B	Off-Campus Dining	D+
Diversity	C	Off-Campus Housing	C-
Drug Safety	C+	Parking	C-
Facilities	B	Transportation	B
Girls	C-	Weather	B-

CP's Student Author On...
OVERALL EXPERIENCE

Cal is a place that draws you in slowly. A lot of people doubt their decision of coming here at first, but, eventually, many alumni find themselves drawn back to Cal with a certain fondness that only comes after being away for a certain period of time. The same people who couldn't stand the place are usually the ones who are aching to get back by the end of their first summer off. There's a personal evolution that makes the entire experience of college different from any other in life; students find out who they are and how they feel about the world, apart from what they've been indoctrinated with their whole lives. California allows a person the freedom to see what's inside of himself.

To be honest, California is a two-star town. It's small and the industry surrounding the area has fallen on hard times. There aren't a lot of bells and whistles, like Starbucks and clubs, to distract you here. The atmosphere allows people to see who they are and what they're made of. For a long time, Cal was most people's second- or third-choice school, but a lot of that has changed, and it's growing and becoming more acclaimed every year. The University is a secret that more and more people are finding out about.

Students Speak Out On...
OVERALL EXPERIENCE

Q Great
"My experience at school has been remarkable. I have met different people from all over the world just about it. I have taken part in productions that I never saw myself indulging in. I can't wait to go back in the fall."

Q Overall
"The campus is nice and would be nicer if there was not construction. I like being able to ride my bike to class even though i live far away from campus. i like being able to walk to the beer distributor, gas station, and restaurants. My favorite thing is to be able to play music as loud as i want without neighbor's complaining"

Q Campus
"Cal's campus is so nice--one of the reasons I came here. On a nice day, it's great to take walks outside."

Q My Feelings
"I loved my first year at cal u. It has taught me a lot of things that i need to do to further my education in hopes of obtaining a career as a physical therapist."

BEST OF CAL U

1. New facilities
2. Powerhouse in Division III sports
3. Dating-wise, there is someone for everyone.
4. Small-town atmosphere conducive to getting work done

Affordable
Tuition is only $11,010, one of the most affordable rates in the country.

Knowledgeable Professors
92% of students surveyed rated the general knowledge of professors as above average.

WORST OF CAL U

1. Campus food is pretty bad.
2. Parking is expensive.
3. Professors are hit or miss.
4. Small-town atmosphere can make students pretty bored.

Students Can't Wait to Get Out of Town
62% of students surveyed said that there's no way they would live here after graduation.

Student Body

African American:	5%	Male Undergrads:	47%
Asian American:	0%	Female Undergrads:	53%
Hispanic:	1%	Living On Campus:	33%
International:	1%	Living Off Campus:	67%
Native American:	0%	Male Athletes:	8%
White:	70%	Female Athletes:	5%
Unknown:	22%	Fraternity Members:	10%
From Out-of-State:	8%	Sorority Members:	10%

Frequently Compared Schools:

Indiana University of Pennsylvania
Penn State
Slippery Rock University
West Virginia University

Students Speak Out On...
EVERYTHING!

ACADEMICS

Very Easy A's

"Here at cal I find it very easy to pull off a 4.0. The classes are VERY easy, and this might be one of the only colleges where you can study for not even an hour the night before a test and still get an A. I know people who drink every other night, and they still pull 4.0's."

Great Professors

"I came to California University because I fell in love with the quaint little town and the friendly atmosphere that surrounds it. The professors here know you by name and most times also know your goals for after college. They are willing to help you in anyway that they can, as long as you make an appointment to see them. I think that by this close relationship that develops, it helps students grow as individuals while in the classroom."

ATHLETICS

Cal Vulcan Football Is Aaaamazing!

"Cal Vulcan football is what every student at Cal U looks forward to on campus! Everyone loves Cal U football!!!! Nothing better on campus than Cal U Football!!! Our school is united as one large, vocal, group positively supporting the activity that brings us all together. I do wish they were stricter about enforcing and looking for alcohol users. We would have just as much fun if fans did not use alcohol."

Good Teams

"I myself am not involved in any form of campus sport, but I hear they do really well at pretty much every sport. So I'm sure the university helps by providing them with adequate workout and practicing things."

CAMPUS DINING

Food

"The cafeteria isn't bad but it could be better and the food court is pretty good but the food is too expensive there for the quantity and the i am not a fan of the meal plan system with restrictions on timing on the use of meals"

Food Is Not the Best.

"Not a whole lot of places to eat at and not too good of food. it is over priced and not a great value"

CAMPUS HOUSING

Dorm Rooms

"Again living in the dorms are great because of how they were built. the have heating and A/C systems and evrything in them. there are also computor labs and a kitchen on the first floor of each dorms."

Beautiful Dorms

"The "dorms" are more like small apartments. They are very newly built (within the last 5 or so years I think) and nice and clean inside and out."

GUYS & GIRLS

Guys N Girls

"The guys and girls are normal. There arent too many weird people here"

Good

"The school has many different looks, not a lot of fashion forward individuals, very average. Alot of athletic people, typical teenage appearance. Interests include parties, friends, working, and extracurriculars."

HEALTH & SAFETY

Completely Safe

"Some crime in the town but students are made aware of any criminal activity and in some cases extra security measures are taken, including locking outside resident hall doors in addition to needing ID to enter front of building and room key to enter wing and dorm door. Typical to see campus police in union and riding around campus every day, all day."

LOOKING FOR MORE?

Check out our full-length guide to this school at collegeprowler.com/california-university-of-pennsylvania/.

Caltech

1200 E. California Blvd.; Pasadena, CA 91125
(626) 395-6811; www.caltech.edu

THE BASICS:

Acceptance Rate: 15%
Yield: 37%
Setting: Mid-sized city
Control: Private Non-Profit
Total Undergrads: 947
SAT Range: 2140–2340*
ACT Range: 33–35

Student-Faculty Ratio: 3:1
Retention Rate: 98%
Graduation Rate: 88%
Tuition: $34,584
Room & Board: $10,872
Avg. Aid Package: $26,164
Students With Aid: 77%

* of 2400

Academics	A+	Greek Life	N/A
Athletics	C-	Guys	C+
Campus Dining	C	Health & Safety	C
Campus Housing	B+	Local Atmosphere	B+
Campus Strictness	A-	Nightlife	C
Computers	A+	Off-Campus Dining	B+
Diversity	A	Off-Campus Housing	D
Drug Safety	A	Parking	B
Facilities	B+	Transportation	C+
Girls	C-	Weather	A

CP's Student Author On...
OVERALL EXPERIENCE

Every school has its pros and cons, but sometimes it feels like Caltech has more cons than pros. Even so, students who have been at Caltech for a while agree that the positives outweigh the negatives. Although students here are always complaining about the workload, the lack of girls, boys who don't shower, non-English proficient TAs, scheduling difficulties, the lack of sleep, and much more, the students here are generally happy. Students who come here know that they are getting a top-notch education for the price of a few years of insanity. They also know what they are getting themselves into before they come—a lot of hard work. Many students here do not want to be anywhere else.... For the rest of this editorial, visit collegeprowler.com.

Students Speak Out On...
OVERALL EXPERIENCE

Q Good

"I have had a pretty good experience. My instructor was very intelligent and strict but i loved it cause it help me be strict with my self also.. This school help me with my ride share and i have had perfect attendance and deans list the whole time. the only thing i did not like was that they did not provide us with student cards and with the proper tools to learn the hands on material."

Q "Caltech is what you make of it. It's the hardest school around, and it will break you. But once you're broken, you'll begin to ask what you really want. For me, it's been a bumpy but profound experience. With all the resources and opportunities here, your motivation is the only limit. I'm glad I came, although I think I might have been happier elsewhere."

Q "I've had a pretty good experience. The workload is really tough, but I found once I got into junior year and into more of the in-major classes, the stress decreased a lot, making it much more enjoyable."

BEST OF CALTECH

1. Tight-knit community
2. Honor Code
3. Research opportunities
4. Location and beauty of campus
5. Intercollegiate sports, without the pressure
6. Traditions

Happy Students
98% of students return after their first year.

Commitment to Teaching
There are 3 students for every member of faculty on campus.

WORST OF CALTECH

1. Difficulty, tough curve, and lots of work
2. Gossip on campus
3. Social awkwardness, some students are socially inept
4. Scheduling issues
5. Unreasonable professors at times

Expensive
Tuition is a steep $34,584, one of the most expensive rates in the country.

AP Credit Wasted
Any AP credits earned in high school aren't eligible for college credit.

Frequently Compared Schools:

Harvard University
Massachusetts Institute of Technology
Princeton University
Stanford University

Students Speak Out On...
EVERYTHING!

ACADEMICS

Understanding and Caring

"What attracted me to the Institute of Technology was the friendly, caring attitude the staff members offered. Any time I have a question or request, I always feel as if I am actually being heard. i like the new building very much and the professors are nice and positive. I also enjoy the small classes, which makes it easier to get one-on-one time with the teacher."

"The teachers are good. They actually enjoy meeting students, and I've found them remarkably willing to explain things outside the classroom if there are questions."

"The teachers are, for the most part, very good. The exceptions are the ones who don't seem to care whether the students do well or just stand in front of the room and lecture without making sure that students understand."

ATHLETICS

Athletics

"there is not really any athletics around the school. there was a way cool things school has perfect team spirit we had a great tail gate thing for super bowl."

"In intercollegiate sports, we always lose, but, on the other hand, you can participate in whatever sport you want without much competition. Interhouse sports are a nice alternative for just having fun."

CAMPUS DINING

Meal Plan

"I am rather pleased there is several snack machines through out the campus and is really close to other resturaunts. I really like the lounge too."

"Sometimes it's good, sometimes it isn't. Breakfast (on the off chance that you are up that early) and lunch are usually better than dinner."

CAMPUS HOUSING

"Campus housing is in fair shape, but it has all the essentials and plenty of storage. For the most part, the rooms are indestructible."

"The South Houses are incredible. They are heavily customized, have murals everywhere, a large number of singles, sinks in each room, porches, balconies, well-equipped kitchens, and oh yeah, they're also falling apart. For example, the roof in Dabney's Alley leaks. Additionally, the metal mesh in the walls degrades cell phone and wireless network transmissions. Many of these issues should be fixed."

GUYS & GIRLS

Students

"All students except new students have to wear their uniform in which area of interest they are studying. Everyone is very friendly. They say hello and good morning. There is a wide variety of people here."

"Men are generally too interested in commitment and lose in the numbers game. Accordingly, women are fairly disinterested in commitment and spend time thinking about things like getting a PhD. In too many relationships, women realize they have control of the situation and take advantage of it, developing a boy-toy. Neither sex is generally experienced at relationships."

HEALTH & SAFETY

Safe and Secure

"At the Institute of Technology, I have always felt safe and secure. There was never any reason to fear for my safety."

"On campus, things are pretty safe, but it's still best to take precautions because people have been accosted near campus."

LOOKING FOR MORE?

Check out our full-length guide to this school at collegeprowler.com/california-institute-of-technology/.

Carleton College

1 N. College St.; Northfield, MN 55057
(507) 222-4000; www.carleton.edu

THE BASICS:

Acceptance Rate: 30%
Yield: 36%
Setting: Town
Control: Private Non-Profit
Total Undergrads: 1,986
SAT Range: 1990–2250*
ACT Range: 29–33

Student-Faculty Ratio: 9:1
Retention Rate: 97%
Graduation Rate: 93%
Tuition: $39,777
Room & Board: $10,428
Avg. Aid Package: $24,326
Students With Aid: 79%

* of 2400

Academics	A	Greek Life	N/A
Athletics	B	Guys	C-
Campus Dining	B-	Health & Safety	A
Campus Housing	B	Local Atmosphere	C+
Campus Strictness	A	Nightlife	C
Computers	B+	Off-Campus Dining	B
Diversity	B-	Off-Campus Housing	C-
Drug Safety	C+	Parking	B-
Facilities	B+	Transportation	C-
Girls	C-	Weather	C-

CP's Student Author On...
OVERALL EXPERIENCE

Given Carleton's high percent retention rate, it's pretty evident that Carls are satisfied with their school. Most people are surprised at how accepting other students at Carleton are and how easy it is to make friends, no matter who you are. As long as you're accepting and understanding, you'll get along just fine. The main reason why people usually end up choosing Carleton is its academics, but the main reason they stay is because of the people. Unlike at larger schools, you will not get lost at Carleton unless you make a conscious effort to do so. Sure, the academics are stressful, but the friendships and life experience you'll gain at Carleton is invaluable.

There's the old cliché that college is the best four years of anyone's life. What makes Carleton unique is that the four years you spend here may be the most challenging and stressful years of your life, but the result will make you a complete, well-rounded, and prepared individual who's ready to go out and face the real world.... For the rest of this editorial, visit collegeprowler.com.

Students Speak Out On...
OVERALL EXPERIENCE

Q Not for Everyone
"This school is definitely not for everyone! If you don't mind the lack of hygiene and the awkward conversation, then this could be the place for you. The classes are also more work than they are worth. Being on the trimester system is extremely stressful and you do not get to take as many different classes than if you went to a semester system college, even though they try to convince you otherwise!"

Q "Carleton is awesome. I've had a great experience, and I think it was the right place for me. It is the right mix of fun and serious study. For the most part, people are cool."

Q "I love Carleton. I feel as though this is a place where one can study really hard during the day, and then relax and party with your friends that night. Carleton is very challenging and also very rewarding."

BEST OF CARLETON

1. The Malt-O-Meal smell
2. Traditions
3. The library
4. The alcohol policy
5. Burton
6. The Arb
7. The Rec Center

Happy Students
97% of students return after their first year.

Commitment to Teaching
There are 9 students for every member of faculty on campus.

WORST OF CARLETON

1. The football team
2. The cold weather
3. Musser
4. The food
5. The Frisbee obsession
6. The workload
7. Bathrooms on a Sunday morning

Expensive
Tuition is a steep $39,777, one of the most expensive rates in the country.

Student Body

African American:	5%	Male Undergrads:	48%
Asian American:	10%	Female Undergrads:	52%
Hispanic:	5%	Living On Campus:	90%
International:	6%	Living Off Campus:	10%
Native American:	1%	Male Athletes:	31%
White:	69%	Female Athletes:	21%
Unknown:	4%	Fraternity Members:	0%
From Out-of-State:	79%	Sorority Members:	0%

Frequently Compared Schools:

Bowdoin College
Macalester College
Middlebury College
Oberlin College

Students Speak Out On...
EVERYTHING!

ACADEMICS

Q **Professors Give More Work Than Necessary**

"The professors here think that they must assign a ton of homework and grade harshly just because it is a highly-esteemed school. You do a lot more work than is necessary. You really do not get enough out of it for how much work you put in."

Q "If the classes are big, then the profs are boring. The bigger the class, the less personal the prof is. Also, no professor really wants to teach intro classes."

Q "The teachers are, for the most part, entirely devoted to teaching and their students. In many classes, they encourage students to take an active role in classes."

ATHLETICS

Q **They Are Better Than They Are Given Credit for**

"Carleton is a academically rigorous school, but that doesn't been we are athletically challenged. The men's basketball and soccer programs are always strong, as is the swimming, cross country and track programs. The women's basketball and football teams are competitive, though their records may not show it. Sporting events are really fun to attend."

Q "Women's basketball. 'Nuff said. Everyone plays Frisbee. Other IMs are very popular."

Q "Varsity sports and IMs are both bigger than religion."

CAMPUS DINING

Q **Environmentally Sustainable Food**

"There are two dining halls. Both have a fair variety of food, although I start to find the menu boring after several weeks on campus. The dining halls make it a point to get food from local sources and food grown with environmentally safe methods. Also, there are always good vegetarian options. There is also a snack bar, open until midnight, where we can buy food such as chips, sandwiches, chicken strips, and more. It's great for a late-night study break."

Q "The dining halls are okay, but they overcharge incredibly. Try to get off board. Other than that, your only option is the Snack Bar, which can be fun if you've got a friend with flex dollars."

CAMPUS HOUSING

Q "Watson is the social tower of power. Burton kids usually suck."

Q "It doesn't matter because as a freshman you're placed into a room and they're all the same. You don't get cable and you pay the same amount for a crappy double in a concrete, bunker-looking building as a senior pays who's living in brand new townhouse with his own bedroom, a kitchen, cable (I think), wood floors, and three or four of his good friends."

GUYS & GIRLS

Q **Eclectic**

"Of course they are a few sore apples, but for the most part everyone is great. There is no "one kind" of person at Carleton, everyone is completely unique. Carleton is not the most attractive college, student body-wise at first, but after a little a while the boys get cute, personality matters."

Q "Girls are not hot. Repeat: girls are not hot."

HEALTH & SAFETY

Q **I Feel Very Safe.**

"I know that, if I went to a big university, leaving my room for even a few minutes would put me at risk for theft. At Carleton, I know that I can trust the people I live near and the people on campus in general. It's a small town, and everyone at the college and in town is really nice, so I never feel uncomfortable."

Q "Carleton is very safe. I don't fear walking alone at night. Security is there, and they'll protect you if something goes wrong. Otherwise, they're in the shadows; they're not intrusive at all."

LOOKING FOR MORE?
Check out our full-length guide to this school at collegeprowler.com/carleton-college/.

Carnegie Mellon University

5000 Forbes Ave.; Pittsburgh, PA 15213
(412) 268-2000; www.cmu.edu

THE BASICS:

Acceptance Rate: 36%
Yield: 28%
Setting: Large city
Control: Private Non-Profit
Total Undergrads: 5,777
SAT Range: 1910–2220*
ACT Range: 29–33

Student-Faculty Ratio: 11:1
Retention Rate: 95%
Graduation Rate: 87%
Tuition: $40,920
Room & Board: $10,840
Avg. Aid Package: $26,552
Students With Aid: 66%

* of 2400

Academics	A	Greek Life	B
Athletics	C+	Guys	B+
Campus Dining	C	Health & Safety	B+
Campus Housing	C+	Local Atmosphere	B
Campus Strictness	B+	Nightlife	B+
Computers	A+	Off-Campus Dining	B
Diversity	A+	Off-Campus Housing	B+
Drug Safety	B-	Parking	C+
Facilities	B	Transportation	B+
Girls	C+	Weather	C+

CP's Student Author On...
OVERALL EXPERIENCE

In appraising CMU, most students are appreciative of the fantastic education they're receiving and the one-of-a-kind experience that the campus offers. At CMU, students have an unprecedented opportunity to explore their fields of study. Sometimes it's hard for students to see all opportunities that Carnegie Mellon gives them. Students who are unhappy with their experience are often frustrated with the sub-par social situation or the massive amount of work.

No matter how fed up students get with the amount of work, the social scene, or the bad weather, students are often glad they came to CMU when they think about the unique experience the school has given them. The academic opportunities you will receive at CMU are astounding, and everyone on campus is truly dedicated to learning. Though the time spent at CMU may not fulfill some students' hopes of living a wild youth, the years spent at Carnegie Mellon can be just as exciting in some ways. It's different. And for people who don't want the same college experience as everyone else, it can be exciting.

Students Speak Out On...
OVERALL EXPERIENCE

Q Great School

"I am extremely happy I chose CMU. I've made great friends here, and it has been easy to get involved in the campus community. Academics are challenging, but there are plenty of resources to help you succeed. Carnegie Mellon has a nice geeky feel to it and some cool traditions."

Q Challanging and Fascinating

"Carnegie Mellon is a great place to go if you want and are willing to work and learn. Overall, this is not a party school, although there are certainly exceptions. Students here know how to have fun, but academics are everyone's top priority. Classes are interesting and challenging, the way high school never was."

Q A Good Academic Environment

"Great academic program. Not enough dorms for students. Not enough off campus housing either. Not enough parking as well. Food is okay if you have low standards. Students not crazy about sports. Next time, I would choose a school that is more "out-going"."

BEST OF CARNEGIE MELLON

1. Carnival
2. Diversity
3. Plays at the Purnell Center
4. Painting the Fence at midnight
5. The $1 movies in the UC
6. Flirting through e-mail &Instant Messenger

Happy Students
95% of students return after their first year.

Proven Success
87% of students will complete their education and graduate with a degree.

WORST OF CARNEGIE MELLON

1. Bagpipes
2. Finding a parking spot
3. Meal plan/dining
4. Sporadic weather
5. The Hub
6. Teachers with heavy accents

Expensive
Tuition is a steep $40,920, one of the most expensive rates in the country.

Expensive Dorms
Living on campus doesn't come cheap, with an average housing price tag of $6,060.

Student Body

African American:	5%	Male Undergrads:	60%
Asian American:	23%	Female Undergrads:	40%
Hispanic:	5%	Living On Campus:	64%
International:	14%	Living Off Campus:	36%
Native American:	1%	Male Athletes:	9%
White:	41%	Female Athletes:	9%
Unknown:	11%	Fraternity Members:	13%
From Out-of-State:	85%	Sorority Members:	9%

Frequently Compared Schools:

Brown University
Cornell University
Northwestern University
University of Pennsylvania

Students Speak Out On... EVERYTHING!

ACADEMICS

Q Expert Teachers, Intelligent Students

"The academics at CMU are grueling, but manageable. You'll learn from professors who know their stuff and you'll be able to work with other bright, motivated students. The biggest problem with academics are that many of the TA's aren't good, but there are many other options for academic help if you're struggling. The general consensus is that if you leave Carnegie Mellon with above a 3.0 GA in engineering or computer science, you're guaranteed to find a decent job."

Q Always Willing to Help

"At Carnegie Mellon you can basically do whatever you want academic wise. The advisors will help you to find majors and minors that fit what you want to do in life and figure out what you need to do to achieve your goals. The professors are incredibly helpful and always available to meet with students to help them with assignments and understanding course material. The workload is heavy, but incredibly helpful in the end."

ATHLETICS

Q People Just Aren't Interested

"Although there are certainly athletic teams for every sport, including many intramural teams and student-organized games, people really don't come to university sports events (i.e. football, etc.). Now that Greek life has gotten involved, more people attend football games, but before that, there were as many people there to see the Kiltie Band as there were to see the Tartans play. The facilities are comfortable, however, and waiting for students to use them."

Q No School Spirit

"Some of the sports teams (Men's Cross Country, tennis, soccer, swimming) are top teams in the NCAA for division 3. But few people care about the sports, which is a shame. The football team is pretty terrible, which kind of sets the standard. Athletic facilities are decent, coaches are good, athletic trainers are horrible. The athletes are not very diverse- most are white christian engineers. Too bad the athletes aren't as diverse as the rest of the community."

CAMPUS DINING

Q Variety

"there is a lot of variety at CMU, tons of choices all around campus, and best of all they all taste great!"

Q New Dining Is Much Better Than Old

"If you read reviews of CMU, you'll often find complaints about bad food. Fortunately, this year a new food company was hired, and the food improved tremendously. Instead of having one main cafeteria, we have many smaller eating places. Some are even run by restaurants in Pittsburgh. So basically, you can get restaurant quality food as part of your meal plan. There's also places that serve typical, greasy college food if that's what you want. The only downside of the meal plan is its cost."

CAMPUS HOUSING

Q Freshman Housing Atmosphere

"Being an RA, I've only lived in freshman dorms for all of college. But I love it. The buildings themselves are not always the nicest or the prettiest, but there is an amazing sense of community in the freshman dorms."

GUYS & GIRLS

Q You Don't NEED Your CMU Goggles

""The odds are good, but the goods are odd" Well...that is kind of true, but hey, normal is boring right?The people are better looking than people think. I mean, we aren't an entire campus of models (although some people definitely could be), but I think we are pretty good looking as a whole.If you want your CMU goggles, it may help, but you definitely don't need them."

HEALTH & SAFETY

Q Safe - but Lock Your Bike

"With CMU students, there are always people walking around campus, even at 3 am, walking back from the library or studios. Very safe on campus. Lock up your bike, though. And if you live off campus, be smart - Pittsburgh IS an urban environment."

LOOKING FOR MORE?

Check out our full-length guide to this school at collegeprowler.com/carnegie-mellon-university/.

Case Western Reserve University

10900 Euclid Ave.; Cleveland, OH 44106
(216) 368-2000; www.case.edu

THE BASICS:

Acceptance Rate: 70%
Yield: 17%
Setting: Large city
Control: Private Non-Profit
Total Undergrads: 4,228
SAT Range: 1830–2130*
ACT Range: 28–32

Student-Faculty Ratio: 9:1
Retention Rate: 91%
Graduation Rate: 81%
Tuition: $36,238
Room & Board: $10,890
Avg. Aid Package: $34,927
Students With Aid: 87%

* of 2400

Academics	B+	Greek Life	A-
Athletics	C+	Guys	B
Campus Dining	B	Health & Safety	C+
Campus Housing	C+	Local Atmosphere	B
Campus Strictness	B+	Nightlife	B
Computers	A	Off-Campus Dining	B
Diversity	B+	Off-Campus Housing	B+
Drug Safety	C	Parking	B-
Facilities	B-	Transportation	A-
Girls	B-	Weather	C-

CP's Student Author On...
OVERALL EXPERIENCE

Case is best-suited for self-motivated, goal-oriented students with a firm grasp on reality. Most students have professional aspirations and a solid idea where they want to be in 10 years. Students tend to be very content with the level of academics and research and learning opportunity. The largest amount of concern from students comes from issues such as social atmosphere and male-female ratio. Students are mostly very happy with their professors and the facilities and resources available for students.

People are wired and "connected," but often very out-of-touch at the same time. It is often interesting to speculate about what cultural analysts from the future would say about the culture on the Case campus. Few students questioned expressed a concern for the amount of student involvement in University or students development or described any need for change in the relationship between departments or between students of different schools within Case. The Case campus offers freedom, and the city of Cleveland affords opportunities; students have the option to carve out their own niche.... For the rest of this editorial, visit collegeprowler.com.

Students Speak Out On...
OVERALL EXPERIENCE

Q Overall, Great

"There is so much to do academically, socially, and athletically. The hospitals (Cleveland Clinic, UH, VA), museums (Natural History, Art, Zoo), businesses (GE, KeyBank, Rockwell) and NASA Glenn are great for research/shadowing/volunteering/internships, the classes are great (though not always easy), the music/art/theater scenes are active, and the students, faculty, and staff are really nice."

Q Case Isn't for Everyone, but I Couldn't Love It More

"When I first arrived I worried that Case wouldn't be where I wanted to spend the next 4 years of my life, but once I got into the swing of life here, I honestly doubt I could be this happy anywhere else. The classes are challenging but rewarding, the people here are nerdy, but so am I, and I never seem to run out of things to do on/off campus."

Q Springfest

"Every spring, the school puts on Springfest, which is basically a celebration involving lots of free food, live music, and fun activities for the whole campus"

BEST OF CASE WESTERN

1. Location
2. Fiber-optic gigabit Ethernet
3. UPB Events
4. Residence hall life
5. Abundant reasearch opportunities for undergraduates

Happy Students
91% of students return after their first year.

Commitment to Teaching
There are 9 students for every member of faculty on campus.

WORST OF CASE WESTERN

1. The student meal plan
2. Parking
3. The Veale Gym weight room
4. Frigid weather
5. Lack of activism and political atmosphere
6. Male-to-female ratio

Expensive
Tuition is a steep $36,238, one of the most expensive rates in the country.

Overly Demanding Course Load
53% of students surveyed rated the manageability of work as below average.

Student Body

African American:	6%	Male Undergrads:	56%
Asian American:	16%	Female Undergrads:	44%
Hispanic:	2%	Living On Campus:	78%
International:	4%	Living Off Campus:	22%
Native American:	0%	Male Athletes:	15%
White:	56%	Female Athletes:	10%
Unknown:	15%	Fraternity Members:	29%
From Out-of-State:	62%	Sorority Members:	28%

Frequently Compared Schools:

Carnegie Mellon University
Cornell University
Northwestern University
University of Michigan

Students Speak Out On...
EVERYTHING!

ACADEMICS

Q The School's Main Draw Doesn't Dissapoint, but the Load May Break Your Back

"At Case, its not the slightest bit unusual to max out your schedule at 19 credit hours, and people overloading their schedule past this maximum isn't uncommon either. Case is a big name in the field of academics, and the rigor of the classes here match, if not, exceed this reputation. Make no mistake, coming to Case entails a lot of work, but ultimately it can be managed and is well worth the effort."

Q Top-Notch

"The professors are good teachers (far from given at a research university) and are more than happy to meet for extra help. The curriculum is open so you can study want you want and double/triple majoring (or switching midway through) is more than possible. There a bunch of internships at the school, and the career center and undergrad studies can help get ones off campus all over the country."

ATHLETICS

Q Support the Spartans

"I've never been a big fan of football, but our football team is very good! For the past few years they have remained undefeated! The Case football team is definitely something to look out for in the fall."

Q They Have Come a Long Way

"Case has a very good division three football that is nationally ranked. We had a national champion wrestler last year. All the sports seem to be improving but most of the student body could care less. The recreational facilities are adequate, and it seems that they are in line for additional funding for some improvements."

CAMPUS DINING

Q Chipotles

"A great place to do work and hang out with friends. Good healthy food choice of local food."

Q Pretty Good

"Usually something good, with the occasional home run or flop mixed in"

CAMPUS HOUSING

Q Dorms

"although there aren't many options for the first two years, once you become upperclassman, you will have plenty of options, including the best housing - the village, in which you get your own room with a queen size bed."

Q Village at 115

"The best dorms you will ever live in. They are modern, new, and right next to the football field. A great location and safe living environment."

GUYS & GIRLS

Q Not Just Dorks

"For a school with lots of engineering and science majors, the guys are often surprisingly not dorks"

Q Case Woman Are Really Ugly. (CWRU)

"So not true. Its funny though. For some reason there is this stigma that Case has just really ugly people. Guys and Girls alike. I know this isn't true. There are tons of pretty girls, loads of slutty ones and a fair share of nerdy ones. Then there are totally hot jock-stupid guys, hot smart ones and ugly smart ones. I think it depends on who you have been burned by and who you hang out with. For the most part, everyone is super smart and ordinary. This isn't USC, but its not MIT either."

HEALTH & SAFETY

Q Saftey

"The security is pretty tight not to many problems to worry about and this is most likely a safe no tolerence enviornment. Everybody here wants to learn and advanced into general society wth their carrers ahead of them."

LOOKING FOR MORE?

Check out our full-length guide to this school at collegeprowler.com/case-western-reserve-university/.

Catawba College

2300 W. Innes St.; Salisbury, NC 28144
(704) 637-4111; www.catawba.edu

THE BASICS:

Acceptance Rate: 70%	**Student-Faculty Ratio:** 16:1
Yield: 40%	**Retention Rate:** 70%
Setting: Town	**Graduation Rate:** 40%
Control: Private Non-Profit	**Tuition:** $23,740
Total Undergrads: 1,324	**Room & Board:** $8,200
SAT Range: 910–1130*	**Avg. Aid Package:** $18,422
ACT Range: 18–25	**Students With Aid:** 100%

* of 1600

This School Isn't Graded Yet!

College Prowler grades are calculated using tons of criteria, including survey responses that come from students at this school.

Unfortunately, we haven't gathered enough student surveys yet for this school to be able to calculate the grades for each section. Stay tuned to *CollegeProwler.com* for grade updates and more!

CP's Student Author On...
OVERALL EXPERIENCE

Every school has its problems, and so does this one. But in the end, looking back on their experiences, many students will tell you that they enjoyed attending Catawba. Many have met some of their closest friends at the College and would jump at the chance to choose this school all over again if they had the opportunity.

As long as students take initiative, they will be well prepared for the "real world" upon graduation. The school is unique for many reasons. Catawba has many athletes, a nationally-ranked music program, and a nationally-ranked theatre program—and these are just a few of its assets. The school continues to grow and change.

Students Speak Out On...
OVERALL EXPERIENCE

Q Great Choice

"I would absolutely choose the school again. My favorite thing about it is that it's really like a big family. Even when you don't know people, they will smile or wave at you, or hold a door open for you. People are just all around friendly."

Q I Love It

"I love this school and I don't want to graduate. I have had the best memories here."

Q LOVE

"Catawba is the perfect mixture of small town charm and big dreams."

Q Experiences

"I think that my overall experiences here at Catawba have been good. It is a small private college but there is a lot to offer. I think the thing that makes our school unique is there we have many types of activities going on. We get free t-shirts, food, ice cream and lots of other other. All of our sport events are free for students."

BEST OF CATAWBA

1. Activities
2. Concern for students
3. People
4. Professors
5. Campus size

Easy Financial Aid Process
75% of students surveyed told us that the financial aid process went smoothly and they received the financial aid they needed.

WORST OF CATAWBA

1. Campus dining
2. Registration
3. Campus size

Good Luck Finding a Part-Time Job
Employment services are not available for students.

Student Body

African American:	16%	Male Undergrads:	46%
Asian American:	1%	Female Undergrads:	54%
Hispanic:	1%	Living On Campus:	72%
International:	2%	Living Off Campus:	28%
Native American:	0%	Male Athletes:	45%.
White:	79%	Female Athletes:	22%
Unknown:	0%	Fraternity Members:	0%
From Out-of-State:	35%	Sorority Members:	0%

Students Speak Out On... EVERYTHING!

ACADEMICS

Q Theatre program is awesome but lots of work

"We have one of the few theatre programs that actually prepares you to work in all areas of theatre. They make sure that you are totally employable by the time you graduate. They also are great at giving real-life advice. However, it is also a ton of work. This isn't a laid-back, all fun and games department. It can be tiring and draining and there are plenty of nights where you'll be in the theatre until 2 a.m. It's definitely only meant for those who really, really want to be theatre majors."

Q They Want You to Do Well

"No matter what you might think, all of the professors want you to do well. They are all more than willing to meet with you after class and help you figure out what it is that you're not getting."

ATHLETICS

Q Catawba Sports

"Catawba sports are the heart and soul of Catawba College. You come here to play sports and we are the best of the best and have the most heart than any other athlete!"

Q Sports Important, Not Top Notch

"Sports are a major reason to come to Catawba, but no more important than the theatre or other on campus activites. pretty good student support."

CAMPUS DINING

Q Healthy but Limited Variety

"The food is good and healthy, but the variety is limited. This is to be expected with the size and enrollment of the school, but there is nothing open past 10:00pm."

Q Average, at best

"I think that the campus dining service needs to take way more pride in their preparation of food in the dining hall. I think most of the time it's a lazy selection, and it doesn't seem carefully prepared. It's average, at best."

Frequently Compared Schools:

Davidson College
Guilford College
University of North Carolina at Charlotte
Wake Forest University

CAMPUS HOUSING

Q Great

"The freshman dorms are a bit dated but every other facility is new."

Q Upperclassman Dorms Are Nice, Others Are Not

"I enjoyed living in Stanback. I did not like either Abernethy or Salisbury-Rowan, but of course Abernethy doesn't exist any more so that's kind of irrelevant. Salisbury-Rowan is cramped and uncomfortable. Stanback is nice."

GUYS & GIRLS

Q Everyone is easy-going

"The students at Catawba are fantastic. Everyone is extremly easy-going and loves to meet everyone. We have a good sample from all places in and out of the country. I have never made so many friends in such a short time."

Q Guys and Girls

"There are all kinds of people, girl or guys. The most prominent type of girl is probably a typical southern girl, and the most common type of guy is probably outspoken and intellectual."

HEALTH & SAFETY

Q Campus Is Comfortably Secure

"I have had no issue whatsoever concerning safety at Catawba. The campus is small and well patrolled by campus police and if any problems ever arise, there are many people that are willing to help you."

Q Campus Is Pretty Safe

"I have personally never felt unsafe on campus. However, if you don't feel comfortable walking across campus late at night, Public Safety will come pick you up and drive you to wherever you're going. Don't be drunk in public and don't steal."

LOOKING FOR MORE?

Check out our full-length guide to this school at collegeprowler.com/catawba-college/.

Catholic University of America

620 Michigan Ave. NE; Washington, DC 20064
(202) 319-5000; www.cua.edu

THE BASICS:

Acceptance Rate: 81%
Yield: 22%
Setting: Large city
Control: Private Non-Profit
Total Undergrads: 3,466
SAT Range: 1520–1830*
ACT Range: 21–27

Student-Faculty Ratio: 10:1
Retention Rate: 81%
Graduation Rate: 71%
Tuition: $31,890
Room & Board: $12,134
Avg. Aid Package: $20,209
Students With Aid: 94%

* of 2400

Academics	B	Greek Life	N/A
Athletics	C-	Guys	A-
Campus Dining	B	Health & Safety	C
Campus Housing	B	Local Atmosphere	B
Campus Strictness	C+	Nightlife	A
Computers	B	Off-Campus Dining	A
Diversity	C+	Off-Campus Housing	B
Drug Safety	B+	Parking	C
Facilities	C+	Transportation	A
Girls	B+	Weather	B-

CP's Student Author On...
OVERALL EXPERIENCE

Catholic University is a good school—plain and simple. It blends the best of both worlds—a small, conservative, Catholic community of religiously devoted students mixed with a liberal arts university smack-dab in Washington, DC. The nation's capital is one of the most exciting cities in the country, if not the world, where students can live up the best years of their lives. Catholic University provides all of the resources necessary to live a spiritual life in college, while still granting the autonomy to students who applied for other reasons, such as the University's exceptional theater, music, architecture, and nursing programs. CUA's biggest problem is the perception that the school's goal is to prep would-be priests and nuns. But this is simply not true. The University's Catholic identity does not hinder or isolate students with different faiths or beliefs. Catholic lives up to the liberal arts curriculum it boasts and does its best to accommodate both those who adore and are apathetic to the Catholic aspect.

When it comes to living the college life, CUA makes good on providing what students are truly looking for.... For the rest of this editorial, visit collegeprowler.com.

Students Speak Out On...
OVERALL EXPERIENCE

Q **The School of Music is amazing.**
"The Music School is one of the best in the country. The music students are so talented ...it is mind blowing."

Q **Diverse Experience**
"Students that need a place to fit in and learn will like Catholic. I've enjoyed my experiences."

Q **amazing school for specific majors**
"nursing architecture musicmusical theatre"

Q **I couldn't have picked a better school**
"It was so important for me to come to a school where people share my values, and I really found it here at Catholic U. And at the same time, I have met others who do not share my values and I have learned from them and vice versa. It has been a really great experience so far, mainly because the student body has been really nice and really reached out to everyone. Overall, I really couldn't have picked a better school."

BEST OF CATHOLIC

1. Catholic University's future is looking so bright right about now, with plans to build additional residence halls and collaborative efforts to improve the city.

Happy Students
81% of students return after their first year.

Commitment to Teaching
There are 10 students for every member of faculty on campus.

WORST OF CATHOLIC

1. Because the University is the official university of the Roman Catholic Church, the strict adherence to Catholic principles is almost always a prerequisite to speaking on campus.

Expensive
Tuition is a steep $31,890, one of the most expensive rates in the country.

Expensive Dorms
Living on campus doesn't come cheap, with an average housing price tag of $7,340.

Student Body

African American:	5%	Male Undergrads:	46%
Asian American:	3%	Female Undergrads:	54%
Hispanic:	6%	Living On Campus:	70%
International:	3%	Living Off Campus:	32%
Native American:	0%	Male Athletes:	20%
White:	65%	Female Athletes:	11%
Unknown:	18%	Fraternity Members:	1%
From Out-of-State:	99%	Sorority Members:	1%

Frequently Compared Schools:

American University
Fordham University
Loyola University Maryland
Villanova University

Students Speak Out On... EVERYTHING!

ACADEMICS

Q Depends on the Department

"At CUA, your workload and the strength of the program really depend on the department. In the most of the humanities departments, professors are really outstanding. Registration is easy and all done online. In some programs, the option is there to do independent study in senior year, which is a very valuable experience. CUA's strongest departments are probably architecture, philosophy, nursing, english, music & musical theater, art history."

Q I Don't Know

"I will be going there in the Fall, so I don't know."

ATHLETICS

Q I absolutely love it

"I absolutely love it. It's a great way to meet people and friends. You have your own little family in your team."

Q College Athletics

"I am an active swimmer with the CUA swim team. Our coach is amazing and really cares about his swimmers. The sports medicine dept is also amazing and is always available to help student athletes with any type of sports related injury. The fitness rm and classes offered are also well planned fun to attend."

CAMPUS DINING

Q In general, the food is pretty good

"I really enjoy the new salad bar because it provides variety of vegetables as well as bread and other condiments. In general, the food is pretty good."

Q An Honest Effort

"Most of the staff is kind and strives to do a good job. They often attempt to get creative with their recipes and the food is decent for the most part. Sometimes they hint a slump and the stuff is the same every week and just not appetizing but overall a good job. I love the hummus!"

CAMPUS HOUSING

Q Depends on What You Want

"There are the residence halls or normal dorms like any other university"

Q South side is more enjoyable

"How is living on-campus? One word: FUN. But really, it all depends on where you lived. If you lived on south side (Spellman, Conaty), you swear up and down how much fun you had but those from north side are indifferent. You decide. And while the north side i.e. Flather, Reagan for freshman are nicer, because they are newer, I cannot stress enough how much more enjoyable south side is despite its lack of luster."

GUYS & GIRLS

Q Guys and girls can be both fun and religious

"The one thing I like about Catholic is that the guys and girls can be both fun and religious. Its totally common to see the very same guys and girls who partied hard on a Saturday night attend mass Sunday morning. They may be hungover, but they are at mass nonetheless."

Q It changes with every grade

"It changes with every grade. For example, the current seniors and freshmen guys are hotter than the girls while the junior and sophomore girls are hotter than the guys. Girls in general are sluttier than the guys, but there are definitely promiscuous guys. You'll know them."

HEALTH & SAFETY

Q Campus is in a rough part of town

"Campus is situated in a rough part of town, but security measures have really been stepped-up over the past two years. The administration takes student safety seriously and, even though crime rates are lower than other schools within the district, they have implemented measures to increase the presence of campus police all over campus at all times of day and night."

LOOKING FOR MORE?

Check out our full-length guide to this school at collegeprowler.com/catholic-university-of-america/.

Centenary College of Louisiana

2911 Centenary Blvd.; Shreveport, LA 71134
(318) 869-5011; www.centenary.edu

THE BASICS:

Acceptance Rate: 54%
Yield: 30%
Setting: Mid-sized city
Control: Private Non-Profit
Total Undergrads: 887
SAT Range: 1480–1830*
ACT Range: 22–27

Student-Faculty Ratio: 11:1
Retention Rate: 74%
Graduation Rate: 59%
Tuition: $22,900
Room & Board: $7,940
Avg. Aid Package: $13,618
Students With Aid: 98%

* of 2400

Academics	B	Greek Life	A
Athletics	B-	Guys	C+
Campus Dining	C-	Health & Safety	B-
Campus Housing	B	Local Atmosphere	B
Campus Strictness	C+	Nightlife	B
Computers	B	Off-Campus Dining	A
Diversity	C-	Off-Campus Housing	C+
Drug Safety	B	Parking	A
Facilities	B	Transportation	B
Girls	B	Weather	B+

CP's Student Author On...
OVERALL EXPERIENCE

Most of the students that enter Centenary are looking for a school where they won't be just a face in the crowd. You can make a name for yourself very easily. Students that have enough drive can accomplish anything they want at Centenary. If you want to take a certain class, but the College doesn't offer it, you can organize an independent study. If you want a certain organization formed, get some signatures and petition the administration. There's a wonderful sense that anything you want to accomplish can be done. Some students complain of being bored at Centenary, but finding your place in the College requires work. Getting involved in an organization is one of the most rewarding things about Centenary, because you have the opportunity to re-create the organization and really leave your mark. Becoming involved at Centenary is essential. Most of the organizations are student-run, and the faculty and staff encourage student input. If you don't participate, the school and city may seem dull.

The most important thing about Centenary, though, is the quality of the academics.... For the rest of this editorial, visit collegeprowler.com.

Students Speak Out On...
OVERALL EXPERIENCE

Q "For the first couple of years, I wanted to transfer, but in retrospect, I'm glad I stayed."

Q "I love Centenary with my whole heart. I feel like I was incredibly lucky to find a school that suits me so well. Besides the Caf, every aspect of the school is great, and I wouldn't want to be anywhere else."

Q "I did leave Centenary for a year, but I missed it and came back. You don't find the kind of attention Centenary gives you and the care anywhere else."

Q "I have always loved Centenary. I suppose I could have gotten some good opportunities at other schools, but I would never want to give up the relationships and the experiences I've had at Centenary. I can't picture myself anywhere else."

Q "I would never trade my experience at Centenary for anything. There were some tough times, but I loved almost all of it!"

BEST OF CENTENARY

1. Small classes
2. Tight-knit community
3. The professors
4. You make great friends
5. You always have the chance to stand out
6. The grounds are gorgeous

Learn from the Best
94% of faculty have earned the highest degree in their field.

Personal Attention
You can expect personal attention with 75% of classes having less than 20 students.

WORST OF CENTENARY

1. Small classes
2. Shreveport gets boring quickly
3. Student apathy
4. The food
5. The girl-to-guy ratio
6. Petty high school behavior

Good Luck Finding a Part-Time Job
Employment services are not available for students.

Want a Job? On Your Own
There aren't any placement services for graduates.

Student Body

African American:	8%	Male Undergrads:	43%
Asian American:	3%	Female Undergrads:	57%
Hispanic:	4%	Living On Campus:	70%
International:	3%	Living Off Campus:	30%
Native American:	0%	Male Athletes:	26%
White:	81%	Female Athletes:	25%
Unknown:	2%	Fraternity Members:	25%
From Out-of-State:	37%	Sorority Members:	25%

Frequently Compared Schools:

Birmingham-Southern College
Chapman University
Claremont McKenna College
Furman University

Students Speak Out On... EVERYTHING!

ACADEMICS

Q "In general, classes are interesting, especially those ones with a discussion-type format; however, some lecture classes can be a bit of a snooze, especially the early morning ones."

Q "The teachers at Centenary are a unique blend of individuals, from the super intellectual to the downright kooky. We have a wonderful staff. Furthermore, it serves to reason with a staff like that, classes are almost always worthwhile and interesting."

Q "The teachers are overworked—the entire history department consists of two professors, who have to teach all the history ever. So if you decide to go into certain majors, you'll have very fried, exhausted—but still fun—teachers. And they do try to keep things interesting."

ATHLETICS

Q **Grade a Sports**

"At Centenary College of Louisiana, varsity sports are a very big part of campus. Most of the students attending here are part of some athletic team. There are so many different sports available and intramural sports! We have great trainers and advisers at our fingertips whenever we need them. All of the students here are so supportive of all of the sports on campus. There is never an event here that is not completely packed."

Q "IM sports are actually a bigger deal than varsity sports. The IM events draw big, noisy crowds."

Q "Varsity sports aren't that big. People rarely come to the baseball and basketball games. As for IM sports, it's always the same groups that put up teams: the fraternities, sororities, choir, and maybe one other."

CAMPUS DINING

Q **How Exactly Is the Food at School?**

"With regards to many factors, my overall views of dining and food at my school are especially pleasant."

Q "Campus food is tolerable as far as taste is concerned. There is a severe lack of healthy food options on campus."

Q "Food is a terrible, awful, greasy, bland, deep-fried, salt-soaked mess."

CAMPUS HOUSING

Q "The dorms are great. If you like to party and live in small rooms, stay in Cline. If you're a guy, you don't have much of a choice until you become a junior."

Q "The dorms are okay, but the RAs seem to think they're running a summer camp. Prepare to have cutesy activities crammed down your throat every single week. James is top pick, since it's the only dorm with a kitchen."

GUYS & GIRLS

Q "There's, like, a two-to-one girl-to-guy ratio. About one-fourth of the males are gay. So there are about seven girls for every straight guy."

Q "You'll find great guys and great girls, as well as terrible guys and terrible girls. More often than not, though, everyone is pretty nice, and there are a lot of hot guys and girls on campus as well. I've only had personal problems with a few people, and they're easy enough to avoid."

HEALTH & SAFETY

Q "I've never had a problem, and DPS will always walk you to wherever you need to go."

Q "Personally, I feel safe on campus. There are enough people around that if something were to happen, I could scream and someone would hear me. However, my car has been broken into once before. The neighborhood around the campus isn't exactly the best."

LOOKING FOR MORE?

Check out our full-length guide to this school at collegeprowler.com/centenary-college-of-louisiana/.

Centre College

600 W. Walnut St.; Danville, KY 40422
(859) 238-5200; www.centre.edu

THE BASICS:

Acceptance Rate: 69%
Yield: 23%
Setting: Town
Control: Private Non-Profit
Total Undergrads: 1,216
SAT Range: 1650–2010*
ACT Range: 26–30

Student-Faculty Ratio: 11:1
Retention Rate: 91%
Graduation Rate: 82%
Tuition: $31,200
Room & Board: $7,800
Avg. Aid Package: $15,809
Students With Aid: 97%

*of 2400

Academics	B+	Greek Life	A+
Athletics	C+	Guys	B
Campus Dining	C	Health & Safety	A-
Campus Housing	B	Local Atmosphere	C
Campus Strictness	B+	Nightlife	C
Computers	B+	Off-Campus Dining	C+
Diversity	D	Off-Campus Housing	D
Drug Safety	B+	Parking	A
Facilities	A-	Transportation	D
Girls	B	Weather	B-

CP's Student Author On...
OVERALL EXPERIENCE

Centre sells itself as an all-around environment; being more than just an academic powerhouse, the school promotes self-growth through service and community involvement. The progression from freshman to senior can seem like just the change of another four years, but Centre's influence over the students is obvious. Centre graduates emerge as well-rounded leaders, activists, and the prominent who's who of their generation. While the College experience is something few would trade, Centre's best asset is the post-graduation benefits of the Centre Mafia of alumni that help graduates score hot jobs.

As far as the overall experience, it's amazing. Merging a great social scene with academics yields rounded individuals who are smart and fun. Centre is a place that takes away all the boring parts of high school but keeps all the spirit and fun. At Centre, each day is a healthy combination of work and play. Centre C is a few hours of class and homework blended with living with or next to your best friends, that hot crush, and your professors. Centre offers a remarkable experience for the whole person.... For the rest of this editorial, visit collegeprowler.com.

Students Speak Out On...
OVERALL EXPERIENCE

Q "It's okay, but I wouldn't do it over if I had to!"

Q "Sometimes, I would complain about how small Centre was, or about anything that seems to bother you when you're going to school there, but now that I've graduated, I'd give anything to go back. I really miss my time at Centre."

Q "It's been pretty cool. I've had some knocks, but I figure I would at any college. I wouldn't want to be anywhere else; it's a good fit for me. You just need to find your fit, and you'll have a blast."

Q "I loved my first few years at Centre, and I wouldn't want to have gone anywhere else. It was the best choice for me."

Q "I loved my Centre experience and wouldn't have changed it for the world. No way have I wished I went elsewhere. And, if you get the chance to study abroad, take advantage of it. You'll regret it if you don't."

BEST OF CENTRE

1. Centre Term
2. All professor-taught classes
3. Photo of the week
4. Nevin
5. Midnight movie
6. Strong academic reputation

Happy Students
91% of students return after their first year.

Proven Success
82% of students will complete their education and graduate with a degree.

WORST OF CENTRE

1. The Registrar's office
2. Interlibrary loan
3. Diversity ratio
4. Nevin
5. Grill prices
6. Classes in Grant
7. Cowan food

Expensive
Tuition is a steep $31,200, one of the most expensive rates in the country.

Not Much Diversity
One of the least racially diverse campuses—only 10% of students are minorities.

Student Body

African American:	4%	Male Undergrads:	46%
Asian American:	2%	Female Undergrads:	54%
Hispanic:	2%	Living On Campus:	98%
International:	2%	Living Off Campus:	2%
Native American:	0%	Male Athletes:	46%
White:	90%	Female Athletes:	30%
Unknown:	0%	Fraternity Members:	34%
From Out-of-State:	38%	Sorority Members:	40%

Frequently Compared Schools:

Denison University
Elon University
Furman University
Rhodes College

Students Speak Out On... EVERYTHING!

ACADEMICS

Good Professors

"The professors are very willing to talk with you about your ideas."

"The professors are corny, but very involved with students. Sometimes, they care a little too much about their particular field, but it's awesome that they get so excited about teaching."

"The teachers are pretty cool, for the most part. They do what they can to make their subject interesting. They will almost always give out their home phone number and are always willing to talk to you about their class, and even things not even remotely related to class. They'll invite you to their houses for class, especially if your class is small, and they've even been known to stop by for a beer or two."

ATHLETICS

"Being a Division III school, varsity sports are not as popular as at a Division I school. However, a good majority of the student population plays sports, and each team likes to come out and support each other. IM sports are also competitive and fun here, although not that many choices are offered."

"Varsity sports are pretty popular, and the people on the teams themselves are exclusive."

"We have an amazing gym that is super nice."

CAMPUS DINING

The Food...

"cowan is pretty terrible, but there are some safe choices that i really like. the grill is almost always good and jazzman's is nice after you finish practice or a workout"

"Eat ramen noodles, Taco Bell, and Huddle House. You should never eat at Cowan, but you will, just like everyone else, every day."

"We're catered by a private company, and frankly, their food isn't the best. They could do much better. Freddie's, Guadalajara, and Applebee's are good places to go to grab some food."

CAMPUS HOUSING

Upperclassman dorms are great

"Depending on what dorm you get, living on campus is great. Upperclassman dorms (PEARL!) are wonderful. The Greek houses also have really large rooms. The dorms in the old quad... not so much.."

Wide Variety

"There is a wide range in quality of dorms. The best dorm is like a resort. The housing process is easy"

GUYS & GIRLS

Pretty Darn Good Looking for a Bunch of Nerds

"Considering that everyone at Centre is extremely smart and dedicated, there are a plethora of hot people to look at."

Pretty Atrractive

"Most people on campus are well dressed and well put together. They like to study and then party. Many attractive people on campus."

HEALTH & SAFETY

Pretty Safe

"Centre's on-campus security, DPS, does a pretty good job at making sure campus safe and welcoming at all times. However, they obviously can't be everywhere, and it's best to be careful, especially at night."

"Highly secure—if you consider five people without guns, handcuffs, nightsticks, Mace, or tazers a police force."

LOOKING FOR MORE?

Check out our full-length guide to this school at collegeprowler.com/centre-college/.

Chapman University

1 University Dr.; Orange, CA 92866
(714) 997-6815; www.chapman.edu

THE BASICS:

Acceptance Rate: 56%	**Student-Faculty Ratio:** 14:1
Yield: 30%	**Retention Rate:** 87%
Setting: Mid-sized city	**Graduation Rate:** 73%
Control: Private Non-Profit	**Tuition:** $36,764
Total Undergrads: 4,476	**Room & Board:** $12,832
SAT Range: 1672–2010*	**Avg. Aid Package:** $17,704
ACT Range: 25–29	**Students With Aid:** 83%

* of 2400

Academics	B	Greek Life	A
Athletics	C-	Guys	A-
Campus Dining	B-	Health & Safety	B-
Campus Housing	B	Local Atmosphere	B
Campus Strictness	C+	Nightlife	B-
Computers	B+	Off-Campus Dining	C+
Diversity	B-	Off-Campus Housing	B-
Drug Safety	C+	Parking	A-
Facilities	B	Transportation	C
Girls	B	Weather	A+

CP's Student Author On...
OVERALL EXPERIENCE

Chapman is perfect for students who are looking for an intimate college setting and the chance to get involved. It's very easy to hold a leadership position on campus by joining Greek life, Associated Students, or a club. And it seems that the more involved a student is, the better his or her experience will be at Chapman. A typical Chapman student is outgoing, friendly, and ambitious. Most have internships or jobs while going to school, and they have specific career goals in mind. Students care a lot about their grades and want to succeed in their classes, so you'll find plenty of students studying during the week, but as soon as Thursday rolls around, most head to the bars or fraternity parties.

The nightlife scene at Chapman isn't comparable to bigger universities, mainly because Chapman is a small school, so there tends to be limited party options. Students like to go to fraternity house parties on the weekends or, if they are 21 or older, to the bars in The Circle. Besides partying, there are lots of fun things to do around Chapman—luckily, it is in the perfect location for students.... For the rest of this editorial, visit collegeprowler.com.

Students Speak Out On...
OVERALL EXPERIENCE

Q Overall Experience: Chapman University

"The professors are amazing and very flexible, the students are easy to get along with, the food is awesome, and the living conditions are pretty good. The professors are the most outstanding part of this school because they really care about all their students, are open to alternative ideas, and are always accessible for extra help."

Q The Best School

"Chapman is the best. It is a small campus and its classes have around only 20 people. Everyone is friendly and kind. The small classes and variety are awesome. Your professors actually know who you are and are very helpful. Some even personally help you. I went to another college before this and it was overcrowded. Space was limited. Some professors never even learned our names. If I would have to choose again, I would have chosen Chapman from the start."

BEST OF CHAPMAN

1. The professors and students
2. Dodge College of Film and Media Arts
3. Small class sizes
4. Sense of community
5. Location
6. The facilities

Happy Students
87% of students return after their first year.

Proven Success
73% of students will complete their education and graduate with a degree.

WORST OF CHAPMAN

1. Lack of school spirit
2. Dining options at the cafeteria
3. Lack of parking for off-campus students
4. No Greek housing
5. Academic advisers don't help students

Expensive
Tuition is a steep $36,764, one of the most expensive rates in the country.

Don't Move Off Campus
Average off-campus housing is a steep $10,816.

Student Body

African American:	2%	Male Undergrads:	41%
Asian American:	8%	Female Undergrads:	59%
Hispanic:	10%	Living On Campus:	41%
International:	2%	Living Off Campus:	59%
Native American:	1%	Male Athletes:	12%
White:	65%	Female Athletes:	7%
Unknown:	11%	Fraternity Members:	26%
From Out-of-State:	39%	Sorority Members:	30%

Frequently Compared Schools:

Loyola Marymount University
Pepperdine University
University of San Diego
University of Southern California

Students Speak Out On... EVERYTHING!

ACADEMICS

Personalized Class Sizes

"Chapman University is a relatively small school, but it allows for more personalized teaching. Most of the professors know who you are personally in their classes and are able to give more one-on-one help."

A Good Student to Teacher Ratio

"Every class that I have taken at Chapman has a good student-to-teacher ratio. This allows the class to interact with the teacher and even create a relationship with the teacher for guidance and reference. Also, this allows teachers to have available office hours to help their students."

ATHLETICS

Supported

"The athletics at Chapman are very much supported, but our football team is not top-notch. I have always been very much a fan of sports. Chapman has a good balance between academics, the arts, and athletics."

There Are Some Awesome Teams

"Our teams are pretty good, for the most part. Football isn't great, but lacrosse, water polo, and baseball are all awesome. Fan support is usually pretty good, as long as the games are advertised so students know about it. Most of our facilities are great, especially the stadium and the pool."

CAMPUS DINING

High Quality, but Slightly Repetitive

"While the quality of our cafeteria and on-campus cafe food is very highly ranked, it does, at times, get repetitive. I think, however, that living on campus and eating only at the cafeteria means some repetition is impossible to avoid, so I truly have no complaints. More weekend/late-night options would be good, though."

Campus Dining

"The cafeteria is open from 7:30 a.m. to 7:30 p.m. Besides that, there are a few places on campus where students can eat, as well as a place in the dorms. The food is really good with lots of different options. There is also vegan and vegetarian food."

CAMPUS HOUSING

Dorms are Incredibly Nice Compared to Other Schools

"Some of the Chapman students do not realize how lucky they are to be living in such nice dorms. The dorms are relatively spacious, so that there is no need for bunk beds unless you get put in Henley. The Henley dorms are smaller, but nicer than most of the other dorms. Sandhu is the best except its rooms are definitely the smallest. It is expensive to live in the dorms, but it is definitely worth it because it is relatively quiet and everything is intact."

Freshman Housing

"I am VERY satisfied and am super spoiled. We are really taken care of here. The rooms are bigger than any other schools' dorms I have seen, and we all have our own bathroom. I love how social the dorms are. I am hardly in my own room because I am constantly visiting my friends!"

GUYS & GIRLS

Girls Are Hot

"Girls are hot, for the most part."

California Girls (and guys)

"Katy Perry's "California Gurls" perfectly describes Chapman's female student body. Chapman probably has as many pretty girls as Harvard has smart girls. The guys are not too shabby either. You can find all the ken dolls at the frat parties or in "Matheletes." This campus definitely does not have a shortage of beautiful people."

HEALTH & SAFETY

Both Very Very Reliable.

"Public Safety is always around campus and will give you a ride anywhere if you call them and express that you want them to give you a ride somewhere. The health services office is right by school and they give you checkups for reasonable prices."

LOOKING FOR MORE?

Check out our full-length guide to this school at collegeprowler.com/chapman-university/.

Chatham University

Woodland Road; Pittsburgh, PA 15232
(412) 365-1100; www.chatham.edu

THE BASICS:

Acceptance Rate: 68%	Student-Faculty Ratio: 10:1
Yield: 30%	Retention Rate: 71%
Setting: Large city	Graduation Rate: 52%
Control: Private Non-Profit	Tuition: $28,088
Total Undergrads: 712	Room & Board: $8,700
SAT Range: 920–1173*	Avg. Aid Package: $12,852
ACT Range: 19–25	Students With Aid: 100%

of 1600

Academics	B-	Greek Life	N/A
Athletics	B-	Guys	B-
Campus Dining	C+	Health & Safety	B-
Campus Housing	A	Local Atmosphere	A-
Campus Strictness	B-	Nightlife	B-
Computers	B	Off-Campus Dining	A-
Diversity	B	Off-Campus Housing	B-
Drug Safety	B-	Parking	B
Facilities	C+	Transportation	B+
Girls	B	Weather	C

CP's Student Author On...
OVERALL EXPERIENCE

Chatham is not a place for everyone. As a small, single-sex institution, the social scene here can be too slow for some, and the same-sex campus might be too stifling for students who would enjoy having male and female students on campus. However, students who choose to adjust to Chatham find that they thrive in its environment, relate well to the people here, and embrace its way of life. Students settle in and find their place among the sports, the schoolwork, and the social life. However, students note that it can be easy to get stuck in the Chatham "bubble," the feeling students get when they feel like they are trapped on campus. But, an outing to any of the surrounding neighborhoods for some shopping, a bite to eat, or a night out can quickly solve this problem. Joining an athletic team can also help students feel more involved and like part of campus, and it also helps students stay in shape to avoid the infamous Freshman 15. Campus safety is also rated high, a facet of the Chatham experience with which students are very pleased. Students say the Public Safety officers are good at their jobs but not overly meddling.... For the rest of this editorial, visit collegeprowler.com.

Students Speak Out On...
OVERALL EXPERIENCE

Q A Good Experience

"Chatham has made my college life exciting. I have dealt with problems any normal student would deal with, and I have adjusted well to them—being at school alone; going to France, twice; getting good grades and studying hard; also making friends, were some of the favorites. Sports kept me in shape and on track."

Q Overall, it's a great school

"Chatham is a great school. I love my professors. Really, the professors here are fabulous, and they make the place worth it. The majority of undergrad students are homosexual, so if you are extremely conservative and not okay with that, then the school is not for you."

Q Favorable

"The food is great and reasonably priced. Living on campus is pretty easy-going, and it is a very safe campus."

BEST OF CHATHAM

1. Chatham is a women's college.
2. Campus is close to the city of Pittsburgh.
3. The dorms are beautiful—many are converted mansions.
4. Small class sizes.

Commitment to Teaching
There are 10 students for every member of faculty on campus.

Low-Stress Course Load
60% of students surveyed rated the manageability of work as above average.

WORST OF CHATHAM

1. A small school can mean classes aren't always offered when you need them.
2. Some of the "behind-the-scenes" employees—admissions, financial aid, and registrar—can be difficult to work with.

Expensive
Tuition is a steep $28,088, one of the most expensive rates in the country.

Life is NOT a Party
80% of students surveyed said it's almost impossible to find a good party.

Student Body

African American:	7%	Male Undergrads:	8%
Asian American:	1%	Female Undergrads:	92%
Hispanic:	1%	Living On Campus:	54%
International:	5%	Living Off Campus:	46%
Native American:	0%	Male Athletes:	0%
White:	60%	Female Athletes:	17%
Unknown:	26%	Fraternity Members:	0%
From Out-of-State:	38%	Sorority Members:	0%

Frequently Compared Schools:

Carnegie Mellon University
Drexel University
Duquesne University
University of Pittsburgh

Students Speak Out On... EVERYTHING!

ACADEMICS

Chatham University - Good to Go

"Most professors at Chatham University are great. They are good at lecturing in class and help out of class with any problems. The curriculum, along with the professors, is good, too. When students first register for classes, the classes are not picked out for them, they get to register for themselves with help from professors and other students. We also have some five-year graduate programs that are great opportunities for many people."

Exercise Science

"We are a small school, and with it comes extremely personal relationships between classmates and professional members of the community."

ATHLETICS

Athletics are Good Here

"The athletics department is good. We have good teams that are hard-working and good coaches and trainers. The athletics facilities are amazing. The only slight negative is fan support, but it has been increasing."

The Athletes Care

"The people who play the sports are kinda cult-like and don't hang out with people who aren't on their teams, so most people don't show up to the games. The intramurals are amazing though; there is a lot of school pride at these games because they are open to everyone, and they are about having fun. Chatham has a fantastic athletic facility that encourages people of all types to get in shape and get involved."

CAMPUS DINING

Dining Hall is Amazing

"Amazing, but we need more veggie options."

Lots of Variety

"There is lots of variety at Chatham University, and if you put on the suggestion slips that you want them to make something, they ALWAYS make it. We even had a meeting with

the executive chef, and he is trying his best to fit our needs. I have never had better college food."

CAMPUS HOUSING

Dorms are spacious and inviting

"My favorite dorm is Woodland, though I believe that every dorm is very spacious and inviting to its inhabitants. The dorms are cleaned daily, and if we need something to be fixed, it will eventually be fixed."

Fickes Dorms Are the Best

"The dorms are spacious and kept clean for the most part."

GUYS & GIRLS

Women's School, but There are Guys!

"We are a women's college, which means that guys are limited. The population is extremely diverse, though. People from all walks of life attend Chatham. However, just because we are a women's college does not mean there are no men. Boys hang around sometimes. Also, there are many other colleges around where you can meet guys."

The People Are Okay.

"There aren't many guys on campus; the ones that are here are graduate students. They seem to be wary of the girls here, but are fun and nice when you get to know them. The girls on campus are a very diverse group. There are many different social circles, but they are friendly, for the most part."

HEALTH & SAFETY

Personal Safety on Campus

"Safety on campus is great. There are many lit areas, we have our own police force, and blue phones are everywhere. There are also bi-semester classes offered on escaping and beating an assailant"

Personal Safety

"I always feel safe on campus, even walking on campus alone in the dark."

LOOKING FOR MORE?

Check out our full-length guide to this school at collegeprowler.com/chatham-university/.

City College of New York

160 Convent Ave.; New York, NY 10031
(212) 650-7000; www.ccny.cuny.edu

THE BASICS:

Acceptance Rate: 37%
Yield: 27%
Setting: Large city
Control: Public
Total Undergrads: 12,836
SAT Range: 890–1140*
ACT Range: —

Student-Faculty Ratio: 13:1
Retention Rate: 79%
Graduation Rate: 37%
Tuition: $10,289
Room & Board: $12,207
Avg. Aid Package: $10,166
Students With Aid: 85%

* of 1600

Academics	B-	Greek Life	C-
Athletics	C+	Guys	A-
Campus Dining	C+	Health & Safety	C+
Campus Housing	C+	Local Atmosphere	B
Campus Strictness	C	Nightlife	B+
Computers	C+	Off-Campus Dining	C
Diversity	A+	Off-Campus Housing	B-
Drug Safety	B-	Parking	C+
Facilities	C	Transportation	B
Girls	B+	Weather	B+

CP's Student Author On... OVERALL EXPERIENCE

City College may be small compared to the other universities in New York City, but it still kicks butt. City has many special attributes that most students won't find anywhere else, including the diversity, the crazy amount of scholarships available, the amazing fellowships and internships, and the professors. It may be a public college, but the professors who teach are still highly qualified. They hail from Ivy League schools and well-known private universities from around the United States to teach a dedicated bunch of City College students—students who are friendly, easy to talk to, and worth making friends with.

Students Speak Out On... OVERALL EXPERIENCE

Q Experience
"my experience so far has been great. i have met good friends, excellent professors"

Q Amazing Expierence
"I love it here. City college has the most amazing campus and there's only so much you can do. everyone is so friendly and there are so many options to choose from. whether you just want to study or spend your free time on campus, city is definitely great."

Q There Is a High Rate of Tolerence Here!
"City college is full of culture. We have a people from all over the world. Every religion is respected to the fullest. People are very nice here and they are willing to help at any momment!"

Q Good
"I like my school, but i just wish that the dorms would be much cheaper."

Q Best Years?
"I am enjoying myself so much more in my final semester than any other and its great!!!"

BEST OF CCNY

1. The fact that you are in Manhattan
2. The diverse population
3. The international students
4. The Rudin Learning Center
5. We're like a mini United Nations in Harlem

Affordable
Tuition is only $10,289, one of the most affordable rates in the country.

Big Dorms
65% of students surveyed felt that dorms were more spacious than average.

WORST OF CCNY

1. No matter how you get to campus, you have to walk up a hill
2. The Administration building
3. The cashiers at the cafeteria
4. Really thick accents you can't understand

Not Everyone Graduates
37% of students do not complete their education or graduate with a degree.

Expensive Dorms
Living on campus doesn't come cheap, with an average housing price tag of $9,250.

Student Body

African American:	24%	Male Undergrads:	48%
Asian American:	16%	Female Undergrads:	52%
Hispanic:	32%	Living On Campus:	3%
International:	10%	Living Off Campus:	97%
Native American:	0%	Male Athletes:	4%
White:	17%	Female Athletes:	2%
Unknown:	0%	Fraternity Members:	—
From Out-of-State:	4%	Sorority Members:	—

Frequently Compared Schools:

Columbia University
CUNY Queens College
Hunter College
New York University

Students Speak Out On...
EVERYTHING!

ACADEMICS

Intro to Legal Process

"The class is an A+ because you learn alot about the United States Supreme Court,how the system works,the judges ideology on law and how law should be interpreted.The class also educates one on the confirmation hearings of the judges. However, the workload is heavy and the professor she is stern on deadline dates for papers. The class is a good class if you are able to meet all deadline dates."

It's on You

"Everything is available as long as you search for it. If you try, you will find the help you need."

Teacher to Student Help

"The teachers are always willing to make time to help the students make sure they understand almost everything."

ATHLETICS

The School Has Many Teams

"The school offers varieties of sport option from which students can choose. In addition there are sufficient facilities available to make sure athletes receive the proper training. As a result CCNY has one of the best athletes in New York."

CAMPUS DINING

Sitting Arrangments

"I think we should have more seats in the dining room"

It Is Expensive

"i ususally eat a bagel and cream cheese, nothing else interest me because i could get the same thing somewhere else for a cheaper price"

Yuck!

"the food at the school is way to expensive the caferteria is mainly used to sit down and eat outside food not food from the cafeteria which does not taste all that great"

CAMPUS HOUSING

Great Things

"to live in campus, it a great thing. Even though i dont dorm in my school, i have heard great things."

The Campus Is Well Equipped.

"I dont live on campus, but if I did Im sure I would love it. The only problem is having to walk several blocks to get to other eatins spots."

Housing on Campus

"I do not live on campus, however, I have friends who do. I believe most of the complaints are general problems with roomates and sharing space. It is expensive to dorm but the benefit is that there is a shuttle bus to drop you off to and from campus, and walking typically takes about 10 minutes."

GUYS & GIRLS

Boys and Girls Behaviors...

"The guys and girls are well mannered overall, very friendly and sociable"

Great Friends to Find

"In city you're always bond to make a friend in any class."

HEALTH & SAFETY

Safe

"You will encounter a policeman at the every entrance of the building. Some seem to be not capable of running after a criminal, but they are sitting there checking everybody's student ID's. Their effort deserves A-"

Security

"well the security to an extent is tight..i def fell safe.."

LOOKING FOR MORE?

Check out our full-length guide to this school at collegeprowler.com/city-college-of-new-york/.

Claflin University

400 Magnolia St.; Orangeburg, SC 29115
(803) 535-5000; www.claflin.edu

THE BASICS:

Acceptance Rate: 36%
Yield: 32%
Setting: Town
Control: Private Non-Profit
Total Undergrads: 1,787
SAT Range: 800–990*
ACT Range: 15–18

Student-Faculty Ratio: 14:1
Retention Rate: 72%
Graduation Rate: 51%
Tuition: $12,666
Room & Board: $6,806
Avg. Aid Package: $13,367
Students With Aid: 95%

* of 1600

Academics	C+	Greek Life	A-
Athletics	C	Guys	B
Campus Dining	C	Health & Safety	C
Campus Housing	C+	Local Atmosphere	D+
Campus Strictness	D+	Nightlife	C
Computers	D+	Off-Campus Dining	C-
Diversity	C+	Off-Campus Housing	B-
Drug Safety	B-	Parking	B-
Facilities	C-	Transportation	D+
Girls	C+	Weather	C+

CP's Student Author On...
OVERALL EXPERIENCE

Claflin University sets itself apart by being a small, family-oriented campus—and you will notice this from the moment you first arrive here. Everyone, from the administrators to the maintenance staff, is always warm, welcoming, friendly, and ready to assist the students. It is very hard to make enemies at this school because everyone respects everyone else and where they came from. The students and faculty come from different backgrounds, yet that does not lead to segregation.

The people here possess genuine Southern hospitality, a trait that never gets old around campus, and everyone takes pride in the rich history they have become a part of at Claflin. Everyone is always focused on their academic success and achieving the desired "Claflin Confidence." The school constantly makes a personal effort to help students achieve all their goals by helping in whatever way they can. When you graduate from Claflin, you will not only leave with your diploma, but you will also leave with a wealth of great friendships and family bonds that you have made with others at the University. It truly is a rewarding experience.

Students Speak Out On...
OVERALL EXPERIENCE

Q Great School
"I absolutely love this place—it's very friendly, and they put an emphasis on academics, which most schools sometimes forget about."

Q Overall Experience
"As a freshman, I have enjoyed my first year at Claflin immensely. I exceeded my goals academically, socially, and artistically. I've made sure the right people know me as a poet. I'm making better grades that I made in high school. My group of friends is diverse and enjoyable to have around."

Q Best Decision I Have Made
"Claflin University is a great university. It has a caring atmosphere and the institution offers a lot of opportunities that are beneficial to the students' futures. The professors are also very helpful and great at building life skills to help the students with their future careers. If I could do it all over again I would still choose Claflin."

BEST OF CLAFLIN

1. Academics
2. Great student-teacher relationships
3. The small family-orientated campus
4. The Honors College
5. The warm, friendly atmosphere

Affordable
Tuition is only $12,666, one of the most affordable rates in the country.

WORST OF CLAFLIN

1. Visitation policy
2. No wireless Internet in the dorms or around campus
3. Same old food at the cafeteria
4. Lack of campus transportation
5. Too many rules on campus

Not Much Diversity
One of the least racially diverse campuses—only 7% of students are minorities.

Student Body

African American:	93%	Male Undergrads:	33%
Asian American:	0%	Female Undergrads:	67%
Hispanic:	0%	Living On Campus:	85%
International:	3%	Living Off Campus:	15%
Native American:	0%	Male Athletes:	20%
White:	1%	Female Athletes:	8%
Unknown:	2%	Fraternity Members:	6%
From Out-of-State:	24%	Sorority Members:	5%

Frequently Compared Schools:

Bob Jones University
Clemson University
College of Charleston
University of South Carolina

Students Speak Out On...
EVERYTHING!

ACADEMICS

My School

"Claflin University is a great school. The people are very friendly and helpful. The teachers make sure you know everything that is taught. If you don't get it in class, then you can have tutoring."

Great School in Christian Environment

"I came to Claflin because it's a great school in a christian environment. The professors are always there when you have a question and are willing to help when you need something."

ATHLETICS

No Football, Bring It on

"Claflin University does not have a football team! Alomst every student has came from a high school where football is the main sport to get fan involvement, but coming to Claflin, will tone the hypeness down. Basketball on the other hand is the only sport that attracts the most people. And the cheerleaders at the game are what gets the crowd coming. The cheerleaders battles other squad and sets the "Bring it On" scenery."

Athletic Panthers

"My school is very small therefore, we do not have a foot ballteam like most colleges. Our school would be alot popular if we had a football team. we do have a basket ball team. they are prety good. although i only been to one game. the students here at claflin do support our althetics department."

CAMPUS DINING

Food for the Panthers.

"The food at Claflin is very fair. They have different varities to choose from. They have a southern hospitality. Our Dinning hall could use a little bit more space. Sometimes there does not be enough room for all the students."

The Paw

"Needs to be open later. Needs a bigger variety of food."

CAMPUS HOUSING

College Life

"It's okay. The college life is an experience that one will never forget. The dorm is not home, but it's not all that bad. I love the social atmosphere."

Resident Experience

"I love Claflin University, and I look forward to giving back to it one day. I am an honors student and have never stayed in the freshman non-honors dorms. All of the dorms are nice. I know in my dorm there are giant bugs that like to lurk from time to time, but it's OK. I have easy access to computer labs, many lounges, laundry facilities, and maintenance is good. I'd rather stay in the honors dorm or the new dorms."

GUYS & GIRLS

Ladies and Guys Panthers

"I love the people at my school. They are so friendly and nice. I have not yet met a mean person ,and i do not plan on it. Most of the students dressed to impress which is a good thing. The girls here where heals almost every day."

Attire

"The men and women at Claflin University are held to a very high standard."

HEALTH & SAFETY

We Are the Best

"Claflin University is one of the most secure campuses when it come to college life. The health services provided here get you the proper attention needed when an injury occurs."

Overall Safety

"Seeing how there is security at both the exit and entrance of the school, as well as always around campus, and they're easily accessible, I must say that I feel really safe on campus. It is not a big campus either, so the enclosed feature that it provides is comforting"

LOOKING FOR MORE?

Check out our full-length guide to this school at collegeprowler.com/claflin-university/.

Claremont McKenna College

500 E. Ninth St.; Claremont, CA 91711
(909) 621-8000; www.claremontmckenna.edu

THE BASICS:

Acceptance Rate: 16%	**Student-Faculty Ratio:** 9:1
Yield: 40%	**Retention Rate:** 94%
Setting: Suburban	**Graduation Rate:** 94%
Control: Private Non-Profit	**Tuition:** $38,510
Total Undergrads: 1,210	**Room & Board:** $12,524
SAT Range: 1920–2220*	**Avg. Aid Package:** $32,151
ACT Range: 29–33	**Students With Aid:** 57%

* of 2400

Academics	A+	Greek Life	N/A
Athletics	C+	Guys	A+
Campus Dining	A+	Health & Safety	B+
Campus Housing	A+	Local Atmosphere	B-
Campus Strictness	A+	Nightlife	B-
Computers	A-	Off-Campus Dining	B
Diversity	B+	Off-Campus Housing	B-
Drug Safety	C	Parking	B+
Facilities	B-	Transportation	B-
Girls	A-	Weather	A

CP's Student Author On...
OVERALL EXPERIENCE

The overall experience for most people at CMC is positive—provided they know what they are getting into. CMC is truly a unique school: this quality makes it heaven for some and extremely limiting and frustrating for others. CMC is not a liberal arts school; it's a preprofessional school with a lot of general education requirements.

While technically you can major in something "liberal artsy" such as literature or history, CMC students are constantly thinking about jobs and their future and mostly stick to government and economics. Haters and lovers alike are happy with their professors and classes at CMC; professors are dedicated to teaching and truly want their students to work hard and challenge themselves. For the most part, if you can't find a class or an activity at CMC, you can head over to one of the other 5Cs. That said, anyone interested in the arts or music should be aware that CMC has no art/music program of any sort, and it can be difficult to get into these classes on others campuses.

CMC students like to have fun. But, for them, having fun involves talking about the economy and a keg.... For the rest of this editorial, visit collegeprowler.com.

Students Speak Out On...
OVERALL EXPERIENCE

ℚ Heaven on Earth
"I love it here. The classes are very tough, but I am learning a ton and I feel myself learning also from all of the worldly insight all of my classmates bring to campus. The social scene is amazing and there is always a party if you are looking for one."

ℚ I LOVE IT HERE
"There truly is no other place like CMC. It's everything I wanted in a school, and it's small enough to feel like a real community. PLUS, I have access to the other Claremont Colleges. It's a truly unique place, and it's the perfect fit for me!"

ℚ Study Hard, Play Hard
"College life at CMC is definitely unique. There are so many bright individuals surrounding you, as it should be, and although viewpoints might run the same way it is still a very open atmosphere where everyone seems to get along. You study all the time Sun-Wed, but once Thursday hits it's on! Make sure to put your drink in a red cup!"

BEST OF CLAREMONT MCKENNA

1. The Athenaeum
2. The professors
3. Parties like Monte Carlo, Superheroes, and the Toga Party
4. WOA! trips
5. Being able to leave your door unlocked 24/7

Happy Students
94% of students return after their first year.

Commitment to Teaching
There are 9 students for every member of faculty on campus.

WORST OF CLAREMONT MCKENNA

1. Small size
2. Story House is OCD about furniture outside.
3. The "fight" song
4. Transportation without a car
5. People seem to get away with just about everything.

Expensive
Tuition is a steep $38,510, one of the most expensive rates in the country.

Expensive Dorms
Living on campus doesn't come cheap, with an average housing price tag of $6,470.

Student Body

African American:	4%	Male Undergrads:	54%
Asian American:	12%	Female Undergrads:	46%
Hispanic:	11%	Living On Campus:	98%
International:	6%	Living Off Campus:	2%
Native American:	0%	Male Athletes:	45%
White:	50%	Female Athletes:	44%
Unknown:	16%	Fraternity Members:	0%
From Out-of-State:	64%	Sorority Members:	0%

Frequently Compared Schools:

Occidental College
Pitzer College
Pomona College
Stanford University

Students Speak Out On... EVERYTHING!

ACADEMICS

Academics

"Academics here at CMC are top-notch. With a very low teacher to student ratio, there is much attention given to each individual to make sure they understand the material and don't struggle. Every professor has lots of office hours where they are always more than happy to give extra help to anyone who wants it. The academics are challenging, but the professors and support network available make it beyond manageable."

Excellent

"Some of the professors are AMAZING, and the academics are challenging but do not overwhelm you with work. In freshman year, most people complete GE's, but you can still register for one or two interesting classes before they fill up. After the first year, people start specialising to their major more and you can usually get what you want, I think. I have heard that the study abroad programs are life-changing."

ATHLETICS

Familiar Faces

"The best thing about CMS Athletics (besides constantly beating our arch-rivals, Pomona-Pitzer), is that you know everyone who's playing. Sure, the games aren't like D-1 games, especially skillwise and the fan support isn't incredible, but you'd go to any game and see your friend playing or realize something like "Woah... I had Lit 10 with the point guard!" For me, that beats any D-1 school."

The sports teams are strong here

"Athletic teams at CMC include students from Scripps and Harvey Mudd, however most of the athletes come from CMC. Sports are a big time commitment for athletes and are very strong for a D3 school. Football resembles that of a high school squad, so don't expect much school spirit at games besides those against rival Pomona-Pitzer. That said, soccer and basketball are highly competitive and popular to watch."

CAMPUS DINING

Food Is Amazing

"There is something for everyone. Lots of fresh fruits and vegetables, as well as delicious pizza, sandwich and salad bars, grilled food, soup, comfort food, fried food, vegan options, and a variety of dessert options. And free snack Mon-thurs with fruit, toast, peanut butter, icecream, and something warm (ex: mozarella sticks, waffles)"

Food Is Fantastic!

"One of the best things about our dining is we can eat at any of the seven dining halls on the Claremont Colleges campuses, for a meal each. The food is done by a catering service, so it's not gross cafeteria food. Because of the multiple locations, there's something for everyone! Personally, I love the food at Scripps, CMC, and Frary (Pomona). CMC also has excellent vegetarian and vegan options!"

CAMPUS HOUSING

Always Things Happening

"Dorms are great! we even have a brand new eco-friendly dorm. However, the best part is the community. Living in the dorms you meet tons of people and you will actually hang out with them and go around campus on thursday-saturday nights to see whats happening. Stuff is always going on and its great!"

Flippin' Awesome

"We have maids. They clean our room. They don't care if there's a bong on the floor. They will clean around you if you are passed out. That is all."

GUYS & GIRLS

Guys and Girls Are Great

"Good looks, Like to party, Like to work hard. Super nice."

HEALTH & SAFETY

Superb Health & Safety

"Campus Safety will give you a ride to your dorm whenever & wherever. They do not overcrowd the campus but they do there jobs very efficiently."

LOOKING FOR MORE?

Check out our full-length guide to this school at collegeprowler.com/claremont-mckenna-college/.

Clark Atlanta University

223 James P. Brawley Drive SW; Atlanta, GA 30314
(404) 880-8000; www.cau.edu

THE BASICS:

Acceptance Rate: 59%	**Student-Faculty Ratio:** 17:1
Yield: 18%	**Retention Rate:** 65%
Setting: Large city	**Graduation Rate:** 45%
Control: Private Non-Profit	**Tuition:** $17,038
Total Undergrads: 3,202	**Room & Board:** $7,192
SAT Range: 810–950*	**Avg. Aid Package:** $10,935
ACT Range: 18–20	**Students With Aid:** 89%

* of 2400

Academics	C	Greek Life	A-
Athletics	B-	Guys	A+
Campus Dining	B-	Health & Safety	C-
Campus Housing	B-	Local Atmosphere	A-
Campus Strictness	C	Nightlife	A
Computers	B	Off-Campus Dining	B-
Diversity	C+	Off-Campus Housing	B
Drug Safety	B	Parking	B-
Facilities	B	Transportation	A-
Girls	B+	Weather	C+

CP's Student Author On...
OVERALL EXPERIENCE

The experience that Clark Atlanta University provides its students is one that is incomparable to any other institution of higher learning. Atlanta is arguably the greatest city for successful African Americans (past and present), and that in itself makes Clark Atlanta University one of the best Historically Black Universities to attend in the U.S. Clark Atlanta has also succeeded in producing some of the top leaders in almost every aspect of the business and social world. The professors are great at teaching in their fields of knowledge, but they're even better at giving life lessons that promote self-esteem, pride, and a sense of belonging. The social bonding that occurs during the matriculation at Clark Atlanta is like no other, and many students find their lifetime friends and significant others while attending Clark.

With all the positive things that can be said about Clark, there is definitely room for growth within this great institution. Patience and organization are two skills that students and parents must hone before they even consider making Clark Atlanta University an option.... For the rest of this editorial, visit collegeprowler.com.

Students Speak Out On...
OVERALL EXPERIENCE

Q WONDERFUL!

"While our institution is not perfect, I absolutely love it here. The professors seem to care about your education and future. The pride in our school is alive. I love hanging out with my friends around the campus and socializing among my peers. My favorite event is Homecoming. During this week there are so many activities to take part in and show our school spirit. In addition, there are many event that you can go to during the year that are informative and fun."

Q Flaws and All

"Clark Atlanta University is a wonderful institution. The teachers are very hands on and I love the school spirit. However, I don't feel as safe as I should being so far from home. The campus isn't a closed off facility ,therefore theres a lot of robberies that take place. If I had to choose I would leave Clark because I'm not safe and my life is very important."

Q Social Life

"mainly meeting the new people on campus has been the best part."

BEST OF CLARK ATLANTA

1. Atlanta
2. Clark Atlanta University pride
3. Developing lifetime friendships
4. School of Business
5. Homecoming events
6. The Strip

Big Dorms
50% of students surveyed felt that dorms were more spacious than average.

Strong Alumni Network
57% of students surveyed said the alumni network is very strong and involved in activities on campus.

WORST OF CLARK ATLANTA

1. Administration
2. Low participation in sporting events
3. On-campus food
4. Male-to-female ratio
5. Sophomores must live on campus
6. Parking

Not Much Diversity
One of the least racially diverse campuses—only 11% of students are minorities.

Student Body

African American:	89%	Male Undergrads:	27%
Asian American:	0%	Female Undergrads:	73%
Hispanic:	0%	Living On Campus:	27%
International:	1%	Living Off Campus:	73%
Native American:	0%	Male Athletes:	14%
White:	0%	Female Athletes:	3%
Unknown:	10%	Fraternity Members:	2%
From Out-of-State:	74%	Sorority Members:	3%

Frequently Compared Schools:

Emory University
Georgia Institute of Technology
Howard University
Spelman College

Students Speak Out On... EVERYTHING!

ACADEMICS

A Wealth of Info

"The professors care about your future and do all they can, going above and beyond to help you where they can."

Fashion Design

"Looking forward to great opportunities for fashion, design and marketing once classes are taken here. Presently in high school."

Professors

"I came to Clark Atlanta University because it is a Historically Black College in Atlanta, Georgia. The professors i get assigned to always make sure you pass. They actually care about your feelings and they are always available for help."

ATHLETICS

School Spirit Is Great

"pretty much all student own cau gear and most students wear it on a normal baisi"

SPORTS

"WE HAVE A VARIETY OF SPORTS HERE AT CAU.I WOULD HAVE TO SAY THE MOST LIKED SPORT HERE IS BASKETBALL."

Sports at CAU Is the Bomb

"Sports at CAU are a big deal, especially football and basket ball. The support is great not only from the faculty but the student body as well. To ecourange sporting activities, the school's president and other important faculty support by attending games and taking fotos with the atletes. The school spirit is seen everyday on campus even if we dont have a game. We just love the CAU Panthers!! Red, Black and Grey is the way to go."

CAMPUS DINING

Its Okay, Could Be Better

"Most of the food is great, if you like eating the same thing over, and over, and over.. there are not enough seats in the dinning area on wednesdays, fried chicken day. but the staff is nice, and with the platnum meal plan u can eat all day."

Food

"The Food is ok.Its way better than high school food but it could use some improvement."

Needs More of a Variety

"I would love if there was more "home cooked meals" type of food."

CAMPUS HOUSING

Clark Campus

"The freshman dorms at Clark Atlanta University are great."

Suite Life!

"Suite Life is the best life. There's a co-ed side and all girls side. Comes with microwave and mini fridge, counter space, sink, private bathroom shared with 3 others. divider wall so own private area. If not Merner hall is best for females, Pheiffer for males."

GUYS & GIRLS

Classmates

"The students on campus are really helpful they are all their for the same reason that I am and that is to get a education and get out of school."

Student Attire

"A lot of the students on campus are bringing back the 80's retro style. Leggings, skinny jeans, Spike Lee glasses, etc. The girls are even bringing the big colorful hair back."

HEALTH & SAFETY

Police and Safety Services

"Public Safety and Clark Atlanta Police are always there when you need them. They are available 24 hours a day and are always at your service."

Safety on Campus

"theres security in every building"

LOOKING FOR MORE?

Check out our full-length guide to this school at collegeprowler.com/clark-atlanta-university/.

Clark University

950 Main St.; Worcester, MA 01610
(508) 793-7711; www.clarku.edu

THE BASICS:

Acceptance Rate: 69%	Student-Faculty Ratio: 10:1
Yield: 21%	Retention Rate: 88%
Setting: Mid-sized city	Graduation Rate: 73%
Control: Private Non-Profit	Tuition: $36,100
Total Undergrads: 2,220	Room & Board: $6,950
SAT Range: 1100–1330*	Avg. Aid Package: $24,581
ACT Range: 24–30	Students With Aid: 85%

* of 1600

Academics	B+	Greek Life	N/A
Athletics	D+	Guys	C-
Campus Dining	C	Health & Safety	B-
Campus Housing	B	Local Atmosphere	C+
Campus Strictness	B	Nightlife	C+
Computers	B+	Off-Campus Dining	B+
Diversity	C	Off-Campus Housing	C
Drug Safety	B-	Parking	B
Facilities	C+	Transportation	B-
Girls	B-	Weather	C-

CP's Student Author On...
OVERALL EXPERIENCE

The students say it best: Clark is a great place to spend four important—perhaps the most important—years of your life. Those who go to Clark report being glad they went. They say that they learned what they wanted to learn in their major, had a lot of fun, and grew up in the process. No campus is perfect, but despite Clark's flaws, students still manage to fall in love with it and pursue their degrees until the end. Clark's strengths lie in its academics, its community, and the city in which it resides. Even though that same city gives rise to some of Clark's largest problems, it also exemplifies the diversity that Clark strives to provide for its students on campus. The city's restaurants also provide a welcome escape from Clark's dreadful meal plan!

Although Clark suffers from a poor social scene, low enthusiasm for organized sports, New England weather, and the double-edged sword of apathy and tolerance, Clarkies leave the school realizing that they have just lived through an incredible academic and social experience.... For the rest of this editorial, visit collegeprowler.com.

Students Speak Out On...
OVERALL EXPERIENCE

Q Clark Is the Best!

"I think Clark is quite possibly the very best school of all time. If it is the right place for you, there is no way you won't have the time of your life. I love the liberal, accepting, and academically challenging environment. I also love spending my days doing school work on our beautiful green with my very best friends. It is hard to imagine my life without this school."

Q Sciences at Clark

"Clark's offerings in the natural sciences are surprisingly good for a small school. Clark has 5th year (Accelerated Bachelors/Master's programs) in Biology, Physics, Chemistry and Environmental Science. All of these programs are free if the student receives at least a 3.00 in their undergraduate major. Clark students can easily do research in preparation for graduate programs given the small size of the University."

BEST OF CLARK UNIVERSITY

1. Clarkies
2. Spree Day
3. Professors
4. Freshman dorms
5. Diversity
6. Local atmosphere
7. Proximity to Boston and Providence

Happy Students
88% of students return after their first year.

Commitment to Teaching
There are 10 students for every member of faculty on campus.

WORST OF CLARK UNIVERSITY

1. Construction noise
2. Worcester winters
3. On-campus food
4. Living in Main South
5. The JC-Sackler wind tunnel
6. 9 a.m. classes
7. Friday classes

Expensive
Tuition is a steep $36,100, one of the most expensive rates in the country.

Student Body

African American:	2%	Male Undergrads:	41%
Asian American:	5%	Female Undergrads:	59%
Hispanic:	3%	Living On Campus:	74%
International:	8%	Living Off Campus:	26%
Native American:	0%	Male Athletes:	19%
White:	67%	Female Athletes:	12%
Unknown:	16%	Fraternity Members:	0%
From Out-of-State:	63%	Sorority Members:	0%

Frequently Compared Schools:

Boston University
Brandeis University
Connecticut College
Northeastern University

Students Speak Out On... EVERYTHING!

ACADEMICS

Psychology Is a Big Major

"Most people at Clark are really into social sciences and psychology, but we still have great programs for the sciences and arts, as well as many others. All of our professors have been out in the field of work, and almost all of them have worked with graduate and undergraduate students in research and writing published papers. So far, I feel very lucky to be able to have a professor who knows exactly what they are doing and how to succeed at their careers."

Environmental Science

"Science majors are pretty common at Clark, but it's still not a science school. Professors are extremely knowledgeable, and you will be blown away by how much you can learn from them if you really want to."

ATHLETICS

Get Less Respect Than They Deserve

"The sports teams here are dedicated and motivated. They earn far less respect or attention than they deserve."

Athletics...Wow.

"The athletics at Clark are really good, but nobody ever really goes to the games unless one of our friends is on the team. We are not the greatest, but everybody is really proud of what they do. We have minimal school spirit for teams, but we do support them. I really like our swim team, but I hate the lacrosse team because all the laxbros are kind of stuck up. We have almost every sport except for football, but nobody really cares because we like our school anyways."

CAMPUS DINING

Options

"Even though there are only three places to eat on our campus, I always feel like I have a multitude of options to choose from, and none of them suck. I think the best place to eat is Higgins Cafe. You can sit there all day and eat buffet style until your heart is content. It opens super early and it doesn't cloes until 8:00. They also have the best vegetarian/ healthy options and the salad bar is open from morning to night."

Food is great

"The review is completely off from what I see in the Caf. There's lots for us vegans, including our own vegan section with beans and whole grains. The food is made from scratch and is usually good. Also, the hours for the caf aren't even right on College Prowler. You're better off going to the caf's own website for information. clarkdining.com"

CAMPUS HOUSING

Good Housing Overall, Some Outdated Buildings.

"Overall the housing is good. The rooms are all a decent size for a college dorm, have wireless and cable, and since it's such a small campus nowhere is necessarily inconvenient to live. The dorms by the street like Wright can get noisy and only Blackstone has elevators, which is really annoying when moving. Laundry rooms are also inconveniently located."

GUYS & GIRLS

Decent

"When it comes to boy girl relationships, Clark isn't so bad. In my opinion, the population isn't bad looking at all, lots of cuties here, and there are lots of cool people on campus. Lots of people are involved in the music scene, so if you're into that, come here. Lots of hipsters and indie kids. A lot of people here are unique in personality, intelligent, and talented. Like any school, there's lots of hooking up, but plenty of people are in relationships as well."

HEALTH & SAFETY

Reasonably Safe/ Improving

"Clark is trying to improve the safety of the neighborhood. However it is still somewhat unsafe off campus. There are frequent "timely warnings" about potential threats. The UP and student EMS are always on campus. Like everywhere, you have to be aware of your surroundings."

LOOKING FOR MORE?

Check out our full-length guide to this school at collegeprowler.com/clark-university/.

Clemson University

201 Sikes Hall; Clemson, SC 29634
(864) 656-4636; www.clemson.edu

THE BASICS:

Acceptance Rate: 58%	**Student-Faculty Ratio:** 16:1
Yield: 36%	**Retention Rate:** 90%
Setting: Town	**Graduation Rate:** 79%
Control: Public	**Tuition:** $25,388
Total Undergrads: 15,291	**Room & Board:** $6,774
SAT Range: 1670–1960*	**Avg. Aid Package:** $10,057
ACT Range: 25–30	**Students With Aid:** 90%

* of 2400

Academics	B+	Greek Life	B
Athletics	A	Guys	A+
Campus Dining	B-	Health & Safety	B
Campus Housing	B	Local Atmosphere	B
Campus Strictness	B	Nightlife	A-
Computers	B+	Off-Campus Dining	A-
Diversity	C-	Off-Campus Housing	A+
Drug Safety	C-	Parking	B
Facilities	B	Transportation	A
Girls	A+	Weather	B

CP's Student Author On...
OVERALL EXPERIENCE

Clemson offers an amazing college experience. Students return for the rest of their lives to see how the campus has changed and to support the Tigers. Although it is located in a small town, the school is big enough that there is never a dull moment, and the location only makes the student body closer to one another. As anyone who has been to Clemson knows, the students' blood here is orange, and the Clemson spirit is contagious for almost anyone who attends.

Students Speak Out On...
OVERALL EXPERIENCE

It's Incredibly Amazing

"Clemson University boasts one of the most friendly and fun campuses in the United States. Everyone at our school shares a family bond that helps us succeed in any situation. Everyone is serious about their education here, while still continuing to have a great time!"

Greek Life and Academics

"Social life is excellent everyone is willing to help anyone get the best grades possible especially instructors. They absolutely just want the best for you!"

A Dream Come True

"Being from far, far away I had no idea what to expect and was a little insecure when I arrived at Clemson, but now I couldn't see myself anywhere else. I have made so many great friends and grown up a lot as a person. Everything about Clemson makes me proud. Proud to wear orange, proud to be a Tiger."

Beautiful Place

"I love the campus, I visited several and Clemson had by far the best. The school does a great job maintaining the campus. The atmosphere on gamedays in amazing."

BEST OF CLEMSON

1. Football Season
2. School Spirit
3. Friendliness of the town
4. Sense of pride and happiness
5. Eye candy
6. Greek Parties
7. Safety

Happy Students
90% of students return after their first year.

Proven Success
79% of students will complete their education and graduate with a degree.

WORST OF CLEMSON

1. Lack of Parking
2. Lack of Diversity
3. Harsh Parking Services
4. Distance from big cities
5. Small town atmosphere
6. No alcohol served on Sundays
7. Rednecks

Lowest Grades
Drug Safety: C-
Diversity: C-
Campus Dining: B-

Student Body

African American:	7%	Male Undergrads:	54%
Asian American:	2%	Female Undergrads:	46%
Hispanic:	1%	Living On Campus:	47%
International:	1%	Living Off Campus:	58%
Native American:	0%	Male Athletes:	4%
White:	81%	Female Athletes:	4%
Unknown:	7%	Fraternity Members:	17%
From Out-of-State:	40%	Sorority Members:	31%

Frequently Compared Schools:
Auburn University
University of Georgia
University of North Carolina
University of South Carolina

Students Speak Out On...
EVERYTHING!

ACADEMICS

Q Amazing
"Excellent educational experience. Professors are willing to help and you will learn at Clemson!"

Q Extra Help Available When Needed
"The thing that I like about Clemson is that they have extra help and tutors available all over, ranging from the library to SI instructors in special classrooms after hours."

ATHLETICS

Q Southern Football
"Clemson is in the south. Football is huge. On gamedays, the population of this rural college town triples. On these days, you'll fully experience the legendary Clemson spirit. Clemson also has basketball, baseball, rowing, swimming, volleyball, and several inter mural sports that any student can play. These range from ultimate frisbee, to flag football, to even field hockey."

Q Ain't Nothing Better
"Clemson was rated the #1 for Jock School by Princeton Review and it is no wonder why since we have good sports teams across the board! Of course Clemson football is a fan favorite and the day of a game Clemson is packed with people. We do have the most exciting 25 seconds in college football when the Tigers run down "the hill". Other big sports are basketball, baseball, and soccer."

CAMPUS DINING

Q Clemson Dining
"Great variety of good-tasting and healthy choices."

Q It's Pretty Good
"I'd say it's pretty good. They just don't stay open long enough. Thats my only complaint."

CAMPUS HOUSING

Q Freshman Dorms Are Great!
"and upperclassmen dorms are even better (especially the apartments)"

Q Love
"I loved the dorms at Clemson, not beautiful but they weren't very strict and if they were it is easy to get around the rules, standard dorms as in small but the girls bathrooms were always clean."

GUYS & GIRLS

Q Be Ready for Good Options
"The guys at Clemson have a reputation for being hot, and they definitely live up to that. There's every kind of guy here: the frat boys, the christian guys, the surfers, the country boys, the adventurers, and every other walk of life. No matter who you are, there's a match for you at Clemson. There's nothing better than a cute southern boy from Clemson!"

Q Fun
"There are many parties on campus and around campus. All race interact with each other peacefully. Everyone gathers for big events such as sports, theatre, and arts."

HEALTH & SAFETY

Q Safety & Security at Clemson
"I have never felt unsafe at any time (night, morning, during the day) on campus."

Q Health and Safety
"The health and safety of the students at Clemson is taken very seriously. The Student Health Center sends out notifications the very SECOND a virus could be likely to spread, or if there is some sort air contamination,etc. The police department also sends out TEXT alerts if there is a crime, an incident or anything type of event that jeopardizes the safety of students."

LOOKING FOR MORE?
Check out our full-length guide to this school at collegeprowler.com/clemson-university/.

Cleveland State University

2121 Euclid Ave.; Cleveland, OH 44115
(216) 687-2000; www.csuohio.edu

THE BASICS:

Acceptance Rate: 64%	**Student-Faculty Ratio:** 16:1
Yield: 40%	**Retention Rate:** 66%
Setting: Large city	**Graduation Rate:** 26%
Control: Public	**Tuition:** $10,713
Total Undergrads: 9,808	**Room & Board:** $9,230
SAT Range: 840–1120*	**Avg. Aid Package:** $8,565
ACT Range: 18–23	**Students With Aid:** 86%

* of 1600

Academics	C+	Greek Life	C+
Athletics	B-	Guys	B+
Campus Dining	B+	Health & Safety	C+
Campus Housing	B+	Local Atmosphere	B+
Campus Strictness	B	Nightlife	B
Computers	B	Off-Campus Dining	B
Diversity	B-	Off-Campus Housing	B+
Drug Safety	C+	Parking	B
Facilities	B	Transportation	B+
Girls	A-	Weather	B-

CP's Student Author On...
OVERALL EXPERIENCE

Cleveland State's motto is "the city is our campus" and with a setting like this, how can a student not enjoy all it has to offer? The city opens doors to many opportunities. No matter what major you are, the teachers are personable and easy to build a rapport with, and, most importantly, they help students gain a better understanding of the real world. With 16,000 students, you get all of the advantages of both large and small campuses, which is hard to find at other schools. The size of the classes helps students better understand the material and makes it easier to become knowledgeable in their desired areas. The city provides plenty of learning experiences that cannot be found at many other colleges.

The majority of students at Cleveland State will probably find a reason to complain about something that has taken place on campus, but the majority of those students, when asked, said they would pick CSU all over again.... For the rest of this editorial, visit collegeprowler.com.

Students Speak Out On...
OVERALL EXPERIENCE

Q Overall Experience
"Love the atmosphere, alot of good caring people, coaches are wonderful and education is very important. I have made so many great friendships!!"

Q Wouldn't Choose Anywhere Else
"A lot of people I know don't give Cleveland State enough credit. It's an amazing facility, and I'm glad I made the decision to go there. The price of tuition is so low compared to other colleges, and I can guarantee you get just as much if not more than one would get elsewhere. The education is outstanding in most cases. Nothing's perfect, but CSU comes pretty close."

Q Everything I've Hoped For
"My overall experience at school has been everything I have pretty much hoped for. Some weekends aren't as great as others, but my roommate and I definitely make fun out of any situation. It's a good time and I love being at school."

BEST OF CLEVELAND STATE

1. The dorms, which are like mini apartments
2. The downtown atmosphere and being in the city
3. The professional sports teams, including the Cleveland Cavaliers, Indians, and Browns

Affordable
Tuition is only $10,713, one of the most affordable rates in the country.

Knowledgeable Professors
91% of students surveyed rated the general knowledge of professors as above average.

WORST OF CLEVELAND STATE

1. Parking
2. The lack of fun that occurs on the weekends for students under 21
3. Dorm rules
4. The school comes with the "Cleveland stigma" attached to it.

Not Everyone Graduates
26% of students do not complete their education or graduate with a degree.

Expensive Dorms
Living on campus doesn't come cheap, with an average housing price tag of $6,700.

Student Body

African American:	20%	Male Undergrads:	44%
Asian American:	3%	Female Undergrads:	56%
Hispanic:	3%	Living On Campus:	8%
International:	3%	Living Off Campus:	92%
Native American:	0%	Male Athletes:	5%
White:	61%	Female Athletes:	3%
Unknown:	9%	Fraternity Members:	1%
From Out-of-State:	6%	Sorority Members:	1%

Frequently Compared Schools:
Case Western Reserve University
Kent State University
Ohio State University
Ohio University

Students Speak Out On...
EVERYTHING!

ACADEMICS

Cleveland State University Curriculum
"The Cleveland State University Curriculums are wonderful chances to enter new programs and meet new people."

Academics at CSU
"I am very pleased with the registration process at Cleveland State University. It is very easy. The professors seem very concerned about graduating capable, well-rounded students. The workload can seem a little heavy at times, but then again, it is graduate school."

Active Learning
"I chose Cleveland State for my undergraduate degree because they encourage students to activly learn by having class discussions, asking questions and because of its convinent downtown location. Going to class seams more like fun and less like work in most classes, regardless of the size. The professors are friendly and open. Also I liked that they had a very strong health science department, and that they have a Occupational Therapy masters program."

ATHLETICS

CSU Althletes
"If there is one thing CSU has plenty of, it's athletes. The school is filled with hundreds of athletes. All of the teams take great pride in their sport and consider it their second job. They also always sport their team jerseys."

Varsity and IM Sports Are Entertaining
"Varsity sports and IM sports at Cleveland State are entertaining. You can relax and have fun without having many worries. IM sports are a good choice when you and all of your friends want to have some fun."

CAMPUS DINING

Dining at Cleveland State Is Excellent
"There is plenty of variety for dining at CSU. Many options are available, and the quality is great."

Food and Dining
"Dining on campus is pretty good. There's Viking dining hall, Fenn Shoppe, Midway and Rascal House. You can either use a meal swipe or your dining dollars to buy food. Fenn Shoppe is personally my favorite, and Viking is usually really good, too."

CAMPUS HOUSING

Fenn Tower!
"They look like mini apartments! They are awesome if you get the quads. kinda pricey though."

Housing is amazing
"The dorms at CSU are amazing. They're really big and everyone gets their own bathroom no matter where you live. It's really nice to not have to worry about using a public bathroom. New dorms are currently being built, and they're just like apartments, which is going to be a great place to live."

GUYS & GIRLS

Guys & Girls
"Majority decent looking guys and girls on and off campus."

Cleveland State University Social Life
"Cleveland State University tries very hard to acknowledge social life, curriculums and interests."

HEALTH & SAFETY

Safe
"There are a lot of homeless people in downtown, but CSU has many cops that are on duty all of the time. They also offer an escort service for people at night walking to their cars. I feel safe walking on campus."

No Worries.
"The only problem that you may run into at CSU is the homeless. Just don't adop a homeless person as your new roommate."

LOOKING FOR MORE?
Check out our full-length guide to this school at collegeprowler.com/cleveland-state-university/.

Coe College

1220 First Ave. NE; Cedar Rapids, IA 52402
(319) 399-8500; www.coe.edu

THE BASICS:

Acceptance Rate: 62%	**Student-Faculty Ratio:** 11:1
Yield: 22%	**Retention Rate:** 83%
Setting: Mid-sized city	**Graduation Rate:** 70%
Control: Private Non-Profit	**Tuition:** $29,270
Total Undergrads: 1,287	**Room & Board:** $7,150
SAT Range: 1608–1888*	**Avg. Aid Package:** $27,000
ACT Range: 23–28	**Students With Aid:** 100%

* of 2400

This School Isn't Graded Yet!

College Prowler grades are calculated using tons of criteria, including survey responses that come from students at this school.

Unfortunately, we haven't gathered enough student surveys yet for this school to be able to calculate the grades for each section. Stay tuned to *CollegeProwler.com* for grade updates and more!

CP's Student Author On...
OVERALL EXPERIENCE

Students who consider academics their main priority will not regret attending Coe. The importance of getting an education often outweighs the prominence of a student's social life, and it is totally up to the student to balance both of these aspects. For many students, their first day of Coe College started with a speech from the school's President, which discussed the essence of having a sound education in writing, critical thinking, and speaking ability. Over the course of four years, students develop these skills, both inside and outside of the classroom. Generally, the liberal arts education students receive at Coe prepares students to work in their desired field after graduation. However, it is of no surprise to see an accounting major working for a health camp in the Peace Corps—you sometimes end up where you least expected to be!

The only reason to ever reconsider Coe would be its location; the small areas of the school and the city are probably the worst of what Coe has to offer. Cedar Rapids is not the best place to be in the United States, but Coe College's good blend of other necessary factors overshadows the darker aspect of the Midwestern region.

Students Speak Out On...
OVERALL EXPERIENCE

Q Nice

"Students are always yearning to learn something new."

Q Best Value

"The whole college experience is worth the money you pay."

Q Valuable Experience

"College experience at Coe provides a great life-time learning experience."

Q Small School With Good Reputation

"The school is small with relatively small student body. This makes a student body more like a family!"

Q Starting to Fit

"So far I have gotten a great education at Coe and have met some wonderful people. I somewhat wish I would have looked at other colleges, but I am beginning to find my place at Coe. There are lots of people for everyone and academics for everyone as well."

BEST OF COE

1. The College appreciates diversity and does provide a good platform for the minorities.
2. Small and friendly community
3. It's easy to approach faculty and administration.
4. Flunk Day

Happy Students
83% of students return after their first year.

Proven Success
70% of students will complete their education and graduate with a degree.

WORST OF COE

1. School spirit among students is missing.
2. Small campus area
3. Surrounding community can be unsafe.
4. Expensive cost of living
5. There's a lot of on-campus drama that's similar to high school.

Expensive
Tuition is a steep $29,270, one of the most expensive rates in the country.

Want a Job? On Your Own
There aren't any placement services for graduates.

Student Body

African American:	2%	Male Undergrads:	46%
Asian American:	1%	Female Undergrads:	54%
Hispanic:	2%	Living On Campus:	84%
International:	4%	Living Off Campus:	16%
Native American:	0%	Male Athletes:	53%
White:	85%	Female Athletes:	21%
Unknown:	4%	Fraternity Members:	25%
From Out-of-State:	43%	Sorority Members:	20%

Frequently Compared Schools:

Clarke College
Cornell College
Grinnell College
University of Iowa

Students Speak Out On... EVERYTHING!

ACADEMICS

Good Liberal Arts Education
"Coe offers many different types of courses, and all are well-instructed. I know my teachers on an out-of-class level, and they are incredibly willing to work with their students. The work is challenging but fitting; it is not unbearable or incredibly simple."

Talented Faculty
"The whole faculty body is really helpful and supportive of the students. They help students both in and out of the class. The best quality is that they don't show partiality towards any student or differentiate anyone."

Practicality on All the Subjects
"The academics of the school is fairly strong and the students are encouraged to work by various methods. In my personal experience I was asked to make a video for economics on one topic towards the end of the course. This adds depth to the whole education experience."

ATHLETICS

Swim Team Is Awesom
"Swimming was great to be part of a co-ed swim team and travel to competitions. The coaches are very supportive and everyone has a great time together. The pressure is not as intense and academics are still the first priority."

Prime Importance
"Many students. including myself, are involved in one or the other athletics. The students respect their football team and the team in return does its effort to bring the glory on the faces of the students."

Not as Big a Part
"The athletics is just a casual participation and part of college."

CAMPUS DINING

Varies
"The cafe is full of variety of food. However, the standard food that is available lacks variety over the weeks, especially on weekends when the food served is almost the same and also has a bad taste."

Oh Sudexo.. You Are Interesting
"We don't have the best food, but it isn't bad either. The rice (which is served at EVERY meal) has no taste and some of the meat is dry. It's pretty decent over all though."

CAMPUS HOUSING

There's Plenty to Do on Campus
"Even though Coe is a small school it is amazingly diverse, economically and socially. You can always find a group with similar interests. Also has that mid-western friendliness."

Good
"Students living in dorms have to take the campus meal plans. This doesnt apply to students who live in the campus apartments."

GUYS & GIRLS

Boring
"Most of the students are average and the more good looking of students, both girls and guys, are internationals."

Not Impressive
"I hardly see anyone attractive. Also, those who are good looking are holding on a relationship with student outside of campus and also long distant relationships."

HEALTH & SAFETY

Best Years of My Life
"I learned so much, made life-long friends, and still go back for Homecoming at every other year. The Professors are superb, always available and take great pride in their students' successes."

Very Safe
"No worries. Small town atmosphere. Security does a great job of keeping us updated as to any concerns."

LOOKING FOR MORE?

Check out our full-length guide to this school at collegeprowler.com/coe-college/.

Colby College

4000 Mayflower Hill Drive; Waterville, ME 04901
(207) 859-4000; www.colby.edu

THE BASICS:

Acceptance Rate: 34%	**Student-Faculty Ratio:** 10:1
Yield: 31%	**Retention Rate:** 94%
Setting: Town	**Graduation Rate:** 90%
Control: Private Non-Profit	**Tuition:** $50,320
Total Undergrads: 1,838	**Room & Board:** $0
SAT Range: 1900–2150*	**Avg. Aid Package:** $32,252
ACT Range: 28–31	**Students With Aid:** 52%

* of 2400

Academics	A	Greek Life	N/A
Athletics	B-	Guys	A+
Campus Dining	A+	Health & Safety	A-
Campus Housing	A	Local Atmosphere	C+
Campus Strictness	A-	Nightlife	B+
Computers	A-	Off-Campus Dining	B
Diversity	B-	Off-Campus Housing	B
Drug Safety	C	Parking	A+
Facilities	A	Transportation	B
Girls	A	Weather	B

CP's Student Author On...
OVERALL EXPERIENCE

Many at Colby feel college is a place for students to grow intellectually and socially. Whether it's in class, conversations around the dinner table, a club, or speaking with another student from a different upbringing, Colby students exemplify this maxim. The community here is one of its defining features, and Colby students (and professors and staff, for that matter) love the College. Most cite the friendly and intellectually engaging people and the pristine new facilities, and although academics can be strenuous, the classes and professors are undeniably wonderful. Students work very hard in and out of the classroom, and most are involved in multiple activities outside of classes.

Many students choose Colby because of the remarkable intimacy between the students, faculty, administrators, and alumni. The school is not for everyone, though. Many Colby students don't have much free time, and some find campus to be claustrophobic at times. Nonetheless, the campus is bolstered by the student body's seemingly endless stores of energy, intellectual curiosity, and optimism.... For the rest of this editorial, visit collegeprowler.com.

Students Speak Out On...
OVERALL EXPERIENCE

Q I LOVE THIS SCHOOL

"The people here are what makes this school different than others. Everyone here is part of a community that fosters incredible growth and generates a feeling of belonging similar to the one that I feel when I am at home. I know that Colby is a place where I am free to think and strive to accomplish the goals that I set for myself."

Q Inviting, Entertaining, and Fun

"Overall, Colby is just a really good time. Studies are important but you always have time for lots of parties and activities. People here couldn't be nicer."

Q Colby Is an All-Around School

"Whether you're a jock or you're a geek, Colby is the perfect school for everyone. Everyone gets along and everyone is considerate of each other. Colby has a one-of-a-kind community that you cannot and will not find at any other institution, no matter how similar the schools may seem on paper. Colby is diverse, Colby is aware, and Colby is social."

BEST OF COLBY

1. Academics
2. The professors—they want every student to succeed and will go out of their way to ensure success.
3. The campus is gorgeous.
4. Everyone is friendly and smart.

Happy Students
94% of students return after their first year.

Commitment to Teaching
There are 10 students for every member of faculty on campus.

WORST OF COLBY

1. Weather, weather, weather
2. Tuition
3. Laundry machines
4. Small size leads to repeat hookups and a vast rumor mill.
5. Security during weekends

Expensive
Tuition is a steep $50,320, one of the most expensive rates in the country.

Student Body

African American:	2%	Male Undergrads:	45%
Asian American:	8%	Female Undergrads:	55%
Hispanic:	3%	Living On Campus:	94%
International:	5%	Living Off Campus:	6%
Native American:	1%	Male Athletes:	48%
White:	69%	Female Athletes:	35%
Unknown:	12%	Fraternity Members:	0%
From Out-of-State:	86%	Sorority Members:	0%

Frequently Compared Schools:

Bates College
Bowdoin College
Hamilton College
Middlebury College

Students Speak Out On... EVERYTHING!

ACADEMICS

Professors are very helpful

"Professors are very helpful, and you will see some of them living in the dorms, such as Heights and Mary Low. They genuinely care about the topics they are teaching, and they want their students to feel the same way. It's pretty easy to get the courses you want. Usually, they might try to create another section to accommodate the extra number of students. Glitches in registration or add/drop are unheard of. Everything runs pretty smoothly."

Rigorous and Rewarding

"The professors give us a lot of work, but they also have many hours in order to help students with the problem sets if they ever need help. The professors are brilliant and demanding, but you get a lot out of the classes. You have to work very hard for an A, and when you get an A you really deserve it. The professors also go out of their ways to help you, and I am already doing research as a sophomore."

ATHLETICS

School Pride

"Though Colby sports may not be the best, Colby students feel a genuine pride toward our athletic teams. Colby-Bowdoin and Colby-Bates football and hockey games are some of the most fun nights on campus."

Fun to Go to!

"School pride is high!"

CAMPUS DINING

Fossilicious

"Every dining hall offers a different vibe, and everybody has a definite favorite. Some days, the food seems much better than others, but the bottom line is that if you want a steak or a hamburger or tofu or ice cream, there's somewhere on campus for you. It's always fresh, healthy, and, depending on the dining hall, it's even exotic."

Foss Is Excellent

"Foss is all-organic dining. It even offers vegetarian options and can accommodate gluten and other allergies. There are three dining halls for only 1,800 or so students. The different dining halls offer options for even the pickiest eaters. Check the menus online before deciding where to eat your next meal. Students can even order food from a variety of different services."

CAMPUS HOUSING

Great, More Spacious Than Most

"Our rooms are a lot bigger than other college dormitories. You can still get one of the best rooms regardless of what year you are in. All years and genders are mixed together, which is nice because it fosters a stronger community."

No Freshmen Dorms

"Colby does a really great job in terms of incorporating everyone and making dorms diverse. There are no freshmen dorms, so the freshmen get to know upperclassmen really well and find out quickly there isn't much of a first-year stigma. Most don't even opt to live off campus because the campus is so active."

GUYS & GIRLS

HOT

"Everyone is good looking! Also very smart, engaging, and ambitious."

HEALTH & SAFETY

Very Safe

"Maine itself is a very safe state, and Colby is pretty insulated. Unlike at other colleges, security is very helpful and kind to students. Among students, we share a climate of trust. We leave our backpacks and coats before we eat in the dining halls and laptops in the libraries. You will not see this in many places."

LOOKING FOR MORE?

Check out our full-length guide to this school at collegeprowler.com/colby-college/.

Colgate University

13 Oak Drive; Hamilton, NY 13346
(315) 228-1000; www.colgate.edu

THE BASICS:

Acceptance Rate: 33%	Student-Faculty Ratio: 10:1
Yield: 33%	Retention Rate: 95%
Setting: Town	Graduation Rate: 91%
Control: Private Non-Profit	Tuition: $41,585
Total Undergrads: 2,901	Room & Board: $10,190
SAT Range: 1890–2180*	Avg. Aid Package: $40,217
ACT Range: 29–32	Students With Aid: 38%

of 2400

Academics	A-	Greek Life	A-
Athletics	A-	Guys	A-
Campus Dining	B+	Health & Safety	A+
Campus Housing	B+	Local Atmosphere	C+
Campus Strictness	B-	Nightlife	B
Computers	B+	Off-Campus Dining	C+
Diversity	C	Off-Campus Housing	C-
Drug Safety	B	Parking	B+
Facilities	A-	Transportation	C-
Girls	A	Weather	D+

CP's Student Author On...
OVERALL EXPERIENCE

Simply put, Colgate students love Colgate. Prospective students pick Colgate as much as Colgate picks them. It is no surprise that the University's retention rate from freshman to sophomore year is 94 percent. It is the best combination of a small liberal arts college and a major university. It has the strong sense of community and warmth of a small college, but the impressive faculty and staff of a major university. Students have a variety of activities to choose from, such as student-run organizations and publications, clubs, and athletic teams. Whatever their interest, Colgate students find their niche and flourish. The University fosters growth and maturity, but most important is the amazing group of individuals living in the dorms and on staff.

Through all the partying and camaraderie, academics and organizations, Colgate grooms its students to become outstanding individuals, soon to be pillars of communities. Students love Colgate, and once you get past the weather, you should be fine. Most students never consider transferring.... For the rest of this editorial, visit collegeprowler.com.

Students Speak Out On...
OVERALL EXPERIENCE

Q Great!

"Colgate is a very unique place in a lot of ways. It's one of the most beautiful campuses in the country and both academic and extracurricular life here are vibrant. The Greek scene's role on campus is debatable and the social system is hedonistic as hell, but I still believe there is more and more of a niche for everyone here"

Q Amazing

"Everything here is amazing. The social scene, classes, professors, and girls are all great. The only negative is the winter."

Q "Trying to decide on a college was possibly the most miserable few months of high school for me. I was absolutely torn between Colgate and Rutgers, for so many different reasons. Finally, I just went with my gut and chose Colgate. I've been here two years now, and I couldn't even imagine being anywhere else."

BEST OF COLGATE

1. The happy medium between an attentive, small liberal arts college with the resources of a major university

Happy Students
95% of students return after their first year.

Commitment to Teaching
There are 10 students for every member of faculty on campus.

WORST OF COLGATE

1. Course registration
2. The hit or miss quality of professors—sometimes the class is great, but the professor is horrible; sometimes the professor is great, but the class is horrible; sometimes both.
3. The bitterly cold winters

Expensive
Tuition is a steep $41,585, one of the most expensive rates in the country.

Student Body

African American:	5%	Male Undergrads:	48%
Asian American:	6%	Female Undergrads:	52%
Hispanic:	6%	Living On Campus:	94%
International:	5%	Living Off Campus:	20%
Native American:	1%	Male Athletes:	25%
White:	75%	Female Athletes:	20%
Unknown:	3%	Fraternity Members:	29%
From Out-of-State:	76%	Sorority Members:	32%

Frequently Compared Schools:

Bucknell University
Cornell University
Hamilton College
Middlebury College

Students Speak Out On...
EVERYTHING!

ACADEMICS

Colgate Polisci

"Engaging faculty are very friendly and willing to help out. Curriculum fair balance of fields taught by professors who have specialties in so many different areas. Workload manageable and classrooms are well equipped."

Overall, Academics are Very Good

"One thing you will not hear Colgate students complaining about is academics. Colgate professors are very available and are happy to talk with you about anything during office hours. There are a few professors people complain about but overall I have been pretty happy with the professors here. The academics are tough, but if you are able to get in here and work hard your grades will reflect it."

ATHLETICS

A Big Part of Our School

"We are a fairly athletic campus, with many students being both scholars and athletes. People go crazy for the hockey and football games -- well, almost every game, actually -- as a lot of the events are spray painted on a sheet of canvas and hung from the dining hall. People wait outside for hours to get hockey tickets: especially against Cornell. All of our athletic teams fare well."

"Varsity sports are huge. We're Division I in everything, I-AA in football. We were the Patriot League champs in football, and have made it to the IAA National Championship game."

CAMPUS DINING

Options Are Limited but Food Is Sufficient

"There is one main dining hall, the grill/sandwich COOP, library cafe, and a sit down cafe on campus. Because Colgate is a small school options are limited, but the staff is very responsive to suggestions and there is always an option for everyone."

Dining Halls

"The food is pretty good. They try to provide food for vegetarians, and have a lot of variety and healthy options."

CAMPUS HOUSING

Dorms

"It all depends on the dorm with the most lenient RA's so you can have people over and drink. Stillman is small and not fun Andrews isn's bad Gatehouse sucks and Curtis is good."

"In the first-year dorms, go for a suite, they offer a lot of space, and up your odds for getting a roommate that you really like."

GUYS & GIRLS

There are few people I have met here who I don't like.

"Everyone actually is pretty nice. There are a fair amount of kids who think they are too cool for school, but I wouldn't call them arrogant by any means. Colgate is NOT as preppy as people make it out to be."

HEALTH & SAFETY

Very safe, fairly healthy

"The reason I know the school is safe is because I never really think about safety. Even girls will say that the thought of something happening never really crosses their mind. I guess you want to be careful about how you act towards townspeople (who don't exactly love Colgate students) especially if it's late and everyone's drunk, but that's about it. As far as health goes Colgate usually offers free vaccines against the flu. Everyone seems to stay pretty healthy."

LOOKING FOR MORE?

Check out our full-length guide to this school at collegeprowler.com/colgate-university/.

College for Creative Studies

201 E. Kirby; Detroit, MI 48202
(313) 664-7400; www.collegeforcreativestudies.edu

THE BASICS:

Acceptance Rate: 39%	**Student-Faculty Ratio:** 10:1
Yield: 42%	**Retention Rate:** 79%
Setting: Large city	**Graduation Rate:** 56%
Control: Private Non-Profit	**Tuition:** $29,985
Total Undergrads: 1,382	**Room & Board:** $7,700
SAT Range: —	**Avg. Aid Package:** —
ACT Range: 18–23	**Students With Aid:** 100%

Academics	B+	Greek Life	N/A
Athletics	D+	Guys	A-
Campus Dining	C	Health & Safety	C
Campus Housing	A-	Local Atmosphere	B-
Campus Strictness	C+	Nightlife	B+
Computers	B	Off-Campus Dining	B
Diversity	B+	Off-Campus Housing	B-
Drug Safety	C+	Parking	A+
Facilities	C+	Transportation	B
Girls	A-	Weather	C

CP's Student Author On...
OVERALL EXPERIENCE

CCS has something that you just can't get at another college or university. There's this feeling in the air, an energy, that makes you feel you finally belong. For the people who knew they were meant for greatness but never really fit in anywhere else, this is the school for them. Once you step foot on campus, you know that this is it. Your life changes. You're given opportunities that you wouldn't find anywhere else.

Detroit itself is an eclectic city, and CCS is where the talent flocks to and where people come to look for talent. There are so many different experiences one can have here that it's hard to narrow it down into one description. You find your bliss here. You get to, and are heavily encouraged to, work on art 24/7. Yes, there are some liberal arts classes, but they make you well-rounded, and CCS gears those classes toward art-minded people. It's the best place for an artist or designer to go for their degree. You will see the most return on your investment. CCS graduates are in high demand.

Students Speak Out On...
OVERALL EXPERIENCE

Q Will Miss It Dearly
"I love my school. I would reccomend to anyone that they come to CCS. The students and staff are so friendly and wonderful, the facilities are plenty, and it is located in the best city in the country. I am almost a Senior, and i am going to be so sad when i graduate!"

Q A Diamond in the Rough
"CCS is a academic Jule that sits across from the DIA. It is filled with kind wonderful people that are easy to get along with. CCS is my home away from home."

Q Invigorating
"I really love CCS. While it challenges you beyond anything you have ever known, it is also best way to grow as a person. If I had to make my decision all over again I would still go to CCS. I realize that I am missing out on parts of the traditional college experience, but I think what CCS offers is more of a real life experience. We are trained to be the best and most successful in our fields, even though the process to the end can be long and stressful."

BEST OF CREATIVE STUDIES

1. Artsy people/environment
2. Demanding
3. Education
4. Experience all four seasons
5. Famous designers and scholars
6. Housing

Commitment to Teaching
There are 10 students for every member of faculty on campus.

Knowledgeable Professors
92% of students surveyed rated the general knowledge of professors as above average.

WORST OF CREATIVE STUDIES

1. Sometimes classes can drag on since they are all three hours long.
2. Cost
3. Sodexo Catering Company
4. Sometimes the work load can seem unrelenting.
5. Crime rate in Detroit

Expensive
Tuition is a steep $29,985, one of the most expensive rates in the country.

Student Body

African American:	7%	Male Undergrads:	56%
Asian American:	4%	Female Undergrads:	44%
Hispanic:	5%	Living On Campus:	29%
International:	6%	Living Off Campus:	71%
Native American:	0%	Male Athletes:	0%
White:	68%	Female Athletes:	0%
Unknown:	8%	Fraternity Members:	0%
From Out-of-State:	17%	Sorority Members:	0%

Frequently Compared Schools:

Michigan State University
Oakland Community College
University of Michigan
Wayne State University

Students Speak Out On... EVERYTHING!

ACADEMICS

Majors

"Ad design, Product/automotive design, fine arts, crafts, and other various cool design/art majors. We have a good liberal arts department. Students get a well rounded creative education that prepares them for life after college. Teachers are not only knowledgable, but most also have been in the business and know what is needed to survive in the creative business world."

Illustration

"It's a lot of commitment and time, but our department is full of students and faculty that are very committed to what they do and helping other students and fostering a network that will last after graduation."

ATHLETICS

We Don't Have Any

"We don't have time, we don't care, nobody wants sports because it is an art school. We have a few athletes but we have a gym, and there honestly isn't time for sports. They get an A+ for being realistic in their expectations. :)"

Athletics?

"We're a very small school and we're an art school so sports aren't top priority here. I actually like the lack of sports at CCS. After going to MSU for two years, it's a nice break from the cult-like following for sports like football and basketball. Although, we do have a hula hooper...."

CAMPUS DINING

Good Cafe Area

"There is not huge cafiteria but they have a great area to grab some food between classes."

Good Expensive Food

"Its good food; But it is too expensive and they serve the same thing alot."

CAMPUS HOUSING

Good

"Dorms are huge, people are friendly...good laundry facilities and the vending machines are fun...24 hour computer labs...very safe....need ID to get in the door and up the stairs...."

Living in the ACB Dorms

"Its very spacious and more like an apartment than a dorm. It is super close to the campus, and fun to live in. Its a little expensive, but worth it for the convenience."

GUYS & GIRLS

Eveyone Is So Friendly

"Everyone on campus is very friendly and open to talk to others and assist others whenever needed. Last year was my first year and I felt very welcome by all guys and girls. No one judges you on your ethnicity or how you dress or anything. They are very accepting of everyone."

Some All Around Cool Cats

"It is an art school so people dress very stylish. There are a lot of people who have the hipster look going for them. Most people I have talked to are super nice."

HEALTH & SAFETY

Maximum Security School

"I feel VERY safe at CCS. The Taubman Center is right across the street from the main Detroit Police station. Getting into the building requires and access card and getting past guards and anywhere you go in the building requires you to use an access card too. Also, Wayne state is in the same area and they have their security as well that patrols our campus as well. I feel very safe walking around this neighborhood. CCS does an excellent job at making sure its students and staff stay safe."

LOOKING FOR MORE?

Check out our full-length guide to this school at collegeprowler.com/college-for-creative-studies/.

College of Charleston

66 George St.; Charleston, SC 29424
(843) 953-5500; www.cofc.edu

THE BASICS:

Acceptance Rate: 64%	Student-Faculty Ratio: 16:1
Yield: 31%	Retention Rate: 82%
Setting: Mid-sized city	Graduation Rate: 64%
Control: Public	Tuition: $21,846
Total Undergrads: 10,146	Room & Board: $9,411
SAT Range: 1700–1940*	Avg. Aid Package: $11,492
ACT Range: 23–26	Students With Aid: 74%

* of 2400

Academics	B	Greek Life	B-
Athletics	C	Guys	B+
Campus Dining	B-	Health & Safety	C-
Campus Housing	B	Local Atmosphere	A
Campus Strictness	B-	Nightlife	A
Computers	C+	Off-Campus Dining	A
Diversity	D+	Off-Campus Housing	B
Drug Safety	D+	Parking	C-
Facilities	B-	Transportation	A
Girls	B+	Weather	B

CP's Student Author On... OVERALL EXPERIENCE

Most students acknowledge the fact that at the College of Charleston, they're experiencing something unique and rare. Not only is the city an interesting and fascinating place, but the years students will spend at CofC will be radically different than they would be at most other schools. Many schools are not located in the heart of a city as Charleston is, and many schools do not preserve the old while combining it with the new, the way the College of Charleston strives to. Although CofC may not have a well-known reputation for superior academics or sports, both the latter and the former are among the greatest in the nation, and many students come to care less and less about the acclaim that Charleston receives.

One cannot truly understand the appeal and rarity of attending the College of Charleston until they have been here awhile, and though students do transfer out for various reasons (including simply not being happy as a CofC student), those who do remain here for all of their college years look back on their memories with nothing but contentment and pride.... For the rest of this editorial, visit collegeprowler.com.

Students Speak Out On... OVERALL EXPERIENCE

Q **Wonderful First Year**
"I couldn't have asked for a better freshman year at the College of Charleston. The campus is beautiful and everyone who comes here is super friendly. You have to work for your grades, but it wont consume every minute of your life. The athletic staff will also encourage and help you while you figure out how to balance both school and athletics."

Q **Pretty Damn Good.**
"I can't complain. The food may not be top notch but the atmosphere makes up for it ten fold. There is always something going on, whether it be a party or a campus event. With 10,000 students you will never be bored. Just make sure to save some time for studying!"

Q **Changing for the Better**
"In the three years that I've been here, I've witnessed the student body growing more open to diversity and progression. It's a beautiful school in the middle of the Bible belt, but there is an acceptance that is prevalent throughout the campus and the city itself."

BEST OF COLLEGE OF CHARLESTON

1. Availability of internships and academic opportunities in the city
2. Charleston!
3. Downtown bars and restaurants
4. Helpful professors
5. Marion Square

Happy Students
82% of students return after their first year.

Knowledgeable Professors
85% of students surveyed rated the general knowledge of professors as above average.

WORST OF COLLEGE OF CHARLESTON

1. Guys from the Citadel
2. Lack of majors
3. Lack of school spirit
4. Not enough boys to go around
5. Parking
6. Strict policies on drug and alcohol violations

Expensive Dorms
Living on campus doesn't come cheap, with an average housing price tag of $6,421.

Student Body

African American:	6%	Male Undergrads:	37%
Asian American:	2%	Female Undergrads:	63%
Hispanic:	2%	Living On Campus:	34%
International:	2%	Living Off Campus:	66%
Native American:	0%	Male Athletes:	5%
White:	82%	Female Athletes:	4%
Unknown:	6%	Fraternity Members:	15%
From Out-of-State:	47%	Sorority Members:	20%

Frequently Compared Schools:

Clemson University
Elon University
James Madison University
University of South Carolina

Students Speak Out On... EVERYTHING!

ACADEMICS

Q Arts Management

"The professors and staff of the department are amazing and supportive!"

Q Lots of Opportunities!

"I am double majoring in theater and communications. There are a lot of opportunities to get internships in these areas. We have different media companies, and we have a lot of theaters where you can audition. I am a freshman this year, so I don't know that much yet, but I am eager to find out!"

ATHLETICS

Q Basketball Makes up for Lack of Football

"The students at CofC are extremely supportive of the basketball team. The games are packed and lively and help to rev up school spirit."

Q Sports Are So So

"Because Charleston doesn't have a football team, sports don't seem to be as prevalent to students. Our basketball team has been doing very well so during basketball season, students usually do their best to attend the games. But soccer and baseball are definitely not as important as basketball. Overall, sports do not encompass a majority of campus activity."

CAMPUS DINING

Q The Wide Variety of College of Charleston's Dining

"The meals on campus are decent. The best place to grab food is at the Stern Center, and the restaurants there accept dining dollars. Chik-fil-a is my favorite and I never could get tired of it. The Liberty cafeteria has decent tasting food, but sometimes the food options get repetitive."

Q Get: OFF CAMPUS MEAL PLAN

"If you get the OFF CAMPUS MEAL PLAN you are able to eat at local restaurants instead of just the on campus ones. OFF CAMPUS MEAL PLAN is the best idea ever!!!! so many choice all around !!!"

CAMPUS HOUSING

Q Dorm Life

"The dorms at CofC are really good. Although there is plenty of opportunity to live off-campus, even as an upperclassman I still live on campus just because the dorms are pretty good. The dorms are like a community, and everyone on your floor knows each other which is really nice. Getting housing is easy and it's not hard to sign up for housing."

Q Nice Dorms

"The dorms at college of Chrleston are hit or miss, but most of them are nice. The only "bad" dorm is Berry, because it has so many people and is supposedly haunted. Most dorms are suite style and you only have to share a bathroom with one or two other people."

GUYS & GIRLS

Q Girls Are HOT

"The girls at Charleston are SEXY. They're all southern belles - thin, in shape, blond-haired, and blue-eyed. And the ratio of girls to guys is great too! There's like 3 girls to every guy."

Q Nice Kids

"A lot of smart girls and bobys, who are for the most part nice and kind"

HEALTH & SAFETY

Q Safety

"I never feel unsafe. It's common sense to not walk alone in sketchy areas or leave doors unlocked."

Q Totally Safe

"The College has great police, fire & EMT staff. There are plenty of security cameras amnd call boxes throughout campus. I have never felt uncomfortable walking back to my dorm room from the library after a late night of studying."

LOOKING FOR MORE?

Check out our full-length guide to this school at collegeprowler.com/college-of-charleston/.

College of Mount Saint Vincent

6301 Riverdale Ave.; Bronx, NY 10471
(718) 405-3200; www.mountsaintvincent.edu

THE BASICS:

Acceptance Rate: 67%
Yield: 25%
Setting: Large city
Control: Private Non-Profit
Total Undergrads: 1,524
SAT Range: 870–1050*
ACT Range: —

Student-Faculty Ratio: 13:1
Retention Rate: 75%
Graduation Rate: 57%
Tuition: $25,710
Room & Board: $9,900
Avg. Aid Package: $9,500
Students With Aid: 96%

* of 1600

Academics	C-	Greek Life	N/A
Athletics	C-	Guys	C+
Campus Dining	C-	Health & Safety	C
Campus Housing	C-	Local Atmosphere	B-
Campus Strictness	B	Nightlife	B-
Computers	D+	Off-Campus Dining	C
Diversity	B	Off-Campus Housing	D+
Drug Safety	C-	Parking	B
Facilities	D+	Transportation	B
Girls	C	Weather	B

CP's Student Author On...
OVERALL EXPERIENCE

After a year of experience at the Mount, I am convinced that this institution is not for me. The small class sizes and close professor-student relationships are qualities that have met only some of my educational standards. Asides from their Nursing program, the Mount has not developed their other programs thoroughly. Some courses have even become a joke, which is the complete opposite of how I feel a college should be. After all, it is only natural to encounter struggles and difficulties throughout a college career. Therefore, passionate Business and Communications majors should not even consider this school. The reasons for this would be their poorly organized programs, unmotivated students, and lack of facilities and equipment. If I were given the opportunity to choose this school over again, unfortunately, I do not think I would.

The limited course options have also put a damper on my confidence in my future. Students are not offered enough variety to be well rounded in different areas, let alone one's specific major. Again, asides from Nursing, I feel like I am not being prepared well enough.... For the rest of this editorial, visit collegeprowler.com.

Students Speak Out On...
OVERALL EXPERIENCE

Q Overall Experience

"My overall experience here so far has been pretty good. I enjoy this place a lot."

Q My Experience at CMSV

"CMSV reminds me of high school because it is really small. I've had my ups and downs, but otherwise, everything seems normal and fine—just as I had expected it to be."

Q Major: Sociology

"I like the professors, but I do not see why it is so expensive—when there are storms the whole school goes out, and sometimes the computers do not even work. I do not go to parties because I do not live in the dorms and I do not live in walking distance."

Q CMSV Is Small.

"A small school has great advantages to learning and being close to your professors. However, it can be like high school when it comes to drama. The students can get pretty cliquey. Sometimes, the students come here just for the parties. However, if you're a nursing student, you probably won't have time for partying."

BEST OF MOUNT ST. VINCENT

1. Nursing program
2. Small class sizes
3. Diversity
4. Tight-knit community
5. Local scenery
6. Spellman is all-you-can-eat

Knowledgeable Professors
60% of students surveyed rated the general knowledge of professors as above average.

WORST OF MOUNT ST. VINCENT

1. Some courses could be more challenging
2. Facilities
3. Dilapidated buildings
4. Lack of equipment in the communications department
5. Poor communication between departments

Disappointed Students
46% of students surveyed would not choose to attend this school if they could do it all over again.

Want a Job? On Your Own
There aren't any placement services for graduates.

Frequently Compared Schools:
Columbia University
Fordham University
Manhattan College
Sarah Lawrence College

Students Speak Out On... EVERYTHING!

ACADEMICS

Interesting

"Nursing is an interesting major. It offers a lot of versatility. We take several science courses that are involved with different aspects of the major. It is also very interactive. We not only learn the anatomy and physiology, but we work with people and dummies, too!"

Nursing at the Mount

"It's extremely difficult, but I feel like it will really help in the long run. The program is designed for success in the future."

Small Classes

"MSV has small class sizes, so it is easy to get help if you want to. Overall, I like the classes."

ATHLETICS

Could Be Better

"Sports aren't a big interest, but the teams do fairly well."

Sports

"It's not the best. We have no fields on campus and the equipment is not great."

What You Expect from a D3 School

"The teams are more like what you would see in a high school. They aren't special, but people play them because they love the sport. There is a group of kids who do attend the sporting events, but nothing huge like you see at D-I schools."

CAMPUS DINING

Benedicts

"Not much variety but food is well prepared."

Food at CMSV

"There are two cafeterias on campus. They're not the best, but good enough, I guess."

Satisfying Most Days

"There are two spots on campus to eat: Spellman dining hall or Benedicts. At Spellman, you use your meal points for the week, while Benedicts charges your Dolphin Dollars. Benedicts is A LOT better than Spellman. Spellman's food is typical and just like any other college's dining halls."

CAMPUS HOUSING

College of Mount Saint Vincent Is One of the Good Colleges Around the Area. the Dorm Buildings Are in the Campus and the Dorm Rooms Are Cool. I Am Loving It!

"College of Mount Saint Vincent, the name says it all. One of the great colleges. Faculty is very helpful, students are friendly and the dorm buildings are good place and the view is excellent."

Dorms

"The dorms at the College of Mount Saint Vincent are very nice. Our dorms are somewhat clean."

GUYS & GIRLS

The People Look Average.

"There is a wide variety of girls and guys."

Guys and Girls at CMSV

"The guys seem to be mostly jocks and musicians. The girls are mostly nurses, entertainers, and teachers, from my perspective. The guys are harder to get along with, and the girls are very friendly and approachable. It's like going through the high school experience with these characteristics."

HEALTH & SAFETY

Safe

"I've never felt unsafe on campus. Security is always on patrol. The campus is not that big, so they are always relatively close by. Some areas around the campus are a little unsafe though."

Comfortable and Safe

"I have never felt unsafe on the CMSV campus. There is only one entrance to the whole campus and there is always a guard present at the entrance gate. Otherwise I don't often see guards around the campus. I am a commuter so I do not really know anything about campus life but from my understanding, I hear that the college instills strict rules pertaining to residents."

College of Notre Dame of Maryland

4701 N. Charles St.; Baltimore, MD 21210
(410) 435-0100; www.ndm.edu

THE BASICS:

Acceptance Rate: 65%	**Student-Faculty Ratio:** 11:1
Yield: 35%	**Retention Rate:** 78%
Setting: Large city	**Graduation Rate:** 62%
Control: Private Non-Profit	**Tuition:** $27,250
Total Undergrads: 1,254	**Room & Board:** $9,100
SAT Range: 900–1160*	**Avg. Aid Package:** $19,708
ACT Range: 18–22	**Students With Aid:** 100%

* of 1600

Academics	B	Greek Life	B-
Athletics	C-	Guys	C-
Campus Dining	C-	Health & Safety	B-
Campus Housing	C+	Local Atmosphere	B-
Campus Strictness	C	Nightlife	B-
Computers	C+	Off-Campus Dining	B
Diversity	B-	Off-Campus Housing	C
Drug Safety	C+	Parking	B
Facilities	C-	Transportation	C
Girls	B-	Weather	C+

CP's Student Author On...
OVERALL EXPERIENCE

Notre Dame is one of those places where you either love it or hate it. For many, it is seen as a mostly academic school. So if you're looking for a huge social life or a "party school," this isn't the place for you. Sure, there are events/activities on campus, but not many that appeal to the students. Often, events that have potential fail because people don't want to participate. School spirit is lacking, so that lessens the excitement and makes us more disjointed as a campus. Academically, students are usually very satisfied with the College. They enjoy the small class sizes and the caring nature of the professors, as well as their teaching styles. General education requirements, though extensive, can be very interesting and even a break from the classes within students' majors. Being a liberal arts college, the College requires extra classes to make students well-rounded in their education.

Notre Dame is not among the most well-known colleges around, even locally. So get used to people mistaking you with the "Fighting Irish" (University of Notre Dame in Indiana) or being recognized as "the one next to Loyola.... For the rest of this editorial, visit collegeprowler.com.

Students Speak Out On...
OVERALL EXPERIENCE

Q Love It!
"School is awesome... a lot of dedicated, like minded individuals, and an amazing staff! Everyone is friendly and welcoming and accepting."

Q Life at CND
"I love CND and all it has to offer. I have transformed into a woman here and the academic life is great. I love the teachers, the class size, the class structure, the people that work here, everyone and everything is good."

Q Stressful, Challenging, but You Learn for Life
"Though I am disappointed with the social life/events on campus, I am very pleased with the classes and professors."

Q Average Experiences
"My experiences here have been a mixture of wonderful and awful. While the classes are small, the professors are amazing, and the campus is beautiful, the administration is ignorant, the dining is atrocious, and the activities/organizations are lacking."

BEST OF NOTRE DAME OF MARYLAND

1. The small size of the student body
2. Interesting classes
3. Kind and reliable teachers
4. Accessible teachers
5. The small class sizes
6. Studying abroad
7. Making lifelong friends

Big Dorms
67% of students surveyed felt that dorms were more spacious than average.

Help to Succeed
The school has academic and career counseling available to help you when you need it.

WORST OF NOTRE DAME OF MARYLAND

1. Lack of events/ activities on campus
2. Very expensive
3. The food quality and options
4. Campus housing
5. Visitation policy for resident students is too strict

Expensive
Tuition is a steep $27,250, one of the most expensive rates in the country.

Life is NOT a Party
80% of students surveyed said it's almost impossible to find a good party.

Frequently Compared Schools:

Goucher College
Johns Hopkins University
Loyola University Maryland
Towson University

Students Speak Out On... EVERYTHING!

ACADEMICS

A Women's College Experience

"I have thoroughly enjoyed my time at Notre Dame. While initially intimidated by the thought of an all women's college, I found that I really enjoyed it. My ideologies were challenged while my pursuits were reinforced. I would not have remained a math major if I had not been in an all women's college."

Its Easy but U Will Have to Transfer

"ALL CLASSES THAT I HAVE TAKEN ARE EASYYYY!! I've taken calc, physics, chemistry, linear algebra, philosphy, and college writing and other stupid classes. I neverrrr have to studyyy!! I'm free everydayy and i hardly ever have any work. I'm getting As in most of my classes. High school was the same way for me too, so it depends on easy high school was for u"

Teachers Actually Care

"The professors at The College of Notre Dame demonstrate genuine care for their students. They are available outside of class and are always willing to provide extra assistance when necessary. Also, the class sizes are small enough that you can get to know your professor and classmates better than at a larger university."

ATHLETICS

Athletics

"We have an active athletic department but it doesn't seem like there are that many athletes. I see many of the same girls on more than one team and the teams themselves are very small. Our athletes are excellent but sometimes I feel that we don't have as much school spirit as we should."

Lacks School Spirit

"The sports are good but the students lack school spirit. Not too many people show up to home games. The athletic facilities definitely need to be renovated."

CAMPUS DINING

MENUS

"I ENJOY THE FACT THAT THERE ARE PLENTY OF SELECTIONS IN THE DINING AREA TO CHOOSE FROM."

Dining on Campus

"Gator Alley has better food than the dining hall but it is much more expensive and you get small portions. The hours of operation are not great. The Dining Hall has good-enough food, generally you can find something, once again, the hours are short."

CAMPUS HOUSING

Meletia

"Meletia is an amazing residence hall to be quite honest. You have high ceilings and hardwood floors. My room senior year had a balcony and I had a shared bathroom with only one other student. Definitely and amazing residence experience!"

Our Dorms Are Awesome

"I like our dorm rooms. The freshmen dorm rooms are somewhat small but we have clean bathrooms and a nice quiet environment. Upperclassmen have bigger rooms and some have rooms with a balcony on it, which is pretty sweet. Suites are offered to upperclassmen, which is also convenient. Those in suites get their own bathroom as well."

GUYS & GIRLS

NO GUYS! AND FULL OF GAY GIRLS

"I wish there were more guys but its a women's college so i should have expected that already. I dont have anything against gay people but if u do then u'll have problems."

HEALTH & SAFETY

Have My Back

"Security is always driving around campus and securing everything so I always feel safe."

Beautiful and Safe

"Notre Dame is situated in a beautiful residential neighborhood of Baltimore, on the crest of gently sloping wooded ridge, punctuated by the ornate landmark tower of Gibbons Hall. It is safe and I have never experienced any problems concerning safty."

LOOKING FOR MORE?

Check out our full-length guide to this school at collegeprowler.com/college-of-notre-dame-of-maryland/.

College of the Holy Cross

1 College St.; Worcester, MA 01610
(508) 793-2011; www.holycross.edu

THE BASICS:

Acceptance Rate: 36%
Yield: 31%
Setting: Mid-sized city
Control: Private Non-Profit
Total Undergrads: 2,933
SAT Range: 1810–2060*
ACT Range: 26–30

Student-Faculty Ratio: 11:1
Retention Rate: 95%
Graduation Rate: 98%
Tuition: $38,722
Room & Board: $10,620
Avg. Aid Package: $29,166
Students With Aid: 62%

* of 2400

Academics	B+	Greek Life	N/A
Athletics	B+	Guys	B
Campus Dining	B+	Health & Safety	A-
Campus Housing	B	Local Atmosphere	C+
Campus Strictness	C+	Nightlife	B
Computers	B	Off-Campus Dining	B+
Diversity	D+	Off-Campus Housing	D
Drug Safety	B-	Parking	C+
Facilities	B	Transportation	C
Girls	B+	Weather	C-

CP's Student Author On... OVERALL EXPERIENCE

Students were mixed, though generally positive, about their overall view of Holy Cross. The social scene seems to be the victim of most criticism, but there is no question that Holy Cross provides all its students with a first-rate education.

Most students are friendly, outgoing, and fun, and making friends is not a problem. However, some students complain about the school's homogeneity. Few students seem to want to do anything that is outside of the norm. In all though, most students are very happy at Holy Cross, as evidenced by the school's unusually high retention rate.

Students Speak Out On... OVERALL EXPERIENCE

Q "Sometimes I wish I were someplace else."

Q "I love it here. I would not want to be anywhere else."

Q "I love it—anyone could find their niche at HC. I wouldn't want to be anyplace else right now, but four years is definitely enough."

Q "I enjoy HC and would not want to be anywhere else. Overall, it's a great academic institution where you will make friends, have fun, and freeze in the winter."

Q "I love it and wouldn't want to be anywhere else."

Q "All I do is party, party, party, so that part is great! But, the school? Eh, I failed three classes, but I got a "C" in one, though!"

Q "I think I'm getting the best education money can buy, but the social life here is really stifling and really boring, especially if you don't want to follow the crowd."

Q "I cannot see myself anywhere else. I really loved the past three years here and can't wait for this one."

BEST OF HOLY CROSS

1. The campus is beautiful.
2. The students are very friendly.
3. The professors are friendly and helpful.
4. The parties are great.
5. Springtime, when it finally comes, is wonderful.

Happy Students
95% of students return after their first year.

Proven Success
98% of students will complete their education and graduate with a degree.

WORST OF HOLY CROSS

1. Worcester is awful.
2. The Worcester police put a damper on everything.
3. A lot of the students can be close-minded.
4. The campus is extremely homogeneous.
5. The school's drinking policies are draconian.

Expensive
Tuition is a steep $38,722, one of the most expensive rates in the country.

Good Luck Finding a Part-Time Job
Employment services are not available for students.

Student Body

African American:	4%	Male Undergrads:	44%
Asian American:	6%	Female Undergrads:	56%
Hispanic:	6%	Living On Campus:	89%
International:	1%	Living Off Campus:	11%
Native American:	0%	Male Athletes:	35%
White:	67%	Female Athletes:	25%
Unknown:	15%	Fraternity Members:	0%
From Out-of-State:	67%	Sorority Members:	0%

Frequently Compared Schools:

Boston College
Fordham University
Providence College
Villanova University

Students Speak Out On... EVERYTHING!

ACADEMICS

Workload

"The workload is way too much. Students are usually over-stressed. Professors should not pile on so much work. It drives students crazy."

"The teachers at Holy Cross are great! They are always willing to provide students with extra help if it is needed. They love students to come and see them!"

"The teachers are about as varied as the classes. I've had some really good ones and some really bad ones. On the whole, I would say that there are more interesting classes than uninteresting ones."

ATHLETICS

Pretty Good for a Small School

"A lot of people actually do go to the games. Hockey is always pretty fun to go to. The football team won the league championships this year, and a few students were drafted into the NFL. Overall, if you really want a team to get behind and become a huge fan of, look elsewhere. Otherwise, there's enough athletic intrigue to keep the average sports fan satisfied."

Too Focused on Athletics

"Holy Cross is too focused on athletics and providing scholarships to athletes"

"Holy Cross is not Notre Dame, but varsity sports are not ignored. The basketball teams—both women's and men's—are at the top of their class and quite competitive. The football team draws a crowd, but this is basically because of tradition's sake and the tailgating—the stands grow sparse after halftime. The soccer team is always solid, as is the women's tennis team."

CAMPUS DINING

Acceptable, but Not Great

"I've found the food pretty decent. The new Science Center Cafe is great, but it's only open for breakfast and lunch on weekdays. The maine dining hall is pretty much on a 2 week cycle, so the same old food there gets old after a while. Also, there are a few healthy options, but not enough to eat well very consistently."

"If you sit in Kimball long enough, you will see the entire campus walk by."

"The food at Kimball can be somewhat repetitive, but there's also Lower and Crossroads to choose from."

CAMPUS HOUSING

Not That Special...

"In comparison with my friends at other schools the housing is really, more or less. Only seniors have the option of getting an apartment, and there are not even enough for everyone. There are plenty of seniors, who in their final year, are still sharing a group bathroom, don't have a kitchen, etc."

Social Atmosphere

"Extremely homogeneous. Same things to do every week"

GUYS & GIRLS

Good Girls...

"The girls at Holy Cross are, generally speaking, very attractive. Plus, considering the "economic status" of the population, the dress well and spring time is always a treat for everyone."

Too Involved in Drinking

"Most students spend too much time hooking up and drinking"

HEALTH & SAFETY

Campus Is Safe

"Public Safety is just out to do their job not go after you. Health services are alright."

"The campus is very safe—Public Safety's tactics ensure that. But watch out! They have been known to run down a student or two with their Public Safety vans—I was a victim!"

LOOKING FOR MORE?

Check out our full-length guide to this school at collegeprowler.com/college-of-the-holy-cross/.

College of William & Mary

102 Richmond Road; Williamsburg, VA 23187
(757) 221-4000; www.wm.edu

THE BASICS:

Acceptance Rate: 34%
Yield: 34%
Setting: Suburban
Control: Public
Total Undergrads: 5,836
SAT Range: 1850–2160*
ACT Range: 27–32

Student-Faculty Ratio: 11:1
Retention Rate: 95%
Graduation Rate: 91%
Tuition: $30,964
Room & Board: $8,382
Avg. Aid Package: $13,703
Students With Aid: 55%

* of 2400

Academics	A	Greek Life	B
Athletics	C	Guys	A-
Campus Dining	C+	Health & Safety	A-
Campus Housing	B	Local Atmosphere	C+
Campus Strictness	B+	Nightlife	B
Computers	A-	Off-Campus Dining	B
Diversity	B	Off-Campus Housing	B-
Drug Safety	C+	Parking	C
Facilities	B+	Transportation	B-
Girls	B+	Weather	C+

CP's Student Author On...
OVERALL EXPERIENCE

To say the least, William & Mary students have a strong affection for their school. They love the sense of history, the size, the faculty, and their fellow students. You hardly ever hear anyone expressing regret for choosing William & Mary. Alumni come back year after year, wishing that they could spend four more years at the place they love all over again. Williamsburg may not be the most bustling hub of city activity, but the students form their own community that cannot be beat.

W&M is definitely academically challenging, but students know all of the hard work is going to add up to a quality education. Most students agree that William & Mary is as close to perfect as they could hope for.

Students Speak Out On...
OVERALL EXPERIENCE

Q I LOVE IT HERE

"It's academia heaven. If you are looking for campus that is beautiful, safe, and condusive to education, this is the place! Everyone here is friendly and wants to learn and succeed. If you are looking for a party school this isn't it."

Q Dream College

"People at William & Mary are in college for the right reasons, with academic enthusiasm and motivation, and the whole institution reflects that. But the focus is not on snobbery or status. The reason I chose William & Mary over its big academic in-state rival, University of Virginia, was the down-to-earth, merit-based attitude of the students and faculty. Completing undergrad at William & Mary is difficult, but incredibly worth it."

BEST OF WILLIAM & MARY

1. The professors and their idiosyncrasies
2. The old brick buildings and the beautiful campus
3. Late night Wawa runs
4. Secret societies, steam tunnels, and other mysterious occurrences

Happy Students
95% of students return after their first year.

Proven Success
91% of students will complete their education and graduate with a degree.

WORST OF WILLIAM & MARY

1. Lack of air-conditioning
2. The gross smell of the tray depository at the SC
3. Finding a seat at SWEM
4. The chaos of course registration
5. The rain
6. Rogers 100

Expensive
Tuition is a steep $30,964, one of the most expensive rates in the country.

Student Body

African American:	7%	Male Undergrads:	45%
Asian American:	8%	Female Undergrads:	55%
Hispanic:	6%	Living On Campus:	74%
International:	3%	Living Off Campus:	26%
Native American:	1%	Male Athletes:	13%
White:	59%	Female Athletes:	9%
Unknown:	16%	Fraternity Members:	26%
From Out-of-State:	38%	Sorority Members:	27%

Students Speak Out On...
EVERYTHING!

ACADEMICS

Q Great Education, Lousy Grades

"I love the education. It's amazing. The professors are phenomenal and really care about what they're teaching. It would be the perfect school were it not for the painful grade deflation."

Q Really Intelligent Professors and Students

"One of my favorite things about William and Mary is the academics; they're great. The professors are helpful, knowledgeable, and for the most part great at relaying their knowledge to the students. Fellow students are surprisingly intelligent (though I've met a few idiots here too). If you're looking for great academics and to really expand your mind, this is a great place to be."

ATHLETICS

Q Surprisingly Good

"The varsity athletics at WM are definitely better than I expected and the fans who do attend events get pretty into it."

Q Rip 'Em up, Tear 'Em up, Give 'Em Hell Tribe!

"That saying describes Tribe athletics. Our football team is getting progressively better, and their is a ton of support from fans and students on campus. Basketball is also another prominent sport on campus, and both men's and women's team are pretty successful. Overall, every sport is pretty successful and has a great following with the people on campus. Gooooooo Tribe!"

CAMPUS DINING

Q Dining Halls OK, but Not the Best

"The food is of good quality, and the eating areas are kept relatively clean. However, the halls get excessively busy and it is sometimes hard to find a place to sit during busy hours. Otherwise, I love the staff and the food is quite good."

Frequently Compared Schools:

Duke University
University of North Carolina
University of Virginia
Wake Forest University

Q Repetitive but Passable

"Dining hall food is repetitive but passable. The Caf is definitely better than the UC. If you get tired of it, you can go to Quizno's or Wawa. Flex dollars are great -- you can use them for any food item anywhere on campus. A great hidden spot is the Dodge Room near the Muscarelle, which serves sandwiches."

CAMPUS HOUSING

Q Good as a College Founded in 1693 Can Get

"Most of the dorm buildings are old and a bit dingy, but the social atmosphere is always upbeat and everyone finds it easy to make friends. The food is good, the showers are gross but bearable, and everything is conveniently located. Everyone always feel safe on campus, and the scenery is absolutely breaktaking!"

Q Totally Depends

"Upperclass dorms are all pretty nice, especially Jamestown. Freshman dorms vary a lot. Barrett is beautiful, Yates and DuPont are more "party" dorms (but keep in mind this is W&M and by no means comparable to other party schools), and Botetourt seems ok until you see other peoples dorms. Then you feel like you drew the short stick. But on the other hand, people in Botetourt tend to hang out in the lounges and be social with each other a lot more than other dorms."

GUYS & GIRLS

Q Guys

"Like every school William & Mary has its attractive, average, and those less fortunate in their level of hotness. For the most part though the guys here are intelligent, kind, personable, and a lot of them are sexy as hell."

HEALTH & SAFETY

Q Very Safe

"Excellent security on campus."

LOOKING FOR MORE?

Check out our full-length guide to this school at collegeprowler.com/college-of-william--and--mary/.

College of Wooster

1189 Beall Ave.; Wooster, OH 44691
(330) 263-2000; www.wooster.edu

THE BASICS:

Acceptance Rate: 59%	Student-Faculty Ratio: 11:1
Yield: 17%	Retention Rate: 87%
Setting: Town	Graduation Rate: 76%
Control: Private Non-Profit	Tuition: $34,950
Total Undergrads: 1,815	Room & Board: $8,950
SAT Range: 1620–1970*	Avg. Aid Package: $18,821
ACT Range: 24–29	Students With Aid: 96%

* of 2400

Academics	B	Greek Life	C
Athletics	B	Guys	B
Campus Dining	B+	Health & Safety	B
Campus Housing	B+	Local Atmosphere	B-
Campus Strictness	C	Nightlife	B
Computers	B-	Off-Campus Dining	B+
Diversity	D+	Off-Campus Housing	D+
Drug Safety	B	Parking	B-
Facilities	B	Transportation	C-
Girls	B	Weather	C+

CP's Student Author On... OVERALL EXPERIENCE

Here's a news flash—the College of Wooster isn't perfect; you can't please everybody. However, in asking students how they honestly felt about Wooster, even if there are things that they can't stand about the school—things that drive them up the wall, frankly—Wooster students are very glad they chose to come to this college above any other. They say that it's something about the atmosphere, something about the personal touches you see all over campus, and something about the friendships you make here that does it for them. They know that they are receiving a great education that will last them far into their future careers, forming friendships that may last longer than even their marriages, gaining a wonderful background for becoming a richer person, and living life to its fullest.

When a college cares about you the person, not just you the student, or you the number, that is when it becomes more than just a college—it becomes a place you can call home. Wooster has shown that to their students even after graduation, even for decades to come. This is the reason why Wooster students wouldn't trade their years there for anything.

Students Speak Out On... OVERALL EXPERIENCE

Q People and Faculty Are Great

"Wooster has an amazing community. Everyone is supportive, friendly and helpful. Teachers make a conscious effort to get to know you, and everyone wants you to succeed. The social scene is diverse. There are parties on the weekends, shopping close-by, and club events running on throughout the week. It's the place to be if you want to get to know your colleagues and professors on a personal level."

Q The People Make It...

"The academic faculty has been quite nurturing to my growth, but truthfully the administration is bunk, promoting a liberal arts education without a liberal arts lifestyle. At the same time you watch the administration ruefully spend your tuition money with no regards to the students, while the president receives one of the highest salaries in the nation. It is quite preposterous. Truly my only enjoyment is derived from the friends I have made here, who are quite diverse and sociable."

BEST OF WOOSTER

1. Small classes
2. The great community
3. Bagpipes
4. Filling the Arch with snow
5. The dorm rooms
6. Strong academic programs
7. The spring

Happy Students
87% of students return after their first year.

Proven Success
76% of students will complete their education and graduate with a degree.

WORST OF WOOSTER

1. No 24-hour food places
2. The crazy Ohio weather
3. The dorm rooms
4. useIT (The computer people)
5. The PEC
6. Stevenson Hall
7. Boy/girl ratio

Expensive
Tuition is a steep $34,950, one of the most expensive rates in the country.

Student Body

African American:	5%	Male Undergrads:	47%
Asian American:	3%	Female Undergrads:	53%
Hispanic:	2%	Living On Campus:	99%
International:	5%	Living Off Campus:	1%
Native American:	0%	Male Athletes:	42%
White:	73%	Female Athletes:	27%
Unknown:	11%	Fraternity Members:	8%
From Out-of-State:	60%	Sorority Members:	12%

Frequently Compared Schools:

Allegheny College
Denison University
Kenyon College
Oberlin College

Students Speak Out On...
EVERYTHING!

ACADEMICS

"Our professors rock! Make sure to pick classes that you are truly interested in, and never take a class because you hear that the professor is easy; you won't get anything out of those classes."

"The professors here at Woo are a ton of fun. All that I have had are interesting, absorbed in their subjects, and interested in me. I feel that they all know me, even though I may not speak individually with all of them. Classes are always interesting, especially the small ones!"

ATHLETICS

Sports Are a Great Option

"Wooster has a great sports program. Our men's basketball program has the winningest program in all of NCAA basketball programs in the past decade. We have a variety of varsity, club and intramural sports team."

"Varsity sports take over some of my friends lives. They get a lot of support from peers, alumni, and faculty, but sports aren't as big a priority as they would be at a D-I school. IM sports get a lot or participants, though."

CAMPUS DINING

Great?

"There are a lot of options if you are creative. The main dining hall offers a lot in terms of 'making' your own food,However, people always complain about them. I just think it really is up to you and your creativity."

Food

"The food here is excellent. We do not use a food service to prepare our food. Everything is made in our kitchens so it is generally very fresh. The place where Wooster loses a few points is that there is not a place that is open 24 hours for food. However there is a place that is open until 3am everyday."

CAMPUS HOUSING

Great

"With a few exceptions, housing here is better than most schools I've seen."

Variety of Housing Options

"The great thing about housing at the College of Wooster is that the college offers a lot of options. It is required that students live on campus for all four years, so there are plenty of different options to keep all four years interesting. In additional to regular residence halls (singles, doubles, triples) there are many special programs including a senior living experience, program houses, language suites, and the cross cultural living experiences program."

GUYS & GIRLS

The Guys Are Hottt-T-Tt-T!!!

"ou'll find all sorts of guys at wooster: city boys,and atl boys. The girls are pretty. They are incredibly hot, for the most part. the fashion styles are pretty cool too! you can check out the woo street style page on facebook!!!!!!!!!!"

Decsent

"I would have to say that not everyone is good looking. I find more of quality people around our campus. The student body is very diverse, so you will be able to find pretty much any kind of people here. People are attractive in many ways"

HEALTH & SAFETY

Just Be Smart.

"Overall, Wooster is such a small town that I can't imagine a safer campus anywhere else-- I feel fine walking home at 3 or 4 in the morning across campus, knowing that nothing will happen to me. If you ever feel nervous or in danger, security has "safe rides"- they're available by phone 24/7 and they will come get you wherever you are (on campus) and take you wherever you need to be with no forms, explanation, or questions."

LOOKING FOR MORE?

Check out our full-length guide to this school at collegeprowler.com/college-of-wooster/.

Colorado College

14. E. Cache La Poudre St.; Colorado Springs, CO 80903
(719) 389-6000; www.coloradocollege.edu

THE BASICS:

Acceptance Rate: 32%
Yield: 33%
Setting: Large city
Control: Private Non-Profit
Total Undergrads: 2,000
SAT Range: 1850–2130*
ACT Range: 28–31

Student-Faculty Ratio: 10:1
Retention Rate: 94%
Graduation Rate: 87%
Tuition: $37,478
Room & Board: $9,624
Avg. Aid Package: $29,412
Students With Aid: 55%

* of 2400

Academics	A-	Greek Life	C
Athletics	B-	Guys	A
Campus Dining	A-	Health & Safety	B-
Campus Housing	B+	Local Atmosphere	B-
Campus Strictness	A	Nightlife	B+
Computers	B	Off-Campus Dining	B
Diversity	C	Off-Campus Housing	B+
Drug Safety	C-	Parking	A
Facilities	B-	Transportation	C+
Girls	A-	Weather	A

CP's Student Author On...
OVERALL EXPERIENCE

The climate, social opportunities, intense academics, and the chance to become involved in a variety of activities (even as a first-year student) sways visitors within moments of stepping onto Colorado College's campus. Incoming students and those planning to apply should drop in for a visit, either for the day or overnight.

More than most other colleges, CC earns respect from its current students and graduates for the training it provides in many areas that serves students well throughout their careers. Aside from social and academic elements, CC brings amazing speakers and activities to campus. Better yet, with all the grants and funding available for student projects, rarely a night passes without a student giving a presentation about his or her adventures hiking in Tibet, helping immigrants survive at the U.S.-Mexico border, or interning in the Antarctic. It's possible to get an education nearly anywhere, but to get a real educational experience, CC is a perfect choice.

Students Speak Out On...
OVERALL EXPERIENCE

Q Work Hard, Play Hard

"The people here are really intelligent, but not flashy about it. In general the atmosphere is really open and people are super friendly. Plus, the vast majority of people are very committed to their study, but know how to throw down on the weekends/ block breaks."

Q The Best School Ever

"My experience at Colorado College does not seem to compare to any of my other friends at other schools. The level of education, the quality of people and the closeness of the school all create a great atmosphere where you can find at no other school!"

Q Rich Experiences

"Colorado College is for independently motivated students who like to try new things and get involved. There are a great variety of courses offered, and a number of incredible people and opportunities. It is easy to get overwhelmed by the block plan and the social scene—but being overwhelmed in college every now and then isn't necessarily a bad thing."

BEST OF COLORADO COLLEGE

1. Block breaks
2. The unique student body
3. The intelligent, caring professors
4. The block plan
5. The Rocky Mountains
6. Beautiful weather
7. Theme parties

Happy Students
94% of students return after their first year.

Commitment to Teaching
There are 10 students for every member of faculty on campus.

WORST OF COLORADO COLLEGE

1. Lack of ethnic diversity
2. Colorado Springs nightlife
3. Residence halls
4. Overcrowded parties
5. Gossip in the small student body
6. Going home for the summer

Expensive
Tuition is a steep $37,478, one of the most expensive rates in the country.

Students Speak Out On...
EVERYTHING!

ACADEMICS

Excellent

"A wonderful phycology and history department highlight a near flawless range in academia. The block plan is brilliant and works for 85% of students."

Acacemics Are Great

"The professors here are very approachable and incredibly smart. Most of them will go above and beyond to help you if you're struggling with something. The sciences at CC are very strong. I don't know much about the other departments, but I've heard similar things about those departments from friends."

ATHLETICS

Um. . . Hockey?

"Being at a small liberal arts school with a D-1, nationally-ranked sports team is really awesome. Tons of people go to hockey games against rival teams like University of Denver. Hockey games are really a point of pride for the school and the town in general. Other sports are fairly unrecognized, unless it's by the players's friends."

D1 Hockey, but No Men's Football Team

"Coming from a state where football is huge, it's weird coming to a school with no football team, but soccer and hockey make up for it. Our hockey team is especially good, one of our few D1 teams, and is nationally ranked. Intramural sports are especially popular here, if you're not able to join a varsity team."

CAMPUS DINING

Food Is Home-Grown, Natural, and Great!

"The food service, Bon Appétit, makes a great effort to have all different choices of food from pasta to salad to a meat dish, and there is even a vegan option for every meal. The fruits and veggies are always fresh, which is my favorite part! The three places to dine on campus all offer unique dishes and good quality food."

Healthy and Earth-Friendly!

"Bon Apetite, Colorado College's campus dining service is incredible. The three eating places on campus: Benji's, Rastall, and the Preserve, offer a wide variety of healthy and earth-friendly foods."

CAMPUS HOUSING

Dorms Pretty Nice Overall

"The freshman dorms are decent, upperclassmen dorms are great. There are decent options for food and the general environment is very welcoming."

On Campus Dorms Are Spacious!

"The freshman dorms are more spacious than other peer schools; it is not difficult to get a single room as well."

GUYS & GIRLS

I Love the CC Look

"Nearly everyone at CC is in good shape and cares about how they look. If you're going to CC, chances are you fit into the range of styles that are prevalent at CC and are probably attracted to people who are similar to you, so you'll find someone. There's someone for most everyone though: bros and the girl equivalent of bros, hipsters, hippies, outdoorsy/rugged types. There is definitely no lack in good looking people at CC."

Rugged Preps

"People at CC are generally really attractive. There is a lot of North Face, Ugg boots, and messy hair, though."

HEALTH & SAFETY

Totally Safe - Some Stray Incidents Beyond Security's Control

"Campus safety watches out for most of us, petty thefts and incidents may be our only worry, its usually safe even at later hours except for when townies want to steal bikes and stuff, so students need to watch out for their stuff."

LOOKING FOR MORE?

Check out our full-length guide to this school at collegeprowler.com/colorado-college/.

Colorado State University - Pueblo

2200 Bonforte Blvd.; Pueblo, CO 81001
(719) 549-2100; www.colostate-pueblo.edu

THE BASICS:

Acceptance Rate: 97%
Yield: 31%
Setting: Mid-sized city
Control: Public
Total Undergrads: 4,825
SAT Range: 840–1050*
ACT Range: 18–22

Student-Faculty Ratio: 18:1
Retention Rate: 66%
Graduation Rate: 33%
Tuition: $15,602
Room & Board: $7,244
Avg. Aid Package: $8,278
Students With Aid: 84%

* of 1600

This School Isn't Graded Yet!

College Prowler grades are calculated using tons of criteria, including survey responses that come from students at this school.

Unfortunately, we haven't gathered enough student surveys yet for this school to be able to calculate the grades for each section. Stay tuned to *CollegeProwler.com* for grade updates and more!

CP's Student Author On...
OVERALL EXPERIENCE

Colorado State University Pueblo is in a small town, so going to this school is a different kind of University experience. Someone who is interested in having large lecture classes, seeing different people every day, or even attending big events all of the time is not going to enjoy this campus and what the University atmosphere is all about. The average class size is about 30 students, and the big lecture classes only hit about 50 people. It's a small community; everywhere you go, you will know at least one other person. The campus size can be compared to a high school, so compared with other colleges, it's not big at all. However, a small campus means less going on all of the time, including shows, speakers, or even weekend parties.

There are advantages to attending a smaller school, though. Closer connections with professors benefit students with their grades as well as with individualized attention during and after class. There is nothing wrong with this school if you are interested in this kind of environment. Also, with a small university, tuition is cheaper.... For the rest of this editorial, visit collegeprowler.com.

Students Speak Out On...
OVERALL EXPERIENCE

Q Positive Overall Experience
"My personal experience with CSU-P is positive so far. They offer events every week for student's weather that is inviting speakers or movie gatherings. You do pay a fee in your tuition, but all the events and facilities are free to the students."

Q Good to Talk to People
"The school is not an amazing school but it is affordable and has exceptable classes. The other students are not incredibly friendly but it's ok."

Q Socializing Over Academics? Not Sure.
"I don't find the standard for academic rigor to be very high. Socializing seems to take priority a lot. Sometimes it feels like high school all over again. I plan on transferring to another school."

BEST OF COLORADO STATE PUEBLO

1. Small classes
2. Tuition
3. Teachers
4. Student activities
5. Athletic events

Help to Succeed
The school has academic and career counseling available to help you when you need it.

WORST OF COLORADO STATE PUEBLO

1. The campus is so isolated.
2. Not much to do except go to Wal-Mart
3. On-campus dining
4. Parking
5. Transportation

Not Everyone Graduates
33% of students do not complete their education or graduate with a degree.

Want a Job? On Your Own
There aren't any placement services for graduates.

Student Body

African American:	7%	Male Undergrads:	43%
Asian American:	3%	Female Undergrads:	57%
Hispanic:	22%	Living On Campus:	19%
International:	2%	Living Off Campus:	81%
Native American:	2%	Male Athletes:	15%
White:	53%	Female Athletes:	6%
Unknown:	12%	Fraternity Members:	1%
From Out-of-State:	11%	Sorority Members:	1%

Frequently Compared Schools:

Boise State University
Idaho State University
Minnesota State University
Missouri State University

Students Speak Out On...
EVERYTHING!

ACADEMICS

Just Show up!

"CSU-P professors truly care about their students. It's really hard to fail a class unless you never show up. They will always make sure the majority of the class did well on the test, or they will go over it and change or curve. Also your grade will not just be all tests. Taking 15 credit semester are no sweat at all."

Psychology Major

"My major is Psychology. The professors here are great at helping you in your search for further schooling and places to get you started into research."

ATHLETICS

Student Involvement

"I feel that going to games of any kind have a good turn out. We support our team and are proud of them win or lose."

CAMPUS DINING

Fair Spit

"The food on campus always a treat. And in truth dinning is spit between three types of services, The Meal Plan; which offers a certain number of meals per week available at the buffet, Thunder Bucks; which encourages student to use specif on campus snack dining areas life the La Cantina, the Pavilion and the Beastro, and finally Dinning Dollar; which allows students to visit anywhere but for a specif amount of money. loaded onto the account at the beginning of the year."

My Hunger Satisfacation

"The food isn't too terrible, but it's definately not home cooked meals. I wish the food was a little better especially since after practice I don't have energy to go make food."

CAMPUS HOUSING

Living at CSU

"Living at CSU is very fun. I get a lot of exercise by walking everywhere because campus is big, but not too big to walk around, and the music building is right near the dorms and dining hall. There are also many different options for living on campus, from living in building with community bathrooms, to having private bathrooms, and even sharing a condo-like facility with a roommate."

On Campus Apartments

"At CSU-Pueblo the dorms are quite nice, however if you would like more privacy the on campus apartments are a much easier to live in. You can live with a select few of your friends instead of an entire hall of people you may not get along with. The apartments are also just as close to campus as the dorms are so it is not a far walk or drive to class."

GUYS & GIRLS

A Diverse Campus

"The students at my school are an incredibly diverse group. There are multiple races, styles, and social classes and CSU-Pueblo. No matter your place of origin there is a group of your peers for you to hang out with."

The Melting Pot

"Anyone you can imagine is located here is Pueblo. We have a large variety of students here. Females are plentiful and guys are just as strong. It's a huge melting pot. We have all types of cultures and backgrounds here."

HEALTH & SAFETY

Safe

"Campus security is doing their job well, as I have always felt safe on campus. We have a branch of the Pueblo Sheriffs department on campus and they have done their job well."

Campus Security

"Pueblo has an acceptable campus security. They are officers all over campus throughout the day. However, there have been some incidences where cars have been broken into and the occasional stolen items. All in all the campus is pretty safe. There has been absolutely no problem with personal attacks. Walking alone is not a problem even at night."

LOOKING FOR MORE?

Check out our full-length guide to this school at collegeprowler.com/colorado-state-university----pueblo/.

Columbia College Chicago

600 S. Michigan Ave.; Chicago, IL 60605
(312) 663-1600; www.colum.edu

THE BASICS:

Acceptance Rate: Open
Yield: —
Setting: Large city
Control: Private Non-Profit
Total Undergrads: 11,592
SAT Range: 880–1110*
ACT Range: 18–24

Student-Faculty Ratio: 11:1
Retention Rate: 63%
Graduation Rate: 34%
Tuition: $18,960
Room & Board: $12,360
Avg. Aid Package: $8,922
Students With Aid: 73%

* of 1600

Academics	B-	Greek Life	N/A
Athletics	D+	Guys	B+
Campus Dining	B-	Health & Safety	C
Campus Housing	B+	Local Atmosphere	A
Campus Strictness	B-	Nightlife	A-
Computers	B	Off-Campus Dining	A-
Diversity	B+	Off-Campus Housing	B+
Drug Safety	C+	Parking	B-
Facilities	B+	Transportation	A+
Girls	B	Weather	B-

CP's Student Author On...
OVERALL EXPERIENCE

Columbia College is Chicago's best-kept secret. The College can be a great asset for many students, but it's important to remember that Columbia is what it is—an art school specializing in media art. It is one of the fastest paced colleges in the United States, with some of the most up-to-date technologies on the market. It is a place that will make or break you. When you come to Columbia, you will either work harder than you have in your entire life and become somebody, or you will realize that you have another dream. Columbia will not joke around with you. Everything here is very real. Everywhere you go on campus unconsciously puts off an energy uttering the phrase, "roll up your sleeves and get to work." In every classroom, faculty member, and assignment, there is truth to your work and how your life will be if you truly want to work in the field you have come to Chicago to study. Coming to Columbia is an investment in your future and worth every penny you shell out of your pocket.

Columbia students work hard. There is passion in what they do.... For the rest of this editorial, visit collegeprowler.com.

Students Speak Out On...
OVERALL EXPERIENCE

Q I Love Columbia College

"In short, I love to wake up every morning and know that I can go to class for something I truly love to do. I could not be some happy with the activities and people I work with every day!"

Q Columbia

"Columbia is truly a great school. I like how the schools allows you to be creative anyway possible. There is no limits on what you can do around the school. The school has plenty of resources around campus to help you. I also realize that Columbia allows you to be yourself at all times."

Q Awesome

"I love Columbia So much!! I wish that they would tighten the acceptance rate and make it a little more prestigious and accept more from their students..because there is so MUCH TALENT HERE!!!!"

BEST OF COLUMBIA COLLEGE

1. The creative student body, churning with inspiration
2. True professionals teaching you everything they know
3. Location, Location, Location—did I mention Location?

Knowledgeable Professors
81% of students surveyed rated the general knowledge of professors as above average.

Low-Stress Course Load
69% of students surveyed rated the manageability of work as above average.

WORST OF COLUMBIA COLLEGE

1. Parking
2. Expensive
3. Urban-based campus life can be intimidating.
4. Housing costs
5. It's easy to feel disconnected if you are living off campus.

Not Everyone Graduates
34% of students do not complete their education or graduate with a degree.

Expensive to Just Get By
68% of students surveyed felt that the amount it costs to live while at school was worse than average.

Student Body

African American:	15%	Male Undergrads:	49%
Asian American:	3%	Female Undergrads:	51%
Hispanic:	10%	Living On Campus:	22%
International:	1%	Living Off Campus:	78%
Native American:	1%	Male Athletes:	0%
White:	62%	Female Athletes:	0%
Unknown:	8%	Fraternity Members:	0%
From Out-of-State:	40%	Sorority Members:	0%

Frequently Compared Schools:
DePaul University
New York University
Northwestern University
University of Chicago

Students Speak Out On... EVERYTHING!

ACADEMICS

Wonderful!!

"I am so happy with Columbia! great teachers,classes and overall campus."

Journalism

"All of the professors have or are still working in the Journalism field and offer relevant, helpful lessons and information that can be practically applied to a career in journalism. I'm really happy with the program."

ATHLETICS

Too Busy for Collegiate Sports!

"Columbia does not compete in any Division sports. We're all too busy creating CHANGE! However, there are on-campus and off-campus clubs you can join if you want to play softball/ baseball, basketball, etc."

Active?

"It may be because I don't make an attempt to get involved in athletics on my campus but my school is not one to be known for its sports, it's known for its arts."

CAMPUS DINING

Optional

"Meal Plans are optional for students. Most students live in apartments with full kitchens. Around campus there are plenty of places to eat such as: Subway,Dunkin Donuts, KFC,Pizza Hut, Thai Spoon, Panera,Epic Burger, Pauly's Pizza, etc. The actual meal plan is also awesome! There is a sushi place, a deli, a burger/chicken place, and a great salad bar so you can't really go wrong."

Just Across the Street

"Being in a large city, Columbia has a wide variety of dining option. I don't live in a dorm, so dining hall food is a mystery. But, just across the street, or around the corner, you will find everything from wings to sushi to curry. And most restaurants offer a student discount."

CAMPUS HOUSING

Highrise Living in Downtown

"Honestly, how many college students get to live in the heart of downtown Chicago? We're privileged. I've had a great experience living on campus and hardly had any problems."

What Can I Say About on Campus Housing

"Expensive! But it is GREAT!!! Upper class or underclass.... They are wonderful."

GUYS & GIRLS

Individuality

"Columbia College Chicago has one of the most diverse student bodies I have ever seen. Not only racially, but people of different socio-economic backgrounds, mindsets, and visions. Most people at Columbia respect themselves as an individual and try to do their own thing, yet also try to contribute to a group in an effort to produce one great piece."

Guys and Girls Are Diverse

"At Columbia the guys and girls are very diverse. You see both genders from all the various cultures around the world that possess unique personalities."

HEALTH & SAFETY

Definitely a Safe Campus!!!

"I haven't been on Columbia's campus yet but I'am certain that the security is very high standard. But students must play a part in keeping themselves safe as well as their personal items by making sure their apartment rooms are locked, their items are secured when unsupervised, and keeping track of who's in and out of their rooms."

LOOKING FOR MORE?
Check out our full-length guide to this school at collegeprowler.com/columbia-college-chicago/.

Columbia University

116 Street and Broadway; New York, NY 10027
(212) 854-1754; www.columbia.edu

THE BASICS:

Acceptance Rate: 11%
Yield: 56%
Setting: Large city
Control: Private Non-Profit
Total Undergrads: 7,693
SAT Range: 2050–2320*
ACT Range: 29–34

Student-Faculty Ratio: 6:1
Retention Rate: 98%
Graduation Rate: 93%
Tuition: $41,316
Room & Board: $10,228
Avg. Aid Package: $34,948
Students With Aid: 57%

* of 2400

Academics	A+	Greek Life	C
Athletics	C	Guys	B
Campus Dining	A	Health & Safety	B
Campus Housing	C+	Local Atmosphere	A+
Campus Strictness	A-	Nightlife	A-
Computers	B	Off-Campus Dining	A
Diversity	A	Off-Campus Housing	C
Drug Safety	B-	Parking	C+
Facilities	A-	Transportation	B+
Girls	B-	Weather	B-

CP's Student Author On...
OVERALL EXPERIENCE

Most students absolutely love Columbia. They discovered the school that filled their academic, social, and professional needs. Since Columbia is so selective, most people who attend are thrilled to be here and would never wish to be anywhere else.

Columbia has the potential to give any student what they are looking for—be it prestige, socialization, culture, or a degree from one of the finest schools in the world. The city is not for the weak-hearted. Those who need hand-holding may not find that kind of support here, but then again, they might, if they look in the right place. It takes time to find and access the things you want and need (and often students discover fulfillment in things they never thought they'd like before like exploring the city late at night or finding joy in Medieval Italian Literature), but if you're willing to work a little bit and leave a little up to chance, you may get more out of college than most of your high school friends who went to smaller, less diverse schools with fewer opportunities.... For the rest of this editorial, visit collegeprowler.com.

Students Speak Out On...
OVERALL EXPERIENCE

Q I Love Columbia
"I couldnt have asked for a better school to be a part of!"

Q Hard, So-So Facilites, but Amazing Resources
"Top-notch programs. Going to have to study hard, but should find moments to kick back."

Q Very Good
"I loved my time in college. You have access to one of the best cities in the world, while still having the security of a campus. Very diverse, so you're sure to find a place somewhere."

Q "I love Columbia. I think I'll force my kids to go (once they are born, of course)!"

Q "All I can tell you is that it is an Ivy League school and a real honor to get into. It has an outstanding academic record. I graduated at the top of my class and had my choices of graduate schools; I chose Columbia."

BEST OF COLUMBIA

1. The Core Curriculum
2. A campus in the heart of New York City
3. Diversity of student body and opinion
4. Access to smart professors and curious peers

Happy Students
98% of students return after their first year.

Commitment to Teaching
There are 6 students for every member of faculty on campus.

WORST OF COLUMBIA

1. The sometimes sluggish bureaucracy
2. Cost of education and cost of living
3. The eternal dilemma - studying or doing something cool and interesting in NYC
4. Cramped housing

Expensive
Tuition is a steep $41,316, one of the most expensive rates in the country.

Expensive to Just Get By
64% of students surveyed felt that the amount it costs to live while at school was worse than average.

Student Body

African American:	9%	Male Undergrads:	51%
Asian American:	15%	Female Undergrads:	49%
Hispanic:	10%	Living On Campus:	94%
International:	10%	Living Off Campus:	6%
Native American:	1%	Male Athletes:	13%
White:	42%	Female Athletes:	11%
Unknown:	14%	Fraternity Members:	7%
From Out-of-State:	79%	Sorority Members:	4%

Frequently Compared Schools:

Brown University
Cornell University
Harvard University
University of Pennsylvania

Students Speak Out On... EVERYTHING!

ACADEMICS

Q Variety-Opportunities-Success

"The academics at Columbia are simple amazing. You will find that the College has many connections to advance careers and one really has to focus to make the best of it. The name Columbia rings a bell with every major company and it has a great reputation. The academics are unlimited and it is very focused and organized. Any student wouould be happy to come here."

Q Great Professors

"Amazing opportunities to meet some of the best minds around."

ATHLETICS

Q Great

"The athletics department at Columbia is great and it offers all types of clubs and student athletics. The team spirit is great here and everyone seems to get involved in a different club. There is alot of diversity here."

Q Not the Greatest Feature of Such a Great School

"I never really associated Columbia with athletics and I still don't. I have not attended 1 sporting event yet and athletics certainly is not one of those factors that unites all the students althought it does during homecoming. Columbia's football and basketball teams are its most famous."

CAMPUS DINING

Q Dining Halls

"The food really is not that bad, but having a mandatory meal plan as a freshman makes it seem awful by the end of the year. I was very content with the dining halls for the first semester, but after not wanting to waste the 15 meals Columbia makes me have a week, I eat there way more than I would like to. Can't wait until next year when don't have a meal plan though!"

Q John Jay Is Good for What It Is: a Dining Hall

"With a variety of options, John Jay Dining Hall is adequate and a popular hangout amongst students. Despite really awkward hours and sketchy food from time to time, John Jay is very reliable. It is noted that students from other schools marvel at hos much better Columbia food is. A meal plan is a good idea. You do, however have NYC at your fingertips. Just keep in mind that it can get pricey."

CAMPUS HOUSING

Q Convenience of Campus Life

"The campus is small enough that your farthest class will be less than a ten minute class and as a freshmen all your dorms are right on campus and easy to get access to. You can stand in the middle of the campus and not know that you are right in the middle of the city. Yet walk outside the gates and anything you need is right there on the street. All different types of food and stores that give you access to college essentials. It makes adjusting to be a college student easy and comfortable."

GUYS & GIRLS

Q Guys N Gals

"Since students live in New York City, everyone has their own personal style. There are preppy people, students who just wear their greek letters all the time, students who wear nothing but black everyday (true to NYC fashion!), and students with other styles as well. Most people are fashionable in some sense of the word, as you won't really find people coming to class in sweats unless they're athletes. Social life is great, we have New York as a playground!"

HEALTH & SAFETY

Q Safety

"the guards are very serious about their jobs and always make sure that people sign in before entering the buildings"

LOOKING FOR MORE?

Check out our full-length guide to this school at collegeprowler.com/columbia-university/.

Concordia College at Moorhead

901 S. Eighth St.; Moorhead, MN 56562
(218) 299-4100; www.cord.edu

THE BASICS:

Acceptance Rate: 79%	**Student-Faculty Ratio:** 13:1
Yield: 32%	**Retention Rate:** 84%
Setting: Suburban	**Graduation Rate:** 5%
Control: Private Non-Profit	**Tuition:** $25,760
Total Undergrads: 2,788	**Room & Board:** $6,275
SAT Range: 1553–1978*	**Avg. Aid Package:** $18,090
ACT Range: 22–28	**Students With Aid:** 100%

* of 2400

Academics	B	Greek Life	N/A
Athletics	C	Guys	A+
Campus Dining	A	Health & Safety	A+
Campus Housing	A-	Local Atmosphere	B
Campus Strictness	C	Nightlife	B-
Computers	B	Off-Campus Dining	B
Diversity	C+	Off-Campus Housing	B+
Drug Safety	B-	Parking	B+
Facilities	B+	Transportation	B
Girls	A	Weather	B

CP's Student Author On...
OVERALL EXPERIENCE

High school seniors are constantly barraged by numerous colleges, all with one basic claim: that they are the best, the cream, the institution with which you not only aspire to be involved, but the institution that fits your exact personality traits. Concordia is no different than the rest of the institutions vying for new freshman classes. However, the college delivers on its promises and, more importantly, does not entice potential students with false or skewed information. You know exactly what you get when enrolling at Concordia, and that is by no means a bad thing. On the contrary, it is nice to know what is explicitly offered.

Some students have their doubts upon applying and accepting freshman status at Concordia, but it is an overall fantastic experience. It is a small, private, liberal arts college that won't consume all of your money, at least not as much as other similar private schools. There are problems—it is definitely not a utopia—but the positives tend to outweigh the negatives.... For the rest of this editorial, visit collegeprowler.com.

Students Speak Out On...
OVERALL EXPERIENCE

Q Amazing School

"Concordia is the ultimate small town environment. You get to know almost everybody and the education is first rate"

Q A+

"It's wonderful! The people are amazing and teachers get to know you super well!"

Q Awesome

"This is a terrific school. There is a wide range of people with different interests, and you get to know the faculty very well. It's a great school."

Q Experience

"I loved everything about Concordia College. Small class sizes are amazing, professors are very helpful, and the students are extremely polite, for the most part. The cost sucks though, I have to be honest here."

Q The Teachers

"The teachers are so helpful and caring. They are able to call on me by name. It is so nice to have supportive teachers."

BEST OF CONCORDIA COLLEGE

1. The people
2. The food
3. Small classes
4. The community
5. The professors
6. Music ensembles

Happy Students
84% of students return after their first year.

Easy Financial Aid Process
73% of students surveyed told us that the financial aid process went smoothly and they received the financial aid they needed.

WORST OF CONCORDIA COLLEGE

1. Cold weather
2. Books are pricey.
3. The Red River floods!
4. There is very little "nightlife."
5. Places are not open 24/7.

Expensive
Tuition is a steep $25,760, one of the most expensive rates in the country.

Not Everyone Graduates
5% of students do not complete their education or graduate with a degree.

Student Body

African American:	1%	Male Undergrads:	39%
Asian American:	2%	Female Undergrads:	61%
Hispanic:	1%	Living On Campus:	67%
International:	4%	Living Off Campus:	33%
Native American:	0%	Male Athletes:	42%
White:	91%	Female Athletes:	20%
Unknown:	1%	Fraternity Members:	0%
From Out-of-State:	33%	Sorority Members:	0%

Frequently Compared Schools:

Davidson College
Gustavus Adolphus College
Harvard University
St. Olaf College

Students Speak Out On... EVERYTHING!

ACADEMICS

One of the Best

"Concordia College has fantastic professors. They always make themselves available and all of the classes that I have had are very interesting."

English Writing/Theatre Arts

"I haven't had too much experience within the courses of my major as I am currently working on getting the required courses done. However, I know the courses are of high quality and taught by excellent professors. The credits required to earn my specific major aren't horrible-less than some other courses-but still quite a load of classes."

ATHLETICS

School Spirit

"Homecoming was simply incredible! I was completely immersed in a sea of cobber colors, where generations of students and alumni were gathered together cheering for our team without badmouthing our opponents."

Hard Workers and Fun Ims

"Anyone can get involved and there are numerous student activities related to sports."

CAMPUS DINING

Easy, Affordable, Cheap

"Three words every college student likes to hear. Also: GOOD! There are numerous options for everyone (including vegetarians) and there is always something different."

Yum

"The food tastes great and there are a lot of options. The hours are nice but they could open earlier on weekends."

CAMPUS HOUSING

Residence Life Staff

"I have gotten to know most of the Resident Advisors in my residence hall, as well as our hall director. They are all positive, helpful people who go above and beyond what I was expecting. Practically every other week my RA organizes a fun event for the floor!"

Living on Campus

"I have really enjoyed my time living on campus. I am in a freshman dorm and have so much fun. The girls on my floor keep their doors open and we socialize with each other a lot. On weekends, there's always something going on. The rooms are a bit small, but I haven't had a problem with the size. My dorm is centrally located on campus, which is very convenient."

GUYS & GIRLS

Relationships Among Students

"The guys and girls at Concordia are all very friendly. That is one thing that I so thouroughly enjoyed when I toured Concordia. The relationships and friendships between not only the students but also between the students and the faculty."

Plenty of Girls

"The girl to guy ratio at Concordia is nearly 2:1 and throwing in Concordia's large gay population, it becomes nearly 3:1 for straight guys. Girls are primarily blonde, and guys range from football hicks to the music students, who are generally smarter, and also dress better."

HEALTH & SAFETY

Completely Safe

"I have never once felt that I was unsafe. Everyone is very welcome and you are bound to find people you are comfortable with!"

Campus Security

"Between RA's on duty, desk workers in every dorm, and on call campus security that are constantly patrolling the campus with a friendly face I never feel endangered or at risk at Concordia."

LOOKING FOR MORE?

Check out our full-length guide to this school at collegeprowler.com/concordia-college-at-moorhead/.

Connecticut College

270 Mohegan Ave.; New London, CT 06320
(860) 447-1911; www.connecticutcollege.edu

THE BASICS:

Acceptance Rate: 37%
Yield: 29%
Setting: Small city
Control: Private Non-Profit
Total Undergrads: 1,908
SAT Range: 1870–2130*
ACT Range: 25–29

Student-Faculty Ratio: 9:1
Retention Rate: 90%
Graduation Rate: 88%
Tuition: $49,385
Room & Board: $0
Avg. Aid Package: $27,515
Students With Aid: 46%

* of 2400

Academics	A-	Greek Life	N/A
Athletics	B-	Guys	B-
Campus Dining	B	Health & Safety	B+
Campus Housing	B+	Local Atmosphere	C+
Campus Strictness	B+	Nightlife	C
Computers	C	Off-Campus Dining	B
Diversity	C	Off-Campus Housing	D-
Drug Safety	B-	Parking	B+
Facilities	B+	Transportation	C
Girls	B+	Weather	C-

CP's Student Author On...
OVERALL EXPERIENCE

Overall, students enjoy their experience at Conn. Some of the most often reasons cited include the amazing professors, strong academic programs, the small size of the school, and the beautiful campus. This is a great school for students who don't know what they want to major in; Conn's General Education requirements make it mandatory to take a variety of courses, and faculty are always available to advise students. Because of this, many come to Conn a tabula rasa, unsure of what to study, and leave as knowledgeable practitioners in a field they genuinely enjoy. The most common complaint among students who don't like Conn is its small size. Because of this, it's important to visit overnight or at least take a tour to try the campus on for size.

Despite the restricted social scene, most students find a core group of friends and have an unforgettable four years. Besides, with a willingness to try new things, students should never be bored on campus.... For the rest of this editorial, visit collegeprowler.com.

Students Speak Out On...
OVERALL EXPERIENCE

Q "I have to say that I was lucky enough to find my core group of friends during freshman year. It was a fun four years that I'll never forget. If I could have gone to Yale or Harvard, speaking from a career standpoint, I wouldn't have come here. However, CC was good to me, and I wish I could do it all over again."

Q "Sometimes I wish I had gone to a bigger school in a bigger city, but on the whole, there's no place I'd rather be than Conn College."

Q "I'm very glad I'm here. If you look for it, the academic environment is there. I've met great people."

Q "I don't really fit in at Conn, but I know so many kids that love it more than anything. I think I would have been happier at a bigger school."

Q "Conn is great. Personally, I should have gone to school in Washington, DC, and I regret not doing so."

Q "I absolutely loved my time at Conn; I couldn't have asked for a more enriching, fun, or stimulating experience."

BEST OF CONN COLLEGE

1. Outstanding professors
2. Student-faculty research opportunities
3. Honor Code/self-scheduled final exams
4. Single rooms (usually) after freshman year
5. Floralia

Happy Students
90% of students return after their first year.

Commitment to Teaching
There are 9 students for every member of faculty on campus.

WORST OF CONN COLLEGE

1. Being stuck in the Middletown Bubble
2. Restricted and predictable social scene
3. Internet blackouts
4. Lack of diversity
5. Lack of public transportation

Expensive
Tuition is a steep $49,385, one of the most expensive rates in the country.

Student Body

African American:	4%	Male Undergrads:	40%
Asian American:	4%	Female Undergrads:	60%
Hispanic:	5%	Living On Campus:	99%
International:	4%	Living Off Campus:	1%
Native American:	0%	Male Athletes:	34%
White:	75%	Female Athletes:	32%
Unknown:	7%	Fraternity Members:	0%
From Out-of-State:	88%	Sorority Members:	0%

Students Speak Out On...
EVERYTHING!

ACADEMICS

Q Great Professors, Challenging but Amazing Classes
"So far all the classes I've had at Conn are great. The professors are incredibly smart and friendly. I'm a French and German double majors and I have to say, if you want to go deep into foreign languages or global focus, Conn is a great great school for you."

Q "Honestly, I don't think that General Education Requirements are hard to fill. It's possible to for people to go aboard, take classes for the centers, double major,and have a minor."

ATHLETICS

Q Lots of Athletes and Many Fans
"There are a lot of athletes on campus, some are varsity level, and many students also participate in club sports. During the soccer games you can find many fans watching on the field and fans support the other teams as well."

Q "It seems like everyone plays a sport. We are an athletic bunch. The people who play truly love what they are doing, so that makes it so much better."

CAMPUS DINING

Q No Variety
"Food at conn started out okay, but once parents weekend hit, it all went downhill. The chefs would often combine a few leftovers into one (obvious) new concoction for dinner. And, the only place for late night was Cro, which offers about 5 different items and closes at 2 on weekends. Harris is always a good option for more selection, but that's if you want to make the trek to the plex."

Q "We have innumerable options in the main dining hall, but the smaller ones are the best for the atmosphere. We also have an all-vegetarian dining hall—Freeman—that does make-your-own stir-fry twice a week."

CAMPUS HOUSING

Q "Lots of people want to live in certain dorms for so many different reasons, but what it comes down to is they all are pretty much the same. You will have the time of your life in any dorm so long as you are with your friends. The people make the dorms great!"

Q "The dorms on north campus at Connecticut College, called the Plex, are nice, but the whole place looks like a hospital. I think it's hard to get around the Plex if you don't live there."

GUYS & GIRLS

Q Conn Guys Are Cute
"Guys at Conn are somewhat feminine and really cute. Most of them tend to be skinny and good looking. As Conn is a school for the richest kids of New England, you prob will see well-dressed preppy guys all around campus."

Q "I think that there are more good-looking girls than guys. This may be because I have a boyfriend already, so I'm not looking at any boys in particular."

HEALTH & SAFETY

Q Health and Safety of CT College
"The safety and health of the college is very safe and sanitary. I believe if you were going to choose a college that followed safety for their students and made sure tehy were out of harms way, it would be Connecticut College."

Q "My experience with Campus Safety was really the only bad experience I had at Conn. They all seem to resent the students and their obvious disdain for me made me feel more unsafe than the possibility of New Londoners coming on campus. They are never helpful and act put out whenever you need anything."

LOOKING FOR MORE?
Check out our full-length guide to this school at collegeprowler.com/connecticut-college/.

Converse College

580 E. Main St.; Spartanburg, SC 29302
(864) 596-9000; www.converse.edu

THE BASICS:

Acceptance Rate: 68%	Student-Faculty Ratio: 10:1
Yield: 38%	Retention Rate: 72%
Setting: Small city	Graduation Rate: 56%
Control: Private Non-Profit	Tuition: $25,230
Total Undergrads: 720	Room & Board: $7,760
SAT Range: 960–1170*	Avg. Aid Package: $22,193
ACT Range: 20–25	Students With Aid: 100%

* of 1600

Academics	B-	Greek Life	N/A
Athletics	C-	Guys	B-
Campus Dining	C+	Health & Safety	B-
Campus Housing	B+	Local Atmosphere	C+
Campus Strictness	C+	Nightlife	C+
Computers	B	Off-Campus Dining	B-
Diversity	B-	Off-Campus Housing	C-
Drug Safety	B+	Parking	A+
Facilities	B+	Transportation	C+
Girls	B+	Weather	B

CP's Student Author On...
OVERALL EXPERIENCE

Converse College is a women's college, but that's not what sets it apart from other schools: it's the students' love for the College that makes it stand out. The school has a lot going for it. Students repeatedly point out that Converse's academics are top-notch, especially its well-known music school. The students also feel that professors are dedicated to their academic advancement inside and outside of class. In addition to its academics, Converse offers an excellent campus community; women generally like and trust one another and feel safe on campus. The community also has many different traditions that make students feel closer to one another, more like sisters than classmates.

However, Converse has its disadvantages, the main one being the limited social life on and off campus. There are few good parties or other events on campus, and to make it worse, most students go home on the weekends. The town of Spartanburg is fine for shopping and food, but it seriously lacks in good places to hang out. The major bar in Spartanburg is Wild Wings, which means that you're pretty limited if you want to get out and party.... For the rest of this editorial, visit collegeprowler.com.

Students Speak Out On...
OVERALL EXPERIENCE

Q **Best Time of My Life!**

"I absolutely adore Converse for so many reasons! I have made many friends here that are sure to be there for me for years to come. I love the traditions around campus, there are so many of them and all of them are tons of fun to take part in! The work load is fair and the classes are definitely worth the price you pay to go to the school."

Q **Extremely Wonderful**

"I love it here. The music program is wonderful. I am able to study as well as have a social life on campus. My friends understand when I can't hang out and don't get upset about it."

Q **Overall Experience**

"Overall, the all girls situation is not that bad. There are some guys here that are grad students, wish there were more though. Wofford College is just seconds away so there are always parties there to go to. There are also a lot of other colleges around and Clemson and USC are really close as well."

BEST OF CONVERSE

1. Campus atmosphere
2. Friendly fellow students
3. Professors
4. Small classes
5. No boys!

Commitment to Teaching
There are 10 students for every member of faculty on campus.

WORST OF CONVERSE

1. Commuting
2. Cost
3. No off-campus housing
4. Limited social life
5. Parking
6. No boys!
7. Strict rules
8. Convocation credits

Students Can't Wait to Get Out of Town
50% of students surveyed said that there's no way they would live here after graduation.

Student Body

African American:	14%	Male Undergrads:	1%
Asian American:	1%	Female Undergrads:	99%
Hispanic:	3%	Living On Campus:	85%
International:	3%	Living Off Campus:	15%
Native American:	0%	Male Athletes:	—
White:	67%	Female Athletes:	—
Unknown:	12%	Fraternity Members:	0%
From Out-of-State:	25%	Sorority Members:	0%

Frequently Compared Schools:
Catawba College
College of Charleston
Occidental College
Rollins College

Students Speak Out On... EVERYTHING!

ACADEMICS

Music Education

"I am very satisfied with my education. The student/teacher ratio is small. The facilities are always clean and nice. Everyone gets along. I have good relationships with my professors. It is alot of work and very time consuming, but well worth the hard work."

Always Encouraging and Interested in Your Acheivment and Development

"The faculty and staff at Converse are invested in their students and care about their students' education and success. All of my professors also act as advisors and are willing to offer support, encouragement, and academic advice."

ATHLETICS

Female Sports Rank Best!

"Since Converse College is a female university, all sports are also single-gendered. There is a nice gym, and workout room for athletics, and also one for the rest of campus. There is a soccer field, and two tennis courts. Our students are very successful in their sport, and there is plenty of fan support!"

Game Day Spirit!

"Athletics at Converse are always top-notch! All the fans are super supportive and students are encouraged to get involved. The facilities on campus are great, too."

CAMPUS DINING

Sodexo Challenge

"I really like the dining here at Converse. I think they try to be healthy, and I think they have a good variety of options. WE actually have six different flavors of ice cream, a variety salad bar, and a neat innovation station, where you can create your own meal. It's overall good:):)"

Campus Dining AKA GEE

"It is very good. It accomodates everyone's preferences by having [options from] vegetarian meals and vegan meals to all meat!!!"

CAMPUS HOUSING

Good but Expensive

"The conditions and atmosphere are excellent. I just wish I could afford it."

Varying Degrees of Awesomeness

"It's not hard to get a dorm. Each dorm has its own flavor and pros and cons. I love Cudd because it feels like a house, but the rooms are either really big or super small. Dexter is the oldest dorm on campus, but it is in the process of renovation. Belk is a suite-style. The best housing is the senior apartments. They are absolutely amazing, but obviously you have to be a senior (academic or social). The senior apartments were just completed, and they are LEED certified."

GUYS & GIRLS

Woman's College

"Converse College is a college comprised almost entirely of women, although there are some male graduate students. Everybody is friendly and most people tend to get along with each other. There are a lot of girls with heavy Southern accents, but it does not take long to get used to!"

All Girls

"Converse is an all girl's school, so get used to not seeing boys on campus. The girls are very friendly, beautiful, and very social!"

HEALTH & SAFETY

Awesome

"Great health professionals who make themselves available in times of acute illness and the security guards are great!"

Completely Secure

"Call booths are located in every parking lot and the police are always willing to help. I feel very safe at the campus even when I'm walking late at night back to the dorms."

LOOKING FOR MORE?
Check out our full-length guide to this school at collegeprowler.com/converse-college/.

Cornell College

600 First St. SW; Mount Vernon, IA 52314
(319) 895-4000; www.cornellcollege.edu

THE BASICS:

Acceptance Rate: 44%
Yield: 26%
Setting: Town
Control: Private Non-Profit
Total Undergrads: 1,142
SAT Range: 1660–1960*
ACT Range: 24–29

Student-Faculty Ratio: 12:1
Retention Rate: 79%
Graduation Rate: 72%
Tuition: $29,580
Room & Board: $7,500
Avg. Aid Package: $25,535
Students With Aid: 97%

* of 2400

Academics	B	Greek Life	B-
Athletics	C	Guys	B-
Campus Dining	C-	Health & Safety	C+
Campus Housing	B	Local Atmosphere	C
Campus Strictness	A-	Nightlife	B
Computers	C+	Off-Campus Dining	C
Diversity	C+	Off-Campus Housing	D+
Drug Safety	C	Parking	B+
Facilities	C+	Transportation	C
Girls	C+	Weather	C+

CP's Student Author On...
OVERALL EXPERIENCE

One Course At A Time (OCAAT) pervades every aspect of the Cornell experience. From the academic schedule and athletics to involvement in organizations and the expected response time to e-mails, OCAAT becomes embedded in Cornell students' way of life. The block plan has a way of distorting time at Cornell. Many students find themselves marking time by the day or week of the block rather than by the actual dates. Though, from an academic standpoint, the block plan isn't for everyone, it does allow the flexibility necessary for learners of all types to be successful in the classroom. Additionally, OCAAT allows most students to at least pick up a minor, while many students double or even triple major. There are valuable internship opportunities around every corner, and several programs and centers focused on helping students thrive. Study abroad experiences are unparalleled and easily affordable, due to the shorter time frame.... For the rest of this editorial, visit collegeprowler.com.

Students Speak Out On...
OVERALL EXPERIENCE

Q Worth the Money

"Met my girlfriend, figured out what I wanted to do with my life, learned to be a better person. Despite what I don't like about Cornell, I still believe I made the right choice in schools."

Q One Course At A Time schedule

"The best thing, in my opinion, about Cornell is the uniqueness of the One Course At A Time schedule. Here, students focus on one class everyday for 18 days, take a 4 day break and begin a new class. This block schedule helps students who have difficulty focusing on more than one thing at a time as well as challenges students to complete work promptly."

BEST OF CORNELL COLLEGE

1. OCAAT
2. Great professors
3. Small class sizes
4. Residential campus/ sense of community
5. Off-campus study opportunities
6. Student organizations

Proven Success
72% of students will complete their education and graduate with a degree.

WORST OF CORNELL COLLEGE

1. Cold winters
2. Dining hall/food
3. Housing
4. Lack of school spirit
5. Campus is located on top of a hill.

Expensive
Tuition is a steep $29,580, one of the most expensive rates in the country.

Student Body

African American:	3%	Male Undergrads:	50%
Asian American:	2%	Female Undergrads:	50%
Hispanic:	3%	Living On Campus:	90%
International:	4%	Living Off Campus:	10%
Native American:	1%	Male Athletes:	49%
White:	80%	Female Athletes:	28%
Unknown:	3%	Fraternity Members:	20%
From Out-of-State:	83%	Sorority Members:	21%

Frequently Compared Schools:
Beloit College
Cornell University
Grinnell College
Lawrence University

Students Speak Out On...
EVERYTHING!

ACADEMICS

Q Cornell Has a Strong Academic Program, Which Drew Me Here

"I really love Cornell academics. Some individual courses or instructors may be extremely challenging, but most courses are both interesting and sufficiently challenging. Cornell's academic reputation is what drew me to this place and I love it here. I love the small group discussions and engaging lectures. I do not love the sometimes "Easy A" classes or majors which get the same grades for doing a lot less work."

Q You Have Lots of Opportunities With Every Major You Are at

"My major is Economics. There is Berry Center which helps Econ students a lot with everything: internships, reading groups, independent study etc. All the professors are very nice and helpful in finding resources for students in their majors. Other majors like Biology, you can do research with your professor throughout the summer. Or Anthropology major, you have chances to travel to study about cultures in different regions or countries"

ATHLETICS

Q Cornell Sports

"Varsity athletics are a part of almost everybody's life. We are a smaller school, so it is easier for students to play sports. We have an excellent sports center to practice and work out. Cornell also offers a lot of IM games throughout the entire year."

Q The RAMS

"I really like watching Basketball. The purple color is cool, the cheer leading team is cool as well. GO RAMS!"

CAMPUS DINING

Q So Many Options

"The set-up of the dining hall at Cornell provides the optimum amount of options. Even when considering how small the school is, there are so many options to choose from that it never gets old. The only downside is the taste of some items really is disgusting."

Q Repetitive Menus

"The food on campus is okay at first, but after awhile it seems like they are just repeating and serving us the same things."

CAMPUS HOUSING

Q Great Housing Options

"Everything is within a 5 minute walk! A very residential campus so most people live in the residence halls. The facilities are up to date, a few buildings are older but even those aren't horrible."

Q Dorms Are Pretty Good for What We've Got Resources for.

"Cornell does well with what resources they have, I think. The buildings are old and would cost an absolute fortune to renovate. Sure, the dorms aren't anything fancy, but they are still pretty nice--spacious, for the most part, too (compared to other colleges)."

GUYS & GIRLS

Q Several students from other countries

"You can probably find students from every state here and several students from other countries. There will always be some that you can relate to."

Q A Variety Show

"Everyone can find someone to connect with here. With students ranging from "preppy" to the most eclectic person you could imagine everyone can find a best friend. We have a lot of people who fall into cliques but there are those individuals that spread themselves out and cross into may different groups. I think anyone can find their niche and a group of core friends here."

HEALTH & SAFETY

Q Safe but Strict

"The fact that the school is in such a small town keeps it from having very much crime. If anything the campus security is annoying in enforcing their policies on the students."

LOOKING FOR MORE?
Check out our full-length guide to this school at collegeprowler.com/cornell-college/.

Cornell University

Ithaca, NY 14853
(607) 255-2000; www.cornell.edu

THE BASICS:

Acceptance Rate: 19%
Yield: 48%
Setting: Small city
Control: Private Non-Profit
Total Undergrads: 13,914
SAT Range: 1930–2230*
ACT Range: 29–33

Student-Faculty Ratio: 12:1
Retention Rate: 96%
Graduation Rate: 93%
Tuition: $37,954
Room & Board: $12,160
Avg. Aid Package: $29,621
Students With Aid: 54%

*of 2400

Academics	A	Greek Life	A+
Athletics	C+	Guys	B
Campus Dining	A	Health & Safety	C+
Campus Housing	B	Local Atmosphere	B
Campus Strictness	B+	Nightlife	A-
Computers	B+	Off-Campus Dining	A-
Diversity	B+	Off-Campus Housing	B+
Drug Safety	C+	Parking	C+
Facilities	A-	Transportation	A-
Girls	B	Weather	D+

CP's Student Author On...
OVERALL EXPERIENCE

Students express both praise and criticism of their overall experience at Cornell University. Positive experiences seem to outweigh negative ones, with most agreeing that even some of the negative aspects of Cornell—the immense workload, competition, dreary weather, and social pressures of a large campus—have taught them valuable life lessons. The large size of the campus can be both a blessing and a curse.Cornell offers a wealth of academic, professional, and personal opportunities, but can also offers the feeling of getting lost in the crowd.

Most students agree that it falls on the individual to make the most out of one's time at Cornell to be outgoing, open to new ideas and experiences, and proactive in pursuit of one's goals. Classes are difficult, and no one can expect to coast, but for those who are willing to work hard, classes can be very fulfilling. Finding a balance between coursework and social activities can be difficult, but if you can manage it, you will find a campus filled with new and interesting activities to get involved in.

Students Speak Out On...
OVERALL EXPERIENCE

Q Best School Ever

"I love this school and it is so worth it to work hard in high school. You really do work with the best and the brightest in every field."

Q Happy~~~~~

"Many lovely places to explore on campus. The clocktower has daily concerts with classical and pop music. Very rainy, but the waterfalls are prettier after the rain. Lots of squirrels and chipmunks. Really good food. Foliage beautiful during autumn. There are many parties but you don't have to go in order to have a good time while at college."

Q Cornell's Overall Experience

"Cornell is an amazing university. It offers so many opportunities and gives you a great education. The university sets up a lot of activities and there are a ton of clubs.The waterfalls and nature scenes are also gorgeous and I see them every weekday on the way to class.Students are friendly so it's easy to find your place and make friends. Also, most professors are very kind and genuinely love what they teach."

BEST OF CORNELL

1. Outdoor scenery, especially in the spring
2. Slope Day
3. Great friends
4. Great food
5. Sledding down Libe Slope on cafeteria trays

Happy Students
96% of students return after their first year.

Proven Success
93% of students will complete their education and graduate with a degree.

WORST OF CORNELL

1. Weather
2. Icy hills and paths
3. Early morning classes
4. Finals week
5. Parking tickets
6. CourseEnroll
7. Fees for the bus, parking, gym, etc.

Expensive
Tuition is a steep $37,954, one of the most expensive rates in the country.

Expensive Dorms
Living on campus doesn't come cheap, with an average housing price tag of $7,210.

Student Body

African American:	5%	Male Undergrads:	51%
Asian American:	16%	Female Undergrads:	49%
Hispanic:	6%	Living On Campus:	57%
International:	9%	Living Off Campus:	43%
Native American:	0%	Male Athletes:	10%
White:	49%	Female Athletes:	9%
Unknown:	15%	Fraternity Members:	32%
From Out-of-State:	72%	Sorority Members:	23%

Frequently Compared Schools:
Brown University
Columbia University
Harvard University
University of Pennsylvania

Students Speak Out On... EVERYTHING!

ACADEMICS

Totally Worth It!

"Most classes at Cornell are intense, but very interesting and in most cases the professors will go out of their way to help you and make sure you understand the material."

Food

"Cornell has some of the best dining options, and the campus itself is gorgeous."

ATHLETICS

Go Big Red! or Not.

"Athletics are encouraged at Cornell, and we do have many wonderful athletic facilities. There is a lot of spirit when it comes to our teams, particularly hockey and basketball (especially after we made it to the Sweet 16 last year!) There are lots of great PE classes too, that I regularly take advantage of. However, the divide between the athletic and non-athletic communities couldn't be starker. I wish that weren't the case."

Tons of School Spirit, but Not That Atheltics Focused

"Don't get me wrong, Cornell pays big bucks to bring in the best athletes, but aside from Basketball, Wrestling, and Hockey, Cornell students don't get too excited over it. The games are all these in state of the art studios, and freshman rush the field for homecoming is a big deal, but it's not the main focus of campus."

CAMPUS DINING

Dining

"There is a large variety-especially for vegetarians/vegans. The food is delicious at all the campus dining halls-you have typical pizza and hot dogs offered, but they always switch it up and offer additional healthy food that is simply amazing."

Ranked #1 for a Reason.

"Cornell's dining facilities are fantastic. Lots of good food, huge variety, and all you can eat. It is very easy to pack on weight at Cornell if you have poor self-control. And the ice cream is FANTASTIC."

CAMPUS HOUSING

In Love With the Housing

"Balch is the most awesome freshmen dorm, girls only. You share a sink room with the neighboring room. Closest dorm to main campus. Beautiful architecture and free ticket giveaways throughout the year. Every Friday there's free edible goodies for the residents. A cool ancient elevator. Really nice people who clean bathrooms and hallway and chat with you about your day. Singles are pretty costly and lonely."

Excellent Housing All-Around

"North Campus is a great environment for freshman-all of the dorms are nice and it has a big community feel. The upperclassman dorms on West are all awesome. They have the best dining halls!"

GUYS & GIRLS

Guaranteed Intelligence Helps :)

"The guys are decently attractive, especially because you know they're definitely intelligent enough to have been accepted.. that helps things a lot"

Hard Prep School Boys

"The Greek Life is huge here so a lot of the boys are "fratty". However, Cornell is not outwardly preppy. The boys are preppy in the way they act and spend their money but for the most part they dress much harder and tougher than they actually are. Handsome boys and most of them have old money and are going places."

HEALTH & SAFETY

Highly Insulated

"The campus is so well protected that when something does happen, the students are so stunned that they react with panic and terror."

LOOKING FOR MORE?
Check out our full-length guide to this school at collegeprowler.com/cornell-university/.

Creighton University

2500 California Plaza; Omaha, NE 68178
(402) 280-2700; www.creighton.edu

THE BASICS:

Acceptance Rate: 82%	**Student-Faculty Ratio:** 11:1
Yield: 27%	**Retention Rate:** 89%
Setting: Large city	**Graduation Rate:** 76%
Control: Private Non-Profit	**Tuition:** $29,544
Total Undergrads: 4,133	**Room & Board:** $8,814
SAT Range: 1570–1910*	**Avg. Aid Package:** $23,916
ACT Range: 24–29	**Students With Aid:** 96%

* of 2400

Academics	B	Greek Life	B+
Athletics	B-	Guys	C+
Campus Dining	B	Health & Safety	C-
Campus Housing	B	Local Atmosphere	B
Campus Strictness	B+	Nightlife	B-
Computers	B+	Off-Campus Dining	A-
Diversity	C-	Off-Campus Housing	B-
Drug Safety	B	Parking	A-
Facilities	B	Transportation	B-
Girls	B	Weather	C+

CP's Student Author On...
OVERALL EXPERIENCE

Whether there's something in the water, brainwashing sound bites being pumped through the heating ducts, or it's genuine, Creighton students overwhelmingly seem to believe they are involved in a passionate love affair with their college. It's tough to blame them, though. You not only take classes, you really grow and develop with the school. The professors, and even administrators, will guide you and offer you support at all times, encouraging you to seek them out in office hours to help you reach your potential.

In some ways, Creighton students seem to fear leaving just because the place is such a fairytale university. Students actually seem to care about one another and the world. As one student said, the Jesuit spirit of service and concern for others really seems to pass from students and teachers, who truly care about one another. Anyone who wants a school where it's impossible to be just a number would find that Creighton is a No. 1 choice.

Students Speak Out On...
OVERALL EXPERIENCE

Q I Love Creighton

"My first year at Creighton was a great experience. It is a very small campus and everyone on campus is very friendly. While the social life isn't really that great, there are always things to do on the weekends."

Q Good Time

"Great Academics, nice people, not bad night life for 21+ students (wet campus). Good times, good memories."

Q It's alright

"I just really wanna get my degree and get out. It's really nice in the summer and early fall, but the rest of the campus during the school year is really ugly."

Q "It's great! I've met a lot of cool people, and Creighton put on a lot of events for its students. It's fun."

Q "I've learned a ton about myself. I have learned who I want to be and how to achieve it."

Q "I love Creighton. Coming here has been the best decision of my life."

BEST OF CREIGHTON

1. Botanical garden-like landscaping
2. Wireless Internet
3. Squirrels
4. Jesuit gardens
5. Wet campus
6. Statues and fountains on campus

Happy Students
89% of students return after their first year.

Proven Success
76% of students will complete their education and graduate with a degree.

WORST OF CREIGHTON

1. Parking
2. Never-ending construction
3. Weather fluctuations
4. Tripping over bricks on the Mall
5. Waiting for shuttles

Expensive
Tuition is a steep $29,544, one of the most expensive rates in the country.

Student Body

African American:	4%	Male Undergrads:	40%
Asian American:	9%	Female Undergrads:	60%
Hispanic:	4%	Living On Campus:	62%
International:	1%	Living Off Campus:	38%
Native American:	1%	Male Athletes:	8%
White:	79%	Female Athletes:	6%
Unknown:	2%	Fraternity Members:	23%
From Out-of-State:	72%	Sorority Members:	21%

Frequently Compared Schools:

Marquette University
Saint Louis University
University of Iowa
University of Nebraska

Students Speak Out On...
EVERYTHING!

ACADEMICS

Pre-Med Program

"Creighton University offers a pre-med course for anyone wanting to go into the medical field. I really like that they offer this course and I feel like it gives me an advantage compared to students who go to other colleges."

Strong

"Ranked the #1 regional school in the Midwest by US News and World Report, Creighton has a very strong academic program. I can see it in the dedication of the teachers and in the hours put in by my fellow students."

"For the most part, I've found that the professors are very approachable and down-to-earth. Most are quirky, and that makes class interesting, even if the subject matter isn't."

ATHLETICS

Lots of Sports

"Could use a football team but other than that it's great"

No Football :(

"Its tough not having a football team but you can try to go to a Nebraska game they are alot of fun. Basketball and volleyball are a lot of fun to go to."

CAMPUS DINING

Skutt Student Center Food Options

"I personally only eat in the Skutt Student Center because I do not live on-campus or have a meal plan. However, they are great for having a quick snack, lunch, or dinner. They have lots of options and a variety of food choices. They even added sushi this year!"

Dining Halls

"The dining halls offer a variety of foods including a pasta, burger, pizza, salad, and sandwich station. However, the quality of food could be improved upon."

CAMPUS HOUSING

Old Market

"Great places to eat and it's close by!"

Dorm Options and Convenience

"The freshman dorms are pretty small, but not bad. After freshman year, there are no more community bathrooms and you get to share a bathroom with roommates. Most of the dorms are very convenient, being at the heart of campus. A few are a little farther away, but there are shuttles from the dorms."

GUYS & GIRLS

Huge Variation

"At Creighton there is a huge variation of people, big city kids, small town kids, kids from all over the country, and even some international kids. Anyone can find someone they feel comfortable with here, because there truely are all kinds present!"

Could Be Better

"There are some definite lookers on campus, but there are some brown baggers too. You'll find your preps, lax bros, laxitutes, and even the occasional Californian or Hawaiian surfer. The 60-40 girl to guy ratio is nice if you're a guy, too."

HEALTH & SAFETY

Health and Safety

"the Campus is a very pretty campus and they care about the Campus and how it works for the students. there has been alittle violence but they try to reach students and protect them with alot of different ways. We have been very happy"

Truely Safe

"I'm just a freshmen here, and I'm not worried at all about anything bad happening to me while I'm on campus"

LOOKING FOR MORE?

Check out our full-length guide to this school at collegeprowler.com/creighton-university/.

CUNY Lehman College

250 Bedford Park Blvd. W; Bronx, NY 10468
(718) 960-8000; www.lehman.edu

THE BASICS:

Acceptance Rate: 32%	**Student-Faculty Ratio:** 14:1
Yield: 24%	**Retention Rate:** 77%
Setting: Large city	**Graduation Rate:** 34%
Control: Public	**Tuition:** $10,300
Total Undergrads: 9,695	**Room & Board:** —
SAT Range: 830–990*	**Avg. Aid Package:** $4,002
ACT Range: —	**Students With Aid:** 90%

* of 1600

Academics	B-	Greek Life	N/A
Athletics	C+	Guys	A
Campus Dining	C	Health & Safety	B
Campus Housing	D+	Local Atmosphere	B
Campus Strictness	C+	Nightlife	B
Computers	B-	Off-Campus Dining	B-
Diversity	A-	Off-Campus Housing	B
Drug Safety	A-	Parking	B
Facilities	B-	Transportation	B+
Girls	B+	Weather	B+

CP's Student Author On...
OVERALL EXPERIENCE

Lehman offers an incredible college experience, despite the fact that it isn't a boarding campus. Lehman's history is rich (it was originally called Hunter Uptown and used to be a site for the UN), and the campus is gorgeous and regularly featured in commercials (the most recent one being a Verizon commercial). Students who wish to succeed academically can do so at Lehman because the professors are dedicated and passionate, and students have the freedom to mold their own curriculum. Each department has its own distinct personality; for example, the English department is known for having quirky students. There are also honors programs in each department (for those who are academica!ly ambitious).

At Lehman, there are so many opportunities to take advantage of, such as the CUNY/Paris Exchange, which is a study abroad program that Lehman students can apply for if they have taken three semesters of French. The cost of tuition is the same as CUNY, and students enroll at the University of Paris and can either rent or do a home-stay.... For the rest of this editorial, visit collegeprowler.com.

Students Speak Out On...
OVERALL EXPERIENCE

Q Experience
"I love this school. There are a variety of things to do on campus like visit the students life building (where you can relax, play some games) and also go to the library or faculty dining room for quiet studying."

Q Good Experience
"Really good experience, love it there, really good professors."

Q Great School Overall
"I highly recommend Lehman to anyone looking for a solid education. Some of the other CUNY schools can have higher tuition and are less accessible, while others cannot compete despite being cheaper. The staff and classmates are all friendly and work with you. The performing arts center also has a lot of great performances from famous artist and is a real treat. Lehman is a great school."

BEST OF LEHMAN COLLEGE

1. Beautiful campus
2. Diversity
3. Location is close to Manhattan.
4. Professors and staff are very helpful.
5. Variety of classes

Affordable
Tuition is only $10,300, one of the most affordable rates in the country.

Help to Succeed
The school has academic and career counseling available to help you when you need it.

WORST OF LEHMAN COLLEGE

1. Buildings are old.
2. Cafeteria food
3. It's a commuter campus.
4. Not enough computer labs
5. Weak social life

Not Everyone Graduates
34% of students do not complete their education or graduate with a degree.

Disappointed Students
27% of students surveyed would not choose to attend this school if they could do it all over again.

Student Body

African American:	30%	Male Undergrads:	30%
Asian American:	5%	Female Undergrads:	70%
Hispanic:	49%	Living On Campus:	0%
International:	5%	Living Off Campus:	100%
Native American:	0%	Male Athletes:	6%
White:	11%	Female Athletes:	2%
Unknown:	0%	Fraternity Members:	0%
From Out-of-State:	2%	Sorority Members:	0%

Frequently Compared Schools:

Baruch College
CUNY Queens College
Hunter College
New York University

Students Speak Out On... EVERYTHING!

ACADEMICS

Physics

"The physics department is very small, which can be good as well as bad. Being small their are alot of opportunities granted to all the students (like research). However, it also means that the classes are not offered as regularly, meaning it could be a hassle to take the classes one needs."

Worth It

"It's great being at Lehman, it has an amazing campus and most of the professors I had were outstanding, they help you no matter what it takes but you need to hold up your end of the bargin."

ATHLETICS

Athletics in Lehman

"Athletics in Lehman are very good. Not only are they good athletics in what they are doing but they also are very good at their academics. Lehman has it's own building for athletics to train and prepare."

Athletic Facilities

"Sports are very important on campus as a means of bringing students together. Official teams encourage school spirit but the variety of facilities and classes, from yoga and salsa classes, to impromptu basketball games and swim meets/ classes, allows students with different interests to pursue a wide array of physical activity. Lehman students are always up for something new."

CAMPUS DINING

Greasy N Dried Leaves

"the food on campus may be good at but wait , actually they are alright. i enjoy the chinese food available at time, and wheni cant take the grease no longer i go for a salad. which often i am dissatisfied with, paticuliarly because of the dried mixture of cheap lettuce, instead of romain, which is know to be way healthier."

Good

"There aren't many options to eat at Lehman, but that is because it is a commuter school. We have the dining room at Carmen, and two at the music building. The prices are overall fairly cheap, tasty food."

CAMPUS HOUSING

Lehman Needs More Student Housing

"The student dorms are located down the block from school. While the location is convenient, they are too small and crowded with too many students, and students on each floor must share restrooms and kitchens. The individual rooms need to be larger and more accomodating."

Housing

"Housing doesn't really exist. This is not a dorming school, it's more of a comuter school, however, we do have frats."

GUYS & GIRLS

Trying to Get Lucky, Will End up Getting You Distracted

"there are plenty of women on campus that i would love to go out with. and it aint like im ugly or anything. its just hard to make that strong intial connection when starting the action and keeping there is so hard. i dont know maybe its because of me putting to much thought in this"

HEALTH & SAFETY

Safe

"I for one feel safe at lehman. There is always an emergency button nearby when you need it and after dark you are allowed to call campus safety to escort you to the nearest transportation station."

LOOKING FOR MORE?

Check out our full-length guide to this school at collegeprowler.com/cuny-lehman-college/.

CUNY Queens College

65-30 Kissena Blvd.; Flushing, NY 11367
(718) 997-5000; www.qc.cuny.edu

THE BASICS:

Acceptance Rate: 38%	Student-Faculty Ratio: 17:1
Yield: 28%	Retention Rate: 86%
Setting: Large city	Graduation Rate: 55%
Control: Public	Tuition: $10,407
Total Undergrads: 15,894	Room & Board: $11,125
SAT Range: 1460–1700*	Avg. Aid Package: $7,500
ACT Range: —	Students With Aid: 71%

*of 2400

Academics	B-	Greek Life	B-
Athletics	C+	Guys	B-
Campus Dining	C	Health & Safety	C+
Campus Housing	B	Local Atmosphere	C
Campus Strictness	B	Nightlife	B-
Computers	C	Off-Campus Dining	C+
Diversity	B+	Off-Campus Housing	B
Drug Safety	A-	Parking	B-
Facilities	C-	Transportation	B
Girls	C+	Weather	B+

CP's Student Author On...
OVERALL EXPERIENCE

Students looking for an affordable college with decent academics may find Queens College to be the place for them. However, students looking for loads of involvement in student life, with a particular sense of community, may not find it at Queens College. The fact that QC is a commuter school causes a lack of communal feeling between the students. For those who are coming to Queens with little or no friends, it is extremely helpful to join a Greek organization. Other students have found themselves to be comfortable and happy on campus with a few close friends. Sometimes it just takes a little work to find your niche.

According to other students, Queens is the ideal place to be—from academics to the social life to adequate facilities to students simply feeling satisfied with their college experience. Queens offers so much and has all that one could ask for as a college student. For students whose desired college experience consists of a large amount of partying and going to bars and pubs, QC is not the best campus for these activities.... For the rest of this editorial, visit collegeprowler.com.

Students Speak Out On...
OVERALL EXPERIENCE

Q Competition

"Although there is absolutely nothing more here except the educational experience, its a good one. The professors are very insightful and there are many good ones here. If you're coming to study, this is the place for you. If you want competition and learn in a very competitive and highly educated environment this is definitely the type of school to hone your academics."

BEST OF QUEENS COLLEGE

1. Student life
2. Events
3. Friends
4. Warm atmosphere
5. Solid education

Affordable
Tuition is only $10,407, one of the most affordable rates in the country.

Happy Students
86% of students return after their first year.

WORST OF QUEENS COLLEGE

1. Early classes
2. Immature students
3. Not enough course sections
4. Not enough student life
5. Parking
6. Public transportation
7. Wireless connectivity

Life is NOT a Party
83% of students surveyed said it's almost impossible to find a good party.

Disappointed Students
25% of students surveyed would not choose to attend this school if they could do it all over again.

Student Body

African American:	9%	Male Undergrads:	40%
Asian American:	23%	Female Undergrads:	60%
Hispanic:	17%	Living On Campus:	2%
International:	6%	Living Off Campus:	98%
Native American:	0%	Male Athletes:	3%
White:	45%	Female Athletes:	2%
Unknown:	0%	Fraternity Members:	10%
From Out-of-State:	2%	Sorority Members:	10%

Frequently Compared Schools:

Hofstra University
Hunter College
New York University
St. John's University

Students Speak Out On... EVERYTHING!

ACADEMICS

Professors Help Us Succeed.

"I love the classes I'm taking. They are so interesting, the topics that are being discussed. Any time I need help the professors are always there for me. The professors are approachable and nice. Some provide additional help for our exams such as practice questions that we can do at home. The department provides information on internships or job opportunities, scholarship information, tutoring and other useful resources."

Major Availiable

"I picked Queens College for a variety of reasons. Mostly because my decided major was availiable and everyone is able to answer my questions i have. Even though some places are to find as far as classes and help go. The overall experiennce is amazing being in college and the campus is great."

Academics

"Professors are usually willing to help during office hours, they really try to encourage you to work hard and get help if needed. They give a lot of opportunities to get help too. The registration process is so difficult and complicated."

ATHLETICS

Awesome

"The athletics is one of the best. Many students have had the chance to be very successful in their sports."

Sports

"Students have the opportunity to tale part in many different sports whatever the area of interest may be. There is also a gym open to students which is amazing."

CAMPUS DINING

Kosher Cafe

"There are plenty of choices which is especially convenient for students keeping Kosher. There are a variety of dishes to choose from which are all tasty."

Fair: Don't Come for the Food

"Always picked up something light, just enough to keep going. This was not part of the college experience that I focused on. Variety is not the greatest, but acceptable. Since students generally do not live on campus, I think this is less of an issue."

CAMPUS HOUSING

They're Chill, but Pricey

"The dorms are vey nice, but too expensive for me. There are also only 300 units,and there is no food on campus at night."

Campus Housing

"The campus housing I heard isn't as everyone expected it to be and there aren't enough dorms to go around. There is also a huge waiting list."

GUYS & GIRLS

All Different Types of People.

"Everyone has their own look and it doesn't matter to us."

Diversity

"The school is pretty diverse with students coming from different cultures and backgrounds. It's pretty cool too because we all sort of come from the same jniour and high schools. All the girls and guys have very unique styles it's great to see that it's almost inspiring"

HEALTH & SAFETY

Guarding Queens College

"Queens college is heavily gaurded by securtiy gaurds and the like. I think they have good scerurity throughout the whole cmpus and I'm not afraid to walk around campus."

I Feel Safe

"I feel totally safe on campus. I have never felt uneasy or afraid"

LOOKING FOR MORE?

Check out our full-length guide to this school at collegeprowler.com/cuny-queens-college/.

Dartmouth College

Hanover, NH 03755
(603) 646-1110; www.dartmouth.edu

THE BASICS:

Acceptance Rate: 13%
Yield: 49%
Setting: Town
Control: Private Non-Profit
Total Undergrads: 4,197
SAT Range: 2000–2320*
ACT Range: 29–34

Student-Faculty Ratio: 8:1
Retention Rate: 98%
Graduation Rate: 95%
Tuition: $38,679
Room & Board: $11,295
Avg. Aid Package: $27,786
Students With Aid: 63%

* of 2400

Academics	A+	Greek Life	A
Athletics	B+	Guys	B
Campus Dining	A+	Health & Safety	A+
Campus Housing	A-	Local Atmosphere	C
Campus Strictness	B	Nightlife	D+
Computers	A	Off-Campus Dining	C-
Diversity	A-	Off-Campus Housing	C-
Drug Safety	B-	Parking	C+
Facilities	B	Transportation	D+
Girls	B-	Weather	C

CP's Student Author On...
OVERALL EXPERIENCE

So the consensus is in—Dartmouth is a great place to go to school! For most students in most situations, it is truly the experience of a lifetime. An overwhelming majority of Dartmouth students fall head-over-heels in love with the place. It is little wonder that Dartmouth has one of the highest alumni giving rates of any college or university in the country. The College is certainly a very unique place to pursue an undergraduate degree, and the academic experience alone is worth its weight in gold. For the most part, Dartmouth professors, administrators, and support staff care deeply about the students and want to do whatever they can to make each student's experience the best it can possibly be.

All that being said, Dartmouth is not for everyone. It is definitely a high-intensity school. The turnaround time between when classes begin and when finals are due each term is pretty rapid, and it's not at all difficult to get snowed under—no pun intended.... For the rest of this editorial, visit collegeprowler.com.

Students Speak Out On...
OVERALL EXPERIENCE

Q Loved every minute

"Dartmouth was the time of my life. Academics were spectacular, and the social life was a blast. Greek life was definitely a large part of the social scene, but I was in a house and loved every minute of it; lots of solid extra-curricular activities."

Q I Have Officially Undergone My Green Blood Transfusion (GBT)

"Dartmouth College is an amazing school, especially for undergraduate education. Hands down, I could not have chosen an institution more fitted to my needs as a student. The remote location of the school is the only drawback that I can personally attest to struggling with at times. The location often prevents you from "getting away," which proves overwhelming and stressful during certain periods, such as midterms and finals."

BEST OF DARTMOUTH

1. Friendly professors
2. The Green on a beautiful day
3. Outdoor opportunities
4. Study abroad opportunities
5. Tight-knit community
6. Three classes

Happy Students
98% of students return after their first year.

Commitment to Teaching
There are 8 students for every member of faculty on campus.

WORST OF DARTMOUTH

1. Isolation
2. Dark winter days
3. The D-Plan
4. Social exclusivity of the Greek system
5. Level of busyness of most students
6. Hanover nightlife

Expensive
Tuition is a steep $38,679, one of the most expensive rates in the country.

Expensive Dorms
Living on campus doesn't come cheap, with an average housing price tag of $6,750.

Student Body

African American:	8%	Male Undergrads:	50%
Asian American:	14%	Female Undergrads:	50%
Hispanic:	7%	Living On Campus:	86%
International:	7%	Living Off Campus:	14%
Native American:	4%	Male Athletes:	28%
White:	55%	Female Athletes:	22%
Unknown:	6%	Fraternity Members:	43%
From Out-of-State:	98%	Sorority Members:	40%

Frequently Compared Schools:
Brown University
Cornell University
Princeton University
Yale University

Students Speak Out On...
EVERYTHING!

ACADEMICS

Q Great Professors, Smaller Classes

"Since Dartmouth College has a pretty small student population, classes are pretty small. Even lecture classes are smaller than most at other schools. This allows for more student/professor interaction, so you're really involved in making the most of your own education. The workload is pretty heavy, but shouldn't be unmanageable if you learn good time management skills."

Q Love It.

"The D-plan is great. Students really get the best internships. The professors are all really friendly and know me personally by name."

ATHLETICS

Q Nowwww It's Good.

"When I was a freshmen, I think all our sports teams collectively won maybe 1 game. Two years later, that's managed to turn around. Our formerly winless football team held their own through overtime, losing by a touchdown to Ivy League favorites, UPenn, which also happens to have almost 3x the undergraduates. Participation is good, everyone does at least some kind of physical activity."

Q Very Athletic Campus

"We have great facilities. I'm not a huge athlete, so I've been on a club team, which is not a large time commitment. Our winter sports are especially great. We have an amazing hockey team which the whole campus follows."

CAMPUS DINING

Q Lots of Variety

"We have everything from local organic produce to chicken nuggets and cheesesteaks. We have a bunch of different dining halls and they all offer different options. There are also dining halls that are open for late-night food. Everyone always has a meal plan."

Q BEAST

"Dining on campus is awesome. I guess it has to be considering there aren't more than two student-friendly restaurants in town."

CAMPUS HOUSING

Q Awesome

"The vast majority of Dartmouth's dorms are very modern and have fantastic social atmospheres. I live in one of the older buildings and I absolutely love it- people are always around and looking for something fun to do, and my room is much larger than the ones my friends at other colleges have. I really can't think of any way that Dartmouth's housing could be better,"

Q Hate This Place

"make sure you get one of the newly built dorms or you will be stuck in b-side old school housing"

GUYS & GIRLS

Q Boy and Girls at Darthmouth

"the students are very friendly and interesting they are very wise and smart."

Q Guys and Girls Are Pretty Good Looking

"I mean, it's an ivy league school so you don't have tons of models here but the majority of the student population is pretty good looking."

HEALTH & SAFETY

Q Safety, as Long as You Follow the Rules

"Dartmouth works really hard to provide a safe environment for it's students and the Safety and Security team is really friendly. Drinking is an environment that is present, but it is extremely easy to avoid or jump into with enthusiasm. Just be safe about it, and the fun will continue."

LOOKING FOR MORE?
Check out our full-length guide to this school at collegeprowler.com/dartmouth-college/.

Davidson College

102 N. Main St.; Davidson, NC 28035
(704) 894-2000; www.davidson.edu

THE BASICS:

Acceptance Rate: 26%	**Student-Faculty Ratio:** 11:1
Yield: 41%	**Retention Rate:** 97%
Setting: Suburban	**Graduation Rate:** 94%
Control: Private Non-Profit	**Tuition:** $35,124
Total Undergrads: 1,744	**Room & Board:** $9,906
SAT Range: 1900–2160*	**Avg. Aid Package:** $21,506
ACT Range: 28–32	**Students With Aid:** 64%

* of 2400

Academics	A	**Greek Life**	A-
Athletics	A	**Guys**	B+
Campus Dining	B+	**Health & Safety**	A
Campus Housing	A-	**Local Atmosphere**	B-
Campus Strictness	B	**Nightlife**	C+
Computers	A-	**Off-Campus Dining**	B-
Diversity	C	**Off-Campus Housing**	C-
Drug Safety	B+	**Parking**	A-
Facilities	A-	**Transportation**	B-
Girls	B	**Weather**	B+

CP's Student Author On...
OVERALL EXPERIENCE

For the majority of Davidson students, the net result of their college experience is highly favorable. Students here do occasionally get frustrated, and there is no question that each and every Davidson student has moaned about his or her workload at some point during his college career, and with good reason. Even so, most realize that the rigorous academics here are what give Davidson its tradition of excellence, and that all their hard work is, in the end, well worth the name on the diploma. Davidson is a work hard/play hard community, and there's no question that you'll put in some substantial hours at the library, but you can also expect to let loose on the weekends.

When assessing whether Davidson is a good school for you, it's important to determine how the pros and cons line up with your own expectations for your college experience. Don't come here expecting the endless beer-fest you'll find at larger state schools like NC State because it's not going to happen. Don't come here expecting a student body with great ethnic diversity because you're not going to find it.... For the rest of this editorial, visit collegeprowler.com.

Students Speak Out On...
OVERALL EXPERIENCE

Q Perfect

"Davidson is a classic liberal arts college in a small town. It is very traditional and the Honor Code is extremely strong. Everyone knows everyone and that makes it great. The faculty and staff are wonderful. The workload is indescribable. It is intense and demanding all the time. You have to go to class and you have to go prepared. It's ironic that I give it an A since no professor will give an A to a student! I love Davidson and I am hoping that graduation day will not come!"

Q "I don't think that I could have found a better place for me. Davidson offers everything that a college should. With the support from the faculty, the student body, and the administration, I believe that it is easier to succeed here than at most places."

Q "I love being at Davidson. There is so much to do here, and I have made wonderful friends. I am quite happy with my choice to go to school there and can never wait to get back when I'm away!"

BEST OF DAVIDSON

1. Accessible and caring faculty
2. Self-scheduled exams
3. Financial aid (grants only; no loans)
4. Spacious, newly renovated dorms
5. Open Party System

Happy Students
97% of students return after their first year.

Proven Success
94% of students will complete their education and graduate with a degree.

WORST OF DAVIDSON

1. Heavy work load
2. Grade deflation
3. Unmistakable homogeneity
4. Claustrophobic dating scene
5. Lack of food variety
6. Limited Dining Hours

Expensive
Tuition is a steep $35,124, one of the most expensive rates in the country.

Good Luck Finding a Part-Time Job
Employment services are not available for students.

Student Body

African American:	6%	Male Undergrads:	48%
Asian American:	4%	Female Undergrads:	52%
Hispanic:	5%	Living On Campus:	94%
International:	4%	Living Off Campus:	6%
Native American:	0%	Male Athletes:	29%
White:	74%	Female Athletes:	19%
Unknown:	6%	Fraternity Members:	40%
From Out-of-State:	78%	Sorority Members:	0%

Students Speak Out On...
EVERYTHING!

ACADEMICS

Q Academics!

"Davidson academics are tough, you have to work hard, to do well. But, Davidson wants you to succeed, and they will be with you through every step of the way. There is the math and science center, speaking center, and writing center, along with many labs, career services, all designed to be student resources. All professors also keep office hours, so its easy to seek help."

Q
"The teachers at Davidson make or break the classes. The student-teacher ratio is such that everyone has the potential to develop a personal relationship with their teachers. My most interesting teachers have taught my most interesting classes; the material shines through whatever lens the teacher wants to show it through."

Q
"What they say about Davidson professors is right: they are unbelievably brilliant, and their classes are endlessly fascinating. I have enjoyed and learned many things from classes outside my English-major interests, like astronomy and other sciences. My experience has shown professors to be warm, engaging, and very open to fostering friendships that often transcend the hierarchical dualism of teacher versus student."

ATHLETICS

Q
"Davidson is one of the smallest schools to participate in Division I athletics, so sports are pretty big. Despite that, admission to all athletic events is free for students."

Q
"While many people at Davidson play sports because the school is Division I, I'd say Davidson is much more academically focused."

CAMPUS DINING

Q
"The cafeteria is good as far as cafeteria food goes, and there is a lot of variety. Not many schools can say that."

Q
"I like Vail Commons because it has lots of choices."

CAMPUS HOUSING

Q Davidson's Atmosphere

"Davidson is great. everyone is friendly and you never feel like an outcast."

Q Quite Better Than Most Colleges

"Davidson College offers large dorms for the most part. Housing is guaranteed for your entire college career. There are options for everyone, whether you want to live close to the campus center or close to the party scene there is a place for you."

GUYS & GIRLS

Q Girls and Guys

"There are a lot of different types of people at Davidson."

Q
"I've been here for four years, and there are no hotties in sight. Maybe they're hiding in their library carrels."

HEALTH & SAFETY

Q The Honor Code in Full Effect.

"There really aren't that many safety or security problems at Davidson, due in large part to the Honor Code. Here, it isn't just a talking point for tours and prospective student literature; it's a way of life. Kids rarely lock the doors to their dormitories because they feel safe, and it's not uncommon to see people post classified ads in our daily email saying, "Someone lost money by [building]. Email me with the amount if it was you.""

Q Playin' It Safe

"I feel completely safe on Davidson's campus. It is walkable in ten minutes, packed with familiar faces, and the school's Honor Code has students leaving their bags around campus with little fear of theft. That being said, be smart. Also, if you're not too belligerent, the cops won't care much if you've gotten your drank on."

Denison University

100 W. College Road; Granville, OH 43023
(740) 587-0810; www.denison.edu

THE BASICS:

Acceptance Rate: 50%	**Student-Faculty Ratio:** 10:1
Yield: 26%	**Retention Rate:** 90%
Setting: Suburban	**Graduation Rate:** 81%
Control: Private Non-Profit	**Tuition:** $36,560
Total Undergrads: 2,267	**Room & Board:** $8,930
SAT Range: 1200–1380*	**Avg. Aid Package:** $27,186
ACT Range: 27–30	**Students With Aid:** 99%

of 1600

Academics	B	Greek Life	A-
Athletics	C+	Guys	B
Campus Dining	B-	Health & Safety	B+
Campus Housing	B-	Local Atmosphere	C+
Campus Strictness	C+	Nightlife	B-
Computers	B	Off-Campus Dining	B-
Diversity	C-	Off-Campus Housing	D
Drug Safety	C+	Parking	B
Facilities	B	Transportation	C
Girls	B+	Weather	C+

CP's Student Author On...
OVERALL EXPERIENCE

Most students who come to Denison absolutely love it. While some students find it a mediocre experience, very few would say they hate it. The quality of education is exceptional, and that alone is enough to convince some students that Denison is the place where they belong. A lot of people also fall in love with the intimate atmosphere that seems to pervade the University. Not only do you live among your peers, but most people are also friends with their professors, which results in a feeling of belonging. No one can deny that being good-naturedly teased by their professor doesn't engender feelings of acceptance. A lot of students also value the safety of the campus. Those students that are unhappy with Denison are generally unhappy with the social scene, lack of diversity, or the exceptional work load. However, your happiness at college is largely a choice. No matter where you go, you will find problems, and you'll deal with them. Nowhere is perfect.

No matter how fed-up students may get sometimes, no one can claim that the academic opportunities at Denison aren't amazing, and that the atmosphere isn't unique.... For the rest of this editorial, visit collegeprowler.com.

Students Speak Out On...
OVERALL EXPERIENCE

Q I LOVE Denison.
"Denison is a great school with challenging academics, a small student body, and enough things to do to keep you busy. There is always something going on around campus, and Columbus is close enough if you want some big-city fun."

Q Denison Is What You Make It
"Denison like any university has it's negatives like the food, people not willing to step outside their groups, and the dominating greek scene, but there are some down to earth, nice people that go to Denison. The academics are great and the professors really care about their students. I don't know if i would have chosen Denison if given another chance. There are a lot of things that go on that bother me, but every experience is what you make of it."

Q "I like it here. I recognize that there are some problems, but all in all, I like the people I have to deal with most of the time, and that makes all the difference in the world."

BEST OF DENISON

1. The teachers. Students love their professors at Denison and really feel like they connect with them, even outside of the classroom.

Happy Students
90% of students return after their first year.

Commitment to Teaching
There are 10 students for every member of faculty on campus.

WORST OF DENISON

1. The nightlife, or lack thereof, can be disappointing.
2. Who knew you could get this much homework?

Expensive
Tuition is a steep $36,560, one of the most expensive rates in the country.

Good Luck Finding a Part-Time Job
Employment services are not available for students.

Student Body

African American:	5%	Male Undergrads:	44%
Asian American:	2%	Female Undergrads:	56%
Hispanic:	3%	Living On Campus:	97%
International:	5%	Living Off Campus:	3%
Native American:	0%	Male Athletes:	36%
White:	81%	Female Athletes:	20%
Unknown:	3%	Fraternity Members:	21%
From Out-of-State:	69%	Sorority Members:	40%

Frequently Compared Schools:

College of Wooster
Dickinson College
Kenyon College
Oberlin College

Students Speak Out On...
EVERYTHING!

ACADEMICS

Q Professors Are Understanding

"At Denison University a student can enter a classroom and explain to his/her professor about a situation they are experiencing and know that the professor will understand. Professor here are like normal regular people they have lives, just as any other colege student and their kindness is shown on a daily basis."

Q

"The majority of the teachers at Denison are very good. Different teachers use different teaching methods so that classes do not become dull and boring. And most of the methods used are very effective. The teachers grade fairly and make their students work hard, which is exactly what I would expect of a school."

ATHLETICS

Q Not Huge, but Present

"Denison attracts scholar athletes, so academics are what Denison is most proud of, but sports are still pretty big on campus. A lot of people I know are on some sort of team ranging from club to varsity sports. School spirit is nothing compared to my high school, but people do attend games, since it is free for students."

Q

"Overall, sports are not big. Rugby is probably the most popular."

CAMPUS DINING

Q Could Be a Lot Better

"More choices are sorely needed in the dining hall. The servers could do a lot better in preparing food, by properly cooking it and containing it. The one bright spot is the alternative choice to dining hall food called meal exchange, but food selection is limited here as well."

Q Not Very Good

"The quality of food here is not very good. You can just tell that the food is low grade. Often the load the food with salt to add taste and therefore you are left feeling bloated and unsatisfied. Recently I found a whole loaf of bread that was moldy. For how much money we pay to go to Denison, the food is absolutely pathetic."

CAMPUS HOUSING

Q You Can't Live Off Campus

"Most of the dorms are pretty nice and in good condition. The only downside is not being able to live off campus. Denison has chosen to make class sizes bigger which means more competition when it comes to housing. DU works on a random lottery system so where you live is based on luck. You can only hope that you will get an apartment senior year with a kitchen, if you aren't so lucky, you'll spend your 4 years at Denison in a dorm."

Q

"Denison really improved Shorney and completely renovated Smith, the two freshman dorms. They just built new Senior apartments, the Elms. They are really sweet. Everyone living on campus is pretty cool. I didn't think I would say that, but it really does create a community."

GUYS & GIRLS

Q Pretty Damn Good

"The guys are pretty hot and intellectual. Most of them are fit too, but sometimes and only sometimes they are overly slutty."

Q Nice but Different

"Coming from a smaller town in Ohio, it took a while to get used to the girls at Denison. Many people are from other states, especially the eastern coast. The styles were slightly different than I was used to at home and it seems like everybody dresses up more on a day to day basis. Overall, a variety of girls and guys."

HEALTH & SAFETY

Q So Secure

"There are safety walks for when you are walking at night to a location. There is plenty of security presence that will assist you if necessary. You can leave your doors open and laptops out and people will not take them."

LOOKING FOR MORE?

Check out our full-length guide to this school at collegeprowler.com/denison-university/.

DePaul University

55 E. Jackson; Chicago, IL 60604
(312) 362-8000; www.depaul.edu

THE BASICS:

Acceptance Rate: 64%
Yield: 31%
Setting: Large city
Control: Private Non-Profit
Total Undergrads: 16,257
SAT Range: 1530–1890*
ACT Range: 21–27

Student-Faculty Ratio: 17:1
Retention Rate: 85%
Graduation Rate: 64%
Tuition: $27,343
Room & Board: $10,617
Avg. Aid Package: $20,459
Students With Aid: 82%

* of 2400

Academics	B	Greek Life	C-
Athletics	B-	Guys	B+
Campus Dining	B	Health & Safety	C-
Campus Housing	A-	Local Atmosphere	A+
Campus Strictness	B-	Nightlife	A-
Computers	B	Off-Campus Dining	A
Diversity	B+	Off-Campus Housing	B+
Drug Safety	C	Parking	B-
Facilities	B+	Transportation	A
Girls	B-	Weather	C+

CP's Student Author On...
OVERALL EXPERIENCE

There is a reason why DePaul students have been voted the happiest college students—they are given a more "real-world" experience, while going to school in a prime spot of Chicago. Freshman move-in day at DePaul doesn't include driving to some campus tucked away in the forest where shopping sprees at Walmart are the highlight of the week. Students here really discover what it's like to live on their own in a big city, and they are given an independence that most college students don't get right away. However, this type of environment is definitely not for everyone, and there is a definite "culture-shock" aspect that goes beyond that of the general college-transitional period.

DePaul students represent the University well by maintaining their diverse beliefs, while keeping an open mind; living the Vincentian model by becoming socially responsible leaders; and striving for academic excellence and lifelong learning. At the end of the day, for better or for worse, most students will stand by their love of the University and its many quirks.... For the rest of this editorial, visit collegeprowler.com.

Students Speak Out On...
OVERALL EXPERIENCE

Q Worth the Money
"Depaul University has teachers that WANT to be there for more than the paycheck. They know what they are teaching!"

Q Experience at Depaul
"So far my experience at DePaul has been great! I love the classroom sizes and professors. The dorms are big and clean. The cafe has great food at decent prices. The campus is located close to the city and there are always interesting events going on that are free for students.I would chose this school again because its location is perfect and the education is well balanced."

Q Get Involved at Depaul
"It is easy to get involved in all types of clubs, activities, volunteer projects, and greek life at DePaul. The music concerts, the bars, the sports... Amazing."

Q Depaul
"DePaul is a great place, professors are accesible and they really care about their students. There are lots of things to do aroung town. Very diverse and small class sizes."

BEST OF DEPAUL

1. City of Chicago
2. FEST
3. Lakefront is within walking distance
4. Open-minded and accepting student body
5. U-Pass

Happy Students
85% of students return after their first year.

Knowledgeable Professors
92% of students surveyed rated the general knowledge of professors as above average.

WORST OF DEPAUL

1. The weather
2. Guy-to-girl ratio (for girls)
3. Cost of tuition
4. Lack of free parking
5. High bookstore prices and inadequate buy-back rates
6. No football team

Expensive
Tuition is a steep $27,343, one of the most expensive rates in the country.

Expensive to Just Get By
50% of students surveyed felt that the amount it costs to live while at school was worse than average.

Student Body

African American:	9%	Male Undergrads:	45%
Asian American:	8%	Female Undergrads:	55%
Hispanic:	13%	Living On Campus:	18%
International:	2%	Living Off Campus:	83%
Native American:	0%	Male Athletes:	2%
White:	56%	Female Athletes:	2%
Unknown:	12%	Fraternity Members:	3%
From Out-of-State:	31%	Sorority Members:	6%

Frequently Compared Schools:

Loyola University Chicago
Northwestern University
University of Illinois
University of Illinois at Chicago

Students Speak Out On...
EVERYTHING!

ACADEMICS

Q Biological Science Major

"Being a science major at DePaul is hard but the professors and teacher assistants are very helpful. The work load is decent because it is a harder major, especially when most students are Pre-med or Pre-dental."

Q Political Science at Depaul Is Great!

"The best part of being a political science major at DePaul is the internship opportunities in Chicago. I have already been offered multiple internships working on campaigns and for research companies. The professors really help the students find internships."

Q Work and School Relations Are Incredible

"I attend DePaul University because this school has a GREAT relationship with my job. One of the ways to receive a promotion is mention that you have a DePaul degree, and it will at least get you an interview.."

ATHLETICS

Q School Spirit

"Our school spirit is great. The basketball games are always roaring with excitement, including students and alumni."

Q Athletics at the University

"DePaul University has excellent athletic facilities and great school spirit!! GO BLUE DEMONS!!"

CAMPUS DINING

Q Very Nice

"The on campus food and dining options is excellent."

Q There Are Many Variety of Food

"There are five stations to get food; deli, mini-store, bakery, soup, asian and soul food. But, after a while of eating the same food everyday, it gets boring."

CAMPUS HOUSING

Q I Don't Know, I Commute

"I hear that the housing is good, but I am a commuter."

Q Living on Campus

"I personally do not reside on campus, but I have heard many students that do are really happy with the campus housing."

GUYS & GIRLS

Q Everyone Is in a Relationship

"If your single here. You won't be for long. Even when you just break-up you can find another partner within that week. There are some who refuse to be in a relationship and we; community do respect them, for their choice. There are many activities here for couples, there are some single activities too. So, the singles won't feel abandon."

Q Respectful

"Students at this institution are all very respectful of one another and get along very well. There is a nice atmosphere almost everywhere you go."

HEALTH & SAFETY

Q Safe

"I have never felt unsafe at DePaul. However there have been several robberies going on. I am confident that if I need assistance, someone will be there for me."

Q Great School

"DePaul University is great! I thoroughly enjoyed my time there. There are 2 primary campuses one in Lincoln Park and on in the Loop. The dorms are great at DePaul and no one is required to ever live on campus. Those looking for traditional Greek life will be disappointed as there are no houses and only 6% participate. Lincoln Park is a great area and many live there while going to DePaul and after college."

LOOKING FOR MORE?

Check out our full-length guide to this school at collegeprowler.com/depaul-university/.

DePauw University

313 S. Locust St.; Greencastle, IN 46135
(765) 658-4800; www.depauw.edu

THE BASICS:

Acceptance Rate: 66%
Yield: 25%
Setting: Town
Control: Private Non-Profit
Total Undergrads: 2,396
SAT Range: 1610–1960*
ACT Range: 24–29

Student-Faculty Ratio: 10:1
Retention Rate: 90%
Graduation Rate: 85%
Tuition: $33,250
Room & Board: $8,740
Avg. Aid Package: $21,238
Students With Aid: 98%

* of 2400

Academics	B	Greek Life	A+
Athletics	B-	Guys	A-
Campus Dining	B+	Health & Safety	A
Campus Housing	B+	Local Atmosphere	C
Campus Strictness	B	Nightlife	C+
Computers	B-	Off-Campus Dining	C+
Diversity	D+	Off-Campus Housing	D
Drug Safety	C+	Parking	A-
Facilities	B+	Transportation	D-
Girls	A	Weather	D

CP's Student Author On...
OVERALL EXPERIENCE

DePauw is definitely home to the quintessential college experience. Students are offered a college town that dominates a small town environment, where full focus is placed on over 2,000 young people who call campus home for nine months of the year. The classes and professors keep students very busy but supply a wealth of knowledge and opportunity.

As with all universities, the experience is what students make of it, but DePauw professors and programs seem to make success especially accessible for those who try. The University is also very conducive to building strong social skills and tight knit friendships that tend to carry on long after graduation. The DePauw network extends across the country and maintains ties between classes, houses, and majors.

A DePauw education has a multitude of benefits, and the allowance to try many different fields and explore areas outside your specific major. The different disciplines teach you how to think, learn, and question.... For the rest of this editorial, visit collegeprowler.com.

Students Speak Out On...
OVERALL EXPERIENCE

I Love Depauw

"I can't imagine going anywhere else. DePauw has a very special Greek community, unique dining places like the Duck and the Den, as well as very friendly students and professors, and I know I would miss that so much if I left. I almost want to spend my vacations at school, I miss it so much!"

Life at Depauw

"Overall, my life at DePauw is pretty good. The dorms and such are clean and close to campus. The campus is fairly small, so it's easy to get to the academic quad and the other buildings on campus. There is no off-campus housing, everything is owned by housing at DePauw. Studying here is a must, but the parties are also epic. I have had a lot of amazing times at DePauw, I'm very happy I chose it for my school."

Horrible

"If I had it all to do over again, I would never have come here. DePauw University was the worst decision of my life."

BEST OF DEPAUW

1. Student and faculty ambition
2. Campus involvement
3. Greek life
4. Travel abroad opportunities
5. Monon Weekend
6. Alumni connections

Happy Students
90% of students return after their first year.

Commitment to Teaching
There are 10 students for every member of faculty on campus.

WORST OF DEPAUW

1. Workload
2. The Gossip Tree
3. Eating disorders
4. Obscurity
5. Competition
6. Lack of an urban center
7. Lack of diversity
8. Shopping

Expensive
Tuition is a steep $33,250, one of the most expensive rates in the country.

Student Body

African American:	6%	Male Undergrads:	43%
Asian American:	3%	Female Undergrads:	57%
Hispanic:	3%	Living On Campus:	95%
International:	6%	Living Off Campus:	5%
Native American:	0%	Male Athletes:	35%
White:	78%	Female Athletes:	19%
Unknown:	1%	Fraternity Members:	78%
From Out-of-State:	61%	Sorority Members:	68%

Frequently Compared Schools:

Denison University
Dickinson College
Indiana University
Northwestern University

Students Speak Out On... EVERYTHING!

ACADEMICS

Math Major

"Being a Math major at my school has been a very rewarding major so far. The teachers are great. THe classes are challenging but doable!"

Over All, Pretty Good

"DePauw prides itself on it's academics, but it has very little monitoring for teachers who aren't excelling at their jobs. The registration process is ridiculous and often results in students not receiving the courses they need or desire."

ATHLETICS

Depauw Never Quits

"I praise the athletic department at DPU. I think they do a good job with keeping their student-athletes committed to their program, and successfully helping them remain students first. Not only do the student athletes do well in the classroom, but on the court/field as well."

Sports Good, for Athletes

"A lot of people are involved in different sports and the university promotes every game. I personally don't attend any games though. All the Greek houses participate in IM sports and it gets pretty competitive. The gym is ok - there are several different machines for weightlifting and a lot of free weights, but the aerobic machines are old and sometimes don't work."

CAMPUS DINING

Food

"I think that the dining halls offer a unique variety of food but after a while you get tired of eating the same type of food. I sometimes wish they offered more healthy options and mixed up the salad bar. The den is nice because it is almost like a market and you can grocery shop there. THe food is also very reasonably priced."

Few Options

"There is a nice amount of options in the hub, however, food in the den gets boring and repetitive."

CAMPUS HOUSING

Excellent Options

"There are lot of housing options on campus and dorms are pretty neat. Many people chose to live in the Greek housing; however, those who do not have dorms or duplexes or houses that they can live in. There is a lottery option that helps award students where they will live next year."

Avoid Hogate and Anderson Street

"The freshman dorms really aren't that bad except for Hogate Hall and Anderson Street Hall. While the South Quad may be more exciting since it is all freshman, North Quad is right in the middle of campus and makes everything easier to get to. Plus North Quad is a mix of freshman and upperclassmen, and much closer to a bunch of the greek houses."

GUYS & GIRLS

Preppy to the Max

"While the personalities of the people may vary, the dress stays very similar. Most girls seemed perfectly coiffed every day. The guys tend to look like they are about to walk into an interview. Most of the people are very preppy. The upside is that everybody is super nice, and even if you don't dress like they do you aren't judged."

HEALTH & SAFETY

Depauw Is Safe

"I have not had any major problems with feeling unsafe and do not know anyone else who has. DePauw is sure to allow the students freedom and to have fun but is also careful that we stay safe. Public safety is good at doing their rounds and Safe Ride is almost always available to give people rides to and from places."

LOOKING FOR MORE?

Check out our full-length guide to this school at collegeprowler.com/depauw-university/.

Dickinson College

College Street & Louther Street; Carlisle, PA 17013
(717) 243-5121; www.dickinson.edu

THE BASICS:

Acceptance Rate: 49%
Yield: 24%
Setting: Town
Control: Private Non-Profit
Total Undergrads: 2,376
SAT Range: 1780–2060*
ACT Range: 26–30

Student-Faculty Ratio: 10:1
Retention Rate: 92%
Graduation Rate: 84%
Tuition: $40,114
Room & Board: $10,080
Avg. Aid Package: $23,286
Students With Aid: 64%

of 2400

Academics	B+	Greek Life	B+
Athletics	B-	Guys	B-
Campus Dining	A-	Health & Safety	A
Campus Housing	C+	Local Atmosphere	C+
Campus Strictness	C-	Nightlife	C
Computers	B	Off-Campus Dining	C+
Diversity	C	Off-Campus Housing	C-
Drug Safety	C+	Parking	C+
Facilities	B+	Transportation	C-
Girls	A-	Weather	C+

CP's Student Author On...
OVERALL EXPERIENCE

When asked, "If you had a chance to do it all over again, would they still come to Dickinson College?", almost every student polled said they would do it in a heartbeat. On the whole, Dickinson is remembered by alumni as a place that provided some of the most incredible opportunities in their lives. The College serves as a starting point for not only career success, but for lifetime happiness, as well.

Students come to school here because they are serious about their futures. Academics are always the top priority and everything else comes second to classes and coursework. Thus, be prepared for Dickinson to push you to your limits academically. Dickinsonians are successful in and outside the classroom, and it is not uncommon for a student to play a sport, participate in a club, have an engaging internship, and still maintain their studying. In addition, you'll learn to expand your social horizons and to indulge the international community through study abroad and a global education at home. Our motto is "Engage the World," and nothing is more focused and concentrated on at Dickinson. A Dickinson College diploma is more than just a degree—it's a way of life.

Students Speak Out On...
OVERALL EXPERIENCE

Q **I've only been here for 3 months...**
"I've only been here for three months, and I absolutely love this school. The professors are great, the students are friendly, and the atmosphere is amazing. I LOVE DICKINSON."

Q **It's a Great Community**
"I love it here. Everyone is very friendly and outgoing, not to mention welcoming, from the professors to the student body. The facilities are great, the campus is beautiful, and the professors are smart, helpful, and flexible. As a freshman, I've had little to no problems getting assimilated into college and almost everyone I know is incredibly happy here. Some people get caught up in drama that seems a little high school, but it's just a small group of people who fall into that category."

BEST OF DICKINSON

1. Engaged and accessible professors
2. Study abroad opportunities
3. Attractiveness of campus
4. Close-knit student body
5. Campus activities and events

Happy Students
92% of students return after their first year.

Commitment to Teaching
There are 10 students for every member of faculty on campus.

WORST OF DICKINSON

1. Rainy, cold weather
2. Limited variety of activities in Carlisle
3. Lack of 24-hour eating on campus and limit of places to use your meal plan

Expensive
Tuition is a steep $40,114, one of the most expensive rates in the country.

Student Body

African American:	5%	Male Undergrads:	45%
Asian American:	5%	Female Undergrads:	55%
Hispanic:	5%	Living On Campus:	92%
International:	6%	Living Off Campus:	8%
Native American:	0%	Male Athletes:	37%
White:	77%	Female Athletes:	18%
Unknown:	2%	Fraternity Members:	16%
From Out-of-State:	79%	Sorority Members:	28%

Frequently Compared Schools:

Bucknell University
Franklin & Marshall College
Gettysburg College
Lafayette College

Students Speak Out On... EVERYTHING!

ACADEMICS

Q Too Much Random Classes

"I have to take more classes that doesn't matter towards my major, but even then, the professors who teaches the random classes are of high quality. Professors are always helpful."

Q Economics

"Very math based material, the courses focus on the economy and how people function around certain inflations or deflations in price and income. The facilities are very nice, they have just been rebuilt this past year. Job opportunities have not been discussed yet for my grade level, but from seeing information on alumni there seems to be great potential in the work force."

ATHLETICS

Q Big Deal

"Sports are a pretty big deal on campus despite the fact that the teams aren't necessarily the best."

Q Sports Are Average

"I feel the student body has little school spirit and that athletics are not too important to the faculty. The school gives little funding to all sport programs and all teams could use new equipment. I feel that my high school took better care of equipment and facilities than my college does, and yet this should be a step up, not a step down. I feel team performances are well deserving of updates in uniforms, facilities and school spirit."

CAMPUS DINING

Q Dining Halls

"We have several options on campus to eat. We have Union Station, the grill/snack bar, the Quarry, our pizza and sandwich joint, the Underground, which serves sushi and vegan/veggie/gluten free options and the regular dining hall, which serves kosher/gf/vegan/hilel options along with a wok up, salad bar, grain bar, sandwich line and daily options."

Q Needs Improvement

"On campus, there are only three options for dinning. The food does not seem to be prepared properly and there is a repatition for the type of food each week. There needs to be more variety and more placed to eat on campus. I feel the best place to eat right now is our grill to go option. Every other dinning is just bland and could use a lot of work."

CAMPUS HOUSING

Q Living on Campus Is Better Than You Think

"On a campus where nothing is more than 10 minutes away, living on campus all four years is a plus. While many students moan about having to stay on campus, the options for seniors are pretty good. Campus Life does their best to make everyone happy, and most of the dorms are either recently renovated (especially in common spaces) or are scheduled to be renovated soon."

Q Housing Is Interesting?

"I've been moderately happy with my dorm (Baird), but that's because I have a single and my roommate lives with his girlfriend. I wish that there was some diversity to the dorms on campus, but they pretty much all look the same. My dorm was freshman housing last year."

GUYS & GIRLS

Q The Student Body Is Very Diverse.

"There are all different types of students at Dickinson College. There are athletes, high academic achievement students, theater people, and foreign students. Everyone finds their place and people generally get along well."

HEALTH & SAFETY

Q I've Never Felt Unsafe

"I've heard a few incidents of people feeling uncomfortable late at night, but during the days and in the evening, I feel perfectly safe walking around alone. DPS distributes their number and makes people aware, but I would suggest walking with at least one other person late at night."

LOOKING FOR MORE?

Check out our full-length guide to this school at collegeprowler.com/dickinson-college/.

Dordt College

498 Fourth Ave. NE; Sioux Center, IA 51250
(712) 722-6000; www.dordt.edu

THE BASICS:

Acceptance Rate: 84%	**Student-Faculty Ratio:** 14:1
Yield: 43%	**Retention Rate:** 76%
Setting: Town	**Graduation Rate:** 69%
Control: Private Non-Profit	**Tuition:** $22,080
Total Undergrads: 1,331	**Room & Board:** $6,010
SAT Range: 1380–1810*	**Avg. Aid Package:** $20,705
ACT Range: 22–27	**Students With Aid:** 100%

* of 2400

Academics	C+	Greek Life	N/A
Athletics	B-	Guys	A-
Campus Dining	C	Health & Safety	B-
Campus Housing	B-	Local Atmosphere	C-
Campus Strictness	C	Nightlife	C+
Computers	B-	Off-Campus Dining	C-
Diversity	C	Off-Campus Housing	C
Drug Safety	B-	Parking	B
Facilities	B+	Transportation	B-
Girls	A-	Weather	C+

CP's Student Author On...
OVERALL EXPERIENCE

The Christ-centered education is evident in the classrooms at Dordt College; the professors not only try to shape your mind around a Christian worldview, but they also try to stretch your imagination and challenge your ideas. Dordt has some quality professors, but the social life is just as important as academics. As a whole, the social life tends to be rather cliquey. You'll want to make sure you find a good social circle where you can be yourself. You can choose to either fit in or stand out, but sometimes it's hard to want to stand out at a place like Dordt because the College is relatively small. Word travels fast, so it makes you a little wary of doing anything too drastic.

The College and town communities can both be a little closed-minded. People say living in Northwest Iowa is as close as you can get to living in a bubble, meaning the community has a tendency to try to shield itself from the outside world. Another way of explaining the community would be to call it sheltered because, in some ways, it is.... For the rest of this editorial, visit collegeprowler.com.

Students Speak Out On...
OVERALL EXPERIENCE

Q Awesome

"I would choose Dordt again in a heartbeat. I love the atmosphere and the people. Going here has been the best decision I've ever made. I haven't regretted it at all."

Q Love it here

"I love the Christ-centered, welcoming atmosphere on campus! Some of my best college memories are of just hanging out with the guys and girls in my dorm. We're like a big family. I had reservations about coming to Dordt, but it was the best decision ever. I've learned so much about my faith and my place in God's world."

Q Amazing

"Dordt is a great place to meet new people as well as study and prepare yourself for a career while developing your relationship with Christ. Social life is equal in importance to academic life here, and students are pretty good at keeping that balance. Because the college is located in a rural area, students are "forced" to make their own fun, but that makes for some awesome memories."

BEST OF DORDT

1. Quality professors and education
2. The professors' willingness to help
3. Smaller class sizes
4. Friendly people
5. The number of study abroad options

Easy Financial Aid Process
75% of students surveyed told us that the financial aid process went smoothly and they received the financial aid they needed.

WORST OF DORDT

1. Visitation hours
2. Parking
3. Meal plan and meal quality
4. Dry campus
5. Not enough events
6. The long winter

Students Can't Wait to Get Out of Town
73% of students surveyed said that there's no way they would live here after graduation.

Student Body

African American:	0%	Male Undergrads:	51%
Asian American:	1%	Female Undergrads:	49%
Hispanic:	1%	Living On Campus:	85%
International:	11%	Living Off Campus:	10%
Native American:	0%	Male Athletes:	34%
White:	85%	Female Athletes:	21%
Unknown:	2%	Fraternity Members:	0%
From Out-of-State:	66%	Sorority Members:	0%

Frequently Compared Schools:

Carnegie Mellon University
Creighton University
Lafayette College
University of South Dakota

Students Speak Out On...
EVERYTHING!

ACADEMICS

Q The Professors at Dordt College Are Understanding and Caring

"Dordt College is a small liberal arts college. Since the college is small, there is a great sense of community. The professors are tough but are very caring and will go out of their way to help you out."

Q Education Program and Christian Worldview

"I chose to come here because the education program had a good reputation. The education professors were friendly and teach with a Christian worldview."

ATHLETICS

Q School Spirit

"Almost everyone comes out for the games and the school encourages school by organizing black out games and stuff like that. Its so fun to go to games there is always tons of people there and fun stuff to do during half time."

Q Teams Do Well

"The sports teams usually do very well. I am impressed with how they compete against much larger schools, often winning."

CAMPUS DINING

Q Dining at Dordt

"I live in the apartments, but I chose to get a declining meal plan this semester to help out with availability of my eating. There is a good variety at the commons, but not the best quality. We also have the Grille which is better, but I don't have the time to go there at all."

Q Repetitive Food

"Food is very repetitive. Commons has ok food but Wednesdays and Fridays are super busy. The Grill offers lots of food and is way better that the Commons."

CAMPUS HOUSING

Q Awesome Community

"Dordt is very intentional about providing opportunities for you to meet people and get involved with what's happening on campus. It's easy to get to know almost everyone if you really want to, and my friends here are the best friends of my life. The new Kuyper apartments are really nice- the older dorms are showing their age, but you haven't lived until you've lived in North!"

Q Housing at Dordt

"I really enjoy the housing situations at Dordt. I like how there are different types of rooms you can pick when figuring out your hosuing arrangements for the upcoming year. I'm excited to live in the apartments junior year with my friends and try that set up of housing."

GUYS & GIRLS

Q Normal Like Any Other School.

"There is a mix of different people. They all look normal, act normal, there is a lot of dating."

Q Get Your MR or MRS Degree at Dordt!

"There is always a running joke of going to Dordt to get your MRS degree or "the Senior Scramble". Dordt students all have the same values, beliefs, and wants in life, so many people find their partner at this college. People engagement at this college probably rate higher than any other typical college, but I think it is a positive thing."

HEALTH & SAFETY

Q Dordt College Is Very Safe

"Dordt College is very safe-almost too safe! Dordt security are always on the prowl during late hours.People trust to have their car doors unlocked and apartment doors open. It is a very safe community."

Q Safe

"I feel very safe on campus. There have been no crimes that I can think of."

LOOKING FOR MORE?

Check out our full-length guide to this school at collegeprowler.com/dordt-college/.

Drexel University

3141 Chestnut St.; Philadelphia, PA 19104
(215) 895-2000; www.drexel.edu

THE BASICS:

Acceptance Rate: 55%	**Student-Faculty Ratio:** 10:1
Yield: 11%	**Retention Rate:** 83%
Setting: Large city	**Graduation Rate:** 62%
Control: Private Non-Profit	**Tuition:** $31,835
Total Undergrads: 13,661	**Room & Board:** $12,681
SAT Range: 1630–1930*	**Avg. Aid Package:** $14,100
ACT Range: 23–28	**Students With Aid:** 99%

* of 2400

Academics	B+	Greek Life	B-
Athletics	B-	Guys	B+
Campus Dining	B-	Health & Safety	C+
Campus Housing	B-	Local Atmosphere	A
Campus Strictness	B	Nightlife	A
Computers	B	Off-Campus Dining	B+
Diversity	B+	Off-Campus Housing	B
Drug Safety	C	Parking	C
Facilities	C+	Transportation	A-
Girls	B	Weather	B-

CP's Student Author On...
OVERALL EXPERIENCE

A lot of students here complain about the "Drexel Shaft" screwing up their scheduling or billing, or how poor their teachers are. The truth is that you will find red tape headaches and poor teachers at just about every university. Even at the top universities, students complain that teachers of freshman-level classes are terrible. I've had first-rate teachers during my time here, even in some 100-level classes. Co-op scheduling can be spoiled by administrative error ("Drexel Shaft") easily, but if you stay on top of things, and be proactive, you can work things out. The Drexel co-op is Drexel's strongest selling point, and many students come here specifically for that program. Some can't wait to graduate and zip through their classes, concentrating more on their co-op, as they feel it gives them more valuable experience. This vocational approach of the student works against the joy of the college learning experience.... For the rest of this editorial, visit collegeprowler.com.

Students Speak Out On...
OVERALL EXPERIENCE

Q **Drexel**
"Even though you have to learn everything in half the time of any other university, there is a lot to take your mind of school here in Phila. It's a college town that caters to young adults. Back on campus, there are over 200 student organizations that a student can get involved in!"

Q **Very Good**
"Joining Greek life is one of the best decisions that I have made, classes are tough but professors are pretty good and care for students for the most part. Made a lot of good friends and Philly is a great city."

Q **Pretty Good**
"The school is expensive and it feels like they are taking more money from you everytime you turn around, but overall, the education is great, class sizes are small, and the people are awesome."

BEST OF DREXEL

1. Hot girls in skimpy outfits during nice weather
2. Much diversity
3. Wireless Internet
4. Cheap basketball tickets
5. Strong biomedical engineering programs

Happy Students
83% of students return after their first year.

Commitment to Teaching
There are 10 students for every member of faculty on campus.

WORST OF DREXEL

1. The Drexel Shaft
2. Characterless, sterile, dungeon-like buildings
3. Sporadic weather
4. Strength of the fundamentalist Christian presence/influence

Expensive
Tuition is a steep $31,835, one of the most expensive rates in the country.

Expensive Dorms
Living on campus doesn't come cheap, with an average housing price tag of $7,602.

Student Body

African American:	9%	Male Undergrads:	54%
Asian American:	11%	Female Undergrads:	46%
Hispanic:	3%	Living On Campus:	35%
International:	7%	Living Off Campus:	65%
Native American:	0%	Male Athletes:	4%
White:	60%	Female Athletes:	4%
Unknown:	9%	Fraternity Members:	4%
From Out-of-State:	56%	Sorority Members:	3%

Frequently Compared Schools:
Boston University
Northeastern University
Penn State
Temple University

Students Speak Out On...
EVERYTHING!

ACADEMICS

Courses at Drexel
"The professors at Drexel are GREAT! They always have time to help with problems or clarifications. I really enjoy my classes"

Specific Major
"I like that my major in health services administration offers several ways of achieving the degree. You can do online, in class room, Saturdays, and co-op."

ATHLETICS

Recreation Center Is Excellent
"the recreation center is really good! there are lots of machine available, and we can running, climbing or do other exercises. and we have many sports clubs, like table tennis, tennis and so on."

Delaware SUCKS!
"Rivalry with Delaware (DELAWARE SUCKS)!Athletics here are awesome.. the teams are good and the games with the Dac Pack are fun as HEEELLLLL!!!"

CAMPUS DINING

Drexel Dragon Dollars
"The dining hall is definitely repetitive with its' stations of pizza, chicken, Chinese, etc. Drexel dining is good, however, in the way in which dining dollars are able to be used towards popular franchises such as Subway and Starbucks as well."

Bland, but Edible
"The Hanshumacher Dining Center has really stepped up their game this year. The breakfast is delicious, the lunch and dinner are mediocre. I guess because they serve a vast variety of people nothing can be seasoned too much, so everything's pretty bland.There's also a Taco Bell, Currito, Chic-Fil-A and Subway which are typically crowded but decent.Ross Commons also has a meal deal that's decent. Pizza, a side, and a drink."

CAMPUS HOUSING

Freshman Dorms
"Living on campus definitely has its pros and cons. I think though that ultimately the pros outweigh the cons. One thing that I love about living on campus is the proximity to a large majority of the freshman population. All of the freshman dorms are within a few hundred yards of each other, and it allows for fun times"

Transfer Process
"Drexel is a great school to transfer to. The financial aid part gets a little complicated if you are changing schools mid-year, so I recommend transfer applicants for the Fall. All the staff is really helpful and offers options though and they explain the process to you."

GUYS & GIRLS

The Same as Every Other College
"The students at Drexel are not that different from most other college settings. Drexel definitely is a melting pot of many students from many cultures ac across the United States and the world."

Good People
"you will find people from all over the country and those from the area...girls are very friendly"

HEALTH & SAFETY

Health & Safety
"Drexel's Public Safety is ranked in the Top 10 nationally"

Drexel's Health & Safety
"Drexel is located in a moderately crime area. There have been a few cases of incidents that put the students at risk but it was rapidly dealt with and told to the students to ward them away to safety."

LOOKING FOR MORE?
Check out our full-length guide to this school at collegeprowler.com/drexel-university/.

Duke University

103 Allen Building; Durham, NC 27708
(919) 684-2813; www.duke.edu

CP's Student Author On...
OVERALL EXPERIENCE

Duke students are generally very happy with their experience, but it's not impossible to find students who imagine they'd be happier somewhere else. Great academics, a vibrant social life, and the beauty of campus make this school an easy choice for many. However, a lot of students are peeved by the top-down social programming they see coming from Duke's administration to counter the fraternity- and sorority-dominated student programming. Students and the administration are still trying to find the right balance of power and a unified direction, but the friendships students have forged with peers and professors easily make up for whatever shortcomings they might perceive.

Duke is one of the top academic schools in the country, but that's not its only hook. You'll never see Harvard's basketball team in the Final Four, or Yale students camping out for weeks to get sports tickets.... For the rest of this editorial, visit collegeprowler.com.

Students Speak Out On...
OVERALL EXPERIENCE

Q Great
"I've enjoyed college because it has helped me learn who I am and who I want to be. Even though the challenges haven't be a joy ride they have helped me grow. What makes make my school unique is the scholastic atmosphere and the passion to represent the school. I would choose Duke because of everything it has given me."

Q Duke
"Duke is just of great school and that is all there is to it."

Q I Love Duke!
"This school is filled with amazing people. Like any high caliber university, nearly everyone is a brilliant and engaged student. What's unique about Duke is that most people are also social and extroverted individuals. "Work hard, play hard" is the mentality every student seems to have and the culture suits me well. Attention all Prom king/queen valedictorians: This is your dream school!"

BEST OF DUKE

1. Cameron Crazies! (college basketball)
2. Caring professors
3. Duke Chapel
4. "Gothic Wonderland" (aka the beautiful campus)
5. Social and smart student body

Happy Students
97% of students return after their first year.

Commitment to Teaching
There are 8 students for every member of faculty on campus.

WORST OF DUKE

1. Catching the bus
2. Greek life with high school-style cliques
3. Some bitter kids who didn't get into Harvard
4. Loafers and pink shorts
5. No air conditioning in some dorms

Expensive
Tuition is a steep $38,741, one of the most expensive rates in the country.

Expensive Dorms
Living on campus doesn't come cheap, with an average housing price tag of $6,285.

Student Body

African American:	9%	Male Undergrads:	50%
Asian American:	20%	Female Undergrads:	50%
Hispanic:	6%	Living On Campus:	83%
International:	6%	Living Off Campus:	17%
Native American:	0%	Male Athletes:	11%
White:	51%	Female Athletes:	8%
Unknown:	7%	Fraternity Members:	29%
From Out-of-State:	86%	Sorority Members:	42%

Frequently Compared Schools:

Brown University
Cornell University
Princeton University
University of Pennsylvania

Students Speak Out On... EVERYTHING!

ACADEMICS

Great!

"Great help from the Econ advisors, renowned faculty, and amazing alumni placement!"

Women's Studies

"The Women's Studies program is extremely interesting and provacative-- not easy courses, but always interesting and cutting edge. I would never consider myself a "feminist" but am considering a WS minor because I loved the classes so much."

ATHLETICS

Amazing

"National Ranked Basketball Champions. A really fun school for basketball lovers."

AWESOME ATHLETIC PROGRAM

"Duke won the NCAA championship this year in both lacrosse and basketball, and sports are a huge part of the Duke community. I spent five weeks in K-ville this past year in order to attend the Duke-Carolina game, and it was fantastic! The feeling of camaraderie with fellow Cameron Crazies is beyond anything I have ever experienced. Duke does a lot for its athletic programs and students are able to go to all varsity sports games without the hassle of buying tickets."

CAMPUS DINING

Wonderful and Varied Options

"Duke has wonderful and varied options for dining on campus. The freshman dining hall provides a welcoming atmosphere that is shared with fellow classmates, and though the food is not top-quality the all-you-can-eat buffet-style makes up for it. Upperclassman options on West are incredible, including both eco-friendly eateries using locally grown ingredients and the favorite McDonalds, high-quality sit-down restaurants and quick hot dog stands."

Theoretically Great

"Though there was clearly a lot of consideration put into dining at Duke, in my experience, it never turns out quite as good as it looks. There are a good number of options for those who live on West campus, but Central and East are pretty lacking in variety. There aren't many inexpensive food opportunities, either."

CAMPUS HOUSING

Worth It!

"For the first three years at least. The freshmen all live together, which is a great experience, but once you're upgraded to West campus, it's absolutely amazing. That's where all the parties are. The dorms are very well-sized and almost all have walk-in closets. If you don't get air conditioning, it can be bad, but I've never had that problem."

West=Wonderful

"Housing on west is fantastic, especially Few/Kilgo/Keohane, but even Edens is not the death sentence some people make it out to be. The freshman community on East is great (but no air conditioning in many dorms is unfortunate)."

GUYS & GIRLS

Everyone's a Social Nerd

"There are definitely more attractive people than unattractive people. You have to remember that everyone's a little bit of a nerd on the inside here, but as far as smart schools go, Duke is hot!"

HEALTH & SAFETY

Duke Is Safe!

"There are often off-campus robberies and such, but on campus, there is seldom ever any crime. It is very safe to be on campus. The Duke police are always somewhere around. Additionally, the bus drivers take great care to make sure that you are safely at your destination when nighttime rolls around."

LOOKING FOR MORE?

Check out our full-length guide to this school at collegeprowler.com/duke-university/.

Duquesne University

600 Forbes Ave.; Pittsburgh, PA 15282
(412) 396-6000; www.duq.edu

THE BASICS:

Acceptance Rate: 76%	**Student-Faculty Ratio:** 14:1
Yield: 28%	**Retention Rate:** 86%
Setting: Large city	**Graduation Rate:** 74%
Control: Private Non-Profit	**Tuition:** $26,468
Total Undergrads: 5,767	**Room & Board:** $9,200
SAT Range: 1540–1810*	**Avg. Aid Package:** $15,268
ACT Range: 23–28	**Students With Aid:** 99%

* of 2400

Academics	C+	Greek Life	B-
Athletics	C+	Guys	A
Campus Dining	C+	Health & Safety	B
Campus Housing	B	Local Atmosphere	B+
Campus Strictness	C+	Nightlife	A
Computers	C-	Off-Campus Dining	B-
Diversity	C	Off-Campus Housing	A-
Drug Safety	C+	Parking	B-
Facilities	B	Transportation	C+
Girls	B+	Weather	C+

CP's Student Author On... OVERALL EXPERIENCE

Students gripe about issues like tuition and parking, but overall, most feel the education and experiences found at Duquesne are worth every penny. Presenting a wide range of majors and programs, the University offers something for prospective students from all walks of life. Most think the campus beautiful, even in its urban setting. Students feel safe, welcome, and challenged here.

Duquesne continuously invests time, effort, and money into improving both the physical surroundings and educational content of the campus. The University emits the feel of a large institution, while still promoting the individuality of each student. Its diverse student body embraces students from all backgrounds. One should never feel lost on this campus. Help is always available for those who need it. The campus's technologically-advanced Living and Learning centers enhance the on-campus learning experience.

Students Speak Out On... OVERALL EXPERIENCE

From an Active Duquesne Students Perspective
"I love it here at Duquesne and I am happy with my decision to attend. The academic classes are top notch and very challenging. The party scene is average but the Universities near by nicely supplement it. I was astonished at how nice and outgoing the students were and feel strongly accepted here. I never could think of attending another college and never want to leave!"

Love It, Just Don't Let the City Overwhelm You!
"Duquesne is perfect for having fun... there is always parties going on in Pittsburgh. Being in a city can be overwhelming so at Duquesne it's kind of a break from the city where students can study.... having good grades is popular here and will earn you respect."

BEST OF DUQUESNE

1. Class sizes are small, despite the size of student body
2. Location of campus
3. Quality of education
4. Easy access to public transportation
5. Friendly atmosphere

Happy Students
86% of students return after their first year.

Proven Success
74% of students will complete their education and graduate with a degree.

WORST OF DUQUESNE

1. Parking
2. On-campus housing
3. High tuition
4. Lack of interest in athletics
5. Social cliques
6. Erratic weather
7. Gym facilities
8. Dorm rules

Expensive
Tuition is a steep $26,468, one of the most expensive rates in the country.

Students Speak Out On... EVERYTHING!

ACADEMICS

Political Science

"My first year at Duquesne was an easy transition to college life. My classes were reasonably demanding, but profs were helpful, understanding. The profs I had for classes within my major were talented, experienced, well educated (Yale, Duke) and well published. My advisor was also a valuable and friendly resource. The bottom line is: you get out of class what you put into class and help is always available."

You Can Buy a Degree

"In programs other than those governed by state certification criteria (i.e. Law, Health Sciences, Education), you can buy the credits you need and work around the system to get your degree. Again with the exception of state rules, GPA requirments for degrees are generally waived by the university after 4 years of tuition dollars are collected, assuming enough credits have been paid for and passed."

ATHLETICS

Red and Blue Crew

"At Duquesne sports are huge. Everyone goes to the football and soccer games because the field in directly in the center of campus. The basketball team seems to be the most popular because some of the games are held at the Consol Energy Center (where the Pittsburgh Penguins play!). Any student can be a part of the Red and Blue Crew, which is the "fan section". You get two t-shirts and free admission for every game."

Sports

"The football team isn't that great, but people always go to the games. Basketball is much more appealing because the team isn't too bad."

CAMPUS DINING

Campus Dining

"The food is very good and we have a good variety. We often have football practice late so it would be nice if they had later hours."

Good Food, but Not Much of a Variety

"The food at Duquesne is good but there isn't much of a variety. There is a place called Options, which surprisingly does't have many options. The food there is great but there are only about seven different things to choose from. There are several places that you can make your own sandwiches, wraps, and burritos. Overall the food is good but there seems to be a pattern as to when certain foods are available."

CAMPUS HOUSING

Dorms Get Better the More You Stay

"The longer you live at Duquesne, the better the housing gets. The freshman dorms are St. Ann's and St. Martins...St. Ann's is better but also more gender separated and strict. Assumption is the honors dorm and is really quiet and boring. Towers is mostly sophomores, and it's a lot of fun cause all of your friends are in one place. Vickroy and Brottier are the upperclassmen dorms, and are really nice. Brottier is more like an apartment, with suite rooms with your own kitchen."

GUYS & GIRLS

Girls Are Hot!

"It's rumored the girls on Duquesne's campus are ranked #3 on PlayBoy's Hottest campuses... and most people would agree. The guys aren't bad themselves, but we have a very attractive class of girls."

HEALTH & SAFETY

I Have Always Felt Safe on Duquesne's Campus

"Duquesne is very safe considering it is right next to a bad area. The Duquesne Police (DuPo) drive, bike, and walk around the campus 24/7. Whenever a crime occurs we get notifiations about very quickly. I have never felt unsafe walking alone. The DuPo are also available for rides if you feel unsafe. The text message alerts are also helpful."

Earlham College

801 National Road W; Richmond, IN 47374
(765) 983-1200; www.earlham.edu

THE BASICS:

Acceptance Rate: 76%	**Student-Faculty Ratio:** 12:1		
Yield: 23%	**Retention Rate:** 81%		
Setting: Town	**Graduation Rate:** 72%		
Control: Private Non-Profit	**Tuition:** $35,164		
Total Undergrads: 1,127	**Room & Board:** $7,160		
SAT Range: 1640–1990*	**Avg. Aid Package:** $16,118		
ACT Range: 24–29	**Students With Aid:** 91%		

* of 2400

Academics	B	Greek Life	N/A
Athletics	C+	Guys	B-
Campus Dining	B	Health & Safety	A
Campus Housing	B	Local Atmosphere	C-
Campus Strictness	C+	Nightlife	C-
Computers	A-	Off-Campus Dining	D+
Diversity	C	Off-Campus Housing	C+
Drug Safety	B	Parking	A-
Facilities	B+	Transportation	C-
Girls	B	Weather	C+

CP's Student Author On...
OVERALL EXPERIENCE

People come to Earlham for the academics, the Quaker principles, and the community. And, for the most part, they fall in love with the off-beat professors and student body. Earlham students are mostly fun, interesting, self-motivated, and incredibly involved on campus. Classes are compelling, and professors have a real love for their subjects and an investment in the students they teach. Quaker beliefs have mostly a positive and constructive presence on campus, helping remind staff and students to be mindful, open, and respectful. The opportunities are endless, and if Earlham's right for you, you're going to have an incredible four years. Surviving the crummy weather and the dismal off-campus dining scene will all be worth it. Most people really love it here, and the positive attitude is contagious. However, be aware that all good things come at a price. If you get claustrophobic in small social scenes or small towns, look elsewhere. The small size is responsible for the best and the worst of Earlham life. Richmond can be quaint and grounding, but after four years, most Earlham students are excited to be off to more exciting destinations.... For the rest of this editorial, visit collegeprowler.com.

Students Speak Out On...
OVERALL EXPERIENCE

Q **Love**

"Earlham is an amazing place because there are so many different people on the campus and we all get along. There are definitely different social groups on campus but people are really open and welcoming that it is easy to be a part of many different groups. Another preat part of Earlham are the professors. They are encouraging, always available, enjoy talking to student outside of class and they are always focused on getting to know every student."

Q "I absolutely love it, and I would never wish myself to be anywhere else. I recommend seriously considering Earlham; it's more than great."

Q "I loved Earlham. I loved it all. It was the most significant experience of my life, and it changed my parents, as well. I think if someone comes away from there without having changed, they were either beautiful to begin with, or too stupid to know when to fall in love."

BEST OF EARLHAM	WORST OF EARLHAM

BEST OF EARLHAM

1. Your professors live next door
2. Farm Day
3. August Wilderness
4. Quaker ideology
5. Shoes are optional everywhere except SAGA

Happy Students
81% of students return after their first year.

Proven Success
72% of students will complete their education and graduate with a degree.

WORST OF EARLHAM

1. Your professors live next door
2. Richmond
3. Dorm drama
4. Radical/liberal infighting
5. Blind rhetoric

Expensive
Tuition is a steep $35,164, one of the most expensive rates in the country.

Student Body

African American:	6%	Male Undergrads:	44%
Asian American:	3%	Female Undergrads:	56%
Hispanic:	2%	Living On Campus:	81%
International:	13%	Living Off Campus:	19%
Native American:	0%	Male Athletes:	32%
White:	65%	Female Athletes:	19%
Unknown:	12%	Fraternity Members:	0%
From Out-of-State:	84%	Sorority Members:	0%

Frequently Compared Schools:
Beloit College
College of Wooster
Macalester College
Oberlin College

Students Speak Out On... EVERYTHING!

ACADEMICS

Hipsters Everywhere
"There are a crap load of dirty hipsters here. If you don't like PBR, find somewhere else."

"I loved my professors, period. By and large they comprise the most brilliant (and hilarious) people I have ever met. In my best classes, professors and students explored complex concepts with insight, humor, and the sheer delight of learning (and interrogating) some really amazing material. Generally speaking, I would not trade my Earlham classes or profs for any others - period. Word to the wise - don't pass up the SoAn department if you don't happen to be a major. You won't regret it."

ATHLETICS

Ha! That's Funny.
"Earlham is not known for its athletics. The athletes are good people, but when it comes to actually playing sports, they're not so good."

"We have lots of IM sports that have many willing and enthusiastic members. I am a varsity tennis player, and I absolutely love it. It is another way to get a close group of friends."

CAMPUS DINING

SAGA Sucks
"The food on campus is often terrible. However, you can skip a meal and go to the cafe, where you can get something for meal exchange, which is often much better."

"Blah! Sorry, freshmen, you can't get away from SAGA. But you have options second semester if you like. Meal exchange is nice if you play sports. The Co-Op is nice, too, with an an interesting crowd of students."

CAMPUS HOUSING

"Bundy, Warren, and Wilson are the nicest, cleanest, and quietest dorms on campus. However, some students like the ancient dorms that have more charisma, drama, and leaky faucets."

"The dorms on campus are fantastic, compared to many other schools I have visited. The nicest dorms are Warren and Wilson, what some call 'the Suburbs,' which are not as centralized as others, but considering how small campus is, they are quite nice. However, the Suburbs are not quite as social as other dorms. For a great social dorm, I would recommend Earlham Hall, Barrett, or Olvey-Andis. They are all a bit loud, but they are great for social atmosphere."

GUYS & GIRLS

"Everyone on campus is great. The guys are nice, and there are some hot ones. There are some gorgeous girls on campus, and they are down-to-earth people."

"Let me just say that Earlham is pretty much the most attractive place that I have ever been. There is an abundance of hot people, both men and women. However, many women complain that there are too few men, since women are easily in the majority on campus. This, though, is one of the best parts of Earlham for many. There are so many hot people all around."

HEALTH & SAFETY

Safe
"I have never felt unsafe on Earlham's Campus. People are respectful and trusting so some people don't even lock their dorm rooms and there usually aren't any problems with theft. Campus Security and the Richmond Police will bust parties if there are noise complaints but they usually just come and break things up."

"Having lived off campus for the majority of my college life, I cannot say much, but I feel that it could be better. There could be more communication between security and the students."

LOOKING FOR MORE?
Check out our full-length guide to this school at collegeprowler.com/earlham-college/.

East Carolina University

1001 E. Fifth St.; Greenville, NC 27858
(252) 328-6131; www.ecu.edu

THE BASICS:

Acceptance Rate: 74%
Yield: 42%
Setting: Small city
Control: Public
Total Undergrads: 21,459
SAT Range: 1360–1640*
ACT Range: 19–23

Student-Faculty Ratio: 18:1
Retention Rate: 79%
Graduation Rate: 54%
Tuition: $15,311
Room & Board: $7,800
Avg. Aid Package: $4,570
Students With Aid: 62%

of 2400

Academics	B-	Greek Life	A-
Athletics	B-	Guys	A-
Campus Dining	B+	Health & Safety	C
Campus Housing	B	Local Atmosphere	B
Campus Strictness	C+	Nightlife	A-
Computers	B+	Off-Campus Dining	A-
Diversity	B-	Off-Campus Housing	A
Drug Safety	C+	Parking	B-
Facilities	A-	Transportation	A-
Girls	B+	Weather	B-

CP's Student Author On...
OVERALL EXPERIENCE

The quality and enthusiasm of the professors who care about their students is what attracts and retains students who could have gone to larger and more prestigious schools. Greenville is quite charming and has such good local food that most skeptics love the area, or at least ECU, by the time they graduate. Although the campus police are friendly, ECU is quite strict, perhaps in an effort to downplay the "party school" reputation. The strictness, however, contributes to student safety and helps reduce the drug presence on campus. Alcohol is a problem for some students, and the clubs are tempting, but the counseling center can help students with their problems. ECU's computer resources are excellent, and the athletic facilities are better than the teams' records. ECU's most enjoyable facilities are the green areas, especially because the weather here is so pleasant—crazy, but pleasant.

Whether living on or off campus, students should join organizations to maximize their college involvement and build leadership experience for their resume.... For the rest of this editorial, visit collegeprowler.com.

Students Speak Out On...
OVERALL EXPERIENCE

Q Great

"East Carlina university is an execellent school for me. As an student I have learn alot. I also swim for the school which sometime is very hard trying to manager going to school and keeping up my grades which I had a gpa of 3.79 as of today and playing a sport at college. I first fell in love with this school first time I seen it, and I am so glad I follow my heart and not my parents who wanted me to stay in Maryland."

Q My Experience at ECU

"I have only been at ECU for two semesters. I love this college! I wish that I would have came here right after high school. I have just had to manage my social life apart from my academics. It is a wonderful college and I would suggest ECU for anyone that wants to pursue an education and have a good time while doing so."

Q Amazing!

"If you don't love ECU, it's because you're not involved! However, if you party too much, that could be a problem."

BEST OF EAST CAROLINA

1. Trees and green spaces
2. Knowledgeable professors
3. Friendly students
4. Easily navigable campus in a comfortable setting
5. Academic, age, and ethnic diversity among students

Knowledgeable Professors
91% of students surveyed rated the general knowledge of professors as above average.

Low-Stress Course Load
60% of students surveyed rated the manageability of work as above average.

WORST OF EAST CAROLINA

1. Sports teams that get more money than their records show they deserve
2. Strictness of campus authorities
3. Students who take partying more seriously than studying

Lowest Grades
Health & Safety: C
Campus Strictness: C+
Drug Safety: C+

Student Body

African American:	15%	Male Undergrads:	42%
Asian American:	2%	Female Undergrads:	58%
Hispanic:	2%	Living On Campus:	25%
International:	1%	Living Off Campus:	75%
Native American:	1%	Male Athletes:	4%
White:	75%	Female Athletes:	2%
Unknown:	5%	Fraternity Members:	7%
From Out-of-State:	18%	Sorority Members:	6%

Frequently Compared Schools:

James Madison University
North Carolina State University
University of North Carolina
University of South Carolina

Students Speak Out On...
EVERYTHING!

ACADEMICS

Popular Study Areas

"East Carolina has wifi on campus and it makes it easier to access the internet if I am unable to get to a computer lab. They have several computer labs and the library has plenty of computers. Both the computer lab and libary are great areas to study. The computer lab that I always go to is very quiet and very peaceful and the libary has designated rooms for late night study or quick cramming."

East Carolina Works Hard to Get You Success

"At ECU I feel that the teachers really do care about you and the academic advisors try to encourage you and attempt to help you acquire employment once you have graduated"

ATHLETICS

Team Sprit

"I didn't attend alot of games this school year, but if I wanted to I would have made sure I got my ticket in a timely manner. The football games were always sold out because the majority of ecu students went and supported the team."

Pirate Atheletics

"Pirate pride is huge in Greenville, the whole town gets behind the sports. You can tell it is definitely a college town. Pirate football is HUGE. there is tailgating for miles. Tailgates are full of free food and drinks, as well as many games you can play. Pirate basketball is on the rise, and Baseball games are extremely fun."

CAMPUS DINING

Dining Halls

"East Carolina has 3 places to dine on campus. I have not had the liberty to enjoy the food because I stay off campus. However, my classmates have told me that the food was affordable and great."

Could Be Healthier

"Overall, the food in the dining halls is pretty delicious, but the nutritional guides available are often blatantly incorrect or have odd portion sizes. The packaged food available around campus is very convenient and generally healthy: from sushi to sandwiches, eating on-the-go is made simple."

CAMPUS HOUSING

Living on Campus

"Living on campus is great, you are close to downtown, close to your classes. The dining halls are right next to where you live. there is always something to do on campus ranging from concerts to laser tag to movies. the only bad part about living on campus is sharing a room. everything else is thoroughly enjoyable no matter where you live."

Campus Living Is the Best

"I lived on campus my freshman year and will be returning this year to the same dorm. It was so convenient to simply fall out of bed and go to class, which was usually in a very close location to my dorm. The dining halls are usually full of good food and the activities on campus are always varied and fun. The cost is expensive but in the long run probably worth it."

GUYS & GIRLS

Girls

"Since I'm a guy, I beleive the girls at East Carolina are amazing. Their smart and beautiful! All of the girls that I met so far are very nice to everyone. Don't be shy to go up and introduce yourself to one of them!"

Ecu People

"Most people at ecu dress fairly nice, when I say most I mean about half. everybody has their own style, i'd say ECU girls are extremely hot though."

HEALTH & SAFETY

Safety on Campus

"The campus is totally safe. Everything is located close to each other. The parking lots are nearby the buildings. The police offers and exceptional service."

LOOKING FOR MORE?

Check out our full-length guide to this school at collegeprowler.com/east-carolina-university/.

Eastern Kentucky University

521 Lancaster Ave.; Richmond, KY 40475
(859) 622-1000; www.eku.edu

THE BASICS:

Acceptance Rate: 72%	**Student-Faculty Ratio:** 17:1
Yield: 48%	**Retention Rate:** 69%
Setting: Town	**Graduation Rate:** 36%
Control: Public	**Tuition:** $17,740
Total Undergrads: 14,008	**Room & Board:** $6,020
SAT Range: 890–1140*	**Avg. Aid Package:** $10,719
ACT Range: 18–24	**Students With Aid:** 96%

* of 1600

Academics	C+	Greek Life	C+
Athletics	C	Guys	B
Campus Dining	C	Health & Safety	B-
Campus Housing	C	Local Atmosphere	B
Campus Strictness	B-	Nightlife	B+
Computers	C+	Off-Campus Dining	B
Diversity	C	Off-Campus Housing	B
Drug Safety	C	Parking	B-
Facilities	C+	Transportation	B
Girls	B	Weather	C-

CP's Student Author On...
OVERALL EXPERIENCE

Eastern has a lot to offer students and prepares them for their future careers through various new programs, technologies, and real world experiences. A lot of the programs require field work to obtain a degree, which helps the student get acclimated to their future career.

The rigor of the University is also becoming more challenging, with a goal of preparing students with writing intensive requirements and new standards in all classrooms. Students are seeing more writing assignments, projects to promote creativity, and advanced communication skills. This is all part of EKU's initiative to promote more effective thinkers. Here professors know your name, and it is rare to have a class with more than 25 people. EKU prides itself on its small class size and individual attention to students. At EKU, you truly are more than just a number.

Students Speak Out On...
OVERALL EXPERIENCE

Q Experiences
"I love the college experience at EKU. So many nice people and programs to be involved in. I would def choose this school again."

Q Best EVER
"I LOVE EKU and am so glad that I went here instead of anywhere else! I thought about going to the University of Kentucky, but ultimately declined because it was too large. EKU is just the right size--small enough that it's easy to make friends and have friends in your classes, but large enough that you are meeting new people all the time. Although it's located in a small town, Lexington is a 25 minute drive away and it has anything that you could ever want to do there (200,000+ population)."

Q EKU Experience
"I would choose EKU all over again because I've had a lot of fun here and met some cool people. The campus has plenty to do outside and lots of scenery which is what I like."

BEST OF EASTERN KENTUCKY

1. Small class sizes
2. Affordable
3. Campus is big, but not too big.
4. Free sporting events
5. Lots of clubs and organizations
6. Nice dorms

Knowledgeable Professors
77% of students surveyed rated the general knowledge of professors as above average.

Low-Stress Course Load
67% of students surveyed rated the manageability of work as above average.

WORST OF EASTERN KENTUCKY

1. Finding a good parking spot
2. Winter weather
3. Two-hour delays instead of cancelling class
4. Computer lab hours
5. Food options on campus

Not Everyone Graduates
36% of students do not complete their education or graduate with a degree.

Not Much Diversity
One of the least racially diverse campuses—only 10% of students are minorities.

Student Body

African American:	5%	Male Undergrads:	42%
Asian American:	1%	Female Undergrads:	58%
Hispanic:	1%	Living On Campus:	29%
International:	1%	Living Off Campus:	71%
Native American:	0%	Male Athletes:	5%
White:	90%	Female Athletes:	2%
Unknown:	1%	Fraternity Members:	8%
From Out-of-State:	17%	Sorority Members:	6%

Students Speak Out On... EVERYTHING!

ACADEMICS

The Academics

"I really enjoy what EKU has to offer opposed to other colleges. My professors are always so kind and very helpful and my workload is just right. I feel like I am able to do what I need to get good grades and further my education with this institution."

EKU

"Professors are extremely helpful and want their students to do well! The workload gets a little overwhelming at times, but it is nothing that I can't handle. I could not imagine myself at any other Univeristy! I love it here!"

ATHLETICS

Athletic Facilities

"Anyone who wants to be involved with athletics can be. My personal opinion is Eastern Kentucky University has the very best gym. It is very clean, open, has a lot of equipment, assessable, spacious, and very nice."

EKU Athletics

"There is something for everyone to participate in at EKU. There are lots of teams that offer scholarships as well as intramurals of all kinds if you just want to have some fun."

CAMPUS DINING

Eastern Kentucky Review

"I love my university. The campus is beautiful and my dorm is awesome."

Powelling

"On campus, we have Lower Powell and Upper Powell. Upper Powell is the cafeteria where we are served a variety of foods. I like that, but I wish that when the food gets cold, they would have fresh food already waiting. Lower Powell has a variety of fast food joints, but I wish it had a Chinese food place inside it as well. I think it would be nice to be able to use flex dollars for payment on everything on campus so long as it could be an option. Right now, Flex can only be used for food."

Frequently Compared Schools:

Morehead State University
Ohio State University
University of Kentucky
Western Kentucky University

CAMPUS HOUSING

Housing

"The housing at Eastern Kentucky University is fairly nice. The dorm which I know most about is Telford which is where I lived. In Telford you have suits. It is two room joined by a private bathroom which you share. This is the only dorm on campus which has this feature, the rest have only 1 bathroom to a floor which everyone uses. Although Telford has this nice quality it is the dorm that is farthest away from everything. The cost is about 3,000 a semester and is worth it!"

Dorms

"I don't mind living in the dorms. The community bathrooms are the worst especially when they aren't cleaned as often as they should be. The cost is relatively low compared to apartments. Living on campus is extremely convenient, that is one reason why I like living on campus."

GUYS & GIRLS

More Girls Than Guys

"Here at Eastern it is about 51 percent girls and 49 percent guys. However, you never really seem to notice it until you join a small social club in which you're hanging out with more girls than guys. Anyway, you will always find a variety of personalities on campus. Eastern is still a lot of fun and I love it more with each passing minute."

HEALTH & SAFETY

Crime

"Most crimes are minor, and security on campus is good. A lot of crimes are alcohol related. If you do get caught doing a crime your name gets put on the police beat in the paper. This is a safe campus and you only get in trouble if you're doing something wrong, the rules are not hard to follow."

LOOKING FOR MORE?

Check out our full-length guide to this school at collegeprowler.com/eastern-kentucky-university/.

Eckerd College

4200 54th Ave. S; St. Petersburg, FL 33711
(727) 867-1166; www.eckerd.edu

THE BASICS:

Acceptance Rate: 72%
Yield: 22%
Setting: Mid-sized city
Control: Private Non-Profit
Total Undergrads: 2,449
SAT Range: 1520–1855*
ACT Range: 22–28

Student-Faculty Ratio: 14:1
Retention Rate: 81%
Graduation Rate: 64%
Tuition: $32,104
Room & Board: $9,058
Avg. Aid Package: $22,743
Students With Aid: 96%

* of 2400

Academics	B	Greek Life	N/A
Athletics	C+	Guys	A-
Campus Dining	C+	Health & Safety	B-
Campus Housing	B-	Local Atmosphere	A-
Campus Strictness	B+	Nightlife	B+
Computers	B	Off-Campus Dining	C+
Diversity	C+	Off-Campus Housing	B
Drug Safety	D+	Parking	B+
Facilities	B-	Transportation	C
Girls	B	Weather	A+

CP's Student Author On...
OVERALL EXPERIENCE

Eckerd is a really unique school with hundreds of quirky and charming dimensions, but it's not for everyone. For some, the school is too small, offers limited major options, and has a somewhat repetitive social scene that can make Eckerd fell less like paradise and more like a very, very small tide pool. But for those who continue on at the College for all four years, there are some great memories to be had and life-long connections with both peers and professors to be made. Profiled in the book "Colleges That Change Lives," Eckerd is a school with a lot of potential, opportunities, and amazing experiences, but it is up to you to get involved and craft your own experience for the next four years of your lives.

However, there's no arguing that the faculty is amazing, the level of interaction is great, and the location is paradise. Eckerd is one of those schools where the world is at your fingertips—students can do everything from participate in a spring break service project overseas to work at the waterfront.... For the rest of this editorial, visit collegeprowler.com.

Students Speak Out On...
OVERALL EXPERIENCE

Q **Amazing School, Amazing Faculty, Amazing Education.**
"I wouldn't trade my undergraduate experience for any other one."

Q **BEST SCHOOL EVER!**
"I couldn't have picked a more perfect school. Eckerd has a very unique atmosphere, with almost everyone sharing a very liberal state of mind."

Q **Love the Florida lifestyle**
"I've really learned to love the Florida lifestyle. Eckerd is great, and I've had a great experience here with most classes and had a great experience at my job on campus."

Q **It Is Exactly as They Describe**
"Eckerd doesn't pretend to be your regular college. Classes are small, teachers are friendly, and the students are unique. It's a unique school, and if you are looking for a different college experience, this is the place to be."

BEST OF ECKERD

1. Waterfront on campus!
2. The Palm Hammocks and hammocks on the beach
3. The beach on campus
4. View from Omega balconies
5. Proximity to both the beach and downtown

Happy Students
81% of students return after their first year.

Easy Financial Aid Process
50% of students surveyed told us that the financial aid process went smoothly and they received the financial aid they needed.

WORST OF ECKERD

1. Limited dining hours
2. Not enough single rooms on campus
3. Café food is always terrible by the end of the semester
4. Nightlife can get repetitive

Expensive
Tuition is a steep $32,104, one of the most expensive rates in the country.

Student Body

African American:	7%	Male Undergrads:	39%
Asian American:	2%	Female Undergrads:	61%
Hispanic:	5%	Living On Campus:	78%
International:	2%	Living Off Campus:	22%
Native American:	1%	Male Athletes:	16%
White:	74%	Female Athletes:	6%
Unknown:	10%	Fraternity Members:	0%
From Out-of-State:	78%	Sorority Members:	0%

Frequently Compared Schools:

Chapman University
Rollins College
University of Miami
University of Tampa

Students Speak Out On... EVERYGTHING!

ACADEMICS

Q Literature Major Have Access to Brilliant Minds

"The Literature professors at Eckerd are the most amazing group of professors. The lit professors are accomplished in their field and brilliant scholars, but so accessible to the students. The Literature department is a small but quality department at Eckerd. The workload is serious; you have reading and writing assignments due every day."

Q Great Experiences

"I came to Eckerd to play tennis and enjoy the small class sizes. What I didn't know is that I would be finding remarkable world-class teachers, engaging course material, and a huge opportunity to study abroad."

Q Teachers Are Easily Accessible

"We have small classes and good teachers."

ATHLETICS

Q Fan Support

"The students all go to the games and are very supportive of our teams, Lots of fan support by students & faculty"

Q Good Variety

"Sports are not very competitive, but there's lots of options."

CAMPUS DINING

Q Othe Ways to Use Your Meal Plan/Flex Dollars

"I like that there are other places to use my flex dollars like the pub."

Q Cafeteria and Pub

"The food is good but very repetitive."

CAMPUS HOUSING

Q Old Dorms but Comfortable

"Relative to other colleges, Eckerd dorms are beautiful, especially the upperclassman apartments. However, for freshmen and sophomores, the traditional housing really could use updating and renovating of both floors. Some of the older dorms are starting to fall apart, and no housing on campus is energy efficient."

Q Living on Campus

"Living in on-campus housing all four years at school is a good decision. Try as hard as you can to get into Omega and try to get a good view. The difference in view is between a parking lot and a view of the bay. Traditional dorms are honestly not bad compared to other schools. Nu is the party dorm. If you wish you were in a frat/sorority, live in Nu."

GUYS & GIRLS

Q Life at Eckerd

"Everyone is very welcoming to all and open to new ideas and ways of thinking—very open-minded, liberal."

Q 3:1 Girls

"Eckerd College, for some reason, is extremely appealing to girls. There is a larger population of girls that guys at the college. There's a wide range of people, from rednecks and country kids to non-shoe wearing hippies and squatters."

HEALTH & SAFETY

Q Thoughts on Campus Safety

"Safety on Tampa West Campus is not an issue. There is security on guard at all times. The guards will walk the ladies to their cars after night classes' end between 8:30pm to 10:30pm, which makes me feel extremely safe. Security codes are turned on after 6:00pm to ensure that unauthorized people don't come into the building."

Q Typical Small Campus Security--Enforcing Rules Case by Case

"Overall, I would say Eckerd's campus is safe and only sparsely littered with crime from students occasionally acting out of line. Campus security picks its battles with drinking games and partying. The security shack at the front gate is ineffective— they are inconsistent with checking in or caring about visitors."

LOOKING FOR MORE?

Check out our full-length guide to this school at collegeprowler.com/eckerd-college/.

Elizabethtown College

1 Alpha Dr.; Elizabethtown, PA 17022
(717) 361-1000; www.etown.edu

THE BASICS:

Acceptance Rate: 75%	Student-Faculty Ratio: 14:1
Yield: 22%	Retention Rate: 79%
Setting: Town	Graduation Rate: 70%
Control: Private Non-Profit	Tuition: $31,800
Total Undergrads: 2,272	Room & Board: $8,150
SAT Range: 1010–1230*	Avg. Aid Package: $22,582
ACT Range: 20–27	Students With Aid: 98%

* of 1600

Academics	B	Greek Life	N/A
Athletics	C	Guys	B-
Campus Dining	B	Health & Safety	A
Campus Housing	B	Local Atmosphere	B-
Campus Strictness	B	Nightlife	B-
Computers	C+	Off-Campus Dining	C
Diversity	C	Off-Campus Housing	C+
Drug Safety	C+	Parking	B+
Facilities	C+	Transportation	C
Girls	B-	Weather	B

CP's Student Author On...
OVERALL EXPERIENCE

Elizabethtown College is quite a wonderful school if one can appreciate a smaller and more personal atmosphere. The faculty and staff at Etown really care and make great efforts to ensure students' comfort and success. Most everyone is friendly, and the college just feels safe. Students don't have to think twice about leaving a purse or expensive phone on the table in the cafeteria; they know that everyone will respect that property. That's the type of community feeling that embodies what it's like to live and learn at Elizabethtown College. It's not 100 percent safe or nice, as every place has its problems with crime and drama, but the people at Etown put a lot of effort into making it the greatest college experience.

There is always something happening, some event or occasion that the College supports and funds in order to make the area not quite so dull. Etown realizes it's not a party school, so it makes an effort to provide entertainment that the students will really enjoy—popular comedians, musicians, movie showings (with free popcorn), concerts, game nights, and more.... For the rest of this editorial, visit collegeprowler.com.

Students Speak Out On...
OVERALL EXPERIENCE

Q Love Etown!

"Elizabethtown is great if you are interested in a small school with a lot of personal attention. Even though we have about 2,000 students, you meet new people all the time. It's a great learning environment and everyone is very nice here."

Q Fantasmic

"It's a small campus, with around 2,000 students, so don't expect raging parties every night. Other than it being a bit too quiet sometimes, I love it here. It's really a friendly atmosphere and beautiful campus. The classes are higher quality because they are so small and taught only by Professors- no teaching assistants."

Q Great Experience.

"I love Etown and would not want to be anywhere else."

Q This is a GREAT school!

"This is a great place to be. It isn't all fun and games. The parties are around if you want them, but you are not pressured to go. The professors really challenge you. For a person who floated through high school, it is a bit of a rough transition, but, in the end, it is that challenge that makes life here great."

BEST OF ELIZABETHTOWN

1. It smells like chocolate sometimes (Mars chocolate factory in town).
2. Close and friendly community
3. Smaller class sizes provides a more personal professor to student interaction.

Easy Financial Aid Process
59% of students surveyed told us that the financial aid process went smoothly and they received the financial aid they needed.

WORST OF ELIZABETHTOWN

1. Expensive meal plan
2. No football team
3. Most dorm buildings are old and haven't been remodeled in a few years.
4. It's a bit difficult to get permission to live off campus.

Expensive
Tuition is a steep $31,800, one of the most expensive rates in the country.

Want a Job? On Your Own
There aren't any placement services for graduates.

Student Body

African American:	4%	Male Undergrads:	36%
Asian American:	2%	Female Undergrads:	64%
Hispanic:	3%	Living On Campus:	87%
International:	2%	Living Off Campus:	13%
Native American:	0%	Male Athletes:	40%
White:	89%	Female Athletes:	17%
Unknown:	0%	Fraternity Members:	0%
From Out-of-State:	35%	Sorority Members:	0%

Frequently Compared Schools:

Dickinson College
Franklin & Marshall College
Gettysburg College
Ursinus College

Students Speak Out On... EVERYTHING!

ACADEMICS

English Major at Etown

"I love the English department here. The professors are wonderful, attentive and brilliant."

Profs Welcome Student Visits Outside of Class

"One of the major reasons I picked Elizabethtown was the fact that the professors are more than happy to have one-on-one interaction with students both in and out of the classroom. I've had discussions with my professors in their offices about academics, extracurriculars, and career related issues. One prof. even introduced me to a local writer, and it's contacts like that which will help me after graduation."

Academics

"Coming from a top notch prep school I was prepared for the academics. They may have been a little easier than I was expecting but i did graduate a few years ago. I think it is continuing to get harder to get in and finish."

ATHLETICS

Good Atheletics

"for a small school good atheletics and support. could use a new facility though."

Small School, Little Participation

"I don't feel like people get too into the sports, but the atmosphere is friendly if you would like to be involved in that."

CAMPUS DINING

Food

"on campus food is excellent. Could use one more snack shop though somewhere."

Not Much Choice

"Because the school is small there are not a lot of different eating facilities. The quality in the cafeteria is alright but gets boring after a while. I would go for the meal plan with more money to spend in the Jays Nest and just one meal swipe a day."

CAMPUS HOUSING

All Dorms Decent Size

"All the dorms are a very decent size, most are approximately the same size. They are bigger than most I have toured. The closet space is great."

Love to Live on Campus

"All dorms at Etown are fantastic. You'll love them and each of the dorm has its unique features. I'll say for the freshmen, Myer is the best dorm, with wide and well-lit hallway, comfortable room and bathrooms, and especially the fact that it is a dorm for student groups. The cost of living on campus is same for all the dorms. You'll just love to stay on campus with the social atmosphere you get there."

GUYS & GIRLS

Students

"The college has mostly women students but there are plenty of guys that attend the school. The male attendees are mostly into athletics. There are city and urban students but there are also those that come from the mountains."

People

"While there are a lot of people with amazing personalities, that doesn't mean that Etown is the dating center of the world. Etown is a mostly girl school, which means it's harder to find boyfriends. But it's okay, there are a lot of worthwhile relationships that can be formed!"

HEALTH & SAFETY

Location, Location, Location!

"Thanks mostly to where Elizabethtown is located, the campus is nested right in a little town. I've never once felt threatened walking from the library to my dorm at two o' clock in the morning, and the campus security office is right in my phone."

So Safe

"The school is in a small town and we have a strong honor policy so it feels very, very safe!!"

LOOKING FOR MORE?

Check out our full-length guide to this school at collegeprowler.com/elizabethtown-college/.

Elmhurst College

190 Prospect Ave.; Elmhurst, IL 60126
(630) 617-3500; public.elmhurst.edu

THE BASICS:

Acceptance Rate: 70%
Yield: 30%
Setting: Suburban
Control: Private Non-Profit
Total Undergrads: 3,145
SAT Range: 1420–1730*
ACT Range: 21–27

Student-Faculty Ratio: 13:1
Retention Rate: 83%
Graduation Rate: 69%
Tuition: $28,600
Room & Board: $8,216
Avg. Aid Package: $21,073
Students With Aid: 92%

* of 2400

Academics	B	Greek Life	C+
Athletics	C+	Guys	B+
Campus Dining	C+	Health & Safety	A+
Campus Housing	B+	Local Atmosphere	A
Campus Strictness	A	Nightlife	B
Computers	A	Off-Campus Dining	A+
Diversity	C+	Off-Campus Housing	A-
Drug Safety	C+	Parking	C+
Facilities	A	Transportation	A+
Girls	A	Weather	B

CP's Student Author On...
OVERALL EXPERIENCE

It's common for students to wonder whether they made the right choice with their college, but this answer cannot be found within a week or two—it takes at least a semester to fully appreciate (or hate) their college. At Elmhurst, orientation can be rather tedious, but once classes start, the campus settles down and thrives. The classes are intriguing and taught by smart yet down-to-earth professors. And through your classes, you will learn about the 100+ different organizations on campus, which is huge considering there are only about 3,000 undergrads here. This makes it easy for students to get involved and begin gaining experiences for their potential careers.

Prestigious graduate programs respect Elmhurst and offer plenty of opportunities to its students. Even though the area has a large concentration of colleges and qualified people, Elmhurst students continually grab top-notch internships with some of the best organizations in the world.... For the rest of this editorial, visit collegeprowler. com.

Students Speak Out On...
OVERALL EXPERIENCE

Q I Love It

"The campus is beautiful, the program is hard but worth it, and the people are very nice and friendly. The professors are helpful. Overall, I love being here!"

Q :D

"Elmhurst is truly my home. I love every aspect of the campus and its residents. I have never met such friendly and kind people in all my experiences."

Q Amazing!

"I love Elmhurst College. It is probably the best thing I've ever done in my life! It's fun here and I've made a lot of friends! Teachers are professional, and mentors and advisors will pull you through any tough academic situation you fall into!"

Q Love It

"I have some problems but it's all good."

Q I Transfered Here and Don't Regret It

"It made me work harder but I can get a good job now because the college is so credible."

BEST OF ELMHURST

1. Perfect location
2. Beautiful campus
3. Smart faculty
4. Plenty of study abroad opportunities
5. Small campus
6. The other students
7. The academic programs

Happy Students
83% of students return after their first year.

Easy Financial Aid Process
64% of students surveyed told us that the financial aid process went smoothly and they received the financial aid they needed.

WORST OF ELMHURST

1. Athletics
2. Lack of diversity—it's mostly in-state suburban students.
3. Parking
4. Residential life
5. Lots of people go home on the weekends.

Expensive
Tuition is a steep $28,600, one of the most expensive rates in the country.

Student Body

African American:	4%	Male Undergrads:	36%
Asian American:	5%	Female Undergrads:	64%
Hispanic:	7%	Living On Campus:	37%
International:	1%	Living Off Campus:	63%
Native American:	0%	Male Athletes:	28%
White:	74%	Female Athletes:	12%
Unknown:	9%	Fraternity Members:	11%
From Out-of-State:	16%	Sorority Members:	10%

Students Speak Out On...
EVERYTHING!

ACADEMICS

Q Better Than I Thought

"Most people come here because they give you lots of money for a smaller school, but the classes are challenging and the professors are amazing. I know the social sciences are great. Take my word for it, it's good."

Q Incredible!

"The music program along with all other classes I've had are so good. The professors know what they are doing and help you out when you struggle."

Q Great College

"The size of the college only helps more. The small classes are great for learning. and the student life is great. They are very helpful in everything you want to do, and when you need academic help too."

ATHLETICS

Q Sports Are Very Nice

"At Elmhurst College, we have a very nice fitness center with different machines. We also have personal trainers who help us look and feel good."

Q Athletics

"The student body gets very involved in all the sporting events. I don't really know how "good" the school really is, but the fans are really supportive!"

Q Good

"I haven't actually attended an athletic game, yet from what I hear, the sports are pretty good."

CAMPUS DINING

Q Cafe and Roost

"You can choose between two places based on what you feel like eating on that particular day."

Q Great Good, Great Conversation

"The Cafe and Roost are great places to just let loose and chat it up with your brothers."

Frequently Compared Schools:

DePaul University
Northwestern University
University of Chicago
University of Illinois at Chicago

CAMPUS HOUSING

Q The College Mall (Quad)

"The college mall is great for socializing and studying when the weather is nice out. During the winter, everyone joins in on the annual first fall of snow snowball fight! The trees, grass, and other plants make it a very beautiful place to relax"

Q Nifty

"They look nice and are comfy."

GUYS & GIRLS

Q Friendly People

"The student body at Elmhurst College, in my opinion, is one of the most friendly groups of people I have ever known. People here make you feel comfortable, like you're at home, and you will be sure to find friends who you will know and cherish for the rest of your life."

Q Chicago's Hottest

"The girls look fine and the guys look finer."

HEALTH & SAFETY

Q Very Safe

"I feel very safe ion Elmhurst College's campus. The campus is small, beautiful, and safe. Since I been here, I never saw a fight or anything inappropriate. I also see police and security around the parking lots, and there are also security cameras."

Q Health and Safety

"Elmhurst is a really safe school. The security is great. They provide an escort service that can be easily accessed by a blue phone located in most of the buildings. With campus security updates via text message or e-mail, you can get the latest news on campus crimes and emergencies. I can proudly say that Elmhurst College is a safe school to attend and live at"

LOOKING FOR MORE?

Check out our full-length guide to this school at collegeprowler.com/elmhurst-college/.

Elmira College

1 Park Place; Elmira, NY 14901
(607) 735-1800; www.elmira.edu

THE BASICS:

Acceptance Rate: 79%	Student-Faculty Ratio: 12:1
Yield: 25%	Retention Rate: 68%
Setting: Small city	Graduation Rate: 61%
Control: Private Non-Profit	Tuition: $34,850
Total Undergrads: 1,430	Room & Board: $10,800
SAT Range: 960–1190*	Avg. Aid Package: $26,911
ACT Range: 22–27	Students With Aid: 99%

* of 1600

Academics	C+	Greek Life	N/A
Athletics	C+	Guys	B
Campus Dining	C+	Health & Safety	C+
Campus Housing	B	Local Atmosphere	D+
Campus Strictness	B-	Nightlife	B+
Computers	C	Off-Campus Dining	C-
Diversity	C+	Off-Campus Housing	D+
Drug Safety	C	Parking	A-
Facilities	C	Transportation	C+
Girls	B-	Weather	B-

CP's Student Author On...
OVERALL EXPERIENCE

Elmira College really allows students to flourish. You can most likely attain every one of your college goals while attending Elmira. If you want to be a leader in government, you can start by getting involved with the student government. If you want to become a sports star, there are plenty of opportunities to train. If you want to become a great writer, you can work alongside the Octagon newspaper and The Sibyl literary magazine. If you have the motivation, you can basically do anything at Elmira. Ambitious individuals are rewarded and recognized for their efforts. More importantly, the type of person that attends Elmira is a decent, caring, fun-loving, and spirited individual. The friendships that are forged add so much to the experience, and meeting others who have the same drive is incredibly rewarding. The faculty, administrators, and staff make sure you are having the kind of experience that you wanted to have. The president of the College goes out of his way to get to know a majority of the students, which is rare at other colleges.... For the rest of this editorial, visit collegeprowler.com.

Students Speak Out On...
OVERALL EXPERIENCE

Q Love It
"people are so nice and accepting to me and there is a place for everyone here. the campus is so pretty and theres always something to do its a great school"

Q I Love It
"I love the small community and the family aspect of the school system"

Q Best Years of my life
"Elmira College has given me the opportunity to become such a strong, independent, and motivated individual. I've been challenged in my classes, learned to write really well, gotten to know a ton of new people, and been taught traditions that I will remember for a lifetime. Club-wise, I've been involved with the same organizations since my freshman year, really strengthening my ties to the college."

BEST OF ELMIRA

1. Elmira College encourages school spirit. There is a strong sense of unity among classmates.
2. The campus is beautiful and well-kept.

Easy Financial Aid Process
70% of students surveyed told us that the financial aid process went smoothly and they received the financial aid they needed.

WORST OF ELMIRA

1. The girl-to-guy ratio is extremely skewed—it's about 2:1 women to men.
2. The city of Elmira does not offer a lot of activities for students—no nightlife.
3. The Freshman Writing Program is very demanding.

Expensive
Tuition is a steep $34,850, one of the most expensive rates in the country.

Student Body

African American:	2%	Male Undergrads:	29%
Asian American:	1%	Female Undergrads:	71%
Hispanic:	1%	Living On Campus:	93%
International:	6%	Living Off Campus:	7%
Native American:	0%	Male Athletes:	40%
White:	69%	Female Athletes:	22%
Unknown:	21%	Fraternity Members:	0%
From Out-of-State:	49%	Sorority Members:	0%

Frequently Compared Schools:

Alfred University
Hamilton College
Ithaca College
Skidmore College

Students Speak Out On... EVERYTHING!

ACADEMICS

Q Great Professors

"The professors here are all really dedicated to what they teach. All the full time professors have their doctorate, so you know they're educated in what they're teaching. They're passionate about what they teach and are willing to help students understand things further."

Q Criminal Justice

"The few classes that I have taken for Criminal Justice have been interesting. The professor actually works in a police force so I am confident that he knows what he is talking about. Overall the classes have been very informative and beneficial."

ATHLETICS

Q Great Athletic Support

"Elmira College treats their athletes very well, not just during game time, but all year round. Athletes have mandated study hall periods, so they don't fall behind in their classes. The student body supports their teams very well. The gym is packed during basketball games and hockey games are crazy. The community supports the hockey team as well. While EC is the D-III school, atheltic teams are supported by the college and treated very well."

Q Sports

"I think the sports here are fantastic. I love how we have team spirit in almost every sport we play such as soccer, and men's hockey being the biggest. They train hard with the coaches and since grades are extremely important here at Elmira if you do not have the grades, you do not play."

CAMPUS DINING

Q Lots of Options

"Dining options include - 1855, Macks, Simeons, Main Dining Hall, and the sautee."

Q Meal Plan

"The dining hall, Mac's, and 1855 offer a good variety of food most of the time, at a decent price. The grill in the dining hall is probably the most convenient and cost effective meal option on campus."

CAMPUS HOUSING

Q Wonderful

"Fantastic. Freshman year was small, but I've had spacey and homey rooms since then."

Q Great

"The freshman dorms are centrally located, and the upperclassman dorms are state of the art and offer everything one would like to have"

GUYS & GIRLS

Q Girls Vs Guys

"The ratio is pretty bad, but guys and girls get along well together here at Elmira. I'm more of a "man's woman" I hunt, fish, get dirty, and all that. Looks wise, well I personally don't pay attention."

Q Elmira Men

"There are not many men at Elmira College but in general they are all quality people. We have a big hockey team, and all the men are incredibly fit. Plus, you have to be pretty smart to get into Elmira, so they are smart too!!"

HEALTH & SAFETY

Q Amazing

"The campus has very good service and is always making students aware of campus happenings."

Q Not Bad!

"There is very little wrong with EC when it comes to health and safety. It isn't handicap accessible really but security is great and the health center is great."

LOOKING FOR MORE?
Check out our full-length guide to this school at collegeprowler.com/elmira-college/.

Elon University

100 Campus Drive; Elon, NC 27244
(336) 278-2000; www.elon.edu

THE BASICS:

Acceptance Rate: 42%	**Student-Faculty Ratio:** 13:1
Yield: 32%	**Retention Rate:** 89%
Setting: Rural	**Graduation Rate:** 78%
Control: Private Non-Profit	**Tuition:** $25,489
Total Undergrads: 4,995	**Room & Board:** $8,236
SAT Range: 1700–1970*	**Avg. Aid Package:** $5,781
ACT Range: 25–29	**Students With Aid:** 74%

of 2400

Academics	A-	Greek Life	A-
Athletics	B-	Guys	A
Campus Dining	B+	Health & Safety	B+
Campus Housing	A	Local Atmosphere	C+
Campus Strictness	B-	Nightlife	B
Computers	A	Off-Campus Dining	B+
Diversity	C	Off-Campus Housing	A-
Drug Safety	C+	Parking	B+
Facilities	A-	Transportation	B-
Girls	A-	Weather	B

CP's Student Author On... OVERALL EXPERIENCE

Elon students enjoy the experience of attending the school, but as with many things there are drawbacks. The community is small and quiet, and other schools are approximately a half hour away. But even though there are drawbacks, and students can sometimes feel like they wish they were somewhere else, they still can't imagine being at anywhere else. Socially, there is a Greek scene, but students also throw parties in their houses and/or apartments. There is also an abundance of nightlife that is in Greensboro, which is only 20–30 minutes away and well worth the trip.

The academic curriculum can be rigorous at times, but the professors are willing to help in any way that they can. Elon's student body is great even though they can be a little difficult to deal with at times; there are not a lot of complaints about the University other than its diversity issues and the size of the town. But don't be fooled by Elon's size—it may not be for everyone, but life at Elon can be a great experience.

Students Speak Out On... OVERALL EXPERIENCE

Q Family

"I just find this campus to be completely gorgeous and everyone is extremely friendly. There are always friends to be made at Elon, and the weather keeps you upbeat and happy. I find that the teachers are helpful and do want you to exceed. Elon is like a big family, and everyone for the most part is looking out for one another. The main objective is to be successful and thats what Elon pries itself on."

Q Transfer

"I just transferred to my school for Spring semester and so far I have loved it. I am from the town it's in so I already had previous experience and knew it was the school for me. It is a private school with a lot of different people from all over the country. The people are so nice and always helpful!"

Q Awesome

"I'm a freshman and Elon paid for me to study abroad to Mexico and create a business plan for a Mexican village. I would choose elon again. Campus is awesome. People are awesome."

Q "I love Elon! It fits my personality completely."

BEST OF ELON

1. One of the best private university study abroad programs
2. The campus is absolutely beautiful

Happy Students
89% of students return after their first year.

Proven Success
78% of students will complete their education and graduate with a degree.

WORST OF ELON

1. Very little diversity on campus.
2. Laundry facilities are sparse, sometimes dirty, and some still charge with quarters, which can be inconvenient.
3. Sports teams are not the most successful.

Lowest Grades
Diversity: C
Local Atmosphere: C+
Drug Safety: C+

Student Body

African American:	6%	Male Undergrads:	42%
Asian American:	1%	Female Undergrads:	58%
Hispanic:	2%	Living On Campus:	58%
International:	4%	Living Off Campus:	42%
Native American:	0%	Male Athletes:	11%
White:	80%	Female Athletes:	7%
Unknown:	7%	Fraternity Members:	18%
From Out-of-State:	75%	Sorority Members:	31%

Frequently Compared Schools:

James Madison University
University of North Carolina
University of Richmond
Wake Forest University

Students Speak Out On...
EVERYTHING!

ACADEMICS

Q Academics Are Outstanding

"The academics at Elon are outstanding. The courses are great and helpful to future careers. The workload varies depending on your year and major. The only downside is that the older students tend to fill up important classes before underclassmen even have a chance to register."

Q Business Majors

"The business program is outstanding, however, it is hard to take the necessary classes because they tend to fill up quickly."

ATHLETICS

Q Very Supportive

"Good fan support and academic support for athletes. Wide variety of sports available at all levels"

Q Great Sports

"Majority of the varsity sports have a team average of 4.0. Most athletes are well liked and friendly. Facilities are outstanding and a lot of students go to the games. We do have a few teams that are really good and are frequently competing for top ranking spots."

CAMPUS DINING

Q Various Options

"There are 3 main dining halls that all give different main menu options everyday. They all have salad bars and food options for vegetarians. There are also 3 deli restaurants on campus as well as a sports bar. All of these can be payed for by the standard meal plan the university offers which makes it very convenient."

Q Dining Options

"Elon has many on-campus dining options that make getting food fast and convenient. With so many options there is a great variety of food at each dining hall. Elon even has Chik Fil A and a smoothie place on meal plans. Whether you are a carnivore or vegetarian, Elon has whatever your stomach of physique desires."

CAMPUS HOUSING

Q Danieley is fun

"Love the housing. Danieley is so much fun because you're on campus but it's like you live in a separate community but are all a part of one giant one. Also, the facilities are super nice and new. Watch out for the RAs though!"

Q Upperclassman Have It Made

"A lot of great options for upperclassmen. Underclassmen still have a fair amount of options, some even single dorms or suite options but not new construction."

GUYS & GIRLS

Q Student Attire

"Elon students are always well-dressed. Girls are usually in nice, preppy attire for class. Not too many people wear sweatpants and roll out of bed for their classes. Guys vary, but a majority do wear nice clothing as well."

Q Hot guys (gay and straight)!

"Even though Elon is 60% girls and 40% guys, there are still a lot of great looking, datable guys. There are also a TON of gays. It is a nice balance. Both girls and guys are really attractive."

HEALTH & SAFETY

Q Completely Safe

"Elon University has no problems with crime because it is surrounded by a small town, which also has a low crime rate. The only problem is there are these random occurences of accidents happening, like a hit and run or a student who got beat up."

Q Very Safe

"Escort service provided when student feels they need it. Locked doos around campus with limited access. Faculty available after hours and friendly"

LOOKING FOR MORE?

Check out our full-length guide to this school at collegeprowler.com/elon-university/.

Emerson College

120 Boylston St.; Boston, MA 02116
(617) 824-8500; www.emerson.edu

THE BASICS:

Acceptance Rate: 42%
Yield: 26%
Setting: Large city
Control: Private Non-Profit
Total Undergrads: 3,696
SAT Range: 1690–1980*
ACT Range: 24–29

Student-Faculty Ratio: 17:1
Retention Rate: 88%
Graduation Rate: 76%
Tuition: $30,063
Room & Board: $12,280
Avg. Aid Package: $16,371
Students With Aid: 60%

* of 2400

Academics	B	Greek Life	D
Athletics	D	Guys	B-
Campus Dining	B+	Health & Safety	B
Campus Housing	B	Local Atmosphere	A+
Campus Strictness	A-	Nightlife	B+
Computers	B-	Off-Campus Dining	A
Diversity	C	Off-Campus Housing	B-
Drug Safety	B	Parking	D
Facilities	B	Transportation	A-
Girls	A-	Weather	C-

CP's Student Author On...
OVERALL EXPERIENCE

Most students are thrilled with Emerson. From the professors to the production equipment to the classes, many students feel they're being well-prepared for the real world. At Emerson, students have more internship opportunities, well-known industry professionals as professors, and quality classes than many larger schools. Since Emerson students come with fervor to learn their trade, they end up bolstering each other in workshops and projects. Some students gripe about the long lines and difficulty dealing with the administrative aspects at Emerson, such as the financial aid office and the registrar. These experiences can obscure the positive parts of the educational experience, but most students agree that something very exciting and positive is going on at Emerson, and there are a lot of resources to take advantage of.

Emerson students are matchless in their excitement to learn, create, and get involved in activities that will better them academically and in character.... For the rest of this editorial, visit collegeprowler.com.

Students Speak Out On...
OVERALL EXPERIENCE

Q I Love It
"Living right on the Boston Commons is like having your own backyard to do whatever you want on while surrounded by a friendly city. People are nice in Boston and there is an open community to all students."

Q Great Place to Get an Education
"Wonderful campus, staff and downtown Boston environment! I love this place and the opportunities Emerson provides."

Q "Emerson is a great academic experience. Financially, I could have made wiser decisions about college. My funding sucks. It often feels as if people are just trying too hard socially, and that is irritating, but I would imagine that the 'traditional' college social scene would have been more maddening."

Q "I would come here again because I don't really party anyways, and apparently, I'm pretty self-destructive when it comes to relationships."

Q "Emerson offers quite a bit, but there is an unequal balance for which majors benefit the most."

BEST OF EMERSON

1. Student organizations
2. WERS-FM
3. The creativity of Emerson students
4. Internship opportunities
5. The Castle and LA programs
6. The professors

Happy Students
88% of students return after their first year.

Proven Success
76% of students will complete their education and graduate with a degree.

WORST OF EMERSON

1. Administrative offices
2. Honors students get first dibs on registration
3. The on-campus comedy troupes
4. The weather
5. Parking and driving in Boston

Expensive
Tuition is a steep $30,063, one of the most expensive rates in the country.

Don't Move Off Campus
Average off-campus housing is a steep $13,950.

Student Body

African American:	2%	Male Undergrads:	42%
Asian American:	4%	Female Undergrads:	58%
Hispanic:	7%	Living On Campus:	49%
International:	3%	Living Off Campus:	51%
Native American:	1%	Male Athletes:	9%
White:	70%	Female Athletes:	6%
Unknown:	13%	Fraternity Members:	3%
From Out-of-State:	81%	Sorority Members:	3%

Frequently Compared Schools:

Boston University
Ithaca College
New York University
Northeastern University

Students Speak Out On...
EVERYTHING!

ACADEMICS

Q Communicaton and the Arts

"The Academics at Emerson College focuses on Communication and the arts. It focuses specifically on Journalism, Acting, Film Diretcting, Communications studies, and amoung others. I came to this school predominately for that reason. Its a great school if you wante to be around the media."

Q "I think for a lot of the teachers, teaching is their passion. Many professors encourage students to come by their office, if not to ask questions about the class, then just to chat."

ATHLETICS

Q Not a Sports School

"Sports aren't very prominent at Emerson, which is fine with me, but people looking for a huge community of sports will be disappointed."

Q If You Want Campus Sports to Be a Big Part of You Life, Go Elsewhere.

"Almost no one at Emerson knows what sports we even have, let alone how our teams are doing. Sports is not a huge deal at Emerson. If you want sports glory, go somewhere else. Unless you love Quidditch."

CAMPUS DINING

Q The Food Is Great

"I enjoy eating lunch and dinner at the Emerson dining hall but i think the breakfast should be altered every other day"

Q Multiple Violations Each Year, Bland, but Nice

"The dining hall itself has been under fire lately for several health violations, but the little convenience stores are all great and well-stocked"

CAMPUS HOUSING

Q Dorms

"The dorms at Emerson are way nicer than most other colleges, but a lot depends on how lucky you are with your room assignments. There are huge doubles as well as tiny ones, and the triples are only slightly bigger than the big doubles. To socialize, especially on the first year, the Little Building is the best dorm, although it is an old building and some of the stuff doesn't work (like the room will either be freezing or super hot)."

Q Dorms at Emerson Are Good, Quiet and Comfortable

"Rooms are comfortable with enough room (not huge) to not feel cramped."

GUYS & GIRLS

Q People Who Are Chill

"The people at Emerson are really artsy for the most part, but very easy to get along with. There is a very active homosexual community, but if you happen to be a straight woman that shouldn't be a concern since the university does happen to be in the middle of Boston. People's dress is relaxed yet fashionable, and the people are attractive, though again, in an "artsy" way. Not a lot of bar hopping or anything like that, but people do have smaller parties."

Q Students

"Almost everyone here is trying to make a fashion statement. If you thought people wore stange clothes in high school, wait til you come here. There are lots of attractive people here, both guys and girls. There is also a strong gay/lesbian community. Everyone here is interested in the arts, and the Oscars was like a holiday."

HEALTH & SAFETY

Q Incredibly Safe School

"Emerson was recently voted the most dangerous campus in the US, but don't be fooled. Nothing could be farther from the truth. The school has to declare all crimes that happen in the Common, Public Garden, and Dowtown Crossing. These never involve Emerson students. Police and R.A.s are a constant, positive presence. I feel very safe here."

LOOKING FOR MORE?

Check out our full-length guide to this school at collegeprowler.com/emerson-college/.

Emory University

201 Dowman Drive; Atlanta, GA 30322
(404) 727-6123; www.emory.edu

THE BASICS:

Acceptance Rate: 27%	Student-Faculty Ratio: 7:1
Yield: 28%	Retention Rate: 96%
Setting: Suburban	Graduation Rate: 87%
Control: Private Non-Profit	Tuition: $38,036
Total Undergrads: 6,980	Room & Board: $10,896
SAT Range: 1960–2240*	Avg. Aid Package: $26,958
ACT Range: 30–33	Students With Aid: 61%

of 2400

Academics	A	Greek Life	A+
Athletics	C	Guys	A-
Campus Dining	B	Health & Safety	A
Campus Housing	A-	Local Atmosphere	A
Campus Strictness	B+	Nightlife	B+
Computers	A-	Off-Campus Dining	B+
Diversity	B+	Off-Campus Housing	A-
Drug Safety	C	Parking	B
Facilities	A	Transportation	A-
Girls	A	Weather	B

CP's Student Author On...
OVERALL EXPERIENCE

Overall, the Emory experience is a good one, albeit very interesting. Emory can be trying at times with its restrictive and sometimes uncooperative administration, cliques, and strange lack of diversity. It can also be very rewarding, with great teachers and classes and a fun, lively city to explore. In evaluating an entire Emory experience, most students note the exceptional education they are receiving from world-class professors. Many also note that they considered transferring once or twice. Like any school, you'll find great teachers and great friends, you just have to do your research and not settle for what seems easiest.

Many students initially wonder if another school would be better for them, a feeling freshmen experience everywhere. Adapting to a new city, a new school, and new people can be tough. Emory's student body, while an impressive selection of students, is truly a mixed bag: sometimes it takes continued effort to find the people that will become your lifelong friends.... For the rest of this editorial, visit collegeprowler.com.

Students Speak Out On...
OVERALL EXPERIENCE

Q Good College in General

"Emory provides your typical college experience with an extra emphasis on academics. Emory tries to take the academic seriousness of an ivy league school, so that can have an effect on you experience if that wasn't something you were looking for"

Q Great School

"So far my experience at Emory has been great. The academics are challenging but completely manageable. The student body is quite diverse, and there are many opportunities to get involved in activities on and off campus. Social and academic lives can both be rich here."

Q Emory Is Great but Plan on Working!

"If you think you can coast by without studying you've got another thing coming."

BEST OF EMORY

1. Atlanta
2. The professors
3. The campus
4. Spring Band Party
5. Dooley's Week and Dooley's Ball
6. Fraternities
7. Clairmont Campus

Happy Students
96% of students return after their first year.

Commitment to Teaching
There are 7 students for every member of faculty on campus.

WORST OF EMORY

1. Cliques
2. New Yorkers
3. Administration
4. Division III varsity
5. No football team
6. Need car and fake ID
7. On-campus food
8. Too many rules

Expensive
Tuition is a steep $38,036, one of the most expensive rates in the country.

Expensive Dorms
Living on campus doesn't come cheap, with an average housing price tag of $6,666.

Student Body

African American:	11%	Male Undergrads:	45%
Asian American:	20%	Female Undergrads:	55%
Hispanic:	4%	Living On Campus:	66%
International:	8%	Living Off Campus:	34%
Native American:	0%	Male Athletes:	7%
White:	51%	Female Athletes:	5%
Unknown:	7%	Fraternity Members:	28%
From Out-of-State:	76%	Sorority Members:	30%

Frequently Compared Schools:
Duke University
University of Pennsylvania
Vanderbilt University
Washington University in St. Louis

Students Speak Out On...
EVERYTHING!

ACADEMICS

Q Great

"Professors are extremely helpful. Classes are very interesting and you learn a lot without being very stressed."

Q Class sizes are great

"The classes are small and allow each student to get personal attention from their professors. Even the largest lectures only have around 50 students. The average classes have about 20-30 students, and smaller intimate discussion or specialty courses have between 10 and 20 students."

ATHLETICS

Q The Teams Are Amazing but the Fans Not So Much

"All of Emory's athletic teams do extremely well regionally and nationally, yet there never seems to be a crowd at any of the sporting events. I think this is due in large part to the lack of a football team and that most people have more important things to do with their time, like study."

Q Lack of Football Team

"Emory doesn't have a football team so we don't have much school spirit compared to larger institutions. However, the Woodruff PE Center (commonly known as the WoodPec) is a great facility that is opened late at night and offers a variety of track fields, swimming pools, tennis courts, and more athletic facilities."

CAMPUS DINING

Q Great Food and Staff, Just a Little Repetitive

"Even though many students get tired of dining at the many locations on campus, it is mainly due to the repetitive nature of these dining locations. The food is well-prepared and the dining offers options for Kosher/Vegans/Vegetarians separately. The staff also attempt to make the experience as enjoyable as possible."

Q Meal Plan

"Anyone living on campus has to have a meal plan and freshman year it is a mandatory unlimited meal plan. This sounds good but the food most freshman eat ends up being from the main cafeteria, which gets pretty boring fast. Overall it is okay though and there are other options in the surrounding areas that are quite nice."

CAMPUS HOUSING

Q Required Freshman and Sophomore Year

"...But this is when you'll be partying the most in campus at Frat houses or getting a cab to Maggies and it helps you bond with people so it's a good set up, plus almost all Freshman dorms are brand new."

Q Almost Every Freshman Dorms Are New Next Year

"Next year, Emory will open a new freshman dorm, which means the class of 2014 gets 4 new dorms. Lucky you."

GUYS & GIRLS

Q Good Looking

"Girls and guys are almost all above average"

Q Prep Prep Prep

"Preppy is the most typical look of both male and female students at Emory University. Also, unique and hippie styles are encouraged. It would be odd to see a male or female dressed as a redneck or punk/goth. It is pretty easy to fit in as long as you are preppy and fratty."

HEALTH & SAFETY

Q Shoddy

"Though its located in a notoriously "bad" nieghbourhood, crime on campus isn't rampant though the security guard is both a joke and a sham"

Q Never Scurred

"Emory has a very safe campus. For those who are afraid to walk home at night (or are too lazy/drunk), you can call the Emory Escort Service and they will pick you up and drive you home (as long as you live relatively close to campus)."

LOOKING FOR MORE?
Check out our full-length guide to this school at collegeprowler.com/emory-university/.

Fashion Institute of Technology

227 W. 27th St.; New York, NY 10001
(212) 217-7999; www.fitnyc.edu

THE BASICS:

Acceptance Rate: 40%
Yield: 66%
Setting: Large city
Control: Public
Total Undergrads: 10,303
SAT Range: —
ACT Range: —

Student-Faculty Ratio: 17:1
Retention Rate: 86%
Graduation Rate: 56%
Tuition: $11,592
Room & Board: $11,248
Avg. Aid Package: $6,815
Students With Aid: 66%

Academics	B-	Greek Life	N/A
Athletics	D+	Guys	B
Campus Dining	C	Health & Safety	C+
Campus Housing	C+	Local Atmosphere	A
Campus Strictness	C-	Nightlife	A-
Computers	C-	Off-Campus Dining	A-
Diversity	A	Off-Campus Housing	C+
Drug Safety	C-	Parking	D+
Facilities	C-	Transportation	B+
Girls	B	Weather	B-

CP's Student Author On...
OVERALL EXPERIENCE

A majority of students at FIT are in agreement that they are receiving a quality education at a fair price in the best city. Most of the teachers have extensive knowledge of their industries and offer their students real-world experiences. Students here are given the chance to expand outside of the classroom with internships, study abroad, and over 70 clubs and organizations. The students that do have a negative view of the college tend to be the ones who are uninvolved and unsure of their career goals.

Even with the lack of a social scene, a real campus, and the overwhelming amount of girls, students still love it here. They forget about these aspects and tend to say they would never have experienced the same cultures and opportunities as they have at FIT. You can live your dream here. If you stay focused and work hard, you will inevitably develop skills and confidence that will lead you to a successful career.

Students Speak Out On...
OVERALL EXPERIENCE

Q Overall Evaluation

"The Fashion Institute was the only practical college for me. I could never see myself anywhere else and I do not know where I would be if I wasn't here. The staff and students are so friendly and welcoming and there is always something to do on campus. ALWAYS. FIT has helped me to adapt to the big city coming from a small town."

Q School Experience

"My experience at school so far has been AMAZING. I love it and honestly never want to leave! You have amazing class, great teachers, and have an amazing social life. This school is a very focused school which I love. I am VERY involved and think that that has made my experience even better. I would not choose any other school but FIT if i had to do this again."

Q My Experience

"FIT has been a great school for me to be in and i do not regret it one bit! The school has so much to offer. Student life is very active and there are so many clubs to join and best of all you meet someone new everyday. I have really enjoyed my time here so far."

BEST OF FIT

1. Classes provide students with real-world experience
2. New York City, where everything is at your fingertips
3. Students who design their own clothes and accessories

Affordable
Tuition is only $11,592, one of the most affordable rates in the country.

Happy Students
86% of students return after their first year.

WORST OF FIT

1. Too many girls
2. Not a typical college campus
3. Some majors require you to take six to eight classes per semester

Life is NOT a Party
59% of students surveyed said it's almost impossible to find a good party.

Student Body

African American:	7%	Male Undergrads:	15%
Asian American:	11%	Female Undergrads:	85%
Hispanic:	10%	Living On Campus:	17%
International:	9%	Living Off Campus:	83%
Native American:	0%	Male Athletes:	2%
White:	39%	Female Athletes:	1%
Unknown:	24%	Fraternity Members:	0%
From Out-of-State:	41%	Sorority Members:	0%

Students Speak Out On... EVERYTHING!

ACADEMICS

Great Fashion School

"FIT has teachers that used to work in the industry, and are very knowleable about the subject. They teach you based on their experience, and not really out of the book. The classes teach you what you really need to know when you get in the industry, and the classes are very revelent to the industry. The workload is alot but not to much where is isnt managable. Its a great school, and I would reccemond anyone to come here."

College Pushes Career and Involvement in Industry EARLY

"At F.I.T. they encourage you and push you to get jobs and/or internships right from first semester. They give you EXCELLENT opportunities with the career center and even volunteering for New York Fashion Week. Here you feel like you have already began your career. You learn the importance in networking very fast. This is how you become the best of the best... get started early & push yourself."

ATHLETICS

Tigers

"Everybody is very into games and support tiger and proud of tiger pride."

Athletics Is Good Especially Fitness Programs

"The gym is great and has all u need but very small. It is scheduled for renovation soon. Athletic office is very helpful offering enough and a variety of classes. The basketball tem is good but not the ideal school for athletes and school spirit."

CAMPUS DINING

Grill/Deli

"The grill & the deli are the stations that I frequent most. I do not usually like what is offered at the 'dinner' station. The deli has plently of breads and toppings to choose from and the grill offers healthy hot food options. Overall, the cafeteria is lacking in variety."

Frequently Compared Schools:

Columbia University
Hunter College
New York University
Rhode Island School of Design

Foooooood

"The food at the cafeteria tastes pretty good but there isn't a wide variety of options for me. I personally would get tired of eating at the cafeteria every day. I do like that you can use your meal plan towards the Starbucks in the cafeteria though."

CAMPUS HOUSING

Alumni and Kaufman Hall

"alumni hall was where i was freshmen year. it was a suite style so we had our own kitchen and bathroom which i really liked. there are two other options for freshmen which are more traditional with a shared bathroom and common room. kaufman hall is the newest addition. the high ceilings make the apartment feel huge. there's large windows, a kitchen, and a bathroom."

Dormlife

"My first two years, I lived in the FIT dorms. I was nervous at first to leave home and live with strangers. However from the very first day forward, I made ever lasting friendships that I will never forget. Dorm life was a unique and interesting experience, mixing cultures and people allowed me to grow as an individual. I wouldn't trade it for anything!"

GUYS & GIRLS

Dress

"The students here are really concerned with how they look, which they should be, going to a fashion school and all. The main thing is not to compare yourself to anyone else, you must create your own identity and don't judge others. Nobody has any idea about another's background or wealth, so just do your own thing and enjoy being in NYC."

HEALTH & SAFETY

Safety

"Safety is amazing, and I wish we could sign in someone at any time, but I rather take the 5 minutes and wait in line and know I'm safe then to let people walk in out and out."

LOOKING FOR MORE?

Check out our full-length guide to this school at collegeprowler.com/fashion-institute-of-technology/.

Ferris State University

1201 S. State St.; Big Rapids, MI 49307
(231) 591-2000; www.ferris.edu

THE BASICS:

Acceptance Rate: 55%
Yield: 35%
Setting: Town
Control: Public
Total Undergrads: 12,592
SAT Range: —
ACT Range: 18–24

Student-Faculty Ratio: 16:1
Retention Rate: 68%
Graduation Rate: 40%
Tuition: $16,770
Room & Board: $8,940
Avg. Aid Package: $15,531
Students With Aid: 93%

Academics	C	Greek Life	C+
Athletics	C+	Guys	B-
Campus Dining	C+	Health & Safety	C+
Campus Housing	C	Local Atmosphere	C-
Campus Strictness	B-	Nightlife	B
Computers	C+	Off-Campus Dining	C+
Diversity	C	Off-Campus Housing	B-
Drug Safety	C-	Parking	C+
Facilities	C+	Transportation	B-
Girls	C+	Weather	C+

CP's Student Author On...
OVERALL EXPERIENCE

According to students, if they were given the option to go to this school again, 69% of students would choose Ferris! The same amount of students surveyed said that they like most everything about the school and would only change a few things. Overall, students find that there are many great people to meet, and it's a good academic college. Though some stress the lack of entertainment and "city" things to do, if a person is content with small-town life, then this would be the best place.

The people and the faculty make Ferris a great experience. The faculty and staff are pretty helpful and understanding if a student needs extra help or is having problems with something. The school and faculty seem to care about the students and take an interest in students getting the help and the experiences they should. As long as the student puts in a decent amount of effort in their classes, faculty will be more apt to help.

Another great factor about the school is that class sizes are small, and there is more individualized attention for each student.... For the rest of this editorial, visit collegeprowler. com.

Students Speak Out On...
OVERALL EXPERIENCE

Q Great Place

"Ferris is a fun place to meet some cool, down to earth people. I love it here. But pretty much the only thing to do is get drunk. Every night. If you let your social life rule your academic life, then it could be trouble. You kind of have to study here; it isn't all parties but it also really depends on your major."

Q Ferris Is Pretty Awesome.

"I like it here. As long as you manage your time well, you will enjoy it I believe."

Q Classes

"In my field, the instructors are very tough, relevant, and knowledgeable."

Q Small Campus, Small Classes, Great School

"Ferris is smaller in size and all the buildings are really close, which is good considering our west Michigan winters. Academics are great, I have been extremely satisfied with the quality of the professors. Classes are almost always under thirty people, I like the personal learning approach, and it's easy to get to know your professor."

BEST OF FERRIS STATE

1. Small class sizes
2. Rare programs
3. Social activities
4. Parties
5. Greek life
6. Nice professors
7. Student-to-professor ratio

Knowledgeable Professors
62% of students surveyed rated the general knowledge of professors as above average.

Low-Stress Course Load
69% of students surveyed rated the manageability of work as above average.

WORST OF FERRIS STATE

1. Parking
2. Small town
3. Not too much to do on the weekends because everyone goes home or leaves town.
4. There are a lot of unintelligent and closed-minded people here.

Cramped Dorms
52% of students surveyed felt that the dorms were less spacious than average.

Student Body

African American:	6%	Male Undergrads:	52%
Asian American:	2%	Female Undergrads:	48%
Hispanic:	2%	Living On Campus:	29%
International:	1%	Living Off Campus:	68%
Native American:	1%	Male Athletes:	5%
White:	80%	Female Athletes:	3%
Unknown:	8%	Fraternity Members:	6%
From Out-of-State:	7%	Sorority Members:	5%

Frequently Compared Schools:

Central Michigan University
Grand Valley State University
Michigan State University
Western Michigan University

Students Speak Out On... EVERYTHING!

ACADEMICS

Q MIMA -- pretty much the coolest organization

"MIMA is amazing. Pretty much the coolest organization on campus. Not gonna lie. And I'm not even biased. I promise. But we...er they rock. Everyone should love them. and know them. They put on awesome shows."

Q Furniture Department at Kendall Collage of Art and Design of Farris

"A fun experience with great teachers and variety of interesting classes. Lots of work but plenty of time to get work done. Tons of opportunities for internships/jobs. I don't know a single senior in this major who doesn't have some kind of internship."

ATHLETICS

Q HOCKEY

"Hockey is amazing but the only sport to watch!"

Q Hockey Is the Biggest Deal Here!

"The hockey games are the only ones worth going to. Classes will tell you to go to a sporting event but the football games don't have many students at them and its to cold most of the year to watch the game with no one around. Go to as many hockey games as you can! That's where the Spirit section (The Dawg Pound) is the biggest. The basketball games are getting bigger now too."

CAMPUS DINING

Q Ferris State University: Campus Dining

"The best place to eat on campus is The Rock, but isn't very accessible if you have classes on the other side of campus. Westview isn't that great and there aren't that many choices."

Q Good Food...Hate Unlimited Meals

"I like the food it's good. It gets old, but having 3 dinning halls makes it a lot better. The selection at each is usually different. I really don't like that we have unlimited meals this year. I don't feel like anyone used all their meals last year and if they did they switched to a bigger one for the next semester. I really

did like that last year we could use meals to buy pizza and snacks, I really dislike the unlimited meal plan."

CAMPUS HOUSING

Q I Lived in Honors Dorms

"If you live in an Honors dorm, then it is a pretty sweet deal! You get your own room, and share a bathroom with a suite mate. Also every dorm is coed by suite, so it's a lot of fun! There are no community bathrooms, each suite shares a bathroom with another suite. There are usually 2 people per suite and 4 per bathroom. Also there are washer/dryers on every floor and a stove."

Q Living in the Dorms

"I lived in the dorms my freshmen and sophomore years. I loved that it was only a couple minutes to walk to eat any meal and the longest walk to classes only took about 10 minutes. I liked all of the activities/events offered in the dorms and while I only attended a handful of them each semester, it got people out of their rooms and interacting with others in the dorms."

GUYS & GIRLS

Q The Crowd -- people from all walks and backgrounds

"It's a college crowd - people from all walks and backgrounds, what more is there to say?"

Q Ferris has a mixture of students on campus

"Ferris has a mixture of students on campus, with many interests ranging from poetry to ice hockey. There's a place for everyone on campus!"

HEALTH & SAFETY

Q Campus Is Safe.

"I have never had any problems on campus, nor have any of my friends. We never have had issues with theft, assault, or anything else."

Q Campus Safety

"I feel very safe on campus. I have never felt threatened or unsafe."

LOOKING FOR MORE?

Check out our full-length guide to this school at collegeprowler.com/ferris-state-university/.

Florida A&M University

1668 S. Martin Luther King Jr. Blvd.; Tallahassee, FL 32307
(850) 599-3000; www.famu.edu

THE BASICS:

Acceptance Rate: 62%
Yield: 53%
Setting: Mid-sized city
Control: Public
Total Undergrads: 10,244
SAT Range: 1220–1490*
ACT Range: 17–21

Student-Faculty Ratio: 18:1
Retention Rate: 78%
Graduation Rate: 41%
Tuition: $15,899
Room & Board: $7,218
Avg. Aid Package: $12,216
Students With Aid: 96%

* of 2400

Academics	C+	Greek Life	B+
Athletics	B-	Guys	A+
Campus Dining	B	Health & Safety	C-
Campus Housing	C+	Local Atmosphere	B
Campus Strictness	C	Nightlife	A-
Computers	C+	Off-Campus Dining	C+
Diversity	C-	Off-Campus Housing	A
Drug Safety	B	Parking	B
Facilities	B-	Transportation	B+
Girls	A	Weather	B-

CP's Student Author On...
OVERALL EXPERIENCE

Florida A&M University will prepare you to excel in your future career. The professors push and encourage their students to go beyond their limits. There are no handouts at the University—you have to work hard and earn your grades. FAMU also offers lots of student organizations, and it's recommended that you get involved with at least one. Many students met some of their best friends through campus organizations.

The University is also unique because it is rich in tradition and culture. Students here bleed orange and green, and their love for the University stays with them after graduation. In fact, FAMU has a huge alumni following, and alumni are constantly coming back to campus for events. Another unique thing about FAMU is the University's award-winning marching band, Marching 100. The band has performed in Super Bowls, appeared on national TV, including CBS News and ESPN College Day, performed with Kanye West and Jamie Foxx at the 2006 Grammys, and was even asked by President Obama to play at one of his events.... For the rest of this editorial, visit collegeprowler.com.

Students Speak Out On...
OVERALL EXPERIENCE

Q Love It
"Every school has its faults, but only us Rattlers can down talk it. THIS IS THE NO. 1 HBCU."

Q Experience
"My experience has been different from others. I have had my good days and my bad days, but the good outweighs the bad."

Q #Represent FAMU
"Florida A&M University is one of the greatest places to study school. We have the reputation for being the strongest partying school in the nation, while still being scholarly and active in the community. We have a great faculty that will work with you and help you if you show that you take your studies seriously and contribute to classroom discussions. All in all we love our school and are proud to be Rattlers. And one this is for sure, FAMU prepares you for life."

Q Set Friday
"A great way to end the week and celebrate with fellow students to some music and free food."

BEST OF FLORIDA A&M

1. FAMU's marching band, Marching 100
2. Student Government Association
3. Greeks
4. Campus safety and campus rules are reasonable.
5. FAMU's history and legacy

Knowledgeable Professors
65% of students surveyed rated the general knowledge of professors as above average.

Low-Stress Course Load
57% of students surveyed rated the manageability of work as above average.

WORST OF FLORIDA A&M

1. Limted parking for games
2. Rude faculty at the beginning of the semester
3. No opposite sex allowed in the dorms
4. Not enough seating in dining facilities
5. Late disbursement of financial aid

Not Much Diversity
One of the least racially diverse campuses—only 7% of students are minorities.

Student Body

African American:	93%	Male Undergrads:	43%
Asian American:	1%	Female Undergrads:	57%
Hispanic:	1%	Living On Campus:	70%
International:	1%	Living Off Campus:	30%
Native American:	0%	Male Athletes:	4%
White:	3%	Female Athletes:	2%
Unknown:	0%	Fraternity Members:	2%
From Out-of-State:	21%	Sorority Members:	3%

Frequently Compared Schools:

Florida International University
Florida State University
Howard University
University of Florida

Students Speak Out On... EVERYTHING!

ACADEMICS

How Easy Work Would Be With a Labtop

"Work is my objective in school, and sometimes it can become a drag trying to use the resources that the school provides because of the clutter of people. I'm not downing my school at all, it's just that I know I would really be more efficient with a laptop. But, all in all, our school facilities are perfect."

Helpful

"Professors in the school of journalism will work extremely hard to educate you and to present you with opportunities. So many professors have real world experience and internships are easy to come by."

ATHLETICS

Overall Very Good

"Every athletic team always keeps us entertained."

FAMU's Athletic Programs.

"FAMU ranks division one for all athletic teams. We have a powerful volleyball team and a strong football team. I have attended some games in the past and the athletes were fit. We have exellent trainers and coaches from all ethnic backgrounds."

CAMPUS DINING

Food Is Good

"The campus dining places at FAMU are very good. They always have a wide selection when it comes to any variety of foods a person may want. The people there are always smiling, which makes it a place for many students to have a healthy social life. I can truly say that campus dining is a good experience for any college student."

GREAT!

"The food at FAMU is excellent and the dining area is amazing. You can sit anywhere you like and there's soft music playing in the background. The ladies and gentlemen who serve you are very friendly. You also have a great variety of foods to choose from."

CAMPUS HOUSING

Freshman Dorms

"The freshman dorms at Florida A&M University are good, but they can have their ups and downs. The faculty is really nice to students, but the students are very quick to take advantage of the rules. I like the dorm room life and I think it can be a good experience for anybody. I encourage any student to live the dorm life; it will give you a sense of freedom."

HOUSING

"Living on campus helps you get to know more people."

GUYS & GIRLS

There Are More Girls Than Men

"There are a lot of sexy ladies here."

Social Life

"You can meet people very easyily around campus and off campus."

HEALTH & SAFETY

Safe and Secure

"While on the campus of Florida A & M University, I have never felt unsafe. It is a nice sized college and all of the rules and regulations are truly enforced. Campus security is really strict about safety!"

Don't Worry About the Crime Outside the Campus

"Every time I have been to Florida A&M University, I have felt safe from all harm and as if I were with family. I have only been a little worried about leaving the campus alone or with young children. However, just be confident and and aware of what is around you."

LOOKING FOR MORE?

Check out our full-length guide to this school at collegeprowler.com/florida-a-and-m-university/.

Florida Atlantic University

777 Glades Road; Boca Raton, FL 33431
(561) 297-3000; www.fau.edu

THE BASICS:

Acceptance Rate: 46%
Yield: 39%
Setting: Small city
Control: Public
Total Undergrads: 21,905
SAT Range: 1440–1700*
ACT Range: 21–25

Student-Faculty Ratio: 18:1
Retention Rate: 79%
Graduation Rate: 39%
Tuition: $14,026
Room & Board: $9,582
Avg. Aid Package: $8,271
Students With Aid: 86%

* of 2400

Academics	B-	Greek Life	C+
Athletics	C+	Guys	B+
Campus Dining	B	Health & Safety	B-
Campus Housing	C+	Local Atmosphere	B
Campus Strictness	B-	Nightlife	B-
Computers	B+	Off-Campus Dining	C+
Diversity	B	Off-Campus Housing	B
Drug Safety	B	Parking	B-
Facilities	B+	Transportation	C-
Girls	B	Weather	A

CP's Student Author On...
OVERALL EXPERIENCE

For most students, FAU was not their first-choice school. While it is a large school, most students are commuters, and it seems as though almost anyone can be accepted. However, once students arrive on campus, they realize that there are many activities and events to get involved with and that maybe their experience will not be so bad after all.

FAU is an up-and-coming school and is growing in students and facilities every year. However, most students do not plan to attend for their entire college career. Many are just using FAU to get their feet on the ground and to get general education classes out of the way. A huge percent of the student population transfers after two years to a larger, more college-town type of school.

Students Speak Out On...
OVERALL EXPERIENCE

Q I Love FAU!

"FAU is the best! We have a great balance of fun and learning. We're a tight-knot community and take care of each other. Assistance is always easy to find. Professors are very knowledgeable and seem to enjoy passing their jobs."

Q We're the OWLS

"Without us there is no other OWLS around plus our Konbit Kreyol [Haitian Students' Association] is the largest student and non-greek organisation on campus so we're on the MAP to becoming just as good and even better than the University of MIAMI"

Q ZERO Complaints!

"Being a sophomore at FAU I have seen and experienced many different things. I love how easy it is to meet new people. All you have to do is walk around or join a club relative to your interests and you are guaranteed to make some new friends."

Q So Far So Good

"FAU is definitely meeting all of my needs, and is a great place to attend school"

BEST OF FLORIDA ATLANTIC

1. Proximity to the beach
2. Diverse student body
3. Beautiful campus
4. Proximity to Miami, Ft. Lauderdale, and West Palm Beach
5. The school is quickly growing.

Knowledgeable Professors
82% of students surveyed rated the general knowledge of professors as above average.

Low-Stress Course Load
67% of students surveyed rated the manageability of work as above average.

WORST OF FLORIDA ATLANTIC

1. Cafeteria food
2. Large number of commuters
3. Too many people go home for the weekend.
4. Parking
5. Small amount of on-campus housing

Expensive Dorms
Living on campus doesn't come cheap, with an average housing price tag of $6,208.

Student Body

African American:	18%	Male Undergrads:	41%
Asian American:	5%	Female Undergrads:	59%
Hispanic:	19%	Living On Campus:	4%
International:	3%	Living Off Campus:	96%
Native American:	0%	Male Athletes:	6%
White:	54%	Female Athletes:	2%
Unknown:	0%	Fraternity Members:	1%
From Out-of-State:	14%	Sorority Members:	1%

Frequently Compared Schools:

Florida International University
Florida State University
University of Central Florida
University of South Florida

Students Speak Out On...
EVERYTHING!

ACADEMICS

Biological Sciences: Ecology

"The science department is incredible! Wonderful professors great laboratories. Being a science major at FAU was a pleasure!!!"

Social Work Major

"At Florida Atlantic University the Social Work teachers have an in depth knowledge of the subject. They are always available for help after class and really care about teaching the material so the students can understand it. I love going to class because I look up to the professors and hope I can be as professional as they are when I become a Social Worker."

ATHLETICS

Lots of Variety of Sports and Team Spirit

"We are a tight-knit community and stand by our teams. There are plenty of sports for us to choose from. Anyone who wants to be involved in a sport, can easily find their calling."

Sports and Spirit

"Our sports get alot of spirit from our school we aren't number one but we definitely support our athletes. In the stands you will see students painted red, white and blue and family cheering on the team. We have a huge fitness center for athletes and students and intermural sports for those who want to play on teams for fun!"

CAMPUS DINING

Caf Food Is Good & Open 'Til Late

"Our cafeteria food is good. There's good variety, great taste and it's all-you-can-eat for about $5 a meal! My two-meals-a-day plan works well and I can space my meals out between classes so I'm never hungry. The caf is usually open until 10 p.m., we can return from work, run errands, etc., and still have dinner there."

Variety & Value

"Never had a problem with the cafeteria. With enough choices you can eat every day for 2-3 weeks something new. There is also a section offering specials, different food served for a change of pace to their permenant menu. The seating area is excellent, so much space you can eat in provacy without a single person within a 15 foot radius."

CAMPUS HOUSING

Campus Living

"Living on campus is very convenient. Classrooms are located near the dorms. Also the food and administrative services are located close to the dorms."

I Do Not Live on Campus

"I do not live on campus but have seen the dorms/apt. They are clean and look relatively new. THey are conveniently on campus. Can't really say how easy the housing process is but i can only imagine it being as painless as possible." •

GUYS & GIRLS

A great amount of different ethnicities

"There is a great amount of different ethnicities around the area. We can find alot of Colmbian Venezuelan and Argentinan people around the school. Its just great because you can compere our culture to other and learn more."

Independent, Determined, Hip

"Students at FAU know their priorities. We have the right balance of partying and studying. The school ensures this balance because they require for us to maintain acceptable GPA's and we know it."

HEALTH & SAFETY

FAU Is an Extremely Safe School

"At FAU I feel safe I've never encountered a situation where a student offered me drugs or alcohol. Or even encountering someone that is on drugs. This campus is more than seventy percent drug safe zone."

LOOKING FOR MORE?

Check out our full-length guide to this school at collegeprowler.com/florida-atlantic-university/.

Florida Southern College

111 Lake Hollingsworth Drive; Lakeland, FL 33801
(863) 680-4111; www.flsouthern.edu

THE BASICS:

Acceptance Rate: 69%	**Student-Faculty Ratio:** 15:1
Yield: 33%	**Retention Rate:** 79%
Setting: Small city	**Graduation Rate:** 52%
Control: Private Non-Profit	**Tuition:** $22,795
Total Undergrads: 2,281	**Room & Board:** $8,242
SAT Range: 1410–1730*	**Avg. Aid Package:** $19,093
ACT Range: 20–25	**Students With Aid:** 98%

* of 2400

Academics	C+	**Greek Life**	B+
Athletics	B-	**Guys**	A
Campus Dining	B-	**Health & Safety**	B
Campus Housing	B+	**Local Atmosphere**	B-
Campus Strictness	C	**Nightlife**	B
Computers	D+	**Off-Campus Dining**	B-
Diversity	B-	**Off-Campus Housing**	B-
Drug Safety	B-	**Parking**	C+
Facilities	B	**Transportation**	D+
Girls	A	**Weather**	A

CP's Student Author On...
OVERALL EXPERIENCE

Students have to be open to the help and advice that is offered at FSC; it's easy when the professors' enthusiasim is contagious. The small community holds options for recent graduates to obtain jobs because the area is riddled with alumni who are more than willing to help out an FSC graduate. Although the amount of different social and academic groups may be fewer than what is available in a larger school, students have many more opportunities to hold leadership positions and gain experience through clubs. The smaller size also gives students more opportunities to participate in campus events, such as free Chick-Fil-A chicken biscuits on certain Fridays.

FSC is unique because of the Frank Lloyd Wright architecture. A point of pride at the school, the buildings have a sense of prestige because they are all exquisite. The absence of bland, boring buildings makes the environment for learning much more appealing. FSC is distinguished as one of the top 10 most beautiful schools in the nation for a reason.

Students Speak Out On...
OVERALL EXPERIENCE

Q Love
"I love everything here from the grounds to the people- it's such a great place to be!"

Q FSC
"My experience as FSC has been awesome so far. I have made a great group of friends and we have so much fun participating in campus activities and laying out in the Florida sun. Our school is so close-knit and personable, it feels like a second home. I would definitely choose Florida Southern again because it meets all my needs academically and personally."

Q It's Great
"There are plenty of activities for students to participate in and plenty of intramural sports. Just about almost every weekend there is something for students to do, wether it is a show or just activities for students to get involved in."

Q Feels Like a Family
"FSC is a smaller community. Coming from a high school that was larger than Florida Southern, I was a little nervous. However the atmosphere is what I enjoy most about my college experience."

BEST OF FLORIDA SOUTHERN

1. Music and entertainment
2. Professors and classes
3. Proximity to other places
4. Lake Hollingsworth is nearby.

Knowledgeable Professors
80% of students surveyed rated the general knowledge of professors as above average.

Big Dorms
79% of students surveyed felt that dorms were more spacious than average.

WORST OF FLORIDA SOUTHERN

1. Lack of food options
2. Not enough parking
3. No football team
4. Limited majors

Lowest Grades
Computers: D+
Transportation: D+
Campus Strictness: C

Student Body

African American:	7%	Male Undergrads:	36%
Asian American:	1%	Female Undergrads:	64%
Hispanic:	6%	Living On Campus:	69%
International:	3%	Living Off Campus:	31%
Native American:	0%	Male Athletes:	24%
White:	64%	Female Athletes:	13%
Unknown:	19%	Fraternity Members:	29%
From Out-of-State:	29%	Sorority Members:	22%

Frequently Compared Schools:
Eckerd College
Florida Gulf Coast University
Florida State University
Rollins College

Students Speak Out On... EVERYTHING!

ACADEMICS

Undeclared

"I'm undeclared. But there are numerous programs on school to help you decide which major is right for you."

Great Professors

"Florida Southern's professors are why students do so well here at FSC. Professors have regular office hours but are also available to answer any questions when in their office because they have an open door policy. Proffessors care about your performance in classes and are willing to answer any questions."

ATHLETICS

Team Performance

"the softball team is one of the best college teams in the polk district. They are a top grade school and so im sure a lot of money is funded into the sport. They are beastly girls who are hardcore about what they do."

FSC Athletics

"Everyone at Florida Southern gets into the athletic scene. There is so much support for all the teams from classmates and friends; it's so inspiring. Our teams do very well in their divisions and we have great facilities for them to use."

CAMPUS DINING

Go to the Grill Master

"Florida Southern has a few options for dining. You can eat in the cafeteria, where there are sandwiches and pizza and other yummy food. Then there is the Underbelly equipped with a Freshens and a place to get hamburgers and fries. There is also Tutus Cafe, which has a Starbucks and a place to get healthy food. Then there is my personal favorite, the Grill Master. They make the best bacon egg and cheese biscuits ever."

Food is good but repetetive

"The places around campus are good. They always have something for everyone to eat. You can get food late at night that still tastes good. Sometimes it gets repetitive, but the food is still good."

CAMPUS HOUSING

Good Campus

"the campus is very nice and evertybody here is friendly"

Campus Life

"Much like other colleges. Get to meet many new people and make great friends."

GUYS & GIRLS

A Friendly Bunch

"Both guys and girls dress nicely but more importantly always carry a smile."

Social Life

"It seems as if everyone knows everyone. It's a nice environment. Everyone is so accepting, I feel so welcome. No one really dresses inappropriate or nasty. It's all pretty nice. There are a couple relationships going around to, but then after it's over they are still friends."

HEALTH & SAFETY

Security 24/7

"On campus, safety officers patrol on golf carts 24/7. They are great at keeping the campus safe but are also willing to give you a ride across campus if needed."

You're in Safe Hands

"I've always felt secure on FSC's campus. Safety regularly patrols the campus in golf carts, and is always on call. Students and faculty are also required to carry "saftey buttons," which, if pushed, send a campus-wide signal alerting the saftey office to your location."

LOOKING FOR MORE?
Check out our full-length guide to this school at collegeprowler.com/florida-southern-college/.

Florida State University

600 W. College Ave.; Tallahassee, FL 32306
(850) 644-2525; www.fsu.edu

THE BASICS:

Acceptance Rate: 61%
Yield: 42%
Setting: Mid-sized city
Control: Public
Total Undergrads: 30,803
SAT Range: 1110–1290*
ACT Range: 24–28

Student-Faculty Ratio: 25:1
Retention Rate: 91%
Graduation Rate: 70%
Tuition: $19,011
Room & Board: $8,000
Avg. Aid Package: $4,107
Students With Aid: 98%

* of 1600

Academics	B	Greek Life	B+
Athletics	A	Guys	A+
Campus Dining	B	Health & Safety	C+
Campus Housing	C+	Local Atmosphere	B+
Campus Strictness	B-	Nightlife	A
Computers	B	Off-Campus Dining	B+
Diversity	B	Off-Campus Housing	B+
Drug Safety	C-	Parking	B
Facilities	A-	Transportation	A
Girls	A+	Weather	B

CP's Student Author On...
OVERALL EXPERIENCE

You would be hard-pressed to find a graduate of Florida State University who doesn't have fond memories of the years they spent on campus. Current students will also agree that they are happy with their decision to attend school here. There is something for everyone, from athletics to academia, and you would have a hard time finding a more comfortable setting than Tallahassee. It has so much to offer, from exciting nightlife to beautiful weather.

Although it bears the reputation of a party school, FSU also has a growing reputation for turning out some of the best and brightest graduates in the entire nation. The school is now turning its focus on research, which should appeal to those interested in science and mathematics. But never fear, FSU also emphasizes the arts through their award-winning film and theater departments. From math and science, to the arts, FSU offers a vast array of eclectic degrees, which will be nothing but helpful later in your life. Choosing which college to attend is not an easy decision, but if you're looking for the perfect combination of a good education and a good time, you can't do much better than Florida State University.

Students Speak Out On...
OVERALL EXPERIENCE

⌕ Awesome
"I really love everything here- from the brick buildings to proximity of everything. I knew from the moment I stepped on the campus, this was where I belonged."

⌕ I Love FSU
"I feel i made an amazing decision on where to attend college. I love FSU and i love tallahassee, i strongly reccomend this university to any incoming freshman."

⌕ I Love FSU
"I love attending FSU. I love how beautiful the campus is and they're always trying to have something fun going on around campus. The people at the school are nice and friendly and it offers a quality education."

⌕ I LOVE FSU
"I wanted to go to UF but I did not get in. If I could do it again, I would not even waste my time applying to UF. I love the campus here, the people...the everything. It is a real college experience and I am proud to be a Seminole!"

BEST OF FLORIDA STATE

1. FSU Seminole football
2. Warm weather
3. FSU Flying High Circus
4. Checking out the "student bodies" on Landis Green
5. FSU Reservation at Lake Bradford

Happy Students
91% of students return after their first year.

Easy Financial Aid Process
59% of students surveyed told us that the financial aid process went smoothly and they received the financial aid they needed.

WORST OF FLORIDA STATE

1. Student parking
2. The humidity in August
3. Airfare in and out of Tallahassee
4. The terrible roads in and around campus
5. Musty buildings

Overextended Faculty
There are 25 students for every faculty member on campus.

Student Body

African American:	11%	Male Undergrads:	45%
Asian American:	3%	Female Undergrads:	55%
Hispanic:	12%	Living On Campus:	19%
International:	1%	Living Off Campus:	81%
Native American:	1%	Male Athletes:	3%
White:	71%	Female Athletes:	2%
Unknown:	1%	Fraternity Members:	14%
From Out-of-State:	11%	Sorority Members:	14%

Frequently Compared Schools:

University of Central Florida
University of Florida
University of Miami
University of South Florida

Students Speak Out On... EVERYTHING!

ACADEMICS

Art History Department

"The art history department is honestly fabulous. Classes are challenging, but professors are always willing to answer questions and love class participation. Internship opportunities are quite common and our advisers do their best to let everyone know as soon as they hear about a new opportunity."

A Great Education

"As an Undergraduate, I have been in courses that everybody has to take. All of them have been great so far. Registration is easy, especially if you're in the honors program. Florida State offers plenty of fun, relevant courses and the professors here are nothing short of excellent. In my first year, I was already able to get recommendations."

ATHLETICS

Athletics

"Florida State University is a very school spirited unviersities with multiple national titles. They have great recruiting and have almost any sport someone would be looking for.Our big sports are football and baseball. On gamedays we have ESPN trailing us on the field and the crowds are usually a sellout. Our IM's are also very good and competitive yet fun. We also have a few club leagues for people not on the college "varsity" level yet they are more competitive than at the IM level."

Noles Hit Goals!

"I'm not too familiar with sports, but the noles are great! I just moved to this little, yet fun-filled college city and although it's a nice change and am enjoying it here, I'm also struggling to get by! I really hope this scholarship comes through for me!!"

CAMPUS DINING

Eating Like a Seminole

"There are plenty of delicious options and varieties to choose from on the great campus of Florida State. Not only are the dining halls full of numerous options, there are also resturants right in the middle of campus! Chilis, Hardees, Pollo Tropical are just to name a few. The campus also features 2 Starbucks, all of which you can use your flex bucks at. There's also a Diner that is open 24 hours, which always stays busy and full of hungry students just waiting to be satisfied."

From Original to Chain

"FSU has the best situation when it comes to o campus dining. There is a starbucks cafe right in the library. The union has chain restaurants such as chilis and Hardies. My favorite place to eat on campus is the 60's diner that serves, quite possibly, the best burger in town."

CAMPUS HOUSING

Summary

"THE COLLEGE DORMS ARE AWESOME... a GREAT ROOM AND EVEN SO MANY GREAT PEOPLE AROUND YOU. tHE ATMOSPHERE OVERALL IS GREAT!!!"

GUYS & GIRLS

Ready to Have a Good Time

"Tallahassee is a party city for college students, but at the same time there are many resources available to help these party animals pass their classes. There are a huge variety of students and even within Greek life the personality of each sorority /fraternity is unbelievably different."

HEALTH & SAFETY

Very Safe

"You will feel totally safe on campus. There are emergency pylons all over campus that will alert the campus police if you're in danger. There's also a nightly cab service for campus only that's free and will get you from one place to the next, just in case you're still not feeling safe. The campus authorities also email announcements to every student if there was a crime or assault in a nearby area along with instructions on what to do if you were ever in the same situation."

LOOKING FOR MORE?

Check out our full-length guide to this school at collegeprowler.com/florida-state-university/.

Fordham University

441 E. Fordham Road; Bronx, NY 10458
(718) 817-1000; www.fordham.edu

THE BASICS:

Acceptance Rate: 50%	Student-Faculty Ratio: 13:1
Yield: 15%	Retention Rate: 90%
Setting: Large city	Graduation Rate: 78%
Control: Private Non-Profit	Tuition: $36,882
Total Undergrads: 7,950	Room & Board: $13,716
SAT Range: 1710–2010*	Avg. Aid Package: $25,258
ACT Range: 26–30	Students With Aid: 94%

of 2400

Academics	B+	Greek Life	N/A
Athletics	C-	Guys	B-
Campus Dining	C-	Health & Safety	B-
Campus Housing	B-	Local Atmosphere	A
Campus Strictness	C+	Nightlife	A-
Computers	B	Off-Campus Dining	A
Diversity	B-	Off-Campus Housing	B-
Drug Safety	C-	Parking	B+
Facilities	B-	Transportation	A
Girls	B+	Weather	B+

CP's Student Author On... OVERALL EXPERIENCE

Neither Rose Hill nor Lincoln Center offers the traditional experience most students associate with stereotypical universities. The Jesuit tradition, the core curriculum, and the vital location of Fordham define the school's base foundation as a hands-on liberal institution. Once you split the University, you'll discover two different worlds: the green college community-feel of Rose Hill and the urban buzz of Lincoln Center. Some students claim that there is a heated rivalry between the two major campuses. Although many Rose Hill students go four years without visiting Lincoln Center (and vice versa), the two campuses complement one another quite nicely. Prospective students, however, will only apply to one of the schools.

At Fordham, the small class sizes and friendly professors create a tight-knit intellectual community. Classes are not about lecture notes, but about the students and how they interpret and mold their own educations. If you think that desks should be equipped with a pull out pillow rest made exclusively for in-class napping, then Fordham is not the college for you.... For the rest of this editorial, visit collegeprowler.com.

Students Speak Out On... OVERALL EXPERIENCE

Q A Whole New World

"Fordham is awesome: brains matter, creativity matters, social conscience matters, friendships matter; professors want you to stretch your brain and welcome questions(and really do answer)-- and people still make time to have lots of fun. If you don't know how to settle down and work hard, you won't last here; if you were a 4.0 in most high schools, you will be shocked at how much it takes to earn an A here. But your mind and spirit will thank you for it."

Q I'm in Love

"Fordham is amazing. The people, education and overall atmosphere are very welcoming and filled with fun"

Q Unique

"The education is great and the proximity to NYC is huge benefit."

BEST OF FORDHAM

1. Location, location, location
2. Free theatre for all students
3. Free laundry!
4. The unprecedented Walsh Library
5. A myriad of internship opportunities

Happy Students
90% of students return after their first year.

Proven Success
78% of students will complete their education and graduate with a degree.

WORST OF FORDHAM

1. The tension between the Rose Hill and Lincoln Center campuses
2. Student apathy regarding school spirit
3. Lack of parking
4. Poor food quality
5. Paying $3 for the Ram Van

Expensive
Tuition is a steep $36,882, one of the most expensive rates in the country.

Expensive to Just Get By
58% of students surveyed felt that the amount it costs to live while at school was worse than average.

Student Body

African American:	6%	Male Undergrads:	44%
Asian American:	7%	Female Undergrads:	56%
Hispanic:	12%	Living On Campus:	56%
International:	2%	Living Off Campus:	44%
Native American:	0%	Male Athletes:	12%
White:	52%	Female Athletes:	7%
Unknown:	21%	Fraternity Members:	0%
From Out-of-State:	53%	Sorority Members:	0%

Students Speak Out On... EVERYTHING!

ACADEMICS

Q The Professors Really Do Want to Help

"I'm still in the underclassmen core programs. The classes aren't that challenging but the grading is tougher. If you make an effort to talk to your professor they will go to any effort to help you. They do care that you are learning."

Q Internships

"There are many available and interesting internships for the business school here because we are so close to NYC."

ATHLETICS

Q Good Effort, Good Crowd

"Fordham trains really hard and brings a lot of fans but its football is kind of weak. Its baseball games are less attending but they have a very strong team."

Q FU Sports, Okay

"Fordham has a pretty good athletics program. The football and basketball teams are not too great, but some of the lesser-watched sports do pretty well. Games are usually fun to watch regardless"

CAMPUS DINING

Q Okay

"The caf food has definitely gotten better than the past, but it still"

Q Getting Better

"The University is working really hard to improve the dining on campus. Undergoing a 5-year overhaul as we speak. Right now, it's too repetitive and just ok quality. Some good, simple fallbacks though"

CAMPUS HOUSING

Q The Higher Your Class, the Better Your Dorm

"Freshmens get stuck in terrible dorms such as North/South. Where there is no central cooling, the lighting is too dim, the halls are dirty and old. However, as to date, Hughes has the nicer dorm with cooling, clean AC, and people are generally

friendlier and more mature, but you have to wait till your sophomore year to get this dorm. New dorms are opening this Fall of 2010 and they even have their own Starbucks and recreation area. Sweet. (Juniors and Seniors only)"

Q Freshman Dorms Are Ok, Upperclassman Ones Are Nicer

"The dorms always have programs and tons of activities going on. The freshman dorms are okay, but the overall quality improves for upperclassmen."

GUYS & GIRLS

Q Diverse

"The crowd fits well with the New York City atmosphere of diversity. There's a good range of all sorts of students roaming the building just depends on your interests and tastes."

Q Good School for the Guys

"In terms of looks, there are some hot looking girls, especially when the weather gets nice and they are tanning on Eddies. Most of them are from the Tri States and some even from Cali. However, the school has a majority of affluent white people who will stick with their white friends. There is a clear social divide between the whites and everyone else. I have met alot of white boys who act stupid because their parents spoiled them."

HEALTH & SAFETY

Q Total Safe

"Fordham is a gated campus, so you must have an ID to enter, which keeps unwanted visitors out. For this I feel completely safe."

Q Security and Health

"The school is always emailing students security alerts and never fails to mention notifications about health related topics. Our campus in Lincoln Center is always closely guarded and I've ever felt like I was in any sort of danger."

LOOKING FOR MORE?

Check out our full-length guide to this school at collegeprowler.com/fordham-university/.

Franklin & Marshall College

415 Harrisburg Ave.; Lancaster, PA 17604
(877) 678-9111; www.fandm.edu

THE BASICS:

Acceptance Rate: 48%
Yield: 25%
Setting: Suburban
Control: Private Non-Profit
Total Undergrads: 2,248
SAT Range: 1230–1390*
ACT Range: 26–30

Student-Faculty Ratio: 10:1
Retention Rate: 92%
Graduation Rate: 79%
Tuition: $42,510
Room & Board: $11,500
Avg. Aid Package: $21,392
Students With Aid: 64%

* of 1600

Academics	B+	Greek Life	A-
Athletics	C	Guys	B
Campus Dining	B+	Health & Safety	B+
Campus Housing	C-	Local Atmosphere	C+
Campus Strictness	B-	Nightlife	C
Computers	B	Off-Campus Dining	B-
Diversity	C	Off-Campus Housing	D-
Drug Safety	B-	Parking	B-
Facilities	A-	Transportation	D+
Girls	B	Weather	C+

CP's Student Author On...
OVERALL EXPERIENCE

Contrary to however much they may complain, Fummers love it here. Once they've found their niche, they're the happiest little bunch of workaholics you'll ever meet. The only regrets come from those people who expected college to be a series of protests and consciousness-raising events. You can have those experiences if you really want to, but in all probability, you'll have to organize them. Another popular complaint is the lack of privacy in the social scene—let's face it, F&M is small, and everyone knows everyone else's business.

The most common F&M experience follows a pattern of coming to know the school, getting to know people, and then having your initial high hopes met with reality. After a brief stint of disillusionment and dissatisfaction (this bit is optional), you'll come to recognize the wonders of F&M and meet the people whom you will hopefully stay close with. You'll close out your experience having grown both academically and socially. Not a bad job for four years!

Students Speak Out On...
OVERALL EXPERIENCE

Q I LOVE IT

"I love this school. It is gorgeous. The boys are generally cute. The girls are nice. The parties are awesome. The professors sincerely want to help you which is huge. For example, I am not a science person. There is 1 lab science required for Gen-Ed requirements. I wasn't doing well in the class but the Professor met with me about 4 times before the final to help me study AND gave me extra credit work to complete in order to bump my grade. I love this school."

Q It's Okay

"There isn't really that much activities to do on campus. The food is pretty good. And the professors are really good here."

Q
"I can picture myself nowhere else. I am a member of a wonderful community. I feel safe, inspired, and enriched—it's a great place!"

BEST OF FRANKLIN & MARSHALL

1. The professors
2. The wireless network
3. Coed halls
4. The ASFC
5. Spring Arts Weekend
6. Flapjack Fest
7. Roschel Performing Arts Center

Happy Students
92% of students return after their first year.

Commitment to Teaching
There are 10 students for every member of faculty on campus.

WORST OF FRANKLIN & MARSHALL

1. The football team
2. The mascot
3. Attacking squirrels
4. Complaining students
5. Rising student apathy
6. The Pit
7. Finals week

Expensive
Tuition is a steep $42,510, one of the most expensive rates in the country.

Expensive Dorms
Living on campus doesn't come cheap, with an average housing price tag of $6,575.

Student Body

African American:	4%	Male Undergrads:	48%
Asian American:	4%	Female Undergrads:	52%
Hispanic:	4%	Living On Campus:	99%
International:	9%	Living Off Campus:	1%
Native American:	0%	Male Athletes:	32%
White:	69%	Female Athletes:	24%
Unknown:	10%	Fraternity Members:	35%
From Out-of-State:	74%	Sorority Members:	20%

Students Speak Out On... EVERYTHING!

ACADEMICS

Helpful Professors

"The professors here are really helpful. If they see that their students are struggling in class, they do whatever it takes to help them."

Freshman courses here are somewhat tough

"The courses here as a freshman are somewhat tough, but there are many Foundation courses you can take that are very easy and can result in a B with minimal effort. My friend is in Bio and Chem though, and he has a ton of work and is up all the time. When I have to study though for a hard test I study anywhere from 5 to 8 hours, so there really are some tough classes. Most of my professors have been very nice and helpful. Their very easy to reach out to."

ATHLETICS

Lots of Opportunities

"Many students are athletes, although it is very easy to not be involved in sports at all--I never went to a varsity game my freshman year. Overall, spirit isn't very high. However, lots of club sports and intramural sports are available for non-varsity athletes who want to participate."

"IM sports like basketball and softball and club sports like rugby and Frisbee are very popular. Varsity sports do not get enough attention from students and profs, in my opinion."

CAMPUS DINING

The Eateries Are Monopolies

"There are essentially two options currently on campus, the dining hall and Pandinis. But after 7:45, the only place to eat is Pandinis. Both eating establishments are below average, besides KIVO the Kosher option on campus which is consistently good. Overall, the food quality is extremely cheap and without hardly any alternate options its impossible to be satisfied."

"My brother went to Hopkins, and they have terrible food. So, in light of what other schools have, it's pretty decent here."

Frequently Compared Schools:

Bucknell University
Dickinson College
Gettysburg College
Lafayette College

CAMPUS HOUSING

It's Horrible

"The rooms are very small small and there tend to be a lot of bugs in the bathrooms and in the dorms."

It Depends on the Person.

"If you are a girl and you dont mind guys being around you all the time, then this place is for you. Or if you want a dorm that is quiet and completely anti-social and where no one says hi to each other, you'll fit in great here. I started moving out, and no one offered to help me even carry my refrigerator down 3 flights of stairs. Theres a lot of smoking and drug use too."

GUYS & GIRLS

Most Come from Families With Money.

"Most people are nice, they are just used to having money as opposed to those of us who do not."

Lax Bro Central

"if you are a lax bro, or if you (for whatever reason) are incredibly attracted to the lax bro, then f&m is the place for you. the girls are pretty easy, very catty (one girl essentially dropped out because of how mean these girls were to her) and the guys are pretty much..well...lax bros."

HEALTH & SAFETY

Safety

"I've never had a problem with safety at Franklin & Marshall. During my entire freshman year, I have only heard of two people being mugged, which is pretty impressive for being in the center of a city. As for Public Safety (the campus security), they are pretty cool. If they find you drunk, they'll just escort you back to your room."

Well...it's good and bad

"You don't really feel unsafe on the campus. The Amnesty policy is used, which is good and bad. At orientation the police give out bottle openers with their numbers on it. If you don't drink, don't come here."

LOOKING FOR MORE?

Check out our full-length guide to this school at collegeprowler.com/franklin--and--marshall-college/.

Freed-Hardeman University

158 E. Main St.; Henderson, TN 38340
(800) 348-3481; www.fhu.edu

THE BASICS:

Acceptance Rate: 99%
Yield: 64%
Setting: Town
Control: Private Non-Profit
Total Undergrads: 1,496
SAT Range: 968–1218*
ACT Range: 20–26

Student-Faculty Ratio: 15:1
Retention Rate: 68%
Graduation Rate: 53%
Tuition: $14,998
Room & Board: $7,090
Avg. Aid Package: $13,942
Students With Aid: 99%

* of 1600

Academics	B-	Greek Life	N/A
Athletics	C+	Guys	A+
Campus Dining	B	Health & Safety	B+
Campus Housing	A-	Local Atmosphere	C+
Campus Strictness	C-	Nightlife	C-
Computers	B-	Off-Campus Dining	C+
Diversity	C	Off-Campus Housing	B
Drug Safety	A+	Parking	B+
Facilities	B+	Transportation	C
Girls	A+	Weather	B+

CP's Student Author On...
OVERALL EXPERIENCE

Almost all FHU students are proud of their school and wouldn't change their college choice. This small campus that is nestled in a small town in Southwest Tennessee is more than a college to its students; it's home and a place where one can feel loved and accepted. FHU focuses on a Christian education as well as an education that will help its students succeed in the business world. The University's mission statement is "Teaching how to live and how to make a living," and the faculty does just that. All of the faculty and staff are members of the Church of Christ and are true examples of what a Christian should be.

Because FHU is such a small campus, it's hard to walk around and not recognize most of the people you pass by. While many college campuses are very large and home to thousands of students, the reason many students come to Freed is because of the small size, along with the Christian atmosphere and endearing faculty. FHU offers a warm feeling to its students, something that is very unique for a university.... For the rest of this editorial, visit collegeprowler.com.

Students Speak Out On...
OVERALL EXPERIENCE

Q Its Awesome Here!
"I love Freed- Hardeman and everything it stands for."

Q FHU Experience
"I would recommend FHU for any students particularly with an interest in doing the Lords work. I can personally vouch for a decent Business school. However, the school is not the most efficient with their money and they have poor spending habits, so tuition can be a bit high for what you are getting."

BEST OF FREED-HARDEMAN

1. Christian fellowship
2. Small classes
3. Social clubs
4. The focus on God
5. Two-dollar movie theater tickets
6. Very approachable staff and faculty

Big Dorms
90% of students surveyed felt that dorms were more spacious than average.

Personal Attention
You can expect personal attention with 52% of classes having less than 20 students.

WORST OF FREED-HARDEMAN

1. Having to get permission to stay overnight at a member of the opposite sex's parent's house
2. Located too far from malls and movie theaters
3. Mandatory curfew
4. No coed visitation in the dorms

Not Much Diversity
One of the least racially diverse campuses—only 10% of students are minorities.

Student Body

African American:	4%	Male Undergrads:	45%
Asian American:	0%	Female Undergrads:	55%
Hispanic:	1%	Living On Campus:	76%
International:	2%	Living Off Campus:	24%
Native American:	1%	Male Athletes:	11%
White:	90%	Female Athletes:	7%
Unknown:	1%	Fraternity Members:	0%
From Out-of-State:	43%	Sorority Members:	0%

Frequently Compared Schools:

Colorado State University - Pueblo
Liberty University
Louisiana State University
Minnesota State University

Students Speak Out On... EVERYTHING!

ACADEMICS

Professors

"The professors at Freed-Hardeman are great! They are very polite and respectful, unlike the stories I have heard from my friends attending other colleges. They are known to invite students to dinner which is great for those of us living far away from home. At FHU, everyone is family. I can't even put into words how instant the feeling of home came to me, after arriving on campus."

Life at Freed-Hardeman

"I am currently undecided on what major I would like to pursue. However, all of the people who helped me come up with a schedule were very helpful and put me in some required classes so that I could get a hang of college life and get in the swing of things."

ATHLETICS

RUGBY!

"Athletics are not the most important aspect at Freed-Hardeman, but it is a good aspect. Our school doesn't have a football team but we pride ourselves in basketball and RUGBY! This year we even have a girls rugby team. We also have ways to be involved in intramural sports."

Sports Are Great

"We have volleyball, soccer, baseball, football, and basketball for guys and girls. Intramural sports are lots of fun too."

CAMPUS DINING

Much Better Than It Used to Be

"The cafeteria has significantly improved this year from years past! The atmosphere is great and the food is usually pretty good too!"

Not Bad

"The food is not to bad. There is a inter-nation bar. A great salad bar. A places to get burgers and fries and pizza etc. I'm a little bet of a health nut so I'm happy to say they have soy milk, yogurt, and lots of fruit and veggies to pick from everyday. There is also a pizza hut located in the same building. Near

buy there is a subway,Mcdonalds (student discount), Taco Bell (student discount), Burger King, Chinese, GREAT mexican restaurant, different diners, and a few others."

CAMPUS HOUSING

I LOVE FREED!

"I love being a student at FHU. It has a great Christian environment and plenty of opportunities to grow closer to God with. We just had our cafeteria Gano completely renovated, the food there is now sooo delicious. We also now have a Pizza Hut and Burger Joint. We have our own movie theater that is exclusively for Freedies. Campus is in a very small town, actually campus is the town. FHU is a great place to meet many new friends."

Hall-Roland

"Hall-Roland is old, but I loved it! Because it only houses around 80 girls, it has such a comfortable, homey feeling. The dorm parents are excellent in Hall-Roland. Hall-Roland is by far the best because they even let you paint the rooms."

GUYS & GIRLS

Variety of Offerings

"Freed isn't just typical christian goody goody people. There are all different kinds of people here. Anything you could possibly want"

Awesome

"The guys and girls are great, Christian, very friendly people. You will always have a friend here."

HEALTH & SAFETY

Great Security

"Chester County has the lowest crime rate in the state of TN. The college has great security. The campus is very well lit. I always feel safe when out on the campus. Just a great place to be."

LOOKING FOR MORE?

Check out our full-length guide to this school at collegeprowler.com/freed--hardeman-university/.

Furman University

3300 Poinsett Highway; Greenville, SC 29613
(864) 294-2000; www.furman.edu

THE BASICS:

Acceptance Rate: 57%
Yield: 30%
Setting: Suburban
Control: Private Non-Profit
Total Undergrads: 2,754
SAT Range: 1760–2050*
ACT Range: 26–30

Student-Faculty Ratio: 11:1
Retention Rate: 92%
Graduation Rate: 85%
Tuition: $36,656
Room & Board: $9,170
Avg. Aid Package: $21,957
Students With Aid: 85%

of 2400

Academics	B	Greek Life	A
Athletics	B-	Guys	B
Campus Dining	B+	Health & Safety	A
Campus Housing	B	Local Atmosphere	B
Campus Strictness	C	Nightlife	C+
Computers	B+	Off-Campus Dining	B
Diversity	D+	Off-Campus Housing	D+
Drug Safety	A-	Parking	B+
Facilities	B+	Transportation	C-
Girls	B+	Weather	B+

CP's Student Author On...
OVERALL EXPERIENCE

Furman students are generally crazy about their school. Although it's not for everyone, the ones who decide to attend usually find it a great match. The academic programs at Furman are a huge draw. Students appreciate the quality of education they are getting and the personal attention they get from their professors. And although the workload can be stressful at times, Furman's idyllic campus makes it difficult to sustain any level of stress for too long.

It's true the Furman bubble may seem out of touch with the real world at times. Sometimes, it seems like you are surrounded by homecoming queens, class presidents, and valedictorians. But despite a few complaints, no one seems to want to leave. Just ask anyone on campus. Furman students love to talk about why they love their school.

Students Speak Out On...
OVERALL EXPERIENCE

Q I LOVE IT

"Furman has kicked my butt academically, but from a student life perspective, it is wonderful. The beautiful view with the lake, the wonderful choirs and other musical performances, the ease to find and make friends make this the best choice of my life. I am happy to be a Paladin, and I will proudly scream our cheer for the rest of my life: "F U ALL THE TIME!""

Q An Overpriced Excuse of a College Experience

"Don't be fooled by the architecture and perfectly manicured grounds. There is a reason why half of the student body leaves on the weekends. Just not the college experience that a UGA or UK could provide you!"

Q "I love it! I could not picture myself anywhere else. I just love the people and atmosphere. I could not go anywhere else after being here for two years."

Q "I absolutely love it, and I'm totally happy. I never had second thoughts about being here, and I have never wished I was anywhere else. Really, it never crossed my mind. I love Furman."

BEST OF FURMAN

1. The Greenville community
2. Professors
3. Research opportunities
4. O-Week/freshman halls
5. Strong academics
6. Friendly students
7. Downtown
8. Friends

Happy Students
92% of students return after their first year.

Proven Success
85% of students will complete their education and graduate with a degree.

WORST OF FURMAN

1. Ever-increasing tuition
2. The Furman "Bubble"
3. Strong Republican mindset
4. Winter weather
5. Parking tickets
6. The construction
7. Lack of dating

Expensive
Tuition is a steep $36,656, one of the most expensive rates in the country.

Student Body

African American:	8%	Male Undergrads:	44%
Asian American:	2%	Female Undergrads:	56%
Hispanic:	2%	Living On Campus:	90%
International:	2%	Living Off Campus:	10%
Native American:	0%	Male Athletes:	20%
White:	79%	Female Athletes:	7%
Unknown:	6%	Fraternity Members:	33%
From Out-of-State:	69%	Sorority Members:	44%

Frequently Compared Schools:

Clemson University
Elon University
University of Richmond
Wake Forest University

Students Speak Out On...
EVERYTHING!

ACADEMICS

ℚ Its Pretty Tough, So That Means Academic Rating Is High...

"Some professors are better than others. Classes are extremely subjective, but if you're not the genius of the class, you may not do so hot. Signing up for classes is not easy, the workload is far more than moderate, and class selection is limited. Special study is pretty good, and the school is flexible with working with other programs to get people where they want to go. Study abroad is popular."

ℚ Small Classes

"small classes equal more accessibility to professors and a more engaged learning experience where teacher and student interactions enhance the overall educational experience. it is a liberal arts college so it allows also, for an all rounded student who has touched upon every academic aspect that will make him/her an asset to any company upon graduating.."

ℚ Mixed bag

"There are quite a few incredible professors here. The small classes are nice, but so far (I'm a freshman) class participation is lacking. However, I think that the academics in general here are quite good."

ATHLETICS

ℚ Sports Not Supported

"Student body tends not to be very supportive of varsity athletics. Not much team spirit"

ℚ Fair Weather Student Crowd

"Sports games are fun to attend if you're into them, but most of the students don't really care. Our football and basketball teams are mediocre, and students tend to leave after halftime. Great student support of the marching band, though!"

CAMPUS DINING

ℚ Awesome Dining

"They have 7 different restaurants that are in the dining hall. For example: Chick-fil-a and Moes."

ℚ Ok

"The food is good, but it does get a little old after a while. The Pden has a good variety of fast food options."

CAMPUS HOUSING

ℚ Awesome

"Upperclassmen dorms and apartments are the best, but compared to other colleges in SC the freshman dorms are great. Everything is nice and clean."

ℚ Opportunities

"many facilities are available for the money you are paying to go here. gym, dining hall, theatre, pools etc. Landscape is gorgeous that if you take time out of your day to relax a bit, you would realise you live on a resort!"

GUYS & GIRLS

ℚ People Are in Love

"The boys and girls of Furman University are strangely attractive. Or rather, there's a large amount of attractive people here. There are weddings on campus monthly, as many as two a week, at times. This seems to be the place to fall in love."

ℚ The Girls, the Boys, and the Beautiful

"A large number of the boys have the southern frat look from the croakies to the RL to the cackies and the sperry's. Most of the girls, apart from the jocks, get dresses up even for 8:30 classes. Most people are really put together and I felt proud to be part of a student body that cared about their appearance."

HEALTH & SAFETY

ℚ Health and Safety

"very safe campus. it's small, gated, and requires card entry to most buildings. also has campus security open 24/7, patrolling the campus frequently"

ℚ FUPO

"They keep you safe and will drive you back to your dorm from the library or Einstine's, but they are super annoying about parking and give out really expensive tickets."

LOOKING FOR MORE?
Check out our full-length guide to this school at collegeprowler.com/furman-university/.

Gannon University

109 W. Sixth St.; Erie, PA 16541
(814) 871-7000; www.gannon.edu

THE BASICS:

Acceptance Rate: 84%	**Student-Faculty Ratio:** 13:1
Yield: 26%	**Retention Rate:** 82%
Setting: Mid-sized city	**Graduation Rate:** 64%
Control: Private Non-Profit	**Tuition:** $24,269
Total Undergrads: 2,978	**Room & Board:** $9,330
SAT Range: 1330–1700*	**Avg. Aid Package:** $19,802
ACT Range: 19–26	**Students With Aid:** 97%

* of 2400

Academics	C+	Greek Life	A+
Athletics	C+	Guys	B
Campus Dining	C	Health & Safety	C
Campus Housing	B	Local Atmosphere	B-
Campus Strictness	C-	Nightlife	A-
Computers	B-	Off-Campus Dining	B-
Diversity	C	Off-Campus Housing	B
Drug Safety	B-	Parking	B-
Facilities	C	Transportation	B
Girls	C+	Weather	C+

CP's Student Author On...
OVERALL EXPERIENCE

While every University has its pros and cons, Gannon students overall are pretty satisfied with their college decision. Gannon's strongest points are some of the most important factors when choosing a college: students, academics/professors, and location/atmosphere. Although Gannon is not perfect, the University does its best to provide what students need.

Gannon students think that the people on campus are one of the best things the University has to offer. Gannon does a phenomenal job of helping students decide what they want to do, pursue and become educated in a field, and then find a corresponding career. The small student-to-faculty ratio allows students to have personal relationships with their professors, who are known for going out of their way to assist students and prepare them for a successful future. The University's urban location, in the heart of Erie, provides students with a slew of experiences, with everything from shopping and entertainment to internships and job opportunities.... For the rest of this editorial, visit collegeprowler.com.

Students Speak Out On...
OVERALL EXPERIENCE

Q I Love College!

"Gannon has a great atmosphere and love for students and achieving their goals. I have a great time learning and being a part of the overall Gannon experience. The university shows how to use this education to my advantage and provide a great future for myself."

Q Overall Great

"Gannon is very small. But with the small factor you get a sense of community. I personally know every one of the professors in my department of study, and I am only a sophomore! I don't know where else I could have went and got an experience like that."

Q In Your Own World

"Gannon is in downtown Erie, PA. While on campus, you forget that you're in a city. Campus is usually quiet and I feel safe as a I walk from building to building. Everything is located within 5 blocks of each other, which makes going from different activities easy. Landscaping is very nice and helps to block out the city noise. Gannon's campus has a way of making you feel at home and forgetting about the outside world."

BEST OF GANNON

1. Professor availability and experience
2. Atmosphere created by students, faculty, and staff
3. Small class sizes
4. Location, city atmosphere
5. Cost

Happy Students
82% of students return after their first year.

Knowledgeable Professors
80% of students surveyed rated the general knowledge of professors as above average.

WORST OF GANNON

1. Food prices and hours
2. Residence hall strictness, freshman rules
3. Location, surrounding neighborhoods, safety concerns
4. Parking
5. Underage drinking policies

Not Much Diversity
One of the least racially diverse campuses—only 13% of students are minorities.

Student Body

African American:	5%	Male Undergrads:	41%
Asian American:	1%	Female Undergrads:	59%
Hispanic:	2%	Living On Campus:	48%
International:	2%	Living Off Campus:	52%
Native American:	0%	Male Athletes:	25%
White:	87%	Female Athletes:	10%
Unknown:	4%	Fraternity Members:	11%
From Out-of-State:	30%	Sorority Members:	10%

Frequently Compared Schools:

Boston College
Drexel University
Duquesne University
Mercyhurst College

Students Speak Out On...
EVERYTHING!

ACADEMICS

Great Academics

"Excellent academics with great professors! They are very knowledgeable on their subjects"

Pre-Med/Biology

"All of the staff are very helpful and accessible. As a student athlete, they are willing to work with me to work around my busy softball season in spring, so I can stay on track. The classes are also very effective for teaching the material contained on the MCATs."

ATHLETICS

Athletics

"I play volleyball and I LOVE my team, coaches, practices, facility and everything about it"

Gannon's Got Great Athletics!!!!

"Gannon may be NCAA Division II, but they have great athletics!!! There are also lots of intramural options for anyone who wants to play!!"

CAMPUS DINING

Food

"I have enjoyed it but know others that don't. I think there's variety, as well as health options."

Variety of Dining Options on Campus

"The dining options on Gannon's campus present a vast variety of options to the students. On campus there is the cafe as well as Doc's, a sandwich shop/mexican restaurant. In addition to that we also have several other places to eat that are located right on campus. Also, we have several off campus options available as well, several restaurants surrounding the area accept GUgold which would be out flex dollars."

CAMPUS HOUSING

Housing

"Freshman dorms are pretty decent although too strict, and sophomores live in apartments which are roomy and clean.

All housing options are close to school buildings, which is convenient."

Get an Apartment!

"Gannon's upperclassmen apartments are pretty nice for college students, and are usually very spacious. Some may be a little farther from campus than one would hope, but hey, at leat its yours!"

GUYS & GIRLS

People at Gannon

"the people at gannon are amazing. I have many friends and i love them all."

Students

"The students are very friendly. They have helped me if I had any problems in classes."

HEALTH & SAFETY

Use Your Head

"There is always room for improvement, but I have never had any problems with safety on campus. Police and safety do their best to make sure all students are safe. John Coleman is not only the best security guard to grace this planet, but he's also always there for the students when they just need someone to talk to. Make sure you pay for your parking pass though, they do like to give out parking tickets!"

A Safe Campus

"Gannon offers its own police force for the safety of its students. Maroon-painted squad cars are always visible on campus. Gannon also sends out campus alerts whenever there is a crime committed on or near campus that the law enforcement feels the student body should know about."

LOOKING FOR MORE?

Check out our full-length guide to this school at collegeprowler.com/gannon-university/.

Geneva College

3200 College Ave.; Beaver Falls, PA 15010
(724) 846-5100; www.geneva.edu

THE BASICS:

Acceptance Rate: 84%	Student-Faculty Ratio: 14:1
Yield: 36%	Retention Rate: 77%
Setting: Suburban	Graduation Rate: 59%
Control: Private Non-Profit	Tuition: $21,400
Total Undergrads: 1,670	Room & Board: $7,770
SAT Range: 1390–1780*	Avg. Aid Package: $17,171
ACT Range: 19–25	Students With Aid: 99%

* of 2400

Academics	C+	Greek Life	N/A
Athletics	C+	Guys	B+
Campus Dining	C	Health & Safety	B-
Campus Housing	B	Local Atmosphere	C
Campus Strictness	C-	Nightlife	C
Computers	C-	Off-Campus Dining	B-
Diversity	C	Off-Campus Housing	B-
Drug Safety	A-	Parking	A-
Facilities	C-	Transportation	C
Girls	B-	Weather	C+

CP's Student Author On...
OVERALL EXPERIENCE

Geneva is more than an institution: it is a lifestyle. Professors are colleagues in learning that strive for students' personal best in education and in life. Fellow students are members of a tight-knit community who wish for each other's well-being. Of course, there are the jocks, geeks, computer nerds, video game junkies, preps, punks, religious dogmatists, and prima-donnas, but we all get along. We all help each other in classes and live together in the dorms. Geneva is an open community that flourishes on the good of man and comes together to support one another's failures.

Obviously there are the aspects of Geneva that few people like, such as the food, some aspects of the administration, the policies, and the parking, but overall, Geneva is a safe place to go for an opportunity to have the best four years of your life. The experience is what you make of it. If you get involved, continue traditions, start some of your own, join some clubs, and partake in the student activities—your experience will be a positive one. Geneva is for students looking for a spiritual influence.

Students Speak Out On...
OVERALL EXPERIENCE

Q Community
"Geneva College has a great sense of community. It is a rather small school and while I don't know everyone, most people are willing to have a conversation and are overall friendly. Everyone at Geneva cares about each other and when something difficult happens, we ban together as a family and are there for each other."

Q Overall Experience
"The Christian atmosphere of the school is the biggest draw for me. The care and compassion of the professors and the sevices available to the students are beyond compare."

Q I Highly Recommend Geneva College
"I love Geneva college; so happy I decided to come here! Great faculty/staff, awesome community in the dorm, reasonable academic standards."

Q Why Geneva Rocks
"The main attraction of this college is the powerful aura of community. It is easy to feel accepted and at home within the residents halls as well as the classrooms. Togetherness is what sets Geneva apart."

BEST OF GENEVA

1. Commited and caring professors
2. Lots of available parking
3. Online registration
4. Professors' availability to students outside of class
5. The student activities department

Easy Financial Aid Process
74% of students surveyed told us that the financial aid process went smoothly and they received the financial aid they needed.

WORST OF GENEVA

1. Strict Residence Life policy
2. Limited facilities
3. Small student body size
4. Humanities core classes
5. The town of Beaver Falls
6. Off-campus living policy

Life is NOT a Party
78% of students surveyed said it's almost impossible to find a good party.

Student Body

African American:	16%	Male Undergrads:	44%
Asian American:	1%	Female Undergrads:	56%
Hispanic:	1%	Living On Campus:	69%
International:	1%	Living Off Campus:	28%
Native American:	0%	Male Athletes:	27%
White:	79%	Female Athletes:	12%
Unknown:	0%	Fraternity Members:	0%
From Out-of-State:	29%	Sorority Members:	0%

Frequently Compared Schools:

Carnegie Mellon University
Grove City College
La Roche College
University of Pittsburgh

Students Speak Out On... EVERYTHING!

ACADEMICS

David Essig, Ph.D.

"Professor Essig has been available for me to visit him personally and answer all of my concerns each time I have visited Geneva. Everyone has worked on a personal level with me and has made it very easy for me to make my college decision."

Student Ministry Life

"Being a Student Ministry major, you get a bad rep. People think that all you do is hang out with kids and write a few reflection papers. Well, I'm here to tell you that I've never been more challenged in my faith or more fascinated with the Lord and the ways He works than I have in the past two years at Geneva, in this major. The professors are poignant and encouraging and they've helped me to develop a specific vision for my future in Urban Ministry."

ATHLETICS

Great Teams

"the sports are not top priority yet the teams are amazing. They have won states many of times and the couches are very nice. Intermerials are also a lot of fun to get involved in."

A Very Christian Environment

"With exceptions, many of the people at Geneva College profess a Christian faith. A step further, there are people from all different denominations, different ethnic backgrounds, different class statuses and simply different ways of life. Aside from the faith connection that most people share at Geneva, there is no description that could account for the varieties of men and women at the school"

CAMPUS DINING

Freedom of Choice

"The dining options on campus are pretty good. The brig is consistant with menu options and food quality, and Alex's sends out emails of what is going to be served so you know what to watch out for. I'd suggest buying the 14-a-week meal plan with flex dollars. You can use flex to buy from the Papa Johns down the street, just make sure you keep track of how much flex you have left."

Alex's

"It's food, and it's forcibly included in the tuition, so I'm paying for it anyway. I'm not going to complain without too much of a reason."

CAMPUS HOUSING

Women Freshmen Housing

"Due to the excessive amount of people that the college accepted, I currently live in what was a lounge with 7 other girls. There are four bunk beds, 8 closets, and 8 bookselves. It sounds annoying. But I love it, as do all my roommates. I am content and satisfied with my housing."

GUYS & GIRLS

Student Friends

"Students are very typical of any school. All races and nationalities, very easy to communicate with and have a good time. They are fun to hang out with and I enjoy some relaxing time takling to them about their families and friends before classes get started. The dress usually seems to be business casual as most of the students do work and are either coming from work to class, or heading to work after class is over. I really enjoy the student life."

HEALTH & SAFETY

The Security of Geneva College

"As far as I know, nothing bad has ever happened on campus. Off campus it can get rowdy, but on campus feels just as safe as home in the country. All the students get along with security, which is great. It brings a great feeling of community."

LOOKING FOR MORE?

Check out our full-length guide to this school at collegeprowler.com/geneva-college/.

George Mason University

4400 University Drive; Fairfax, VA 22030
(703) 993-1000; www.gmu.edu

THE BASICS:

Acceptance Rate: 63%
Yield: 31%
Setting: Suburban
Control: Public
Total Undergrads: 19,700
SAT Range: 1520–1840*
ACT Range: 23–27

Student-Faculty Ratio: 16:1
Retention Rate: 85%
Graduation Rate: 61%
Tuition: $24,008
Room & Board: $7,650
Avg. Aid Package: $11,991
Students With Aid: 65%

of 2400

Academics	B	Greek Life	C
Athletics	B-	Guys	B+
Campus Dining	B	Health & Safety	A-
Campus Housing	B-	Local Atmosphere	B-
Campus Strictness	B-	Nightlife	B
Computers	B-	Off-Campus Dining	B
Diversity	A	Off-Campus Housing	B-
Drug Safety	C+	Parking	C-
Facilities	B	Transportation	A-
Girls	B-	Weather	B-

CP's Student Author On...
OVERALL EXPERIENCE

Let's get brutally honest for a minute: Mason's not for everybody. For students dreaming of wild house parties and a 24-7 drinking fest akin to scenes in "Animal House," they might be better off at a school with a bigger party reputation than Mason. But just because Mason isn't what people stereotypically associate with a college experience, doesn't mean students don't get a real college experience nonetheless. As one of the most diverse schools in the nation, Mason offers students a unique college experience and plentiful opportunities to get involved in different organizations or groups and meet a lot of different people while doing so. Not to mention the campus's central location, just 20 minutes outside of Washington D.C., which gives students access to museums, clubs, restaurants, and popular attractions like the monuments. So what if students can't walk next door and do a keg stand? They have the opportunity to mold their very own college experience around Mason's numerous clubs, events, and classes.

It might sound a little cliché, but Mason truly offers the best of both worlds.... For the rest of this editorial, visit collegeprowler.com.

Students Speak Out On...
OVERALL EXPERIENCE

Q Diversity and Friendship

"Coming to Mason has changed my life, I absolutely love it. I have met the women who will be my bridesmaids in my wedding one day, have met so many diverse people and have had so many crazy experiences that I would never forget in a million years. What makes Mason unique is how we are so diverse. You can never go a whole day without seeing your friends or making new ones. I'm actually really upset that my time is coming to an end at Mason and I have decided to make Fairfax my home!"

Q Experiences

"Mason was not my top choice coming out of high school, but after four years, I've enjoyed meeting the people and being part of a unique university."

Q Wonderful Atmosphere

"Whether you are looking for camping, a club scene, or a relaxed suburban area, George Mason can provide it all. You are in close proximity to Washington, D.C. yet can still get into the mountains and enjoy the rural, mountainous regions that surround the area."

BEST OF GEORGE MASON

1. The weather in Fairfax is great, students get to experience the best of all four seasons.

Happy Students
85% of students return after their first year.

Knowledgeable Professors
77% of students surveyed rated the general knowledge of professors as above average.

WORST OF GEORGE MASON

1. Mason doesn't have a football team and not all students attend basketball games, so there's not as much school spirit as you see at schools with Division I football teams.

Don't Move Off Campus
Average off-campus housing is a steep $11,680.

Student Body

African American:	7%	Male Undergrads:	47%
Asian American:	15%	Female Undergrads:	53%
Hispanic:	6%	Living On Campus:	26%
International:	4%	Living Off Campus:	74%
Native American:	0%	Male Athletes:	5%
White:	42%	Female Athletes:	4%
Unknown:	25%	Fraternity Members:	7%
From Out-of-State:	21%	Sorority Members:	6%

Frequently Compared Schools:

American University
James Madison University
University of Virginia
Virginia Tech

Students Speak Out On...
EVERYTHING!

ACADEMICS

The Conflict Analysis and Resolution Program Is Gold!

"I am a conflict analysis and resolution major with an emphasis in community/organization issues, and the program is fantastic. It is small enough to where I know all of the professors in my major, and they are willing to meet on a one-on-one basis to help with anything you could imagine. I can't imagine being a different major."

School of Management

"Great program! It very challenging, competitive and useful."

ATHLETICS

Extreme Support

"Everyone is very supportive and has school spirit."

I've enjoyed attending sporting events

"I've enjoyed attending sporting events at George mason. My favorite part is the social atmosphere of these events. The school really goes all out to keep the fans interested. They have many free giveaways, t-shirts, pizza, foam hats, school logo items...I'm not a very sports minded person but I enjoy going because of how the school promotes school spirit."

CAMPUS DINING

George Mason's Dining

"The dining on campus is good but not excellent. I find that half way through the semester I feel like all my options really are not that great and that I would rather spend my money eating off campus than on it. My friends and I really do enjoy the late night dining place Ikes because it is a place we can go to when we get out of class late or whenever we are hungry late at night when we pull all nighters."

My Opinion

"They are extremely delicious and nearly everything is homemade."

CAMPUS HOUSING

Living in the Dorms

"Living on campus this year was the best decision. I was able to make so many new friends I wouldnt have met if I had commuted and my experience as a whole was amazing. Everyone on my floor was friendly and we all hang out and most of us plan on rooming together next year. It was pretty affordable and even though we don't have much here, it's enough to get us through the year and to help us with our college career."

I Don't Live on Campus

"I don't live on campus, but the dorms are pretty nice. They're a bit far from the campus but they seem excellent if someone wants a quiet atmosphere."

GUYS & GIRLS

An Eclectic Scene

"The Mason student body is very diverse and very accepting. People are not afraid to be themselves, dress a little differently or start their own trends. There are cliques, but people can find small groups of close friends for themselves. You won't feel alone."

Lots of ethnic diversity

"Lots of ethnic diversity, large groups of Asians, Indians, African-Americans, and Middle Easterners."

HEALTH & SAFETY

Tight-Knit Community

"George Mason is a dry campus which substantially decreases the amount of tomfoolery and "pranks gone bad" that are so stereotypical of college. The people there are outgoing and friendly and would not hesitate to help someone out whether it be telling them where a class room is or calling the police."

LOOKING FOR MORE?

Check out our full-length guide to this school at collegeprowler.com/george-mason-university/.

George Washington University

2121 I St. NW; Washington, DC 20052
(202) 994-1000; www.gwu.edu

THE BASICS:

Acceptance Rate: 37%	Student-Faculty Ratio: 13:1
Yield: 34%	Retention Rate: 91%
Setting: Large city	Graduation Rate: 81%
Control: Private Non-Profit	Tuition: $41,655
Total Undergrads: 10,505	Room & Board: $10,120
SAT Range: 1790–2070*	Avg. Aid Package: $22,321
ACT Range: 26–30	Students With Aid: 57%

* of 2400

Academics	A-	Greek Life	B
Athletics	C-	Guys	C+
Campus Dining	B	Health & Safety	C
Campus Housing	B+	Local Atmosphere	A
Campus Strictness	A-	Nightlife	A
Computers	B-	Off-Campus Dining	A-
Diversity	B+	Off-Campus Housing	B-
Drug Safety	C-	Parking	C-
Facilities	B	Transportation	A
Girls	C-	Weather	B-

CP's Student Author On... OVERALL EXPERIENCE

Students at GW tend to complain a lot about the pricey tuition, lack of school spirit, perhaps unnecessary new facilities, and excessive nickel-and-diming. However, most students stay at GW for four years—GW's retention rate is 91 percent. Many students are also upset about how GW compares academically to other schools, and that the science labs and facilities are run-down and old. GW students want the best and sometimes the University does not live up to their expectations.

Although GW provides students with a large variety of entertaining on-campus activities, students can also go off campus and enjoy the city. The University's location in DC makes most GW students' experiences worthwhile and interesting. GW would not be the same, nor as wonderful, if it were not located in DC. The city adds life, variety, and uniqueness to the campus environment. Students have the opportunity to land incredible internships while taking classes. The city also offers countless off-campus shows, productions, sporting events, restaurants and bars, museums, and (of course) the monuments to visit.... For the rest of this editorial, visit collegeprowler.com.

Students Speak Out On... OVERALL EXPERIENCE

Q Overall Experience
"Overall experience is great. I just want to do well and further my education."

Q Amazing Experience
"I always enjoy being here. It is at the heart of DC, so there's definitely a lot to do. There are also many people who enjoy partying as well as studying when the time calls for it. While the cafeteria food can be sucky sometimes, the variety of other food places in the area make up for it. The classes are amazing, as long as you keep up with them."

Q "I would not come here again, not in this lifetime. If you're a rich kid with money to burn and no desire to do any work other than to get drunk and party, GW's the place. If you actually want to go to school with students who care about learning, find a different school."

BEST OF GEORGE WASHINGTON

1. Located in Washington, DC
2. Internship opportunities
3. College campus feel, in the middle of the city
4. Top-of-the-line facilities and dorms
5. Great bars, clubs, and restaurants nearby

Happy Students
91% of students return after their first year.

Proven Success
81% of students will complete their education and graduate with a degree.

WORST OF GEORGE WASHINGTON

1. High tuition
2. Lack of school spirit
3. The fairly common spoiled rich students
4. Cost of city living
5. Red tape and bureaucratic procedures
6. Slow 4-RIDE service

Expensive
Tuition is a steep $41,655, one of the most expensive rates in the country.

Expensive to Just Get By
64% of students surveyed felt that the amount it costs to live while at school was worse than average.

Student Body

African American:	8%	Male Undergrads:	45%
Asian American:	10%	Female Undergrads:	55%
Hispanic:	7%	Living On Campus:	64%
International:	6%	Living Off Campus:	36%
Native American:	0%	Male Athletes:	5%
White:	56%	Female Athletes:	4%
Unknown:	13%	Fraternity Members:	19%
From Out-of-State:	99%	Sorority Members:	18%

Students Speak Out On... EVERYTHING!

ACADEMICS

Q Masters in Public Health

"Great! There are great opportunities for internships and other professional enhancement opportunities for students. The curriculum is structured well and provides students with a solid foundation."

Q GW Professors

"GW professors are some of the best in he country. They are very informative, understand their topics, and look beyond theory. Every professor I have encountered love the subject they teach and make an effort to extend that love to their students."

Q

"The professors are generally good. You really need to research the professors for the classes you want to take. You will find a lot of professors with amazing experiences, but others won't have so much."

ATHLETICS

Q Misunderstood

"We have some great athletic programs, however, the one's that get the most publicity are the sports that are struggling (boys basketball). I also think the fan support is a rough, we are not always good sports when we are playing other teams."

Q Too Busy

"People at GW have so much going on, it's hard to form unity through sports teams."

Q Not the Focus.

"Sports are not really the focus at GWU and not many attend the basketball games and the team really is not too good. We need to make this more of a focus to increase campus pride."

CAMPUS DINING

Q Only Two Places

"there are only two places on campus, marvin center and ivory tower. Basically, what GW does is contract out spaces to whoever wants to buy them (independent franchises or corporations) and students who go to those places can choose

between the contracted spaces or the food provided by the university."

Q Blah

"J Street closes on weekends, which is really annoying. The food is also unhealthy and overpriced."

CAMPUS HOUSING

Q Dorms

"Very spacious. However quite expensive. Thurston, while the most fun dorm, is a complete s--t hole. I lived there last year and my ceiling fell in... twice."

Q

"Most of the dorms are nice. It depends on what you're looking for in a dorm, because some of the freshman dorms tend to have different personalities. The upperclassman dorms are incredibly nice, like the Dakota and City Hall. They're also building some new ones. I think that GW has the best housing in the United States. Second to academics, housing is the best thing."

GUYS & GIRLS

Q Average

"Everyone here is pretty average... There are very few 'smokin' people..."

Q Guys Are Average

"Guys at GW are often skinny, Jewish, and generally unattractive. Many girls date guys from Georgetown. A lot of the Jewish girls are stuck up."

HEALTH & SAFETY

Q Security

"I live in D.C. there is a ton of security from the secret service to the regular campus police."

Q Safety

"There are a lot of thefts but it seems that the UPD is doing a good job at preventing and recovering the stolen objects."

Georgetown University

37th Street & O Street NW; Washington, DC 20057
(202) 687-0100; www.georgetown.edu

THE BASICS:

Acceptance Rate: 19%
Yield: 45%
Setting: Large city
Control: Private Non-Profit
Total Undergrads: 7,196
SAT Range: 1310–1490*
ACT Range: 26–33

Student-Faculty Ratio: 10:1
Retention Rate: 96%
Graduation Rate: 93%
Tuition: $39,036
Room & Board: $12,506
Avg. Aid Package: $29,000
Students With Aid: 58%

* of 1600

Academics	A	Greek Life	N/A
Athletics	B	Guys	A+
Campus Dining	A	Health & Safety	C
Campus Housing	B+	Local Atmosphere	A
Campus Strictness	B	Nightlife	A-
Computers	C	Off-Campus Dining	A
Diversity	B+	Off-Campus Housing	B-
Drug Safety	D+	Parking	C
Facilities	B+	Transportation	A-
Girls	A	Weather	B

CP's Student Author On...
OVERALL EXPERIENCE

Georgetown is a great university doing its best to become the Stanford of the East Coast—a non-Ivy that still gets the kids who got into Harvard. It has a long way to go. The academics are top-notch, but the school is still in the throes of transitioning from a regional Catholic university to a nationally-known research institution. In many cases, Georgetown's reputation has begun to outstrip its resources; in almost every category except academics, you're going to get better bang for your buck at a state school. Perhaps it seems silly to "discount" academics, but the truth is that they're assigning the same books at Harvard and Yale as they are at Georgetown (and as they are at Ohio State). Whether or not you read them is up to you.

At the end of the day, it's almost impossible to predict whether or not Georgetown is the right school for you. The best you can do is to think about your priorities and decide if they and the school intersect. Whatever you do, do not come to Georgetown simply because you didn't get into Princeton, or Berkeley, or wherever else.... For the rest of this editorial, visit collegeprowler.com.

Students Speak Out On...
OVERALL EXPERIENCE

Q Amazing

"Best, most interesting people. The most unlikely people can surprise you with the most incredible life stories."

Q Unforgettably Amazing

"Going to Georgetown University was one of the best decisions of my life. I have a great group of friends, interesting classes, and a bright future. Living in just outside downtown DC makes this place the perfect area to learn, socialize, and explore. I'm a Hoya for life!"

Q Great

"There are plenty of activities for all types of students here. A lot of campus programs are free or fairly cheap and accommodating for students. Many professors are genuinely out to help you learn and are willing to explain difficult concepts."

BEST OF GEORGETOWN

1. International students and teachers
2. Washington, DC
3. Awesome speakers and presenters on campus
4. Cherry Tree season
5. The Exorcist stairs

Happy Students
96% of students return after their first year.

Commitment to Teaching
There are 10 students for every member of faculty on campus.

WORST OF GEORGETOWN

1. Sporadic weather
2. Meal plans
3. Parking
4. No Metro stop
5. Hoya Football
6. Student Health Center
7. Cost – overall and tuition
8. No wireless in dorms

Expensive
Tuition is a steep $39,036, one of the most expensive rates in the country.

Expensive to Just Get By
62% of students surveyed felt that the amount it costs to live while at school was worse than average.

Student Body

African American:	6%	Male Undergrads:	47%
Asian American:	8%	Female Undergrads:	53%
Hispanic:	5%	Living On Campus:	71%
International:	11%	Living Off Campus:	29%
Native American:	0%	Male Athletes:	16%
White:	55%	Female Athletes:	10%
Unknown:	16%	Fraternity Members:	0%
From Out-of-State:	97%	Sorority Members:	0%

Frequently Compared Schools:

Boston College
Brown University
George Washington University
University of Pennsylvania

Students Speak Out On... EVERYTHING!

ACADEMICS

Academics
"Good liberal arts school. If one has any problems with just about anything, someone is always there to help."

Classes
"Are challenging but doable if you are focused. Every professor pushes you to suceed."

ATHLETICS

WE ARE GEORGETOWN!
"The school spirit surrounding men's basketball is amazing! The other sports teams are not as popular, but many are also very successful. The only downside is that our football team isn't very big and never wins. Intermural and club sports are also very popular!"

Good, Not Great.
"Small school, basketball is HUGE, but others don't have very good resources"

CAMPUS DINING

Not Bad After Hearing Campus Horror Stories
"After always hearing from people (from different colleges) that campus food is not the best, I had pretty low expectations. I was pleasantly surprised by the food at Leo's, the dining hall. There was a ton of variety, and the food was great too!"

Centralized Options but Better Than Average Selection
"Georgetown only has one main dining hall: Leo's. It's not gourmet food, but it's better than most dining halls and there are many foods I enjoy eating there. There are other good eateries around campus, but you cannot use your weekly meal allowance at these."

CAMPUS HOUSING

Leo's Is Great
"Leo O'Donovan Hall ("Leo's") is the main dining hall for students and it is excellent...no kidding. It is routinely ranked very high for vegetarian options, and it caters to palates of all types. No complaints...I have had a meal plan for 4 years and love it."

Dorms
"The best dorms for underclassmen are Village C and New South. The worst would be Darnell. But it is being currently renovated."

GUYS & GIRLS

Prep Central
"Everyone is attractive, but in a homogeneous way. Northfaces, UGGs, and Longchamp bags predominate campus fashion. People are very preppy and have too much similar style choices"

Students
"Here you will find just about everything and anything. Some very preppy, others laid back and chill. It all depends on who you hang out with."

HEALTH & SAFETY

Georgetown Health & Safety
"I am a new student at Georgetown University and I was very apprehensive at first. All of my classes are at night so I had no idea what to expect, especially with being located in Washington, DC. I am proud to say that the campus police officers are around road intersections after classes watching out for the students well-being and safelty."

DOPS Looks After Hoyas
"I would say that Georgetown is a pretty safe place. DOPS (the Department of Public Safety) responds quickly to emergency situations and we have SafeRides which transports us from Georgetown neighborhood to GU. Convenient but not always on time."

Georgia State University

33 Gilmer St.; Atlanta, GA 30303
(404) 413-2000; www.gsu.edu

THE BASICS:

Acceptance Rate: 41%
Yield: 68%
Setting: Large city
Control: Public
Total Undergrads: 21,770
SAT Range: 1450–1740*
ACT Range: 20–24

Student-Faculty Ratio: 19:1
Retention Rate: 83%
Graduation Rate: 44%
Tuition: $25,708
Room & Board: $9,030
Avg. Aid Package: $8,393
Students With Aid: 88%

of 2400

Academics	B-	**Greek Life**	B-
Athletics	C+	**Guys**	A-
Campus Dining	B-	**Health & Safety**	B-
Campus Housing	B+	**Local Atmosphere**	A-
Campus Strictness	C+	**Nightlife**	B+
Computers	B	**Off-Campus Dining**	B
Diversity	A	**Off-Campus Housing**	B-
Drug Safety	B-	**Parking**	C+
Facilities	B	**Transportation**	B
Girls	A	**Weather**	B-

CP's Student Author On...
OVERALL EXPERIENCE

Attending Georgia State is truly a unique college experience, with the University being in the heart of a huge city, amongst not just students and academia, but thriving businesses, corporations, and music and art scenes. Yes, the school has its shortfalls—its reputation academically isn't consistent, and it still struggles with the "back-up school" label—but because of GSU's size and status as one of the few research universities within the state of Georgia, it is constantly being affiliated with other top state schools like the University of Georgia and the Georgia Institute of Technology. The students that complain don't take advantage of the many opportunities that the school provides. Given the metropolitan area, students will most likely be able to find a job or internship applicable to any area of study. Because the campus is in the city, students who choose to go to GSU should be prepared for more than just a few classroom buildings on a green-lawned campus.

Students who get involved with student organizations get to know the University a lot better than those who don't take advantage of such opportunities.... For the rest of this editorial, visit collegeprowler.com.

Students Speak Out On...
OVERALL EXPERIENCE

Q LOVE IT
"I love GSU. The staff, people, and activities are all AWESOME"

Q Living in the Heart of the City
"Georgia State does not resemble the average college campus, which makes it stand out more. A lot of networking takes place in a large city such as Atlanta, and it can be beneficial. Although robberies take place more often, the police force do an outstanding job taking care of the issues. Living in the city has taught me to appreciate the quite suburbs, but Atlanta has taken my heart and there is no other place I'd rather be."

Q Best Time of My Life
"Before I joined the Music School at GSU my life felt pointless. Before GSU I knew no one who shared my passion for music. Life was lived day by day in a dreary...sorrowful state. I would never change my choice. I'm proud to be where I am."

Q Ga State
"Ga state is unique in its diversity and the fact its in the heart of the city."

BEST OF GEORIGA STATE

1. Advantageous and fun location in the heart of Atlanta
2. Diversity of the student body
3. Many programs and majors to choose from

Happy Students
83% of students return after their first year.

Knowledgeable Professors
75% of students surveyed rated the general knowledge of professors as above average.

WORST OF GEORIGA STATE

1. Outsiders committing crimes against students (mostly theft or robbery)
2. The traffic going in and out of the city
3. The lack of school spirit
4. Always having to pay for (expensive) parking
5. Handicap accessibility

Expensive Dorms
Living on campus doesn't come cheap, with an average housing price tag of $6,746.

Student Body

African American:	31%	Male Undergrads:	40%
Asian American:	11%	Female Undergrads:	61%
Hispanic:	5%	Living On Campus:	13%
International:	3%	Living Off Campus:	88%
Native American:	0%	Male Athletes:	2%
White:	33%	Female Athletes:	2%
Unknown:	17%	Fraternity Members:	1%
From Out-of-State:	6%	Sorority Members:	1%

Students Speak Out On... EVERYTHING!

ACADEMICS

Amazing

"The professors understand what they are doing and are helpful, this is why I want to goto this school."

African American Studies

"My major has opened up many doors to me, and has not only given me knowledge but a greater sense of pride. The department takes take to nourish each student in the department with individual treatment and guidance. Many opportunities are available to graduates of the program because of how dedicated the facutly is to furthering students."

ATHLETICS

GA State Football

"2010 Georgia state begins a new years with a new foot ball team."

Football Creates School Pride!

"Georgia State University has created its first football team ever in the school's history. The games have brought the student together and raised morale. Student pride is at a all time high."

CAMPUS DINING

In the Heart of Atlanta

"Georgia State is located downtown Atlanta. The dining options within walking distance of the campus are excellent. From deli to fast food to a hookah/ethnic cafe. There are a host of Greek, Asian and Pizza joints. The school eatery is also good and I spend many lunches dining on campus due to convenience and reasonable prices."

We Breathe, So We Must Eat.

"There are so many different variety's of food in downtown where GA State is. You could never go hungry! Most places have a student discount too, which is nice since we are most always broke. It helps that Atlanta is so diverse there is something for everyone!"

Frequently Compared Schools:

Emory University
Georgia Institute of Technology
Georgia Southern University
University of Georgia

CAMPUS HOUSING

Commons

"Campus housing is great at the Commons...they are apartment like"

To Dorm or Not to Dorm.

"I live off campus because housing is too expensive."

GUYS & GIRLS

Georgia State's Diverse Population

"The student population is extremely diverse in all areas: There is not one typical look at Georgia State, student's express themselves any way they please. So many different languages take place in the classrooms. Sometimes people speak spanish, chinese, japanese, and etc. In addition, people come from all over which different accents and morals. With a few exceptions the students are welcoming, and develop friendly relationships."

Very Diverse Community

"The people at gsu tend to be very nice and diverse. You find many people for all kinds of walks of life here."

HEALTH & SAFETY

Very Safe

"GSU's campus is located all over the city of Atlanta. While some people may feel nervous about that, I feel perfectly safe. There are blue boxes that have a phone to call the campus police if needed. The city police are also a short walk from the campus if you ever need them. Dorm security is fairly tight. You have to access cards to get in through the main gates and into the dorm. There also people who check your ID before you are allowed to enter the individual dorms."

In Geat Hands

"Our campus security is wonderful. We are an open campus but we have our own police force which helps to guarantee or safety. There are thefts around campus but they are rare, and we even have an escourt system in place to help out our crime prevention tactics."

LOOKING FOR MORE?

Check out our full-length guide to this school at collegeprowler.com/georgia-state-university/.

Georgia Tech

225 North Ave.; Atlanta, GA 30332
(404) 894-2000; www.gatech.edu

THE BASICS:

Acceptance Rate: 61%	**Student-Faculty Ratio:** 18:1
Yield: 42%	**Retention Rate:** 93%
Setting: Suburban	**Graduation Rate:** 77%
Control: Public	**Tuition:** $25,716
Total Undergrads: 13,516	**Room & Board:** $8,204
SAT Range: 1840–2100*	**Avg. Aid Package:** $10,475
ACT Range: 27–31	**Students With Aid:** 77%

* of 2400

Academics	B+	Greek Life	B
Athletics	A	Guys	B
Campus Dining	C+	Health & Safety	C
Campus Housing	C	Local Atmosphere	B+
Campus Strictness	B	Nightlife	B+
Computers	A	Off-Campus Dining	B+
Diversity	B	Off-Campus Housing	B-
Drug Safety	C	Parking	C+
Facilities	B	Transportation	A-
Girls	C-	Weather	C+

CP's Student Author On...
OVERALL EXPERIENCE

It is true that many Tech students might sometimes wish that they had chosen another, less demanding school for college. Georgia Tech is very academically demanding, to an extreme that alienates many students and parents. Many see the school as a sort of "proving ground" for professional life.

However, the size of the student body is not overly large, and it is easy for one to get involved socially and academically without straining your GPA. The rigorousness of academic life at Georgia Tech instills a rare motivation in the students there that will prepare them well for professional life. Most students feel that an education at Tech was worth all the work.

Students Speak Out On...
OVERALL EXPERIENCE

Q Diverse and Good Reputation

"GA Tech is extremely diverse allowing people to learn about other cultures. It also has a stellar reputation that has stuck with me since I graduated"

Q I Love Georgia Tech

"It was a close decision for me, and I ended up deciding on Georgia Tech, but I am so glad that I did. I've found three activities to get involved with as well as a research position, and I'm very happy where I am. If I could do it over again, I'd make the same choice."

Q I'm Having a Great Time

"Although I am not the most sociable guy here, I still have fun with all of my friends I've met during orientation and such."

Q Very Good

"I really enjoy Georgia Tech . I love the classes, the people and the layout of the school. The schoolwork is hard and you have to study but it is worth it."

BEST OF GEORGIA TECH

1. Academic reputation
2. State-of-the-art facilities
3. Sunny weather
4. Athletics
5. Greek life
6. Friendly atmosphere
7. Atlanta nightlife
8. Local restaurants

Happy Students
93% of students return after their first year.

Proven Success
77% of students will complete their education and graduate with a degree.

WORST OF GEORGIA TECH

1. Parking
2. Dining hall food
3. Professors are sometimes more interested in their research than teaching
4. Public transportation
5. Theft on campus
6. Hot weather

Overly Demanding Course Load
80% of students surveyed rated the manageability of work as below average.

Cramped Dorms
50% of students surveyed felt that the dorms were less spacious than average.

Student Body

African American:	7%	Male Undergrads:	70%
Asian American:	16%	Female Undergrads:	30%
Hispanic:	5%	Living On Campus:	59%
International:	5%	Living Off Campus:	41%
Native American:	0%	Male Athletes:	4%
White:	64%	Female Athletes:	5%
Unknown:	1%	Fraternity Members:	23%
From Out-of-State:	39%	Sorority Members:	31%

Students Speak Out On...
EVERYTHING!

ACADEMICS

Rigorous but Worth It

"Georgia Tech is one of the best schools in the nation - and works hard to earn it. Its curriculum raises the bar for all students and can leave them stressed, but also prepares them for the work place. All of this hard work does pay off, as graduates are often offered the best starting salaries in the best vocations. In addition, all professors are willing to work with students as well as offer them wonderful research opportunities. Attending Tech has definitely been one of my best decisions."

Advisors Very Helpful; Students Friendly

"I attend the Georgia Institute of Technology, and am enrolled in the Civil Engineering program. So far, my advisors have been extremely helpful in finding classes for me, and they also do a wonderful job of emailing job and internship opportunities to the Civil students. I transferred from another school and the workload is way bigger here, but I definitely enjoy it!"

ATHLETICS

Excellent Atheletics Program

"GIT has exceptional recreational sports facilities. The pools were created for the 1996 Olympics."

Good Competition to Watch

"Sports are very competitive. The sport that interests me the most is tennis and I enjoy going to the matches and cheering on my college. There is always a group of friends to go with to show support."

CAMPUS DINING

Tech Square

"There are a variety of restaurants that you can eat at, such as Waffle House, Moe's, Tin Drum, Ray's Pizza, and 5th Street Ribs & Blues."

Frequently Compared Schools:
Cornell University
Purdue University
University of Georgia
University of Illinois

Pretty Good

"The cafeteria is pretty good food, but after a while it gets old. Luckily there is the student center where there are tons of fast food places to mix it up with."

CAMPUS HOUSING

Social Life on Campus

"The Campus offers many different options for freshmen including Freshmen Experience which has great social get-togethers"

Good Choices

"Dorms are just that, dorms. Nothing special, but usually not terrible. Rooms are an acceptable, if a bit small size. Apartments come pretty equipped and are better. Furniture is not that great. Cost is pretty cheap, and locations are fairly convenient."

GUYS & GIRLS

Very International

"There are lot of students from different countries like India, China, Korea, and others. You can find bona fide geeks, southern boys and city boys, etc. The ratio tells me girls are few but as a girl I don't really feel that way at all."

All Types from Athletes to Nerds

"Every type of student at Tech. Mainly on the smarter side."

HEALTH & SAFETY

Very Safe

"Georgia Tech always sends out email alerts whenever there's been an on or off campus robbery or attack. You still need to be careful walking around at night, but cops usually patrol the area well."

Somewhat Safe

"There are plenty of police driving around campus and they seem to be doing there job. I would like to see more police on campus as I am walking. I don't want to push a warning button that signals the police."

LOOKING FOR MORE?

Check out our full-length guide to this school at collegeprowler.com/georgia-institute-of-technology/.

Gettysburg College

300 N. Washington St.; Gettysburg, PA 17325
(717) 337-6000; www.gettysburg.edu

THE BASICS:

Acceptance Rate: 40%
Yield: 34%
Setting: Town
Control: Private Non-Profit
Total Undergrads: 2,520
SAT Range: 1220–1380*
ACT Range: 27–30

Student-Faculty Ratio: 11:1
Retention Rate: 90%
Graduation Rate: 83%
Tuition: $39,140
Room & Board: $9,360
Avg. Aid Package: $23,388
Students With Aid: 74%

*of 1600

Academics	B	Greek Life	A
Athletics	B-	Guys	B
Campus Dining	B+	Health & Safety	B+
Campus Housing	B	Local Atmosphere	C+
Campus Strictness	B	Nightlife	B-
Computers	B	Off-Campus Dining	B
Diversity	D+	Off-Campus Housing	D
Drug Safety	C+	Parking	B+
Facilities	B+	Transportation	D-
Girls	B	Weather	C+

CP's Student Author On... OVERALL EXPERIENCE

Four years may seem like a long time to spend at one place, particularly a place as geographically and numerically small as Gettysburg College. And while it may at first seem simultaneously overwhelming and underwhelming, Gettysburg has a way of growing on you. The key to getting the most out of Gettysburg is to understand what it is and what it isn't, and to embrace the former and accept the latter. Gettysburg will never be a UNC or Ohio State in terms of diversity, class offerings, or athletics. Then again, you'll never be in a class of 350 people, and you will never feel lost and or ostracized. The faculty is, for the most part, awesome. You have the chance to get to know your professors, as well as your classmates. The academics are challenging and rewarding. The more you put in, the more you get out. The study abroad, career development, and alumni services are incredibly useful, and they make what can normally be complicated and difficult processes exceedingly straightforward.

In the end, the two most important things you will take with you are your degree and your friends.... For the rest of this editorial, visit collegeprowler.com.

Students Speak Out On... OVERALL EXPERIENCE

Q **Kids in the Background Going Craaaaazay**
"Been here one month and its unbelievable. Classes aren't to bad and the workload is sporadic. HANSON 3 BABBAY!! Only freshman dorm with AC and the rooms are huge. Weekends are awesome, as long as you have girls you get into almost any frat"

Q "I personally had a fantastic experience at Gettysburg in every aspect and would do it all again in a heartbeat."

Q "I guess, in general, I like going to GC. Sometimes, it's fun, sometimes it's really hard work, and sometimes I get annoyed at stupid people. But, for the most part, it's been a good experience. I've learned a lot both inside and outside of the classroom. I can't really imagine myself being anywhere else."

Q "I love Gettysburg College. It's the perfect school for me. I've had so many incredible opportunities, met amazing people, and made connections with a number of staff and faculty. I would do it again in a heartbeat."

BEST OF GETTYSBURG

1. Springfest
2. The students - roommates, classmates, neighbors, and co-workers
3. The beautiful campus
4. The faculty
5. The food

Happy Students
90% of students return after their first year.

Proven Success
83% of students will complete their education and graduate with a degree.

WORST OF GETTYSBURG

1. The location of the school - backwater Pennsyltucky
2. Lack of diversity
3. Math/science requirements for humanities majors
4. Humanities requirements for math/science majors

Expensive
Tuition is a steep $39,140, one of the most expensive rates in the country.

Not Much Diversity
One of the least racially diverse campuses—only 16% of students are minorities.

Student Body

African American:	5%	Male Undergrads:	46%
Asian American:	1%	Female Undergrads:	54%
Hispanic:	3%	Living On Campus:	94%
International:	2%	Living Off Campus:	6%
Native American:	0%	Male Athletes:	36%
White:	84%	Female Athletes:	19%
Unknown:	5%	Fraternity Members:	38%
From Out-of-State:	78%	Sorority Members:	26%

Frequently Compared Schools:

Dickinson College
Franklin & Marshall College
Lafayette College
Muhlenberg College

Students Speak Out On... EVERYTHING!

ACADEMICS

The Truth About Gettysburg College Academics

"The academic aspect of Gettysburg College is most certainly an understanding one. The vast majority of teachers give you ample time to finish papers and tests. That is not to say that there are not teachers who do the opposite; there are, but most teachers are helpful. The suggestions that I would give the school is to make the most popular classes offered more, hire more teachers for the theatre department and make sure that students understand about school requirements."

"This school was the best thing that has ever happened to me! While it was stifling at first—and quite a culture shock—I emerged a stronger, more well-rounded person. I feel prepared and enabled to tackle whatever awaits me upon graduation this May because of the past four years spent at Gettysburg College. Also, Greek life takes quite a rap from its detractors but it gives GC a social edge it would otherwise lack."

ATHLETICS

Meh

"Not too many sports teams get much attention from the student body. Yes, many of Gettysburg's students play sports on the College's teams, but games aren't usually attended by a lot of people. I wish there was more support for the sports programs, though. Lacrosse and football are pretty big here."

"Varsity sports are pretty sad. The best sports as far as competition are the club sports. Varsity athletes think they're incredible except they're absolutely horrible. Intramurals are the same as in high school. Fun but nothing exceptional."

CAMPUS DINING

It's Decent

"The food here isn't that bad at all. I went to a boarding school in CT before coming here and I'd say the food is better than it was there. But the food is the only good thing here. :("

Just Ok, Sometimes Better Than

"The menu is ok. There are some ethnic options sometimes, but not too often. The salad menu is always the best in my opinion. I think the menu needs a bit more work."

CAMPUS HOUSING

They Are Okay.

"The dorms are decent. I live in Hanson Hall which is the only dorm with air conditioning, but I live on the all girls floor, which sucks. they call use the "B**ch Ditch". I live in the basement with a lot of freaking dust which sucks, but other than that my living arrangement is fine."

Social Scene

"Very Fraternity oriented campus. If you are not a member of a fraternity it can be boring at times. Virtually all campus parties are located at frat houses."

GUYS & GIRLS

Typical Student

"Dress is typically very "preppy." Most students have come from prep schools and act in a somewhat stereotypical "prep" manner. If you went to a private high school, you will fit right in, but campus isn't all that diverse."

Guys and Girls on Campus

"There is some diversity amongst guys and girls at Gettysburg. With this young generation, you will see enough variety to differentiate who is who and what is what. There are city guys and girls, country guys and girls, rocker chicks and rocker guys, religious guys and girls."

HEALTH & SAFETY

Okay

"not extremely good, not very bad. a lot of assaults happen"

LOOKING FOR MORE?

Check out our full-length guide to this school at collegeprowler.com/gettysburg-college/.

Gonzaga University

502 E. Boone Ave.; Spokane, WA 99258
(509) 328-4220; www.gonzaga.edu

THE BASICS:

Acceptance Rate: 78%
Yield: 28%
Setting: Mid-sized city
Control: Private Non-Profit
Total Undergrads: 4,528
SAT Range: 1090–1280*
ACT Range: 24–29

Student-Faculty Ratio: 10:1
Retention Rate: 92%
Graduation Rate: 81%
Tuition: $29,675
Room & Board: $8,246
Avg. Aid Package: $20,339
Students With Aid: 95%

* of 1600

Academics	B+	Greek Life	N/A
Athletics	A-	Guys	A+
Campus Dining	C+	Health & Safety	B
Campus Housing	A-	Local Atmosphere	B
Campus Strictness	B	Nightlife	A-
Computers	B	Off-Campus Dining	B+
Diversity	C-	Off-Campus Housing	B-
Drug Safety	B	Parking	A
Facilities	B	Transportation	B-
Girls	A	Weather	B

CP's Student Author On...
OVERALL EXPERIENCE

Most students at Gonzaga are very happy to be here. Few would argue that Gonzaga isn't flawed. Common complaints include that it isn't strong enough academically, classes are too big, it's too Catholic or not Catholic enough, and Spokane is a lousy city for a college student. But most students admit their love for it anyway. Perhaps the primary reason for this is the tightness of the Gonzaga community and the relaxed and friendly atmosphere that comes with it. One can cope with shortcomings more easily when living in a comfortable and friendly environment. Students' workload fluctuates wildly depending on field of study, but few are completely overwhelmed or obsessed with studying. Another major draw to many Gonzaga students is the school's study abroad program. Almost a quarter of Gonzaga students study overseas, the majority attending Gonzaga's well-established Florence program.

The biggest challenge facing Gonzaga over the next few years will be the resolution of these various transition-related problems. If Gonzaga truly wants to establish itself as an elite school, growing pains still need to be resolved.... For the rest of this editorial, visit collegeprowler.com.

Students Speak Out On...
OVERALL EXPERIENCE

Q I Love It
"Gonzaga is a great school. It has a wonderful community and great professors."

Q Worth It
"I am glad I chose this school. I definitely feel like I am getting as much out of my education I should. Academics are definitely important, but it is really more the community that makes Gonzaga so great. Students can balance their social life with their studies, for the most part. Also, basketball is a way of life here, and it is a great thing that brings the campus together. Being a small school, you really get individualized attention from your professors."

Q Legit School
"I like Gonzaga. It is a vibrant college where people are very active in the surrounding community and are generally friendly. The environment is semi-conservative, but if you find the right group of friends it's super awesome."

BEST OF GONZAGA

1. Basketball games at the MAC
2. Fall colors
3. The strong sense of community
4. Walking along the river to downtown

Happy Students
92% of students return after their first year.

Commitment to Teaching
There are 10 students for every member of faculty on campus.

WORST OF GONZAGA

1. Bone-numbing wind
2. COG food and meal plan prices
3. Insultingly easy and boring classes
4. The University's frequent misrepresentations and mishandling of its Catholic identity

Expensive
Tuition is a steep $29,675, one of the most expensive rates in the country.

Frequently Compared Schools:

Santa Clara University
Seattle University
University of Oregon
University of Washington

Students Speak Out On... EVERYTHING!

ACADEMICS

All Jesuit, All the Time

"During my year at Gonzaga, I have been challenged academically, spiritually, and emotionally by my professors. They always push me to strive for more than I thought I could do and I have already learned so much about being a citizen of the world from the classes that I have taken in my first year."

Friendliness of Professors

"The professors here are awesome. They are all extremely gifted teachers and are very willing to help at anytime."

ATHLETICS

Athletics

"Athletics are great at Gonzaga. Although we are mostly known for our basketball team, in fact all sports teams are very successful. We also have amazing athletic facilities and fans so its an awesome place to be able to play sports."

Basketball

"Gonzaga is a major basketball school. A majority of students attend games and get dressed in school colors."

CAMPUS DINING

Limited Plans but Descent Food

"The meal plan options are rather limited with only three options as of 2010, but the food they provide is good and usually has a wide selection. The flex is high but so are the prices of the to-go food, so it is easy to spend it quickly. The staff is very friendly and accommodating to vegetarians and vegans who require certain food made separately. I wish there were more staple vegan options as well as more meal plan flexibility."

Not Many Options, but Decent Food

"There is only one cafeteria, but it is buffet style, which is nice. There are several on campus restaurants that take flex as well as a couple places off campus that take flex. Meal plans that offer the most amount of flex are generally the bet, as the cafeteria can get tedious and crowded at times."

CAMPUS HOUSING

Social Life in the Dorms

"Living on campus is fun and a great way to meet new people. Many dorms are close to food services and other popular hangouts which makes things convenient for students."

All Housing Is Pretty Good, Minus CM.

"At Gonzaga the main freshman dorm is Catherine Monica and is quite the hang out for underclassman. However, if you are one that needs quiet, CM is not the place to live. The Kennedy apartments are really new and super nice as well. Coughlin houses freshman and sophomores and is new as well as really clean."

GUYS & GIRLS

Boys and Girls Come from All Over the US

"Boys are from all over. They are generally smart and good looking. Girls are friendly in general and dress well. Good students."

Everyone Is in Shape

"With the cold weather, most people are bundled up, but once the sun comes out it's clear that all the guys and girls on campus work out hard, because everyone is in great shape at Gonzaga, and once the weather is good they aren't afraid to show it."

HEALTH & SAFETY

Gonzaga Safety

"GU does well in informing student about security incidents and does its best to prevent any crime that might go on on campus. Their campus security officers are extremely nice and helpful. I feel safe walking around campus at night."

Do I Feel Safe on Campus?

"I feel extremely safe on Gonzaga's campus. It is very relaxing and quiet. It is always smart to keep your belongings to yourself to avoid petty theft."

LOOKING FOR MORE?

Check out our full-length guide to this school at collegeprowler.com/gonzaga-university/.

Goucher College

1021 Dulaney Valley Road; Baltimore, MD 21204
(410) 337-6000; www.goucher.edu

THE BASICS:

Acceptance Rate: 64%
Yield: 14%
Setting: Small city
Control: Private Non-Profit
Total Undergrads: 1,484
SAT Range: 1550–1930*
ACT Range: 23–27

Student-Faculty Ratio: 9:1
Retention Rate: 75%
Graduation Rate: 64%
Tuition: $33,785
Room & Board: $10,008
Avg. Aid Package: $22,285
Students With Aid: 75%

* of 2400

Academics	B	Greek Life	N/A
Athletics	C-	Guys	C
Campus Dining	B	Health & Safety	B+
Campus Housing	C+	Local Atmosphere	B+
Campus Strictness	B	Nightlife	B+
Computers	B+	Off-Campus Dining	A-
Diversity	D	Off-Campus Housing	D
Drug Safety	B-	Parking	C
Facilities	C+	Transportation	C-
Girls	B-	Weather	B-

CP's Student Author On... OVERALL EXPERIENCE

Goucher provides an atmosphere for students to grow, learn, and expand their views on the world without being restricted or criticized. With an attentive and experienced faculty, freedom to design one's major, endless leadership opportunities, and a stimulating series of lectures, discussions, and performances, the Goucher experience is one-of-a-kind. Goucher is also the first school in the country to require that all students complete a study abroad experience. Despite complaints on parking, public transportation, the social scene, and campus facilities, the majority of Goucher students have great overall experiences. The quality and variety of the academics, study abroad programs, and the close-knit community are among the contributing factors to their experiences.

Students who transferred or wish they did disliked the atmosphere of student apathy toward on-campus events, clubs, and athletics. They felt that Goucher's small community was too small for them and that it didn't provide enough options when it came to both academic and social life.... For the rest of this editorial, visit collegeprowler.com.

Students Speak Out On... OVERALL EXPERIENCE

Q :)
"Goucher university is an amzing place to go to school. with their huge variety of vegetarian food and the really nice people that live and go to school their. the teacher ratio of 1:10. i can think of any where else id rather be."

Q Be Careful
"I would recommend that anyone that is considering Goucher do an overnight visit. You can get a taste for the student life and decide if it is really a good fit for you. It is not a campus that provides everything in a college experience for you, so you have to create it yourself. Looking back, I probably would not have chosen to come here again. It's too isolated and not a very exciting place to be. I am not challenged here at all and everyone seems very much the same."

BEST OF GOUCHER

1. Gorgeous campus
2. You're within walking distance of everything you need
3. Open-minded community
4. Free cable, Internet, and laundry
5. Student performance

Commitment to Teaching
There are 9 students for every member of faculty on campus.

Personal Attention
You can expect personal attention with 75% of classes having less than 20 students.

WORST OF GOUCHER

1. Incestuous hookups
2. Lack of convenient parking
3. Food pricing in Pearlstone
4. Lack of public transportation
5. Unpredictable weather
6. Parking tickets

Expensive
Tuition is a steep $33,785, one of the most expensive rates in the country.

Expensive Dorms
Living on campus doesn't come cheap, with an average housing price tag of $6,156.

Student Body

African American:	6%	Male Undergrads:	32%
Asian American:	3%	Female Undergrads:	68%
Hispanic:	4%	Living On Campus:	86%
International:	2%	Living Off Campus:	16%
Native American:	0%	Male Athletes:	24%
White:	68%	Female Athletes:	14%
Unknown:	17%	Fraternity Members:	0%
From Out-of-State:	76%	Sorority Members:	0%

Students Speak Out On... EVERYTHING!

ACADEMICS

Professor Availability

"Professors here are always available and will work with you to find a way to accomplish your goal."

Elementary Education at CCBC

"It is very nice to be an elementary education major at my school. The professors are extremely helpful and want to help you succeed. The program consists of many classes taken in any order you please which makes it easy to make your schedule fit your life outside of school. Everyone there is also very understanding, in the matter that they understand our lives do not consist of just school. I thoroughly enjoy being an elementary education major at the Community College of Baltimore County."

ATHLETICS

Sports?

"Goucher Athletes stick out like sore thumbs. They tend to stick together and are very cliquey. They think very highly of their sport and they aren't so bad at it. Equestrian is really big on campus, and male Lax is growing. If its your thing, you can totally get involved. Goucher has a number of intermural sports that are really fun if you don't want to play so seriously. Ultimate Frisbee is our biggest club sport."

Bad athletics

"There are not many serious sports here which sucks but intramural sports are fun if you are just looking to make some friends"

CAMPUS DINING

Awesome food!

"The food at Goucher is really good! There is usually something good for everyone on campus. There are healthy options and vegetarian and vegan options. Alice's is new this year and it has improved but they are new so I'm giving them a chance. They are open until 3 am and have such good smoothies and pastries!"

Frequently Compared Schools:

American University
Clark University
Hampshire College
Skidmore College

For a College, the Food Is Great.

"No, Goucher College dining halls are not 5 star restaurants, but the food is much better than most colleges. There are two main dining halls (Stimson & Huebeck), a cafeteria for burgers, fries, and fried chicken (Pearlstone), a coffee kiosk in an academic building (The Van), and Alice's Restaurant, located in the bottom floor of the library and open until 3am."

CAMPUS HOUSING

Stimson

"loud, smelly, mouse/bug-infested, rooms are waaay too crowded, bad lighting, basically feels like a prison."

"There is a huge disparity in dorm quality and no reduction in price. If you're a freshman, chances are that you will be put in Stimson, which is mouse infested and deemed the 'ghetto.'"

GUYS & GIRLS

People

"Some attractive and some unattractive, just like any other school."

Guys Are a Precious Commodity

"Due to the shortage of straight males on Goucher's campus, girls are either quite promiscuous or really clingy. Guys are usually taken by someone or are jerks."

HEALTH & SAFETY

Goucher Is Safe

"I've worked a midnight to 4AM shift on campus and I have never once been afraid of returning to my dorm alone. There are plenty of Public Safety officers, the dorms can only be entered by swiping your student ID and some dorms are closed only to students who live in the building. Goucher is relatively safe and there aren't many incidents"

LOOKING FOR MORE?

Check out our full-length guide to this school at collegeprowler.com/goucher-college/.

Grambling State University

403 Main St.; Grambling, LA 71245
(318) 247-3811; www.gram.edu

THE BASICS:

Acceptance Rate: 33%	Student-Faculty Ratio: 19:1
Yield: 64%	Retention Rate: 56%
Setting: Small city	Graduation Rate: 36%
Control: Public	Tuition: $9,902
Total Undergrads: 4,538	Room & Board: $7,168
SAT Range: 1170–1410*	Avg. Aid Package: $6,800
ACT Range: 16–19	Students With Aid: 96%

of 2400

This School Isn't Graded Yet!

College Prowler grades are calculated using tons of criteria, including survey responses that come from students at this school.

Unfortunately, we haven't gathered enough student surveys yet for this school to be able to calculate the grades for each section. Stay tuned to *CollegeProwler.com* for grade updates and more!

CP's Student Author On...
OVERALL EXPERIENCE

Grambling State University is an accredited HBCU that is full of opportunities—you just have to be ready take advantage of them. The University has a good academic reputation and an influx of companies—including IBM, Tyson, and Wal-Mart—come to recruit students annually. These companies offer internships, as well as full-time positions to students who fit their requirements. The social life at Grambling State is satisfactory. There are several party venues, and Plush is 5 minutes from campus. Other than that, the Yard is always a fun place to be between classes. You'll regularly see the fraternities and sororities hanging out on the Yard and there will sometimes even be a stroll off. There are dorm parties every weekend, as well as off-campus parties. However, sometimes you'll need to drive a bit, so a car is a necessity.

Some people say Grambling State is horrible because of its location, but if you know the right people who can tell you where all the fun is and if you have a form of transportation, you'll be fine. The overall experience is good and acceptable for a university of its size. There are wonderful experiences just waiting for you to explore them.

Students Speak Out On...
OVERALL EXPERIENCE

Q Why Gram Is Great
"I think Grambling is great. My major is Criminal Justice, one of the largest major on campus, and we have good programs of opportunity for Criminal Justice majors"

Q My Time Here
"Grambling is an okay school but it is not the best. However, the cost and the benefits of being a student is wonderful. There are very rewarding activities to take part in."

Q Lack of Respect
"The faculty and staff could be more respectful toward students and more prompt at getting business handled in a professional way."

BEST OF GRAMBLING STATE

1. Traditions, like spring festivals and homecoming
2. The overall atmosphere on campus is soothing and calming.
3. Campus parties
4. Football
5. The athletic facilities

Affordable
Tuition is only $9,902, one of the most affordable rates in the country.

Big Dorms
50% of students surveyed felt that dorms were more spacious than average.

WORST OF GRAMBLING STATE

1. The food in the cafeteria
2. Campus life can be monotonous.
3. Lack of healthy food options
4. Classroom buildings
5. Some dorms need to be renovated.

Not Everyone Graduates
36% of students do not complete their education or graduate with a degree.

Not Much Diversity
One of the least racially diverse campuses—only 12% of students are minorities.

Student Body

African American:	88%	Male Undergrads:	40%
Asian American:	0%	Female Undergrads:	60%
Hispanic:	0%	Living On Campus:	53%
International:	9%	Living Off Campus:	47%
Native American:	0%	Male Athletes:	8%
White:	2%	Female Athletes:	4%
Unknown:	0%	Fraternity Members:	6%
From Out-of-State:	53%	Sorority Members:	6%

Frequently Compared Schools:

California University of Pennsylvania
Florida A&M University
Jackson State University
Missouri State University

Students Speak Out On... EVERYTHING!

ACADEMICS

GOOD OVERALL

"The academics offered at the school are very diverse and prepares an individual for the outside world. Professors are very knowledgeable and competent. The registration process could be a little easier at times, but it is generally swift. Popular study areas include the library and JTS building."

Loyal to History and Traditional Aspects

"I attend Grambling State University for nursing. When I first came to GSU, I did not know much about the history of the school. Thank god for the FYE (First Year Experience) classes that helped and progressed my knowledge of the school, helped me to understand the aspects of GSU, and keep traditional purposes sacred."

It's Alright, I Can Say.

"It's great and I am loving it."

ATHLETICS

GSU I Thought You Knew

"There is a lot of school spirit, not only from students and faculty but also from neighboring areas. Football games are the biggest sporting events of the fall semester. If you don't go to at least one football game at Grambling, you're missing the whole Grambling "Experience.""

Grambling Pride

"School spirit at Grambling State is always prevalent, even when the teams' performances aren't their best. Sporting events are always a big deal on campus because the area surrounding the university isn't very interesting. The largest events are always the football games. People come from all around to see the world-famed Grambling Tiger marching band and football team."

CAMPUS DINING

The Menus

"It's sometimes good but the quality of chicken is not very good. I recommended African-type chicken be prepared—it's more tasty than the American chicken. The juice also need to be changed—the same kind of juice every day makes it bore."

Wide Diversity Needed

"The University needs to offer healthier foods to students."

CAMPUS HOUSING

The Housing Is Good Enough

"The housing can be considered good! There are facilities available to the students to make them feel like they are at a home away from home."

I Prefer Upperclassman Dorms Over Freshman Dorms

"The freshman dorms at Grambling State University are fine, but the upperclassman dorms are the way to go. As an upperclassman, I wouldn't want to stay in freshman dorms."

GUYS & GIRLS

Relaxed Setting

"Most of the guys at Grambling are mostly Southern guys who don't really care about how they look. Some of them have manners, but others are unbelievably rude. The girls all look same, following whatever trend is in the media."

Needs Improvement

"At Grambling, there are a lot of girls who let loose and a lot of boys who take advantage of that, so be aware of those people. But, there are boys on campus who are respectable, well-dressed, and upperclassmen. And if a girl is pretty at Grambling, she is rare and steals all the boys."

HEALTH & SAFETY

Awesome Safety

"The safety and security on campus is very good. They're quick and very responsive. For instance, when a student was hurt or sick they had an ambulance on the scene within minutes."

Personal Safety

"There is police present all the time, so I feel safe."

LOOKING FOR MORE?

Check out our full-length guide to this school at collegeprowler.com/grambling-state-university/.

Grand Valley State University

1 Campus Drive; Allendale, MI 49401
(616) 331-2020; www.gvsu.edu

THE BASICS:

Acceptance Rate: 81%	**Student-Faculty Ratio:** 17:1
Yield: 35%	**Retention Rate:** 83%
Setting: Suburban	**Graduation Rate:** 56%
Control: Public	**Tuition:** $13,402
Total Undergrads: 20,850	**Room & Board:** $7,478
SAT Range: 1480–1840*	**Avg. Aid Package:** $8,760
ACT Range: 22–26	**Students With Aid:** 95%

* of 2400

Academics	B-	**Greek Life**	B+
Athletics	B-	**Guys**	B+
Campus Dining	B+	**Health & Safety**	B-
Campus Housing	A-	**Local Atmosphere**	B
Campus Strictness	B-	**Nightlife**	B
Computers	A-	**Off-Campus Dining**	C+
Diversity	C+	**Off-Campus Housing**	A-
Drug Safety	B-	**Parking**	B
Facilities	A	**Transportation**	A-
Girls	B	**Weather**	C-

CP's Student Author On...
OVERALL EXPERIENCE

There are very few students who do not adore Grand Valley. Many appreciate the country setting and closeness to a big city. The diversity and range of activities and organizations here ensures that everyone finds their niche, although for some students it takes a year, while others put in little effort and find their place. This is similar to the academic experience of many students: Some find passing classes to be no problem, while others have to study often. The professors and staff are excellent at helping students who need additional academic assistance and seek it out. Everyone is different at Grand Valley, a fact that is embraced and understood by all students and faculty.

In general, students agree that Grand Valley is an experience they would never trade. Organizations offer a social life, networking opportunities, and depending on the organization, academic help. It is important that students take an occasional break from the stress that inevitably comes with homework and deadlines. Club meetings, eating out, or seeing a movie with friends is a great way to take a short break from school.... For the rest of this editorial, visit collegeprowler.com.

Students Speak Out On...
OVERALL EXPERIENCE

Q Everyone is Friendly!

"I really like it here because the people are friendly. Also, there are always random events going on. There are also many things to get involved in. The people who don't like it here are the people who don't get involved."

Q Green School

"GVSU was selected as a "Green College" by the Princeton Review. There is a campus-wide appreciation for environmental awareness, and the small campus and nightly events make getting to know people very easy."

Q Very Nice School

"The campus is beautiful and everything is new. The teachers and advisers here actually seem to want to help you and don't treat you like just another number. The athletics here are all very good. I'm playing for the roller hockey team, and it's a good time. Most of the places to live are well-kept; I haven't seen any terrible places yet. I feel very safe on and off campus. So far, I'm very happy here."

BEST OF GRAND VALLEY STATE

1. Small feel although the student body is relatively large
2. A very large and diverse selection of student organizations
3. Friendly students, professors, and faculty

Happy Students
83% of students return after their first year.

Knowledgeable Professors
93% of students surveyed rated the general knowledge of professors as above average.

WORST OF GRAND VALLEY STATE

1. Parking, especially for commuters
2. Themes (general education requirement)
3. Frigid winter wind
4. Some of the housing is outdated.
5. Limited number of on-campus jobs

Not Much Diversity
One of the least racially diverse campuses—only 14% of students are minorities.

Student Body

African American:	5%	Male Undergrads:	41%
Asian American:	3%	Female Undergrads:	59%
Hispanic:	3%	Living On Campus:	25%
International:	1%	Living Off Campus:	75%
Native American:	1%	Male Athletes:	6%
White:	86%	Female Athletes:	3%
Unknown:	2%	Fraternity Members:	—
From Out-of-State:	5%	Sorority Members:	—

Students Speak Out On... EVERYTHING!

ACADEMICS

Q TOP OF THE LINE

"The professors and their curriculums at GVSU are second to none; I learn something new every lecture, and the professors are readily available and more than willing to talk if I have a question about something. As far as the strength of the academics, courses are definitely challenging, but with hard work, they can be conquered."

Q Excellence in Management

"I feel the Management College at GVSU is excellent."

ATHLETICS

Q Athletics

"I don't really know much except we're a really good Division II school."

Q Excellent

"GVSU is one of the top performing schools in Division II across the board. All the sports perform well and student involvement and support is incomparable. The athletic facilities are top notch."

CAMPUS DINING

Q YUM

"Food on campus is great! Plenty of places to go with plenty of options. You usually don't have to pay a thing either with a meal plan. They are very useful to have."

Q A Lot of Options

"There are quite a few different options for grabbing something to eat on campus. I live off campus and never invested in a meal plan, but I have heard most students are fairly happy with the food on campus."

CAMPUS HOUSING

Q So Nice

"Campus housing is great, probably some of the nicest dorms around."

Frequently Compared Schools:

Central Michigan University
Michigan State University
University of Michigan
Western Michigan University

Q Dorm Life

"Living in Grand Valley Dorms is a great overall experience. If you get traditional style, expect older and smaller, but very manageable, rooms. You will become very close to your floormates as long as you open up. There are tons of great people here as gvsu is a very friendly college and has an inviting atmosphere to it."

GUYS & GIRLS

Q GVSU STUDENTS

"The students who attend Grand Valley State University, whether they are male or female, are great people. They are classy and intelligent and determined about their future. They are all also very friendly and helpful and mindful of others. It is a wonderful place to attend school because the social and educational environment is so great to be around."

Q Friendly

"The students at Grand Valley are generally very friendly, and also dress very well. They wear fashionable clothes, and as per usual for a group of roughly 20 year olds, most are pretty attractive."

HEALTH & SAFETY

Q Very Safe

"I have never felt unsafe on GVSU's Allendale campus, no matter the time of day. Campus police are visible and present throughout the day, and crime is typically limited to petty theft, though they're more crimes of opportunity than viciousness. Grand Rapids campus has more crime, and students should walk in groups at night due to the higher crime rate of the city and the homeless people who hang around the garbage bins behind the dorms."

Q Definitely Safe

"I feel very safe on campus. There is always security around and available to call. It is also nice that Grand Valley is a dry campus because the use of alcohol is constantly being looked for, which will prevent accidents from happening."

LOOKING FOR MORE?

Check out our full-length guide to this school at collegeprowler.com/grand-valley-state-university/.

Grinnell College

1121 Park St.; Grinnell, IA 50112
(641) 269-4000; www.grinnell.edu

THE BASICS:

Acceptance Rate: 34%
Yield: 34%
Setting: Town
Control: Private Non-Profit
Total Undergrads: 1,688
SAT Range: 1220–1460*
ACT Range: 28–32

Student-Faculty Ratio: 9:1
Retention Rate: 95%
Graduation Rate: 85%
Tuition: $36,476
Room & Board: $8,536
Avg. Aid Package: $30,751
Students With Aid: 91%

* of 1600

Academics	A-	Greek Life	N/A
Athletics	C+	Guys	C+
Campus Dining	B	Health & Safety	A-
Campus Housing	B+	Local Atmosphere	C
Campus Strictness	A	Nightlife	C+
Computers	B+	Off-Campus Dining	C+
Diversity	B	Off-Campus Housing	C+
Drug Safety	C	Parking	A-
Facilities	B+	Transportation	D-
Girls	C+	Weather	C+

CP's Student Author On...
OVERALL EXPERIENCE

A vast majority of Grinnell students love it. Students who choose to come here love the challenge they get from academia and their peers, and they love the amount of freedom that the administration gives them (mostly through self-governance). Grinnell students are free to learn and grow into responsible, conscientious adults, and the students here are thankful that the school they've chosen has given them the opportunity to thrive. Some students can't even imagine what it would be like if they'd ended up somewhere else.

Yeah, Grinnell students complain sometimes about the things that aren't available to them that would be at their disposal at a larger, city school. We gripe about excess construction, bogus administration policies, and the things that fellow Grinnellians do that just plain bug everyone. Overall, though, most of the students here are happy with the decisions they've made and the direction they're going in their lives, and a lot of them have the Grinnell faculty, students, and townspeople to thank for that.... For the rest of this editorial, visit collegeprowler.com.

Students Speak Out On...
OVERALL EXPERIENCE

Q **Grinnell Offers a Lot in a Small Bubble!**
"I've had great classes, great interactions with all sorts of peers, great friends. Grinnell's great financial aid brought me here but I would stay anyway. The attitude here is unique, visit to see for yourself."

Q **Liberal**
"The Iowan winters really do affect the atmosphere of the college. It gets unbearably cold--coming from someone who lived in the tropics. The seasonal affectedness disorder is prevalent. However, the community becomes closer because of the doldrums you face. Grinnell has a great social atmosphere, almost everyone is respectful, curious, and kind."

Q "My experience has been great! You'd be hard-pressed to find a school where more freedom is granted than Grinnell. The college really makes you feel alive!"

Q "Grinnell has its perks and jerks, but I wouldn't change schools for the world. I'm getting a great education, and I'm constantly meeting people who teach me about the world. My peers are the men and women who really are going to make a difference someday."

BEST OF GRINNELL

1. Amazing and caring professors
2. Titular head
3. Phynd
4. Waltz
5. Block Party
6. Sexual promiscuity
7. Bob's Underground Café

Happy Students
95% of students return after their first year.

Commitment to Teaching
There are 9 students for every member of faculty on campus.

WORST OF GRINNELL

1. Poor dining hall food
2. Rude high school townies
3. Long, cold winters
4. Walking to class in the middle of winter
5. Social claustrophobia
6. Immature drunks on weekends

Expensive
Tuition is a steep $36,476, one of the most expensive rates in the country.

Student Body

African American:	5%	Male Undergrads:	47%
Asian American:	7%	Female Undergrads:	53%
Hispanic:	6%	Living On Campus:	87%
International:	11%	Living Off Campus:	13%
Native American:	0%	Male Athletes:	46%
White:	62%	Female Athletes:	29%
Unknown:	8%	Fraternity Members:	0%
From Out-of-State:	89%	Sorority Members:	0%

Frequently Compared Schools:

Carleton College
Kenyon College
Macalester College
Oberlin College

Students Speak Out On... EVERYTHING!

ACADEMICS

Independent Research Projects

"In the summer between my junior and senior years at Grinnell, I developed and carried out an independent research project with the help of one of my professors. It was a great opportunity to get to know a professor well, and really experience what research is like. Additionally, because I completed my MAP (Mentored Advanced Project) over the summer, Grinnell provided me with a stipend that covered my living expenses, because I was too busy to have a job."

"Most of the professors I've had truly invested themselves in the students and the material. They also had high expectations for their students."

ATHLETICS

Meh

"Grinnell doesn't offer any athletic scholarships. Most people I knew took pride in how bad the football team was."

Team Performance

"The teams other than cross country are not very good, Football, basketball, and baseball are not very good and those are the three main sports that most people pay attention to."

CAMPUS DINING

Great Dining Hall That Really Reaches Out to Students

"One (very) central dining hall makes it a melting pot for all of campus. Workable hours plus Outtakes lets you use dining plan to its fullest. Variety is always offered in great salad bar, vegan bar, soups, pizza, cereal, and changing menus of special sections."

One of the Best

"Our Dinning Hall has been recognized as one of the best campus dinning halls. They have a rotation so that every month there isn't a repetition of dinner foods and so forth. They do a great job at incorporating new foods in the menu and decorate/make new food during events such as the Chinese New Year."

CAMPUS HOUSING

Students Respect Sub-Free Housing

"One aspect I always appreciated about Grinnell was that even though it was a very wet campus, people generally respected "sub-free" housing, which, like every other residential aspect about Grinnell, was completely self-governed."

"The dorms are quite good. There really are no dorms to avoid."

GUYS & GIRLS

Lots of Support

"Everyone is pretty open to everyone around them. There is a lot of campus community especially when biased motivated incidents occur. There are a lot of hipsters on campus and athletes, but there is also the average looking person. Dress is mostly jeans and a buttoned shirt. Social life is very accepting, there are always parties during the weekend, concerts, and great bonding activities. Relationships seem to be very serious."

Social Life

"There are parties every Friday and Saturday night and since Grinnell is a wet campus, underage drinking isn't really enforced. There aren't too many other things to do on those nights that I've found other than go out and drink."

HEALTH & SAFETY

I Mean, It's Iowa

"I feel incredibly safe on campus. Security isn't a huge presence in my day to day life (which is good since it makes me uneasy when cop-type figures are around), but I know they're there. Plus, it's Iowa dude. Very occasionally, someone's laptop or something will be stole, but this is pretty rare. Most people I know don't lock their doors."

LOOKING FOR MORE?

Check out our full-length guide to this school at collegeprowler.com/grinnell-college/.

Grove City College

100 Campus Drive; Grove City, PA 16127
(724) 458-2000; www.gcc.edu

THE BASICS:

Acceptance Rate: 64%
Yield: 56%
Setting: Town
Control: Private Non-Profit
Total Undergrads: 2,530
SAT Range: 1131–1367*
ACT Range: 25–30

Student-Faculty Ratio: 16:1
Retention Rate: 93%
Graduation Rate: 84%
Tuition: $12,590
Room & Board: $6,824
Avg. Aid Package: $6,345
Students With Aid: 68%

* of 2400

Academics	B+	Greek Life	C
Athletics	C+	Guys	B
Campus Dining	C	Health & Safety	A+
Campus Housing	B-	Local Atmosphere	C
Campus Strictness	D-	Nightlife	D+
Computers	B-	Off-Campus Dining	C+
Diversity	D-	Off-Campus Housing	N/A
Drug Safety	A	Parking	B
Facilities	B-	Transportation	D+
Girls	C+	Weather	C

CP's Student Author On...
OVERALL EXPERIENCE

Freshmen might be a little skeptical about the "Grove City family" lingo that they hear during orientation and opening convocation. However, by graduation, many undergrads admit that Grove City College is a second family. Like almost any real family, Grove City College has its unpopular rules, its rebels, its squabbles, and its quirks. But also like a real family, there's a bond—despite the blemishes. Not everyone is in love with their college family, but Grovers have no excuse to feel like just one of the crowd.

Some students complain their way through four years of killer academics, narrow-mindedness, and local boredom, but by the time most of them actually finish, they have enjoyed Grove City College, despite their gripes. In contrast, many students rave about the school right from the start. They thrive on the academic challenges, accept Christian values, and change the local atmosphere with their passionate desire to serve God and others. The popularity of activities like Orientation Board, Homecoming Committee, and tour guiding are sure signs that students love their school.... For the rest of this editorial, visit collegeprowler.com.

Students Speak Out On...
OVERALL EXPERIENCE

Q Love the People
"It's definitely not for everyone..However, if you are the 'right' type, you will love it in this college."

Q What Could Be Better
"This is a place with great balance of studying and social life."

Q "After thinking long and hard, I am glad I stayed at Grove City. It has provided a little net for me. It held me accountable, so I didn't get in to too much trouble, but I was also able to grow up a bit while at college. The academics are incredible and I love the challenging scene."

Q "My experience so far has been that it is a very narrow-minded demanding school. But I love the friends I have made and the experiences I have gained. Honestly, for as much as people complain about the school and all the hard work that is expected of us, I think I'm happy I chose Grove City College. I have asked my friends who are about to graduate if they could do it again, would they? And they all surprisingly said yes. You meet a lot of nice people at GCC."

BEST OF GROVE CITY

1. Low tuition costs
2. Impromptu praise and worship time with friends
3. Ice cream at Geedunk
4. Ultimate Frisbee in the rain and mud
5. The President's open office hours

Affordable
Tuition is only $12,590, one of the most affordable rates in the country.

Happy Students
93% of students return after their first year.

WORST OF GROVE CITY

1. Lack of diversity
2. 21-meal plan only
3. FitWell
4. Rumors about dating after one date
5. $125 for a parking permit
6. Temperamental computer systems

Not Much Diversity
One of the least racially diverse campuses—only 6% of students are minorities.

Student Body

African American:	1%	Male Undergrads:	50%
Asian American:	2%	Female Undergrads:	50%
Hispanic:	1%	Living On Campus:	93%
International:	1%	Living Off Campus:	7%
Native American:	0%	Male Athletes:	23%
White:	94%	Female Athletes:	14%
Unknown:	1%	Fraternity Members:	15%
From Out-of-State:	53%	Sorority Members:	19%

Frequently Compared Schools:

Geneva College
Penn State
University of Pittsburgh
Wheaton College - Illinois

Students Speak Out On... EVERYTHING!

ACADEMICS

Q Mathematics With a Certification in Secondary Education

"I love my major, but it is definitely one of the most demanding behind the engineering programs. The professors are extremely helpful and willing to stay after hours to help on concepts. However, the classes are very difficult and there have been many, many late nights studying in order to be able to pass a test. I think the education I am getting and the efforts I'm making to succeed will pay off well in the end."

Q Competitive Yet Engaging

"Every student is motivated to do well, and this is reflected in the classroom environment, where it is relatively difficult if not impossible in many cases to excel. However, the academics at GCC promote growth and a greater understanding and love for the course work."

ATHLETICS

Q Everything but Football?

"All the sports (either IM, Club, or Varsity)are pretty well organized and rank off pretty well.The only sport that does not necessarily meet this evaluation is probably football."

Q IM Sports Are Great

"Some people are really into athletics, while others don't really pay attention. I fall into the latter category. Our football team isn't great, but our lacrosse team is really good. Intramural sports are a big deal. There are tons of them and they're really fun."

CAMPUS DINING

Q Some of the Best College Food!

"Grove City's dining options are better than most college's I have experienced. The dining halls are nice, and they always have a good amount of food options. For students who are more health oriented, the dining halls always have a large salad bar with a variety of items. Soup, pizza and sandwiches are always available. There are also some nice restaraunts nearby in case you want a break from cafeteria food."

Q GCC Food

"its okay. Not the greatest not the worst. Space is tight though. I would appreciate a bigger dining hall. the SAC is open though and is an okay alternative"

CAMPUS HOUSING

Q Overall Pretty Nice, a Short Walk to Classes.

"The freshman girls just got brand new dorms this summer, which are efficient, stylish and great. The upperclassmen female dorms are well furnished, and comfy.The dorms are all (except the Apartments)a 5-8 minute walk from the class buildings. That's especially wonderful on rainy/snowy days."

Q "All of the guys dorms are generally the same. It is what you make of the situation; who you live around is more important than freshly-painted walls."

GUYS & GIRLS

Q Get Married Before You Graduate.

"Most students in the college share similar world-views due to its unity in Christianity.Most students are also very fit due to variety of different IM sports available throughout the seasons."

Q Social Life

"The social life of students is conservative but fun"

HEALTH & SAFETY

Q Personal Safety

"Grove City College's campus safety is really good at making rounds often enough through out the day and they take their job very seriously. I have never felt unsafe on campus and the campus is well lit at night."

Q Safe and Boring

"Yes this school is pretty safe. There have been some armed robberies at local convenience stores, but the school is very safe. Campus security has a very overbearing yet useless presence."

LOOKING FOR MORE?

Check out our full-length guide to this school at collegeprowler.com/grove-city-college/.

Guilford College

5800 W. Friendly Ave.; Greensboro, NC 27410
(336) 316-2000; www.guilford.edu

THE BASICS:

Acceptance Rate: 62%
Yield: 19%
Setting: Large city
Control: Private Non-Profit
Total Undergrads: 2,846
SAT Range: 1360–1780*
ACT Range: 20–26

Student-Faculty Ratio: 15:1
Retention Rate: 80%
Graduation Rate: 58%
Tuition: $27,850
Room & Board: $7,560
Avg. Aid Package: $20,232
Students With Aid: 98%

of 2400

Academics	B-	Greek Life	N/A
Athletics	C-	Guys	B-
Campus Dining	C-	Health & Safety	B+
Campus Housing	B-	Local Atmosphere	B
Campus Strictness	C+	Nightlife	B
Computers	B	Off-Campus Dining	A-
Diversity	B-	Off-Campus Housing	C
Drug Safety	C	Parking	B+
Facilities	B	Transportation	B
Girls	B+	Weather	B+

CP's Student Author On...
OVERALL EXPERIENCE

Guilford is a wonderful place to be if you are looking for a small liberal arts college experience. Guilford does not attract the types of people who go to standard, huge state schools with flourishing Greek scenes and near-professional football programs. In many different respects, students adore their school, the atmosphere, and their peers. Guilford allows (and expects) you to be independent academically, but you must be willing to work to get the most out of your education here. Although it is a good bit harder to "slip through the cracks" at Guilford, it is certainly possible to fail out. The majority of students feel sufficiently and appropriately challenged academically, although some say it all really depends on your department. Others don't bother to do the work, or take the easiest classes possible and end up taking extra years to graduate, then complain about it all the while. Those who are happy tend to make the most out of their time on campus. Get involved in the Guilford community, have fun, and try to do most of your work.

Guilford students are good at voicing their opinions.... For the rest of this editorial, visit collegeprowler.com.

Students Speak Out On...
OVERALL EXPERIENCE

Q **Been Pretty Good**
"Experience has been good, but not great. There are many cliques and it gives a feeling of exclusivity. Once people have a group of friends, they don't feel the need to interact outside of that group. Academics has been good. The professors are nice, but don't always know as much as they claim. The campus itself is beautiful. Trees and greenery everywhere."

Q "Guilford has its problems; some of them need serious attention. But it's still a great school with great faculty. I couldn't imagine spending my four years anywhere else."

Q "I love the campus, the teachers, and the students. Guilford is a really unique place, and I can't imagine being happier at another college."

Q "I sometimes wish that the school administration would get its act together, since they seem very confused about the school's identity. However, there are really awesome teachers and classes here, and it's not hard to get in. We're lucky."

Q "I used to love it, but now I just want to be left alone by the administration."

BEST OF GUILFORD

1. Professors
2. The beautiful campus and grounds
3. Small classes
4. Friendly, interesting people
5. All four seasons
6. Clubs and organizations

Happy Students
80% of students return after their first year.

Personal Attention
You can expect personal attention with 61% of classes having less than 20 students.

WORST OF GUILFORD

1. Meal plan food
2. Construction noise and inconvenience
3. Campus Life's mothering complex
4. Lack of convenient public transportation
5. Party ban

Expensive
Tuition is a steep $27,850, one of the most expensive rates in the country.

Student Body

African American:	24%	Male Undergrads:	40%
Asian American:	2%	Female Undergrads:	60%
Hispanic:	3%	Living On Campus:	41%
International:	1%	Living Off Campus:	20%
Native American:	1%	Male Athletes:	30%
White:	64%	Female Athletes:	10%
Unknown:	5%	Fraternity Members:	0%
From Out-of-State:	63%	Sorority Members:	0%

Frequently Compared Schools:

Earlham College
Elon University
Oberlin College
Wake Forest University

Students Speak Out On... EVERYTHING!

ACADEMICS

Q Registration Process

"Registering for classes can be overwhelming when attending a new school. Guilford College had easy to follow instructions that were not only helpful but made registration fast and rewarding."

Q First Year Intended Health Sciences/ Relgious Studies Major

"Freshman year experience/ orientation feels like a waste of time, but other than that I find the overall population to be extremely friendly and classes to be okay. The sense of "community" that is often mentioned seems to be lacking a bit and students don't seem to whole-heartedly get into activities on campus. The Health Sciences coordinator is extremely helpful and very easy to communicate with. She makes sure everyone in the major know about every oppertunity in the community."

ATHLETICS

Q The Quakers

"they do well above what one would expect from a division III school."

Q "Some believe Guilford is divided between athletes and non-athletes more than between races. So sports have a presence on campus, but it is not as big as it is in state schools, by any means."

CAMPUS DINING

Q Meal Plan Options

"There is usually something edible. Lots of fresh fruit in the dining hall, but meat dished could use improvement. Also, dining hours are inconvenient and too early in the day. Grille food is too greasy and does not encourage healthy eating. Luckily, the smoothie stand is quite good and the pastries are delicious."

Q Two Campus Dining Options

"the caf - which is only good on wednesday's (when they encourage professors to go) and the grill - which has super slow service and extremely greasy food. But they do have all the vegan and organic you could want, if your into that sort of thing"

CAMPUS HOUSING

Q Milner Living

"milner is one of the two freshman dorms and it's great. everything is kept clean (as clean as possible for college) and most people keep their doors propped open when they're in so there's lots of opportunity to meet new people and socialize."

Q "I would recommend staying out of Bryan; it's a nice place to visit, but a hard to place to live."

GUYS & GIRLS

Q Guilford Kids

"The guys at guilford are generally laid back hippies or hipsters but there is a huge range we really have all types of men here, most are pretty mature but also love to have a good time. The girls are pretty much the same."

Q Guilford Family.

"Almost everyone in Guilford is friends with one another, they are all accepting of who and what you are. Also. there are no pressures on students to look or dress a particular way, for all we care you could show up in rags, we would still accept you. all in all, there is always a helping hand when it is needed."

HEALTH & SAFETY

Q Hippies Feel Safe Enough to Leave Their Doors Unlocked

"The hippies leave their doors unlocked but I guess that's because the normal kids worry about the "hips" so I guess the hippies have nothing to worry about. But yes the hippies here will steal your stuff"

LOOKING FOR MORE?

Check out our full-length guide to this school at collegeprowler.com/guilford-college/.

Gustavus Adolphus College

800 W. College Ave.; Saint Peter, MN 56082
(507) 933-8000; www.gustavus.edu

THE BASICS:

Acceptance Rate: 74%
Yield: 29%
Setting: Town
Control: Private Non-Profit
Total Undergrads: 2,478
SAT Range: 1145–1370*
ACT Range: 24–29

Student-Faculty Ratio: 11:1
Retention Rate: 91%
Graduation Rate: 83%
Tuition: $31,760
Room & Board: $7,900
Avg. Aid Package: $23,652
Students With Aid: 95%

of 1600

Academics	B-	Greek Life	B-
Athletics	B	Guys	B+
Campus Dining	A-	Health & Safety	B
Campus Housing	C+	Local Atmosphere	C
Campus Strictness	B-	Nightlife	C+
Computers	B	Off-Campus Dining	C-
Diversity	D-	Off-Campus Housing	C
Drug Safety	C+	Parking	B+
Facilities	A-	Transportation	D+
Girls	A-	Weather	D

CP's Student Author On...
OVERALL EXPERIENCE

Regardless of the times of frustration, stress, and anger, students always seem to firmly believe that Gustavus was the right choice for them, and they live and breathe the school and the campus traditions. As the often-repeated saying goes, you will become a Gustie for life. Students who enter Gustavus know many of the "downfalls" before they enroll: the small-town atmosphere, limited majors, and the social politics that will be involved by attending a college the size of many high schools. However, the benefits of the small school experience that come with Gustavus are experienced right away: small class sizes, personal attention from professors, and the ability to meet and befriend a number of fellow students. Students who stick through the four years at Gustavus come away with a changed outlook on themselves, life, and the world around them.

While Gustavus may lack many of the things that come with attending large schools, there are plenty of opportunities to make the four years something to treasure: activities are plentiful, the curriculum challenging, and the chance for self-exploration abounds.... For the rest of this editorial, visit collegeprowler.com.

Students Speak Out On...
OVERALL EXPERIENCE

Q **Everyone is so nice**
"Love the school, every one is so nice and friendly. It is a small campus, but that is what makes it so great."

Q "I loved Gustavus—everything about it—even the bad stuff like the wind, the funky smells from the farms, and parking tickets. It was fantastic, and I would do it again in a heartbeat if someone would let me."

Q "I am very satisfied with my college experience and would pick Gustavus again if I had the choice. On our campus, there is a strong sense of pride and community among the students. I was challenged in the classroom, and I had a lot of freedom to turn my education into what I wanted it to be. I was not only able to build lasting friendships with my peers but also with my professors and other staff I worked with throughout my four years. It really was the best four years of my life!"

Q "I absolutely loved Gustavus, and if I had to do it over again, I would have been a Gustie. I made lifelong friendships with the faculty, professors, and with students. Even though all of my friends do not live in Minnesota, I know we will be friends for life!"

BEST OF GUSTAVUS

1. Close-knit community
2. Annual Nobel Conference
3. High standards of excellence
4. Brand new workout facilities in Lund
5. The Caf food

Happy Students
91% of students return after their first year.

Proven Success
83% of students will complete their education and graduate with a degree.

WORST OF GUSTAVUS

1. Do something stupid on Friday night? The kid you've never talked to in French class will undoubedly know by Monday morning.
2. Living in a rural community

Expensive
Tuition is a steep $31,760, one of the most expensive rates in the country.

Not Much Diversity
One of the least racially diverse campuses—only 11% of students are minorities.

Student Body

African American:	2%	Male Undergrads:	43%
Asian American:	5%	Female Undergrads:	57%
Hispanic:	2%	Living On Campus:	81%
International:	1%	Living Off Campus:	19%
Native American:	0%	Male Athletes:	45%
White:	89%	Female Athletes:	24%
Unknown:	1%	Fraternity Members:	11%
From Out-of-State:	18%	Sorority Members:	12%

Frequently Compared Schools:
Luther College
Macalester College
St. Olaf College
University of Minnesota

Students Speak Out On...
EVERYTHING!

ACADEMICS

Gustavus Profs

"The professors are very accessible, and are always willing to help and write references. They really try to get to know you."

Psychology Major

"I haven't taken that many psychology classes at Gustavus yet because I am just starting my second year of college. The class that I have taken there was interesting. The professor was very flexible about retaking things that I missed because of sports."

"I love the professors at Gustavus. This is a staff that is truly passionate about their jobs. They go out of their way to help you because they genuinely want you to succeed."

ATHLETICS

Gustavus Sports

"The fans in the Gustavus community are amazing. They are so supportive of all the sports. One thing that I believe Gustavus does very well is strive to have good sports teams while encouraging and making sure us student athletes know academics come first."

Good Support for a DIII School

"We have some kick ass teams and some not so good teams. Tennis is big as is hockey. Fan support for the major sports like football, basketball, and hockey is high and even cross country and gymnastics have fans. The facilities are pretty new and I haven't heard any complaints. There are a lot of coaches for teams, and teams recieve good support from the school."

CAMPUS DINING

Convenient

"I don't think one appreciates the Caf until you leave and are on your own for meals. I don't know of another college cafeteria that will make omelets or steak to order. It's only once a week, but pretty amazing. You don't have to eat at traditional meal times and can always grab something "to-go." The fresh fruit has been a welcome addition."

"The cafeteria doesn't have enough overall variety to keep the kids shoving in with the same enthusiasm they had moving from disgusting high school cafeterias to eating in the big world."

CAMPUS HOUSING

"Dorms are crappy, but where are they nice? They can be fun no matter where you are. I would say avoid Complex in general, because it smells really bad, but I never lived there, so I don't really know."

"All of them have their bad points. Going into GAC, at first I loved Norelius (a.k.a. Coed) because it was always happening, and there were always people around to hang out with or study with."

GUYS & GIRLS

Guys and Girls

"There is all kinds of people at Gustavus. There are some boys and girls who are nice to talk to AND look at, and there are those who are good to do one of the two things with. But people here like to interact with each other and are pretty friendly all the time."

Typical Midwestern Variety

"We're pretty normal at GAC. Students don't spend a whole lot of time on their appearance and everyone's pretty relaxed. That's not to say there are not hot people, girls and boys alike. There are unique dressers and quirky personalities that shine through in their clothing choices."

HEALTH & SAFETY

Extremely Safe

"The Campus Safety officers are very willing to work with students and maintain a friendly relationship with them through communication. They are concerned with the safety of students, which includes the risks of drinking."

"For the most part, I felt safe, but not always; it seems like S&S takes its job too leniently."

LOOKING FOR MORE?
Check out our full-length guide to this school at collegeprowler.com/gustavus-adolphus-college/.

Hamilton College

198 College Hill Road; Clinton, NY 13323
(800) 843-2655; www.hamilton.edu

THE BASICS:

Acceptance Rate: 29%
Yield: 33%
Setting: Suburban
Control: Private Non-Profit
Total Undergrads: 1,882
SAT Range: 1950–2190*
ACT Range: 29–32

Student-Faculty Ratio: 9:1
Retention Rate: 95%
Graduation Rate: 91%
Tuition: $40,870
Room & Board: $10,890
Avg. Aid Package: $27,347
Students With Aid: 50%

* of 2400

Academics	A	Greek Life	B-
Athletics	B-	Guys	A
Campus Dining	A	Health & Safety	A
Campus Housing	B	Local Atmosphere	B-
Campus Strictness	A-	Nightlife	B+
Computers	B+	Off-Campus Dining	B-
Diversity	B-	Off-Campus Housing	C+
Drug Safety	C-	Parking	A-
Facilities	A+	Transportation	C+
Girls	A	Weather	C+

CP's Student Author On...
OVERALL EXPERIENCE

As long as you don't ask a Hamilton student about how much they love their school in the dead of winter, you are likely to receive an overwhelmingly positive response. Complaining about the school can sometimes appear to be the new cool thing to do and becomes increasingly more popular as the days grow darker, and homework and snow seem to endlessly pile up. But, if you listen to what students say, it's more than likely you will find a strong undertone of affection for life at Hamilton College. This school offers its students an incredible opportunity to take advantage of an intellectual faculty and student body through small classrooms, supportive computer networks, and fairly magnificent campus facilities. While attending school, Hamilton students can sleep like royalty—as long as their lottery number is decent enough to score a nice dorm room—eat great food both on and off campus, and have snowball fights for more than half the year. Yet, in order to take advantage of their four years at Hamilton, they must be able to make the best of what can often be a trying and narrow life outside of academics.... For the rest of this editorial, visit collegeprowler.com.

Students Speak Out On...
OVERALL EXPERIENCE

Q THE BEST
"Students love Hamilton. Professors love Hamilton. The administration loves Hamilton. Alumni love Hamilton. People are happy here. Students graduate with wonderful friends, passions, and the ability to communicate effectively."

Q Love this place
"Couldn't imagine spending four years anywhere else"

Q LOVE IT
"Hamilton in general is full of smart, athletic, involved students who are very successful yet don't take themselves too seriously. They have a great balance of work and play and are generally really down to earth and fun-loving. Generally a great community with amazing academics but also great people."

Q "When I first got here, I hated the place, but over the past year, I have come to love it. Hamilton is beautiful, the classes are challenging, and there are a lot of cool people here."

BEST OF HAMILTON

1. The first warm day of spring
2. Community feel of the school
3. Inspirational professors
4. Students who get creative to make their own fun
5. Class and Charter Day/Senior Week

Happy Students
95% of students return after their first year.

Commitment to Teaching
There are 9 students for every member of faculty on campus.

WORST OF HAMILTON

1. The weather
2. Stereotypical fraternity brothers
3. Vast nothingness of Central New York
4. Party monotony
5. The Commons catwalk
6. Spontaneous fire alarms

Expensive
Tuition is a steep $40,870, one of the most expensive rates in the country.

Student Body

African American:	4%	Male Undergrads:	47%
Asian American:	7%	Female Undergrads:	53%
Hispanic:	5%	Living On Campus:	98%
International:	5%	Living Off Campus:	2%
Native American:	1%	Male Athletes:	42%
White:	70%	Female Athletes:	31%
Unknown:	9%	Fraternity Members:	34%
From Out-of-State:	70%	Sorority Members:	18%

Frequently Compared Schools:

Bowdoin College
Colby College
Colgate University
Middlebury College

Students Speak Out On...
EVERYTHING!

ACADEMICS

Work Hard, Play Hard.

"Students at Hamilton are hard-working, motivated, and focused during the week, but also enjoy kicking back and relaxing during the weekend. The professors at Hamilton are exceptional and always willing to go the extra mile. Classes are engaging and exciting!"

Sharp

"Challenging courses and the professors are very available. Most classes are small and discussion based."

ATHLETICS

Go Blue!

"As a student athlete I cannot say enough great things about the athletics at Hamilton. My teammates are some of my closest friends and everyone come out t cheer for games. Athletic events are a huge part of the social scene at hamilton."

GREAT!!

"There are tons of ways to get involved in athletics at Hamilton. In generally the student body is very active and students take part in all sorts of activities ranging from very competitive varsity to sports, to more relaxed club sports, to goofing around on the rock-climbing wall."

CAMPUS DINING

Yum

"The best part is the diner that is open till 5am on weekends, 12am during the weeks. Red booths, a jukebox, and delicious diner foods. There are lots of options at the 2 dining halls. The cafes on campus have great baked goods and coffee, as well as lunch. The pub on campus is a nice alternative for lunch. For the number of students, there are lots of places to eat."

Unique Hamilton

"One claim to fame is our varsity streaking team. They are always a good source of laughter during stressful finals (or accepted students day), if you don't mind seeing a little more of your friends than you'd expected."

CAMPUS HOUSING

Beautiful Dorms

"27 different residence halls. Many living options and fantastic facilities."

Campus Housing

"I love the housing on campus. There are 28 residence halls, which gives Hamilton students a great variety of living spaces. You can live with up to 5 roommates in suite-style housing, or with as few as zero roommates in one of the easily-acquired singles. I have been completely satisfied with my housing options, living in two of the older and wonderfully renovated residence halls."

GUYS & GIRLS

Unique

"I don't think there is a way to characterize Hamilton students. I think that in general the student body is active, easy-going, motivated, and enthusiastic."

Work Hard, Play Hard.

"There is really no way to describe a "typically" Hamilton student because there is no such thing; however, I do believe that most Hamilton students share a generally mentality. We like to let lose and have fun on the weekends, but are very focused and motivated during the week."

HEALTH & SAFETY

Friendliest People

"Hamilton students are incredibly friendly, passionate, active, and supportive. When you walk across campus, students smile and stop to chat. They love to talk about Hamilton and how happy they are to be at such a wonderful school."

Completely Safe

"There is practically no crime on campus. I feel comfortable leaving my computer unguarded in the library because I know that in such a small, tight knit community people would notice if someone tried to steal a computer."

LOOKING FOR MORE?

Check out our full-length guide to this school at collegeprowler.com/hamilton-college/.

Hampshire College

893 West St.; Amherst, MA 01002
(413) 549-4600; www.hampshire.edu

THE BASICS:

Acceptance Rate: 63%
Yield: 24%
Setting: Town
Control: Private Non-Profit
Total Undergrads: 1,435
SAT Range: 1720–2070*
ACT Range: 25–29

Student-Faculty Ratio: 12:1
Retention Rate: 87%
Graduation Rate: 67%
Tuition: $39,912
Room & Board: $10,433
Avg. Aid Package: $32,910
Students With Aid: 86%

* of 2400

Academics	B	Greek Life	N/A
Athletics	F	Guys	B-
Campus Dining	B-	Health & Safety	B+
Campus Housing	B+	Local Atmosphere	C+
Campus Strictness	A-	Nightlife	C+
Computers	B-	Off-Campus Dining	B
Diversity	C	Off-Campus Housing	D+
Drug Safety	C	Parking	A-
Facilities	C+	Transportation	C+
Girls	B-	Weather	C+

CP's Student Author On...
OVERALL EXPERIENCE

It's true, Hampshire students have no shortage of complaints about the place, but the harshest critics are also likely to be the most vocal advocates of the College. There are few, if any, places quite like Hampshire, and the love-hate relationship many have with the College is based on the passion with which they view alternative, experimental education. Criticize they may, but most students would be quick to defend the College if someone dismissed it. Hampshire students don't have a reputation as talkers for no reason.

This is a place where you get your hands dirty, whether that is out on the farm testing sustainable farming practices, out in the field researching or developing new technology, or embroiled in a campus debate over the College's policies. To mirror the idealism that runs through this campus, Hampshire is place where people learn to make a difference in their immediate surroundings and the broader world. This is not a place for everyone, but it is home to serious academics turned off by the ivory tower's strict disciplinary boundaries.... For the rest of this editorial, visit collegeprowler.com.

Students Speak Out On...
OVERALL EXPERIENCE

Q "I'm grateful for the place and the friends I've made, and I already miss the school, but I would have gone somewhere else if I could do it over again."

Q "There are a lot of things I could complain about, and believe me, I love to complain, but this is a great school and I love it here. I can't wait to go back for classes. Sometimes I wonder whether I'd try to lengthen my college experience to eight years. The best part of Hampshire is definitely the people. Where else would I find so many mad geniuses?"

Q "I think knowing what I know now about the school's lack of money, I might have considered going elsewhere. But I adore my teachers, and I love how flexible I can be with my studies. Hampshire is so unique in giving me the place to forge my own intellectual destiny. I can't see that happening anywhere else, but this place is far from perfect and has a lot of trouble addressing its weaker aspects."

BEST OF HAMPSHIRE

1. Academic freedom
2. Accessible, helpful professors
3. Creative and intelligent students
4. Five College Consortium
5. No tests, no grades

Happy Students
87% of students return after their first year.

Personal Attention
You can expect personal attention with 66% of classes having less than 20 students.

WORST OF HAMPSHIRE

1. Difficulty in enrolling in high-demand classes
2. Disorganization of faculty, staff, and students
3. Financial aid problems

Expensive
Tuition is a steep $39,912, one of the most expensive rates in the country.

AP Credit Wasted
Any AP credits earned in high school aren't eligible for college credit.

Student Body

African American:	4%	Male Undergrads:	42%
Asian American:	3%	Female Undergrads:	58%
Hispanic:	7%	Living On Campus:	90%
International:	5%	Living Off Campus:	10%
Native American:	1%	Male Athletes:	0%
White:	73%	Female Athletes:	0%
Unknown:	7%	Fraternity Members:	0%
From Out-of-State:	82%	Sorority Members:	0%

Students Speak Out On... EVERYTHING!

ACADEMICS

ℚ Chinese

"I have been satisfied with my major so far. I am being taught Chinese by a native speaker, which is a lot easier than being taught by a non native speaker. Not only am I learning the Chinese language, but also the Chinese culture."

ℚ Hampshire Requires So Many Small Details It Can Make Graduation Difficult to Attain

"With the Division process comes a lot of checkpoints which at first sound amazing but when you are in the trenches and need guidance from professors it can be difficult to peg anyone down. It could be a great school if students and professors alike had good work ethic, but if you actually want to achieve and are a motivated student- this is virtually impossible."

ℚ "For the most part, Hampshire professors are spectacular. Sure, there will be the occasional flaky hippie who is incapable of evaluating a single paper, but most professors are willing to lavish a great deal of personal attention on students."

ATHLETICS

ℚ We Have Frisbee.

"Hampshire is not known for it's athletics. Though we only have one organized sport, frisbee, we have a great outdoor recreation program called OPRA. Through this program students can ice climb, mountain bike, take trips to high ropes courses or even go kayaking in the caribbean."

ℚ "There are few sports teams, and they all pretty much suck. But anyone can join, and they have a lot of fun, so I dont' think anyone really cares."

CAMPUS DINING

ℚ Saga, or: Canadian Prison Food Isn't Too Bad

"Yeah, I honestly haven't a problem with Saga or The Bridge. I make it a point not to eat there often. Most students make that point. =)Sodexo is, factually, a Canadian prison caterer... perhaps in being sympathetic to the plight of Canadian prisoners, we live relatively. xD. I dunno. Besides being cooked with laxatives, the food is genuinely sufferable."

ℚ "The main dining hall, Saga, is okay. Most people complain about it, but it's institutional food. You can't expect much."

CAMPUS HOUSING

ℚ "Enfield has a very suburban feel. The buildings look like townhouses."

ℚ "I would advise first-years to live in the dorms as opposed to mods. Being a first-year in a mod isn't easy."

GUYS & GIRLS

ℚ Everyone Is Different...

"I find everyone to be very passionate about what they are involved in or just at Hampshire for the party scene. The guys are very scruffy (not in a bad way) and down-to-earth for the most part. They can also be very into their looks if they fit into the hipster category (i.e. hilarious shoes and glasses, tight pants). The girls have similar styles, just in a feminine way. Social life is mostly centered on-campus."

ℚ "With the possible exception of Smith College, no educational institution is quite as uniquely disgusting as Hampshire. That aside, there is no dating scene at this college. There are drunken hookups, and that is the extent of our romantic intrigues."

HEALTH & SAFETY

ℚ I Feel Completely Safe on Hampshire Campus.

"Hampshire has trained public safety and highly qualified Emergency Medical Technicians (EMTs) always on call. The students are all here for the same reasons, to learn and to enjoy the experience of college. There are rarely ever fights or thefts on campus and if there is, it is usually people that do not attend Hampshire. I have never felt scared or unsafe on Hampshire's campus."

ℚ "I've never felt unsafe on campus, but more call-boxes to Public Safety wouldn't hurt."

LOOKING FOR MORE?

Check out our full-length guide to this school at collegeprowler.com/hampshire-college/.

Hampton University

100 E. Queen St.; Hampton, VA 23668
(757) 727-5000; www.hamptonu.edu

THE BASICS:

Acceptance Rate: Open
Yield: 34%
Setting: Mid-sized city
Control: Private Non-Profit
Total Undergrads: 4,430
SAT Range: 937–1182*
ACT Range: 17–26

Student-Faculty Ratio: 13:1
Retention Rate: 77%
Graduation Rate: 51%
Tuition: $17,212
Room & Board: $7,664
Avg. Aid Package: $2,893
Students With Aid: 64%

of 1600

Academics	C+	Greek Life	C+
Athletics	C	Guys	A-
Campus Dining	D+	Health & Safety	C-
Campus Housing	D+	Local Atmosphere	C+
Campus Strictness	D+	Nightlife	B-
Computers	C	Off-Campus Dining	C-
Diversity	C-	Off-Campus Housing	B
Drug Safety	C	Parking	C-
Facilities	D+	Transportation	D+
Girls	B+	Weather	B-

CP's Student Author On...
OVERALL EXPERIENCE

Hampton University requires an acquired patience and has issues you would probably not endure at another university. The financial aid mix-ups, runaround, and the registrar's office's inability to provide answers can make any Hamptonian want to pack their bags and transfer elsewhere. The crazy weather, poor transportation and parking, and the never-ending hunt for something to do at night, while frustrating, can also lead to some interesting memories and experiences. It can even make for a good story or two. On the other hand, the educational experience students receive is one of the best in the HBCU system, full of inspirational teachers and awesome classes. The friends you make and relationships you build at Hampton make any student or alumni proud to live out a Hampton University experience. Many meet their lifetime mates either while attending Hampton, or by meeting a Hampton alumni later in life at a job or other event. Hampton students and alumni are everywhere and can tell you about the good times and bad times they spent at the University.

The HU experience is definitely one-of-a-kind.... For the rest of this editorial, visit collegeprowler.com.

Students Speak Out On...
OVERALL EXPERIENCE

Hampton's "The Standard of Excellence"

"There is no gray area at Hampton. You either love or hate it. I fell in love with Hampton first sight of it. We have a beautiful campus, wonderful traditions, a diverse student body to be an HBCU and excellent people. I wouldn't change anything about my decision. Coming from a large city it takes a minute to get familiar with the surroundings but it was manageable. I love my school!"

H.U. Campus

"The campus of Hampton University is very beautiful, and fulfilling to the eyes. It is wonderful to walk around, and the distance from place to place is not very far."

I Love Hampton

"I love that fact that i attend hampton. I have a great social life, i love the people, the academics is great, and the teachers can relate to the students!"

BEST OF HAMPTON

1. Professors know your name.
2. You make lifetime friends.
3. School name is very popular among the business world.
4. Excellent chances of employment

Knowledgeable Professors
86% of students surveyed rated the general knowledge of professors as above average.

Low-Stress Course Load
67% of students surveyed rated the manageability of work as above average.

WORST OF HAMPTON

1. Dorm living
2. Food
3. Ratio of males to females
4. Credibility of particular programs is dropping
5. Facilities are not up-to-par
6. Parking and transportation

Students Can't Wait to Get Out of Town
63% of students surveyed said that there's no way they would live here after graduation.

Student Body

African American:	96%	Male Undergrads:	37%
Asian American:	1%	Female Undergrads:	63%
Hispanic:	1%	Living On Campus:	59%
International:	0%	Living Off Campus:	41%
Native American:	0%	Male Athletes:	11%
White:	2%	Female Athletes:	4%
Unknown:	0%	Fraternity Members:	5%
From Out-of-State:	78%	Sorority Members:	4%

Students Speak Out On... EVERYTHING!

ACADEMICS

Professional Atmosphere

"Hampton University has a very professional atmosphere. The professors stress the importance of appropriate dress, work habits and speaking as if you were out in the real world. They are focus, expect respect and provide encouragement to all students."

The Best

"The academic program at hampton university is great. The staff is always available to answer any questions and to assist stdents when possible. the staff is friendly and warm."

ATHLETICS

Football

"We are the Pirates. Footbal season on campus is awesome. The band, cheerleaders and the dance team really show their support for the team. The people on campus and surrounding neighbors show their excitement during and after the games."

Winners

"The athletic department is the best and the staff members are friendly people. The faciities are not up to date but the athletes make the best of it and they are winners."

CAMPUS DINING

The Simple Campus Dining

"The food is not that good especially Friday through Sunday. Holiday dinners are the best especially Thanksgiving. People wait on line an hour before the cafeteria opens just to eat. Sunday brunch is always good and every Wednesday is fried chicken Wednesday."

OK Dining Halls, Great Menus, Good Flex Dollars.

"Unfortunately at Hampton we only have two Dining Halls and they close at 7:00pm. It would be really helpful if they stayed open later to at least 9:00pm due to some peoples class schedules. However the Menus of the Dining Hall on most days are Delicious! Also if I don't want cafe food I can always go to the Student Center to purchase something to eat using my 'Pirate Card' or "Flex Dollars"."

Frequently Compared Schools:

Howard University
Old Dominion University
Spelman College
Virginia Commonwealth University

CAMPUS HOUSING

I Enjoyed My Time

"I enjoyed my time living on campus at Hampton University. It allowed me to experience the ups and downs of being a college freshman."

Campus Is Cool

"Campus is cool. Visitation is necessary."

GUYS & GIRLS

Many Diverse People

"Although its an HBCU, the campus is very diverse. There are people from all over they world, from many different backgrounds/cultures, most of whom happen to share a similar skin tone."

Fashion Show

"Although there are more girls than guys that attend Hampton it is still diverse. Mostly African American students attend Hampton because it is a top HBCU. We do have other ethnicities that also attend. This is a "fashion show" school. You will always see girls in heels walking to class and showing off their personal styles. Hampton students have required to have atleast one business suit."

HEALTH & SAFETY

It Is Safe

"it is a very safe campus and surrounding area in southern virginia. Noting to worry about"

Very Safe.

"There are police everywhere around Hampton University. That definitely ensures students that they're safe."

LOOKING FOR MORE?

Check out our full-length guide to this school at collegeprowler.com/hampton-university/.

Hanover College

359 LaGrange Road; Hanover, IN 47243
(812) 866-7000; www.hanover.edu

THE BASICS:

Acceptance Rate: 61%
Yield: 16%
Setting: Town
Control: Private Non-Profit
Total Undergrads: 938
SAT Range: 1460–1790*
ACT Range: 22–28

Student-Faculty Ratio: 10:1
Retention Rate: 80%
Graduation Rate: 59%
Tuition: $26,350
Room & Board: $7,900
Avg. Aid Package: $20,509
Students With Aid: 73%

* of 2400

Academics	B	Greek Life	A-
Athletics	C	Guys	B+
Campus Dining	C	Health & Safety	C
Campus Housing	B-	Local Atmosphere	C-
Campus Strictness	B-	Nightlife	B-
Computers	C+	Off-Campus Dining	C
Diversity	C	Off-Campus Housing	D+
Drug Safety	C	Parking	A
Facilities	B+	Transportation	C
Girls	B	Weather	B

CP's Student Author On...
OVERALL EXPERIENCE

Hanover is the perfect fit for students who push themselves academically, treasure close friendships, and wish to be a part of a college community where everyone actually stays on campus. If you are looking for a difficult academic school that is revered in the region and is among the top schools in the United States, Hanover is for you. There are many ways to be involved here, and the more involved you are, the more you will enjoy your time, follow your interests, and make great friends. The relationships gained with faculty, administrators, and alumni will last as long as you keep the ties going. There are faculty members at this school who are hidden treasures and have much wisdom to offer students who make the extra effort. While there is some disconnect between what students want and what the administration does, everyone at Hanover works together to make it the best college experience possible. When talking to Hanover alumni, you get a sense that the College changed and shaped them into better people during their time here.... For the rest of this editorial, visit collegeprowler.com.

Students Speak Out On...
OVERALL EXPERIENCE

Q Pick It Again

"I'm in my senior year at Hanover, and every experience I've had so far I would gladly do again. I feel prepared for my future and through my time here I've met amazing people who I'm sure I'll be in contact with for many years in the future."

Q HC Experience

"Hanover has offered me a lot of great opportunities. One of the things I would say they are best at is making studying abroad easy and fun to do. I definitely love all the traveling opportunities I was given."

Q Hard to Explain

"I would choose to come here again. It's hard to describe, but the people here are amazing and the professors are very personable. It's a great small school feel."

BEST OF HANOVER

1. Greek life
2. The friends you'll make
3. The classes and class sizes
4. Hinkle's
5. The Point
6. Frat theme parties
7. The small size, which forces you to get involved

Happy Students
80% of students return after their first year.

Commitment to Teaching
There are 10 students for every member of faculty on campus.

WORST OF HANOVER

1. It's in the middle of nowhere
2. It's cold in the winter
3. There's no city life
4. Most people know one another
5. Minimal course offerings

Expensive
Tuition is a steep $26,350, one of the most expensive rates in the country.

Not Much Diversity
One of the least racially diverse campuses—only 14% of students are minorities.

Student Body

African American:	1%	Male Undergrads:	45%
Asian American:	2%	Female Undergrads:	55%
Hispanic:	1%	Living On Campus:	93%
International:	3%	Living Off Campus:	7%
Native American:	1%	Male Athletes:	55%
White:	86%	Female Athletes:	25%
Unknown:	5%	Fraternity Members:	32%
From Out-of-State:	33%	Sorority Members:	39%

Students Speak Out On... EVERYTHING!

ACADEMICS

Q Professors Truly Care

"Most of the professors at Hanover College want to see their students succeed. They are always willing o meet to discuss things and will say hello to you when you are walking around. They seek to develop friendships with their students and will help you out whenever they can."

Q Advantage of Small

"There are only about 30 majors but most of them are challenging and backed by good professors. You can learn a lot in classes because they are usually only around 10-20 students and you can get extra help if needed. You can also get to know your professors for this same reason."

ATHLETICS

Q Fun

"Hanover may not be on the same level as Division I schools, but I love that the people I watch play are my friends and classmates. I run cross country and I love my teammates and coach. We push hard but also have fun. A lot of teams at Hanover are in the top three in the conference and both the basketball and golf teams are ranked nationally."

Q Top Athletic Facilities

"Hanover College has versatile athletic facilities. The Horner Center has many pieces of workout equipment available for everybody. It also has open courts, rooms, and tracks available to play sports if someone does not want to simply lift weights or run on a treadmill."

CAMPUS DINING

Q Improving Machine!

"I am so happy to finally be eating out of my Greek house because now I can be a vegetarian again. There are tons of options for me at the campus center, and I am happy for that. Also, it seems to improve each time I go there. I am glad that there is such a receptive staff there."

Frequently Compared Schools:

Centre College
Indiana University
Kenyon College
Miami University

Q Pretty Good Variety on Campus

"The main dining hall has a variety of different kinds of food everyday, including a themed cuisine that changes everyday, soup and salad bar. There is another location that specialized in take out items, and an on-campus location that serves alcohol and bar/grill food."

CAMPUS HOUSING

Q Dorms

"Hanover makes living on campus pretty enjoyable. The only thing that could improve with upperclassman dorms is to have more activities for the halls like they did freshman year."

Q Some Good, Some Bad

"Of the housing on campus, those that have just been redone are in great conditions, but some, such as Katherine Parker, badly need redone."

GUYS & GIRLS

Q Social Life at Hanover College

"The size of the campus allows the students to get to know their classmates really well which helps build lasting friendships."

Q Friendly Crowd

"In my experience at Hanover, everyone is very friendly and helpful. Students would help me find my classes or take me there themselves."

HEALTH & SAFETY

Q Safest Community This Side of the Ohio River

"The are always security vehicles driving about campus and there are emergency phones around the outskirts of campus. There is rarely any crime on campus and there is never a need to take special security measures in order to feel safe. In the dorms, we are all like a family and I could leave my door wide open and nothing would be disturbed."

LOOKING FOR MORE?

Check out our full-length guide to this school at collegeprowler.com/hanover-college/.

Harvard University

12 Holyoke St.; Cambridge, MA 02138
(617) 495-1000; www.harvard.edu

THE BASICS:

Acceptance Rate: 7%	**Student-Faculty Ratio:** 7:1
Yield: 80%	**Retention Rate:** 98%
Setting: Mid-sized city	**Graduation Rate:** 98%
Control: Private Non-Profit	**Tuition:** $37,012
Total Undergrads: 10,200	**Room & Board:** $11,856
SAT Range: 2070–2350*	**Avg. Aid Package:** $32,850
ACT Range: 31–34	**Students With Aid:** 81%

* of 2400

Academics	A	Greek Life	D
Athletics	B+	Guys	B
Campus Dining	B+	Health & Safety	C+
Campus Housing	A+	Local Atmosphere	A+
Campus Strictness	A-	Nightlife	B+
Computers	A-	Off-Campus Dining	A
Diversity	A	Off-Campus Housing	D-
Drug Safety	B+	Parking	C
Facilities	A-	Transportation	A
Girls	B-	Weather	C-

CP's Student Author On...
OVERALL EXPERIENCE

Challenging, rigorous, and positive all describe students' overall experience at Harvard. The academic challenge initially seems daunting to many students, but the intellectual growth facilitated by this academic powerhouse leaves students pleasantly surprised. The social life of most Harvard students acts as a counterbalance to the intellectual challenge, and not surprisingly, students forge lifetime memories and friends throughout their four years at Harvard.

The Harvard experience leaves most students yearning for more. The University provides undergraduates with a rich history, unparalleled cultural diversity, and intellectual rigor that challenge each student to fulfill every ounce of their potential. Students leave the College satisfied, prepared, and as a stronger, more aware global citizen than when they entered.

Students Speak Out On...
OVERALL EXPERIENCE

Q I Love It

"I joined an a-capella group with some of the nicest people I know in it. We have a blast touring together. My roomates and I get along fine. I love the area. My classes are very interesting, as are the guest speakers who come to campus."

Q Wouldn't Choose Differently

"I had chosen Harvard over UC Berkeley and it was one of the best decisions I've made. It definitely is a different experience having to fly across the country to go to school. Many of my friends at Berkeley go home often."

Q So Eclectic

"this is a great place for people who have far ranging interests. yet its possible to find people just as committed to some oddball thing just as you are. just sometimes, there doesnt seem to be enough of them."

Q "I don't wish I were anywhere else. Even though there's a fair share of dorks, I love the place."

BEST OF HARVARD

1. Access to the best professors and minds of our time.
2. The student motivation and ambition on campus is contagious.
3. The opportunity to pursue literally any interest you might have.

Happy Students
98% of students return after their first year.

Commitment to Teaching
There are 7 students for every member of faculty on campus.

WORST OF HARVARD

1. People often focus too much on future careers and making money, and sometimes lose track of enjoying the present.

Expensive
Tuition is a steep $37,012, one of the most expensive rates in the country.

Expensive Dorms
Living on campus doesn't come cheap, with an average housing price tag of $7,248.

Student Body

African American:	7%	Male Undergrads:	47%
Asian American:	14%	Female Undergrads:	53%
Hispanic:	6%	Living On Campus:	98%
International:	13%	Living Off Campus:	2%
Native American:	1%	Male Athletes:	19%
White:	47%	Female Athletes:	14%
Unknown:	12%	Fraternity Members:	1%
From Out-of-State:	86%	Sorority Members:	1%

Frequently Compared Schools:

Brown University
Princeton University
University of Pennsylvania
Yale University

Students Speak Out On...
EVERYTHING!

ACADEMICS

It's Alright.

"Heavy workload. Decent faculty interaction. Great facilities and work opportunities. The student center does not exist though."

It's What You Expect

"I'm a science concentrator and pre-med, so my workload is pretty heavy. But I expected that because I go to Harvard. However, it's not difficult to find classes that are easy and interesting. Students have access to their professors (who teach the classes by the way) and TFs. All teaching staff provide students with support and help when asked for."

"The professors I've had have almost all been really great. I've had one professor, so far, who I found not so great, but the others have been amazing . . . some of the best lecturers I've ever heard."

ATHLETICS

Athletics at Harvard

"There are many kinds of sport facilities at Harvard, at campus there are sport courts and students can use them every day. I think it is a great oppurtunity to relax after lessons"

Not Enough Spirit

"Our teams are quite competitive in a lot of Ivy League sports, but too few students get out to support the teams."

Great Niche Sports

"Not a big deal here except for the Harvard-Yale Football Game."

CAMPUS DINING

Dining Halls Great

"Great place to socialize and catch up with friends. I think the food is great (definitely better than anything I could cook!) and the dining hall staff is very friendly"

Menu

"food comes from either the home or from a vending machine. Other than that every day a couple students come by in the evening and sell some food that they make."

CAMPUS HOUSING

Harvard Is the Best!

"HARVARD IS THE BEST COLLEGE IN THE HISTORY OF HISTORY. THERE IS NO DENYING!"

Upperclassman Houses

"Living in one of Harvard's 12 upperclassman houses is one of the best things about attending Harvard. House life and house community really make being a school a home away from home"

GUYS & GIRLS

So and So

"People got in here for their brains, not beauty. The 10% of students who are wealthy legacies or athletes tend to look very attractive, but the vast majority are average to ugly. The few bombshells are invariably shallow and conceited, as well as remarkably vapid."

Girls Are Bad

"It is hard to find a good looking girl who can hold a conversation"

HEALTH & SAFETY

Very Safe!

"The Harvard University Police Department does an excellent job of protecting students. Cambridge is relatively safe at all hours of the day and night, and the rules are generally enforced well."

"I always feel safe, and I've never heard of anything bad happening. It's a city, so you have to use common sense, but I've never been uncomfortable, not even once."

LOOKING FOR MORE?

Check out our full-length guide to this school at collegeprowler.com/harvard-university/.

Harvey Mudd College

301 Platt Blvd.; Claremont, CA 91711
(909) 621-8000; www.hmc.edu

THE BASICS:

Acceptance Rate: 32%	Student-Faculty Ratio: 8:1
Yield: 28%	Retention Rate: 91%
Setting: Suburban	Graduation Rate: 90%
Control: Private Non-Profit	Tuition: $38,467
Total Undergrads: 757	Room & Board: $12,570
SAT Range: 2083–2330*	Avg. Aid Package: $26,737
ACT Range: 32–35	Students With Aid: 85%

* of 2400

Academics	A	Greek Life	N/A
Athletics	C+	Guys	B-
Campus Dining	A	Health & Safety	B
Campus Housing	A	Local Atmosphere	B-
Campus Strictness	A	Nightlife	B-
Computers	A-	Off-Campus Dining	C
Diversity	B	Off-Campus Housing	D-
Drug Safety	A-	Parking	A-
Facilities	A-	Transportation	C-
Girls	C	Weather	A

CP's Student Author On...
OVERALL EXPERIENCE

Everyone agrees that attending school at Mudd is both a gift and a curse. The workload is immense, the tests are sometimes impossible, and a two question homework assignment can take all night. The reason most of us came to Mudd has a lot to do with the academic integrity of the College (we have one of the lowest grade inflation rates out of any college in the U.S.) and a lot more to do with the community. The professors here are amazing and the deans know students by name. The students are generally respectful of and helpful to each other.

One of the main reasons that Mudd is such a strong community is the Honor Code. The Honor Code is a way of life for students and is created and governed by students. Students here take it to heart. It means closed-book, closed-notes, take-home finals; being able to leave your possessions unguarded when you take a coffee break; 24-hour access to any academic building; having your wallet returned to you if you lose it in lab; and not having to lock your door, even if you go home for the weekend. Mudd has a trusting community. People look out for each other.... For the rest of this editorial, visit collegeprowler.com.

Students Speak Out On...
OVERALL EXPERIENCE

Q "If you're looking particularly for a great place to learn, I don't think you could go anywhere else and be as well off as I am here."

Q "I love Mudd. It has hurt me, time and time again, but like a puppy, I keep crawling back to be kicked. There's a real love-hate relationship here, but I would never go to another school, ever—Mudd is the best."

Q "I ended up here partially by accident, and I'm really happy I did. I've had a far better experience here than I think I could have gotten at any other school. The professors are amazingly dedicated, and the environment is great."

Q "Ask me Sunday night and I'll tell you that Mudd is horrible. Ask me on a Friday and I'll tell you that Mudd is heaven on earth. I guess the right answer is more like a Wednesday—Mudd is hard as anything, but loads of fun."

BEST OF HARVEY MUDD

1. The Honor Code. It's great to have so many students committed to a policy of honesty. Harvey Mudd has a more than well-developed sense of community, even when compared to other small schools.

Happy Students
91% of students return after their first year.

Commitment to Teaching
There are 8 students for every member of faculty on campus.

WORST OF HARVEY MUDD

1. Sleep deprivation--fun and easy! Mudd students don't breeze through classes, and that kind of workload leaves little room for sleep. Say goodbye to your pillow when you get here.

Expensive
Tuition is a steep $38,467, one of the most expensive rates in the country.

AP Credit Wasted
Any AP credits earned in high school aren't eligible for college credit.

Student Body

African American:	2%	Male Undergrads:	64%
Asian American:	21%	Female Undergrads:	36%
Hispanic:	8%	Living On Campus:	98%
International:	3%	Living Off Campus:	2%
Native American:	1%	Male Athletes:	16%
White:	57%	Female Athletes:	13%
Unknown:	9%	Fraternity Members:	0%
From Out-of-State:	64%	Sorority Members:	0%

Frequently Compared Schools:

Claremont McKenna College
Massachusetts Institute of Technology
Pomona College
Stanford University

Students Speak Out On...
EVERYTHING!

ACADEMICS

Q "It's hard to get used to not being the best in your class, but being around so many intelligent people makes up for it. If I never get another 'A' again, it will have been worth it."

Q "Work! Work! Work! If you don't like academics, it's impossible to survive here. All of the students were the top in high school. Having a curve that high means you have to work like crazy to succeed."

ATHLETICS

Q **Not Fantastic.**
"Not really any kind of fan support or school spirit for athletics teams. Student involvement in the sports teams is very limited. However, ballroom dance, as both a social dance and a competition dance, is quite popular amongst many Mudders. Just about everyone at Mudd is a dancer her/himself or knows someone personally who is a dancer."

Q "Those part of the Claremont-Mudd-Scripps teams are very committed to their sport. It takes a lot of discipline to maintain a Mudder's academic schedule while doing the necessary practices. Intramural sports are huge, especially inner tube water polo!"

CAMPUS DINING

Q **Lots of Variety**
"There are 5 colleges, with each college having at least one dining hall, as well as some sort of store. Needless to say, this makes it pretty easy to get some variety. People learn which dining halls they like for which meals and tend to follow a pattern; for example, the sandwich bar at lunch at Pitzer is amazing, while the Mudd dining hall's best meal is breakfast."

Q "Mudd's dining hall is probably the best out of all of the other Claremont colleges, which is definitely a plus. Other campus' dining halls aren't bad either, so it's good to get around and have a little variety when Mudd food gets repetitive."

CAMPUS HOUSING

Q **Awesome Campus**
"Most Mudders live on-campus for the first two years. Everything is very close by: walking to the academic buildings on-campus from dorms takes about 10-15 minutes if you're from Outer Dorms, 2-5 minutes on a skateboard or unicycle. A wide number of living arrangements are available, depending on which dorm building you pick during the room draw process. There are doubles, singles, and suites of various sizes. Each dorm as a distinct social atmosphere."

Q "After spending a summer in a state school dorm, I realized that the dorms here are pretty awesome."

GUYS & GIRLS

Q **These Girls Are Not a C**
"As a guy at Mudd, I have to say that the girls in Suite Booty in Linde Dorm are pretty hot. They are a legacy suite that throws parties such as Lingerie, Anything But Clothes, and Red Light District. Those girls alone can change the grade for girls at Harvey Mudd from a C to an A!"

Q "It may be my love of nerds, but I think the guys here are so much hotter than at the other colleges. You can actually have conversations with them. It's a big turn-on."

HEALTH & SAFETY

Q **Very Safe, Just Be Responsible**
"The only real problem we have is theft, which generally occurs when people leave things outside and unsecured. Campus Safety is generally very helpful in supporting a positive environment."

Q "I know if anything ever happened here, other Mudders would be there to protect me. It's a very nice feeling to know that you can trust your fellow students, and that there really is nothing to be afraid of."

LOOKING FOR MORE?

Check out our full-length guide to this school at collegeprowler.com/harvey-mudd-college/.

Hastings College

710 N. Turner Ave.; Hastings, NE 68901
(402) 463-2402; www.hastings.edu

THE BASICS:

Acceptance Rate: 74%
Yield: 26%
Setting: Town
Control: Private Non-Profit
Total Undergrads: 1,104
SAT Range: 990–1250*
ACT Range: 20–27

Student-Faculty Ratio: 10:1
Retention Rate: 73%
Graduation Rate: 64%
Tuition: $21,782
Room & Board: $6,000
Avg. Aid Package: $14,901
Students With Aid: 99%

of 1600

Academics	A-	Greek Life	B
Athletics	A-	Guys	B+
Campus Dining	C	Health & Safety	B+
Campus Housing	A-	Local Atmosphere	B-
Campus Strictness	C	Nightlife	C+
Computers	B+	Off-Campus Dining	C+
Diversity	D-	Off-Campus Housing	B+
Drug Safety	B	Parking	B+
Facilities	B+	Transportation	C
Girls	B+	Weather	B-

CP's Student Author On...
OVERALL EXPERIENCE

Students at Hastings College are part of a family that has been growing for more than 125 years, along with the College's strong foundation of education and excellence. Hastings College's motto is "Pursue Your Passion." It's true that HC students are usually high achievers, and there are many things to take advantage of on campus. J-Term, a one-month class session in January, features many weeklong (or longer) class trips to places including Australia, Africa, New York, Hawaii, and Puerto Rico. Not many students choose to study abroad, but the option is available. Through connections with past students who've studied abroad and by brainstorming with professors, students can come up with a number of options for international study. Students can also take advantage of a personalized program, which is created with the help of a professor and presented to the Board of Trustees for approval. The possibilities are endless, and not only in academics. Hastings College offers more than 70 student organizations. Students have to try hard not to find something to their liking to get involved in on campus.... For the rest of this editorial, visit collegeprowler.com.

Students Speak Out On...
OVERALL EXPERIENCE

Q **Pursuing your passions**

"I think there are so many aspects of Hastings College that make it great: the academics, teachers, students, activities, facilities, you name it. My teachers in the departments from both of my majors work with each other to make being a double major easy for me, which is really helpful. I still have time to participate in many of the extra-curricular activities. Hastings is also about "Pursuing your Passion," but for me and a lot of students I know, it's more like "Pursuing your Passions.""

Q **My experience has been great**

"I love Hastings College, and my experience here has been great. The professors have been immensely helpful with helping me pick a major and pursue grad school. I would most definitely come here again! My favorite things here have been dorm life, being an RA, and being part of the Greek system."

Q **Before I came here, I wish I would have known...**

"Before I came here, I wish I would have known that it would be completely awesome."

BEST OF HASTINGS

1. Professors are helpful and available to students outside of class.
2. Students and faculty are friendly and welcoming.
3. Wide selection of organizations to be a part of and events offered on campus

Commitment to Teaching
There are 10 students for every member of faculty on campus.

WORST OF HASTINGS

1. Sodexo cafeteria food (options offered, cost, limited hours, and meal plan requirements for residents in the dorms and honors houses)
2. Three-year on-campus living requirement

Not Much Diversity
One of the least racially diverse campuses—only 11% of students are minorities.

Student Body

African American:	3%	Male Undergrads:	53%
Asian American:	1%	Female Undergrads:	47%
Hispanic:	4%	Living On Campus:	73%
International:	1%	Living Off Campus:	27%
Native American:	1%	Male Athletes:	59%
White:	89%	Female Athletes:	33%
Unknown:	0%	Fraternity Members:	20%
From Out-of-State:	33%	Sorority Members:	30%

Frequently Compared Schools:
Grinnell College
Hanover College
Lawrence University
University of Nebraska

Students Speak Out On... EVERYTHING!

ACADEMICS

Q Music and education programs
"As I was looking at colleges, I heard many great things about HC's music and education programs. Having been through them both, I have to agree that both programs are very strong and really prepare you for your career."

Q Very nice biology department
"We have a very nice biology department. Our new science building is currently being built and will offer a lot of exciting technology throughout the building. As far as other majors, I honestly can't think of a department that isn't that great."

ATHLETICS

Q School Spirit Hoorah
"There is so much support for our athletics. There is always a nice big crowd to cheer our teams on. The pep and marching band definitely adds to the aesthetics of the games and meets. It's a hype like you've never seen."

Q Education always comes first
"There is the stereotype that Hastings College is an athletic school. As far as that stereotype being true, I feel education always comes first at HC. A large number of our student athletes and sports teams have received honors for their academic achievements."

CAMPUS DINING

Q The food is actually very good and healthy
"The food on campus, contrary to the popular belief, is actually very good and healthy. There are almost Subway-quality sandwiches made to order at lunch and dinner. Sodexo provides nutritious meal options for students."

Q Not fine-dining, but it works
"The cafeteria is certainly not fine-dining, but it works. The chicken strips are usually a good bet and probably one of the best things on the menu. The ice cream is also pretty good, and the deli is great."

CAMPUS HOUSING

Q The dorms are great!
"The dorms are great! I highly recommend dorm life. Taylor is the nunnery; they are really strict there. Babcock has mostly female athletes, Weyer has male music majors, Bronc is smelly and full of male athletes, and Altman is the really awesome co-ed dorm. Altman is great because it has three nice lounges, a brand new kitchen, and a mix of all kinds of people and personalities from all different majors. And DUH, it's co-ed."

Q If you love living with a hundred babbling girls...
"If you love living with a hundred babbling girls, then the dorm life is for you!!! It is also where you meet some of your best friends. It is parent free except for your dorm mom or dad, and you will have some of your best memories in the dorms!"

GUYS & GIRLS

Q Very involved student body
"Both guys and girls at Hastings College are usually involved in a sport or music ensemble. All in all everyone is really friendly, and we all have a great time. Hastings is also a campus where everyone knows everyone. I think it's obvious that HC students love to be involved in their school!"

Q Guys are very well mannered
"Most of the guys are well mannered. They open doors, say hi, and are pretty respectful. You can tell a lot of HC guys were raised in small towns where manners were a must. Your typical HC student is very busy being involved in sports, music, or clubs. Most of us are in a variety of those things; we are all well rounded."

HEALTH & SAFETY

Q Health and Safety
"Crime is virtually non-existent, personal safety is of utmost importance and everyone looks out for each other. Campus security is always on alert, dorms are locked at all times and require a special key to gain entry. The local police and sheriff's office is located within a safe distance to the college and everyone always feels secure being there."

LOOKING FOR MORE?
Check out our full-length guide to this school at collegeprowler.com/hastings-college/.

Haverford College

370 Lancaster Ave.; Haverford, PA 19041
(610) 896-1000; www.haverford.edu

THE BASICS:

Acceptance Rate: 25%	**Student-Faculty Ratio:** 11:1
Yield: 37%	**Retention Rate:** 97%
Setting: Suburban	**Graduation Rate:** 94%
Control: Private Non-Profit	**Tuition:** $39,085
Total Undergrads: 1,190	**Room & Board:** $11,890
SAT Range: 1960–2240*	**Avg. Aid Package:** $31,701
ACT Range: 30–33	**Students With Aid:** 62%

* of 2400

Academics	A-	Greek Life	N/A
Athletics	C+	Guys	B-
Campus Dining	B	Health & Safety	B+
Campus Housing	A-	Local Atmosphere	B
Campus Strictness	A	Nightlife	C
Computers	B	Off-Campus Dining	B+
Diversity	B	Off-Campus Housing	D-
Drug Safety	B+	Parking	B+
Facilities	B+	Transportation	C+
Girls	B-	Weather	B-

CP's Student Author On...
OVERALL EXPERIENCE

On the whole, students are satisfied with their experience at Haverford. Most seniors look back on their Haverford education with a distinctive appreciation. It is a fondness that comes from understanding how profoundly the College has changed them. Haverford teaches its students more than just school subjects: it teaches them to lead honorable lives. Students feel that they have learned just as much from each other and the Haverford community as they have from their courses and professors. Many alumni do not realize the scope of their education until years later, but the impact is almost always felt. In this way, Haverford is unique.

Academically, the school has a spirit of reflective intellectualism that discourages students from becoming too detached from the real world. Social relations are guided by honor and civility. The student body generally has a sense of purpose and perspective and knows how to relax while tackling a challenging school curriculum. Granted, Haverford is not for everyone. Extreme partiers will not be happy here, nor will those who have no thirst for learning.... For the rest of this editorial, visit collegeprowler.com.

Students Speak Out On...
OVERALL EXPERIENCE

Q "I've had a good time at Haverford. I've never really wished to be anywhere else—that could be because I don't know what anything else is like, but it also could be because I'm happy at Haverford."

Q "I love Haverford. The students are amazing, passionate, interesting people from diverse backgrounds, who come together to create a school community based on trust and respect, which is amazing to live in for four years. People say its unrealistic to live under the Honor Code for four years because it's not like the real world, but that's why were here, to try to change the real world to make it more like the 'Ford.'"

Q "I'm having the time of my life."

Q "I love it here. The professors are great, and the campus is wet; I only wish that golf were varsity."

Q "I couldn't have made a better choice than Haverford. I love the people, the campus, the classes, and the social scene here. I clicked with Haverford, and I wouldn't go anywhere else for the world. (Well, for the world, yes. For a Klondike bar? No!) I love Haverford!"

BEST OF HAVERFORD

1. The people
2. Charming Quaker history
3. The wealth of extracurricular activities
4. Haverfest
5. Professors
6. The Bi-College News
7. Lenient alcohol policy

Happy Students
97% of students return after their first year.

Proven Success
94% of students will complete their education and graduate with a degree.

WORST OF HAVERFORD

1. Students' shyness
2. Short, hairy guys named Dan
3. Mandatory meal plan
4. Inconsistent weather
5. Dealing with the locals
6. No cable TV in some dorms

Expensive
Tuition is a steep $39,085, one of the most expensive rates in the country.

Expensive Dorms
Living on campus doesn't come cheap, with an average housing price tag of $6,750.

Student Body

African American:	8%	Male Undergrads:	46%
Asian American:	10%	Female Undergrads:	54%
Hispanic:	9%	Living On Campus:	99%
International:	3%	Living Off Campus:	1%
Native American:	1%	Male Athletes:	60%
White:	67%	Female Athletes:	38%
Unknown:	0%	Fraternity Members:	0%
From Out-of-State:	86%	Sorority Members:	0%

Frequently Compared Schools:
Amherst College
Bowdoin College
Swarthmore College
Wesleyan University

Students Speak Out On... EVERYTHING!

ACADEMICS

Ok

"We're supposed to be known for sciences, but my freshman chemistry and math classes were taught by very new professors and were poorly structured. I would have rather had a TA at least overseen by a more senior professor. Professors do however make themselves available for questions after class."

"The professors are incredibly helpful. Almost all of the classes have discussion sections so that if you don't understand something, there is much less pressure to ask a question than if it were in front of a class of 100. The classes I'm taking really suit my interests, and they're very exciting."

ATHLETICS

Awesome

"Haverford consistently wins championships despite its tiny student body."

"Varsity sports at Haverford? I wouldn't say they are a priority. I don't think anyone comes here specifically to play on one of our teams. But I would say that some teams have some kind of a redeeming quality to them: lacrosse, baseball, basketball, and fencing. We have an awesome cricket team!"

CAMPUS DINING

"The food gets repetitive after the first month. The DC spices it up occasionally with themed nights, but it is pretty bland overall. The Coop is great for late-night breadsticks, though!"

"There is only one dining hall on campus, called the Haverford College Dining Center, and a small eatery located in the Campus Center, called the Coop. While most students bond on how terrible the Dining Center food is, it really isn't that bad. Unfortunately, all students, including upperclassmen, must be on the meal plan, unless you live in the college-owned Haverford College Apartments or live off campus."

CAMPUS HOUSING

Housing Is Great!

"Freshman housing is wonderful-if you want a single on a floor of people you will get to know very well, Haverford is for you. Over 60% of the rooms on campus are singles, organized into suites or halls ready for your group of friends to move in. Also great are the apartments, which house from two to four people who share a kitchen, common room, and bathroom. This is the best option if you like having a ton of space and 24 hour availability to your own cooking space."

"Avoid the Apartments at all costs! They are far away from everything and an awful place to do work. Frosh should try to get Barclay because of the big hallways."

GUYS & GIRLS

"The Haver-male (short, hairy, and named Dan) is not a myth, but is not very prevalent. The campus is slightly shorter than the average population of the country. The guys are typically pretty good looking, and most are stand-up gentlemen. The girls are gorgeous—all of us."

"Ha! It's tough to define hot. Like at any other school, we have beautiful, pretty, normal, ugly, and hideous people. It depends on your taste. We are kind of a nerd school, so we have a lot of dorks. I mean that in a good way. Or maybe I don't."

HEALTH & SAFETY

"The Haverford College campus is very safe, but that has to do with the area the school is in, not the Haverford Safety and Security Department, which is pretty incompetent. They don't have to do much and have no idea what's going on."

"Safety and Security is amazing. The environment rarely has problems and is very safe and comforting. We call it the 'Haverbubble' because of the sense of security on campus."

LOOKING FOR MORE?

Check out our full-length guide to this school at collegeprowler.com/haverford-college/.

Hofstra University

100 Hofstra University; Hempstead, NY 11549
(516) 463-6600; www.hofstra.edu

THE BASICS:

Acceptance Rate: 53%	Student-Faculty Ratio: 14:1
Yield: 16%	Retention Rate: 76%
Setting: Suburban	Graduation Rate: 54%
Control: Private Non-Profit	Tuition: $30,130
Total Undergrads: 7,937	Room & Board: $11,330
SAT Range: 1090–1270*	Avg. Aid Package: $11,210
ACT Range: 23–27	Students With Aid: 90%

* of 1600

Academics	B+	Greek Life	B-
Athletics	C-	Guys	B
Campus Dining	B-	Health & Safety	C+
Campus Housing	C	Local Atmosphere	C
Campus Strictness	B	Nightlife	B+
Computers	B-	Off-Campus Dining	B-
Diversity	B-	Off-Campus Housing	B-
Drug Safety	C-	Parking	B+
Facilities	B	Transportation	C+
Girls	B-	Weather	B-

CP's Student Author On...
OVERALL EXPERIENCE

How any particular student feels about the school depends on a number of things— classes, people, money, etc.—but most people like it here, minus the high tuition. Hofstra's academic credibility has definitely gone up in recent years. Whenever Hofstra students tell people where they go to school, people usually say, "I've heard that's a really good school." When this happens, students feel some "Hofstra Pride." Even though Hofstra doesn't have a football team anymore, they've still got some pretty good sports for people who are interested in them. Hofstra also has great academic programs and good professors. Overall, Hofstra students really do have a lot of good things going for them.

To make the best of your time here, try to get involved in different clubs and activities. Go to a midnight movie, play pool down in the game room, and utilize the newly-renovated Recreation Center. There is a lot more to do here than most people realize, and once you know everything Hofstra has to offer, it makes the experience that much better.

Students Speak Out On...
OVERALL EXPERIENCE

Q Free Trips or Cheap Trips

"i really like all of the free and reasonable trips available on campus. There are school sponsored trip into NYC and the area often, and there are lots of choices to appeal to everyone."

Q Loves the Students.

"Advisors seem to actually care about the students...but hey, I guess that's what you get when you go to a private college!"

Q Great School

"This is a great school with a fantastic journalism program."

Q A Different Experience

"Very beautiful scenery especially in the fall and spring. Good professors, small classes, friendly people. A little difficult to make friends and not many people come to events held by clubs."

BEST OF HOFSTRA

1. Club sports
2. Dutch, Italian, and Irish festivals
3. Music Fest with great artists for free
4. Homecoming Parade
5. Jones Beach when the weather gets nice

Knowledgeable Professors
88% of students surveyed rated the general knowledge of professors as above average.

Low-Stress Course Load
75% of students surveyed rated the manageability of work as above average.

WORST OF HOFSTRA

1. Living in the Towers
2. Commuter parking situation
3. Campus food/meal plan
4. Non-competitive sports teams
5. Icy and freezing winters
6. Traffic

Expensive
Tuition is a steep $30,130, one of the most expensive rates in the country.

Expensive to Just Get By
62% of students surveyed felt that the amount it costs to live while at school was worse than average.

Student Body

African American:	10%	Male Undergrads:	48%
Asian American:	5%	Female Undergrads:	52%
Hispanic:	8%	Living On Campus:	47%
International:	1%	Living Off Campus:	53%
Native American:	1%	Male Athletes:	6%
White:	60%	Female Athletes:	4%
Unknown:	15%	Fraternity Members:	6%
From Out-of-State:	50%	Sorority Members:	8%

Students Speak Out On... EVERYTHING!

ACADEMICS

Communications School

"I love having my major at my school. Hofstra offers a great communications program. The professors and advisers really help out as much as they can. Internships are always difficult, but I found my information through job/internship fairs at Hofstra, which made the process easier."

AWESOME.

"ITS AN AWESOME SCHOOL FOR COMM.THIS IS ONE OF THE BEST SCHOOLS IN NY. ONLY THING THAT SUCKS IS THE REGISTRATION FOR CLASSES...ITS A BITCH OTHER THAN THAT ITS GREAT"

ATHLETICS

Sports Are Very Good

"Varsity sports at Hofstra are very well known. There are various clubs and intramurals for less competitive atheltes as well."

No More Football

"Our athletics departments are excellent. Not being a part of any athletic activities I would have to go by what I hear, and I hear that our basketball teams have been doing well and that our lacrosse team is pretty decent."

CAMPUS DINING

Very Good Food

"Excellent variety and good tasting food. There are normal, healthy, kosher, and other cultural options. Great and convenient hours."

Decent but Could Improve

"Although Hofstra has a lot of different options for food, they all relatively serve the same thing. It'd be nice if each place had their own selection of food so students didn't get bored with the food choices after a month."

Frequently Compared Schools:

Fordham University
St. John's University
Stony Brook University
Syracuse University

CAMPUS HOUSING

Honors Housing

"I live in the Honors Housing on campus and it is amazing! There is carpeted floor and it is really spacious. There is a lot of social meetings so you meet everyone on your floor and make friends with them quickly"

Pretty Decent

"If you're a freshmen, enjoy the first year of your dorm life. Hofstra isn't as nice to the upperclassmen, but the upperclassmen dorms aren't too bad, just not as good as for the freshmen."

GUYS & GIRLS

A Place for Everyone

"Hofstra is very diverse, despite what rumors may float around, and that's why I love it here. There are your typical guidos and guidettes, but there are so many other types of people that go to this school, and that keeps it always interesting. There are artistic kids, very driven kids, athletes, dancers, hipsters; you name the group, it's here at Hofstra."

Variety

"There are a diverse group of students. You can find many different looks, interests,social life and relationships."

HEALTH & SAFETY

Campus Safety Issue

"The Campus Safety police are very efficient I would say on Hofstra Campus because if they feel there are any kind of safety threats no matter what it is they pretty much will warn the student and if they can't reach them by telephone they do send out saftey warnings. They are always visible and if you need one of the campus police they are not hard to find."

LOOKING FOR MORE?

Check out our full-length guide to this school at collegeprowler.com/hofstra-university/.

Hollins University

7916 Williamson Road NW; Roanoke, VA 24020
(540) 362-6000; www.hollins.edu

THE BASICS:

Acceptance Rate: 88%
Yield: 32%
Setting: Suburban
Control: Private Non-Profit
Total Undergrads: 796
SAT Range: 1450–1850*
ACT Range: 22–28

Student-Faculty Ratio: 10:1
Retention Rate: 76%
Graduation Rate: 59%
Tuition: $28,115
Room & Board: $10,040
Avg. Aid Package: $17,913
Students With Aid: 99%

of 2400

Academics	B	Greek Life	N/A
Athletics	C	Guys	N/A
Campus Dining	B	Health & Safety	A+
Campus Housing	A	Local Atmosphere	B-
Campus Strictness	B+	Nightlife	C
Computers	B-	Off-Campus Dining	B-
Diversity	C-	Off-Campus Housing	D+
Drug Safety	B+	Parking	A-
Facilities	A-	Transportation	C
Girls	B+	Weather	B

CP's Student Author On...
OVERALL EXPERIENCE

Hollins students love their school. Many become very sentimental and enthusiastic in expressing this. If you are looking for a school that can evoke that kind of feeling, Hollins might very well be what you're looking for. Some fear that Hollins might not fare well as single-sex institutions lose popularity. This inspires many students to sing the praises of Hollins so that more women will give the University a chance. Due in large part to its devoted alumnae recruiting system, Hollins remains poised to succeed in the future. Students also express the need to reach more minority students, as the student body is overwhelmingly white.

When it comes to stimulating classes, caring professors, interesting students, and beautiful surroundings, Hollins has it made. Students have a lot of say in what and how much they want to put into their educations. If flexibility and individuality are important to you, you'll appreciate the academic environment. If you crave academic structure, Hollins might not provide you with what you are looking for.... For the rest of this editorial, visit collegeprowler.com.

Students Speak Out On...
OVERALL EXPERIENCE

Q **Best School!**
"Hollins is the best school I've ever attended. Excellent and diverse classes, beautiful campus, accessible staff and faculty, and a very happy family among my fellow students. I wish the printers were more reliable, but if that is the biggest issue, there is no place like Hollins."

Q "It's funny: Hollins attracts a lot of weirdos and a lot of clean-cut kids. We end up with a unique balance in our social atmosphere. If you're up for a change, come to Hollins. Just don't expect the expected."

Q "I love Hollins, and I wish I could stay forever. I am so happy and know that this is where I belong."

Q "Hollins is welcoming and warm. I feel at home here. I would not trade it for anything. The campus is beautiful, and the people are as friendly as they get. There is hardly any competition among students. We all want each other to do well. I have heard stories about how some students at other institutions will tear out important pages in library books to sabotage other students and to give themselves an advantage. That is the complete opposite of the attitude here."

BEST OF HOLLINS

1. Encouragement of new ways of thinking
2. Friendly professors
3. Tinker Day
4. Freya
5. The study nooks in the library
6. On-campus parties

Commitment to Teaching
There are 10 students for every member of faculty on campus.

Learn from the Best
99% of faculty have earned the highest degree in their field.

WORST OF HOLLINS

1. Downed networks
2. The printers
3. Noisy heaters
4. Lack of fun local bars
5. Parking tickets
6. The walk from Siberia
7. The lack of treadmills
8. Cliques

Expensive
Tuition is a steep $28,115, one of the most expensive rates in the country.

Expensive Dorms
Living on campus doesn't come cheap, with an average housing price tag of $5,965.

Student Body

African American:	8%	Male Undergrads:	0%
Asian American:	2%	Female Undergrads:	100%
Hispanic:	3%	Living On Campus:	89%
International:	4%	Living Off Campus:	11%
Native American:	1%	Male Athletes:	0%
White:	82%	Female Athletes:	14%
Unknown:	0%	Fraternity Members:	0%
From Out-of-State:	56%	Sorority Members:	0%

Students Speak Out On... EVERYTHING!

ACADEMICS

Q Hollins Cares

"Hollins has the best resources and professors that really help and care for each student that attends Hollins University."

Q Biochemistry

"I'm really just getting started on all of the requirements for this major. My course load is going to be pretty heavy for the rest of the time that I'm at school."

Q "I never feel as though I can't speak during class. Whenever I have something to say, I say it. I never felt like this in high school. Would it be cheesy to say that I feel as though Hollins has liberated me in a way?"

ATHLETICS

Q OK I Guess

"I'm not personally involved in any, so I can't give any personal stories."

Q "Sometimes I'll be walking around the loop, and I'll see a team out in the field. I can't tell if it's a game or a practice, because no one goes to the games."

Q "Intramural sports aren't around as of yet. We do have some club sports teams that play other IM teams from other colleges. Most other sports that aren't varsity are taught in PE class. Varsity sports are taken very seriously, especially tennis and riding, which place very high in the ODACs every year."

CAMPUS DINING

Q Repetitive and Limited

"It's a small campus so there aren't a lot of choices. There are a few stand outs but a lot of it is pretty basic."

Q "There's only one dining hall, where all your meals are included in your room-and-board fee, so you don't have to worry about running out of money on a card or anything. There's a snack bar that's open late where you can grab snacks, sandwiches, smoothies, and so on."

Frequently Compared Schools:

Guilford College
James Madison University
Susquehanna University
University of Virginia

CAMPUS HOUSING

Q "Compared to most other schools, Hollins has awesome dorms. Some of my friends who went to universities where they had to live in huge, industrial buildings with tons of other kids got homesick so quickly. This was not a problem for me."

Q "All of the dorms are really nice and very beautiful. Tinker is the only dorm with air conditioning. West, Main, and East are the oldest and all sit around Front Quad. They all have high ceilings."

GUYS & GIRLS

Q Women

"I don't really like girls. Never have. Turns out I love the company of women. And that puts Hollins apart."

Q "If you think Lily Pulitzer dresses and pearls are hot, you'll find someone. If you think Harry Potter capes are hot, you'll find someone."

HEALTH & SAFETY

Q Gererally Safe

"The only real problem that I've ever heard when it comes to campus safety is one person had their car vandalized. Campus safety called her at 3 in the morning and stayed in the parking lot with her and helped her clean her car for and hour though."

Q "We have a campus safety office located centrally on campus. Generally the officers are very helpful. There have been a few thefts in some of the academic buildings, but I have not seen too many problems with crime on campus. We have some blue-light emergency posts around campus, and we have an emergency alert system that sounds from a central location on our (small) campus. We also have text messaging alerts for emergencies or to notify us of campus closings."

LOOKING FOR MORE?

Check out our full-length guide to this school at collegeprowler.com/hollins-university/.

Hood College

401 Rosemont Ave.; Frederick, MD 21701
(301) 663-3131; www.hood.edu

THE BASICS:

Acceptance Rate: 72%
Yield: 22%
Setting: Small city
Control: Private Non-Profit
Total Undergrads: 1,432
SAT Range: 1440–1790*
ACT Range: 20–25

Student-Faculty Ratio: 11:1
Retention Rate: 83%
Graduation Rate: 65%
Tuition: $28,170
Room & Board: $9,440
Avg. Aid Package: $21,889
Students With Aid: 91%

* of 2400

Academics	B-	Greek Life	N/A
Athletics	C	Guys	B
Campus Dining	C	Health & Safety	B-
Campus Housing	B-	Local Atmosphere	B
Campus Strictness	C+	Nightlife	B
Computers	C-	Off-Campus Dining	B+
Diversity	C+	Off-Campus Housing	B
Drug Safety	C+	Parking	B
Facilities	C	Transportation	C+
Girls	B	Weather	C+

CP's Student Author On...
OVERALL EXPERIENCE

Four years endlessly stretch out ahead of you when you're miles away from home, in an unfamiliar area, living with a stranger, and surrounded by hundreds of people you don't know. For many, just trying to adjust to a new style of education while being away from home can make a student feel like turning around and going back to what they know. But it helps when your family is by your side, right? And that's how people describe Hood: as a big friendly family. There are some loose screws and oddballs, but that's what makes a family unique. However, no matter what happens, your family is always behind your back and will support you. So when a tragedy hits someone at Hood, faculty, staff, and students are all prepared to do whatever they need to do to help out. Roommates frequently become best friends, and professors become valuable mentors, filled with a wealth of knowledge for students. In addition, the numerous exciting opportunities for internships, jobs, and clubs leave many students living a busy and hectic lifestyle—which most choose to embrace.... For the rest of this editorial, visit collegeprowler.com.

Students Speak Out On...
OVERALL EXPERIENCE

Q HOOD

"I love Hood because its perfect for me! I love that everyone if friendly, the professors care, and that it is small so I don't get lost!"

Q I'm Excited to Start

"I just received my acceptance letter and I'm very excited to start this upcoming Fall. The campus is beautiful and every representative I've met with has been both friendly and helpful. It's right in town and I've always wanted to stay local."

Q A Great, Friendly Small School

"I chose Hood because they gave me a large scholarship, and I fell in love with the feeling. Almost everyone you meet here is friendly and open, and will stop to say hi (as long as they're not too busy). The professors take an invested interest in their students, and after 3 years here, Frederick feels like a second home and the people of Hood are my second family."

BEST OF HOOD

1. Very friendly and accepting students
2. CAB events

Happy Students
83% of students return after their first year.

Easy Financial Aid Process
73% of students surveyed told us that the financial aid process went smoothly and they received the financial aid they needed.

WORST OF HOOD

1. Dining hall food/ lack of on-campus late-night food
2. Everyone knows everyone.
3. Gossiping
4. Lack of campus housing/ small dorm rooms
5. Lack of parking

Expensive
Tuition is a steep $28,170, one of the most expensive rates in the country.

Student Body

African American:	10%	Male Undergrads:	31%
Asian American:	3%	Female Undergrads:	69%
Hispanic:	3%	Living On Campus:	54%
International:	2%	Living Off Campus:	46%
Native American:	0%	Male Athletes:	31%
White:	74%	Female Athletes:	16%
Unknown:	7%	Fraternity Members:	0%
From Out-of-State:	24%	Sorority Members:	0%

Frequently Compared Schools:

Colgate University
Franklin & Marshall College
Lafayette College
Oberlin College

Students Speak Out On... EVERYTHING!

ACADEMICS

Q Hood College, Tiny Classes, Big Heart

"I came to Hood College because of its beautiful campus, its small class sizes, and because everyone seems to know everyone. The professors are easily accessible and always willing to help."

Q Communications Is Awesome

"I love being a communications major. Most of the classes I have taken I have really enjoyed and I have had the same professor's for multiple classes, so students can build personal relationships with the professor. Communication majors have the option to have a concentration in different fields, and in picking PR I have had the same classes with the same people for the past three semesters."

Q Two Majors - Psychology and Law

"Law is difficult because most of the classes are offerred in the fall. I transferred in as a junior so this was difficult with schedule classes for me to graduate in time. Psychology is ok thus far, classes are tough but will help in the future."

ATHLETICS

Q Sports

"i know there are a lot of sports and i know a lot of members from the community are involved with the sports."

Q On the up and up

"Teams are getting better but at a real cost academically. We are letting in athletes who do not have the GPA for this school."

CAMPUS DINING

Q Average

"Hood isn't a big school, so the dining options are limited. There is only one dining hall. However, there is a pretty good variety of food, in addition to many specialty nights where they offer better food. The Blazer, the only on campus option other than Coblentz, has fairly decent food, but is overpriced."

Q OK but a Little Expensive

"Hood has pretty good dining options, but the prices are a little high."

CAMPUS HOUSING

Q Sunset Apartments Are Excellent

"On campus housing is all right. The dorms are old, and they've got the feeling of having a lot of history. Most of the rooms are slightly larger than your average dorm. The setup of the residential quad is great for getting that "togetherness" feeling, but the nicest rooms are in the Sunset Apartments for upperclassmen."

Q Dorms

"The dorms are all comfortable and each have their own unique aspects to them."

GUYS & GIRLS

Q Everyone Seems Nice

"Everyone seems nice, i have met a few friends who i have become close with and it is easy to meet new people."

Q Not Very Outgoing

"girls at school are bounded within their packs.There is not a lot of socialization around the campus expect at the parties."

HEALTH & SAFETY

Q Very Safe

"I have always felt very safe while on Hood's campus. The security is always around and they can be seen keeping campus safe 24-7. I never feel alone after dark, and Hood's security even has arangments if students need to be walked to their cars after dark while on campus. Safety and security are great!"

Q I Feel Secure

"I feel secure and safe on and around Hood College's campus."

LOOKING FOR MORE?

Check out our full-length guide to this school at collegeprowler.com/hood-college/.

Howard University

2400 Sixth St. NW; Washington, DC 20059
(202) 806-6100; www.howard.edu

THE BASICS:

Acceptance Rate: 54%	**Student-Faculty Ratio:** 11:1
Yield: 32%	**Retention Rate:** 83%
Setting: Large city	**Graduation Rate:** 65%
Control: Private Non-Profit	**Tuition:** $16,075
Total Undergrads: 6,952	**Room & Board:** $7,966
SAT Range: 1330–1980*	**Avg. Aid Package:** $16,473
ACT Range: 19–29	**Students With Aid:** 91%

* of 2400

Academics	B-	Greek Life	B+
Athletics	C-	Guys	A+
Campus Dining	C	Health & Safety	C-
Campus Housing	C+	Local Atmosphere	B+
Campus Strictness	B-	Nightlife	A
Computers	D+	Off-Campus Dining	B
Diversity	B-	Off-Campus Housing	B
Drug Safety	C+	Parking	B-
Facilities	C-	Transportation	A
Girls	A	Weather	B-

CP's Student Author On...
OVERALL EXPERIENCE

Students are more than satisfied with the quality of education that they are receiving at Howard. Students seem to have no trouble meshing with their peers, as well as the faculty. In fact, the only qualm that students seem to have is experiencing the difficulties of dealing with HU administration. The bureaucracy and red tape involved with getting anything done at the administrative level is nothing short of nerve racking, and the race to ensure that your financial aid is administered on time and paperwork properly entered into the system is probably more effective for rapid weight loss than any weight loss program currently being advertised. But even with all the little frustrations that come with dealing with the administration, there is a firm consensus among the students that there is no better place for them to be than where they are now. From the quality of the relationships they have formed to the quality of the education that they are receiving, as well as the numerous opportunities made available to them, HU students are pretty darn happy.... For the rest of this editorial, visit collegeprowler.com.

Students Speak Out On...
OVERALL EXPERIENCE

Q Great
"This school is amazing. You would have to go here to understand. If I could do it all over again I would."

Q So Many Stories..
"I picked Howard because of the money, but i have learned since being here that you cant put a price on the experience. Sure grades come first but if you can balance the two, you can have a blast over here. From the greek life to the consistent party scene, Howard has something for everyone being in DC."

Q I'm So Glad I Go to Howard U
"Howard is definitely what you make it. There are so many academic, professional, and social opportunites at Howard that you can enjoy that will enrich your college experience. The resources are there and it's up to the student to determine how they live their college lives. The thing I will miss the most is being with my friends in D.C."

BEST OF HOWARD

1. Sense of pride
2. Faculty
3. Academics
4. Celebrity-filled seminars
5. Networking
6. Career Opportunities
7. School Spirit
8. Cultural Significance

Happy Students
83% of students return after their first year.

Knowledgeable Professors
83% of students surveyed rated the general knowledge of professors as above average.

WORST OF HOWARD

1. The Administration Building
2. Campus food
3. Shortage of campus housing
4. Facilities
5. Athletics
6. Technology

Lowest Grades
Computers: D+
Facilities: C-
Athletics: C-

Student Body

African American:	64%	Male Undergrads:	34%
Asian American:	1%	Female Undergrads:	66%
Hispanic:	1%	Living On Campus:	55%
International:	5%	Living Off Campus:	45%
Native American:	0%	Male Athletes:	10%
White:	0%	Female Athletes:	3%
Unknown:	29%	Fraternity Members:	2%
From Out-of-State:	98%	Sorority Members:	1%

Frequently Compared Schools:

Georgetown University
Hampton University
Spelman College
University of Maryland

Students Speak Out On...
EVERYTHING!

ACADEMICS

HU Accounting Program

"Accounting is one of the toughest majors within the School of Business. However, companies and firms heavily recruit for accounting and finance, so it's worth it."

Sports Medicine

"It is alright. We focus on the sciences; chemistry, organic chemistry, biology, physiology, etc. The workload is heavy. I also work full time at Georgetown University Hospital, which I would not recommend doing well being a full time student."

ATHLETICS

School Spirit

"We have EXCELLENT school spirit, but dont expect us to win anything."

School Spirit Is Very High

"The students are great with supporting school sports. Team performance is not very good but the students continue to support them any way."

CAMPUS DINING

Eats at the Real HU

"Good eats around campus. McDonalds, subway, carribbean food, thai food, mexican. you name it. The cafe is good, lots of options to choose from: pizza, pastas, sandwiches, burgers n fries, home-styled meals."

Fine Dine

"Howard University offers a variety of dining options on campus. The food is often good, but not the best. Dining halls on campus are: The Cafe, the annex cafe, etc. I enjoy eating at both cafeterias although the cafe is more entertaining because there are a variety of people and both sexes."

CAMPUS HOUSING

Campus Involvement

"I had many opportunities to be involved on campus. That level of involvement helped me to build my character and become a more well-rounded individual. The people I've met as a result and the activities in which I participated made interviewing for jobs easier as I was able to relay those experiences and make a better case as to why I should be hired"

Off Campus Living.

"I have never lived on campus. I dont know a lot about it, but according to my friends, they love it, they can easily have fun, but one think that I consider bad is that it is very easy to sneak into dorms. Plus it is hard to get on campus housing because of the small amount of available rooms compared to the number of students."

GUYS & GIRLS

Pretty Girls

"Howard is full of beautiful girls and a large variety of all different types. Everyone can dress really well too. It's like a daily fashion show on campus."

HOT HOT HOT

"Howard definitely lives up to expectation when it comes to the notion that the school is one great fashion show. You will not be at a loss for gorgeous, fashionable women on campus. Sometimes, the guys are even more glamorous than the girls. In any case, dressing up to class is a MUST."

HEALTH & SAFETY

9

"Safty of students is always of primery concern to students -I had no bad experiences"

Howard Safety!

"Howard University is pretty good when it comes to safety and campus security. Since I've been here, I haven't heard of any campus crimes, and that makes me feel safe on campus. On the site of the University, there are lit poles that you can run to and call for help if you are in danger, there are campus police patrolling around the clock, and there are escorts available to decrease the amount of students walking around at night."

LOOKING FOR MORE?

Check out our full-length guide to this school at collegeprowler.com/howard-university/.

Hunter College

695 Park Ave.; New York, NY 10065
(212) 772-4000; www.hunter.cuny.edu

THE BASICS:

Acceptance Rate: 28%
Yield: 26%
Setting: Large city
Control: Public
Total Undergrads: 15,957
SAT Range: 990–1190*
ACT Range: —

Student-Faculty Ratio: 15:1
Retention Rate: 84%
Graduation Rate: 42%
Tuition: $10,359
Room & Board: $11,755
Avg. Aid Package: $5,121
Students With Aid: 79%

of 1600

Academics	B	Greek Life	N/A
Athletics	C+	Guys	B
Campus Dining	C+	Health & Safety	B-
Campus Housing	C	Local Atmosphere	A-
Campus Strictness	B+	Nightlife	B+
Computers	B-	Off-Campus Dining	B-
Diversity	A	Off-Campus Housing	C
Drug Safety	B-	Parking	D+
Facilities	C-	Transportation	B+
Girls	B	Weather	B+

CP's Student Author On...
OVERALL EXPERIENCE

With 20,000 students, opinions vary greatly on what it means to go to Hunter College. Students may exhaust themselves working full time and going to school full time, others may overload on credits to graduate early (or on time), while others may become dedicated to the school and join a dozen clubs, become student ambassadors, and take on administrative positions within the school. There are those that despise getting off the subway at 68th Street, others can't wait to get to school.

As an overwhelming number of students commute to school, a lot of the student body fears they are missing out on the "traditional" college experience, if traditional means living on campus with parties every day of the week and buckets of school spirit. A lot of students went to Hunter specifically to avoid that environment, though; their life isn't focused on, nor does it depend on, the school. On the whole, it can be safe to say that the students who attend Hunter feel very fortunate to be there, and they work very hard to stay there. They appreciate the education they are receiving, and don't allow the red tape or any other inconvenience to put a damper on their experience

Students Speak Out On...
OVERALL EXPERIENCE

Q Student life is great if you look into it
"I love it here. They say student life isn't that great but it is if you look into it. I've been to three colleges and Hunter is my favourite."

Q Overall Experience
"My experience at Hunter has been an interesting one. The professors are hard and easy at the same time. Most of the professors I have had so far have been extremely supportive and wonderful at teaching."

Q Diversity
"Hunter's diversity makes it an experience I would want to repeat."

Q I'm Pretty Satisfied
"There is a definitely a good mix of people at Hunter, the problem is getting to know one another (this applies to professors as well). I really like that I wouldn't come out of college in debt and I get the experience with a dorm and study abroad."

BEST OF HUNTER

1. New York City
2. Diversity
3. Tuition
4. Central Park
5. Boy-to-girl ratio (for guys)
6. Food trucks
7. Campus has own subway stop

Affordable
Tuition is only $10,359, one of the most affordable rates in the country.

Happy Students
84% of students return after their first year.

WORST OF HUNTER

1. Big classes
2. Cafeteria food
3. Boy-to-girl ratio (for girls)
4. Social scene
5. Construction at the dorm
6. Red tape
7. Limited dorm

Life is NOT a Party
63% of students surveyed said it's almost impossible to find a good party.

Don't Move Off Campus
Average off-campus housing is a steep $10,382.

Student Body

African American:	12%	Male Undergrads:	33%
Asian American:	19%	Female Undergrads:	67%
Hispanic:	19%	Living On Campus:	2%
International:	9%	Living Off Campus:	98%
Native American:	0%	Male Athletes:	5%
White:	40%	Female Athletes:	2%
Unknown:	0%	Fraternity Members:	0%
From Out-of-State:	4%	Sorority Members:	0%

Frequently Compared Schools:

Baruch College
Columbia University
New York University
Stony Brook University

Students Speak Out On...
EVERYTHING!

ACADEMICS

Amazing Academics

"Going to a large, public university, I was surprised at how small all my classes were, and how attentive and willing to help my professors were. They encourage us to come to their office hours and really help you if you ask for it!"

Great Academics

"Classes are really exciting. Lots of hands on experience and most professors really take the time out to help you whenever you need it. Hunter also offers a wide variety of classes which keeps things interesting."

ATHLETICS

They Have a Lot of Different Varieties of Sports

"Hunter College has a great variety of sports with all kinds of people. The thing that I love most about it, is the fact that you don't have to be in the best shape or be super athletic to be on a team. Like track team, you just need to responsible, and take it seriously. I'm not the most athletic person out there, but if I had the time I would definitely join track; there is no physical requirements."

Sports for Everyone

"The sports opportunities at hunter seem to be endless. The spirit of sportsmanship is prevalent throughout the school and there is always something exciting to see. Our facilities are way more than OK and there are sports for every type of student!"

CAMPUS DINING

Cafeteria Blues

"The cafeteria on the 3rd floor is disappointing. The sushi roll aren't bad but a little expensive. The cafeteria prices are not so good on a whole, but if you put money on your student ID card there's no tax on the food. Around campus there areplenty of pizza places, food carts, deli's, diners...basically plenty of choices. You just have to walk a little."

Dining Experience at Hunter

"Food in the cafeteria is somewhat expensive if you're planning to eat there every day. It would be better to either bring your own food or buy something from a different part of Manhattan. There is an easy commute to different parts of Manhattan."

CAMPUS HOUSING

Brookdale Life

"Living at Brookdale as a part of MHC is like a dream come true, and a fantastic experiment for all of the young people involved."

Hunter Campus

"At our current situation, housing is only offered off campus to Hunter's Macauley Honors Program students."

GUYS & GIRLS

Something for Everyone

"There is a lot of diversity and many different types of guys and girls. If it exists, you will find it here."

Diverse and Lots of Women

"There are people from all over the world in New York and at Hunter. It used to be a women's school and it seems like it still mostly is. I am not sure of the numbers, but it there are a lot more women than men there."

HEALTH & SAFETY

Safety

"with our new turnstiles, there is a great sense of security in the campus."

Health & Safety Review

"The safety in school is very well maintained. I have visited the health center and they seem pretty helpful."

LOOKING FOR MORE?

Check out our full-length guide to this school at collegeprowler.com/hunter-college/.

Idaho State University

921 S. Seventh Ave.; Pocatello, ID 83209
(208) 282-3620; www.isu.edu

THE BASICS:

Acceptance Rate: 80%
Yield: 60%
Setting: Small city
Control: Public
Total Undergrads: 11,258
SAT Range: 910–1185*
ACT Range: 18–24

Student-Faculty Ratio: 16:1
Retention Rate: 60%
Graduation Rate: 26%
Tuition: $14,770
Room & Board: $5,050
Avg. Aid Package: $5,987
Students With Aid: 90%

of 1600

Academics	B-	Greek Life	C-
Athletics	B-	Guys	B-
Campus Dining	B	Health & Safety	A+
Campus Housing	C+	Local Atmosphere	B
Campus Strictness	C	Nightlife	C+
Computers	B	Off-Campus Dining	B
Diversity	D+	Off-Campus Housing	A+
Drug Safety	A-	Parking	B-
Facilities	A-	Transportation	B-
Girls	B+	Weather	B-

CP's Student Author On...
OVERALL EXPERIENCE

ISU is what someone might call one of a kind. It has the city setting without actually being in a huge city. It is an institution with diverse programs, qualified professors, and a field of interest for any student. And although it is an Idaho university with an Idaho environment, out-of-state and international students are welcome and included. There is a club or student organization for everybody, and if that isn't your cup of tea, there is always the great Idaho outdoors to enjoy. ISU has a wonderful hometown feel with multiple opportunities available. The student experience at ISU, and probably any college or university, really comes down to what the student wants out of it. Pocatello can be viewed as an amazingly boring town, or it can be a fun, chill place to just lay back and enjoy life. That is definitely the word for Pocatello and ISU life in general—chill. For the most part, students and professors are laid-back and easy-going. The ISU experience is what students make of it, but most likely that experience will be one of great memories and good times in good ol' Idaho.

Students Speak Out On...
OVERALL EXPERIENCE

Q Comfortable
"I felt comfortable and enjoyed the campus setup and town. I would choose again if had choice."

Q Doubt You'll Graduate on Time
"The school is ok. I really do like the professors i think they care about what they are teaching. Its the administration that is ridiculous at the school and they make so people can never graduate on time because they don't offer the needed classes every semester."

Q ISU IS GREAT but..
"I had great experience with the students. I had a hard time getting funding approved through the office of financial aid. They raised the fee alot. Everything is expense but if you have the money then go ahead and go to school there."

Q "For the most part, ISU is awesome! The academic programs are awesome, and the social life is out there if you want one! You definitely will make memories."

BEST OF IDAHO STATE

1. Outdoor activities
2. Teachers
3. Diverse students
4. Hometown community
5. Location
6. Relatively low gas prices
7. State of the art facilities

Personal Attention
You can expect personal attention with 66% of classes having less than 20 students.

WORST OF IDAHO STATE

1. Tuition keeps going up
2. Decrease of grants and aid
3. Old buildings
4. Parking
5. Old dorms
6. Not a lot of support for all athletics

Not Everyone Graduates
26% of students do not complete their education or graduate with a degree.

Student Body

African American:	1%	Male Undergrads:	43%
Asian American:	2%	Female Undergrads:	57%
Hispanic:	5%	Living On Campus:	6%
International:	1%	Living Off Campus:	94%
Native American:	1%	Male Athletes:	6%
White:	74%	Female Athletes:	4%
Unknown:	16%	Fraternity Members:	1%
From Out-of-State:	9%	Sorority Members:	1%

Frequently Compared Schools:

Boise State University
Montana State University
University of Montana
University of Utah

Students Speak Out On...
EVERYTHING!

ACADEMICS

Nursing

"Well, I am still doing prerequisites, so I haven't applied to the program yet."

"There's no way to really describe all of the teachers because they are all so different. Most, however, are eager to help if you have questions regarding their classes."

"For the most part, the teachers at ISU are willing to help any student. Most know what they are teaching. They all teach in different ways, so it's hard to compare, but I haven't had a teacher yet that I despise!"

ATHLETICS

Athletics

"The athletic programs are decent, but the teams performance depends on the sport. The football team doesn't win many games, but the women's basketball team does pretty good. They have a new gym facility to work out in, which is way nice."

"Sports are pretty big wherever you go! The varsity sports teams may not be the best in the state, but they do try hard, so it's worth it to go. The intramural sports are fun and crazy! There is quite a variety to choose from, and they get quite competitive."

"Varsity sports are big on campus. Many students attend all of the home football games in our indoor stadium, and both the football and basketball teams receive good fan support. They are almost always exciting to attend. There are IM teams for almost every sport you can think of. Flag football and basketball get very competitive."

CAMPUS DINING

Not Enough Variety

"I enjoy a few of the places around campus, but feel like it becomes a rut to eat at the same halls. I feel like there needs to be a variety of ethnic food choices to add some creative taste."

Okay

"Not exactly the best place to eat. The food is poor quality and I hardly ever eat there at all now. The food is also over priced. menus and variety are okay."

CAMPUS HOUSING

Campus Apartments

"I lived in University Courts at ISU. They were not the best because they were small and I could not imagine sharing the area with someone, but they are convenient to get to classes and it is nice to have campus security driving by as a single woman. The cost was a little steep, but getting to them after being a sophomore was easy."

Been a While Since I Have Lived on Campus.....

"They just completed the Rendezvous building about 2 years ago. From what I hear the place is awesome-but I haven't been in there for a while."

GUYS & GIRLS

Average

"most of the guys and girls at this university are just average students. you will see some who are older or who are parents just trying to finish their schooling. its a pretty relaxed environment and not a huge party school."

Supper Guy to Girl Ratio

"There are at least 3 girls for every guy, its heaven."

HEALTH & SAFETY

A Safe Campus

"ISU is a safe campus. There is good lighting, safety officers, capmus security, fire drills, alerts, quick response by police."

Never Felt Unsafe on Campus

"I have never felt unsafe on campus, there are posts set up aver so often should you need help immediately, I have never heard of anyone using them either.."

LOOKING FOR MORE?

Check out our full-length guide to this school at collegeprowler.com/idaho-state-university/.

Illinois State University

100 N. University St.; Normal, IL 61790
(309) 438-2111; www.ilstu.edu

THE BASICS:

Acceptance Rate: 62%
Yield: 35%
Setting: Small city
Control: Public
Total Undergrads: 18,389
SAT Range: —
ACT Range: 22–26

Student-Faculty Ratio: 19:1
Retention Rate: 85%
Graduation Rate: 70%
Tuition: $16,561
Room & Board: $7,882
Avg. Aid Package: $8,618
Students With Aid: 68%

Academics	B-	Greek Life	B
Athletics	C	Guys	A
Campus Dining	B	Health & Safety	C-
Campus Housing	B-	Local Atmosphere	B
Campus Strictness	C	Nightlife	A-
Computers	B	Off-Campus Dining	A-
Diversity	C+	Off-Campus Housing	B-
Drug Safety	C-	Parking	B-
Facilities	B	Transportation	B+
Girls	A	Weather	C+

CP's Student Author On...
OVERALL EXPERIENCE

One thing that students notice at ISU is that each professor cares about the students and wishes them to succeed as individuals. Illinois State University is unique because the relationship between students and teachers is powerful. The students have the will to learn, and the teachers provide the necessary tools to prepare students for the real world after college. Each major offers an internship adviser that has resources specifically for students. Teachers dedicate themselves to their classes and make sure that students understand the material. From the outside, ISU may seem like a typical state school, but once you're here you realize the unique character it possesses. Students are proud to say that they are from Illinois State University.

Students Speak Out On...
OVERALL EXPERIENCE

Q Illinois State is AWESOME!

"I love Illinois State University! I have learned a lot about myself and what I want to do in the future. I have made great friends."

Q Im So Happy I Chose ISU!

"Coming here was the best decision of my life. I met new people, learned more about myself, and became a new and improved person."

Q A Great Ride

"I'll be finishing my life at ISU at the end of the fall semester, 2010. It's been an interesting ride. Met nice people, had great classes with good teachers. I feel at home in this town and will look back fondly."

Q I Love ISU!

"I love Illinois State University! I have met so many wonderful people from all walks of life. My classes are leading me to what I hope is a great career in Special Education. It's only 2-1/2 hours from home, so it's close, but not too close ;) if you know what I mean ..."

BEST OF ILLINOIS STATE

1. Laying out on the Quad
2. The bar scene
3. The campus
4. Weekends
5. Watterson Towers
6. Football on the Quad
7. Becoming independent
8. Comfortable atmosphere

Happy Students
85% of students return after their first year.

Proven Success
70% of students will complete their education and graduate with a degree.

WORST OF ILLINOIS STATE

1. Lack of school spirit
2. Mandatory living on campus for two years
3. Excess amount of cornfields
4. No 18-and-older bars
5. The guy/girl ratio
6. Strong winds in the winter

Not Much Diversity
One of the least racially diverse campuses—only 16% of students are minorities.

Student Body

African American:	5%	Male Undergrads:	44%
Asian American:	2%	Female Undergrads:	56%
Hispanic:	4%	Living On Campus:	33%
International:	1%	Living Off Campus:	67%
Native American:	0%	Male Athletes:	3%
White:	84%	Female Athletes:	2%
Unknown:	4%	Fraternity Members:	8%
From Out-of-State:	1%	Sorority Members:	8%

Students Speak Out On... EVERYTHING!

ACADEMICS

Communication Major

"The teachers are great at helping and explaining things. Many of the journalism teachers have had a lot of good experience in the field they teach. Also, ISU's Alumni Magazine is a great internship for anyone pursuing a career in journalism."

Professors Are Helpful

"If you have a question it is a good idea to talk to your professor because they can always help you. It is also better to have the name to face recognition from a professor if you are in a lecture hall class."

ATHLETICS

HUGE

"There is so much team spirit at Illinois State! Everyone enjoys going to the athletic games especially against the rival schools. Students also like to be involved in try outs for sports too."

Spread the Red

"We have a campaign called Spread the Red (I know, it sounds kind of funny), but what it is is that every Friday students wear a school shirt and at times, especially during the beginning of the year, people have give aways if they see students wearing their shirts."

CAMPUS DINING

Always an Option

"There are a lot of options when it comes to campus dining. Usually you will be able to find exactly what you are hungry for. Sometimes the people working can be mean but a lot of people try to sneak in guests without paying."

The Dining Halls Are Good... to Good.

"The flex dollar system is a wonderful program that should never change. The dining halls, on the other hand, need to focus a bit more on offering less unhealthy food options as everyday options and incorporating more healthy choices as everyday options."

Frequently Compared Schools:

Illinois Wesleyan University
Northern Illinois University
University of Illinois
University of Iowa

CAMPUS HOUSING

Tri Towers Are the Best

"The tri towers are the best dorms for anyone. They are the farthest away from campus, but it has the best cafeteria and is the most fun. Friendly people and all three dorms are connected underground."

Many Dorm Choices

"There are different dorms all around campus. The farthest ones are the Tri-Towers, which is where most of the student athletes live. Most of them are close to campus, but some can be ditty."

GUYS & GIRLS

Girls at ISU

"The girls are a big positive here, but they generally only go for the cocky guys....typical. As the for the guys at ISU...there isn't much to talk about."

Girls Are Pretty and Sexy

"In ISU, you find the girls are all charming. They have awesome appearance. They have blue eyes, blonde hair and evil shape of body! They are undeniably hot and sexy. They wear shorts and tubes sometimes even to class. They hair nice-painted nails and accessories on their bodies. And one more, they do not feel shy to kiss by the roadside and they start a relationship in days."

HEALTH & SAFETY

Uuuber Secure

"I have never even thought about feeling un-safe at the College of DuPage. Police officers are always around, and there are call stations everywhere. Nothing ever happens, which makes me wonder... "why even have so much security?""

LOOKING FOR MORE?

Check out our full-length guide to this school at collegeprowler.com/illinois-state-university/.

Illinois Wesleyan University

1312 N. Park St.; Bloomington, IL 61702
(309) 556-1000; www.iwu.edu

THE BASICS:

Acceptance Rate: 54%
Yield: 29%
Setting: Small city
Control: Private Non-Profit
Total Undergrads: 2,069
SAT Range: 1170–1400*
ACT Range: 26–30

Student-Faculty Ratio: 11:1
Retention Rate: 93%
Graduation Rate: 83%
Tuition: $33,982
Room & Board: $7,776
Avg. Aid Package: $25,006
Students With Aid: 95%

of 1600

Academics	B+	Greek Life	A
Athletics	B-	Guys	B-
Campus Dining	B+	Health & Safety	A-
Campus Housing	B	Local Atmosphere	B
Campus Strictness	B+	Nightlife	B
Computers	B	Off-Campus Dining	B-
Diversity	D	Off-Campus Housing	B
Drug Safety	B	Parking	A
Facilities	B+	Transportation	C+
Girls	B	Weather	C+

CP's Student Author On...
OVERALL EXPERIENCE

As most students realize by their second or third year at Illinois Wesleyan, this school is exactly what it claims to be: a small, liberal arts school. This small student body facilitates intimate peer relationships but prevents social interaction on a large scale. The liberal arts approach to education is meant to introduce new ways for students to approach problems, as well as expose students to fields of study they may not otherwise experience. These gen ed requirements can be burdensome for music majors, theater majors, or students with a double major, who already need to overload on classes.

For many students, IWU could be substituted with a more affordable institution. For business majors, there are more sensible options. The business and economics school at IWU is respectable, but not worth the amount of tuition as compared to state schools. The atmosphere at IWU benefits from a mix of academia, down-to-earth students, and intelligent students with strong opinions. Conversations and colloquiums on campus are informed and debated, but pretension is popular.... For the rest of this editorial, visit collegeprowler.com.

Students Speak Out On...
OVERALL EXPERIENCE

Q Positive Experience Overall
"I'm happy with my choice. The faculty needs to help students more in terms of career guidance, etc. Sports are dominant and fun. There's parties if you want them."

Q Overall Experience
"Overall...the education you hear about is overrated, the food sucks, parking can be a nightmare, and facilities are average, however, greek life and partying can be good."

Q "At first, I was bummed I didn't get into University of Chicago or Washington University, but from what I've now learned about those institutions, I'm thankful for the smaller community and atmosphere here."

Q "I don't wish I were anywhere else, because I plan to go to grad school. IWU is a great launching point for further education."

Q "I thought about transferring my freshman year until I realized that everyone has an awkward first year. I enjoy it here and look forward to graduating in the spring."

BEST OF ILLINOIS WESLEYAN

1. Classes: the combination of small class sizes and knowledgeable professors
2. Outspoken and opinionated students
3. Community atmosphere fostered by cross-curricular exposure

Happy Students
93% of students return after their first year.

Proven Success
83% of students will complete their education and graduate with a degree.

WORST OF ILLINOIS WESLEYAN

1. The likelihood of never leaving the Wesleyan bubble
2. The small and unimpressive main quad
3. The difficulty in meeting new people when you know everyone on campus

Expensive
Tuition is a steep $33,982, one of the most expensive rates in the country.

Student Body

African American:	6%	Male Undergrads:	41%
Asian American:	4%	Female Undergrads:	59%
Hispanic:	3%	Living On Campus:	76%
International:	4%	Living Off Campus:	24%
Native American:	0%	Male Athletes:	39%
White:	78%	Female Athletes:	21%
Unknown:	5%	Fraternity Members:	33%
From Out-of-State:	17%	Sorority Members:	25%

Frequently Compared Schools:

DePauw University
Illinois State University
Northwestern University
University of Illinois

Students Speak Out On... EVERYTHING!

ACADEMICS

Q "The teachers here all have a passion for what they do, so their enthusiasm makes going to class interesting. Some classes only permit so much flexibility in teaching style, given the subject matter, like economics and math."

Q "The teachers are well-educated, but not all of them can teach. It's up to you to find classes that sound interesting. The selection is not bad because even lower-level classes offer diverse subject matter."

Q "The majority of the faculty is well-qualified and professional. It varies from class to class, but generally there is a nice balance between interesting subject matter and enthusiastic professors."

ATHLETICS

Q **Lame**

"If you are looking for fun college sports, tailgating, and rivalry, do not come here. I have been to like one football game in all 3 years here and not a single basketball game and I am not out of the ordinary. I go to a lot of soccer games but that is because I know a lot of people of the teams and used to play myself. Sports are absolutely not a priority here unless you are actually on the team."

Q "Varsity sports are huge at Wesleyan. There are a lot of athletes who attend. Intramural sports are pretty big also. There's just about anything you're looking for here."

CAMPUS DINING

Q **Food**

"the food here isn't very good, except on a few nights and a few menu options. I'm being pretty merciful with this C actually. Not a lot of healthy options at all...lots of fried food"

Q "Food is not too bad. They have rotating menus at Commons, so it's never the same thing night after night. Tommy's is excellent but a little pricey."

CAMPUS HOUSING

Q **Pretty Good**

"There are some really nice living options, and there are some not so nice living options. Most of the dorms are conveniently located except for one which is way off-campus and quite isolated. The dorms appear to be a bit overpriced for what one gets."

Q **Campus Housing**

"dorms are pretty nice, but they don't have wireless and the regultions heating and cooling of the buildings can be annoying"

GUYS & GIRLS

Q **Guys and Girls**

"The girls here are terrible. They generally are not attractive and not good company. For the most part they are intelligent. The guys are also for the most part intelligent, and while not trying to sound bias guys (mostly in greek life) are good looking and appealing. So really, in this grade guys would get a B+ and girls i would give a D"

Q "You can find some real winners on campus because the majority of the students here are intelligent and have good manners. The girls aren't all done up and fake-looking like they are at some colleges. There's pretty much someone for everyone here."

HEALTH & SAFETY

Q **Pretty Safe**

"While I have never felt unsafe on campus and we have plenty of Emergency lights on our small campus we do get periodical emails about attacks or threats that happen near campus although none of them are major crimes."

Q "Security is good on campus. We have plenty of blue-light security poles, and our security staff is well-trained and physically fit."

LOOKING FOR MORE?

Check out our full-length guide to this school at collegeprowler.com/illinois-wesleyan-university/.

Indiana University

107 S. Indiana Ave.; Bloomington, IN 47405
(812) 855-4848; www.iub.edu

THE BASICS:

Acceptance Rate: 73%
Yield: 31%
Setting: Small city
Control: Public
Total Undergrads: 32,490
SAT Range: 1570–1910*
ACT Range: 24–29

Student-Faculty Ratio: 19:1
Retention Rate: 89%
Graduation Rate: 73%
Tuition: $26,160
Room & Board: $7,546
Avg. Aid Package: $7,544
Students With Aid: 77%

* of 2400

Academics	B	Greek Life	B-
Athletics	A-	Guys	A
Campus Dining	B+	Health & Safety	B-
Campus Housing	B+	Local Atmosphere	B+
Campus Strictness	B	Nightlife	A
Computers	B+	Off-Campus Dining	A-
Diversity	B	Off-Campus Housing	A-
Drug Safety	C-	Parking	C+
Facilities	A-	Transportation	B+
Girls	A-	Weather	C+

CP's Student Author On...
OVERALL EXPERIENCE

IU is a well-rounded school, excelling in everything from academics to athletics. The fact that it offers something for almost everyone is the testimony given by the student body; over 40,000 kids from all over the world found IU and have made it their home for four years or more. IU's campus is an original place in an isolated little town, and while it may be in the middle of nowhere, it doesn't take long for most students to find something that makes it feel a little more like home.

Most of the complaints about IU involve its large size, and if you're looking for the kind of school where everybody knows everyone else's names, this isn't the right place for you. However, the faculty, staff, and general population of Indiana University all work together to make an otherwise intimidating atmosphere feel a bit more accepting. There are so many opportunities here that your experience at IU is undoubtedly what you make of it.... For the rest of this editorial, visit collegeprowler.com.

Students Speak Out On...
OVERALL EXPERIENCE

Q Come to Indiana University!

"Indiana University is located in a great college town. The quality of education is outstanding. The student body is diverse and dynamic. There is always something to do here whether it's going to the bars or attending a lecture."

Q Best Place on Earth!

"Indiana University is the best school on Earth to attend college. When you picture college you picture IU. From the beautiful campus, college town vibe, amazing social scene, outstanding academics in every field imaginable, a good-looking and friendly student body, students from all walks of life, amazing athletics and an insane amount of school spirit... IU is just perfect."

Q I Love Being a Hoosier!

"I love Indiana University. You meet a variety of people, and get a great eduaction at the same type. You have to stay focused, because there are over 40,000 students, which means there is always something to do. I would recommended IU to two of my friends and they are both here enjoying it as well!"

BEST OF INDIANA UNIVERSITY

1. Campus in spring
2. Hoosier basketball
3. Little 500
4. Having so many classes to choose from
5. The guys
6. The girls

Happy Students
89% of students return after their first year.

Proven Success
73% of students will complete their education and graduate with a degree.

WORST OF INDIANA UNIVERSITY

1. No parking!
2. Walking to class in the snow
3. Walking to class in the rain
4. Walking to class when it's 90 degrees
5. Overcrowded and somewhat outdated gyms

Expensive
Tuition is a steep $26,160, one of the most expensive rates in the country.

Student Body

African American:	5%	Male Undergrads:	49%
Asian American:	4%	Female Undergrads:	51%
Hispanic:	2%	Living On Campus:	36%
International:	7%	Living Off Campus:	64%
Native American:	0%	Male Athletes:	3%
White:	80%	Female Athletes:	2%
Unknown:	2%	Fraternity Members:	16%
From Out-of-State:	36%	Sorority Members:	18%

Frequently Compared Schools:

Purdue University
University of Illinois
University of Michigan
University of Wisconsin

Students Speak Out On... EVERYTHING!

ACADEMICS

Always More to Learn

"Most of the people here are here to learn. The campus and professors provide the resources for students to get whatever education they want from the school."

Kelley School Experience

"As a direct admit I have had the luxury of working with the amazing staff at the Kelley School of Business. All of the staff including advisors to professors create an experience that is both manageable and challenging. Thus far I have had great experiences with all of my business courses."

ATHLETICS

Little 500

"Indiana University promotes sports and athletic events. World famous bicycle race is held annually on campus. Many students passionately exercise for an extended amount of time in order to prepare for this competition. Millions of dollars are generated by the students to benefit community during this event. IU has a fantastic gym on campus. That is both appealing in modern technology as well as fun physical group exercises and activities."

Big Ten

"It can't get any better than IU. Students have a lot of school pride. Basketball is king, but Football is on the upswing."

CAMPUS DINING

I-Bucks and Dining Halls Are Great!!

"The food is always fresh and outstanding with all kinds of options to eat. Eating on campus never gets old from all you can eat to a-la-carte to vegan/vegetarian options! And my I-bucks roll over into my sophomore year! I can even eat in Ballantine Hall on my I-Bucks."

Best Places

"Best dinings halls include Read Food Court and Collins Food Court. Read has great waffles, burritos, and sandwiches. Collins offers vegetarian, vegan, and other alternative options to the standard food court fare."

CAMPUS HOUSING

Social Atmosphere at IU Is Incredible

"In a bustling town like Bloomington, IN there is always something going on to do. The social atmosphere is always great between the exciting basketball and football games to the many concerts playing throughout the town. IU is a busy campus and there are many events to keep all the students entained."

Campus Life

"Freshman year I had no problem meeting other people and getting around campus. Everything is accessible at almost all times, and there is a great support system with your RAs and with the people in your dorm, even if it is a big school."

GUYS & GIRLS

The Peeps Around B-Town

"People are amazing in Bloomington. Friendly, energetic, talkative people all around the campus. And trust me gentlemen if you are looking for an attractive lady, COME TO IU! The women at IU are B-E-A-UTIFUL. There is always something you can get involved with other people in and everyone is friendly and ready to meet new people."

Talk About Diversity

"Indiana University is among the most diverse and cultured campuses in the country. There are students of every walk of life and ever country on earth. You can walk the campus every day and find someone of a different race, culture or walk of life every day."

HEALTH & SAFETY

IU Feels Just as Safe as Home

"IU's campus is very safe. Police patrol alot everyday."

Safety

"There always seems to be security officers in the parking lots, and at nighttime the campus walkways and parking lots are sufficiently lit. I feel safe on campus."

LOOKING FOR MORE?

Check out our full-length guide to this school at collegeprowler.com/indiana-university/.

Indiana University of Pennsylvania

1011 South Drive; Indiana, PA 15705
(724) 357-2100; www.iup.edu

THE BASICS:

Acceptance Rate: 64%

Yield: 44%

Setting: Town

Control: Public

Total Undergrads: 12,291

SAT Range: 1310–1600*

ACT Range: —

Student-Faculty Ratio: 18:1

Retention Rate: 75%

Graduation Rate: 50%

Tuition: $15,645

Room & Board: $8,558

Avg. Aid Package: $10,032

Students With Aid: 90%

of 2400

Academics	B-	Greek Life	B-
Athletics	C	Guys	B-
Campus Dining	B	Health & Safety	C
Campus Housing	B	Local Atmosphere	C-
Campus Strictness	C+	Nightlife	B+
Computers	B-	Off-Campus Dining	B-
Diversity	C+	Off-Campus Housing	B-
Drug Safety	D+	Parking	C
Facilities	B-	Transportation	B+
Girls	B-	Weather	C-

CP's Student Author On...
OVERALL EXPERIENCE

Picking the right college often leaves students stranded between two choices: sacrificing a well-rounded education for a cheaper school, or ponying up the cash for a private education with a lot of extras. In a way that many other public schools simply aren't, Indiana University of Pennsylvania is honestly the best of both worlds. IUP students get a quality education that rivals many smaller private colleges at the public university price. Although Indiana isn't a major city, and the small-town atmosphere is something that students have to take into consideration, the town is picturesque and fun if you know where to look. Be sure to come visit before you commit to IUP, and keep an open mind when you come. Indiana has a way of growing on you.

The student body at IUP is fairly diverse, but every student can find his niche. Although 15,000 seems like a lot of students, the campus itself doesn't feel that large.... For the rest of this editorial, visit collegeprowler.com.

Students Speak Out On...
OVERALL EXPERIENCE

Q If I Had to Chose Agian I Would Still Pick IUP

"I love IUP. IUP is a great school. Professors are nice and willing to help you. The campus is beautiful. The students at IUP are friendly and I have met some of my closest friends at IUP."

Q Unique

"iup is different because the housing is all new and its petit and very tidy in terms of campus setting"

Q Excellent Experience

"I love IUP! I don't think I would have found a place quite like the atmosphere at here in the honors college. You can find places to have a good time regardless of whether or not you drink."

Q Yeop

"Its a nice school. The campus is incredibly beautiful, much more than any of the other 14 or so campuses I visited. Classes are usually fun or at least interesting, and the dorms are quite nice. The biggest issue is really the mandatory Health Class (which you will most likely NOT want to attend) and the on-campus food, which is terrible. Even so, it's a good place. Very pretty, albeit slower than east coast life. I'd still do it again."

BEST OF IUP

1. The Oak Grove
2. The Commonplace Coffee House
3. Bands and comedians performing on campus
4. Homecoming festivities
5. Scenery, especially in the fall

Knowledgeable Professors
86% of students surveyed rated the general knowledge of professors as above average.

Low-Stress Course Load
57% of students surveyed rated the manageability of work as above average.

WORST OF IUP

1. Parking
2. Poor weather conditions
3. Scheduling classes
4. Lack of (legal) nighttime activities
5. Partying/public drunkenness

Students Can't Wait to Get Out of Town
67% of students surveyed said that there's no way they would live here after graduation.

Student Body

African American:	11%	Male Undergrads:	45%
Asian American:	1%	Female Undergrads:	55%
Hispanic:	2%	Living On Campus:	33%
International:	3%	Living Off Campus:	67%
Native American:	0%	Male Athletes:	5%
White:	76%	Female Athletes:	4%
Unknown:	7%	Fraternity Members:	9%
From Out-of-State:	8%	Sorority Members:	8%

Frequently Compared Schools:

Penn State
University of Pittsburgh
West Chester University of Pennsylvania
West Virginia University

Students Speak Out On... EVERYTHING!

ACADEMICS

MUSIC, MUSIC, MUSIC

"My college is all about music and that is my major and my plan for my life...music education."

My First Year

"I have been satisfied so far with my college's curriculum upon my major. Although I am only a freshman and is not yet eligible for the internship/job opportunities, I am pleased with how often they are around. The workload is not much, and easy to complete due to my interest within the subject."

ATHLETICS

Okay School Spirit

"basketball games just now and then. stadiums are not full but has enough supporters and fans. IUP team performance has been great.supportive students buy merchandise."

Sports on Campus

"I don't pay attention to sports for the most part, but I do attend volleyball games. The team is very good, and the fans that go (which is sometimes somewhat limited) tend to be really into the games. The field house they play in is pretty nice and there is an even nicer athletic center being built."

CAMPUS DINING

Food and Dining Options

"The dining halls are very well put together. They have a variety of food options for people to choose from. There are three total dining halls to eat and they are average with the cost of meals. You can use your flex money at each of those locations and it is easy to get lunch in between classes. I wouldn't complain about any of the food because it is good, quality food."

Good

"The food no matter what your going to get tired of it, but the food is exceptable and its good."

CAMPUS HOUSING

Residential Revival

"I love IUP's Housing. It is the primary reason why I chose this school. The rooms are spacious and inviting. They are a bit expensive, but the convenience definitely makes them worth every penny."

Social Atmosphere

"Campus as a great social atmosphere because every one knows every one and there are always a lot of social event on campus housing"

GUYS & GIRLS

Girls and Guys Are All Different

"The campus is made up of mostly white and black students, but there are Indian, Arabic, Asian, etc. races and everyone in those categories tends to dress like each other. White girls tend to dress preppy or hipster, and there are a lot of girls that wear NorthFace and Uggz. Guys tend to dress in sweats or preppy collared shirts. The Black community dresses similarly, too, with a certain style and often certain brands."

A Taste of the Upper Class

"The guys make it a habit of only wearing clothes in the latest new jersey style, or they choose to dress in the typical stoner fashion. The girls on the other hand will wear remarkably little if its sunny, or leggings as pants if its remotely cold. Typical day in the IUP life would include skipping class in the morning and attending no less than three frats at night. Most relationships here are lucky to last more than a night."

HEALTH & SAFETY

Good

"great security i feel safe theres almost too much that i feel like theyre trying to take over the campus and start a kind of mini army"

LOOKING FOR MORE?

Check out our full-length guide to this school at collegeprowler.com/indiana-university-of-pennsylvania/.

Iowa State University

2415 Union Drive; Ames, IA 50011
(515) 294-5836; www.iastate.edu

THE BASICS:

Acceptance Rate: 87%	**Student-Faculty Ratio:** 16:1
Yield: 42%	**Retention Rate:** 84%
Setting: Small city	**Graduation Rate:** 67%
Control: Public	**Tuition:** $17,871
Total Undergrads: 22,521	**Room & Board:** $7,277
SAT Range: 1040–1330*	**Avg. Aid Package:** $4,440
ACT Range: 22–28	**Students With Aid:** 88%

* of 1600

Academics	B	Greek Life	A
Athletics	A-	Guys	A-
Campus Dining	A-	Health & Safety	B+
Campus Housing	B	Local Atmosphere	B
Campus Strictness	B-	Nightlife	B+
Computers	B+	Off-Campus Dining	B+
Diversity	B-	Off-Campus Housing	B+
Drug Safety	C	Parking	B
Facilities	A-	Transportation	A+
Girls	B-	Weather	C+

CP's Student Author On...
OVERALL EXPERIENCE

For the most part, students enjoy their Iowa State experience. Iowa State is a large school with a beautiful campus and a reasonably diverse population. The first year can be difficult for many students, especially those who are not from the Midwest and are away from their families. It can be hard adjusting to college life, but once friends are made, the experience improves. Lifelong friendships are formed at Iowa State. Ames is a town that supports the college atmosphere, and students can quickly feel at home here. Iowa can have a few too many seasons for students not used to such dramatic weather, but students who can survive the first year find that the rest of their time at ISU gets easier.

Iowa State is a university of science and technology, so students in other fields may want to thoroughly investigate their fields of study before enrolling at Iowa State over another institution. You get out of college what you put into it. No matter where you are, if you are determined to learn, to make friends, and to succeed, your college experience will be fun.... For the rest of this editorial, visit collegeprowler.com.

Students Speak Out On...
OVERALL EXPERIENCE

Q Lovin' the Life

"I love college life, as my mom told me I would. She knows best!"

Q Unique Experience

"There are so many ISU traditions that make everything about college fun. You would have to be and cyclone to know what I'm talking about. Ames is awesome."

Q Loving Ames

"I love this school, its a great place to get an education. Ames has an active night life but studies do take priority. The athletic events are always fun and there is great tailgating opportunities. The Veishea festival in the spring is a great time to enjoy what the university has to offer along with career fairs every semester."

Q I Love It

"Iowa State is a great place to go to school. The classes are difficult and generally require studying in order to get a good grade. The campus is beautiful and I love walking around it. After I was adjusted to the size of the campus it had much more of a small college feel to it than I had expected."

BEST OF IOWA STATE

1. The people
2. Ethernet
3. VEISHEA events
4. The beautiful campus
5. Campaniling
6. Sports
7. The strong academic reputation

Happy Students
84% of students return after their first year.

Knowledgeable Professors
91% of students surveyed rated the general knowledge of professors as above average.

WORST OF IOWA STATE

1. Finding a place to park
2. Tuition hikes
3. Walking to class in the winter
4. The Ames City Council's lame ordinances
5. Budget cuts
6. Parking tickets

Lowest Grades
Drug Safety: C
Weather: C+
Diversity: B-

Student Body

African American:	3%	Male Undergrads:	56%
Asian American:	3%	Female Undergrads:	44%
Hispanic:	3%	Living On Campus:	39%
International:	6%	Living Off Campus:	61%
Native American:	0%	Male Athletes:	3%
White:	81%	Female Athletes:	3%
Unknown:	4%	Fraternity Members:	14%
From Out-of-State:	34%	Sorority Members:	17%

Frequently Compared Schools:

Purdue University
University of Illinois
University of Iowa
University of Minnesota

Students Speak Out On...
EVERYTHING!

ACADEMICS

Iowa State Is Amazing

"Iowa State has been the best choice I have ever made. There science and technology school of engineering is amazing with great professors and a very detailed curriculum. Plenty of internships and study abroad opportunities are made available. The work load is pretty heavy being a technology school."

I Love My Major!

"I'm in Dietetics and I really like it so far. All the teachers that I have are amazing and I'm always excited to learn new things about nutrition. Being healthy is really important to me so I can teach by example. I want to help others to learn more about what the right choices are and how to make their favorite recipes with healthy alternatives."

ATHLETICS

Sports Is Pretty Good

"We have a lot of school spirit for sure and our basketball has potential to be amazing. Football is the big thing at Iowa State even though our team is great. All of the athletic facilities are top notch though with great rec centers."

School Spirit

"Excellent school spirit. Every body dresses up in their red and gold for tailgating and any sporting event. It is all in good spirit."

CAMPUS DINING

Very Good and Varied

"Iowa State offers a number of options around campus to eat. Naturally, students get tired of eating at the same dining hall every day, but there are several options to expand your dining experience. The food is very good and you can almost always expect the schedule to be varied enough to enjoy your favorites but to also try something new."

Season's

"The food is great!! The have many different options everyday and those options change throughout the day and the week. If you need something to eat between classes than its great too because you can go in and git a to go container of whatever you can fit in the container."

CAMPUS HOUSING

Dorm Living Is the Life for Me!

"I love the contact with other students. There's always someone to do things with."

Very Comforatable

"The dorms at Iowa State University are relatively good size and are a safe place to stay. There is a great variety of housing options for both underclassmen and upperclassmen."

GUYS & GIRLS

Engineers and Agriculture

"There are engineers and plenty of country kids. Iowa is an agricultural school,it's great."

Diverse!

"At a school as big as Iowa State you will see students of all kinds. And when I say all kinds, I really mean it! Not to be racist, but we have a heavy population of chinese students. We have our jocks, our nerds, and everything in between. Iowa State really is a diverse campus as far as looks, interests, dress, social life, and relationships go."

HEALTH & SAFETY

Safe

"In the past year it has only become not that safe I guess, this guy named John Luacina I think it was, disappeared for about 3 months and they found him dead in a barn the was going to be torn down. And then a month later some girl got pushed on to railroad tracks and got ran over. But before this year it has been really safe, I blame the freshman. No not really, that was a joke."

Personal Safety

"As far as I am concerned, this place is very safe and I don't need to worry about any safty problem."

LOOKING FOR MORE?
Check out our full-length guide to this school at collegeprowler.com/iowa-state-university/.

Ithaca College

953 Danby Road; Ithaca, NY 14850
(607) 274-3011; www.ithaca.edu

THE BASICS:

Acceptance Rate: 74%	**Student-Faculty Ratio:** 12:1
Yield: 21%	**Retention Rate:** 86%
Setting: Suburban	**Graduation Rate:** 77%
Control: Private Non-Profit	**Tuition:** $32,060
Total Undergrads: 6,440	**Room & Board:** $11,780
SAT Range: 1585–1900*	**Avg. Aid Package:** $17,353
ACT Range: 23–28	**Students With Aid:** 91%

* of 2400

Academics	B+	Greek Life	D+
Athletics	C	Guys	A-
Campus Dining	A-	Health & Safety	A-
Campus Housing	C	Local Atmosphere	A-
Campus Strictness	B	Nightlife	B+
Computers	B-	Off-Campus Dining	A+
Diversity	B-	Off-Campus Housing	B+
Drug Safety	C-	Parking	B-
Facilities	B+	Transportation	B-
Girls	A-	Weather	C+

CP's Student Author On...
OVERALL EXPERIENCE

In evaluating their overall experience at IC, students often look to what has happened beyond the classrooms. IC offers countless opportunities to learn outside of class, and the students who take advantage of those offers are generally more pleased with their education. Many students love IC because of its size. It's hard to walk anywhere on campus without bumping into someone you know. With its great location, IC offers much off campus as well. The most common complaints are how much it costs to attend IC and the bitterly cold winter months that students have to endure.

With many things in life, students' experiences with IC are simply what they make of them. If you sit in your dorm room for four years, you will be miserable. If you experience the life Ithaca has to offer outside of the four walls of your room, you most likely won't regret your decision to attend IC. The school's high retention rate proves this. IC offers a great mix of academics and everything else the college life should offer—friends, fun, and a time to learn and grow.

Students Speak Out On...
OVERALL EXPERIENCE

Q GO HERE!
"I love the school. There are some kinks, but it really is a great experience with so much to offer. From parties to great theatre and academics, I love IC!"

Q Fulfilling
"Ithaca is a great place with fun real people. Classes are super fun because they are small and engaging. People at this school are down for a good time, but are also serious about school. Its the perfect balance."

Q Love It
"IC is such a great place to be. The people are very friendly, professors are awesome, and the campus is gorgeous. There is always an event or activity going on hosted by one of the couple hundred student organizations. I would absolutely recommend getting involved with an activity on campus, whether it be a student organization, performing arts group, or academic group, there are so many opportunities to make your college experience richer at IC."

BEST OF ITHACA

1. The friendly people
2. Many extracurricular activities
3. Cortaca Jug
4. Fitness Center, Park, science buildings, residence halls
5. Living in a college town

Happy Students
86% of students return after their first year.

Proven Success
77% of students will complete their education and graduate with a degree.

WORST OF ITHACA

1. The winter weather
2. Since IC is on a hill, climbing all the stairs
3. The price
4. Many professors are hit or miss
5. No big name performers or comedians come to campus

Expensive
Tuition is a steep $32,060, one of the most expensive rates in the country.

Expensive Dorms
Living on campus doesn't come cheap, with an average housing price tag of $6,238.

Student Body

African American:	3%	Male Undergrads:	44%
Asian American:	4%	Female Undergrads:	56%
Hispanic:	4%	Living On Campus:	70%
International:	2%	Living Off Campus:	30%
Native American:	0%	Male Athletes:	20%
White:	74%	Female Athletes:	13%
Unknown:	13%	Fraternity Members:	1%
From Out-of-State:	59%	Sorority Members:	1%

Frequently Compared Schools:

Boston University
Northeastern University
Syracuse University
University of Vermont

Students Speak Out On... EVERYTHING!

ACADEMICS

Q Depends on the School

"If you are a student in the Park School of Communications, School of Music, physical therapy program, or theatre department you will be getting a top-notch education. Our theatre department is consistently ranked as one of the top 10 in the country. Alumni are extremely helpful in job/internship searches, as well."

Q Some Classes Fill Up Fast

"Some classes fill up quickly, especially theatre and communications, mainly because of their high demand and stature as one of the best in the country."

ATHLETICS

Q Everyone Jogs

"Every time I look out the window someone is jogging. Every time I try and play volley ball people are already there. Even though Ithaca College is division III it seems like athletics have a huge influence on campus and people regularly visit the fitness center or are seen outside."

Q Growing Rapidly

"IC just built a new state-of-the-art facility for athletics which is supposed to be done within a year. We don't a have a HUGE student athlete population, but it is pretty big and there are more and more student athletes every year. We have some of the top-rated teams in the country (like our Women's Rowing and Lacrosse teams). Fans are really loyal (esp. during Cortaca) and will fight to defend IC against Cortland."

CAMPUS DINING

Q Top Notch

"While there isn't much variety, the quality of the food is excellent. Almost all produce is grown organically and locally."

Q Pretty Good

"IC has 3 dining halls, 2 small shops, a food court and a few kiosk type things in some of the buildings. The food is fine and there is quite the variety. Eventually you'll run out of different things to eat, but there is more than enough so you shouldn't get too sick of something if you don't want to."

CAMPUS HOUSING

Q Different Options for Everyone

"There are tons of choices for housing on campus. From studio apartments to double dorm rooms to independant appartments, the choices never end"

Q Convenient Quads

"The upper and lower quads aren't as modern-looking as the Terraces or as cool as the Towers, but they're much closer to everything on campus, and the rooms are usually bigger and nicer. Terraces has more single rooms and suites, but it's a bit of a hike from main campus. Upperclassmen housing like Gardens and Circles are both excellent, but you have to factor in distance and cost of living."

GUYS & GIRLS

Q Friendly

"Everyone at Ithaca college is very friendly and accepting of others. I have yet to find a crew of mean spirited or just negative people."

Q Not Many Straight Guys but Girls and Gay Guys Have Their Pick

"Straight girls may find it hard to find a steady relationship but the amount of homosexual couples on campus is astonishing. Many people are looking for a quick hook up so finding a lasting relationship can be hard."

HEALTH & SAFETY

Q Blue-Light Systems Almost Everywhere

"It is impossible to walk around campus without seeing at least two or three blue-light security systems. Student security workers also keep the campus safe, along with Ithaca city police."

LOOKING FOR MORE?

Check out our full-length guide to this school at collegeprowler.com/ithaca-college/.

IUPUI

425 University Blvd.; Indianapolis, IN 46202
(317) 274-5555; www.iupui.edu

Academics	C+	Greek Life	C
Athletics	C+	Guys	B-
Campus Dining	C	Health & Safety	B-
Campus Housing	C-	Local Atmosphere	B+
Campus Strictness	B	Nightlife	B
Computers	A-	Off-Campus Dining	B+
Diversity	B	Off-Campus Housing	B
Drug Safety	C+	Parking	C
Facilities	B	Transportation	B
Girls	C+	Weather	C+

CP's Student Author On...
OVERALL EXPERIENCE

Overall, IUPUI has a lot to offer to a lot of different people. The diversity of students at IUPUI is an illustration of what the University has to offer. Everyone is catered to in some way, whether it is through ESL learning, studies abroad, 24-hour computer facilities, wireless access, Dr. Martin Luther King Jr. service projects, resume assistance, and so much more. IUPUI may not be a traditional campus with frat parties and hookups, but students really seem to appreciate its function and purpose, which is to promote professionalism, diversity, and urban learning.

With praise comes the reality—students shouldn't go to a college thinking that everything will always be great. As with any university, IUPUI has its major flaws. As far as the physical campus itself is concerned, athletic facilities are not yet to the standard that the students can accept, parking is way below the needs of the students, and campus food is not worth the paper plates that it is served on. Too harsh? Maybe, but through the student reviews, they have shown how much they truly value their school.... For the rest of this editorial, visit collegeprowler.com.

Students Speak Out On...
OVERALL EXPERIENCE

Q **Great School**

"IUPUI is a good school with great programs. It is a commuter school and therefore has a lot of diversity. Most people feel comfortable here and fit in easily."

Q **Excellent**

"I am really glad I chose this school because I was reluctant on transferring but I love this school and I can always visit the other ones. I just wish people were friendlier and we had more campusy feel to it. Like more frats and stuff like that."

Q **Good Fit**

"I think IUPUI provides a great campus experience, but since it's a commuter campus it's what you make of it. The get the most out of it you really need to attend events or join a club, and if possible get into on-campus housing. IUPUI is diverse and always evolving."

Q **Experience**

"I really enjoy the experience IUPUI has to offer. They have all kinds of fun and sociable events. Also, many of the events that IUPUI offer will help you academically."

BEST OF IUPUI

1. Service learning
2. Diversity of students
3. Minimal partying and more learning
4. Campus in the heart of Indy
5. Multicultural festivals and activities

Easy Financial Aid Process
52% of students surveyed told us that the financial aid process went smoothly and they received the financial aid they needed.

WORST OF IUPUI

1. Parking
2. Lack of student involvement in extra-curriculars
3. Food on campus
4. Not enough dorms
5. Some apathetic part-time professors

Not Everyone Graduates
33% of students do not complete their education or graduate with a degree.

Life is NOT a Party
50% of students surveyed said it's almost impossible to find a good party.

Student Body

African American:	10%	Male Undergrads:	42%
Asian American:	3%	Female Undergrads:	58%
Hispanic:	2%	Living On Campus:	3%
International:	3%	Living Off Campus:	97%
Native American:	0%	Male Athletes:	2%
White:	78%	Female Athletes:	2%
Unknown:	3%	Fraternity Members:	1%
From Out-of-State:	4%	Sorority Members:	1%

Frequently Compared Schools:

Ball State University
Indiana University
Purdue University
University of Michigan

Students Speak Out On... EVERYTHING!

ACADEMICS

Professors

"I feel that the professors at IUPUI are extremely efficient in their subjects, and are always willing to help in any way possible."

Place of Impact

"IUPUI is certainly a place of impact. The classes are not easy but the class sizes are smaller for more individual attention. There are many chances to get involved on campus and in your community. There are study abroad fairs and career fairs that connect you to places and people outside of the college to get you going in the right direction."

ATHLETICS

Basketball Games Are Awesome

"they are always pumped up and have lots of energy in the building and i love coach Hunter when he does his annual, game without shoes, so it makes people aware of the fact that there are kids without shoes out there."

Basketball Is Boss

"I would have to say that basketball is the most popular sport at IUPUI. There is a huge student following for both the men's and women's basketball teams. The students have a lot of spirit."

CAMPUS DINING

How Will I Survive?

"There will mostly be fast food."

Dining

"The dining options at IUPUI are great there is a maximum amout of choices in food courts and the surrounding areas so you have many choices and reasonable prices available to you."

CAMPUS HOUSING

Campus Apartments

"I don't know too much about campus living because I live off campus but my freshman year I made a lot of friends who lived in the dorms and the campus apartments. They were nice and we were able to have fun with in reason. The apartments located next to campus that are not exactly housed by IUPUI is where most partying was done. I had a good time and felt safe. Those were the days....seven years ago."

Apartments

"They are very convenient but a little pricey. It is nice to have your own bedroom, bathroom, a full kitchen, and a washer and dryer."

GUYS & GIRLS

Everyone Has Their Own Style

"There is a multitude of diverse students at IUPUI. Despite the diverstity everyone gets along great and there is a great sense of teamwork. It's cool because there is a lot that is learned from each other and all of the different backgrounds of the students."

Normal

"I love IUPUI for the diversity. Many, many different kinds of people go to IUPUI. Young, old, white, black, athletes, science majors, etc."

HEALTH & SAFETY

I've Never Really Thought About It, but I Feel Safe.

"I really don't know much about crime that goes on on the campus. I've never been raped or murdered, so I suppose it's a pretty secure place."

Very Safe

"There are emergency buttons and lights all over campus. If you ever feel unsafe, just call the campus security for a vehicle escort. The campus intersects many busy roads and because it's downtown there is always someone around."

LOOKING FOR MORE?

Check out our full-length guide to this school at collegeprowler.com/indiana-university--purdue-university-indianapolis-(iupui)/.

Jackson State University

1440 J.R. Lynch St.; Jackson, MS 39217
(601) 979-2121; www.jsums.edu

THE BASICS:

Acceptance Rate: 48%
Yield: 20%
Setting: Mid-sized city
Control: Public
Total Undergrads: 6,803
SAT Range: —
ACT Range: 16–20

Student-Faculty Ratio: 18:1
Retention Rate: 76%
Graduation Rate: 43%
Tuition: $11,358
Room & Board: $5,693
Avg. Aid Package: —
Students With Aid: 89%

Academics	C+	Greek Life	A
Athletics	B-	Guys	A
Campus Dining	B	Health & Safety	C+
Campus Housing	B+	Local Atmosphere	C-
Campus Strictness	C	Nightlife	B+
Computers	B	Off-Campus Dining	C+
Diversity	C	Off-Campus Housing	C+
Drug Safety	C+	Parking	C
Facilities	B-	Transportation	B-
Girls	B	Weather	B

CP's Student Author On... OVERALL EXPERIENCE

Jackson is the home of many, and the future home of many to come. Prospective students always want to know: Why choose JSU? Choosing Jackson State is one of the best choices a student can make in his or her life. Many people are quick to judge this University because of its HBCU title. Once you're here, though, you receive a reward that will be remembered. Every school has it down sides, some more than others, but this does not characterize the University's ability and what it can do for you.

Students at JSU strive to raise the standards and live above the stereotype set out for JSU. They show love for their school through sports, academics, and community service. Attending JSU teaches you to respect others and use common sense. If you did not know who you were before entering, you will know upon graduation.

The professors are very encouraging, and they care about their students. The knowledge they instill in one is different but comprehension. Many professors have personal relationships with their students, and it makes the college ride a smooth sailor.... For the rest of this editorial, visit collegeprowler.com.

Students Speak Out On... OVERALL EXPERIENCE

Q My Dear Old College Home

"Jackson Fair, Jackson Dear thee I love my dear old college home!!! My Jackson State University is the ONLY place to be. Here, a student that manages their social life with their academics will always prevail and enjoy this beckon of education that is Jackson State University! I love this school!!!"

Q It's My Heart

"There is no other place like it. The campus is one big family. There is something for everybody here. A place where academics and fun are perfectly balanced"

Q The Best Decision

"Choosing Jackson State has been the highlight of my life. I came here knowing no one and now i have friends for a lifetime. there is so much to do and get involved in. i am a member of Tiger P.r.i.d.e. connections where i currently serve as a member of the executive board. my school has the best of the best we get our work done and reward ourselves with various activities."

BEST OF JACKSON STATE

1. Advisers
2. Community service
3. Faculty and staff
4. Family atmosphere
5. Greeks
6. Open mic
7. Plays
8. Social gatherings

Affordable
Tuition is only $11,358, one of the most affordable rates in the country.

Big Dorms
67% of students surveyed felt that dorms were more spacious than average.

WORST OF JACKSON STATE

1. Food – Wal-Mart will be your best friend.
2. Parking – the early bird gets the worm, literally.
3. Visitation – strictly enforced hours

Not Much Diversity
One of the least racially diverse campuses—only 5% of students are minorities.

Student Body

African American:	95%	Male Undergrads:	37%
Asian American:	0%	Female Undergrads:	63%
Hispanic:	0%	Living On Campus:	31%
International:	0%	Living Off Campus:	69%
Native American:	0%	Male Athletes:	10%
White:	4%	Female Athletes:	4%
Unknown:	0%	Fraternity Members:	11%
From Out-of-State:	34%	Sorority Members:	19%

Frequently Compared Schools:

California University of Pennsylvania
Florida A&M University
Grambling State University
Louisiana State University

Students Speak Out On...
EVERYTHING!

ACADEMICS

A 3 Word Summary

"I came to Jackson State University because my parents are both alumni. I am currently majoring in business marketing, which Jackson States staff is very helpful with assistance. When I need any help the business department is great about giving me the tools I need to complete a task, or comprehend something."

Biomedical Science Is #1 at JSU

"Science majors at Jackson State are very competitive, the teachers are willing to help you if you want to help yourself. There are plenty opportunities for internships and jobs."

ATHLETICS

JSU Athletes a+ - F-

"Our football team was not very successful last semester however, our boys basketball team was great! The made it very far in the SWAC championship. The games are always sold out and it gives people a chance to enjoy themselves legally!"

Involvement

"The students are very involved in athletics, but the faculty seems to not care as much."

CAMPUS DINING

The Legacy

"The legacy is very nice and sanitary! Also the seating arrangements are pretty well!!!"

Food Is Okay but Sometimes Repetitive

"we get a good variety of food but some days the food kind of repeats."

CAMPUS HOUSING

Dorm Life

"In each of the dorms, all students are equipped with the essentials..i.e.bed, desk, cable ready, telephone service(one time service fee), internet ports and wireless capabilities. Safety is a plus within the dorms as they're cameras located throughout the building and the only way someone can gain access inside the building is by using they're id cards which are activated to the student's particular dorm specified at the time of housing registration."

Dorm Living

"I believe living on campus is a a learning experience. I say this because you have to live in the dorm in which you are classified, whether you like it or not. Not only that but you have to share a bathroom with three other females, so getting to the bathroom first is always a hassle. However, it does keep you abreast of what is going on campus and keeps you socially attatched to the campus life."

GUYS & GIRLS

Relationships

"Who's dating who and How long are they going to last is the hot topic on campus. It is important to find the one in college, so that you may be able to grow."

HEALTH & SAFETY

Safe

"I have always felt safe when i stepped on JSU's campus. Campus police patrol daily and are serious about their job."

Don't Feel Safe

"As a student on campus we have a lot security officers, and police officers but I still don't feel safe on campus. We have a places on campus where security guards are not located at night like by the library, and other buildings where students go for study time. I strongly believe that they should secure the entire campus instead of part of the campus."

LOOKING FOR MORE?

Check out our full-length guide to this school at collegeprowler.com/jackson-state-university/.

James Madison University

800 S. Main St.; Harrisonburg, VA 22807
(540) 568-6211; www.jmu.edu

THE BASICS:

Acceptance Rate: 65%
Yield: 63%
Setting: Small city
Control: Public
Total Undergrads: 17,281
SAT Range: 1580–1870*
ACT Range: 22–26

Student-Faculty Ratio: 16:1
Retention Rate: 92%
Graduation Rate: 82%
Tuition: $19,376
Room & Board: $7,386
Avg. Aid Package: $7,891
Students With Aid: 55%

* of 2400

Academics	B-	Greek Life	B
Athletics	B-	Guys	A-
Campus Dining	A	Health & Safety	C+
Campus Housing	B+	Local Atmosphere	B
Campus Strictness	B-	Nightlife	B+
Computers	B	Off-Campus Dining	B
Diversity	C+	Off-Campus Housing	A+
Drug Safety	C-	Parking	C
Facilities	A-	Transportation	B+
Girls	A	Weather	B-

CP's Student Author On...
OVERALL EXPERIENCE

Students note that Harrisonburg comes up short, as far as bars and nightclubs go. As a result, apartments and houses have become the main party venues. Some students complain about the fact that most of JMU's students are heavily involved in the party scene. On Monday morning, as you dodge empty kegs and red plastic cups on your walk from the apartments to campus, it's hard to believe that not everyone takes part in the weekly hullabaloo. However, if you choose to abstain, even the most dedicated of drinkers will most likely respect your choice.

Although students will lodge some minor complaints about the excessively flourishing festivities, the whimsical weather, the perpetual parking pitfalls, and the lack of notable nightlife, the overall consensus is that JMU is a lovely location to live. With JMU's beautifully landscaped campus, the close proximity of the luscious Shenandoah Valley, the knowledgeable professors, friendly staff, and warm-hearted student body, it's not a huge surprise that students spend four or more very happy years at James Madison University.... For the rest of this editorial, visit collegeprowler.com.

Students Speak Out On...
OVERALL EXPERIENCE

Q JMU = AMAZING

"JMU has been my home for four years and I would recommend the school to anyone. There are extracurriculars for every person, the professors genuinely love being there, and the food is incredible. LOVE this school!"

Q <3 <3 Love JMU!!!!

"I loved living in a dorm (may sounds strange, but my hallmates are literally my best friends). I guess this may make JMU different. JMU has lots of parties on weekends, all with no cover charge and pretty nice about letting random strangers into them. This does get sort of annoying though. There is nothing else to do on weekends except drink."

Q I Love JMU!

"JMU is a fantastic school, and I enjoy ever minute I spend here. The campus is gorgeous, the people are friendly (everyone holds the door for everyone!), the classes are challenging but not impossibly so, the food is #3 in the nation! Overall I really enjoy being here."

BEST OF JAMES MADISON

1. The Quad
2. JMU Marching Band
3. UREC
4. The Breeze, JMU's student newspaper
5. Free movies, at Grafton or hosted by clubs

Happy Students
92% of students return after their first year.

Proven Success
82% of students will complete their education and graduate with a degree.

WORST OF JAMES MADISON

1. Saturday make-up days for inclement weather
2. Winter weather in the springtime
3. The guy/girl ratio
4. Lack of bars and nightclubs
5. The Modular Building

Lowest Grades
Drug Safety: C-
Parking: C
Diversity: C+

Student Body

African American:	4%	Male Undergrads:	41%
Asian American:	5%	Female Undergrads:	59%
Hispanic:	2%	Living On Campus:	36%
International:	1%	Living Off Campus:	64%
Native American:	0%	Male Athletes:	3%
White:	81%	Female Athletes:	4%
Unknown:	6%	Fraternity Members:	10%
From Out-of-State:	34%	Sorority Members:	12%

Frequently Compared Schools:

Penn State
University of Delaware
University of Virginia
Virginia Tech

Students Speak Out On...
EVERYTHING!

ACADEMICS

Great Atmosphere

"Everything around is so pretty and the people are so incredibly nice. Wonderful!"

Health Sciences/Health Studies Concentration

"I love my major. Other than a few classes, I've thoroughly enjoyed the subjects I've studied and the professors who've taught me. The class size is usually reasonable, so the professors and students are able to interact more 1-on-1 and collectively than the larger classes. Its important to get to know your professors, especially since many of them teach multiple courses that Health Science majors are required to take."

ATHLETICS

Not Great, but Fun

"Our football and our basketball teams are not great, but still really fun to watch. People are not crazy about our teams, but do show our support at the games. We are getting a new stadium. Overall, I like how JMU does sports. Basically, they are fun when nothing else to do, but not a lifestyle."

Everyone Can Go to Games

"We dont have the best teams but we everyone can go to all the games. There is so much school spirt and everyone is envoled on game days!"

CAMPUS DINING

Yummm

"amazing. thers so many choices and its so delicious!"

Fantastic. Something for Everyone.

"The two main dining halls on campus always have fantastic food with plenty of variety. There are options for every style of diet. Huge salad bars, home-cooked style meals, and a bakery make any diner a happy camper."

CAMPUS HOUSING

On Campus Housing: Access to Everything!

"I chose to live on campus for two years at James Madison University because the freshman and sophomore dorms were close to my classes and allowed me the opportunity to meet new people. I felt extremely connected to campus and all it had to offer."

Off Campus Life

"James Madison University has plenty of stuff for people, like me, who live off campus. Not everything is restricted to people in the dorms. They have great transit system that reduces my driving considerably."

GUYS & GIRLS

Girls Girls Girls

"JMU has 60% female, 40% male ratio. All generally attractive, but some are stereotypical college girls. Most of them are pretty easy to talk to. There are guys here too. Most fit the typical frat-boy kinda deal. But there are some who are not. Again, most are pretty chill and are easy enough to get along with"

Guys and Girls

"The guys are a little bit tougher to find because it's 60-40 girls to guys. Alot more pretty girls than good looking guys but there are definitely more good looking guys that have come in."

HEALTH & SAFETY

Amazing!

"Before you start freshman year, the school has you take this fun online course called "AlcoholEdu". The object is to make you more aware about alcohol intake. Also they've given out flu shots."

Great Safety

"There is a great sense of safety on campus. There are emergency phones all over campus and I've very often walked back from the library very late at night and felt completely safe."

LOOKING FOR MORE?

Check out our full-length guide to this school at collegeprowler.com/james-madison-university/.

John Carroll University

20700 N. Park Blvd.; Cleveland, OH 44118
(216) 397-1886; www.jcu.edu

THE BASICS:

Acceptance Rate: 81%
Yield: 24%
Setting: Suburban
Control: Private Non-Profit
Total Undergrads: 2,986
SAT Range: 1430–1760*
ACT Range: 21–26

Student-Faculty Ratio: 13:1
Retention Rate: 83%
Graduation Rate: 80%
Tuition: $28,840
Room & Board: $8,330
Avg. Aid Package: $23,033
Students With Aid: 99%

* of 2400

Academics	B	Greek Life	C+
Athletics	C	Guys	A-
Campus Dining	C+	Health & Safety	C+
Campus Housing	B	Local Atmosphere	B-
Campus Strictness	B-	Nightlife	B
Computers	B	Off-Campus Dining	B
Diversity	C-	Off-Campus Housing	B
Drug Safety	C+	Parking	B
Facilities	C+	Transportation	B
Girls	B+	Weather	B-

CP's Student Author On...
OVERALL EXPERIENCE

Overall, students love being students at John Carroll, but it is important to remember that there are always things that could be better—no matter the university. However, most John Carroll students said that they would pick JCU again if they had the chance to do it all over. The close community at John Carroll is really one of the University's biggest pluses. You will never love everything about the school that you choose, but it is important to pick a school based on what is important to you.

A lot of students tell freshmen that if they don't get involved in things on campus, they will miss out on a lot of great opportunities, fun times, and wonderful people. This is true. College is mostly what you make it. It is about meeting new people, growing as a person, and taking advantage of experiences and opportunities that are readily available to you. John Carroll will become your home and your friends will become your family. It is a wonderful feeling to be at what you feel is "the right school" for you.

Students Speak Out On...
OVERALL EXPERIENCE

Q So Much to Do So Little Time..

"I came to John Carroll not excited at all really about college. As soon as I got active on campus this has been the best two years of my life so far! If I had to choose all over again it would totally be John Carroll."

Q Great Campus, Students, Faculty, and Facilities

"This is a great place to go to college. There are events for evryone put on by the programming board and of course there are parties. Sometimes they get out of hand, but overall it's a great place!"

Q The Truth

"I love going to JCU. It's a small community and people are friendly. The truth of the matter though is, you only get out of it what you put in. You will be bored if you do not do anything. Take advantage of the opportunities and clubs on campus. I have yet to meet anyone from a department on campus that hasn't been friendly."

BEST OF JOHN CARROLL

1. Close shopping areas
2. Clubs and student organizations
3. Friends
4. The newspaper (The Carroll News)
5. The people
6. Residence life

Happy Students
83% of students return after their first year.

Proven Success
80% of students will complete their education and graduate with a degree.

WORST OF JOHN CARROLL

1. Cafeteria meal prices and dining variety
2. Cliques
3. Distribution of athletic funding
4. High tuition
5. No variety of majors
6. A lot of gossip

Expensive
Tuition is a steep $28,840, one of the most expensive rates in the country.

Student Body

African American:	6%	Male Undergrads:	49%
Asian American:	2%	Female Undergrads:	51%
Hispanic:	3%	Living On Campus:	46%
International:	0%	Living Off Campus:	54%
Native American:	0%	Male Athletes:	26%
White:	78%	Female Athletes:	14%
Unknown:	11%	Fraternity Members:	8%
From Out-of-State:	31%	Sorority Members:	14%

Frequently Compared Schools:

Loyola University Chicago
Marquette University
Miami University
Ohio State University

Students Speak Out On... EVERYTHING!

ACADEMICS

Teachers Rock

"The teachers on campus really care about the students."

Political Science

"My specific major offers a lot of help, interesting classes, and also a wide range of classes to take to fulfill the requirements. Also, all of the professors within the department are very helpful and help make the study of politics very interesting."

ATHLETICS

Athletic Facilities

"The athletic facility at JCU is decent, however I feel that it is too small at times. There is a good variety of machines but I often find myself having to do something else while I wait for the machine that I want to use; which is annoying when I have a time-limit. The main times that this is true is when there are sports teams that are there all together."

Cross Country Gets Minimum Funds

"All sports compete at a D3 level. Some teams are the best in the conference. Others aren't. It's all about how hard the athletes are willing to work. The distance running team does not receive adequate funding compared to the football team in order to provide equipment to the athletes, but the close social group on the team is worth it."

CAMPUS DINING

May Need to Be a Little Inventive..

"The food is pretty good on campus, but the variety is not huge. You may need to be creative in forming your dishes. The Einstein's Bros. Bagels and Inn Between on campus are yummy!"

Better Than Most

"JCU's dining hall offers food on a 4-week rotation, meaning the meals are the same every four weeks. There is a wide variety of food offered every day, and also gives options for vegetarians. There is only one dining hall on campus, so the food does get repetitive after awhile. Be ready for waits in line exceeding 10 minutes during high traffic hours."

CAMPUS HOUSING

Pricey but You Get What You Pay for!

"Even though John Carroll is known for being a pretty big expense, you can get your moneys worth. There are so many volunteer opportunities, on-campus activities and cultural events to participate in! So as long as you take advantage of all it has to offer this is a great place for the price."

Dorms

"I've lived in a dorm the whole time I've been here and I find the dorm atmosphere very fun. I could have possibly just lucked out, but the floors I lived on my first couple years on campus were awesome. However, now that I'm a junior I'd rather live off-campus, but overall the dorms are a great experience."

GUYS & GIRLS

Unsure

"This will be my first semester back into this school since 2001, I do not know what the guys and gals look like or how they behave or what they're interest are or seem to be."

Dress and Looks

"Guys wear polo and J-Crew clothes and there are not a lot of blonde-haired guys. The girls are good looking and dress well, not trashy."

HEALTH & SAFETY

Personal Safety

"I have never been scared for my personal safety on or around campus."

Campus Safety Services

"Our campus safety services are reliable and they work hard to keep our campus safe. They could do more walking rounds around the campus instead of driving during the day and night!"

LOOKING FOR MORE?

Check out our full-length guide to this school at collegeprowler.com/john-carroll-university/.

Johns Hopkins University

3400 N. Charles St.; Baltimore, MD 21218
(410) 516-8000; www.jhu.edu

THE BASICS:

Acceptance Rate: 28%
Yield: 31%
Setting: Large city
Control: Private Non-Profit
Total Undergrads: 5,831
SAT Range: 1940–2230*
ACT Range: 29–33

Student-Faculty Ratio: 11:1
Retention Rate: 96%
Graduation Rate: 89%
Tuition: $39,150
Room & Board: $12,040
Avg. Aid Package: $31,130
Students With Aid: 60%

of 2400

Academics	A-	Greek Life	A
Athletics	C+	Guys	B+
Campus Dining	B	Health & Safety	B+
Campus Housing	A-	Local Atmosphere	B
Campus Strictness	B+	Nightlife	B+
Computers	B+	Off-Campus Dining	B
Diversity	A-	Off-Campus Housing	A-
Drug Safety	D+	Parking	C+
Facilities	B+	Transportation	A
Girls	B-	Weather	C+

CP's Student Author On...
OVERALL EXPERIENCE

Students who love Hopkins and students who hate it both recognize that JHU isn't the school for everyone. Many students believe that classes at JHU are just as hard as Ivy League schools, but they complain that Hopkins' professors grade much harder. Many students wish that Hopkins offered grade inflation, as other top schools do, since even people who work hard sometimes end up with low grades. This influences some students to put studying above any social activity in hopes of being one of few people in a class who receives an "A." Hopkins offers a variety of social programming, but no one forces students to participate, and there's no one holding your hand and leading you to fun activities. Even though students complain, most say that they've enjoyed being challenged by their experiences at Hopkins.

Hopkins presents a well-rounded experience for most students, but not every student takes advantage of the academic, social, and extracurricular opportunities.... For the rest of this editorial, visit collegeprowler.com.

Students Speak Out On...
OVERALL EXPERIENCE

ℚ Play Hard, Work Hard(Er)

"I love JHU and most things about it. However, it does come with a lot of stress and competition. We work our butts off during the week, party on weekends, and get ready for hell week again on Monday."

ℚ It's a Wonderful School

"John Hopkins is an experience greatly deserved. To come hear is like being in the mist of some Americas great leaders. The environment is friendly, people are awesome (diversity craze), teachers are caring yet strict disciplinarians, and school has many programs to get into. It's a wonderful place to be."

ℚ Great Choice

"I would definitely choose Hopkins again. Although the athletic scene is lacking, most of the rest of the activities are great."

BEST OF JOHNS HOPKINS

1. Research opportunities abound. If you want to do research as an undergraduate, Hopkins is a great choice.

Happy Students
96% of students return after their first year.

Proven Success
89% of students will complete their education and graduate with a degree.

WORST OF JOHNS HOPKINS

1. Many students feel that professors are more concerned with their own research than with helping the students they teach.

Expensive
Tuition is a steep $39,150, one of the most expensive rates in the country.

Expensive Dorms
Living on campus doesn't come cheap, with an average housing price tag of $6,882.

Student Body

African American:	7%	Male Undergrads:	49%
Asian American:	21%	Female Undergrads:	51%
Hispanic:	6%	Living On Campus:	56%
International:	7%	Living Off Campus:	44%
Native American:	1%	Male Athletes:	16%
White:	49%	Female Athletes:	10%
Unknown:	9%	Fraternity Members:	24%
From Out-of-State:	90%	Sorority Members:	23%

Frequently Compared Schools:
Brown University
Columbia University
Cornell University
University of Pennsylvania

Students Speak Out On...
EVERYTHING!

ACADEMICS

ℚ Academic Excellence
"The history department is great. The professors really care, and are always there to help you. The academic level is very impressive, with a lot of students involved in research in addition to their classroom work."

ℚ Nursing
"The program is VERY intense. You always have a large workload and studying to do."

ATHLETICS

ℚ School Spirit
"Students at JHU are crazy about lacrosse!! They are also very supportive of other teams. However, the majority of students attends only lacrosse games."

ℚ No School Spirit
"The athletic teams at Johns Hopkins are very good and competitive, but the student body as a whole doesn't support them all that much however. The football team made it to the elite eight for D3 NCAA tournament this year, and hardly anyone came to the games other than family members of the players."

CAMPUS DINING

ℚ Better Than Expected
"I have eaten at several different colleges, and Hopkins has been the best so far. There is a great variety of meals, and many options are available for those with special dietary needs. The staff at the dining facilities are very helpful, and they are happy to get you a to-go box if you don't have time to eat-in. Everything is fresh and of good quality."

ℚ Eat Off Campus!
"Baltimore has tons of great restaurants! Don't waste your time and money at the dining hall, venture out and discover great food!"

CAMPUS HOUSING

ℚ It Depends
"Its more expensive to stay on campus, but it is safer, funner, and closer. Freshman dorms are the closest, but they are small and only include a room. Upperclassman get a lot more."

ℚ Fine for the First Year
"Then move! It's more fun and spacious to find off-campus housing and prices are reasonable."

GUYS & GIRLS

ℚ General Review of Students at Johns Hopkins
"There are a wide variety of students at Hopkins, with a similarly wide variety of associated interests, both academic and extra curricular. It is certainly possible to find a group or groups of people who are interested in the same kinds of things as you. The pre med students can be somewhat crazy at times with respect to their studying, but in general people are able to find time and balance studying, sleeping, and socializing."

ℚ People
"mostly girls, very few males and everyone is very focused on school."

HEALTH & SAFETY

ℚ There Are Uniformed Police Officers on Every Corner
"Hopkins makes sure to keep security as a major priority. in the couple blocks just off campus there are still police officers and cars. But once you get past a couple blocks, you're on your own. There are blue lights in some neighborhoods and if you see those blue lights it means you're in a bad neighborhood and should leave the area immediately."

LOOKING FOR MORE?
Check out our full-length guide to this school at collegeprowler.com/johns-hopkins-university/.

Juniata College

1700 Moore St.; Huntingdon, PA 16652
(814) 641-3000; www.juniata.edu

THE BASICS:

Acceptance Rate: 71%	Student-Faculty Ratio: 13:1
Yield: 27%	Retention Rate: 85%
Setting: Town	Graduation Rate: 80%
Control: Private Non-Profit	Tuition: $31,550
Total Undergrads: 1,532	Room & Board: $8,650
SAT Range: 1100–1310*	Avg. Aid Package: $17,035
ACT Range: 24–28	Students With Aid: 100%

* of 1600

Academics	B	Greek Life	N/A
Athletics	B-	Guys	B-
Campus Dining	C+	Health & Safety	A+
Campus Housing	B	Local Atmosphere	B-
Campus Strictness	A-	Nightlife	C-
Computers	B	Off-Campus Dining	B-
Diversity	D	Off-Campus Housing	C+
Drug Safety	A-	Parking	B+
Facilities	A-	Transportation	D-
Girls	B	Weather	C

CP's Student Author On... OVERALL EXPERIENCE

Too good to be true? Possibly, but overall, most Juniata students really do love Juniata. They don't always like it, but most of the time they do. Why do they love it, and why do they not? Because Juniata is a small college in a small town. Yes, it has its advantages, and it has its drawbacks. If something's going to kill your experience, it's bound to be its smallness. But overall and overwhelmingly? Well, you've just read it. Students and professors are warm, welcoming, and largely open-minded. Opportunities on campus and around the world are literally endless and growing.

The College is not perfect, but if something's wrong or broken, the administration does its best to fix it. Students appreciate that. As with anything you love, it's true that sometimes you just don't like whatever it is you say you adore, but that doesn't change your feelings in the end. That pretty much sums up the Juniata experience. Students work hard, have fun, find their passions, and prepare for the world and the future. They also occasionally pull their hair out from claustrophobia. But in the end, they do appreciate Juniata, both while they're there and after they graduate.... For the rest of this editorial, visit collegeprowler.com.

Students Speak Out On... OVERALL EXPERIENCE

Q **WOO**
"I love my school and I would never leave it. My professors are amazing, my friends are genuine people, and my small mindedness is quickly being remedied by hours of hard work. There is no room for slacking here, but that is exactly what I wanted in a school, and that is exactly what i got from Juniata."

Q "I don't know how I got here, but I'm here and it fits. I wouldn't trade it unless I was accepted to Princeton. Everyone is helpful and most people are very nice."

Q "I absolutely loved Juniata—beautiful campus, friendly, interested (and interesting) professors, cute little town, and so many cool people I met while I was there. If I had to choose again, I'd definitely pick Juniata. On the other hand, since I've never attended a different college, I don't have that much to compare it to, really, and maybe if I'd picked somewhere else, I would have thought that was the 'best place ever,' too."

BEST OF JUNIATA

1. Your peers
2. Your profs
3. The individual POE
4. Mountain Days
5. Madrigal-both tenting out and the dinner/dance

Happy Students
85% of students return after their first year.

Proven Success
80% of students will complete their education and graduate with a degree.

WORST OF JUNIATA

1. The lack of a student center
2. The lack of diversity
3. Finding a place to park
4. The Sodexho food
5. The bathrooms in Sherwood
6. J's closing

Expensive
Tuition is a steep $31,550, one of the most expensive rates in the country.

Not Much Diversity
One of the least racially diverse campuses—only 14% of students are minorities.

Students Speak Out On... EVERYTHING!

ACADEMICS

Q Intl Politics

"This is one of the best academic class at my school It is very tough. You have to study as hard as possible. Otherwise, you'll get a bad grade. You have to write a four-page essay with more than forty sources in the class. This is very tough, but in the end you would know a great grasp of the topic."

Q

"Generally, the teachers are very helpful. It is rarely a problem to meet after class or in their office for extra help. Classes are small, so in-class discussion is useful, plus it helps keep the classes interesting."

ATHLETICS

Q Juniata Sports and Recreation

"Juniata isn't known for our football team, we're not known for our baseball team, and we're not really all that well known for our soccer teams. What people do know about Juniata, is that we hold our own in volleyball. If the varsity sports aren't your thing, there are many more club sports that students can become involved in."

Q Sports Not Top Priority

"Sports are not huge at Juniata College. The football team was pretty pathetic, but it has been improving a lot. Volleyball and Basketball are very good, and have a lot of support from the students. Other schools don't like playing at Juniata because we support our teams so strongly. I do not think the other sports teams get as much support. The athletic facilities are pretty great. There are many intramural and club sports, rugby and frisbee are very popular."

CAMPUS DINING

Q

"We have Baker and Muddy Run. If the food in Baker sucks (our main cafeteria), you can always go to Muddy Run and get a burger and fries or a sub."

Q

"The food at Juniata is okay, not the best, but not horrible either. Eventually, you acquire a taste for it and maybe grow to like it. I really had no huge complaints about it, although at times, it gets a bit crowded in the cafeteria. Meals at Juniata

were always a great time to get together with friends and share the ups and downs of college life. Muddy Run Café is a nice choice if you get sick of Baker. Jitters also has Starbucks coffee and some good snacks."

CAMPUS HOUSING

Q If Your Not an Upper Classman, Dorms Suck

"The lowerclassman dorms are small, dark, and have a completely cold feel to them. It doesn't matter how nicely one tries to cover it up, the fact ifs the the dorms feel more like prison cells than comfortable rooms to live and learn in. The only exception ot this are the upperclassman dorms, but most of these are also the furthest for the academic buildings, thus forcing the students to choose between comfort and convenience."

Q

"The dorms are pretty nice compared to other campuses I've seen. Avoid North and Sherwood at all costs. Girls, Lesher has the biggest rooms and biggest closets. South is always fun."

GUYS & GIRLS

Q

"I've noticed the girls coming in behind me were rather shallow, self-centered, and materialistic. I mean, do you really need to take your cell phone into the dining hall? I don't think so. And then you wonder why you're eating all by yourself. The guys are pretty split. They are either pretty mature for college guys and hold the doors open for the ladies, or they act like five year olds."

Q

"Most everyone is friendly and pretty cool. There are plenty of hot people on our campus."

HEALTH & SAFETY

Q I Feel Safe

"I feel very safe on campus. I can leave my backpack in the library, unwatched, for hours at a time and know that nothing will happen to it. There is a comforting sense of trust with the other students. There have been a few vandalism acts with bicycles though...other than that it is a very safe campus."

Kansas State University

Anderson Hall; Manhattan, KS 66506
(785) 532-6250; www.k-state.edu

THE BASICS:

Acceptance Rate: 98%	Student-Faculty Ratio: 20:1
Yield: 45%	Retention Rate: 79%
Setting: Town	Graduation Rate: 58%
Control: Public	Tuition: $17,577
Total Undergrads: 18,774	Room & Board: $6,752
SAT Range: 1470–1890*	Avg. Aid Package: $7,033
ACT Range: 21–26	Students With Aid: 81%

of 2400

Academics	B	Greek Life	A+
Athletics	A	Guys	B+
Campus Dining	B+	Health & Safety	B
Campus Housing	B	Local Atmosphere	B
Campus Strictness	C+	Nightlife	B+
Computers	B	Off-Campus Dining	B+
Diversity	C+	Off-Campus Housing	B
Drug Safety	C	Parking	B
Facilities	A-	Transportation	B+
Girls	B	Weather	B-

CP's Student Author On... OVERALL EXPERIENCE

You can laud it as Middle America magic, or you can write it off as institutional brainwashing, but there's no denying that Kansas State has a way of winning the hearts of its students. Not everyone is thrilled to matriculate, but by the time graduation rolls around, all but a handful of curmudgeons are smitten with the school. Exactly why this occurs is not immediately apparent. Odds are it's not the parking. Or the clement weather. And tasty as Call Hall ice cream is, the "Yum!" factor goes only so far.

But maybe it has something to do with the people behind the ice cream counter—and behind the Hale reference desk and behind the classroom podiums. The welcome, the warmth, and the willingness to help a freshman track down an article on Parkinsonian ataxia from a 1928 issue of an out-of-print medical journal the night before his psych paper is due are all part of what makes K-State great. Or maybe it's the town—after the initial resignation to Manhattan's limited offerings, students learn to swear by its bars and coffeeshops. Or maybe it's that transcendent cream pie at the end of the dinner line.... For the rest of this editorial, visit collegeprowler.com.

Students Speak Out On... OVERALL EXPERIENCE

Q Great Environment!

"Really educational and I would love to continue my education on this campus, because of the size of the classes which are mostly small, and teacher are alway willing to help during office hours. I would recommend this school to anyone ready for college, also for international student like me who have learned English just here and now can speak and write almost as a native speaker!"

Q Phenomenal

"I have really enjoyed the 5 semesters I have been here. The students, faculty, and Manhattan locals are very friendly and welcoming. People look out for each other. The classes are pretty good. There is a great push for education, and focusing on success past college. The resources provided for students are very helpful, and changes are made based on what students need. I would choose to come her again in a heartbeat."

BEST OF K-STATE

1. ASI 601: Physiology of Lactation
2. Bosco Plaza's water "feature"
3. Wrist-wrestling Intramurals
4. The option of declaring a major in horticultural therapy

Easy Financial Aid Process
50% of students surveyed told us that the financial aid process went smoothly and they received the financial aid they needed.

WORST OF K-STATE

1. Bacon cheeseburger pizza
2. George Strait on repeat
3. Purple
4. White
5. Together
6. Sunday morning shower tiles
7. Dead Week – it's ALIVE!

Lowest Grades
Drug Safety: C
Diversity: C+
Campus Strictness: C+

Student Body

African American:	4%	Male Undergrads:	52%
Asian American:	2%	Female Undergrads:	48%
Hispanic:	3%	Living On Campus:	37%
International:	4%	Living Off Campus:	63%
Native American:	1%	Male Athletes:	3%
White:	83%	Female Athletes:	3%
Unknown:	4%	Fraternity Members:	20%
From Out-of-State:	20%	Sorority Members:	20%

Frequently Compared Schools:

University of Kansas
University of Missouri
University of Nebraska
University of Oklahoma

Students Speak Out On... EVERYTHING!

ACADEMICS

Hale Library Is a Great Place to Study

"I live out of town and Hale Library is a great place to go for those long hours in between classes. It has all the resources you will need and even has a 24 hour study lab. It makes things so much more convenient."

The Professors at Kansas State University

"The professors at Kansas State University are very hands on and helpful. They are willing to make extra time in their schedules to work with you on learning the information. During finals there are always opportunities to attend review sessions and work on study guides. They welcome anyone with open arms and are egar to help students when they need it."

ATHLETICS

Awesome Athletes

"Our sports rock, although we might not be the number one seed, the crowd is loud and proud, and every game is chuck full of fun and entertainment, not to mention our basketball team made it to the elite eight!"

Kansas State Salina Athletics

"The athletics at Kansas State Salina are growing in numbers. This campus has basketball, cheer leading, baseball, and many other sports and sport like activities. Kansas State of Salina has a bran new athletics department that has weights, a walking path, a basketball court, televisions, classes, and many other incentives. The best part is that as a student use of the facility is FREE!"

CAMPUS DINING

Great Selection

"The food on campus is great and several choices for everyone. They have healthy choices as well as selections for those with allergies or specific diets."

Derby Dinning Center

"Lots of variety, good food, and healthy choices also."

CAMPUS HOUSING

Interesting Yet Fun

"Living on campus is very convienient. When I lived in the dorms I was very close to everything, and the food was good. I always had somebody to help me out with just about anything. Now I live in the on campus apartments, and they are awesome. There is a shuttle to campus, and I have the same support here as I did in the dorms. It is nice to live around students, it helps me to feel more welcome. I love it, otherwise I wouldn't have lived here for the past 3 years"

Goodnow, Marlatt, Jardine, Haymaker.......!

"The residence halls are great at Kansas State. There is a distinct sense of community on each of the different floors and I know that on my floor I have made some great lifelong friends. They are close to campus and are not too small. Perfect for freshman and cost efficient for every student!"

GUYS & GIRLS

Sea of Purple

"Everyone dresses how they want. You see a sea of purple though. The Wildcat support is phenomenal! We have amazing team support and cheer on our Wildcat athletes at every sporting event! People are friendly and helpful"

HEALTH & SAFETY

Campus Is as Safe as You Make It

"As long as you are careful and demonstrate some situational awareness, there is little to worry about. As a man I never feel scared or intimidated to walk about campus at night, I have also noticed that the female population doesn't seem to be feel threatened while walking alone at night. The campus is well lit and if you are safe you need not worry about any personal harm."

LOOKING FOR MORE?

Check out our full-length guide to this school at collegeprowler.com/kansas-state-university/.

Kent State University

800 E. Summit St.; Kent, OH 44242
(330) 672-3000; www.kent.edu

THE BASICS:

Acceptance Rate: 74%
Yield: 39%
Setting: Suburban
Control: Public
Total Undergrads: 19,918
SAT Range: 900–1150*
ACT Range: 19–24

Student-Faculty Ratio: 20:1
Retention Rate: 78%
Graduation Rate: 49%
Tuition: $16,418
Room & Board: $7,940
Avg. Aid Package: $8,492
Students With Aid: 90%

*of 1600

Academics	C+	Greek Life	C+
Athletics	B-	Guys	A-
Campus Dining	B+	Health & Safety	C+
Campus Housing	B-	Local Atmosphere	B
Campus Strictness	B-	Nightlife	B+
Computers	B	Off-Campus Dining	B
Diversity	C+	Off-Campus Housing	B
Drug Safety	C-	Parking	B-
Facilities	B+	Transportation	B
Girls	A-	Weather	C-

CP's Student Author On...
OVERALL EXPERIENCE

Kent State is the university that everyone loves to pretend to hate. But at the end of the day, there are very few students who would trade their college experience for anything else. Other universities are fun to visit on the weekends, but Kent State has an atmosphere that is welcoming to students and feels like a home away from home. If you ask an alumni of Kent State about his or her college years, most will think back on them fondly, and some will even say they were the best years of their life.

Kent State is known for its parties, but it's obvious that drinking is not all that matters to the students here. Year by year, Kent State is gaining more and more prestige in the university world by improving its programs and facilities. Most of its staff members are experts in their fields and have years of experience, which they are happy to pass down to budding students. The majority of the students at Kent State have moved past the liberal, in-your-face attitude from the '70s that put KSU in the history books. They're just trying to get their degree, move on to the next phase in their lives, and have a little fun while doing so.

Students Speak Out On...
OVERALL EXPERIENCE

Q **Excellent School**

"i would recomend this school to anyone looking to start their education. it is a great school with many advantages, and also opportunities."

Q **I Love Kent!**

"Besides the occassional mishap, I have absolutely loved everything about Kent State. We have a great atmosphere, and a great variety of majors and people. A lot of people dub Kent as "dumb", but we have excellent Fashion, Medical, Architecture, Nursing, Psychology, and several other programs."

Q **Loving Kent**

"Kent is a great school for me. Its a very social school and very very diverse. Its alot of orginazation join and come become apart off. If you love diversity then you will love kent. Draw backs alot of the black girls and guys like to clique up and never branch out and the asian kids stick together but if your not shy you can penatrate any group and be well accepted. =)"

BEST OF KENT STATE

1. The Rec
2. Black squirrels
3. The abundance of clubs
4. Friendly people
5. Student publications
6. Safe campus
7. You can walk anywhere on campus

Knowledgeable Professors
88% of students surveyed rated the general knowledge of professors as above average.

Big Dorms
63% of students surveyed felt that dorms were more spacious than average.

WORST OF KENT STATE

1. The weather
2. Parking
3. The football team
4. 05/04/09
5. The bus system
6. Lack of beef
7. Too many frats
8. Small Group

Lowest Grades
Drug Safety: C-
Weather: C-
Diversity: C+

Student Body

African American:	9%	Male Undergrads:	42%
Asian American:	2%	Female Undergrads:	58%
Hispanic:	2%	Living On Campus:	35%
International:	2%	Living Off Campus:	65%
Native American:	0%	Male Athletes:	4%
White:	82%	Female Athletes:	2%
Unknown:	4%	Fraternity Members:	1%
From Out-of-State:	0%	Sorority Members:	1%

Students Speak Out On... EVERYTHING!

ACADEMICS

Q Great Environment With Helpful Staff

"Kent State University has a great music faculty who are always there to support and help you throughout your musical career, whether it is advising related or just general encouragement. The professors are friendly and work with you throughout your registration process, and they always keep in mind what your workload will be when registering your classes as well as keeping your interests and preferences a top priority."

Q Broad Spectrum of Study Areas

"I specifically came to Kent State because of the high ranked graphic design program that they have. It is one of the most difficult majors because of the heavy course work and workload. I wanted to go to one of the best schools so that is why I came here."

ATHLETICS

Q Kent State Athletics

"I play baseball at Kent state currently and have been very impressed with the state of the art fitness center and other facilities Kent offers its athletes."

Q Well Supported and Well Maintained

"The athletics here at Kent State University are not only well maintained and up-kept, but also well supported by the student body. Game attendance is usually fairly high and the spirit drowns out the opposing team. Sports facilities are taken care of and the players themselves do a great job of maintaining the facilities they use."

CAMPUS DINING

Q Rosie's: Tri-Towers Necessity

"Rosie's Diner at Kent State University is a great place to order food. In addition, Rosie's is also a great place to shop for groceries while you wait for your order. It is located in the Tri-Towers building, so if you live in a dorm nearby, I would suggest stopping by for a nice meal at Rosie's."

Frequently Compared Schools:

Miami University
Ohio State University
Ohio University
University of Cincinnati

Q Awesome With Variety

"There are so many places to choose from. You can buy food and make it or sit down and eat. We have many well known places to eat such as Damon's Grill, Subway, Einstein Brother's Bagels, and Arthur Treacher's. The grocery stores are awesome and you can use your meal plan like a debit card, it has dollars on it."

CAMPUS HOUSING

Q Many Living Places

"There are a variety of places to live on campus with different set ups. There are older dorms and there are brand new dorms. They are all of good quality and space. My dorm hall is one of the oldest buildings on campus and I still really like my living space."

Q Housing

"The better options house upperclassmen. The new dorms are gorgeous, and right in the middle of campus."

GUYS & GIRLS

Q Fashion Majors Are Everywhere

"Since Kent State University is ranked third in the country and 13th in world, there are many girls who attend Kent State to pursue a career in fashion. The women are always dressed nice, present themselves with class and are extremely attractive. There is not a day that goes by that I do not meet a new female in the fashion department."

Q Diversity

"There is a lot of diversity. There are all types of guys and girls."

HEALTH & SAFETY

Q Excellent.

"Any time an incident occurs, campus security and city police [if necessary] are on top of taking care of it. Whether referring students to support services, investigation or arrest and expulsion."

LOOKING FOR MORE?

Check out our full-length guide to this school at collegeprowler.com/kent-state-university/.

Kenyon College

103 College Drive; Gambier, OH 43022
(740) 427-5000; www.kenyon.edu

THE BASICS:

Acceptance Rate: 39%	**Student-Faculty Ratio:** 10:1
Yield: 30%	**Retention Rate:** 91%
Setting: Rural	**Graduation Rate:** 88%
Control: Private Non-Profit	**Tuition:** $40,980
Total Undergrads: 1,618	**Room & Board:** $7,260
SAT Range: 1850–2130*	**Avg. Aid Package:** $26,969
ACT Range: 28–32	**Students With Aid:** 67%

* of 2400

Academics	A-	Greek Life	B
Athletics	C+	Guys	B-
Campus Dining	B	Health & Safety	A-
Campus Housing	B	Local Atmosphere	C+
Campus Strictness	B-	Nightlife	D+
Computers	B-	Off-Campus Dining	C-
Diversity	C-	Off-Campus Housing	D
Drug Safety	C+	Parking	B
Facilities	B	Transportation	C-
Girls	B-	Weather	C+

CP's Student Author On...
OVERALL EXPERIENCE

Kenyon College is a small school in rural Ohio. There is no student union, the "town" is one block long, the weather is unpredictable at best, and half the dorms are said to be haunted. English, the most popular department, sends out its majors to work at supermarkets. However, you still wouldn't be able to ask any current student or alum, "Do you like Kenyon?" without setting aside at least 45 minutes for the answer. Kenyon casts a spell on everyone who passes through it—all the things that might initially make it sound unappealing are, in the end, what make the place so special. No one else will ever have a college experience quite like a Kenyon student. Everyone at Kenyon is there for the simple reason that they want to be. They have not come for the glamour of a big city, and they have not come because of an Ivy League name to drop at parties. They have chosen Kenyon in spite of all its deficiencies, or perhaps because of them. Kenyon's isolation simply means that there is nothing to distract students from learning and from each other.... For the rest of this editorial, visit collegeprowler.com.

Students Speak Out On...
OVERALL EXPERIENCE

Q Love It
"It's been the best years of my life in almost every respect."

Q Raging Party Scene and Good Academics
"Students here really work hard and play hard. The social scene is dictated by the Greeks who host large, noisy, drunken parties but the academics more than make up for the lack of social variation."

Q "Kenyon has poisoned me forever. I desperately want to get on with my life, and I never, ever want to leave. This place is perfect and deeply dysfunctional. It is not in any way, shape, or form like real life, and why should it be? It's college."

Q "The people are incredible and have made my college experience wonderful. Kenyon is the perfect college for anyone who is serious about their studies, and life in general. And of course, you'll have an incredible time."

BEST OF KENYON

1. The people
2. The campus
3. Easy connection with professors
4. Getting a great education without getting it forced down your throat
5. The isolation of the hill

Happy Students
91% of students return after their first year.

Commitment to Teaching
There are 10 students for every member of faculty on campus.

WORST OF KENYON

1. Facilities
2. Being surrounded by cornfields
3. Parking
4. Language classes that meet nine times a week
5. The isolation of the hill

Expensive
Tuition is a steep $40,980, one of the most expensive rates in the country.

Students Speak Out On...
EVERYTHING!

ACADEMICS

Amazing

"Challenging, interesting classes in all departments (except American Studies and Sociology, the two easiest departments). Great professors who genuinely care about their students, with many being available almost 24/7. Intellectual atmosphere throughout campus (recently witnessed an argument between two frat boys about the morality behind British colonialism in the KAC weightroom)."

Political Science

"While the vast majority of Kenyon's student body is liberal, including myself, Kenyon's Political Science department is well known its conservative leanings (ex. Straussian Political Philosophy). While this could be a source of tension, they overwhelmingly promote debate through completely understanding all sides of an issue. Professors David Leibowitz, Fred Baumann, and Pam Jensen are all outstanding. The Political Science department is widely regarded as one of Kenyon's best departments."

ATHLETICS

Swimming and the KAC

"The KAC is in a class of it's own among D3 athletic centers. If a small college in this country has a better training center, I've never heard of it. The sports teams are average in strength as a whole, but the school has an amazing legacy in swimming. It's been more than three decades since the lords of the water managed to disappoint."

"The two highest profile sports are football and men's basketball. Football, which has heightened importance because of Kenyon's location in Ohio, and men's basketball has had three coaches in the past six years, regularly only draw 300 to 400 people to a weekend game. Those numbers put us near the bottom of our conference."

CAMPUS DINING

AVI and Peirce

"The renovation of Peirce, Kenyon's beautiful dining hall, were completed two years ago, and the dining experience at Kenyon has improved dramatically since. Nevertheless, there's not a lot of variation, and the single location dining system means that a meal requires a decent walk for most students."

Dining Hall Only

"The dining hall food is pretty good, but it's the only option available to students. Since campus is so remote, there aren't restaurants nearby."

CAMPUS HOUSING

Few Options

"Housing is limited on campus, which is made worse by the fact that off-campus housing doesn't exist. Unlike at a lot of colleges, Kenyon has very few suite style rooms and most dorms are much more traditional. The nicer housing--such as suites--is cost prohibitive because scholarships only cover the most basic double room in a dormitory."

"Caples, an upperclass dorm, is a nine-story pencil, and it is generally considered the least desirable dorm on campus."

GUYS & GIRLS

Odd and Interesting!

"There are plenty of pretty girls here! And they are all interesting!"

Girls Are Terrible

"A common lament of Kenyon men that can be heard throughout campus is the lack of attractive girls. The fact is that attractive girls are few and far between. The majority of girls are mediocre in terms of attractiveness, personality, interests etc. Many girls will freely admit that the girls are nowhere as attractive as the men on campus. If you are a decent looking girl with a good personality, you can clean up at Kenyon."

HEALTH & SAFETY

Very Safe

"Kenyon is in the middle of nowhere in Ohio. There isn't much crime happening."

LOOKING FOR MORE?

Check out our full-length guide to this school at collegeprowler.com/kenyon-college/.

La Roche College

9000 Babcock Blvd.; Pittsburgh, PA 15237
(412) 367-9300; www.laroche.edu

THE BASICS:

Acceptance Rate: 68%	**Student-Faculty Ratio:** 12:1
Yield: 33%	**Retention Rate:** 60%
Setting: Suburban	**Graduation Rate:** 64%
Control: Private Non-Profit	**Tuition:** $21,638
Total Undergrads: 1,230	**Room & Board:** $8,756
SAT Range: 1170–1510*	**Avg. Aid Package:** $13,000
ACT Range: 17–22	**Students With Aid:** 97%

* of 2400

Academics	B-	**Greek Life**	N/A
Athletics	C-	**Guys**	B
Campus Dining	D	**Health & Safety**	B-
Campus Housing	A-	**Local Atmosphere**	B+
Campus Strictness	A	**Nightlife**	B-
Computers	C	**Off-Campus Dining**	B+
Diversity	C	**Off-Campus Housing**	B+
Drug Safety	B+	**Parking**	B-
Facilities	B+	**Transportation**	C
Girls	B+	**Weather**	C+

CP's Student Author On... OVERALL EXPERIENCE

La Roche is a small campus, but it has plenty of resources. With a library full of books and a spacious student union area, there's something for everyone. The teachers and students here have a very personal connection, and everybody knows your name. To most students, this is what their ideal college is all about. However, La Roche is very expensive and doesn't offer many of the things that larger schools have—Greek life, an on-campus health clinic, 24-hour dining services, and campus bars and restaurants to name a few—which turns a lot of people away from this beautiful campus.

It would be hard for someone at La Roche to go their entire career without meeting someone from the other side of the world. La Roche's international students set it apart from other schools. The people make this college. From the students, traditional and non-traditional, to the college activities directors who will be at every function dancing and partying with students, everyone is friendly.... For the rest of this editorial, visit collegeprowler.com.

Students Speak Out On... OVERALL EXPERIENCE

Q "I have a feeling when I graduate from La Roche I will have confidence in my new skills to be successful in my career."

Q "The education here is great, but the La Roche campus is socially boring."

Q "I like that my teachers know my name. They know what sports I play, and they care about my grades. That's really nice."

Q "You really have a chance to stand out and be part of clubs without getting lost."

Q "I hate this place. I don't like the administration or the way everything seems to be a big secret."

Q "I love the small community atmosphere of this school. Teachers are always there for you, and you never get lost in a mass of nameless faces."

Q "I get a ton of personalized attention at La Roche, which I am just thrilled with."

BEST OF LA ROCHE

1. Small campus community
2. Dorms with bathrooms in every room
3. The bookstore
4. Proximity to Pittsburgh
5. The Booze Cruise
6. Personable and knowledgeable faculty

Personal Attention
You can expect personal attention with 74% of classes having less than 20 students.

WORST OF LA ROCHE

1. The long wait for public safety to respond to a call
2. Lighting in the parking lots
3. Bad public transportation
4. High tuition that keeps rising

Lowest Grades
Campus Dining: D
Athletics: C-
Computers: C

Student Body

African American:	5%	Male Undergrads:	35%
Asian American:	1%	Female Undergrads:	65%
Hispanic:	1%	Living On Campus:	36%
International:	11%	Living Off Campus:	64%
Native American:	0%	Male Athletes:	22%
White:	71%	Female Athletes:	11%
Unknown:	11%	Fraternity Members:	0%
From Out-of-State:	25%	Sorority Members:	0%

Students Speak Out On... EVERYTHING!

ACADEMICS

Q "The education I have been—and still am—receiving at La Roche College is wonderful. I feel as though I'm truly being prepared for the professional business world."

Q "I cannot imagine a better education from a higher education institution."

Q "The teachers here tend to encourage their students to reach their goals. They will go to any length to help their students achieve anything they want."

ATHLETICS

Q "Wait a second—do we actually have sports teams at La Roche? Wow, you learn something new every day!"

Q "The jocks think they are so much better than everyone, and that's funny because they suck at sports."

Q "To be honest, I don't even know if we have sports on campus."

CAMPUS DINING

Q "The food in the caf is hit or miss. Some days it's really good, and some days you're stuck with cereal for dinner. I recommend the demo cooking."

Q "The food's bad. Period."

Q "The cafeteria has the worst food I've ever encountered in my life."

CAMPUS HOUSING

Q "If you have an emergency or need help with something, such as a new light bulb for the bathroom, be prepared to wait."

Q "The dorms are nice, but there are too many little things that go wrong."

Frequently Compared Schools:

Carnegie Mellon University
Duquesne University
Penn State
University of Pittsburgh

Q "The best part of La Roche College is the dorms. They're much nicer than any of the dorms at other colleges I visited."

GUYS & GIRLS

Q Girls Are Prissy...Guys Are Mostly Foreign

"Most girls are kind of stuck up, but they are cute. The one's that are more friendly, aren't as great looking. There are exceptions. Guys usually are baseball players or from other countries. Usually you can find a few friends that make good buds."

Q "There really aren't that many great-looking guys. They're all very scrawny and have the stereotypical punk-rocker look to them. The girls are really snobby."

Q "The baseball team has a bad reputation, but most of them are actually pretty cool guys."

HEALTH & SAFETY

Q "La Roche is considered one of the safest campuses in the nation. That seems safe to me."

Q "No one has died, and nothing has hit major news, so I think our campus is pretty safe."

Q "I think students feel safe here. I do. Nothing bad ever really happens. Since everyone knows everyone else's business, it's hard to get away with things."

LOOKING FOR MORE?

Check out our full-length guide to this school at collegeprowler.com/la-roche-college/.

Lafayette College

Quad Drive; Easton, PA 18042
(610) 330-5000; www.lafayette.edu

THE BASICS:

Acceptance Rate: 42%	Student-Faculty Ratio: 11:1
Yield: 26%	Retention Rate: 95%
Setting: Suburban	Graduation Rate: 89%
Control: Private Non-Profit	Tuition: $38,490
Total Undergrads: 2,406	Room & Board: $11,799
SAT Range: 1750–2060*	Avg. Aid Package: $25,063
ACT Range: 26–30	Students With Aid: 64%

* of 2400

Academics	B+	Greek Life	A
Athletics	B	Guys	B+
Campus Dining	B-	Health & Safety	B+
Campus Housing	B+	Local Atmosphere	C
Campus Strictness	B-	Nightlife	C
Computers	B	Off-Campus Dining	B-
Diversity	C-	Off-Campus Housing	D
Drug Safety	C+	Parking	C
Facilities	A-	Transportation	D-
Girls	B+	Weather	C+

CP's Student Author On...
OVERALL EXPERIENCE

For the Leopards who take the time to meet people, get to know their professors, and dive into their academics, Lafayette can be a very rewarding place. One of the best qualities of the college is its community atmosphere; in certain aspects, it is definitely a family. Like at any school, students support one another, and spend almost every waking moment together, and this close comfort is a benefit instead of a detriment. Lafayette College students know how to work hard. They all know what they are getting into with the intense course load, but they also love to have fun with their friends and it shows. The Greek system and nightlife are popular (karaoke on Wednesdays!), and social organizations are thriving.

There is a good balance, and that makes for some exciting college memories. It may sound cliché, but many of the students knew that Lafayette was the place for them as soon as they stepped onto the campus. The school has that effect on people; it clicks, and once they realized that it was a match, they find they can't let go.... For the rest of this editorial, visit collegeprowler.com.

Students Speak Out On...
OVERALL EXPERIENCE

Q Experience

"amazing school. would definitely attend if i had to do it all over again. professors are easy to get in touch with and almost everyone are very helpful and accommodating. the administration is very flexible and will accommodate you if you have any problems. there arent much stuff to do off campus but thats not very important for me. overall, i love it here"

Q Would NEVER GO HERE Again

"I wanted a real college experience and was strongly disappointed. Very immature population with high school drama. Definately not what I was looking for in college."

Q "I think if I went to a larger school, I might be having an even better time, but Lafayette is excellent for its academics, teaching staff, location (not too far from NYC or Philly), and campus."

Q "Overall, I have enjoyed my time at Lafayette, and I know that I am receiving an excellent education."

BEST OF LAFAYETTE

1. Professors
2. Smart, social students that get more worldly and diverse each year
3. The beautiful campus
4. Lehigh/Lafayette football
5. Career Services
6. Small classes

Happy Students
95% of students return after their first year.

Proven Success
89% of students will complete their education and graduate with a degree.

WORST OF LAFAYETTE

1. Parking
2. Location
3. Food
4. Price
5. Diversity
6. Paths across Quad are no longer practical

Expensive
Tuition is a steep $38,490, one of the most expensive rates in the country.

Expensive Dorms
Living on campus doesn't come cheap, with an average housing price tag of $7,105.

Student Body

African American:	5%	Male Undergrads:	54%
Asian American:	4%	Female Undergrads:	46%
Hispanic:	5%	Living On Campus:	96%
International:	6%	Living Off Campus:	4%
Native American:	0%	Male Athletes:	28%
White:	71%	Female Athletes:	23%
Unknown:	9%	Fraternity Members:	26%
From Out-of-State:	81%	Sorority Members:	45%

Frequently Compared Schools:

Bucknell University
Colgate University
Lehigh University
Villanova University

Students Speak Out On...
EVERYTHING!

ACADEMICS

Smart School

"The acedemics are tough but most of the professors are very available and helpful. Not an easy acedemic school at all."

"The professors are very interested in the involvement of the students. They are always willing to put in the extra time with a struggling student, or they simply help you stay on track. It's easy to lose focus with other things going on, but professors always stay on top of you."

ATHLETICS

I Could Care Less About the Leopards

"... and apparently a lot of fellow students feel the same way. I rarely was aware of a football game except for the game against Lehigh and Homecoming."

"Sports are really big. I feel like I might just be the only person on campus that isn't an athlete. I still take classes at the gym to make up for it, though."

CAMPUS DINING

Too Much of the Same

"There are two major dining halls on campus; Marquis and Farinon. Marquis, thought to be the better of the two, specializes in home-style meals, but hours are limited. Additionally, there is not much seating, so it can be hard to find a spot. Farinon has more options than Marquis, but burgers and fries tend to be the staples of lunch."

Decent Fare, Lackluster Variety at Certain Dining Halls

"The variety is poor at upper and lower farinon, but the food is usually good. Marquis has a better selection and much more variety. Gilbert's and simons are always good. Lines are long at lower farinon during peak hours."

CAMPUS HOUSING

Most new, a few older, but all cute!

"Lafayette has a whole section of campus containing newly built beautiful dorms with great sized rooms and all the modern conveniences! A few of the dorms, mostly by Farinon student center, are a little older, but certainly full of architectural charm! All the dorms are safe and kept clean, even with college-guys roaming around."

Most Great, Some Okay

"Though most dorms tend to have a lot of space and nice amenities, a few dorms (Gates Hall in particular) are run-down and are well in need of a refurbishment. Some dorms have been recently refurbished and they look better than ever before."

GUYS & GIRLS

"Lafayette has a very wide spectrum of students. They have a very large amount of attractive girls and guys. Most people are very nice and outgoing, and they're willing to meet you and talk. There are people that are rather shy and geeky, but that's expected in every school environment."

"Guys can be summed up like this: Abercrombie, Abercrombie, Abercrombie. Girls can be summed up like this: Tiffany's, Tiffany's, Tiffany's, pink sweatpants with some cute Greek letters, and something Von Dutch. Nalgene bottles, Reef sandals, and anything North Face apply to all. Lafayette has its lookers; Playboy won't be calling any time soon, though. A lot of kids are self-centered, upper-middle-class, but there are also a lot of amazing people here, mostly outside the Greek scene."

HEALTH & SAFETY

Safety

"its a pretty safe campus. there will always be people who steal stuff but you have to be responsible yourself for your things. the campus itself is pretty safe othewise."

Safety and Security at Lafayette College

"Excellent safety and security, provided by the private Public Safety department."

LOOKING FOR MORE?

Check out our full-length guide to this school at collegeprowler.com/lafayette-college/.

Lawrence University

115 S. Drew St.; Appleton, WI 54911
(920) 832-7000; www.lawrence.edu

THE BASICS:

Acceptance Rate: 69%
Yield: 20%
Setting: Rural
Control: Private Non-Profit
Total Undergrads: 1,495
SAT Range: 1800–2080*
ACT Range: 25–30

Student-Faculty Ratio: 9:1
Retention Rate: 87%
Graduation Rate: 75%
Tuition: $34,596
Room & Board: $7,053
Avg. Aid Package: $26,800
Students With Aid: 94%

* of 2400

Academics	B+	Greek Life	B
Athletics	C+	Guys	C+
Campus Dining	C+	Health & Safety	A+
Campus Housing	A-	Local Atmosphere	B-
Campus Strictness	A	Nightlife	C+
Computers	B	Off-Campus Dining	A-
Diversity	C+	Off-Campus Housing	D-
Drug Safety	B	Parking	B-
Facilities	B	Transportation	C-
Girls	C+	Weather	C

CP's Student Author On...
OVERALL EXPERIENCE

It is easy for a college student to complain about the school they attend. Lawrence has a unique environment, and it has its oddities and drawbacks, but most students can't imagine being anywhere else. At other small liberal arts colleges, many students complain about the confines in academics and often too-true stereotypes of a campus full of spoiled rich kids. Nothing could be further from the truth here. The opportunities in both the college and the conservatory are exceptional for any school, and a student can achieve as much he or she aspires for. The college attracts an impressively diverse assortment of students, a trait they hold highly, and it does as much as it can to keep finances from being a deterrent to enrollment. The campus consists of future classical pianists, marine biologists, poets, hockey players, jazz trumpet players, and doctors. With dedication, motivation, and straight-up hard work, they can achieve their goals.

So the food is terrible, the town is dull, and your wild party fantasies may remain unfulfilled. But it's all part of the school the students love to hate and hate to love.... For the rest of this editorial, visit collegeprowler.com.

Students Speak Out On...
OVERALL EXPERIENCE

Q Not Really Enjoying Myself...
"I'm transferring from Lawrence for a variety of reasons. The students are overall unmotivated, even though the professors are amazing. The general lack of amenities is absurd considering how expensive the education is. The social scene is virtually non-existent. The Lawrence bubble is overwhelming. Isolation is terrible, and suffocation is common."

Q "I really love Lawrence. The students are smart and talented. i think everyone leaves feeling like they made great friends, not to mention received a great education."

Q "At times I have wished that I went to a bigger school, but then I realize that the small classes and individualized attention teachers can give at a small school is extremely rewarding."

Q "My time here has been awesome. As long as you have a healthy relationship with your advisor and listen to his advice, classes will be beneficial. If there isn't a specific class offered, you can do a tutorial or internship under a professor that has knowledge in that area of interest."

BEST OF LAWRENCE

1. Professors
2. Convocations
3. Conservatory
4. Free concerts
5. Community
6. Size
7. Jazz Celebration Weekend

Happy Students
87% of students return after their first year.

Commitment to Teaching
There are 9 students for every member of faculty on campus.

WORST OF LAWRENCE

1. Everyone knows everyone else's business
2. Small campus
3. Wisconsin winters
4. Parking
5. Friends get too busy to hang out
6. Mediocre food

Expensive
Tuition is a steep $34,596, one of the most expensive rates in the country.

Students Speak Out On...
EVERYTHING!

ACADEMICS

Great Faculty, Terrible Students

"Academically the professors are quite good, yet the quality of student is far below what I would have expected. In general, the attitude academically is "that will do", very few people seemed genuinely interested in learning. I would consistently see professors 'pulling teeth' to get answers from students during class discussions. I would say it was the most average collection of people imaginable."

"I find most of my classes to be quite interesting. Lawrence is good about letting you take things when you want, so you don't need to do all your gen-eds right away, allowing for more fun classes that are tailored to your major."

ATHLETICS

Not a Sporty School

"Sports are not a huge part of campus life at Lawrence. Very few students attend the games of any sport, and our sports teams are nothing to write home about."

We Have Athletics?

"Other than having one friend on the track team, I virtually never hear about athletics at Lawrence. The football team is sad, especially considering I was raised to worship the pigskin. If you're looking for exciting athletics, Lawrence is not the place for you."

CAMPUS DINING

Variety and Quality

"Lawrence University has a great selection of food at the main dining hall, cafe, and corner store. Food quality is high and the desserts are delicious!"

Okay

"Lawrence has three places to eat. There's a grill where you can get food during most of the day, there's a store, and a cafeteria. Those are all good, but the meal plan is really expensive ."

CAMPUS HOUSING

All Dorms Are in a Convenient Location

"The freshman dorms are big compared to others I've seen, and the options for upperclassmen are awesome. All the dorms are close to something because the campus is so small, so everyone has their own opinions on which residence hall is the best."

"The dorms at Lawrence are way bigger than dorms at other colleges. Each has a unique history and unique characteristics that fit a variety of personalities."

GUYS & GIRLS

VARIETY

"You'll find a wide variety of people at LU from nerds and musicians to jocks and greeks. Many do recognize the SAFE atmosphere created at Lawrence with groups such as G.L.O.W (gay, lesbian or whatever). There is are more woman then men on campus but overall you will find all walks of life."

Guys Are Okay

"They are a few catches, but for the most part, everyone is fairly mediocre. Many of the guys are either in sports or music."

HEALTH & SAFETY

Security Is Always There!

"Lawrence's security staff is top-notch. They are always present around campus and respond quickly to every call they get regarding safety of the students, unlocking doors, and petty theft. I have never felt unsafe on campus and Appleton is generally a very safe city to live in."

Very Safe

"The campus is small and I would not be afraid walking around after dark. However, you will want to make sure your door is locked to avoid theft (for example there has been instances of computers being stolen)."

Lehigh University

27 Memorial Drive W; Bethlehem, PA 18015
(610) 758-3000; www.lehigh.edu

THE BASICS:

Acceptance Rate: 33%
Yield: 33%
Setting: Small city
Control: Private Non-Profit
Total Undergrads: 4,809
SAT Range: 1220–1390*
ACT Range: 27–31

Student-Faculty Ratio: 10:1
Retention Rate: 94%
Graduation Rate: 85%
Tuition: $38,630
Room & Board: $10,200
Avg. Aid Package: $31,611
Students With Aid: 62%

* of 1600

Academics	A-	Greek Life	A+
Athletics	A-	Guys	A-
Campus Dining	B+	Health & Safety	B
Campus Housing	B	Local Atmosphere	C
Campus Strictness	C+	Nightlife	B-
Computers	B+	Off-Campus Dining	B
Diversity	C	Off-Campus Housing	B
Drug Safety	C+	Parking	C+
Facilities	B+	Transportation	C-
Girls	B	Weather	C+

CP's Student Author On...
OVERALL EXPERIENCE

There's nothing quite like being an undergraduate at Lehigh University. There's a reason why many people call college "the best four years of your life," and that statement applies to Lehigh perfectly. It may not be in the greatest town in the world—the winters can be harsh, and the student body is incredibly homogenous, but Lehigh students love their school. The professors are mostly knowledgeable and friendly, and academics play a huge role in any college student's experience, but the friendships forged and the outstanding social life are what make Lehigh students fall head over heels for their school. Freshmen enter Lehigh unsure of what awaits them and emerge four years later wishing there was a way they could stay for another four years. You're thrown together in various dorms in hopes that you'll be able to coexist with one another, and for the first time in your life, you have unlimited freedom—you take classes you hate and eat horrible meals in the dining halls, but the Hill still has an intriguing, almost otherworldly aura about it.... For the rest of this editorial, visit collegeprowler. com.

Students Speak Out On...
OVERALL EXPERIENCE

It"S the Greatest!
"I love Lehigh! There is so much to do but plenty of quiet space when needed."

Practically Perfect in Every Way
"There's no better place than Lehigh University. There are so few places where the academics are so strong in every department, athletics and the arts thrive, transportation to Philadelphia and New York is readily available, and has a healthy social scene. I only applied to Lehigh and I know a lot of my friends did too. We live Lehigh and if you come around, you'll quickly see why."

Conformity
"My least favorite part about Lehigh is the conformity. Everywhere you look, everyone looks the same. Our diversity level barley exists, and much of the campus consists of the rich, white kids who all join Greek life. As an athlete at Lehigh this is easy to see, because most students seem to either join a Fraternity/ Sorority, or join an athletic team. My favorite experiences all come from being a part of Lehigh Athletics."

BEST OF LEHIGH

1. Greek life
2. Playing Beirut
3. Forging incredibly close friendships
4. Fraternity parties
5. Tailgates
6. Sociable students

Happy Students
94% of students return after their first year.

Commitment to Teaching
There are 10 students for every member of faculty on campus.

WORST OF LEHIGH

1. Parties frequently getting busted by cops
2. Parking tickets
3. Bethlehem winters
4. Sporadic weather
5. Bethlehem
6. Drunken hookups
7. Upper UC food court

Expensive
Tuition is a steep $38,630, one of the most expensive rates in the country.

Expensive Dorms
Living on campus doesn't come cheap, with an average housing price tag of $5,910.

Student Body

African American:	3%	Male Undergrads:	59%
Asian American:	6%	Female Undergrads:	41%
Hispanic:	5%	Living On Campus:	69%
International:	4%	Living Off Campus:	31%
Native American:	0%	Male Athletes:	15%
White:	73%	Female Athletes:	17%
Unknown:	8%	Fraternity Members:	30%
From Out-of-State:	79%	Sorority Members:	34%

Frequently Compared Schools:

Bucknell University
Cornell University
Lafayette College
Villanova University

Students Speak Out On... EVERYTHING!

ACADEMICS

Great School

"I came to Lehigh because is has a great variety of academic majors to choose from, an excellent reputation, and I love the campus. I joined a sorority my second semester and have made many friends. Tha sports programs are excellent too. Lehigh has the best of both worlds - academics and social!!!"

Economics Major in the Business School

"It's possible to major in Economics three different ways at Lehigh but for the business school, it's easy although the lack of ability to graduate with honors can be frustrating since curriculum here does not work the same function as the College of Arts and Sciences but the class options are diverse and all interesting."

ATHLETICS

Always Fun

"I love attending our schools games. Football is always in high attendance especially for the big rivalry game Lehigh/Laff."

Good

"Although the football team is poor at best, we are excellent at wrestling, and basketball isn't bad either. Occasionally, other sports like crew or soccer will step up to the challenge and perform. Overall, we aren't the best, but we don't suck completely either."

CAMPUS DINING

Gooood Stuff

"The dining halls offer a variety of foods each meal which make it almost difficult to decide what to eat. The food is good quality and you always eat till your drop. Aside from the dining halls the fast food places are also very good and easy to get in and out. There is a little cafe that is also open late for those who stay out studying late or on the weekends need a snack after a fun party."

Dining

"on-campus foods are ok. Upper UC has better food. The meal plan that freshmen are required to have is kind of large---we don't need that much, but we have to choose one, I would choose a smaller meal plan once I could."

CAMPUS HOUSING

Senior/Junior Dorms Are Awesome!

"The freshman dorms are kind of small but the building is nice and vintage. The senior ones are really cool and spacious. The walk is a little farther than the underclassmen dorms but its worth it with the quality of the rooms."

"The dorms are great. None of them should be avoided; they all have a certain something."

GUYS & GIRLS

Lehigh Guys and Girls

"There are way more guys here at Lehigh than girls, which some guys complain about. Most of the guys here are nerdy and socially awkward. There are a few good looking guys but they are almost always asses. The guys on sports teams who are not in frats are the best guys here"

Typical

"The guy to girl ratio has gotten a lot better, but the most of the guy population is either losers or nerds. The females are either athletes or sorority chicks."

HEALTH & SAFETY

Pretty Safe

"On campus I feel completely safe; however, going off campus at night can be a bit scary in Bethlehem and the cops are usually busy up on the Hill. Generally though, if you stay in a group and don't wander alone nothing bad will happen to you at Lehigh."

"Lately, there's been a decent amount of e-mails from police about people getting mugged in the middle of the day on campus by the dorms. It's pretty unnerving."

LOOKING FOR MORE?

Check out our full-length guide to this school at collegeprowler.com/lehigh-university/.

Lewis & Clark College

0615 SW Palatine Hill Road; Portland, OR 97219
(503) 768-7000; www.lclark.edu

THE BASICS:

Acceptance Rate: 65%	**Student-Faculty Ratio:** 12:1
Yield: 14%	**Retention Rate:** 83%
Setting: Large city	**Graduation Rate:** 71%
Control: Private Non-Profit	**Tuition:** $35,233
Total Undergrads: 1,988	**Room & Board:** $9,320
SAT Range: 1810–2080*	**Avg. Aid Package:** $22,536
ACT Range: 27–30	**Students With Aid:** 81%

* of 2400

Academics	B+	Greek Life	N/A
Athletics	C-	Guys	A
Campus Dining	A	Health & Safety	A-
Campus Housing	B	Local Atmosphere	B+
Campus Strictness	A-	Nightlife	B+
Computers	A-	Off-Campus Dining	A
Diversity	B-	Off-Campus Housing	A
Drug Safety	C	Parking	A-
Facilities	B+	Transportation	A-
Girls	A-	Weather	B

CP's Student Author On...
OVERALL EXPERIENCE

Lewis & Clark has a lot to offer, but it depends on the student's motivation and ability to work hard. Some students just sail by with average grades, living it up and smoking up a lot, without really challenging themselves. However, there are many students who are very active and make the most of the opportunities that are available at such a small school. The weather can be depressing and the social atmosphere can be stifling at times. However, if you find your niche at LC, you'll love what you're doing, and a little rain and gossip won't bother you.

There is so much talent to be found in many different areas. Everyone is always willing to help you. It's a common practice for professors to invite you over to their houses for dinner. Most classes are incredibly small and intimate, and open discussion runs rampant. The liberal atmosphere is one that everyone is bound to feel comfortable in. All are encouraged to voice opinions, even if they aren't part of the mainstream way of thinking. Students are encouraged to take action with the issues that mean something and to see outside of the box.... For the rest of this editorial, visit collegeprowler.com.

Students Speak Out On...
OVERALL EXPERIENCE

Q SOAWESOME

"I live in SOA which actually really Awesome: therefore I title my summary as SOAwesome. I make really good and lifetime friends at LC! I am in Love with this place, even when I go back home I count my day left for LC! LOVE IT LOVE IT LOVE IT! MUAW :)"

Q I Love This Place

"I love this place. The professors are some of the nicest, smartest and most helpful people you will ever meet. They teach you and during their office hours they will sit with you and not let you leave until they are sure you know the material. The campus is absolutely gorgeous. The classes are challenging and the food, although college food, is pretty above par. The cultural experience is wonderful and downtown Portland is a kick!"

BEST OF LEWIS & CLARK

1. Great professors
2. Beautiful campus
3. Overseas study opportunities
4. Library open 24 hours during the week
5. Pioneer Express Shuttle
6. The city of Portland

Happy Students
83% of students return after their first year.

Proven Success
71% of students will complete their education and graduate with a degree.

WORST OF LEWIS & CLARK

1. Feels like summer camp with boring Friday nights.
2. Rumors spread like wildfire
3. Unbalanced boy-to-girl ratio
4. Dreary winter weather
5. Food gets repetitive

Expensive
Tuition is a steep $35,233, one of the most expensive rates in the country.

Student Body

African American:	2%	Male Undergrads:	40%
Asian American:	6%	Female Undergrads:	60%
Hispanic:	4%	Living On Campus:	66%
International:	9%	Living Off Campus:	34%
Native American:	1%	Male Athletes:	19%
White:	57%	Female Athletes:	16%
Unknown:	22%	Fraternity Members:	0%
From Out-of-State:	91%	Sorority Members:	0%

Frequently Compared Schools:

Reed College
University of Puget Sound
Whitman College
Willamette University

Students Speak Out On... EVERYTHING!

ACADEMICS

Professors

"They are all intelligent and informative while keeping topics interesting and allow for the students to interact with subjects."

Interesting and Challenging

"Classes are usually discussion based, and it's interesting to learn from your peers just as much as from professors. Professors make their subjects applicable to real life. Professors are available for school help and want to get to know you. I love going to class at Lewis and Clark."

ATHLETICS

Not That Great

"We have good teams and there is a focus in the administration to improve them, but the majority of the students don't really care."

Athletes Are Great but Need More Fans

"There are several sports and athletes work hard to excel in their sports but most of the student body doesn't pay attention to sports."

CAMPUS DINING

Great for Vegetarians/Vegans

"The menu can get a bit repetitive, but the overall quality is great. One of the cafeteria's is open until midnight, which many find helpful. There are a lot of options for vegans and vegetarians, and many ingredients come from local farms."

Ideal for Vegan/Vegetarian Crowd

"Compared to most on-campus dinning, LC is where it's at. The Bon, as well call it, has really great vegan, vegetarian, gluten-free and more general options. The choices vary from day to day, but there's always something good."

CAMPUS HOUSING

Stewart Is the Best

"I live in the wellness dorm on campus, Stewart. It is a great place to study, very comfortable living, and very inviting atmosphere. The worst dorm on campus is Copeland, although I've never lived there it is very noise, and often there are lots of parties there."

Live on Campus!!

"Living on campus completes the 'college experience' here at Lewis and Clark. The convenience of being so close to downtown Portland and all of your classes makes life a breeze. As for making friends, you couldn't find it easier anywhere else."

GUYS & GIRLS

There's a Bit of Everything

"Even though Lewis and Clark is a small school, if you want something there is probably someone out there the fits the bill. It can be tough finding them though."

The Split

"There is a split between the athletes and the hippies. The hippies hang out together and the athletes are together. There is some intermingling between a few people. There is no tension between the two but each likes to party with its own crowd"

HEALTH & SAFETY

Great

"I never locked my dorm room or my car, or my locker and not once had any privacy incidents. Basically most people in Portland are good people and it makes anyone that goes there want to be that way."

Health Services

"I have never felt unsafe on campus. The infirmary is good for small ailments and OHSU is nearby for more serious things. The hours can be a little inconvenient"

LOOKING FOR MORE?

Check out our full-length guide to this school at collegeprowler.com/lewis--and--clark-college/.

Linfield College

900 SE Baker St.; McMinnville, OR 97128
(503) 883-2200; www.linfield.edu

THE BASICS:

Acceptance Rate: 82%
Yield: 31%
Setting: Town
Control: Private Non-Profit
Total Undergrads: 1,677
SAT Range: 1430–1780*
ACT Range: 21–27

Student-Faculty Ratio: 12:1
Retention Rate: 81%
Graduation Rate: 73%
Tuition: $29,054
Room & Board: $8,280
Avg. Aid Package: $19,168
Students With Aid: 94%

of 2400

Academics	B+	Greek Life	B
Athletics	B-	Guys	A-
Campus Dining	C+	Health & Safety	A-
Campus Housing	A-	Local Atmosphere	B-
Campus Strictness	B	Nightlife	B
Computers	B	Off-Campus Dining	B
Diversity	B-	Off-Campus Housing	B-
Drug Safety	C-	Parking	A-
Facilities	A-	Transportation	C+
Girls	A-	Weather	B-

CP's Student Author On...
OVERALL EXPERIENCE

The majority of students states that Linfield College is excellent if you're looking for smaller classes, individual attention, and a focus on academics with the opportunity to enjoy sports and extracurricular activities. Linfield has excellent professors who really care about students; the only drawback is that the school is located in a small rural town, where it can sometimes seem boring. However, if students are willing to look hard enough, there is always something to do, no matter what students' interests are. Generally, everything is accessible, and there are plenty of resources. It's relatively easy to find your niche.

Linfield is an excellent college for those who are looking for a small school with a focus on academics, access to professors, and a strong emphasis on the study abroad program. The College is perfect for students who want a balance between academics and developing leadership skills through civic events in the community, internships, as well as having the time to participate in extracurricular activities. The College's mantra is that "Linfield is a place of connecting learning, life, and community.... For the rest of this editorial, visit collegeprowler.com.

Students Speak Out On...
OVERALL EXPERIENCE

Q Great

"Always something to do, no matter what you like. Everything is accessible and you have so many resources for it all. Easy to find your niche."

Q Love It!!!

"Plenty of scholarships, great community of friends from all around the country, strong academics, great connections with employers, individual attention from high-degree teachers, very strong Division III athletics."

Q Great Place to Grow

"Linfield is a place to find yourself and grow with friends who are of similar focus as you are. You can experience the party side of college while having the feeling that you matter to staff due to the smaller class sizes, you are not just a number at Linfield"

BEST OF LINFIELD

1. Strong academics
2. Great professors
3. Small classes, personalized attention
4. Excellent study abroad program
5. Lots of organized activities and events happening on campus

Happy Students
81% of students return after their first year.

Proven Success
73% of students will complete their education and graduate with a degree.

WORST OF LINFIELD

1. Parking during special events is difficult.
2. Food gets tiresome.
3. Need a car to get to rural areas
4. Not many 24-hour restaurants nearby
5. Rainy season

Expensive
Tuition is a steep $29,054, one of the most expensive rates in the country.

Student Body

African American:	1%	Male Undergrads:	44%
Asian American:	8%	Female Undergrads:	56%
Hispanic:	5%	Living On Campus:	74%
International:	5%	Living Off Campus:	26%
Native American:	1%	Male Athletes:	47%
White:	69%	Female Athletes:	24%
Unknown:	9%	Fraternity Members:	22%
From Out-of-State:	50%	Sorority Members:	27%

Frequently Compared Schools:

Lewis & Clark College
Seattle University
University of Puget Sound
Willamette University

Students Speak Out On... EVERYTHING!

ACADEMICS

I Appreciate Linfield Even More Now That I Am a Grad Student

"There is no doubt in my mind that my Linfield education gave me a solid education that has served me well as I continue on through my MA and in all likelihood my PhD. The liberal arts tradition is alive and well at Linfield and the international program opportunities are legion. The professors, with VERY few exceptions, were fantastic and I really grew as a person and a scholar while attending this college. Like all educational opportunities however, you get out of it what you put into it."

Program and Curriculum

"I'm a finance major, the business department does a very good job of making sure that you have a good fundamental base in general business and then by junior year you narrow it down. By taking the general classes it helps narrow down an otherwise very broad subject."

ATHLETICS

Athletics at Linfield Are Huge

"Athletics at Linfeld are extremely professional, and have a huge following not only by Linfield students, but is also supported by the community. There is a lot of enthusiasm and excitement at the football, basketball, and baseball games. There is usually a good turn out and the teams at Linfield are extremely competitive. Linfield's football team had 53 consecutive winning seasons which has been the most in NCAA history."

Thumbs up

"Great athletics. I love going to the games. I was on the JV volleyball team too, it was very fun."

CAMPUS DINING

Comfortable Dining

"The dining hall is a really comfortable setting to eat and be in. The menus are varied enough, and there is large support for healthy choices.Plans consist of a set of Dinners (all you can eat style), and then a declining balance for the rest of your meals/snacks across campus. Great plan, allows students to add more to the declining balance throughout the year."

Has Its Moments

"Mostly the cafeteria food is good, sometimes though they serve awful food but for the most part the food is fresh, has vegetarian options. The coffee shop is really good, but could have better hours."

CAMPUS HOUSING

Each Housing Option Has Its Perks

"All the dorms on campus hold their own perks. None of the dorms have tiny rooms, and are sized well to comfortably fit at least two people to a room. There is a range from smaller dorms to larger ones and on campus apartments for upperclassmen. A quick look through the campus housing link on the schools website describes the amenities each dorm/apartment holds."

GUYS & GIRLS

Linfield High...

"There is really something for everybody. There does seem to be an absence of minority students from both genders but as far a classifying people, dont try. I have seen almost every type of group possible and somehow they seem to get along just fine. The greek system does make up about 1/3 of the campus population and athletics are abundant."

HEALTH & SAFETY

Campus Safety

"There were only a handful of incidences this year at most, and campus safety was quick to respond in a professional and friendly manner, they also give rides to class upon request. I have nevber felt unsafe, it is a smaller, beautiful campus."

LOOKING FOR MORE?

Check out our full-length guide to this school at collegeprowler.com/linfield-college/.

Louisiana College

1140 College Drive; Pineville, LA 71359
(318) 487-7011; www.lacollege.edu

THE BASICS:

Acceptance Rate: 51%
Yield: 46%
Setting: Suburban
Control: Private Non-Profit
Total Undergrads: 1,036
SAT Range: 1240–1800*
ACT Range: 17–24

Student-Faculty Ratio: 16:1
Retention Rate: 65%
Graduation Rate: 38%
Tuition: $12,530
Room & Board: $4,450
Avg. Aid Package: $10,014
Students With Aid: 100%

of 2400

Academics	C+	Greek Life	D+
Athletics	C+	Guys	B+
Campus Dining	C-	Health & Safety	B-
Campus Housing	C	Local Atmosphere	C
Campus Strictness	C	Nightlife	D+
Computers	D+	Off-Campus Dining	C-
Diversity	C	Off-Campus Housing	C-
Drug Safety	B-	Parking	A+
Facilities	D+	Transportation	B
Girls	B+	Weather	A-

CP's Student Author On...
OVERALL EXPERIENCE

The Louisiana College experience is definitely unique. The school stands out from other universities in the area, but before you apply, you should make sure LC fits your interests. The first thing you need to know is that LC is a Baptist college. The college is strict compared to most schools, and you should be prepared for the academic challenge, the small campus size, and the residence life atmosphere. And be sure to buckle your seatbelt for your first semester of classes! Transitioning from high school to college is always difficult, but making the leap to the high academic standards of LC can be tough. Talk to current students to figure out which professors you should take for your core classes. Some professors will give you an easy A, but others want to "refine you with fire," to use some Baptist lingo. But don't stress if you're struggling: the professors are all on your side. Small class sizes give you a direct line of contact with your professor. If you're still having trouble, get tutored.

The campus is also small enough to walk across in five or ten minutes.... For the rest of this editorial, visit collegeprowler.com.

Students Speak Out On...
OVERALL EXPERIENCE

Q **It's small and easy to get around**
"I love the place! It's small and easy to get around, and everyone is so friendly, and there's always something to do. :)"

Q **My Experience So Far**
"My experience has been great. I love the classes, and the teachers are really nice. They are always helpful when you get confused. There are no parties because it is a Christian college, so we worship God and focus on our studies."

Q **I enjoy my school**
"I enjoy my school. The debate team is awesome, and the professors help you out. Other than that, nothing stands out that much."

Q **New student's experience**
"So far I have really enjoyed school. The first semester took some getting used to, but that's with any adjustment from high school. The professors here are great. Most of them really want to work with you to help you achieve. The facilities are not amazing, but the atmosphere is inviting."

BEST OF LOUISIANA

1. Small class and campus size
2. School spirit at football games
3. Late night sand volleyball
4. Genuinely helpful professors
5. Ultimate Frisbee in Wildcat Stadium

Affordable
Tuition is only $12,530, one of the most affordable rates in the country.

WORST OF LOUISIANA

1. Gaining the Freshman 15 (and beyond) from local Southern cuisine
2. Unreliable Internet
3. Only one campus facility open 24 hours
4. Lack of variety at Hattie B's (watch out for the meatloaf)

Not Everyone Graduates
38% of students do not complete their education or graduate with a degree.

Student Body

African American:	15%	Male Undergrads:	50%
Asian American:	2%	Female Undergrads:	50%
Hispanic:	1%	Living On Campus:	52%
International:	2%	Living Off Campus:	48%
Native American:	1%	Male Athletes:	55%
White:	78%	Female Athletes:	21%
Unknown:	1%	Fraternity Members:	11%
From Out-of-State:	10%	Sorority Members:	18%

Frequently Compared Schools:

Jackson State University
Louisiana State University
Millsaps College
Tulane University

Students Speak Out On...
EVERYTHING!

ACADEMICS

Good variety of academics

"They give a good variety at our school from religion to art. Would like to see even more varity of majors to expand the schools."

Louisiana College Professors Love Their Jobs

"I am a history major at Louisiana College and I can honestly say that I have never had a bad experience with a professor. The history department is small, but the professors love what they do and enjoy teaching their content to students. They are highly qualified in what they do. They know their students by name and will stop in the hall to have a normal, non-school related conversation."

ATHLETICS

No Exceptions

"Most of the Athletes that start as a Freshman do not make it to their spring semester at Louisiana College. Louisiana College is a tough private school, and they don't make allowances for the athletes just because they're on varsity. They have to do their classwork just like everybody else. The coaches enforce good grades and Christian conduct. For the players that make it past their freshman year, I believe that they have an excellent experience at Louisiana College."

Wild for the Wildcats

"Our student body loves our athletics. The football team finally had two winning seasons, and we all go hardcore in blue and orange. Our new stadium was packed out this season."

CAMPUS DINING

Few Dining Options, but the Food Is Good

"There's one main dining hall for meal plans and declining balances, and a fast food place for declining balance only. Fast food tends to be greasy and there are few inexpensive fruit/ vegetable options. Dining hall fare offers more variety, but they tend to serve the same staples repeatedly. There are custom cooking stations in the dining hall and a well-stocked salad bar that I take advantage of on a regular basis."

Pretty Good.

"Even if I don't like what's being served, there's always other food to grab, and I usually do like what's being served, so no problem! The cooking staff is great."

CAMPUS HOUSING

Campus Life

"It is really expensive to live on campus. The dorms are not the best and it could be better for the cost of the school. The social atmosphere is ok. The cost of the school to me is too much for the quality of the food we get in the cafe, the dorm, etc."

Campus Quarters

"The dorms and apartments are in need of improvement, but the atmosphere is quite pleasant."

GUYS & GIRLS

LC Is Great

"LC is a small Christian school, with a small number of students. With only around 1400 students, the atmosphere is more like a family. you get to know so many people. Most students attend LC because this is where they feel that God has lead them. Also the acedemic quality at LC is much greater than other state schools in our area. Several medical grad schools look for LC students because they know we have received a good education."

HEALTH & SAFETY

This Campus Is One of the Safest Places I Have Ever Been.

"I have seen students leave purses, backpacks, books, and other personal items in classrooms or the cafeteria, and then go back the next day and find them right where they left them. You can't do that just anywhere!"

LOOKING FOR MORE?

Check out our full-length guide to this school at collegeprowler.com/louisiana-college/.

Louisiana State University

3357 Highland Road; Baton Rouge, LA 70803
(225) 578-3202; www.lsu.edu

THE BASICS:

Acceptance Rate: 73%	**Student-Faculty Ratio:** 20:1
Yield: 46%	**Retention Rate:** 84%
Setting: Mid-sized city	**Graduation Rate:** 61%
Control: Public	**Tuition:** $14,383
Total Undergrads: 23,012	**Room & Board:** $7,738
SAT Range: 1560–1880*	**Avg. Aid Package:** $6,219
ACT Range: 23–28	**Students With Aid:** 95%

* of 2400

Academics	B-	Greek Life	B
Athletics	A+	Guys	A-
Campus Dining	A-	Health & Safety	B
Campus Housing	B	Local Atmosphere	B+
Campus Strictness	B+	Nightlife	A
Computers	A-	Off-Campus Dining	B+
Diversity	C+	Off-Campus Housing	B
Drug Safety	C	Parking	B-
Facilities	A	Transportation	B+
Girls	B+	Weather	A-

CP's Student Author On...
OVERALL EXPERIENCE

Sure LSU students gripe about everything from parking to the weather to questions about academics and more, but rarely will you meet a student who will actually tell you they wish they had gone somewhere else. The overall experience of LSU outweighs any factor students could imagine. There is an overwhelming sense of pride and allegiance to the University that unites all LSU students. The phrase, "I bleed purple and gold," holds more true than anyone could imagine.

LSU is all about experiences. It's the experiences of community, whether it be through football games, through nightlife, through more academic organizations, or through living on campus. Students appreciate the fact they are at something far bigger than themselves. The size of the University presents students with opportunities to do so much from getting involved academically to finding a boyfriend or girlfriend. It's about the experiences of involvement from joining a frat to working on campus to not doing anything at all. LSU seems to offer anything any student could imagine.... For the rest of this editorial, visit collegeprowler.com.

Students Speak Out On...
OVERALL EXPERIENCE

Q Love It

"While I have had some disciplinary issues from partying, I enjoy being here more than any other place I've been in my entire life. It's just all around the best experience I could imagine. The people are great, the school is great, the atmosphere is fantastic... I just don't know what more you could ask for."

Q Woderful

"accepting, friendly people, and always a good party!"

Q It's LSU

"I have loved every minute at LSU and I do not think anyone would be disappointed with there choice."

Q Live Your Life

"LSU is such a diverse campus, encompassing all nationalities and academic concentrations. I love encountering different people and having fun with them. I have no regrets coming here, and will always try to sway people to bleed purple and gold."

BEST OF LOUISIANA STATE

1. Football season
2. The party-school atmosphere
3. Really attractive coeds
4. Hurricane parties when school is cancelled
5. Walking the lakes

Happy Students
84% of students return after their first year.

Knowledgeable Professors
100% of students surveyed rated the general knowledge of professors as above average.

WORST OF LOUISIANA STATE

1. The size
2. Parking on campus
3. The pollen that gets on everything in the spring
4. Teachers that have difficulty with the English language
5. Waiting for the CATS bus that may never come

Lost in the Crowd
Expect to take at least a few classes in a lecture hall—36% of classes have more than 50 students.

Don't Move Off Campus
Average off-campus housing is a steep $12,834.

Student Body

African American:	10%	Male Undergrads:	49%
Asian American:	3%	Female Undergrads:	51%
Hispanic:	3%	Living On Campus:	23%
International:	2%	Living Off Campus:	77%
Native American:	0%	Male Athletes:	4%
White:	79%	Female Athletes:	2%
Unknown:	3%	Fraternity Members:	12%
From Out-of-State:	25%	Sorority Members:	18%

Students Speak Out On... EVERYTHING!

ACADEMICS

Very fantastic sports!!

"I love the feelings here in a football or baseball match. Very fantastic!"

Enjoyable Learing Experience

"Professors are nice. They do their best to make more A's in the classes. They are very accessible if classes are small."

ATHLETICS

Amazing Athletics!

"Athletics are the reason I chose LSU! Football, baseball, basketball and volleyball are my favorite sports to watch and LSU has the best in all of them!! LSU takes great pride in Athletics and students get free or reduced price tickets for everything! It's amazing. The REC center has great intermural sports!"

Geaux Tigers!

"The athletics at LSU are AMAZING! Not only is football season a great time to be on LSU's campus, but we, the students, also enjoy supporting other sports as well, such as basketball, baseball, and gymnastics. The fan spirit is out of this world. Everyone should come and experience a weekend in Death Valley. It's a once in a lifetime experience."

CAMPUS DINING

Awesome New Facilities and Great Variety

"Awesome variety. State of the art, new facilities."

Student Union

"The Student Union has just been update and you can find a wide range of choices. The use of PawPoints and TigerCash is great because it gives you the freedom to use your student ID like a debit card. If you are in a time crunch between classes and cannot walk back to the dining halls, then the Union is the best place for a quick bite. A CC's Community Coffee (which is a great local coffee shop) and Starbucks are a great place for a quick cup of coffee to help give you a caffeine boost."

Frequently Compared Schools:

University of Alabama
University of Georgia
University of Mississippi
University of Texas

CAMPUS HOUSING

Evangeline Hall Was Nice & Comfortable

"I like my first year living in Evangeline hall because the quiet study environment it provided. Furnitures are nice and stable. Lobby at the first floor are for friends to hangout and chatting."

LSU Life

"LSU offers its students a wide variety of activities to participate in as well as club, frat life, ROTC, and of course Athletics!"

GUYS & GIRLS

Great, Absolutely!

"The guys are kind, friendly, and helpful. Those girls are just so lovely and frisky hot !!!"

Social Scene Is Important!

"Greek life, clubs and sports are the main vein of the LSU student life. The dress is a mix of preppy frat clothes, khakis, to LSU shirts. The girls wear a lot of running shorts and t shirts to classes and ugg boots in the winter. The athletes wear their LSU athletic clothes, mostly. The social scene is very big. Always a party going on somewhere."

HEALTH & SAFETY

LSU Health & Safety

"I feel very safe on campus, and am not scared at night to walk home in the dark from bars or the rec. Having id cards makes me feel safer because I know not anyone can get into my dorm. My favorite about campus safety is that a bus is never more than 5 minutes away it seems when I need to get home."

KHS

"OUR SERCURITY ON CAMPUS IS ALWAYS AROUND FOR OUR PORTECTION. THE KEEP US SAFE AND FROM HARM."

LOOKING FOR MORE?

Check out our full-length guide to this school at collegeprowler.com/louisiana-state-university/.

Loyola Marymount University

1 LMU Drive; Los Angeles, CA 90045
(310) 338-2700; www.lmu.edu

THE BASICS:

Acceptance Rate: 59%	Student-Faculty Ratio: 11:1
Yield: 25%	Retention Rate: 88%
Setting: Large city	Graduation Rate: 79%
Control: Private Non-Profit	Tuition: $35,419
Total Undergrads: 5,833	Room & Board: $12,025
SAT Range: 1610–1910*	Avg. Aid Package: $16,337
ACT Range: 24–28	Students With Aid: 80%

* of 2400

Academics	A-	Greek Life	B
Athletics	C+	Guys	A-
Campus Dining	B-	Health & Safety	B
Campus Housing	B+	Local Atmosphere	A
Campus Strictness	B	Nightlife	B+
Computers	B	Off-Campus Dining	C+
Diversity	B	Off-Campus Housing	B+
Drug Safety	C+	Parking	A-
Facilities	A	Transportation	C+
Girls	B	Weather	A

CP's Student Author On...
OVERALL EXPERIENCE

Students here are quick to point out that LMU differs from its neighbors USC and UCLA. Overall, LMU is quiet and intimate. Palm trees dot the courtyards between the small buildings. On the exterior, LMU looks like an expensive school. The grounds are neatly manicured and constantly maintained. The school lacks the concrete sterility of a major university, but it possesses the advantages of a big city school—theaters, museums, and celebrities. The biggest contributor to student satisfaction is the size. Students cite a small student body and close ties with professors as the main advantages to an LMU education. Another plus is the lavish facilities, especially the Burns Rec Center with its state-of-the-art fitness center. The academics programs are also a highlight with students. The film school is growing in size and notoriety, while programs in political science, business, and communications are strong points.

On the negative side, a small university still possesses the same problems as a large university. Students repeatedly report problems with a disorganized administration, especially financial aid.... For the rest of this editorial, visit collegeprowler.com.

Students Speak Out On...
OVERALL EXPERIENCE

Q I Love It!

"LMU is great because it makes students feel at home. Students, faculty, and staff help develop a strong sense of community. There seems to always be something going on whether it's a concert, dance, comedy night, philanthropy event, forum, or some other sort of event. Students are given the opportunity to learn about themselves and meet others who have the same goals. I feel like LMU is helping me reach my full potential."

Q Amazing

"You will have the time of your life because everything balances each other."

BEST OF LOYOLA MARYMOUNT

1. The Bluff
2. The weather
3. Los Angeles
4. Small class sizes
5. Burns Recreation Center
6. Friendly students
7. University Hall

Happy Students
88% of students return after their first year.

Proven Success
79% of students will complete their education and graduate with a degree.

WORST OF LOYOLA MARYMOUNT

1. Tuition and housing hikes
2. Inadequate financial aid
3. Parking shortage
4. Constant complaints from Westchester area residents
5. Campus food
6. Lack of school spirit

Expensive
Tuition is a steep $35,419, one of the most expensive rates in the country.

Expensive to Just Get By
54% of students surveyed felt that the amount it costs to live while at school was worse than average.

Student Body

African American:	8%	Male Undergrads:	43%
Asian American:	12%	Female Undergrads:	57%
Hispanic:	20%	Living On Campus:	49%
International:	2%	Living Off Campus:	51%
Native American:	1%	Male Athletes:	8%
White:	55%	Female Athletes:	8%
Unknown:	2%	Fraternity Members:	15%
From Out-of-State:	32%	Sorority Members:	23%

Frequently Compared Schools:

Pepperdine University
Santa Clara University
University of San Diego
University of Southern California

Students Speak Out On...
EVERYTHING!

ACADEMICS

Film

"Everyone loves the film majors. There are many opportunities to work on student projects and you receive emails every week about internships in the city."

Academics

"There are some great study options here at LMU. There are interesting classes and a challenging curriculum. The registration process is not that difficult and if you email your teachers or speak with your advisor you can usually get into the classes you want. The professors are amazing and are available in office hours to help you with whatever you need."

ATHLETICS

Great Support

"LMU doesn't always have the best teams but we have a lot of school spirit for most sports. For basketball, everyone gets together to support the team and it's a huge event sine we don't have a football team. We have pretty diverse teams for most sports although some teams could use more diversity."

No Football Team, We Love Our Men's Basketball Team

"men's basketball is the team to watch, school spirit. We also have competitive water polo teams. The workout center is new and very popular, great place to hang."

CAMPUS DINING

Campus Dining LMU

"There are several dining areas on campus which offer all types and varieties of food. There are also several meal plans to choose from depending on your needs and budget. Flex dollars on the OneCard can be used for some off-campus eateries as well."

The Best Dining Hall

"Roski's is the better of the two dining halls on campus. They have good wraps, sandwhiches, and breakfasts. At the other dining hall, The Lair, the best options are the sushi, the burritos at the Mexican station, and the baked potatoes at The Market Place."

CAMPUS HOUSING

Living on Campus

"I am a junior transfer student and I absolutely love the pristine campus at Loyola Marymount University. Everything on campus, from dormitories to the Hannon Library, is first class. I feel like I go to school on a resort. The upperclassman dorms such as Levy's and Hannon are the most popular living areas. All other living arrangements on campus are convenient and safe. I highly recommend living on campus if you attend this university."

Great Experience-Highly Recommended

"I have lived on campus my whole time at LMU and it has provided the best experience. The freshman dorms are the worst, but even then they are not bad. Once you get into the oncampus apartments, you cant go wrong!"

GUYS & GIRLS

Guys Are Strong and Athletic, but Not Enough of Them

"Wish there were more guys. The beach attracts some pretty cute guys and it's a great spot to do some additional checking."

HEALTH & SAFETY

Health and Safety

"Loyola Marymount University is one of the safest campus in the United States. During night you never feel in danger. There are emergency stations all over campus. The few times there was a problem on campus the on campus public safety fixed the problem right away. Public safety is very strict regarding drinking and drugs. Overall public safety at LMU is in my opinion one of the best i've ever seen. I always feel safe on campus."

LOOKING FOR MORE?

Check out our full-length guide to this school at collegeprowler.com/loyola-marymount-university/.

Loyola University Chicago

1032 W. Sheridan Road; Chicago, IL 60660
(312) 915-6000; www.luc.edu

THE BASICS:

Acceptance Rate: 78%
Yield: 15%
Setting: Large city
Control: Private Non-Profit
Total Undergrads: 10,077
SAT Range: 1610–1940*
ACT Range: 24–29

Student-Faculty Ratio: 17:1
Retention Rate: 85%
Graduation Rate: 66%
Tuition: $30,656
Room & Board: $10,885
Avg. Aid Package: $21,689
Students With Aid: 93%

* of 2400

Academics	B	Greek Life	C+
Athletics	C	Guys	B+
Campus Dining	B	Health & Safety	C
Campus Housing	B-	Local Atmosphere	A
Campus Strictness	C+	Nightlife	A-
Computers	B+	Off-Campus Dining	B-
Diversity	B	Off-Campus Housing	B
Drug Safety	C-	Parking	B+
Facilities	B-	Transportation	A
Girls	B-	Weather	B

CP's Student Author On...
OVERALL EXPERIENCE

Loyola's students are quick to point out the school's faults. There is little sugar-coating in their appraisal of the school as a financial mess that is so rife with incompetence that it is hard to accomplish even the simplest administrative tasks without putting up a fight. That said, most Loyolans love their school. They see its faults as nothing more than additional challenges they must face on their way to graduation. The majority of students would prefer to look past all the talk of budget cuts and program eliminations they hear during the course of their academic careers and focus on the positives. Loyola offers a quality education for those who are willing to work at it.

Are the administrative problems at Loyola disruptive to a student's studies? Definitely. Should this scare you away from Chicago's Jesuit institution? No. Loyola is starting to come slowly out of its period of financial distress. Fewer cutbacks are expected as incoming class sizes grow in size. Outside of the classroom, the University is actually growing and improving by the day.... For the rest of this editorial, visit collegeprowler.com.

Students Speak Out On...
OVERALL EXPERIENCE

Q I Love College!

"I have got to say that the city is a great place to attend school. It is welcoming and always busy which I love. I love the constant crowds on the street and the many students to talk to. I also have family at Loyola."

Q Amazing

"I love Loyola. I'm from a small town and moving to a big city like Chicago is epicness. So many amazing experiences and meeting new people. Really happy with my classes and all Loyola offers. Clubs, events, and more."

Q Nothing but Love for Loyola

"Loyola has been wonderful. The people that make up the Loyola community are friendly, unique, and welcoming. There is a nice balance of both social and academic aspects of life, which is the perfect fit for me."

Q Experience

"My experience has been wonderful, I enjoy it very much."

BEST OF LOYOLA CHICAGO

1. Lake Michigan
2. Chicago
3. The Rome Center and Study Abroad
4. Guy-to-girl ratio for guys
5. Student-to-teacher ratio
6. Service learning programs

Happy Students
85% of students return after their first year.

Knowledgeable Professors
100% of students surveyed rated the general knowledge of professors as above average.

WORST OF LOYOLA CHICAGO

1. Administrative red tape
2. Programs constantly downsized or eliminated
3. Guy-to-girl ratio for girls
4. Lake Shore Dining Hall
5. No football team
6. Lack of positive fraternity presence

Expensive
Tuition is a steep $30,656, one of the most expensive rates in the country.

Expensive Dorms
Living on campus doesn't come cheap, with an average housing price tag of $7,160.

Student Body

African American:	5%	Male Undergrads:	35%
Asian American:	11%	Female Undergrads:	65%
Hispanic:	9%	Living On Campus:	39%
International:	1%	Living Off Campus:	61%
Native American:	0%	Male Athletes:	4%
White:	59%	Female Athletes:	2%
Unknown:	15%	Fraternity Members:	6%
From Out-of-State:	42%	Sorority Members:	5%

Frequently Compared Schools:
DePaul University
Marquette University
Northwestern University
University of Chicago

Students Speak Out On...
EVERYTHING!

ACADEMICS

Easy Double Major

"I love International Studies because it's so easy to make classes for Core or other majors count towards it and they have no limits on "double dipping" like this. It's a nice major to start out with and then you still have plenty of time to add a second major your freshman or sophomore year."

Worldly Professors

"Most of my classes are like story time. I always struggled paying attention in high school, but my profs are so interesting in college that I have no trouble staying on top of the lectures. Most of the professors I've had teach as a second job or began teaching once they retired from their amazing, incredibly interesting career."

ATHLETICS

Athletic Facilities

"We have great athletic facilities at Loyola. Whether for athletes or regular students you can find a place to work out on campus."

FUN FUN FUN!

"We have a lot of athletics. Although we do not have a football team, we have fun sports like soccer, basketball, volleyball, track, QUIDDITCH! We have pride for our sports team"

CAMPUS DINING

A very good dining hall

"A very good dining hall, lots pf good things to choose from. the pizza especially ios very good, once i tried carmelized pottatoes, AMAZING. no othe word for it."

8/10

"The campus has a good selection of food and location. MOST of the time the food is great quality but it has its bad days. The menu selection is good for people of all tastes. Prices are high but I suppose most campus are."

CAMPUS HOUSING

So Many to Choose from

"While i don't yet attend Loyola I was very impressed with their dorm selection. There are options that fit every type of student."

Housing

"most housing is pretty nice. i never lived in a freshmen dorm so i can't say i know anything about that but upperclassmen halls are pretty nice. there are a lot of apartments that are affordable within walking campus of campus"

GUYS & GIRLS

Girls and Guys Are Well Dressed

"i feel like everyone on campus is very much preppy and/or unique in the way they dress"

Very Different

"Lots of different people here, either culturally different or even socially different. People hailing from various countries, states, suburbs, etc... The usual skaters, preps, stuck up snobs, emos, theater geeks, etc... Overall the people here are alright, more girls than guys, and most girls are hot."

HEALTH & SAFETY

Safe

"There's always emails about major outbreaks, and Loyola Campus Police and 8-Ride are on duty to pick students up/keep students safe."

Safety on Campus

"Despite our location near the city, one always feels safe walking on campus. Traveling at night alone is still not recommended, but if necessary, there are plenty of safety precautions taken. In my experience, I have noticed campus security cars patrolling campus and emergency call boxes are located throughout campus. Campus safety always seems to be on top of things, especially parties."

LOOKING FOR MORE?
Check out our full-length guide to this school at collegeprowler.com/loyola-university-chicago/.

Loyola University Maryland

4501 N. Charles St.; Baltimore, MD 21210
(410) 617-2000; www.loyola.edu

THE BASICS:

Acceptance Rate: 66%
Yield: 16%
Setting: Large city
Control: Private Non-Profit
Total Undergrads: 3,757
SAT Range: 1610–1910*
ACT Range: 24–28

Student-Faculty Ratio: 12:1
Retention Rate: 89%
Graduation Rate: 86%
Tuition: $37,610
Room & Board: $10,200
Avg. Aid Package: $25,360
Students With Aid: 70%

* of 2400

Academics	B	Greek Life	N/A
Athletics	B	Guys	A-
Campus Dining	B+	Health & Safety	B
Campus Housing	A+	Local Atmosphere	A-
Campus Strictness	B-	Nightlife	B
Computers	B+	Off-Campus Dining	A
Diversity	D+	Off-Campus Housing	C
Drug Safety	C+	Parking	C-
Facilities	A-	Transportation	A-
Girls	A+	Weather	B-

CP's Student Author On...
OVERALL EXPERIENCE

For freshmen everywhere, the first few weeks, maybe even semesters, of college life can be a daunting experience. Sharing a room with a total stranger, making a whole new circle of friends, and learning how to cope with professors and lecture classes can be enough to make anyone rethink the decision to go away to school. Fortunately for students at Loyola, these anxieties are quickly replaced by school pride and affection for the intelligent professors, gorgeous dormitories, and exciting nightlife. The opportunities at Loyola are endless. You can take part in student government groups and get hands-on experience with politics. If you're more of a sports star, there are intramural and club sports to join. And as Loyola students love to do, there's always a bar nearby for taking a break from the books.

While Loyola has a great list of pros, there are some cons to life on campus. There is little diversity among the student body, which for some is a major downfall. You won't get exposed to many different walks of life unless you actively seek out people who are different from you. However, in a city like Baltimore, there will definitely be opportunities for this.... For the rest of this editorial, visit collegeprowler.com.

Students Speak Out On...
OVERALL EXPERIENCE

Q **Awesome**
"Great place to go for 4 years. Baltimore is a really cool city; you just need to see past its reputation as a hotbed of crime. Good academics, hot girls, decent sports, and convenient location. Just be prepared to find a job on your own after school as the career center is nothing to write home about"

Q **You'll Meet Good Friends, but at a Price.**
"The academics at Loyola are really great, and are very hands-on. If you don't get involved in clubs and other organizations, most likely you will be spending the majority of your weekends at the bars off campus. Loyola is definitely a bar school... meaning you have to have the extra money to spend if you want to have any social life at all."

Q "I wouldn't change my choice for anything. I have had a great experience at Loyola thus far."

Q "I made a great choice. I think Loyola is a really good school."

BEST OF LOYOLA MARYLAND

1. Beautiful dorms
2. Relaxed RAs
3. The dining hall and cleaning employees are friendly
4. Small class sizes
5. Lots of snow days
6. Varied weather

Happy Students
89% of students return after their first year.

Proven Success
86% of students will complete their education and graduate with a degree.

WORST OF LOYOLA MARYLAND

1. Very expensive to have a social life at Loyola
2. NO on-campus parties
3. Superficial peers
4. The laundry situation sucks
5. No school spirit
6. No pets

Expensive
Tuition is a steep $37,610, one of the most expensive rates in the country.

Expensive Dorms
Living on campus doesn't come cheap, with an average housing price tag of $8,720.

Student Body

African American:	4%	Male Undergrads:	42%
Asian American:	3%	Female Undergrads:	58%
Hispanic:	4%	Living On Campus:	79%
International:	1%	Living Off Campus:	21%
Native American:	0%	Male Athletes:	12%
White:	85%	Female Athletes:	13%
Unknown:	3%	Fraternity Members:	0%
From Out-of-State:	83%	Sorority Members:	0%

Frequently Compared Schools:

Boston College
Northeastern University
Providence College
Villanova University

Students Speak Out On... EVERYTHING!

ACADEMICS

Q I Love Attendinf Loyola University Maryland

"I am a Speech Pathology major. All of the professors in the department are very welcoming and eager to help the students. For my major, I am only taking one introductory class. I find this class very interesting and I am excited to take more classes involved with my major. So far, I found that the cirriculum is challanging and helps me to become a better learner. There are a lot of opportunities that Loyola offers its students. One thing that I love about Loyola is the opportunity to do service."

Q General Academics

"Usually the workload is a good size, the teachers are nice and offer out of class time to help, and what you learn is important. The teachers are actually able to involve students and I haven't had many experiences at all with bad teachers."

ATHLETICS

Q Loyola Athletics Are Not Too Bad

"Loyola Athletics have very little school spirit, but we have a few sports, Men's soccer and lacrosse specifically, which are consistantly national championship contenders."

Q Not a Lot of School Spirit

"Our teams usually do fairly well, and sometimes people go to the games, but it isn't a priority for most people. The athletic facilities are nice, but I wish there was more fan support and school spirit for our teams."

CAMPUS DINING

Q Not Much of a Selection but...

"The food is good, don't get me wrong. However, there are only 3 different venues to choose from in the "new" Boulder Cafe, and it gets old, fast. If you want variety, go to Primo's but it'll cost you about $12 per visit, which gets pricey. The Indian and Sushi places are fantastic, and an average price. Off campus dining is better once you can have your car on campus, but it still gets annoying."

Q Pretty Boring

"The food is okay, but it gets really old after first semester and it is hard to eat healthy unless you go to the salad place 3 times a day."

CAMPUS HOUSING

Q Amazing

"The dorm rooms are huge and you get apartments with living rooms and kitchens after freshman year. Flannery O'connor is an all freshman dorm and is definately the nicest because it's only a few years old."

Q Dorms Are Great

"Loyola's housing is really amazing. Only some freshman live in standard doubles, which are all pretty good sizes, and everyone else lives in an apartment. Upperclassmen housing is fantastic, and most upperclassmen choose to stay on campus all four years."

GUYS & GIRLS

Q Girls Are Absolutely Gorgeous

"The ratio is something crazy. I think the school is something like 66% female and many are very very attractive."

Q There Are Definitely Some Good Looking Girls

"Loyola is known for consistently having a large population of hot girls. Usually high maintenance though."

HEALTH & SAFETY

Q Baltimore

"Baltimore can be a little sketchy at times so be careful at night and always travel in groups. But, on campus, I have never felt unsafe and the campus security doesn't give any problems usually."

Q Campus Is Very Safe, but Be Careful in Baltimore

"If you plan on going into the city on the weekends, make sure you go in groups and have street smarts. Baltimore has a high crime rate. The campus is very safe though."

LOOKING FOR MORE?

Check out our full-length guide to this school at collegeprowler.com/loyola-university-maryland/.

Luther College

700 College Drive; Decorah, IA 52101
(563) 387-2000; www.luther.edu

THE BASICS:

Acceptance Rate: 70%
Yield: 27%
Setting: Rural
Control: Private Non-Profit
Total Undergrads: 2,519
SAT Range: 1520–1950*
ACT Range: 23–29

Student-Faculty Ratio: 12:1
Retention Rate: 89%
Graduation Rate: 72%
Tuition: $32,290
Room & Board: $5,380
Avg. Aid Package: $23,487
Students With Aid: 99%

* of 2400

Academics	B	Greek Life	C-
Athletics	C+	Guys	C+
Campus Dining	B-	Health & Safety	A+
Campus Housing	B-	Local Atmosphere	C
Campus Strictness	B+	Nightlife	C
Computers	B	Off-Campus Dining	B-
Diversity	D+	Off-Campus Housing	C-
Drug Safety	B	Parking	B
Facilities	B	Transportation	D+
Girls	B	Weather	C

CP's Student Author On...
OVERALL EXPERIENCE

The Luther bubble does a wonderful job of creating an experience that is not duplicated anywhere else, and many students hold that near to their hearts. The campus's small size allows for plenty of bonding and gives students support and a sense of community and common purpose. The College's "liberal" bent has less to do with politics and more to do with personal choice. The College allows students to be creative and experiment on their own terms without punishing them for being different sexually, personally, or in terms of viewpoint. In the same way, professors at Luther are not about pushing their own ideas onto other students; they would rather present multiple viewpoints to you and let you make your own decision based on what you've learned. The community is also present outside of academics, and everyone is in the same boat at Luther. Despite the existence of a small Greek system, there is no real hierarchy at Luther over who rules the roost. If you're looking for an Animal House-type experience or plan on living and dying based on the basketball team, you'll be out of luck at Luther.... For the rest of this editorial, visit collegeprowler.com.

Students Speak Out On...
OVERALL EXPERIENCE

Q **A Few Bad Spots but Mostly Good.**
"Professors are wonderful. Food service isn't. Luther has a bit of an aura--not stuck up like St. Olaf, but a little weird. For most of us here, it kind of describes us. You can tell a Luther grad from it, and we love it--for those of us who realize it. It's a small town with not much to do, but there are plenty of places to go on a date in town and enough bars to support the campus."

Q "Your Luther experience is what you make it. There are a ton of people who leave here disappointed, but there are just as many who have a great time."

Q "My Luther experience has been fine. I'm happy with where I've wound up. I looked at other schools and almost transferred at one point, but I know I'm not going anywhere now because of the friendships I've made and the memories we've created."

Q "I think the best part of Luther was meeting my friends. I have met so many great people. We have so much fun and love to be with each other. There are just too many great memories!"

BEST OF LUTHER

1. Great academic programs
2. Friendly student body
3. Beautiful, spacious campus
4. Quick walks to essential student areas
5. Safety of a small town

Happy Students
89% of students return after their first year.

Proven Success
72% of students will complete their education and graduate with a degree.

WORST OF LUTHER

1. Required on-campus housing for four years
2. Outdated dorms for majority of students
3. The price tag
4. Lack of nightlife in Decorah
5. "Luther Bubble," isolation from the rest of the world

Expensive
Tuition is a steep $32,290, one of the most expensive rates in the country.

Want a Job? On Your Own
There aren't any placement services for graduates.

Student Body

African American:	1%	Male Undergrads:	42%
Asian American:	2%	Female Undergrads:	58%
Hispanic:	2%	Living On Campus:	88%
International:	4%	Living Off Campus:	12%
Native American:	0%	Male Athletes:	42%
White:	83%	Female Athletes:	21%
Unknown:	7%	Fraternity Members:	3%
From Out-of-State:	71%	Sorority Members:	4%

Frequently Compared Schools:

Gustavus Adolphus College
Macalester College
St. Olaf College
University of Minnesota

Students Speak Out On... EVERYTHING!

ACADEMICS

LOTS of Work.

"Luther College is hard work. However, the profs and the advisors are willing to help out at all times. There are lots of opportunities for special study options, like study abroad. J-term offers an in depth look into your field."

"I love the Monday/Wednesday/Friday and Tuesday/Thursday format. If you have a professor you really don't enjoy, try to take their class on a Tuesday/Thursday block for an hour and a half, instead of Monday/Wednesday/Friday for an hour. You'll see them less during the week, and have more time to work on their assignments as long as you don't procrastinate."

ATHLETICS

Division III

"This is a school where 1000 out of the 2500 students are involved in music whether it be choir, band, orchestra, voice lessons or anything in between. Our sports players play for the joy of the game. There are many sports teams, Luther probably has the sport you are interested in playing.But basically they're just not really a big deal compared to the music program."

A Few Are Ok

"Swimming and diving and cross country are top-notch. Too bad no one cares about them. Everything else isn't so great."

CAMPUS DINING

Life Sustaining Ok

"Oneta Market is the best, cafe is so-so on rare occasions they might have something good. Otherwise lots of stir fry and cereal."

"I know many students don't like it, but I think the Caf is actually really good; it's far better than any state school I've ever been to, and much better than many colleges of our size as well."

CAMPUS HOUSING

You Really Just Sleep There

"The dorms at Luther are not beautiful, but they sure are fun. My freshman year was the year that two of the freshman dorms were re-done. Looking back, these dorms are some of the best I've seen at many colleges. Even Towers is an experience, and still bigger than most rooms at NYU. The Key to succeeding in the housing is to know what you want, and to be organized when room draw comes around."

"Sophomores and juniors really get the shaft from Luther. Seeing the freshman dorms makes you think that dorm living won't be so bad, but that's because those got remodeled and are actually fit to live in."

GUYS & GIRLS

Good Variety

"There's a good variety of students at Luther and plenty of attractive ones. Many are involved in music (especially choir) and the everyone on campus is so welcoming and friendly."

"The typical guy is something hard to define, but I guess a typical guy is nice with a good sense of humor. Girls can be really hot, and some aren't. For the most part, they are attractive in one way or another."

HEALTH & SAFETY

Like Your Own Private Security Team

"Like it or not, these guys are attentive. The security on campus is effective and visible and easily reached. They take care of everything from security issues to providing nighttime escorts home from the library."

Safe and Relaxed

"i never feel nervous or uneasy at Luther, totally safe community on and off campus. Gorgeous area and great place to learn and study."

LOOKING FOR MORE?

Check out our full-length guide to this school at collegeprowler.com/luther-college/.

Macalester College

1600 Grand Ave.; Saint Paul, MN 55105
(651) 696-6000; www.macalester.edu

THE BASICS:

Acceptance Rate: 46%
Yield: 27%
Setting: Large city
Control: Private Non-Profit
Total Undergrads: 1,985
SAT Range: 1910–2170*
ACT Range: 29–32

Student-Faculty Ratio: 11:1
Retention Rate: 94%
Graduation Rate: 87%
Tuition: $38,174
Room & Board: $8,768
Avg. Aid Package: $25,376
Students With Aid: 76%

* of 2400

Academics	A-	Greek Life	N/A
Athletics	B-	Guys	A-
Campus Dining	A	Health & Safety	B
Campus Housing	B	Local Atmosphere	A-
Campus Strictness	A	Nightlife	B+
Computers	B+	Off-Campus Dining	B+
Diversity	B+	Off-Campus Housing	A-
Drug Safety	C	Parking	A
Facilities	B	Transportation	B-
Girls	B+	Weather	C

CP's Student Author On...
OVERALL EXPERIENCE

You'll be hard-pressed to find a student at Macalester who doesn't want to be there. The intimacy of the small Macalester campus gives students a sense of community and support, yet the liberal spirit of the College gives students the space and independence they need to make their own decisions and experiences. The professors and the College staff at Mac are not there to draw conclusions for students or to tell them what to think; rather, they are there to help undergrads make their own choices. If you're interested in getting a fantastic education and meeting some very amiable and interesting individuals along the way, Macalester is the right school for you. If you're looking to join a fraternity and party after all of the major football games, however, most Mac students will agree that you're probably better off somewhere else. Macalester is a very small campus, so whether you like it or not, you're never going to get lost in the crowd here. As soon as you step foot on campus, you become part of a very welcoming community.... For the rest of this editorial, visit collegeprowler.com.

Students Speak Out On...
OVERALL EXPERIENCE

Q Four Years Isn't Enough

"There's so much going on around campus that you'll get through your four years and wish you had four more. Even though Mac's a small school there's so many fun and interesting classes to choose between, countless student orgs, and all the good sports/cultural/political events that we have here in the Twin Cities."

Q Perfect

"Professors are engaged, care about the world and don't want to just be academics. Students are equally engaged and dynamic. Macalester is a place that exudes positive social values and challenges suffering in the world. And hey, it's fun, too."

Q Pretty Fun

"Professors are first-rate. The administration's been getting progressively more conservative. We got Dan Deacon for Springfest. It's a great place to be gay or heterosexual. Don't regret coming here."

BEST OF MACALESTER

1. International diversity
2. Small classes
3. The large variety of friendly people
4. Fast walks to class
5. Professors with a sense of humor

Happy Students
94% of students return after their first year.

Proven Success
87% of students will complete their education and graduate with a degree.

WORST OF MACALESTER

1. Freezing cold walks to class
2. Scorching hot walks to class
3. Outdated athletic facilities
4. Required on-campus housing for two years
5. Required cafeteria food for two years

Expensive
Tuition is a steep $38,174, one of the most expensive rates in the country.

Student Body

African American:	4%	Male Undergrads:	42%
Asian American:	8%	Female Undergrads:	58%
Hispanic:	4%	Living On Campus:	67%
International:	11%	Living Off Campus:	33%
Native American:	1%	Male Athletes:	30%
White:	67%	Female Athletes:	19%
Unknown:	5%	Fraternity Members:	0%
From Out-of-State:	83%	Sorority Members:	0%

Frequently Compared Schools:

Carleton College
Middlebury College
Oberlin College
St. Olaf College

Students Speak Out On... EVERYTHING!

ACADEMICS

Mac Academics

"Macalester is known for its high and challenging academic program. The professors are absolutely wonderful, providing individual attention and always there to answer questions and help. The class sizes are small (the largest class I had was 30 students), and courses are discussion-based."

No Strong Opinions Either Way.

"If you have any kind of mental health or medical issue that might require you to miss more than two classes per semester, don't expect a lot of understanding. Courses are interesting (in some cases) but few were life-changing or particularly exciting for me personally."

ATHLETICS

Something for Everyone

"I'm not into organized sports but there are lots of intramural options and classes you can take even if you're not an athlete. I've taken yoga, pilates, zumba, step aerobics, and swimming here. The new athletic facilities are AMAZING and people there are really friendly and nice. Lots of room to study and hang out as well."

Smart Athletes

"I think that Macalester's orientation towards academics and not so much towards sports attracts intelligent athletes to the campus. Athletes do the sport because they want to do it for pleasure more than starting a professional athlete career."

CAMPUS DINING

Freshmen 25

"The food at Mac is super varied and there are lots of options like Italian, all-American, Asian, Mexican, salad bar, cold meats, omelets made to order, gluten-free and veggie options... you name it. Also, this year Mac has really worked to make flex dollars useful around the neighborhood and so you can use your meal plan money to go to all the popular cafes around here like Coffee News, which has become a Mac obsession. Oh, and they work with the vending machines too."

Repetitive but Good

"Food at Cafe Mac can sometimes be repetitive but nevertheless it's good. I know many students who don't like to eat at the cafeteria, but compared to other colleges, I would say that the food and the food service at Macalester is above average."

CAMPUS HOUSING

Off Campus

"Macalester is situated in a really nice neighborhood in the middle of St. Paul. Off campus housing is cheap, there are plenty of options, and the neighbors are usually great. It's safe, close to campus, and a great way to adjust to living on your own before graduation."

Upper Classman Dorms Are the Best

"These dorms are right at the center of Macalester which is really nice. Also, all the dorms are suites which is perfect for on campus privacy."

GUYS & GIRLS

Diverse

"Well, there's hipsters, hippies, businessmen, artists, etc. Everyone has a crowd but people are generally inquisitive of who they are and their effect on the world. There is decent "hotness" and nearby schools have your coach totting blonde chicks if that's what you really want...."

HEALTH & SAFETY

Safety and Security

"We live in a really great neighborhood in St. Paul. The people are friendly and I never feel unsafe walking home from campus at night. It is a city, so there are some problems with theft, but those cases are rare occasions. The on-campus security are also really friendly and great people and really look out for students."

LOOKING FOR MORE?

Check out our full-length guide to this school at collegeprowler.com/macalester-college/.

Manhattan College

4513 Manhattan College Parkway; Bronx, NY 10471
(718) 862-8000; www.manhattan.edu

THE BASICS:

Acceptance Rate: 65%
Yield: 21%
Setting: Large city
Control: Private Non-Profit
Total Undergrads: 3,024
SAT Range: 1490–1785*
ACT Range: 21–25

Student-Faculty Ratio: 13:1
Retention Rate: 86%
Graduation Rate: 72%
Tuition: $26,718
Room & Board: $10,160
Avg. Aid Package: $16,839
Students With Aid: 87%

* of 2400

Academics	B	Greek Life	D
Athletics	B	Guys	B+
Campus Dining	C+	Health & Safety	B+
Campus Housing	B	Local Atmosphere	A
Campus Strictness	C-	Nightlife	A+
Computers	B-	Off-Campus Dining	B+
Diversity	C	Off-Campus Housing	B-
Drug Safety	B-	Parking	C
Facilities	B-	Transportation	A+
Girls	B+	Weather	B-

CP's Student Author On...
OVERALL EXPERIENCE

Manhattan College is a small college located in the greatest city in the world. Because of the school's size, students have the opportunity to know half of their college, which is something that isn't possible at many other institutions. There is a great student-to-faculty ratio, so teachers generally know students by their first names. The professors care about the students and make sure that they graduate and are prepared to succeed in the "real world." There are some things that are missing from the College, like a football team, but Manhattan still has a lot of energy and life.

The best part of the College is the people. The trick is getting to know them. If you do, you can see just how cool and fun everyone is. The professors are intense in the classroom, but outside of class, they are really chill and are always looking to help you. There are students that are slackers and there are students that are really hardworking, but the majority of the school is somewhere in the middle.... For the rest of this editorial, visit collegeprowler.com.

Students Speak Out On...
OVERALL EXPERIENCE

Q I love MC
"I love MC I love how it's small, I love how all the teachers know your name and generally care about you and succeeding in life, it's a wonderful experience, I would come here again and again, my favorite part is the freedom we get, my least favorite part will be saying goodbye to this wonderful place. MC is my home away from home."

Q I have had a great time at this school
"I personally have had a great time at this school as well as experiences. I have met many great people and would definitely come here again if I had the chance. The guys on my floor in Jasper freshman year were all great and I will always remember them."

Q I have had an incredible time at MC
"I have had an incredible time at MC, from the teachers, to the academics, to the people I've met and experiences I've had. I would definitely do it again."

Q I would definitely come here again
"Yes. This school for the most part is wonderful and I would definitely come here again."

BEST OF MANHATTAN

1. Caring professors
2. Graduation
3. Great people
4. Great school tradition
5. Internship opportunities
6. New York City
7. Rooting for a Division I sports team

Happy Students
86% of students return after their first year.

Proven Success
72% of students will complete their education and graduate with a degree.

WORST OF MANHATTAN

1. Athletic facilities
2. Having to explain why Manhattan College is called Manhattan but located in the Bronx. Because it is!
3. New York City winter weather (can be dreadfully cold)

Expensive
Tuition is a steep $26,718, one of the most expensive rates in the country.

Don't Move Off Campus
Average off-campus housing is a steep $10,160.

Student Body

African American:	3%	Male Undergrads:	52%
Asian American:	3%	Female Undergrads:	48%
Hispanic:	11%	Living On Campus:	70%
International:	0%	Living Off Campus:	30%
Native American:	0%	Male Athletes:	18%
White:	73%	Female Athletes:	15%
Unknown:	7%	Fraternity Members:	7%
From Out-of-State:	29%	Sorority Members:	5%

Frequently Compared Schools:

Fordham University
New York University
Northeastern University
Villanova University

Students Speak Out On... EVERYTHING!

ACADEMICS

Q Advisors Help Students With Internship Opportunity

"Manhattan College really helps students with internship opportunities. Every semester an advisor goes to all the classses and discusses with students all the internship programs that are available. They help with resumes and train the students for the interviews. At the same time they have career fairs and students get the chance to meet with professionals for potential job opportunities."

Q All the teachers are very helpful

"All the teachers are very helpful and want you to pass. They know what they are talking about and if they say something you should listen because they know what they are talking about. Our school is in the top 5 for engineering. I know they do a lot of work but, every subject can be easy or hard, it's just about the effort you put into it, and if you want to succeed in life. But MC is definitely the right college for anyone who wants to be something in life."

ATHLETICS

Q Varsity sports at Manhattan College are good

"The varsity sports at Manhattan College are good here. I like the fact that there are so many athletes on campus. I think that if your team is successful then the team will get a lot of support from the student body. Intramural basketball is very popular at our school and it is very competitive."

Q Manhattan is Division 1 in all sports

"Manhattan is Division 1 in all their sports so they are good. I really don't know about the intramurals."

CAMPUS DINING

Q Best Places

"Here we have four dinning cafes. Lockes is the most common buffet style. It provides students with endless choices and endless amounts of food. My personal favorite is platos. It's open late hours of the night and has fresh grill options, such as the classic bacon egg and cheese!"

Q Average

"Dinning at Manhattan College is OK. The dining hall is pretty descent. Some of the food is made right in front of you but the taste is not all that great. It is a good thing the school is located near other fast food restraunts."

CAMPUS HOUSING

Q Dorms Are Fun

"The dorms at Manhattan College are great and there is good atmosphere. You are protected 24/7 with security around the entire campus and the rooms have plenty of space."

Q Jasper, Horan, Overlook

"I have lived in Jasper, which is a pretty nice dorm. It allows you to really meet people as many people leave their doors open. Horan includes a lot of security and you aren't able to meet many people outside your own suite mates. I have lived in Overlook for 2 years and have enjoyed it. The rooms are more of an apartment type setting."

GUYS & GIRLS

Q Everyone at the school is pretty good

"Everyone at the school is pretty good. You have the diversity of everyone so it is a good environment."

Q Ah Boys Boys Boys

"The boys at this college are nice when you need something from them. most of them are from Yonkers and New Jersey so they have a Northern attitude about everything. be careful."

HEALTH & SAFETY

Q Security is very good

"Security is very good, all the guards are extremely nice, and are around 24/7, and most students know them on a 1st name basis. They really crack down on crime."

LOOKING FOR MORE?

Check out our full-length guide to this school at collegeprowler.com/manhattan-college/.

Manhattanville College

2900 Purchase St.; Purchase, NY 10577
(914) 694-2200; www.manhattanville.edu

THE BASICS:

Acceptance Rate: 53%
Yield: 21%
Setting: Suburban
Control: Private Non-Profit
Total Undergrads: 1,842
SAT Range: 1530–1860*
ACT Range: 22–26

Student-Faculty Ratio: 13:1
Retention Rate: 75%
Graduation Rate: 60%
Tuition: $32,760
Room & Board: $13,500
Avg. Aid Package: $26,779
Students With Aid: 89%

* of 2400

Academics	B	Greek Life	N/A
Athletics	B-	Guys	B
Campus Dining	B	Health & Safety	A
Campus Housing	B	Local Atmosphere	B+
Campus Strictness	B	Nightlife	A-
Computers	A-	Off-Campus Dining	B+
Diversity	A-	Off-Campus Housing	D-
Drug Safety	B	Parking	B+
Facilities	A-	Transportation	A
Girls	B+	Weather	B-

CP's Student Author On...
OVERALL EXPERIENCE

Manhattanville is a college that many students usually love or hate—the first step in a college student's career, but not necessarily the last. After a few semesters, some students are not happy, nor are they doing well at Mville, and they often transfer. For their friends, it is sad to see them go, but their happiness and well-being take top priority. For some students who stay, they end up loving the atmosphere, the people, and, of course, the Castle. Not many schools have castles, and that is one thing that makes Mville so unique. The students who stick it out believe that they made the right decision and are happy with their education, even if it was a slow transition. Many students find getting involved on campus to be very important to the adjustment process. By staying active, students meet students who introduce them to other students. Many students become happier and more comfortable with Manhattanville as their circle of friends grows.

There is also a good number of students who transfer to Manhattanville.... For the rest of this editorial, visit collegeprowler.com.

Students Speak Out On...
OVERALL EXPERIENCE

Q I love it
"I love it. The people and atmosphere are amazing...and we have a castle. You don't really need anything else. The teachers really care and classes are small, which is wonderful. While the small size does limit options, it creates a very familial atmosphere that is very welcoming. I would never change my mind."

Q I made the right choice coming to Manhattanville
"I made the right choice coming to Manhattanville. I like the people, the professors and the campus is beautiful. I'd be crazy if I ever decided to leave!"

Q It's the perfect place for me
"There is nothing I don't like about this school. It's the perfect place for me."

Q Good times at Mville
"I have had nothing but good times at Mville, but it was hard to see some of my friends transfer after freshman year. It's too bad that they didn't find their perfect school right away like I did."

BEST OF MANHATTANVILLE

1. 200, 100, and 50 Nights
2. The affordable weekend trips to NYC for musicals, sporting events, etc.
3. Being able to see NYC from the quad
4. The Castle
5. Fall Fest and Quad Jam

Learn from the Best
96% of faculty have earned the highest degree in their field.

Personal Attention
You can expect personal attention with 73% of classes having less than 20 students.

WORST OF MANHATTANVILLE

1. The Pub closes at 2 a.m.
2. There isn't a football team.
3. The high tuition costs
4. Certain athletic teams are more idolized than others.
5. The lack of school spirit
6. Male-to-female ratio

Expensive
Tuition is a steep $32,760, one of the most expensive rates in the country.

Expensive Dorms
Living on campus doesn't come cheap, with an average housing price tag of $8,000.

Student Body

African American:	7%	Male Undergrads:	34%
Asian American:	2%	Female Undergrads:	66%
Hispanic:	13%	Living On Campus:	82%
International:	10%	Living Off Campus:	18%
Native American:	0%	Male Athletes:	34%
White:	48%	Female Athletes:	15%
Unknown:	20%	Fraternity Members:	0%
From Out-of-State:	53%	Sorority Members:	0%

Frequently Compared Schools:

Hofstra University
Sarah Lawrence College
Stony Brook University
University of San Francisco

Students Speak Out On... EVERYTHING!

ACADEMICS

Q Teachers overall are very good

"Teachers overall are very good and comprehensive of student life. Some professors curve grades and have different scales for grading, which can sometimes work on your advantage."

Q I'm getting a great education here

"I'm getting a great education here and I don't feel bad that my parents are spending so much money to send me here."

Q I really like Mville

"I transferred to Mville because I wasn't doing well at my other school. This is the place for me. My grades have improves significantly and I am happy with my progress."

ATHLETICS

Q The soccer team are the nicest

"I love the soccer team. Those boys are the nicest male team and they are genuine people."

Q I love supporting the athletes

"I love going to all the games. There isn't one sport that I haven't watched. I enjoy seeing my peers work hard and win on the court/field."

Q I enjoy going to the games

"I enjoy going to the games. The Valiants are the best and work so hard to do as well as they do."

CAMPUS DINING

Q No problems being a vegetarian

"I don't eat meat and I never have a problem finding food in FLIK. That was something that I was scared about when I came to college."

Q The Pub is very convenient

"The Pub is quick. I have back-to-back classes, so the Pub is very convenient."

Q Very Good

"The areas that provide food and dining are very good. Well organized, clean, and offer great service."

CAMPUS HOUSING

Q Spellman was amazing

"Spellman was amazing. I miss it so much! If I could live there all four years, I would."

Q I love Spellman!

"I love Spellman! I can't even put into words how happy I am living in Spellman."

Q I enjoy living in the suites

"I enjoy living in the suites. They are like apartments without a kitchen and I like the feel of living there."

GUYS & GIRLS

Q I love that there are so many girls here

"I love that there are so many girls here. It gives me a chance to keep my options open."

Q Manhattanville has a wide range of boys and girls

"Manhattanville has a wide range of boys and girls from the geeky to the jocks and everything in between. It makes the campus very diverse and enjoyable to be in."

HEALTH & SAFETY

Q Security is very vigilant

"Security is very vigilant. Crime can be said to be pretty much nonexistent inside our campus. I feel very safe in our campus and confident with the job that our Campus Safety staff performs."

Q Campus Safety is always on top of everything

"Campus Safety is always on top of everything. They make me feel comfortable when I am on campus and I know that if anything became dangerous, they would be ready to take care of the situation."

LOOKING FOR MORE?

Check out our full-length guide to this school at collegeprowler.com/manhattanville-college/.

Marlboro College

2582 South Road; Marlboro, VT 05344
(802) 257-4333; www.marlboro.edu

THE BASICS:

Acceptance Rate: 71%
Yield: 23%
Setting: Rural
Control: Private Non-Profit
Total Undergrads: 312
SAT Range: 1700–2010*
ACT Range: 24–30

Student-Faculty Ratio: 8:1
Retention Rate: 79%
Graduation Rate: 64%
Tuition: $33,660
Room & Board: $9,220
Avg. Aid Package: $16,745
Students With Aid: 91%

of 2400

Academics	B	Greek Life	N/A
Athletics	F	Guys	B-
Campus Dining	C+	Health & Safety	A-
Campus Housing	B	Local Atmosphere	B-
Campus Strictness	A+	Nightlife	C+
Computers	C+	Off-Campus Dining	B
Diversity	D+	Off-Campus Housing	C
Drug Safety	C+	Parking	A-
Facilities	B	Transportation	C-
Girls	B	Weather	D

CP's Student Author On...
OVERALL EXPERIENCE

There is one thing you can be certain about: Marlboro College is not for everyone. It takes a certain person to come here and challenge themselves to an independently-created education. To give a student freedom and endless opportunity is often a scary concept. Additionally, to create a project that reflects four years of rigorous learning is quite the undertaking. But once embarked upon, a journey through Marlboro has infinite rewards.

Consistently growing in its respectable reputation, this school will forever strive to keep the learning process focused on and around the students. Walter Hendricks wanted to make education a conversation, and that's what Marlboro College continues to do. The College has yet to change its approach to learning. As a student at Marlboro, you can expect to be tossed around, treated like an adult, and taken to new heights. Not everything is possible at Marlboro, but once a student graduates, they have the power to imagine anything and act upon their dreams.

Students Speak Out On...
OVERALL EXPERIENCE

Q "There are good people here, and I know they will always be part of my life. I can't think of any place closer to a utopia than Marlboro College."

Q "It has been said that at Marlboro, you either love it, or you hate it. The reason this college causes such a dramatic reaction in its students cannot be easily explained. It lies somewhere between the moody weather and the students that embrace that weather by playing four-square or Frisbee in the sun and rain. It is a mix of great atmosphere and philosophical conversations over an oily lunch. There is something about the place, an essence, that makes it 'Planet Marlboro.'"

Q "A college is supposed to be a place of intellect and social development, but it is only when the college makes the student want to be a better and more complete person that the college has truly succeeded in its mission. I'm sure I could find a more well-rounded college, with more teachers and a greater variety of classes, but I don't think I would be able to find myself as well as I have at Marlboro College."

BEST OF MARLBORO

1. Dedicated community
2. Professors
3. Diverse interests and personalities
4. Conversations
5. Weekend brunch
6. Open-mindedness of the student body

Commitment to Teaching
There are 8 students for every member of faculty on campus.

Personal Attention
You can expect personal attention with 94% of classes having less than 20 students.

WORST OF MARLBORO

1. Friday night dinner
2. Snow following 70-degree weather
3. The price of tuition
4. The hike to the library
5. Deciding on your Plan
6. Finding your flashlight in a blackout

Expensive
Tuition is a steep $33,660, one of the most expensive rates in the country.

Student Body

African American:	1%	Male Undergrads:	51%
Asian American:	5%	Female Undergrads:	49%
Hispanic:	4%	Living On Campus:	80%
International:	1%	Living Off Campus:	20%
Native American:	1%	Male Athletes:	0%
White:	81%	Female Athletes:	0%
Unknown:	9%	Fraternity Members:	0%
From Out-of-State:	86%	Sorority Members:	0%

Students Speak Out On... EVERYTHING!

ACADEMICS

"The teachers are characters. They are some of the most interesting people I've ever met. Even in classes I am bored by, I can tell that the teachers really care about the subject."

"One of the unique things you'll find at Marlboro is teachers that are committed to learning. Most teachers would say teaching is a heuristic process. They're probably learning right along with the students. One of my favorite teachers could probably make the phone book interesting."

ATHLETICS

Not Much

"If you're into athletics you shouldn't come here. You can start any kind of club you want but there is no competition."

"Ha ha! Seriously, though, if competitive athletics are your thing, Marlboro may not be the place for you. We have a soccer team composed of students and professors that has won about two games in the last 10 years. We do have an active fencing community, though."

CAMPUS DINING

Dining at Marlboro

"The kitchen at Marlboro is constantly accused of stashing money away and not giving enough food to keep students running. Luckily, this has caused students to get more involved in the kitchen, and in the 2010-2011 year our food provider has to re-bid, so things to change. Students are also starting a business of a coffee shop/cafe on campus, which as I understand it is a lot cooler than what other college's can offer."

"Since Gene is cooking for so few people, the kitchen can put more time into everything. Sometimes it sucks, because there are limited options, but there's always something, if not in the dining hall then in the Campus Center."

CAMPUS HOUSING

"Dorms are nice. Avoid whichever dorm is going to be the 'sketchy' dorm. From what I hear, it goes back and forth between Schrader and Happy Valley."

"I think the dorms tend to be the most rundown buildings on campus (probably because Marlboro's major donors never have to see them). There are some pretty nice ones, though. In my opinion, Out of the Way is by far the best, but it's also a bit of a hike from the center of campus. Housing preferences are given according to number of credits, so upperclassmen are much more likely to get what they want."

GUYS & GIRLS

Marlboro Students

"Students at Marlboro are interested in and participating in a wide variety of things. They can party but it is not the main event. People are focused on their education."

"Marlboro is such an insular and intense environment, both academically and socially, that it's easy to start relying on one or just a few people to fulfill all of your emotional needs. Codependency is rampant on campus."

HEALTH & SAFETY

Safety & Security at Marlboro College

"well is supper safe, we are on a mountain. accidents do happy when people are intoxicated, and it seems like it is much more of a big deal then it is because of the small amount of students hear. every one keeps there doors unlocked, and things don't get stolen. you can also just leave your things around and its fine. sometimes there will be petty theft, but everyone gets very angry about it and it ends shortly after it begins."

"There's some guy in a security uniform. He doesn't do much, and the only thing he seems to bust people for is sleeping in the library."

Marquette University

615 N. 11th St.; Milwaukee, WI 53233
(414) 288-7710; www.marquette.edu

THE BASICS:

Acceptance Rate: 66%	**Student-Faculty Ratio:** 14:1
Yield: 17%	**Retention Rate:** 89%
Setting: Large city	**Graduation Rate:** 76%
Control: Private Non-Profit	**Tuition:** $29,096
Total Undergrads: 8,081	**Room & Board:** $9,680
SAT Range: 1610–1940*	**Avg. Aid Package:** $21,428
ACT Range: 24–29	**Students With Aid:** 86%

* of 2400

Academics	B+	**Greek Life**	C+
Athletics	B	**Guys**	B
Campus Dining	C+	**Health & Safety**	B-
Campus Housing	C+	**Local Atmosphere**	B+
Campus Strictness	C+	**Nightlife**	A-
Computers	B-	**Off-Campus Dining**	C
Diversity	D+	**Off-Campus Housing**	B+
Drug Safety	C+	**Parking**	B-
Facilities	B-	**Transportation**	A
Girls	B-	**Weather**	C-

CP's Student Author On...
OVERALL EXPERIENCE

It is almost unanimous—Marquette students could not be more satisfied with their experience here. Almost every student who looks back at their experience says they would make the same decision all over again if they could. Even if a student experienced uneasiness or uncertainty at the start, they almost never regret their decision in the end. Yes, money may be an issue, the campus is not all that diverse, and studying hard is a must, but hey, no school is perfect. Marquette can offer more than you may expect, like a welcoming atmosphere, distinguished faculty, and a noteworthy academic reputation.

During the college selection process, Marquette is often a top pick among prospective college students due to a number of factors. Sure, students are quick to recognize the drawbacks, but most acknowledge the beneficial qualities Marquette can provide, such as the strong academic foundation, top-quality professors, and an endless amount of entertainment opportunities in a major city location. Most of all, a feeling of small-town community togetherness makes Marquette feel unique to the students here.... For the rest of this editorial, visit collegeprowler.com.

Students Speak Out On...
OVERALL EXPERIENCE

Q Frickin Love It!

"As an Engineering Student, I couldn't ask for anything better!"

Q It's Completely Awesome

"The academics are supurb. I have struggled to completely immerse with numerous crowds, which I wish was more possible. I love it and wouldn't want to be anywhere else! The sports games and school run activities are a ton of fun."

Q Marquette Is the Best

"My experience at Marquette has been phenomenal. I can honestly say I haven't met a bad person here and everyone truly cares for one another. If you want a decent-sized school that is in a major athletic conference, Marquette is the best choice. GO MU!"

Q I Love Marquette

"I love the atmosphere at Marquette. The people and city are inviting and welcoming."

BEST OF MARQUETTE

1. Academics
2. Off-campus restaurants, bars, and clubs
3. Friendly atmosphere
4. Sense of community
5. The professors
6. Safety and security is great.

Happy Students
89% of students return after their first year.

Proven Success
76% of students will complete their education and graduate with a degree.

WORST OF MARQUETTE

1. Dining and meal plan options
2. High-priced expenses/tuition
3. Unpredictable weather
4. No diversity
5. City noise

Expensive
Tuition is a steep $29,096, one of the most expensive rates in the country.

Expensive Dorms
Living on campus doesn't come cheap, with an average housing price tag of $6,230.

Student Body

African American:	6%	Male Undergrads:	47%
Asian American:	4%	Female Undergrads:	53%
Hispanic:	6%	Living On Campus:	54%
International:	2%	Living Off Campus:	46%
Native American:	0%	Male Athletes:	3%
White:	81%	Female Athletes:	3%
Unknown:	1%	Fraternity Members:	8%
From Out-of-State:	66%	Sorority Members:	12%

Frequently Compared Schools:

Loyola University Chicago
Northwestern University
Saint Louis University
University of Wisconsin

Students Speak Out On... EVERYTHING!

ACADEMICS

Real Estate & Finance

"There are great professors, many internship/job opportunities, tough workload yet not impossible, and state-of-the-art facilities. Also, the alumni network is phenomenal. They really care about trying to help you out in the job market."

Challenging, but Worth It

"The classes are definitely challenging, but most professors do their best to make classes interesting and manageable. You definitely get your money's worth out of each class. TAs are often from foreign countries and have accents that make them difficult to understand, but they clearly know the material and you rarely deal with them outside of lab and discussion sections anyway."

ATHLETICS

Marquette Basketball Is AMAZING!

"Marquette Basketball never disappoints its fans! GO GOLDEN EAGLES!"

Basketball

"Our basketball team is bombbbb. The games are so much fun to go to, definitely a lot of school spirit. Also I played for some club teams, depending on which team there are practices ranging from twice a week - five times a week. A great way to meet people with a mixture of competition with other rival schools like madison and fun. I believe our womens club soccer team made it to nationals in arizona this year."

CAMPUS DINING

Good Food!

"I think the food on campus is actually really good. There is a good variety of options; from sushi to italian to healthy food to a 50's style diner. All of the food is of good quality. The dining halls are so different that you don't have to worry about eating the same meals continuously."

Food Options

"There are a variety of food options. I live in Cobeen Hall and that has the best traditionaly dining on campus. You can order meals or they always have a variety of entrees ready. There are always vegan choices available as well."

CAMPUS HOUSING

Living on Campus

"I love living on campus. There are plenty of campus activities and safe things to do on weekends. There are movies, bowling, and sports. I love my dorm. I am in a triple and I have my own bathroom. The people are welcoming and I felt right at home my first day on campus."

Dorms at MU

"I hate that they make you live in the dorms for two years—I'm so sick of being babysat. The rules are ridiculously Catholic, and I just want out. No boys, no late visitors, you have to check everyone into the dorm, and swipe every time you enter. The actual facilities are very nice, but the overall atmosphere is uptight and uncomfortable. They are also incredibly expensive—almost $10,000 for a year."

GUYS & GIRLS

Fun

"There are a lot of fun guys at Marquette. They are really friendly and always welcome. We have movie nights and go out on weekends."

HEALTH & SAFETY

Limo

"On our campus security is very important since we are in the heart of Milwaukee. We offer limos to students between the hours of 5:30 p.m. and 3 a.m., so if you are alone, you don't have to go anywhere by yourself. There are also blue-light phones all around campus that dial directly to DPS when picked up."

LOOKING FOR MORE?

Check out our full-length guide to this school at collegeprowler.com/marquette-university/.

Maryville University

650 Maryville University Drive; Saint Louis, MO 63141
(800) 627-9855; www.maryville.edu

THE BASICS:

Acceptance Rate: 65%	**Student-Faculty Ratio:** 12:1
Yield: 48%	**Retention Rate:** 82%
Setting: Suburban	**Graduation Rate:** 56%
Control: Private Non-Profit	**Tuition:** $20,994
Total Undergrads: 2,934	**Room & Board:** $8,210
SAT Range: 940–1090*	**Avg. Aid Package:** $17,959
ACT Range: 22–27	**Students With Aid:** 97%

* of 1600

This School Isn't Graded Yet!

College Prowler grades are calculated using tons of criteria, including survey responses that come from students at this school.

Unfortunately, we haven't gathered enough student surveys yet for this school to be able to calculate the grades for each section. Stay tuned to *CollegeProwler.com* for grade updates and more!

CP's Student Author On...
OVERALL EXPERIENCE

Getting involved on campus at the beginning of your college career is crucial to meeting new people and building a foundation for the next four years or more. It gives you a better knowledge of the school and helps you become familiar with all of the opportunities there are for Maryville students. The smaller size of the University makes it easier for everyone to make friends, join clubs, and even have a better connection with their teachers. The friendliness and warmth makes the students want to relieve their experiences again and be thankful Maryville was their college of choice. If you immerse yourself from the start and take full advantages of the opportunities the University offers, you'll experience many wonderful moments during your time here.

The school's values are very strong, the wisdom of many is incredible, and the lessons you will learn everyday while surrounded by individuals who care about the souls of the students is astonishing. The overall experience at this school is beyond amazing. Maryville is one of the most positive, thrilling, relaxed, and closely knit private universities in St.... For the rest of this editorial, visit collegeprowler.com.

Students Speak Out On...
OVERALL EXPERIENCE

Q A Great School

"I am very comfortable here, there are many events, the environment is friendly the staff and students are very helpful. I really recommend this school to anyone who is seriously considering attending or is curious."

Q I Can't Complain

"I'm giving my experience a solid B because I have nothing that is very bad about it but at the same time I haven't had the easiest time there either."

Q A Commuter Campus

"Personally Maryville isn't for me. If you want to commute from the STL area this is probably the school for you."

BEST OF MARYVILLE

1. The administration
2. The atmosphere is breathtaking.
3. The closeness to the shopping centers and eateries
4. Free T-shirts at events
5. The friendly faces

Happy Students
82% of students return after their first year.

Personal Attention
You can expect personal attention with 67% of classes having less than 20 students.

WORST OF MARYVILLE

1. Cost of tuition
2. The geese
3. It's a commuter school
4. Need more residence halls
5. No football team
6. Outdated residence halls
7. Student diversity

Student Body

African American:	7%	Male Undergrads:	24%
Asian American:	2%	Female Undergrads:	76%
Hispanic:	1%	Living On Campus:	21%
International:	0%	Living Off Campus:	79%
Native American:	0%	Male Athletes:	25%
White:	83%	Female Athletes:	8%
Unknown:	5%	Fraternity Members:	0%
From Out-of-State:	18%	Sorority Members:	0%

Frequently Compared Schools:

Saint Louis University
University of Missouri
Washington University in St. Louis
Western Illinois University

Students Speak Out On... EVERYTHING!

ACADEMICS

Q Professors Are Very Close to Their Students

"The first time I visited Maryville University, I talked to many students and a few teachers on campus. They all said that students have professor's cell phone numbers and they are able to call them if they ever need anything. Not only are they there for extra help, but they are their if you need someone to talk to about problems going on in your life."

Q Education Program

"I came to Maryville University for their education program. You get into the school early so that you get more experience in your career choice. I also loved how you got your Masters Degree in 5 years."

Q Being a Music Therapy Major Is Exceptional

"I'm at Maryville University and I have been so thrilled with the music therapy program I am enrolled in as well as all the other classes I have gotten to participate in this year. The program has a lot of great one on one time with professors and many opportunities to get to know different things that I can do with a music therapy degree."

ATHLETICS

Q Fun to Watch

"Athletes are talented and fun to watch."

CAMPUS DINING

Q Dining Hall, Cafe, Kahldi's

"options include:one card- ID card in which you put money on to use wherever on campus, like a credit carddining plan- you get a set number of meals per semester, or you pay $6.10 to eat at dining hallcafe is usually opened and food is good, little expensive but good"

Q Not Cheap but Is Good

"The places on campus that serve food have a lot of variety, but the prices are pretty steep."

CAMPUS HOUSING

Q Small Campus...Feels Like Home Everywhere.

"The campus is so small and comfortable. It feels like "coming home" no matter where you are."

Q Most Bang for Your Buck in Apartments

"Mouton is the better of the two dorms, but the apartments are your best bet. With the apartments, you get your own room, a kitchen, and a living room for close to the same cost as the residence halls."

GUYS & GIRLS

Q Majority of students are preppy

"The majority of students (male and female) are very preppy. The university is located in an affluent area and it shows. The ratio of girls to guys is completly skued. There is an abundance of girls compared to guys."

Q No Diversity

"Maryville isn't very diverse so if you're looking for a little diversity in a relationship, its not the best place for that."

HEALTH & SAFETY

Q Excellent Safety and Security

"The safety and security on campus is excellent! I never would have expected as much care and dedication out of the security. The employees are also very friendly. I never felt unsafe on campus, especially walking to my car at night. The best aspect of the campus safety and security is the campus wide email alerts that are sent out to inform everyone associated with the school about anything unusual happening on campus."

Q The Campus Is Small and Safe

"I feel extremely safe at Maryville University. We are like "one big family"."

LOOKING FOR MORE?

Check out our full-length guide to this school at collegeprowler.com/maryville-university/.

Massachusetts College of Art & Design

621 Huntington Ave.; Boston, MA 02115
(617) 879-7000; www.massart.edu

THE BASICS:

Acceptance Rate: 51%	**Student-Faculty Ratio:** 10:1
Yield: 38%	**Retention Rate:** 88%
Setting: Large city	**Graduation Rate:** 65%
Control: Public	**Tuition:** $24,400
Total Undergrads: 2,216	**Room & Board:** $11,288
SAT Range: 1480–1810*	**Avg. Aid Package:** $10,262
ACT Range: 20–25	**Students With Aid:** 75%

* of 2400

Academics	B-	Greek Life	N/A
Athletics	C-	Guys	A-
Campus Dining	C+	Health & Safety	D+
Campus Housing	B	Local Atmosphere	B
Campus Strictness	B+	Nightlife	B+
Computers	B-	Off-Campus Dining	C-
Diversity	B+	Off-Campus Housing	C+
Drug Safety	C-	Parking	C
Facilities	C-	Transportation	B+
Girls	B	Weather	C

CP's Student Author On...
OVERALL EXPERIENCE

MassArt is a small school. The size of most classes here allows students and teachers to get to know each other and communicate on more personal level. The education in arts here is wonderful; however, MassArt lacks organization. Often they don't give students enough information, when it comes to registering for classes. A lot of times, even for freshman, people at the registrar's office just assume that the students know when and where to get their registration packets with all the requirements. Unfortunately, some students come here because they expect art school to be easy, but soon they realize that this is not the case. Students here probably have a bit more control than other schools over how hard it is, but that doesn't make it easy.

With all the advantages that art school can offer, the setbacks seem unimportant. MassArt is in a great location, which allows teachers to have classes at the Museum of Fine Arts. Student life here is fun and full or strange and very interesting art projects. Taking risks, thinking outside the box, and exploring the unknown is what students do and enjoy doing here.

Students Speak Out On...
OVERALL EXPERIENCE

Q **Experience**
"I love MassArt! People at my high school thought i was weird, but everyone is weird here, we r all artists!"

Q **The Best, and Most Affordable, Place to Be an Artist!**
"Massachusetts college of art comes with the most affordably price tag in the country for an art college, and not because of any lacking qualities! MassArt has incredible, passionate teachers and an intensive freshman program that forces its students to excel at a rapid rate. With these sorts of programs and teachers, MassArt earns its place in my heart."

Q **Best School Ever!**
"I am very glad I ended up going here! Its fun but hard. All of my professors are very good."

BEST OF MASSACHUSETTS ART & DESIGN

1. Free technology resources (cameras and other equipment)
2. Printing lab
3. Fenway Cash allows you to use your ID as a debit card
4. Art supply and book store on campus

Happy Students
88% of students return after their first year.

Commitment to Teaching
There are 10 students for every member of faculty on campus.

WORST OF MASSACHUSETTS ART & DESIGN

1. Only freshmen are guaranteed housing
2. It's expensive to live off campus
3. Living on campus is even more expensive then off campus
4. The Green Line is slow
5. Parking

Expensive to Just Get By
50% of students surveyed felt that the amount it costs to live while at school was worse than average.

Student Body

African American:	3%	Male Undergrads:	33%
Asian American:	5%	Female Undergrads:	67%
Hispanic:	4%	Living On Campus:	23%
International:	2%	Living Off Campus:	77%
Native American:	0%	Male Athletes:	—
White:	53%	Female Athletes:	—
Unknown:	33%	Fraternity Members:	0%
From Out-of-State:	31%	Sorority Members:	0%

Frequently Compared Schools:

Boston University
Emerson College
Northeastern University
Rhode Island School of Design

Students Speak Out On...
EVERYTHING!

ACADEMICS

Q Academics

"They are good here. The Class sizes are perfect, and the teachers help alot. sometimes some teachers are not good but are great artsits..and that can be frustrating."

Q I Love Massart!

"All the professors i've had are great, and the workload is to be expected. If you're not prepared it can be difficult. Every professor works with their student individually."

ATHLETICS

Q Enough to Be Fit

"We have access to free gym at Wentworth and a pool at Simmons. I think for someone who just wants to stay fit its enough."

Q Sports

"MassArt does offer sports, but its not big at all. Most people who like sports just go to gym or jog. We don't have time for these things."

CAMPUS DINING

Q Clever Title

"MassArt has two main places to dine, with access to Wentworth's dining commons if you have the fancy Fenway Cash. They do seem to slack off in at the end of spring semesters, though. I end up spending all of my money on cereal in the C-Store for lack of delicious options that provide me with awesome variety like in the fall semesters. It offers a full meal plan for freshman, but a half meal plan alternative for sophomores and upperclassmen living in the dorms."

Q Food Is Ok

"There is always a wide array of pizza and specials each day that come with a free med. fountain drink. The specials are usually good and provide a nice change in pace."

CAMPUS HOUSING

Q Dorms

"Its really nice that all dorms have workrooms and rooms themselves are larger then a standard dorm rooms."

Q One Dorm Is Great, Other Is Gross

"The Artist Res is a great dorm, but there are students from SMFA here and I do not think that they should get part of our dorm. Smith Hall is gross and far too cramped. The Artist Res is much better kept up and it is much easier to live in, the only issue is that its pretty expensive to live here, so after freshman year, most people move off campus to live somewhere half the price of it."

GUYS & GIRLS

Q Guys

"Guys at MassArt are SO COOL! They know how to dress and a lot of them have an interesting style. Not just sweatshirts and sweat pants like some schools next to us."

Q Girls

"MassArt girls take a better care of their looks then a lot of other surrounding colleges."

HEALTH & SAFETY

Q Safe

"Public Safety officials patrol the school at all hours. If people are in the building working after a certain time they are required to sign in at the public safety office so the office knows who is in the building and where. If anyone wants to leave the building between 11pm and 5am they are REQUIRED to take a taxi, and a $10 voucher is given to cover all or part of the taxi ride, depending where the student is going."

LOOKING FOR MORE?

Check out our full-length guide to this school at collegeprowler.com/massachusetts-college-of-art--and--design/.

McGill University

845 Sherbrooke St. W; Montreal, QC
(514) 398-4455; www.mcgill.ca

THE BASICS:

Acceptance Rate: 46%	Student-Faculty Ratio: —
Yield: 46%	Retention Rate: —
Setting: Large city	Graduation Rate: —
Control: Public	Tuition: $15,420
Total Undergrads: 24,065	Room & Board: $6,800
SAT Range: 1870–2020*	Avg. Aid Package: $6,145
ACT Range: 26–29	Students With Aid: —

* of 2400

Academics	B+	Greek Life	D
Athletics	D+	Guys	B-
Campus Dining	B	Health & Safety	B-
Campus Housing	B	Local Atmosphere	A+
Campus Strictness	A+	Nightlife	A-
Computers	C	Off-Campus Dining	A+
Diversity	B	Off-Campus Housing	A
Drug Safety	B+	Parking	C-
Facilities	C+	Transportation	A-
Girls	A-	Weather	C-

CP's Student Author On...
OVERALL EXPERIENCE

Looking at the school as a whole, most students would say that they are pretty content to call McGill their university. It can be pretty hard to pin down the overall atmosphere here; it's a large school in a large city, and where there is one trend on campus, it is not hard to find the exact opposite happening somewhere else. This can be a great asset. It's so easy for students to do their own thing and find someone who does something similar, too. However, it can also be troublesome if you don't know what your thing is yet. It's so easy to get overwhelmed with decisions about majors, where to live, when to study, and when to party, that succeeding here can seem unlikely at best. To top it off, McGill's bureaucracy is obscene, there are a million policies and guidelines buried in the Web site, and administration likes to be as unhelpful as possible enforcing these guidelines.

However, despite the red tape and faceless crowds, McGill is an amazing opportunity for those who want to make it one. It really is a school that you can mold to fit your needs.... For the rest of this editorial, visit collegeprowler. com.

Students Speak Out On...
OVERALL EXPERIENCE

ℚ Great Party and Academic School

"McGill University is in the great city of Montreal, QC. The parties are great because the drinking age is 18, so clubs/bars are free range for all students including freshman. No sneaking or hiding alcohol and parties needed. The academics are also top notch. It is rated the best school in Canada and is deemed the Harvard of Canada. It is a great school and a lot of fun. Great place to be."

ℚ Highs and Lows

"McGill is a very competitive environment which can feel overwhelming sometimes. However, from an academic point of view it's a very good school. I had the opportunity to study from professors who are summities in their chosen subjects. In addition I have met some interesting people and Montreal offers a wide variety of activities to partake in with said interesting people, even though the winters here are very cold."

BEST OF MCGILL

1. Montréal
2. Being treated like an adult
3. School-sponsored drinking
4. The campus
5. Low tuition
6. Legal drinking age is 18
7. The profs

Learn from the Best
95% of faculty have earned the highest degree in their field.

WORST OF MCGILL

1. Bureaucracy
2. The weather
3. The hills
4. 8:30 a.m. classes
5. Laundry cards and printing cards
6. No fine arts programs
7. Labs

Lost in the Crowd
Expect to take at least a few classes in a lecture hall—77% of classes have more than 50 students.

Student Body

African American:	—	Male Undergrads:	40%
Asian American:	—	Female Undergrads:	60%
Hispanic:	—	Living On Campus:	8%
International:	19%	Living Off Campus:	92%
Native American:	—	Male Athletes:	4%
White:	—	Female Athletes:	2%
Unknown:	82%	Fraternity Members:	1%
From Out-of-State:	43%	Sorority Members:	1%

Students Speak Out On...
EVERYTHING!

ACADEMICS

Q Don't go anywhere else

"Great university, great teachers, and excellent internship opportunities. I am currently competing with top 3-Ivy League undergrad. students, and I thank McG U for everything I was taught there."

Q Teachers With Knowledge on Topics That Interest Students

"At my school, teachers know how to do their job while incorporating pieces of information that we hear from the radio or television. They always offer to give us extra help and are willing to sacrifice their time so we can get what we need. They give rewards when we are good and know when to discipline us when we misbehave."

ATHLETICS

Q Not Much to Say

"Hockey. I wouldn't say its a big deal, but its the only sport that really qualifies as a deal here as far as general participation-interest go. The fitness center, while inexpensive, is pretty limited."

Q Not Much School Spirit

"The school is very big, and while students will run around chanting McGill's battle cry during the first week of Frosh, thats about as good as it gets. I went to one football game last year (the first one that only cost $1), and the seats were barely full, and the game was kind of boring. The games after that were even worse. Hockey games do tend to get more attendance but its not a school wide thing like it is in a lot of American schools."

CAMPUS DINING

Q Macdonald Campus Food Service

"They closed the only cafeteria on campus so now we have a small cafe that is only open for a few hours in the afternoon and cannot support the number of students who want to eat there."

Q

"I have not really experienced much of the food on campus. I think that compared to other universities, McGill has far fewer places to eat. Indeed, there are snack bars in just about every building, and there are several cafeterias, but if I am going to spend my money, I would much rather go one step off campus and get something at one of my favorite restaurants. McGill is at the heart of downtown Montréal, so there are tons of great, interesting places just steps away."

CAMPUS HOUSING

Q Off-Campus Housing Is Great

"While first year students at McGill tend to stay in dorms, most move out to surrounding off campus housing after the first year. I got my first hint of it recently and I am very excited. The cost is fantastic, much less than the already average McGill housing cost and there are many very close to campus, closer than McGill residences. The freedom and quality of what is around makes off-campus housing at McGill a great option."

Q Laird Hall

"Not glamorous but great way to make friends and learn how to cook. I liked not having to rely on a meal plan for my food. The rooms have plenty of storage space too."

GUYS & GIRLS

Q Guys and Girls Like to Party

"In Montreal the legal drinking age is 18. Needless to say many students love to take advantage of this fact and party hard from thursday to sunday. As soon as thursday night hits, the weekend starts early and students are running out to house parties, clubs and bars to have a lot of fun."

HEALTH & SAFETY

Q Safer Than Safe

"I've been living in NYC & London, but Montreal brings the "s" in "safety". It remains a "hipster-city", with very fashionable students on campus, and a trendy neighborhood that will make you feel at ease in no time."

LOOKING FOR MORE?

Check out our full-length guide to this school at collegeprowler.com/mcgill-university/.

Mercer University

1400 Coleman Ave.; Macon, GA 31207
(478) 301-2700; www.mercer.edu

THE BASICS:

Acceptance Rate: 62%
Yield: 20%
Setting: Small city
Control: Private Non-Profit
Total Undergrads: 4,457
SAT Range: 1595–1895*
ACT Range: 24–29

Student-Faculty Ratio: 13:1
Retention Rate: 83%
Graduation Rate: 57%
Tuition: $30,360
Room & Board: $8,788
Avg. Aid Package: $31,192
Students With Aid: 99%

* of 2400

Academics	B+	Greek Life	A
Athletics	C+	Guys	B+
Campus Dining	C	Health & Safety	B+
Campus Housing	C+	Local Atmosphere	B-
Campus Strictness	C	Nightlife	B+
Computers	C+	Off-Campus Dining	B
Diversity	B	Off-Campus Housing	B-
Drug Safety	C+	Parking	B
Facilities	B-	Transportation	C+
Girls	B-	Weather	C+

CP's Student Author On...
OVERALL EXPERIENCE

Mercer provides a great overall experience for its students. It offers a good social environment, as well as an exceptional academic environment. However, it is also difficult. Even if you easily received A's in high school, you will have to put substantial time and effort into your work here if you want to continue to get grades like that.

The professors at Mercer are passionate and often create classroom environments that are open-minded and thought-provoking. This sense of engagement and candidness can make your courses seem more exciting and worthwhile. Overall, the majority of Mercer students say they would not trade their experience at Mercer for anything.

Students Speak Out On...
OVERALL EXPERIENCE

Q Me and Mercer

"So far I love my colllege experiance at Mercer U I have met alot of people and made many friends. Dorm life was a shock but it has been a wonderful learning experience and I have friends for life."

Q A Nice Small School

"If you're looking for that small, private liberal arts school feeling with plenty of individual attention without a lot of the pretension, Mercer holds up quite well. The faculty is wonderful and truly cares about the students. It may not have as many things to offer as a large school does, but Mercer does well in meeting its student's needs."

Q It's Ok

"There can be way too much drama at times. People are always trying to force their views on others and make them conform into who they want to be."

BEST OF MERCER

1. Aesthetic beauty of campus
2. Discussion-based courses
3. Greek life
4. Professors
5. Sense of community
6. Small size
7. The other students

Happy Students
83% of students return after their first year.

Easy Financial Aid Process
59% of students surveyed told us that the financial aid process went smoothly and they received the financial aid they needed.

WORST OF MERCER

1. Campus tends to empty out on weekends.
2. The current dry campus policy
3. High cost of a private education
4. Lack of "green" efforts
5. Lack of late-night food options on campus

Expensive
Tuition is a steep $30,360, one of the most expensive rates in the country.

Student Body

African American:	32%	Male Undergrads:	30%
Asian American:	4%	Female Undergrads:	70%
Hispanic:	2%	Living On Campus:	68%
International:	3%	Living Off Campus:	32%
Native American:	0%	Male Athletes:	9%
White:	49%	Female Athletes:	5%
Unknown:	9%	Fraternity Members:	19%
From Out-of-State:	18%	Sorority Members:	25%

Frequently Compared Schools:

Clemson University
Emory University
Georgia Institute of Technology
University of Georgia

Students Speak Out On...
EVERYTHING!

ACACEMICS

Q The Registration Process Is Really Easy

"I chose Mercer University because of the convenience of location, the ease of registration, the course offerings, and the cost of tuition at the time. The entire process was very easy and the system is very user friendly for any non-traditional college student."

Q An Ivy League-Level Education

"Mercer University is rightly famous for its high standards in liberal arts, medicine, law, and engineering."

Q Mercer's Academics

"Mercer is a wonderful university with amazing faculty."

ATHLETICS

Q Let's Go Mercer Let's Go

"The sports at Mercer are exciting events and bring everyone on the campus together to hangout with friends and family. They are a great stress-reliever and they really make the campus appealing."

Q Basketball Is Exciting but....

"Mercer basketball is the only sport that really gets any attention."

Q Basketball

"Very involved on campus good fan support with rallys and events"

CAMPUS DINING

Q The Student Lounge

"There is a student lounge available with vending machines that allow you to use your student ID card or cash. Chick-fil-A also comes and serves hot and cold food, salads and desserts."

Q Good Variety for Small School

"There is a great variety for dining options at Mercer. The Caf is always a good place for unlimited eating, while Bear Necessities has coffee and snacks. The UC Food Court is great when you want a meal on the go or different choices than the Caf. All-around good selection with a variety of payment options."

CAMPUS HOUSING

Q Campus Housing

"Campus housing has its ups and downs. The underclassman dorms have their wear and tear, but they are in the best location for classes. I have not had any trouble being late to class because of where my room is located."

Q Better With Age

"The room options get better after freshman year, but the office of residence life is pretty uncooperative about issues that arise."

GUYS & GIRLS

Q Wide Variety

"There are many groups and stereotypes. Most everyone is friendly, but everyone has their own group they tend to stay with. Guys and girls go to class in everything from pajamas to the clothes they were wearing the night before. Most people either go out weekly (some nightly) or not at all. It's easy to find someone you have something in common with."

Q Guys & Girls

"The guys and girls seem to get along very well at Mercer. There is a very big ratio of interests, dress, social life, and relationships across the board for both girls and guys."

HEALTH & SAFETY

Q Indeed

"I have no problems with walking from one end of the campus to the other, since I pass by at least three MERPO vehicles on the trek."

Q Pretty Safe

"I never had any problems with security, but I know people who did. No problems during the day, but the campus isn't as well lit as it could be at night."

LOOKING FOR MORE?

Check out our full-length guide to this school at collegeprowler.com/mercer-university/.

Mercyhurst College

501 E. 38th St.; Erie, PA 16546
(814) 824-2000; www.mercyhurst.edu

THE BASICS:

Acceptance Rate: 74%
Yield: 31%
Setting: Mid-sized city
Control: Private Non-Profit
Total Undergrads: 4,045
SAT Range: 1400–1710*
ACT Range: 21–25

Student-Faculty Ratio: 17:1
Retention Rate: 81%
Graduation Rate: 72%
Tuition: $24,351
Room & Board: $9,069
Avg. Aid Package: $19,803
Students With Aid: 99%

* of 2400

Academics	C+	Greek Life	N/A
Athletics	C	Guys	B
Campus Dining	B-	Health & Safety	C
Campus Housing	B-	Local Atmosphere	B-
Campus Strictness	C	Nightlife	B-
Computers	B-	Off-Campus Dining	C
Diversity	C+	Off-Campus Housing	C+
Drug Safety	C+	Parking	B+
Facilities	B-	Transportation	C+
Girls	C+	Weather	C+

CP's Student Author On...
OVERALL EXPERIENCE

With the great student-to-professor ratio and the beautiful campus, it's hard not to be happy at Mercyhurst. Classes are small, so getting to know the people and professors is easy, which makes classes more enjoyable. However, for many MC students, one drawback to the College is the weather. Although the weather at Mercyhurst can be harsh and wear down some students, you can usually find ways to get through the long winter and even enjoy it. Students tend to complain about the weather, but many times all it takes is a glimpse around campus, and they can't help but stop and admire the beautiful and fresh Lake Erie snow.

MC students have plenty of things to do around campus. The SAC (Student Activities Council) events on campus are well planned and well attended. The events are fun and keep students busy. Also, if you like theatre, consider being a part of the Mercyhurst College student-run musicals, which are always fun and present students with a chance to learn about theatre and meet new people.... For the rest of this editorial, visit collegeprowler.com.

Students Speak Out On...
OVERALL EXPERIENCE

Q Enjoyable

"I really enjoyed my time spent here at Mercyhurst, the campus is beautiful and there was always something for me to do. I always felt safe with either the gates and police and safety. Everyone is very welcoming and professors are there whenever you need them."

Q Size Uniqueness

"I really love Mercyhurst, and a lot of it has to do with the size and the people I have met. With small classes, professors are always available to help and it is much easier to get to know people. You can find your group of friends almost instantly, and luckily, it's not all work. I have a lot of fun at school and even tend to dread the summer."

Q I Love It Here!

"Although Mercyhurst does have some downsides, overall I love this place and can't picture myself anywhere else. I have made great friends that I know will last a lifetime, found a boyfriend who I love, and I really feel prepared for my career after school."

BEST OF MERCYHURST

1. Academic programs
2. Awesome library
3. Beautiful campus
4. Close-knit community
5. Friends
6. Hockey games
7. Location
8. Professors

Happy Students
81% of students return after their first year.

Proven Success
72% of students will complete their education and graduate with a degree.

WORST OF MERCYHURST

1. Apartments
2. Availability of parking
3. Cold weather
4. Cost
5. Food
6. Housing sign-ups
7. Lack of flexibility
8. Older dorms

Lowest Grades
Campus Strictness: C
Off-Campus Dining: C
Health & Safety: C

Student Body

African American:	6%	Male Undergrads:	41%
Asian American:	1%	Female Undergrads:	59%
Hispanic:	2%	Living On Campus:	52%
International:	4%	Living Off Campus:	48%
Native American:	0%	Male Athletes:	25%
White:	76%	Female Athletes:	11%
Unknown:	10%	Fraternity Members:	0%
From Out-of-State:	43%	Sorority Members:	0%

Frequently Compared Schools:

Duquesne University
Gannon University
Siena College
Slippery Rock University

Students Speak Out On... EVERYTHING!

ACADEMICS

Mercyhurst Academics

"Mercyhurst College is home of excellent academics. It is a small school and the professors are extremely available to students. Students are never a number and it is very personal and comfortable in the classroom."

Internship/Job Opportunities

"I am an elementary and special education major at Mercyhurst, and I love that there are always plenty of opportunities for me to go visit a classroom and get involved. I know that some people from other colleges that I know have not had nearly as much experience in the classroom as I have, and this makes me feel very confident that I will be able to find a job once I graduate."

ATHLETICS

Hockey

"Even the least sports oriented student is going to have so much pride when it comes to our hockey teams. We are the best and there is so much energy at the hockey games."

Sports Is Pretty Big

"We have a great recreational center. Sports at Mercyhurst is pretty big. We have a very good hockey team."

CAMPUS DINING

Grab a Bite at the Bookstore

"Although I do not have a meal plan at Mercyhurst I often frequent the Bookstore, which offers Starbucks coffee, smoothies, pastries, sandwiches, and other treats. They have THE BEST cookies on the planet, and the staff always greets you with a pleasant hello."

Egan Dining Hall

"As a freshman, you have an unlimited meal plan, which is great! I always stopped in the cafeteria on my way to the library to pick a cup of coffee or snack, and the unlimited plan I had allowed me to just swipe my card and get food at anytime. The dining services always did themed weeks featuring ethnic foods, and always decorated for the holidays-it was really cool that they made the extra effort!"

CAMPUS HOUSING

Living on Campus

"Living on campus is very comfortable and convenient. I lived in Warde Hall and enjoyed all the benefits the dorm offers including the C-store on the first floor, the media and work-out rooms on the second floor, and the study rooms on all of the floors. The social atmosphere was also nice. If I ever needed anything I could walk down the hall and knock on anyone's door. It is also nice to live on campus because you can walk anywhere on campus within five minutes."

Campus Dorms = Nice!

"The campus dorms for freshman are in good shape. I lived in Warde Hall my freshman year and the rooms were huge!! My roommate and I could even fit a futon in our room. The only problem is the lack of communal options. Everyones doors automatically shut and there was no way for us to socialize communally."

GUYS & GIRLS

School

"You'll find lots of good kids at Mercyhurst. A lot of foreign kids give the campus a wide diversity, making sure you'll meet lots of cool kids. The guys are nice a lot of kids are into intermural sports as are the girls. Did I mention that its a 70% to 30% girls to guy ratio??"

HEALTH & SAFETY

Perfect

"Mercyhurst is probably one of the safest campuses there can be. I have never felt threatened and it's like our own little community."

LOOKING FOR MORE?

Check out our full-length guide to this school at collegeprowler.com/mercyhurst-college/.

Messiah College

1 College Ave.; Grantham, PA 17027
(717) 766-2511; www.messiah.edu

THE BASICS:

Acceptance Rate: 68%	**Student-Faculty Ratio:** 13:1
Yield: 34%	**Retention Rate:** 87%
Setting: Suburban	**Graduation Rate:** 77%
Control: Private Non-Profit	**Tuition:** $26,700
Total Undergrads: 2,766	**Room & Board:** $7,880
SAT Range: 1530–1880*	**Avg. Aid Package:** $18,236
ACT Range: 23–28	**Students With Aid:** 100%

* of 2400

Academics	B	Greek Life	N/A
Athletics	B	Guys	A-
Campus Dining	B	Health & Safety	B+
Campus Housing	B	Local Atmosphere	B-
Campus Strictness	C-	Nightlife	C
Computers	B	Off-Campus Dining	B-
Diversity	C-	Off-Campus Housing	D+
Drug Safety	B+	Parking	B+
Facilities	A-	Transportation	C+
Girls	B+	Weather	B-

CP's Student Author On...
OVERALL EXPERIENCE

Messiah College is what you make of it. Because of the school's distinct beliefs and traditions, no student is going to love every aspect of the College. The rules will bind some but will set others free. A positive attitude and an open mind are definitely needed to be happy at this school. A passion for helping others and feeling connected will also make your years here more enjoyable because Messiah's commitments to service and community are what make this school unique. The College greatly encourages service to others by presenting many service opportunities throughout the year, and there is a service requirement in the general education curriculum. As a freshman, be prepared to hear the word "community" repeated very often in chapel, class, and from your RA and RD.

Messiah wants to have an intentional community across campus, and promotes it through every aspect of student life. However, all of this community and togetherness sometimes drives people apart and into cliques and groups, and Messiah definitely has a problem with rumors, snobbery, and generally mean and exclusive behavior.... For the rest of this editorial, visit collegeprowler.com.

Students Speak Out On...
OVERALL EXPERIENCE

Q **Great Christian Community**

"I am so happy I chose to come to Messiah—I love it here. The great academics, the bonding community, and the Christian atmosphere are all top-notch. The campus is beautiful. I can't find any problems with Messiah!"

Q **Recommend to Any Serious College Student**

"I thought that my time at Messiah College was very enjoyable. You get to meet a lot of great people, get a really good education, improve your faith by a ton, and you tend to stay out of trouble and become a better person. I definitely wouldn't recommend it to party animals, but to anywho want a really good experience, I would recommend Messiah."

Q **Overall Experience**

"Messiah is great. Everyone on campus is so nice and while there's not really too much to do, you can find things to do for entertainment. It is a very good environment."

BEST OF MESSIAH

1. Beautiful campus and grounds
2. Caring and attentive professors
3. Excellent academics
4. Incredibly safe campus
5. Soccer!

Happy Students
87% of students return after their first year.

Proven Success
77% of students will complete their education and graduate with a degree.

WORST OF MESSIAH

1. Visitation hours
2. Male-to-female ratio—girls far outnumber guys
3. Mandatory chapel
4. Lack of nightlife

Expensive
Tuition is a steep $26,700, one of the most expensive rates in the country.

Life is NOT a Party
77% of students surveyed said it's almost impossible to find a good party.

Student Body

African American:	2%	Male Undergrads:	37%
Asian American:	2%	Female Undergrads:	63%
Hispanic:	1%	Living On Campus:	87%
International:	3%	Living Off Campus:	13%
Native American:	0%	Male Athletes:	21%
White:	84%	Female Athletes:	10%
Unknown:	6%	Fraternity Members:	0%
From Out-of-State:	44%	Sorority Members:	0%

Frequently Compared Schools:

Elizabethtown College
Grove City College
Penn State
University of Pittsburgh

Students Speak Out On... EVERYTHING!

ACADEMICS

Great Community in HDFS

"I am a senior Human Development and Family Science major at Messiah College. I love that I know all of my professors, and they are very personable. Plus, we have a small to medium number of students in our department, so I've developed close friendships with several fellow major students."

Several Diverse Majors and Quality Education

"As an Accounting major, it is important that the Accounting program has been rated No. 1 in Pennsylvania and No. 7 in the country (based on the CPA passage rate). The classes are small and the professors truly care. We have a strong community."

ATHLETICS

Excellent

"Messiah College has a very successful athletic program. Most programs receive student support and excitement. Fans especially enjoy special events, such as white outs and rival games. There is usually a fun and competitive atmosphere at games. Most student-athletes seem to work hard academically too, which yields more support and respect."

Love the Athletics

"I love the athletics we have at Messiah. We have such a great fan support, and the team performances make me proud to say that I go to Messiah!"

CAMPUS DINING

All You Can Eat

"You can get an unlimited meal plan and eat at a buffet from 7 a.m. to 7:30 p.m. You can also get food at the student union until 11 p.m. The meal plan gives you extra money for the Union and other places around campus, as well as your meals at the main dining hall, which is buffet-style."

Great Food, Limited Variety

"The food all around campus is really good. The only problem is that you have very limited options for where to spend your flex dollars."

CAMPUS HOUSING

Residence Life; an Essential Part of the College Experience

"Residence Life at Messiah College is the backbone of the institution. Here, you will find a place to become your own person and to matter as an individual."

Wit-Wit!

"I love my first-year dorm. I am truly blessed to have such an excellent RA who is always there for me. I can go to her anytime if I have a question, a concern, or even if I just need someone to talk to. The girls on my floor are very nice and fun. I love walking past all of the open doors and being able to peek in and say hi to the girls. My roommates are great, as well. None of us thought we would end up in a quad but have grown to love one another over the course of the semester."

GUYS & GIRLS

Very Attractive Ladys

"All sorts of guys and girls exist on campus. There are many attractive ones (girls). I met my wife at Messiah. They are all genuine real people, and they don't party, which is nice."

Messiah College Boys

"They are always a notch above the rest. They're amazing men with amazing potential."

HEALTH & SAFETY

Campus Is Extremely Safe

"Messiah College is very safe—on every level. Campus crime is pretty much non-existent, my personal safety is never an issue, and police and safety services are always available if needed."

LOOKING FOR MORE?

Check out our full-length guide to this school at collegeprowler.com/messiah-college/.

Miami University

500 High St.; Oxford, OH 45056
(513) 529-1809; www.muohio.edu

THE BASICS:

Acceptance Rate: 79%
Yield: 24%
Setting: Town
Control: Public
Total Undergrads: 14,872
SAT Range: 1060–1280*
ACT Range: 24–28

Student-Faculty Ratio: 17:1
Retention Rate: 89%
Graduation Rate: 81%
Tuition: $26,988
Room & Board: $9,786
Avg. Aid Package: $11,374
Students With Aid: 72%

* of 1600

Academics	B	Greek Life	B+
Athletics	B-	Guys	A
Campus Dining	A-	Health & Safety	B-
Campus Housing	B	Local Atmosphere	B-
Campus Strictness	C	Nightlife	A-
Computers	B	Off-Campus Dining	B+
Diversity	D+	Off-Campus Housing	B
Drug Safety	D+	Parking	B-
Facilities	B	Transportation	A
Girls	A-	Weather	B-

CP's Student Author On... OVERALL EXPERIENCE

There's an old saying that goes, "You can make a big school small, but you can't make a small school big." The overall experience at Miami University is different for every student, but most seem to have enjoyed their time here, and most will agree that the former part of this statement is representative of Miami. Miami is not a huge school, but it is large enough to feel like a big university without being overwhelming. It is essential to find a niche when you arrive; otherwise, you may get lost in the shuffle. One of the best ways to determine if you will like Miami is to take into consideration what is important to you in a school and to really weigh your options. Visit the campus and ask questions—this is the next four or five years of your life. If Miami does not fulfill an important need you have, it probably isn't the school for you, and there are people here who feel like they don't belong.

Nobody enjoys school 100 percent of the time, but the students at Miami have a plethora of options, both social and academic, at their doorsteps.... For the rest of this editorial, visit collegeprowler.com.

Students Speak Out On... OVERALL EXPERIENCE

Q I Wouldn't Go Anywhere Else

"I can't imagine myself anywhere else."

Q AMAZING!!!

"Miami has so many opportunities for students to get involved, further their academic career, and do amazing things! The fact that we are a smaller school really helps make one's education that much better. The teachers really get to know who you are. Plus, the social life is great here. There may not be a ton to do when looking at the city of Oxford, but you find things to do with your friends. There really is something for everyone here."

Q Amazing

"I love Miami University. I love the people, I love the atmosphere, I love the classes, I love the environment, I love my new friends, I love the activities, I love the trees, I love the classes, I love the dorms, I love it all."

BEST OF MIAMI

1. The lifelong friends you make
2. Exceptional professors you stay in contact with
3. Watching the beautiful campus change with the seasons

Happy Students
89% of students return after their first year.

Proven Success
81% of students will complete their education and graduate with a degree.

WORST OF MIAMI

1. Finding parking tickets on your windshield
2. Feeling isolated from the rest of the world
3. Tuition for out-of-state students
4. Trying to schedule for classes

Expensive
Tuition is a steep $26,988, one of the most expensive rates in the country.

Student Body

African American:	4%	Male Undergrads:	47%
Asian American:	3%	Female Undergrads:	53%
Hispanic:	2%	Living On Campus:	49%
International:	2%	Living Off Campus:	51%
Native American:	1%	Male Athletes:	4%
White:	84%	Female Athletes:	4%
Unknown:	4%	Fraternity Members:	23%
From Out-of-State:	33%	Sorority Members:	22%

Frequently Compared Schools:

Indiana University
Ohio State University
Ohio University
University of Michigan

Students Speak Out On... EVERYTHING!

ACADEMICS

⟨Q⟩ Political Science

"It's very interesting and relative to day-to-day life, especially in times of revolution, such as in Tunisia and Egypt."

⟨Q⟩ Get Involved

"Being an education major at Miami University has so far been a great experience. During my freshman year, I learned the basics and then next year in my cohort, I will actually get to work in classrooms! I can't wait—the experience will be so helpful in my future."

ATHLETICS

⟨Q⟩ Great Sports

"All of the sports teams here are talented and fun to watch. Hockey games are wild and the team is tops in the nation, but other great sports exist and are well supported too"

⟨Q⟩ Fan Support at Miami

"For the majority of our sports, our students have a pretty large fan support system. Our football team did really well this season, and the students helped support them by attending games. Our hockey team is very well known and probably the biggest sport at Miami. Our hockey team is very good and the games are always fun to attend."

CAMPUS DINING

⟨Q⟩ Excellent and Variety

"There are dining halls and markets all over campus. There's lots of variety, including stir-fry, sushi, Mexican, and burgers. Quality of food is far above average, especially when compared to other colleges. I'm a senior and still have a small meal plan because I love the food!"

⟨Q⟩ Miami Has a Wide Variety of Food for Everyone.

"The most popular meal plan at Miami is the Diplomat. It acts like a debit card and you can use it anywhere on campus. There are on-campus restaurants where you can use your card, as well as many dining halls with all different types of food."

CAMPUS HOUSING

⟨Q⟩ Thomson Hall Is the Best

"My dorm is amazing. We have the largest number of international students on this part of Western Campus, along with American students that just love other cultures. We always participate in events. It's amazing!"

⟨Q⟩ Freshman Dorms Are the Best Experience

"Freshman dorms each have a different theme and are focused on creating an inclusive community. The "Living Learning Communities" range between focuses on health, history, language, culture, and music. I had a wonderful time getting to know my fellow students and resident life assistants, and I wouldn't have traded the experience for a different one."

GUYS & GIRLS

⟨Q⟩ Hot Hot..... HOT

"If you want to be a big fish in a small pond regarding your looks, don't come to this school. People here are great looking but not because they put outrageous amounts of time into their looks. Yes, people dress up to go out at night but jeans or running shorts are what you will mostly see in your classes. In the end, everyone just looks like they care about themselves and you have lots of eye candy. There are lots of hookups, but by junior year dating is far more popular."

⟨Q⟩ Guy and Girls Dress Well

"Guys wear polos or jeans to class. They present themselves well. They are city boys. Girls dress alike; they are always up to date on the fashion trends."

HEALTH & SAFETY

⟨Q⟩ Safety on Campus

"The campus is incredible safe. I have never felt in danger anywhere. I can walk on back streets late at night by myself and still feel safe. There are occasional break-ins at houses but that is pretty much it."

LOOKING FOR MORE?

Check out our full-length guide to this school at collegeprowler.com/miami-university/.

Michigan State University

College Road; East Lansing, MI 48824
(517) 355-1855; www.msu.edu

THE BASICS:

Acceptance Rate: 72%	Student-Faculty Ratio: 17:1
Yield: 40%	Retention Rate: 91%
Setting: Rural	Graduation Rate: 75%
Control: Public	Tuition: $27,343
Total Undergrads: 36,489	Room & Board: $7,444
SAT Range: 1490–1880*	Avg. Aid Package: $6,378
ACT Range: 23–27	Students With Aid: 85%

of 2400

Academics	B	Greek Life	B
Athletics	A	Guys	A
Campus Dining	B+	Health & Safety	C+
Campus Housing	B+	Local Atmosphere	B
Campus Strictness	C+	Nightlife	B+
Computers	B-	Off-Campus Dining	B+
Diversity	B	Off-Campus Housing	B
Drug Safety	C	Parking	C+
Facilities	B	Transportation	A
Girls	A	Weather	C+

CP's Student Author On...
OVERALL EXPERIENCE

Most students are very satisfied with their decision to attend Michigan State University. New students sometimes complain that the size of MSU can be overwhelming and that it's pretty easy to get lost while walking to classes; however, it only takes a few weeks before the campus starts to look familiar and feels more like home. Many students say they have made great friends and have been able to handle the challenging workload.

A university as large as MSU provides students with countless opportunities to excel academically, develop unforgettable social ties, and prepare themselves for a meaningful career and future. Unique research opportunities allow students to work closely with professors while gaining experience in their field of study. Many students take advantage of the wide range of study abroad experiences that are available every semester. With over 500 student groups and more than 200 programs of study, there is something for everyone at MSU. Program- and hobby-related groups are a fun way to meet new people. Make an effort to talk to people and keep up with schoolwork.... For the rest of this editorial, visit collegeprowler.com.

Students Speak Out On...
OVERALL EXPERIENCE

Q **Michigan State Student Life**
"To be a Spartan is somthing I am very proud of; i wouldn't choose another school to represent who I am. I love the cold winter and enjoy the rainy summer. I grew independent considering I came to Michigan from Texas."

Q **My School Is Unique**
"My school is unique because their are a viraety of people"

Q **I Love You MSU**
"I can describe the the way I feel about my svhool in one word; love."

Q **I love MSU!!!**
"I love my school and couldn't imagine going anywhere else. The school spirit, academics, athletics, and social environment are hard to beat and the opportunities here are endless."

Q **MSU Is Great**
"MSU is great! People are generally nice, and campus is beautiful."

BEST OF MICHIGAN STATE

1. The gorgeous walking trails on campus
2. Friendly students
3. The parties
4. Fall colors on campus
5. School spirit
6. Tailgating

Happy Students
91% of students return after their first year.

Proven Success
75% of students will complete their education and graduate with a degree.

WORST OF MICHIGAN STATE

1. Limited parking spaces and endless parking tickets
2. Cafeteria food
3. Walking long distances to classes, especially in six inches of snow
4. Crowded buses

Expensive
Tuition is a steep $27,343, one of the most expensive rates in the country.

Student Body

African American:	8%	Male Undergrads:	47%
Asian American:	5%	Female Undergrads:	53%
Hispanic:	3%	Living On Campus:	43%
International:	6%	Living Off Campus:	57%
Native American:	1%	Male Athletes:	3%
White:	75%	Female Athletes:	3%
Unknown:	2%	Fraternity Members:	8%
From Out-of-State:	20%	Sorority Members:	7%

Students Speak Out On... EVERYTHING!

ACADEMICS

Great Professors and Classes!

"Michigan State University has great professors that are always looking to make sure you do well in the class and learn as much as possible. The class schedules are flexible and the classes are interesting!"

Criminal Justice

"I'm not going to college just yet but I will in a few months. I've visited Michigan State many times and what I have seen was awesome. There is so much to do on campus and everyone seemed very friendly. I was planning on going to college in California but after I visited Michigan State's campus, I changed my mind."

ATHLETICS

MSU Basketball

"Final four!! MSU just won elite 8, and going to final four. I always cheered for MSU basketball team. I can't wait to watch our SCHOOL to become a national champion again! I will always support our team and always support for our school."

Sports Are Huge

"Michigan State varsity sports are very popular. Students love tailgating and attending games, and there is a ton of school spirit. IM sports are also very popular, but I have never participated in any so can't really give any information on them."

CAMPUS DINING

Campus Food

"Many different cafeterias, each having unique foods. food quality is good and selection diverse."

Wide Selection And Delicious

"Food here is very good over-all, Sny-Phi currently has the the best food, but the freshman dorms will have a new huge cafeteria with 11 different restaurants. There many options and there mostly all very tasty."

Frequently Compared Schools:

Ohio State University
Penn State
Purdue University
University of Michigan

CAMPUS HOUSING

The Social Atmosphere

"The social atmosphere of campus is incredible. There are so many people to meet with and the people on campus are very diverse"

Dorms Aren't Bad, Apartments Are Awesome!

"Dorms aren't bad at all. They're not big but you get used to it. They're all clean and you can personalize them to your liking. Apartments and houses are awesome!"

GUYS & GIRLS

Girls are STUNNING

"I've never been to a college with so many attractive people, in such great shape."

Diversity Personified

"There are many different types of people at Michigan State University, guys and girls. In particular because we have the largest percentage of international students in the United States, You can find people from all walks of life and all nations of the world. MSU is a real melting pot."

HEALTH & SAFETY

Safety

"Michigan State has their own campus police. I feel very safe because of the safety boxes that you can find all over campus. If you feel in trouble you push the button and they come right away."

Safe

"I have always felt safe at Michigan State University. I live on campus and just outside my door is a green phone that I can use in case of an emergency. There are also phones all over campus we can use in needed. The fire department and police station are close by and arrive fast."

LOOKING FOR MORE?

Check out our full-length guide to this school at collegeprowler.com/michigan-state-university/.

Middle Tennessee State University

1301 E. Main St.; Murfreesboro, TN 37132
(615) 898-2300; www.mtsu.edu

THE BASICS:

Acceptance Rate: 70%
Yield: 54%
Setting: Mid-sized city
Control: Public
Total Undergrads: 22,299
SAT Range: 910–1160*
ACT Range: 20–25

Student-Faculty Ratio: 20:1
Retention Rate: 73%
Graduation Rate: 45%
Tuition: $17,916
Room & Board: $6,754
Avg. Aid Package: $5,396
Students With Aid: 94%

* of 1600

Academics	C+	Greek Life	B
Athletics	B-	Guys	B
Campus Dining	B-	Health & Safety	B-
Campus Housing	B-	Local Atmosphere	B+
Campus Strictness	B-	Nightlife	A-
Computers	A-	Off-Campus Dining	B+
Diversity	B-	Off-Campus Housing	B+
Drug Safety	B-	Parking	B-
Facilities	B	Transportation	B+
Girls	B	Weather	C+

CP's Student Author On...
OVERALL EXPERIENCE

Not everyone is keen on the town of Murfreesboro, but almost everyone loves MTSU—it's a safe and rewarding environment. One key to a stress-free experience here is to plan ahead so you're not running late for class all the time. Stress can be tough, and a few stitches in time can help you avoid a lot of headaches. Once students graduate, many seem to leave with a bigger impression of the people who helped them learn, rather than the actual material they studied. Lots of students also comment that they have made great friends at MTSU and are grateful for the experience and opportunities. There is something for everyone in Murfreesboro, and if you make an effort to look around the corner, you may find the solution to a problem you didn't even know you had.

The outdoor environment around MTSU is personally rewarding. There are local parks everywhere and major state parks as close as a 30-minute drive in any direction. Anyone who chooses to become active in outdoor pursuits will not be let down.... For the rest of this editorial, visit collegeprowler.com.

Students Speak Out On...
OVERALL EXPERIENCE

Q Lovely School ,Nice Teacher ,Good Student

"I have been there my first semester at mtsu after 15 years,i love it ,teachers are great ,they try very hard to help you,they want you to succeed, Mtsu have very good repatation."

Q What a Wonderful School

"I have enjoyed my overll school experience at MTSU. There is always activities to participate in and numorous services such as campus recreation center, campus events and school sporting events. The education I have recieved has been stellar and well worth the price of admission. I am proud and privileged to have had the opportunity to attend Middle Tennessee State University."

Q I Love This School!

"MTSU has everything that I could ask for in a school. It is close to home, plenty of room on the campus, and great housing. I love it here!"

Q Mtsu

"awesome. a lot of school pride amongst the students. Go Blue Raiders!!!"

BEST OF MIDDLE TENNESSEE

1. Beautiful environment.
2. Student opportunities are varied and plentiful.
3. Availability of help in all areas of student life.
4. Starbucks.
5. Homemade muffins.
6. 24-hour computer labs.

Knowledgeable Professors
85% of students surveyed rated the general knowledge of professors as above average.

Low-Stress Course Load
60% of students surveyed rated the manageability of work as above average.

WORST OF MIDDLE TENNESSEE

1. Parking and driving anywhere on campus.
2. Tuition increases every year, while financial aid availability does not.
3. Any amount of sexual assault.

Lowest Grades
Weather: C+
Academics: C+
Diversity: B-

Student Body

African American:	15%	Male Undergrads:	48%
Asian American:	3%	Female Undergrads:	52%
Hispanic:	2%	Living On Campus:	15%
International:	1%	Living Off Campus:	85%
Native American:	0%	Male Athletes:	3%
White:	78%	Female Athletes:	2%
Unknown:	1%	Fraternity Members:	9%
From Out-of-State:	5%	Sorority Members:	11%

Frequently Compared Schools:

Belmont University
Tennessee State University
University of Tennessee
Vanderbilt University

Students Speak Out On... EVERYTHING!

ACADEMICS

Q Academic Schooling

"I'm in the University of Middle TN, and I really like their academics. I'm currently studying chemistry and they teach it really good. Some of the teachers are good some of them don't give a s**t about you, but some of them are just great. I'm looking forward to finish my college career at Mtsu."

Q Nursing

"We have our own building, and special curriculum.There is study groups and they have a dorm dedicated to nursing majors so you can live near fellow students and help each other study. All The professors are license holding Nurses with masters and higher."

ATHLETICS

Q Favorite Sports

"The most famous sporting events you hear about are football and basketball. Those are the two most school spirited sports on campus. Everybody comes to the games whether it's a good game or not. The teams are supported by everybody and the facilities are very nice to enjoy the victories we achieve."

Q Athletics of MTSU

"Our athletic department is great. They seem to be team players, and are good at what they do. Its always great to be a part of the raiders! GO BLUE!!"

CAMPUS DINING

Q Campus Dining

"There is such a variety of dining options that I haven't even seen them all! They are placed all around campus and are very efficient and fast. I am able to get food between classes within minutes! To my knowledge there are: Pizza Hut, Subway, Cafeterias, Starbucks, Chick-Fil-A, burger king, another burger place, a chinese place, and so many more!"

Q Lots of Choice

"MTSU has a lot of choices. They have several dining halls, food courts, and a very reasonable meal plan with flex dollars. They have a variety of restaurants in the food courts including Chick-fillet and chinese food. Also, they have healthy options for health concious students. They even have special things at their Rec Center like strawberry protein shakes. It's perfect after a hard work out."

CAMPUS HOUSING

Q MTSU Life

"I personally do not live on campus, but I have seen the dorms and social places and they are great. MTSU has a great social life and good food in the Student Union. The school is conveniently located for me because I live 30 minutes away."

Q I Do Not Live in the Dorms.

"I do not live in the dorms, however I have been inside a few. They are cozy, and are usually shared. The bathroom is also shared. Overall the dorms are not bad at all."

GUYS & GIRLS

Q State Melting Pot

"There is a diverse group of people who attend Middle Tennessee State University. The girls out number the guys, which makes for a wonderful experience for a single male. Being a state university, a variety of ethnicities, nationalities, and cultures can be found among students."

HEALTH & SAFETY

Q Safety

"I feel absolutely safe at MTSU because we are surrounded by 3 different police stations in the city of murfreesboro,TN. The police are awesome and know how to do their job."

LOOKING FOR MORE?

Check out our full-length guide to this school at collegeprowler.com/middle-tennessee-state-university/.

Middlebury College

14 Old Chapel Road; Middlebury, VT 05753
(802) 443-5000; www.middlebury.edu

THE BASICS:

Acceptance Rate: 17%	**Student-Faculty Ratio:** 9:1
Yield: 42%	**Retention Rate:** 97%
Setting: Rural	**Graduation Rate:** 93%
Control: Private Non-Profit	**Tuition:** $49,210
Total Undergrads: 2,455	**Room & Board:** $0
SAT Range: 1940–2230*	**Avg. Aid Package:** $35,640
ACT Range: 30–33	**Students With Aid:** 41%

* of 2400

Academics	A	Greek Life	N/A
Athletics	B	Guys	A-
Campus Dining	A	Health & Safety	A+
Campus Housing	A-	Local Atmosphere	B-
Campus Strictness	B+	Nightlife	D
Computers	B+	Off-Campus Dining	C+
Diversity	B	Off-Campus Housing	D
Drug Safety	B	Parking	B+
Facilities	A	Transportation	C-
Girls	A-	Weather	C-

CP's Student Author On...
OVERALL EXPERIENCE

Most people you talk to who are still in school at Middlebury are more than satisfied with their college experience or else they wouldn't be doling out the high tuition to come here. The academics are outstanding, though you may wonder where they'll take you later. Students often wish they toiled less at the books and more at the booze, but the pristine facilities tend to distract from scholastic misery. Professors are brilliant, witty, and sympathetic, although there are some haughty bumps in the road. The on-campus social scene is lively and shot through with school spirit. The athletics put Middlebury at the top of its division, and the area is quaint ("quaint," unfortunately, being the opposite of any adjective suggestive of "nightlife").

Middlebury provides an incredibly varied experience—an opportunity to stick your paintbrush in all shades of colors, so to speak. Students can leave Middlebury with seven different areas of study, visits to 10 foreign countries, and/or stories of rock climbing in New Zealand under their belts.... For the rest of this editorial, visit collegeprowler.com.

Students Speak Out On...
OVERALL EXPERIENCE

Q Overall Experience at Middlebury

"Middlebury is an amazing place to go to college. Yes it is in the middle of nowhere, but you are isolated among 2000+ incredibly intelligent people. The Snow Bowl is quick, free shuttle ride away. The academic environment is challenging and led by incredibly talented professors. The campus is beautiful and the town perfectly quaint. I am so happy that I chose to go to Middlebury."

Q Great Academics; Bad Party Scene.

"You can find out about academics on their website. What detracts from the Midd experience is the lack of nightlife even though campus police don't do anything. This is a nerd's paradise, but if you want party, look elsewhere."

Q Why Go to Middlebury

"Middlebury is amazing. I love it here. The professors are wonderful and easily accessible, and the student body is incredibly diverse and entertaining. But you have to study here, and because it is in a rural area, you have to figure out how to have your own fun."

BEST OF MIDDLEBURY

1. Athletic facilities
2. Dining hall food
3. Small classes
4. Generally helpful professors
5. Outdoor activities
6. Easy-going student body

Happy Students
97% of students return after their first year.

Commitment to Teaching
There are 9 students for every member of faculty on campus.

WORST OF MIDDLEBURY

1. Overachievers
2. Overly-competitive students
3. Pretentiousness
4. Stress
5. Security and parking
6. The study abroad office

Expensive
Tuition is a steep $49,210, one of the most expensive rates in the country.

Student Body

African American:	2%	Male Undergrads:	48%
Asian American:	6%	Female Undergrads:	52%
Hispanic:	6%	Living On Campus:	97%
International:	10%	Living Off Campus:	3%
Native American:	0%	Male Athletes:	38%
White:	67%	Female Athletes:	30%
Unknown:	9%	Fraternity Members:	0%
From Out-of-State:	95%	Sorority Members:	0%

Frequently Compared Schools:

Bowdoin College
Brown University
Colby College
Williams College

Students Speak Out On...
EVERYTHING!

ACADEMICS

Great Professors in All Departments

"I'm not entirely set on a major, because I am interested in so many. I will probably do Economics however, and the professers have been great thus far. There is a lot of work, but it is rarely overwhelming... it is still possible to have a social life. Academic facilities are great, a lot of the buildings are brand new and state of the art. Job opportunities after graduation are great. Midd's alumni network is also very strong. They are also a top feeder school to graduate school programs."

Top Notch Academics

"Middlebury is a tough school. There is a lot of work, but it seems to come in waves, as there are definitely weeks that I have a lot of free time. The teachers are very helpful and approachable. It's rare that you'll take a boring class, I've found myself interested in subjects I had never liked before thanks to the teachers. It's hard deciding a major because I have become interested in so many fields. Registration is relatively painless, it's usually possible to get into the classes you want."

ATHLETICS

Varsity Sports Are Among the Best D-III

"Midd's varsity teams have won many NCAA championships and even more NESCAC titles. Most of our teams are very good and there is a lot of school spirit. The athletic facilities are also impressive. IM sports are available, fun and somewhat popular, but they are not a major part of campus life."

Go Panthers?

"The athletics are pretty good. Hockey games are fun (or so I hear...). There's definitely not the type of school spirit you see at big universities."

CAMPUS DINING

Now Thats What I Am Talking About!

"Watch out freshman fifteen. At first one would assume that the average Middlebury kid should be fat, but alas, they are all as fit as could be. The food they provide dictates that there should be a much larger number of fat people, but the quality and health of the food allows you to pig out and still shape up."

"The food on campus is really outstanding, especially at the Grille. However, if you want to eat in the dining halls, there is always plenty of choice—particularly at Ross."

CAMPUS HOUSING

Housing Is Great

"The housing at Middlebury is much better than average and only gets better as an upperclassman. Junior and Senior house is extremely nice and the options are plentiful."

Nothing Special.

"The availability of campus housing for all years is quite impressive, but the housing options themselves are nothing to write home about.Freshman dorms are impossible small and cramped while upperclassman dorms range from closet-sized singles to spacious suites and houses."

GUYS & GIRLS

Good Looking Student Population

"In generally, Midd kids are good looking, well dressed kids."

Clichy Just Like High School.

"While not as bad as high school, the attractive students generally associate themselves with other attractive students. Dating is almost non-existent; people prefer casual sex although the girls tends to be prude and are afraid of being judged.Again, like high-school, girls looking for casual sex prefer athletes, not just for physical attractiveness, but for status.Overall, girls are attractive and so are the guys; everyone here is obsessed with fitness and are generally in shape."

HEALTH & SAFETY

As Safe as Possible

"The campus is extremely safe, there is almost no crime and the town is equally safe. The role of Public Safety is effective and same with the Health Center."

LOOKING FOR MORE?

Check out our full-length guide to this school at collegeprowler.com/middlebury-college/.

Millsaps College

1701 N. State St.; Jackson, MS 39210
(601) 974-1000; www.millsaps.edu

THE BASICS:

Acceptance Rate: 74%	Student-Faculty Ratio: 10:1
Yield: 29%	Retention Rate: 78%
Setting: Mid-sized city	Graduation Rate: 68%
Control: Private Non-Profit	Tuition: $26,240
Total Undergrads: 1,017	Room & Board: $9,252
SAT Range: 1030–1280*	Avg. Aid Package: $17,774
ACT Range: 23–29	Students With Aid: 100%

* of 1600

Academics	B	Greek Life	A+
Athletics	C+	Guys	B+
Campus Dining	C+	Health & Safety	C
Campus Housing	C	Local Atmosphere	B-
Campus Strictness	B	Nightlife	B-
Computers	B-	Off-Campus Dining	B
Diversity	C	Off-Campus Housing	C-
Drug Safety	B+	Parking	A+
Facilities	C+	Transportation	C+
Girls	B	Weather	A-

CP's Student Author On...
OVERALL EXPERIENCE

Despite all their qualms with the academics, the facilities, and the social aspects of Millsaps, many students look on their years here as a great personal investment. For young adults that need challenges, they will find them. For those who need nourishment, there will be enough of that as well. The administration is truly committed to this. With 12 students to each faculty member, the school gives higher education a personal touch that distinguishes success from failure. Of course, no student who wished to stay forever could be considered a success, and most students are extremely eager to begin their futures. Sometimes, these ambitions become evident in the highly political, possibly even malevolent, maneuvering of on-campus gossip.

The student body is respectfully conservative—there will be little in the form of bitter disputes of beliefs. Millsaps College prides itself on being a transformative experience, and many students come back more thoughtful, more liberal, and more mature.... For the rest of this editorial, visit collegeprowler.com.

Students Speak Out On...
OVERALL EXPERIENCE

Q "Coming to Millsaps and working in the Jackson community really opened my eyes. I discovered how maladjusted our collegiate system is and decided that working in that bureaucracy was misguided at best."

Q "Everybody has a 'Millsaps moment': a time when the critical thinking and diverse education that you receive at Millsaps comes in handy in the workaday world we live in. Mine was when I was interviewing for an internship, and there was a strange appearance in the corner of some venting problem. From the knowledge that I had learned in a superscience course, which integrates many different fields, I deduced the problem in an aside in the interview and got the job."

Q "Setting up for your future is fairly easy here. Practically every department has internships. I think a Millsaps degree goes far in the eyes of grad schools and employers. I certainly have met a tremendous amount of people here that will do great when they move on, wherever they move on to."

BEST OF MILLSAPS

1. The personal touch
2. Strong academic programs
3. Exceptionally well-maintained facilities
4. The natural beauty of campus
5. The safe environment

Commitment to Teaching
There are 10 students for every member of faculty on campus.

Learn from the Best
97% of faculty have earned the highest degree in their field.

WORST OF MILLSAPS

1. The administration
2. The dorms
3. Gossip
4. The lack of diversity
5. Gloomy seasonal weather
6. Meal plan requirements
7. The rising cost of tuition
8. Lack of good athletics

Expensive
Tuition is a steep $26,240, one of the most expensive rates in the country.

Student Body

African American:	11%	Male Undergrads:	49%
Asian American:	4%	Female Undergrads:	51%
Hispanic:	2%	Living On Campus:	81%
International:	1%	Living Off Campus:	19%
Native American:	0%	Male Athletes:	46%
White:	79%	Female Athletes:	17%
Unknown:	2%	Fraternity Members:	49%
From Out-of-State:	64%	Sorority Members:	51%

Frequently Compared Schools:

Birmingham-Southern College
Louisiana State University
Rhodes College
Tulane University

Students Speak Out On... EVERYTHING!

ACADEMICS

Q **Awesome**

"Millsaps is absolutely awesome. I could not imagine going anywhere else. They have a liberal arts promgram which allows you to have a major or have 4 minors to make a major. Any and every course you could ever imagine is offered and the professor are wonderful. They are always there and willing to help with everything. The workload is managable but they do expect a lot of their students. And registration has always been pretty much hassle free."

Q "I wish students within majors were more interconnected. I have met more people in my major from parties than from classes. Most people enjoy the company of their fraternity brothers more than their fellow majors. Whenever I do get into a conversation, it's about how easy this professor is or how sexist this one is."

ATHLETICS

Q "The sports diversity isn't really there. Students want to get a rugby team started, and I would join a swimming team, but Millsaps isn't really interested in getting either going."

Q "Students are lackadaisical in their support of teams. As a result, a ton of players don't take the games very seriously. It works out well because it is just a game, and people that just want to go out and have a cultivated and well-rounded life can do it without having sports consume them."

CAMPUS DINING

Q "Avoid the Caf' when you get the chance. That way, it won't be poison by the time you gear up for finals. Better yet, ignore my advice; by the second semester, every student learns that lesson."

Q "I had the same experience as every one else. As a freshman, I was surprised by how good it was. As a sophomore, I ate more fast food than I ate on campus. By my junior and senior years, everyone asked me whether I had transferred because they never saw me in the Caf' or Kava

House. By the seven thousandth chicken breast or ham and cheese sandwich, I needed a serious change."

CAMPUS HOUSING

Q "It should be criminal to place rational beings in Ezelle. It's a dump and a major downgrade from Franklin, which I lived in my first year."

Q "There's a high premium on some dormitories, like New South, but all of them are pretty good quality. It's a lot better than having to hunt for an apartment and deal with your friends' financial arrangements. Plus, in Jackson, if there are more than four girls to an apartment it is legally considered a bordello, and there are some sort of sanctions."

GUYS & GIRLS

Q **Mix of Looks**

"Guys are either the typical frat guy (meaning ones with the shorts and polos with visors or khaki pants and button up oxford shirts) or have the look of "I really don't care". Most are really nice, with a southern gentleman charm. There are PLENTY of athletes on campus so there is definite eye candy. Girls have either the studious look or the trendy/grunge look. Plenty of sorority girls that have to dress up all the time. In the end, looks don't say much about personality"

Q "My rule has always been to avoid relationships at Millsaps. The guys are so much like big brothers to me, and as nice as a lot of them are, they're as gossipy as old lady spinsters."

HEALTH & SAFETY

Q "When someone gets robbed, it's a big deal. That's how infrequent assaults are here. If you need to have some minor medical issue taken care of, you can drop in to the health center between classes, and red tape is extremely rare."

LOOKING FOR MORE?

Check out our full-length guide to this school at collegeprowler.com/millsaps-college/.

Minnesota State University

228 Wiecking Center; Mankato, MN 56001
(507) 389-1866; www.mnsu.edu

THE BASICS:

Acceptance Rate: 89%	Student-Faculty Ratio: 23:1
Yield: 42%	Retention Rate: 77%
Setting: Town	Graduation Rate: 52%
Control: Public	Tuition: $12,861
Total Undergrads: 13,046	Room & Board: $6,322
SAT Range: —	Avg. Aid Package: $8,130
ACT Range: 20–24	Students With Aid: 83%

This School Isn't Graded Yet!

College Prowler grades are calculated using tons of criteria, including survey responses that come from students at this school.

Unfortunately, we haven't gathered enough student surveys yet for this school to be able to calculate the grades for each section. Stay tuned to *CollegeProwler.com* for grade updates and more!

CP's Student Author On...
OVERALL EXPERIENCE

MSU is definitely a school to look into if you want academics mixed with the typical college experience. Many students say they would choose to come here all over again if they had to make the decision again. The professors here love their subjects and are really understanding about any problems that may come up. The social scene is unimaginable, with something to do around every corner. The size of the campus is perfect for anyone from a small school because it allows you to be a person instead of a just a number.

MSU is known as a party school, but that's not necessarily the true reality. MSU doesn't have bigger drinking issues than any other school, but the local residents and police call more attention to it than other places. Either way, this should not influence your decision about coming to Minnesota State. Overall, this University is a great place for everyone, the people and professors are extremely nice, and the experiences that students gain here are unforgettable. Any future Maverick will be welcomed with open arms!

Students Speak Out On...
OVERALL EXPERIENCE

Awesome Place

"mankato state is the best place ever. there are a lopt of diversity and the students are so much friendly and outgoing that it makes the atmosphere nice. also the teachers makes sure that you understand the materials given to you and there are a lot of activities and social networks that will make you enjoy the campus."

Method of Teaching

"MSU has a great method of teaching. The class rooms are very convinient for learning. Instructors are very friendly and make sure to carry each student along during lecture. It is indeed a best way of learning."

I Will Always Choose MSU

"My experience at college has really helped me grow as a person and academically. I love the wide variety of classes and majors to choose from. My favorite experience so far is welcome week.The campus really welcomed me in, I meet so many new people and found out so much new information about campus.Campus life is so much fun!"

BEST OF MINNESOTA STATE

1. Good atmosphere
2. Updated technology
3. There are lots of students clubs, and it's easy to start a new one.
4. Variety of people
5. Variety of classes
6. Free laundry

Affordable
Tuition is only $12,861, one of the most affordable rates in the country.

WORST OF MINNESOTA STATE

1. Cafeteria
2. Lack of comfy furniture
3. Number of foreign professors who are hard to understand
4. You see people you don't want to see all the time.
5. Auditorium seating

Student Body

African American:	4%	Male Undergrads:	48%
Asian American:	2%	Female Undergrads:	52%
Hispanic:	1%	Living On Campus:	25%
International:	4%	Living Off Campus:	75%
Native American:	1%	Male Athletes:	5%
White:	83%	Female Athletes:	5%
Unknown:	5%	Fraternity Members:	3%
From Out-of-State:	16%	Sorority Members:	3%

Frequently Compared Schools:

East Carolina University
Missouri State University
Saint Cloud State University
University of Minnesota

Students Speak Out On... EVERYTHING!

ACADEMICS

Major...?

"I just declared my Graphic Design major today, so I'm unsure what the program is like. The head of the Art Department, however, said it took them about four years to find another professor good enough to join the Graphic Design faculty, so I'm bound to be impressed... I hope!"

I Am Not in College Anymore

"I would like to get into the U of Minnesota however I am too scared to take the next step in my college degree to sign up for that college."

ATHLETICS

Student Athletes

"I am a student athlete at MSU and have enjoyed my experience 100%. The school provides the support we need to succeed in both academics and athletics. In addition, the fans are very enthusiastic and make being a maverick one of the best experiences of my life!"

Go Mavs Go

"Our student involvement and support for our sports teams is great! The majority of our teams are winners. Our football team had an ok season and our mens basketball team made it to the Final Four this season. I believe that we have great school spirit. our facilities are pretty good too."

More Involvement

"although games are a big issue, I have never been involved. I feel more involvement in sports at residence halls would be benifical"

CAMPUS DINING

Could Include More Options

"The food is good, but often the menu is the same week after week. I think if more options were included more students would want to eat there."

CAMPUS HOUSING

Like It on Campus

"I would have to say that I like to live on campus a lot. Its very convenient and clean and everyone seems to get along just fine. There are always activities going on to keep the atmosphere pleasant as well."

Dorm Life

"I believe that living in the dorms is a great experience here at MSU. Gage Residence Community houses a large amount of the freshman students and does an excellent job on getting the students involved in oppurtunies and provides a great deal of academic assistance. The only downside I see with living in the dorms in the cost. The convience to campus is nice but living on campus all four years would be way to expensive for any college student."

GUYS & GIRLS

Attractive All Around

"Here at MNSU there are hot guys and girls from all different groups of people. This year we even had the most eligible bacholer in Minnesota attending school here! What else do you need?"

HEALTH & SAFETY

Personal Safety

"i feel really safe on cam pus because everywhere i go, i see security guards around surveying the areas and at night, they are always walking around and whenever they see students they always make sure they are safely in their dorms"

Campus Security

"When I was a freshman and I was afraid to walk across campus alone after a night class, or home from a party I had a campus security officer would come meet me at the University building and walk me back to my dormitory."

LOOKING FOR MORE?

Check out our full-length guide to this school at collegeprowler.com/minnesota-state-university/.

Minnesota State University - Moorhead

1104 Seventh Ave. S; Moorhead, MN 56563
(218) 477-4000; www.mnstate.edu

THE BASICS:

Acceptance Rate: 77%
Yield: 47%
Setting: Suburban
Control: Public
Total Undergrads: 6,949
SAT Range: 870–1090*
ACT Range: 19–24

Student-Faculty Ratio: 19:1
Retention Rate: 67%
Graduation Rate: 41%
Tuition: $6,598
Room & Board: $6,242
Avg. Aid Package: $8,172
Students With Aid: 91%

* of 1600

Academics	C+	Greek Life	C
Athletics	C	Guys	B
Campus Dining	B-	Health & Safety	C+
Campus Housing	B	Local Atmosphere	B-
Campus Strictness	C+	Nightlife	B
Computers	B+	Off-Campus Dining	B
Diversity	C+	Off-Campus Housing	B+
Drug Safety	C+	Parking	B+
Facilities	B	Transportation	B
Girls	B	Weather	C

CP's Student Author On...
OVERALL EXPERIENCE

MSUM is focused on academics. Countless former students have reported being happy they chose this college, but there are always ways to make a good experience better. Just like anything in life, college is what one puts into it. The more students become involved and study, the more they take out of it. As long as a student doesn't become trapped in the tendency to go out and party or not do their homework, then they'll be fine. There are many different ways to become active. Most students who have joined clubs and organizations and have become active have reported that it has made their college experience much better.

Fargo-Moorhead is a fun community with many events going on. Fargo alone has over 40 parks so students can always go and take a walk along the river, play catch at any of the parks, or gawk at the sunbathers. The main problem with Fargo-Moorhead is the weather. The winters are brutal, and summers are too short. However, the University does a great job of keeping students warm and entertained during the long winter months.

Students Speak Out On...
OVERALL EXPERIENCE

Q Overall Review

"MSUM is a WONDERFUL community to be apart of. Everyone is so accepting and helpful one feels right at home. It's also very easy to become involved and meet people."

Q AMAZING

"I rate my experience the highest you could. I have met some great people and I am doing something that I love! Being a member of the football team here is everything I thought it would be. I have met people that will be friends for the rest of my life."

Q I Love MSUM!

"I absolutely love it at MSUM. I come from a small town, so the diversity at campus was a lot more than I was used to, but it's a good thing. You are responsible for a lot of work, so you have to make sure you make time for your homework and don't party all the time."

BEST OF MINNESOTA STATE MOORHEAD

1. Affordable tuition
2. Friendly people
3. Helpful professors
4. Large variety of degree choices
5. Many student organizations and clubs
6. Pleasant community

Affordable
Tuition is only $6,598, one of the most affordable rates in the country.

Knowledgeable Professors
85% of students surveyed rated the general knowledge of professors as above average.

WORST OF MINNESOTA STATE MOORHEAD

1. Weather. It is often below freezing.
2. Dragon Core is the program that every student has to follow to graduate. Many students feel like they have to take classes that don't pertain to them.

Lowest Grades
Greek Life: C
Athletics: C
Weather: C

Student Body

African American:	2%	Male Undergrads:	43%
Asian American:	1%	Female Undergrads:	57%
Hispanic:	2%	Living On Campus:	21%
International:	6%	Living Off Campus:	79%
Native American:	1%	Male Athletes:	10%
White:	82%	Female Athletes:	6%
Unknown:	4%	Fraternity Members:	0%
From Out-of-State:	36%	Sorority Members:	1%

Frequently Compared Schools:

Gustavus Adolphus College
Minnesota State University
University of Minnesota
University of South Dakota

Students Speak Out On... EVERYTHING!

ACADEMICS

Q Psychology/Biology Majors

"As a multiple major student going into pre-med, the science facilities were very important to me. I could not be happier with the tools I have been given at MSUM to further my academic career. In many of my science classes are students from other universities in the area who came to MSUM to take classes because of the great resources that are not offered at other schools, such as a cadaver lab for anatomy and NMR for chemistry."

Q Most Liberal School Within 150 Mile Radius

"Very progressive school. We have lots of art work on campus that is progressive, such as sculptures and drawings of nude men and women, and sculptures of penises that are very beautiful and realistic. If you are gay, there are lots of dating opportunities, such as if you are straight. We have transgender students too. Our diversity is better than the surrounding schools. We also have the best arts programs with 150 miles as well."

ATHLETICS

Q Home of the Dragons

"Dragon athletics are average, with some fairly impressive teams. However, I think the most notable and important part of our school's athletic involvement is the fan support and school spirit. The Dragon fans are incredibly positive and excited about our school. Even if the game or event does not bode well, the fans will never stop cheering or having a good time."

Q Team Performance

"since the school is more of a commuter school beucase there isnt weekend offerings to keep students around, fan support is horrible. athletics needs more funding and better coaching to propel athletics to an area of interest"

CAMPUS DINING

Q Mmm, Yummy

"I really love the food they offer on campus. It is at a decent price and tastes great. I was so surprised that they even have tofu for my stir fry! I am a vegetarian and am really glad that MSUM has a lot of delicious food that I can eat. I usually stuff myself silly when I eat on campus."

Q Options

"There are a lot of options on campus of places to eat. A lot of time they have the same thing at the same shop but you can go some where else and see what they are having."

CAMPUS HOUSING

Q Dorm Life

"It was really nice living on campus. The dorms are pretty nice and up to date and the RA's are trained to create a family with the people/students living on the floor. From what I've heard, the dorms here at MSUM have more of a social life because of the RA's interaction with the residents."

Q Living

"It's a great place to start out your college experience. You never feel alienated by anyone, and everyone is very accepting. I would recommend living in the dorms the first semester if not year, because of all the friends you can make. It was an incredible time for me."

GUYS & GIRLS

Q Diversity.

"There is someone here for everyone. SO many different cultures, whether you are gay, lesbian, straight, bisexual, or transgender there is someone here for you, who is like you. You WILL find friends very easily, midwesterners are known for their friendly attitudes and with 3 major colleges in the area, along with the tri-college program, you will find someone."

HEALTH & SAFETY

Q Very Safe!

"I always felt safe walking on campus, even at 2 am. There were a few incident of campus going on lockdown, but it was preventative, and the people we're just near campus. Security is nice and helpful...don't do anything stupid and you'll be good."

LOOKING FOR MORE?

Check out our full-length guide to this school at collegeprowler.com/minnesota-state-university---moorhead/.

Misericordia University

301 Lake St.; Dallas, PA 18612
(570) 674-6400; www.misericordia.edu

THE BASICS:

Acceptance Rate: 69%
Yield: 36%
Setting: Suburban
Control: Private Non-Profit
Total Undergrads: 2,368
SAT Range: 950–1120*
ACT Range: 20–25

Student-Faculty Ratio: 13:1
Retention Rate: 85%
Graduation Rate: 67%
Tuition: $24,050
Room & Board: $10,050
Avg. Aid Package: $16,738
Students With Aid: 99%

* of 1600

Academics	B	Greek Life	N/A
Athletics	C-	Guys	B
Campus Dining	C-	Health & Safety	A-
Campus Housing	B	Local Atmosphere	C
Campus Strictness	C+	Nightlife	B
Computers	C+	Off-Campus Dining	B-
Diversity	C-	Off-Campus Housing	C+
Drug Safety	B-	Parking	B-
Facilities	B	Transportation	C+
Girls	B	Weather	C-

CP's Student Author On...
OVERALL EXPERIENCE

All in all, the University definitely prepares students for future success in their chosen fields. One aspect that students find unique to Misericordia is the great amount of hands-on learning. Classes aren't just focused on lectures and reading from a book; through demonstration, students gain a better understanding and are able to handle whatever is thrown at them. Academics are Misericordia's strong point. Another factor that makes Misericordia unique is the amount of individualized attention students receive so that they can excel inside and outside of the classroom. The professors are caring, friendly, and their quality of teaching is above average. Most of the professors that work at Misericordia have worked full-time in their fields at high-end companies and organizations, so the pointers and tips they give for success are especially helpful.

Obviously, students come to college to pick a major and try to succeed in their field of study both inside the classroom and well after they graduate. Well, that is exactly what Misericordia prepares students for: success.... For the rest of this editorial, visit collegeprowler.com.

Students Speak Out On...
OVERALL EXPERIENCE

Q I Love Misericordia :)

"Ever since I first started school here, I loved it. Everyone is so nice and always willing to help. On campus, I am part of Cougar Cast, our school's cable show and it's so much fun! Everyone involved is so fun and awesome. It's like a small family there."

Q I Love Misericordia

"The best part of my college experience has been my class instructors. They're very good, and what makes them special is that they encourage you to meet them individually if you're having trouble with something. I like that they know our names."

Q Miseri Fun

"Misericordia University is a great time for college students and it all depends on what the student makes of it. If you don't get involved with activities outside of classes then chances are your college years will be a flop. If you are very involved with clubs and different activities then your social and academic life in college will be awesome!"

BEST OF MISERICORDIA

1. Active campus that participates in community service projects
2. Safe campus
3. Newly renovated workout area provides students with the latest gym equipment.

Happy Students
85% of students return after their first year.

Big Dorms
53% of students surveyed felt that dorms were more spacious than average.

WORST OF MISERICORDIA

1. Classes aren't very demanding.
2. Commuters aren't treated as fairly as resident students.
3. Finding a parking spot is difficult during the day, and there are rarely any spots available.

Not Much Diversity
One of the least racially diverse campuses—only 4% of students are minorities.

Student Body

African American:	1%	Male Undergrads:	29%
Asian American:	1%	Female Undergrads:	72%
Hispanic:	1%	Living On Campus:	37%
International:	0%	Living Off Campus:	63%
Native American:	0%	Male Athletes:	41%
White:	96%	Female Athletes:	20%
Unknown:	0%	Fraternity Members:	0%
From Out-of-State:	24%	Sorority Members:	0%

Frequently Compared Schools:

Muhlenberg College
Temple University
University of Pittsburgh
Wilkes University

Students Speak Out On... EVERYTHING!

ACADEMICS

Professors

"Every professor I have this semester and in the past semesters at Misericordia, was willing to offer extra help with what they were covering in class."

Speech

"The Speech program at Misericorida is very good. It is a tough major but will definitely be worth it in the end. The professors are great and are always willing to help."

ATHLETICS

Sports

"Athletics is a main priority at MU. I think that it is an important part of college life, but is not essential. Other activities should get the same amount of press but never do."

Sports Are the IT Factor.

"Sports at Misericordia are a big deal and everyone participates. It seems that if you don't do a sport it is hard to fit in. Sports are popular here and the practices take up more time than classes. The ganes are fun and everyone goes to support the different teams. We don't have great workout facilities but it gets the job done. Mens Basketball and Baseball are pretty huge here along with swimming."

CAMPUS DINING

I've Enjoyed the Foods at School...

"I don't eat much at school, but when I have, I really liked the variety and quality. The prices are decent, too. I never got a meal plan since I'm not on campus that often, but I have eaten in the cafeteria, and I did like it."

Food at Misericordia

"I never really eat in the cafeteria. Iusually eat at the Cougar's Den. The food in the Cougar's Den is good, but they need a new variety of foods because the options have been the same for almost 2 years. I really like that the Cougar's Den also has equivalency options for students who can't make it to the dining hall or choose to eat something different. It is $6.00

to use for equivalency without being charged with our flex dollars."

CAMPUS HOUSING

Dorms on Campus Are Like Home Sweet Home

"The dorms on campus are great with a variety to pick from. Freshman aren't able to pick where they want to live during there first year, but Sophomores, Juniors, and Seniors have many options. The most popular place to live are the townhouses, which include 2 bathrooms, 2 double bed rooms, 2 single bed rooms, a living room, a kitchen and a joint closet in the hall way. I will be living in the townhouses next year with 5 of my friends. The other buildings are nice as well."

Housing

"The dorms are all pretty nice. They are kept clean and renovated. I wish I could stay here forever"

GUYS & GIRLS

Very Nice

"I am an adult student, but what I have witnessed with the younger generation is all positive. I am encouraging my daughters to go here and live on campus. There is a mixture of all different type of kids."

The Students Are Diverse

"There are only a few diverse students on campus. Some kids are into skateboarding and others just like to study and are consdered preppy."

HEALTH & SAFETY

Safer Then Safe

"I hava never felt unsafe at Misericordia. All of the buildings are close together and students are always outside so there is never a reason not to feel safe. I have lived on campus for two years and have never had one incident that I feel I was in danger. The Campus Safety Department is close to all of the buildings and are ALWAYS there to meet a students needs."

LOOKING FOR MORE?

Check out our full-length guide to this school at collegeprowler.com/misericordia-university/.

Missouri State University

901 S. National; Springfield, MO 65897
(417) 836-5000; www.missouristate.edu

THE BASICS:

Acceptance Rate: 52%
Yield: 57%
Setting: Mid-sized city
Control: Public
Total Undergrads: 17,269
SAT Range: 990–1230*
ACT Range: 21–27

Student-Faculty Ratio: 20:1
Retention Rate: 76%
Graduation Rate: 53%
Tuition: $11,556
Room & Board: $5,952
Avg. Aid Package: $7,307
Students With Aid: 84%

of 1600

Academics	B-	Greek Life	B+
Athletics	B-	Guys	B
Campus Dining	B	Health & Safety	C
Campus Housing	B-	Local Atmosphere	B
Campus Strictness	C	Nightlife	B+
Computers	B+	Off-Campus Dining	A-
Diversity	C+	Off-Campus Housing	A-
Drug Safety	B-	Parking	B-
Facilities	A-	Transportation	A-
Girls	B-	Weather	D+

CP's Student Author On...
OVERALL EXPERIENCE

Missouri State University is a great experience for many students. Overall, the campus is really fun and always has activities going on. The classes are challenging, but spark many students' interests, many times in topics students normally wouldn't give a second thought. The classes definitely prepare students for their professions of choice and the real world, in general.

If students could have a "do over," many would take it in a second and go through freshman and sophomore years all over again. Not only is there knowledge gained in the classroom, but through "real life" experiences and student organizations, as well. The specific courses greatly prepare students for their future careers. Missouri State is so unique because the campus size itself is rather small, but there is a large amount of students (and a large amount of spirit).

Students Speak Out On...
OVERALL EXPERIENCE

Q **Friendly Faculty and Staff**
"The staff and Faculty at Missouri State was surprisingly friendly. I took one class my freshman year with the dean of the honors college and he still remembers my name! The campus is beautiful and is maintained regularly."

Q **Perfect Fit**
"I love this school. The parties are great, and the students are all very nice. The professors understand the students are going because they want to.. and dont treat me like a child, which is always good."

Q **I Love It.**
"The classes aren't extremely difficult but you will need to study. All of the teachers I've had so far are great and they understand that you can't always make it to class and everyone has bad days. The campus is beautiful and there are always plenty of things to do when you have free time."

BEST OF MISSOURI STATE

1. Small campus, very easy to get around
2. Beautiful campus
3. Great location
4. Great professors
5. Lots of extracurriculars available/stuff to do
6. School pride/school spirit

Affordable
Tuition is only $11,556, one of the most affordable rates in the country.

WORST OF MISSOURI STATE

1. Drainage system in Springfield—it floods when it rains.
2. Springfield Police
3. Parking and parking tickets
4. Cafeteria food is not the best.
5. Scholarships are limited.

Not Much Diversity
One of the least racially diverse campuses—only 14% of students are minorities.

Student Body

African American:	3%	Male Undergrads:	45%
Asian American:	2%	Female Undergrads:	55%
Hispanic:	2%	Living On Campus:	26%
International:	2%	Living Off Campus:	74%
Native American:	1%	Male Athletes:	3%
White:	86%	Female Athletes:	3%
Unknown:	5%	Fraternity Members:	11%
From Out-of-State:	12%	Sorority Members:	13%

Students Speak Out On... EVERYTHING!

ACADEMICS

Q The Plethora of Knowledge

"The amazing amount of information at Missouri State is absolutely endless. They have such a wide variety within their curriculum, and they do an absolutely incredible job educating their students in all that they teach."

Q Academics at Missouri State

"I transferred from a local community college to Missouri State because they provide a degree in Professional Writing, which is an uncommon degree program in the area."

ATHLETICS

Q Athletic

"There are plenty of Athletic here on campus basketball, football, soccer, cheerleading, track & field and many more."

Q My School Athletics

"The Fans Are Great and very Supportive. Everyone shows up for games. Its Just the best thing to experience. MAROON MADNESS!!! GO BEAR!!"

CAMPUS DINING

Q Great Dining Services

"There is a wide variety of food services conveniently available for students to eat at. They have hours that are flexible for students and provide plenty of seating."

Q Good but Not Great

"There are only a few dining halls on campus, but they aren't bad. Some days there are lots of tasty things to eat, and some days you have to resort to cereal. Most of the dorms require a meal plan, and freshman are required to live in dorms for their first year, so start at a smaller meal plan and upgrade if you need it."

CAMPUS HOUSING

Q Wells Hall

"I've had an awesome experience and the people are great."

Q Res. Halls on Campus

"MSU has a pedestrian campus, with clearly marked bike and walking paths. Landscaping is well-done. Of the dorms, Scholars House is the newest and best, as rated by many students. However, many of the dorms are being revamped this summer. The dining halls are reasonably priced and have pretty good food. They are conveniently located throughout campus. Residence Assistants are helpful and friendly, and put a lot of work into making the dorms into positive, friendly communities."

GUYS & GIRLS

Q Split Personality

"Missouri State has a lot of diverse personalities. Some people wear casual clothes everyday. Some go for the surfer/skater look. Some wear jeans and cut off shirts. In the business classes, there are a lot of Chinese people. MSU have a little bit of everything."

Q Social Life

"Many students here are apart of the Greek life and are very actively involved in school activities"

HEALTH & SAFETY

Q Healthy and Safe

"There is very rarely crime on campus, and when there is, it is sexual harassment between people who already know each other. There are constant policemen watching out for us on campus, and we can even phone one to walk us to our dorms at night. The entire campus is relatively small and very well lit at night as well."

Q Safety on Campus

"Safety is not a concern for me. The campus is well lit and there are always Univeristy police driving around. Springfield police ride their bikes around sometimes too. There are emergency buttons located throughout campus if you find yourself in a sticky situation."

MIT

77 Massachusetts Ave.; Cambridge, MA 02139
(617) 253-1000; web.mit.edu/student

THE BASICS:

Acceptance Rate: 11%	Student-Faculty Ratio: 8:1
Yield: 64%	Retention Rate: 97%
Setting: Mid-sized city	Graduation Rate: 94%
Control: Private Non-Profit	Tuition: $37,782
Total Undergrads: 4,232	Room & Board: $11,360
SAT Range: 2030–2320*	Avg. Aid Package: $32,437
ACT Range: 32–35	Students With Aid: 86%

of 2400

Academics	A+	Greek Life	A+
Athletics	B+	Guys	B-
Campus Dining	B	Health & Safety	C+
Campus Housing	B-	Local Atmosphere	A+
Campus Strictness	B-	Nightlife	A
Computers	A+	Off-Campus Dining	A
Diversity	A+	Off-Campus Housing	D-
Drug Safety	A-	Parking	C+
Facilities	B+	Transportation	A
Girls	C+	Weather	C-

CP's Student Author On...
OVERALL EXPERIENCE

MIT students have a love/hate relationship with the school. They love the people and the atmosphere and hate the boatloads of work. Correction: Some people like the work and learning things, but most people hate being ignored by certain "research-oriented" professors. Most students who come to MIT had some tough decisions to make about schools before making a final decision, like "Should I go to Harvard or MIT?" and "Should I go to this in-state school with a full scholarship and a free computer or go to MIT and pay for almost everything?" Overall, every student, at some point, will think that they made the wrong decision, but it's the fact that these people made the decision to attend MIT that sets them apart from the rest. Whether they knew what MIT was like or not, students here were willing to take the chance. As a result, the people at MIT are the most creative, helpful, brilliant, and unique in the world. MIT admissions doesn't admit people accidentally—no matter how dumb you may feel when you fail your first exam. Everyone at MIT is incredibly down-to-earth, and everyone has the potential to do great things, even if everyone is deprived of sleep.... For the rest of this editorial, visit collegeprowler.com.

Students Speak Out On...
OVERALL EXPERIENCE

Q Challenging Yet Rewarding

"If you are ready for a challenge academically, but still want to have a good college experience, this is the perfect place. You will meet some the most amazing people and learn so much over your years here. You can play sports, be in a sorority or fraternity, and do well in school and have a life if you budget your time well enough. It was the perfect place for me."

Q It's MIT

"It's unlike most top tier schools. Less stuck-up people and more fun and chill ones to hang out with. We work hard, but party just as hard. At first, it may be hard to find that balance, but you will quickly enough."

Q "I love MIT, and I love Boston. The only thing that would make this place better is better-looking women."

Q "I'm satisfied with my college experience. I'm not satisfied with my academic experience. I'm leaving here pretty burnt-out and somewhat unsure of my abilities in the real world. MIT arms you with a lot of educational tools and the ability to learn, but it takes about four years to regain your confidence and self-esteem."

BEST OF MIT

1. Outstanding professors
2. Student-faculty research opportunities
3. Career and academic network prospects
4. The incredible student body
5. The city of Boston and all of its resources

Happy Students
97% of students return after their first year.

Commitment to Teaching
There are 8 students for every member of faculty on campus.

WORST OF MIT

1. GIRs
2. Intense workload
3. Level of difficulty
4. Realizing that you might not be the smartest anymore
5. Scarcity of free time

Expensive
Tuition is a steep $37,782, one of the most expensive rates in the country.

Expensive Dorms
Living on campus doesn't come cheap, with an average housing price tag of $6,850.

Students Speak Out On... EVERYTHING!

ACADEMICS

Academics... Fml

"There is a wide range of classes offered. The workload will keep you very busy, and students often have extra-curricular activities that keep them even busier. There is a lot of help offered, though office hours and tutoring services. There is even a Reading Room, which is a quite room of tables and desks to study."

Advisors Have Your Best Interest at Heart

"While I have not officially started classes in my major (Mechanical Engineering), I have already met with my academic advisor and spoken with other various professors in the MechE field regarding my classes. They were all extremely attentive and helped me work out my class schedule for this semester and the semesters to come"

ATHLETICS

Sports Not in Spotlight

"While there is a good variety of sports, and a solid athletic program, unlike most schools, athletics are not as big of a deal here. They're visible, but not a top priority. However, among the people you meet are still a large number of athletes. IM sports are more common across the general population."

"Varsity sports don't draw large crowds. On the whole, MIT sports rarely excel. Intramural (IM) sports are more popular because they are dorm or club organized, and there is no demand for practice time."

CAMPUS DINING

Food

"Food is not a problem but it isn't a great thing either."

No Meal Plan

"Dining options are not very good. The dining halls are only open for dinner from 5:30-8:30. Only two are open on Fridays and Saturdays. Although the meals themselves are good and accommodate nearly every dining style, students have to pay by meal, which costs about $8. I suppose students have the

option to save money by cooking for themselves but when in a time crunch, its not very convenient."

CAMPUS HOUSING

Awesome and Totally Dependent on Culture

"It's great. Each dorm has its own culture and that really helps freshmen determine where they belong."

Housing on Campus

"each dorm on campus has its own community, making it easy for students to find where they fit in. although not all of the dorms have dining halls, there are campus food options within walking distance. some of the dorms are situated a little far from main campus, which is rough during the winter."

GUYS & GIRLS

More Diverse Than Meets the Eye

"The students are not all nerds, but you can find an inner geek in most students, even the hard-core partyers. The dorms each have a very unique culture."

Odds Are Good, but the Goods Are Odd.

"Most people at MIT are very open-minded and very easy to get along with, but not all are good-looking. Lots of girls sacrifice fashion due to the workload, but on weekends people dress up to go to parties. The best part though is that if you're looking for hot girls we have BU across the river."

HEALTH & SAFETY

MIT Is a Very Safe Campus

"Make no mistake, the Cambridge/Boston area can be dangerous at times, as all city areas are. However, MIT Campus police are physically around enough that I feel very safe at all hours of the night, and they are very willing to help out. They are also very accessible to contact by phone."

Be Aware, but Don't Be Paranoid

"I have always felt safe. Some people lock their doors, others don't feel the need; it depends on your dorm. There are occasional reports of robbery, etc. but that is not unexpected."

LOOKING FOR MORE?

Check out our full-length guide to this school at collegeprowler.com/massachusetts-institute-of-technology/.

Montana State University

S. Seventh Avenue; Bozeman, MT 59717
(406) 994-0211; www.montana.edu

THE BASICS:

Acceptance Rate: 67%	Student-Faculty Ratio: 16:1
Yield: 50%	Retention Rate: 72%
Setting: Town	Graduation Rate: 48%
Control: Public	Tuition: $17,651
Total Undergrads: 10,762	Room & Board: $7,380
SAT Range: 1000–1250*	Avg. Aid Package: $9,834
ACT Range: 21–27	Students With Aid: 83%

of 1600

Academics	B-	Greek Life	C
Athletics	B-	Guys	A-
Campus Dining	C+	Health & Safety	B+
Campus Housing	B-	Local Atmosphere	B+
Campus Strictness	B	Nightlife	B
Computers	B-	Off-Campus Dining	A-
Diversity	C+	Off-Campus Housing	B+
Drug Safety	C	Parking	B-
Facilities	B	Transportation	A-
Girls	B+	Weather	A-

CP's Student Author On...
OVERALL EXPERIENCE

Many students at MSU, mainly those from out-of-state, are surprised that they ended up here. What they find even more surprising is that they never want to leave. Academics find a great research university and exceptional learning environment. Skiers look out their windows to see countless backcountry and ski hill opportunities. Coffeeshop connoisseurs could sample different drinks for weeks, and young philosophers could sit around for hours throwing ideas out to one another. Where the school is lacking, the town and surroundings compensate, and vice versa. An education should consist of more than sitting in a classroom, and MSU realizes this.

Attracting people who love life and are happy in their current situations, MSU and Bozeman have a pleasant atmosphere. The only problem with this is the unwillingness to change, which causes a lot of issues to stagnate in the community. Overall, MSU is a place where the happiness is infectious, as is the relaxed state of mind. Everyone is accepted, and people from different backgrounds love to mix.... For the rest of this editorial, visit collegeprowler.com.

Students Speak Out On...
OVERALL EXPERIENCE

Q I Love It Here!

"I love Montana! If you're into the outdoors it is absolutely perfect! The scenery is gorgeous, and there is great skiing, hiking, camping, rafting, climbing, just minutes off campus. I have made many great friends here and the photography program is amazing."

Q MSU Is the Place to Be

"MSU is the best place on earth. They have numerous hiking trails, rafting, skiing/snowboarding, Yellowstone is just a short drive away, they also have numerous hot springs that you can chill in after a long week at school. I wouldn't trade this campus life for anything. I love it here. Just like with any college though what you put into it your going to get out of it. So make sure to study but also make sure you take time for yourself."

Q Great Choice of College

"I have only spent one year there, but it was one of the best years of my life. There are so many kind pepole to get to know from all over the country other studnets, professors, and staff. It is easy to make friends. Plus the outdoor adventure is great!"

BEST OF MONTANA STATE

1. The mountain setting
2. The laid-back attitude
3. The duck pond
4. People-watching on the Mall on a sunny day
5. Gathering with friends to discuss life at the Brewed Awakening

Big Dorms
92% of students surveyed felt that dorms were more spacious than average.

Highly Satisfied Students
100% of students surveyed would make the same school choice if they could do it all over again.

WORST OF MONTANA STATE

1. Lack of public transportation
2. Food service
3. Near-complete focus on the sciences and engineering
4. The totally apathetic attitude

Not Much Diversity
One of the least racially diverse campuses—only 13% of students are minorities.

Student Body

African American:	0%	Male Undergrads:	54%
Asian American:	1%	Female Undergrads:	46%
Hispanic:	2%	Living On Campus:	25%
International:	3%	Living Off Campus:	75%
Native American:	3%	Male Athletes:	5%
White:	87%	Female Athletes:	4%
Unknown:	4%	Fraternity Members:	2%
From Out-of-State:	38%	Sorority Members:	1%

Students Speak Out On...
EVERYTHING!

ACADEMICS

College of Agriculture

"In the college of agriculture there are so many things to do and clubs to be involved in. Currently I am involved in the horsemans club, the pre-veterinary club and the IHSA team."

Great Program!

"The premed programs allows to choose what electives you would like to take your junior and senior year. This allows to direct your studies to the area of your chosing."

ATHLETICS

Sports

"The biggest rivalry ever: MSU Bobcats v UM Grizzles. The most attended game of the year & the most enjoyable!"

School Spirit

"The school spirit in Bozeman is amazing and everyone living in the area are all huge supporters. The spirit on campus is just as great and games of all kinds are always full of support."

CAMPUS DINING

Dining Halls

"The dining halls on campus are pretty good. The food is always yummy and there is always a variety to choose from. The campus has four dining halls and they all offer something different as well as a different atmosphere."

The Dining Halls Provide Many Different Options and Are Good Quality

"Two of the dining halls are good. One of them is way too overcrowded and the food is poor quality. So the students just need to know where to go."

CAMPUS HOUSING

The Hedges

"If your going to MSU you want to Shoot for one of the Hedges sky rises they're coed, always have something going on, and overall just fun. the people you will meet are well unforgettable."

Frequently Compared Schools:

University of Colorado
University of Montana
University of Oregon
University of Washington

Roskifarian

"The freshman dorms are split on opposite sides from each other. In my opinion the North and South hedges along with Roskie are where to be. If herb and partying hard is part of your lifestyle you need to be in Roskie. Noone parties harder than Roskie with its 70% out of state residents."

GUYS & GIRLS

Ratio Is 3:1 Guys to Girls

"Being a girl at MSU has many advantages as it is considered an engineering school so there are many guys to choose from and a large diversity as well."

They All Look Good

"Yes the boys and girls here all look really good. A lot of us are active, since that is a huge reason kids come to college here and Bozeman has been rated one of the top cities to raise outdoor and healthy kids. We are all nice and will talk. Its easy to meet people here."

HEALTH & SAFETY

Not Worried at All

"I fell incredibly safe on campus, I have never been worried once. I can't say about the campus police beacsue I have never needed them, but see them all the time, between classes or even in the dining hall."

Completely Safe

"I have never felt unsafe on Montana's campus. It's an awesome campus, they always have UPD out roaming the campus making sure everything is safe. UPD on this campus tries in many ways to make the students of the campus feel safe. It could be from them providing escorts to your car or dorm, or just giving you a ride back to where you need to be. There always there to help. I've ever felt safe than I do on MSU's campus."

LOOKING FOR MORE?

Check out our full-length guide to this school at collegeprowler.com/montana-state-university/.

Montclair State University

1 Normal Ave.; Montclair, NJ 07043
(973) 655-4000; www.montclair.edu

THE BASICS:

Acceptance Rate: 47%	Student-Faculty Ratio: 17:1
Yield: 33%	Retention Rate: 83%
Setting: Suburban	Graduation Rate: 62%
Control: Public	Tuition: $17,685
Total Undergrads: 14,139	Room & Board: $10,838
SAT Range: 1350–1640*	Avg. Aid Package: $9,217
ACT Range: —	Students With Aid: 75%

of 2400

Academics	B	Greek Life	B+
Athletics	C+	Guys	B+
Campus Dining	C+	Health & Safety	C+
Campus Housing	C	Local Atmosphere	C+
Campus Strictness	C+	Nightlife	B-
Computers	B-	Off-Campus Dining	B
Diversity	A-	Off-Campus Housing	C
Drug Safety	C+	Parking	C-
Facilities	B-	Transportation	B-
Girls	B	Weather	B-

CP's Student Author On...
OVERALL EXPERIENCE

Montclair State University is not the first choice for a lot of people. Some students choose the University for its education program, the proximity to their hometown, or the chance to play a sport, but others come because they can't afford anything else or they got in here and not many other places. In the end, though, Montclair offers a good education at a great price.

While any college can only prepare a student as much as they are willing to work, Montclair isn't lacking in its offerings. Many of the programs are very good, and there are opportunities that MSU offers to build upon what is offered in the classroom. Some majors require cooperative education, while all others make it available and help students find internships for the semester or break. Besides that, there are opportunities to do research, go abroad, and participate in organizations that give real world experience. Yes, some students coast through MSU and leave unprepared for any type of job by the time they get their degree, but other students also work hard and are ready to get a good job at the end of four years.... For the rest of this editorial, visit collegeprowler.com.

Students Speak Out On...
OVERALL EXPERIENCE

Q Montclair's Experience

"Montclair State University is great environment for knowledge. They have a solid staff faculty members that actually help you in a way to achieve your goal in life."

Q I Love It!

"I wasn't sure about MSU when I first got here, but after three years I love it! I even live here during the summer. It's great—I love my classes, professors, what I've been learning, the dorms, the social scene, Greek life, and all the clubs! If you don't get involved you'll hate it, so get involved! Live on campus! And have fun! Also, take advantage of the great staff/ job opportunities/career builders/free workshops/free gym!/ everything!"

Q Good

"There's a lot of different ways to get involved at school here. There are various clubs, fraternities and sororities, sports, and events. I like it."

BEST OF MONTCLAIR STATE

1. Cheap tuition
2. Close to New York City
3. Good summer course offerings
4. Great professors
5. Lots of activities
6. No. 1 public university in New Jersey

Happy Students
83% of students return after their first year.

Knowledgeable Professors
87% of students surveyed rated the general knowledge of professors as above average.

WORST OF MONTCLAIR STATE

1. At times, the shuttles can get off schedule or be very full.
2. Communication between departments sometimes breaks down.
3. Constant construction
4. La Quinta Inn
5. Lack of school spirit

Expensive Dorms
Living on campus doesn't come cheap, with an average housing price tag of $7,088.

Don't Move Off Campus
Average off-campus housing is a steep $10,640.

Student Body

African American:	9%	Male Undergrads:	38%
Asian American:	6%	Female Undergrads:	62%
Hispanic:	19%	Living On Campus:	26%
International:	7%	Living Off Campus:	74%
Native American:	0%	Male Athletes:	
White:	52%	1246%	
Unknown:	7%	Female Athletes:	3%
From Out-of-State:	3%	Fraternity Members:	5%

Frequently Compared Schools:

Penn State
Ramapo College of New Jersey
Rutgers University
Seton Hall University

Students Speak Out On... EVERYTHING!

ACADEMICS

Q Fine Arts Program

"I came to MSU because it has a Fine Arts Program. I love MSU and living on campus and my professors have been good."

Q Family and Child Studies

"It's an extremely easy curriculum. The professors are great."

Q Well-Educated and Helpful Professors

"The nutrition program is a lot of work—it follows strict ADA coursework. The professors in the program are really knowledgeable and helpful. Most of them have a lot of experience in the field. The "listserv" provides access to a lot of job opportunities in the area and abroad."

ATHLETICS

Q School Spirit

"At Montclair State, it seems as if the school spirit comes more from student organizations and fraternities and sororities than sports. I don't mind, but I guess it sucks for the athletes."

Q RED HAWKS!!!!

"Varsity sports in Montclair are great. We have a great school spirit and compete in the competitive levels of the NCAA."

CAMPUS DINING

Q Comida

"There are over 7 places to eat on campus, each wonderful in it's own way. There is sushi for a reasonable price, pretty good pizzeria that also serves Jamaican beef patties, the Campus Diner is amazing, and several cafes."

Q Campus Dining Is Good

"I'm glad that Montclair offers so many different food and dining options. In every building they have a little store where they serve hot and cold food, where food is always fresh. The prices for the most part are affordable, and the best part is that you can be hungry any time of the day like the early morning or very late night and still be able to feed your hunger."

CAMPUS HOUSING

Q I Love Living on Campus

"A lot of people say that living on campus is way too expensive, but it is actually better. I am never late to class because it's so convenient. I don't care how much debt I have because I had such amazing experiences here on campus living in the dorms."

Q Living on Campus

"I lived on the honors floor of Freeman Hall, and it was the greatest experience of my college career thus far. I have made so many wonderful friends that I know I will have for the rest of my life, and it's all because I chose to live on campus. The Village is awesome once you're an upperclassman, and the shuttles aren't nearly as bad as they seem like they will be."

GUYS & GIRLS

Q Social Life

"Students at Montclair State University are very active. There are always events on campus for anyone and everyone to participate in. Students are very involved in clubs, intramural sports, Greek life, and various other activities all throughout the year."

Q So Much Variety

"I enjoy seeing people from all over—I love seeing so many different cultures. I never feel like a minority because everyone is one. I've never had an issue with race either."

HEALTH & SAFETY

Q Very Safe

"Campus is well lit with six police officers on duty on a relatively small campus at all times. There are rape phones throughout campus."

Q Campus Safety/Security

"I am aware of a strong, at times overbearing yet non-hostile, police presence on campus."

LOOKING FOR MORE?

Check out our full-length guide to this school at collegeprowler.com/montclair-state-university/.

Mount Holyoke College

50 College St.; South Hadley, MA 01075
(413) 538-2000; www.mtholyoke.edu

THE BASICS:

Acceptance Rate: 58%	Student-Faculty Ratio: 9:1
Yield: 32%	Retention Rate: 90%
Setting: Suburban	Graduation Rate: 82%
Control: Private Non-Profit	Tuition: $39,126
Total Undergrads: 2,273	Room & Board: $11,450
SAT Range: 1835–2120*	Avg. Aid Package: $31,459
ACT Range: 27–31	Students With Aid: 76%

of 2400

Academics	A	Greek Life	N/A
Athletics	C-	Guys	C-
Campus Dining	A	Health & Safety	B+
Campus Housing	A-	Local Atmosphere	B-
Campus Strictness	B+	Nightlife	C+
Computers	A	Off-Campus Dining	C+
Diversity	A+	Off-Campus Housing	C-
Drug Safety	C+	Parking	B+
Facilities	A+	Transportation	B
Girls	A-	Weather	C-

CP's Student Author On...
OVERALL EXPERIENCE

It seems that students come to Mount Holyoke for the academics and stay for the community. Women who come here either quickly discover that they hate it and transfer out, or fall in love with the school and become unable to imagine going anywhere else. The overall sense students have about the College is that it's more than just a school, and it's more than a place to study for four years, get your diploma, and be set free—MHC becomes a second home. Its close-knit environment allows students to explore their own boundaries in safety, perhaps try on a few lifestyle changes, and maybe even find a few that stick. You will undoubtedly be exposed to new influences during your time here, as you would at almost any college, but here, you won't be afraid to call some of those new influences your friends—especially the ones who scared you at first.

Part of what's so wonderful and unique about this school is the sense that students are really cared about as individuals.... For the rest of this editorial, visit collegeprowler.com.

Students Speak Out On...
OVERALL EXPERIENCE

Q Moho Review
"I love Mount Holyoke! It's awesome. Most of the classes are small sizes, but the only disadvantage is that some classes are not offered every semester. Also the campus is beautiful, the professors are amazing, the dorms are awesome, and the dining options are a lot."

Q Make an Effort to See the Bigger World
"This college indeed provides students awesome education and environment. Great professors, classes (also you can take classes at other 5-colleges), library, resources. Also it has beautiful campus, dorm, dining halls. However, the school is tiny, has only 2200 students (you'll see same people everywhere) and very much isolated. While you struggle to use plentiful resources from the college, you should make an effort to take yourself out of this small world."

Q "My education was amazing, and the friends I made were all wonderful. It was a home away from home. This was the nurturing environment I wanted, and the opportunities I had going to MHC have shaped, and will always shape, my life. I just really loved it, from day one to graduation."

BEST OF MOUNT HOLYOKE

1. The beauty of the campus
2. The sense of community
3. The inspiring and warm professors
4. The rigorous academics
5. The open and tolerant attitude most students have

Happy Students
90% of students return after their first year.

Commitment to Teaching
There are 9 students for every member of faculty on campus.

WORST OF MOUNT HOLYOKE

1. Widespread academic burnout
2. The length of the winters
3. That almost everything closes at 9 p.m.
4. The lack of guys
5. Forced meal plan, even if you don't plan to eat all your meals on campus

Expensive
Tuition is a steep $39,126, one of the most expensive rates in the country.

Student Body

African American:	5%	Male Undergrads:	0%
Asian American:	11%	Female Undergrads:	100%
Hispanic:	5%	Living On Campus:	94%
International:	18%	Living Off Campus:	6%
Native American:	1%	Male Athletes:	0%
White:	48%	Female Athletes:	11%
Unknown:	12%	Fraternity Members:	0%
From Out-of-State:	83%	Sorority Members:	0%

Frequently Compared Schools:

Bryn Mawr College
Smith College
Vassar College
Wellesley College

Students Speak Out On... EVERYTHING!

ACADEMICS

Classroom Experience

"The classes are small and the discussions insightful. The professors are there to guide you, not hammer their own beliefs into you. Like in any other school, you will have your easy professors and hard professors. The difference is that unlike other "easy" professors, the ones in Mount Holyoke actually help you grow inside and outside of the classroom."

Professors Are AMAZING

"Being in the psychology and education department has so many positive perks. The professors really like to get to know you, the classes are extremely engaging and the students are intelligent (overall) to be around. Workload is not overwhelming and there are so many ways to get involved in independent studies or research with professors."

ATHLETICS

Sports

"I have never being one with sports. Some of my friends even tell me I lack school spirit. Regardless of that I know that the athletic facilities are amazing!!! They were just remodeled last year and everything is state of the art. The only reason I go to the gym now is to catch up on my daily dose of tv trash. I can run and watch tv at the same time. Unlike me, I know a lot of students who feel strongly about sports and if not involve in a team are fans cheering at the sidelines!"

Uhhh

"To be honest, I've gone to 2 games since I've been at MoHo. I heard the fans are great though and always cheer on their friends who are playing. As far as how good they are, it's D3 so I wouldn't expect to see and Lisa Leslies or Mia Hamms on the court or field. But everyone on the athletic teams seem to be good friends which is great if you're the type who views your team as a second family."

CAMPUS DINING

Best Mashed Potatoes Ever

"Relatively healthy, balanced meals for breakfast, lunch and dinner. Sad that they got rid of made-to-order breakfast. That said, North and South Rockefeller halls have the best mashed potatoes in the world."

Better

"The options we have at Mount Holyoke for dining is better than most schools, so i've heard. We have several different dining halls that all offer different foods each night. Many meals are carb loaded, though. Blanchard center has a wide variety of snacks, sandwiches and burgers. And it closes at midnight. Each semester we get $30 to either use on a guest during dining or at the coffee shop, Uncommon Grounds."

CAMPUS HOUSING

New Dorm or No Dorm

"Best dorm is New Dorm. Although it's not at all soundproof, so if you want to sleep at an unusual hour or at weekends, this is not a good place. Wilder and Mead are both good dining halls. The rest are dirty or old. The best place for food is Blanchard or Wilder. Changing rooms in the middle of the semester is difficult, and near impossible. But between semester moves are easily arranged."

"The dorms are nice, especially Safford."

GUYS & GIRLS

Go Girls!

"Well, this IS a women's college but most people I've spoken to don't seem to mind, since we're so close to UMass and Amherst College (no one cares about Hampshire). If students here want to find a guy elsewhere, it's not difficult to do. The girls here are great though. Honestly, it's a very preppy (in the good sense of the word) student body overall. We're not Smith so we actually look like women."

HEALTH & SAFETY

Small and Safe

"At Mount Holyoke, which is an all-women's college, the campus feels safe and secure. There are plenty of public safety officers on patrol, especially at night, by car and on foot."

LOOKING FOR MORE?

Check out our full-length guide to this school at collegeprowler.com/mount-holyoke-college/.

Muhlenberg College

2400 Chew St.; Allentown, PA 18104
(484) 664-3100; www.muhlenberg.edu

THE BASICS:

Acceptance Rate: 45%	**Student-Faculty Ratio:** 12:1
Yield: 29%	**Retention Rate:** 92%
Setting: Mid-sized city	**Graduation Rate:** 86%
Control: Private Non-Profit	**Tuition:** $36,990
Total Undergrads: 2,517	**Room & Board:** $8,440
SAT Range: 1670–1970*	**Avg. Aid Package:** $19,928
ACT Range: 26–30	**Students With Aid:** 78%

* of 2400

Academics	B+	**Greek Life**	B
Athletics	C	**Guys**	A
Campus Dining	A	**Health & Safety**	C+
Campus Housing	B+	**Local Atmosphere**	B-
Campus Strictness	B	**Nightlife**	B-
Computers	B-	**Off-Campus Dining**	B-
Diversity	C	**Off-Campus Housing**	A-
Drug Safety	C	**Parking**	A-
Facilities	A	**Transportation**	B-
Girls	A	**Weather**	B-

CP's Student Author On...
OVERALL EXPERIENCE

The student body is notorious for its overwhelming praise for Muhlenberg. Despite whatever complaints you may hear about the housing lottery or parking, the majority of students graduates with nothing short of adoration for their 'Berg experience. The professors make classes rewarding and challenging, and the overall community is supportive; these two things together help students find their ideal home-away-from-home. There are some students who dislike the school's small size, saying that with a limited party scene, the weekends become uneventful. Others say they believe the community is warm, close-knit, and active because of the small size. Students are as dedicated to their clubs as they are to friends and schoolwork, so there is always some student-run activity on campus. If you look in the right places, there is always something to do.

The majority of the student body does love Muhlenberg, but that does not mean the school is for everyone. Muhlenberg is a small campus and is not exactly in the most metropolitan location.... For the rest of this editorial, visit collegeprowler.com.

Students Speak Out On...
OVERALL EXPERIENCE

I Love It Here

"What makes Muhlenberg unique is the exceptional friendliness of the students. Everywhere you go people are extremely nice and helpful. A student can make great friends here. Also, the professors are very committed to teaching their students. There are no TA's and the professors have convenient office hours and are constantly available by email. Overall I have had a great experience thus far at Muhlenberg, learned a lot and made great friends!"

School Overall

"I think Muhlenberg is a great college for its academics and programs in the performance arts. I have made some amazing friends and my professors are very helpful and knowledgeable in the subjects they teach. Allentown is also a wonderful area that is both urban and suburban. However, I wish there were more things to do on campus and clubs were more proactive"

BEST OF MUHLENBERG

1. Desserts
2. Free entertainment and food in Seegers and on the lawn
3. Friendly staff
4. Hanging out on the lawn on a nice day

Happy Students
92% of students return after their first year.

Proven Success
86% of students will complete their education and graduate with a degree.

WORST OF MUHLENBERG

1. Clique-y fraternities/ sororities
2. Finding a parking spot
3. Housing lottery
4. How much everything costs on campus
5. Lack of diversity
6. Library hours of operation

Expensive
Tuition is a steep $36,990, one of the most expensive rates in the country.

Student Body

African American:	2%	Male Undergrads:	41%
Asian American:	2%	Female Undergrads:	59%
Hispanic:	4%	Living On Campus:	92%
International:	0%	Living Off Campus:	8%
Native American:	0%	Male Athletes:	41%
White:	83%	Female Athletes:	15%
Unknown:	9%	Fraternity Members:	15%
From Out-of-State:	81%	Sorority Members:	18%

Frequently Compared Schools:

Dickinson College
Franklin & Marshall College
Gettysburg College
Lafayette College

Students Speak Out On... EVERYTHING!

ACADEMICS

It's a Smart School

"but I hate homework. I'd rather learn in class than have to do stuff outside of it"

Amazing Academics

"Muhlenberg is known for having strong academics, and for good reason. As with any school, each different professor has different teaching styles. Class sizes are small and many of the classes encourage open discussion. Generally, Muhlenberg faculty does a great job of fostering an open learning environment and giving lots of support to their students."

ATHLETICS

Not Bad for Division 3

"Sports aren't really a huge deal at Muhlenberg. We have almost every kind of team you can think of and it there are plenty of opportunities to play. People love going to the games as much as they like any of the other activities on campus but it just doesn't dominate the campus scene."

There's Definitely School Spirit

"At all of the football games, you see a crowd of Muhlenberg students dressed from head to toe in school gear.. but its nothing like a big state school. If you have friends on the team, you're more likely to go. Teams advertise games in Parents Plaza near Seegers, but a lot of people choose not to go."

CAMPUS DINING

Better but Not Great.

"The new dining hall improved on campus dining, but it can still get repetitive and the lines in Campus Restaurant are LONG. The new meal plan system makes eating at some of the better eating options more expensive. Overall, it's alright."

"Sometimes I get really sick of the food here, but then I kind of miss it when I go home! Pasta Day in GQ is my favorite."

CAMPUS HOUSING

A Welcoming Atmosphere

"There is always something to do and people with whom to be friends. Whether a person likes to party or not, he/she will always find someone similar. Everyone is friendly and considerate."

It Depends

"The dorms in general are very inconsistent. You really have to do your research to find out which buildings are the best. For freshmen, the best dorms are Walz and Brown (the all girl's building). Try to avoid Prosser Hall if at all possible."

GUYS & GIRLS

Average

"There's not too many super good-looking guys, but there are some decent ones."

Muhlenfamily

"People at Muhlenberg are, in general, very friendly. Since it is a small school, you will know mostly everyone by face or name. The size of the school makes for a tight-knit community, and you will form a very close group of friends quickly. Although there are a lot of preppy and quirky theater people, there really is a large variety when it comes to style, personality, and hobbies."

HEALTH & SAFETY

Pretty Safe, Just Be Smart

"I haven't personally had a safety problem on campus. We are in a city so sometimes robberies occur. You just need to be smart about things. Don't walk alone at night!"

Crime Happens Everywhere

"There are occasional crimes on or near campus, but I think the number is fairly small despite the fact that Muhlenberg is in the third largest city in PA. The campus has an alarm, text, and email alert services, so you're always well informed when something happens."

LOOKING FOR MORE?

Check out our full-length guide to this school at collegeprowler.com/muhlenberg-college/.

New College of Florida

5800 Bay Shore Road; Sarasota, FL 34243
(941) 487-5000; www.ncf.edu

THE BASICS:

Acceptance Rate: 53%	**Student-Faculty Ratio:** 10:1
Yield: 29%	**Retention Rate:** 86%
Setting: Small city	**Graduation Rate:** 63%
Control: Public	**Tuition:** $26,386
Total Undergrads: 825	**Room & Board:** $7,783
SAT Range: 1820–2100*	**Avg. Aid Package:** $12,018
ACT Range: 27–30	**Students With Aid:** 100%

* of 2400

Academics	B+	Greek Life	N/A
Athletics	F	Guys	B-
Campus Dining	C+	Health & Safety	A-
Campus Housing	A-	Local Atmosphere	B-
Campus Strictness	B-	Nightlife	B
Computers	B+	Off-Campus Dining	B-
Diversity	C-	Off-Campus Housing	C+
Drug Safety	B	Parking	A-
Facilities	C+	Transportation	B-
Girls	B	Weather	A

CP's Student Author On...
OVERALL EXPERIENCE

New College is a special place. You cannot think of it as just another small liberal arts school in the South. There is not a single aspect of New College that can be considered traditional. From the progressive academics to the alternative social culture, it is a unique setting. This intensity does not bode well for everyone. Many come to New College expecting a Utopia and are shocked when the rigorous academics and insularity kick in. Others come because of its academic reputation, oblivious to the fact that it requires a certain type of personality and drive. Not everyone can hack it; many fail out, and many transfer.

New College students feel they have made a frugal, strategic choice that will land them in their desired graduate program. While this choice involves many seemingly undesirable trade-offs, it is ultimately worth it for those who are free-spirited, independent, and serious about academics. On one hand, New College is small. It has limited financial resources and doesn't have the household prestige that high-caliber students crave. On the other hand, it is a bargain.... For the rest of this editorial, visit collegeprowler.com.

Students Speak Out On...
OVERALL EXPERIENCE

Q Great!
"I loved this place, I wouldn't have gone anywhere else for undergrad. All science students have to do research which prepares students very well for grad school/research jobs. Combined with the work hard play hard attitude this makes NCF an amazing place."

Q "I don't really regret anything about the academic program I have taken, except for a couple classes I didn't like. I have spread myself across the board, and this school has allowed me to do that. It's a very good school."

Q "If you've already chosen a career, New College is not a great idea. If you are undecided, I would very much recommend coming here. Our strong academics will surely help you decide what you want to do with your future and let you give many different things a try."

Q "New College is very low-key socially and very stressful academically. It is inexpensive, and there is a high likelihood of getting into a good grad school."

BEST OF NEW COLLEGE

1. Palm Court Parties (PCPs)
2. The free table
3. Towne Meetings
4. The student e-mail forum
5. The Four Winds Café
6. Walls
7. No red tape

Happy Students
86% of students return after their first year.

Commitment to Teaching
There are 10 students for every member of faculty on campus.

WORST OF NEW COLLEGE

1. Townies interfering at Walls
2. Getting capped out of classes
3. Poor food in dining halls
4. Sub-optimal relations with surrounding community
5. No nightlife on weekdays

Expensive
Tuition is a steep $26,386, one of the most expensive rates in the country.

Student Body

African American:	2%	Male Undergrads:	38%
Asian American:	3%	Female Undergrads:	62%
Hispanic:	10%	Living On Campus:	75%
International:	0%	Living Off Campus:	25%
Native American:	1%	Male Athletes:	0%
White:	79%	Female Athletes:	0%
Unknown:	5%	Fraternity Members:	0%
From Out-of-State:	25%	Sorority Members:	0%

Students Speak Out On... EVERYTHING!

ACADEMICS

Everything Is Flexible

"One thing I love about New College is that the entire system is designed to work with you. Mini classes let you get a feel for what the class will entail before you decide to register. The contract system keeps you in control with your academic progress."

"You will develop a close relationship with your professors and adviser. This is one of the best aspects of academic life at New College."

"The academics are strong, which is the main reason I chose New College over the other state schools. Academic respectability and cost were important factors, and the Bright Futures scholarship allowed me to come here for free."

ATHLETICS

....Athletics?

"Well our football team has been undefeated since 1960."

"Athletics would disrupt the academic focus. Athletic programs are nice for larger places, but I'm glad we don't have that. The fitness center is fine. We have fun with racquetball, fencing, Aikido, and a lot of other sports."

CAMPUS DINING

The Food

"the food is so good and tasteful. it a big place and its remind me of highschool."

Small College, Small Options

"The food from Ham Center is generally not too bad during the school year during the weekdays, when most of the student body is there. During Orientation, Finals week, ISP, and the breaks, the food deteriorates in variety and quality. The Four Winds is a student-run cafe on the bay side of campus that has great food, and has a great atmosphere. Unfortunately, it's not part of the meal plan, so you can either transfer your "Ham Money" over, or pay cash."

Frequently Compared Schools:

University of Central Florida
University of Florida
University of Miami
University of South Florida

CAMPUS HOUSING

Overpriced to Say the Least.

"Housing on campus is overpriced, and generally the new dorms were poorly designed and corners were cut while building them."

"I've visited a lot of other colleges, and honestly, these are like luxury suites. For the price, it's definitely worth it. Plenty of other schools pay double what we do for a fourth of the space."

GUYS & GIRLS

Guys Are Stylish!

"Very stylish guys! People are very accepting of all types of dress. Most guys dress metropolitan, and relaxed, and kind of unique. Not really many preppy guys here."

"There is a better chance of hooking up than finding a relationship. New College is kind of incestuous. There is a Facebook group called New College Sex Web because so many people are connected. The guys here think they are smarter than they really are. The girls here range from being hard workers who aren't intelligent to the other way around."

HEALTH & SAFETY

New College Cops Are the Best!

"The campus police are your friends. They aren't there to bust students for underage drinking or the like, they're there to protect the student body and to keep the campus safe."

Campus Is Pretty Safe

"There were some problems my first year but the rest of my time here that have not been any incidents"

LOOKING FOR MORE?

Check out our full-length guide to this school at collegeprowler.com/new-college-of-florida/.

New York University

70 Washington Square S; New York, NY 10012
(212) 998-1212; www.nyu.edu

THE BASICS:

Acceptance Rate: 38%	**Student-Faculty Ratio:** 11:1
Yield: 35%	**Retention Rate:** 91%
Setting: Large city	**Graduation Rate:** 85%
Control: Private Non-Profit	**Tuition:** $38,765
Total Undergrads: 21,759	**Room & Board:** $13,228
SAT Range: 1830–2140*	**Avg. Aid Package:** $24,507
ACT Range: 27–31	**Students With Aid:** 64%

* of 2400

Academics	A-	**Greek Life**	C-
Athletics	D+	**Guys**	A
Campus Dining	A-	**Health & Safety**	B-
Campus Housing	C+	**Local Atmosphere**	A
Campus Strictness	B	**Nightlife**	A+
Computers	B-	**Off-Campus Dining**	A
Diversity	A-	**Off-Campus Housing**	C+
Drug Safety	C+	**Parking**	D+
Facilities	B	**Transportation**	B+
Girls	A-	**Weather**	B-

CP's Student Author On...
OVERALL EXPERIENCE

Students say that the best part about attending NYU is living in New York City. Students' biggest complaint is the large tuition. Other complaints were that there is not much of a campus or student bond, and that the school is run too much like a business. But in general, those who go to NYU cite many benefits of living in the city, such as great nightlife, food, and internship opportunities.

NYU requires a certain taste and is not for everyone. Those who love city life and the arts tend to do best here. For those who prefer keg parties and large organized student events, such as sports and Greek life, this is probably not the right place. Whatever you're thinking when you apply to this school, just remember that if you attend, you should be prepared for a mix of demanding academics and wild experiences in the city. Finding a balance between the two is key at this big-city school.

Students Speak Out On...
OVERALL EXPERIENCE

Q My Overall Experience

"Excellent. The teachers are great. We receive our education from full time professors who are well published and know. We do not receive our lectures from graduate students as many schools do."

Q Great Grad School

"undergrad? I dunno, the financial aid for undergrad and even 1st yr. grads kinda sucks"

Q The Best

"Academics are challenging and that sometimes affects your social life, but it's all worth it in the end. Coming to NYU is the best decision I ever made. Living in the city is so much fun, and if you take the initiative to make friends, you'll never be alone."

BEST OF NYU

1. Great location
2. Internship opportunities
3. Abundant nightlife
4. Skilled professors and well-constructed curriculum
5. Subways
6. The independence

Happy Students
91% of students return after their first year.

Proven Success
85% of students will complete their education and graduate with a degree.

WORST OF NYU

1. High tuition $$$
2. Housing lottery
3. Lack of boyfriend/ girlfriend material
4. No school spirit
5. Cranky security guards
6. Spoiled people
7. Eccentric roommates

Expensive
Tuition is a steep $38,765, one of the most expensive rates in the country.

Expensive to Just Get By
70% of students surveyed felt that the amount it costs to live while at school was worse than average.

Student Body

African American:	4%	Male Undergrads:	39%
Asian American:	18%	Female Undergrads:	61%
Hispanic:	8%	Living On Campus:	52%
International:	6%	Living Off Campus:	48%
Native American:	0%	Male Athletes:	3%
White:	44%	Female Athletes:	2%
Unknown:	20%	Fraternity Members:	1%
From Out-of-State:	75%	Sorority Members:	2%

Frequently Compared Schools:

Boston University
Columbia University
Cornell University
Northeastern University

Students Speak Out On... EVERYTHING!

ACADEMICS

In Anticipation of New York

"I have just recently been accepted into NYU's college of Nursing. NYU is known for having a great nursing program and I have heard great things about what New York has to offer from great entertainment, the diversity of the people and delicious food."

Biology

"It is very interesting to be Biology major in an area that is very inclined to the arts. There is however loads of internship and research opportunities here."

Academics

"NYU offers a wide range of major and demanding curriculums"

ATHLETICS

Football Isn't Everything

"Sure NYU doesn't have a football team, but good for me that I don't like football. On the other hand, NYU has a variety of sports that I consider more sophisticated. We have a good swimming team, basketball team, and even a fencing team. There is even an equestrian team. Anything is possible, even in the city. The athletic facilities are also nice. There are two places to work out and there is everything from indoor swimming pools to rock walls, and top notch equipment."

Athletic at NYU

"It's big to a cetain extent, but due to the fact that most sports are indoors, sport at NYU aren't as popular as they could be in there were more athletic facilities outdoors, especially in the summer. On a plus side, it's always cool inside, and the free pizza, and T-shirts during sports rally don't hurt."

CAMPUS DINING

Endless Choices of Delicious Affordable Food

"NYU cafeteria at Kimmel Center is great. you have just about everything to choose from: sushi to pizza, salad to stir fries etc. But what's even better is that we're surrounded by restaurants all around, since its NYC after all. There is literally just about every cuisine out there and many affordable choices for students. Many of the restaurants also take part in the NYU flex dollars, so it's great."

Good Variety and Placed Near Most Dorms

"good food, lots of choices and placed near or in dorms around the city. the main campus around washington square has a few different dining halls for variety as well."

CAMPUS HOUSING

It's New York

"I really don't think you can do better than New York here. There's not really any student events of notice, but thats irrelevant when you can see shows for 20 bucks and Broadway."

Possible Free Ride for Dorms!

"The cost is expensive just like any other school. But they offer RA positions which will cover room and board and meal plans! (if chosen as the RA after the "workshop training")."

GUYS & GIRLS

Guys&Girls

"The guys and girls at NYU are trendy and very outgoing."

Interesting, Diverse Students

"The students here are all over the spectrum- in terms of style, ethnicity, interests, and majors. There's a large population of artsy kids, which is cool but some are pretentious. Most people are attractive, and well-dressed."

HEALTH & SAFETY

Student Campus Safety

"They have security at every entrance and everyone must show identification including swiping in."

Crowded but Protected

"NYU Public safety works around the clock to ensure the well being of students at all times."

LOOKING FOR MORE?

Check out our full-length guide to this school at collegeprowler.com/new-york-university/.

North Carolina A&T State University

1601 E. Market St.; Greensboro, NC 27411
(336) 334-7500; www.ncat.edu

THE BASICS:

Acceptance Rate: 53%	Student-Faculty Ratio: 16:1
Yield: 55%	Retention Rate: 77%
Setting: Large city	Graduation Rate: 38%
Control: Public	Tuition: $13,553
Total Undergrads: 8,844	Room & Board: $5,659
SAT Range: 1190–1490*	Avg. Aid Package: $6,361
ACT Range: 17–22	Students With Aid: 92%

of 2400

Academics	C+	Greek Life	B
Athletics	B-	Guys	B+
Campus Dining	B-	Health & Safety	C-
Campus Housing	C+	Local Atmosphere	B
Campus Strictness	C	Nightlife	A-
Computers	C+	Off-Campus Dining	B
Diversity	C	Off-Campus Housing	A-
Drug Safety	C+	Parking	C+
Facilities	B	Transportation	A-
Girls	B	Weather	C+

CP's Student Author On...
OVERALL EXPERIENCE

North Carolina A&T State University is "that" school. A large number of Aggies have dreamed about attending A&T since they were young, and once you visit, it is hard not to see why. Everyone who comes here learns so much about themselves, their capabilities, and how to be leaders by the time they graduate. A&T is recommended for anyone looking to enjoy their college experience (and can find something they want to major in among the many degree offerings).

The classes are enjoyable, and the people and professors are very helpful. Students can have active social lives because there are plenty of parties here, but just like at any school, you will have to learn how to balance your social and academic lives. Some alumni say they regret that they weren't more involved at A&T, so don't make the same mistake they did and do your best to be active. Go to homecoming, join organizations, have fun, and excel in your classes! Ask any graduate if they would do it all again and see if you do not get a resounding "yes." Aggie pride!

Students Speak Out On...
OVERALL EXPERIENCE

Q A Shared Journey

"I love the fact that my school is full of people that I can relate to. Not just the fact that they are African American for the most part, but the fact that we have similar backgrounds. It's like we take on the journey of college together."

Q The Best School Ever

"NC A&T State University has the best school spirit ever!!! It is like a really close-knit family atmosphere. Shortly after I arrived, I immediately considered A&T my home away from home. We have great, skilled, diverse professors. It is obvious the University is going to continue to grow and change for the better."

Q College Experience

"My overall experience on campus has been great. The faculty and students are very friendly. Also our school is very family oriented. We like to help each other and be their for one another. I would choose my school again cause it has offered me many opportunities and have me grow a lot as a person."

BEST OF NC A&T

1. "The Greatest Homecoming on Earth"
2. The University's rich history
3. School spirit
4. The people
5. Social life
6. Campus activities

Knowledgeable Professors
80% of students surveyed rated the general knowledge of professors as above average.

Low-Stress Course Load
82% of students surveyed rated the manageability of work as above average.

WORST OF NC A&T

1. Parking
2. Café food
3. Financial aid system
4. Football team
5. Lack of scholarships for some majors
6. Not as well known as it should be

Not Everyone Graduates
38% of students do not complete their education or graduate with a degree.

Not Much Diversity
One of the least racially diverse campuses—only 11% of students are minorities.

Student Body

African American:	89%	Male Undergrads:	48%
Asian American:	1%	Female Undergrads:	52%
Hispanic:	2%	Living On Campus:	10%
International:	1%	Living Off Campus:	90%
Native American:	0%	Male Athletes:	4%
White:	6%	Female Athletes:	2%
Unknown:	2%	Fraternity Members:	—
From Out-of-State:	18%	Sorority Members:	—

Students Speak Out On... EVERYTHING!

ACADEMICS

Great Engineering Curriculum

"North Carolina A&T has one of the greatest HBCU engineering programs on the east coast; the coursework is very fast paced but easy to get the hang of. Also there are upperclassmen hired by the professors that are available to help with your work at any time. Most professors take pride in knowing exactly who their students are at a personal level and try to be as helpful as they can inside and outside of the classroom."

Passion for Fashion

"It takes talent and patience to be a fashion major. Some people think it is an easy major to breeze by, but they should know this cannot be any further from the truth."

Business Marketing

"The Business College is very well put together. There have been a lot of meetings so far just to introduce the professors and get an overall good feel for the school."

ATHLETICS

Athletics Diversity

"The school's athletic department consists of a diverse group of coaches and assistant coaches who work very hard to be a winning factor at the university."

AGGIE PRIDE

"When it comes to athletics, the Aggies are always down to support any team, any time, any place! But, the best part of it all is when all Aggies come together at the football games to cheer on the football team!"

CAMPUS DINING

Fried Chicken Fridays

"Williams Memorial Cafeteria has many food options every day. Everyone can be satisfied with our all-you-can-eat meal plans, including vegetarians and vegans. Also, each meal has an info card with its nutritional facts."

Ok but Gets the Job Done

"I do not really eat in the cafe, but when I do, I get my money's worth! There are plenty of options, so there should be something for you to find. The student union also has options that can fit your needs along with the dining spots beside the cafeteria. There are plenty of options, so you will not go hungry on campus at all!"

CAMPUS HOUSING

The Suits Are the Best

"The best dorm for any classman to live is the Aggie Village. It promotes great college life and a positive study environment."

Life on Campus

"Most dorms have everything you need and are very positive and happy enviroment."

GUYS & GIRLS

Social Life

"The girls at our school mostly likes to party, its gets really good during the summer. They love to club"

Diverse Group

"The school is an HBCU, so there are beautiful shades of black and brown everywhere. The guys are good looking, and the women are pretty."

HEALTH & SAFETY

Campus IS Safe for the Most Part

"People are mostly affected by crime if they set themselves up for it. For example, leaving doors unlocked or walking alone after dark is setting yourself up for failure. Unfortunately, others are just random victims of crime."

A&T Campus Life

"My school has an on site health facility and on campus police department. Things rarely happen on campus but sometimes things happen around on campus && the schools ends us emails && text alerts to let us know what is going on and whether or not we should stay indoors."

North Carolina State University

2101 Hillsborough St.; Raleigh, NC 27695
(919) 515-2011; www.ncsu.edu

THE BASICS:

Acceptance Rate: 56%
Yield: 46%
Setting: Large city
Control: Public
Total Undergrads: 25,398
SAT Range: 1590–1890*
ACT Range: 22–27

Student-Faculty Ratio: 17:1
Retention Rate: 91%
Graduation Rate: 71%
Tuition: $17,960
Room & Board: $7,966
Avg. Aid Package: $7,426
Students With Aid: 62%

* of 2400

Academics	B+	Greek Life	C+
Athletics	A-	Guys	B+
Campus Dining	B-	Health & Safety	B-
Campus Housing	B-	Local Atmosphere	B+
Campus Strictness	C	Nightlife	B+
Computers	A-	Off-Campus Dining	B
Diversity	B-	Off-Campus Housing	B+
Drug Safety	C+	Parking	C+
Facilities	B-	Transportation	A-
Girls	B-	Weather	B-

CP's Student Author On...
OVERALL EXPERIENCE

Overall, the students' experience with NCSU is that it provides them with a rich learning environment. Students learn to balance play and work. Some come to NC State because of family tradition, to get away from the cold, or because of the College of Engineering—but whatever the reason is for the individual, positive feedback always finds its way out. Professors at the University will go above and beyond their call of duty. You make lifelong friends, and you have a huge list of organizations to partake in. Whether you're involved in a college sport, student government, or the Agribusiness Club, you will find your niche here among the thousands of students. Some professors will take you under their wing, and you will learn enormous amounts of information from them. These professors will also become lifelong connections who will probably end up writing letters of recommendation for you when it is time for you to find a job.

NC State wants its students to succeed not only in academics, but in life, too. Here you learn important lifelong skills that are essential to your survival in the real world.... For the rest of this editorial, visit collegeprowler.com.

Students Speak Out On...
OVERALL EXPERIENCE

Q **AWESOME**

"BEST SCHOOL IN THE WORLD. I didn't want to leave Raleigh for the summer I loved it so much. Academics and social life are great but you have to know how to balance everything - it is possible. It took me a semester to figure that out but FYC helped and it's been the best year of my life so far!"

Q **Loving My School**

"I grew up in a small town so coming to Raleigh was a very big change. But my school is perfect. It is for one beautiful, it has a lot of nature surrounding it and all the flowers and trees that bloom in the Spring are beautiful. My roommate and I get along great which helps a lot. I have met so many new people and I would definitely choose my school again to be able to relive the great experiences I have already had here."

Q **Experiences**

"Excellent place to be for the ambience of a learning environment. It inspires me to be a better person."

BEST OF NC STATE

1. We're not UNC-Chapel Hill
2. The large, diverse student body
3. Intramural sports
4. Research symposia
5. College of Textiles
6. College of Engineering

Happy Students
91% of students return after their first year.

Proven Success
71% of students will complete their education and graduate with a degree.

WORST OF NC STATE

1. Tailgating restrictions
2. Greek life directors
3. Parking
4. The distance to the stadium
5. Construction
6. Most bars aren't within walking distance

Lowest Grades
Campus Strictness: C
Drug Safety: C+
Greek Life: C+

Student Body

African American:	9%	Male Undergrads:	55%
Asian American:	5%	Female Undergrads:	45%
Hispanic:	3%	Living On Campus:	34%
International:	2%	Living Off Campus:	66%
Native American:	1%	Male Athletes:	3%
White:	77%	Female Athletes:	3%
Unknown:	3%	Fraternity Members:	8%
From Out-of-State:	12%	Sorority Members:	10%

Students Speak Out On...
EVERYTHING!

ACADEMICS

Nuke Is the Best!

"NC State has one of hte best engineering programs in the country and Nuclear Engineering rocks. It is super challenging but the professors are there to get you through it...with a couple of exceptions. If you go this major you WILL have 2-5 job offers up to 8 months before you graduate. Expect $55k for a B.S., $65k for a M.S. and $80k+ for a Ph.D. Eat that art history!"

Top Notch Engineering School

"Not that there are many school with nuclear engineering programs, but I would not have picked anywhere else to do my doctorate than NCSU's Nuke Department. All of the engineering school's here are great. I hear some of the undergrad classes are very large though."

ATHLETICS

School Spirit

"There is a high level of school spirit at NC State University. The football games are always packed as well as the basketball. Our school has formed many rivalries with surrounding schools. A vast majority of studnets keep up with athletics"

Good Times

"Our teams may not always win, but the fans are always having a great time."

CAMPUS DINING

Plenty of Dining Options!

"Beyond the three main dining halls where food is good, although repetitive, you can go to the Atrium or Student Center to find the Wolve's Den for burgers or chicken strips, a Sub Shop, Taco Bell, Chic-Fil-A and even a pizza and wrap station as well as multiple coffee shops."

Frequently Compared Schools:

Clemson University
University of North Carolina
University of South Carolina
Virginia Tech

Love the Dining Halls

"Most people hate the dining halls (Clark, Fountain, Case) but I absolutely love them. They serve a varied and nutritious menu that when I eat there, I am extremely content and happy after a meal!"

CAMPUS HOUSING

NCSU Dorm Life

"I live in the Tucker FYC dorm and I really enjoy it. The rooms are big enough for my roomate and I to share and not too cramped. All the dorms are close to central campus and is only a short walk from any class or dining option."

Lower Class Man Life.

"The dorms are average here at North Carolina State University. However, the life her isn't so great. There isn't to much to get out and do apart from the gym and food. There needs to be more social events. The beginning of the semester was just fine, but the campus seems to be lacking of life throughout the rest of the year."

GUYS & GIRLS

People

"Everyone seems pretty average. Good social life, near downtown so something is always going on. Made some really good freindships this past yeat."

Definitely Some Lookers

"There is quite the mix of social scenes, and I love walking through the brickyard so I can see all the people. There are definitely some hot guys around. ;) The girls, mostly dress nice and they look nice, but personality tends to leave a bit to be desired."

HEALTH & SAFETY

Safe

"Personally, I feel completely safe on campus all the time. There are always campus police circling around campus. Many blue light emergency things are also available if needed. I haven't heard too much about campus crime."

LOOKING FOR MORE?

Check out our full-length guide to this school at collegeprowler.com/north-carolina-state-university/.

North Central College

30 N. Brainard St.; Naperville, IL 60540
(630) 637-5100; northcentralcollege.edu

THE BASICS:

Acceptance Rate: 68%
Yield: 29%
Setting: Mid-sized city
Control: Private Non-Profit
Total Undergrads: 2,522
SAT Range: 1410–1846*
ACT Range: 22–27

Student-Faculty Ratio: 16:1
Retention Rate: 77%
Graduation Rate: 63%
Tuition: $26,916
Room & Board: $8,379
Avg. Aid Package: $20,623
Students With Aid: 97%

* of 2400

Academics	B-	Greek Life	N/A
Athletics	B-	Guys	B
Campus Dining	C+	Health & Safety	B+
Campus Housing	B-	Local Atmosphere	B+
Campus Strictness	B-	Nightlife	B+
Computers	B-	Off-Campus Dining	A-
Diversity	C	Off-Campus Housing	B
Drug Safety	C+	Parking	C+
Facilities	B-	Transportation	B-
Girls	B-	Weather	C+

CP's Student Author On...
OVERALL EXPERIENCE

North Central College is not perfect, but it does what it promises. The College's mission is to "prepare students to be informed, involved, principled, and productive citizens and leaders over their lifetime." North Central College accomplishes this mission by providing lots of personal interaction with staff and faculty while still leaving the education largely up to each individual student. All professors have office hours, but students have to take the initiative to visit during these hours or set up appointments to meet at another time. The faculty goes out of its way to help and get to know students, but students have to do their part to get the most out of the experience. Additionally, there are events and programs, both academic and non-academic, going on; students just have to make the choice to go to them.

If given the chance to do it all over again, most students would not change their decision to attend North Central. The College's academics are good, and the academic adviser program aligns students with professors in their fields of study and their future occupation.... For the rest of this editorial, visit collegeprowler.com.

Students Speak Out On...
OVERALL EXPERIENCE

Q North Central, Where You Are Central

"The campus is beautiful--tons of trees and flowers. Nothing is not accessible to any student here--freshman get offers to research with professors. They give out Richter Grants, which is basically money they give out to help someone explore something they are interested in. We have stuff to do every weekend, including good, clean, fun, and there's never a dull moment here."

Q Pretty Goooooood

"I love north central. I just wish I could afford to live on campus. I feel as though there is almost a sort of discrimination of commuters."

Q Love It!

"It's a small school. Be prepared for that. Love the small class sizes, professors are awesome, and have really come to enjoy it!"

BEST OF NORTH CENTRAL

1. Being located in downtown Naperville
2. Small class sizes
3. Friendly and respectful classmates
4. No teaching assistants (TAs)
5. Lots of discussion-based classes

Easy Financial Aid Process
74% of students surveyed told us that the financial aid process went smoothly and they received the financial aid they needed.

WORST OF NORTH CENTRAL

1. Parking
2. Lack of diversity
3. High tuition costs
4. Required meal plan
5. Technical glitches and failures

Expensive
Tuition is a steep $26,916, one of the most expensive rates in the country.

Student Body

African American:	4%	Male Undergrads:	45%
Asian American:	4%	Female Undergrads:	55%
Hispanic:	5%	Living On Campus:	55%
International:	1%	Living Off Campus:	45%
Native American:	0%	Male Athletes:	45%
White:	78%	Female Athletes:	18%
Unknown:	8%	Fraternity Members:	0%
From Out-of-State:	13%	Sorority Members:	0%

Frequently Compared Schools:
DePaul University
Northwestern University
University of Chicago
Wheaton College - Illinois

Students Speak Out On... EVERYTHING!

ACADEMICS

Q Good for Everyone, Great for Future Teachers

"The professors are great people, always willing to make time to meet you outside of office hours. The campus is well-located, and compact, so you don't have to walk far to get anywhere, whether to a class or to go shopping downtown. If you are going to be a teacher, this place is especially great due to the availability and diversity of school districts surrounding it."

Q Marketing

"I am very satisfied thus far. Classes are unique and challenging, and North Central fosters growth an learning."

ATHLETICS

Q Sports Are HUGE!

"Sports here at North Central are quite a big deal - and our teams often take down everyone else in their division. We are lucky to have state-of-the-art facilities for our teams as well."

Q Athletics = Awesome

"I run for the best Cross Country and Track and Field Program in that nation. Al Carius is like a second father to me and is an icon to the sport of running. The programs tradition and alumni support is second to none in the nation. The members of the team are like my brothers. This is the best program I have been involved with in my life"

CAMPUS DINING

Q Kaufman and the Cage

"The Cage is good but too expensive, flex dollars get used up so fast even on the plan with the most of them. Kaufman needs more options (one day it was all Mexican food, and no other options if you don't like that)"

Q Nothing Special but Not Awful Either

"There are certain days at Kaufman that are better than others, panini day or grilled cheese and tomato soup day are always good. Breakfast is consistently good at the main dining hall and there's always an omelette bar. Unless you are extremely busy or like to cook for yourself stick with the middle meal plan for a good balance of dining hall swipes and flex dollars to use at the Cage and the BoilerHouse Cafe."

CAMPUS HOUSING

Q Upperclassmen Dorms Are the Best

"There are multiple dorms that the freshman can stay across campus. They are not the best since they are old but you get free internet and cable, and you can control your own heat and air conditioning. The upperclassmen dorms are nice. If you get your application in on time you can stay at Naper Place Apts in downtown Naperville or the town houses on campus."

Q Living at NCC

"North Central College is a great school, and I enjoy living here. I currently live on the female Honors floor in Geiger Hall, and it's been a great experience. The dorm is toward the south end of campus, but it's right by the dining hall, so it's pretty convenient. However, sometimes the dorm is pretty quiet because people are busy and/or at home on the weekends."

GUYS & GIRLS

Q 60% Ladies Yeaaa

"There are a lot of good looking girls here and it is easy to meet someone"

Q Rich Naperville

"The location of my school is near downtown naperville, so, most students who are from the area are decently weathly and dress the part. Over all, the students are good looking, well dressed, but not always well behaved (this goes for the jocks)"

HEALTH & SAFETY

Q Very Safe

"Campus security is always driving around their patrol cars, and they have, to my experience, responded quickly to incidents. They will drive to and from class if you feel unsafe walking at night or even pick you up from the train station if you have a train that gets in late"

LOOKING FOR MORE?

Check out our full-length guide to this school at collegeprowler.com/north-central-college/.

Northeastern University

360 Huntington Ave.; Boston, MA 02115
(617) 373-2000; www.northeastern.edu

THE BASICS:

Acceptance Rate: 41%	**Student-Faculty Ratio:** 15:1
Yield: 20%	**Retention Rate:** 91%
Setting: Large city	**Graduation Rate:** 70%
Control: Private Non-Profit	**Tuition:** $35,362
Total Undergrads: 19,129	**Room & Board:** $12,350
SAT Range: 1780–2040*	**Avg. Aid Package:** $17,877
ACT Range: 27–31	**Students With Aid:** 86%

* of 2400

Academics	B+	Greek Life	C+
Athletics	C+	Guys	B+
Campus Dining	B+	Health & Safety	C+
Campus Housing	B	Local Atmosphere	A
Campus Strictness	B-	Nightlife	A-
Computers	B	Off-Campus Dining	B+
Diversity	B+	Off-Campus Housing	B-
Drug Safety	C-	Parking	C+
Facilities	B+	Transportation	B+
Girls	B	Weather	C+

CP's Student Author On...
OVERALL EXPERIENCE

Student complaints about Northeastern are generally the same complaints students have anywhere else: the advisors don't care enough, people slack off in their jobs, etc. Like any school, Northeastern has its setbacks, but these are easy to overlook, given the many advantages the University has to offer.

The city of Boston offers an unparalleled experience for students. The Northeastern faculty is among the best you'll find anywhere, and student life on campus is fun and vibrant. Students may take issue with trivial matters here and there—parking's hard to find, the University can be too strict—but it's unlikely you'll find anyone who feels that Boston is boring, or that the University doesn't prepare students for post-college life. When it comes down to it, most students are happy to be here.

Students Speak Out On...
OVERALL EXPERIENCE

Q Amazing - Don't Regret It
"I absolutely love it here. Boston is amazing city, classes are hard but you learn alot. Depending on the major you have to study otherwise you will fail."

Q Being a Transfer....
"I transferred here from a school in the middle of nowhere and the transition has been fantastic. The campus is beautiful as well as the facilities. The people are extremely nice here and the teachers are here to help. The dining hall is above par (we even have a sushi bar!!) I can't wait to co-op next semester!"

Q Northeastern
"I love it here. If you let your social life rule your academic life, then it could be trouble. You have to study here; it isn't all parties. I had a rough time before I came here."

Q Work Hard, Play Hard
"Not the most relaxing campus but that can be a good thing. Party life is crazy and academics it a challenge. Job connections, great professors and the co-op program will give you the industry knowledge of a mid career worker on graduation day."

BEST OF NORTHEASTERN

1. Co-op program
2. Beautiful campus
3. Location, location, location! Boston is the ultimate college city!
4. Northeastern is gaining more recognition each year
5. Feeling of diversity

Happy Students
91% of students return after their first year.

Knowledgeable Professors
90% of students surveyed rated the general knowledge of professors as above average.

WORST OF NORTHEASTERN

1. Expensive tuition
2. The NU Shuffle
3. The cold weather
4. Expensive off-campus housing
5. Difficulty in course registration and getting into the classes you need

Expensive
Tuition is a steep $35,362, one of the most expensive rates in the country.

Expensive to Just Get By
70% of students surveyed felt that the amount it costs to live while at school was worse than average.

Student Body

African American:	6%	Male Undergrads:	49%
Asian American:	8%	Female Undergrads:	51%
Hispanic:	5%	Living On Campus:	47%
International:	8%	Living Off Campus:	53%
Native American:	0%	Male Athletes:	4%
White:	55%	Female Athletes:	3%
Unknown:	18%	Fraternity Members:	4%
From Out-of-State:	68%	Sorority Members:	4%

Frequently Compared Schools:

Boston College
Boston University
Cornell University
New York University

Students Speak Out On... EVERYTHING!

ACADEMICS

WOW

"The business school is just great, proffesors care and even in my frist year I felt that I have learned alot."

Business Academics are great

"Since day 1 in freshman yr., you get real world experience by making a business plan for a business where you can help them improve revenue...This is just great!"

ATHLETICS

Hockey!

"Sports are a huge part of Northeastern life. We are known for our hockey team. Hockey games are always fun to attend and bring friends/family to. Along with our usual seasonal games, we compete in the Beanpot each year against our rivals, BC and BU, and there is always a lot of excitement and competition surrounding the events."

Husky Pride

"You go to any hockey or basketball game and you'll see nothing but red and black (unless there's a blackout game) and hear nothing but our good 'ol chants. The games are outrageous and we have tons of fun before and after them. Marino is one of the historic venues that the Boston Bruins first played at. We don't have football anymore, but that's alright... We got plenty of other sports teams to go see and cheer on."

CAMPUS DINING

Many Options

"There are a lot of different places to eat around campus. The student center offers many popular options and satisfies a wide variety of food preferences."

Variety

"Northeastern U. has four dining halls, with a wide variety in food from good old pizza and burgers, to Indina cuisine, sushi, and much more. We also have a number of local eateries which take 'Husky dollars'."

CAMPUS HOUSING

Avoid White

"Housing changes every year but most dorm culture is great. Freshmen housing is okay, but upper classmen housing is superb."

Honors Housing

"Freshman honors housing has been pretty awesome. Aside from a few broken things here and there its been clean and convenient to have your own bathroom"

GUYS & GIRLS

Handsome Men

"Northeastern has plenty of beautiful people for everyone. Just smile and look around... enjoy the scenery."

Hotness

"With over 15,000 girls and guys on campus, you're bound to find your ultimate hottie(s). Plus between all of the parties and social events on campus, it's really easy to meet new people all the time. If something doesn't work out, well, you go to a big school, so it's not like you'll be doing the walk of shame down university ave over here. Everyone here, is extremely chill and just down for a good time. All the Greek life members are sexy."

HEALTH & SAFETY

UHCS

"UHCS is extremely helpful their staff doctors and nurses have always been extremely helpful and nice."

Very Safe Campus

"I always feel very safe on campus. Although the NUPD are very friendly and generally stay out of your way, however they have enough of a presence to make you feel that they are watching out for your safety."

LOOKING FOR MORE?

Check out our full-length guide to this school at collegeprowler.com/northeastern-university/.

Northern Arizona University

S. San Francisco Street; Flagstaff, AZ 86011
(928) 523-9011; home.nau.edu

THE BASICS:

Acceptance Rate: 73%	Student-Faculty Ratio: 19:1
Yield: 19%	Retention Rate: 72%
Setting: Small city	Graduation Rate: 53%
Control: Public	Tuition: $17,858
Total Undergrads: 18,301	Room & Board: $7,872
SAT Range: 1390–1730*	Avg. Aid Package: $4,879
ACT Range: 20–25	Students With Aid: 79%

of 2400

Academics	B-	Greek Life	B-
Athletics	C	Guys	B+
Campus Dining	B	Health & Safety	B-
Campus Housing	B	Local Atmosphere	B+
Campus Strictness	B	Nightlife	B
Computers	B-	Off-Campus Dining	B
Diversity	B-	Off-Campus Housing	B
Drug Safety	C	Parking	B
Facilities	B+	Transportation	B
Girls	B-	Weather	B+

CP's Student Author On...
OVERALL EXPERIENCE

When asked to reflect back on their time at NAU, the overwhelming majority of students give it the thumbs up. Most will tell you that they love Flagstaff and would recommend NAU to anyone. The small class sizes and beautiful location make it a perfect spot to learn and develop within the confines of higher education. It's too bad that many people write the school off as nothing more than a gathering of hippies. When you peel the stereotypes away, you find that it's a school where you'll get a pretty good education, lots of opportunities, and maybe a few lifelong friends on the way. Flagstaff itself is a town of great history, great food, and a decent amount of things to see.

Northern Arizona University is not perfect by any means. The school will be hit drastically by the recent budget cuts passed by the state legislation to the Arizona public universities. While the administration and President are very active in dealing with the slashed budget, extracurriculars will be cut, and class size is bound to go up. The people here are nice and friendly and usually will return your hello if you offer it.... For the rest of this editorial, visit collegeprowler.com.

Students Speak Out On...
OVERALL EXPERIENCE

Q Welcome to NAU

"The atmosphere is fantastic from meeting new people to the way teachers treat their students. Adjusting to college life is an easy process."

Q AMAZIN!

"NAU is the greatest university any senior seeking a college is looking for. It is in state and the academics, people, as well as teh overall campus is friendly and there is a great diversity on campus so there is something for everyone to do."

Q My School Has Pride

"Pima is student oriented and staff take a lot of pride in their fields, working hard to put on excellent plays, dance and opera performances, successful sport teams, and many exercise classes. When class sizes are 25-30 students, I get to know my Professor really well and make new friends."

BEST OF NORTHERN ARIZONA

1. Small class sizes
2. Friendly people
3. Snowy, postcard-worthy landscapes
4. Guy-to-girl ratio (if you're into girls)
5. Flagstaff culture

Knowledgeable Professors
89% of students surveyed rated the general knowledge of professors as above average.

Low-Stress Course Load
80% of students surveyed rated the manageability of work as above average.

WORST OF NORTHERN ARIZONA

1. Dining halls
2. Parking
3. Lackluster performances from sports teams
4. Lack of recognition campared to other state schools
5. The area can be boring at times

Lowest Grades
Drug Safety: C
Athletics: C
Diversity: B-

Student Body

African American:	3%	Male Undergrads:	41%
Asian American:	3%	Female Undergrads:	59%
Hispanic:	13%	Living On Campus:	40%
International:	2%	Living Off Campus:	60%
Native American:	6%	Male Athletes:	4%
White:	70%	Female Athletes:	3%
Unknown:	2%	Fraternity Members:	3%
From Out-of-State:	31%	Sorority Members:	2%

Frequently Compared Schools:

Arizona State University
San Diego State University
University of Arizona
University of Oregon

Students Speak Out On... EVERYTHING!

ACADEMICS

Q NAU Sets up Ways to Help You Succeed.

"Northern Arizona Univeristy is located in Flagstaff, Arizona. It is a college town with beautiful sourrounding scenery. The campus is great with many things near by. Depending on your studies of interest the coursework may be tough, however NAU offers many options to help you succeed, such as free tutoring, or late night library options. You have the option of meeting with academeic advisors to ensure you are on the right track."

Q They Want You to Succeed

"Northern Arizona University has professors that truly care how well you do in their class and offer plenty of help whenever you need it."

ATHLETICS

Q Nau Has Good Sports

"They dont compete with any of the top schools very much but they are able to put on good games agianst the other teams in the big sky. Nau has a very good school spirit you can find clothes in the walmart and in ohter stores."

Q Supported but Not Played

"Varsity sports are a big deal at Northern Arizona University, however not many people seem to participate in them. There is huge fan support and school spirit however. Most of the campus enjoys watching rather than playing."

CAMPUS DINING

Q Great

"The food selection is fairly reasonable. The prices are great on all the cooked food, but the pre-packaged food is pricey. The dining area is spacious and a great hang-out spot."

Q Food Is Good and a Big Selection

"There are many places to get food up there and they have a big dinning hall where they have food stands all over. They have places that are open late for those who are staying up late studying."

CAMPUS HOUSING

Q Living on Campus a Must as a Freshman

"Applying for housing was easy and access to campus is convenient. I would recommend all freshman live on campus so that you can connect with a variety of people right away."

Q On Campus Housing

"The freshmen doors are over crowded but the upper class doorms and apartments are great."

GUYS & GIRLS

Q Guys/ Girls at Nothern Arizona Unviersity

"To be honest, College is like high school but there is more responsibility. The girls/ guys dress the same as they were before high school or having a more relax look. Social life is excellent because there is no parents. Be careful of who you are in a relationship with."

Q Different Than California Girls

"Coming from California where the girls try to wear as little as possible, it's quite a change to see girls bundled up in layers of clothing. However it's a nice change, creates more allure and allows for more creativity on the typical standard of attractiveness. So far most of the guys in the area I've met have quite different attitudes than I'm used to and it's quite nice, not so many thick jock headed types."

HEALTH & SAFETY

Q Campus Is Very Safe

"The town is a small town so you dont really have to worry about anyone attacking you. Security is very good they will protect all the students and they are always around."

Q NAU Police Does Their Job Well

"The NAU police is very helpful in a lot of cases. They care about safety and rules. If you need help with something, they will help you."

LOOKING FOR MORE?

Check out our full-length guide to this school at collegeprowler.com/northern-arizona-university/.

Northern Illinois University

1425 W. Lincoln Highway; Dekalb, IL 60115
(800) 892-3050; www.niu.edu

THE BASICS:

Acceptance Rate: 59%
Yield: 29%
Setting: Suburban
Control: Public
Total Undergrads: 18,277
SAT Range: 1330–1740*
ACT Range: 19–24

Student-Faculty Ratio: 17:1
Retention Rate: 72%
Graduation Rate: 51%
Tuition: $18,410
Room & Board: $8,112
Avg. Aid Package: $9,910
Students With Aid: 81%

of 2400

Academics	B-	Greek Life	B
Athletics	B-	Guys	A+
Campus Dining	B-	Health & Safety	B
Campus Housing	B-	Local Atmosphere	C+
Campus Strictness	B-	Nightlife	B+
Computers	B+	Off-Campus Dining	B
Diversity	B-	Off-Campus Housing	B+
Drug Safety	C+	Parking	B
Facilities	C+	Transportation	B+
Girls	A	Weather	C

CP's Student Author On...
OVERALL EXPERIENCE

NIU isn't for everybody. It's a school in the middle of nowhere with a large student population and a less-thanstellar academic reputation. Make no mistake: there are times you will feel like crap if you come to NIU. They will often be spurred by observing or attempting to talk to the meatheads who come to college to party and dropout in a year or two. It can be tough to avoid being affected by that mindset, or the parking, or some of the ancient facilities, or the difficulty of registering for classes, or the—well, you get the idea. The toughest part is getting through the first year. Dorm life can be hell, with small rooms and obnoxious floor mates. On top of that, you can't take classes in your major until late in your second year. You will probably end up thinking of transferring or quitting school all together at least once. However, in the end, the positives far outweigh the negatives. The people are down-to-earth and not the stuck-up brats you might find at a school like Northwestern. There is always a bar or party or concert to go to, no matter the day of the week. It's also remarkably affordable when compared to other schools in Illinois and nationwide. Oddly enough, NIU can grow on you.... For the rest of this editorial, visit collegeprowler.com.

Students Speak Out On...
OVERALL EXPERIENCE

Q Unexplainable

"I never thought i would love this school so much. It has been the best experience of my life and i have only attended it for almost a full year. This school is unique because no other place is like it. It feels like home and almost every person that attends Northern is bright and polite. I would chose this school over and over if i had the chose to start over. It has taught me so much and i plan to learn way more."

Q Great quality

"NIU has good quality programs at a great price. Many of my professors were great at teaching and very respected in their fields. Students are fun, smart, and down to earth. I would highly recommend going here and getting involved on campus. Huskie football is awesome. Work hard, and take advantage of everything NIU has to offer."

Q Best decision I made!

"I love NIU and I would have never thought this was the school for me. I used onlineeducation.com to help me match up and I couldn't be happier. Go Huskies!"

BEST OF NORTHERN ILLINOIS

1. The people
2. Being independent from your parents
3. Tailgating
4. The football team
5. Thursday nights
6. The Recreation Center

Knowledgeable Professors
70% of students surveyed rated the general knowledge of professors as above average.

Low-Stress Course Load
55% of students surveyed rated the manageability of work as above average.

WORST OF NORTHERN ILLINOIS

1. Finding a parking spot
2. Winter weather
3. NIU's academic reputation outside the region
4. Registering for classes
5. Suitcase students
6. Residence hall floor fines

Students Can't Wait to Get Out of Town
50% of students surveyed said that there's no way they would live here after graduation.

Student Body

African American:	13%	Male Undergrads:	49%
Asian American:	6%	Female Undergrads:	51%
Hispanic:	7%	Living On Campus:	33%
International:	1%	Living Off Campus:	67%
Native American:	0%	Male Athletes:	3%
White:	67%	Female Athletes:	3%
Unknown:	6%	Fraternity Members:	19%
From Out-of-State:	3%	Sorority Members:	11%

Students Speak Out On...
EVERYTHING!

ACADEMICS

Q Pre-Physical Therapy

"With my major you are a health and human sciences major as well. The major that I am interested in is very competitive and you have to have at least a 3.5 GPA. You have your work cut out for you in this major, but everyone that has succeed has been happy and encourage it. It is worth it in the end, is what I'm told. Also there are many different resources that help you in your major, you just have to go out and find them."

Q Great Business Program and Professors

"The business program is top knotch and professors are truly interested in success of the students."

Q Speech Pathology at Northern Illinois

"Being a Speech Path major is amazing! The advisors are so helpful, and the professors know what they are talking about. After my first year in major classes, I am so confident in the rest of my years because of the help and support I have gotten already at Northern Illinois, Health and Human Sciences!"

ATHLETICS

Q The Rec Center

"The rec center is where I go to mellow out. It is spacious and provides us with morernized equipment to continue to stay in good physical condition. The basketball court is my favorite andran well by the staff."

Q Northern

"Northern Illinois Universtiy athletic teams are the best. The games are exciting. The team is full of energy and ready to play and represent NIU!"

CAMPUS DINING

Q Boring

"Yes, the food is good; there just doesn't seem to be much to choose from. There are plenty of places around, including the dining halls, but eating the same food so often gets, well, boring."

Frequently Compared Schools:

Illinois State University
Northwestern University
University of Illinois
University of Iowa

Q Cheeseburgers

"buns on top and bottom with the burger inside with ketchup"

CAMPUS HOUSING

Q Stevenson Suite

"Living in a suite allows communication toward your roommates"

Q Dorms Are Decent

"Everyone is pretty much nice and very respectful when it came to living in the dorms I had little or no problems what so ever."

GUYS & GIRLS

Q Huskie Pride

"Everyone on campus from jocks to computer whizs, cheerleaders to normal women, instructors to staff members all wear Northern Illinois University athletic and school wear to show their love for the college especially when games such as football and volleyball happen on campus."

Q Guys and Girls

"The students at Northern Illinois are very friendly outgoing. They love to meet new people and trey new things."

HEALTH & SAFETY

Q Completely Safe

"I never feel unsafe on NIU's Campus I walk up and down the streets at all hours .There are always campus police at hand."

Q NIU Police

"I feel safe when on campus. The NIU police do a great job and their presence is obvious on the campus. They are willing to walk one to their car, class, etc. The late night ride service also means never having to walk home in the dark."

LOOKING FOR MORE?
Check out our full-length guide to this school at collegeprowler.com/northern-illinois-university/.

Northwestern College - Saint Paul

3003 Snelling Ave. N; Saint Paul, MN 55113
(651) 631-5100; www.nwc.edu

THE BASICS:

Acceptance Rate: 96%
Yield: 43%
Setting: Suburban
Control: Private Non-Profit
Total Undergrads: 2,967
SAT Range: 980–1260*
ACT Range: 21–27

Student-Faculty Ratio: 16:1
Retention Rate: 79%
Graduation Rate: 58%
Tuition: $23,180
Room & Board: $7,426
Avg. Aid Package: $16,842
Students With Aid: 97%

* of 1600

Academics	B-	Greek Life	N/A
Athletics	B-	Guys	B+
Campus Dining	B-	Health & Safety	B-
Campus Housing	A-	Local Atmosphere	B+
Campus Strictness	C	Nightlife	C+
Computers	B-	Off-Campus Dining	A-
Diversity	D+	Off-Campus Housing	B
Drug Safety	A+	Parking	B+
Facilities	B-	Transportation	B
Girls	B+	Weather	B-

CP's Student Author On...
OVERALL EXPERIENCE

As a whole, Northwestern is loved by its students. The faculty, programs, students, staff, community, and environment create an atmosphere of love, comfort, and respect. A high level of satisfaction exists because most students chose the College for the high level of Christian education that Northwestern offers.

Northwestern is a place where professors and faculty do not shut down when they go home at night. Professors make themselves available to help and support students all the time, many of them even giving out their home numbers to students in case they should ever need to talk. Nearly all students that attend Northwestern have a deep passion for their faith and are on fire for the Lord. Students and faculty have such welcoming and sincere personalities, which makes it easy to get to know people. Friendships created at NWC are something cherished by everyone. There's not a place on campus where you won't receive a smile or salutation. The light created by the Lord is apparent on this campus and in its students.

Students Speak Out On...
OVERALL EXPERIENCE

Q Love Northwestern!

"Northwestern is a great school. It's a comfortable place to live, the academic programs are amazing, and the people are wonderful. I've made many friends and memories that will last forever."

Q Northwestern

"Love Northwestern. Such a great Christian School. You have to study because they challenge students academicly and spiritually."

Q It's Ok

"Good school with good education and teachers, but it's just not for me. Too far from home (1500miles) and the weather makes me feel depressed, always overcast, cold, and windy. I want my 95 degree plus and only a month of winter."

BEST OF NORTHWESTERN SAINT PAUL

1. Beautiful campus and great location
2. Daily chapel
3. Academically challenging
4. Caring and understanding professors
5. The Christian community

Big Dorms
93% of students surveyed felt that dorms were more spacious than average.

Highly Satisfied Students
90% of students surveyed would make the same school choice if they could do it all over again.

WORST OF NORTHWESTERN SAINT PAUL

1. Cost
2. Little diversity
3. The disconnect to the real world
4. Parking
5. Visitation hours
6. Food

Expensive to Just Get By
57% of students surveyed felt that the amount it costs to live while at school was worse than average.

Life is NOT a Party
82% of students surveyed said it's almost impossible to find a good party.

Student Body

African American:	3%	Male Undergrads:	42%
Asian American:	3%	Female Undergrads:	58%
Hispanic:	2%	Living On Campus:	69%
International:	0%	Living Off Campus:	31%
Native American:	0%	Male Athletes:	26%
White:	91%	Female Athletes:	10%
Unknown:	0%	Fraternity Members:	0%
From Out-of-State:	30%	Sorority Members:	0%

Frequently Compared Schools:
Carleton College
Macalester College
St. Olaf College
University of Minnesota

Students Speak Out On... EVERYTHING!

ACADEMICS

Biology Major
"It is so wonderful, the teachers are super helpful and always answer my questions with great detail. I feel like I have already learned so much!"

Marketing/Accounting
"The entire business department is very rigorous and goes very in-depth into the study of business. The professors are all very knowledgeable and have real life experience working in their specific areas of business."

Depends on Your Major
"The overall quality of academics is very good. the instructors are knowledgeable in their fields."

ATHLETICS

Sport
"Sports at Northwestern are always exciting. There are always fans supporting and parents are always there. It's like one family. The school takes sport seriously but they also make sure students take care of their class work first before sports."

A Place to Belong
"Northwestern is in the process of joining Division 3, our basketball teams are very competitive and recieve a lot of support from the students, the best part of atheletics are the coaches that strive to create community and a nurturing place for students to grow on and off the field."

Decent Sports Involvement
"Most people would not come to this school to play sports. While very adequate all around and an exceptional basketball team, sports are not one of the primary focus points of the school."

CAMPUS DINING

Food
"I love how great the staff is and how there are a lot of healthy choices at every meal."

CAMPUS HOUSING

Dorms Are Great!
"The dorms are very spacious and have mini kitchenette with oven, stove, and fridge. They also include a bathroom with a vanity."

Great Dorms
"The dorms at Northwestern are awesome. I have visited other college's dorms, either on a visit or to see friends, and I have yet to find dorms that even come close to NWC. Even though 3 people share a room in the main dorms and 8 in the other dorms, there is plenty of space. I visited a friend at a different college and his dorm is literally half the size and they have the 3 people. NWC's dorms have a bathroom, kitchenette, and vanity (except for Arden). Great dorms."

GUYS & GIRLS

Conservative Might Explain It
"Northwestern is a Christian school. The girls cover their cleavage, and the boys do not walk around with there shirts off. Friends with benefits is not in the vocabulary. The girls are modest and polite, while the guys are gentlemen; which is word not used very often in society. At Northwestern you'll find kids from private, home, and public schools."

Guys and Girls
"At Northwestern, you have a variety of people from all different places! Most people are genuine and very welcoming!"

HEALTH & SAFETY

Northwestern Security
"I've never felt unsafe on campus. Campus Security is always available and clearly present. The small campus and sense of community helps me feel safe there."

Totally Safe
"Campus Security does a great job of making people feel safe on campus!!"

LOOKING FOR MORE?
Check out our full-length guide to this school at collegeprowler.com/northwestern-college---saint-paul/.

Northwestern University

633 Clark St.; Evanston, IL 60208
(847) 491-3741; www.northwestern.edu

THE BASICS:

Acceptance Rate: 26%
Yield: 32%
Setting: Small city
Control: Private Non-Profit
Total Undergrads: 9,914
SAT Range: 2030–2280*
ACT Range: 30–33

Student-Faculty Ratio: 7:1
Retention Rate: 97%
Graduation Rate: 94%
Tuition: $38,463
Room & Board: $11,703
Avg. Aid Package: $29,411
Students With Aid: 54%

* of 2400

Academics	A	Greek Life	A
Athletics	B+	Guys	B+
Campus Dining	B	Health & Safety	B-
Campus Housing	B	Local Atmosphere	B-
Campus Strictness	B-	Nightlife	B+
Computers	B	Off-Campus Dining	A
Diversity	B	Off-Campus Housing	B-
Drug Safety	C	Parking	C
Facilities	B+	Transportation	B+
Girls	B+	Weather	D+

CP's Student Author On...
OVERALL EXPERIENCE

At Northwestern, you'll spend plenty of time throwing yourself into your schoolwork. But once you get past that, it's not all about the papers and exams here—you'll see that you'll be able to kick back and have some fun, too. If you were chosen by Admissions to get into NU, then you definitely have enough skills to get through all the work and still find the fun at the end of the tunnel.

The percentage of Northwestern freshmen who return for their sophomore year is very high, hovering near 100 percent on a consistent basis—and this is one of those cases where the numbers pretty much speak for themselves. At NU, students find plenty to complain about—bad weather, tough classes, insensitive professors, and lack of sleep are probably common places to start—but at the end of the day, everyone chose this school for a reason, and that because it's one of the best in the country. Don't get it twisted—no school is perfect, and neither is Northwestern—but there's also plenty to appreciate here.

Students Speak Out On...
OVERALL EXPERIENCE

Q Favorite Place EVER!
"Northwestern is by no means an easy school in academics or extracurricular activities, but the people here are amazing, the teachers are passionate, and there are opportunities for anyone and everyone to do anything they are interested in on campus. I love this place!"

Q All-Star University
"It's filled with all-stars, and it has all-star amenities. Close to the greatest city in the country, picturesque and on the beach, tons of athletic events that actually receive national attention, more diversity and cultural enrichment than anywhere else, and let's face it: People work extremely hard. You will meet the most interesting and driven people you ever have, and chances are, you're one of them, too!"

Q Great People
"Everyone I have met here has been really talented and driven. The social life is better than at most top universities, and if you want to go out, you definitely can. Academic work is pretty challenging but that is to be expected."

BEST OF NORTHWESTERN UNIVERSITY

1. Academics overall, but especially the Medill School of Journalism, Theatre Program, and dual-degree options
2. Proximity to Chicago
3. Dillo Day
4. The Lakefill

Happy Students
97% of students return after their first year.

Commitment to Teaching
There are 7 students for every member of faculty on campus.

WORST OF NORTHWESTERN UNIVERSITY

1. Winter in Chicago
2. Dorky guys
3. Dining hall food
4. Suffering social scene
5. Pressure to succeed
6. Expensive
7. No U-Passes (free CTA passes)

Expensive
Tuition is a steep $38,463, one of the most expensive rates in the country.

Expensive Dorms
Living on campus doesn't come cheap, with an average housing price tag of $6,657.

Student Body

African American:	5%	Male Undergrads:	48%
Asian American:	17%	Female Undergrads:	52%
Hispanic:	6%	Living On Campus:	65%
International:	6%	Living Off Campus:	35%
Native American:	0%	Male Athletes:	6%
White:	55%	Female Athletes:	5%
Unknown:	11%	Fraternity Members:	32%
From Out-of-State:	75%	Sorority Members:	38%

Frequently Compared Schools:

Brown University
Cornell University
University of Pennsylvania
Washington University in St. Louis

Students Speak Out On...
EVERYTHING!

ACADEMICS

Professors

"Most professors are amazing here! Almost every prof I've had here has cared so much for the students, for their future success, and for their work in the class. They don't care so much about their paycheck, it's about the student."

Theatre

"I'm hoping to get into the musical theatre certificate program (we audition in the spring of frosh and soph years) and so I'm currently preparing for that. Most of my classes were challenging without being impossible, though one professor was kind of a washout. We tend to get to know the profs extremely well, which helps whenever you have questions about the industry or even another class."

ATHLETICS

Spirit Is ... Lacking

"Football season is fun, but beyond that, people don't really care about the other sports that happen, and I know maybe two or three people who go to games. People really get excited about football, though."

Decent Big Ten Sports

"It's awesome going to such a prestigious school that still has Big Ten sports. We play against some of the best teams in the country, and actually usually do decently against them. The best part about going to only a decently good school is when you beat big teams (like Iowa). Often people will forgo going to games for studying, but there's always really spirited crowds that go to every game, making them really fun to go to."

CAMPUS DINING

Above Average, Even for a Celiac

"There are numerous dining halls on North and South campus, and there are many high-quality, varying options at each hall. There are several convenience stores across campus for late-night snack fixes or even for on-the-run meals."

Food in Dining Halls

"I use nearly every dining hall or other café food options on campus. I like how each dining hall offers varieties of food. Lisa's is good if you need a quick sandwich, while Norris is good if you have a little more time to sit and eat. The dining halls offer omelets, sandwiches, salads, etc., as well as soups and burgers. They are a great place to meet up and shoot the breeze with friends."

CAMPUS HOUSING

Residential Collegs Are Great

"I live in a non-thematic residential college, and I love it. I love the atmosphere and the events. The rooms are huge too. However, several of my friends have been unhappy in their dorms for several other reasons."

Dorms at Northwestern

"Generally, dorms at Northwestern are pretty good but are generally dumping grounds for freshmen. Upperclassmen tend to live off-campus, in sorority/fraternity houses, or in the higher quality upperclassmen dorms. Residence halls are another option for those wishing to enter a closer knit community. Many people stay in their residence halls throughout their college career."

GUYS & GIRLS

Diversity

"I find that there is a wide diversity of what kind of people are at northwestern. Boys can be flamboyantly gay, dancers, and theater majors, or athletes, engineers, or social sciences or some combination of them all. Girls are very similar in those respects, though I find that majors tend to show a dominating sex."

HEALTH & SAFETY

Super Safe

"well-lit campus, visible campus police, you can walk around at 3am. a blissful bubble."

LOOKING FOR MORE?

Check out our full-length guide to this school at collegeprowler.com/northwestern-university/.

Oakwood University

7000 Adventist Blvd. NW; Huntsville, AL 35896
(256) 726-7000; www.oakwood.edu

THE BASICS:

Acceptance Rate: 56%	**Student-Faculty Ratio:** 13:1
Yield: 49%	**Retention Rate:** 72%
Setting: Mid-sized city	**Graduation Rate:** 39%
Control: Private Non-Profit	**Tuition:** $13,834
Total Undergrads: 1,830	**Room & Board:** $8,764
SAT Range: 760–1020*	**Avg. Aid Package:** $6,500
ACT Range: 16–21	**Students With Aid:** 92%

* of 1600

Academics	C-	Greek Life	N/A
Athletics	C+	Guys	A-
Campus Dining	C+	Health & Safety	B-
Campus Housing	C	Local Atmosphere	B-
Campus Strictness	C-	Nightlife	C+
Computers	C+	Off-Campus Dining	C+
Diversity	C+	Off-Campus Housing	B
Drug Safety	C+	Parking	A+
Facilities	D+	Transportation	C
Girls	B	Weather	D+

CP's Student Author On...
OVERALL EXPERIENCE

The overall experience for Oakwood is exemplary. It may take a while to get settled and understand how Oakwood operates, but when they do, Oakwood becomes a wonderful experience. It is like looking at the cup as half full rather than half empty. If one focuses on the negative things of Oakwood, they will not have a good experience, but if one looks at the positive things, their experience can be promising.

Being a freshman and waiting in long registration lines may seem rough and uncomfortable at first, but in the long run, it is worth it. It is worth the relationships you build. It is worth the spiritual life that you gain. It is worth the amazing classes you take and the experiences you have. Oakwood is not a perfect school, and it definitely lacks in some areas, but it is all worth it compared to what you are given. The friends that are made and the experiences that are had will be things that students wouldn't trade for the world. Many people focus on the destination, but at Oakwood, it is not so much the destination that matters but the journey you take to get to that destination. Future students can be assured that Oakwood University is a great journey.

Students Speak Out On...
OVERALL EXPERIENCE

Q It's a Wonderful Social and Spiritual Atmosphere
"I love the atmosphere. It abides by what it stands for and the aim of the school is accomplished. There are alot of outreach programs, social and religious activities, and connections with the area's local universities! We try very hard as well to connect with our sister institutions to keep a diverse atmosphere. The international population is also well represented, hence it lends to a culturally diverse and culturally sensitive campus."

Q Oakwood Is GREAT!
"The life at Oakwood is a great one, from friends to the campus personal. Oakwood is a very warm and welcoming school and everyone there will totally love the experience and miss it once it is over!"

Q Oakwood Is Great
"This school is great. The students are really nice, and the spiritual aspect makes it even better. The school spirit is high, and that is a huge part in making the O.U. experience worthwhile."

BEST OF OAKWOOD

1. The merciful teachers
2. The unity
3. The people
4. The music
5. The spiritual life

Knowledgeable Professors
73% of students surveyed rated the general knowledge of professors as above average.

Low-Stress Course Load
50% of students surveyed rated the manageability of work as above average.

WORST OF OAKWOOD

1. Weather
2. Costs
3. Dumpsters are too far
4. Dorms
5. Dinner
6. Deans

Life is NOT a Party
80% of students surveyed said it's almost impossible to find a good party.

Not Much Diversity
One of the least racially diverse campuses—only 11% of students are minorities.

Student Body

African American:	89%	Male Undergrads:	41%
Asian American:	0%	Female Undergrads:	59%
Hispanic:	1%	Living On Campus:	68%
International:	7%	Living Off Campus:	32%
Native American:	0%	Male Athletes:	2%
White:	0%	Female Athletes:	1%
Unknown:	3%	Fraternity Members:	0%
From Out-of-State:	90%	Sorority Members:	0%

Frequently Compared Schools:

Birmingham-Southern College
Middle Tennessee State University
Samford University
Vanderbilt University

Students Speak Out On... EVERYTHING!

ACADEMICS

Health Science Major
"Health Science is already an interesting major in itself. Here at Oakwood its just that much better. There are many things to get involved in pertaining to health. Opportunites such as NAPS,an organization that does missionary work locally as well as internationally. The workload is manageable and can be tolerated if you are organized."

The Purpose of Our Education.
"While Oakwood is a learning institution; math, history and science have their place. However, nothing surpasses the need for Christ in our lives and our teachers understand that. We pray before every class and sometimes we even have devotion before the lesson. Yes academics are important, but our classes offer so much more. That's why I appreciate my school."

Heavy Workload
"The workload at Oakwood University can be heavy at sometimes but it is all about managing your time and knowing what your priorities are."

ATHLETICS

Decent Athletics
"We have a decent athletic program but its isnt NCAA, so for me they dont get that much respect."

School Spirit
"Oakwood University offers few sports, but when there is a game going on, the school spirit is very high. The students at Oakwood supports their school in sports. Basketball is the biggest sport on campus. There is no football team, however, there is inter-mural flag football. The gymnasium is a bit small and can be redecorated to be more modernized."

CAMPUS DINING

The Healthy Way
"Oakwood University promotes a healthy life style and it follows a strict healthy diet"

The Food is Good
"The food is good but it is mainly vegetarian. It could make more provisions for the students who are vegan but it has a good variety of vegetarian meals. The dining hall is very lovely. It has a beautiful set up. The waiting line can be pretty long, depending on what time one reaches the dining hall. There could be more variety for the take out line and during breakfast and dinner time. However, Lunch is the best time to get a meal for there is so much variety for both vegans and vegetarians."

CAMPUS HOUSING

Holland Hall
"Holland Hall is o.k. It is not the greatest dorm. It should be co-ed."

Dorm Life
"Life at the dorms is pretty good. There are lots of great social activities, the environment is friendly, and most of the classes are nearby. Still, laundry could be cheaper."

GUYS & GIRLS

Great
"Everyone is nice and caring."

Christian Love
"Oakwood is a school based on Christian principles. When it comes to relationships our school varies from many public universities. For example, the dress, interest, and trends of our school vary from others schools. We focus on more Christian focused events instead of parties like other universities."

HEALTH & SAFETY

Campus Is Safe
"Petty theft is really your only worry."

Security and Health Issues
"I personally feel safe moving around the campus as often as I vist. The health measures that they embark on is in the best interest of the school and the student."

LOOKING FOR MORE?

Check out our full-length guide to this school at collegeprowler.com/oakwood-university/.

Oberlin College

70 N. Professor St.; Oberlin, OH 44074
(440) 775-8411; www.oberlin.edu

THE BASICS:

Acceptance Rate: 34%
Yield: 33%
Setting: Suburban
Control: Private Non-Profit
Total Undergrads: 2,889
SAT Range: 1920–2200*
ACT Range: 28–32

Student-Faculty Ratio: 9:1
Retention Rate: 93%
Graduation Rate: 84%
Tuition: $40,004
Room & Board: $10,480
Avg. Aid Package: $26,912
Students With Aid: 83%

of 2400

Academics	A-	Greek Life	N/A
Athletics	C	Guys	A
Campus Dining	A	Health & Safety	A-
Campus Housing	B+	Local Atmosphere	B-
Campus Strictness	A+	Nightlife	B
Computers	B	Off-Campus Dining	A-
Diversity	B+	Off-Campus Housing	A
Drug Safety	C	Parking	B+
Facilities	A-	Transportation	B
Girls	A-	Weather	D+

CP's Student Author On...
OVERALL EXPERIENCE

No matter how critical Oberlin students tend to be, they rarely deny the quality of education they receive. In fact, most students are more than appreciative of the unique academic and cultural opportunities Oberlin offers, and are hard pressed to think of a school they'd rather be at. Students who are frustrated with their experience often complain about the small, insular environment, long, cold winters, and the heavy workload. Those who thrive with Oberlin's stimulating academics and interesting student body are those willing to accept the challenges inherent to attending a small, liberal arts institution. Here you won't experience the aspects of a state university education, such as Greek life, large sports, a lot of hotties, or packed classes. But that is the point--Oberlin prides itself in being everything that a state university is not.

Many students take for granted the fact that Oberlin, for an undergraduate institution of its size, has one of the most impressive library and art collections in the country, and that the Conservatory provides students with a constant repertoire of world-class music.... For the rest of this editorial, visit collegeprowler.com.

Students Speak Out On...
OVERALL EXPERIENCE

Q Really Great
"I love Oberlin. I feel at home here. There's good people, good classes. I'm from New York, so it was a bit of a transition to a small town, but I've never regretted my decision to come here."

Q Amazing
"Oberlin is my favorite place in the world, I wouldn't trade my time here for anything. From the academics to the people to the parties, everything is wonderful."

Q Overall a Good Experience
"The people I've met are awesome, I like that the sports offered are fun and competitive but also really accessible. The club teams are full of wonderful people and the varsity teams aren't about to take the nation by storm, but they're still great to go watch. If you can get over your initial distaste for hipsters and accept that a lot of people here are a little strange, you'll have a great time. Come here if you're open-minded. The only downer so far is the location."

BEST OF OBERLIN

1. Music scene
2. Clean environment
3. Art museum
4. Library system
5. Student radio
6. Co-ops
7. Lack of sororities and fraternities

Happy Students
93% of students return after their first year.

Commitment to Teaching
There are 9 students for every member of faculty on campus.

WORST OF OBERLIN

1. Dating scene
2. Campus Dining Services (CDS)
3. No music store
4. Weather
5. Intellectual snobbery
6. Too few bars
7. ResLife

Expensive
Tuition is a steep $40,004, one of the most expensive rates in the country.

Student Body

African American:	6%	Male Undergrads:	45%
Asian American:	7%	Female Undergrads:	55%
Hispanic:	5%	Living On Campus:	75%
International:	6%	Living Off Campus:	25%
Native American:	1%	Male Athletes:	18%
White:	75%	Female Athletes:	11%
Unknown:	0%	Fraternity Members:	0%
From Out-of-State:	91%	Sorority Members:	0%

Frequently Compared Schools:

Kenyon College
Macalester College
Vassar College
Wesleyan University

Students Speak Out On... EVERYTHING!

ACADEMICS

Q Brilliant! a+

"I'm a Harvard professor, and have taught students at Cambridge, Cornell, Columbia, London, Paris, Wesleyan, Swarthmore, and Yale. Oberlin is a jewel in the crown of American intellectual life. Nowhere does one find a better equipped environment, from libraries, to musea, to music, for stimulation of the life of the mind, and the students are genuine, extremely capable, inquisitive, adventurous. An intellectual's heaven. The best place in the country."

Q Professors Very Interactive

"I am a history an environmental studies major and all the professors I have had have been very helpful and accessible. They know how to accommodate each students needs and the classes are interactive and interesting. While classes are challenging I have had the help of my professors to make sure I can get through and do my personal best."

ATHLETICS

Q Former Varsity Athlete

"It was a really wonderful experience for me to play a varsity sport at Oberlin. That being said, I obviously did not continue to play. This was mainly because there are a lot of other extracurricular activities so it was hard to manage varsity athletics with my other commitments. Many of my friends continue to be athletes and have been able to balance other commitments better than I was able to."

Q Good of It's Kind

"If you are looking for a very athletic school, you'd have to be stupid to consider Oberlin. But for a small, Division III liberal arts school, the athletics are pretty good - and can be good fun. The football team is pretty good and we have soccer. However, we also have Ultimate Frisbee (both a guys and a girls' team) and Quidditch, both of which can be very fun and good exercise without being too serious."

CAMPUS DINING

Q Great Food Always

"There are always vegetarian and vegan options. Ingredients are fresh. Lots of variety."

Q Co-Ops

"Amazing option. We have one of the largest co-op systems of any college. The food is much better than cafeteria food, and there's a lot of options for people who have dietary restrictions (i.e. kosher, vegetarian, vegan, gluten free) It's also cheaper to join."

CAMPUS HOUSING

Q Overall a Good Experience

"I live in the brand new freshman dorm, so my experience isn't necessarily very representative of overall campus quality. Still, if you get into it, the Kahn building is amazing, and way too nice for freshmen. The campus is pretty and nothing is terribly far away, but I really don't dig this rural Ohio business. However, I imagine that at any other college you would end up spending a ton of time on campus so it's not a big deal. Cleveland is maybe half an hour to forty-five minutes away, anyway."

Q Good Community

"The freshman dorms aren't superb to live in but you make a lot of great friends and it's a really nice community to live in."

GUYS & GIRLS

Q Creative, Adventurous, Sexually Intense

"Oberlin has an extremely creative student population...in all domains...One can be maximally sexual, or not at all. An atmosphere of tremendous freedom prevails!"

HEALTH & SAFETY

Q Rideline!

"I have never felt unsafe on this campus. I can bike or walk around at all hours.Rideline is also the best thing, a student-operated shuttle from 9pm-2am, every day of the week. Great for when it's cold!"

LOOKING FOR MORE?

Check out our full-length guide to this school at collegeprowler.com/oberlin-college/.

Occidental College

1600 Campus Road; Los Angeles, CA 90041
(323) 259-2500; www.oxy.edu

THE BASICS:

Acceptance Rate: 43%	**Student-Faculty Ratio:** 9:1
Yield: 22%	**Retention Rate:** 91%
Setting: Large city	**Graduation Rate:** 86%
Control: Private Non-Profit	**Tuition:** $38,935
Total Undergrads: 1,972	**Room & Board:** $10,780
SAT Range: 1810–2080*	**Avg. Aid Package:** $28,325
ACT Range: 28–32	**Students With Aid:** 78%

* of 2400

Academics	B+	Greek Life	D
Athletics	C+	Guys	B
Campus Dining	B	Health & Safety	B+
Campus Housing	A-	Local Atmosphere	A+
Campus Strictness	B	Nightlife	A
Computers	B-	Off-Campus Dining	A+
Diversity	A	Off-Campus Housing	C-
Drug Safety	B-	Parking	A-
Facilities	C+	Transportation	B-
Girls	B+	Weather	A

CP's Student Author On...
OVERALL EXPERIENCE

For a small liberal arts college, Occidental does very well. The academic programs are strong, the support network for students is huge, there is a lot to do both on and off campus, and the diverse community really brings people together. Most students who go to Oxy love the school and are incredibly glad that they came. There are some who did not like it because of the kind of school it is, and others who disliked the way certain programs are treated at the school. It is a highly diverse school in terms of those who attend as well as the multitude of academic and extracurricular options available to all students. It also has a very tight community, both between the students amongst themselves as well as students and the administration. Many students have received direct assistance from their professors in ways that could never occur at a larger institution where there are 300 people in one class.

There is a plethora of things to do on and off campus as well, and for those looking for a change or looking for a variety in culture or entertainment, there is nothing lacking in Los Angeles.... For the rest of this editorial, visit collegeprowler.com.

Students Speak Out On...
OVERALL EXPERIENCE

Q **Personal Growth Through a Lot of Fun, a Lot of Work**
"At oxy, the general thought is that you have school work, sleep, and a social life and you only get to choose two. Most people choose school work and a social life. Participation and involvement in the community is a huge part of living at Oxy. The academics are challenging but worth it. You can't slip by under the radar but its great because you're encouraged by your peers, professors and yourself to be the best you can be."

Q "I love the diversity, the people, and the classes—Oxy rules!"

Q "I really enjoy Oxy, even though there are some problems. I wish the school had more money, or at least spent what they had better. Maybe then I could get some new equipment for my projects."

Q "It's not perfect, but the community and the academics together make me glad I came."

BEST OF OCCIDENTAL

1. The people
2. The diversity
3. Being in Los Angeles (beaches, things to do)
4. The entertainment
5. Cultural possibilities of LA (museums, concerts)
6. The weather

Happy Students
91% of students return after their first year.

Commitment to Teaching
There are 9 students for every member of faculty on campus.

WORST OF OCCIDENTAL

1. Being in Los Angeles (smog, traffic)
2. Being secluded
3. Needing a car
4. Small size
5. Internet connection
6. Distance from most major areas in LA

Expensive
Tuition is a steep $38,935, one of the most expensive rates in the country.

Expensive Dorms
Living on campus doesn't come cheap, with an average housing price tag of $6,130.

Student Body

African American:	6%	Male Undergrads:	45%
Asian American:	15%	Female Undergrads:	56%
Hispanic:	14%	Living On Campus:	76%
International:	2%	Living Off Campus:	24%
Native American:	1%	Male Athletes:	31%
White:	57%	Female Athletes:	17%
Unknown:	3%	Fraternity Members:	10%
From Out-of-State:	54%	Sorority Members:	16%

Frequently Compared Schools:

Claremont McKenna College
Pitzer College
Pomona College
University of Southern California

Students Speak Out On... EVERYTHING!

ACADEMICS

Professors

"Oxy has a pretty difficult workload, but the classes are worth the effort. I've only had a couple professors that weren't that great, but most of the professors I've had have been amazing and completely dedicated to their studies AND their students."

Good, but Could Be Better

"The professors are great; they really know their stuff and are easy to approach and willing to help. There is a lack of academic extracurricular activities, and the degree you earn could be stronger"

ATHLETICS

Small but Very Present

"Most students are involved in sports, whether varsity or club. We make up in spirit what we lack in size and talent pool to draw from. School spirit is pretty high. Team performances vary across the board. Because it is a small school, fan support is great because students come out to support their friends."

"The swimming pool is open quite a bit, and that's how I get my exercise. It's really fun to work out with such a tight group of students, faculty, and administrators. It really makes me feel like a part of the campus community."

CAMPUS DINING

Good but Expensive

"The food here is very good, but prices for non-campus produced food are exorbitant. Not considering financial aid, it costs me about $56,000 to go here, yet they feel the need to charge us 2x the amount we would have paid for the same product off campus. We're students, we're broke. It needs to stop trying to profit off its students."

"The food is pretty good, but I'd like more options. I always find myself eating the same stuff over and over again, mostly because there are only three or four things at each station that they rotate through."

CAMPUS HOUSING

Good Atmosphere

"Students are required to live on campus for three years so there is a great social atmosphere. The dorms arent too bad as long as youre in one that has AC."

"Lower campus is the place to be. All the dorms are better, and you're really close to everything important on campus. Nobody goes to upper campus unless there's a party or they have to."

GUYS & GIRLS

Great Range

"You can find a range of people at Occidental. Everyone can find a niche."

Guys Look Better the Longer You Stay on Campus

"The people here are awesome and really different. It can be obnoxious sometimes because there are so many loud opinions flying around but if you learn to appreciate that all those opinions came from a different childhood in a different place it is pretty cool. Also, because it is such a small school, people start becoming more attractive the longer you are around them and no one else..."

HEALTH & SAFETY

Campus Safety

"Campus Safety are good at responding if you have a problem, and I feel like campus is generally a safe place to be. However, there are occasional thefts etc, same as everywhere..."

Campus Is Safe, but Don't Be Careless!

"Very safe on campus, no fights. There are a good amount of theft, though a lot of it has to do with people being careless. Have been numerous incidents of muggings very close on campus, even during the day. Even though the town is pretty safe, good to be carefull and go in pairs. Besides that, Campus Safety are (usually) trying to keep you safe."

LOOKING FOR MORE?

Check out our full-length guide to this school at collegeprowler.com/occidental-college/.

Oglethorpe University

4484 Peachtree Road NE; Atlanta, GA 30319
(404) 261-1441; www.oglethorpe.edu

THE BASICS:

Acceptance Rate: 42%
Yield: 11%
Setting: Suburban
Control: Private Non-Profit
Total Undergrads: 1,013
SAT Range: 1570–1900*
ACT Range: 23–27

Student-Faculty Ratio: 16:1
Retention Rate: 75%
Graduation Rate: 62%
Tuition: $26,650
Room & Board: $9,990
Avg. Aid Package: $26,500
Students With Aid: 99%

of 2400

This School Isn't Graded Yet!

College Prowler grades are calculated using tons of criteria, including survey responses that come from students at this school.

Unfortunately, we haven't gathered enough student surveys yet for this school to be able to calculate the grades for each section. Stay tuned to *CollegeProwler.com* for grade updates and more!

CP's Student Author On...
OVERALL EXPERIENCE

Oglethorpe is unusual but only in the best of ways. The education is great, and the environment is supportive, but a stay at Oglethorpe requires hard work. Some parties are fun, but some are boring, and there are many nice people but also some cliques. However, most everyone is welcoming and not afraid to be themselves —eccentricities are the norm on campus. If someone's looking for fun, they'll eventually find it.

While many scholarships are available, it can prove hard to maintain the GPA required to keep them. This makes studying very important, and it can sometimes interfere with the social scene. For others, though, the curriculum is not so bad, and there is plenty of time to enjoy themselves both on an off campus.

Oglethorpe is a safe and nurturing environment where a student can expect to be treated as an individual. The classes are tiny but by no means lacking in comparison to courses at other schools. In fact, an advantage of Oglethorpe is the one-on-one treatment a student can expect from teachers.... For the rest of this editorial, visit collegeprowler.com.

Students Speak Out On...
OVERALL EXPERIENCE

Q Best Time of My Life

"Everything from challenging academics amazing people and an awesome sense of civic engagement make Oglethorpe the best place Ive ever been"

Q We're a Strange Group

"I love Oglethorpe because we're miles away from the usual. We have some of the craziest traditions ever and we're home to the second most unusual mascot in America. We're also like one big family here. Everyone knows everyone. But, this school is definetly not for the faint of heart. We have fun here but we also work our butts off. Studying is not an option and midterms are not play time."

Q Perfect Fit for Me!

"I wouldn't trade the tiny class sizes, individual attention, and sense of community here for anything! I am being challenged, yet I don't feel completely overwhelmed like some of my friends at other schools seem to be. I feel like I matter and that I am a person, not just a number. This is a place where I feel comfortable enough to explore any opportunity I desire. I wouldn't want to go anywhere else!"

BEST OF OGLETHORPE

1. Friendly atmosphere
2. A unique, "Hogwarts-esque" style campus
3. Professors who actually care about students
4. Scholarship opportunities
5. Small class sizes

Easy Financial Aid Process
56% of students surveyed told us that the financial aid process went smoothly and they received the financial aid they needed.

WORST OF OGLETHORPE

1. Very competitive atmosphere
2. Walking up the hills to get to classes
3. Alcohol use
4. The cafeteria had a case of food poisoning.
5. Unpredictable, sometimes very hot weather

Expensive
Tuition is a steep $26,650, one of the most expensive rates in the country.

Don't Move Off Campus
Average off-campus housing is a steep $10,190.

Student Body

African American:	23%	Male Undergrads:	40%
Asian American:	4%	Female Undergrads:	61%
Hispanic:	4%	Living On Campus:	61%
International:	4%	Living Off Campus:	39%
Native American:	1%	Male Athletes:	32%
White:	48%	Female Athletes:	19%
Unknown:	15%	Fraternity Members:	33%
From Out-of-State:	31%	Sorority Members:	25%

Frequently Compared Schools:
Emory University
Georgia Institute of Technology
Georgia State University
University of Georgia

Students Speak Out On... EVERYTHING!

ACADEMICS

As a Psych Major
"The psych teachers that I've had have been so helpful, and have shown that they really want to work with me and other students. One thing that I really appreciate is that when you are struggling, the professors try to help you work to reach the level you should be at, rather than demoting you to an easier level."

Could Be Better
"The reason I chose Oglethorpe University was because of its small class sizes, and apparently nice professors. Now, having experienced this first hand, I have learned that many of the professors don't care who you are, even with such small class sizes. It is also apparent that the Admissions offices really don't care about you and do little to help with their own errors."

Economics
"Interesting class, but it is important to read and understand material before you go to class."

ATHLETICS

Sports Are Pretty Intense.
"Even though we're a division three school, the sports get pretty crazy; everyone on campus has the Stormy Petrel spirit."

We're a Small School
"We've got the teams, but not such a big turnout. No Football."

Don't Know Too Much About Sports.
"I've never really been into sports, but we have a good baseball and volleyball team. Attendance is fairly average, but I'm not the person to ask about the subject."

CAMPUS DINING

Food and Dining
"Though we don't have a wide variety of food in our dining hall, I'm picky so the value and the taste outweigh the lack of choices."

The Norovirus
"The food comes with the dorm tuition. After hearing praise during the tour given, I was hopeful about the food amenities. It was a fallacy, the food service repeatedly serves dishes that no one wants, are tasteless, and often carry diseases. It has been three times now that there has been widespread norovirus pandemic."

Ew
"They try way too hard to be fancy. Most students live on cereal."

CAMPUS HOUSING

Better Than Others
"The dorms do have some bugs, but other than that, they are roomy with private bed and bath after freshman year. Freshman dorms are not bad either"

GUYS & GIRLS

People
"At OU, we ARE diversity. From goths to preps, you can find anyone. And everyone cares about the same thing: education."

There's a High Variety of Pretty Girls.
"There are a lot of girls and other people who are willing to be friendly and have fun all around campus."

HEALTH & SAFETY

Campus Always Feels Very Safe
"There have been a few car break-ins on campus, but that's almost impossible to avoid when you live in Atlanta. I always feel safe on campus. The campus safety officers respond quickly to any incident, even things as small as getting locked out of your building."

Campus Safety
"Campus safety is pretty lax and not very evident. I've never had any run-ins with them. They're good about giving you warnings before giving you parking tickets."

LOOKING FOR MORE?
Check out our full-length guide to this school at collegeprowler.com/oglethorpe-university/.

Ohio State University

190 N. Oval Mall; Columbus, OH 43210
(614) 292-6446; www.osu.edu

THE BASICS:

Acceptance Rate: 65%
Yield: 49%
Setting: Large city
Control: Public
Total Undergrads: 41,349
SAT Range: 1660–1980*
ACT Range: 25–30

Student-Faculty Ratio: 15:1
Retention Rate: 92%
Graduation Rate: 73%
Tuition: $22,251
Room & Board: $9,468
Avg. Aid Package: $10,225
Students With Aid: 89%

of 2400

Academics	A-	Greek Life	B-
Athletics	A+	Guys	A-
Campus Dining	A-	Health & Safety	B
Campus Housing	B-	Local Atmosphere	A-
Campus Strictness	B+	Nightlife	A
Computers	B	Off-Campus Dining	A
Diversity	B-	Off-Campus Housing	B
Drug Safety	D+	Parking	B-
Facilities	A+	Transportation	A
Girls	B+	Weather	C+

CP's Student Author On...
OVERALL EXPERIENCE

There is a reason the Buckeye Nation is considered to be so devoted; an overwhelming love for OSU is evident in student responses, and in the loyalty of alumni to their alma mater. Each person has his or her own reasons for loving the University, and there are quite a few of them. Some students feel that the academics are top-notch and have found exactly the programs they wanted; others lean toward the athletic success of the Buckeye teams, while some just feel that the friendships and bonds they have made are enough to make their tenure at OSU worthwhile. At any rate, everyone can agree that being a Buckeye creates a special bond between you and nearly 50,000 other students, which you will carry with you for the rest of your life.

Once you get past the sheer size of the University, it will really become a second home. After only a quarter of classes, you won't be able to cross the Oval without seeing someone you know. Ohio State is truly the smallest large university you will find.... For the rest of this editorial, visit collegeprowler.com.

Students Speak Out On...
OVERALL EXPERIENCE

Q We Are the BUCKEYES!

"I love that when I graduate, it'll be with a degree from THE Ohio State University. It can be hard getting adjusted to such a large university when you first get here, but it's pretty easy to make friends from classes, and I wouldn't trade having classes with my favorite professors for anything. OSU has so many different clubs and student organizations, everyone will find something to love here."

Q O-H-I-O

"This is the best place on Earth. It is like one gigantic family here. The total college experience. So many opportunities things to do here."

Q I Never Want to Leave.

"I never want to leave Ohio State. Everyone is so nice and I love the nightlife. The classes are hard but I love the school spirit. Go Bucks!"

BEST OF OHIO STATE

1. Football Saturdays
2. Michigan Week and jumping into Mirror Lake
3. The Oval when it's nice and sunny out
4. Parties
5. School spirit

Happy Students
92% of students return after their first year.

Proven Success
73% of students will complete their education and graduate with a degree.

WORST OF OHIO STATE

1. Parking
2. Completely unpredictable weather
3. Occasional rioting
4. Crime
5. Minimal Greek scene
6. Panhandlers on High Street

Lowest Grades
Drug Safety: D+
Weather: C+
Greek Life: B-

Student Body

African American:	7%	Male Undergrads:	53%
Asian American:	5%	Female Undergrads:	47%
Hispanic:	3%	Living On Campus:	24%
International:	4%	Living Off Campus:	76%
Native American:	0%	Male Athletes:	3%
White:	78%	Female Athletes:	3%
Unknown:	3%	Fraternity Members:	6%
From Out-of-State:	18%	Sorority Members:	7%

Frequently Compared Schools:
Miami University
Ohio University
Penn State
University of Michigan

Students Speak Out On... EVERYTHING!

ACADEMICS

Q Study Options

"There are so many educational options at OSU. So if you decide to change your major it can be easily done and you won't have to transfer."

Q Working Towards a Goal

"I'm in the School of Allied Medical Professions, and only those who are accepted are allowed to be within the school. A lot of work is involved in order to pursue the professions within the school, since many plan on going onto Graduate School. The classes are smaller then the lecture halls and you get to work with professors one on one. We work right in the OSU medical center, so we have many options for jobs and hands on clinicals."

ATHLETICS

Q Can't Beat Ohio State Football

"Ohio State's varsity sports (especially football) are unmatched. The entire city of Columbus comes alive when the Buckeyes are at play. There is a feeling of community and unity that you just can't find anywhere else, especially when Carmen Ohio plays and you link arms with complete strangers to sing. Its just something you have to experience."

Q Sports in General

"Sports at Ohio State are definitely a huge part of student life. As a student, you are first and foremost a Buckeye. The school spirit is phenomenal!"

CAMPUS DINING

Q Vegeterian Friendly Options

"Great dining options with a wide variety of fresh food. I'm a vegeterian and there are many available options for me."

Q Dining Halls

"There are only a few cafeteria-type, because there are SO many up-to-date, cool, fresh, delicious options! You don't have to feel stuck in a routine. You can go somewhere different for like 2 weeks. The food never gets old."

CAMPUS HOUSING

Q Dorms Are Where You Meet People

"The dorms are defintely where you meet people your freshman and sophmore years. Become close with your neighbors and roomate(s). They will end up becoming some of your closest friends in college. Rooming assignments can be difficult, but rememeber to think positive. Rooming randomly is the best way to meet new people and expand your horizons."

Q Great Social Climate

"I stay at Morrison Tower and everyone is very friendly. There is a lot to do and everyone helps each other out."

GUYS & GIRLS

Q Incredible Variety

"Ohio State's size results in incredible diversity, there are students from all around the world at this school and tons of pretty people everywhere you look. If you're looking to meet people with similar interests then you must join a few of our student organizations, there are over 900 by the way, that cater to practically any interest. Meeting people is definitely not an issue here at Ohio State."

Q Interests

"Ohio State has many diverse interests and events to attract anyone. Everyone can find something to belong to."

HEALTH & SAFETY

Q Great Work

"There are Emergency "booths" scattered all over campus, where a student, if in danger, could press the emergency button and be immediately connected to the OSU police. Standing at one, you can always see another spot, which was a great move by the university."

LOOKING FOR MORE?

Check out our full-length guide to this school at collegeprowler.com/ohio-state-university/.

Ohio University

1 Park Place; Athens, OH 45701
(740) 593-1000; www.ohio.edu

THE BASICS:

Acceptance Rate: 82%
Yield: 35%
Setting: Town
Control: Public
Total Undergrads: 18,166
SAT Range: 1440–1790*
ACT Range: 21–26

Student-Faculty Ratio: 19:1
Retention Rate: 82%
Graduation Rate: 70%
Tuition: $17,937
Room & Board: $9,408
Avg. Aid Package: $7,738
Students With Aid: 81%

* of 2400

Academics	B	Greek Life	B-
Athletics	B-	Guys	A+
Campus Dining	B	Health & Safety	B-
Campus Housing	B-	Local Atmosphere	B+
Campus Strictness	B	Nightlife	A+
Computers	B	Off-Campus Dining	A
Diversity	C+	Off-Campus Housing	B
Drug Safety	C-	Parking	B-
Facilities	A-	Transportation	B+
Girls	A+	Weather	C+

CP's Student Author On...
OVERALL EXPERIENCE

The majority of OU students can never envision themselves going to any other school but Ohio University. Whether it's the unique atmosphere, great classes, people they've met, or a combination of several factors, Bobcats are passionate about their school and feel confident about the choice they made. Once they graduate, it's inevitable they will return more than once to recapture the feeling of strolling along Court Street and hanging out with great friends over a beer or game of pool.

Though students may gripe over Friday afternoon classes, strict resident assistants, or how they can't seem to get any work done because they live above a bar, students are still happy to be there and know that the good times will greatly outnumber the bad. It's safe to say that OU is an excellent choice because it doesn't just offer a first-rate education, but also provides students with the necessary life skills needed to survive out in the real world.... For the rest of this editorial, visit collegeprowler.com.

Students Speak Out On...
OVERALL EXPERIENCE

Q **Ohio University Is Simply Amazing**

"I love everything about Ohio University. The campus is beautiful, Athens is a diverse and interesting town, I always feel safe, there's never a shortage of things to do on the weekends, and professors are consistently helpful and knowledgable."

Q **I'm Still New**

"I have only been here for a week. So far it has been good. Staff and students all seem freindly."

Q **Good**

"The college lifestyle is great and so freeing. However it is easy to get side tracked from school because of social life. Yet studying is still important."

BEST OF OHIO UNIVERSITY

1. Court Street is the epitome of fun in Athens. It's the reason that the city gets its reputation as a transplanted Mardi Gras and why OU is known as a top party school.

Happy Students
82% of students return after their first year.

Proven Success
70% of students will complete their education and graduate with a degree.

WORST OF OHIO UNIVERSITY

1. Parking is without a doubt the worst thing at OU. You're better off driving some sort of tunneling machine than trying to find a spot sometimes.

Students Can't Wait to Get Out of Town
53% of students surveyed said that there's no way they would live here after graduation.

Student Body

African American:	5%	Male Undergrads:	51%
Asian American:	1%	Female Undergrads:	49%
Hispanic:	2%	Living On Campus:	44%
International:	3%	Living Off Campus:	56%
Native American:	0%	Male Athletes:	3%
White:	88%	Female Athletes:	3%
Unknown:	0%	Fraternity Members:	10%
From Out-of-State:	11%	Sorority Members:	14%

Frequently Compared Schools:

Miami University
Ohio State University
Penn State
University of Cincinnati

Students Speak Out On... EVERYTHING!

ACADEMICS

Q Academics at OU

"The program for my major at OU has been wonderful. The professors are very helpful and eager to get to know the students. The curriculum and facilities are excellent. I have also been very satisfied with the job opportunities. I was able to easily find a job con campus and I have been very satisfied with it"

Q Photojournalism Classes

"OU's photojournalism program is a wonderful program. The professors are knowledgable and professional and work in the field. They are helpful and create amazing classes for students to learn. The students are talented and helpful to one another."

ATHLETICS

Q Fan Support/School Spirit

"Our athletic team st Ohio University have a very strong fan base that includes students and the Athens community. There are usually many people supporting the teams at their games in all kinds of different weather. Also, the O-Zone has many students involved who attend almost all of the games."

Q Athletics at OU

"There is so much school spirit at OU! THe school really comes together to support its athletic teams. This was especially noticable this year when our basketball team want the farthest it has in decades in the NCAA tournament.All of the facilities are maintained very well, and there are plenty of opportunities to get students involved with supporting teams, and participating in club and intramural activities."

CAMPUS DINING

Q Adding New Things

"They are adding new dining halls and switching up the food options to keep students interested and happy."

Q Shively Is the Best

"Dining on campus is alright if you know where to go and at what times. Shively is the most crowded but by far has the best food and bets variety of options. You can get any type of entree you want here."

CAMPUS HOUSING

Q My Home at OU

"I am in a freshman only dorm that only offers quad style rooms. This has helped me make multiple new friends, and to learn how to coexist with other people. Most of the rooms on campus are spacious enough for everyone to have a little bit of their own space, but they aren't much bigger than that. The dorms are all close to dining halls and laundry services, and there is a building to go through so that you don't have to walk up the huge hills on campus."

Q Renovated Dorms Rule!

"I lived in a renovated dorm on campus and it was a wonderful place. We had sinks in our room and a shared bathroom for 20-ish girls. Rooms were large and had decent space."

GUYS & GIRLS

Q Diversity

"OU is a very diverse school. You have all different types of people. Everyone can find a group to fit into."

HEALTH & SAFETY

Q Safety at OU

"I have often taken advantage of the Safe Ride Program that the university police department offers. The campus is very safe, but as a freshman,I am still weary of walking across campus late at night."

LOOKING FOR MORE?

Check out our full-length guide to this school at collegeprowler.com/ohio-university/.

Ohio Wesleyan University

61 S. Sandusky St.; Delaware, OH 43015
(740) 368-2000; www.owu.edu

THE BASICS:

Acceptance Rate: 64%
Yield: 18%
Setting: Town
Control: Private Non-Profit
Total Undergrads: 1,895
SAT Range: 1040–1320*
ACT Range: 23–29

Student-Faculty Ratio: 11:1
Retention Rate: 81%
Graduation Rate: 63%
Tuition: $35,030
Room & Board: $8,808
Avg. Aid Package: $27,761
Students With Aid: 100%

* of 1600

Academics	B	Greek Life	A
Athletics	C+	Guys	B+
Campus Dining	B+	Health & Safety	B-
Campus Housing	B	Local Atmosphere	B-
Campus Strictness	C+	Nightlife	B
Computers	B	Off-Campus Dining	B+
Diversity	C-	Off-Campus Housing	D+
Drug Safety	C+	Parking	B+
Facilities	B+	Transportation	C-
Girls	B+	Weather	C+

CP's Student Author On... OVERALL EXPERIENCE

An Ohio Wesleyan student truly appreciates the opportunities that are given to them at this small liberal arts school in Delaware. There is something special about OWU that the rankings seem to overlook, and only the students experiencing it know what that is. An OWU student is given the advantage of being personally taught by a group of one of the greatest faculty in America, a group that is not concerned with research, but with instilling knowledge in the best way possible. In addition, the endless leadership opportunities on campus give OWU students another chance for growth and development as a person that will help them in their future endeavors. The students appreciate an Ohio Wesleyan education because it focuses on every aspect of character and knowledge and not just what is taught in the classroom. OWU students do not just learn about facts and equations; they learn how to think, and that is what sets them apart.... For the rest of this editorial, visit collegeprowler.com.

Students Speak Out On... OVERALL EXPERIENCE

Q Depends on How You Look at It

"A lot of students dislike owu because of the administration, which is sometimes warranted. However, the school is much more then bad reslife policies etc. The students and especially the professors make the school. Something almost any student here can agree on is how wonderful our professors are, they genuinely care about their students and are extremely helpful both in and outside of class (especially those that live in delaware)."

Q "It's not that I wish I were somewhere else, but I will say that Ohio Wesleyan was not my number-one choice. After not getting into my number-one choice, I was happy to come to OWU, but I cannot help but wonder 'what might have been.' Instead, I know I should be wondering, 'what still might be!'"

Q "Overall, I am very happy here, and yes, I'll admit that I have from time to time thought about what if I went to a large school or stayed in the East Coast. However, we all do that. The truth is, I am happy at school. I have been very happy with the last two years, and I look forward to the next two."

BEST OF OHIO WESLEYAN

1. Ridiculously high acceptance rate
2. Delaware is not a college town
3. Off-campus living policies
4. No off-campus food points
5. Sometimes excessively strict campus police

Happy Students
81% of students return after their first year.

Genders Equally Represented
A male-to-female ratio of 48/52 means there's a pretty even balance of students on campus.

WORST OF OHIO WESLEYAN

1. Ridiculously high acceptance rate
2. Delaware is not a college town
3. Off-campus living policies
4. No off-campus food points
5. Sometimes excessively strict campus police

Expensive
Tuition is a steep $35,030, one of the most expensive rates in the country.

Student Body

African American:	4%	Male Undergrads:	47%
Asian American:	2%	Female Undergrads:	53%
Hispanic:	1%	Living On Campus:	87%
International:	9%	Living Off Campus:	13%
Native American:	1%	Male Athletes:	34%
White:	81%	Female Athletes:	20%
Unknown:	2%	Fraternity Members:	39%
From Out-of-State:	50%	Sorority Members:	26%

Students Speak Out On... EVERYTHING!

ACADEMICS

Q Great Science Department

"The science department at Ohio Wesleyan is amazing. The professors are very approachable and helpful, and there are many opportunities for research. The curriculum is tough, but it prepares you well for graduate or professional school. The science department and the school in general seems to have a great reputation."

Q Ohio Wesleyan Professors

"The professors at OWU are very helpful and active in students' lives. They are always available and willing to help students, and they are very active in campus activities. Some professors even offer special activities/meetings to further promote their topics of interest and engage in discussions with students."

ATHLETICS

Q Not Sure

"i'm not in sports so i'm not sure, but i heard it's pretty good."

Q Sports Are Good

"there are a lot of student athletes. some of the teams arent that great, football is pretty bad but we have done very well in other sports like track and field, basketball and field hockey. most student athletes are very dedicated and teams seem to be close with eachother."

CAMPUS DINING

Q Greek Life

"Fraternity house has personal chef, food is plentiful, varied and I feel I have great options for snacks."

Q Not Bad

"There are options in almost every area of campus. The main dining area gets very crowded at lunch and it would be nice if it were a bit larger. There are many different options, and some days seem to be better than others with food choices. As a senior, I would say the food has improved since I've been here and will probably continue to do so."

Frequently Compared Schools:

College of Wooster
Denison University
Kenyon College
Oberlin College

CAMPUS HOUSING

Q

"All but two of the dorms are configured in a suite-style, where two to four people share one bathroom, depending on whether you're in a quad or a double. Singles are available but highly coveted with most of them going to students with senior status. If you're looking for quieter dorm, you should consider Welch Hall, which is substance-free and is also the honors dorm."

Q

"The dorms really range from pretty nice to pretty decrepit. Welch, the honors dorm, has the cleanest (and quietest) halls and rooms. Smith offers typical quads and has always been a personal favorite because of the partitioned rooms within the quads."

GUYS & GIRLS

Q Unique

"For being such a small school we have a pretty diverse campus with a lot of truly interesting people, guys and girls."

Q Diverse

"lots of different people on campus with different looks, styles interests and backgrounds."

HEALTH & SAFETY

Q Is It Really the Small Town Charm?

"I personally have never run into anything bad, but there have been stories... I figured it would be a relatively safe place because of the small town feel, but it is still a college campus and things can happen. I feel pretty safe here, but you should have a good head on your shoulders and know to contact public safety so you do not walk around alone at night."

Q

"What I can say personally is that it is really up to you to be in good company and in good hands, especially during party nights. There have been isolated incidents regarding security of girls on campus, but to the best of my knowledge, they have been kept under control."

LOOKING FOR MORE?

Check out our full-length guide to this school at collegeprowler.com/ohio-wesleyan-university/.

Old Dominion University

5115 Hampton Blvd.; Norfolk, VA 23529
(757) 683-3000; www.odu.edu

THE BASICS:

Acceptance Rate: 72%	Student-Faculty Ratio: 21:1
Yield: 39%	Retention Rate: 80%
Setting: Mid-sized city	Graduation Rate: 49%
Control: Public	Tuition: $15,862
Total Undergrads: 18,260	Room & Board: $7,634
SAT Range: 1430–1710*	Avg. Aid Package: $7,597
ACT Range: 18–23	Students With Aid: 71%

of 2400

Academics	B-	Greek Life	B-
Athletics	B-	Guys	A-
Campus Dining	B+	Health & Safety	C+
Campus Housing	B	Local Atmosphere	B
Campus Strictness	B	Nightlife	B+
Computers	C+	Off-Campus Dining	B-
Diversity	B-	Off-Campus Housing	B-
Drug Safety	C+	Parking	B
Facilities	B+	Transportation	B
Girls	B	Weather	B

CP's Student Author On...
OVERALL EXPERIENCE

Students gripe about workload and professors just like at any other university; they may also feel distant from their surroundings because they are in eternal flux, but in the end, graduates are more than content with the choices they've made. Old Dominion provides its students with so many opportunities to explore the world with study abroad programs, internship opportunities, and hands-on job experience that it is almost impossible for a student to fail in anything that they do—be it academic, athletic, or social. Old Dominion can simply be an institution for education, but most of the student body does not treat it as that.

Overall, there are a lot of changes going on at Old Dominion University. The school is currently transitioning from a commuter school to a residential campus, meaning there is constant construction and landscape work. At the same time, the school is searching for a new president to replace the old one, Roseann Runte. That being said, ODU is an exciting school to attend. There is always something going on somewhere, and it is a range of diverse activities.... For the rest of this editorial, visit collegeprowler.com.

Students Speak Out On...
OVERALL EXPERIENCE

Q Loving ODU
"I love going to ODU so far. I feel like college is easier than high school. I like that the school always has activities that students can attend.For example they have shut-ins with themes, pep rallies, homecoming events. It is just cool."

Q My Favorite Experiences
"My favorite part of college is definitely marching band. It allowed me to make lots of friends while doing something I enjoy."

Q I Like It So Far.
"I am a new transfer student, only been at the school for 6 months. But so far I have enjoyed the campus and the people."

Q Grown on Me
"Old Dominion University isn't exactly a prestigious school, but they do have good programs - the thing that I value above all, however - the people here. As long as you can find good people, it doesn't matter where you go - and that's what I've found here."

BEST OF OLD DOMINION

1. Amiability of professors
2. Clean campus
3. Proximity to the beach
4. Wi-fi access in nearly all buildings
5. Great academic programs
6. Good chance of finding an internship

Happy Students
80% of students return after their first year.

Knowledgeable Professors
90% of students surveyed rated the general knowledge of professors as above average.

WORST OF OLD DOMINION

1. It's constantly being worked on (construction)
2. Trying to find a parking space and never succeeding
3. Getting parking tickets for absolutely no reason at all
4. Having to drive mostly everywhere

Lowest Grades
Drug Safety: C+
Computers: C+
Health & Safety: C+

Student Body

African American:	23%	Male Undergrads:	45%
Asian American:	5%	Female Undergrads:	56%
Hispanic:	4%	Living On Campus:	29%
International:	2%	Living Off Campus:	71%
Native American:	1%	Male Athletes:	4%
White:	61%	Female Athletes:	3%
Unknown:	5%	Fraternity Members:	4%
From Out-of-State:	8%	Sorority Members:	3%

Students Speak Out On...
EVERYTHING!

ACACEMICS

Q Academics at ODU
"Old Dominion University is beautiful inside and outside. The teachers are friendly yet challenging."

Q Still Not Sure What I Want My Career to Be
"I've only completed one year, but it has been good so far. The advisors are very helpful in aiding me to pick my classes. The workload is hefty, but it's not overwhelming."

Q Exercise Science
"I'm in the Education College, and I enjoy the program. I feel like the workload is just right, it preparing up for the realworld."

ATHLETICS

Q Talent
"Our sports teams are a group of very talented individuals."

Q I Bleed Blue and Silver
"Fall 2009 marks the comeback of Monarch football at Old Dominion University. After nearly 70 years with no football team, they have built a state of the art stadium and gym. The fan support for the season was exceptional. Student tickets were hard to come by and the stadium was always packed. Winning 9 games and losing only 2 set the ODU football team apart from other start up teams and left other schools talking."

CAMPUS DINING

Q The Cafe
"They always have a lot to choose from. And, it is always good and the people who work there are seem to enjoy what they do. They are very polite and helpful to all of the students."

Q Variety
"There are so many options when it comes to dining at ODU. I don't know about anyone else, but I, for one, hate eating the same food everyday. I like to mix it up. If I feel like eating the equivalence of home cooking, then I would go to 1201, but if I'm in the mood for Chinese, then I just order in."

Frequently Compared Schools:
James Madison University
University of Virginia
Virginia Commonwealth University
Virginia Tech

CAMPUS HOUSING

Q Housing Is Awesome
"The dorms at Old Dominion are amazing. It is an awesome Social area where many friends can be met. Everyone works together to study and everyone are friends with each other. Great environment."

Q Quad Dorms Are Wonderful
"I really like the Quad dorms at ODU. My freshman year I stayed in a brand new freshman only dorm, and my sophomore year I stayed in a brand new upperclassmen dorm. They're very clean and the staff are extremely concerned about safety."

GUYS & GIRLS

Q Great Group of People
"The people are great and have wonderful personalities. It is very diverse and there is always a group that you will fit into."

Q Different
"The guys and girls at ODU are all different. You have people from all walks of life so it's a nice change from what one may be used to."

HEALTH & SAFETY

Q Exercise Science
"I'm in the Education College, and I enjoy the program. I feel like the workload is just right, it preparing up for the realworld."

Q Feels Safe to Be Here
"I feel safe being at ODU. Every once in a while I do get e-mails about safety incidents, about students/nonstudents getting robbed on and off campus, but that occurs normally in the late night/early morning... between 11:00 p.m. and 5:00 a.m. I think you'll be perfectly fine if you're inside before then. Make smart decisions and you'll be good. Always lock your doors, that's just common sense."

LOOKING FOR MORE?
Check out our full-length guide to this school at collegeprowler.com/old-dominion-university/.

Oral Roberts University

7777 S. Lewis Ave.; Tulsa, OK 74171
(918) 495-6161; oru.edu

THE BASICS:

Acceptance Rate: 65%
Yield: 49%
Setting: Large city
Control: Private Non-Profit
Total Undergrads: 2,595
SAT Range: 940–1210*
ACT Range: 20–25

Student-Faculty Ratio: 14:1
Retention Rate: 75%
Graduation Rate: 54%
Tuition: $19,106
Room & Board: $7,916
Avg. Aid Package: $18,724
Students With Aid: 96%

of 1600

Academics	B-	Greek Life	N/A
Athletics	B-	Guys	A+
Campus Dining	B-	Health & Safety	A+
Campus Housing	A-	Local Atmosphere	B
Campus Strictness	C	Nightlife	B
Computers	B-	Off-Campus Dining	A
Diversity	B+	Off-Campus Housing	B
Drug Safety	A+	Parking	A+
Facilities	B-	Transportation	B+
Girls	A+	Weather	B

CP's Student Author On...
OVERALL EXPERIENCE

Nearly everyone at ORU said that if they had to make their college decision all over again, they would still choose this university. Students give high marks to the strong Christian community here, and say that the professors and students are approachable, kind, and helpful. Another positive is the size of the school—it's easy enough to get personal attention from the teachers, but the school is still large enough that you'll regularly be able to meet lots of new, unique people.

Overall, Oral Roberts University is a great place for anyone who has a strong desire to become spiritually awake, intellectually alert, physically disciplined, professionally competent, and socially adept!

Students Speak Out On...
OVERALL EXPERIENCE

Q ORU Is Great!

"I love being at ORU. I am so glad I chose to come here. The overall experience is great. The best part about the campus is the spiritual atmosphere."

Q A Good Balance

"Overall, this university has a very positive uplifting atmosphere. At times it can be a little annoying, but for the most part it's fairly nice."

Q ORU=Awesome

"ORU is the greatest place on earth. I love it here. If you let your social life rule your academic life, then it could be trouble. You have to study here; it isn't all fun. I had a rough time before I came here. Six colleges later, I ended up at Oral Roberts University, where my heart, and God told me to go."

Q Private Schooling

"I love going to a private school, because we get chapel and the student to teacher ratio is very low which I feel is important."

BEST OF ORAL ROBERTS

1. The kindness displayed by nearly everybody involved with ORU
2. Christian community
3. Student-teacher relationships
4. Community outreach
5. Beautiful campus

Easy Financial Aid Process
53% of students surveyed told us that the financial aid process went smoothly and they received the financial aid they needed.

WORST OF ORAL ROBERTS

1. All the rules
2. Curfew
3. Dress code
4. Lack of dining options
5. No coed dorms
6. Some buildings are old.
7. Visitation hours
8. Weather

Life is NOT a Party
85% of students surveyed said it's almost impossible to find a good party.

Student Body

African American:	17%	Male Undergrads:	43%
Asian American:	2%	Female Undergrads:	57%
Hispanic:	6%	Living On Campus:	75%
International:	8%	Living Off Campus:	25%
Native American:	3%	Male Athletes:	15%
White:	57%	Female Athletes:	8%
Unknown:	9%	Fraternity Members:	0%
From Out-of-State:	69%	Sorority Members:	0%

Frequently Compared Schools:

Clemson University
Liberty University
Oklahoma State University
University of Oklahoma

Students Speak Out On...
EVERYTHING!

ACADEMICS

Q Never better

"The courses offered at ORU are great! They are always trying to help the students do the best and not just to get a name for themselves. The teachers go above and beyond to get people to grow in their field."

Q Something for Everyone

"ORU offers a variety of studies, every field is top notch, and the professors are incredible."

Q New Testament

"My major is very specific and there are only a few students that have the same one. Our program is a very valuable because our teachers are varied. Their area of expertise is specific. They have different denominations, which gives us diversity."

ATHLETICS

Q Basketball is the best

"Basketball is amazing. All other sports are pretty good."

Q Awesome!

"Oral Roberts athletics are great."

Q Great Enviorment

"its a great place to go to school at really friendly people. a true college experience for modern day christians"

CAMPUS DINING

Q Oral Roberts Food

"There is a huge variety of food. You can basically get anything you want, anytime you want. It's great!"

Q Food Is... Interesting at Times

"Saga isn't always the best, but there's always Chick-fil-A."

Q Variety of Dining

"The campus provides a variety of food, flexible meal plans, and several dining options both on and off campus. However, the Saga dining hall and late night stop by Chick-Fil-A can get old sometimes but one of the nearby restaurants can satisfy your desire for something different."

CAMPUS HOUSING

Q Small but Cozy

"There are plenty of different choices of dorms that you can choose from no matter your grade level. There are basic dorms where you have a roommate. You can also choose to live in the basic dorms, but pay extra to have your own room. There are larger rooms, and rooms with their own bathrooms, all of which you have to pay extra for. But whatever you're used to living with, ORU has something for you."

Q Convenience

"Oral Roberts University is in a convenient location. It is not too close to the busy city but it is close enough to everything you may need including Walmart, a restaurante strip, jobs, churches, and parks."

GUYS & GIRLS

Q Well Rounded

"The ORU student body encompasses a persona of excellence and spiritual and physical awareness."

Q Good Picks

"There are many guys and girls available, and it may even seem like people come here to find a future mate. There are many good picks for those who are searching."

HEALTH & SAFETY

Q My Campus Safety

"Security is everywhere all the time. I can never escape from them!"

Q Clean and Safe

"I've never felt secure living anywhere as much as I do at Oral Roberts University. It is a smaller campus but everything is well watched even during non-school hours. Everyone is very understanding and always there to help no matter what the problem is."

LOOKING FOR MORE?

Check out our full-length guide to this school at collegeprowler.com/oral-roberts-university/.

Pace University

1 Pace Plaza; New York, NY 10038
(212) 346-1200; www.pace.edu

THE BASICS:

Acceptance Rate: 75%	**Student-Faculty Ratio:** 15:1
Yield: 24%	**Retention Rate:** 77%
Setting: Large city	**Graduation Rate:** 55%
Control: Private Non-Profit	**Tuition:** $32,816
Total Undergrads: 7,800	**Room & Board:** $11,560
SAT Range: 980–1170*	**Avg. Aid Package:** $28,055
ACT Range: 21–26	**Students With Aid:** 98%

* of 1600

Academics	B-	Greek Life	B
Athletics	D+	Guys	B+
Campus Dining	B-	Health & Safety	C+
Campus Housing	B-	Local Atmosphere	A-
Campus Strictness	C+	Nightlife	A-
Computers	B	Off-Campus Dining	B+
Diversity	B+	Off-Campus Housing	B
Drug Safety	C-	Parking	B-
Facilities	C-	Transportation	B+
Girls	C+	Weather	C+

CP's Student Author On... OVERALL EXPERIENCE

For most students, they either love or hate Pace University. The people who love Pace probably like it for its generous financial aid package, location, and co-op opportunities. The students who would love to torch the establishment to the ground probably dislike it for its lack of financial support and crummy services. A lot of students have a strong dislike for the food and the Office of Student Aid (OSA). This office has misplaced many student files, causing many time delays for students to register for classes. The academic staff is very encouraging, which makes classes bearable.

Some students feel that the money they are paying to enroll should result in better and more efficient services that make the process of earning an education easier. While there are a good amount of wonderful people, there are just as many that are petty, acting like they still belong in high school. They can't seem to tolerate opinions other than their own. A few years ago, people obsessed over the now-defunct Web site called Juicy Campus, which was a virtual place where people established hurtful rumors about other students.... For the rest of this editorial, visit collegeprowler.com.

Students Speak Out On... OVERALL EXPERIENCE

Q Pace
"I absolutely love my school. i am a nursing student so there are so many great resources to help us out and we are truly like a family. I'm so happy i am apart of the Pace community and the class of 2011. =)"

Q Pace
"The only reason I chose this school was because they gave me the most financial help, but I wouldn't have chosen to stay here if it sucked. I like it a lot so far."

Q The End Result
"I love the acting/performing profs but opportunities are somewhat limited at Pace due to the economic duress"

Q Overall Experience
"some excellent unique instructors and classes; some were horrific--change grading policies, etc."

BEST OF PACE

1. Location
2. Easy access to alcohol
3. Co-op opportunities
4. Friendliness
5. Business school
6. Teachers
7. Liberalness
8. Free stuff!

Big Dorms
69% of students surveyed felt that dorms were more spacious than average.

Help to Succeed
The school has academic and career counseling available to help you when you need it.

WORST OF PACE

1. Excessive drinkers
2. The fitness center
3. The food
4. The guidos
5. Maria's Tower
6. The pollution
7. The poorly dressed
8. The RAs

Expensive
Tuition is a steep $32,816, one of the most expensive rates in the country.

Expensive to Just Get By
67% of students surveyed felt that the amount it costs to live while at school was worse than average.

Student Body

African American:	10%	Male Undergrads:	41%
Asian American:	8%	Female Undergrads:	59%
Hispanic:	11%	Living On Campus:	45%
International:	8%	Living Off Campus:	55%
Native American:	0%	Male Athletes:	9%
White:	41%	Female Athletes:	3%
Unknown:	22%	Fraternity Members:	5%
From Out-of-State:	44%	Sorority Members:	5%

Frequently Compared Schools:
Fordham University
Hofstra University
New York University
St. John's University

Students Speak Out On...
EVERYTHING!

ACADEMICS

Major
"I think the Academics at Pace all depends on your major. Some teacher's are terrible and others are great. The workload is manageable as long as you do all your work. My one advice is to take one easy class per semester."

Good Once You Enter Your Major
"When I was taking my core classes I was extremely upset about the professors. No other words to describe them besides HORRIBLE. For how much tuition is, some of the teachers were just terrible. Once i got into my major though, it improved significantly. The registration process is stressful, be prepared to have back-up courses because the classes fill up extremely fast."

ATHLETICS

Not an Athlete, Not Aware
"Unless you are an athlete, the only event that students go to is homecoming. other sporting events seem to be lost in the shuffle of campus life."

Not Really
"Athletics aren't really happening much at the NYC campus. Once in a while, the basketball team from the Pleasantville campus will come to the city for a game or two, and maybe the girls volleyball team. Other than that, its really nothing. I mean there is a gym where you can play b-ball but if its athletics your looking for, Pace University in NYC is not for you!"

What Athletics?
"The campus that I attend (NYC Campus) has very little to do in the athletic department. However, I cannot speak for the Pleasantville Campus, for it has all of the athletics. At the NYC Campus I would group the gym/athletics in with that of a high school P.E Class."

CAMPUS DINING

Price Versus Taste.
"There are three different areas that sell food at my campus, one is a large cafeteria and the others are small cafes. The food is adequate but nothing in a four star restaurant. But there is a large variety of different options, however the price is rather upsetting for those of us with a small meal plan."

Mixed Feelings
"The food is okay. Expect to gain a lot of weight during your first semester. Most of the options include some sort of fried food which is not very healthy. Food also doesn't make you feel very good. Most of it doesn't taste too bad, good variety and packaged food options."

CAMPUS HOUSING

Campus Life in the Big Apple
"For freshman year, it is best to live in Maria's tower. Here is where the most socializing goes and where lasting friendships are made. The building is quite old, however the rest of Pace's housing facilities are all fairly new and offer great space and amenities."

GUYS & GIRLS

Its a Melting Pot
"The girls at Pace come from different walks of life, parts of the country and other countries at well. Hipsters, club-rats, geeks, theater kids we have them all. Overall given the girl to guy ratio and the general quality of the women here I would rate them high."

HEALTH & SAFETY

Safe
"Pace is sooo safe nothing will happen to you, the school is closed and is only one building there are only 3 Entrances and you wont get it with out you pace id.also my freshman year i had a dorm and never locked the door and nothing happened."

Security
"I've never felt unsafe at Pace University. The security is amazing here."

LOOKING FOR MORE?
Check out our full-length guide to this school at collegeprowler.com/pace-university/.

Penn State

201 Old Main; University Park, PA 16802
(814) 865-4700; www.psu.edu

THE BASICS:

Acceptance Rate: 51%	**Student-Faculty Ratio:** 17:1
Yield: 36%	**Retention Rate:** 93%
Setting: Small city	**Graduation Rate:** 85%
Control: Public	**Tuition:** $25,946
Total Undergrads: 37,988	**Room & Board:** $8,820
SAT Range: 1100–1300*	**Avg. Aid Package:** $9,698
ACT Range: 24–29	**Students With Aid:** 70%

* of 1600

Academics	B+	Greek Life	B-
Athletics	A	Guys	A+
Campus Dining	A-	Health & Safety	B+
Campus Housing	B	Local Atmosphere	B
Campus Strictness	B	Nightlife	A
Computers	B+	Off-Campus Dining	B+
Diversity	C+	Off-Campus Housing	B
Drug Safety	C-	Parking	C+
Facilities	A-	Transportation	A+
Girls	A	Weather	C

CP's Student Author On...
OVERALL EXPERIENCE

Despite common reservations about the location and climate, most Penn State students are fiercely loyal to their alma mater. Penn State boasts one of the largest alumni populations in the United States; graduates are proud of their degrees, and employers recognize the University's name immediately. Although the campus is located in a very rural area, school is technologically up-to-date and on the cutting-edge of current research.

Aside from academics, PSU is also known for its social scene, especially in relation to sports and parties. Nittany Lion football—home of the 2008 Big Ten Champions—is a national draw and a point of pride for both the University and the town of State College. For anyone interested in playing or watching varsity sports, PSU is a top choice. Penn State has also been ranked highly by many polls and "party school" surveys as one of the top party schools in the nation. While it certainly isn't the wildest town, these rankings are definitely accurate.... For the rest of this editorial, visit collegeprowler.com.

Students Speak Out On...
OVERALL EXPERIENCE

Q The Absolute Perfect College Experience

"Penn State is your stereotypical college experience. It is everything that most people think that college will be. The social scene is amazing, academics are great, and if youre the kind of student who likes to work hard AND play hard too, this is your school. From the moment I visit campus, I knew I would go to PSU. It really says something when you want summer and holiday's to end so that you can go to back to school. They don't call it the happiest valley on earth for nothing."

Q Penn State

"Penn State is by far the perfect college experience. It has everything you could want in a school. Its in a great location that is based around the college. It has every major you could ever want. There are thousands of new people to meet and always something going on. I am never bored. The professors are great too! Although you may have some huge classes, you get your share of small size classes where professors get to know you! I couldn't imagine going anywhere else!"

BEST OF PENN STATE

1. Academics balanced with partying
2. Enormous school spirit
3. Penn State football: "The Greatest Show in College Sports" – Sports Illustrated
4. The beautiful central Pennsylvania surroundings

Happy Students
93% of students return after their first year.

Proven Success
85% of students will complete their education and graduate with a degree.

WORST OF PENN STATE

1. Isolated rural location
2. Sparse, expensive, and difficult parking
3. Frigid winters
4. Lack of diversity
5. Tough to develop relationship with teachers

Expensive
Tuition is a steep $25,946, one of the most expensive rates in the country.

Student Body

African American:	4%	Male Undergrads:	55%
Asian American:	6%	Female Undergrads:	45%
Hispanic:	4%	Living On Campus:	37%
International:	4%	Living Off Campus:	63%
Native American:	0%	Male Athletes:	2%
White:	78%	Female Athletes:	2%
Unknown:	5%	Fraternity Members:	13%
From Out-of-State:	34%	Sorority Members:	11%

Students Speak Out On... EVERYTHING!

ACADEMICS

Q You Earn Your Degree Here

"The classes here are hard. The teachers will help you learn but you have to do your share. This is what makes a Penn State degree valuable to employers because they know that you really worked hard to get your degree."

Q Friendly

"Becoming an adult student was a hard decision but now that I'm there I love it. The staff is extremely helpful and the students are great."

ATHLETICS

Q Never a Dull Moment

"Penn State clearly has one of the best athletic departments in the country. Fans are abundant and football game days are a can't miss."

Q School Spirit Is #1

"If there is one thing that Penn State can do more than any other school, its this - How to throw a party for the athletic teams! Between our 3-time consecutive NCAA Championship Women's Volleyball team and our White Out crowd supported Nittany Lion Football team, we have school spirit above the rest! IM sports are also incredibly popular, including a full tournament bracket for certain sports!"

CAMPUS DINING

Q Simply Exquisite, Highly Recommend

"There is a huge variety, food is great quality, excellent service, convenient and accesible locations and very well affordable with the campus meal plan. The planners of Penn State food services are brilliant."

Q South Halls

"In South Halls you can have stir-fry, Chinese, everything imaginable for breakfast, made-to-order subs! Not to mention a salad bar, burgers and fries and other occasional specialties!!"

Frequently Compared Schools:

University of Delaware
University of Maryland
University of Michigan
University of Pittsburgh

CAMPUS HOUSING

Q Well, What Is There to Say...

"I'm not quite sure I understood the qualifications for this award, I am not attending Penn state, i would like to attened Penn State. I's love to imagine that the dorms at Penn state will be amazing."

Q Living on Campus

"Living on campus has a great advantage. Your near so many facilities like the library and the computer labs. If you do not feel like walking the bus rout is right outside the buildings. If your ever afraid of walking alone at night there is campus security that will escort you to your destination."

GUYS & GIRLS

Q Penn State Students

"You can find many different types of students at Penn State. Although there is an extremely large variety of race and ethnicity of the students, everyone is very helpful and kind."

Q Many Options

"There are so many people at Penn State no matter what you are looking for you will find it!"

HEALTH & SAFETY

Q Campus Is Nice and Safe.

"Abington campus is pretty safe place. "No Place for Hate" campus!"

Q Always Safe

"I have never felt unsafe and have even frequently wandered around the campus at 4 a.m.or later. Blue lights on campus are abundant and State College was even named one of the safest cities. Many people i know don't even lock their doors and i personally never locked my dorm room door."

LOOKING FOR MORE?

Check out our full-length guide to this school at collegeprowler.com/penn-state/.

Penn State Altoona

3000 Ivyside Park; Altoona, PA 16601
(814) 949-5000; www.aa.psu.edu

THE BASICS:

Acceptance Rate: 75%	**Student-Faculty Ratio:** 17:1
Yield: 32%	**Retention Rate:** 85%
Setting: Small city	**Graduation Rate:** 64%
Control: Public	**Tuition:** $19,078
Total Undergrads: 4,013	**Room & Board:** $8,820
SAT Range: 1350–1650*	**Avg. Aid Package:** $8,735
ACT Range: 20–23	**Students With Aid:** 80%

* of 2400

This School Isn't Graded Yet!

College Prowler grades are calculated using tons of criteria, including survey responses that come from students at this school.

Unfortunately, we haven't gathered enough student surveys yet for this school to be able to calculate the grades for each section. Stay tuned to *CollegeProwler.com* for grade updates and more!

CP's Student Author On...
OVERALL EXPERIENCE

The overall experience at Penn State Altoona is a great one for most, and many say that the campus has exceeded their expectations. The smaller campus is great—and if you're concerned about a smaller campus equaling a small-minded student body, don't be. The Penn State Altoona campus is a perfect balance of size and personality, and the atmosphere allows for people to get to know one another in a number of situations. This is a place where friendships bloom and flourish to their fullest extent, and are then kept up long after graduation.

The professors at Penn State Altoona are all very open about their research, and each one is excited to be teaching. All the professors are real intellectuals, and they have such an abundance of knowledge in their field, as well as many other topics. And they are helpful to all students, regardless of whether you know them well or are taking one class with them. At college, students learn the most from the people who assign the textbooks, not the actual textbooks themselves (although some professors at Penn State Altoona write their own textbooks), and this University is no different.

Students Speak Out On...
OVERALL EXPERIENCE

Q Why I Would Pick Altoona Again.

"The campus here is small, yet big enough. Your professors know who you are and are fairly easy to talk to and see in person. They respond quickly to e-mails and are helpful as well as just about all the staff on campus. You seem to be able to always find what ya need, if you go to the wrong place you are directed the right way. Also the campus is safe and fun to be on. It's easy to get around. You get the full college experience."

Q Perfect Balance of Size and Personality

"Penn State Altoona is a great place with awesome professors who actually care about their students. It's a smaller campus that allows you to be as involved as you want. It's the perfect place to create lasting friendships and to receive a stellar Penn State education!"

BEST OF PENN STATE ALTOONA

1. Being able to take in the beauty of nature while studying
2. Cheaper than private school
3. Friendly professors
4. Intimate atmosphere
5. Knowledgeable teachers

Happy Students
85% of students return after their first year.

Genders Equally Represented
A male-to-female ratio of 53/47 means there's a pretty even balance of students on campus.

WORST OF PENN STATE ALTOONA

1. No late-night food options
2. No late-night activities
3. Campus dining gets repetitive.
4. Dry campus
5. Lack of nightlife, especially for underage students

Don't Move Off Campus
Average off-campus housing is a steep $10,242.

Student Body

African American:	7%	Male Undergrads:	50%
Asian American:	2%	Female Undergrads:	50%
Hispanic:	3%	Living On Campus:	22%
International:	1%	Living Off Campus:	78%
Native American:	0%	Male Athletes:	6%
White:	83%	Female Athletes:	5%
Unknown:	4%	Fraternity Members:	2%
From Out-of-State:	21%	Sorority Members:	4%

Students Speak Out On...
EVERYTHING!

ACADEMICS

Q It's a Team Effort

"As a whole, everyone works hard to see you succeed. And that's rare."

Q Intimate Classes

"I like the classes because the teachers really take the time for each student. They make it easy for students to contact them with office hours, phone numbers, and e-mail. The classes are intimate and the teachers hold a lot of group discussions."

Q Criminls Justice

"good field, enhance your learning abilities in law enforcement only if you are interested criminal law. professors helps a lot and makes it easy to help when ever needed."

ATHLETICS

Q Athletes

"The athletes at Penn State are cool. They hang out together and you will occasionally see them at parties, but they are all friendly. I am friends with a few, and they are really nice guys and girls."

Q Penn State Sports Rock

"Sports at Altoona is a very serious subject. Athletes are respected and the enthusiasm is huge. We're close enough to University Park, so we have the best of both worlds. Facilities are top of the line and the fans are very supportive."

Q Poor Fans

"Due to the popularity and our proximity to the University Park campus, Altoona's sports are very much over looked. There is not very much fan support for the students on campus."

CAMPUS DINING

Q Food Is Okay but Too Expensive

"There is a variety but the food is expensive. There is only one dining hall on campus. Sheetz is down the street, as well as an Indian restaurant and a Chinese restaurant."

Q Port

"It's alright for the first few weeks. Then it's repetitive and you turn to fast food"

CAMPUS HOUSING

Q Dorms

"There are 4 dorms which are all close to classrooms and even closer to the dining hall. Cedar is the newest, hotel like. Spruce is also good. Oak and Maple are for freshmen, Oak is older but the social situation is unlike any other dorm."

Q Dorms

"Oak sucks. Maple is pretty good. Spruce and cedar are for upperclassmen and are pretty nice but no one socializes in those"

GUYS & GIRLS

Q Guys and Girls

"There is a wide variety of people at PSA. You have your popular kids, arts kids, goth kids, smart kids. Just like in high school. If you are very social you will make some friends but everyone usually goes to PSA with their friends from high school."

Q Everything!

"Pretty much any walks of life can be found at Penn State Altoona, and most are extremely friendly."

HEALTH & SAFETY

Q Campus Security

"I feel totally safe on campus. There are campus police available and patrolling the campus 24 hours a day!"

Q Very Safe

"The campus is usually very populated. Police patrol all day and there are emergency phones located throughout campus. Campus is bare at night, but still police patrol campus. Police is almost a nuisance."

Pepperdine University

24255 Pacific Coast Highway; Malibu, CA 90263
(310) 506-4000; www.pepperdine.edu

THE BASICS:

Acceptance Rate: 34%
Yield: 33%
Setting: Suburban
Control: Private Non-Profit
Total Undergrads: 3,440
SAT Range: 1660–2010*
ACT Range: 24–29

Student-Faculty Ratio: 13:1
Retention Rate: 90%
Graduation Rate: 81%
Tuition: $37,850
Room & Board: $10,900
Avg. Aid Package: $32,908
Students With Aid: 74%

* of 2400

Academics	B	Greek Life	B+
Athletics	B-	Guys	A
Campus Dining	B-	Health & Safety	B+
Campus Housing	B+	Local Atmosphere	B
Campus Strictness	D	Nightlife	B
Computers	B+	Off-Campus Dining	B
Diversity	B+	Off-Campus Housing	C-
Drug Safety	B+	Parking	B+
Facilities	A-	Transportation	C-
Girls	A+	Weather	A+

CP's Student Author On...
OVERALL EXPERIENCE

Most Pepperdine students are happy with the college they picked, their minor critiques of particulars giving way to an overall appreciation of the experience and benefits Pepperdine has granted them that no other school could. Students who don't gush forth wholehearted and unwavering words of love usually cite the school's size and social climate as the source of whatever dissatisfactions they may have. When people decide to transfer from Pepperdine, it isn't because of the lack of dining halls and parking availability, or some qualms they have about student housing; it's because of the other Pepperdine students and the community environment they create. For example, some religious students are dismayed to discover that many don't share their Christian enthusiasm. Others, in contrast, find the Christian atmosphere to be overwhelming.

Many students complain that the high schools they attended were larger and less strict than Pepperdine, with more to do on the weekends, while others with similar high school experiences find Pepperdine a welcome respite.... For the rest of this editorial, visit collegeprowler.com.

Students Speak Out On...
OVERALL EXPERIENCE

Q Love Every Minute of It
"Pepperdine has been the perfect fit for me. The community here and the people who surround you are absolutely amazing and it's great to have a solid group of friends who have their heads in the right place. The school is conducive to building strong relationships and academics, but also just enjoying life in the beauty of Malibu."

Q Greatest Place on Earth
"This is the most beautiful place on the planet. I love it here and am definitely cannot see myself anywhere else. Living in Malibu is expensive, but totally worth it. The atmosphere is unbeatable. The study abroad programs are DEFINITELY a must -- you won't find better ones anywhere else. There's so much to do and see nearby and the people are the greatest."

Q It's Been Okay.
"There are lots of GE's and lots of events to attend."

Q "It's an amazing place, but it feels like a bubble most of the time."

BEST OF PEPPERDINE

1. The view
2. International programs
3. Friendly community
4. Location
5. Religious atmosphere
6. Attractive people
7. Great Books program
8. The dorms

Happy Students
90% of students return after their first year.

Proven Success
81% of students will complete their education and graduate with a degree.

WORST OF PEPPERDINE

1. Astronomical Malibu living expenses
2. Overly strict Ras
3. Monotonous and expensive nightlife
4. Lack of parking
5. Stairs, stairs, and more stairs

Expensive
Tuition is a steep $37,850, one of the most expensive rates in the country.

Expensive Dorms
Living on campus doesn't come cheap, with an average housing price tag of $8,380.

Student Body

African American:	7%	Male Undergrads:	46%
Asian American:	9%	Female Undergrads:	54%
Hispanic:	10%	Living On Campus:	67%
International:	6%	Living Off Campus:	33%
Native American:	1%	Male Athletes:	9%
White:	59%	Female Athletes:	9%
Unknown:	8%	Fraternity Members:	18%
From Out-of-State:	48%	Sorority Members:	33%

Frequently Compared Schools:

Loyola Marymount University
Santa Clara University
University of San Diego
University of Southern California

Students Speak Out On... EVERYTHING!

ACADEMICS

Q "I found most teachers to be easily accessible and more than willing to help you with the class and its related material—except for the general education classes with hundreds of people in them. Teachers in these classes seemed annoyed with student questions, and they'd shun their TAs."

Q "Some of the English teachers are wackos (which goes along with the major), but most of them really want you to succeed and do well, and with the small class sizes, they have the ability to give one-on-one help. I even had a professor who would cry while reading Shakespeare. Religion classes were not interesting—ever. They are, however, required."

Q "Most of the teachers have their quirks, and some are downright quirky. All take a sincere interest in their students' learning."

ATHLETICS

Q Decent

"Sports are good at Pepperdine but for a division 1 school they aren't that great. The school spirit lacks a little because we don't have a football team and the basketball team isn't that great. Volleyball is awesome though and fun to watch!"

Q Sports Are Decent

"The athletics at Pepperdine are not as competitive and big as I wished them to be. But when there is a home game, there are good amount of fans. There are 2 gyms. One gym is big and nicely done but its only available for Division 1 athletes at fixed time. The second one is for all students but it's a small gym and sometimes, it gets crowded."

CAMPUS DINING

Q Dining

"The food could be better. It's pretty expensive for what it is and the portions are very small."

Q Good

"Its great food but pretty expensive if you want to eat there for every meal"

CAMPUS HOUSING

Q Palatial Dorms

"After living off campus post-graduation, you will find nothing cleaner and more spacious with ocean views."

Q Brings a Social Atmosphere

"People here get a lot of social interaction by living on campus. Even though the food costs a lot, the dorms are close to each other and to classes."

GUYS & GIRLS

Q Where Gorgeous People Reign

"Some diversity, lots of christians, republicans and blondes. People here are generally more beautiful than other places"

Q Girls and Guys of Pepperdine

"The girls on campus are extremely nice and beautiful. They are willing to get to know anyone and everyone. Most girls are involved in Greek-Life. The guys on campus are all really cool and love to party. They are for the most part all active in sports and are also active in Greek-Life."

HEALTH & SAFETY

Q Very Safe

"very safe, i am totally comfortable walking by myself at night with no worries"

Q Safe

"it's a small school in a relatively small town with a lot of families nearby, so it would be pretty hard to feel unsafe here. the security is pretty laid back but i haven't heard of very many vandalism or theft incidents on campus."

LOOKING FOR MORE?

Check out our full-length guide to this school at collegeprowler.com/pepperdine-university/.

Pitzer College

1050 N. Mills Ave.; Claremont, CA 91711
(909) 621-8000; www.pitzer.edu

THE BASICS:

Acceptance Rate: 20%	Student-Faculty Ratio: 11:1
Yield: 31%	Retention Rate: 89%
Setting: Suburban	Graduation Rate: 69%
Control: Private Non-Profit	Tuition: $39,330
Total Undergrads: 1,043	Room & Board: $11,440
SAT Range: 1140–1330*	Avg. Aid Package: $29,182
ACT Range: 25–30	Students With Aid: 59%

* of 1600

Academics	A	Greek Life	N/A
Athletics	C	Guys	A
Campus Dining	A+	Health & Safety	B+
Campus Housing	A	Local Atmosphere	B+
Campus Strictness	A+	Nightlife	B+
Computers	B+	Off-Campus Dining	A
Diversity	B+	Off-Campus Housing	A-
Drug Safety	C-	Parking	A+
Facilities	A-	Transportation	B-
Girls	A	Weather	A

CP's Student Author On...
OVERALL EXPERIENCE

Pitzer continues to grow every year and is no longer "the baby" of the Claremont College Consortium. You know you've stepped foot on Pitzer's campus when almost every student greets you with a smile, and has the drive and passion to change the world for the greater good.

All students have their pet peeves and things they wish were different on campus, but, overall, students have enjoyed the five campus setup, the state-of-the-art Keck Joint Science Center, the political activism, the social responsibility, the study abroad opportunities, the friendships, the professors, and just about everything else. Surprisingly, although Pitzer is an extremely active campus politically, some are not big fans of the political activism that is played out.

When it comes down to it, the only largely-accepted complaint is cost, which is understandable for one of the most expensive colleges in the nation. Yet, Pitzer offers relatively good financial aid that only continues to improve, as well as an array of work-study and non-work-study jobs and programs.... For the rest of this editorial, visit collegeprowler.com.

Students Speak Out On...
OVERALL EXPERIENCE

New Experiences
"Learn from top noch professors about a wide range of topics you'll never think about. Meet many people and professors from 5-C colleges. You can eat at each 5-C college cafertia."

5C Community Is Great
"so many more options because of unique claremont colleges community + pitzer has a lot to offer. tight-knit community, small classes, good social life, proximity to la, ca sunshine"

Amazing Lifestyle, We Like to Call It Camp Pitzer
"Pitzer has an amazing balance of academic and social life. Pitzer students are engaged and interested in their studies but don't let that dictate their social lives. Classes aren't competitive or focused on grades. The general atmosphere on campus is very laid back, but still academically enriching and intellectual."

BEST OF PITZER

1. 5C resources
2. Beautiful weather
3. Always something to do
4. Great study abroad programs
5. Accessibility to professors
6. The laid-back vibe

Happy Students
89% of students return after their first year.

Knowledgeable Professors
100% of students surveyed rated the general knowledge of professors as above average.

WORST OF PITZER

1. Finding an empty study room
2. Tuition costs
3. Pollution
4. Financial Aid
5. Claremont
6. Pitzer is losing its hippie spirit.

Expensive
Tuition is a steep $39,330, one of the most expensive rates in the country.

Expensive Dorms
Living on campus doesn't come cheap, with an average housing price tag of $7,240.

Frequently Compared Schools:

Claremont McKenna College
Occidental College
Pomona College
Scripps College

Students Speak Out On... EVERYTHING!

ACADEMICS

Exceptional Studies

"One can challenge ones self as much has one wants. I have loved the ability to take courses at other colleges including Pomona, Claremont McKenna, Scripps, and Harvey Mudd."

Small Classes

"My biggest class is Political Studies, which has about 50 students in it. My smallest class has about 12 students. The teachers usually know everyone by name within a month or so, and they are extremely helpful. Use their office hours, or make an appointment to meet with them and they will always be there to help."

ATHLETICS

Small but Mighty

"Like most division 3 schools, athletics do not encompass all of our time at Pitzer. Nevertheless, athletics are extremely fun here and we do a good job of putting out very competitive teams across the board in every sport usually coming in the top 3 of our conference nearly every year in almost every sport. Our gym is smaller than a bigger institution but all that does is make our presence known even louder."

Fun If You Go

"The Pomona-Pitzer Sagehens fans are not the most ardent supporters, which is kind of strange considering our proficiency at a multitude of sports. Our basketball team lost in the championship round last year, our baseball team was crowned champion, as was waterpolo. In addition, our 5C rugby teams had to be placed in a special D-1 premier class because they were so good. If you have an interest you can find some talented young athletes, but don't expect massive crowds."

CAMPUS DINING

You're Crazy If You Think the Food Is Bad!

"Due to the fact that Pitzer is apart of the Claremont Consortium, we not only have access to one amazing dining hall, but 7 of them! All of the Claremont College's dining halls are top notch, but in particular Pitzer specializes in locally grown and organic and vegan food options. Most days I think the meals I eat on campus are better than the meals I have at home."

Seven Dining Halls, All Great!

"Students can eat at all seven dining halls around the five colleges. All of them are far above the average college dining hall food quality."

CAMPUS HOUSING

Life on Campus Is Awesome!

"Living on campus builds a really strong sense of community here at Pitzer College. In my opinion, all the dorms are worth living in. Holden and Mead halls give you the best old-school Pitzer vibe - there's something really endearing about the age factor. I'm not a fan of the newer dorms that were constructed recently. I feel they're a little sterile and demonstrate how Pitzer's trying too hard to become the other colleges."

PAS Dorms Are Wonderful

"our dorms are environmentally friendly and highly sustainable. nice big bathrooms and enough room space."

GUYS & GIRLS

"Pitzer Pretty"

"So many girls here are natural beauties. They're stylish and unique. We call it "Pitzer pretty" because they're not the typical "hot" sorority girls but they're beautiful and real and different. Boys are still boys. They're still growing, physically and emotionally. There are lots of fun parties on campus across the Claremont Colleges, like Groove at the Grove. There are as many serious relationships as random hookups."

HEALTH & SAFETY

I've Never Felt Threatened.

"Who would attack someone on Pitzer's campus? Kids here couldn't be more peaceful and the Village doesn't exactly host criminals either."

LOOKING FOR MORE?

Check out our full-length guide to this school at collegeprowler.com/pitzer-college/.

Pomona College

550 N. College Ave.; Claremont, CA 91711
(909) 621-8131; www.pomona.edu

THE BASICS:

Acceptance Rate: 16%
Yield: 39%
Setting: Suburban
Control: Private Non-Profit
Total Undergrads: 1,550
SAT Range: 2090–2320*
ACT Range: 31–34

Student-Faculty Ratio: 7:1
Retention Rate: 97%
Graduation Rate: 95%
Tuition: $37,017
Room & Board: $12,651
Avg. Aid Package: $29,600
Students With Aid: 62%

* of 2400

Academics	A	Greek Life	D
Athletics	C+	Guys	B-
Campus Dining	A	Health & Safety	B
Campus Housing	B-	Local Atmosphere	B-
Campus Strictness	A	Nightlife	B
Computers	B+	Off-Campus Dining	C
Diversity	B+	Off-Campus Housing	D-
Drug Safety	B-	Parking	B
Facilities	B+	Transportation	C-
Girls	B-	Weather	A

CP's Student Author On...
OVERALL EXPERIENCE

Just about any Pomona student will tell you that they truly enjoyed their college experience. And it's not just the free booze that makes Pomona one of the happiest colleges in the country. It helps, but the booze alone couldn't make everyone so darn genuinely happy, day in and day out. After all, some people don't even drink, and they seem just as happy as everyone else. it's not the location either. The classes are good, and the professors are great, and that certainly plays its part, and it's an open, friendly campus, which is nice. But there is some other factor which makes people like this place so much. There are some people who were dead set on hating it. Why, you might wonder, did they go in the first place? One reason was parental pressure. Another was students, who by the end, had to grudgingly admit that they had enjoyed themselves. They might still claim that they don't have an affectionate place in their heart for their alma mater, but they can't deny that the experience was worthwhile.

The question is, "Why are Pomona students so unabashedly jolly?" There are only two feasible answers.... For the rest of this editorial, visit collegeprowler.com.

Students Speak Out On...
OVERALL EXPERIENCE

Q Pomona Is Great!
"Pomona is a great community full of an awesome and diverse (in many ways) group of people. It is a fairly tight-knit community that is a lot of fun. The academic experience is challenging but rewarding and the professors are engaging and knowledgeable. Whenever I leave campus I can't wait to get back. Pomona offers a great mix of academic and social lives."

Q The Best Years of My Life
"We study hard and play harder. We are curious, creative, and fun. Many of us are socially ajusted nerds, even in the sciences. There is a true sense of community and belonging to the school. When you meet alums of the school, you automatically feel a connection in most cases."

Q
"I wish Pomona were in LA. I miss being in a city. Pomona lets you have cars your freshman year, which is great, but getting in and out of LA is a pain in the rear. Other than that, I honestly could not have asked for more from a college."

BEST OF POMONA

1. The caring and nurturing environment. Oh, yeah, and did I mention the free beer?
2. Climbing the flag pole
3. Free strawberry-flavored condoms!
4. Table Manners
5. Sneaking into Frary

Happy Students
97% of students return after their first year.

Commitment to Teaching
There are 7 students for every member of faculty on campus.

WORST OF POMONA

1. Claremont
2. Chino winds
3. The network going down when, and only when, it is most inconvenient

Expensive
Tuition is a steep $37,017, one of the most expensive rates in the country.

Expensive Dorms
Living on campus doesn't come cheap, with an average housing price tag of $7,415.

Student Body

African American:	8%	Male Undergrads:	50%
Asian American:	14%	Female Undergrads:	50%
Hispanic:	11%	Living On Campus:	98%
International:	4%	Living Off Campus:	2%
Native American:	0%	Male Athletes:	19%
White:	47%	Female Athletes:	10%
Unknown:	15%	Fraternity Members:	5%
From Out-of-State:	73%	Sorority Members:	0%

Frequently Compared Schools:

Brown University
Claremont McKenna College
Pitzer College
Stanford University

Students Speak Out On...
EVERYTHING!

ACADEMICS

Q "Obviously, the Pomona barrel contained some bad apples, but even my average experience was good, and I had some outstanding and very supportive teachers."

Q "The teachers were smart, but apathetic about pushing students academically."

Q "My teachers, in the humanities at least, were altogether pathetic. They inspired a level of mediocrity in their students which I have not encountered before or since. I think they accomplished this by not really expecting anything in the way of hard work or independent thought from their students, and then by giving more than half of them As anyway."

ATHLETICS

Q Sports Are There, but Not a Priority

"We share our athletic department with Pitzer College. Sports are not a super big deal at Pomona College. If you play them, that's great, but the turn out to watch them isn't very large unless it's a game against our rivals, CMS (Claremont McKenna, Harvey Mudd, and Scripps share athletic departments). That said, there are a lot of talented athletes that attend the school; athletics just isn't their number one priority. The games are fun to attend."

Q Athletics

"We are a Division III school, so our sports aren't very good. Our most talented competitive organization is the Claremont Colleges Ballroom Dance Company, and our most talented sport is men's water polo. Pomona is a college of brainiacs rather than jocks, though, and I don't think many people actually care about our sports teams."

CAMPUS DINING

Q Wide Variety and Usually Pretty Good.

"On campus dining is pretty good. You have 2 dining halls on Pomona that you can eat at plus the Coop Fountain. The always have salads, sandwiches, pizzas, the basics... then you get some cool 'exhibitions' like steaks, sushi, and burritos. The best part about the dining is that you can go to any of the other Claremont Colleges if you get tired of Pomona's."

Q "The food at Pomona is not terrible, but it's nothing to rave about."

CAMPUS HOUSING

Q Pretty Good

"Dorms vary, but generally they're nothing to complain about, especially compared to other college dorms. As you get older, the dorms get nicer. They're also building a new dorm that looks like it's going to be ridiculously nice. The kitchens aren't too nice on South Campus, especially. Parties often happen in dorm rooms. Room draw is crazy, but fair. Lots of options."

Q "The dorms are anywhere from really nice to really terrible. Clarks are nice, and South Campus isn't so nice."

GUYS & GIRLS

Q Awkward Much?

"I'll be honest... most guys are at least semi-awkward at Pomona. They're mostly nice, but generally not the most conventionally attractive bunch."

Q "My boyfriend's really hot, but the rest of the student body is mainly middling. If you have a fetish for pale, weedy intellectuals, you're in luck. My boyfriend's pale and intellectual, but he's not weedy."

HEALTH & SAFETY

Q Bike Thefts Common

"I have never felt unsafe on Pomona's campus. It is a small campus bordered by an affluent community. However, bike thefts are very common, so invest in a U-lock. Also, students have had laptops stolen, though I have never worried about any of the students taking my things."

Q "Dude, don't ever go to Baxter Health Center for anything; they always take one look at you and say, 'well, it's either Mono or you're pregnant.'"

LOOKING FOR MORE?

Check out our full-length guide to this school at collegeprowler.com/pomona-college/.

Princeton University

110 W. College Road; Princeton, NJ 08544
(609) 258-3000; www.princeton.edu

THE BASICS:

Acceptance Rate: 10%
Yield: 60%
Setting: Suburban
Control: Private Non-Profit
Total Undergrads: 5,069
SAT Range: 2090–2360*
ACT Range: 31–35

Student-Faculty Ratio: 6:1
Retention Rate: 98%
Graduation Rate: 96%
Tuition: $35,340
Room & Board: $11,680
Avg. Aid Package: $30,242
Students With Aid: 58%

of 2400

Academics	A+	Greek Life	N/A
Athletics	B+	Guys	B
Campus Dining	A-	Health & Safety	B+
Campus Housing	B-	Local Atmosphere	B-
Campus Strictness	B+	Nightlife	C
Computers	A-	Off-Campus Dining	B
Diversity	A+	Off-Campus Housing	D-
Drug Safety	B-	Parking	B-
Facilities	B+	Transportation	B-
Girls	B	Weather	B-

CP's Student Author On...
OVERALL EXPERIENCE

Once students get past the relative isolation of Princeton, they immerse themselves in the multitude of campus academic and social activities, from political and humor publications to debate societies to eating clubs. The academic program is demanding, which students appreciate, and it prepares students for not only the work force but also top-notch graduate schools. The historic buildings and eating clubs give Princeton its own sort of feel that may not mesh well with all students but certainly provide Princeton undergrads with a plethora of traditions and opportunities that are characteristically Princeton.

Princeton is not just a school, it is an experience. Students who take full advantage of what Princeton has to offer have the opportunity to work with some of the most talented professors and scholars in the world on an idyllic campus. They graduate with one of the best undergraduate educations in the country and with all the connections the alumni experience has to offer.... For the rest of this editorial, visit collegeprowler.com.

Students Speak Out On...
OVERALL EXPERIENCE

Q **Princeton Is Amazing**
"I love everything about Princeton--the people, the classes, the campus, alumni, etc. I honestly could not see myself happier at any other university."

Q **You Just Gotta Love It**
"Even though the work is incredibly hard sometimes, they really take care of you at Princeton once you get in. The sense of community is incredible-once you are in, you are in, and people will do everything they can to help you succeed."

Q "I love Princeton. If you have the opportunity, come to school here."

Q "It has been, by far, the best time of my life, both socially and intellectually. I really wish I could stay here forever."

Q "I loved Princeton so much that I found it difficult to maintain friendships from high school, because my old friends simply did not understand the combination of the rigorous academic program with the fantastic social life. They could not look beyond what they thought as Princeton's nerdy students to see some of the most dynamic people I have ever known."

BEST OF PRINCETON

1. Strong academic program
2. Focus on campus undergraduate life
3. Renovated dorms
4. Tradition and strong alumni programs
5. Sunday brunch at Forbes

Happy Students
98% of students return after their first year.

Commitment to Teaching
There are 6 students for every member of faculty on campus.

WORST OF PRINCETON

1. The relative isolation of the town
2. Rainy springs
3. Old, outdated dorms
4. Crowded Stephens Fitness Center
5. Rare Big Three Bonfires

Expensive
Tuition is a steep $35,340, one of the most expensive rates in the country.

Expensive Dorms
Living on campus doesn't come cheap, with an average housing price tag of $6,340.

Student Body

African American:	9%	Male Undergrads:	53%
Asian American:	15%	Female Undergrads:	47%
Hispanic:	8%	Living On Campus:	98%
International:	10%	Living Off Campus:	2%
Native American:	1%	Male Athletes:	24%
White:	51%	Female Athletes:	16%
Unknown:	7%	Fraternity Members:	0%
From Out-of-State:	86%	Sorority Members:	0%

Frequently Compared Schools:
Brown University
Harvard University
University of Pennsylvania
Yale University

Students Speak Out On...
EVERYTHING!

ACADEMICS

Q Incredible
"-Registration is done online and is fairly easy. -Workload is very tough and demanding.-Professors are brilliant-Wide variety of course offerings"

Q Incomparable
"Princeton professors are nothing short of brilliant. Your teacher may be (probably will be) pioneers in his or her field. However, some lecturers have their shortcomings, and academic prowess is no guarantee of a good lecturer. Nevertheless, Princeton students are privileged to be the recipients of a vigorous intellectual experience. The workload though is nothing short of Herculean."

ATHLETICS

Q Greattttt
"Walked on-to Varsity Crew without ever rowing a boat in my life before. Lots of opportunities. NOt a huge student fan base but still a decent, fun size."

Q Alumni Spirit
"Current Princeton undergraduates don't typically go to every athletic event on campus, however, they always sport their orange and black shirts, scarves, sweatshirts, etc all over campus. The athletic facilities are all state-of-the-art and are fantastic. If anything, it seems like Princeton alumni care more about some sporting events than students."

CAMPUS DINING

Q Dining Is Fantastic
"The food at Princeton is fantastic, simple as that. As a freshman and sophomore, you typically eat in one of the residential college dining halls. The food in the dining halls is generally the same across the board and is very good. As an upperclassmen, you can choose to join one of 10 Eating Clubs."

Q Yummm
"The food at the cafeterias can get repetitive and boring, but there are other options such as the Frist Campus Center and various cafes that add variety. Also, late meal (look it up) is a life-saver."

CAMPUS HOUSING

Q Great Dorms
"The dorms at Princeton have really improved over the last 4-5 years. With the addition of Whitman College, and the complete reconstruction of Butler Colleges, the quality of residential life has exponentially increased. The dorms all have heating, and in some cases air conditioning, and the newer dorms have private bathrooms or bathrooms steps outside of your door. However, in some of the older dorms, you may end having to walk down 3-4 flights of stairs to use the bathroom or do laundry."

Q Full Spectrum
"It really depends on where you live. Everything has its pluses and minuses, but no one complains - in fact, a lot of people brag."

GUYS & GIRLS

Q Guys and Girls
"There are a bevy of cute girls at Princeton; however you'll never see more than a handful crawling out of the woodwork during the day. During the night though you see a pretty eclectic range of lookers from leggy blondes to ample-figured brunettes. That being said the average girl is exactly that: average.The guys are pretty much the same; some would say a marginally better crop than the girls."

HEALTH & SAFETY

Q Safe
"Campus is safe and getting medical treatment is quick and easy."

LOOKING FOR MORE?
Check out our full-length guide to this school at collegeprowler.com/princeton-university/.

Providence College

1 Cunningham Square; Providence, RI 02918
(401) 865-1000; www.providence.edu

THE BASICS:

Acceptance Rate: 60%
Yield: 19%
Setting: Mid-sized city
Control: Private Non-Profit
Total Undergrads: 4,304
SAT Range: 1600–1910*
ACT Range: 23–28

Student-Faculty Ratio: 13:1
Retention Rate: 91%
Graduation Rate: 86%
Tuition: $33,120
Room & Board: $11,360
Avg. Aid Package: $17,583
Students With Aid: 75%

* of 2400

Academics	B	Greek Life	N/A
Athletics	A-	Guys	B+
Campus Dining	B	Health & Safety	B
Campus Housing	B+	Local Atmosphere	B+
Campus Strictness	B-	Nightlife	B+
Computers	C+	Off-Campus Dining	A-
Diversity	D+	Off-Campus Housing	C-
Drug Safety	B-	Parking	B-
Facilities	B	Transportation	A-
Girls	A-	Weather	C

CP's Student Author On...
OVERALL EXPERIENCE

Looking back on their time at PC leaves students glowing with fond memories. Most appreciate the stimulating academics and whirlwind social scene that PC offers. While the occasional person complains that it is too much of the same thing, a copious number of students say that they couldn't imagine being anywhere else, and if they had to do it all over again, they would absolutely make the same choice to come to PC. The overwhelming majority look on their time spent at PC as a phenomenal learning experience that has helped them develop into the intellectually, emotionally, and socially well-rounded beings that they are today.

The brilliance of the education at PC is that it extends itself outside of the classroom. A student's experience at PC can be anything that they want to make it. If you want to focus on academics, you can, and you will find a group of people who feel exactly the same way you do. If you want an education in socializing or just want your college years to be the wild and crazy ones you've heard they can be, PC has that, too.... For the rest of this editorial, visit collegeprowler.com.

Students Speak Out On...
OVERALL EXPERIENCE

Q The Sense of Community Is Great

"The students that attend PC are very similar, but are different enough that it is still a very fun place. Everyone is sociable, and most have the same goals for their time at PC. Everyone in my dorm gets along great. I enjoy social life everyday, not only on the weekends. I know I've made some friendship here that will last a lifetime."

Q Overall Great Experience

"You will definitely have a great time at PC. Besides the academics, which I have found to be very challenging, the social scene is amazing. PC somehow manages to attract the most out-going kids, many of whom were varsity athletes in high school. Drinking on the weekends is very popular, but there are always options for those choose not to drink, and no one will pressure you to do so."

Q Too Conventional Without Enough Options

"Unless you are a devout Catholic or an extreme partier you should look elsewhere. The curriculum is very strict and does not allow for individual thinking. There is not a great variety in student organizations or things to do on the weekends."

BEST OF PROVIDENCE

1. Being in a city
2. Restaurants
3. Bars and ticket parties
4. Civ scream
5. Rejects on the rise
6. Movies on Slavin lawn
7. SOB/JRW
8. Blackfriars Theater

Happy Students
91% of students return after their first year.

Proven Success
86% of students will complete their education and graduate with a degree.

WORST OF PROVIDENCE

1. Diversity
2. Parking
3. Ray food
4. Windtunnels
5. Nautilus weight room
6. Civ
7. Parietals
8. Boy/girl ratio

Expensive
Tuition is a steep $33,120, one of the most expensive rates in the country.

Expensive Dorms
Living on campus doesn't come cheap, with an average housing price tag of $6,560.

Student Body

African American:	2%	Male Undergrads:	44%
Asian American:	2%	Female Undergrads:	56%
Hispanic:	3%	Living On Campus:	78%
International:	1%	Living Off Campus:	22%
Native American:	0%	Male Athletes:	12%
White:	75%	Female Athletes:	10%
Unknown:	16%	Fraternity Members:	0%
From Out-of-State:	88%	Sorority Members:	0%

Students Speak Out On... EVERYTHING!

ACADEMICS

Q Great!

"The Creative Writing Major is amazing! A dream come true!"

Q Math Department Is Very Good

"When I arrived at PC I didn't know what I was going to be. My first math class turned out to be a great experience. Since, I've always been interested in math, I decided to continue. My next teacher was even better than the first one. I'm excited to be a part of the PC math department."

Q Professors Really Care

"I came to PC not having a clue what i want to do in the future, and all of my professors really care and really want you to succeed. They push class discussions and the development of the students ideas rather than talking at you in a big lecture. I even call all of my professors by their first names!"

ATHLETICS

Q "It's hard to make a team at PC, but the school spirit is pretty amazing."

Q "PC men's basketball is the team of Rhode Island, so even non-students and alumni get really hyped up for the basketball season. Go Friars!"

Q "Because there aren't that many team sports on campus, intramurals are huge. There are also a variety of competitive clubs such as rugby, golf, and sailing."

CAMPUS DINING

Q Food

"It's a college campus to the food isn't anything spectacular. However the dining staff tries to ensure a variety of foods and dining options. There is always something that you can find."

Q It Is What It Is.

"Basically, it's what you'll get anywhere else when it comes to Ray. You can get tired of the food, but there's always Slavin or Jazzman's, and there's tons of places to eat closeby in the city."

CAMPUS HOUSING

Q Better Than Expected

"I lived in a forced quad and didn't even realize it. Our room was huge! Plenty of room for four, and it was only meant for three. For freshman girls, Ray is the best!"

Q Options for Everyone

"Pretty much everyone at PC lives on campus and you can't move off until your junior year. While some people do move off campus, the houses are practically on Providence college grounds. The freshman buildings are nothing special, but it is possible to live in the suites and apartments as early as sophomore year."

GUYS & GIRLS

Q All Similar Looks

"Good looking student body but everyone seems to reflect what they see others looking like on campus. A lot of Lax Bros and preppy girls but you do get the odd hipster...very rarely. I have hardly seen any overweight people on campus."

Q Very Specific Type of People

"The school has many people with a lot of money flashing around. Everybody is very friendly once you get to know them, but many people can be cold at first. The guys seem to be more friendly and down to earth than the girls at the school but there are plenty of other schools in the area so there's always a group for everyone"

HEALTH & SAFETY

Q Completely Safe

"There are security guards at every gate that provides an entrance to the school that prevents anyone from getting in. There are shuttles that take students around campus at night."

Q Security is incredible

"The security guards are incredible, and there is no theft on campus."

LOOKING FOR MORE?

Check out our full-length guide to this school at collegeprowler.com/providence-college/.

Purchase College

735 Anderson Hill Road; Purchase, NY 10577
(914) 251-6000; www.purchase.edu

THE BASICS:

Acceptance Rate: 27%	Student-Faculty Ratio: 16:1
Yield: 30%	Retention Rate: 82%
Setting: Suburban	Graduation Rate: 51%
Control: Public	Tuition: $14,365
Total Undergrads: 4,065	Room & Board: $10,230
SAT Range: 1500–1830*	Avg. Aid Package: $9,728
ACT Range: 21–25	Students With Aid: 81%

* of 2400

Academics	B-	Greek Life	N/A
Athletics	C	Guys	B
Campus Dining	B	Health & Safety	C+
Campus Housing	C	Local Atmosphere	C+
Campus Strictness	B	Nightlife	B+
Computers	C	Off-Campus Dining	C+
Diversity	B-	Off-Campus Housing	C
Drug Safety	D+	Parking	B
Facilities	C+	Transportation	B+
Girls	C	Weather	B-

CP's Student Author On...
OVERALL EXPERIENCE

The level of enthusiasm and talent in classmates and professors at SUNY Purchase is something normally found at a small liberal arts school. Being around the conservatory students and seeing the dedication and long hours that go into perfecting and crafting an art helps motivate and influence fellow students. Sometimes, the policies that the administration enforces can be frustrating, and there is the occasional professor who has no idea what he or she is talking about; however, the strongest part of the University and what makes it so unique is the people. A lot of the learning that takes place at Purchase is up to the individual. It is tempting for students to simple classes, get average grades, and graduate early, but the students who take the time to challenge themselves will grow so much more than the students who seek the easy way out. The professors have such a big impact on students, so having a good professor is essential. Plus, the most interesting classes are always those where the professor is most passionate.

Purchase is the type of place where it is up to the student to go out and meet other people.... For the rest of this editorial, visit collegeprowler.com.

Students Speak Out On...
OVERALL EXPERIENCE

Q Love It
"My favorite part of Purchase is the fact that the students are always extremely friendly and just happy overall. There's never a time when someone would walk around campus and feel any hostility or judgement."

Q Rate and Review the Overall Experience at State University of New York - Purchase College
"I can't explain it, but my life would be a lot worse and I may not have even known it if I had never come to Purchase. It really is my home, and as much as I hate it, and some of thier policies. I love it."

BEST OF PURCHASE COLLEGE

1. "The Stood" or student center
2. Cheese club
3. Culture shock
4. Proximity to New York City
5. The conservatories
6. The courses

Happy Students
82% of students return after their first year.

Highly Satisfied Students
83% of students surveyed would make the same school choice if they could do it all over again.

WORST OF PURCHASE COLLEGE

1. All of the bricks
2. Dining areas close too early.
3. Housing is expensive.
4. Lack of available men
5. Large commuter population
6. Small dorms

Professors Are Still Learning
Only 49% of faculty have earned the highest degree in their field.

Student Body

African American:	7%	Male Undergrads:	45%
Asian American:	3%	Female Undergrads:	55%
Hispanic:	9%	Living On Campus:	67%
International:	2%	Living Off Campus:	33%
Native American:	0%	Male Athletes:	6%
White:	46%	Female Athletes:	5%
Unknown:	33%	Fraternity Members:	0%
From Out-of-State:	24%	Sorority Members:	0%

Frequently Compared Schools:

Ithaca College
New York University
State University of New York at New Paltz
Syracuse University

Students Speak Out On... EVERYTHING!

ACADEMICS

Q Professors

"I've had the luck of having really great professors so far. They're always available when you need help. They have great office hours and answer emails very quickly."

Q Purchase Has Some Amazing Faculty

"There are a few bad eggs here and there, but professors in the Literature department in particular have a level of understanding and expertise you'd expect to find at an Ivy League school."

ATHLETICS

Q Sports

"Definitely nothing compared to great universities, but the teams we do have all play very well together. Students on this campus are extremely friendly, which provides happier teams."

Q School Spirit

"Unfortunately because we're more of an art school we don't have a big athletic section and it's not D1 so there is very little school spirit when it comes to sports on our campus"

CAMPUS DINING

Q Dining Halls

"The main dining hall is pretty terrible. There's no variety and the food isn't prepared very well. The hub has better food, but not that big of a selection. Tera Ve is the best place. It's the vegetarian dining place on campus. The food is always very fresh and different."

Q Food

"the food on campus is good compared to other campuses, however it gets old really fast. you find yourself getting the same food over and over again"

CAMPUS HOUSING

Q Big Haus

"Big Haus is a relatively old building with little to no class or style. It's not comfortable and I inhaled pounds of dust over the course of the year. What made it a home to me were the inhabitants inside. I loved the people."

Q Housing at Purchase

"Try not to live in the dorms. Definitely try to get an apartment or Purchase will suck."

GUYS & GIRLS

Q Extremely Diverse

"I don't think you can find a campus as diverse as SUNY Purchase. There are people from every walk of life in all sorts of arts, sciences, athletics, and you see the whole campus co-exist in a great way. It tends to get a little cliquey, but for the most part everyone hangs out with everyone else. When it comes to looks and styles: that shoots the gamut as well. The girls are gorgeous and there are a lot of them. You have a rising athletic student body so there are enough guys to go around."

Q Haha

"Absolutly no greek life which is wonderful, the school is very diverse and most people are friends or simply friendly with each other. The majority of students are artsy, but there is still a fair share of non-arts students."

HEALTH & SAFETY

Q Campus Security

"I feel really safe on campus. The whole place is pretty well lit up, and there are campus security officers that are available. Most of the night life is pretty close to each other. The campus is kind of secluded so people who don't have some connection with the college don't walk around campus. And if there is a problem that needs to be dealt with by campus security they are very thorough."

Q Good Guys

"The police on campus are actual state police, but they're real cool guys. Every time I've had to deal with a UPD officer they have been extremely helpful."

LOOKING FOR MORE?

Check out our full-length guide to this school at collegeprowler.com/state-university-of-new-york---purchase-college/.

Purdue University

610 Purdue Mall; West Lafayette, IN 47907
(765) 494-4600; www.purdue.edu

THE BASICS:

Acceptance Rate: 73%
Yield: 31%
Setting: Suburban
Control: Public
Total Undergrads: 32,499
SAT Range: 1530–1880*
ACT Range: 23–29

Student-Faculty Ratio: 14:1
Retention Rate: 87%
Graduation Rate: 72%
Tuition: $25,118
Room & Board: $8,710
Avg. Aid Package: $9,426
Students With Aid: 70%

* of 2400

Academics	B	Greek Life	B
Athletics	A	Guys	A-
Campus Dining	A	Health & Safety	B+
Campus Housing	B+	Local Atmosphere	B+
Campus Strictness	B-	Nightlife	A-
Computers	B+	Off-Campus Dining	B
Diversity	B	Off-Campus Housing	B+
Drug Safety	C	Parking	B-
Facilities	B	Transportation	A-
Girls	B	Weather	B-

CP's Student Author On...
OVERALL EXPERIENCE

All hail to the old gold and black! Students could not have been more glowing in their praise about their time at Purdue University. Boilermakers unanimously appreciate all the opportunities that are afforded to students at a Big Ten university. From the thriving social scene to the academics, to the prestige of a Purdue diploma to the lifelong friends, Purdue students are grateful for their time in the heartland of the Midwest, and none could dream of having attended school anywhere else. As with anything in life, there are positives and negatives to any situation, but it appears that the benefits of being a Boilermaker greatly outweigh everything else.

The sheer size of Purdue may intimidate those students who feel that they will never be more than a number at Purdue, but as students have pointed out, there's a niche here for everyone. If the chance to be top dog is what you desire from a college, you won't find that here.... For the rest of this editorial, visit collegeprowler.com.

Students Speak Out On...
OVERALL EXPERIENCE

Q Caring Teachers and Tas

"Treat your teachers and TAs with respect and they will go out of their way to help you. For example, instead of not showing up to class if you know you're going to be out, let them know that you will be absent. They will absolutely work with you to make sure that you don't miss anything!"

Q Dream Come True

"Purdue is my dream school. I've completely found my niche of people and wouldn't trade it for anything. Even though it's a bigger school, all the programs offered make everything seem so much cozier. There is something for everyone here, whether its the greek scene, marching band, athletics, or clubs for everything imaginable! Boiler up!"

Q Diversity Is the Key

"My expirence so far has been great purdue has opened my eyes to the world. I love the people here because everybody is nice to each other, i would do it ll over again an again"

BEST OF PURDUE

1. Fountain runs
2. The awesome Big Ten athletics
3. The beautiful campus--so pretty, and so easy to navigate that it must have been designed by an engineer
4. Grand Prix

Happy Students
87% of students return after their first year.

Proven Success
72% of students will complete their education and graduate with a degree.

WORST OF PURDUE

1. The extreme boredom of the Lafayette/West Lafayette surroundings
2. Traffic during home games
3. The Midwestern weather
4. Foreign TAs
5. Dead Week

Lowest Grades
Drug Safety: C
Weather: B-
Campus Strictness: B-

Student Body

African American:	4%	Male Undergrads:	58%
Asian American:	5%	Female Undergrads:	42%
Hispanic:	3%	Living On Campus:	40%
International:	8%	Living Off Campus:	60%
Native American:	1%	Male Athletes:	2%
White:	80%	Female Athletes:	2%
Unknown:	0%	Fraternity Members:	18%
From Out-of-State:	36%	Sorority Members:	17%

Frequently Compared Schools:

Indiana University
Penn State
University of Illinois
University of Michigan

Students Speak Out On... EVERYTHING!

ACADEMICS

Q Great for academics

"I say Purdue is excellent for academics but that is probably because I was in the science and engineering field. The classes I took in the liberal arts schools were terrible. The instructors in those classes just didn't care and really didn't know the material either. But in science and engineering the professors are amazing. They know their subjects and most know how to get the information across really well. This is where Purdue excels more than any other category."

Q Life Is Good!

"Purdue works hard at making Freshmen feel welcome and at home. Boiler Gold Rush is their orientation. You are put in small groups and do activities together, learn your way around and shop for supplies. They have parties and other get-togethers so you meet lots of people."

Q Nursing at Its Finest

"Nursing at Purdue is a great major. The faculty really do their best job in teaching the material and it is a prestigious occupation. Last year, the incoming nursing students even had a higher high school GPA than the engineering students!"

ATHLETICS

Q Amazing

"Athletics are HUGE! The football games are always packed, and the basketball team will be ranked top in the nation this year. The games are so fun and always exciting!"

Q Soccer

"The programs here are the best. I played soccer for the womens club team and they are great! We even made it to Nationals this year and we traveled to Arizona for our games. It was awesome!!"

CAMPUS DINING

Q Always Something New.

"The food is great. There is always something different on the menu and you can never get bored. If you don't like the items offered at one dining court, you can always walk a block and

have something completely different. There is always plenty to eat, too, so you will never be hungry. Be sure to watch out for the freshman 15!"

Q Menus

"menus are very diverse. purdue has received awards for its food."

CAMPUS HOUSING

Q All Dorms Are Equal

"Freshman dorms are very modern and there are alot of different options to choose from. Upperclass men dorms have many great options as well"

Q Very Nice

"The University housing is quite nice - some of the the halls are a bit older, but everything is kept very clean and in good working order."

GUYS & GIRLS

Q Moderate and Tolerant

"Students here for the most part are fairly moderate and pretty tolerant."

Q Lots of Diversity

"There is a lot of diversity between students here. Tons of clubs that cater to just about everyone out there."

HEALTH & SAFETY

Q Campus Safety Is a Plus

"Campus is surrounded with emergency boxes and campus police arrive with less than 5 minutes. Never have to worry about danger."

Q Safety Is #1.

"They have lots of call boxes where you walk. There is also an escort service if you don't want to walk alone."

LOOKING FOR MORE?

Check out our full-length guide to this school at collegeprowler.com/purdue-university/.

Radford University

801 E. Main St.; Radford, VA 24141
(540) 831-5000; www.radford.edu

THE BASICS:

Acceptance Rate: 71%
Yield: 33%
Setting: Town
Control: Public
Total Undergrads: 7,773
SAT Range: 1370–1640*
ACT Range: 19–23

Student-Faculty Ratio: 18:1
Retention Rate: 78%
Graduation Rate: 60%
Tuition: $16,568
Room & Board: $6,970
Avg. Aid Package: $9,394
Students With Aid: 63%

of 2400

Academics	B-	Greek Life	A
Athletics	C	Guys	B
Campus Dining	B-	Health & Safety	A
Campus Housing	B	Local Atmosphere	B-
Campus Strictness	C-	Nightlife	C+
Computers	B+	Off-Campus Dining	A-
Diversity	D	Off-Campus Housing	A
Drug Safety	B-	Parking	D+
Facilities	B	Transportation	D
Girls	B+	Weather	B

CP's Student Author On...
OVERALL EXPERIENCE

Radford University offers an incredibly unique experience in a small-town environment. The small size of the University allows for a much more personal connection with the faculty and other students. Professors make it their mission to create an engaging learning environment, going above and beyond when a student makes the effort to ask for help. Professors are more than willing to write recommendations, assist in classroom issues, and be fantastic sounding boards for academic advancement. The goal of Radford academia is to better the students at all costs. The social life is also a bonus of attending such a small school. With a small population, the majority of students knows one another fairly well. They party together, go to classes together, and spend quality time together during campus activities. The nightlife is a legend among the colleges of Virginia, and the parties are incredible. But, even if you don't like to drink until you can't stand up, there are plenty of things to do like bowling, playing pool or pingpong, or checking out a movie.

The town of Radford is small, but within miles of several hotspots for action.... For the rest of this editorial, visit collegeprowler.com.

Students Speak Out On...
OVERALL EXPERIENCE

Q I love it here
"I love it here. If I could start over as a freshman, I would do it in a heartbeat."

Q I have loved my experience at Radford
"I have loved my experience at Radford. I'd come here again if I had to do it over. The study abroad programs here are top notch. We have study abroad programs with something like 30 different countries and universities. I went to England and Scotland to study history for a summer. Most wonderful experience ever. I made some really good friends on that trip."

Q My overall experience has been amazing
"My overall experience has been amazing, I've made wonderful friends that I wouldn't trade for the world. I wouldn't imagine going anywhere else. One of those memories that just sticks out every time I think about Radford is the Theatre picnic at the beginning of each year. Everyone has been away from each other for the summer, and to be able to come back and see everyone again is always a great feeling."

BEST OF RADFORD

1. One-on-one relationships with professors
2. Nightlife
3. The variety of places to eat
4. The friendliness of the students
5. Variety of on-campus activities

Help to Succeed
The school has academic and career counseling available to help you when you need it.

WORST OF RADFORD

1. Lack of recycling
2. Lack of public transportation
3. Strictness of campus policies
4. Dining hall food
5. Not a lot to do in the town of Radford

Good Luck Finding a Part-Time Job
Employment services are not available for students.

Want a Job? On Your Own
There aren't any placement services for graduates.

Student Body

African American:	6%	Male Undergrads:	43%
Asian American:	2%	Female Undergrads:	57%
Hispanic:	3%	Living On Campus:	37%
International:	1%	Living Off Campus:	63%
Native American:	0%	Male Athletes:	5%
White:	86%	Female Athletes:	5%
Unknown:	2%	Fraternity Members:	9%
From Out-of-State:	8%	Sorority Members:	11%

Students Speak Out On... EVERYTHING!

ACADEMICS

Teachers all have a lot of personality

"The teachers at Radford University all have a lot of personality, at least all the teachers that I have had. Most have an attendance policy because they want you to be able to enjoy and get the full experience of the class in order to get the students involved."

Professors are extremely intelligent

"In my experience, the professors at Radford University have been extremely intelligent, as well as available for their students. Radford is known for its party scene, but when it comes to academics, I'd say that the education, psychology, nursing, dance and theatre departments are what we are known for. The professors in these areas are the best in their craft and it shows through the students."

Workload varies with professors

"The workload varies with professors, but I have yet to feel so bogged down by a class that it becomes unbearable. I admire a professor who can go beyond expectations of a syllabus and can find ways to really aid a student in their journey through academia."

ATHLETICS

Basketball, soccer, and rugby are big

"Basketball, Soccer, and Rugby are big at Radford. We do have many club offers in sports and from what I've heard they are fun. During the winter I joined the snowboarding club and those were some of the best times of my life, but being in the club was so expensive."

Pretty Good

"we do not have a football team...although some are trying to get one, but since we are so close to VT not sure how that will go"

Varsity sports are pretty good

"The varsity sports are pretty good. The women's team are better then the men's teams, based on past/presents records and statistics, but of course the men get praised more. We have lots of intramural sports from Rugby to volleyball."

CAMPUS DINING

Food

"The food is great, and a large selection is available."

Nice

"nice variety in the two dining halls (which are relatively close together) we have chinese and mexican in the bonnie. oh and also a starbucks :)"

CAMPUS HOUSING

The Dorms Are Lovely

"I enjoy the dorms a lot. The are very convenient and cozy, as long as you don't end up in a triple!"

Madison and Jefferson are nice

"The nice ones are Madison, where you get your own bathroom to only share with one roommate. I like Jefferson, where they have suites, and it's only three floors so it's not that noisy."

GUYS & GIRLS

Very relaxed, fun people

"The guys and girls at Radford are very relaxed, and fun people. They are easy to get to know and from what I've seen most are outgoing."

The guys I hang out with are AMAZING!

"The guys that I hang out with are AMAZING! I love them and wouldn't trade them for anything. The girls are fun I am in a social sorority and I absolute love it."

HEALTH & SAFETY

Security and safety is excellent

"Security and safety is excellent. The most crime that occurs on and off campus is property crime."

Great university police department

"The school has a great University Police department and the Radford City Police does well in maintaining order on the weekends."

LOOKING FOR MORE?

Check out our full-length guide to this school at collegeprowler.com/radford-university/.

Ramapo College of New Jersey

505 Ramapo Valley Road; Mahwah, NJ 07430
(201) 684-7500; www.ramapo.edu

THE BASICS:

Acceptance Rate: 51%
Yield: 36%
Setting: Suburban
Control: Public
Total Undergrads: 5,776
SAT Range: 1520–1800*
ACT Range: —

Student-Faculty Ratio: 18:1
Retention Rate: 86%
Graduation Rate: 70%
Tuition: $18,771
Room & Board: $10,949
Avg. Aid Package: $8,002
Students With Aid: 73%

* of 2400

This School Isn't Graded Yet!

College Prowler grades are calculated using tons of criteria, including survey responses that come from students at this school.

Unfortunately, we haven't gathered enough student surveys yet for this school to be able to calculate the grades for each section. Stay tuned to *CollegeProwler.com* for grade updates and more!

CP's Student Author On...
OVERALL EXPERIENCE

Ramapo generally does a good job of setting people up with roommates, as long as each person has an open mind and is willing to be friendly with different types of people. However, no two students are likely to have the same experience at Ramapo, and a negative side of the people on campus is dealing with the administrative offices, many of which look at students as an obstacle involved with their job. In order to get things accomplished, students must constantly nag, with unyielding tenacity. Like the administrative people, even student workers in the offices seem required to be surly and uninformed about important matters.

The classes were interesting and necessary, with a few exceptions. While it's important to get a well-rounded education, many students grow tired of the general education requirements after a while. However, once they get into courses within their major, students' interests in the education aspect of the College increase significantly.... For the rest of this editorial, visit collegeprowler.com.

Students Speak Out On...
OVERALL EXPERIENCE

Q Chose Again

"I wouldn't chose another college to go to. Ramapo is convinent and has great professors."

Q Great School, Great People

"I have made a great number of friends while at ramapo and i would definitely pick ramapo again. Ofcourse there are some drawbacks but i feel the positive outweighs the negative. Overall i feel good about the education i am receiving"

Q Love My School!

"I honestly could not picture myself anywhere else. The school is beautiful, the academics are great and greek life is awesome! I am so happy that I got to spend four years of my life here!"

Q Great, for What It's Costing Me

"I am at Ramapo on scholarship, so I am only paying about $2,000 a year for it. If I was paying more, I might be dissapointed with the school's lack of organization and problem prevention. Lots of technical problems... And many of the professors are difficult to deal with and/or grade erratically and unfairly. But I am still learning alot. and the dorms ROCK!"

BEST OF RAMAPO NEW JERSEY

1. "Experiential component" of courses
2. Good sources of transit in the area
3. Printing is free.
4. Professors
5. Proximity to NYC
6. Ramapo Reservation

Happy Students
86% of students return after their first year.

Big Dorms
100% of students surveyed felt that dorms were more spacious than average.

WORST OF RAMAPO NEW JERSEY

1. Administration
2. Alcohol is prohibited in most areas.
3. Commuter campus
4. Hilly terrain in winter
5. Lack of off-campus housing options
6. No football team

Expensive Dorms
Living on campus doesn't come cheap, with an average housing price tag of $8,200.

Student Body

African American:	6%	Male Undergrads:	42%
Asian American:	5%	Female Undergrads:	58%
Hispanic:	8%	Living On Campus:	57%
International:	3%	Living Off Campus:	43%
Native American:	0%	Male Athletes:	10%
White:	77%	Female Athletes:	7%
Unknown:	1%	Fraternity Members:	10%
From Out-of-State:	5%	Sorority Members:	13%

Frequently Compared Schools:

Montclair State University
Rutgers University
The College of New Jersey
William Paterson University of New Jersey

Students Speak Out On... EVERYTHING!

ACADEMICS

Many interesting things offered

"My school offers a lot of interesting things such as co-op programs, interships, and many other things."

Great Professors

"I have had a good relationship with all of my professors in the psychology and law and society fields. they are always available for meetings and are very flexible with students who do the work on time."

Excellent

"Each and every teacher (with a few exceptions) is knowledgable, friendly, and willing to help you go the extra mile to make sure you do well in the class and understand the course material."

ATHLETICS

Athletics Are Average

"They're not the best in the country but there is a wide selection of them and they're good to get involved in."

Options but Little Drive

"the ramapo college of new jersey has several options when it comes to sports, but not much push to be on a team. they have options that range from team sports to groups of friends playing pool. there is not much organization or information on how to join leagues, one has to find out how to join on their own."

Terrible School Spirit

"Being a D3 school with no football team, there is absolutely no school spirit on campus. People rarely attend sporting events and leave early on the off chance they do."

CAMPUS DINING

Dining Needs

"The dining options at Ramapo are very diverse meeting all kinds of meal needs"

It's Just Okay.

"The food here is alright, there is not much variety in the things and places you can eat. There are only two dining halls, the Pav and Birch. The Pav is definitely the better of the two. You can use your Flex dollars at the Atrium, which has pretty good food."

CAMPUS HOUSING

Ramapo Housing

"Great! Stay on top of your grades so you can have a high gpa and select housing first. Better than all the other Jersey state schools' housing options."

GUYS & GIRLS

Girls are normal

"The guys and girls on my campus are just like those at any other campus. Girls dress, look, and act like any others do."

Excepting

"Most of the school has very likeable personalities. There tend to be cliques but everyone is very excepting of others for the most part."

HEALTH & SAFETY

Public Safety

"I've never been concerned for the safety of me or any of my belongings on campus. Besides that, Public Safety has always been kind and courteous and have done all that was in their power to help make my college experience a good one. However, they are pretty zero tolerance on parties, so be warned."

Public Safety

"The safety of the Campus is very good; I always feel safe. They don't have a fence around campus though and there is no one checking who comes into the dorms. I always feel secure though!"

LOOKING FOR MORE?

Check out our full-length guide to this school at collegeprowler.com/ramapo-college-of-new-jersey/.

Reed College

3203 SE Woodstock Blvd.; Portland, OR 97202
(503) 771-1112; www.reed.edu

THE BASICS:

Acceptance Rate: 41%	**Student-Faculty Ratio:** 10:1
Yield: 29%	**Retention Rate:** 88%
Setting: Large city	**Graduation Rate:** 78%
Control: Private Non-Profit	**Tuition:** $39,700
Total Undergrads: 1,452	**Room & Board:** $10,250
SAT Range: 1930–2210*	**Avg. Aid Package:** $29,930
ACT Range: 29–33	**Students With Aid:** 56%

* of 2400

Academics	A-	Greek Life	N/A
Athletics	D-	Guys	C+
Campus Dining	C+	Health & Safety	B+
Campus Housing	A	Local Atmosphere	A-
Campus Strictness	A	Nightlife	B
Computers	A-	Off-Campus Dining	A-
Diversity	C+	Off-Campus Housing	B-
Drug Safety	C	Parking	A
Facilities	B+	Transportation	A
Girls	B	Weather	B-

CP's Student Author On... OVERALL EXPERIENCE

Looking back upon the person I was when coming to Reed three years ago is like looking through an opaque window. I still see the frame and some features from my old self in who I am now, but the greater part of who I am rests on this side of the mirror, having been tempered by my experiences at Reed. I suppose that my reasons for coming to Reed, after examination and time, still hold up: I desired a small school with an intimate academic setting, a liberal and open culture to present numerous facets of the world, and a community of mostly-nice and genuine individuals who would be friendly. I did not want to be another face in the crowd at a large state school, and I wanted to experience the traditional collegiate rites of passage with members of the Reed community. I could state that I have lost love, found love, done drugs, studied hard, been arrested, and snuck onto a golf course at night, but any student at any college could very well have done the same. Empirically, Reed's commitment to making critical thinkers and writers out of its students separates it from other academic institutions.... For the rest of this editorial, visit collegeprowler.com.

Students Speak Out On... OVERALL EXPERIENCE

Q The Reed Experience
"The academics at Reed are great--but I would not recommend this college to anyone who feels that extracurriculars are very important. There is plenty to do on campus, and the area is great, but the workload is very overwhelming, and it is very difficult to find time for anything besides schoolwork, but I guess that's what you sign up for when you go to Reed."

Q "Although this place is not without its flaws, and there is an alienating cultish mentality to being a 'Reedie,' I am happy here. I do not know of a place where I would rather be."

Q "I love Reed. It's been great for me, and I feel very prepared for graduate school."

Q "Reed is amazing. You will know if Reed is for you."

BEST OF REED

1. The academics, professors, and literature
2. Reed's campus
3. Renn Fayre
4. The Honor Principle
5. Reed student organizations

Happy Students
88% of students return after their first year.

Commitment to Teaching
There are 10 students for every member of faculty on campus.

WORST OF REED

1. The levels of stress associated with Reed
2. Reed's lack of diversity
3. The difficulty of managing time while remaining sane
4. Portland's weather
5. The copious amounts of work

Expensive
Tuition is a steep $39,700, one of the most expensive rates in the country.

Student Body

African American:	3%	Male Undergrads:	44%
Asian American:	9%	Female Undergrads:	56%
Hispanic:	7%	Living On Campus:	64%
International:	6%	Living Off Campus:	36%
Native American:	1%	Male Athletes:	0%
White:	56%	Female Athletes:	0%
Unknown:	19%	Fraternity Members:	0%
From Out-of-State:	92%	Sorority Members:	0%

Students Speak Out On... EVERYTHING!

ACADEMICS

Top Notch Academics.

"The academics at Reed are fabulous. Professors are generally brilliant and sincerely dedicated to helping students meet the very high expectations put on them. Students are seriously engaged in their studies and classes provide a rich forum for articulation and exchange of ideas."

"My professors are all great. At first, it was strange to be taught by people who a) had mastered their subjects, b) could present it well, and c) actually enjoyed teaching! It's crazy. I love it. And all my classes are interesting. I wish I had time to take all of them (well, okay, except math and science)."

ATHLETICS

Athletics at Reed

"While there are not any sort of formal athletics at reed, there are certainly many opportunities to stay active. Students are required to take at least 6 PE courses (1 course lasts a quarter) during their time at Reed. There are many options such as yoga, rock climbing, juggling, fencing, ultimate frisbee, etc."

"There are quite a few athletic people on campus, so you can definitely play sports. Read the sports column in the Quest newspaper and you'll get the picture. There's absolutely no pressure to be cool and be a jock or any stuff like that."

CAMPUS DINING

Nicely Distributed Resources

"After commons, you have the bookstore (called Homer's hut after 3 on weekends) to buy food and such, and there are three coffee shops (that DON"T take points) at two opposite corners as well as the center of campus"

"Commons is the only place on campus that consistently has perishable food that is not frozen. The food at Commons is usually pretty good. The menu offers some variety, but the same food items tend to circulate back onto the menu, so the menu can eventually seem a bit unoriginal. There are days when nothing looks appetizing and other days when there are too many good things to choose from."

Frequently Compared Schools:

Brown University
Lewis & Clark College
University of Puget Sound
Whitman College

CAMPUS HOUSING

"The dorms at Reed are some of the best I've seen at any college. Even the older dorms are nice! Steele and Sullivan are the most aesthetically-pleasing dorms. The Old Dorm Block may get a bad rap, but even those dorm rooms are cozy and large."

"There are pretty dorms, like Bragdon and Anna Mann, and there are dorms that look like they were erected in about three months and should really have been replaced a couple of decades ago, like Woodbridge and Chittick. Still, there's running hot water, heating, electricity, and Ethernet in all dorms, and you can't really ask for much more than that."

GUYS & GIRLS

"People tend to be much more concerned with their academic lives—men and women both. Hotness tends to clump in groups, so you must seek them out."

"Depends on your tastes, but there are plenty of beautiful people here, and the upside is they're all smart! The only problem is that some Reedies are a little lacking in the social skills department, and this is due to a preference for books over people."

HEALTH & SAFETY

Campus Feels Very Safe.

"I've never felt unsafe on campus. Security officers are around but you hardly notice them."

"The campus safety officers are never far away when you need them. Even if you've just locked yourself out of your room or are uncomfortable walking back to the dorm at two in the morning, they're always there to help out."

LOOKING FOR MORE?

Check out our full-length guide to this school at collegeprowler.com/reed-college/.

Regis University

3333 Regis Blvd.; Denver, CO 80221
(800) 388-2366; www.regis.edu

THE BASICS:

Acceptance Rate: 80%
Yield: 24%
Setting: Large city
Control: Private Non-Profit
Total Undergrads: 5,706
SAT Range: 1450–1800*
ACT Range: 22–26

Student-Faculty Ratio: 14:1
Retention Rate: 71%
Graduation Rate: 64%
Tuition: $29,700
Room & Board: $9,400
Avg. Aid Package: $15,333
Students With Aid: 62%

* of 2400

This School Isn't Graded Yet!

College Prowler grades are calculated using tons of criteria, including survey responses that come from students at this school.

Unfortunately, we haven't gathered enough student surveys yet for this school to be able to calculate the grades for each section. Stay tuned to *CollegeProwler.com* for grade updates and more!

CP's Student Author On...
OVERALL EXPERIENCE

Regis is a close-knit community because it is so small that you know a majority of the student body, which is great when you are walking through campus, saying "Hi!" to most of the people you see. It gives you a sense of togetherness. The professors are amazing at Regis. They are experienced and knowledgeable about their subjects, and they want you to know and understand as much as you can about their subject, so they will do whatever it takes to accomplish this goal.

Students Speak Out On...
OVERALL EXPERIENCE

Q Memorable and Valuable

"Regis is extremely academically focused. The honors program, ministry programs, and faculty are phenomenal. However, the organizations on campus and the student government are committed to planning and providing quality entertainment weekly. There are many creative, academic people on this campus that are dedicated to giving students an experience that will shape the whole person into successful professionals, and wonderful, balanced people."

Q Overall Experience

"Regis University makes it possible for working mothers to achieve a higher degree. They are very supportive."

BEST OF REGIS

1. Being close to the Rocky Mountains for outdoor activities
2. Being so close to downtown Denver and the nightlife that comes with it

Help to Succeed
The school has academic and career counseling available to help you when you need it.

WORST OF REGIS

1. Colorado weather—you never know what you will get.
2. The food selection on campus is not very broad.
3. No football team
4. The parking situation for people living off campus

Expensive
Tuition is a steep $29,700, one of the most expensive rates in the country.

Want a Job? On Your Own
There aren't any placement services for graduates.

Student Body

African American:	6%	Male Undergrads:	37%
Asian American:	3%	Female Undergrads:	63%
Hispanic:	10%	Living On Campus:	50%
International:	1%	Living Off Campus:	50%
Native American:	1%	Male Athletes:	12%
White:	64%	Female Athletes:	7%
Unknown:	15%	Fraternity Members:	0%
From Out-of-State:	35%	Sorority Members:	0%

Frequently Compared Schools:

Gonzaga University
Santa Clara University
University of Colorado
University of Denver

Students Speak Out On... EVERYTHING!

ACADEMICS

Online BSN Program

"The whole process of registration and completing courses has been a breeze. The online advisors are amazing, the content has enhanced my professional life, and the professors are supportive. I highly recommend Regis University."

Academics at Regis

"With Regis being a Jesuit college, hard work is a must. The workload can be heavy but if you properly apply yourself this isn't a problem. With the exception of one professor, I have found all professors and staff at Regis very willing to assist in any way they can."

ATHLETICS

We Did It All Without a Football Team

"We may not have a football team but our soccer teams always make it far in the playoffs. We also offer basketball, baseball, lacrosse, tennis, swimming, hockey, rugby, softball, cross country, among others. Some are club sports but the university does recognize these teams in some instances."

Athletics

"Regis is great in supporting its various teams whether on the field or in the classroom. It is just hard sometimes to make it to all the games due to timing issues and rough when the commendear some of the fields normally used by students to have fun."

CAMPUS DINING

Sodexo

"The locally owned restaurants are good because the people who own them want and expect their food to be good. There are also many food chains around campus. The food provided in the cafeteria could be better. The cafeteria offers pizza, salad bar, sandwich line, and a grilled food area. But the different meals offered at lunch and breakfast are "cafeteria food" (which means it could be better). But overall, you will be satisfied."

Campus Dining

"The dining hall is always clean, the options for though food are repetitive and slim. There is not enough fresh friut and vegetables."

CAMPUS HOUSING

On Campus Housing

"The freshman dorms at Regis University are phenomenal and essential to student life, but after freshman year, dorms are not as fun because student life expands past the dorm life because everyone knows each other. A better option is the townhomes where you still live with and around your classmates, but life is more independent."

GUYS & GIRLS

Variety

"There are people of all sorts at Regis, and you are sure to find someone who piques your interest, but finding them could take some time. Also, because it's a small school, odds are someone else on campus has already dated or hooked up with them"

Variety

"There is a wide variety of students that attend Regis. There are the athletes, the acedemics, and many laid back. Everyone here is here to get an education."

HEALTH & SAFETY

Completely Safe

"Campus Safety is always around and present in their blue coats and car and with all the monitoring that goes on on the small campus, it is hard not to feel safe. Plus the entire campus is gated so it feels like the outside world with all its theft and crime is kept outside campus limits. This doesn't mean though that you still should not lock up you dorm or car to prevent vandalism and from anything being stolen by others."

LOOKING FOR MORE?

Check out our full-length guide to this school at collegeprowler.com/regis-university/.

Rensselaer Polytechnic Institute

110 Eighth St.; Troy, NY 12180
(518) 276-6000; www.rpi.edu

THE BASICS:

Acceptance Rate: 42%
Yield: 26%
Setting: Small city
Control: Private Non-Profit
Total Undergrads: 5,525
SAT Range: 1850–2130*
ACT Range: 25–30

Student-Faculty Ratio: 16:1
Retention Rate: 91%
Graduation Rate: 83%
Tuition: $39,165
Room & Board: $11,145
Avg. Aid Package: $30,635
Students With Aid: 99%

* of 2400

Academics	B+	Greek Life	A-
Athletics	B-	Guys	B
Campus Dining	B+	Health & Safety	B
Campus Housing	B	Local Atmosphere	C
Campus Strictness	B	Nightlife	B-
Computers	A+	Off-Campus Dining	C+
Diversity	C+	Off-Campus Housing	B
Drug Safety	A-	Parking	C
Facilities	B+	Transportation	C+
Girls	C+	Weather	D

CP's Student Author On...
OVERALL EXPERIENCE

RPI provides many advantages to its students—the most important of those are the prospects post-graduation. This is perhaps the most compelling reason to come to RPI—although the economy has been slow in the past few years, most graduates find their way into the workforce with decent entry-level jobs. The school itself is very challenging and provides an education and a name that few other universities can match (especially in the science and engineering fields). The social life isn't what you can find at other schools, but there are still fun things to do if you're willing to look for them; students who get into the social scene tend to remain friends with the people they meet, even after graduation.

Before deciding if RPI is where you want to spend your college years, be sure to take into account a few important points. The first is that this is not a party school—work comes first. Partying is fine, but not at the expense of schoolwork. If you can't manage your time well, you won't be staying in Troy for long. The second thing to remember is the male-to-female ratio is three to one.... For the rest of this editorial, visit collegeprowler.com.

Students Speak Out On...
OVERALL EXPERIENCE

Q It's Amazing Here
"RPI is an amazing place, I love it. You have to be able to find a balance between going out and studying in order to get high grades, however sources are available if you need help."

Q Pretty Fun but Definitely Hard Work
"If you leave your room there is plenty to do between clubs, student organizations and greek life. Parties are pretty good and easy to get into if you know the brothers or are a female. Classes and professors can be extremely tough and require 30+ hours of studying every week. But if you are willing to do the work you can blow off steam on the weekends and RPI on your resume or CV looks very impressive."

BEST OF RPI

1. Education
2. Computer network
3. Fraternity parties
4. Big Red Freakout
5. GM Week
6. Senior Week
7. Mueller Center
8. Intramural sports

Happy Students
91% of students return after their first year.

Proven Success
83% of students will complete their education and graduate with a degree.

WORST OF RPI

1. Parking
2. Male-to-female ratio
3. Weather
4. Anti-social student population
5. Campus Dining
6. Lack of things to do
7. One-sided administration

Expensive
Tuition is a steep $39,165, one of the most expensive rates in the country.

Expensive Dorms
Living on campus doesn't come cheap, with an average housing price tag of $6,300.

Student Body

African American:	4%	Male Undergrads:	72%
Asian American:	11%	Female Undergrads:	28%
Hispanic:	6%	Living On Campus:	53%
International:	2%	Living Off Campus:	47%
Native American:	0%	Male Athletes:	10%
White:	75%	Female Athletes:	16%
Unknown:	2%	Fraternity Members:	25%
From Out-of-State:	71%	Sorority Members:	18%

Students Speak Out On... EVERYTHING!

ACADEMICS

Tutors on Hand

"In my major of mechanical engineering there are many resources available if you're having trouble with physics, or engineering classes."

Science to Engineering Major

"I started as a chemistry major and I can say that once you get into the sophomore chem classes that it becomes really tight knit and the professors are very accessible. I cant speak much for the engineering courses, as I just started taking them but overall I feel that this school provides a quality education. Workload is tough though."

ATHLETICS

Sports Are Not a Priority

"Hockey games are a lot of fun, and our only D1 sport. Otherwise, very few people go to games, but those that do have a lot of school spirit."

Hockey

"We have Div 1 Hockey which the whole school gets behind. Also, our intramural league sports program is awesome. It has different leagues for all skill levels."

CAMPUS DINING

Good!

"Sage and Blitman are both dining halls with really good food. Commons is the main dining hall but it sucks so try and avoid it. You can eat in the Union which has really good food but you have to use your flex or rad dollars. We have a Ben and Jerrys which only takes cash and credit."

New....But Then Boring

"At first all the food is really good but I guess after a while it seems boring, but occassionally theres some special and its delicious. They normally have good desserts too."

Frequently Compared Schools:

Carnegie Mellon University
Cornell University
Massachusetts Institute of Technology
Rochester Institute of Technology

CAMPUS HOUSING

Dorms Are Good Overall

"RA's can be annoying and they are way overpriced but very good quality anyway. Stacwyck all the way."

General on-Campus Living

"If you are a freshmen or a sophomore, the on-campus living system is great because you are both guaranteed on-campus housing, and required to live on-campus. If you are an upperclassmen, good luck finding housing. The dorms are pretty average, but can especially get crowded in Quad. The hill is virtually identical dorms."

GUYS & GIRLS

Mostly Nerds

"As this is a primarily engineering school, it attracts a certain type of person. This is where the geeks and nerds reign supreme. I would say about half of the male population are socially awkward and stay in their rooms. But the other half are normal happy people so its not so bad."

The Ratio

"The ratio of guys to girls at RPI is notoriously high. This is usually balanced out by the fact that 1/4 of those guys spend most of their time playing video games anyway and the all-girls school down the hill. As for the looks, some people try to look good every day and usually do, but the majority of people just roll out of bed and into lecture. But on weekends, nearly everyone usually gets all made up and goes out and lets loose all the stress caused by our huge workload."

HEALTH & SAFETY

Health and Safety at RPI

"Campus safety at RPI is extremely important and always present for students. There are often squad cars patrolling at all times throughout the day and I believe they do an excellent job to ensure student and faculty safety. There are sometimes crimes on campus but overall, I feel very safe on the RPI campus. It is definitely "my home away from home.""

LOOKING FOR MORE?

Check out our full-length guide to this school at collegeprowler.com/rensselaer-polytechnic-institute/.

Rhode Island School of Design

2 College St.; Providence, RI 02903
(401) 454-6100; www.risd.edu

THE BASICS:

Acceptance Rate: 35%	**Student-Faculty Ratio:** 10:1
Yield: 46%	**Retention Rate:** 95%
Setting: Mid-sized city	**Graduation Rate:** 86%
Control: Private Non-Profit	**Tuition:** $36,659
Total Undergrads: 1,940	**Room & Board:** $10,846
SAT Range: 1690–2050*	**Avg. Aid Package:** $11,800
ACT Range: 22–29	**Students With Aid:** 51%

* of 2400

Academics	B+	Greek Life	N/A
Athletics	D-	Guys	C+
Campus Dining	B	Health & Safety	B
Campus Housing	B	Local Atmosphere	A-
Campus Strictness	B+	Nightlife	B
Computers	B+	Off-Campus Dining	A-
Diversity	B+	Off-Campus Housing	C
Drug Safety	C+	Parking	C-
Facilities	B-	Transportation	A-
Girls	B+	Weather	C

CP's Student Author On... OVERALL EXPERIENCE

Many students love and hate RISD at the same time. The workload may be extremely demanding, but RISD students are not coming to receive the typical college experience. They are coming to get in touch with a community of artists that will enrich their understanding of art as a medium. RISD students come to gain access to an amazing amount of resources and equipment, which enable them to push their art form as much as possible. They aren't looking for the big party school or a Greek scene—they are coming here to find themselves, to be individuals, and excel in their individual talents.

RISD students work very hard and are rewarded in the end. Many feel they are prepared to enter some sort of job or pursue a way to become active professionals in their field. In many ways, RISD is like boot camp for art, but it's also an amazing opportunity for students to make the work that they want, while learning about themselves and their surroundings in the process.... For the rest of this editorial, visit collegeprowler.com.

Students Speak Out On... OVERALL EXPERIENCE

Q Artist Community

"Rhode Island School of Design is a great environment for artists. The people that surround you everyday are all different and creative which inspires individual creativity and motivation. Everyone is passionate about what they do and work so hard, our work is our life."

Q It's Got Its Ups and Downs

"Organization needs attention. With the budget the school has they seem to not always have the best teachers for the "less important" courses. Students teaching students is probably one of the best aspects of this school. You are surrounded by students who work until they cant stand. And there are always great demos and lectures going around."

Q "Art school is the biggest joke and the best thing ever. Don't take it too seriously."

Q "I love it—I wouldn't want to be anywhere else."

Q "RISD is a school that is academically and personally rigorous and challenging."

BEST OF RISD

1. The versatility and originality of art and design projects
2. The growth in the way one develops an idea and its construction
3. The professors
4. Preparation for future careers

Happy Students
95% of students return after their first year.

Commitment to Teaching
There are 10 students for every member of faculty on campus.

WORST OF RISD

1. A large workload
2. Stinginess in financial aid
3. There's no official double-major program
4. The segregation among departments
5. A lethargic reaction to extracurricular activities

Expensive
Tuition is a steep $36,659, one of the most expensive rates in the country.

Expensive Dorms
Living on campus doesn't come cheap, with an average housing price tag of $6,120.

Student Body

African American:	2%	Male Undergrads:	33%
Asian American:	13%	Female Undergrads:	67%
Hispanic:	4%	Living On Campus:	70%
International:	14%	Living Off Campus:	30%
Native American:	0%	Male Athletes:	0%
White:	35%	Female Athletes:	0%
Unknown:	32%	Fraternity Members:	0%
From Out-of-State:	95%	Sorority Members:	0%

Students Speak Out On... EVERYTHING!

ACADEMICS

Q Interior Architecture

"The program is based on the study of sustainability and adaptive reuse in the architectural design, using concept, green design and. The undergraduate program prepares students with an in depth understanding of the reuse of the building in this day in age with courses in structure, human factors and other areas to prepare the student with the understanding of design to both work with the artistic approach and the effect on the user."

Q

"Almost the only teachers that I have had that I would consider bad were in Foundation Year. Everything is less specialized, and it doesn't seem they're quite as into the class. But then again, it really depends on what teachers you happened to get."

Q

"There are too many RISD alumni as teachers. However, if you get into the right class, it's very interesting."

ATHLETICS

Q Haha... What?

"Hahaha. Athletics? Barely. It's more of a joke. There is a Hockey team and a basketball team. There is intermural soccer. Fans are crazy in the stands, even if we're losing really really badly. It's a fun crowd, but sports are not the main focus at risd."

Q Athletics Are Humerous at RISD

"RISD has a few informal sports teams. The school also has a very interesting Mascot. However, RISD students are allowed to participate in Brown University sports and recreational activities"

CAMPUS DINING

Q Taste of the World

"There are new food to try everyday. Almost unlimited choices and combination of food choices, even for the vegetarians!"

Q

"The breakfast menu at the cafeteria never changes, and the eggs are not real, but it's very sanitary."

CAMPUS HOUSING

Q Living on Campus

"it's expensive. From 4,500- 12,000 a year for on campus housing. You can get off campus housing for as little as 300 a month if you look hard enough."

Q

"Compared to other colleges, RISD has good housing, even for freshmen. To RISD students, the Quad seems horrible, but just for one year. After freshman year, the housing on campus is almost luxurious."

GUYS & GIRLS

Q Guys and Gals

"Not to disappoint the girls, but you have to understand one thing about RISD- its an art school, and an art school is bound to have less guys than girls. I'd say 80% girls, 20% guys, and of the 20%, half would be qualified as gay. But no worries! RISD is located in close proximity to Brown, and there are plenty of opportunities for us girls to attend Brown parties. As for RISD girls, alot of them look and dress like models."

Q

"The guys and girls are hot, fun, and smart. There are too many gay guys, bummer, but they make great friends. There are plenty of good girlfriends."

HEALTH & SAFETY

Q Very Safe

"Rhode Island School of Design's campus security is run by Public Safety. They have emergency call stations spread throughout campus and also monitor the campus personally. I have never felt unsafe on campus."

Q Health and Saftey

"School Health serviced are pretty basic. They could really try to do walk ins since the school gives us such busy schedules. Security is not bad even though it is pretty spread out. The school has a great "RISD RIDES" shuttle service from 7pm to 330am. Pretty helpful and makes being in studio late helpful"

LOOKING FOR MORE?

Check out our full-length guide to this school at collegeprowler.com/rhode-island-school-of-design/.

Rhodes College

2000 North Parkway; Memphis, TN 38112
(901) 843-3000; www.rhodes.edu

THE BASICS:

Acceptance Rate: 42%
Yield: 20%
Setting: Large city
Control: Private Non-Profit
Total Undergrads: 1,689
SAT Range: 1730–2060*
ACT Range: 26–30

Student-Faculty Ratio: 10:1
Retention Rate: 90%
Graduation Rate: 72%
Tuition: $33,710
Room & Board: $8,314
Avg. Aid Package: $29,144
Students With Aid: 91%

* of 2400

Academics	B+	Greek Life	A-
Athletics	C-	Guys	A-
Campus Dining	C	Health & Safety	A-
Campus Housing	B+	Local Atmosphere	B
Campus Strictness	B+	Nightlife	A-
Computers	B	Off-Campus Dining	A
Diversity	C+	Off-Campus Housing	B+
Drug Safety	C-	Parking	A
Facilities	B+	Transportation	C
Girls	B+	Weather	B

CP's Student Author On...
OVERALL EXPERIENCE

When assessing their college experience, most students feel that Rhodes is the right place for them and wouldn't want to be anywhere else. The incredible academics, boundless opportunities, and one-of-a-kind atmosphere make it hard to be disappointed. At Rhodes, students are constantly challenged to reach their potential, explore their interests, and take advantage of their talent. In the beginning, it's sometimes difficult for students to take all of this in. Students who are unhappy at Rhodes and decide to transfer often don't find their niche right away. They get frustrated with the hefty workload or unnerved by other students' unbridled ambition, and ultimately decide to leave. The best things about Rhodes are discovered after spending time as a student, as a leader, as a teacher, and realizing who you love being and what you love doing.

At some point during their time at Rhodes, students are going to dislike something about the college—the massive amount of work, the social scene, the food, and even the weather. But overall, most students are very satisfied with their decision to attend Rhodes.... For the rest of this editorial, visit collegeprowler.com.

Students Speak Out On...
OVERALL EXPERIENCE

Q No Regrets

"I absolutely love Rhodes. It is definitely hard work- you have to study a fair amount to stay on top, but it's totally worth it. There is always plenty to do other than academics as well, and the people are all really friendly. Greek life does not dominant the social scene; there are plenty of non-Greek related things to do. The professors are wonderful and the campus is beautiful. I love everything about this school."

Q Amazing here

"It's amazing. I love it. You learn so much and have so much fun."

Q Love

"I've loved my time at Rhodes. Even though they ended up not having a specific major for what I wanted to go into, I was able to make up for it by taking a class or two at CBU and also taking certain other classes in other disciplines. It's been challenging, but in a good way."

BEST OF RHODES

1. The Honor Code
2. Professor-student relationships
3. Strong academic programs
4. Close-knit student body
5. Gothic architecture
6. The squirrels

Happy Students
90% of students return after their first year.

Commitment to Teaching
There are 10 students for every member of faculty on campus.

WORST OF RHODES

1. Meal plan/dining options
2. Lack of diversity
3. Tuition
4. Athletics
5. The class registration "Tree"
6. Erratic weather and/ or random flooding

Expensive
Tuition is a steep $33,710, one of the most expensive rates in the country.

Student Body

African American:	7%	Male Undergrads:	42%
Asian American:	5%	Female Undergrads:	58%
Hispanic:	2%	Living On Campus:	76%
International:	2%	Living Off Campus:	24%
Native American:	0%	Male Athletes:	35%
White:	79%	Female Athletes:	20%
Unknown:	4%	Fraternity Members:	45%
From Out-of-State:	77%	Sorority Members:	53%

Frequently Compared Schools:

Furman University
University of Richmond
Vanderbilt University
Wake Forest University

Students Speak Out On... EVERYTHING!

ACADEMICS

Academics

"Small class sizes. Small department sizes. Limited course offerings. Work load is rigorous and mostly involves memorization. Professors vary greatly. Some are fantastic and inspiring, some are actually more boring than the text book."

Neuroscience

"I am a neuroscience major and I would say that it is extremely hard. The professors are tough but interesting. You will definitely learn how to think like a neuroscientist and be challenged. Science courses are some of the toughest in general so pre-med students will definitely be prepared."

ATHLETICS

Rhodes Athletics

"Athletics at Rhodes are ok. I mean it is division III, so you cant really compare it to D1 athletics. but the majority of the students are seen tailgating before the home football games. However, you only really attend the games, if you are another athlete, or have a friend/roommate on the team. The teams in general are pretty good. Field Hockey and baseball usually go to NCAA. Oh, and were just about to get a lacrosse team too"

No Fans

"A high portion of students participate in athletics, but the school spirit for athletics is incredibly low compared to a state school."

CAMPUS DINING

Actually Pretty Good

"I think the on-campus dining options are pretty good! If you don't like what the main dish is, you can always get pizza, sandwiches, salad, and stir-fry. And who doesn't love the pub? Beers with your professors is a lot of fun!"

Dining Halls

"The food places aren't bad, but since there are only two you kind of get sick of them. However, there are good places to eat within walking distance of campus."

CAMPUS HOUSING

Pretty Good

"Don't listen to what people say..WILLIFORD IS AWESOME. there's a great sense of community. you will love it. the rooms are pretty tiny but just bring underbed storage..it's no big deal. But seriously. Williford is like a huge family."

Living on Campus Is Convenient and Fun

"I love living in the dorms. The girls that I was placed on a hall with could not have been more fantastic and my friends and I worked with the system to all live in the same dorm next year. Because campus is so small it's very convenient to live on campus. The dorms are nice and most upperclassmen dorms are pretty roomy. I like that a lot of dorms with hall bathrooms have sinks in the room."

GUYS & GIRLS

Very Attractive Campus

"definitely a very attractive campus overall. a lot of people do dress up for class but you do see everything."

Girls and Guys

"Here at Rhodes College you can find someone from each social group imaginable. There is a good bit of diversity on the Rhodes campus, which is something that I really like. You can find people that are just like you while you can also meet people who you might have never considered being friends with in high school."

HEALTH & SAFETY

Totally Safe

"I have never felt unsafe on Rhodes's campus. It is a small, beautiful, safe place to be. Keep your doors locked to avoid petty theft or late-night pranks. And be warned that Campus Security isn't too happy 'bout drinking games, so keep your Beirut games under control."

LOOKING FOR MORE?

Check out our full-length guide to this school at collegeprowler.com/rhodes-college/.

Rice University

6100 S. Main St.; Houston, TX 77005
· (713) 348-0000; www.rice.edu

THE BASICS:

Acceptance Rate: 22%	Student-Faculty Ratio: 8:1
Yield: 36%	Retention Rate: 97%
Setting: Large city	Graduation Rate: 93%
Control: Private Non-Profit	Tuition: $32,057
Total Undergrads: 3,342	Room & Board: $11,230
SAT Range: 1970–2270*	Avg. Aid Package: $19,565
ACT Range: 30–34	Students With Aid: 85%

* of 2400

Academics	A	Greek Life	N/A
Athletics	B	Guys	B
Campus Dining	B	Health & Safety	B+
Campus Housing	A	Local Atmosphere	A-
Campus Strictness	A-	Nightlife	A-
Computers	A-	Off-Campus Dining	A+
Diversity	A-	Off-Campus Housing	C
Drug Safety	B+	Parking	B
Facilities	B+	Transportation	C
Girls	B-	Weather	B

CP's Student Author On...
OVERALL EXPERIENCE

Overall, Rice students are highly satisfied with their college experiences. While they complain about some of the negative aspects of Houston (pollution, transportation, traffic, panhandlers), they also admit that there are many positive aspects to Rice's location (cultural and social opportunities of a big city, great restaurants!). Similarly, students have gripes about the University, including rising prices, the increasingly bleak parking situation, and a somewhat repetitive social scene (the same parties every year). Many aspects of Houston and Rice can be seen as both positive and negative. Houston weather is warm and temperate for the winter months, but it is oppressively hot and humid in the summer. Rice's small campus and student body are nice because they create a personal environment and allow students to meet more people and not just feel like faces in the crowd. However, students also claim that it begins to feel confining at times.

Rice students love the residential college system. They also find their coursework to be challenging, but manageable.... For the rest of this editorial, visit collegeprowler.com.

Students Speak Out On...
OVERALL EXPERIENCE

Q **Unique and Fantastic**

"There's no where else I can imagine going to school. I can spend a week pulling all-nighters designing heart valves and reviewing biomechanics with some of my best friends, and the next week filling water balloons in the gorgeous March weather, drinking with some of the most brilliant people I know in preparation for Beer Bike. There's such a thrilling combination of stimulation here: Houston has a ton of experiences to offer, but my peers here are what make Rice special."

Q **It's Awesome**

"You hear that a lot about fantastic schools like Rice, but I'm telling you from somebody who's visited friends at peer schools like Columbia, Stanford, Penn, and Yale that the college experience at Rice is unparalleled. If you get in, definitely come check it out for yourself."

BEST OF RICE

1. The residential college system
2. Tremendous faculty and challenging academics
3. The alcohol policy/ wet campus
4. The honor code
5. Willy Week/Beer Bike

Happy Students
97% of students return after their first year.

Commitment to Teaching
There are 8 students for every member of faculty on campus.

WORST OF RICE

1. Parking and tickets
2. Overachiever attitude
3. Repetitive/monotonous social life
4. Some professors consider teacher as second string
5. Honor code
6. Public transportation

Expensive
Tuition is a steep $32,057, one of the most expensive rates in the country.

Expensive Dorms
Living on campus doesn't come cheap, with an average housing price tag of $7,510.

Student Body

African American:	7%	Male Undergrads:	52%
Asian American:	20%	Female Undergrads:	48%
Hispanic:	12%	Living On Campus:	80%
International:	6%	Living Off Campus:	20%
Native American:	1%	Male Athletes:	18%
White:	49%	Female Athletes:	13%
Unknown:	5%	Fraternity Members:	0%
From Out-of-State:	53%	Sorority Members:	0%

Frequently Compared Schools:

Duke University
Stanford University
University of Pennsylvania
Vanderbilt University

Students Speak Out On... EVERYTHING!

ACADEMICS

Great Academics

"The academics are very estimable here at Rice. As a freshman, I have not found the transition from public high school to classes here at Rice to be unmanageable."

Top Notch

"The student to teacher ratio at Rice is 5:1. That's lower than nearly all the Ivys. It means that there are a ton of opportunities to get involved in research and further engage in the material during office hours and such. The class registration system is pain free, and each department here is great, unlike some schools that only have one good program (think Georgetown SFS). Students are interested in their work, and the general campus attitude is geared towards somebody who wants to learn."

ATHLETICS

Not Such a Big Deal

"Although there is moderate interest in IM sports, few people care about varsity sports. The student section at football games is just laughable, while basketball games aren't much better. Baseball gets the most attention, but is still not a hugely significant event for most students. However, Rice athletes are ranked highly academically; Rice prides itself on putting the "student" first in "student athlete", and this is something to be commended, I feel."

"Varsity sports aren't too big at Rice, but we won the National Championship in baseball recently, so it could be on the upswing!"

CAMPUS DINING

Clean and Fresh

"Nearly all the dining facilities (we call them serveries) at Rice are new. That allows food to be fresh and delicious. For example, the pizza at West Servery is better than any take out around town. Rice also employs real chefs -- not food industry workers. There are people with white chef suits on, inspecting the food, and making sure students are enjoying every meal.

The food at Rice compared to other universities is truly top notch."

Poor Choices for Vegetarians

"Every servery is different, so the food choices vary greatly. At north servery, there is really good vegetarian food only on tuesday lunch, but the rest of the week is rather lacking. however, other serveries sometimes have better options, but they are on like the opposite side of campus, so its generally not worth the walk."

CAMPUS HOUSING

Wiess College

"It depends on the residential college, but Wiess, where I am at, is very nice. It's cleaned by a crew every morning, and bathroom is kept clean every week. It's also very spacious with a suite-style living and a nice "living room" type common area per room. A large yard is also available as well as recording rooms, movie rooms, dance rooms, etc and a large common area for social reasons. There is also a computer lab on each college."

GUYS & GIRLS

There's One for Everyone

"You'll find a variety of nice, good looking educated guys. The girls are hot and educated too. Everyone has something unique about them and you will meet your soulmate here."

HEALTH & SAFETY

Rice University Police Dep't = the Best

"Unlike some schools with just a public safety department, Rice employs its own police department. They're affectionately called RUPD here on campus. The officers are not out to get students, only outside criminals. In fact, RUPD officers regularly eat lunch in the colleges with students. I feel totally safe on campus and on the outskirts of campus too."

LOOKING FOR MORE?

Check out our full-length guide to this school at collegeprowler.com/rice-university/.

Rider University

2083 Lawrence Road; Lawrenceville, NJ 08648
(609) 896-5000; www.rider.edu

THE BASICS:

Acceptance Rate: 75%
Yield: 19%
Setting: Suburban
Control: Private Non-Profit
Total Undergrads: 4,891
SAT Range: 1400–1720*
ACT Range: 19–24

Student-Faculty Ratio: 13:1
Retention Rate: 79%
Graduation Rate: 58%
Tuition: $29,060
Room & Board: $10,720
Avg. Aid Package: $14,338
Students With Aid: 96%

* of 2400

Academics	B	Greek Life	B
Athletics	B-	Guys	B
Campus Dining	B	Health & Safety	B
Campus Housing	B	Local Atmosphere	B+
Campus Strictness	C	Nightlife	B
Computers	B+	Off-Campus Dining	B
Diversity	B	Off-Campus Housing	B-
Drug Safety	C	Parking	A-
Facilities	B	Transportation	C+
Girls	C+	Weather	B-

CP's Student Author On...
OVERALL EXPERIENCE

Rider University has a lot going for it. It is a small school, which can offer a personal college experience to students. The class sizes are small, so you will get to know the professors and your voice will be heard. The professors are generally more than willing to help students if they need additional help with their academics or even if they're having a non-academic problem. The advisers here are extremely helpful, as well—they offer great assistance when scheduling your classes and are there to help you find your way after Rider.

A small student body means everyone pretty much recognizes every face on campus. This can provide a sense of comfort, but some people say this leads to a lack of privacy because everyone knows everyone else's business. But, there is a bunch of nearby towns if you want to escape campus for awhile. Rider is also a very safe place because the University does all it can to keep students safe on campus.

Students Speak Out On...
OVERALL EXPERIENCE

Q Great Mix

"We have a great mix of students for the arts, student athletes, etc. It is a country-club-like setting in a beautiful part of the state with every amenity available very quickly."

Q Rider Is Small, but I Like It

"Even though Rider is a small college, I feel that it's great. I love knowing a lot of people on campus, and I enjoy the small class sizes."

Q Rider Experience

"It's a great experience. The professors are very helpful, and the students very friendly. It's not a big campus; everything is walking distance. It's in a great location, only a 15-minute drive to Princeton, 45-minutes drive to Belmar Beach, and a 45-minute drive to Philadelphia."

Q Great Services

"The classes are small, and if you need help, professors are willing to help. For almost every course there is a tutoring session available a couple times a week. The classes have good equipment."

BEST OF RIDER

1. Academics
2. Activities offered
3. Advisers are easy to talk to.
4. Close-knit community
5. It is easy to double major.
6. Local food options
7. Location

Big Dorms
85% of students surveyed felt that dorms were more spacious than average.

WORST OF RIDER

1. Campus floods easily when it rains.
2. Housing lottery system
3. Lack of late-night food options
4. Lots of people go home every weekend.
5. Most rooms don't have air conditioning.

Expensive
Tuition is a steep $29,060, one of the most expensive rates in the country.

Expensive to Just Get By
50% of students surveyed felt that the amount it costs to live while at school was worse than average.

Student Body

African American:	9%	Male Undergrads:	39%
Asian American:	4%	Female Undergrads:	61%
Hispanic:	5%	Living On Campus:	56%
International:	1%	Living Off Campus:	44%
Native American:	0%	Male Athletes:	10%
White:	70%	Female Athletes:	6%
Unknown:	10%	Fraternity Members:	4%
From Out-of-State:	28%	Sorority Members:	9%

Students Speak Out On... EVERYTHING!

ACADEMICS

Q Westminster Choir College Is Always Challenging

"Students at WCC are expected to constantly be practicing (an hour a day for voice primary and three hours a day for piano primary). This alone is demanding. On top of that, the professors demand your best effort and all your attention in each of their classes. The Music Education Department especially puts its students through a rigorous academic and musical experience."

Q Secondary Education

"Almost all of the education professors are awesome. They are very nice and are always there to help. The workload is sometimes a lot—some people even complain that it's too much—but in reality, they are just preparing future educators for the real world. They get you in the classroom as early as your sophomore year, so you'll know very early on if teaching is the right career choice for you."

ATHLETICS

Q School Spirit

"There is high support for the athletes."

Q Awesome Sports

"The women's soccer team is the best I have ever seen at this college so far. Every sport here is Division I, and everything is just wonderful. There is no unsportsmanlike conduct on the teams, and all the people at the college support their friends and athletes to keep up the Rider spirit."

CAMPUS DINING

Q Varied and Balanced

"The school provides a variety of vegetarian and healthy alternatives."

Q Great

"There's a good selection for all appetites. I thoroughly enjoy the dining and have never been bored of it."

Frequently Compared Schools:

Drexel University
Lafayette College
Rowan University
Rutgers University

CAMPUS HOUSING

Q Satisfying Experience

"My freshman dorm was brand new and in excellent condition. This year, I am in an older dorm but there is no decrease in my standard of living."

Q Greek Housing

"I live in a sorority "house," which is basically a glorified dorm because we all get to live together, have carpeting, a kitchen, and can put up shelves, and I really love it here! I just wish the outside looked as pretty as the inside and not like a normal dorm."

GUYS & GIRLS

Q Variety!

"There are so many different kinds of people here on campus, and sometimes it makes me wish I were single when I got here! There are your typical jocks, preps, and jokers, but there are also plenty of guys who are genuine sweethearts, and there are plenty of nerds that you can relate to if you have a ton of schoolwork. In general, it's an ocean in a pond!"

Q The Guys Are Hot

"They guys here have different taste. They all have their own sense of style, all look different and alot of them are HOT! there are guys with spiky hair, guys with "justin beiber" type hair, or guys with short hair. There is a variety and that is one reason i love it!"

HEALTH & SAFETY

Q Crime Rate Is Very Low

"The crime rate at Rider is very low to nonexistent. I've never heard of a crime being committed on campus or in the surrounding town. Public Safety often looks bored and only tends to have to deal with people parking in the wrong places."

LOOKING FOR MORE?

Check out our full-length guide to this school at collegeprowler.com/rider-university/.

Robert Morris University

6001 University Blvd.; Moon Township, PA 15108
(800) 762-0097; www.rmu.edu

THE BASICS:

Acceptance Rate: 92%
Yield: 21%
Setting: Suburban
Control: Private Non-Profit
Total Undergrads: 3,701
SAT Range: 1350–1660*
ACT Range: 20–24

Student-Faculty Ratio: 15:1
Retention Rate: 78%
Graduation Rate: 56%
Tuition: $20,560
Room & Board: $10,370
Avg. Aid Package: $16,548
Students With Aid: 99%

of 2400

Academics	B-	Greek Life	C+
Athletics	C+	Guys	B+
Campus Dining	C	Health & Safety	A
Campus Housing	C-	Local Atmosphere	B+
Campus Strictness	C	Nightlife	B-
Computers	B	Off-Campus Dining	C
Diversity	C+	Off-Campus Housing	C+
Drug Safety	B-	Parking	B-
Facilities	B+	Transportation	B+
Girls	B-	Weather	B-

CP's Student Author On...
OVERALL EXPERIENCE

RMU goes above and beyond to prepare students for future careers, with career fairs, career expos, and the never-ending help from the Career Center. RMU's ColonialTRAK is also incredibly helpful, and even after graduating, students are allowed to use it, just as they are allowed to use the Career Center. RMU has very high placement rates for alumni (94 percent for undergraduates). And the RMU Web site states that "one of the ultimate outcomes for an institution like RMU, whose curriculum is centered upon applied knowledge, is the willingness of employers to hire its graduates."

RMU has about 5,000 students, so it's not a huge campus, but a good enough size to meet plenty of people and have a good time. It's not overwhelming, but it's also not underwhelming. The amount of time professors take with helping students is a huge advantage. There is personal attention that comes along with the 16-to-1 student-to-faculty ratio. Classes are not lecture halls; they are interactive and group discussions are always encouraged.... For the rest of this editorial, visit collegeprowler.com.

Students Speak Out On...
OVERALL EXPERIENCE

Q I Love It
"Robert Morris is awesome. The people there are so friendly. I love the students, the instructors, and the programs!!"

Q RMU
"I loved RMU! The part I loved the most was the amount of one-on-one time I received with my professors."

Q Great School If You're Focused on Your Future.
"Sometimes the nights can be quite boring, but I knew that if I went to a crazy party school, then I would get absolutely no work done. It is really great school and the professors are always willing to help you with class work."

Q Great
"Overall, I enjoy RMU, I especially like the academics, and the people."

Q Pretty Good
"It is a pretty good experience. Your teachers will make sure that you are successful and will do whatever they can to help. Not much to do on campus though and can be very boring from a social life stand point."

BEST OF ROBERT MORRIS

1. Academics
2. Athletics
3. People
4. Ability to stand out
5. Professors

Easy Financial Aid Process
58% of students surveyed told us that the financial aid process went smoothly and they received the financial aid they needed.

WORST OF ROBERT MORRIS

1. The cost of tuition
2. Lack of things to do on campus
3. Parking
4. Everyone goes home on the weekends.
5. If you don't have a car, you can't go anywhere.

Disappointed Students
30% of students surveyed would not choose to attend this school if they could do it all over again.

Student Body

African American:	8%	Male Undergrads:	55%
Asian American:	1%	Female Undergrads:	45%
Hispanic:	1%	Living On Campus:	32%
International:	2%	Living Off Campus:	68%
Native American:	0%	Male Athletes:	17%
White:	83%	Female Athletes:	16%
Unknown:	4%	Fraternity Members:	3%
From Out-of-State:	22%	Sorority Members:	4%

Frequently Compared Schools:

Duquesne University
Kent State University
Penn State
University of Pittsburgh

Students Speak Out On... EVERYTHING!

ACADEMICS

Q Wonderful

"I like meeting new people in my classes and forming study groups."

Q Accounting Teachers

"The Teachers at Rober Morris University are incredible. They spend one-on-one time with each student if need be. The teachers do no try to rush you out of their door but instead will spend as much time that is needed for you to understand the information."

Q Awesome

"The academics here are awesome. Theres something about RMU's academics that makes it a great experience."

ATHLETICS

Q Athletics

"Our varsity sports has a excellent performance well participated by students and followed by fans. With outstanding practice and workout facilities."

Q Good Entertainment

"I think the athletics are good, but there is usually very little interest unless a team is very successful."

Q Excellant Opportunity to Compete at the Div 1Aa Level

"varsity sports as well as the intramural sports are top notch in the country"

CAMPUS DINING

Q Romo Food Court

"Our food court in very good, a little pricey but good food, wish they were open later."

Q It Is All Good to Me

"I have no real complaints about the dining on campus. Granted it is not the best, it could always be better, but it is not the worst either. RMU has given the students a lot of variety and offer good times before they close. The dining hall does their best to change things up and keep us wanting more. Since I am not a picky eater, I like it all."

Q Sufficent

"Fast, convenient, with an array of dining choices from healthy to fattening."

CAMPUS HOUSING

Q I Think the Dorms Are Amazing

"I dont really live on campus, but I've been in there and heard many stories. The dorms are clean, but the rooms arent very spacious. The building is very clean."

Q Need Updated

"Housing could use updates: dorms didn't even have AC when I went there. The new apartments are very nice though."

Q Robert Morris University Cost

"the Cost of the Tuition at RMU is near $33,000/year. The housing runs a near $10,000/year with this kind of cost and limited parking it is very inconvient if you live on campus and have a vehicle."

GUYS & GIRLS

Q Gender Mix

"There is a ggood ratio of girl to guy count on campus. They're also some cute girls."

Q School Social Life

"Great group of students here, no creeps(well maybe 1 or 2) but overall a higher standard of students."

HEALTH & SAFETY

Q Campus Safety

"I felt very safe while I was on campus never once did I feel unsafe."

Q Very Safe and Healthy University

"RMU is very safe and promotes a healthy lifestyle through nutrition and exercise."

LOOKING FOR MORE?

Check out our full-length guide to this school at collegeprowler.com/robert-morris-university/.

Rochester Institute of Technology

1 Lomb Memorial Drive; Rochester, NY 14623
(585) 475-2411; www.rit.edu

THE BASICS:

Acceptance Rate: 62%	**Student-Faculty Ratio:** 12:1
Yield: 32%	**Retention Rate:** 85%
Setting: Suburban	**Graduation Rate:** 62%
Control: Private Non-Profit	**Tuition:** $29,283
Total Undergrads: 12,980	**Room & Board:** $9,642
SAT Range: 1610–1930*	**Avg. Aid Package:** $19,800
ACT Range: 25–30	**Students With Aid:** 92%

* of 2400

Academics	B+	Greek Life	B
Athletics	C+	Guys	B
Campus Dining	B	Health & Safety	B
Campus Housing	B-	Local Atmosphere	B
Campus Strictness	B	Nightlife	B
Computers	A+	Off-Campus Dining	B
Diversity	B-	Off-Campus Housing	B+
Drug Safety	C-	Parking	B-
Facilities	B	Transportation	A-
Girls	B-	Weather	D+

CP's Student Author On... OVERALL EXPERIENCE

RIT does its best to provide students with a wealth of information, great facilities, top-notch academics, and a pretty good athletic program. Living in Rochester for four years teaches students a lot about who they are and what they want out of life (with the lack student-oriented activities, you'll have a lot of time to think). Many choose to drop out or transfer schools, due to the strenuous quarter system and the arduous work hours that come along with it. Many students who come to RIT on academic scholarships end up on academic probation. Many choose to do the drunken-college-student bit, and many choose the studious-bookworm role; but in the end, many students realize that classwork may not always be the most important thing. Most students here will, at one time or another, disagree with their roommates, RAs, bursars, registrars, and their departments. These are all facts of life, though. No two people can see eye to eye on everything.

In the end, four years and one degree later, many RIT students will tell you that they would willingly do it all over again.... For the rest of this editorial, visit collegeprowler.com.

Students Speak Out On... OVERALL EXPERIENCE

Q My School Is Awesome

"I love RIT. I do not think I would be this happy anywhere else. RIT does have some quirks, but what school doesn't? RIT is on a trimester system, which makes school seem a lot easier and faster. They are also on an A, B, C grading system, which makes it easy to get good grades if you try. RIT is a perfect mix of school and fun. There are many different social things you can do - sports games, parties, fundraisers. It is just a complete blast and I am so glad I chose it."

Q Overall Experience

"The school is just wonderful. Teachers are nice and offer lots of support. there are plenty of study supports for the students as well. There is alot of school pride in everything and slowly becoming recognized as a really good school. The social and academic life balance each other out really nicely. Glad I went to this school."

Q Not Too Bad

"I am going for an education so I am pretty satisfied. Met a lot of friend and had some good times"

BEST OF RIT

1. Getting professional experience from co-ops
2. The strongly focused academic environment
3. Number of various club and events on campus
4. The variety of wellness courses

Happy Students
85% of students return after their first year.

Easy Financial Aid Process
52% of students surveyed told us that the financial aid process went smoothly and they received the financial aid they needed.

WORST OF RIT

1. The poor girl-to-guy ratio
2. The unpredictable weather
3. Lack of (legal) parking all around campus
4. Lack of school spirit at sporting events (other than hockey)

Expensive
Tuition is a steep $29,283, one of the most expensive rates in the country.

Student Body

African American:	5%	Male Undergrads:	67%
Asian American:	5%	Female Undergrads:	33%
Hispanic:	4%	Living On Campus:	65%
International:	5%	Living Off Campus:	35%
Native American:	0%	Male Athletes:	6%
White:	70%	Female Athletes:	7%
Unknown:	10%	Fraternity Members:	5%
From Out-of-State:	50%	Sorority Members:	5%

Students Speak Out On...
EVERYTHING!

ACADEMICS

Special Study Options

"I plan on working with the Deaf/Hard of Hearing and RIT offers one of the BEST programs in the country for English Interpreting"

Amazing Program for My Major

"Computer Engineering here is really amazing. The advisors and professors always make time for you and the facilities are great. Theres a place to be tutored for everything and with the difficulty of the major, you will need them. The Co-Op program is said to be one of the bests. I haven't done a co-op, but I am sure it will be really fun, and not too difficult to get one."

ATHLETICS

Go RIT Tigers!

"RIT doesn't really have any major teams aside from the hockey team... but the hockey team is absolutely fantastic. Also, the school allows all the students access to all the athletic facilities with just a swipe of your ID, which is great and incredibly useful if you and your friends want to go ice skating or swimming."

HOCKEY

"Highly popular with Hockey both men and women. Division I Men Hockey in Frozen Four of 2010. Women Hockey of 2010-11 with high record! Hockey rink always full and planning to buy a new and bigger hockey rink on campus for future fans!"

CAMPUS DINING

Dining

"The campus has many dining choices and at the cafeterias there are many different choices in foods to eat. The food is in a large veriety."

Many Eateries, Varying Menues, Food Is Generally Tasty.

"As a freshman, the main dinning hall can get repetitive, but overall food quality is above average. After freshman year food offerings are extremely varied on campus as each of the campus eateries and stores have an independent manager.

This allows for the various campus offerings to all use the same meal plans but offer significantly differing types of dining experiences."

CAMPUS HOUSING

Freshman Housing

"The dorms were so much fun. I was put in a suite style dorm, so i had to share a bathroom with 6 people, while my friends (living in the building next to mine) had to share with the whole floor. It was fun being around people all the time though, and all the dorms were connected in underground tunnels, so you didn't have to walk outside in the winter. The tunnels also connected to two food places and a convenient store."

Campus

"The RIT campus is very nice and very modern. The facilities are beautiful. The school costs a lot so it should be nice."

GUYS & GIRLS

A Bunch of Awesome People, but Mostly Guys

"RIT had gained a bit of a rep for being a nerd school, and while not everyone there is a 'nerd,' many of them are. Everyone is pretty individual in their style and people come from everywhere. Still, the school has a 70/30 split between guys and girls, so the testosterone gets a bit overwhelming at times."

HEALTH & SAFETY

Safety on Campus

"During the tour, one could see at any given point on campus, at least 2 "blue lights" frowhere they stood. These blue lights are actually direct connections to campus safety in the form of 27 new York state trained public safety officers who will do everything from escort you to a destination, to help jumpstart your car in the winter. Aside from this, every residence hall on campus as well as academic buildings, require ID card access. This being said, I felt very safe on campus."

LOOKING FOR MORE?
Check out our full-length guide to this school at collegeprowler.com/rochester-institute-of-technology/.

Rollins College

1000 Holt Ave.; Winter Park, FL 32789
(407) 646-2000; www.rollins.edu

THE BASICS:

Acceptance Rate: 62%
Yield: 25%
Setting: Suburban
Control: Private Non-Profit
Total Undergrads: 2,581
SAT Range: 1650–1940*
ACT Range: 23–28

Student-Faculty Ratio: 10:1
Retention Rate: 82%
Graduation Rate: 69%
Tuition: $36,220
Room & Board: $11,320
Avg. Aid Package: $25,245
Students With Aid: 71%

* of 2400

Academics	B	Greek Life	A
Athletics	B	Guys	B+
Campus Dining	B+	Health & Safety	B-
Campus Housing	C+	Local Atmosphere	A-
Campus Strictness	B	Nightlife	A-
Computers	B	Off-Campus Dining	B+
Diversity	C	Off-Campus Housing	C
Drug Safety	C-	Parking	B
Facilities	A-	Transportation	B-
Girls	A	Weather	A

CP's Student Author On...
OVERALL EXPERIENCE

Rollins has a way of growing on you. This seems to be the general consensus among students, as even those who may have been dubious at first find themselves happy with their college choice in time. Starting college can be a major change, and entering Rollins feels a little like entering another world. Maybe it has something to do with the paradise-like setting, or the constant notion of being at an expensive country club. Whatever the cause may be, Rollins is different from most other colleges. The small size of Rollins is generally considered a major plus, academically. Students praise the fact that they are never a number. At Rollins, you can expect one-on-one attention, no TAs, and inspired teachers who really want to impart their knowledge. Many students spoke of their high regard for the professors and gratitude for the many opportunities afforded them through the college. Academically, Rollins doesn't disappoint and frequently exceeds the expectations of entering freshmen.

In regards to social life, the small size of Rollins is not always considered a plus.... For the rest of this editorial, visit collegeprowler.com.

Students Speak Out On...
OVERALL EXPERIENCE

Q I Love Rollins.

"I have loved every minute on campus. I am not much of a partier but the few that I have attended were load of fun and the people there were great. The schools beauty and smallness make it unique. I am not a number here and teachers know me by name. They have small classes and amazing teachers. I would definately choose my school over again if I had the chance to go all over again."

Q It's Awesome Here!

"Rollins is the greatest campus around. I love the campus and the facilities, not to mention the lake it's on, the park it's near, and the downtown within walking distance. The best part is the international programs department as they make studying abroad the easiest and most painless opportunity! It also doesn't cost any extra! The tuition is the same for Winter Park Florida as it is for Shanghai, China! Rollins is amazing."

BEST OF ROLLINS

1. Fox Day
2. The weather
3. Downtown Orlando
4. The pool
5. Strong academics
6. Park Avenue
7. Frat parties
8. Drink specials

Happy Students
82% of students return after their first year.

Commitment to Teaching
There are 10 students for every member of faculty on campus.

WORST OF ROLLINS

1. Parking
2. Small student body
3. Lack of diversity
4. Winter Park Police
5. Late nights in the 24-hour lab
6. The dorms
7. Materialism

Expensive
Tuition is a steep $36,220, one of the most expensive rates in the country.

Expensive Dorms
Living on campus doesn't come cheap, with an average housing price tag of $6,660.

Student Body

African American:	6%	Male Undergrads:	42%
Asian American:	3%	Female Undergrads:	58%
Hispanic:	11%	Living On Campus:	75%
International:	4%	Living Off Campus:	25%
Native American:	1%	Male Athletes:	24%
White:	70%	Female Athletes:	14%
Unknown:	5%	Fraternity Members:	38%
From Out-of-State:	57%	Sorority Members:	40%

Frequently Compared Schools:

Elon University
Stetson University
University of Central Florida
University of Miami

Students Speak Out On... EVERYTHING!

ACADEMICS

Excellent Professors and Interesting Classes

"The professors at Rollins are so helpful! They are continually checking up with their students to see if they need any help or point out something of the student's interest. The classes offered are extremely interesting, especially for your physical education requirements. For example, I took ballroom dance and power yoga my first year and absolutely loved it!"

Art History

"I absolutely love my major. The professors know what they are talking about and encourage students to bring their own opinions to the table. They schedule new and different classes that inspire their students. The work load is hard with multiple research papers and readings for every class, but they encourage one on one meetings for assistance. The only thing I would change would be to add more professors to the major. There are only two at this current time."

ATHLETICS

Different Sports but Always Exciting!

"Varsity sports at Rollins college are a pretty big part of campus life, although not as big as other schools. There is no football team, yet there are so many more other sports that keep the student body busy. The training facilities are also awesome and open to everyone on campus! The student body really gets into attendance at most games and really shows their support. IM sports are also great and diverse as even students get into Ultimate Frisbee!"

Sutdent Involvement

"the sports are not a huge deal at Rollins and not alot of events are attended by students."

CAMPUS DINING

Good Variety, Clean, Nice Workers, Expensive

"There are lots of places on campus to eat, and lots of variety. There's not much if you're diabetic or hypoglycemic or a vegetarian. Dave's Down Under is open late, but is the only one that's available in the middle of the night. Dominoes pizza accepts your meal plan, though, so if you're in the mood for pizza, you can spend that money you're not using in the cafeteria."

Pretty Good...Better Than Regular Cafeteria Food

"The food is really pretty good! The food in the dining halls is customized and made to order. However, after a while, the food can become repetitive however. Freshman living on campus are required to have a meal plan."

CAMPUS HOUSING

Pretty Good Housing, on-Campus Apartments the Best

"The freshman dorms depend on which dorm you get. Rex Beach is said to be the worst, but they have a kitchen that they all use and is pretty small. McKean is the biggest and is pretty okay. Ward Hall just got refurbished and is the best underclassmen dorm. As for upperclassmen, Sutton Apartments is the best but you need to apply early. Elizabeth Hall is also really nice for upperclassmen--the rooms are huge."

GUYS & GIRLS

Country Club

"While I love Rollins College and have many friends, the best way to describe the majority of the students on campus is that of a Country Club. It is not uncommon to see the latest fashions on campus, despite the price. In regards to relationships, since the College is so small, gossip and news travels quickly around college. If you are looking for a good time and good parties with the elite, this college is perfect."

HEALTH & SAFETY

Safe

"Security, while not always visible on campus, is available at any time to drive you across campus to either your dorm or car."

LOOKING FOR MORE?

Check out our full-length guide to this school at collegeprowler.com/rollins-college/.

Rowan University

201 Mullica Hill Road; Glassboro, NJ 08028
(856) 256-4000; www.rowan.edu

THE BASICS:

Acceptance Rate: 68%	Student-Faculty Ratio: 15:1
Yield: 31%	Retention Rate: 82%
Setting: Suburban	Graduation Rate: 65%
Control: Public	Tuition: $18,308
Total Undergrads: 9,665	Room & Board: $9,958
SAT Range: 1430–1740*	Avg. Aid Package: $8,793
ACT Range: —	Students With Aid: 73%

of 2400

Academics	C+	Greek Life	B+
Athletics	B+	Guys	C
Campus Dining	C	Health & Safety	B
Campus Housing	C+	Local Atmosphere	C
Campus Strictness	B-	Nightlife	C+
Computers	B	Off-Campus Dining	C+
Diversity	C+	Off-Campus Housing	C-
Drug Safety	B-	Parking	C-
Facilities	B+	Transportation	C-
Girls	B+	Weather	B-

CP's Student Author On...
OVERALL EXPERIENCE

Rowan University is more than you'd expect from a New Jersey state university. With a student body of close to 10,000 students, the University is a great size—it has a close-knit feel, but you'll still probably meet someone new every day. With a nationally acclaimed engineering program, the University attracts some of the best and brightest. The Rowan experience exists far beyond the classroom though. On any given weekday night, there is always something to do. Whether it's a University-planned event, bingo at Rowan After Hours, or a fraternity party, there is something for everyone.

Rowan is home to a humble student body, so if you put yourself out there, there's a good chance you'll meet some of the greatest friends you will ever make. As far as academics go, if you put in a lot of work, you'll get a lot back. The professors genuinely care about the students' success and often encourage everyone to share their opinions in class.... For the rest of this editorial, visit collegeprowler.com.

Students Speak Out On...
OVERALL EXPERIENCE

Q I would do it all over again

"I would do it all over again, hands down. I am so glad that I've come to meet such a diverse student body and faculty that is open to student opinions, which ultimately allows creativity. Being able to have found a Christian organization just shows Rowan's open arms to diverse cultures and ideas."

Q I Love Rowan

"Rowan is a great school. I am so glad I attend Rowan. The experience is great, the people are friendly, and the parties are crazy and fun—before they get out of hand. The professors and advisors really want to see you succeed. Rowan is everything someone looks for in a school. We aren't the most popular and don't have the biggest party scene or the best sports teams. But what we do have makes your 4(+) years here wonderful! I would recommend Rowan to everyone I know."

Q My overall experience was great

"My overall experience was great. I learned who I was while being here, and I would definitely do this again."

BEST OF ROWAN

1. Marketplace Cafeteria
2. Genuine people
3. Boro Bucks (money placed on the RowanCard that can be used at local businesses)
4. Caring professors
5. Large amount of student clubs and organizations

Happy Students
82% of students return after their first year.

Big Dorms
70% of students surveyed felt that dorms were more spacious than average.

WORST OF ROWAN

1. Parking
2. Location
3. Loud partygoers
4. Diversity could be better
5. It rains a lot.
6. Local bus service
7. Local nightlife

Expensive Dorms
Living on campus doesn't come cheap, with an average housing price tag of $6,248.

Student Body

African American:	9%	Male Undergrads:	47%
Asian American:	3%	Female Undergrads:	53%
Hispanic:	7%	Living On Campus:	34%
International:	2%	Living Off Campus:	66%
Native American:	0%	Male Athletes:	7%
White:	76%	Female Athletes:	5%
Unknown:	2%	Fraternity Members:	5%
From Out-of-State:	5%	Sorority Members:	6%

Frequently Compared Schools:

Rutgers University
Temple University
The College of New Jersey
University of Delaware

Students Speak Out On... EVERYTHING!

ACADEMICS

Q Biology

"I came to Rowan University because it has a very good biology program which I'm interested in. My adviser, Dr. O'Brien, has been very helpful. He is always available to answer any questions I have."

Q Most teachers are highly qualified

"Most of the teachers at Rowan are well informed and highly qualified. The only workload that has been intense was in my practicum for elementary education. The engineering and education programs are well known at Rowan."

Q Workload is a bit heavy

"The teachers here are serious about the subjects they teach. The workload is a bit heavy."

ATHLETICS

Q Athletics

"Eventhough we are a DIII school the athletics are great. Alot of students are involved and more students come out to support."

Q Intramural sports are great year round

"Intramural sports are great year-round with a plethora of activities to choose from. Varsity football has been exceptional in recent years."

Q Great baseball, football, and swim teams

"We have great baseball, football, and swim teams."

CAMPUS DINING

Q Great Variety and Get Your Moneys Worth

"The dinning hall has an all you can eat buffet for lunch and dinner which has a lot of food for the price and a lot of different varieties to choose from. The Grill and Deli has combo deals which you get a side and a drink with your sandwich. You can create your own and everything is made to order."

Q Food Here Is Pretty Good

"The main dining hall isn't bad at all. The food options are varied, and for the most part, tastes pretty good. The only downside is that the pizza is very powdery, the salad bar gets redundant, and the cookies all have that same cafeteria taste after a while. There are a bunch of other faster food options to choose from, too."

CAMPUS HOUSING

Q Building new dorms

"We have new dorms that only house seniors. You have to earn your way there."

Q Biggest rooms are in Evergreen Hall

"The biggest rooms are in Evergreen Hall, which is a freshman dorm. The rooms are large enough for two individuals."

GUYS & GIRLS

Q Rowan Girls/Guys

"Rowan is a popular school for students that are from Brick/Ocean. Majority of the guys are the beach/surfer type. No offense but about 60% of the girls are easy. With that aside, I would have to say that the campus is pretty good looking because it's full of people who are conceited and like to take care of themselves."

Q Decent

"There's a good assortment of girls. They're good looking for the most part, and their interests vary."

HEALTH & SAFETY

Q The Health Center Is Great

"I get free vaccinations and can have fun at school without worrying about getting sick."

Q Safe Enough

"In the beginning of the semester, a lot of bad things were happening, but I have never felt truly unsafe on or off campus."

LOOKING FOR MORE?

Check out our full-length guide to this school at collegeprowler.com/rowan-university/.

Russell Sage College

45 Ferry St.; Troy, NY 12180
(518) 244-2000; www.sage.edu

THE BASICS:

Acceptance Rate: 76%	**Student-Faculty Ratio:** 11:1
Yield: 35%	**Retention Rate:** 84%
Setting: Small city	**Graduation Rate:** 73%
Control: Private Non-Profit	**Tuition:** $27,790
Total Undergrads: 749	**Room & Board:** $9,670
SAT Range: 1080–1180*	**Avg. Aid Package:** $31,024
ACT Range: 24–25	**Students With Aid:** 100%

*of 1600

Academics	C+	Greek Life	N/A
Athletics	C	Guys	B-
Campus Dining	D+	Health & Safety	C-
Campus Housing	A-	Local Atmosphere	C
Campus Strictness	C+	Nightlife	B-
Computers	C-	Off-Campus Dining	B-
Diversity	C+	Off-Campus Housing	C+
Drug Safety	C+	Parking	B-
Facilities	C-	Transportation	B+
Girls	B	Weather	C+

CP's Student Author On...
OVERALL EXPERIENCE

What's great about Russell Sage College is the friendly atmosphere, the variety of courses, and the professors who actually want to see students succeed. One problem that some students have encountered is the changing curriculum for certain majors, which causes student schedules to become altered and completely messed up. However, problems like this one are usually fixable by speaking with an adviser. Overall, the College greatly prepares students for their future careers through student involvement in extracurricular activities and community service. When students volunteer with companies in their fields of study, they make connections with people who they could potentially work for someday, through opportunities like internships and job shadowing.

Russell Sage College is unique because it is an all-women's college, and all women who attend Sage end up having the power to change the world. Sage wants all of its students to make a difference, and many other schools do not focus as much on the power and influence of women as Sage does.... For the rest of this editorial, visit collegeprowler.com.

Students Speak Out On...
OVERALL EXPERIENCE

Q Sage Is Right for Me

"There are a lot of students who say that Sage is too boring and there is not enough for them to do, but I believe it is exactly the right fit for me. It allows me to get my work done and have safe fun with my friends. I am involved in many clubs, work studies, and other on campus organizations. The general atmosphere of the student body is very friendly and accepting of all types of people. It is a great place to make the transition into an adult."

Q Russell Sage Experience

"I like that the campus is small, and it is pretty easy to find classes. I also like that everyone knows almost everyone else. I do not like the drama that is caused by it being a womans college."

Q Russell Sage

"Overall a good school. Needs some changes in ways things are done here. I love the traditions but the student life is DEAD"

BEST OF RUSSELL SAGE

1. Academic programs
2. The atmosphere is welcoming.
3. Campus is very walkable.
4. Friendly environment
5. Gator Pit
6. Great professors
7. Lots of clubs to join

Happy Students
84% of students return after their first year.

Proven Success
73% of students will complete their education and graduate with a degree.

WORST OF RUSSELL SAGE

1. Athletic teams are hard to join.
2. Big workload
3. Dining hall food
4. Financial aid office
5. Heating/cooling systems in the housing on campus

Expensive
Tuition is a steep $27,790, one of the most expensive rates in the country.

Frequently Compared Schools:

Dartmouth College
Rensselaer Polytechnic Institute
Simmons College
Union College

Students Speak Out On... EVERYTHING!

ACADEMICS

Fine Arts Major, Illustration Minor

"There is a considerable amount of work but it is doable. The faculty is usually very helpful and available since class size is small."

Workload

"Workload can be heavy at times but it is for the students best interest in succeeding."

Political Science

"I love my professor for my specific program. I see them as my confidants. I give Political Science at Sage a B+ because it there are not enough classes concerning political science specifically. Many surround the law aspect."

ATHLETICS

Athletics

"equipment is always brand new. coaching/athletic training staff is excellent."

Quality Athletes

"The athletes are dedicated and talented. Home games are somewhat attended by the student body. Away games are not highly attended by our students."

CAMPUS DINING

Best Bistro

"Although some things are very repetitive in the Dining Hall, the Bistro always has something great to offer. Meals are made to order. starbucks coffee helps!! Smoothies and salads and lots of sandwiches are always available. As a commuter student, I can always find something great to eat."

Flex Dollars/Dining Halls

"Card money can't be used anywhere except for in buchman so it would be nice if we could use money somewhere else but we can't. The dining hall food can be repetitive but it is okay."

CAMPUS HOUSING

Dorms and Social Atmosphere

"The dorm rooms at Sage are big compared to other school's that I have visited and the social atmosphere is amazing. Everyone gets along socially and there are usually no problems between people. The freshmen dorm rooms are definately the most crowded but the location is awesome."

Flexibility of Housing

"The dorms themselves may not be state of the art, but they absolutely provide an immense amount of space and storage for each resident. Students have a huge say in who they room with and where they live. Many of the dorm buildings are restored brownstones that really connect students to the history of the area. Roommate conflicts are serious business and students can relatively easily switch their room or roommate throughout the semester."

GUYS & GIRLS

All Girl School

"All varieties of girls and interests. Some guys are exceptions!!"

Girls Only

"It is a girls only school. i think that everyone seems to get along here. There are a lot of people with the same intrests. It seemslike everyone is very social."

HEALTH & SAFETY

Safety

"Russel Sage College is patrolled by off duty police of the area. The area is a fairly decent area and I feel relatively safe."

Public Safety

"Cars were broken into in the parking lot for 2 weeks. I think that should have been monitored beter. Besides that i feel very comfortable because i see officers walking around on campus all the time."

LOOKING FOR MORE?

Check out our full-length guide to this school at collegeprowler.com/russell-sage-college/.

Rutgers University

83 Somerset St.; New Brunswick, NJ 08901
(732) 932-1766; www.rutgers.edu

THE BASICS:

Acceptance Rate: 61%	**Student-Faculty Ratio:** 14:1
Yield: 33%	**Retention Rate:** 91%
Setting: Small city	**Graduation Rate:** 75%
Control: Public	**Tuition:** $23,058
Total Undergrads: 29,095	**Room & Board:** $10,676
SAT Range: 1600–1940*	**Avg. Aid Package:** $10,709
ACT Range: —	**Students With Aid:** 94%

* of 2400

Academics	B+	Greek Life	B-
Athletics	A	Guys	A-
Campus Dining	B	Health & Safety	C
Campus Housing	C+	Local Atmosphere	C+
Campus Strictness	B	Nightlife	A-
Computers	B+	Off-Campus Dining	B+
Diversity	B+	Off-Campus Housing	B-
Drug Safety	C-	Parking	C+
Facilities	B	Transportation	A-
Girls	B+	Weather	C+

CP's Student Author On... OVERALL EXPERIENCE

The courses are tough at Rutgers. TAs mainly don't speak English, and you can never find a parking spot. However, despite these things, after the first week of your freshman year, you realize Rutgers is different than other schools. Diversity is definitely something that makes Rutgers stand out—the friends you will meet at Rutgers will make you realize that you like Indian music and Persian food, and you'll go to friends houses during their Jewish holidays. Students will learn to live with all different people, despite different backgrounds, and smile and laugh the nights away in the dorms.

It is a very large university, and professors won't realize or care if you are failing a course. However, students remark that they wanted to attend a large university because it makes them grow up. At Rutgers, no one holds your hand as you pick courses (and there's 4,000 to choose from), and they don't make sure you are taking the courses necessary for your major. Everything is done by the actions of the students. If you want real life experiences instead of a college resembling your high school, you'll find it here.

Students Speak Out On... OVERALL EXPERIENCE

Q Best College Ever !
"Rutgers is the best college. It was my number one college and I would definitely recommend it to everyone. The diversity is awesome and so are the academics."

Q Rutgers
"Rutgers has something for everyone. Its party scene is great if you know where to go, its academics are fantastic and nationally ranked, the people are diverse and friendly, and its big enough to keep things interesting but organized so that you feel just at home."

Q Enjoyable to Everyone
"Rutgers is such a diverse school in every aspect. It can be for anybody, it offers dozens of clubs, majors, and ways to meet new people. It wasn't hard adjusting at all. The dining hall food isn't too bad either. Whether you're a party animal or a comic book junkie there's something to do for you."

BEST OF RUTGERS

1. Diversity
2. Getting the small school feel, because of the different campuses, even though you are at a large university
3. Division I sports
4. Being so close to Manhattan and Philly

Happy Students
91% of students return after their first year.

Proven Success
75% of students will complete their education and graduate with a degree.

WORST OF RUTGERS

1. The RU Screw - bureaucratic red tape that gets in the way of anything you want to do
2. Parking
3. Not knowing what classes to take on your APA Day
4. The Rutgers buses in the snow or rain

Expensive Dorms
Living on campus doesn't come cheap, with an average housing price tag of $6,526.

Don't Move Off Campus
Average off-campus housing is a steep $14,409.

Student Body

African American:	9%	Male Undergrads:	51%
Asian American:	24%	Female Undergrads:	49%
Hispanic:	10%	Living On Campus:	47%
International:	2%	Living Off Campus:	53%
Native American:	0%	Male Athletes:	3%
White:	49%	Female Athletes:	3%
Unknown:	6%	Fraternity Members:	—
From Out-of-State:	9%	Sorority Members:	—

Students Speak Out On... EVERYTHING!

ACADEMICS

Q Sports Management

"My major is great! its a major that has a lot of potential, as you learn many different things, from economics to psychology to marketing, your job choices are tremendous. the staff is great, and try as best they can to help you out. they have many great opportunities for students like guest speakers and even a major club."

Q Rutgers University Offers a Diverse Group of Staff and Professors Aimed at Developing Students Into Their Full Potential.

"Rutgers have a large and diverse campus full of people from all walks of life all unified by one common goal, education and success."

ATHLETICS

Q Student Involvement

"There are over 350 student organizations on campus which provide opportunities for involvement, whether it's being a member or officer of an organization or attending an event sponsored by a student organizeation. The groups are ranged from academic to social action organizations to leisure organizations and some include the student government of the university of Rutgers."

Q Sports Are Hidden "12Th Man"

"Rutgers has great facilities to get in shape and be fit. But it has great fan support with many non-college fans and affiliates that is able to lift the team's spirit to win and motivate others. We have diverse teams from Football to water polo. Sport season, especially in the fall, are extremely popular and part of the college life. Gong to one of "Scarlet Knights" games is a must!"

CAMPUS DINING

Q Best Places

"Neilson is the best dining hall on campus. It always has fresh and good tasting food. Sbarro's is also a nice pizza place on Livingston where we can use meal swipes. The DCC and CCC are good places if you want to get food for later."

Q Pretty Good

"The variety is usually excellent, and the quality is very good. I never go hungry, and even sometimes look forward to the meals."

CAMPUS HOUSING

Q Douglass College Housing

"Douglass college housing is a women's only option. The dorms are spacious and there isn't a huge price tag on housing. Douglass campus dorms are conveniently located near the dining hall, campus center, and bus stops. It's easy to get around campus and off campus from Douglass."

GUYS & GIRLS

Q Diversity

"Both the guys and the girls at Rutgers are diverse and very open minded. The best part is the combination of different religions and cultures. Everyone is interested in something different and at the same time students can find others who have common interests. Around campus you don't feel hated or discriminated against."

HEALTH & SAFETY

Q Completely Safe

"Rutgers has sign in/out sheets at every dorm, the students aren't in danger of one aonther or of other outstiders to the campus. There are police kiosks at every corner and street. Here you can push the button and be helped in less than 30 seconds. The security will either escort you to your dorm or they will solve whatever problem you have. I feel extremely safe here."

Sacramento State

6000 J St.; Sacramento, CA 95819
(916) 278-6011; www.csus.edu

THE BASICS:

Acceptance Rate: 67%
Yield: 22%
Setting: Large city
Control: Public
Total Undergrads: 24,389
SAT Range: 830–1070*
ACT Range: 17–22

Student-Faculty Ratio: 26:1
Retention Rate: 79%
Graduation Rate: 42%
Tuition: $16,060
Room & Board: $11,332
Avg. Aid Package: $6,007
Students With Aid: 65%

* of 2400

Academics	C+	Greek Life	B-
Athletics	B-	Guys	B+
Campus Dining	B+	Health & Safety	B-
Campus Housing	C+	Local Atmosphere	B+
Campus Strictness	B-	Nightlife	B+
Computers	B+	Off-Campus Dining	B
Diversity	B+	Off-Campus Housing	B
Drug Safety	B-	Parking	B-
Facilities	B-	Transportation	B
Girls	B	Weather	B+

CP's Student Author On...
OVERALL EXPERIENCE

Most students appreciate Sac State because it's pleasant, but they often wish it had more school spirit. The ones who are satisfied with it usually haven't been to other four-year universities, so they don't have anything major to compare it to from first-hand experience. Those who wish for more excitement usually mention wilder Bay Area campuses. A majority of people who attend Sac State just want a degree so they can get out. They know not to expect the typical college experience that makes for legendary times and awesome memories. Too many of them commute. If Sac State were more of an on-campus school, there would be more student satisfaction socially. If you decide to study here and want campus community, seek clubs or other social organizations as soon as possible. If you're laid-back and don't mind coming to a school where everyone just comes to a get a grade and a job, make yourself at home.

Many students would be blown away if they knew how hard their education could be, but a lot of them are fine with Sac State's current academic level. Most assignments are easy, and it's surprising what students worry about.... For the rest of this editorial, visit collegeprowler.com.

Students Speak Out On...
OVERALL EXPERIENCE

Q Nothing Better
"I feel like i have made some life long friends. I love my team I love the party atmosphere. Im successful in school. what could go wrong?"

Q Sac State Experience
"Sac State has a lot to offer. I love being able to take different classes such as dance, yoga and more because beyond just taking class for a major i got to learn new things and have fun. This school is unique because its truly for the students and their success. If I could do it all over again I would choose this school because without the help of the staff here i would be as far as I am today. Sac State provides students with what they need to reach their dreams."

BEST OF SAC STATE

1. Tuition
2. Diversity
3. State holidays-- no school!
4. Closeness to a lot of food and shopping venues
5. Wireless Internet
6. Laid-back atmosphere
7. Health services

Easy Financial Aid Process
52% of students surveyed told us that the financial aid process went smoothly and they received the financial aid they needed.

WORST OF SAC STATE

1. Parking
2. Student government
3. Dorms
4. Communal bathrooms in dorms
5. Lack of campus community
6. Student-to-computer ratio

Overextended Faculty
There are 26 students for every faculty member on campus.

Expensive Dorms
Living on campus doesn't come cheap, with an average housing price tag of $6,358.

Student Body

African American:	7%	Male Undergrads:	43%
Asian American:	19%	Female Undergrads:	57%
Hispanic:	14%	Living On Campus:	5%
International:	1%	Living Off Campus:	95%
Native American:	1%	Male Athletes:	3%
White:	40%	Female Athletes:	3%
Unknown:	17%	Fraternity Members:	5%
From Out-of-State:	2%	Sorority Members:	4%

Frequently Compared Schools:
San Diego State University
San Francisco State University
San Jose State University
University of California - Davis

Students Speak Out On...
EVERYTHING!

ACADEMICS

Programs ·
"I enrolled in Sac State because it has a great business department, and a great accounting department. The pass rate for the CPA exam is very good."

Committed
"All of my professors are completely committed to their jobs and their students success. They always want to help in any way to see us succeed in grasping the material and outside of the classroom."

Sac State Guidance
"The Business program at Scramento State is one of the best programs and I have received helpful guidance from both my bussiness major advisor and academic advisor. Plenty of information is given and I am thankful for their help."

ATHLETICS

School Spirit
"I love the atmosphere of the football games, all I see when I look at the stand is the color green and gold and its a great feeling. There is spirit and support coming from the stands."

Force
"The athletics in sacramento state is engertic and full of determination"

CAMPUS DINING

Dining on Campus
"They have a lot to choose from like Round Table, a 5-star restaurant, crepe, togos, subwya, sushi the list goes on"

Cheap and a Variety
"There are many places where you can find cheap lunches/food. The dorm food also offers a variety. Good overall."

CAMPUS HOUSING

The Housings
"well i haven't actually live there yet but i assume that it is a good place if not, it is livable and there are housings nearby and even though students don't live nearby there is the lightrail and transportation that is accessible and easy to use. so i guess the housings are good."

Cost Is a Little High
"The dorms at Sac State are a little expensive especially when you have to get the meal plan. It is worth it all to be able to live in the dorms and get food, but the cost is just a little too much for my taste. The atmosphere around the dorms is great though and it is easy to get a dorm. it is full of amenities like wi-fi and T.V."

GUYS & GIRLS

Very Good Looking People
"The girls in Sacramento are very attractive and there are not allot of over-weight people. The girls are from all over California so it is very eclectic and very cool. There are a variety of types of guys in Sacramento from the smart masses to the not so smart. But the women are very HOT."

Typical Students
"There is so much diversity on campus, you will see rockers, athletes, country boys and girls. There is just so much different types of people."

HEALTH & SAFETY

Safe
"I have never felt unsafe walking around campus at Sac State. I have heard of many instances of people's personal property being stolen from places such as the library, but in my opinion this was due to the neglect of the owners because they left their property unsupervised. I just make sure to keep everything with me at all times and I feel fine."

Seems Good
"From the information Ive seen the school demonstrates excellent health and safety."

LOOKING FOR MORE?
Check out our full-length guide to this school at collegeprowler.com/sacramento-state/.

Saint Francis University

117 Evergreen Drive; Loretto, PA 15940
(814) 472-3000; www.francis.edu

THE BASICS:

Acceptance Rate: 75%
Yield: 36%
Setting: Rural
Control: Private Non-Profit
Total Undergrads: 1,705
SAT Range: 940–1160*
ACT Range: 21–27

Student-Faculty Ratio: 14:1
Retention Rate: 84%
Graduation Rate: 56%
Tuition: $25,554
Room & Board: $8,716
Avg. Aid Package: $17,053
Students With Aid: 100%

* of 1600

Academics	B-	Greek Life	B+
Athletics	C-	Guys	B
Campus Dining	B	Health & Safety	B-
Campus Housing	C	Local Atmosphere	C-
Campus Strictness	C	Nightlife	C+
Computers	B+	Off-Campus Dining	C-
Diversity	C-	Off-Campus Housing	D+
Drug Safety	C+	Parking	B
Facilities	B-	Transportation	C-
Girls	A-	Weather	C

CP's Student Author On...
OVERALL EXPERIENCE

Saint Francis University has its strengths and its weaknesses, but the flaws of the University are tremendously outweighed by the assets. The rural setting of the campus may not be for everyone, but most students appreciate the beauty, safety, and seclusion of the campus while still being able to take advantage of the city life that is only a short drive away. A larger campus may be preferred by some, but the small class sizes and personal relationships make Saint Francis students feel important and always supported. Some buildings may be outdated, but state-of-the-art renovations are constantly being made around campus to ensure that it is always exciting and accommodating. Saint Francis is a small, rural university, but every aspect of the school itself is outstanding.

The strong sense of community is what draws students to Saint Francis and keeps them attached throughout their college experience. Students say they are completely comfortable at Saint Francis, and they truly feel like the University community is their home away from home.... For the rest of this editorial, visit collegeprowler.com.

Students Speak Out On...
OVERALL EXPERIENCE

Q First Year Experience
"My first year at Saint Francis was a lot of fun. I met great people and learned a lot."

Q Great Overall
"Saint Francis has a very well-rounded environment. Its isolation may actually come in handy, because there are not as many distractions when studying is necessary. It is a college campus, however, so there are always others looking for fun and for activities to take part in. I personally have loved my years at Saint Francis so far."

Q A Great Time
"I've had a great time the entire time I've been at school."

Q Can't Imagine Being Anywhere Else
"While the social scene isn't the greatest, I love the environment of Saint Francis. Its small size makes it very easy for all students to get involved and also gives all students the opportunity to succeed academically. Every student really gets the special attention that he wants and is made to feel special and important."

BEST OF SAINT FRANCIS

1. Beautiful campus and scenery
2. Excellent academic programs
3. Friendly people
4. Open-door policy with advisers and professors
5. Small class sizes

Happy Students
84% of students return after their first year.

Highly Satisfied Students
80% of students surveyed would make the same school choice if they could do it all over again.

WORST OF SAINT FRANCIS

1. Outdated buildings
2. Removed location
3. Strict policy enforcement
4. Winter weather
5. Only one dining hall
6. Inconvenient and limited parking
7. Lack of school spirit

Not Much Diversity
One of the least racially diverse campuses—only 15% of students are minorities.

Student Body

African American:	5%	Male Undergrads:	42%
Asian American:	1%	Female Undergrads:	58%
Hispanic:	1%	Living On Campus:	75%
International:	0%	Living Off Campus:	25%
Native American:	0%	Male Athletes:	37%
White:	85%	Female Athletes:	22%
Unknown:	7%	Fraternity Members:	10%
From Out-of-State:	29%	Sorority Members:	10%

Frequently Compared Schools:

Bucknell University
Duquesne University
Penn State
Saint Joseph's University

Students Speak Out On... EVERYTHING!

ACADEMICS

Physical Therapy

"This is an excellent program that fully prepares you to be a professional in the field. There are a lot of opportunities to become close with not only your classmates, but teachers and older classmates, as well. I love my major and couldn't see myself doing anything else."

Professors Are Wonderful

"Academic advisers and professors are always willing to help students however they can. They give every student the opportunity to succeed academically."

ATHLETICS

SFU — Quaint School

"Athletics aren't the best, but the teams are building. I personally love SFU. It is small and personal, all of my professors know me, and I get to develop relationships with pretty much everyone on campus, even if it's just a quick hello while passing in the campus mall."

Athletics

"They were not doing too well, but the teams are getting a lot better. The fan base is getting better, as well!"

CAMPUS DINING

Dining Halls

"The dining hall is very spacious for the amount of students at the University. Every food station is spread out around the facility, so there is no line backup. The tables and chairs are arranged in a spacious way."

One Dining Hall, One Restaurant

"There is only one dining hall at Saint Francis—Torvian. While it gets busy at certain times of the day, it's spacious and has tons of options for food. If you don't want to eat there, you can always go to Frankie's, our campus's little restaurant."

CAMPUS HOUSING

Housing

"The dorms are small but they're very clean. The RAs do a great job hosting events, and the cleaning service is great. The dorms are very safe and are a fun place to live."

Not All That Bad

"The dorm system is trying to improve at Saint Francis. There are not many options for upperclass housing, but the school is starting to provide more University-sponsored off-campus housing. But as far as living on campus, the rooms are pretty small, and the school tends to try and cram as many people in dorms as possible. It's not terribly uncomfortable, but it could be improved."

GUYS & GIRLS

Guys Will Be Guys

"The guys here at USF are like the guys I went to high school with. Some are nice, where the rst can be real jerks. Her on campus, I can start a conversation with some guys, like about school, and in the middle, they will start talking about sex and the like. Why can't there ever be a guy that will talk about what I want to."

Life at SFU

"Even though there is an unfair 3:1 ratio of girls to guys at Saint Francis, everyone is very nice, and it is very easy to make friends at school."

HEALTH & SAFETY

Extremely Safe

"I've always felt completely safe walking around campus at any time of day or night. Also, the dorm buildings are extremely safe. The buildings' doors are locked 24/7, and you can only get into them by swiping your student ID card. I've never run into any incidents of theft, vandalism, etc. Campus police does an excellent job patrolling the campus at all hours of the day and is available whenever you need them."

LOOKING FOR MORE?

Check out our full-length guide to this school at collegeprowler.com/saint-francis-university/.

Saint Joseph's University

5600 City Ave.; Philadelphia, PA 19131
(610) 660-1000; www.sju.edu

THE BASICS:

Acceptance Rate: 82%	**Student-Faculty Ratio:** 14:1
Yield: 22%	**Retention Rate:** 86%
Setting: Large city	**Graduation Rate:** 79%
Control: Private Non-Profit	**Tuition:** $34,090
Total Undergrads: 5,408	**Room & Board:** $11,800
SAT Range: 1530–1830*	**Avg. Aid Package:** $17,132
ACT Range: 21–26	**Students With Aid:** 92%

* of 2400

Academics	B-	Greek Life	C+
Athletics	B-	Guys	B+
Campus Dining	C	Health & Safety	C+
Campus Housing	B	Local Atmosphere	B
Campus Strictness	B-	Nightlife	B+
Computers	C+	Off-Campus Dining	B
Diversity	D+	Off-Campus Housing	B+
Drug Safety	D+	Parking	B-
Facilities	C	Transportation	B
Girls	B-	Weather	B

CP's Student Author On...
OVERALL EXPERIENCE

To fully understand St. Joe's, you have to appreciate the people who run it. There's a uniform vibe amongst the faculty, staff, and students here that's unique to the school. A large number of students end up sticking around the area or moving to Philly for job offers after graduation. While it's true many grads pack up and head to D.C. or NYC for jobs, it's because of the time and effort they put in at St. Joe's that got them there. Also, it's not uncommon for St. Joe's students to stick around the University with campus jobs in certain departments or as housing advisors.

Everyone at St. Joe's takes the school with a small sense of humor. There are some who love it and a small percentage who pretend they hate it, but most people agree this quirky school in an even quirkier city is endearing. The biggest complaint is the cost of attending; however, this is often offset by the large amount of scholarships given out. The running theme through the school is Hawk pride. A lot of students have the "grass is greener" syndrome when reflecting on their time here. However, ask a St. Joe's student if they would rather be down the road at UPenn or Villanova, and you might get a fat lip.

Students Speak Out On...
OVERALL EXPERIENCE

Q The Best Years of Your Life!

"There is a wonderful welcoming spirit at Saint Joe's. It so so easy to meet people if you are involved with activities, and the faculty are very accomadating. Like almost everywhere, your school experience is what you make it."

Q Saint Joseph's Is the Best!!

"Everyone is really nice, the school is tough but very good I feel like i have learned a lot. Parties aren't the best but they are still fun. I have so many great memories of Saint Joe's and I am so glad I went here, I would never choose anywhere else!!!"

Q Solid University!

"Great atmosphere, great people, beautiful campus, and a curriculum that is relevant to my interests. The crunch times really do come on strong, so remember to buckle down when you need to."

BEST OF ST. JOE'S

1. Freedom Festival/ Softball Tournament
2. Trips to Madison Square Garden for basketball
3. One o'clock walk
4. Last free period
5. The school radio station
6. Formals and date parties

Happy Students
86% of students return after their first year.

Proven Success
79% of students will complete their education and graduate with a degree.

WORST OF ST. JOE'S

1. Parking
2. The smell of the "poop-berries" in the trees in the fall
3. Sourin
4. How Hawk's Nest is so expensive
5. Small school gossip

Expensive
Tuition is a steep $34,090, one of the most expensive rates in the country.

Expensive Dorms
Living on campus doesn't come cheap, with an average housing price tag of $7,320.

Student Body

African American:	9%	Male Undergrads:	47%
Asian American:	3%	Female Undergrads:	53%
Hispanic:	4%	Living On Campus:	63%
International:	2%	Living Off Campus:	37%
Native American:	0%	Male Athletes:	11%
White:	79%	Female Athletes:	9%
Unknown:	4%	Fraternity Members:	8%
From Out-of-State:	60%	Sorority Members:	13%

Frequently Compared Schools:

Drexel University
Temple University
University of Delaware
Villanova University

Students Speak Out On... EVERYTHING!

ACADEMICS

Q Workload Makes Sense

"I am not overloaded, nor do I think I am wasting my time. I feel like the amount of work I put into my classes is exactly reflected in my grades."

Q Academics

"I believe that there is some sort of major here for every body. There is a lot of flexibility with adding double majors or minors, which is helpful for your career. Majority of teachers are always there for you however, sometimes it may take a while to track them down. But, when you do track them down, they have valuable knowledge to share with you."

ATHLETICS

Q SJU Sports

"The sports really are not that good, except for mens cross country, the basketball team which the school puts the most effort into, has won like 3 games this season. But the brand new Hagan Arena is really nice. SJU also has a wide range of clubs sports, too."

Q Athletics

"Nice, Spirt, Energetic"

CAMPUS DINING

Q Solid and Good Variety

"For a small school there is plenty of variety at SJU. There are plenty of places to eat and as far as quality, it is just as good if not better than your average college cafeteria. In addition, you can use your declining balance (flex dollars) at Starbucks and Cosi which are located right off campus."

Q What Do You Expect? It's College Food!

"Campion has completely remodeled its appearance in the past few years. It definitely looks up to date and modern, but let's just say the appearance is better than the actual food quality. The variety has gotten better since last year, but it's still typical college food. Don't expect a gourmet meal from this place, but it isn't the worst I've ever eaten either. The choices for vegans and vegetarians is definitely lacking."

CAMPUS HOUSING

Q Best freshman dorms

"Go with McShain. I picked LaFarge because I thought I wanted to live in a suite, but you meet tons of people either way. McShain, for girls at least, is much better because there are really nice closets and wardrobes, whereas in LaFarge, it's just a combo dresser and closet. All the dorms have their ups and downs, but Moore is by far the worst because it's really far off campus (you do get your own bathroom though)."

Q Mcshain Is the Best Freshman Housing Option!!!

"McShain is the best for freshman; The rooms are spacious especially first floor which has high ceilings and seem to be wider than the rest. Sourin and Lafarge are great if you like the suite style of living it definitely helps with meeting new people. Depending on your RA your hall can be very sociable and fun but most people venture onto other halls to meet more people."

GUYS & GIRLS

Q Lax Bros

"it seems like the majority of the boys at sju are either lax bros or are trying to be... most girls typically dress in skin tight outfits at night and cheesy outfits or are fans of the sweatpants or class look..."

Q Dress

"The clothes here are very preppy, but you do not have to be preppy to fit in. There are enough people in the school to offer a good variety."

HEALTH & SAFETY

Q Campus Is Safe but Watch Your Back

"Don't do anything stupid in the surrounding area and you should be fine. Campus police are almost always around"

Q Pretty Safe

"There are always public safety officers around campus."

LOOKING FOR MORE?

Check out our full-length guide to this school at collegeprowler.com/saint-joseph's-university/.

Saint Leo University

33701 State Road 52; Saint Leo, FL 33574
(352) 588-8200; www.saintleo.edu

THE BASICS:

Acceptance Rate: 78%	Student-Faculty Ratio: 15:1
Yield: 31%	Retention Rate: 68%
Setting: Rural	Graduation Rate: 39%
Control: Private Non-Profit	Tuition: $18,200
Total Undergrads: 1,862	Room & Board: $9,120
SAT Range: 1330–1610*	Avg. Aid Package: $21,992
ACT Range: 20–24	Students With Aid: 99%

* of 2400

Academics	B-	Greek Life	B-
Athletics	C+	Guys	B
Campus Dining	C	Health & Safety	B+
Campus Housing	B	Local Atmosphere	C
Campus Strictness	B-	Nightlife	B-
Computers	A	Off-Campus Dining	C
Diversity	B	Off-Campus Housing	C+
Drug Safety	C-	Parking	C+
Facilities	C+	Transportation	C
Girls	C+	Weather	A

CP's Student Author On...
OVERALL EXPERIENCE

The overall experience at Saint Leo University is decent. You make friends, have fun, go to school, and live in the sun—although the small size does limit some of the resources normal college students have access to. There are no big football games with huge tailgating parties, and you won't see a big school band; nor is SLU the place for your typical social scene run by Greek life. The location is quaint, simple, and actually quite beautiful, but there just isn't a whole lot going on in the area. Yet, at the same time, you are only a 25-minute drive from the city of Tampa. Most students fall in love with the Bay atmosphere while they are here, and the roaring tourist economy of Orlando is only an hour away.

Your experience at this school will be greatly enhanced if you have a car. It's just not the place you can find everything you need within walking distance, and public transportation down here hardly exists.... For the rest of this editorial, visit collegeprowler.com.

Students Speak Out On...
OVERALL EXPERIENCE

Q Saint Leo Life

"Saint Leo really isn't that bad when it comes to the social life. It is only the drama that bothers most people like myself. They have a very successful Education program here and that is why I am continuing to move forward."

Q Best Times

"I have had alot of fun times on campus. I am on the soccer team so traveling is always fun. We also have fun in the dorms too. Watching sports, enjoying company, and laughing with friends really makes me enjoy college."

Q Small School

"There are some things I wish I would've partook in but overall, being here and continuing my education at this Institution has been a very good experience. It's all about what you make of it and how you perceive your experience."

BEST OF SAINT LEO

1. Great weather
2. Lots of golfing
3. You know your professors, and they care about your success.
4. Eight-week terms
5. Small class sizes

Knowledgeable Professors
93% of students surveyed rated the general knowledge of professors as above average.

Low-Stress Course Load
80% of students surveyed rated the manageability of work as above average.

WORST OF SAINT LEO

1. Cafeteria food
2. Financial aid
3. Greek life

Not Everyone Graduates
39% of students do not complete their education or graduate with a degree.

Want a Job? On Your Own
There aren't any placement services for graduates.

Student Body

African American:	31%	Male Undergrads:	43%
Asian American:	2%	Female Undergrads:	57%
Hispanic:	8%	Living On Campus:	71%
International:	1%	Living Off Campus:	29%
Native American:	1%	Male Athletes:	6%
White:	41%	Female Athletes:	3%
Unknown:	17%	Fraternity Members:	18%
From Out-of-State:	44%	Sorority Members:	13%

Frequently Compared Schools:

Florida Gulf Coast University
Florida International University
University of Central Florida
University of South Florida

Students Speak Out On... EVERYTHING!

ACADEMICS

Pro-Fessors

"Saint Leo University has the most professional professor's i've ever met. They are willing to stay late, work with you after class or before, will schedule an appointment with you and do all they can to get you the help and resources you need to succeed."

Adult Learners

"The adult learners and online programs are fantastic. I can't imagin going back to school at my age any other way."

Small Classes are Great

"I couldn't handle sitting in a lecture class with 200+ students and just be a number. Here, the class sizes are very small, and you get one-on-one time with professors. You also get a chance to make great friendships since everyone knows everyone."

ATHLETICS

Students are involved

"The students are very involved and competitive in the intramural teams."

My Opinion

"I believe the student involvement on campus is average in relation to atheletics."

Sports Are Well Maintained

"The athletic department is well funded and is good to its student athletes."

CAMPUS DINING

Food is good

"The food on campus is really good, but it does kinda get old after a while."

Decent When I Go

"Only been there a few times, but they have good variety in their foods"

CAMPUS HOUSING

Great Friendly Campus!

"Living on campus is an amazing experience. The dorms are a nice size and very clean. There is enough room to bring everything you need to live on campus. There's also enough bathroom stalls and shower for everyone at all times because each hall has their own restrooms. The staff is always cleaning and making sure that the buildings are spotless. The social atmosphere is great. There are always things to do on and off campus."

On Campus Housing or Off Campus

"I do not live on campus, I am an adult learner and have my home, which makes St. Leo's distance learning and classes held in differnt campus so wonderful for me. Working a full time job and four children, I would not be able to stay on campus."

GUYS & GIRLS

Friendly People

"Everyone is very helpful. No one hesitates to lending a helping hand."

St Leo Students

"The typical student are part of the military culture. They either are in the military or are affiliated with it. Students are very friendly and are willing to help each other out. Most of them are full time parents or recent HS graduates."

HEALTH & SAFETY

Excellent

"The school I am attending is on a military base. So it is very safe."

Safe Campus

"This campus is pretty safe. Nothing to big ever happens here."

LOOKING FOR MORE?

Check out our full-length guide to this school at collegeprowler.com/saint-leo-university/.

Saint Louis University

221 N. Grand Blvd.; Saint Louis, MO 63103
(314) 977-2222; www.imagine.slu.edu

THE BASICS:

Acceptance Rate: 71%
Yield: 23%
Setting: Large city
Control: Private Non-Profit
Total Undergrads: 11,169
SAT Range: 1110–1340*
ACT Range: 25–31

Student-Faculty Ratio: 13:1
Retention Rate: 85%
Graduation Rate: 74%
Tuition: $31,342
Room & Board: $9,590
Avg. Aid Package: $18,359
Students With Aid: 91%

* of 1600

Academics	B	Greek Life	B-
Athletics	C+	Guys	A
Campus Dining	B-	Health & Safety	C
Campus Housing	B-	Local Atmosphere	A-
Campus Strictness	B-	Nightlife	B+
Computers	C+	Off-Campus Dining	B
Diversity	C	Off-Campus Housing	B+
Drug Safety	D+	Parking	B-
Facilities	B+	Transportation	B+
Girls	A-	Weather	C+

CP's Student Author On...
OVERALL EXPERIENCE

SLU gets largely positive reviews from students, and few have complaints about the academics or the campus itself. It's certainly safe to say that no one attends for the cheap tuition, so the size of the student body speaks for itself. Above all else, however, it's important to understand that you get out what you put in at SLU. Of course, this can be said for any college, but given the large commuter population at St. Louis, it's especially applicable here. The worst feelings toward the University tend to come from students who haven't been involved with much during their time on campus; ironically, these are the students who complain about the lack of things to do. SLU is definitely a university that needs to be experienced through its many clubs, service opportunities, and extracurricular programs.

If you do choose to attend SLU, take some time to find your way around the campus and meet as many people as possible. It's also a good idea to explore the city itself, though this can be a lot more interesting with a group of friends. School and city alike offer a wealth of things to become involved with, or just ways to kill time; these can be as important to college life as any classroom.

Students Speak Out On...
OVERALL EXPERIENCE

Q **Good So Far**

"There were plenty of parties Freshman year. The party scene is weird since we are in a city. Anything Health Care related, SLU is great for. The people are so nice and really friendly. Honestly I am glad I go here but like every college, you have to put the effort forth to find happiness."

Q **Sallie Mae, Say What??**

"Tuition is ever increasing and it will continue to do so every year, and SLU is no exception. Although I have a schlorship I am still having to take out ennormous loans that will take me years to pay off and question my abilty to attend graduate school. It is much too expensive and I have not had the great experience that is suposed to come with the quality private school education, more like getting owned by teachers and having to accept whatever they say or do."

Q **Not So Good**

"For as much money as it costs to go here I am not that fond of SLU. The neighborhood isn't that great and there's not much to do besides party and drink. My car has already been broken into and I scared to leave my dorm at night."

BEST OF SAINT LOUIS

1. The abundance of clubs, organizations, and activities
2. Knowing (or at least recognizing) everyone on campus
3. Laying around "studying" at the clock tower

Happy Students
85% of students return after their first year.

Proven Success
74% of students will complete their education and graduate with a degree.

WORST OF SAINT LOUIS

1. Signing up for on-campus housing
2. The network crashes on the morning of class registration
3. Accidentally getting sprayed by the water jets underneath the clock tower

Expensive
Tuition is a steep $31,342, one of the most expensive rates in the country.

Student Body

African American:	8%	Male Undergrads:	40%
Asian American:	5%	Female Undergrads:	60%
Hispanic:	2%	Living On Campus:	53%
International:	4%	Living Off Campus:	47%
Native American:	0%	Male Athletes:	6%
White:	74%	Female Athletes:	5%
Unknown:	6%	Fraternity Members:	18%
From Out-of-State:	69%	Sorority Members:	23%

Students Speak Out On... EVERYTHING!

ACADEMICS

Q A Good School

"Intelligent and knowledgable professors, challenging classes, weight on academics"

Q Saint Louis University Parks College of Engineering

"What makes SLU's engineering school (Parks) so great is the hands-on experience. So many universities are really lacking in experiential learning. Not the case with SLU Parks."

Q Love It

"I came to Saint Louis University for the Top 10 nationally ranked health management program. I've really enjoyed all my classes, and the teachers try & make all your classes enjoyable."

ATHLETICS

Q Athletic Facilities

"The athletic facilities of this campus is in superb form."

Q SLU Athletics

"SLU has good athletics. Good sports, good coaches. The students really come together to support their teams."

Q Bleed Blue

"We all are a family, no matter what team we play for. We give it our all, and hope for the outcome we want. The fans are there supporting us, with their bodies painted and their air horns blowing. Our school spirit is at top notch, for walking around campus you will see that everyone is wearing something of our school. Our facilites are at top notch and are as clean as you could get them. Our teams have a mode and that is, THIS IS OUR HOUSE."

CAMPUS DINING

Q Many Options, but Hours Are Inconvenient

"If you are a vegetarian, you have no need to worry about finding food. There is a cafe that is strictly vegetarian and delicious. I eat lunch there everyday. However, the hours aren't the greatest. Most places are only open until 7:00, although there is one food court that is open until 2:00a.m.

There is a lot of variety though -- we have Chik-Fil-A, Subway, Salsaritas, Au Bon Pain, and quite a few sandwich/wrap/pizza places on campus."

Q Not Too Shabby

"Lot's of options, which is great. I love Salsaritas!"

CAMPUS HOUSING

Q Reinert Hall Is Not as Bad as People Think

"The freshmen Reinert Hall dorms are considered "off-campus" and too far away - when in reality it's a 5 minute walk max to the lecture halls. Plus, it comes with its own bathroom!"

Q Pretty Good

"As a freshman, try to get a room in Reinert if you can. The rooms are HUGE, each room had its own bathroom, and the floors are co-ed. It is three to a room. Honestly, it's not that far of a walk. Suck it up. And "Shady" Shell isn't really shady at all, it's where the cops get their doughnuts."

GUYS & GIRLS

Q Student's Relationship

"The relationship among the students is highly encouraging despite the diversity in race and background"

Q They Are Nice, Helpful, Attractive

"You make some great friends when joining a learning community"

HEALTH & SAFETY

Q Good

"They spend millions on safety."

Q Pretty Safe but Be Smart

"Alot of break-ins happen around the holidays. Behind Village Housing is not very safe since the parking lot is kind of sketch. Honestly, walk in groups and take campus escort and you'll be fine. I feel pretty safe at SLU>"

LOOKING FOR MORE?

Check out our full-length guide to this school at collegeprowler.com/saint-louis-university/.

Salem College

601 S. Church St.; Winston Salem, NC 27101
(336) 721-2600; www.salem.edu

THE BASICS:

Acceptance Rate: 60%
Yield: 44%
Setting: Mid-sized city
Control: Private Non-Profit
Total Undergrads: 734
SAT Range: 1440–1810*
ACT Range: 22–28

Student-Faculty Ratio: 10:1
Retention Rate: 75%
Graduation Rate: 53%
Tuition: $21,380
Room & Board: $11,210
Avg. Aid Package: $18,755
Students With Aid: 97%

of 2400

This School Isn't Graded Yet!

College Prowler grades are calculated using tons of criteria, including survey responses that come from students at this school.

Unfortunately, we haven't gathered enough student surveys yet for this school to be able to calculate the grades for each section. Stay tuned to *CollegeProwler.com* for grade updates and more!

CP's Student Author On...
OVERALL EXPERIENCE

Students have mixed feelings about Salem, although most never regret their time here. Some of the best things about this school are the friendships that students make with peers and the close relationships that develop with faculty members. However, some feel that Salem's sense of community almost makes it too sheltered and insular. There are plenty of opportunities for leadership and participation, but a small group of active students often end up in charge of many big clubs and stretch themselves to the point of exhaustion. Students sometimes feel a disconnect with newer members of the administration who are less familiar with Salem College's traditions; if newcomers try to "standardize" the school to the point of losing that sense of community, it really upsets the crowd.

Salem does try to mold students into independent thinkers because that's the best thing the College can offer. Since Salem is a small, all-women's school, it can't offer everything larger colleges might, which forces students to take initiative and take control of their academic lives.... For the rest of this editorial, visit collegeprowler.com.

Students Speak Out On...
OVERALL EXPERIENCE

Q Experience
"Salem is good, not much activity on the the weekend."

Q I Would Chooseit Again.
"Its affordable,very enthusiastic, and relaxing in campus.I get to meant lots of friendly people. Plus Salem is an historical place, great teachers, safe city.i cant wait for the summer to end so i can go back."

Q Life in General
"It hasn't been horrible i guess. i don't really have another college experience to compare it to though. I don't like the women's college thing, and visitation is kinda ridiculous"

BEST OF SALEM

1. Excellent faculty/staff who also care about you personally
2. Sense of community/ sisterhood
3. Traditions and rich history
4. Pretty campus
5. Friends

Commitment to Teaching
There are 10 students for every member of faculty on campus.

Learn from the Best
89% of faculty have earned the highest degree in their field.

WORST OF SALEM

1. Food
2. Insular/sheltered/ isolated/boring
3. Lack of privacy/ cliquishness
4. Limited course offerings/majors
5. Poor public transportation

Student Body

African American:	19%	Male Undergrads:	4%
Asian American:	1%	Female Undergrads:	96%
Hispanic:	4%	Living On Campus:	52%
International:	8%	Living Off Campus:	48%
Native American:	0%	Male Athletes:	0%
White:	60%	Female Athletes:	12%
Unknown:	6%	Fraternity Members:	0%
From Out-of-State:	33%	Sorority Members:	0%

Frequently Compared Schools:

Emory University
University of North Carolina
Wake Forest University
Warren Wilson College

Students Speak Out On... EVERYTHING!

ACADEMICS

Workload

"Salem is a much more difficult school than people give it credit for. Each class is required to have "14 hours of work in and out of class per week." Multiplied by four or five classes makes a tough work load. There are always professors who are easier than this however. Overall the academics are rigorous especially in classes that aren't considered "gen ed.""

Most Teachers Are Amazing at Salem

"Most of the teachers are available for help all the time. The class sizes are small. The workload is usually not too bad. There are not a ton of different majors offered but that can be expected since it's such a small school."

ATHLETICS

There Are Good Athletics

"The school is small so athletics are not as large as at other schools but they are pretty fierce and perform well. All of the athletes I know are very content."

Great Teams and Fitness Center

"Due to Salem being an all womens college, it doesn't offer certain sports. With that being said, the sports at Salem are excellent. The teams are so dedicated to their sport, and the fan support is tremendous. We have some of the best sports teams at Salem, and their team performance shows it. The athletic facilities are some of the best out there. The fitness center is easy to access and there is always an available student to help you if you are having trouble with the machines."

CAMPUS DINING

Food

"Food at the "RAT" the refectory is usually good, and there is some variety of food available. Sometimes I feel like I am going to die as a vegan! :P"

The Food Is Average

"At Salem College there is an exclusive dining option. You do not have a meal plan. You pay a certain amount at the beginning of the year and you can eat as much as you want as many times a day as you want."

CAMPUS HOUSING

Living on Campus

"Cheap-everything like food is included. There are a lot of free or cheap events always going on to attend. Everything is within walking distance. Gramley is a great first year dorn becasue it has nicer furntiure that can be stacked."

GUYS & GIRLS

Salem Is an All Girls College

"There are every type of girl at Salem College. Athletes, Preps, Nerds, etc. They are all powerful leaders and strong academics, and lot's of fun."

Arts/Womens School

"Salem is a womens college so only males 23 and older can attend. Going to class in the mornings, people just role out of bed, some do not even change out of pjs. Most people at Salem are some what arts minded so they dress somewhat alternatively. Hardly anyone wears expensive clothes. Everyone wears jeans and a t-shirt most of the time."

HEALTH & SAFETY

Wonderful Safety

"The campus is downtown of a semi large city so people take precautions even though there has never been a incident of crime (I have been here 2 years now). It is very safe. The public safety officers really do there job. At all events, they are there making sure nothing happens."

LOOKING FOR MORE?

Check out our full-length guide to this school at collegeprowler.com/salem-college/.

Salisbury University

1101 Camden Ave.; Salisbury, MD 21801
(410) 543-6000; www.salisbury.edu

THE BASICS:

Acceptance Rate: 54%
Yield: 32%
Setting: Suburban
Control: Public
Total Undergrads: 7,557
SAT Range: 1570–1820*
ACT Range: 21–26

Student-Faculty Ratio: 17:1
Retention Rate: 80%
Graduation Rate: 69%
Tuition: $15,114
Room & Board: $8,070
Avg. Aid Package: $7,027
Students With Aid: 79%

* of 2400

Academics	B	Greek Life	C+
Athletics	B-	Guys	B
Campus Dining	A-	Health & Safety	D+
Campus Housing	B	Local Atmosphere	C
Campus Strictness	C+	Nightlife	B
Computers	B-	Off-Campus Dining	B-
Diversity	C+	Off-Campus Housing	B+
Drug Safety	C	Parking	C+
Facilities	A-	Transportation	B+
Girls	B-	Weather	C

CP's Student Author On...
OVERALL EXPERIENCE

Salisbury University's homepage proclaims the school as "A Maryland University of National Distinction," and rightly so. For the past dozen years, SU has been ranked as one of the top universities not only in the state of Maryland, but also in the country. Students at Salisbury are attracted to the relatively small class sizes that afford them personal attention from professors, as well as the availability of other academic resources, such as computers. In addition, SU has a great financial aid and scholarship program, which, coupled with the modest fees, makes college more affordable to a larger number of students. Together, the available academic resources and financial aid options make Salisbury a very attractive institution, especially for those planning on careers in education or business, two of SU's strongest programs.

In addition to the academic advantages, the biggest draw of Salisbury is the social atmosphere. Every day is a chance to meet someone new. It is not uncommon for students to simply sit down at an occupied table in the Commons and introduce themselves.... For the rest of this editorial, visit collegeprowler.com.

Students Speak Out On...
OVERALL EXPERIENCE

Q I Love Being a Seagull

"I love salisbury. I have wanted to go here all my life. the atmosphere is really chill and there are a good amount of students; not too many not too few. the teachers tend to be pretty relaxed and understanding. the vibe of the place is laid back but offers a great education. There is a local party scene but i really dont get into it. for the most part the students are here for education and there isn't a lot of bull. everyone i've come across is really friendly."

Q It's the Only Place I Wanted to Go, and I Love It

"Salisbury is the only school I really visited and wanted to go to. A few other people from my small, private high school attended here the same year as I, and they all are still here. It's such a pleasant school and a great education, but the only downfall is the awful, dangerous surrounding community."

BEST OF SALISBURY

1. Small class sizes
2. Affordable tuition
3. Great education program
4. Great professors
5. Large amount of AP credits accepted
6. Close to several beaches

Happy Students
80% of students return after their first year.

Big Dorms
54% of students surveyed felt that dorms were more spacious than average.

WORST OF SALISBURY

1. Hard to get parking
2. Not a well-stocked library
3. Lots of rain
4. Not much to do around town
5. High fines for dorm room violations

Lowest Grades
Health & Safety: D+
Local Atmosphere: C
Weather: C

Student Body

African American:	12%	Male Undergrads:	45%
Asian American:	3%	Female Undergrads:	55%
Hispanic:	3%	Living On Campus:	37%
International:	1%	Living Off Campus:	60%
Native American:	1%	Male Athletes:	11%
White:	80%	Female Athletes:	5%
Unknown:	2%	Fraternity Members:	5%
From Out-of-State:	18%	Sorority Members:	5%

Frequently Compared Schools:

James Madison University
Towson University
University of Delaware
University of Maryland

Students Speak Out On... EVERYTHING!

ACADEMICS

Amazing Professors

"The professors in the Physical Education Teaching Education program at Salisbury University are phenomenal. They are very experienced and passionate about what they are teaching students because they know what we will learn will help us teach the future of tomorrow. The teachers are fun and skilled, they help students whenever problems occur and they are great to work with!"

Professors Are Great

"All of the professors I have had were awesome. They were truly in tune with their field and they were also very friendly and eager to help any student in need."

ATHLETICS

Well Known for Athletics

"Our school is basically known majorly for it's athletic department. There's sports fields, gyms and facilties all over the place. No matter where you are on campus or what time of day you can always see people running and biking around."

Great Teams

"Our sports teams are pretty big but not as big as a division 1 campus. Our football team is not very good so going to Saturday football games is not a huge deal. Guys and girls lacrosse are big sports on campus, along with baseball, womens field hockey and basketball. The campus treats us very well with facilities and training staff. Inter-mural and club sports are huge at Salisbury."

CAMPUS DINING

Best Food!!

"Salisbury has the best on campus food one could ask for. They always have a variety of choices on top of the usual food everyday. On campus satellite dinning areas are provided and are equally as good as our commons. Off campus there are many good places to eat. Lots of fast food but also places like Chili's and Ruby Tuesdays. A lot of the off campus dinning places accept your gullcard as form of payment which is very nice."

Good Food Choices

"The on-campus dining facilities are pretty nice. Sometimes the dining hall gets a little old, but they have a good variety. There are a lot of healthy choices, which definitely helps keep those freshman 15 off."

CAMPUS HOUSING

Never Lived on Campus

"I commute and like living at home---it's cheaper."

New and Improved

"The residential services recently has rebuilt four dorms and they have much bigger rooms. The campus is small but not too small, and everything is easily accessible."

GUYS & GIRLS

Typical Looks

"At Salisbury University there is a vast array of students but it represents the typical American. You may see the guy in flip flops and tee and the girl in a casual skirt and top to a typical African dress. All the student blend and mesh regardless of their dress."

Hot Would Be an Understatement

"There are a numerous variety of girls here at Salisbury University from country girls to city girls. There is a great social life here, everyone is willing to meet new people."

HEALTH & SAFETY

It's Very Safe

"There are emergency blue lights and campus police around."

LOOKING FOR MORE?

Check out our full-length guide to this school at collegeprowler.com/salisbury-university/.

Sam Houston State University

1806 Avenue J; Huntsville, TX 77340
(936) 294-1111; www.shsu.edu

THE BASICS:

Acceptance Rate: 57%
Yield: 25%
Setting: Town
Control: Public
Total Undergrads: 14,569
SAT Range: 900–1090*
ACT Range: 18–22

Student-Faculty Ratio: 20:1
Retention Rate: 75%
Graduation Rate: 21%
Tuition: $14,825
Room & Board: $6,744
Avg. Aid Package: $4,340
Students With Aid: 67%

of 1600

Academics	C+	Greek Life	B
Athletics	B-	Guys	B
Campus Dining	C+	Health & Safety	B
Campus Housing	C	Local Atmosphere	C+
Campus Strictness	B-	Nightlife	B
Computers	B+	Off-Campus Dining	C-
Diversity	B-	Off-Campus Housing	B+
Drug Safety	C+	Parking	C+
Facilities	B	Transportation	B-
Girls	C+	Weather	B+

CP's Student Author On...
OVERALL EXPERIENCE

With the end of high school growing closer by the minute, many questions may be filling your head. "What career will I pursue?" or "Do I want to stay near home or go far away?" or "What will college be like?" Sam Houston State does a great job helping students find their calling and pursue their dreams with confidence. For any student looking for a school that offers a great overall experience, SHSU not only lives up to this but also exceeds it. Sam Houston is a fun school where it is easy to make life-long friends, while receiving a quality education from instructors who care.

Freshmen come in with a lot of unanswered questions and always receive competent answers. The professors do a good job of teaching valuable life lessons along with sharing their experiences in their field. The faculty at SHSU cares about its students and keeps their best interests in mind by offering guidance and knowledge to all those who seek it. This is made possible because of the great faculty-student interaction, which is pretty unique for such a big university.... For the rest of this editorial, visit collegeprowler.com.

Students Speak Out On...
OVERALL EXPERIENCE

Q Peace

"their are many locations in the campus where one can sit and relax with shade. there is peace and a great atmosphere to study outdoors or just chill with friends. computer labs are great and can be found all over campus."

Q Sam Is Awesome!

"i love sam for its diversity and its daily activities. there is always something going on!"

Q Education at Sam

"I transferred into Sam Houston and I love it education wise. I have learned more than I ever did at my old school."

Q Sam Houston State

"I wouldn't change my school for the world. I go to every football game and tailgate party here on campus, i go to every rugby game i can and i love that there is always something to be involved in. Everyone is friendly and ready to help you with whatever you need."

BEST OF SAM HOUSTON

1. School spirit
2. Low student-to-professor ratio means professors actually know their students.
3. The small-town feel of Huntsville and the proximity of campus to its surroundings

Knowledgeable Professors
83% of students surveyed rated the general knowledge of professors as above average.

Low-Stress Course Load
65% of students surveyed rated the manageability of work as above average.

WORST OF SAM HOUSTON

1. No matter what part of campus you are heading toward, you will be walking up a very steep hill.
2. SHSU is a "suitcase college," meaning lots of students go home or leave on weekends.

Not Everyone Graduates
21% of students do not complete their education or graduate with a degree.

Student Body

African American:	15%	Male Undergrads:	44%
Asian American:	1%	Female Undergrads:	56%
Hispanic:	13%	Living On Campus:	22%
International:	1%	Living Off Campus:	78%
Native American:	1%	Male Athletes:	4%
White:	69%	Female Athletes:	2%
Unknown:	0%	Fraternity Members:	3%
From Out-of-State:	1%	Sorority Members:	1%

Frequently Compared Schools:

Texas State University - San Marcos
Texas Tech University
University of Houston
University of Texas

Students Speak Out On...
EVERYTHING!

ACADEMICS

Shsu

"The professors are very close to the students and are easy to have a conversation with. I really enjoy the open campus allowing me to walk where ever I need to."

Professors and School Placement Helpful

"The professors are very helpful with explaining any material you have questions over and always make sure to make themselves available through email or phone when outside of class. The workload while it can be difficult is not impossible to keep up with and keep a good grade. The school has a great placement rate for finding jobs and there are often internship opportunities given to all students throughout the year."

ATHLETICS

Athletics

"Athletics here are awesome. I love going to all sporting events. The fans are crazy and always keep you on your toes. Also are facilities I feel, are really nice too."

Athletics at SHSU Are Great!

"There are always games taking place at SHSU, from football to soccer to lacrosse to Quidditch! The support and spirit of the students is always vibrant and exciting. Orange is everywhere especially during games. The players are great and always winning games, especially in football. The gym at SHSU is one of the best and most interesting to be at."

CAMPUS DINING

Dining Areas

"There are alot of diffrent food choices around the dining areas. Always very clean and many staff working to help you. The dining areas are also wi-fi so you can multi task."

Belvin Cafe

"The Belvin cafe is magnificent. It's similar to other campus buffet meal plans but much better than anywhere else I have been. It also has special days too. For example, on Wednesdays, in addition to the regular menu, they also serve Buffalo chicken wraps...yum! Buy the meal plan that gives you a set number of meals for the semester. If you get the meals per week, you are sure to waste them and then you can't bring people in with you!"

CAMPUS HOUSING

Campus Living

"There are plenty of places for entertainment with easy access from the school. The gym is available with convenient hours for all students and the food in the cafeteria is not bad. Most of the dorms smell like old gym socks but that is typical of college dorms anyhow."

Can't Let You Do That

"The dorms I've stayed at were all fine, providing the necessary furniture for proper living, but the rules and the punishments for them seem needlessly severe. You must throw all trash out in the dumpster's outside of the dorm or you get a fine. If you lock yourself out, you get fined. No extra refrigerators or cooking supplies or you are fined, etc."

GUYS & GIRLS

The Students

"There are beautiful girls, and most of them dress appropriately. Some guys are rowdy though at dinnertime at Belvin. Overall, everyone is friendly."

SHSU LIFE

"the life at SHSU is very lively. There are constantly events happening somwhere on campus keeping the students involved with school spirit and open to creating new friendships."

HEALTH & SAFETY

Huntsville Crime

"Security is strictly enforced at Sam Houston. One reason is huntsville has a total of nine prsions. The other is for the safety of students and staff. I feel same walking on campus."

LOOKING FOR MORE?

Check out our full-length guide to this school at collegeprowler.com/sam-houston-state-university/.

Samford University

800 Lakeshore Drive; Birmingham, AL 35229
(205) 726-2011; www.samford.edu

THE BASICS:

Acceptance Rate: 84%	**Student-Faculty Ratio:** 12:1
Yield: 38%	**Retention Rate:** 82%
Setting: Suburban	**Graduation Rate:** 77%
Control: Private Non-Profit	**Tuition:** $20,420
Total Undergrads: 2,908	**Room & Board:** $6,624
SAT Range: 1040–1295*	**Avg. Aid Package:** $15,037
ACT Range: 21–28	**Students With Aid:** 78%

* of 1600

Academics	B-	Greek Life	B+
Athletics	C-	Guys	A-
Campus Dining	C+	Health & Safety	C
Campus Housing	B	Local Atmosphere	B
Campus Strictness	C	Nightlife	B
Computers	A-	Off-Campus Dining	B+
Diversity	D+	Off-Campus Housing	B
Drug Safety	B	Parking	B+
Facilities	B	Transportation	C
Girls	B-	Weather	B

CP's Student Author On...
OVERALL EXPERIENCE

Samford can be a wonderful experience for students. While the first semester can be extremely difficult, with students being away from their families and friends for the first time, things become easier with perseverance. Students first need to get out of their comfort zones and invest in the hilarious, wonderful people who make up the Samford population.

That being said, the people make the experience worthwhile, and there are always opportunities to meet new people, whether it's free concerts on the quad, chilling next to the fountain in Ben Brown Plaza, renting the Vail movie room for "Glee" nights, Step Sing, or worshiping at RUF (Reformed University Fellowship). These are just some of the many things students can experience at Samford. Plus, the caring professors instill in students not only knowledge, but wisdom, preparing men and women for the future every time they step into the classroom. The liberal arts aspect prompts many to draw endless comparisons and similarities between different classes, teaching students to see the "big picture.... For the rest of this editorial, visit collegeprowler.com.

Students Speak Out On...
OVERALL EXPERIENCE

Q Breath of Fresh Air!

"I love Samford and I wouldn't want to have gone to any other school. There are so many activities (sometimes it's so hard to choose which ones to go to!), but at the same time the academics are great. I don't have enormous classes, which I love; the professors can actually get to know us."

Q I Love My Samford U

"Choosing Samford was one of the best decisions I've ever made. I've never regretted coming here, and I'm reminded daily of why I love this school so much. The people here are so amazing and I've made so many lifelong relationships. I would definitely pick Samford again, as well as recommend it to anyone considering coming here."

Q Experience

"So far my experience has been great. I have made a ton of new friends and I couldn't be happier."

BEST OF SAMFORD

1. Campus scenery
2. Harry's Coffeehouse
3. Free printing
4. Greenbelt across the street
5. Step Sing
6. The Underground
7. Concerts on the Quad

Happy Students
82% of students return after their first year.

Proven Success
77% of students will complete their education and graduate with a degree.

WORST OF SAMFORD

1. Tuition cost
2. Not much diversity
3. Caf food on the weekends
4. Food court hours on the weekends
5. Different class credits that are hard to transfer to other schools

Not Much Diversity
One of the least racially diverse campuses—only 13% of students are minorities.

Student Body

African American:	7%	Male Undergrads:	36%
Asian American:	1%	Female Undergrads:	64%
Hispanic:	1%	Living On Campus:	67%
International:	1%	Living Off Campus:	33%
Native American:	0%	Male Athletes:	28%
White:	87%	Female Athletes:	9%
Unknown:	2%	Fraternity Members:	21%
From Out-of-State:	68%	Sorority Members:	29%

Students Speak Out On... EVERYTHING!

ACADEMICS

Q Profs Very Accommodating

"Our professors are incredibly accommodating, they ask us how we learn best and will try to gear the curriculum to suit our learning styles. They are always available to assist with studying for tests, questions on homework, talking about life in general, and finding jobs. They really do whatever they can to help us succeed."

Q LOVE

"Samford has a 12:1 student to faculty ration. The professors are always willing to help in any way that they can."

Q Excellence

"Many classes are rigorous to provide a vast amount of knowledge to everyone. Samford does have the right to withdraw a student if they go below a 2.0 average and show no signs of improving their GPA in order to maintain its reputation of being a high quality school."

ATHLETICS

Q Athletics

"You don't come to Samford for the exciting sports atmosphere."

Q School Spirit

"School spirit can be really great on big games, but non-existent for others."

CAMPUS DINING

Q Caf and Food Court

"The Caf is a popular place for great food and socializing"

Q Pretty Good for a School Cafeteria

"Yes, the cafeteria gets repetitive like most cafeterias, but you can always be creative and find something new to eat. Also, the cafeteria staff are very interested in fulfilling any requests for new food items that students have. I have seen several changes this year. There are several places close by to eat off-campus and, of course, the food court is always tasty!"

CAMPUS HOUSING

Q Samford University Life

"Samford Life is awesome. You live on a beautiful campus with great workout facilites, great professors, wonderful students, and so many opportunities to get involved with!"

Q Social Life at Samford

"Samford provides opportunities to have fun with fellow classmates. Our class decided to have a Rave, and it was one of the best nights I've had here at Samford this year. The time I spend to socialize with most people is when I eat in the caf. You are able to see almost all of your friends then."

GUYS & GIRLS

Q Guys Are Gentlemen, and Everyone Is Friendly!

"The guys may not always ask you out, but if they see a girl coming, they will typically wait for her and hold the door open for her! Everyone is very nice and friendly and don't judge you or look down upon people because they are different. It's an atmosphere that is so awesome!"

Q Wide Range of Guys and Girls

"There are all types of people at Samford, from the typical preps and Southern belles to punks."

HEALTH & SAFETY

Q Campus Safety

"I have never felt unsafe on Samford's campus. It has a very clean and safe atmosphere. Campus security is always around and willing to help in any way possible. We also have call boxes conviently located all over campus in case of emergency."

Q Campus Safety

"I always feel safe on Samford's campus. It is gated, and after 10 p.m. you must enter through the gates by the guardhouse and either show your student ID or have the Samford decal on your car. There are Campus Police that patrol constantly. It is in a super safe suburb of Birmingham!"

LOOKING FOR MORE?
Check out our full-length guide to this school at collegeprowler.com/samford-university/.

San Diego State University

5500 Campanile Drive; San Diego, CA 92182
(619) 594-5200; www.sdsu.edu

THE BASICS:

Acceptance Rate: 31%	**Student-Faculty Ratio:** 26:1
Yield: 28%	**Retention Rate:** 81%
Setting: Large city	**Graduation Rate:** 61%
Control: Public	**Tuition:** $16,062
Total Undergrads: 26,796	**Room & Board:** $11,485
SAT Range: 930–1170*	**Avg. Aid Package:** $8,500
ACT Range: 20–25	**Students With Aid:** 81%

* of 2400

Academics	B	Greek Life	B+
Athletics	B-	Guys	A-
Campus Dining	B+	Health & Safety	B-
Campus Housing	B-	Local Atmosphere	A
Campus Strictness	B-	Nightlife	B+
Computers	B	Off-Campus Dining	B
Diversity	B+	Off-Campus Housing	B-
Drug Safety	C+	Parking	B-
Facilities	B	Transportation	B+
Girls	A-	Weather	A+

CP's Student Author On...
OVERALL EXPERIENCE

Nearly all San Diego State students are pleased with their decision to attend school here. They find that SDSU offers the perfect mix of stellar academics and a booming social life. With the beauty of the campus, the quality of the teaching, and the fun social environment, it is difficult to dislike much about the school, but some do. Those who tend to dislike San Diego State have reservations about the social scene, which is heavily conducive to partying and Greek life. This is a misconception. SDSU offers a lot, including partying, and the school is truly what you make of it. As long as people don't hold a grudge against the sort of environment that offers partying as an activity many choose to participate in, they will enjoy their time here. San Diego State is a very well-rounded school that has a lot to offer to a variety of students, but if you are searching for a strictly academic experience in a university with a prestigious reputation, you should look elsewhere.

San Diego State is essentially defined by its social culture, and if students relate to it, they love the school, and if they don't, they can loathe their time here.... For the rest of this editorial, visit collegeprowler.com.

Students Speak Out On...
OVERALL EXPERIENCE

Q I Love SDSU

"If I could do it all over again I would. Despite even the smallest things that may irk me like the on campus bar, I love San Diego and all it has to offer. SDSU has become my home"

Q Why My School.

"SDSU is a very frendly environment. It's easy to make friends and is highly diverse. While studying is a must there is also time for fun. SDSU is a very accepting place for all races and well as sexualities. I have never had a problem with anyone on campus."

Q I Love It

"It has worked out for me well so far. Good teachers, good classes and close to where i live."

Q A for Amazing

"I love San Diego State University. It has prestigious programs, which are dedicated to finding you a great career, but does not lack on the social scene. One of the biggest party schools in the nation."

BEST OF SAN DIEGO STATE

1. Good looking people
2. Friendly atmosphere
3. Clean environment
4. Architecture
5. Perfect weather
6. Nightlife
7. Great social scene
8. Accessible professors

Happy Students
81% of students return after their first year.

Knowledgeable Professors
88% of students surveyed rated the general knowledge of professors as above average.

WORST OF SAN DIEGO STATE

1. Out-of-date dormitories
2. The strictness of RA policy
3. Party school reputation
4. Trying to get the classes you need
5. Lack of parking during peak hours
6. Too much construction

Overextended Faculty
There are 26 students for every faculty member on campus.

Don't Move Off Campus
Average off-campus housing is a steep $10,388.

Student Body

African American:	4%	Male Undergrads:	43%
Asian American:	16%	Female Undergrads:	57%
Hispanic:	22%	Living On Campus:	15%
International:	3%	Living Off Campus:	85%
Native American:	1%	Male Athletes:	2%
White:	44%	Female Athletes:	2%
Unknown:	10%	Fraternity Members:	9%
From Out-of-State:	9%	Sorority Members:	7%

Students Speak Out On... EVERYTHING!

ACADEMICS

Q Good Professors

"the professors are very well versed in their subjects and are eager to teach"

Q If Only I Were Committed

"My major program would be great if I were committed. I frequently receive contact from my college president and various criminal justice programs. However, I am not fully set on being a criminal justice major so I haven't taken full advantage of all the opportunities offered"

ATHLETICS

Q SDSU: Athletic Support

"San Diego State is a large and involved school that supports its athletic teams though they do not always excel. The fans are spirited and enjoy athletic attendance. The athletic facilities are in great condition which facilitate the imporvment of the athletes."

Q Sports Are Everything

"For those who attend San Diego State University.. Aztec Pride is a way of life. Regardless of the sport, the students here back their team 100%! On any given day you will encounter hundreds of students wearing Red & Black, and you'll find a countless number of other students who will be talking about how well the basketball, baseball or football team is doing. Who has spirit? The Aztecs do! We've got spirit!! How about you?!"

CAMPUS DINING

Q Diverse and Convenient

"No matter what you're craving, there is a spot on campus (or immediately around it) that can satisfy that craving. There are spots for comfort food as well as health food, with mini-convenience shops throughout campus whenever we need a quick between-class snack."

Frequently Compared Schools:

California Polytechnic State University
California State University - Long Beach
University of California - San Diego
University of California - Santa Barbara

Q Best Places

"I love San Diego State UniversitySan Diego is the place to be for college students, or for anyone looking for a great place to live. Trujillo's is a great place to grab a bite to eat, then you got Rubio's and Chipotle as well."

CAMPUS HOUSING

Q Atmosphere

"The atmosphere in the dorms is great. Everyone gets along and it feels like a family away from home."

Q Great Experience for Underclassmen

"The dorms are mostly close together and are a great way to meet friends. If you are looking for the complete college experience, it can't better than living in the dorms. Not only do you meet tons of new people, but you are close to campus and there are great resources. Most students move to off-campus housing by the end of their second year, though."

GUYS & GIRLS

Q Girls Are Hot!

"There are so many gorgeous girls on this campus. Any where you turn you will always see a hot girl."

Q Dimes

"there are some fine ladies but its very superfical and clicky, more about looks than personality, but there are exeptions of course"

HEALTH & SAFETY

Q Safety

"The campus feels completely safe and in the case that anyone is in need there is always available help."

Q Health & Safety

"I feel really safe here at SDSU. The atmosphere is really lively and I don't feel any unwanted discomforts at all."

LOOKING FOR MORE?
Check out our full-length guide to this school at collegeprowler.com/san-diego-state-university/.

San Francisco State University

1600 Holloway Ave.; San Francisco, CA 94132
(415) 338-1111; www.sfsu.edu

THE BASICS:

Acceptance Rate: 66%
Yield: 18%
Setting: Large city
Control: Public
Total Undergrads: 25,430
SAT Range: 1330–1700*
ACT Range: 19–24

Student-Faculty Ratio: 25:1
Retention Rate: 75%
Graduation Rate: 44%
Tuition: $15,900
Room & Board: $11,970
Avg. Aid Package: $10,668
Students With Aid: 53%

* of 2400

Academics	C+	Greek Life	C
Athletics	C	Guys	B+
Campus Dining	B-	Health & Safety	B-
Campus Housing	B-	Local Atmosphere	A-
Campus Strictness	B	Nightlife	B+
Computers	C	Off-Campus Dining	C
Diversity	A	Off-Campus Housing	B-
Drug Safety	C+	Parking	C+
Facilities	C	Transportation	A
Girls	B-	Weather	B+

CP's Student Author On...
OVERALL EXPERIENCE

During their first year at San Francisco State, many students may be saddened and lonely, as it may seem hard to find the right social group outright. But when it is finally time to leave for good, the tears are sure to come flowing. With so much one can explore and experience within the seven-mile stretch of San Francisco, SFSU offers much more than what other universities and areas offer in longer mile stretches. The trendy piercing/tattoo shops of Haight Street, the tourism of Powell, the swell relaxation and jogging atmosphere of Embarcadero—they all combine to create an experience unlike any other city. The majority of students would still choose to go to SFSU rather than transfer or go to another school, mainly due to the culture.

San Francisco is one of the rare places where just about anyone who spends time in the city can at some point reach within themselves and find an aspect that runs parallel with the city. Even as a commuter student, one is sure to be able to soak up the fog and feel out the city. Take a moment to revel in all you have seen and heard. The experience is there—a growth from lowly student to man or woman.

Students Speak Out On...
OVERALL EXPERIENCE

Q Really Fun Experience

"I have had fun with the time of going to SFSU. At first you may think it's all fun and games, but you have to make sure you get your work done and have it successful."

Q Great Experience

"I recently just transferred here and it's been everything i wanted about a college; Very diverse, Very involved and inspiring teachers, Awesome activities to involve oneself in on campus and off campus through campus. The bureaucracy here is pretty annoying. However the overall experience has been what i wanted for college and wish i was here the whole time."

Q High Tuition

"The university itself is very good. I like the campus, people, professors. The only thing is that tuition for international students are much higher than for domestic students, and there are no discounts."

BEST OF SAN FRANCISCO STATE

1. The Village Market being open until 12 a.m.
2. The amount of cool majors available
3. Ease of getting an on-campus job
4. Quality of teachers
5. Student discount with Muni passes

Knowledgeable Professors
92% of students surveyed rated the general knowledge of professors as above average.

Low-Stress Course Load
75% of students surveyed rated the manageability of work as above average.

WORST OF SAN FRANCISCO STATE

1. The awful wind during the months of December and July
2. The meter maids
3. Lack of school spirit
4. Shortage of uncommitted students looking for relationships

Overextended Faculty
There are 25 students for every faculty member on campus.

Expensive to Just Get By
63% of students surveyed felt that the amount it costs to live while at school was worse than average.

Student Body

African American:	6%	Male Undergrads:	41%
Asian American:	29%	Female Undergrads:	59%
Hispanic:	16%	Living On Campus:	50%
International:	7%	Living Off Campus:	89%
Native American:	1%	Male Athletes:	1%
White:	29%	Female Athletes:	1%
Unknown:	12%	Fraternity Members:	—
From Out-of-State:	4%	Sorority Members:	—

Frequently Compared Schools:

California State University - Long Beach
San Diego State University
San Jose State University
University of California - Santa Cruz

Students Speak Out On...
EVERYTHING!

ACADEMICS

Q Better Eduation

"I like education given at Cameron University. My University is small so I can get better information and knowledge about my degree. Also our professors are really helpful and ready to help students in any course matter. I am not bound only with the course work but other exciting educational things as well. Teaching have been always part of entertainment for me at Cameron University."

Q Geology   Great Professors

"I am a geology major. Its great here every class generally has one major field trip longest I have done so far was a 4 day trip to Nevada to visit gold mines. Awesome right. We camp party at night and then work during the day.   Its not a major for the faint of heart.   The classwork does get technical."

ATHLETICS

Q School Spirit

"Amazing spirit at campus for sports and other activities."

Q The Sports We Do Have

"Here at San Francisco State its fair to say for a Division II school, 100% of our athletes compete with a Division I attitude. We are like jaguars on the soccer field, WNBA and NBA players on the court, contortionists on the mat, Ken Griffey Jr's at the plate, and personal dust feeders on the track. What else can I say about that Gator pride welcome to the swamp."

CAMPUS DINING

Q The Food Is Delicious for the Most Part.

"All the places there is to eat in the student center are good. There is healthy food,asian food, latin food, italian food,etc. There is everything."

Q Meals at Cesar Chavez Building

"This building has to be one of the hot spots at San Francisco State University for meals purchase. They offer a variety of cuisines, and different menu options. I personally love eating breakfast there, chowing on some really tasty and delicious omelets."

CAMPUS HOUSING

Q Social Atmoshere

"Social atmosphere is great at the university. Its a happening place with lots of activities going on eveyrday"

Q Campus Beauty

"Living on campus is accessible. The muni is at the top of campus and that makes it easy to get anywhere. The dorms are nice and well kept. The campus in general is incredibly beautiful with student art work and sculptures and many, many trees. The food on campus is satisfactory. Wherever you live is good, all the places are suitable and nice. At night the campus is usually buzzing with excitement."

GUYS & GIRLS

Q Students on Campus

"SFSU is ethnically diverse, which really finalized my choice on attending SFSU. It is really easy to acquaint people, because many are open and friendly."

Q SFSU

"There is a variety of students there, different races and from different parts of the world."

HEALTH & SAFETY

Q Health and Safety

"Well SFSU is in San Francisco, one of the cleanest and greenest cities in the United States. It is a city there are some crimes, but SFSU is located in a safe district, its just like any other place to live, if you practice general safety, you will be safe."

LOOKING FOR MORE?

Check out our full-length guide to this school at collegeprowler.com/san-francisco-state-university/.

Santa Clara University

500 El Camino Real; Santa Clara, CA 95053
(408) 554-4000; www.scu.edu

THE BASICS:

Acceptance Rate: 58%
Yield: 21%
Setting: Mid-sized city
Control: Private Non-Profit
Total Undergrads: 5,159
SAT Range: 1120–1330*
ACT Range: 25–30

Student-Faculty Ratio: 13:1
Retention Rate: 92%
Graduation Rate: 85%
Tuition: $36,000
Room & Board: $11,400
Avg. Aid Package: $21,337
Students With Aid: 84%

* of 1600

Academics	A-	Greek Life	N/A
Athletics	B-	Guys	A-
Campus Dining	B+	Health & Safety	B+
Campus Housing	A	Local Atmosphere	B
Campus Strictness	B-	Nightlife	B+
Computers	B	Off-Campus Dining	B
Diversity	B-	Off-Campus Housing	B
Drug Safety	D+	Parking	A-
Facilities	A-	Transportation	B
Girls	B+	Weather	A+

CP's Student Author On...
OVERALL EXPERIENCE

Inspired by its Jesuit roots, Santa Clara's mission to educate the whole person by engaging the mind, body, and spirit encourages its students to maintain a healthy balance between work and play. Santa Clara's diverse academic, extracurricular, and community service opportunities make it easy for students to do what they love and to tailor their SCU experience accordingly. Though many students initially have a tough time adjusting (typical for most college freshmen), taking advantage of the resources provided by the strong campus community can help make the transition process easier. Thriving at Santa Clara requires finding your niche, which can take awhile, but is worth it once you do.

Most students cite weather, location, and academics as Santa Clara's greatest strengths, and they appreciate the active and supportive community on campus. While many students agree that they would change certain aspects of the school if they could (the cost of tuition taking priority), most feel pretty satisfied with their Santa Clara experience.

Students Speak Out On...
OVERALL EXPERIENCE

Q Love It

"I love my friends and my education here. I have gotten so many opportunities to get a jump start on my career and have met so many networking channels. I definately came here for my education and it has met all my expectations in that regard!"

Q Love It!

"I am so glad I decided to come to Santa Clara. The campus is beautiful and the classes are challenging, and I've made some of the best friends of my life!"

Q Great Community Feel

"The best part about SCU has been the strong sense of community. I always felt as though there were many resources for support, and the people and professors generally seemed very down-to-earth. Work was challenging, but not overwhelming. Aside from that, the weather was to die for!"

BEST OF SANTA CLARA

1. Beautiful campus
2. Sunny and warm, even in February
3. Close-knit campus community
4. Fall quarter doesn't start until the end of September
5. Small classes

Happy Students
92% of students return after their first year.

Proven Success
85% of students will complete their education and graduate with a degree.

WORST OF SANTA CLARA

1. No football team
2. Housing is expensive.
3. Lack of diversity
4. Spring quarter doesn't end until mid-June.
5. Tuition is expensive.
6. Lame nightlife

Expensive
Tuition is a steep $36,000, one of the most expensive rates in the country.

Expensive to Just Get By
74% of students surveyed felt that the amount it costs to live while at school was worse than average.

Student Body

African American:	4%	Male Undergrads:	47%
Asian American:	17%	Female Undergrads:	53%
Hispanic:	13%	Living On Campus:	48%
International:	3%	Living Off Campus:	52%
Native American:	1%	Male Athletes:	7%
White:	46%	Female Athletes:	6%
Unknown:	16%	Fraternity Members:	0%
From Out-of-State:	42%	Sorority Members:	0%

Frequently Compared Schools:

Loyola Marymount University
University of California - Santa Barbara
University of San Diego
University of Southern California

Students Speak Out On... EVERYTHING!

ACADEMICS

Q Accounting: Great Job Security

"accounting major is a very difficult major with the most class requirements of any other major. However, we have a great accounting association that works really hard at getting students internships and jobs."

Q Amazing Tiny Classes With Personal Attention

"Academics win here! I had many classes with only 8 students and our professor. It creates opportunities to form relationships and have good dialogues."

ATHLETICS

Q Academics Are Valued More at SCU

"I guess we have a pretty decent athletic program here at Santa Clara. Although we don't dominate in every sport, we have our ups and downs and overall, it's not bad. We have a nice facility, open to all faculty and students populations, which houses our workout room, a multi-purpose room (where we have fitness classes everyday on different things like cardio kick boxing and zumba and yoga), and also indoor courts where intramural games are held. We also have a swimming pool."

Q Athletics

"All the sports at Santa Clara are supported widely by many of the students. Every basketball game and soccer game I have attended has shown school spirit as well as a large amount of attendees."

CAMPUS DINING

Q Good but Repetitive

"The food on campus is really good, but gets kinda repetitive after awhile. Definitely a lot better than the food on most other college campuses."

Q Good, but the Food Can Get Old Fast

"The food is delicious, it just is really repetitive after awhile."

CAMPUS HOUSING

Q Rlcs Are Awesome

"The residence halls at SCU are divided by learning community. Each building has a different theme and each has it's own unique personality. Incoming freshmen always freak out about where they are going to be placed, but mostly everyone loves their freshman experience. Every building is differnt, but they all have something to offer. Campus is small, so distance and location isn't really a factor."

Q Wonderful Dorm Communities

"The dorms at Santa Clara University have a strong emphasis on community, and I think that they do a great job facilitating it. The buildings themselves vary in quality, but overall they are comfortable and clean."

GUYS & GIRLS

Q Girls Are Pretty Attractive.

"Girls at Santa Clara are generally really attractive. A lot of them won't talk to me because they can be really stuck-up if you are not in a frat. They are still nice to look at even though they are snobs."

HEALTH & SAFETY

Q A+ Safety

"There has never been a time when I did not feel completely safe on or around campus. There is never a shortage of campus safety patrolling the grounds and when you need them they respond quickly to any and all emergencies. The Santa Clara Police Department also faces the school and there are many other emergency medical response agencies surrounding the school or not far from campus. Santa Clara is definitely one of the safest campuses I have ever visited."

LOOKING FOR MORE?

Check out our full-length guide to this school at collegeprowler.com/santa-clara-university/.

Sarah Lawrence College

1 Mead Way; Bronxville, NY 10708
(914) 337-0700; www.slc.edu

THE BASICS:

Acceptance Rate: 60%	**Student-Faculty Ratio:** 9:1
Yield: 28%	**Retention Rate:** 82%
Setting: Suburban	**Graduation Rate:** 73%
Control: Private Non-Profit	**Tuition:** $41,968
Total Undergrads: 1,367	**Room & Board:** $13,370
SAT Range: 1160–1350*	**Avg. Aid Package:** $28,686
ACT Range: —	**Students With Aid:** 63%

* of 1600

Academics	B+	Greek Life	N/A
Athletics	D+	Guys	C+
Campus Dining	C+	Health & Safety	C+
Campus Housing	B	Local Atmosphere	B-
Campus Strictness	B	Nightlife	C+
Computers	B-	Off-Campus Dining	B
Diversity	C-	Off-Campus Housing	D
Drug Safety	C-	Parking	C+
Facilities	B-	Transportation	B-
Girls	B+	Weather	B-

CP's Student Author On...
OVERALL EXPERIENCE

SLC is a magnet for students who want, above all other things, to be well-educated. Careers, money, and business are seen as secondary in comparison to the joy of learning. The one-of-a-kind curriculum gives you the freedom to choose what you want to learn and how you want to learn it. Many students come to Sarah Lawrence unsure of their futures, and many graduate feeling no less disoriented. Yet, it's agreed that the SLC program, with its distinctive philosophy of academics, is a life-changing experience. After all, being a student here equals spending four years immersed in a community of intellectual young people and world-renowned professors.

What students report as the biggest setback is the anemic social scene. Nightlife is nearly nonexistent. Traditionally, SLC students are introspective, private, and socially-awkward people. Loners are abundant, as are small, insular cliques. The severe lack of ethnic or political diversity means that there may be too many like-minded people for the college's own good.... For the rest of this editorial, visit collegeprowler.com.

Students Speak Out On...
OVERALL EXPERIENCE

Q I Love SLC!

"Sarah Lawrence is great for me. I couldn't be happier or more at home. If I could pick it again I would - the individualized learning experience is worth every penny, and the good financial aid office makes it so those pennies are few and far between."

Q Unique

"SLC is definitely like no other college. It's a very artsy school with a lot of hipsters. The kids here are very smart though and very passionate about their studies. The professors are dedicated and brilliant for the most part. It's a very free and open school, in terms of thinking, the social aspect, and academic pursuits. There's quite a large gay community here and everyones okay with it."

BEST OF SARAH LAWRENCE

1. Small, intimate classes
2. Independent study
3. The approachability of the professors
4. Bacchanalia
5. Quick access to NYC
6. Black squirrels
7. Campbell Sports Center

Happy Students
82% of students return after their first year.

Commitment to Teaching
There are 9 students for every member of faculty on campus.

WORST OF SARAH LAWRENCE

1. The New Dorms
2. No air conditioning
3. Laundry facilities
4. Long winters
5. Kimball Avenue
6. Reckless drinking
7. Hipsters

Expensive
Tuition is a steep $41,968, one of the most expensive rates in the country.

Expensive to Just Get By
62% of students surveyed felt that the amount it costs to live while at school was worse than average.

Student Body

African American:	3%	Male Undergrads:	27%
Asian American:	5%	Female Undergrads:	73%
Hispanic:	5%	Living On Campus:	86%
International:	3%	Living Off Campus:	14%
Native American:	0%	Male Athletes:	9%
White:	65%	Female Athletes:	9%
Unknown:	18%	Fraternity Members:	0%
From Out-of-State:	81%	Sorority Members:	0%

Students Speak Out On... EVERYTHING!

ACADEMICS

One on One System Helpful

"At Sarah Lawrence, you would have to try really hard to not establish a relationship with your professors. Most are well-connected and knowledgeable. Lots of face time means lots of opportunities to excel. However, a lot of classes are heavily literature based. Students spend nearly all of their time reading - and still don't finish everything."

Professors Are Fantastic

"Academics is one thing that I am satisfied with Sarah Lawrence. The professors are very efficient about their work and very devoted.It is also a fantastic place to build a one on one relationship with the professors because of our conference system. The professors really know their fields and are helpful in many ways."

ATHLETICS

Cute, Fun and Laid Back

"Sarah Lawrence Sports are fun, and anyone can participate. We really emphasize team-spirit, not necessarily winning. Our sports center is beautiful, but we're not the most athletic student body. Our PE credit come from things like playground games and bocci club."

Not a Sporty School

"You don't go to Sarah Lawrence because of its athletics. That being said, most of the teams are competitive in the division they're in, especially crew, boys' basketball, girls' tennis, and equestrian. Not many people go to games, but they're around if you want to watch and show your support. A great opportunity to try playing a sport you've never played before; no one who wants to play is turned away, generally speaking."

CAMPUS DINING

OK

"As a vegetarian it gets a little difficult to find food that is interesting...i.e. not only salad and pasta. Bates is probably the best option in terms of value but it's at the far end of campus from many dorms. The Pub's good but it's always crowded during meal times."

Its College..

"The food at Sarah Lawrence is not as bad as people have said..Compared to other schools, the food here is pretty good. The places to eat are Bates dinings hall, the Pub (which has food to go as well as dine-in), The Atrium Cafe, and Hill To Go (which has groceries, laundry products, etc). I don't mind the food at all. Sure, its not gourmet, but I don't know how good college food can really be.."

CAMPUS HOUSING

It Really Depends on Where You Are.

"It really depends on where you are. Most upperclassmen (sophomores and above) get great housing and the kind of housing they want to have. Many first years get stuck in triples in more traditional style dorms. If you can tough that out for a year, you're good to go."

GUYS & GIRLS

Kind of Hipster Still

"While the ratio of hipsters to science and math kids has shifted dramatically, there are still a lot of hipsterish-looking kids who are at Sarah Lawrence as a stepping stone into Brooklyn."

HEALTH & SAFETY

Safety at Sarah Lawrence College

"I feel very safe at Sarah Lawrence, Bronxville is incredibly safe and I never lock my door at night because there is no reason to (my dorm is also really safe and I trust the people in it). Yonkers is less safe but as long as you don't walk alone late at night then your fine. The security staff is always patrolling and there is a night time shuttle that students can take around campus or to the train station."

LOOKING FOR MORE?

Check out our full-length guide to this school at collegeprowler.com/sarah-lawrence-college/.

Scripps College

1030 N. Columbia Ave.; Claremont, CA 91711
(909) 621-8149; www.scrippscollege.edu

THE BASICS:

Acceptance Rate: 33%
Yield: 30%
Setting: Suburban
Control: Private Non-Profit
Total Undergrads: 898
SAT Range: 1900–2160*
ACT Range: 27–32

Student-Faculty Ratio: 9:1
Retention Rate: 88%
Graduation Rate: 83%
Tuition: $38,700
Room & Board: $11,850
Avg. Aid Package: $28,865
Students With Aid: 40%

of 2400

Academics	A-	Greek Life	N/A
Athletics	C-	Guys	N/A
Campus Dining	A	Health & Safety	B+
Campus Housing	A	Local Atmosphere	B-
Campus Strictness	B+	Nightlife	B-
Computers	A-	Off-Campus Dining	C
Diversity	C+	Off-Campus Housing	D-
Drug Safety	B+	Parking	B-
Facilities	A-	Transportation	C-
Girls	A-	Weather	A

CP's Student Author On...
OVERALL EXPERIENCE

Scripps is definitely a very unique place that is not for everyone. Luckily, it is the perfect place for some. Academics are a first and foremost concern in looking at colleges, and I feel that this is also the leading concern of Scripps and its student body. Classes and faculty provide an intimate setting for in-depth learning and the personal pursuit of knowledge. The emphasis on learning, the openness to exploration, and the acceptance of what is different and exceptional are all things that students love about the school, and things that contribute to positive overall growth and development, as well as self realization. The physical comforts and beauty of the college are nothing compared to the mental challenges and the amazing student body. From classes to activities, students are taught to work beyond the bare necessity and think beyond the mere possibilities. The atmosphere here has a sense of healthy competition that encourages students to feed off each other and mature together.... For the rest of this editorial, visit collegeprowler.com.

Students Speak Out On...
OVERALL EXPERIENCE

Q "I think that I have learned a lot about myself and the world around me. Scripps has helped me to expand my thinking and mature mentally."

Q "It's hard to transition in, but after sophomore slumps, it's a lot better. Just be comfortable with yourself."

Q "I love this school, not only for its people, but for the experiences it has brought to me. The workload is hard enough that I'm not bored and the classes are challenging and interesting—sometimes downright quirky. I think that's pretty universal all over, but the community here is something unique, and the opportunities provided by attending a consortium is beyond any that I would get from any other university."

Q "I have had a great experience being here at Scripps. Getting involved was the key to adapting quickly and taking advantage of the opportunities that abound here. Although I did not originally want to or plan on actually coming to Scripps, I am thankful I did. I know this is where I am supposed to be."

BEST OF SCRIPPS

1. The women
2. Beautiful Campus
3. Intimate and small
4. Tradition-bound
5. Humanities focus
6. Attentive faculty
7. Individual growth based, lack of competitiveness

Happy Students
88% of students return after their first year.

Commitment to Teaching
There are 9 students for every member of faculty on campus.

WORST OF SCRIPPS

1. Its small size
2. Cost
3. Limited course selection
4. Difficult to get an A
5. Lack of nearby off-campus social scenes
6. Lack of space
7. Lack of diversity

Expensive
Tuition is a steep $38,700, one of the most expensive rates in the country.

Expensive Dorms
Living on campus doesn't come cheap, with an average housing price tag of $6,400.

Student Body

African American:	4%	Male Undergrads:	1%
Asian American:	13%	Female Undergrads:	99%
Hispanic:	8%	Living On Campus:	96%
International:	2%	Living Off Campus:	4%
Native American:	1%	Male Athletes:	0%
White:	49%	Female Athletes:	15%
Unknown:	23%	Fraternity Members:	0%
From Out-of-State:	60%	Sorority Members:	0%

Students Speak Out On... EVERYTHING!

ACADEMICS

Q Interdisciplinary Studies

"The academic load at Scripps college is rigorous, but do-able. The great thing about it is that so many of the classes cross-examine other aspects of your studies. Registrations is fair, with time slots being assigned randomly and there are tons of opportunities to take classes at any of the other four Claremont Colleges."

Q

"Teachers do more than encourage discussion, they demand it. Classes are always interesting and educational, both in the material they examine and the way in which we discuss and apply it."

Q

"Individual experiences with instructors vary, but all depend upon one's willingness to participate both during and outside of class time."

ATHLETICS

Q

"Although we may hear the roar of a football game at CMC, most Scripps students don't keep track of sports unless they or their friends are involved. In general, your interest determines your level of involvement."

Q

"Cross-country and track are pretty big. Also, the lacrosse team increases its prestige each season. However, most Scripps students don't focus on athletics. Scripps students are more likely to get involved in IM sports."

Q

"Anyone can possibly join a sport here and have fun, whether with the official school team or just a club."

CAMPUS DINING

Q Food Is Great!!

"The food is really good!! There are a lot of options for vegans and vegetarians. The kitchen staff also take suggestions! I love the food!!"

Q LOVE LOVE LOVE the D-Halls

"There are 7 dining halls, each with their own delicious menus each night, which are posted on the school sites. The dining halls are also beautiful places to catch up with friends, and there is outdoor dining all year long."

CAMPUS HOUSING

Q GJW

"These dorms are amazing. They are spacious and comfortable. Events organized for us in the dorms make the experience more like a community. Everyone is really friendly and make you feel at home."

Q

"The 'old dorms' built in the 1930s are some of the most beautiful places I've ever been to, and even the newer dorms, built around the 1970s, are palatial compared to any other college's dorms."

GUYS & GIRLS

Q Guys When You Want Them.

"I have plenty of guy friends (don't worry if you don't make them first semester) and dating prospects, but the close community of women in my dorm is so vital to my college experience."

Q Every Possibility

"Since Scripps is in a 5-College consortium, you can find every type of guy or girl here, the athletic people, hippies, the cute geeks, average, the partiers, and just relaxed people."

HEALTH & SAFETY

Q Fairly Safe

"The school doesn't do much to actively protect the students, but the location doesn't warrant any further protection."

Q

"Any suspicious activity on the campuses is reported to the student body rapidly, no matter how insignificant. I've never feared for my safety here."

Seattle Pacific University

3307 Third Ave. W; Seattle, WA 98119
(206) 281-2000; www.spu.edu

THE BASICS:

Acceptance Rate: 93%	**Student-Faculty Ratio:** 14:1
Yield: 37%	**Retention Rate:** 87%
Setting: Large city	**Graduation Rate:** 64%
Control: Private Non-Profit	**Tuition:** $27,810
Total Undergrads: 3,015	**Room & Board:** $8,544
SAT Range: 1500–1850*	**Avg. Aid Package:** $25,349
ACT Range: 22–28	**Students With Aid:** 96%

* of 2400

This School Isn't Graded Yet!

College Prowler grades are calculated using tons of criteria, including survey responses that come from students at this school.

Unfortunately, we haven't gathered enough student surveys yet for this school to be able to calculate the grades for each section. Stay tuned to *CollegeProwler.com* for grade updates and more!

CP's Student Author On...
OVERALL EXPERIENCE

Seattle Pacific University is unique. Students do not have to fit a specific prototype to find their experience rewarding and worthwhile. While SPU does not boast a particularly diverse student body, the education and experience offered truly could accommodate one. For those who seek spiritual growth, there are loads of activities and classes to nurture their souls. For those who aren't interested, a few Christian scripture classes with surprisingly open-minded professors will suffice. Unlike many religiously-affiliated universities, SPU does not have mandatory chapel services.

Scholarships are distributed generously, which means it won't take a miracle to finance school if the attendee is comfortable with moderate school loans upon graduation. Plus, students can complete their degree in four years—no sweat. For students who desire a close-knit community, small class sizes and on-campus housing are available and ready to smother them with warm fuzzies. For the more independent, adventurous type, there is a bustling city full of character to be explored—just a walk or bus ride away.... For the rest of this editorial, visit collegeprowler.com.

Students Speak Out On...
OVERALL EXPERIENCE

Q Wonderful!

"SPU is awesome; words can't even describe how great it is; and as cheesy as it sounds, our motto: engage the culture, change the world, is true with the way of life here at SPU."

Q I Love SPU

"SPU is great place to go to school. Even though they are a Christian University, they do not force religion on you but instead give you the choice and opportunity to shape your faith and discover what you believe in. The campus is beautiful, the people are great, and I love the city of Seattle. There's is so much to discover here, and SPU provides the way. I LOVE IT."

Q Love It!!

"SPU is really a great place to be. It's a pretty tight-knit community with lots of activities going on. If you're looking for a party school, you might want to look somewhere else (although honestly, we're in Seattle, so a good party is never far away), but if you're looking for an excellent all around experience and you know how to have fun without the aid of recreational substances, you should definitely check it out."

BEST OF SEATTLE PACIFIC

1. "Orangemen of 6th Ashton"
2. Great classes for those who seek spiritual growth
3. No real crime problem in Queen Anne neighborhood
4. Not as strict as other Christian universities

Happy Students
87% of students return after their first year.

Easy Financial Aid Process
73% of students surveyed told us that the financial aid process went smoothly and they received the financial aid they needed.

WORST OF SEATTLE PACIFIC

1. "Lifestyle Expectations"
2. Commuter parking can be cutthroat.
3. Dating scene
4. Due to lack of crime, security is more apt to hand out parking tickets.

Expensive
Tuition is a steep $27,810, one of the most expensive rates in the country.

Student Body

African American:	2%	Male Undergrads:	32%
Asian American:	6%	Female Undergrads:	68%
Hispanic:	3%	Living On Campus:	54%
International:	1%	Living Off Campus:	46%
Native American:	1%	Male Athletes:	9%
White:	74%	Female Athletes:	9%
Unknown:	13%	Fraternity Members:	0%
From Out-of-State:	43%	Sorority Members:	0%

Frequently Compared Schools:

Seattle University
University of Puget Sound
University of Washington
Whitworth University

Students Speak Out On... EVERYTHING!

ACADEMICS

Professors and Classes Are Great

"There is a wide variety of classes offered at this school. I am planning to be an Interior Designer and I am pleased with the courses offered for this major. The professors here are wonderful. They genuinely care about their students. It's great to have smaller class sizes because we can get more help from professors."

Small Class Size and Availability of Professors

"Professors know individual students and are available to them. Communication was a great degree that prepares you for work in any area. I also minored in Education which was a great program and I student taught in the Seattle area. I was hired before I graduated by the top district in the state."

ATHLETICS

School Spirit

"Varsity Sports are pretty great. We don't have football here, so people really take pride in our soccer and basketball. We also have cross country, volleyball, gymnastics, track and field, and Rowing. Women's soccer took an NCAA title in 2009. We have really strong teams and there is a lot of support from the school at games. We really support our teams."

Avergae

"It is exciting to go and watch the games but there are not many different varieties of teams."

CAMPUS DINING

Variety

"needs more variety!!! and the SUB food locations should be open on weekends!"

CAMPUS HOUSING

Hill Hall

"I live in hill hall as a sophmore and I absolutely love it. I would live in it next year, but most people live off campus their Junior and Senior Year. There is so much community. It is like a brotherhood. Everyone leaves all their stuff in the bathrooms being able to trust others not to use their stuff. Aren't the nicest dorms, but will keep you so busy and entertained with events and a nice Christian Community."

Ashton

"I would have to give the dorms, and mine in particular a B+ because it is very fun to live here however, it is expensive and some renovations could be made like more lofts being made available to the students. It would also be nice to have free laundry as well. But overall, the atmosphere is great to live in, the people are very kind and welcoming and my floor is very tight-knit. The community of the dorms is great!"

GUYS & GIRLS

Slanted Proportions

"Although the ratio of girls to guys is not ideal, the people who are here are great. Not to mention good looking. Something about Seattle makes people dress way better than they did in my hometown. Everyone is really friendly and there is a huge variety of "types.""

The Guys to Girl Ratio at SPU Is 2:1.

"Almost all of your classes will have more girls than guys, but I haven't noticed it too much. When it comes to dress, I've noticed that hardly anyone wears sweats or pajamas to class; people typically dress up more, though there is no formal dress code."

HEALTH & SAFETY

Definitely Safe

"The safety and security on campus is reassuring. The campus is not very big, so it doesn't seem very dangerous. But if someone loses a key or something, it is very easy to contact safety and security."

Campus Seems Safe, but Is Close to Downtown Seattle

"Feels like a safe community, but with Seattle right over the hill, there is always the possibility for crime."

LOOKING FOR MORE?

Check out our full-length guide to this school at collegeprowler.com/seattle-pacific-university/.

Seattle University

901 12th Ave.; Seattle, WA 98122
(206) 296-6000; www.seattleu.edu

THE BASICS:

Acceptance Rate: 66%	Student-Faculty Ratio: 13:1
Yield: 21%	Retention Rate: 90%
Setting: Large city	Graduation Rate: 71%
Control: Private Non-Profit	Tuition: $29,340
Total Undergrads: 4,306	Room & Board: $8,805
SAT Range: 1570–1900*	Avg. Aid Package: $24,468
ACT Range: 23–29	Students With Aid: 96%

* of 2400

Academics	B	Greek Life	N/A
Athletics	C+	Guys	B-
Campus Dining	B	Health & Safety	B
Campus Housing	B	Local Atmosphere	A-
Campus Strictness	C+	Nightlife	B+
Computers	B-	Off-Campus Dining	A
Diversity	B+	Off-Campus Housing	B+
Drug Safety	B	Parking	C+
Facilities	B	Transportation	A
Girls	A-	Weather	C-

CP's Student Author On...
OVERALL EXPERIENCE

It would be difficult to find someone who didn't enjoy his or her time at Seattle University and would not be willing to do it all over again. Of course, there are some gripes, and some genuine difficulties, but none of them have ever really been large enough to make people regret their decisions to come here. The professors who teach here are top-notch, and it is easy for students to form a close relationship with them, and not just because of the small class sizes. Of course, the size of the campus itself, and the kind of community that surrounds it, prevents there from ever being a traditional "college-town" feel like you would get around the UW and the Ave, but with all of the options around First Hill and on Broadway up on Capitol Hill, you won't be lacking for anything to do.

The city itself is a wonderful place to live and play, with a vibrant cultural life in many different areas like music, theater, and cuisine, and despite recent issues, it is a generally safe place to live. It's the kind of dynamic place that is essential to explore if you want to have a fully developed college experience.... For the rest of this editorial, visit collegeprowler.com.

Students Speak Out On...
OVERALL EXPERIENCE

Q Holistic School

"I've gotten more than an academic education at SU; I've really grown as a person. The core Jesuit values help with that, but it's mostly because of the people that go here. They're caring and awesome. You're just as likely to hear an engaging conversation as you are hearing about a raging kegger."

Q I Love It!

"I love Seattle University. The campus is beautiful, it's close to nearly anything you could want to do in Seattle, and the teachers are amazing. The rain gets old after a while, but it's made me appreciate the sun that much more."

Q A Great Catholic School

"My time at Seattle University has been excellent. The teachers are amazing and it really is a great place for academics. I've felt that it has been time and money well spent. I am a Catholic and that was important in choosing a school. Although the student body can be at times a little to liberal and out of step with Catholic teaching, the school does make an effort to maintain its Catholic identity."

BEST OF SEATTLE UNIVERSITY

1. The atmosphere
2. Location, location, location
3. The diversity
4. The sense of community
5. WiFi across campus
6. Hanging out in the Quad

Happy Students
90% of students return after their first year.

Proven Success
71% of students will complete their education and graduate with a degree.

WORST OF SEATTLE UNIVERSITY

1. Awful parking
2. Weird dining hours
3. Limited computer lab use
4. Lack of upperclassman housing
5. Not enough athletic facilities
6. Meal plan requirement

Expensive
Tuition is a steep $29,340, one of the most expensive rates in the country.

Student Body

African American:	5%	Male Undergrads:	39%
Asian American:	19%	Female Undergrads:	61%
Hispanic:	7%	Living On Campus:	39%
International:	9%	Living Off Campus:	61%
Native American:	1%	Male Athletes:	9%
White:	51%	Female Athletes:	8%
Unknown:	7%	Fraternity Members:	0%
From Out-of-State:	51%	Sorority Members:	0%

Frequently Compared Schools:

Gonzaga University
Reed College
University of Puget Sound
University of Washington

Students Speak Out On...
EVERYTHING!

ACADEMICS

Your Not Just a Number

"Seattle University is not only in a great location, but the school is small enough that you are never just a number in class. Class sizes are small and professors always know who you are and are available to help in their office hours or over email. Resources are always available if you are struggling and the classes are always worth your time."

Nursing

"I haven't done much in the way of Nursing classes yet, however I find the advisors and professors at Seattle University to be some of the nicest most helpful people I've met! The classes are challenging and always eye-opening."

ATHLETICS

Athletics Are Dumb

"No one really goes to the super-hyped basketball games. There are lots of fun intramural & club sports to join, though, like soccer. Volleyball games are fun to watch if you're more of a spectator"

Athletics Popularity Growing

"Seattle University recently made the move back to D-1 athletics and this has proved a mixed bag of success. Some of the smaller programs have demonstrated results; however, basketball has mostly floundered during the season. Athletes are given certain special treatment and prestige and sometimes seem resented by some of the students on this more academically progressive school."

CAMPUS DINING

Mmm

"the food at SU is pretty amazing, if you want to be spoiled food wise, come here. they offer lots of choices and vary from week to week. theres one station at the main food court that does custom omelets in the morning and custom pasta at night. the food is good quality so its really easy to maintain a healthy diet. they also do a good job at providing vegetarian selection"

Decent

"The food is, overall, pretty decent and has a good variety, but after a while, it gets pretty old. The food is a little on the pricy side, but it's good food for the money."

CAMPUS HOUSING

Dorm Life

"Living on campus at Seattle University is a great experience for everyone. Every dorm has something to contribute to the campus and it makes it easy to meet new people and create new friendships."

On Campus Housing

"Living on campus is fun for the first two years. They are quiet, clean, and you have the opportunity to make a lot of new friends. Everything is close to classes and food so you cant lose living on campus. It is expensive; however, it is also expensive to live off campus, get a bus pass, and figure out that sort of schedule. I have enjoyed living off campus as an upperclassmen, but strongly suggest to live on campus the first year or two."

GUYS & GIRLS

The Students

"Most students at Seattle University are there to work hard and complete their education. All of the individuals are unique in their own way which attributes the schools upbeat and trending feeling."

HEALTH & SAFETY

Reactionary, Not Proactive

"Public Safety tends to be more reactionary than proactive on the Seattle University campus. Though once a problem arises, the staff seems able to take care of things, they do not seem to plan head to prevent problems from occurring. Having the Night Hawk, a safety shuttle, is a huge bonus."

LOOKING FOR MORE?

Check out our full-length guide to this school at collegeprowler.com/seattle-university/.

Seton Hall University

400 S. Orange Ave.; South Orange, NJ 07079
(973) 761-9000; www.shu.edu

THE BASICS:

Acceptance Rate: 79%
Yield: 13%
Setting: Suburban
Control: Private Non-Profit
Total Undergrads: 5,209
SAT Range: 1420–1730*
ACT Range: 20–25

Student-Faculty Ratio: 14:1
Retention Rate: 82%
Graduation Rate: 61%
Tuition: $30,470
Room & Board: $10,514
Avg. Aid Package: $14,664
Students With Aid: 95%

* of 2400

Academics	B	Greek Life	B
Athletics	B+	Guys	A-
Campus Dining	A-	Health & Safety	C
Campus Housing	B+	Local Atmosphere	C
Campus Strictness	C+	Nightlife	B
Computers	A	Off-Campus Dining	B
Diversity	B+	Off-Campus Housing	B-
Drug Safety	C+	Parking	B
Facilities	A-	Transportation	B+
Girls	A-	Weather	B

CP's Student Author On...
OVERALL EXPERIENCE

Part of your education is being around people from different walks of life, and no place is better for that than Seton Hall, one of the most diverse campuses in the country. The social scene at Seton Hall is very trendy and fast-paced. The school is full of rich kids with all the money in the world to burn, and they normally burn it on clothes and bars. Seton Hall's education is good depending upon your major. Business, nursing, computer science, and diplomacy are what make Seton Hall a Tier II school. The people you meet here, and the friendships that you form, make this school a community. After an academically-tough freshman year, the only thing that kept me from transferring were the friends that I would miss. Another good reason to attend Seton Hall is its proximity to New York City, which is an endless bank of great internships, and possibly jobs. The Career Center on campus works very hard to obtain Seton Hall students positions in places like Wall Street, and as the saying about NYC goes, if you can make it there, you can make it anywhere.... For the rest of this editorial, visit collegeprowler.com.

Students Speak Out On...
OVERALL EXPERIENCE

Q Love It

"The school offers alot. It is what you make of it. The parties are there, the professors are there, and the cafe has always been my home away from the dorms."

Q Amazing

"My experience at Seton Hall has been amazing up-to-date. From the atmosphere to the students and faculty, I have never been so involved in campus life. Every individual has been extremely helpful and influential making my experience one-hundred times better."

Q Why the School Is Unique.

"this school is unique because a lot of people complain about professors, cleanliness, and area. the school is really great. there are lots of professors that care about you doing well, the campus is always clean and the grass is freshly cut always, and the area is great. there is a nice downtown area that is open until reasonable times and cops and security are always around for your need."

BEST OF SETON HALL

1. The parties
2. The guys/girls
3. Student organizations
4. Laptops with wireless Internet
5. Basketball games
6. Boland hall
7. Hanging on the Green

Happy Students
82% of students return after their first year.

Knowledgeable Professors
82% of students surveyed rated the general knowledge of professors as above average.

WORST OF SETON HALL

1. Financial aid office
2. Fire safety regulations
3. High tuition $$$
4. Monotonous campus food
5. Campus is a ghost town on weekends

Expensive
Tuition is a steep $30,470, one of the most expensive rates in the country.

Expensive Dorms
Living on campus doesn't come cheap, with an average housing price tag of $7,548.

Student Body

African American:	12%	Male Undergrads:	43%
Asian American:	6%	Female Undergrads:	57%
Hispanic:	11%	Living On Campus:	45%
International:	3%	Living Off Campus:	55%
Native American:	0%	Male Athletes:	9%
White:	48%	Female Athletes:	7%
Unknown:	20%	Fraternity Members:	5%
From Out-of-State:	30%	Sorority Members:	3%

Frequently Compared Schools:

New York University
Rutgers University
Syracuse University
Villanova University

Students Speak Out On...
EVERYTHING!

ACADEMICS

Seton Hall Cirriculum

"The Seton Hall University cirriculum is extremely rigigorous. The expectations for incoming freshman is high and requires many of them to engage in different facets of university life. I absolutely love the English program at Seton Hall because students are not required to study one aspect of literature, but rather delve into all of the wonderful genres. The professors are brilliant, and they encourage to learn as much as I can and always remain open-minded."

Great Program

"The Occupational therapy program is a unique program at Seton Hall. Unlike many other colleges, Seton Hall students are eligible to enter the program as soon as they graduate high school. If the student meets the requirements they can enter a 3 + 3 program. This means the student will earn a master's degree after completing 3 years of undergraduate schooling and 3 years of graduate schooling."

ATHLETICS

Seton Hall Pirates

"GO PIRATES! Seton Hall University is well known for their fantastic basketball team. The school spirit surrounding our team is not only one of great enthusiam, but also one of great spirit and pride. A very large percentage of students purchase season tickets every year and join in on the pirate fun."

Go Pirates

"The Basketball games are sick at the Prudential Center. Also head to the ironbound section of newark to pregame with some San Garia"

CAMPUS DINING

All You Can Eat

"There is a ton of variety which is usually pretty good and the employees are friendly. I spend more time talking with Eugene and Aunt Gene then my friends. I like the spicy tuna sushi and the flank steak for carvery."

Very Good

"I really enjoy the dining hall. It can be really cramped at times, but the food is really good. I really like the sushi, rotisserie chicken, and Pizza it is always really good. There are a ton of options it took me 3 months just to learn everything there. I thank Essie for showing me how to cook my own omelet. My parents were impressed. Valentines day was really cool I loved the chocolate fountain and hand passed hors devourers. I really like Pirates Cove and mostly all the staff is really nice."

CAMPUS HOUSING

Seton Hall Has Great Kids on Campus

"its great because my friends are here the elevators are broke alot and the food is campus food so what can I say there is great chinese takeout.It is expensive but the kids are worth it."

Dorms

"Dorms are pretty good having your own bathrooms are clutch compared to other schools."

GUYS & GIRLS

Seton Hall Live

"there is a diverse member at seton hall. people from all over attend. we have californians, floridians, people from up north, down south or out west. being from a small town it is new to see so many different races and relgions. its a great place to be with great people. everyone is so friendly and outgoing."

Fun Times

"Girls all have great personalities, most are very attractive. Some of the girls in Greek life are very stuck up, but for the most part everyone gets along well and has a great time being around each other"

HEALTH & SAFETY

Health Services

"I went there once when I was sick. They were very friendly and took great care of me."

LOOKING FOR MORE?

Check out our full-length guide to this school at collegeprowler.com/seton-hall-university/.

Simmons College

300 The Fenway; Boston, MA 02115
(617) 521-2000; www.simmons.edu

THE BASICS:

Acceptance Rate: 57%	**Student-Faculty Ratio:** 13:1
Yield: 18%	**Retention Rate:** 75%
Setting: Large city	**Graduation Rate:** 73%
Control: Private Non-Profit	**Tuition:** $31,450
Total Undergrads: 1,969	**Room & Board:** $12,050
SAT Range: 1500–1800*	**Avg. Aid Package:** $14,473
ACT Range: 21–26	**Students With Aid:** 94%

* of 2400

Academics	B	Greek Life	N/A
Athletics	C-	Guys	N/A
Campus Dining	B-	Health & Safety	A-
Campus Housing	B-	Local Atmosphere	A+
Campus Strictness	B+	Nightlife	B+
Computers	B+	Off-Campus Dining	A
Diversity	C	Off-Campus Housing	B-
Drug Safety	B	Parking	D+
Facilities	B	Transportation	A-
Girls	B+	Weather	C-

CP's Student Author On...
OVERALL EXPERIENCE

It is the mix of extracurriculars, academics, environment, and nurturing that leads Simmons women to enjoy their experience. The surprising amount of transfers into the College supports the claims of students. Students who have survived their first year, with all its ups and downs and acclimations, seem to be happy with their decision. Dix Scholars, the older undergraduates on campus, are welcomed just as much as students coming into school at the traditional age. Community is valued, and the support benefits all undergraduates. Close-knit relationships with faculty and instructors catapult students into their professions and evoke tears when it comes time to graduate and say good-bye.

Being in Boston provides professional opportunities for its students when it comes to picking internships and finding jobs after graduation. The urban environment fills a social gap that the absence of Greek life or men on campus could create. The winters pose a challenge to out-of-state students not used to the area's rough and extremely cold Nor'easters.... For the rest of this editorial, visit collegeprowler.com.

Students Speak Out On...
OVERALL EXPERIENCE

Q Not Great
"I have not had a good experience here. People are not accepting in the right ways and there is not enough freedom to become independent. The majority of teachers are not great. I intend on transferring."

Q "I am really glad I chose Simmons as my college; I can be myself and still explore so many areas of life."

Q "I have loved Simmons since I first got on campus. There are certainly some times where I wish it was coed, because, as we all know, being around all girls all the time can get a little tough. But I have no doubt that I am receiving an excellent education at a great location."

Q "I love Simmons! It took some getting used to, but what doesn't? I think it was the best decision I could have made. I love who I have become at Simmons."

Q "School rocks. If you balance work and play well, you'll have an excellent experience, and remember, the first semester or two is all about learning this balance, so don't be too hard on yourself."

BEST OF SIMMONS

1. Living in Boston
2. Small class sizes
3. Caring and attentive professors
4. All-women environment
5. Constant improvements
6. Networking possibilities
7. Intelligent students

Proven Success
73% of students will complete their education and graduate with a degree.

WORST OF SIMMONS

1. Parking
2. Freezing winters
3. Only one dining hall on campus with limited choices
4. All-women environment
5. Boston drivers
6. Required meal plan

Expensive
Tuition is a steep $31,450, one of the most expensive rates in the country.

Don't Move Off Campus
Average off-campus housing is a steep $12,050.

Student Body

African American:	6%	Male Undergrads:	0%
Asian American:	6%	Female Undergrads:	100%
Hispanic:	4%	Living On Campus:	55%
International:	3%	Living Off Campus:	45%
Native American:	0%	Male Athletes:	0%
White:	68%	Female Athletes:	7%
Unknown:	13%	Fraternity Members:	0%
From Out-of-State:	41%	Sorority Members:	0%

Frequently Compared Schools:

Boston University
Emerson College
Northeastern University
Smith College

Students Speak Out On... EVERYTHING!

ACADEMICS

Academics

"I really like all the professors I have had, which is the only reason I'm giving Simmons a B+. The course options are limited, and I feel like the options are becoming fewer and fewer, and they are letting go of a lot of teachers. This semester it was almost impossible for me to create a good schedule because of all the conflicting times and lack of courses offered in my major."

"The reasons I decided to come to Simmons were based on the art administration program and the classes it offered. The classes at Simmons are like no other."

ATHLETICS

Athletics and Dynamics

"Simmons College Athletics are D3, making school top priority. The athletic staff is very understanding when school related detriments cause one to miss practice; no one will make you repent. The facilities are fairly new, clean, and staffed with coaches, maintenance and trainers that'll help one throughout their athletic career. The Spirit at Simmons is closely knit; the way a "sisterhood" should be."

"What sports? Our sports teams are fun to go watch, but we are definitely a D-III school."

CAMPUS DINING

Average

"Meals can be expensive without meal plans. Good at times and not so good others."

"Bartol is pretty run-of-the-mill college food, I would say. They have a pretty decent selection of food: big salad bar, sandwich bar, cereal, and so on. And they do try to offer healthy low-fat entrees and things along with whatever else they are cooking. But as anything does, the food gets boring after a few months. The Fens (on main campus) has excellent food, but is not covered by your meal plan—you must use extra points or cash there."

CAMPUS HOUSING

Living at Simmons

"I loved living in a dorm at Simmons. Everyone is nice and very helpful. There are plenty of activities to get involved in, and the residence campus is just beautiful. It's like it's own little community right in the heart of Boston. Also, even though the academic campus is a block away, it serves as a little bit of exercise every morning. However, I give it an A- because even though I loved living on campus, it is very costly. Therefore, I was only able to experience dorm life for one year."

Nothing to Write Home About.

"The dorms at Simmons College are far from glamorous, but they serve their purpose and are in a safe, gated and clean environment footsteps away from Fenway Park. The freshman dorms are small, and a little congested but there are much better options for upperclassmen. Unlike most urban schools, each dorm looks out onto a large grassy common where many students study, play frisbee and build snowmen."

GUYS & GIRLS

They're All the Same

"The LGBT community sticks together, as well as the Crew team, the nursing students, student gov, and the black student organization. As a freshman, everyone is welcoming and willing to help you out, for the first semester. After that, to each his own. Most students are either preppy, ugg-wearing girls from Maine, or they are uniquely different or eclectic."

"Unfortunately, there are not any guys, unless they are grad students, students from other schools, security officers, staff, or someone else that is not an undergrad."

HEALTH & SAFETY

Reliable

"I have never felt unsafe. Public safety always notifies when something's going on around campus."

LOOKING FOR MORE?

Check out our full-length guide to this school at collegeprowler.com/simmons-college/.

Skidmore College

815 N. Broadway Ave.; Saratoga Springs, NY 12866
(518) 580-5000; www.skidmore.edu

THE BASICS:

Acceptance Rate: 42%
Yield: 25%
Setting: Suburban
Control: Private Non-Profit
Total Undergrads: 2,666
SAT Range: 1730–2030*
ACT Range: 26–30

Student-Faculty Ratio: 9:1
Retention Rate: 95%
Graduation Rate: 81%
Tuition: $40,420
Room & Board: $10,776
Avg. Aid Package: $32,204
Students With Aid: 47%

* of 2400

Academics	B	Greek Life	N/A
Athletics	B-	Guys	B-
Campus Dining	B	Health & Safety	B+
Campus Housing	A-	Local Atmosphere	C+
Campus Strictness	B-	Nightlife	C+
Computers	B	Off-Campus Dining	B-
Diversity	C	Off-Campus Housing	D+
Drug Safety	C	Parking	B
Facilities	B+	Transportation	B-
Girls	B+	Weather	D

CP's Student Author On...
OVERALL EXPERIENCE

Skidmore has its down points. It is cold for most of the school year, the total student body is small enough to breed gossip, and there isn't always a lot of excitement for students under 21. Campus apathy is not uncommon around sophomore year when "the slump" kicks in for a while. However, most upper-class students can attest to the fact that Skidmore grows on you. You will inevitably find your niche of friends, and your passions and interests will develop as you do as a person. College is a tough time for most people, as you are in a state of figuring out what the heck you want to do with your life. Luckily, Skidmore has a great deal of potential in helping you do this. Its strongest points are the closeness you will find in friends, classmates, and very importantly, professors. These people are rooting for you! They will surprisingly help lead you in the right direction because Skidmore offers a strong sense of family. You are not just a number here. You are Jane/John Doe, for goodness sake! Another strong point is flexibility. If you are unsatisfied with any aspect of the College, there is almost always room for change.... For the rest of this editorial, visit collegeprowler.com.

Students Speak Out On...
OVERALL EXPERIENCE

Q You Get Used to It
"Skidmore sucks at first but once you find a good group of friends, it's a great place. The professors are very helpful, kind, and intelligent. The classes can be easy so it's really up to the students if they want a challenging four years."

Q "I love Skidmore. There might be some policies and priorities I would change, but I do not prefer to be anywhere else, and I value the education I am getting, both inside and outside of the classroom."

Q "I've had a wonderful time at Skidmore. There are definitely some downsides, but nothing that makes me wish I was somewhere else."

Q "I am glad that I went to Skidmore. It is a great place to grow, especially for the independent. Skidmore is the perfect place for someone who does not quite know what one wants to do in life. Skidmore gives its students a chance to try many different fields of study."

BEST OF SKIDMORE

1. Huge dorm rooms
2. Window seats (North Quad)
3. Not sharing a bathroom with a whole floor
4. Both the apathetic and the hardworking can find a niche

Happy Students
95% of students return after their first year.

Commitment to Teaching
There are 9 students for every member of faculty on campus.

WORST OF SKIDMORE

1. Meal plan/dining
2. Snow snow snow
3. Men/women ratio
4. Library hours
5. Getting stuck in the "Skidmore bubble"
6. Townies' stereotypes of Skidmore students

Expensive
Tuition is a steep $40,420, one of the most expensive rates in the country.

Expensive Dorms
Living on campus doesn't come cheap, with an average housing price tag of $6,376.

Student Body

African American:	3%	Male Undergrads:	40%	
Asian American:	8%	Female Undergrads:	60%	
Hispanic:	5%	Living On Campus:	85%	
International:	3%	Living Off Campus:	15%	
Native American:	1%	Male Athletes:	19%	
White:	63%	Female Athletes:	13%	
Unknown:	17%	Fraternity Members:	0%	
From Out-of-State:	71%	Sorority Members:	0%	

Frequently Compared Schools:

Connecticut College
Hamilton College
Vassar College
Wesleyan University

Students Speak Out On... EVERYTHING!

ACADEMICS

Pick the Right Major/Professors.

"Skidmore emphasizes teaching and professor ability so it has some really amazing professors, but you have to pick them carefully as some of them can be really bad despite the schools best efforts. Also, some majors are extremely easy whereas others are very challenging and very stimulating."

Friendly and Helpful Department

"All around the professors in the Psych department have been really helpful, and a lot of fun. It's one of the bigger departments on campus, so you don't get as much of a feel of a tight-knit group as some of the smaller majors, but it works out fine. The classes are fun and the professors are helpful. If you get involved you can do your own experimental work using our labs, and the opportunities for internships are there if you look for them."

ATHLETICS

Athletics

"Students are somewhat involved with athletics. People will show up to games, but that is more dependent on the team. Lots of people go to Men's hockey, but few go to Women's lacrosse. There is not a lot of school spirit. The athletic facilities are excellent and are well kept. Most of the teams have very good records."

Ok

"Some teams are good, some are bad, but no one really cares either way."

CAMPUS DINING

Great Food

"The dining hall is awesome, especially if you are a vegetarian or have special dietary needs."

"Campus food is campus food. It is hard to make food good for over 2,000 kids. If you are creative, you can make some good meals from bits and pieces of what they offer."

CAMPUS HOUSING

Social Atmosphere

"a very diverse community providing random room allocation, which permits cultural understanding. Even though there may be difficult due to the cultural differences, with time the social atmosphere becomes more and more appreciable."

"For the most part, the dorms are really nice, much nicer than some of the other colleges I visited. I think the nicest dorm I have stayed in is Wait, and I think the one to avoid is Penfield."

GUYS & GIRLS

Art Students, Hipsters and... Jocks?

"There's a weird dichotomy at Skidmore between the more liberal artsy students and jocks, who for some reason decide Skidmore would be a good place for them. It's a little bizarre, but you learn to deal with it."

Guys and Girls

"There are a lot of good looking people and with 61% of the students being girls, there are a lot of pretty girls."

HEALTH & SAFETY

Safe and Sound

"Skidmore is not a place where security is an issue, or where students typically find themselves feeling unsafe. It is one of the safest places I know. Even so, the blue light system is everywhere on campus, and the week you arrive on campus as a freshman, Campus Safety requires that everyone puts the campus safety # in their cell phones. If there are ever any safety threats in the area, Campus Safety takes care of them immediately."

LOOKING FOR MORE?

Check out our full-length guide to this school at collegeprowler.com/skidmore-college/.

Slippery Rock University

1 Morrow Way; Slippery Rock, PA 16057
(724) 738-9000; www.sru.edu

THE BASICS:

Acceptance Rate: 59%	**Student-Faculty Ratio:** 20:1
Yield: 45%	**Retention Rate:** 81%
Setting: Town	**Graduation Rate:** 59%
Control: Public	**Tuition:** $10,116
Total Undergrads: 7,825	**Room & Board:** $8,554
SAT Range: 1370–1670*	**Avg. Aid Package:** $7,842
ACT Range: 19–24	**Students With Aid:** 84%

* of 2400

Academics	B-	Greek Life	B+
Athletics	C	Guys	A-
Campus Dining	B-	Health & Safety	B-
Campus Housing	A-	Local Atmosphere	C
Campus Strictness	C	Nightlife	B
Computers	B-	Off-Campus Dining	C-
Diversity	C	Off-Campus Housing	A
Drug Safety	C+	Parking	B
Facilities	A-	Transportation	B+
Girls	B	Weather	C

CP's Student Author On...
OVERALL EXPERIENCE

Picking a college is a tough decision and nobody expects you to have your whole life charted out upon high school graduation. Fortunately, Slippery Rock can help you find yourself by exposing you to a laundry list of opportunities and organizations. Sure, students gripe about Weisenfluh food, the miserable weather, and the Ticket Nazi, but SRU students are in it together. Here, you are not treated as a number, but, in many cases, as a family member. Most students agree that the people are what make this place. You will not only make lifelong friendships and connections with fellow students but with professors and local townspeople, as well. It is highly difficult to find a school where professors sincerely care about you, and not just about their research and side projects.

In recent years, Slippery Rock has been trying to overcome the party school stigma that has overshadowed its sophisticated academic programs. Known for many programs, including education, physical therapy, and parks and recreational management, Slippery Rock offers high quality at a low price.... For the rest of this editorial, visit collegeprowler.com.

Students Speak Out On...
OVERALL EXPERIENCE

Q I LOVE IT!!!

"Slippery Rock is very friendly. Its small and comfortable, exactly what I was looking for in a school. The classes aren't too big, every professor will know your name before the end of the semester. And the dorms are amazing."

Q What Make Your School Unique

"Slippery rocks dorms are new and great. The layout of the dorms creates an atmosphere of independence but also promotes socialization."

Q I Love College

"I love meeting people, and getting to experiencing new things. While it was hard at first, I'm ready to come back after a weekend home."

Q Slippery Rock Is Awesome, but Don't Forget to Study!

"Slippery Rock is a great place, that you can figure out who you want to be. Any student can break away from just being a number, and the professors are very personable. I would definitely choose Slippery Rock all over again, because of the great opportunities it provides."

BEST OF SLIPPERY ROCK

1. The people
2. Off-campus parties
3. The low cost of tuition
4. No TAs
5. The ARC
6. Greek life
7. The outlet mall

Affordable
Tuition is only $10,116, one of the most affordable rates in the country.

Happy Students
81% of students return after their first year.

WORST OF SLIPPERY ROCK

1. Lack of school spirit
2. The miserable weather
3. The local police
4. Lack of a true nightclub nearby
5. Students' laziness
6. The parking ticket Nazi

Lowest Grades
Off-Campus Dining: C-
Diversity: C
Campus Strictness: C

Student Body

African American:	5%	Male Undergrads:	44%
Asian American:	1%	Female Undergrads:	56%
Hispanic:	1%	Living On Campus:	36%
International:	1%	Living Off Campus:	64%
Native American:	0%	Male Athletes:	8%
White:	83%	Female Athletes:	8%
Unknown:	9%	Fraternity Members:	5%
From Out-of-State:	12%	Sorority Members:	5%

Frequently Compared Schools:

Grove City College
Penn State
Siena College
University of Pittsburgh

Students Speak Out On... EVERYTHING!

ACADEMICS

Q Everyone Seems Helpful

"everyone from the advisors, professors, and CA are readily available to help you out. Transition to college was an important factor to the college. Open doors all the way"

Q Lots of Work Will Help in the Long Run...

"I am a dance major at a liberal arts college. I have met and enjoy working with all of my professors in my specific major. The workload can test your nerves but I know that this will all pay off for me because I know going into the performing arts I will be able to handle the workload in the future. I think this will defiantly help with my future."

ATHLETICS

Q Athletics Are Adequate

"Athletics at Slippery Rock are probably what they should be for a school this size. A decent amount of students attend football and basketball games, but the attendance for other sports seems to be lacking."

Q Athletics

"the athletics aren't nationally ranked for the most part, but it is still fun to go out to a football game or some other type of game to hang out with your friends"

CAMPUS DINING

Q Dining

"3 places to eat on campus. If you get sick of one, there are other options, plus plenty of places in town to eat."

Q Food at the Rock

"The dining halls have good quality food with lots of options. The multiple cafes around campus are nice but everything closes early generally and there is no availability on the weekends."

CAMPUS HOUSING

Q Excellent New Suites

"Within the past few years they built all new residence halls.

They are so nice to live in! The dining hall and all the classroom buildings are in walking distance which is nice."

Q Residential Suite Buildings Are Amazing

"The Residential Buildings A-F on campus are amazing. i guess the traditional halls on the other side of the campus are ok, but If you like to have your own space and do everything how and when you want to the new Buildings are for you. They are state of the art"

GUYS & GIRLS

Q WOW

"There is a small diversity of girls but you will definitely find just about any girl from any ethnicity. But, they're predominantly white girls. Lookswise, well I want to say that if you walk around campus, about 6 out of every 10 girls are at least a 7 or up. And yes there are some 10s, quite a few. Overall, the girls here are extremely sexy."

Q Variety

"The university attractets all types of people from international students to locals in the area. It offers all kinds of majors so it isnt hard to find the type of people you fit right in with."

HEALTH & SAFETY

Q Personal Safety on Campus

"As a student at Slippery Rock University, I feel safe when I walk back to my dorm room from my night classes. I have never felt unsafe in my entire time at the University. I see the University Police Officers patroling / driving around campus daily and the crime rate on campus is very low in my opinon."

Q Safe, I'd Say.

"They (campus police, staff, etc.) make sure that incoming freshman know about the safety on campus. There is emergency call posts all over. I've never felt threatened on campus. I still wouldn't leave my books unattended in the middle of the quad, but who would?"

LOOKING FOR MORE?

Check out our full-length guide to this school at collegeprowler.com/slippery-rock-university/.

Smith College

7 Elm St.; Northampton, MA 01063
(413) 584-2700; www.smith.edu

THE BASICS:

Acceptance Rate: 47%	**Student-Faculty Ratio:** 9:1
Yield: 35%	**Retention Rate:** 91%
Setting: Suburban	**Graduation Rate:** 88%
Control: Private Non-Profit	**Tuition:** $37,758
Total Undergrads: 2,614	**Room & Board:** $12,622
SAT Range: 1760–2090*	**Avg. Aid Package:** $34,524
ACT Range: 25–31	**Students With Aid:** 70%

* of 2400

Academics	A	Greek Life	N/A
Athletics	C+	Guys	C
Campus Dining	A-	Health & Safety	B
Campus Housing	A	Local Atmosphere	B+
Campus Strictness	B+	Nightlife	B
Computers	C+	Off-Campus Dining	A+
Diversity	B+	Off-Campus Housing	C-
Drug Safety	C-	Parking	B-
Facilities	A+	Transportation	A-
Girls	A-	Weather	C

CP's Student Author On...
OVERALL EXPERIENCE

One thing is for sure, Smith is not for everyone. One person's favorite part of the school could be another's most-hated aspect. Some cannot handle the single-sex environment, while others find it to be their favorite part of Smith. Some are miserable with the social scene and feel limited in their options, while others are perfectly content. It's a college of extremes, and when talking to Smith students, you'll probably find that most have an ambivalent relationship with the school. However, when it comes down to it, the education received at Smith is top-notch. The small classes and wide range of academic opportunities ensure that students are engaged and challenged. Moreover, Smith is committed to providing opportunities that most students don't get until graduate school, such as independent research with professors in their first year or writing graduate-level theses.

Smith is not a huge party school and it's not a stereotypical college experience, but, for most Smith students, that's exactly the way they like it.... For the rest of this editorial, visit collegeprowler.com.

Students Speak Out On...
OVERALL EXPERIENCE

Q Smithies Are Unique Women

"Smith is amazing, for the right kind of woman. And no, despite what the admissions brochure may tell you, it's not easy to find datable guys around here. You have to be smart, strong, open minded, liberal, and community oriented to thrive here. We have a lot of traditions that only women's colleges can offer. It's like belonging to a secret society. I would choose Smith again in a heartbeat."

Q It Has the Perfect Balance of Everything!

"I love Smith. People here work hard and play hard. Everyone is engaged and excited about whatever they're doing, and it is easy to learn new things, as well as dive deeper into a subject. I wouldn't want to be anywhere else!"

BEST OF SMITH

1. No guys
2. Everyone is open and nice.
3. The academics, including no gen-ed requirements
4. House community and great living accommodations

Happy Students
91% of students return after their first year.

Commitment to Teaching
There are 9 students for every member of faculty on campus.

WORST OF SMITH

1. No guys
2. Long winters
3. Bridge traffic
4. Instead of using salt, they put down this soy-sauce-like substance to melt the ice—it doesn't work well, and it smells.

Expensive
Tuition is a steep $37,758, one of the most expensive rates in the country.

Expensive Dorms
Living on campus doesn't come cheap, with an average housing price tag of $6,320.

Student Body

African American:	7%	Male Undergrads:	0%
Asian American:	13%	Female Undergrads:	100%
Hispanic:	7%	Living On Campus:	94%
International:	7%	Living Off Campus:	6%
Native American:	1%	Male Athletes:	0%
White:	43%	Female Athletes:	9%
Unknown:	23%	Fraternity Members:	0%
From Out-of-State:	83%	Sorority Members:	0%

Frequently Compared Schools:

Bryn Mawr College
Mount Holyoke College
Vassar College
Wellesley College

Students Speak Out On...
EVERYTHING!

ACADEMICS

Great English Program

"The English professors at Smith are such amazing people. They're truly passionate about their subjects, and they care a lot about the students. There are so many wonderful courses to choose from—it's a lot of fun. My only quibble with the program is that there is a huge reliance on British literature and a major shortage of American literature. However, Amherst has some really great American literature classes, so that mostly makes up for it."

Loving Like a Parent

"Smith professors give you a TON of support and guidance, even if you don't ask for it. This can be a wonderful thing if you want to delve into academics, do special studies, etc.—they are all ears. If you want to slack off, forget it. They will know, much like when your overbearing mother caught you sneaking out of the house! DON'T SKIP CLASS!"

ATHLETICS

Super School Spirit

"I've heard there are lots of different sports."

Not a Huge Sports School, but Still Really Fun!

"I'm not really into sports, so I really enjoy the atmosphere we have at Smith. There are a ton of fitness resources, and there are plenty of fun games to watch, but no one is super intense about it. Our rugby team is awesome, and soccer games between houses are great. It's just really laid-back and fun. Plus, the first women's basketball game was played at Smith, so it's cool to feel that historical connection."

CAMPUS DINING

Good Food and Lots of Variety

"Food is good, and the dining staff is willing to accommodate students needs."

Food Is Great but on a Tight Schedule

"Each house offers a different meal each night, so it doesn't get boring and feels like home. Since there's no "meal plan," you can eat as much as you want at as many dining halls as you want for the length of dinner–but dinner is only an hour and a half long. So if you happen to be busy during that time, you tend to be out of luck for finding food on campus the rest of the night."

CAMPUS HOUSING

House System

"All Smithies are required to live on campus in houses. It is expensive to pay for on campus housing all four years, but the community you build within your house is priceless. Each house on campus has an entirely unique personality that changes with the women that live there. It's amazing."

It's Awesome

"Most of the houses are well kept and beautiful with more than decent-sized rooms. I've had a wonderful experience with each room I've had and have had a single since my sophomore year at Smith."

GUYS & GIRLS

It's a Women's College

"There's a whole spectrum of people here, and the students are rad. Both awesome and radical. Intelligent and fun."

Liberal, No Guys

"The girls are varied and interesting. It is an all-girls school."

HEALTH & SAFETY

It Is an Unbelievably Safe Community

"I feel extremely safe on and around campus. I haven't even heard of petty theft on campus, not that I encourage leaving your stuff all over the place. Our Public Safety is incredibly attentive and offers to escort you any time that you may feel uncomfortable walking by yourself. They also are more into making sure we're safe than trying to police us."

LOOKING FOR MORE?

Check out our full-length guide to this school at collegeprowler.com/smith-college/.

Southern Methodist University

6425 Boaz St.; Dallas, TX 75275
(214) 768-2000; www.smu.edu

THE BASICS:

Acceptance Rate: 53%
Yield: 30%
Setting: Suburban
Control: Private Non-Profit
Total Undergrads: 6,228
SAT Range: 1700–2000*
ACT Range: 25–30

Student-Faculty Ratio: 11:1
Retention Rate: 88%
Graduation Rate: 74%
Tuition: $35,160
Room & Board: $12,360
Avg. Aid Package: $28,130
Students With Aid: 77%

* of 2400

Academics	A-	Greek Life	A
Athletics	B-	Guys	B+
Campus Dining	B+	Health & Safety	B+
Campus Housing	A	Local Atmosphere	A+
Campus Strictness	B	Nightlife	A
Computers	C+	Off-Campus Dining	A-
Diversity	C+	Off-Campus Housing	A-
Drug Safety	C	Parking	B-
Facilities	A	Transportation	B+
Girls	A	Weather	B+

CP's Student Author On...
OVERALL EXPERIENCE

While some SMU students will gladly tell you that this school was their first choice, there are plenty of others that will admit that they're not sure how they got here. For several, SMU was a last-minute decision that turned into a remarkable one. SMU offers individual schools and majors that are praised nationwide. Students are able to test several interests before choosing a particular major. While there are many other things to brag about, like the study abroad programs, the social scene is a key aspect of SMU. This school offers introverts an environment where they can become extroverts in a small community that fosters socializing. Among the community, students get the hookups for internships and jobs by networking with friends and alumni.

An exuberant school spirit in terms of athletics might be missing, but SMU pride in the sense of academic excellence and social atmosphere is highly evident. Students get irritated with parking and other little issues, but in the long run, most of them are satisfied with their level of education and their experience.... For the rest of this editorial, visit collegeprowler.com.

Students Speak Out On...
OVERALL EXPERIENCE

Q Life After SMU

"It looks very promising and one of the great things about SMU is the connections and reputation of this place. Dallas is a great place to be and will be a great place to life thanks to all good things that this school represents in the real world."

Q It Is Awesome!

"I have enjoyed my experience at SMU so far. I have been able to get involved in the many activities on campus and enjoy the different things that SMU has to offer. I don't think that I would choose a different school if I were to do it all over again, because I think at such a small school, I would get lost and not be able to find my group of friends easily. One thing is that it is hard to study with so much going on, but you have to find time to do it!"

Q Good Overall Experience

"The campus is beautiful, the faculty are first-rate scholars, and the libraries are up-to-date and expansive."

BEST OF SOUTHERN METHODIST

1. Small classes and teachers that know your name
2. Tailgating
3. Brown Bag in Meadows
4. Study abroad program
5. Tate Lecture Series
6. Local SMU bar specials
7. The attractive campus

Happy Students
88% of students return after their first year.

Proven Success
74% of students will complete their education and graduate with a degree.

WORST OF SOUTHERN METHODIST

1. Parking
2. The Cinco Center
3. Ongoing construction
4. Overwhelmingly conservative
5. Desolate stands during soccer and football games
6. Community bathrooms

Expensive
Tuition is a steep $35,160, one of the most expensive rates in the country.

Expensive to Just Get By
55% of students surveyed felt that the amount it costs to live while at school was worse than average.

Student Body

African American:	5%	Male Undergrads:	47%
Asian American:	6%	Female Undergrads:	53%
Hispanic:	8%	Living On Campus:	31%
International:	6%	Living Off Campus:	69%
Native American:	1%	Male Athletes:	7%
White:	74%	Female Athletes:	7%
Unknown:	1%	Fraternity Members:	23%
From Out-of-State:	54%	Sorority Members:	31%

Frequently Compared Schools:

Baylor University
Texas A&M University
Texas Christian University
University of Texas

Students Speak Out On... EVERYTHING!

ACADEMICS

If you arent doing well, you're pathetic

"smu is really easy academically. study before youre test, attend class and take notes and with minimal effort you should be able to hold a b to b+ average. The business and econ schools require teachers to have atleast a B+ class average, so generally the classes are curved in your favor at the end of the semester. also take advantage of the free tutors. they help"

Sacred Music Degree

"The sacred music program is a perfect curriculum for preparing students for the world of church music. It is a balance of music, theology, and specifically sacred music courses. All the classes have different demands on your mind and schedule, but they hang in a nice balance."

ATHLETICS

Sports

"Now that the football team is kicking butt its really fun to hit up the games. Madd tailgatin' before is great! The rich P's know how to do it! SMU is on the way to greatness again .... get out of the frat house more and watch"

On the rise

"SMU is coming back! More students all the time at the games. Soccer, BBall and football are great to watch. Cannot beat the Boulevard before a FB game. Pony Up!"

CAMPUS DINING

Food!

"yum! there are many dining options at smu. the main cafeteria has so many sections including, organic bar, spa cuisine, pizza and pasta bar, huge salad bar, home cooking section, omlette bar and bakery! they give you fresh baked warm cookies from the oven!"

Eats

"Pretty good.......the school is close to great places to eat so its never a prob. to find something"

CAMPUS HOUSING

There Are Great Differences in Dorms

"There are a great amount of differences from dorm to dorm, which is good because there is something for everybody. However, some of the dorms don't have regular housekeeping. There are.some that are also really far from the rest of campus, but it is all based on the preference that you want."

Dorms Are Dorms.

"Although Dorms are still dorms, SMU's housing is not too bad. It is clean and most building get taken care of really well, if not there is consequences for the residents such as fines. There are suite bathrooms as well as community. I know currently they are thinking about even building more new dorm halls."

GUYS & GIRLS

Preppy

"Many of the students on this campus are from wealthy families and dress in very preppy clothing."

Girls/Guys

"The girls are rich and pretty. The guys are rich and ugly."

HEALTH & SAFETY

SMU is completely safe (even for girls)

"I've been at SMU for three years. As a girl I regularly walk home from the library, home with from the frat houses and have never felt unsafe at night. While I wouldn't suggest leaving your wallet and purse out in public places, if you practice reasonable street smarts, you'll be fine. You're in the nicest area of Dallas- where Dallas' wealthiest families choose to live, so honestly its really not that unsafe."

Campus Crime

"The police dept. at North Lake College is fantastic. I recently had my backpack stolen, and the police found the guy within 2 weeks. I received everything back including my expensive books."

LOOKING FOR MORE?

Check out our full-length guide to this school at collegeprowler.com/southern-methodist-university/.

Southwestern University

1001 University Ave.; Georgetown, TX 78626
(512) 863-6511; www.southwestern.edu

THE BASICS:

Acceptance Rate: 63%
Yield: 24%
Setting: Town
Control: Private Non-Profit
Total Undergrads: 1,301
SAT Range: 1140–1350*
ACT Range: 25–30

Student-Faculty Ratio: 10:1
Retention Rate: 84%
Graduation Rate: 75%
Tuition: $30,220
Room & Board: $8,800
Avg. Aid Package: $16,577
Students With Aid: 93%

of 1600

Academics	B	Greek Life	A
Athletics	C	Guys	B-
Campus Dining	B-	Health & Safety	A
Campus Housing	B+	Local Atmosphere	B
Campus Strictness	C+	Nightlife	B+
Computers	B	Off-Campus Dining	B
Diversity	C-	Off-Campus Housing	C-
Drug Safety	B+	Parking	B+
Facilities	B	Transportation	C-
Girls	B+	Weather	A-

CP's Student Author On...
OVERALL EXPERIENCE

How much a student likes Southwestern depends entirely on the personality and upbringing of the individual student. For many, Southwestern is a collegiate paradise. The school feels safe, close-knit, and supportive. This is particularly true for those students that come from other small Texan towns similar to Georgetown. To others, the school feels constricting, bland, and homogenous. If you would rather live in a relaxed, affluent, (though academically rigorous) environment instead of one that regularly pushes your comfort-zone boundaries, you may very well be the ideal Southwestern student. There are very few students who are in the middle about their feelings towards Southwestern; they either love it or hate it. Many of those that dislike Southwestern came in with poor attitudes, often because Southwestern was not their first choice. However, as the popularity and prestige of Southwestern grows, so does the number of students coming here because it's where they want to be.

Essentially, Southwestern provides top-notch and unique educational opportunities for its students.... For the rest of this editorial, visit collegeprowler.com.

Students Speak Out On...
OVERALL EXPERIENCE

Q **EPIC**
"Though Southwestern is small, there is always something to do for everyone. Georgetown may be small, but let me tell you, the night life here is unbelievable. Georgetown, Texas is where the party is at, especially over in Sun City."

Q **I Love Jesus**
"God has exploded in my life since coming to Southwestern, not because Southwestern encourages my faith (on the contrary, the liberal faculty teach you to hate God) but because of the amazing friends and fellowship with the small Christian community on campus. Academics are ridiculously hard and there is a large workload, but I learn a lot. The atmosphere is hostile to Christianity and Republicans, but overall a nice, small community :)"

Q "I like it here. I wish some other kids were somewhere else."

Q "Southwestern is the kind of place that you wish you never came to, but now that you are here, you don't want to go through the hassle of leaving."

BEST OF SOUTHWESTERN

1. Dedicated professors
2. Wednesday night study breaks on Frat Row
3. Strong Fine Arts department
4. Impeccably green and beautiful surrounding that is the SU campus
5. Close proximity to Austin

Happy Students
84% of students return after their first year.

Commitment to Teaching
There are 10 students for every member of faculty on campus.

WORST OF SOUTHWESTERN

1. Mouthwestern
2. Georgetown being a non- and almost anit-college town
3. Lack of diversity
4. Boy/girl ratio
5. High workload
6. Lack of name recognition

Expensive
Tuition is a steep $30,220, one of the most expensive rates in the country.

Student Body

African American:	3%	Male Undergrads:	40%
Asian American:	4%	Female Undergrads:	60%
Hispanic:	15%	Living On Campus:	81%
International:	0%	Living Off Campus:	19%
Native American:	1%	Male Athletes:	29%
White:	75%	Female Athletes:	17%
Unknown:	2%	Fraternity Members:	29%
From Out-of-State:	10%	Sorority Members:	30%

Frequently Compared Schools:

Texas A&M University
Texas Christian University
Trinity University
University of Texas

Students Speak Out On...
EVERYTHING!

ACADEMICS

Q Tough Profs That Stick With You Till You Get It

"Professors here are tough. They make you learn more and deeper than you would at other schools. That being said, they'll also help you out until they're sure you understand it. And they're nice about it too!"

Q "My teachers seem like interesting people, but aside from FYS (first-year seminar), I feel that my presence in class is not valued very much. In other words, most classes are a 'sit down and listen' type format with little room for students' views."

ATHLETICS

Q There but Kind of Dead

"We have lots of very talented students on our sports team, but it often seems that many SU students don't recognize this or even care. SU is already pretty unified thanks to the size of our school, but even though I am not an athlete, I feel like our school athletes deserve way more credit and praise, especially given their success athletically along with their success academically."

Q Basketball Games Are Fun

"My roommate is on the basketball team so I go to every game, which are pretty fun, I would say that those games get higher attendance than any other sporting team. Although people come to SU for academics and the atmosphere, not to have an Awesome football team."

CAMPUS DINING

Q Commons Could Improve Greatly

"I love the cafeteria workers; they put a smile on my face each time I go, but the food really could improve. At special dinners like Thanksgiving and other holidays the food is excellent, but the food on a daily basis is mediocre to poor."

Q Eek

"Don't touch the entrees here. The Commons will inspire you to eat vegetarian. There's a nice salad bar and vegan bar, which I go to whenever I have to eat there. However, since the second semester I've been preparing my own food mostly.

You're also forced to buy the meal plan (minimum 12/week), so that wasted a lot of my money."

CAMPUS HOUSING

Q No Bad Dorms

"All of the dorm are nice including apartments for upperclassmen, but they're expensive."

Q Nice

"rooms are small and structures very old but the maids clean very well"

GUYS & GIRLS

Q Intellectual Frats & Sororities?

"Fraternities and sororities are an extremely central part of Southwestern U. I hate it and think its rather counterproductive to the pursuit of a college degree, but it exists nonetheless. Most guys are respectful and nice, except for the Sigs who are notoriously rude and sloppy. There is a small community of Christian guys who are awesome. There are a good deal of sorority girls, most of which are nice for the most part. There is a small community of Christian girls who are awesome."

Q Under-Par Appearance

"The girls at Southwestern are below average and generally prude. Their looks are disturbing and whoever views their application photos needs to take off their beer goggles and be a little bit more shallow."

HEALTH & SAFETY

Q Great Health and Safety

"SU has a great health services program and has organizations like Student Health Advisory Council that promote student health on campus. Speaking to safety, SU is extremely safe, some times it almost appears that the SUPD are overly protective."

LOOKING FOR MORE?

Check out our full-length guide to this school at collegeprowler.com/southwestern-university/.

Spelman College

350 Spelman Lane SW; Atlanta, GA 30314
(404) 681-3643; www.spelman.edu

THE BASICS:

Acceptance Rate: 35%	Student-Faculty Ratio: 11:1
Yield: 26%	Retention Rate: 84%
Setting: Large city	Graduation Rate: 80%
Control: Private Non-Profit	Tuition: $20,926
Total Undergrads: 2,220	Room & Board: $10,062
SAT Range: 960–1120*	Avg. Aid Package: $7,000
ACT Range: 20–24	Students With Aid: 93%

* of 1600

Academics	B	Greek Life	B
Athletics	D-	Guys	N/A
Campus Dining	C+	Health & Safety	B+
Campus Housing	B	Local Atmosphere	A
Campus Strictness	D	Nightlife	A-
Computers	B	Off-Campus Dining	A
Diversity	D+	Off-Campus Housing	B-
Drug Safety	A	Parking	C-
Facilities	B-	Transportation	B+
Girls	B+	Weather	B+

CP's Student Author On...
OVERALL EXPERIENCE

Spelman students generally embrace both the good and the bad elements of their college experience and emerge with a positive overall view. The sisterhood, challenges, and nurturing environment are aspects of their time at Spelman that they cherish the most. Many express a love for Spelman that one could conclude transcends the educational experience and speaks more to a bond formed with the institution, the faculty, and their peers. Spelman is definitely a small school, so there are a few students who may feel like they missed out on the advantages of a big, coed, institution. For others, they like the fact that they had the access to the other campuses of the Atlanta University Center but were always able to return to the gates of Spelman. Spelman is seen as a journey into womanhood for many young ladies. It is also an opportunity for many students to meet other women of color like themselves, for the first time in their lives. As was mentioned in the Diversity section, Spelman brings together a plethora of women who might not otherwise have met or ever discovered the common bonds they share despite their different upbringings and backgrounds.... For the rest of this editorial, visit collegeprowler.com.

Students Speak Out On...
OVERALL EXPERIENCE

Q **The Spelman Woman Is an Anamoly- Above the Rest.**
"If you are looking for legitimate sisterhood, a sincere community of supporters, dynamic social scene, and an education that will certainly improve the way to see the world, this may be the place for you."

Q **I Wouldn't Change**
"I absolutely love my overall experience at Spelman College. Because it is located in the Atlanta University Center, I am able to make friends with people from many different schools. I love being able to take classes at Morehouse College and Clark Atlanta University."

Q **Good Experience**
"my college journey so far as been great i have made new friends and i am doing well academically. I love the spelman college for all that it stands for and their devotion to molding strong african american females."

Q "I'm happy that I chose Spelman. From my experience there and around the AUC, I'm a better person. I met a lot of lifelong friends, and hopefully my daughter will be able to attend!"

BEST OF SPELMAN

1. Homecoming
2. In the heart of the Atlanta University Center
3. Unique traditions that are a part of the rich history of the school
4. Market Friday
5. The Grill

Happy Students
84% of students return after their first year.

Proven Success
80% of students will complete their education and graduate with a degree.

WORST OF SPELMAN

1. Your car getting towed off campus
2. Parking sucks!
3. Dorms with no air conditioning
4. Controlled male visitation
5. Convocation-mandatory for freshmen

Not Much Diversity
One of the least racially diverse campuses—only 9% of students are minorities.

Student Body

African American:	91%	Male Undergrads:	0%
Asian American:	0%	Female Undergrads:	100%
Hispanic:	0%	Living On Campus:	62%
International:	4%	Living Off Campus:	38%
Native American:	0%	Male Athletes:	0%
White:	0%	Female Athletes:	3%
Unknown:	2%	Fraternity Members:	0%
From Out-of-State:	79%	Sorority Members:	5%

Students Speak Out On... EVERYTHING!

ACADEMICS

THE BEST THAT YOU COULD ASK

"EVERYTHING IS ONLINE AND YOU HAVE PROFESSORS WHO ARE INTERESTED IN YOU AS A PERSON. THEY TREAT YOU AS IF YOU BELONG TO THEIR FAMILY. ALSO YOU HAVE THE OPTION OF ATTENDING OTHER CAMPUS'S IF YOU NEED CLASSES WHEN NOT OFFERED ON MY CAMPUS"

Rigorous Academics

"Spelman College has done it's best to guarantee students a great education. Every major has an advisor of whom students can refer to for their individual academic planning. There are also opportunities for students to meet with various representatives in order to better prepare for graduate school applications."

ATHLETICS

Rising Basketball Player

"The varsity sports at spelman college are very interesting. the coaches are on point and motivates their players for the win."

Spelman Athletics Are Average

"Although Spelman is an all girl school, many young women do participate in athletics. However, the support that they receive and the school spirit regarding athletic events could be better. Spelman does have nice athletic facilities, though they could be better and definitely bigger. Spelman school spirit in general is huge because of the pride and sisterhood."

CAMPUS DINING

ITS OK!

"The places around campus are good. I guess you get kind of tired of eating at dining halls, but when you need something to eat between classes, you can't complain. Spelman College dining hall food is not all that bad, it just gets old sometimes. So I retreat to the Grill for a little variety. I suggest not buying a huge meal plan after freshman year."

Frequently Compared Schools:

Clark Atlanta University
Emory University
Hampton University
Howard University

Ugh.

"Food is food. I've never been on to complain, but oh my, some of the food that Spelman puts together is just weird. One night last semester, the main line served nachos, collard greens, and honey glazed tofu. Go ahead and eat from the main line of you want, and end up sick...The pasta line is the best though. Mr. Stanley (Hey!) makes the best pasta for us, and the sandwich line is pretty good too."

CAMPUS HOUSING

Options Options

"The most popular freshmen dorm is Howard Herald (HH). All of the older dorms are absolutely beautiful. The Suites are by far the best place to stay on campus but they are reserved for juniors and seniors who opt to stay on campus. LLC 1 is the only freshmen dorm with air conditioning. It is the best for group studying and has a few independent study halls."

GUYS & GIRLS

Diversity Lies on the Inside

"Though Spelman College is comprised of predominantly African American women, our diversity lies in our hometowns, our families and our heritage, and how we interact with others. Throughout the three years I have been at Spelman, I have met women from all across the country and the largest thing they brought with them was the music. My music library is probably the craziest it has been."

HEALTH & SAFETY

Incredibly Safe

"I live on a small gated campus where our security guards take their jobs very seriously and come equipped with, not only weapons, but care for the students whom they are securing. It is practically impossible for trespassers to sneak on and we even see our police down the street, so we can feel safe even walking to the fast food restaurants up the street."

LOOKING FOR MORE?

Check out our full-length guide to this school at collegeprowler.com/spelman-college/.

St. Edward's University

3001 S. Congress Ave.; Austin, TX 78704
(512) 448-8400; www.stedwards.edu

THE BASICS:

Acceptance Rate: 66%
Yield: 38%
Setting: Large city
Control: Private Non-Profit
Total Undergrads: 4,368
SAT Range: 1530–1840*
ACT Range: 22–27

Student-Faculty Ratio: 15:1
Retention Rate: 82%
Graduation Rate: 62%
Tuition: $24,440
Room & Board: $8,196
Avg. Aid Package: $20,039
Students With Aid: 90%

* of 2400

Academics	B	Greek Life	N/A
Athletics	C	Guys	A
Campus Dining	B-	Health & Safety	B-
Campus Housing	A	Local Atmosphere	A+
Campus Strictness	C	Nightlife	B+
Computers	B	Off-Campus Dining	A
Diversity	A-	Off-Campus Housing	B
Drug Safety	B	Parking	B
Facilities	B	Transportation	B+
Girls	A	Weather	A-

CP's Student Author On...
OVERALL EXPERIENCE

St. Edward's is truly a unique place. The location of the campus itself—perched on the top of a picturesque hill overlooking one of the most vibrant cities in the country—is reason enough for many students to say they would come back time and time again. But, the personalization of the education students receive here is what makes the University so unique in comparison to its peers.

St. Ed's students are taught to view the world with a balanced perspective and to analyze things thoroughly. The University puts a heavy emphasis on global education and provides students the opportunity to study abroad, especially through its new sister campuses in France and Scotland. Studying abroad fosters a global sense of understanding for many students on campus. The University's motto is "Learn to Think," and by striving to provide students with an education that fosters an aware and ethical understanding of the world, the school helps many achieve just that.

Students Speak Out On...
OVERALL EXPERIENCE

Q Small Community

"What you want from a small college St. Edward's has to offer. The teachers are really helpful and encourage you to go to them for help. It's a good school for those seeking a small college."

Q I Love St. Edward's

"I would recommend St. Edward's to anyone looking at going to a private Texas liberal arts school. The atmosphere, location, community, and faculty are amazing. They really have your best interest in mind. They offer a little of everything for everyone. I am person who likes a smaller environment when it comes to classes but loves the big active city, so St. Edward's really offers me the best of both worlds."

BEST OF ST. EDWARD'S

1. Small classes
2. Degrees offered
3. Close-knit interaction between faculty and students
4. Size of campus (It only takes 15 minutes to walk from one side to the other.)

Happy Students
82% of students return after their first year.

Easy Financial Aid Process
56% of students surveyed told us that the financial aid process went smoothly and they received the financial aid they needed.

WORST OF ST. EDWARD'S

1. Food is generally overpriced.
2. Limited food service hours—the only option after 8 p.m. is the nauseatingly greasy tacos at The Huddle.
3. Parking!

Life is NOT a Party
57% of students surveyed said it's almost impossible to find a good party.

Student Body

African American:	5%	Male Undergrads:	40%
Asian American:	3%	Female Undergrads:	60%
Hispanic:	31%	Living On Campus:	38%
International:	3%	Living Off Campus:	62%
Native American:	1%	Male Athletes:	8%
White:	53%	Female Athletes:	5%
Unknown:	5%	Fraternity Members:	0%
From Out-of-State:	10%	Sorority Members:	0%

Frequently Compared Schools:

Texas A&M University
Texas Christian University
Texas State University - San Marcos
University of Texas

Students Speak Out On... EVERYTHING!

ACADEMICS

Psychology Student

"St. Edward's has a challenging curriculum, and all students must satisfy it in order to continue. The school does offer various services in order to guarantee the students' success."

English

"I'm very appreciative of the internship opportunities."

ATHLETICS

Hill Raisers

"Our teams on campus are a family. All the athletes consider themselves a family. The games are always fun to go to. A school spirit association called Hill Raisers are at every event, cheering on the team. The facilities themselves are in great shape. However, the school workout gym is small and crowded and not very clean."

Supporting Our Athletes

"There is no St. Edward's football team, so school spirit is sometimes lacking. However, there is huge support for basketball, soccer, and the many other sports. Although the budget was cut and our cross country team was eliminated, our school does support athletics in every way it can by holding many intramural activities throughout the year and remodeling the workout facilities. The coaches and athletic department faculty and staff are a great aid to the St. Edward's school spirit."

CAMPUS DINING

St .Edward's Food

"It's great. I'm so happy they have vegetarian choices!"

Dining

"The food at St. Edwards is really delicious. Not only is it organic, it is also from local farms."

CAMPUS HOUSING

Dorms

"dorms are fancy unless you get stuck with a small room. i love the new residents hall."

I Love Where I Live but Not All Dorms Are Great

"I personally really enjoy living on campus. I'm a freshman and happen to love my dorm, my room, my suitemates, and my roommate. I really have nothing to complain about. I have, however, been to Teresa Hall, and thought it was pretty bad. It's so old and tiny; I would hate to live there. Although this school is pricey, I think it's worth it, and I'm really happy with where I am."

GUYS & GIRLS

A Golden Ratio

"As a guy, I absolutely love the ratio of guys to girls; it's 3:1 at least. And the women are the most diversely beautiful in Austin. There are hippies, scene girls, rockers, athletes, bombshells, hipsters, ravers, go-go girls, southern belles—the list goes on and on. If you want a bunch of dumb blond sorority bimbos, go to UT. If you like beauty and brains, SEU all the way. They're not prudes, but you'll have to work for it, and it makes the sugar all the sweeter."

Typical Student's Style

"People who attend St. Edward's University are typical Austin folks. You never know what type of clothing they will throw at you next. However, it is usually super cute and extremely unique."

HEALTH & SAFETY

Reality on Campus

"After living in a small town, Austin was a scary place at first, until I started living on campus and noticed all the patrolling security. Knowing I have someone to call to walk me back to my dorm at night if I feel unsafe makes me feel at home."

St. John's University

8000 Utopia Parkway; Queens, NY 11439
(718) 990-6161; www.stjohns.edu

THE BASICS:

Acceptance Rate: 46%
Yield: 18%
Setting: Large city
Control: Private Non-Profit
Total Undergrads: 14,806
SAT Range: 970–1190*
ACT Range: —

Student-Faculty Ratio: 18:1
Retention Rate: 78%
Graduation Rate: 60%
Tuition: $30,040
Room & Board: $13,140
Avg. Aid Package: $17,371
Students With Aid: 96%

* of 1600

Academics	B-	Greek Life	B-
Athletics	B	Guys	A
Campus Dining	B	Health & Safety	B+
Campus Housing	B+	Local Atmosphere	A-
Campus Strictness	C+	Nightlife	B+
Computers	B+	Off-Campus Dining	B+
Diversity	A-	Off-Campus Housing	B+
Drug Safety	C	Parking	B+
Facilities	B+	Transportation	A-
Girls	B	Weather	B-

CP's Student Author On...
OVERALL EXPERIENCE

St. John's has its ups and downs, but most students agree, sometimes reluctantly, that the bad outweigh the good. Some argue that with the high tuition cost, students should receive better student services and facilities. The school's motto is, "We are St. John's," but does the administration listen when students speak? They need more dorm rooms, better computers, better safety and security, and more people ready to help them instead of giving them the run around or transferring their calls to someone else. These things are not luxuries, but rather necessities to keep the students and the institution running smoothly.

Going to St. John's is a good experience, and the name only seems to impress many people, which is a good trademark to use in the workforce. (What's in a name? Apparently a lot if that name is St. John's.) The overwhelming majority of teachers care about their students and know what they were teaching. Check out St. John's extensively before attending to see if it can meet your needs, especially monetary wise. In 1870, when St.... For the rest of this editorial, visit collegeprowler.com.

Students Speak Out On...
OVERALL EXPERIENCE

Q I Like Them Boys They Be Hottttt
"hotties errrywhere. they can be a lil stuck up but in the end know how to treat a woman right"

Q Happy at St John's University
"St John's University, Excellent Study Abroad Program, I had the pleasure of being accepted to the Discover The World which involved Spain, Rome Italy (St. John's Have a Campus on Site) and Paris, France. I love all countries but Paris, France was my favorite. The academic is wounderful, I love SJU."

Q St. John's University (Queens)
"I love the majority of my classes at St. John's. I have been lucky enough to have good professors, however if you don't do your work, any professor can be a bad one. As long as you are focused, and get your work done, the school is good and I love the school of education."

BEST OF ST. JOHN'S

1. Different backgrounds are incredibly valuable.
2. Manhattan is just a short trip away.
3. The school supports a large number of student organizations.
4. New York has a great system of transportation.

Big Dorms
64% of students surveyed felt that dorms were more spacious than average.

WORST OF ST. JOHN'S

1. Tuition is high and it keeps going up.
2. The cost of room and board is high, and it keeps going up.
3. Sometimes financial aid just isn't there for those who need it.

Expensive
Tuition is a steep $30,040, one of the most expensive rates in the country.

Expensive Dorms
Living on campus doesn't come cheap, with an average housing price tag of $8,250.

Student Body

African American:	14%	Male Undergrads:	45%
Asian American:	15%	Female Undergrads:	55%
Hispanic:	14%	Living On Campus:	23%
International:	4%	Living Off Campus:	77%
Native American:	0%	Male Athletes:	3%
White:	41%	Female Athletes:	3%
Unknown:	10%	Fraternity Members:	6%
From Out-of-State:	35%	Sorority Members:	7%

Students Speak Out On... EVERYTHING!

ACADEMICS

Q RED STORM ALL DAY BABY

"WE BACK wit steve lavin headin our bball team we goin to the tourny this year fo sho. errybody gonna be chantin LETS GO JOHNNIES"

Q School Psychology

"I chose the School Psychology program at St. John's because of the faculty. They are doing cutting edge research and are always available to students. Other schools are using the textbooks that my professors have written. The faculty in my program remain humble, and it is clear that their main goal is to help their students and encourage us to succeed."

ATHLETICS

Q Good

"St. John's is known for our Athletics. We have a renowned Men's basketball team. All the other sports are good too or decent."

Q Too Much Pride!

"I must say, the students have A LOT of pride in this school. Everywhere you go, people have St. John's sweatpants, sweatshirts, t-shirts, and even sandals. You can tell people have a lot of school spirit. As for the teams, I believe all the sports are NCAA Division I, especially basketball, which is the most notable sport in thte school."

CAMPUS DINING

Q Decent and Lots of Variety

"Dining here is alright. There is a lot of variety and good places to eat such as Burger King and Taco Bell. The actual dining hall can get boring and only has food at certain times, but usually its not bad."

Q Decent Dining

"The food selection is pretty good except you'll need to carry a good amount of money all the time. After that, just burn it all off at the gym. That way you won't maintain the freshman 15."

Frequently Compared Schools:

Fordham University
Hofstra University
New York University
Stony Brook University

CAMPUS HOUSING

Q Fun

"You get to meet everyone because when the commuters go home it's quite small of a community. The downside it's pretty expensive and you have to buy a meal plan and are forced to eat at Montgoris which is ok with food but not grand. Make sure you have a big bank account and are good at saving money because it all goes quickly"

Q Dorms

"The dorms are very nice to live in and and very convenient. The suite style dorms allow for a combination of both a social and studious environment depending on your needs."

GUYS & GIRLS

Q Guys Be Poppin Girls Be Trippin.

"them boys are hott. Them girls are not, but think they are. when them boys be staring its cause they like u ugly not u hott"

Q Diversity

"I never imagined a college could be so diverse. I cannot even say it's predominantly white, black, asian, spanish, etc."

HEALTH & SAFETY

Q St Johns Security

"I feel that st johns is very sevure in the fact that take pride in allowing students to have a safe secure environment with many oppurtunities"

Q Safe If You Are Smart.

"The city can be a dangerous and daunting place for those that have never experienced anything like it, but if you travel in numbers and don't look for any trouble then you will be completely fine. Campus security is also on hand every second and has trained members that know how to handle every situation."

LOOKING FOR MORE?

Check out our full-length guide to this school at collegeprowler.com/st.-john's-university/.

St. Lawrence University

23 Romoda Drive; Canton, NY 13617
(315) 229-5011; www.stlawu.edu

THE BASICS:

Acceptance Rate: 39%
Yield: 31%
Setting: Town
Control: Private Non-Profit
Total Undergrads: 2,295
SAT Range: 1050–1250*
ACT Range: —

Student-Faculty Ratio: 12:1
Retention Rate: 92%
Graduation Rate: 76%
Tuition: $39,765
Room & Board: $10,160
Avg. Aid Package: $37,509
Students With Aid: 85%

* of 1600

Academics	B+	Greek Life	C
Athletics	B-	Guys	A-
Campus Dining	A-	Health & Safety	A-
Campus Housing	B	Local Atmosphere	C-
Campus Strictness	A-	Nightlife	B
Computers	A-	Off-Campus Dining	C
Diversity	C+	Off-Campus Housing	C-
Drug Safety	C-	Parking	B+
Facilities	A+	Transportation	C+
Girls	A-	Weather	C+

CP's Student Author On...
OVERALL EXPERIENCE

One of the University's biggest detractors is its location; Canton is in the middle of farmland, and the nearest city is Montreal, at about two hours away. However, the location contributes to the community feel on campus, since students are there all of the time, and opens up opportunities for trips to Canada or the Adirondacks over breaks. Even so, many mourn the lack of off-campus entertainment and the difficulty of getting anywhere. Because of St. Lawrence's location and strong campus community, there is a tendency for students to get caught in the "SLU bubble." To resolve that problem, students should make a point to volunteer or take advantage of other opportunities in the surrounding area. Some classes have a community-based learning component, which gets students volunteering in the community in a way that contributes to their class experience. SLU expects students to not only be able to memorize facts, but to also be able to apply them to real world experiences. Volunteerism, study abroad, research opportunities, and internships are all part of SLU's hands-on approach to learning and a major focus of academics at the University.... For the rest of this editorial, visit collegeprowler.com.

Students Speak Out On...
OVERALL EXPERIENCE

Q Uniqueness
"I love St. Lawrence and wouldn't choose any other school."

Q Having Too Much Fun
"Great friends, great people, perfect balance of learning and fun"

Q Everything I Want
"I love SLU: parties, good students and high academic standards, good food, great location near the Adirondacks, plenty of things to do outdoors, students who love the outdoors."

Q Great Choice
"I have greatly enjoyed my time here at SLU. Period."

Q Fantastic School!
"I love it here at SLU. I found that it was incredibly easy to get involved. I wish I had been more prepared for the weather, though. It rains a lot more than I thought it was and gets pretty cold!"

BEST OF ST. LAWRENCE

1. Tightly-knit community
2. Broad range of academic options
3. The professors
4. Small campus and class sizes
5. Johnson Hall of Science

Happy Students
92% of students return after their first year.

Proven Success
76% of students will complete their education and graduate with a degree.

WORST OF ST. LAWRENCE

1. Negative temperatures start in November; winters are COLD.
2. Isolated campus
3. Lack of student diversity
4. No convenient transportation to and from campus

Expensive
Tuition is a steep $39,765, one of the most expensive rates in the country.

Student Body

African American:	3%	Male Undergrads:	45%
Asian American:	2%	Female Undergrads:	55%
Hispanic:	3%	Living On Campus:	97%
International:	6%	Living Off Campus:	3%
Native American:	1%	Male Athletes:	50%
White:	66%	Female Athletes:	28%
Unknown:	20%	Fraternity Members:	5%
From Out-of-State:	59%	Sorority Members:	17%

Students Speak Out On... EVERYTHING!

ACADEMICS

Q Underrated English Dept.

"The English department here is fantastic--many opportunities for summer fellowships, attentive faculty, strong mentorship relationship with professors. If you invest yourself into this department, you will absolutely get even more out than you put in."

Q Caring Profesors

"In every class, your teacher makes sure you feel comfortable and does everything possible to help you succeed."

Q Close Personal Bonds

"I came to St. Lawrence because it is a small, liberal arts school where I would have the ability to study many different subjects, have small classes, and have professors that know my name. Also, classes are more discussion based rather than lecture based which is excellent for learning."

ATHLETICS

Q Amazing

"It is amazing how many people, like faculty, students, parents come together at sporting events and support the athletes."

Q Awesome Facilities

"new renovations just completed. new tennis courts, new field house, new track, new turf, what more could you want? oh yeah, we have an 18 hole golf course, too, with greens fee discounts for students."

Q School Spirit

"Great attendance at all athletic events; everyone feels included even if not on the team, and great facilities as well!"

CAMPUS DINING

Q I Love the Food!!

"The pub is delicious and Dining Services caters to our desires."

Frequently Compared Schools:

Hobart & William Smith Colleges
Syracuse University
Union College
University of Vermont

Q Excellent Variety

"Nutritious food and a variety of fresh produce. It seems a little difficult to get away from more fatty foods because there's not as much healthy things to choose from, but overall it's terrific!!"

CAMPUS HOUSING

Q Whitman Dorm

"I've lived in Whitman for 3 years and I think it's one of the best dorms on campus. It's close to everything, has a great computer lab, and the Center for Civic Engagement, HEOP and a few other academic offices are right in the building."

Q Cottage Theme House

"I live in a cottage theme house and greatly enjoy it. I am still living on campus, which is unfortunate because there are limitations and regulations, but for living on campus, I feel I am at a great advantage, having space to cook and live."

GUYS & GIRLS

Q Guys Are Sexy

"The athletes here are so fine! And the smart ones are even hotter!"

Q Social Life

"There is a good variety of students and everyone seems to get along and find someone they like to be with."

HEALTH & SAFETY

Q I Feel Very Safe.

"There are safe walks available and the local police work very closely with campus security, but we're in such a small town a secure campus is easy to maintain. The key-card doors and combination locks to rooms are really nice too."

Q Super Safe.

"St. Lawrence is such as safe campus. Let me put it this way: I am the only child son to a full-blood Italian woman... if she felt comfortable leaving me here anyone's parents would as well."

LOOKING FOR MORE?

Check out our full-length guide to this school at collegeprowler.com/st.-lawrence-university/.

St. Mary's College of Maryland

18952 E. Fisher Road; Saint Mary's City, MD 20686
(240) 895-2000; www.smcm.edu

THE BASICS:

Acceptance Rate: 52%	**Student-Faculty Ratio:** 12:1
Yield: 32%	**Retention Rate:** 91%
Setting: Rural	**Graduation Rate:** 75%
Control: Public	**Tuition:** $22,718
Total Undergrads: 2,016	**Room & Board:** $10,250
SAT Range: 1720–2020*	**Avg. Aid Package:** $7,500
ACT Range: 24–29	**Students With Aid:** 75%

* of 2400

This School Isn't Graded Yet!

College Prowler grades are calculated using tons of criteria, including survey responses that come from students at this school.

Unfortunately, we haven't gathered enough student surveys yet for this school to be able to calculate the grades for each section. Stay tuned to *CollegeProwler.com* for grade updates and more!

CP's Student Author On...
OVERALL EXPERIENCE

St. Mary's looks like it's going to be a boring campus in the middle of nowhere with nothing to do for fun. But most students find that this impression is wrong once they stay on campus for a bit and meet everyone. The friendly students and faculty make St. Mary's a warm and inviting place where everyone feels right at home. Students enjoy hanging out by the water or lazing around on the grass, taking a stroll through Historic St. Mary's City, and going swimming down by The Point. While enjoying what is supposedly the best four years of their lives, students receive a quality education that will take them further in life than they ever imagined. Graduating students are excited for their futures to unfold but also regretful that they must leave St. Mary's, a place lovingly called "home" for so long.

St. Mary's facilitates learning through incredible faculty, amazing course offerings, and a general atmosphere that broadens horizons and fosters growth within students. Students who attend St. Mary's arrive as children and leave as adults, having been given the opportunity to experience new things and learn so much through these experiences.

Students Speak Out On...
OVERALL EXPERIENCE

Q I Love It Here

"I love it at St. Mary's. All of the students have a great work ethic since it is an honors college, but they still know how to have a good time on the weekends. It is definitely not your typical college since the population is very small, but knowing most of your schoolmates gives St. Mary's a cozy atmosphere."

Q Consider Your Priorities Carefully

"SMCM is very isolated. The area is rural and lower class. If you go for a walk, you'll see the river, some suburban neighborhoods, and plenty of farms. Hardly any places to go off campus. The school tries hard to bring events and people to the campus to keep things interesting, but social life revolves primarily around the party and drinking scene, especially on the weekends. Academics are okay, but not particularly inspiring."

BEST OF ST. MARY'S COLLEGE MD

1. Buildings are a mixture between the past and the present.
2. Drugs aren't a problem on campus.
3. Good college food from Bon Appétit
4. Good reputation as a "Public Honors College"

Happy Students
91% of students return after their first year.

Proven Success
75% of students will complete their education and graduate with a degree.

WORST OF ST. MARY'S COLLEGE MD

1. Parking
2. Transportation in the area
3. Not a lot to do in St. Mary's City
4. Campus lacks in diversity
5. Influx of "yuppie" kids

Want a Job? On Your Own
There aren't any placement services for graduates.

Student Body

African American:	8%	Male Undergrads:	41%
Asian American:	4%	Female Undergrads:	59%
Hispanic:	4%	Living On Campus:	85%
International:	2%	Living Off Campus:	19%
Native American:	1%	Male Athletes:	19%
White:	77%	Female Athletes:	14%
Unknown:	4%	Fraternity Members:	0%
From Out-of-State:	21%	Sorority Members:	0%

Students Speak Out On... EVERYTHING!

ACADEMICS

Q Academics

"The professors are overall really good. Very smart and very nice. But some suck, even ones who may be the head of a department."

Q Major

"My major itself isn't so bad. The workload isn't terrible, and all of the teachers are really neat people. I'm interested in possibly pursuing a minor in Neuroscience and that really increases my workload though. The school sends out notifications about internship and job opportunities, but I haven't been able to look into them much."

Q If You Study Hard, It Will Pay Off

"I've learned my lesson about missing class and i have concluded that whenever i do show up I get good grades on my test and I am more willing to study hard once i get home."

ATHLETICS

Q Water Water Everywhere

"If you're into sailing, crew, or windsurfing, this is the place for you. Because we're right on the water, water sports are definitely a strong point here. Lacrosse, soccer, field hockey, and rugby have a pretty strong prescience on campus as well. Sports events are pretty well attended with the exception of sailing regattas which (because it's difficult to tell which boat is sailing for SMC at any given time) are less so."

CAMPUS DINING

Q Just Desserts!

"The main place to get food is ok, sometimes very repetitive. However sometimes, the campus spices it up and the desserts are always delicious n made fresh everyday! I don't usually eat very often at the great room so if you can switch your meal plan to gain more flex's and less blocks. You can always use a first-year's plan. =)"

CAMPUS HOUSING

Q The Walk

"Being able to walk barefoot to class without worries was pretty sweet. Though, nowadays, the paths aren't nearly as feet friendly as they were when I was around."

Q Dorm Life:SMCM Style

"The dorms are incredibly overcrowded. Until you reach upperclassman status, there aren't a lot of premium living options. I prefer North Campus, because the dorms are the nicest and most attractive."

GUYS & GIRLS

Q So Many Lesbians! and a Few Hippies Too!

"There seems to be quite a large number of lesbians at St. Mary's. However, there are still straight girls, and every woman comes in a great variety: geeky, preppy, punk, you name it and we've probably got it. The boys are a little bit toned down, usually they're very chivalrous and hold the door open for others and such, usually very nice guys that are quite handsome."

HEALTH & SAFETY

Q Extremly Safe

"I have never felt unsafe on campus. Even in the dark areas in the woods where they haven't replaced the lights. The health center seems to be hit and miss though on how they help though"

St. Mary's University

One Camino Santa Maria; San Antonio, TX 78228
(210) 436-3011; www.stmarytx.edu

THE BASICS:

Acceptance Rate: 76%
Yield: 29%
Setting: Large city
Control: Private Non-Profit
Total Undergrads: 2,438
SAT Range: 1400–1720*
ACT Range: 20–25

Student-Faculty Ratio: 16:1
Retention Rate: 80%
Graduation Rate: 59%
Tuition: $21,320
Room & Board: $7,090
Avg. Aid Package: $20,138
Students With Aid: 91%

* of 2400

Academics	B	Greek Life	B-
Athletics	C+	Guys	B
Campus Dining	C+	Health & Safety	B+
Campus Housing	B+	Local Atmosphere	B
Campus Strictness	B-	Nightlife	B-
Computers	C	Off-Campus Dining	D+
Diversity	B-	Off-Campus Housing	B-
Drug Safety	B-	Parking	B+
Facilities	C	Transportation	D+
Girls	B	Weather	A

CP's Student Author On...
OVERALL EXPERIENCE

A majority of St. Mary's students have loved their time here and would not change a thing. The most common regret from students is that they did not go to a larger university. Students often reflect on administrative politics and control as something that has also restricted them in some ways. Nonetheless, students find themselves loving the education and relationships that they have gained here and are glad they made the decision that they did. Some had first choices other than St. Mary's, but they generally say that they would not trade their experiences here for anything. Students appreciate the attention and challenges that professors and their courses have offered, and most feel more than prepared after graduation.

The relationships you form at a small, friendly university cannot be duplicated at a larger university where students are just a number when they walk into class. Creating bonds with faculty helps you get more out of the classroom experience and makes learning more enjoyable overall. This solid structure also means more career resources and advice for the future.... For the rest of this editorial, visit collegeprowler.com.

Students Speak Out On...
OVERALL EXPERIENCE

Q I've Never Been to Such a Wonderful Place

"St. Mary's University is the place to be, albeit it is a private catholic school. If I had to start over, I would not even consider going to any other college. I'm glad I went there and I hope all my kids and cousins go there in the future!!"

Q I Love College

"I have really enjoyed my time at my school. I love the classes and have made some amazing friends. I love San Antonio."

Q Social Paradise, Academic Coin Flip

"Socially, St. Mary's is top of the list. Everyone is accepted by everyone else. Academically, if you luck into choosing professors that care if you succeed, you will succeed. If not, it takes a lot of self-discipline to do most of the work yourself."

BEST OF ST. MARY'S

1. Ambitious students
2. Campus safety
3. Committed and caring faculty
4. Fiesta Oyster Bake
5. The friendly people and community feel

Happy Students
80% of students return after their first year.

Big Dorms
54% of students surveyed felt that dorms were more spacious than average.

WORST OF ST. MARY'S

1. Administrative control over student organizations and publications
2. Cliques
3. Fewer people in the dating pool
4. The immediate neighborhood is not the nicest in town.

Lowest Grades
Off-Campus Dining: D+
Transportation: D+
Computers: C

Student Body

African American:	4%	Male Undergrads:	40%
Asian American:	3%	Female Undergrads:	60%
Hispanic:	68%	Living On Campus:	55%
International:	4%	Living Off Campus:	45%
Native American:	0%	Male Athletes:	11%
White:	18%	Female Athletes:	8%
Unknown:	2%	Fraternity Members:	22%
From Out-of-State:	6%	Sorority Members:	16%

Frequently Compared Schools:

Santa Clara University
Trinity University
University of San Diego
University of Texas at San Antonio

Students Speak Out On...
EVERYTHING!

ACADEMICS

Biology Department

"St. Mary's is well known to have a strong Biological Sciences curriculum. They have professors who are always around for help. the courses are challenging, however they are only preparing you for your career."

Personal Attention

"Every professor gets to know you on a first name basis. Even the school President go out to the campus coffee house and shares a table with students just to hang out! The class sizes are small and the courses are tough, but you learn a lot. The educational expreience is invaluable."

Biology Major

"I love it here. The teachers really work with the students and there are many programs offered that will help with what happens after I graduate."

ATHLETICS

Athletics

"At St. Mary's there is no football team. Them major sports teams here are basketball, vollyball, and soccer. We have a variety of other sports but those are the top ones through out the university. That being said, there is a lot of support for these teams and good turn outs for the games."

Athletics at STMU

"It appears to me that the athletes get a pretty good scholarship deal and are very dedicated to their training activities. I think St Mary's university has done a pretty good job on keeping a nice structure that allows the students to practice whatever they want to."

CAMPUS DINING

Very Good but Only Certain Stuff Open at Certain Times/ Gets Repetitive

"The campus food is very good, but we mainly have the same thing because not all the other places are open. The only thing that is constantly open is "Grill Works" and their food does get repetitive. If more of the food places in the cafe were open like grill works it would be better. It is very good though and whenever you need food its there and easy to buy since you use your st. mary's rattler card. One easy swipe and thats it."

Unhealthy but Healthy

"Food is all right some of the time. It's pretty unhealthy too, seeing all the fried food. Also, the lines take a really long time, and they need a better system for serving the food. Prices are also jacked up."

CAMPUS HOUSING

Very Convenient and Comfortable

"I've never lived on campus, but my friends tend to have a good time there haha"

Campus Overall

"it is a beautiful campus! words can not describe what i really feel."

GUYS & GIRLS

Attractive Girls :P

"There is a good amount of attractive girls here at St.Marys. A majority of them are short Hispanic girls. For the most part, mini-shorts are a staple for StMU girls."

Guys & Girls

"You can find just about all types."

HEALTH & SAFETY

Safe on Campus

"I feel somewhat safe on campus. It's small and gated and there is always police on watch. But I wished there more were cameras. There have been robberies and trespassers before."

Gated Community

"St. Mary's is a gated community and that helps keep the neighors out of the University. Surrounding the university there is a whole other percentage of crime. The most I have heard is an occasional break in of a car because someone left there valuables sitting out in their car."

LOOKING FOR MORE?

Check out our full-length guide to this school at collegeprowler.com/st.-mary's-university/.

St. Olaf College

1520 St. Olaf Ave.; Northfield, MN 55057
(507) 786-2222; www.stolaf.edu

THE BASICS:

Acceptance Rate: 57%
Yield: 35%
Setting: Town
Control: Private Non-Profit
Total Undergrads: 3,099
SAT Range: 1180–1400*
ACT Range: 26–31

Student-Faculty Ratio: 12:1
Retention Rate: 93%
Graduation Rate: 86%
Tuition: $35,500
Room & Board: $8,200
Avg. Aid Package: $22,743
Students With Aid: 83%

of 1600

Academics	B+	Greek Life	N/A
Athletics	C+	Guys	B+
Campus Dining	A	Health & Safety	A
Campus Housing	B+	Local Atmosphere	B-
Campus Strictness	C+	Nightlife	D+
Computers	A-	Off-Campus Dining	B+
Diversity	D	Off-Campus Housing	D+
Drug Safety	B	Parking	B-
Facilities	A	Transportation	C-
Girls	A+	Weather	C-

CP's Student Author On...
OVERALL EXPERIENCE

t's not uncommon at St. Olaf to run into second-, third-, or even fourth-generation Oles. This fact, coupled with the school's outstanding 94 percent retention rate, shows that there is obviously something that keeps drawing current students, alumni, and their children back to the Hill. Sure, if you ask current students walking across campus in mid-February about their overall experience of St. Olaf, they probably won't extol many praises. But if you catch them when it's over 45 degrees, you're sure to hear nothing but great things.

Despite the long winters, the course work, and the stress of life in general, campus is an extraordinarily happy place to be—and it shows. The zombification of students that occurs at other schools (bags under the eyes, clammy hands desperately clutching coffee tumblers, etc.) is a rarity at Olaf. Even in the dead of winter, most Oles are good-humored, friendly people who seem overjoyed to be right where they are. St. Olaf really offers students a wholesome four years, and I don't mean "wholesome" in the cheesy 7th Heaven way.... For the rest of this editorial, visit collegeprowler.com.

Students Speak Out On...
OVERALL EXPERIENCE

Q **A Perfect Fit!**
"I love St. Olaf. Teachers really care about you, and the campus is small enough to get around quickly but large enough to see new people every day. The food is awesome!!! I love that I've been able to customize my own major. If you want to party, you can, but if you want to avoid it, it's really easy. I feel in LOVE with the library. I also met my boyfriend here. Music majors are so wonderful, and there are lot of them here!"

Q **Awesome**
"The School is an awesome atmosphere. The majority of the people are friendly and the safety is quite high. For music people, the St Olaf Choir and Band are spectacular with highly prestigious professors such as Dr. Aspaas and Dr. Arstrong. The theatre department is quite top notch as well."

Q "Sometimes I do wish I were somewhere else, but the whole college choice thing is mostly a wash anyway. It doesn't really matter where you go, just what you bring with you."

Q "I would recommend it to anyone. I'm forcing my kids to go here."

BEST OF ST. OLAF

1. The people
2. The classes
3. The music
4. All the opportunities to study abroad
5. Sledding
6. The food
7. Campus Culture

Happy Students
93% of students return after their first year.

Proven Success
86% of students will complete their education and graduate with a degree.

WORST OF ST. OLAF

1. The wind
2. The long winters
3. The homogeneity
4. The isolation of the Hill
5. Everything closes at midnight
6. The dating problem
7. The dry campus

Expensive
Tuition is a steep $35,500, one of the most expensive rates in the country.

Want a Job? On Your Own
There aren't any placement services for graduates.

Student Body

African American:	1%	Male Undergrads:	45%
Asian American:	5%	Female Undergrads:	55%
Hispanic:	2%	Living On Campus:	96%
International:	2%	Living Off Campus:	4%
Native American:	0%	Male Athletes:	33%
White:	83%	Female Athletes:	20%
Unknown:	7%	Fraternity Members:	0%
From Out-of-State:	51%	Sorority Members:	0%

Frequently Compared Schools:

Carleton College
Macalester College
Oberlin College
University of Minnesota

Students Speak Out On... EVERYTHING!

ACADEMICS

Admissions Process

"The admissions at St. Olaf are streamlined and easy, and the staff is friendly as can be. From the beginning, I felt at home."

Definitely Not a Slacker Major

"As a St. Olaf music major, I've been able to grow quite a lot as a musician. Professors are very caring and quite reachable (sometimes, they'll put their phone numbers on the board!). While the music building is cramped at times, I believe they are expanding it in the next few years. It's a conservatory-quality education without all the garbage that goes with that sort of environment. Absolutely wonderful!"

ATHLETICS

Supportive Team Members

"The teams are very supportive of the team members. Even though students of color are scanty on the teams, the white athletes are very nice and supportive."

Great Team Spirt

"As an Ole you always feel a great pride for your team, and we do fairly well athletically"

CAMPUS DINING

Excellent Food, Friendly Service!

"We have an excellent dining experience at St. Olaf. Our food is great quality and there are both reliable and healthy options as well as a rotating menu to chose from. Food is served with a smile!"

Inflexible

"The food in the caf is excellent, or as excellent as eating the same food for 4 years can be. The problem is that one is required to have a meal plan all four years. The price is the same no matter how many meals one actually eats and there is no half-plan option when living on campus."

CAMPUS HOUSING

Variety!

"No matter what kind of dorm you want: a classic old building with huge fire places and fancy couches, or a more modern tower-style dorm with suite style rooms where you and your friends can dominate an entire floor, St. Olaf has it! Freshmen dorms tend to have some issues, like a leaky window here and there, but overall they're good. Upperclassmen dorms are wonderful, and the communities found in all the dorms are really close-knit and welcoming."

Dorms Vary Enormously

"The room sizes and amenities of the dorms vary widely at St. Olaf, from the tiny rooms in Kil where freshmen share a closet, to the huge rooms in Hill with their own sinks and walk-in closets. But the buildings are all maintained very well, and any problems that you tell maintenance about are taken care of quickly."

GUYS & GIRLS

Smart!

"The guys at St. Olaf are extraordinarily smart. There is a great diversity...LOVE the music majors! (But there are a lot of gay guys on campus) Girls are smart too, and there are a lot of artsy dressers."

Preppy or Artsy

"The people here are either really involved in the music and arts scene, or they are really interested in the sports (mostly hockey and cross country skiing or track), and they show it proudly. While there are some people in the middle, they are few and far between."

HEALTH & SAFETY

Pretty Good!

"Health services are decently fast and relatively inexpensive. Campus security is EXCELLENT. I feel very safe on campus and people feel comfortable leaving their bags in the hallway outside the cafeteria."

LOOKING FOR MORE?

Check out our full-length guide to this school at collegeprowler.com/st.-olaf-college/.

Stanford University

450 Serra Mall; Stanford, CA 94305
(650) 723-2300; www.stanford.edu

THE BASICS:

Acceptance Rate: 8%	**Student-Faculty Ratio:** 6:1
Yield: 70%	**Retention Rate:** 98%
Setting: Suburban	**Graduation Rate:** 94%
Control: Private Non-Profit	**Tuition:** $38,676
Total Undergrads: 6,532	**Room & Board:** $11,463
SAT Range: 2010–2300*	**Avg. Aid Package:** $33,108
ACT Range: 30–34	**Students With Aid:** 75%

* of 2400

Academics	A+	Greek Life	B
Athletics	A	Guys	A
Campus Dining	A+	Health & Safety	B
Campus Housing	A	Local Atmosphere	B
Campus Strictness	A	Nightlife	B
Computers	A+	Off-Campus Dining	B
Diversity	A+	Off-Campus Housing	C
Drug Safety	B-	Parking	B
Facilities	A+	Transportation	B+
Girls	A+	Weather	A

CP's Student Author On...
OVERALL EXPERIENCE

The verdict is in: most students are overwhelmingly happy with their Stanford experience. The combination of challenging academics, undergrad-oriented faculty, diversity, beautiful weather, and a fairly social campus environment all combine to make for a great four years of college. Students, particularly those in engineering or sciences, might find the workload to be especially heavy at times, but most students are capable and want to work hard in the first place. Perhaps the biggest challenge students face at Stanford is just dealing with the other students, who range from hippies to hyper-competitive pre-meds. It makes for an interesting environment, but also a stressful one. However, if you immerse yourself in it long enough, it will eventually start to feel reasonably normal.

Despite the problems that Stanford students find with the University, they overwhelmingly agree that Stanford is "their place," and they can't imagine being anywhere else. It seems all the hype and the hefty price tag are well justified by the experiences that students can, and will, have here.... For the rest of this editorial, visit collegeprowler.com.

Students Speak Out On...
OVERALL EXPERIENCE

Q Overall Experience

"The weather is amazing. No snow. Chilly but not freezing. Sunny but not burning. Laid back and so surprisingly fun. Quirky."

Q Can't Have Picked a Better School

"My time at Stanford has been amazing. I've met incredible people and had the best experiences of my life. My fellow students have never seized to amaze me with their curricular AND extra-curricular endeavors. My time abroad through the Bing Overseas Studies Program in Florence was a highlight of my undergraduate career and I am ever so thankful to Stanford for the amazing opportunities it has, and continues, to offer me."

Q Overall Experience

"Stanford is my home away from home... and I come from Hawaii! Honestly, I am happy with my choice and very grateful to have the chance to be here. It's balanced in every regard, and that makes it almost better than home."

BEST OF STANFORD

1. Beautiful campus/ beautiful weather
2. Getting a job
3. Great athletics/ extracurricular activity options
4. San Francisco
5. Talented, compassionate professors

Happy Students
98% of students return after their first year.

Commitment to Teaching
There are 6 students for every member of faculty on campus.

WORST OF STANFORD

1. Cost of living
2. "The Stanford Bubble"
3. Competitive
4. Large campus
5. The quarter system
6. Bike accidents
7. Palo Alto

Expensive
Tuition is a steep $38,676, one of the most expensive rates in the country.

Expensive to Just Get By
56% of students surveyed felt that the amount it costs to live while at school was worse than average.

Student Body

African American:	9%	Male Undergrads:	51%
Asian American:	21%	Female Undergrads:	49%
Hispanic:	11%	Living On Campus:	91%
International:	9%	Living Off Campus:	9%
Native American:	2%	Male Athletes:	16%
White:	35%	Female Athletes:	15%
Unknown:	13%	Fraternity Members:	—
From Out-of-State:	60%	Sorority Members:	—

Frequently Compared Schools:

Harvard University
Princeton University
University of Pennsylvania
Yale University

Students Speak Out On... EVERYTHING!

ACADEMICS

Political Science

"The political science department has the teachers and tools to get you the education and connections you need to be successful."

Fun Yet Chalenging

"Professors are available and helpful and the programs are great in pretty much every field. Other students are realy fun, and there are lots of extra-curricular options. The workload is, as is probably true anywhere, as hard as you make it, but the work is not busywork."

ATHLETICS

Athletics

"Athletics is unrivaled and EXCELLENT. People could be paid for their team spirit, which is tops. All in all, the school treats athletes well so they play at the highest levels and win championships annually. Naturally, the student body gets behind them and the whole school is united in its sports pride."

Top Collegiate Athletics

"Stanford is home to some top sports teams, such as our varsity football team and women's basketball team. Varsity athletes, even in smaller sports such as sailing, get high-quality treatment at the school. Athleticism of all kinds is definitely encouraged, no matter if it's running with your friends twice a week or taking home a national championship."

CAMPUS DINING

Great Food

"The food is definitely better than other colleges that I've visited."

Yay, Food!

"The food at the dining halls is good, but there are also a lot of non-dining hall options available. Many places, like the Axe & Palm, Union Square, Subway, etc. accept meal plan dollars - which is nice :)."

CAMPUS HOUSING

Frosoco Is the Place to Be

"Frosoco is the best freshman/sophomore dorm ever. Our remoteness makes this place great for quiet studying but also lots of mingling and socializing happens, due to the crazy nature of the people here and also all the great events that the dorm sponsors or subsidizes for us."

All the Dorms Are Pretty Nice, Inside and Out

"The outside of the dorms, as with most buildings on-campus, look really nice. The rooms are definitely much larger than average college dorm rooms. Most of the furniture is pretty new too. The social atmosphere is wonderful. A unique aspect here is the amount of dorm spirit. As a freshman, most of the people you meet will be those in your dorm. Amenities include computer clusters and a dining hall near the dorm."

GUYS & GIRLS

See the Entry on Diversity

"Considering the wide range of students here, it shouldn't be too hard to find someone who has physical compatibility and personality compatibility. There are plenty of opportunities to get to know girls (and guys)."

The People Are Great

"Stanford people in general are the best part of the campus experience. Everyone has a different background and is very interested or passionate about something. Anyone can find a guy or girl they would like here."

HEALTH & SAFETY

Safety: Not an Issue

"I always feel safe when I'm on campus. Whether it's in broad daylight or walking back to my dorm from the library at 4 am in the morning."

LOOKING FOR MORE?

Check out our full-length guide to this school at collegeprowler.com/stanford-university/.

Stetson University

421 N. Woodland Blvd.; DeLand, FL 32723
(386) 822-7000; www.stetson.edu

THE BASICS:

Acceptance Rate: 53%
Yield: 20%
Setting: Suburban
Control: Private Non-Profit
Total Undergrads: 2,162
SAT Range: 1460–1790*
ACT Range: 21–26

Student-Faculty Ratio: 11:1
Retention Rate: 76%
Graduation Rate: 67%
Tuition: $31,770
Room & Board: $8,934
Avg. Aid Package: $12,981
Students With Aid: 99%

* of 2400

Academics	B	Greek Life	A-
Athletics	B	Guys	B+
Campus Dining	C-	Health & Safety	B+
Campus Housing	B-	Local Atmosphere	B
Campus Strictness	C+	Nightlife	B
Computers	A	Off-Campus Dining	B-
Diversity	C+	Off-Campus Housing	C
Drug Safety	B	Parking	C+
Facilities	B	Transportation	B-
Girls	B+	Weather	A

CP's Student Author On...
OVERALL EXPERIENCE

The overall experience of Stetson University can be described as intimate. The campus itself isn't big, so of course that has its pros and cons. The pros are the fact that students get to know one another well, and finding and walking to classes is easy. Of course, if it's a really rainy or hot day, then it can be a hassle. However, with a small campus, students are able to get to know their professors well, which is great. On the downside, if you miss a class, the professor will notice. Some professors here will curve grades based on attendance. Another contributing factor of the overall experience is the small class size. Small class sizes are nice for those who like it, but they correlate with a higher tuition rate. I feel that for every pro, there is a con of some sort. The overall experience will differ for each student. Some move on to other universities; others like it here and stay. It all comes down to whether a student will take the good with the bad. I can say for myself that, since Stetson is always looking to improve, they will listen. Since they will listen, the bad things about Stetson become tolerable and make it a decent school all around.... For the rest of this editorial, visit collegeprowler.com.

Students Speak Out On...
OVERALL EXPERIENCE

Q My Stetson Experience

"My Stetson experience has been amazing. The campus is so beautiful and I have made some great friends and met awesome professors. Stetson provides an atmosphere that is very comforting, one in which you are allowed to be whoever you are and will be embraced regardless of race, ethnicity, religion, or any of these factors. It's because of these things that I would definitely choose Stetson again if I could do it all over."

Q "As a music student, my overall experience has been music. That's not necessarily a good thing. I love music, but I'm always devoting my time and energy to the music school. I don't get enough time to go out and experience any fun with my friends. My free time is vital to me, and I take it to unwind. The music school is very demanding. They don't ease you into anything. Your freshman year is a minimum of 18 credit hours, and that's heinous."

BEST OF STETSON

1. Small classes
2. Approachable professors
3. Small town atmosphere
4. Location
5. Beautiful campus
6. Small campus
7. Green campus
8. The lecture series

Learn from the Best
92% of faculty have earned the highest degree in their field.

Personal Attention
You can expect personal attention with 60% of classes having less than 20 students.

WORST OF STETSON

1. The limited dining services options
2. Dorms
3. Attendance policies
4. Professors notice when you're absent
5. Limited funding for clubs

Expensive
Tuition is a steep $31,770, one of the most expensive rates in the country.

Student Body

African American:	5%	Male Undergrads:	43%
Asian American:	2%	Female Undergrads:	57%
Hispanic:	10%	Living On Campus:	72%
International:	3%	Living Off Campus:	18%
Native American:	0%	Male Athletes:	14%
White:	73%	Female Athletes:	12%
Unknown:	6%	Fraternity Members:	29%
From Out-of-State:	21%	Sorority Members:	23%

Frequently Compared Schools:

Rollins College
University of Central Florida
University of Florida
University of Miami

Students Speak Out On...
EVERYHING!

ACADEMICS

Tuition

"I love this school theteachers are nice and workable. The tuition is so high it its hard to focus on schoolwork but the education is wonderful here."

"They try to make well-rounded students, but I think that they try too hard. There are a lot of general education requirements that preclude me from focusing on my major and interests."

"I think the general requirements need a major overhauling of who teaches them because they get tenured professors who are no longer fresh in their field."

ATHLETICS

The Heart of Stetson

"Though are sport's teams are small, they have great heart. School spirit is mediocure but all the sports team's are supported by the school and are encouraged to be the best they can be."

Division I for Real?

"Stetson University is very small, yet our athletics are Division I. Too much funding goes to athletics."

CAMPUS DINING

Leftovers?!

"They food is rather creative seeing that they make a variety of different meals from the leaftover food! However, you are lucky when you catch the special day's on campus when the food is especially good."

Main Dining Hub

"The food doesn't change. EVER. They rip us off on prices and meal plans. I worked there long enough to know that stetson allows Sodexo to rape us for food. They have almost no vegetarian or Vegan options and the only time we get new or good high quality food is when prospective families come. Nice to know they stop caring once you agree to go there."

CAMPUS HOUSING

A Little Bit of Everything

"The newer dorms are farther away from campus, so they're not as convenient as the older dorms. The best thing about dorms at Stetson is the free laundry!"

Newer Dorms Are Your Best Bet

"If you have allergies, the newer dorms are your best option. I lived in one of the oldest dorms my first year and was always sick. Since upgrading I've enjoyed a healthly year and a half."

GUYS & GIRLS

Greeks Run Stetson

"If you aren't Greek, you don't do anything, and you contribute little. Greeks are in SGA, FOCUS, Intramurals, political groups, club sports, residential life, EVERYWHERE. and the best part is, they do a great job at it."

"I think the girls on campus are a little too uptight, and they need to be a little less judgmental on whether they're a part of a clique or not."

HEALTH & SAFETY

Safe

"They have public safety and they are very kind. I give them an A+ because they are on there job 24/7 doinhg there work and getting the job done. They have an amazing response time to any situation. I love this schools safety."

Very Secure

"I have always felt at ease with the security on campus. Also, the Public Safety officers are extremely friendly and willing to lend a helping hand!"

LOOKING FOR MORE?

Check out our full-length guide to this school at collegeprowler.com/stetson-university/.

Stevenson University

1525 Greenspring Valley Road; Stevenson, MD 21153
(410) 486-7000; www.stevenson.edu

THE BASICS:

Acceptance Rate: 57%
Yield: 22%
Setting: Suburban
Control: Private Non-Profit
Total Undergrads: 3,198
SAT Range: 1350–1680*
ACT Range: 18–22

Student-Faculty Ratio: 15:1
Retention Rate: 79%
Graduation Rate: 58%
Tuition: $20,644
Room & Board: $9,345
Avg. Aid Package: $14,124
Students With Aid: 94%

* of 2400

Academics	B-	Greek Life	N/A
Athletics	C+	Guys	B
Campus Dining	C	Health & Safety	B
Campus Housing	B+	Local Atmosphere	B-
Campus Strictness	B	Nightlife	B-
Computers	C+	Off-Campus Dining	B
Diversity	B-	Off-Campus Housing	B-
Drug Safety	C+	Parking	A+
Facilities	C+	Transportation	B
Girls	B-	Weather	B-

CP's Student Author On...
OVERALL EXPERIENCE

Stevenson University offers students a great experience, both academically and personally. However cliché it may sound, the school really is like a big family. The teachers develop close bonds with their students that just cannot be found at other schools. Even though the school is growing in leaps and bounds, the closeness of the school will never be gone because the administration actually cares about students' futures. There is a good reason this school is the most up-and-coming University in the state of Maryland: the people are great.

Stevenson University offers students an opportunity to grow. However, it is important to note that the University gives students back only what the students put in. It is possible to attend Stevenson University, do "just enough" to graduate, and get a job. It is possible to try "just enough," and just be another student in a desk. However, students like this usually drop out in the first year. Why? This University is designed for people who want to push themselves and help push each other to succeed. "Just enough" isn't good enough for most who attend here.... For the rest of this editorial, visit collegeprowler.com.

Students Speak Out On...
OVERALL EXPERIENCE

Q I love it here
"I absolutely love this school. The people here are amazing; the faculty and staff make it all worthwhile."

Q I Love College
"Stevenson University overall has been an eye opening experience for me. I enjoy the freedom, space, the rooms, as well as the facilities on campus. The school provides you with any thing you might need to better yourself in the future. I love the two campuses, but dislike the distance between them. On the weekends it's very quiet because there are a lot of commuters that attend Stevenson. I love quiet environments, and the fact that Stevenson is centrally located between Towson, and UMBC"

Q Love It!
"Stevenson is small, but slowly growing. Classes stay pretty small, around 30 students. Most professors try and kept their schedule open so they can meet with students. Stevenson is expensive but very challenging and a great tool for future prep for the real world. There isn't too many distractions that keep you from your goals."

BEST OF STEVENSON

1. Campus housing is modern and swanky.
2. Teachers are always available to help.
3. The campuses are close to Baltimore City, where there's always something to do.

Knowledgeable Professors
100% of students surveyed rated the general knowledge of professors as above average.

Low-Stress Course Load
60% of students surveyed rated the manageability of work as above average.

WORST OF STEVENSON

1. The campus becomes a ghost town on weekends.
2. There is very little diversity among the students.
3. Res Life enforces the school's alcohol policy with a vengeance.

Expensive Dorms
Living on campus doesn't come cheap, with an average housing price tag of $6,750.

Student Body

African American:	16%	Male Undergrads:	28%
Asian American:	3%	Female Undergrads:	72%
Hispanic:	2%	Living On Campus:	41%
International:	0%	Living Off Campus:	59%
Native American:	1%	Male Athletes:	20%
White:	70%	Female Athletes:	7%
Unknown:	9%	Fraternity Members:	0%
From Out-of-State:	10%	Sorority Members:	0%

Students Speak Out On... EVERYTHING!

ACADEMICS

Stevenson University

"I am hoping to attend Stevenson University (SU) to study for a degree in Criminal Justice. SU offers state-of-the-art education in criminal justice, addressing the needs of the students as they move toward their future career. SU instills values such as service to the community, which is very important to me. SU promotes student learning through a commitment to continuous improvement. I would be proud to one day be an alumnus of the Criminal Justice program at SU."

Getting to Know the Teacher and Making the Effort Goes a LONG Way

"Once you get to know the teachers and they you and as long as you make a point to show some effort and have any interest whatsoever, things get much easier"

ATHLETICS

SU Has Spirit

"Stevenson is doing a great job at having athletics being a highlight of the school. For a D3 school, lacrosse and soccer are big at SU. With the construction of a new gym, and a football team being formed, stevenson is on their way to great things"

Sports at Stevenson

"The sports arena at Stevenson is growing. We are getting a football team in fall 2011."

CAMPUS DINING

Dining at Stevenson

"I love the dining halls at Stevenson. Additionally, we are now allowed to use our flex dollars at some restaurants off campus."

Campus Dining

"Since I am a commuter I do not use the colleges on campus dining but I do know they have great food and several for the on campus students. I was able to try the food on the day to check out the university."

Frequently Compared Schools:

Salisbury University
Towson University
University of Maryland
University of Maryland - Baltimore County

CAMPUS HOUSING

Awesome Housing

"The dorms are roomy, great and relatively new and they are awesome. I feel like I am living in my own apartment, not dorms on a college campus. Highly recommend."

Dorms

"I absolutely loved living in the dorms, it was a great way to meet people and have a full college experience. It also gave me the feeling of being an adult, living on my own."

GUYS & GIRLS

Girls and Guys at School

"Great people. There are at least 7 to 1 girls vs guys ratio. High class white population. Young atmosphere for daytime students"

Diverse Campus

"There's all types of girls and guys everywhere on campus. People from all around the U.S. Social life a lot of people do like to start drama for no reason at all. something to get used to i guess."

HEALTH & SAFETY

Security on Campus

"I can say, with no doubt, that I feel absolutely safe on campus. There are cameras everywhere, and the security guards who stay during the night are always watching the cameras and making sure everyone is safe. There is a gate at the entrance of the campus, where there is a security guard. One must also scan their student ID to be able to enter. I feel that I can walk around campus at any time of the day and feel totally safe."

I Feel Safe Here

"I have never felt unsafe on campus. Security is always close by, it is well lit, and everyone minds their own stuff. I have left my bag laying around and doors unlocked and never had a problem with anything missing from the apartments."

LOOKING FOR MORE?

Check out our full-length guide to this school at collegeprowler.com/stevenson-university/.

Stony Brook University

100 Nicolls Road; Stony Brook, NY 11794
(631) 632-6000; www.stonybrook.edu

THE BASICS:

Acceptance Rate: 40%	**Student-Faculty Ratio:** 19:1
Yield: 25%	**Retention Rate:** 89%
Setting: Suburban	**Graduation Rate:** 61%
Control: Public	**Tuition:** $14,388
Total Undergrads: 16,395	**Room & Board:** $9,590
SAT Range: 1620–1910*	**Avg. Aid Package:** $8,115
ACT Range: 24–28	**Students With Aid:** 79%

* of 2400

Academics	B	Greek Life	B-
Athletics	C+	Guys	B-
Campus Dining	B-	Health & Safety	B-
Campus Housing	B-	Local Atmosphere	C+
Campus Strictness	B-	Nightlife	B-
Computers	B+	Off-Campus Dining	C+
Diversity	A	Off-Campus Housing	B-
Drug Safety	C	Parking	B
Facilities	C+	Transportation	B+
Girls	C+	Weather	C+

CP's Student Author On...
OVERALL EXPERIENCE

Stony Brook is definitely the kind of place where you really need to put in the effort to make friends and actively participate in the social scene. If you keep to yourself during your first semester, you may be wishing you were back home or even consider transferring. However, by the second semester when you start going out more, you will be much happier now. There are so many ways to meet people and get involved on campus, and that is really the trick to being happy. Even if your classes are really stressful, you can always work on your homework with classmates—something that definitely makes it less stressful. Finding a balance between academia and a social life is not hard to do, but it isn't easy either. It is very easy to get lost in the shuffle sometimes. The campus is absolutely dead on the weekends, since most people live locally and go home. Stony Brook is widely known as a commuter school for that reason. Attending Stony Brook will hold true the cliché that college is what you make of it.

The classes themselves also vary. Some will overload you with work, and others will have you excited to learn.... For the rest of this editorial, visit collegeprowler.com.

Students Speak Out On...
OVERALL EXPERIENCE

Q It's Grrreat.

"Stony Brook is awsome. The people are nice; there are many groups and clubs to join; Most of the faculty are great professionals. Stony Brook is not far from the city (New York), and there are a lot of activities to keep me active."

Q I Love Stony Brook

"Stony Brook has a great atmosphere. There are lots of good people! Everyone I've met is super nice. The sport events are great. They have a huge turn out and there is tons of school spirit! Also, the academics are great. It is a very tough school academically but it is renowned for it's biology program and pre health. Most students are bio majors and pre health (which is premed) If you want to be a doctor or explore the medical field, Stony Brook is a smart choice."

BEST OF STONY BROOK

1. Makes you appreciate home cooking so much more
2. Kelly breakfasts
3. Real life experiences
4. The scandalous and scantily clad women
5. Great people-watching opportunities

Happy Students
89% of students return after their first year.

Knowledgeable Professors
70% of students surveyed rated the general knowledge of professors as above average.

WORST OF STONY BROOK

1. Appreciating home cooking so much that you actually want to go home to get some, which only forces you to remember why you decided to go away to college in the first place
2. Food

Expensive Dorms
Living on campus doesn't come cheap, with an average housing price tag of $6,112.

Don't Move Off Campus
Average off-campus housing is a steep $11,288.

Student Body

African American:	7%	Male Undergrads:	50%
Asian American:	20%	Female Undergrads:	50%
Hispanic:	8%	Living On Campus:	52%
International:	8%	Living Off Campus:	48%
Native American:	0%	Male Athletes:	4%
White:	34%	Female Athletes:	3%
Unknown:	22%	Fraternity Members:	2%
From Out-of-State:	16%	Sorority Members:	3%

Frequently Compared Schools:

Binghamton University
Cornell University
University at Albany
University at Buffalo

Students Speak Out On... EVERYTHING!

ACADEMICS

Amazing Professors With Real Life Experience

"All of my professors at Stony Brook are experts in their field of study. My professors have written textbooks on their subjects and particpated in real life political situations. I have professors that are special advisors to the UN. You know here at Stony Brook You will be ready and prepare for the real world."

Professors are amazing

"All the professors are very friendly and approachable. They love to talk and interact with students. They are very open and understanding. Also, all our academic programs are amazing. People think we are only good in Biology and engineering but all our programs are strong. The Poltical science, Economics, and Business fields at Stony Brook is very underrated. The number one major at Stony Brook is Business Management."

ATHLETICS

Seawolves!!!

"Our Athletic program at Stony Brook is very underated.All our programs are Division 1. Our football team won their second straight conference title. Our lacrosse, Rugby and hockey team are rank in the top 25 in the country. Our basketball team had a rough year this year but it is getting better."

Athletics at Stony Brook University

"Athletics is very important part of the academic for all student. Athletics at Stony Brook is very famous and many student are involvement either in athletics or in clubs. Performance of Stony Brook athletics teams show the team work. Communication between fan support and encourage the athletics team. In addition, to encourage the team Stony Brook have a cartoon character, Wolfie."

CAMPUS DINING

Where to Eat Next?

"There are many choices on campus to satisfy any need or craving."

Good but Not Healthy

"The food at the dining halls is good, and I would say has a large variety of mostly everything that you would want. The food is actually much better than I expected, and the only problem I would say that it is not the healthiest. There are enough options to go about eating healthy but the main food is not the best, but it's a college campus so you can't expect much else."

CAMPUS HOUSING

Very Good

"Clean dorms, respectful and quiet suit-mates, close to campus dining hall. Cost a bit much."

Most Dorms Are Great

"Most dorms are close to classes and there is always a bus passing by every quad to pick up students. The upperclassman dorms, which are optional to live in, are the farthest away from classes. This is still not a big problem since a buss passes by there every 5-10 minutes."

GUYS & GIRLS

Nice

"There's definitely a diverse population in stony brook, though most people believe it's a university filled with asian people, theres more to it then that."

Whatever You Want

"It's pretty chill at Stony Brook. Lots of girls dress up everyday and others just wear sweats. There is no pressure to dress up which is nice.There are lots of really nice girls and lots of really nice guys. Nice people in general."

HEALTH & SAFETY

Safety and Security on Campus

"Have never seen or heard of any major problems. Security personnel patrol campus all day and night, cops are on duty as well."

LOOKING FOR MORE?
Check out our full-length guide to this school at collegeprowler.com/stony-brook-university/.

SUNY Fredonia

280 Central Ave.; Fredonia, NY 14063
(716) 673-3111; www.fredonia.edu

THE BASICS:

Acceptance Rate: 52%	Student-Faculty Ratio: 17:1
Yield: 35%	Retention Rate: 81%
Setting: Town	Graduation Rate: 63%
Control: Public	Tuition: $14,159
Total Undergrads: 5,375	Room & Board: $9,630
SAT Range: 1010–1190*	Avg. Aid Package: $8,119
ACT Range: 21–26	Students With Aid: 87%

* of 1600

Academics	B-	Greek Life	B
Athletics	C+	Guys	A-
Campus Dining	C+	Health & Safety	A-
Campus Housing	B-	Local Atmosphere	B
Campus Strictness	B	Nightlife	A-
Computers	B	Off-Campus Dining	B-
Diversity	C+	Off-Campus Housing	B-
Drug Safety	C-	Parking	B-
Facilities	B-	Transportation	A
Girls	B+	Weather	C+

CP's Student Author On...
OVERALL EXPERIENCE

SUNY Fredonia becomes a second home to almost all of its students. Because the campus is relatively small, it is easy to develop close friendships with other students, which is extremely important when living away from home. If given the chance, many students would choose SUNY Fredonia again over any other school. It is rare for students to decide to leave the school because they did not like the atmosphere or the school. SUNY Fredonia is not just a place to meet lifelong friends, but it is also a place to develop as a person and discover what to do in life. This is where the school's professors come into play.

The professors at SUNY Fredonia genuinely want the students to succeed. Both the professors and the school make sure that students are prepared for their chosen career fields before they graduate. There are endless options to ensure that this happens, from internships to academic adviser guidance. It is unusual to hear pending graduates say that they feel unprepared for the real world.... For the rest of this editorial, visit collegeprowler. com.

Students Speak Out On...
OVERALL EXPERIENCE

Positive!

"There is so much to do within the campus community. There are clubs, intramural sports, places to hang out and many activities to keep you busy. I would never think of going to another school! There is so much green-space that makes the campus beautiful and the teachers really try and get to know you. So far my experience has been a very positive one that I believe will keep on building."

Best Four Years of My Life

"From the first day of freshman year to graduation weekend I was in love with Fredonia. I met some of the craziest and quirkiest people who became my amazing friends. One of my favorite things about Fredonia was the music scene. There was never any shortage of house shows or bar performances to attend, and it exposed me to a wide variety of musical talent. Fredonia is a friendly, creative school with plenty of opportunities to explore your talents and become involved."

BEST OF SUNY FREDONIA

1. The campus is just the right size, so it doesn't feel too small or too large.
2. Class sizes are small, so students get more one-on-one time with professors.

Happy Students
81% of students return after their first year.

Big Dorms
60% of students surveyed felt that dorms were more spacious than average.

WORST OF SUNY FREDONIA

1. The bookstore closes at 5 p.m. during the week and isn't open on the weekends.
2. The cost of meals/food is expensive without a meal plan.

Not Much Diversity
One of the least racially diverse campuses—only 9% of students are minorities.

Student Body

African American:	3%	Male Undergrads:	44%
Asian American:	1%	Female Undergrads:	56%
Hispanic:	3%	Living On Campus:	52%
International:	1%	Living Off Campus:	48%
Native American:	1%	Male Athletes:	10%
White:	91%	Female Athletes:	7%
Unknown:	0%	Fraternity Members:	3%
From Out-of-State:	4%	Sorority Members:	3%

Frequently Compared Schools:

State University of New York at Geneseo
State University of New York at Oswego
State University of New York College at Brockport
State University of New York College at Oneonta

Students Speak Out On... EVERYTHING!

ACADEMICS

English

"Wonderful faculty, very close. Of course every apple has its seeds. The program is challenging but do-able with a great honors program."

ATHLETICS

Sports

"I didn't play any sports at Fredonia. I know we have a really good hockey team, and the swimming and diving team does well. It would have been fun if we'd had a football team. I went to a few lacrosse practices but being involved in the theatre department it was hard to do both. Everyone was very welcoming on the team though."

Athletics

"I am not on any sport teams at SUNY Fredonia, but I have been on many intramural sports. They are a lot of fun and less competitive. There are a ton to chose from and it is so much fun. The fans of the sports teams on campus are awesome. We are pretty good at the Divison 3 sports."

Fun

"The hockey games were tons of fun to go to. The crowds really got into it."

CAMPUS DINING

Good Eats

"Cranston is always good, Erie is Ponderosa, and Willy C is good, but you need to mix it up a little. My only concern is nothing is open past midnight, something should be open as long as the library even if its just a coffee shop."

Food

"There are two buffet type dining halls at Fredonia and one that is like a food court. The meal plans seem to change every semester, but just try to figure out the best way to use it at the beginning of the semester so you aren't wasting all your extra dollars/points at the end. Cranston (the newest hall) is often busy all the time, and the food isn't as great as everybody

claims it is. Erie needs more of an overhaul to be great like it once was, and the newly renovated Willy C is decent now."

CAMPUS HOUSING

Dorming, What's to Say?

"The dorms aren't bad. Corridor style dorms are nicer than the suite style, but in the suites you become closer and better friends with the people you live with."

Upperclass Dorms Were Better, but Not That Different

"The dorms were fine, had to take a lot of effort to make them feel more like home than a small room. The suites offered more space and better access to a bathroom with more privacy. Housing selection was a pain."

GUYS & GIRLS

Girls and Guys

"The girl to guy ratio is that there are more girls than guys on campus. The looks at SUNY Fredonia are unique beacuse there are differnt types of people from all over the country and the world. We are a libral school and we are really into the arts. The social life is great."

Pretty Diverse

"Lots of hippies, preps, guido-ish, sports. Pretty much everyone drinks, obviously, greek life maybe a bit more than normal. Girls are generally all the same."

HEALTH & SAFETY

Feeling Safe on Campus

"I always feel safe on campus because the police are always around and the cars and building security is great. Also it's a small town and a college town so things run very safe."

Cat Beat It

"Security on campus is great, its strict in the areas it needs to be, but also lenient in other areas so that students can feel safe but not so much that they feel tense."

LOOKING FOR MORE?

Check out our full-length guide to this school at collegeprowler.com/state-university-of-new-york-at-fredonia/.

SUNY New Paltz

1 Hawk Drive; New Paltz, NY 12561
(845) 257-7869; www.newpaltz.edu

THE BASICS:

Acceptance Rate: 39%
Yield: 24%
Setting: Town
Control: Public
Total Undergrads: 6,516
SAT Range: 1550–1820*
ACT Range: 23–27

Student-Faculty Ratio: 15:1
Retention Rate: 88%
Graduation Rate: 69%
Tuition: $13,981
Room & Board: $9,202
Avg. Aid Package: $9,748
Students With Aid: 73%

*of 2400

Academics	B	Greek Life	B-
Athletics	C	Guys	A
Campus Dining	B	Health & Safety	A
Campus Housing	B+	Local Atmosphere	B+
Campus Strictness	B+	Nightlife	A
Computers	B+	Off-Campus Dining	A
Diversity	A-	Off-Campus Housing	B+
Drug Safety	C-	Parking	B
Facilities	B	Transportation	A-
Girls	B	Weather	B-

CP's Student Author On... OVERALL EXPERIENCE

When it comes to overall experience, the common phrase people say is, "I love New Paltz!" There is always something to do, whether it's on campus or in town. But you can't slack off and party all of the time; you really have to do your work. And the reverse goes for those students who do nothing but study: you have to enjoy the little things sometimes. Even when student schedules are pretty hectic, you should still make a point to sit down with friends for a meal every day. Many students find that their friends act more like family on campus. It's a new experience, living away from home, and it can be lonely, which is why it's important to have a support system.

They say college is the best four years of your life; when it comes to New Paltz, many students will agree with this statement. Despite the hardships students encounter, SUNY New Paltz can be an amazing experience if students let it! You'll meet a lot of great people, and you'll learn so much about life, yourself, and others.

Students Speak Out On... OVERALL EXPERIENCE

Q Big Fan

"i am a huge fan of new paltz. i couldn't see my self being at any other school. there are so many different breeds of people yet everyone gets along so well. love love love suny new paltz"

Q New Paltz Experience

"new paltz is really laid back and it doesnt really matter where you came from. a lot of the students are from the city but im from a really small town upstate. i feel like nobody cares that im not from the same place as them and dont have the same background. The experience you get from going to new paltz cannot be replicated anywhere else. the professors are awesome; i'm good friends with a few of my professors. they genuinely care about their students."

Q Experience

"new paltz is an extremely diverse place with tons of things to do"

BEST OF SUNY NEW PALTZ

1. Blue and Orange Weekend
2. The Career Resource Center
3. The eco-friendly environment
4. EOP advisers
5. The fashion shows

Happy Students
88% of students return after their first year.

Big Dorms
87% of students surveyed felt that dorms were more spacious than average.

WORST OF SUNY NEW PALTZ

1. Allergy season because of the trees all around
2. The bumblebees that surround the bridge when it's warm
3. The cold temperatures during the winter
4. The ducks

Expensive Dorms
Living on campus doesn't come cheap, with an average housing price tag of $6,020.

Student Body

African American:	5%	Male Undergrads:	34%
Asian American:	3%	Female Undergrads:	66%
Hispanic:	9%	Living On Campus:	45%
International:	7%	Living Off Campus:	55%
Native American:	0%	Male Athletes:	6%
White:	53%	Female Athletes:	4%
Unknown:	22%	Fraternity Members:	4%
From Out-of-State:	7%	Sorority Members:	3%

Frequently Compared Schools:

Binghamton University
State University of New York College at Oneonta
Stony Brook University
University at Albany

Students Speak Out On... EVERYTHING!

ACADEMICS

Q Fun but Tiring

"being an arts major is very time consuming, but i'm sure it's like that at any school. all of the students are also very friendly and help you with your projects. the workload is very large though"

Q History

"Many of the professors are hit or miss, but it's a matter of finding the good ones and sticking to them."

Q New Paltz Academia

"liberal arts, art, theatre, music, teaching"

ATHLETICS

Q Athletics

"The athletic facility at the school is excellent. although there are a fair amount of people involved in athletics school spirit for athletic events isn't very high."

Q The Gym Is Great

"Our fitness center is great. it is big and accomodating. It offers programs and classes and activities and does very well at advertising these things."

Q Not for Athletes

"SUNY New Paltz doesn't have a football time or a hockey team so there's not a lot of school spirit floating around. I don't think we're ranked very high at all."

CAMPUS DINING

Q Hazbrouck Dining Hall

"I love hazbrouck and have be going there for dinner everyday for the past 3 years. I love the options the friendly enviornment. It is clean and the food is always good."

Q Transfer Student

"I'm a transfer student. The only experience that i had with the cafeteria food was decent, no complaints."

CAMPUS HOUSING

Q All the Halls Are Great for Different Reasons.

"I live in Lenape Hall at SUNY New Paltz....it's a pretty long walk to get to anything on campus aside from the gym, but nothing insane. Lenape is one of two halls with air conditioning, and it's the only residence hall with private bathrooms, a major perk. Each hall has its own character and each hall is a great hall to live in for different reasons."

Q Best Dorms on Campus

"As long as you stay far away from college & shango hall your in the clear. They seem to have issues like running out of hot water. Crispell and Lenape are the nicest halls on campus."

GUYS & GIRLS

Q Description of New Paltz

"It doesn't seem like the students here are much into looks. It's a hippie town and a hippie school."

Q Guys and Girls

"The number of females outweighs the males. Students all seem interested in class discussions and presentations. This school has a laid back atmosphere where dress is casual. There are many social events and organizations that students can be a part of."

HEALTH & SAFETY

Q Very Safe

"New Paltz is a very save school. It has one of the lowest crime rates of any school. It has its own police who are very nice and helpful if you ever need anything. There's also escorts for people who do not want to walk alone at night."

Q Overdone

"Health and safety is something that the school does an amazing job on. Cops are everywhere on campus, you feel safe walking back at 2 or 3 am in the morning. Their are blue light booths everywhere in case your scared and escort services as well."

SUNY Oswego

7060 State Route 104; Oswego, NY 13126
(315) 312-2500; www.oswego.edu

THE BASICS:

Acceptance Rate: 47%
Yield: 28%
Setting: Town
Control: Public
Total Undergrads: 7,362
SAT Range: 1050–1190*
ACT Range: 21–25

Student-Faculty Ratio: 18:1
Retention Rate: 80%
Graduation Rate: 57%
Tuition: $14,056
Room & Board: $10,870
Avg. Aid Package: $10,744
Students With Aid: 87%

of 1600

Academics	C+	Greek Life	C+
Athletics	B-	Guys	B-
Campus Dining	B+	Health & Safety	C+
Campus Housing	C-	Local Atmosphere	B-
Campus Strictness	B+	Nightlife	B+
Computers	B-	Off-Campus Dining	C
Diversity	C	Off-Campus Housing	C+
Drug Safety	C-	Parking	B-
Facilities	C+	Transportation	B
Girls	C+	Weather	C+

CP's Student Author On...
OVERALL EXPERIENCE

SUNY Oswego truly prepares students for the real world through the countless opportunities offered to students, including travel and world exploration experiences. SUNY Oswego also encourages students to think critically about the world around them, through resources like the Global Living and Learning Center in Hart Hall. Through such programs, the University motivates students to learn the importance of making a difference in the world, as individuals helping out their local communities. This motivation is also instilled in students by the great faculty that makes up SUNY Oswego.

If students ever had to choose again, most would definitely choose SUNY Oswego a second time because the University is not only a beautiful campus, but also carries exceptional faculty mentors, never to be forgotten by students for the rest of their lives.

Students Speak Out On...
OVERALL EXPERIENCE

Q My Experience at Oswego

"I really love SUNY Oswego. I received my Bachelor's Degree here in May of 2009 and decided to saty to pursue a Master's Degree in School Counseling. The classes are great and informative and fun. The campus is safe and appealing and the lake is beautiful not to mention the awe-inspiring sunsets."

Q Really Solid Overall.

"A great well-rounded and diverse school, but you have to get out there yourself to get the most of what it has to offer. That's key. The faculty and courses are 8 for 10, in my opinion -- in terms of good classes and professors, combined. The lake is also so beautiful, and I feel lucky to be a student here."

BEST OF SUNY OSWEGO

1. The beautiful sunsets and lake
2. Campus Center
3. Friendly and helpful people
4. Study abroad program is excellent.
5. Internship and resume help

Happy Students
80% of students return after their first year.

Learn from the Best
88% of faculty have earned the highest degree in their field.

WORST OF SUNY OSWEGO

1. The weather can become a pain.
2. Cost
3. No late-night venues
4. Not a lot to do
5. Strict drinking rules
6. Parking

Expensive Dorms
Living on campus doesn't come cheap, with an average housing price tag of $6,890.

Don't Move Off Campus
Average off-campus housing is a steep $10,670.

Student Body

African American:	4%	Male Undergrads:	47%
Asian American:	2%	Female Undergrads:	53%
Hispanic:	4%	Living On Campus:	58%
International:	1%	Living Off Campus:	42%
Native American:	0%	Male Athletes:	9%
White:	89%	Female Athletes:	6%
Unknown:	0%	Fraternity Members:	7%
From Out-of-State:	3%	Sorority Members:	6%

Frequently Compared Schools:

State University of New York College at Buffalo
State University of New York College at Oneonta
University at Albany
University at Buffalo

Students Speak Out On...
EVERYTHING!

ACADEMICS

Q Psychology Major

"I really love my major. It keeps things interesting and the course load can vary. Depending on the classes you take each semester determines the level of difficulty. If you take a bunch of difficult courses in one semester you're going to drive yourself insane. Spread out the more difficult classes with a bunch of the easier required electives."

Q My Major

"To be an education major at my school is fairly new to me. I just recently switched majors from Business Administration to Adolescent Education. I still have courses that need to be fulfilled and learn more of the possible opportunities."

Q Depending on Professor

"Some professors do not know how to teach, if failing a class take it with another professor results are 10X better. Alot of major opportunities yet advisors may not explain all details, must find out on yourself. Class rooms aren't crowded which is great! With that said, workload depends on class level."

ATHLETICS

Q Athletics

"The only sport that is actually division 1 is hockey. When there is a hockey game everyone attends."

Q Hockey

"Hockey seems to be the big draw for students, faculty and the community."

CAMPUS DINING

Q Pretty Darn Good

"Each dining hall has its own "specialty" for example one dining hall will has an ice cream bar, another has a Chinese food bar etc. which is really nice. They consistently have two to three main menu choices which is good for picky eaters. They have a wonderful salad bar and they always offer soups of the day. For the price you pay, you get a lot of food and you are allowed to take two items to go. I'd say it's pretty good food."

Q Some Are Better Than Others

"Each dining all is a little different which is really nice to not have the same thing everytime."

CAMPUS HOUSING

Q Life on Campus

"There are a lot of fun things to do on campus. One of my favorite dorms is Funnelle Hall because of how it feels like you live in an apartment. I feel people are able to get to know each other a lot easier. The cost is great for me, since it is a state school and offers so much."

Q My Hall

"The dorms are a good size. awesome view. lots of friends. friendly."

GUYS & GIRLS

Q Venus & Mars

"The guys at my school mostly stick to themselves.THe girls are flirtatious"

Q Ehhh What Ever

"Most guys are douchbags, not that many "hot" girls....BUT i made amazing friends. Theres a type of person for everyone, so its very diverse. Its not great BUT not bad."

HEALTH & SAFETY

Q Police

"the police on campus are very present they see you all the time and you can do anything without them right around the corner. i had never had to call the police but i am sure if needed they would be there quick fast and in a hurry.. there is really not that much campus crimes but if there is they are tooken care of in the best mannor."

Q The Campus Is Safe.

"It's not that cops are everywhere and there are things of that nature, it's just the campus is safe. People are not very violent."

LOOKING FOR MORE?

Check out our full-length guide to this school at collegeprowler.com/state-university-of-new-york-at-oswego/.

Susquehanna University

514 University Ave.; Selinsgrove, PA 17870
(570) 374-0101; www.susqu.edu

THE BASICS:

Acceptance Rate: 73%
Yield: 28%
Setting: Town
Control: Private Non-Profit
Total Undergrads: 2,231
SAT Range: 1510–1810*
ACT Range: 23–28

Student-Faculty Ratio: 13:1
Retention Rate: 87%
Graduation Rate: 82%
Tuition: $32,450
Room & Board: $8,800
Avg. Aid Package: $17,336
Students With Aid: 96%

* of 2400

Academics	B	Greek Life	B-
Athletics	C+	Guys	A-
Campus Dining	B	Health & Safety	A
Campus Housing	B	Local Atmosphere	C+
Campus Strictness	C	Nightlife	C
Computers	B+	Off-Campus Dining	C+
Diversity	D	Off-Campus Housing	B-
Drug Safety	B-	Parking	A
Facilities	A	Transportation	D+
Girls	A-	Weather	C+

CP's Student Author On...
OVERALL EXPERIENCE

Susquehanna is an amazing place to go to school. While some people see it as their worst nightmare, for those who want a small liberal arts school, there aren't many better places to go than SU. The academics are impressive, the faculty is caring, and the atmosphere created by the students is amazing. A good motto for SU students is "work hard, play hard." Everyone is here to succeed, but having fun never hurt anyone. While there are always a couple of students who forsake the work part, the majority of campus has its priorities straight. It's easy to strike a balance between work and a social life.

While there are shortcomings on the SU campus, they pale in comparison to the positives. There are a lot of catch-22s. Campus security is really strict, but at the same time, the campus is incredibly safe. Professors live close so there are rarely snow days, yet they care deeply about their students and open up their homes to them. As already mentioned, if you are looking for a city atmosphere or a large campus, then SU would not be your ideal spot.... For the rest of this editorial, visit collegeprowler.com.

Students Speak Out On...
OVERALL EXPERIENCE

Q School or Fun?

"Your experience here in Susquehanna University really depends on why you are attending college in the first place. If you came to get a good education, then this place deserves an A. If you came to party and half fun, out of all seriousness, this place deserves a D. I gave it an A- because although I came for a good education, it can get really boring sometimes."

Q DONT GO HERE

"Do not go to the school. It is over priced, and in the middle of nowhere with nothing to do. If you have a social life and want a "college expirence" attend a different school. I only went here for a year and I am transfering out because i could not take it anymore. If you enjoy going to partys, drinking, look to join a frat, or having fun in general do not go here."

Q "I've loved my time at Susquehanna, but I also remember how it used to be before it got strict. I wouldn't change anything; I love my friends and the memories—but if I were applying to colleges now, I don't think I'd go here. The feeling I got when I walked on this campus three years ago is not the feeling that the campus gives off now."

BEST OF SUSQUEHANNA

1. Amazing relationships between faculty and students
2. Always seeing familiar faces
3. The variety of student organizations

Happy Students
87% of students return after their first year.

Proven Success
82% of students will complete their education and graduate with a degree.

WORST OF SUSQUEHANNA

1. Teachers all live close, so classes rarely get cancelled for snow
2. Crazy weather with lots of rain
3. No microwaves allowed in dorm rooms
4. Fire alarms at 2 a.m.

Expensive
Tuition is a steep $32,450, one of the most expensive rates in the country.

Not Much Diversity
One of the least racially diverse campuses—only 12% of students are minorities.

Student Body

African American:	3%	Male Undergrads:	45%
Asian American:	2%	Female Undergrads:	55%
Hispanic:	2%	Living On Campus:	74%
International:	1%	Living Off Campus:	26%
Native American:	0%	Male Athletes:	40%
White:	88%	Female Athletes:	23%
Unknown:	4%	Fraternity Members:	13%
From Out-of-State:	51%	Sorority Members:	20%

Students Speak Out On... EVERYTHING!

ACADEMICS

Q Interesting and Flexible

"The professors at Susquehanna University generally keep classes small and lively. They are always available and willing to help. Depending on your program, the coursework can be demanding. But I've had a class that I didn't find useful. Also, The registrar's office is incredibly flexible if you decide to change majors or minors. I know this having changed my own five times."

Q

"Classes are very relative. I find the classes that I like interesting whereas others are boring. I like science classes, so I find them interesting. I like most of the classes though."

ATHLETICS

Q Don't Pay Attention

"We have sports but I do not attend many of the sport stuff."

Q

"Varsity sports aren't a big deal on campus. They don't usually draw big crowds, except for football or soccer on the weekends. IM sports are very popular; most people play at least one IM sport. It's a lot of fun and a good way to meet people."

CAMPUS DINING

Q Lots of Variety, Not Much Change

"There are several places to eat on campus, and the offer a decent amount of variety. However, they don't change up the menu a lot, so you're liable to get tired of eating the same thing all the time. The food is decent. My favorite places on campus are Clyde's and Charlie's. Clyde's is out of the way, and keeps weird hours, but it serves really healthy food. Charlie's is the campus coffehouse, and is open in the evenings."

Q

"At first I did not think that the food at SU was very good. Anything compared to my mom's home cooking is, at best, mediocre. When I tasted food at other schools though, SU food seems amazing. For cafeteria food, SU's is definitely the best I've tasted."

Frequently Compared Schools:

Dickinson College
Gettysburg College
Muhlenberg College
Ursinus College

CAMPUS HOUSING

Q Close to Class

"All the dorms are pretty decent, but the best options are Seibert and West Village. They aren't available for freshmen, though, so a newcomer's best option is either Reed or Aikens. No matter which dorm you're in, it will never take you more that 15 minutes to get to class."

Q Conveinent Dorms

"Aikens hall is near the campus center which houses three food locations and a computer lab. Reed hall is close to the campus center and music building. Smith hall is near the gym. Hassinger hall is inbetween the gym and library, but the dorm rooms are the smallest. Seibert hall is closest to the science buildings. North hall is closest to the newest science building, but has thin walls."

GUYS & GIRLS

Q More Intellectual Place

"Most of the students want to learn but also enjoy meeting one another. We do a lot in study groups. The campus has lots of activities, so you really do not even need to leave campus. Girls are high class!"

Q SU Students - Go Crusaders!

"Both boys and girls are average looking. Most students are from Pennsylvania, New Jersey, or other nearby New England states and come from upper to middle-class families. Relationships come and go, but it all depends on what type of relationship you're looking for. Students range from wild party animals to studious nerds."

HEALTH & SAFETY

Q Pretty Safe

"I never get nervous walking though Susquehanna's Campus. It's quiet and safe, and public saftey keeps a fairly close eye on things. I recommend keeping your dorm room locked to protect your stuff, but on campus you never have to worry about someone taking your things."

LOOKING FOR MORE?

Check out our full-length guide to this school at collegeprowler.com/susquehanna-university/.

Swarthmore College

500 College Ave.; Swarthmore, PA 19081
(610) 328-8000; www.swarthmore.edu

THE BASICS:

Acceptance Rate: 17%
Yield: 41%
Setting: Suburban
Control: Private Non-Profit
Total Undergrads: 1,524
SAT Range: 2010–2290*
ACT Range: 30–33

Student-Faculty Ratio: 8:1
Retention Rate: 99%
Graduation Rate: 92%
Tuition: $39,260
Room & Board: $11,900
Avg. Aid Package: $36,571
Students With Aid: 63%

of 2400

Academics	A+	Greek Life	C
Athletics	C	Guys	A-
Campus Dining	B	Health & Safety	A+
Campus Housing	A-	Local Atmosphere	B
Campus Strictness	A+	Nightlife	C+
Computers	A-	Off-Campus Dining	C+
Diversity	A+	Off-Campus Housing	B+
Drug Safety	B-	Parking	B-
Facilities	A	Transportation	A-
Girls	B	Weather	B

CP's Student Author On...
OVERALL EXPERIENCE

Swarthmore is not for everyone. However, students who find their niche here are generally happy they came. So, what type of student is Swarthmore College suited for? Well, in the broadest sense, someone who is open-minded, ultra-liberal, and possesses a true passion for intellectual stimulation tends to thrive here. This leads to another important question that must be addressed. What type of student should stay away from Swarthmore? Anyone who considers their normality a personal virtue, conservatives (and most moderates, for that matter), reckless individuals who constantly choose their social lives over academics, students longing for a true big name/big game athletic experience, and anyone who doesn't care to make a difference in their (and others') lives probably won't feel as comfortable here.

With that being said, Swarthmore at its worst can make you feel claustrophobic, inept, apathetic, and extremely frustrated. You might even be tempted to heave your laptop out the window of the library at the height of finals week.... For the rest of this editorial, visit collegeprowler. com.

Students Speak Out On...
OVERALL EXPERIENCE

Q I Love Swat :)

"This place is great. I am loving my classes, my profs, my classmates, my roommate, my hallmates, and my teammates. You definitely need to work—a lot. Homework piles up fast, and papers and exams are always looming. If you let it build up you WILL struggle. But if you work hard, you play hard. Relaxing and partying and being social really make the experience great."

Q Very Unique Place

"It is a whole different world at Swarthmore. There are so many unique and intriguing people. The atmosphere is really welcoming, and I feel welcome here."

Q Great but Can Be Better!

"The academics and stuff are great here. But if the nightlife and party scene here can improve. It'd be perfect!"

BEST OF SWARTHMORE

1. Arboretum and a beautiful campus
2. Close-knit, family-like campus community
3. Free parties (free alcohol)
4. Administration and Public Policy officers are there to help you, not get you in trouble.

Happy Students
99% of students return after their first year.

Commitment to Teaching
There are 8 students for every member of faculty on campus.

WORST OF SWARTHMORE

1. The feeling of being drowned by the workload
2. No Wawa (the Philly area's most popular convenience store)
3. Lack of dining options (only one main dining hall)

Expensive
Tuition is a steep $39,260, one of the most expensive rates in the country.

Expensive Dorms
Living on campus doesn't come cheap, with an average housing price tag of $6,018.

Student Body

African American:	9%	Male Undergrads:	48%
Asian American:	17%	Female Undergrads:	52%
Hispanic:	11%	Living On Campus:	88%
International:	7%	Living Off Campus:	12%
Native American:	1%	Male Athletes:	30%
White:	44%	Female Athletes:	27%
Unknown:	12%	Fraternity Members:	13%
From Out-of-State:	89%	Sorority Members:	0%

Frequently Compared Schools:

Amherst College
Brown University
Haverford College
Williams College

Students Speak Out On...
EVERYTHING!

ACADEMICS

Q Excellent Academics

"The unique and incredible academic experience had at Swarthmore is unmatched in any other liberal arts school in the country and focuses a lot more on personalized results and attention than at Ivy leagues and other similar schools. Not only is the academic curriculum at the school unparalleled, its top-notch facilities and professors strive to keep the atmosphere at its best."

Q Very Demanding and Engaging

"The professors are awesome and sometimes they expect a whole lot from you. This can be overwhelming, but most Swarthmore students enjoy it because that is the reason we applied in the first place. It is a common occurrence to correct textbook solutions and answers during problem sessions. Professors do not strictly abide by their office hours because they are available even outside these hours. In all, Swarthmore is a perfect setting for the academically inclined mind."

ATHLETICS

Q Swat Sports Are Pretty Good

"Swarthmore isn't a big school, and the focus is on academics. But we still find time for the fun of sports. Unfortunately, Swarthmore discontinued football about 10 years ago. I would have really loved to have that part of the college experience. But the student body attends other sporting events (for free!), and soccer games are particularly crowded. As an athlete myself, I find the facilities to be pretty good; not world-class but more than sufficient."

Q Sports Are Underappreciated but Still Good

"Playing lacrosse, it sometimes feels as if the students on campus don't appreciate the sports teams. The administration, on the other hand, always tries to provide the sports teams with the very best."

CAMPUS DINING

Q Outdated Infrastructure but Quality Food

"The infrastructure of the main dining hall is old and thus can only go so far, but what they produce is better than you would expect from such an old facility. Other dining options are available at the coffee bars, and as long as you plan right, you can eat your fill and it's all relatively healthy and tasty, compared to other college dining halls. The meal plan is expensive but flexible and includes money to spend at any school food place."

Q Good Ideas, Decent Execution

"The menus are planned out well, but it seems like the cooks can't execute the food really well. There are some good days though, and the salad bar/deli is always a good go-to option."

CAMPUS HOUSING

Q Housing Is Above Average

"I'm satisfied with the dorm I live in but am apprehensive about where I might live next year. Many sophomores tend to be housed off campus, which may be inconvenient in terms of what is accessible."

Q Not Bad

"There are a variety of dorm options. The only campus housing that I would utterly despise is ML. It's just not my type and too far from campus, but some people love it. I live in Willets this year and I actually like it a lot, though it gets a bad rap from the rest of campus."

GUYS & GIRLS

Q Everyone Is Special

"From an academic's perspective, the variety here is great. The student pool is so diverse in background and interests, and there are so many unique personalities that you're bound to find someone who's right for you, guy or girl. Most students, both girls and guys, aren't particularly high-maintenance, but beauty is in the eye of the beholder."

HEALTH & SAFETY

Q Health and Safety

"I doubt any campus is safer than Swat's."

LOOKING FOR MORE?

Check out our full-length guide to this school at collegeprowler.com/swarthmore-college/.

Syracuse University

700 University Ave.; Syracuse, NY 13244
(315) 443-1870; syr.edu

THE BASICS:

Acceptance Rate: 60%
Yield: 26%
Setting: Mid-sized city
Control: Private Non-Profit
Total Undergrads: 13,736
SAT Range: 1570–1900*
ACT Range: 23–28

Student-Faculty Ratio: 15:1
Retention Rate: 91%
Graduation Rate: 80%
Tuition: $34,926
Room & Board: $12,374
Avg. Aid Package: $24,710
Students With Aid: 79%

* of 2400

Academics	B+	Greek Life	A-
Athletics	A+	Guys	B+
Campus Dining	C+	Health & Safety	C+
Campus Housing	C+	Local Atmosphere	B-
Campus Strictness	B	Nightlife	A-
Computers	B+	Off-Campus Dining	B
Diversity	B	Off-Campus Housing	B
Drug Safety	C-	Parking	B-
Facilities	B	Transportation	B+
Girls	B-	Weather	D+

CP's Student Author On...
OVERALL EXPERIENCE

SU has a laundry list of good qualities about it and very few flaws. The main thing to remember is that SU and its students refuse to be pigeonholed. There are so many varying interests at Syracuse University, as well as a broad array of extracurricular activities. People can't even agree on what major is the most prestigious (although many claim communications or architecture). Still, although there is a broad range of people at SU, there usually is a consensus on one thing: people at Syracuse University really like it. Sure, there are different reasons, but almost everyone who spends a few years at SU enjoys it.

Some like the choices in classes, while others like the prominent sports teams on campus. Some like the appeal of a real college campus in the middle of a big city. No one comes for the weather. And besides the few reasons a student will specifically seek out Syracuse University, there are a broad number of factors that keep students here. The on-campus and off-campus housing is excellent, the computer facilities are top-notch, and the nightlife can be a major draw.... For the rest of this editorial, visit collegeprowler.com.

Students Speak Out On...
OVERALL EXPERIENCE

Q It's a Great Place to Study

"Syracuse is really great. I mean you don't really have any issues -the campus is really relaxing and there aren't that many distractions around. You are able focus on your academic studies and you don't usually get involved in anything unless you want to."

Q I Love It

"I love Syracuse University. I've made so many awesome friends and it's a totally different experience than when I grew up. There's something here for everyone and the one thing everyone has in common is orange pride!"

Q I Would Choose This School All Over Again

"I love the atmosphere of Syracuse. I like the fact that I have so much freedom here."

Q It's Been Cool

"It's been alright. I met great inspiring and talented people, friends as well as proffesionals. Classes are interesting and sometimes a bit challenging."

BEST OF SYRACUSE

1. Midnights on Marshall Street
2. Kimmel Food Court at 2 a.m. on a Saturday night
3. SU's nine prestigious undergrad colleges
4. The national championship-winning basketball team

Happy Students
91% of students return after their first year.

Proven Success
80% of students will complete their education and graduate with a degree.

WORST OF SYRACUSE

1. Windy afternoons on Marshall Street
2. Dining hall food
3. Teaching assistants who barely speak English, and part-time professors who don't like their jobs
4. The very average football team

Expensive
Tuition is a steep $34,926, one of the most expensive rates in the country.

Student Body

African American:	5%	Male Undergrads:	43%
Asian American:	6%	Female Undergrads:	57%
Hispanic:	5%	Living On Campus:	75%
International:	3%	Living Off Campus:	25%
Native American:	1%	Male Athletes:	8%
White:	40%	Female Athletes:	5%
Unknown:	39%	Fraternity Members:	18%
From Out-of-State:	57%	Sorority Members:	21%

Students Speak Out On... EVERYTHING!

ACADEMICS

Awesome Archi. Program

"Architecture at Syracuse University is awesome and challenging. Your classmates will become your closest friends."

Varies

"It has many great programs with high standing such as Whitman school of Business, School of Visual and Performing Arts, and Newhouse. The coursework depends on your major. ITstudents have it easy while design students barely sleep. But the people who have graduated from some of the schools are working for top cooperations so the hard work is worth it. Tutoring is available as well as academic counselors."

ATHLETICS

Excellent School Spirit, Facilities

"Very competitive but also provides many additional sports clubs and organization"

Wild Cuse Spirit

"Sports are big big big big big here. Even if you're not a big sports fan, it's hard not to feel at least a little proud of our school :)"

CAMPUS DINING

Supercard Money

"SUpercard money is part of meal plans offered here that offer a unique opportunity to use this money on your id card to buy snacks and meals at various on campus dining centers and vending machines"

Where to Eat

"The Food is healthy for the most part and depending on which dining hall you go to, there's a lot of variety. But in the big dining halls such as Ernie, there's so many people to feed that they don't really take care in cooking the food and stuff ends up lukewarm at times. Shaw is a good dining hall though, it's smaller and with a good variety, they take care with the food there too."

Frequently Compared Schools:

Boston University
New York University
Northeastern University
Penn State

CAMPUS HOUSING

Flint Hall Was the Best

"As an Acting major I had the option of living in a Learning Community floor, but I chose not to and to just live in a regular coed Hall. My floor had a variety of different people with different interests and hobbies and meant more networking for me. This will definitely benefit me as an aspiring actor looking for his next producer or one who remembers his friend who lived right next door to Spielberg."

Campus Housing

"The dorms at Syracuse University are pretty nice. Some dorms location aren't as good as others but overall the dorms are very social and quite expensive. There are quite a few dorms with laundry rooms on floors, TVs, a small gym, and small shopping store."

GUYS & GIRLS

Diverse Guys and Girls from Different Ethnicities Who Are Very Friendly

"In Syracuse University, there are a vast majority of guys from all backgrounds. There are the shy ones, funny outgoing ones, sweet ones, and the studs. The girls are very pretty and come from different places also such as from New York all the way from Texas. The international students are also very nice and interesting in the way they dress. Most of the people wear Syracuse gear and people are overall friendly and easy to talk to."

HEALTH & SAFETY

Syracuse University Safety

"On campus, I have never felt that my security was in any way at risk. There are public safety officers around campus, and at night, you can even get a public safety escort home if you feel unsafe. The only real crimes I've been aware of recently have been thefts, which could have been prevented by locking doors or by traveling in groups."

LOOKING FOR MORE?

Check out our full-length guide to this school at collegeprowler.com/syracuse-university/.

Taylor University

236 W. Reade Ave.; Upland, IN 46989
(765) 998-2751; www.taylor.edu

THE BASICS:

Acceptance Rate: 83%
Yield: 30%
Setting: Town
Control: Private Non-Profit
Total Undergrads: 2,436
SAT Range: 1500–1910*
ACT Range: 24–31

Student-Faculty Ratio: 13:1
Retention Rate: 85%
Graduation Rate: 78%
Tuition: $25,396
Room & Board: $6,708
Avg. Aid Package: $18,002
Students With Aid: 93%

* of 2400

Academics	B+	Greek Life	N/A
Athletics	B-	Guys	A
Campus Dining	C+	Health & Safety	A-
Campus Housing	A-	Local Atmosphere	B-
Campus Strictness	C+	Nightlife	D+
Computers	B-	Off-Campus Dining	C-
Diversity	C+	Off-Campus Housing	B+
Drug Safety	A+	Parking	A+
Facilities	B-	Transportation	C+
Girls	A	Weather	B

CP's Student Author On...
OVERALL EXPERIENCE

"It takes a village to raise a child," quotes an ancient African proverb. This old cliché closely describes the overall student experience at Taylor University. As one retired professor commented, "students come to Taylor as kids and leave Taylor as adults." While this process happens at most universities, nowhere can students find a group of scholars, faculty, and staff more willing to invest in one another than at Taylor University. Taylor's mission statement incorporates three basic principles: intentional community, global engagement, and the integration of faith and learning. The goal of Taylor is not to produce successful students who can accomplish the American dream, but rather to mold holistic people who can be successful for the Kingdom of God.

According to president emeritus and advocate of Taylor, Jay Kesler, in his 25 years of being connected to Taylor, he has only heard one student give a negative review of his or her overall experience. Of 75 Taylor students polled, 100% said that if they had to reapply for college all over again, they would still pick Taylor University.... For the rest of this editorial, visit collegeprowler.com.

Students Speak Out On...
OVERALL EXPERIENCE

Q "Community"

"Taylor is renowned for its campus community, and after four years, I couldn't agree more. The residence life program is fantastic, and the hall directors really care about the people in their residence halls. Professors are personable and highly qualified. If I could do college over again, I would pick Taylor University."

Q Love It Here!

"I absolutely love it here at Taylor! It has such an open and friendly atmosphere and there is a genuine passion for Christ on campus. I would highly recommend the university to anybody considering coming here!"

Q I LOVE THIS PLACE!!!!!!!!!!!!!!!

"Professors are fun, amiable, and available to help. Girls and guys alike are more often than not the friendliest you'll meet. And the campus is gorgeous. Sure, the programs can be rigorous, but it's totally worth coming!"

BEST OF TAYLOR

1. The people are extremely friendly.
2. Integration of faith and learning is what Taylor's all about.
3. Chapel
4. Good relationships with professors

Happy Students
85% of students return after their first year.

Proven Success
78% of students will complete their education and graduate with a degree.

WORST OF TAYLOR

1. No dancing allowed!
2. Upland is in the middle of nowhere—except for cornfields, that is.
3. The weather—it's so unpredictable.
4. High tuition and board costs

Life is NOT a Party
92% of students surveyed said it's almost impossible to find a good party.

Not Much Diversity
One of the least racially diverse campuses—only 9% of students are minorities.

Student Body

African American:	2%	Male Undergrads:	45%
Asian American:	3%	Female Undergrads:	55%
Hispanic:	2%	Living On Campus:	39%
International:	2%	Living Off Campus:	61%
Native American:	0%	Male Athletes:	22%
White:	91%	Female Athletes:	10%
Unknown:	0%	Fraternity Members:	0%
From Out-of-State:	67%	Sorority Members:	0%

Frequently Compared Schools:

Ball State University
Cedarville University
Indiana University
Wheaton College - Illinois

Students Speak Out On... EVERYTHING!

ACADEMICS

The best in the midwest

"The academics here at Taylor are the best in the midwest. Period. Students will get a quality well-rounded education unrivaled in the U.S."

The academics are top of the line

"The academics are top of the line here at Taylor. One couldn't ask for a better school."

Professors are great

"professors are great."

ATHLETICS

Lots of people attend the sporting events

"Taylor athletics are good. Lots of people attend the sporting events, including people from the Upland community. Sports are important and fun for the school but not focused on too much. They have a perfect balance."

Fantastic Sports

"School Spirit is great at Taylor and and the teams are good too. Athletic facilities are constantly being updated and anyone can use them, even if you don't participate in a sport."

Athletics are on the up side

"Athletics are on the up side. The football, soccer and basketball teams are all exciting to watch. Many students attend as many games as they can"

CAMPUS DINING

Yum Yum Yum!!

"Taylor's Dining Commons is diversified and delicious!! They have different bars that are always there but with different options everyday (such as mexican, italian, american, etc.) and great desserts too! Healthy, wholesome food is easy to find as well as sweets :)"

Food in DC

"The food here at Taylor is average: just as good as at any school. The variety is great though."

CAMPUS HOUSING

Why My Dorm Is the Best.

"Living in English was the best choice for me because it is an all girl dorm, you can study here and also hang out with the sisters here. There is a great sense of community in this dorm and girls really care about you. Other girls dorms are hard to study in which is not right for me. Mixed gender dorms are not right for me either because i like to have privacy and time away from boys. However, it is nice to see boys on the weekends in their gender specific dorms."

On Campus Living

"THe dorms are great. plenty of community and everyone is very loving"

GUYS & GIRLS

Guys and Girls at Taylor

"Taylor has lots of quality people that are very friendly. On average they come from upper middle class families from the midwest. It's a very fit campus with lots of attractive individuals (especially for the small number of students even on campus)."

Chivalrous Men

"While this can't be applied to 100% of situtions, it is generally true that men at Taylor practice chivalry. Doors are opened for me all around campus. It's really great to live in a place where you can find some really sweet guys."

HEALTH & SAFETY

Safety

"One is very safe on Taylor's campus"

You are always safe

"There is no problem with lack of security at Taylor. You are always safe"

LOOKING FOR MORE?

Check out our full-length guide to this school at collegeprowler.com/taylor-university/.

Temple University

1801 N. Broad St.; Philadelphia, PA 19122
(215) 204-7000; www.temple.edu

THE BASICS:

Acceptance Rate: 61%
Yield: 37%
Setting: Large city
Control: Public
Total Undergrads: 26,618
SAT Range: 1500–1810*
ACT Range: 21–26

Student-Faculty Ratio: 16:1
Retention Rate: 88%
Graduation Rate: 62%
Tuition: $21,634
Room & Board: $9,198
Avg. Aid Package: $13,961
Students With Aid: 85%

* of 2400

Academics	B-	Greek Life	C+
Athletics	B-	Guys	B+
Campus Dining	B	Health & Safety	C+
Campus Housing	B-	Local Atmosphere	B+
Campus Strictness	B-	Nightlife	A-
Computers	A-	Off-Campus Dining	C+
Diversity	B+	Off-Campus Housing	B-
Drug Safety	C-	Parking	B-
Facilities	B+	Transportation	A-
Girls	B	Weather	B-

CP's Student Author On...
OVERALL EXPERIENCE

Overall, Temple has its ups and it has its downs, but students seem to love it all the same. On the downside, there can be some head-butts with tyrannical teachers, unfriendly cafeteria workers, and the always-frustrating financial aid office. Housing can cause an enormous hassle, and those commuting have to battle with parking or public transportation. Some people don't feel as though they are prepared for the real world once they leave campus, but others say it's been an incredible learning experience. Those students that love their experience at Temple all have their own reasons. Some love the atmosphere and found it to be a lot of fun. Others found it to be a great place to grow up and discover themselves. Lots of students take away more from living in a big city than they do from the University. But one thing it seems most all students agree upon is that the people at Temple University are what really make it a worthwhile experience.

In general, students coming into Temple have big expectations from both the school and the city.... For the rest of this editorial, visit collegeprowler.com.

Students Speak Out On...
OVERALL EXPERIENCE

Q Experience Unavailible Anywhere Elsee
"Temple is the real world not a bad imitation of it. Its fun, a good learning environment, and a great place to be."

Q Temple Pride!
"I bleed cherry and white! I love everything about Temple: basketball games, parties, classes; it's all just great! If you're looking for a great time, in a big city, where you'll NEVER be bored...COME to TU!"

Q Overall Review of Temple
"I believe temple is the college of my dreams. The pre-professional programs are well set-up, the campus is very fun and vibrant, and it's my number one choice."

Q Its a Great Place
"Temple is a great place to attend. i love the social and academic life. A business school that caters to the needs of the business students."

BEST OF TEMPLE

1. Diversity
2. Bar on campus
3. Spring Fling/ Homecoming
4. Aeropostle box sales
5. Choice between city campus and suburban campus

Happy Students
88% of students return after their first year.

Knowledgeable Professors
92% of students surveyed rated the general knowledge of professors as above average.

WORST OF TEMPLE

1. Staff attitudes
2. Not enough computers
3. Financial aid office screwing you over
4. Teachers screwing you over
5. Malls are far away

Expensive Dorms
Living on campus doesn't come cheap, with an average housing price tag of $6,126.

Don't Move Off Campus
Average off-campus housing is a steep $10,100.

Student Body

African American:	17%	Male Undergrads:	46%
Asian American:	10%	Female Undergrads:	54%
Hispanic:	4%	Living On Campus:	20%
International:	3%	Living Off Campus:	80%
Native American:	0%	Male Athletes:	4%
White:	57%	Female Athletes:	3%
Unknown:	9%	Fraternity Members:	1%
From Out-of-State:	25%	Sorority Members:	1%

Frequently Compared Schools:
Drexel University
Penn State
University of Pennsylvania
University of Pittsburgh

Students Speak Out On... EVERYTHING!

ACADEMICS

Q Academic Offered
"Excellent school wonderful reputation for its wide variety of academics offered"

Q Study Areas
"Temple University's study areas are extremely peaceful and quiet at all times. If you want to get some studying or reviewing done between classes you are able to do so anywhere on campus. There are also many places you could go whether it is the library, computer labs, or simply outside on the grass for example."

ATHLETICS

Q Sports Are Awesome!
"The different sports teams at Temple University are great. The sporting events are fun to attend and the teams are very good. There are many events where students can meet the athletes and can have a great time with all the different sports."

Q T for Temple U!
"Temple is a very big sports school. There are many things to be involved in and many sports to go watch. There are also many sports clubs you can be a part of. I have gone to football and basketball games at Temple. The atmosphere is unreal when you are there. The fans are very supportive towards the athletes and the school"

CAMPUS DINING

Q Diamond Dollars
"Temple's dining plans includes a $150 charge for 150 Diamond Dollars. Diamond dollars is money in an account and can be used to buy food at area restaurant, books, clothes in the clothing store, electronics at the local Radio Shack and other items."

Q Campus Foods
"There are lots of places to find food on campus and as a college student that is extremely useful."

CAMPUS HOUSING

Q Freshman Dorms Are Not Good but Everything Else Is Great
"The freshman dorms are not the best but the upperclassman housing is better containing a kitchen and more space."

Q Campus Housing Isn't So Bad.
"The Freshmen dorms are generally pretty small, but livable. Most of them are doubles although many athletes and honors students live in suites. Upperclassmen housing is better and apartment style, but are a little bit further away on the edges of campus."

GUYS & GIRLS

Q Diversity Galore!
"Temple is probably known for one of the most diverse student body in the world. There are literally so many different people from different backgrounds, ethnicities, cultures, and even countries, that you could not possibly describe them all. Of course with such diversity you'll get a lot of cute guys and pretty girls, but also a lot of guys and girl who aren't as nice to look at. Most everyone has a great personality, though, once you get to talk to them."

Q Diversity
"this is a very diverse campus and people have an array of styles; a lot of artsy people as well as athletic people mixed into one crowd"

HEALTH & SAFETY

Q On Campus Your Are Safe Without a Doubt
"Being about as bright as times square at night with cameras everywhere definitely deters crime. Campus is safe."

LOOKING FOR MORE?
Check out our full-length guide to this school at collegeprowler.com/temple-university/.

Tennessee State University

3500 John Merritt Blvd.; Nashville, TN 37209
(615) 963-5111; www.tnstate.edu

THE BASICS:

Acceptance Rate: 65%	Student-Faculty Ratio: 16:1
Yield: 43%	Retention Rate: 67%
Setting: Large city	Graduation Rate: 36%
Control: Public	Tuition: $17,342
Total Undergrads: 6,827	Room & Board: $8,790
SAT Range: 1163–1463*	Avg. Aid Package: $7,546
ACT Range: 16–20	Students With Aid: 97%

* of 2400

Academics	B-	Greek Life	B
Athletics	B-	Guys	B
Campus Dining	C	Health & Safety	C+
Campus Housing	C	Local Atmosphere	B+
Campus Strictness	B-	Nightlife	A-
Computers	C	Off-Campus Dining	B+
Diversity	C	Off-Campus Housing	A-
Drug Safety	B+	Parking	C+
Facilities	B	Transportation	B+
Girls	A-	Weather	B

CP's Student Author On...
OVERALL EXPERIENCE

Students at TSU seem to be happy with their experiences thus far. The school has its issues, such as parking and problems with administration, but on the whole, students feel it is a good school and they have no regrets. The University's motto is "Students Matter Most," and they truly try to aid students in any way they can. The teachers are excellent; although some could be a little more outgoing, the majority really tries to help students to get the education they are paying for. There is a good balance between academics and socializing as well, and TSU students know when to party and when to study. There are a few exceptions, but most students do not allow their social lives to interfere with their grades because their education is important to them. However, students are not afraid to blow off class for the fall and winter breaks to go home early, and they are not shy about heading out early on a Friday for a Tigers road game! There are a few improvements that could be made such as parking, registration, and some building renovations, but most of TSU's drawbacks are related to the same problems the city itself has.... For the rest of this editorial, visit collegeprowler.com.

Students Speak Out On...
OVERALL EXPERIENCE

Q Great Experienced Instructors
"I have had great teachers that can explain the work well and open for discussion when I have needed help. They seem to be dedicated and like their jobs."

Q Caution
"Tennessee State University has an open acceptance policy. This means that if you apply, you get in. This also means that if a student couldn't get in anywhere else, this is where they end up. It is most visible in the faculty attitude. Of course, not all instructors act like they hate their job, but enough of them do that there are very few students that respect the staff. If there were another engineering program in the area I would leave this school in an instant. Unfortunately there is not."

Q Wouldn't Chose My School Again
"My experience overall is just not what I expected or worth the amount of money paid in out of state expenses."

Q "I like my school, but I wish we could pick it up and put it in downtown Nashville. I wish we were around more things like Vandy. (I kind of want to go to Vandy.)"

BEST OF TENNESSEE STATE

1. The Band
2. The Parties
3. Football games
4. The Food
5. The Campus
6. The Greek Parties
7. The Courtyard
8. The coffee shop

Help to Succeed
The school has academic and career counseling available to help you when you need it.

WORST OF TENNESSEE STATE

1. Parking
2. Financial aid
3. Crime
4. The lack of school spirit at football games
5. The football team losses
6. The STD rumors
7. The locals

Not Everyone Graduates
36% of students do not complete their education or graduate with a degree.

Student Body

African American:	79%	Male Undergrads:	37%
Asian American:	1%	Female Undergrads:	63%
Hispanic:	1%	Living On Campus:	34%
International:	0%	Living Off Campus:	66%
Native American:	0%	Male Athletes:	8%
White:	17%	Female Athletes:	2%
Unknown:	1%	Fraternity Members:	12%
From Out-of-State:	33%	Sorority Members:	12%

Frequently Compared Schools:

Howard University
Middle Tennessee State University
University of Tennessee
Vanderbilt University

Students Speak Out On...
EVERYTHING!

ACADEMICS

Q Faculty That Care

"I came to Tennessee State University because it is an accredited institution and has the necessary tools that I need to become successful in my field of study, which is Business. The faculty and staff care a great deal about the students and will work day and night to help students with whatever they need assistance with."

Q Opportunities

"The workload is level out to your schulde, also internship/job are avaiable for you."

Q Workload

"The workload is spaced enough that it does not become over whellming, but should be alittle more engaging"

ATHLETICS

Q Tn State Athletes

"Sports at tennessee state is very active on and off the field/court. all the athletes are very friendly"

Q Most Students Can't Get Information.

"Students don't know where to get information on althletics. Tsu does not try to give it out."

Q

"Sports are pretty decent as far as being made a big deal of, but the Aristocrat of Bands (the marching band) is where it's at. They get down!"

CAMPUS DINING

Q Food and Dining Options on Campus

"The places are good around campus. Easy to find locations. Great location and area. Great atmoshere."

Q DINING

"The dining hall on campus, is pretty good the works make sure you get what yo ask for, but i personally do not eat on campus. But i see classmates eating and it looks and smells really good. It is very loud, but i guess its not bad if you do not have anywhere to go."

CAMPUS HOUSING

Q Campus Life

"The campus life at Tennessee State University is very fulfilling! There is a high rate of student involvement not only with other students, but faculty as well. Whether students are in the student center, library, or even just hanging around outside, students are very cohesive. Tennessee State University has the best school pride and spirit."

Q The Library Is the Biggest Building.

"Most of the new students can't find their classrooms. The library helps them to find out where they are."

GUYS & GIRLS

Q Student Body

"One of the characteristics I like best about TSU is the freedom of expression. You dont have to dress a certain way or drive a certian car to be sccepted."

Q There Are Many Varieties of Guys and Girls.

"An extremely positive quality that Tennessee State University has, is that its filled with a diverse group of guys and girls. students come from all over the nation to attend TSU; you'll encounter many different ethnicities, styles, and personlities to go along with such great people."

HEALTH & SAFETY

Q Secure Security

"Tennessee State's campus is a homely campus. Never have I felt out of place or unsecure inside their grounds. The campus police are always doing their jobs and always on the scence if something even small is going on."

Q Problems at Health Center

"The health center at Tennessee State University could use some more improvement. Sometimes there is only one nurse working with patients. There should be more nurses treating patients. Also, they do not work up to speed and sometimes have students miss class and other activities."

LOOKING FOR MORE?

Check out our full-length guide to this school at collegeprowler.com/tennessee-state-university/.

Texas A&M International University

5201 University Blvd.; Laredo, TX 78041
(956) 326-2001; www.tamiu.edu

THE BASICS:

Acceptance Rate: 53%	Student-Faculty Ratio: 21:1
Yield: 40%	Retention Rate: 63%
Setting: Rural	Graduation Rate: 40%
Control: Public	Tuition: $11,387
Total Undergrads: 5,315	Room & Board: $6,918
SAT Range: 1220–1480*	Avg. Aid Package: $5,062
ACT Range: 15–20	Students With Aid: 96%

* of 2400

Academics	C	Greek Life	C+
Athletics	C+	Guys	B
Campus Dining	C+	Health & Safety	B
Campus Housing	B+	Local Atmosphere	C-
Campus Strictness	B	Nightlife	C+
Computers	B	Off-Campus Dining	C
Diversity	C	Off-Campus Housing	C+
Drug Safety	C	Parking	B-
Facilities	C+	Transportation	B-
Girls	B-	Weather	B-

CP's Student Author On...
OVERALL EXPERIENCE

Texas A&M International University is a young, vibrant school that is still growing. However, the majority of current students will probably tell you that TAMIU doesn't necessarily provide them with the complete college experience because there is little social unity on campus and a lack of school spirit. But, on the upside, the University is still in the process of constructing efficient buildings and obtaining up-to-date equipment for educational purposes. While students may seem a bit disappointed with the lack of activities around campus, the school is still relatively new, is starting to show signs of growth, and has enormous potential. Right now, most students tend to do their own thing around campus, as opposed to spreading social unity. While it is true that the city of Laredo is not the most enjoyable atmosphere for students, the University's academics more than make up for this.

The overall experience at TAMIU could be improved if organizations did a better job promoting the University and if TAMIU organized pep rallies to bring some school spirit back on campus.... For the rest of this editorial, visit collegeprowler.com.

Students Speak Out On...
OVERALL EXPERIENCE

Q Love It!

"It's so sophisticated here. There's good food, nice people, and the professors are great. There's awesome parties, and you get a great education, as well."

Q Fun

"I love TAMIU. The variety of people here is awesome, and the landscape and wildlife on campus make it fun to be around."

Q Good School

"It is not the traditional university, but it is always fun if you find your way in. The teachers are nice, but you might have trouble understanding all their different accents."

Q Good Campus for Those Who Want to Mind Their Own Business.

"It is a small and good campus; however, it has a lot of features typical of Laredo's society: isolated, close minded, conservative. It is not a bad place to concentrate on your studies, but you'll sacrifice a decent social life here at Laredo in exchange for a better education."

BEST OF TEXAS A&M INTERNATIONAL

1. Everyone on campus is friendly.
2. Diversity
3. The campus is well-kept, green, and up-to-date.
4. The cost
5. Rec Center

Affordable
Tuition is only $11,387, one of the most affordable rates in the country.

Big Dorms
86% of students surveyed felt that dorms were more spacious than average.

WORST OF TEXAS A&M INTERNATIONAL

1. Financial aid confusion
2. Lack of adequate parking
3. Parking
4. Skunks that come out late at night
5. The professor (sometimes)
6. Lack of computer labs
7. Lack of school spirit

Life is NOT a Party
58% of students surveyed said it's almost impossible to find a good party.

Student Body

African American:	1%	Male Undergrads:	39%
Asian American:	1%	Female Undergrads:	61%
Hispanic:	92%	Living On Campus:	12%
International:	3%	Living Off Campus:	88%
Native American:	0%	Male Athletes:	9%
White:	2%	Female Athletes:	4%
Unknown:	0%	Fraternity Members:	1%
From Out-of-State:	2%	Sorority Members:	1%

Students Speak Out On...
EVERYTHING!

ACADEMICS

Q Major: Biology. Minor: Creative Writing

"The biology curriculum is not something too hard for me; however, at moments, it does get difficult because I am a creative writing minor, and I am constantly switching from being very artistic to being very technical. The only reason I am a bio major is to learn and apply as much as I can to my fiction writings. Overall, I enjoy biology but I am not interested in job opportunities or internships because my goal is to get a PhD in Creative Writing."

Q TAMIU

"At TAMIU, the academic support is endless. The professors, with the exception of a few, are always willing to provide help to those who need it. The classes are not large in number, and the upside is that the professors get to provide those who need extra examples during class the help they need. There is an academic relationship that can be developed with professors here."

ATHLETICS

Q Athletes

"At TAMIU, the athletes (from what I can see) are very outgoing people and are always involved with the school. They are the first to volunteer and the last to leave."

Q A for Athletics

"Texas A&M International University has an outstanding gym facility and trainers, great coaches, and dedicated athletics. The fields for the sports are always clean and ready for any game."

CAMPUS DINING

Q Not Much Variety of Food on Campus

"On campus, there is only a diner, a pizzeria, and a Subway where one can go and have lunch after class. However, most of the students that attend this university live at home, so it isn't a complete and total necessity."

Frequently Compared Schools:

Baylor University
Texas Tech University
University of Texas
University of Texas at Dallas

Q Average Dining

"There is not much of a variety of food's to choose from; nevertheless, the food that is avaiable is pretty good, such as Subway and the Pizza diner."

CAMPUS HOUSING

Q The Dorm's Are Just Right.

"The dorms are not small but average. The privacy is great and but it's a good walk from the campus."

Q Could Be Better

"The dorms are usually good, but the classrooms seem to be a little outdated."

GUYS & GIRLS

Q Girls Are Friendly

"I have found every girl that I've met to be really easy to get along with. You find girls from a lot of places."

Q Campus Life

"The students are friendly, and it's usually easy to start a conversation with a stranger. TAMIU is diverse as far as the people that attend. Most are Hispanic and have the ghetto look in Laredo, but on campus there's a little of everything."

HEALTH & SAFETY

Q Safe!

"Campus safety is excellent at TAMIU. I have never felt unsafe, even in the late hours of the night. Campus PD is always on the lookout, and they are always kind enough to escort you to your car, help you change a flat tire, and many other things. There is wildlife, such as deers and skunks, roaming around campus. But, this isn't something to be worried about. Accidents with the wildlife are not common."

Q Safety Is a Concern

"At TAMIU, safety is of utmost importance. Campus police is always available and can be found monitoring the parking lots. I've never witnessed any crime take place on campus, and I've never felt as safe as I do when I'm at TAMIU."

LOOKING FOR MORE?

Check out our full-length guide to this school at collegeprowler.com/texas-a-and-m-international-university/.

Texas A&M University

401 Joe Routt Blvd.; College Station, TX 77843
(979) 845-3211; www.tamu.edu

THE BASICS:

Acceptance Rate: 67%
Yield: 53%
Setting: Small city
Control: Public
Total Undergrads: 38,958
SAT Range: 1580–1910*
ACT Range: 24–30

Student-Faculty Ratio: 19:1
Retention Rate: 93%
Graduation Rate: 78%
Tuition: $22,606
Room & Board: $8,039
Avg. Aid Package: $14,665
Students With Aid: 75%

* of 2400

Academics	B	Greek Life	B
Athletics	A	Guys	A+
Campus Dining	B+	Health & Safety	B-
Campus Housing	B-	Local Atmosphere	B+
Campus Strictness	B-	Nightlife	A-
Computers	A-	Off-Campus Dining	B+
Diversity	C+	Off-Campus Housing	A
Drug Safety	B-	Parking	B-
Facilities	A-	Transportation	A-
Girls	A+	Weather	B+

CP's Student Author On...
OVERALL EXPERIENCE

Most students either love or hate A&M, and those who hate it usually transfer out their first year. A&M offers an incredible educational and life experience that most students thoroughly enjoy. If you have a problem with life at A&M, it's most likely because you haven't found a niche and you still feel lost in the crowd. At a school this big, it's not hard to feel as though you've vanished. It can be difficult to find people with common interests that you really click with, but if you get involved in student organizations and your classes, you'll figure it out. It can be intimidating at first, but don't give up. Going away to college is a big change, and it can take a while to get adjusted and find your place, no matter what kind of person you are.

Aggies have an overwhelming pride in their school, and the age-old traditions can seem annoying to a new student who has never been a part of them. However, the consistency of the traditions that carry over from year to year offers a timeless experience that you can share with any other A&M grad.... For the rest of this editorial, visit collegeprowler. com.

Students Speak Out On...
OVERALL EXPERIENCE

Q Traditions

"Texas A&M University is a very special place in which traditions are very much alive all throughout the school. There is not a day that goes by in which a tradition is not met. I love all the traditions that A&M has, many of them help you to be more active with the school."

Q Traditions Are Amazing

"This campus has the best traditions and they are used widely throughout the campus. The best times are at the football games."

Q Wonderful Experience

"Overall, Texas A&M provides a great college experience. Get involved! We have a huge selection of student organizations, so there is something for everyone. The traditions are so interesting and provide us all with a way to bond with each other, as well as the thousands of Aggies before us. Great university. Thanks and Gig 'Em!"

BEST OF TEXAS A&M

1. Traditions
2. Unity
3. Chivalry
4. Respect for history
5. Freebirds
6. Northgate
7. Football
8. School spirit

Happy Students
93% of students return after their first year.

Proven Success
78% of students will complete their education and graduate with a degree.

WORST OF TEXAS A&M

1. Parking
2. Transportation officers
3. Standing up for the entire football game
4. Getting towed during football games
5. Alumni are treated better than current students.

Lowest Grades
Diversity: C+
Health & Safety: B-
Drug Safety: B-

Student Body

African American:	3%	Male Undergrads:	52%
Asian American:	5%	Female Undergrads:	48%
Hispanic:	14%	Living On Campus:	24%
International:	2%	Living Off Campus:	76%
Native American:	1%	Male Athletes:	2%
White:	76%	Female Athletes:	2%
Unknown:	0%	Fraternity Members:	5%
From Out-of-State:	4%	Sorority Members:	12%

Frequently Compared Schools:
Baylor University
Texas Christian University
Texas Tech University
University of Texas

Students Speak Out On... EVERYTHING!

ACADEMICS

Education Is Excellent

"I came to Texas A&M University as a transfer student during my undergrad and fit right in. This University is one of the most welcoming universities I visited and its education is awesome. I have learned an incredible amount of knowledge and love this place so much that I am now pursuing my master's."

Major

"Well, I absolutely love my major! My program requires 125 hours to graduate—35 hours of psychology classes, and the rest is basics, which a lot of them you can take at a community college. The workload is okay; it requires a lot of reading though. There are many internship and study abroad opportunities. The advisors are really helpful."

ATHLETICS

We May Not Always Win, but We Have the Best Time at Games!

"Texas A&M football is not the best in the country, but it certainly is the most fun to watch! The spirit and traditions present at not only football games but all other athletic games is unbelievable. One of the most amazing aspects of Texas A&M athletics is the great support that the student community shows for the athletics. Whether we lose or win, we all have a wonderful time watching our team play and cheering them on. There's no doubt that our fans are the best in the country!"

Spirit of Texas a&M

"The spirit that Texas A&M University possesses cannot be matched with any other school. We say that looking in, you can't understand it but form the inside looking out, you can't explain it. Once you are an aggie, you are always an aggie and the brotherhood that comes with being a committed student to Texas A&M never ends. The students and alumni support every sporting event the school holds with whole hearts."

CAMPUS DINING

The food is really good

"The food is really good for on campus and since it's on Northside if the food gets boring you can just walk across the street to get Freebirds, Potbelly, Sushi, pizza, and countless other things."

Sbisa

"The best places to eat on campus include Sbisa and the Ag Cafe. Sbisa is the university's biggest dining hall and includes buffet-style dining. No matter if it is breakfast time or dinner time, the cafeteria is always full of variety and options. The Ag Cafe offers several different types of food including Chick-fil-A, Which Which and a Tomato Bar Express. So, no matter what you're in the mood for, they have you covered."

CAMPUS HOUSING

Very Community-Oriented

"As a student living on the north side of campus, it's a very refreshing to have a nice community atmosphere. The only thing I really don't care for is the pervasiveness of the tradition here. It sometimes seems like you can't walk around a corner without having to yell some weird collection "whoops" or "hey!" While that can be good for some people, it's not the ideal environment."

A&M

"Everything you could need is on campus. It is great."

GUYS & GIRLS

Students

"Guys here are super hot. :)"

Unique people who go here

"The people who go here are so nice and considerate. I had a fear that they would be overbearing and stubborn to any opposing beliefs but if you take the time to talk to any one, they're willing to listen."

HEALTH & SAFETY

Health and Safety

"It is very safe. You are provided with a 24 hour escort whenever needed."

LOOKING FOR MORE?
Check out our full-length guide to this school at collegeprowler.com/texas-a-and-m-university/.

Texas Christian University

2800 S. University Drive; Fort Worth, TX 76129
(817) 257-7000; www.tcu.edu

THE BASICS:

Acceptance Rate: 59%	**Student-Faculty Ratio:** 13:1
Yield: 26%	**Retention Rate:** 86%
Setting: Large city	**Graduation Rate:** 69%
Control: Private Non-Profit	**Tuition:** $28,298
Total Undergrads: 7,640	**Room & Board:** $9,810
SAT Range: 1570–1910*	**Avg. Aid Package:** $19,570
ACT Range: 23–28	**Students With Aid:** 77%

* of 2400

Academics	B	Greek Life	A
Athletics	B	Guys	B+
Campus Dining	B	Health & Safety	B
Campus Housing	A-	Local Atmosphere	A
Campus Strictness	B+	Nightlife	A-
Computers	B	Off-Campus Dining	B+
Diversity	C+	Off-Campus Housing	A
Drug Safety	C-	Parking	C+
Facilities	A	Transportation	B
Girls	B	Weather	B+

CP's Student Author On...
OVERALL EXPERIENCE

Most students at TCU are pleased with their education and the opportunities presented to them. While diversity continues to be an issue on campus, strong academics, good facilities, and countless organizations play a larger role in student life. To most students, TCU offers a strong academic foundation in a lively setting. Fort Worth and Dallas provide endless entertainment, while campus police and Froggie Five-O do their best to protect and serve the students on TCU's campus. Students have a wide variety of living options, providing them with a great environment while earning their educations.

Don't be fooled by the name: TCU isn't a stuffy church school. It's a place where students are encouraged to try new things and branch out. A few numerous organizations—Greek ones in particular—tend to discriminate between social groups, but the overall student body is quite friendly. Academically, students are eager to learn, and a small student-faculty ratio allows students to interact closely with each of their professors.... For the rest of this editorial, visit collegeprowler.com.

Students Speak Out On...
OVERALL EXPERIENCE

Q Overall Great

"I've loved my time at TCU and I don't think I would have had such a great experience anywhere else. People can say what they wanted but I've had an amazing college experience and I wouldn't trade it for the world"

Q TCU is Awesome

"I love the atmosphere. It is small but in a great part of Texas. It is very nice, and the people are friendly. there are plenty of parties and plenty of people to hang around if you chose not to. Football games are fun and our team is awesome! There are so many opportunities."

Q School

"i love TCU. i've never been so happy in all my life. i love all of the opportunities we have at school. every friday night is movie night in the Bluu and a bunch of my friends get together for a free movie. Last week was The Social Network. I love it. The food is amazing. i just wish i had applied sooner so that i could obtain more scholarships my school is extremely expensive."

BEST OF TEXAS CHRISTIAN

1. The teachers
2. Nice city, close to Dallas and a major airport
3. Small classes
4. Good facilities
5. Clean campus
6. Friendly people
7. Modern technology

Happy Students
86% of students return after their first year.

Big Dorms
75% of students surveyed felt that dorms were more spacious than average.

WORST OF TEXAS CHRISTIAN

1. No parking
2. High tuition
3. Lack of diversity
4. Emphasis on athletics instead of academics
5. Everything (food, printing) is expensive

Expensive
Tuition is a steep $28,298, one of the most expensive rates in the country.

Expensive Dorms
Living on campus doesn't come cheap, with an average housing price tag of $6,180.

Student Body

African American:	5%	Male Undergrads:	41%
Asian American:	3%	Female Undergrads:	59%
Hispanic:	8%	Living On Campus:	46%
International:	5%	Living Off Campus:	54%
Native American:	1%	Male Athletes:	10%
White:	74%	Female Athletes:	4%
Unknown:	4%	Fraternity Members:	37%
From Out-of-State:	31%	Sorority Members:	39%

Frequently Compared Schools:

Baylor University
Southern Methodist University
Texas A&M University
University of Texas

Students Speak Out On... EVERYTHING!

ACADEMICS

Q Academics at TCU

"The class sizes are all relatively small, even for the general classes ie english, history etc. The classes are all taught by professors that seem to have a vested interest in having the students succeed. The classes are challenging but there is ample opportunity to meet with the professor outside of the classroom to get additional help when needed."

Q Great Education

"Strong accounting program. Excellent placement. Multiple opportunities for internships."

ATHLETICS

Q TCU Sports and School Spirit

"From volleyball games to intramural flag football games, there is a tremendous amount of pride and sportsmanship for each game. As a student-athlete, I signed a contract to always have good sportsmanship. Our workout facilities and trainers are awesome and we are always in shape, not to mention the thousands of fans that are at each game."

Q The Athletics

"Great facilities. Excellent fan base and fan support. Quality training. Excellent team performance."

CAMPUS DINING

Q Food Is Great

"There are so many things to choose from, you can't get tired of it. The lounges are especially made so that you can eat and study any hours of the day or to just chill with your friends."

Q Food Is Good

"there is a variety of food in the dining hall. the dining hall also has healthy food choices."

CAMPUS HOUSING

Q Honors Dorm Is Awesome

"The Milton Daniel Honors dorm is newly renovated and quite arguably the best lower classmen dorms on campus. Staff is

nice and the atmosphere is conducive to both studying and socializing."

Q All Newly Redone

"every residence hall has been redone within the last 10 years and they are very nice. Average size and great community feel"

GUYS & GIRLS

Q Pretty Even and Diverse

"There are high standards of what the school allows but it is very diverse."

Q Pretty goodlooking

"The girls are really attractive for the most part, usually the goodlooking girls are in sororities though. The guys are not bad. Most dress alike (southern preppy/fratty). There seems to be a lot of hooking up if you're involved in the party/Greek scene. If you go out and are decent looking, you definitely don't have to go home alone."

HEALTH & SAFETY

Q Campus is safe

"I personally have never felt unsafe. They have had a couple of problems but what college campus doesnt? Froggie Five-0 gives rides to girls anywhere on campus after dark so they dont have to walk by themselves."

Q Pretty Safe Except at Night

"I feel overall really safe when i am on campus, except at night i think the school could use more lightning. Cops are everywhere to be seen there is always one when you need one."

LOOKING FOR MORE?

Check out our full-length guide to this school at collegeprowler.com/texas-christian-university/.

Texas Lutheran University

1000 W. Court St.; Seguin, TX 78155
(830) 372-8000; www.tlu.edu

THE BASICS:

Acceptance Rate: 66%
Yield: 49%
Setting: Small city
Control: Private Non-Profit
Total Undergrads: 1,387
SAT Range: 1320–1650*
ACT Range: 18–23

Student-Faculty Ratio: 14:1
Retention Rate: 67%
Graduation Rate: 52%
Tuition: $21,910
Room & Board: $7,100
Avg. Aid Package: $19,049
Students With Aid: 91%

* of 2400

This School Isn't Graded Yet!

College Prowler grades are calculated using tons of criteria, including survey responses that come from students at this school.

Unfortunately, we haven't gathered enough student surveys yet for this school to be able to calculate the grades for each section. Stay tuned to *CollegeProwler.com* for grade updates and more!

CP's Student Author On...
OVERALL EXPERIENCE

Most people who first look at this small school have doubts about its overall size. But it is not about the buildings or the square footage of campus that's important: it's the people. TLU's slogan is, "Small Classes, Big Difference." This is very true. Students have a lot of interaction with professors, and the one-on-one attention is key. Getting to know professors helps light a fire for many students because they want to be the best they can be for the professors. Many students say that TLU helped them realize what they're interested in, what they enjoy learning, and what they want to do with their life. As a small private school, TLU doesn't have the same bells and whistles as a lot of large, state-funded schools, but TLU has an atmosphere that makes students feel right at home.

This is a small school, so if you come in with the wrong attitude, you will obviously leave with one. With a positive attitude, most students leave with a solid educational foundation and a solid social circle.... For the rest of this editorial, visit collegeprowler.com.

Students Speak Out On...
OVERALL EXPERIENCE

Q Amazing Expereince

"Great place to go to school, great academics, people, everything. I would never go anywhere else."

Q AWESOME

"When I first came to TLU, I underestimated it because it was a very small school. Little did I know, the small classes made a huge difference. Also, one is able to connect so much easier with other people versus at a big school. I loved my freshman year, and I'm looking forward to next year."

BEST OF TEXAS LUTHERAN

1. Close to San Antonio and Austin
2. Great professors who want students to succeed
3. Lots to do on campus
4. Parking isn't a problem.
5. Small campus

Genders Equally Represented
A male-to-female ratio of 50/50 means there's a pretty even balance of students on campus.

WORST OF TEXAS LUTHERAN

1. Not a big sports scene
2. Not many public transportation options around town or campus
3. Off-campus housing is inconvenient.
4. Restrictions on parties thrown by social groups (Greek life)

Student Body

African American:	10%	Male Undergrads:	49%
Asian American:	1%	Female Undergrads:	51%
Hispanic:	20%	Living On Campus:	62%
International:	1%	Living Off Campus:	38%
Native American:	0%	Male Athletes:	34%
White:	64%	Female Athletes:	15%
Unknown:	3%	Fraternity Members:	30%
From Out-of-State:	3%	Sorority Members:	54%

Frequently Compared Schools:

Abilene Christian University
Angelo State University
Baylor University
Southern Methodist University

Students Speak Out On... EVERYTHING!

ACADEMICS

Awesome Professors That Will Help You Anytime

"All the professors really know there information in the business department, and they are very willing to help you with concepts you don't understand in class and with career advice. Their doors are almost always open for students to drop by who have any questions. The program is top notch, and although the workload can get intense at times they do a very good job of preparing you for your future."

Changes That Are Happening

"When I came to TLU I thought that it was going to be a great experience. Socially it has been a great experience but academically there have been changes that many students don't agree with. With changes in faculty, cutting back in different majors and minors, and also the lack of improvement with the apartments as well as many students complaining about the campus."

ATHLETICS

On the Rise

"TLU isn't really known for having great athletic programs. However, this past year has been amazing for a couple of the athletic teams. The women's basketball team made history, and the track team won the district tournament. We are a small school, on the rise to becoming great."

TLU Athletics

"The school athletics vary in performance with the baseball team being exceptional and the football team having a losing record of 0-11. The teams don't have separate workout facilities and instead share with the general school population. the student body does a good job of supporting the football, men's basketball and baseball teams but the rest of the teams aren't equally supported."

CAMPUS DINING

Good Food at TLU

"There is a good variety of food choices at the dining hall and Lucky's Kennel. Many of the meals in the dining hall are chicken based though."

CAMPUS HOUSING

When It Rains...

"I find it incredibly ridiculous that the campus has not adapted to the innovation of the storm drain. While I know it has only been 4,000 years since the creation, still."

GUYS & GIRLS

Very Friendly and Personable Campus

"On campus generally everyone knows each other, and everyone is very helpful. There is a lot of variety of people on campus since its a liberal arts college, so generally anyone can find a group where they will fit in."

HEALTH & SAFETY

Safetown

"It's a nice campus not too big, small classes open area, and 24 hour police rounds. I do believe there has not been an act of violence in over a decade on campus."

Needs Light

"The Campus has a low crime rate, however its location in the town of Seguin is not so safe. The lack of sufficient lighting makes me nervous to walk alone at night."

LOOKING FOR MORE?

Check out our full-length guide to this school at collegeprowler.com/texas-lutheran-university/.

Texas State University - San Marcos

601 University Dr.; San Marcos, TX 78666
(512) 245-2111; www.txstate.edu

THE BASICS:

Acceptance Rate: 76%
Yield: 40%
Setting: Town
Control: Public
Total Undergrads: 26,011
SAT Range: 1430–1710*
ACT Range: 21–25

Student-Faculty Ratio: 20:1
Retention Rate: 79%
Graduation Rate: 54%
Tuition: $12,816
Room & Board: $7,310
Avg. Aid Package: $14,974
Students With Aid: 71%

* of 2400

Academics	B-	Greek Life	B-
Athletics	B-	Guys	A+
Campus Dining	B	Health & Safety	B+
Campus Housing	B-	Local Atmosphere	B+
Campus Strictness	B	Nightlife	A-
Computers	A	Off-Campus Dining	B
Diversity	B	Off-Campus Housing	A-
Drug Safety	C	Parking	C+
Facilities	A-	Transportation	A-
Girls	A	Weather	A-

CP's Student Author On...
OVERALL EXPERIENCE

Texas State is such a friendly, open, accepting university. It's not a super huge college, so the people aren't stuck-up or cocky like you might find at bigger universities. It's very relaxed on campus, and there's a very chill atmosphere surrounding the city of San Marcos, as well. You can feel at home at Texas State, and you'll be surprised to find how easy it is to make friends.

Texas State is superb in making sure its students are offered the opportunities they need to gain skills that will make them the most competitive in their field. Being a smaller university makes it even easier for academic advisers and professors to take the extra time to talk to students one-on-one about their future career paths. The professors and advisers are always eager to help.

Students Speak Out On...
OVERALL EXPERIENCE

Q **Texas State University - San Marcos: Overall Experience**

"My overall experience here at Texas State University in San Marcos has been amazing! I have really fallen in love with not only the campus, but the town of San Marcos. This is a place where you can be yourself and find great friends. It is an amazing school."

Q **Awesome**

"Texas State is amazing. I love it and wouldn't change my experience so far at all."

Q **I Would Chose Texas State Everytime!**

"Texas state is the best school. I have loved every minute of this place. I would make the choice over again to come here. I hear it every time, "the party" school but thats not true. This is a great place you just have to keep your priorties intact."

BEST OF TEXAS STATE

1. Beautiful scenery/the river
2. Diversity
3. Friendly people
4. Great professors/ strong academics
5. Nightlife
6. San Marcos community
7. School spirit

Affordable
Tuition is only $12,816, one of the most affordable rates in the country.

WORST OF TEXAS STATE

1. Availability of some classes
2. Lots of stairs on campus
3. Parking
4. Reinstitution of Friday classes
5. Smokers are everywhere.

Lowest Grades
Drug Safety: C
Parking: C+
Greek Life: B-

Student Body

African American:	6%	Male Undergrads:	45%
Asian American:	2%	Female Undergrads:	55%
Hispanic:	24%	Living On Campus:	24%
International:	1%	Living Off Campus:	76%
Native American:	1%	Male Athletes:	3%
White:	67%	Female Athletes:	1%
Unknown:	1%	Fraternity Members:	5%
From Out-of-State:	2%	Sorority Members:	5%

Students Speak Out On...
EVERYTHING!

ACADEMICS

Q Education Program

"I came to Texas State because they one of the best education programs in Texas. Texas State was once a school for just education students. The teachers are very knowledgeable, and are willing to help whenever possible."

Q Wonderful

"The Texas State University theatre department is, by far, one of the best departments I have had the pleasure of working with. The professors are fantastically talented and helpful, always looking to better the experience and polish the talents of the student."

ATHLETICS

Q School Spirit

"The main reason I selected texas state. Go bobcats!"

Q Tons of Team Spirit!

"Everyone wears Texas State t-shirts and is proud of it."

CAMPUS DINING

Q Awesome Dining Facilities

"The dining halls all have awesome food and the facilities are beautiful. There is also fast food options on campus that you can use your meal plan for."

Q Great

"The restaurants around campus are great! The Bobcat Bucks are able to be used at a majority of them which is also a plus. The dining options between classes are also beneficial because there are an array of choices. I don't normally buy a large meal plan because I prefer to cook at home so I am glad that they offer commuter meals for those students who are not living on campus but need a quick bite to eat in between classes."

Frequently Compared Schools:

Texas A&M University
Texas Tech University
University of North Texas
University of Texas

CAMPUS HOUSING

Q Restaurants/Square

"I really enjoy the new restaurant Chimeys. It is a great place to go before going out to the square."

Q Texas State

"Dorm life isn't bad. You get sick of eating dining hall food all of the time but when you go home you appreciate home cooked meals more!"

GUYS & GIRLS

Q Students at San Marcos Are Awesome

"There is a great variety of people attending this university. There are people from all over the world who are very interesting and have a lot to offer"

Q Diversity Is Everywhere

"We have a huge diversity of both males and females here. Most of the ladies are very attractive even though some are preppy and others are more conservative. Most males are in very good shape. Males are more diverse than women when it comes to their outfits. There are some who dress as thugs, some in suits, while others don't appear to care about how they dress."

HEALTH & SAFETY

Q Nothing to Worry About

"I have never felt unsafe walking around campus, I used to walk home to my dorm from all the way across campus at 2am and never had any problems. There are a lot of police that run around San Marcos and their favorite thing to do is break up parties or catch speeders on Aquarena Springs. Be warned, during the summer most of the city leaves so they are super bored and their numbers seem to double."

Q Personal Safety

"I have never felt unsafe on campus at Texas State. The campus security has always been timely when handling matters. The campus is well lit and has always felt safe to me."

LOOKING FOR MORE?

Check out our full-length guide to this school at collegeprowler.com/texas-state-university----san-marcos/.

Texas Tech University

2500 Broadway Ave.; Lubbock, TX 79409
(806) 742-2011; www.ttu.edu

THE BASICS:

Acceptance Rate: 68%
Yield: 41%
Setting: Mid-sized city
Control: Public
Total Undergrads: 24,236
SAT Range: 1460–1770*
ACT Range: 21–26

Student-Faculty Ratio: 22:1
Retention Rate: 81%
Graduation Rate: 57%
Tuition: $12,858
Room & Board: $7,688
Avg. Aid Package: $7,424
Students With Aid: 73%

* of 2400

Academics	B-	Greek Life	B
Athletics	A	Guys	A-
Campus Dining	A-	Health & Safety	B
Campus Housing	B+	Local Atmosphere	B+
Campus Strictness	B-	Nightlife	A
Computers	A-	Off-Campus Dining	B+
Diversity	C	Off-Campus Housing	A-
Drug Safety	C	Parking	B+
Facilities	A	Transportation	A+
Girls	B+	Weather	A-

CP's Student Author On...
OVERALL EXPERIENCE

The reviews of Tech from outsiders looking in are usually mixed or negative. It's stereotyped as a party school in the middle of nowhere, where going to class takes a backseat to having a beer. Although Thursday nights are big in Lubbock, students who attend Tech get not only a great education but a chance to explore who they are and what they are good at in a laid-back environment. Texas Tech has it all, or all you need anyway. Whether you want to load each semester with 18 hours and be done a semester early, or you choose to take a fifth-year victory lap, Tech is as challenging as each individual wants to make it. Four years will fly by, and students who leave with only a head full of facts have only taken in a small percentage of what Tech has to offer. Even though Lubbock may not be huge, the network of people it brings together is. The relationships built in Lubbock while studying for finals or just hanging out easily transfer to post-college life. More importantly, these relationships make the time you spend in college unforgettable and irreplaceable.

A major aspect of any college experience is road trips…. For the rest of this editorial, visit collegeprowler.com.

Students Speak Out On...
OVERALL EXPERIENCE

Q I LOVE Texas Tech

"No matter what you're involved in or what your interests are, there's always a place for you to fit in. Everyone is friendly and most people just want to have a good time while furthering their education."

Q Love It Here

"Campus is beautiful; great for biking, running and the rec center is great."

Q WHAT a GREAT PLACE TO BE

"I LOVE LUBBOCK AND I LOVE TEXAS TECH! THERE IS NO BETTER PLACE TO BE. IM FROM EAST TEXAS. HERE BETTER WEATHER AND BETTER PEOPLE"

Q I Chose Texas Tech

"I am planning on being a health care professional. Most people who want to be doctors go to Baylor if they got accepted, which I did, but I chose Tech. The campus is all in one spot and it's beautiful and administration is always willing o help. I love Lubbock and I love the students. Texas Tech has helped me learn how to do what I need to do to reach my goals as easily as possible. I wouldn't go anywhere else."

BEST OF TEXAS TECH

1. The people
2. The facilities
3. Sunny days
4. Freshman year
5. The attractive campus
6. Arbor Day
7. Game Day
8. Greek life

Affordable
Tuition is only $12,858, one of the most affordable rates in the country.

Happy Students
81% of students return after their first year.

WORST OF TEXAS TECH

1. Traveling to Tech (the Highway 84 stretch)
2. Walking to class during wind and dust storms
3. Parking
4. Unruly fans
5. Campus's proximity to cattle slaughterhouses

Lowest Grades
Diversity: C
Drug Safety: C
Campus Strictness: B-

Student Body

African American:	4%	Male Undergrads:	56%
Asian American:	3%	Female Undergrads:	44%
Hispanic:	14%	Living On Campus:	24%
International:	1%	Living Off Campus:	76%
Native American:	1%	Male Athletes:	3%
White:	76%	Female Athletes:	2%
Unknown:	1%	Fraternity Members:	14%
From Out-of-State:	5%	Sorority Members:	18%

Frequently Compared Schools:

Texas A&M University
Texas Christian University
University of Oklahoma
University of Texas

Students Speak Out On...
EVERYTHING!

ACADEMICS

Q Texas Tech Business School Is Really Exciting

"The Texas Tech business program is both exciting and demanding. I have spoken with several professionals in the field and they concur that a degree from Texas Tech is coveted. I feel that I am accomplishing my goals and hope to ensure a successful future for myself."

Q Texas Tech

"Texas Tech has a wide range of subjects in their curriculum. Students choose one college within the university to be in depending on the major of their choice. There are many very interesting classes. A lot are very difficult and need determination and great study habits to make an A in them, but there are some classes, depending on dept. that have very easy classes. The one downfall is the math department where almost every professor is foreign and you can't understand them."

ATHLETICS

Q Everybody Is a Fan.

"One of the best parts of attending Texas Tech University is the not only school spirit but complete town spirit for varsity sports."

Q Fan Support/School Spirit

"As Red raiders, we value and respect our athletic teams and the hard work the athletes, sponsors, and supporters put in each and everyday. For that reason, our campus is incredibly dedicated and makes sure to attend as many games as they can. We paint up, get loud and crazy and always support them no matter what the score is."

CAMPUS DINING

Q Dining at Texas Tech

"There are several different dining halls at all of the dorms, and they all serve very good food. The only problem I ever had is that I started to get pretty tired of the food they served near the end of the year; however you are going to get that at any college where you live on campus. The best place on campus to get food would be in The Market in between the Stangel and Murdough dorms."

Q Good Variety

"Food and dining plans at Texas Tech are very flexible and easily accessible. There are options on campus for almost type of food."

CAMPUS HOUSING

Q My Life in the Dorms

"I love it! It is great as a freshman to know how great it is to live somewhere else besides your parents home. Great life experience and all you have to do is get involved and be part of your school to enjoy your life in the dorms. Everything has been positive."

Q Mediocre Food With a Hospitable Atmosphere

"The staff on campus are great they come to fix your problems with no grumbling and complaining like most other apartments. They also always have a smile one. The food is pretty average as far as it goes but it is edible. The upperclassmen dorms are nice because you can use as much air conditioning and electricity as you want without having to pay over for it."

GUYS & GIRLS

Q Classy

"Almost everyone is very pretty! The guys and girls alike dress in a preppy type style. However, everyone is accepted! The social life is great and many people have relationships. It is just a classy school environment!"

HEALTH & SAFETY

Q Safety First

"Tech is a very safe school. there are emergency phones located all over campus. Campus police are always on duty to make sure everything is running smoothly. Alcohol is not allowed on campus. Twenty mph Speed limits are strictly enforced upon cars and bikers. Those of us who walk to class never have to worry about getting run over."

LOOKING FOR MORE?

Check out our full-length guide to this school at collegeprowler.com/texas-tech-university/.

Thomas College

180 W. River Road; Waterville, ME 04901
(207) 859-1111; www.thomas.edu

THE BASICS:

Acceptance Rate: 82%
Yield: 40%
Setting: Rural
Control: Private Non-Profit
Total Undergrads: 814
SAT Range: 1270–1490*
ACT Range: 15–19

Student-Faculty Ratio: 20:1
Retention Rate: 66%
Graduation Rate: 51%
Tuition: $20,440
Room & Board: $8,410
Avg. Aid Package: $18,009
Students With Aid: 98%

of 2400

This School Isn't Graded Yet!

College Prowler grades are calculated using tons of criteria, including survey responses that come from students at this school.

Unfortunately, we haven't gathered enough student surveys yet for this school to be able to calculate the grades for each section. Stay tuned to *CollegeProwler.com* for grade updates and more!

CP's Student Author On...
OVERALL EXPERIENCE

Thomas College has a very warm atmosphere with friendly faces and someone always there to help. It is a small campus with numerous resources, and it does not take long to get to know the faculty and staff. Students here are treated with respect, and you will learn all you need to in order to start a successful career. Thomas students grow and learn every day, and the importance of building a professional attitude is a big focus. The greatest part about the College is its size—you can easily get involved, professors know you by name, and you are not just a number in a classroom. The classes are also small, with an average of 20 students or less. This is a popular reason why students choose Thomas College.

Everyone is here to help at Thomas. Starting as early as Orientation, first-year students will see first-hand how helpful and enthusiastic everyone is in the Thomas community. It is very easy to stay busy on campus, as well. There are multiple organizations and clubs that meet weekly with a focus on making the Thomas community a better place for all.... For the rest of this editorial, visit collegeprowler.com.

Students Speak Out On...
OVERALL EXPERIENCE

Q **Suitable**

"Thomas is a good place to settle into your education and get a start on your career. It's not the best place for the other aspects of college, i.e. drinking, partying, etc."

Q **Thomas Overall**

"Athletics definitely run this school, as well as drinking at night and on weekends. If I had to do it again, I think I would choose a bigger city over the school because there would be more things to do off campus."

BEST OF THOMAS

1. Professors
2. Campus is small and walkable.
3. Class sizes
4. Clubs and organizations
5. Free printing on campus
6. Lots of different events and activities on campus

Genders Equally Represented
A male-to-female ratio of 51/49 means there's a pretty even balance of students on campus.

WORST OF THOMAS

1. Food
2. Cafeteria hours
3. Sometimes there's not enough to do.
4. Nightlife options
5. Not much to do in Waterville
6. Some RAs are strict.

Not Much Diversity
One of the least racially diverse campuses—only 12% of students are minorities.

Student Body

African American:	2%	Male Undergrads:	50%
Asian American:	1%	Female Undergrads:	50%
Hispanic:	1%	Living On Campus:	64%
International:	0%	Living Off Campus:	36%
Native American:	0%	Male Athletes:	38%
White:	88%	Female Athletes:	29%
Unknown:	8%	Fraternity Members:	—
From Out-of-State:	21%	Sorority Members:	0%

Frequently Compared Schools:

Bates College
Bowdoin College
Colby College
University of Maine

Students Speak Out On... EVERYTHING!

ACADEMICS

Professors

"Our professors are great. Each and every one of them cares about how well you do. If you are struggling they will do everything within their power to help you improve your grade. They know your name, and you see them around campus."

Plenty of Resources

"I have lived on campus for 2+ years now, and each year, I have discovered more and more about the opportunities for help if a student is struggling. Apart from teachers being available at most times, there are a lot of students who are available for help in many different areas of college life."

Interesting

"At Thomas, all the professors are interested in seeing the students succeed and have the knowledge and contacts to help them achieve their goals."

ATHLETICS

Thomas Athletics

"The athletics at Thomas are structured very well. They express the importance of being active and also doing your studies. The athletic director tracks academic progress and makes plans for tutors or other help. They schedule matches around classes and MOST coaches encourage academics over athletics."

Athletics

"Student involvement in athletics is pretty high, and team performance is average. Fan support is really only great during basketball games and school spirit is not very recognized. Facilities could be improved; could maybe be bigger."

CAMPUS DINING

The Food and Surroundings

"The area, amount of cleanliness, and satisfaction of food is good. All the students get a choice whether to buy meal tickets or not. We can have the choice of breakfast every morning before class. As for lunch and dinner, we eat whenever we get hungry. The cleanliness is well. They are constantly cleaning up messes in the kitchen after a long day."

Thomas Dining Center

"The pastries and desserts are really good. Sometimes the dinner is greasy, but they usually have a pretty good variety of choices for each meal."

CAMPUS HOUSING

Dorms Will Be Dorms

"There is really nothing special here dorm-wise. The first-year dorms are rather old and plain. When you get to the upperclassman dorms, there is more of a change; however, the townhouses were just put in a few years ago, and they already have significant problems with them. I do enjoy the locations of the dorms compared to the academics buildings. Nothing is too far of a walk, even during the harsh winters of Maine."

GUYS & GIRLS

Thomas Student Body

"The student body at Thomas College is divided along lines. There are the hicks, there's descent population size of African Americans on campus. Most of them being players on our soccer and basketball teams. The girl at the school physically fit and very body conscience. There are very few homosexuals on campus. It is a very heterosexual campus. Sometimes a little to much heterosexual which in return makes the few homosexual individuals feel uncomfortable to be who they are."

HEALTH & SAFETY

Really Safe

"I feel very safe. The students carry around passes with codes on them for each building, and the cards are the only way to get into the buildings. What I really like about the college is that there are two security guards in each dormitory who watch over the area to make sure no one gets hurt and that no one sneaks anyone in and out."

LOOKING FOR MORE?

Check out our full-length guide to this school at collegeprowler.com/thomas-college/.

Towson University

8000 York Road; Towson, MD 21252
(410) 704-2000; www.towson.edu

THE BASICS:

Acceptance Rate: 63%
Yield: 25%
Setting: Small city
Control: Public
Total Undergrads: 17,148
SAT Range: 1483–1750*
ACT Range: 21–24

Student-Faculty Ratio: 17:1
Retention Rate: 84%
Graduation Rate: 66%
Tuition: $18,232
Room & Board: $8,670
Avg. Aid Package: $8,991
Students With Aid: 72%

* of 2400

Academics	B-	Greek Life	C
Athletics	C	Guys	B+
Campus Dining	B	Health & Safety	C+
Campus Housing	B-	Local Atmosphere	B+
Campus Strictness	C+	Nightlife	B+
Computers	C+	Off-Campus Dining	B+
Diversity	B-	Off-Campus Housing	A-
Drug Safety	C+	Parking	C+
Facilities	B-	Transportation	A-
Girls	B	Weather	B-

CP's Student Author On...
OVERALL EXPERIENCE

Towson is the type of school that, if you find the right people, you will have a wonderful experience. For those who have trouble making friends, it is highly recommended to get involved on campus. There are many organizations and sports teams that thrive in Towson and are strongly recommended in order to assist students in finding a solid group of friends. Some students love Towson so much that they just cannot pinpoint exactly what it is that they love so much. Perhaps it is the attentive faculty at Towson or the nightlife that has so much to offer. Maybe they just enjoy the small, comfortable campus setting that allows them to pass by familiar faces every day.

Towson is a school that becomes what you make of it. It is clear that the students who are engaged in their work or are interested in an organization gain a greater sense of appreciation for Towson. Some students express how rewarding their experiences at Towson have been while acknowledging the fact that the University is not for everyone.

Students Speak Out On...
OVERALL EXPERIENCE

Q If I Could Do It All Again I'd Still Pick Towson

"The friendships that I have made at Towson will last me a lifetime. I have participated in a few clubs and have always felt welcome where ever I wanted to participate. I have met the love of my life at this school and wouldn't have it any other way."

Q Love It

"I love Towson and I would definitely pick it all over again. The campus is pretty and small, so you never have to walk to far. There is always plenty to do since it is so close to Baltimore. And there is a mall, movie theater, and lots of other things right up the road."

Q Overall, It's Worth It!

"Overall, Towson's a good school. The constant construction of new addition may be annoying to on-campus students, and the budget reductions for certain majors may cause schedule inconveniences, but I never felt that anyone would leave Towson just because of any of those reasons. It's a great place to learn!"

BEST OF TOWSON

1. Going Uptown
2. Going Downtown
3. The Patuxent
4. Tiger Fest
5. Towson Hot Bagel
6. Towson Town Center
7. The Inner Harbor
8. The boys' lacrosse team

Happy Students
84% of students return after their first year.

Knowledgeable Professors
82% of students surveyed rated the general knowledge of professors as above average.

WORST OF TOWSON

1. Parking on campus
2. The Glen
3. Res Tower
4. Lack of school spirit
5. Last call starts before 2 a.m.
6. York Road traffic
7. Academic advising

Lowest Grades
Athletics: C
Greek Life: C
Computers: C+

Student Body

African American:	12%	Male Undergrads:	41%
Asian American:	4%	Female Undergrads:	59%
Hispanic:	3%	Living On Campus:	22%
International:	3%	Living Off Campus:	78%
Native American:	0%	Male Athletes:	5%
White:	68%	Female Athletes:	3%
Unknown:	10%	Fraternity Members:	7%
From Out-of-State:	30%	Sorority Members:	7%

Frequently Compared Schools:

James Madison University
Penn State
University of Delaware
University of Maryland

Students Speak Out On...
EVERYTHING!

ACADEMICS

Q Towson University

"Well, the registration process was quick and easy. Not too hard to understand either. They give you tons of class choices as well."

Q Kinesiology Staff Is Always Helpful

"The Kinesiology staff is very helpful and always there to lend a helping hand. They are extremely knowledgeable and work around the clock to answer the tough questions/criteria that come along with the already difficult major."

ATHLETICS

Q School Support

"Its so great how all the students go out and support the school and their friends."

Q Excenllent Student Involvement

"THe greatest thing about Towson students is that they are agressive to join in student involvement"

CAMPUS DINING

Q Great Food

"Towson University has great food consistently and in every dining hall. The meal point is also pretty wonderful as you get to spend the points you don't use that week on snacks and other groceries."

Q Dining Halls

"The best dining all is ptux or susquhanna in the university union. They have healthy food choices and all the food tastes good."

CAMPUS HOUSING

Q Underclassman Dorms = Center to Student Life

"The freshman and sophomore dorms at Towson University are located at the heart of the school. This is where the union is nearby as well a neutral point to various classroom buildings. There's also the biggest dining hall situated directly in front of them. Perfect place to be when you're just starting out and don't have a clue where everything is."

Q Dorms

"The dorms are a great place to meet friends and thats where most of the social life starts. I think the residence halls are great, the common rooms are convient, and spacius."

GUYS & GIRLS

Q Girls Are Sexy

"Very hot and come in all shapes and sizes. Any type of girl you could want."

Q The Girls Are Great, the Guys...

"The girls here are your typical Ugg/North Face wearers--which is just fine! For the most part, they're pretty hot. The guys leave more to be desired, though."

HEALTH & SAFETY

Q Security is everywhere

"There is a ton of police everywhere. The University is in between two of the best hospitals in Baltimore so in case of any emergency, help is close. There is a police station on campus, and plenty of dorm security. Every night at 11 a guard takes the over night shift, but to get into any building you need a One card and proof of residency, which is the assigned sticker to your building. Unfortunately you sometimes catch the guards asleep-but there isn't much action going on anyway."

Q Pretty Safe.

"I've gone here for over a year now, and I've never felt unsafe on campus. I've walked around at all hours, after dark, and by myself around midnight. Still take normal precautions like locking your doors and everything, but it's pretty good."

LOOKING FOR MORE?

Check out our full-length guide to this school at collegeprowler.com/towson-university/.

Trinity College

300 Summit St.; Hartford, CT 06106
(860) 297-2000; www.trincoll.edu

THE BASICS:

Acceptance Rate: 41%
Yield: 31%
Setting: Mid-sized city
Control: Private Non-Profit
Total Undergrads: 2,292
SAT Range: 1810–2080*
ACT Range: 26–30

Student-Faculty Ratio: 9:1
Retention Rate: 91%
Graduation Rate: 86%
Tuition: $40,840
Room & Board: $10,560
Avg. Aid Package: $26,982
Students With Aid: 47%

* of 2400

Academics	A-	Greek Life	A
Athletics	B-	Guys	A
Campus Dining	C+	Health & Safety	C
Campus Housing	B-	Local Atmosphere	D+
Campus Strictness	A-	Nightlife	B+
Computers	B-	Off-Campus Dining	C+
Diversity	C+	Off-Campus Housing	C+
Drug Safety	D+	Parking	B
Facilities	B	Transportation	B-
Girls	A-	Weather	C+

CP's Student Author On...
OVERALL EXPERIENCE

Everyone seems to experience a similarly hard freshman year; Trinity is not perfect. Once you accept that, you can begin settling down, grow comfortable, and view this little oasis in the middle of Hartford as a home for the next four years. Quite a few Trinity students can't wait for the beginning of September just to get back to school. Another experience everyone else seems to have in common at Trinity is a fierce loyalty to their alma mater—the love for the Bantam is only one example.

Well, now that you're hip to all the facts and opinions about Trinity College, you without a doubt have a head start on all the other incoming freshmen. Whether you decide to spend the next four years of your life at Trinity or choose another college, learn to accept the college or university that you selected. Don't be quick to give up or transfer. If half of the students who felt frustrated initially chose to leave Trinity, they never would have discovered what a great place it really is.

Students Speak Out On...
OVERALL EXPERIENCE

Q Loving Life at Trinity

"Trinity is an amazing liberal arts college. I applied here ED and haven't once looked back. I couldn't have imagined a greater fit for me. It is such a seamless balance between my academics, sports and social life."

Q Great

"Trinity is a get what you put in college. A lot of students put in no effort, and get bad grades, and get nothing out of it. Students that use everything that Trinity provides get a huge amount out of it."

Q Great Now and Later

"Great while you're there, and the benefits last both directly after graduation and long after graduation"

Q Find Your Niche

"It may take some time but you should be able to find your niche within the Trinity community. Time management is key to making it through Trinity. Once you find that balance between your academic and social life, you should be set. I've had a great time."

BEST OF TRINITY

1. The quad in the spring
2. The kind and compassionate professors
3. The small campus - all your friends live within a two-minute walk

Happy Students
91% of students return after their first year.

Commitment to Teaching
There are 9 students for every member of faculty on campus.

WORST OF TRINITY

1. Budget cuts
2. The location (Hartford)
3. No parking - anywhere!
4. The horrendous campus food
5. The awful weather
6. The flipped-up polo shirt collars

Expensive
Tuition is a steep $40,840, one of the most expensive rates in the country.

Student Body

African American:	7%	Male Undergrads:	49%
Asian American:	6%	Female Undergrads:	51%
Hispanic:	6%	Living On Campus:	95%
International:	4%	Living Off Campus:	5%
Native American:	0%	Male Athletes:	39%
White:	60%	Female Athletes:	25%
Unknown:	17%	Fraternity Members:	20%
From Out-of-State:	84%	Sorority Members:	16%

Students Speak Out On...
EVERYTHING!

ACADEMICS

Q Academics

"All of the professors only have undergrads and not all do too much research, so they are really helpful and have long office hours. Teachers want students to do well"

Q Academic Options

"While I have not formally picked a major yet, there are a wide range of options, including some cool interdisciplinary majors. The professors and advisors are dedicated and easily accessible. Class sizes are also small which provides access again to professors. In my freshman year my largest class was 40 students."

Q Great Professors and Classes

"We have very small classes and a lot of individual attention. You know your professors very well here and most of the classes are set up in the seminar discussion style."

ATHLETICS

Q division 1 powerhouse

"best squash in the world, undisputed"

Q Sports Are Top-Grade

"We may be a small school, but in terms of sports, we rock our bantam pride to the fullest! We have wonderful training and workout spots like the gym."

Q SQUASH

"Our men's squash team is the best college athletic team in the country in US history. Enough said."

CAMPUS DINING

Q Great Food

"I am a vegetarian student, and before I came to Trinity I was concerned. However there are always vegetarian and vegan options at all three dinning locations! Additionally there are healthy choices as well as fast food type choices so theres something for everyone!"

Frequently Compared Schools:

Connecticut College
Hamilton College
Tufts University
Wesleyan University

Q Buffet Style in the Main Dining Hall

"There are a lot of options in our main dining hall and it is buffet style so you can always find something to eat. I personally really like the food but some people get bored with it."

CAMPUS HOUSING

Q Campus Housing

"Freshman year dorms aren't great, but lottery system makes it fair. Upperclassmen dorms look like classy hotels"

Q Check Out Theme Housing

"Freshman dorms are typically the "worst" dorms at Trinity. Upperclassmen dorms are usually better, with a variety of theme housing options if you are seeking a specific type of community (students can apply to create new theme housing options each year)."

GUYS & GIRLS

Q the best

"trin has the best girls in the nescac"

Q best in the nescac

"every girl always makes sure she looks great despite the day of the week"

HEALTH & SAFETY

Q Trinity College Has a Secure Campus

"For the most part, Trinity College has a very safe campus. Security patrols the campus during night hours to make sure that students get their destinations safely. I personally have no experience of feeling unsafe on Trinity's beautiful campus."

Q I Have Never Had a Safety Problem at Trinity

"A - I have never personally felt unsafe on Trinity's campus. It is a very comfortable campus, and I feel very safe here. At night I always make sure to walk with a friend and not listen to my Ipod is its dark and i'm alone, but those rules are pretty general for wherever you live."

LOOKING FOR MORE?

Check out our full-length guide to this school at collegeprowler.com/trinity-college/.

Trinity University

One Trinity Place; San Antonio, TX 78212
(210) 999-7011; www.trinity.edu

THE BASICS:

Acceptance Rate: 59%	Student-Faculty Ratio: 9:1
Yield: 26%	Retention Rate: 89%
Setting: Large city	Graduation Rate: 81%
Control: Private Non-Profit	Tuition: $28,452
Total Undergrads: 2,487	Room & Board: $9,760
SAT Range: 1790–2060*	Avg. Aid Package: $21,149
ACT Range: 27–31	Students With Aid: 90%

* of 2400

Academics	B	Greek Life	B+
Athletics	C+	Guys	B+
Campus Dining	B+	Health & Safety	B+
Campus Housing	A	Local Atmosphere	A-
Campus Strictness	B+	Nightlife	A-
Computers	B	Off-Campus Dining	A-
Diversity	C	Off-Campus Housing	C+
Drug Safety	B	Parking	B+
Facilities	B	Transportation	B-
Girls	A-	Weather	B

CP's Student Author On...
OVERALL EXPERIENCE

Most students that come to Trinity find a niche and have a wonderful four years at the University. The experience can be as exciting or as mundane as you make it, but no matter what you do outside the classroom, the academic standards never fall. You will find that there is a lot of work to do, but the education you get makes it all worthwhile. It is really important to put yourself out there to benefit from the Trinity community, because they offer so many opportunities for you to find your niche.

Students on every campus are going to find something to complain about. At Trinity, it's the common complaints that make everyone laugh and complain some more, but no one ever actually takes measures to change things. Why? Because when it comes down to it, the people that come to Trinity enjoy the four or five years that they spend here and wind up happy that they worked hard and gave up sleep for an educational experience that prepares them for the future.... For the rest of this editorial, visit collegeprowler. com.

Students Speak Out On...
OVERALL EXPERIENCE

Q **Respectful Students and Staff Make a Difference**
"I have enjoyed meeting people of many different ethnicities and cultural and religious backgrounds at Trinity. Students are very friendly and welcoming. The lectures are often very thought provoking and entertaining and are for the most part well attended by students. It is very clear that all of the staff are trying to make the students happy. The weekly or monthly events such as Nacho hour and Cheesecake Tuesday are icing on the cake."

Q **Good Place to Be**
"I am very glad I came to Trinity--it is a very supportive environment, and pretty rigorous academically. The art building here is great, as are the teachers. Also, it's a beautiful campus."

Q **Diversity is pretty good**
"Coming from a foreign country, it was really welcoming and reassuring to find people from different nationalities. My overall experience has been pleasant both due to the quality of faculty and the social environment encountered at Trinity"

BEST OF TRINITY TEXAS

1. Dorm life
2. Professors
3. The network
4. Coates
5. Mudwrestling in the rain
6. Finals study breaks
7. Proximity to Mexico
8. Athletic facilities

Happy Students
89% of students return after their first year.

Commitment to Teaching
There are 9 students for every member of faculty on campus.

WORST OF TRINITY TEXAS

1. Parking
2. Computer lab hours
3. Student Court
4. Lack of diversity
5. Thomas Hall
6. Cardiac Hill
7. Abercrombie clothes everywhere

Expensive
Tuition is a steep $28,452, one of the most expensive rates in the country.

Expensive Dorms
Living on campus doesn't come cheap, with an average housing price tag of $6,690.

Student Body

African American:	4%	Male Undergrads:	47%
Asian American:	7%	Female Undergrads:	53%
Hispanic:	11%	Living On Campus:	95%
International:	6%	Living Off Campus:	5%
Native American:	1%	Male Athletes:	29%
White:	60%	Female Athletes:	12%
Unknown:	12%	Fraternity Members:	20%
From Out-of-State:	37%	Sorority Members:	16%

Frequently Compared Schools:

Rice University
Southwestern University
Texas Christian University
University of Texas

Students Speak Out On... EVERYTHING!

ACADEMICS

Q Professors Are Engaging and Interested in Student Progress

"At Trinity most of the professors take a lot of interest in the students and are available for discussion outside of class. The class sizes also promote a lot of discussion, at least in the English department, so that student interaction is a huge part of education."

Q Neuroscience

"It's great because I meet professors from all departments. Everyone is very friendly and eager to contribute ideas."

ATHLETICS

Q Quality D-III Athletics

"Athletics are pretty great for a Division III school. Sports aren't die-hard, but the teams are all ranked quite well. Students turn out for many different sports events, including baseball, football, soccer, and lacrosse in order to support their friends."

Q Sports at Trinity

"There's a wide variety of sports and involvement is encouraged but there is not enough fan support for sports that aren't football or basketball"

CAMPUS DINING

Q Generally Good.

"Campus food is generally good. There are always fresh options, everything is prepared when you order it, and it's five-star quality compared to many other schools."

Q Food Good but Expensive

"The meal plan is based on real dollars and not meals or points so many students run out quickly. There are a variety of options but the food isn't always the freshest or healthiest. I'm sure it's much better than a lot of other schools though."

CAMPUS HOUSING

Q BEST DORMS

"Trinity U is well known for its amazing dorms, rating top in the nation. One room is shared by 2 students, and 2 rooms share a bathroom. Dorms such as Mclean ar super duper good, and upperclassmen dorms are just great. The students within one dorm groups also bond very well, and usually they become the few of your best friends in university."

Q "The dorms are generally very good. Of the freshman dorms, Winn is the most social, Murchison is the best if you are lazy or perpetually late (it's closer to all the classes), and Herndon has the worst mold. Upperclassmen dorms are generally better. Thomas and Lightner are known for drunken frat boys and vandalism, Prassel is a palace, but farther from the rest of campus, and McLean is best for oddballs and those who like to live near the food."

GUYS & GIRLS

Q Diverse

"The diversity of Trinity University is incredible. The amount of cultural background on this campus is truly inspiring."

Q A Lot of Different Kind of Guys and the Girls Are Usually Hot

"The guys at Trinity are generally pretty good lookin' and nice guys. There are a few you have to watch out for. We have the good boys, the frat boys, and a range. The girls are usually very attractive and intelligent but a lot of them are taken already. So you just have to be on the look out... they are really fun."

HEALTH & SAFETY

Q DCS

"I feel incredibly safe walking alone at night because there are cops stationed in most of the parking lots and security phone lines placed strategically around campus."

Q I Feel Quite Safe

"Overall, the campus security officers seem very on the ball. Many of them are also nice. I like that there are emergency telephones on campus--makes me feel a bit safer."

LOOKING FOR MORE?

Check out our full-length guide to this school at collegeprowler.com/trinity-university/.

Troy University

University Avenue; Troy, AL 36082
(334) 670-3100; www.troy.edu

THE BASICS:

Acceptance Rate: 66%
Yield: 73%
Setting: Rural
Control: Public
Total Undergrads: 22,064
SAT Range: —
ACT Range: 18–23

Student-Faculty Ratio: 22:1
Retention Rate: 72%
Graduation Rate: 39%
Tuition: $9,556
Room & Board: $5,441
Avg. Aid Package: $4,485
Students With Aid: 82%

Academics	C+	Greek Life	B
Athletics	B-	Guys	A-
Campus Dining	B-	Health & Safety	B-
Campus Housing	B-	Local Atmosphere	B-
Campus Strictness	C+	Nightlife	C+
Computers	B	Off-Campus Dining	C
Diversity	B+	Off-Campus Housing	B
Drug Safety	C+	Parking	B
Facilities	B	Transportation	B+
Girls	B	Weather	B-

CP's Student Author On...
OVERALL EXPERIENCE

The overall experience at Troy is wonderful. There is not much to during the spring semester because football season is over, but the local cities have activities for students. Montgomery has several sit-down restaurants, malls, and cultural activities, and Dothan has its annual Peanut Festival and a large selection of shops to choose from, including a mall. There are also activities that take place on campus, also such as comedy shows, recitals, and theater performances.

The University does a lot to help its students succeed academically, as well. Professors are always willing to help whenever possible, and many students even develop relationships with their professors that later help with references and jobs. Overall, Troy is a great school, and anyone would enjoy their experience here!

Students Speak Out On...
OVERALL EXPERIENCE

Q AMAZING

"Troy has been like a home to me. Almost all of the teachers I've had care about my future, and they'll help you in anyway they can."

Q College Life

"Troy is a cool place. Of course, academics are a must, but there are certain times to have fun. I'm pleased with the campus and all of the events going along with it."

Q Small Knit Community=Limited Distractions

"I chose Troy University because of the closeness of the campus and the small-town feel. Troy is small enough so that stores are in walking distance, and if you don't feel like walking, the shuttle is available. It's a great school with great opportunities to offer. I love it here!"

Q Troy University Is Great.

"Troy is sort of small but yet has a big school feel with the Trojan Big time football. The University has many possible top degree choices with the advantage of smaller classes. The city doesn't offer much in the way of outside activities...so don't plan on much entertainment."

BEST OF TROY

1. Small campus means you won't have to walk far to class.
2. Football games
3. Nice campus
4. Welcoming and helpful faculty
5. Campus activities

Affordable
Tuition is only $9,556, one of the most affordable rates in the country.

Knowledgeable Professors
90% of students surveyed rated the general knowledge of professors as above average.

WORST OF TROY

1. Parking
2. Some dorms, especially Hamil and Alumni halls
3. The cafeteria
4. Wireless connection at times
5. Lack of places to go out
6. Lack of food choices

Not Everyone Graduates
39% of students do not complete their education or graduate with a degree.

Student Body

African American:	39%	Male Undergrads:	44%
Asian American:	1%	Female Undergrads:	56%
Hispanic:	4%	Living On Campus:	30%
International:	2%	Living Off Campus:	70%
Native American:	1%	Male Athletes:	6%
White:	49%	Female Athletes:	3%
Unknown:	4%	Fraternity Members:	14%
From Out-of-State:	34%	Sorority Members:	15%

Frequently Compared Schools:

Auburn University
Mississippi State University
University of Alabama
Washington State University

Students Speak Out On... EVERYTHING!

ACADEMICS

Troy Academics

"Troy's academics are excellent! The teachers put forth their best and they are always available for help. I have never had a professor that was not willing to help. The university makes it known what is expected of their students."

Great

"I came to Troy in Montgomery because Im a parent and the offer night classes."

Professors Care About the Success of the Students

"At Troy University, professors go above and beyond the call of duty by making themselves more available to the students. Also, professors encourage students to get involved in class discussions, as well as their involvement through on-campus activities. I could not have chosen a better place and environment to attend college."

ATHLETICS

Athletics

"The sports are good."

Amazing Athletics

"Our football team is amazing. The past couple of years we have won the Sun Belt Conference back to back. The fans love to watch some action-packed football on Saturdays."

Troy Athletics

"Troy University has a great athletic department."

CAMPUS DINING

Dinning Hall

"I gave it a B because I would prefer a larger dining hall with more seating and lighting areas."

Good Job Troy

"There are many dining options on campus and off, but the cheaper route to getting food would be the cafe, although it's not always the best."

Dining

"The dining area is okay for now."

CAMPUS HOUSING

Campus Housing

"Campus housing gets better after freshman year."

Campus Houing

"I would prefer to stay on campus, due to everything being at a gret convience."

Dorms

"The dorms at Troy are all very nice with the exception, in my opinion, of Alumni."

GUYS & GIRLS

Life of Guys and Girls

"at troy university we all get together. the girls are all different most are in sororities. the guys are in frats. the school comes together.."

Society at Troy University

"At Troy, you will find all sorts of ethnicities and styles. Just like at any other school, you have the preps, rednecks, goths, city boys, athletes, and your Southern belles. There are a great deal of relationships in Troy and also different styles, too."

HEALTH & SAFETY

Police and Safety Services

"I always feel safe on this campus because the police station is close to my dorm."

Security

"The security here is alert and is always riding around making sure students are safe."

LOOKING FOR MORE?

Check out our full-length guide to this school at collegeprowler.com/troy-university/.

Truman State University

100 E. Normal St.; Kirksville, MO 63501
(660) 785-4000; www.truman.edu

THE BASICS:

Acceptance Rate: 72%	Student-Faculty Ratio: 16:1
Yield: 40%	Retention Rate: 84%
Setting: Town	Graduation Rate: 69%
Control: Public	Tuition: $11,543
Total Undergrads: 5,468	Room & Board: $6,590
SAT Range: 1100–1320*	Avg. Aid Package: $6,056
ACT Range: 25–30	Students With Aid: 98%

of 1600

Academics	B	Greek Life	A-
Athletics	C+	Guys	B-
Campus Dining	B-	Health & Safety	A+
Campus Housing	B-	Local Atmosphere	C+
Campus Strictness	B	Nightlife	C+
Computers	B+	Off-Campus Dining	C+
Diversity	D+	Off-Campus Housing	A
Drug Safety	B	Parking	B+
Facilities	B+	Transportation	D+
Girls	C+	Weather	C+

CP's Student Author On... OVERALL EXPERIENCE

If you ask a Truman student why he or she is at Truman, as opposed to a different college, chances are you'll hear, "It was the money." For in-state kids, Truman is a fabulous deal, especially because the school gives out so many scholarships. When push comes to shove, that's why a majority of students initially enroll. But however majestic the buildings are, how impressive and wonderful the professors are, or how many scholarships are awarded, it's the other students who make or break the college experience. Truman students are a pretty motivated, involved, and accepting bunch of people.

If you choose Truman, be prepared to delve whole-heartedly into college life because there's not much to do outside of the University. But there is always something to do on campus: movie nights, plays, concerts, karaoke, lectures, and demonstrations for every interest under the sun. A lot of colleges claim to be involved in student life, but Truman definitely makes good on its own assertion.... For the rest of this editorial, visit collegeprowler.com.

Students Speak Out On... OVERALL EXPERIENCE

Q **"A Bunch of Friendly Geeks"**
"I loved Truman after my first year. An older friend who graduated the same year I was a freshman described the school to me as "a bunch of friendly geeks." And that's exactly what it is. For the most part, students really embrace each other's differences and have a good time together. In a nutshell, Truman is a community of unique and intelligent young people living and learning together."

Q **Favorite Experiences**
"Truman is a great campus for a variety of activities. Academics are very important and social lives are hard to keep sometimes but there are lots of opportunities to hang out with people."

Q "Sometimes I think about the places I didn't go, but overall I am very happy and satisfied with my decision to come to Truman. I also think that very few people are dissatisfied with Truman when they leave here."

Q "I love this school. I feel that I fit in from the start. Sometimes I wish that the location of the school were different, but I love Truman."

BEST OF TRUMAN STATE

1. The faculty
2. The value
3. Impromptu snowball fights in winter and the big trees on campus in the fall
4. SAB Concerts
5. KTRM and the Index

Affordable
Tuition is only $11,543, one of the most affordable rates in the country.

Happy Students
84% of students return after their first year.

WORST OF TRUMAN STATE

1. Sodexo
2. Walking to class in the snow
3. Re-lofting your dorm room bed
4. DPS
5. Location, location, location

Lowest Grades
Diversity: D+
Transportation: D+
Weather: C+

Student Body

African American:	4%	Male Undergrads:	42%
Asian American:	2%	Female Undergrads:	58%
Hispanic:	2%	Living On Campus:	48%
International:	6%	Living Off Campus:	52%
Native American:	1%	Male Athletes:	15%
White:	80%	Female Athletes:	6%
Unknown:	4%	Fraternity Members:	31%
From Out-of-State:	20%	Sorority Members:	22%

Frequently Compared Schools:

Saint Louis University
University of Kansas
University of Missouri
Washington University in St. Louis

Students Speak Out On... EVERYTHING!

ACADEMICS

Q Business School

"Overall, I think the business school at Truman State University is very professional and does a pretty good job. I am a management major and the variety of classed you must take for the liberal arts degree is extensive. There are also a lot of very exclusive company opportunities given to us through our career center and particularly for business majors, so I do think that we are recognized for excellent by employers."

Q It's the Harvard of the Midwest

"My academic advisor explained Truman's academics as this: "there are two kinds of kids that come to Truman...those who easily coasted through high school with excellent grades, and those who had to work their butts off just to do well. Those who coasted will learn the meaning of hard work here and those who already work hard are going to have to work even harder.""

ATHLETICS

Q The Bulldogs

"There is a very great team spirit among all Truman Students. We, including top management members of the school board like the President, give all the teams great support and come all out in mass to support them at their games which is why do very well at these games."

Q Equestrian Team

"I am on the Equestrian Team at Truman and it's awesome. Definitely the best sport there. We have our own barn, breeding program, riding herd, indoor and outdoor arena. We made it to nationals last year. Football on the other hand... not so much. So join e-team! No need to have any riding experience, just come play with the horses."

CAMPUS DINING

Q Dining Halls

"Dining on campus isn't as bad as many make it out to seem, it's just easy to get burned out on. Sodexo isn't the best but you do have choices when you go to eat dinner. Usually there are 2-3 entrees to choose from and then of course there is always pizza and the salad bar and hot bar. There are lots of cereal choices as well every day. Premium night is the best. People from off campus without meal plan will come back and have a friend swipe them on premium night."

Q Only Really Good Place to Eat Is the Mainstreet Market

"Dining Hall food is ok but it is repetitive the only why most people eat there is because it is cheap and only costs 1 meal for a buffet. The best night is steak night its one of the nights we look foward to. The SUB is the best place to eat on campus but is expensive so people cant eat there alot"

CAMPUS HOUSING

Q Living on Campus at Truman

"Truman is great. Don't let the small town fool you. There is plenty of activities and places you can do/or go if you open yourself up!"

GUYS & GIRLS

Q Students

"The students here are very open minded and friendly. Most students come from the city, like St. Louis or Kansas City. I found almost everyone is involved in an organization on campus."

HEALTH & SAFETY

Q Rape Polls!

"Truman's campus has those emergency polls all over the place-and I've never seen or heard of one ever needing to be used. Truman has it's own police department with jurisdiction over campus. And our dorms have recently been outfitted with perimeter access systems to monitor who goes in and out..."

LOOKING FOR MORE?

Check out our full-length guide to this school at collegeprowler.com/truman-state-university/.

Tufts University

4 Colby St.; Medford, MA 02155
(617) 628-5000; www.tufts.edu

THE BASICS:

Acceptance Rate: 27%
Yield: 33%
Setting: Suburban
Control: Private Non-Profit
Total Undergrads: 5,162
SAT Range: 2040–2300*
ACT Range: 30–33

Student-Faculty Ratio: 9:1
Retention Rate: 96%
Graduation Rate: 92%
Tuition: $40,342
Room & Board: $10,746
Avg. Aid Package: $28,512
Students With Aid: 48%

* of 2400

Academics	A	Greek Life	C
Athletics	C	Guys	C+
Campus Dining	A-	Health & Safety	B+
Campus Housing	B-	Local Atmosphere	A-
Campus Strictness	B+	Nightlife	B+
Computers	B	Off-Campus Dining	A
Diversity	B+	Off-Campus Housing	C
Drug Safety	B	Parking	B-
Facilities	B	Transportation	B
Girls	C+	Weather	C-

CP's Student Author On...
OVERALL EXPERIENCE

Most students who make the decision to attend Tufts are happy with their experience. Overall, Tufts has so many programs and activities, it's impossible for one student to take advantage of everything the school has to offer in four short years, but since there are so many different types of students at Tufts all with different interests, there is definitely something for everyone. The biggest complaint coming from the students seems to be adjusting to the new lifestyle and environment, whether at the school itself or the Boston area in general.

The Tufts experience goes far beyond the classroom, and provides students easy access to the ideal academic and social surroundings. The combination of school opportunities and local culture give Tufts its own distinctive flavor that allows students to grow in ways they never could have imagined. Most of the negative experiences that Tufts students gripe about are also good growth experiences, such as dealing with the weather or actually having to get around without a car. Ultimately, graduates are proud of their education and their school.... For the rest of this editorial, visit collegeprowler.com.

Students Speak Out On...
OVERALL EXPERIENCE

Q **I Love the Work Hard, Play Hard Mentality**
"Students here study very hard during the week, but are rewarded with vast knowledge on a subject. We do know how to have fun though and the combination of studying and partying ensures that I am always busy and always enjoying myself. I couldn't imagine a better school!"

Q "I'd advise going anywhere but Tufts, or you'll regret it. I actually left Tufts last year, and I am going to UCLA as a junior this fall. I was pretty miserable after my first year—a popular sentiment among the students, especially those from the West Coast."

Q "Going to Tufts was the biggest mistake of my life. It seems very hard to have a positive experience unless you're a rich, white male student. Tufts is all talk about protecting or supporting its students, but if you run into any little bit of trouble or difficulties (i.e. being sexually assaulted by another student), it seems like the school is more concerned about covering its own butt than helping a victim."

BEST OF TUFTS

1. The Library roof (you'll understand when you get here)
2. Getting to know your professors
3. A cappella
4. Spring Fling
5. Opportunities to do research

Happy Students
96% of students return after their first year.

Commitment to Teaching
There are 9 students for every member of faculty on campus.

WORST OF TUFTS

1. Being referred to as "Jumbo" all the time
2. Walking uphill to class
3. Trying to make brown and blue match
4. Parking tickets
5. Elitists - students who have "something to prove"

Expensive
Tuition is a steep $40,342, one of the most expensive rates in the country.

Student Body

African American:	6%	Male Undergrads:	49%
Asian American:	11%	Female Undergrads:	51%
Hispanic:	6%	Living On Campus:	66%
International:	5%	Living Off Campus:	34%
Native American:	0%	Male Athletes:	21%
White:	56%	Female Athletes:	19%
Unknown:	15%	Fraternity Members:	15%
From Out-of-State:	77%	Sorority Members:	4%

Frequently Compared Schools:

Brown University
Cornell University
University of Pennsylvania
Wesleyan University

Students Speak Out On...
EVERYTHING!

ACADEMICS

Q Dynamic, Rigorous, Excellent

"Now I only take classes in the English department. Some of my English professors are at the absolute top of their fields, in queer studies, film studies, and American poetry, for instance. And most of the ones that aren't eminent are fantastic teachers anyway. Professors can't get hired by our English department unless they are truly, truly amazing."

Q As good as you make them

"All the professors are briliant, and the academics are the main focus of the faculty. Professors genuinely care about you and your education. Truly one of the top schools in the country in terms of undergraduate education."

ATHLETICS

Q Sports

"The people who are involved in sports are the same people who support others who play sports. Although we do not have a huge sports culture here and rarely have fans, usually just those who play sports show up, the teams work really hard. The athletic facilities are not that great, however we are getting a new facility in the near future. We do have some pretty great teams at Tufts. Outside of athletics the athletes typically hang out and party with each other."

Q "Sports? Tufts has sports teams? Oh! That's what they were doing on that field! No, seriously, the best sports at Tufts are the club sports, like skiing and ultimate Frisbee. They mesh well with the college lifestyle and are a lot of fun—competitive, without cramping your style. If you are big into varsity athletics, just be prepared to not have too many fans at the games."

CAMPUS DINING

Q State of the Art

"Tufts is known for its food. The two dining halls on campus serve a variety of high quality food themed from all over the world, and offer a variety of options for students with special dietary needs. All in all, Tufts dining is equivalent to a restaurant."

Q Good Food, Healthy Options

"The food is very good on campus, and dining dollars can be used at various restaurants off campus, which adds to the variety of food available in the area."

CAMPUS HOUSING

Q Campus

"The campus is beautiful. There are trees everywhere, and it's very green. The surrounding area is a little sketchy, though, which detracts from the experience."

Q Wren

"I am currently living in Wren Hall. I live with 9 other people. Wren is a dorm where social interactions with your friends is very easy. There are four double rooms and two singles, with a common area and bathroom. It is a really nice place to live if you have ten other people who you know you will be able to get along with."

GUYS & GIRLS

Q Someone for Everyone.

"Tufts has most of the social groups you'd expect on a college campus - Greek community members, hippies, gamers, quiet study nerds. Unfortunately for those of us looking to have a really fun weekend, the latter prevails. Maybe about 20% of the Tufts population likes to have creative fun outside of either their dorm room or Greek House."

Q Girls Are Solid

"I came expecting the worst and was pleasantly surprised. The girls here cover a wide range but there are a lot of attractive ones for sure. Way better than expected, and I would say above average for a good school."

HEALTH & SAFETY

Q "Although there are reports of petty crimes here and there, overall, campus feels very safe. While I am wary of dangers, as a girl, I am not nervous about walking home alone at night."

LOOKING FOR MORE?
Check out our full-length guide to this school at collegeprowler.com/tufts-university/.

Tulane University

6823 Saint Charles Ave.; New Orleans, LA 70118
(504) 865-5000; www.tulane.edu

THE BASICS:

Acceptance Rate: 26%	**Student-Faculty Ratio:** 8:1
Yield: 14%	**Retention Rate:** 91%
Setting: Large city	**Graduation Rate:** 74%
Control: Private Non-Profit	**Tuition:** $40,584
Total Undergrads: 7,133	**Room & Board:** $9,520
SAT Range: 1870–2110*	**Avg. Aid Package:** $32,565
ACT Range: 28–31	**Students With Aid:** 81%

*of 2400

Academics	B+	Greek Life	A-
Athletics	C+	Guys	B+
Campus Dining	B-	Health & Safety	C
Campus Housing	B-	Local Atmosphere	A-
Campus Strictness	B-	Nightlife	A
Computers	B	Off-Campus Dining	A+
Diversity	B	Off-Campus Housing	A-
Drug Safety	B-	Parking	C+
Facilities	B+	Transportation	B+
Girls	B+	Weather	B

CP's Student Author On...
OVERALL EXPERIENCE

Tulane is an acquired taste. Some people take to it instantly, but for others it can take more than a semester to fit in and enjoy the university system. All of the students questioned said that they love Tulane and love being here. Living in such a culturally rich environment creates a unique learning opportunity that many kids who go to different schools will never get a chance to experience.

It takes a very intelligent and well-balanced person to attend Tulane. The nightlife and 24/7 party scene can tempt students
to blow off classes and just have a good time. Finding the right balance of partying and school work makes for the best experience. Remember, this isn't high school glorified; college is actually going to be a lot of work. Even the so-called "blow-off classes" that you take for humanities credit will make you read one long-winded book after the other and write 10–15 page research papers by the end of the semester. You'll see a lot of people come in for the fall semester that won't come back after Christmas.... For the rest of this editorial, visit collegeprowler.com.

Students Speak Out On...
OVERALL EXPERIENCE

Q Tulane Is Awesome

"My first year at Tulane has been the best of my life so far. I've met some simply amazing people and had some awesome experiences. The academics are rigorous, but there's still time to have fun, and tons of it. From the Oak Street Po Boy festival to Jazzfest there's always an excuse to party in New Orleans."

Q Great School

"Overall, this is a great school to attend because there are many academic and social options (as well as a beautiful campus). Most likely you will enoy your time here be it a long or short stay."

Q Love

"Despite how ridiculous it is sometimes, I absolutely LOVE Tulane. I don't feel like they help us out for the most part, but if I were to apply all over, I would still come here, no doubt."

Q Not So Great

"Don't come here if you want to just relax and have a fun weekend booze free (trust me, I tried). it's really hard to actually get to know people here because all anyone talks about is how drunk they were last night."

BEST OF TULANE

1. The city of New Orleans
2. The weather—it's hardly ever below 40 degrees!
3. The unique culture and people
4. The nightlife (both on and off campus)
5. The music scene

Happy Students
91% of students return after their first year.

Commitment to Teaching
There are 8 students for every member of faculty on campus.

WORST OF TULANE

1. General requirement courses
2. The rain and humidity
3. Safety around/off campus
4. Tuition!
5. Lack of communication between students and the administration

Expensive
Tuition is a steep $40,584, one of the most expensive rates in the country.

Student Body

African American:	11%	Male Undergrads:	46%
Asian American:	5%	Female Undergrads:	54%
Hispanic:	4%	Living On Campus:	48%
International:	2%	Living Off Campus:	52%
Native American:	2%	Male Athletes:	7%
White:	68%	Female Athletes:	4%
Unknown:	7%	Fraternity Members:	25%
From Out-of-State:	84%	Sorority Members:	30%

Students Speak Out On... EVERYTHING!

ACADEMICS

International Development

"The professors are extremely involved in what they teach. They have a lot of experience. The classes are taught by multiple professors who are experts in the areas they teach on. Grades are mainly based on a few papers and the midterm and final. The papers are relatively easy to write but require a certain amount of research and interpretation."

Workload

"The workload at Tulane is challenging, but not to the point of being exhausting. You do need to work for grades, but you are not constantly pushed over the edge for an A in each class."

ATHLETICS

Sports? Who Knew?

"While Tulane has many very good sports teams (basketball, baseball, etc.), the student body very rarely or ever takes time to go to the games or show up to sporting events. The workout facilities are great, but many students are here to study, not show their school spirits or to get in shape."

Sports....

"Our football team is not good and most people don't bother going to the games."

CAMPUS DINING

Food Is Okay

"Tulane offers a lot of different dining options such as Panda Express, Einsteins Bagels, Sushi, Quiznos, Byblos Greek Food, Taco Bell, Smoothies, and WoW! in our student center. We also have the main dining hall and a "green" alternative cooking restaurant. Overall the food does get repetitive especially if you're a picky eater."

Dining Hall

"The food is a lot better than other dining halls that I have been to. They try to switch up the menu so it doesn't get to repetitive."

Frequently Compared Schools:

Emory University
University of Miami
University of Michigan
Vanderbilt University

CAMPUS HOUSING

Josephine Louise

"I live the all girl dorm making it hard to meet people of the opposite sex if you are an introvert. It is a beautiful dorm though and the rooms are really spacious. The bathrooms are always clean and you never have to worry about all the showers being taken."

Deming

"Deming is not a place you live. Though it is conveniently located near Tidewater, the windows don't open, and roaches never go away, the rooms are tiny, and there's no social atmosphere."

GUYS & GIRLS

Really Attractive

"Some of the girls are a little too Jappy, but other than that Tulane girls are pretty hot. Typical dress around campus might be a white v-neck with sorority pin, tote bag, nike shorts, and colorful rain boots. Guys can be fratstars, with flip-flops or boat shoes."

Preppy Hippies

"Most people that come here have parents with money and you can tell. Although, many students come from middle class America as well. The guys range from super preppy to weirdos who don't shower. A lot of people are really into fitness."

HEALTH & SAFETY

Police Presence on Campus Is Reassuring

"New Orleans is a high-crime city, but Tulane's police force does a good job of keeping us safe. I never feel unsafe on campus, even alone after dark. Be warned, TUPD is just a harsh on pot smokers as they are on actual criminals."

Very Safe

"I feel completely safe on campus save for the few incidents of people entering the dorms that did not belong anywhere near campus."

LOOKING FOR MORE?

Check out our full-length guide to this school at collegeprowler.com/tulane-university/.

UC Berkeley

110 Sproul Hall; Berkeley, CA 94720
(510) 642-6000; www.berkeley.edu

THE BASICS:

Acceptance Rate: 21%
Yield: 41%
Setting: Mid-sized city
Control: Public
Total Undergrads: 25,534
SAT Range: 1800–2170*
ACT Range: 25–32

Student-Faculty Ratio: 16:1
Retention Rate: 96%
Graduation Rate: 90%
Tuition: $31,022
Room & Board: $15,308
Avg. Aid Package: $16,914
Students With Aid: 66%

* of 2400

Academics	A	Greek Life	A-
Athletics	A	Guys	A-
Campus Dining	B+	Health & Safety	C+
Campus Housing	B-	Local Atmosphere	B
Campus Strictness	B+	Nightlife	B
Computers	B	Off-Campus Dining	A-
Diversity	A-	Off-Campus Housing	C+
Drug Safety	C-	Parking	C+
Facilities	A-	Transportation	B+
Girls	B	Weather	B+

CP's Student Author On...
OVERALL EXPERIENCE

Generally, students have positive things to say about going to school here. Students who want to focus solely on academics or Cal's prestigious name leave here satisfied with their educations. Those who come to "Berzerkeley" for its radicalism (or drug scene) are excited to see that the school is still carrying on its Free Speech Movement reputation. The students who chose Berkeley because it was the best college they got into are happy to know that Cal doesn't have to be too weird. And anyone looking for good conversation will want to stay here forever.

Cal definitely has the ups and downs of being a public school. The large class sizes and lack of personal attention are the two major gripes. Being "just a number" makes it easy to become lonely, and many people see Berkeley as a place that's difficult to make friends. While there is minimal hand-holding, the University teaches students to be independent and proactive. Most students at Cal are proud to be at a school that doesn't spoil its students.... For the rest of this editorial, visit collegeprowler.com.

Students Speak Out On...
OVERALL EXPERIENCE

Q The Best for All
"Theres everything you need to enjoy college from huge libraries to huge parties all you have to do is find what you like and enjoy it."

Q Plentiful and Enlightening
"Wonderful place to attend, professors are respectful and extremely knowledgeable, along with the rest of Berkeley's staff."

Q Sound Education
"UCB is a fine institution and any student will recieve a top notch educution. It is rated as the top public school in the nation, and it deserves this title."

Q It's Definitely a College Experience Worth Having!
"Berkeley is one in a kind. There is SO much to do in the Bay Area and San Francisco is only a short trip away. You will find people here from all over the world. It's truly unlike any place I've ever seen. I think it's the best town to spend your college days at!"

BEST OF UC BERKELEY

1. Huge, diverse, and intellectually-driven student body
2. World-renowned and inspiring faculty
3. Large and abundant academic and athletic facilities

Happy Students
96% of students return after their first year.

Proven Success
90% of students will complete their education and graduate with a degree.

WORST OF UC BERKELEY

1. Quality and price of off-campus housing
2. High academic pressure
3. Homeless population around campus
4. An overly accepted drug culture
5. Rainy weather in the winter

Expensive
Tuition is a steep $31,022, one of the most expensive rates in the country.

Expensive to Just Get By
65% of students surveyed felt that the amount it costs to live while at school was worse than average.

Student Body

African American:	4%	Male Undergrads:	47%
Asian American:	41%	Female Undergrads:	53%
Hispanic:	12%	Living On Campus:	35%
International:	4%	Living Off Campus:	65%
Native American:	1%	Male Athletes:	5%
White:	31%	Female Athletes:	3%
Unknown:	8%	Fraternity Members:	10%
From Out-of-State:	12%	Sorority Members:	10%

Students Speak Out On... EVERYTHING!

ACADEMICS

Q Eye-opening and incredibly rewarding

"Attending Berkeley means attending the premier public university in the world, and I feel that the academics here live up to this name. I have the opportunity to study with experts in nearly every academic field, which means my eyes are opened to new things each day. The classes are competitive and time consuming, but this means I will be uniquely prepared to survive in the "real world" come graduation."

Q Eye-opening and incredibly rewarding

"Attending Berkeley means attending the premier public university in the world, and I feel that the academics here live up to this name. I have the opportunity to study with experts in nearly every academic field, which means my eyes are opened to new things each day. The classes are competitive and time consuming, but this means I will be uniquely prepared to survive in the "real world" come graduation."

ATHLETICS

Q Big School, Big Spirit

"The variety and talent of our sports teams make UC Berkeley a great place to study if you're an athlete. We have winning teams in a bunch of college sports like Basketball and Football, and the Golden Bears definitely have a huge fan base. We are currently building a new training center near the stadium, so sports are a priority at Cal despite it's other well-known scholastic attributes."

Q The Best!!!

"If you went to a high school where football or basketball for example were very popular and your school had a ton of school spirit, Berkeley is the place for you. We win numerous championship titles, we're ranked in the Pac-10, and we our school spirit is uncanny. Football and basketball games are so much fun and unites the student body as a whole."

CAMPUS DINING

Q Delicioso!

"The food on campus is delicious. With many options and dining facilities, i never get bored and I'm definitely not

looking forward to returning to my home cooking come winter break."

Q It's Awesome

"The dining halls offer really great food. They have a variety of selections. They have typical American food, Indian food, Chinese food, Thai food and much more. Sometimes they offer special menu which includes sushi and seafood. The best place, I think, is crossroads. It's the most convenient dinging hall and the workers there are very friendly. I also have many options about using the meal plan dollars, such as teapot, lotions, cups, and study materials."

CAMPUS HOUSING

Q Great Dorms

"The dorms seem perfectly fine to me. A little crowded, but it is really ok."

Q Everything You Want Just a Few Minutes Away.

"There are a lot of options for housing, restaurants and social atmosphere. You can find cheap apartments, but most housing is expensive and very worn-out. There are brand new apartments with great amenities but I think they are too pricey for any college student."

GUYS & GIRLS

Q Women

"WOmen here at berkeley consists of main skinny asians and white women. I love women and to me they are all beautiful. except if you say the wrong things then these women are no longer beautiful. but never give up they love to chat and learn from them"

HEALTH & SAFETY

Q Safety Is Paramaount

"As with any Institute of Higher Learning, safe students are happy students."

LOOKING FOR MORE?

Check out our full-length guide to this school at collegeprowler.com/university-of-california----berkeley/.

UC Davis

1 Shields Ave.; Davis, CA 95616
(530) 752-1011; www.ucdavis.edu

THE BASICS:

Acceptance Rate: 53%
Yield: 23%
Setting: Suburban
Control: Public
Total Undergrads: 24,420
SAT Range: 1560–1940*
ACT Range: 22–28

Student-Faculty Ratio: 16:1
Retention Rate: 92%
Graduation Rate: 81%
Tuition: $32,027
Room & Board: $12,361
Avg. Aid Package: $12,574
Students With Aid: 70%

* of 2400

Academics	B	Greek Life	B-
Athletics	B-	Guys	A-
Campus Dining	A	Health & Safety	A-
Campus Housing	A-	Local Atmosphere	B
Campus Strictness	C+	Nightlife	B
Computers	B	Off-Campus Dining	A
Diversity	B	Off-Campus Housing	B+
Drug Safety	C+	Parking	B
Facilities	B+	Transportation	A+
Girls	A	Weather	B-

CP's Student Author On...
OVERALL EXPERIENCE

Overall, students seem to really enjoy their time at the University of California at Davis. Students are granted unprecedented opportunities to excel academically alongside expert professors who exhibit genuine interest in sharing their knowledge. With such a friendly campus and competitive academics, many enjoy the dynamic between the bustling, active University and the laid-back college town. Some even get a little fond of the cows after a while!

Despite the frustratingly intense course load, fizzling nightlife, and blazing summers, students usually leave UC Davis feeling glad they came. Studying at Davis is a unique experience, and the education you leave with remains with you for the rest of your life. Not only are you likely to leave Davis with a priceless diploma and a starting salary that makes up for all those weekends spent in Shields, you'll also leave with friends, memories, and the experience of a lifetime. Sure, there are some things here that are somewhat different.... For the rest of this editorial, visit collegeprowler.com.

Students Speak Out On...
OVERALL EXPERIENCE

Q Great Fit

"Although I've only been here for 2 quarters, I know that I made the right decision coming to UC Davis. I'm excited to join things next quarter and become more apart of the school and the experience."

Q Unique

"I loved that Davis was very spacious. Every lecture hall had a new feel to it and was different. The school is unique because we have so many farm animals which is really cool. What other schools have cows that you can pet in the middle of the night? Davis was my top choice because the small-town environment and the friendly people and I would definitely choose it again."

Q Best Choice I Ever Made

"Choosing to go to school at UC Davis was honestly the best decision I have ever made and I couldn't be happier."

BEST OF UC DAVIS

1. The people
2. The campus
3. Downtown
4. School spirit, Picnic Day, and the Whole Earth Festival
5. The educational opportunities

Happy Students
92% of students return after their first year.

Proven Success
81% of students will complete their education and graduate with a degree.

WORST OF UC DAVIS

1. Parking
2. Dealing with administration
3. Off-campus housing prices
4. Late charges on registration fees
5. Open container law

Expensive
Tuition is a steep $32,027, one of the most expensive rates in the country.

Student Body

African American:	3%	Male Undergrads:	44%
Asian American:	41%	Female Undergrads:	56%
Hispanic:	13%	Living On Campus:	25%
International:	2%	Living Off Campus:	75%
Native American:	1%	Male Athletes:	4%
White:	34%	Female Athletes:	3%
Unknown:	7%	Fraternity Members:	5%
From Out-of-State:	3%	Sorority Members:	6%

Frequently Compared Schools:

University of California - Berkeley
University of California - Los Angeles
University of California - San Diego
University of California - Santa Barbara

Students Speak Out On... EVERYTHING!

ACADEMICS

Greatest

"The professors are amazing at UC Davis. Anthropology to genetics to animal science- everything has top grade professors."

Professors Are Amazing

"I have had so many professors who have gone above and beyond my expectations in so many ways. extremely intelligent, approachable and eager to help."

ATHLETICS

EXCELLENT

"I LOVE THE SPORTS HERE. IT IS CRAP THAT 9 TEAMS ARE GETTING CUT. THEY ARE WHAT HELPS DAVIS SUCCEED!"

Fan Support

"In the University of California, Davis, the fan based more commonly known as the Aggie Pack is a huge support at sports games. The students wear a Aggie Blue shirt and they all sit at the student section and are standing up and cheering during the whole game."

CAMPUS DINING

State of the Art

"The dining commons are excellent! There are plenty of them and they are usually not very crowded. The variety is impressive, and you are guaranteed to find something you like. Very vegetarian/vegan friendly as well. Late night dining options with fresh baked cookies= amazing."

Dining Option

"Davis have a variety of food that has to offer to student. Everyday they try to come up with new ideas so that student doesn't get sick of it too easily, but the dessert menu seems to be the same most the time. Overall, the food is quite good and seems pretty healthy."

CAMPUS HOUSING

Off Campus Is Great

"There is a lot to do and look forward too by living off campus."

The Dorms Are a Great Community!

"Most students choose to live off campus after their freshman year because housing in the Davis is community is easy to find and cheap. This is great for all involved because, as a freshman, you will be surrounded by your peers all of whom are trying to meet as many people as you are. Students will often form IM sports teams with the people on their floor and it's a great, easy way to hang out and meet people right off the bat in Fall."

GUYS & GIRLS

GUYS AND GIRLS

"The guys at Davis range from surfer dudes to intellectuals and party animals. Most of them are intelligent and fun at the same time which is great. Very different from high school, engaging and fun to be with. The girls at Davis range as well most of them are studious but like to have a good time and fun to be around. Not too much drama."

Girls and Guys at Davis

"Overall, both the girls and the guys like to get out and party. everyone is outgoing and friendly but when it is time to study, they get down to business."

HEALTH & SAFETY

Safety

"I never feel unsafe on campus. Even when it's late at night and there is no one on campus I always know that if I don't feel safe or comfortable biking back to my room alone I can always call the escort service and they will come pick me up wherever I am on campus. I never have to worry about not being safe on campus because there is always campus police around."

LOOKING FOR MORE?

Check out our full-length guide to this school at collegeprowler.com/university-of-california---davis/.

UC Irvine

University Drive; Irvine, CA 92697
(949) 824-5011; www.uci.edu

THE BASICS:

Acceptance Rate: 49%
Yield: 22%
Setting: Mid-sized city
Control: Public
Total Undergrads: 21,952
SAT Range: 1590–1900*
ACT Range: 23–28

Student-Faculty Ratio: 19:1
Retention Rate: 94%
Graduation Rate: 81%
Tuition: $31,387
Room & Board: $10,655
Avg. Aid Package: $10,733
Students With Aid: 62%

* of 2400

Academics	B+	Greek Life	B-
Athletics	B-	Guys	B
Campus Dining	B+	Health & Safety	B+
Campus Housing	B	Local Atmosphere	A-
Campus Strictness	C+	Nightlife	B-
Computers	B	Off-Campus Dining	B-
Diversity	B-	Off-Campus Housing	A-
Drug Safety	C+	Parking	C+
Facilities	B+	Transportation	A-
Girls	B	Weather	A

CP's Student Author On...
OVERALL EXPERIENCE

Many students here will admit that UCI wasn't their first choice or even their second. While UCI still doesn't live up to the prestige of UCLA or UC Berkeley—leading to some serious inferiority complexes among some students—it's increasingly gaining respect. It may not have a football team, an infinite number of majors, a true college town atmosphere, an abundance of parking spots, or even a reputable mascot, but the administration is still growing and expanding the campus with the public funds and donations that it gains.

Despite being strong in academics and fair in athletics, there are still some heavy skeptics in a group of would-be happy, shiny people. No university, no matter how good, can please everyone. Whether you enjoy UCI will be based on what you make of it through your own perceptions. With enough imagination, you should never be bored, and there is no pressure to do anything you don't want to. The minimum courseload is light, and most people take at least one class beyond the minimum required for full-time status.... For the rest of this editorial, visit collegeprowler.com.

Students Speak Out On...
OVERALL EXPERIENCE

ℚ The Quiet Weekend

"The weekends are quiet except if someone has a party. We are surrounded by residential areas, and Irvine is a very safe city that runs like clockwork. Sprinklers go on every morning at 3 am. The weekend is the perfect time to hang out with friends, catch up on work, study, or go home."

ℚ I'd Do It Again

"UCI is a great college for students looking to get ahead. It is quarter system which is nice because you get more classes out of the way faster and it makes you focus more because tests come up fast. The teachers are pretty cool and very willing to help. It's a great campus."

BEST OF UC IRVINE

1. High-profile research professors
2. Famous alumni
3. Frequent high-profile guest speakers, including the Dalai Llama and Governor Schwarzenegger

Happy Students
94% of students return after their first year.

Proven Success
81% of students will complete their education and graduate with a degree.

WORST OF UC IRVINE

1. The solicitors
2. Parking hell
3. Increased student fees
4. High cost of textbooks
5. Difficult to find things to do
6. Commuter school
7. High cost of living

Expensive
Tuition is a steep $31,387, one of the most expensive rates in the country.

Student Body

African American:	2%	Male Undergrads:	48%
Asian American:	52%	Female Undergrads:	52%
Hispanic:	13%	Living On Campus:	36%
International:	3%	Living Off Campus:	64%
Native American:	0%	Male Athletes:	3%
White:	23%	Female Athletes:	2%
Unknown:	7%	Fraternity Members:	9%
From Out-of-State:	11%	Sorority Members:	8%

Students Speak Out On... EVERYTHING!

ACADEMICS

Many opportunities

"The Undergraduate Research Opportunities Program (UROP) allows current undergrads to pursue research with senior faculty while earning their bachelor's degree. Many interesting and important things have been discovered at this school, the 14th best research institution in the nation."

Great Professors and Campus!

"The professors are very helpful and encouraging and love it if students visit their office hours. The campus is great because there is so many different great study areas. One can choose to study outside with shade and fresh air or inside a library."

ATHLETICS

Sports Are Not That Important

"Sports at UCI are not as important when compared to UCLA or USC. We do have a great baseball team and some less popular sports. We are known for our academic performance rather than the athletic's."

Soccer and Baseball at UCI

"UCI has a great soccer team and a baseball team. A lot of students attend these games because they are pretty intense but also fun to watch."

CAMPUS DINING

Dining Hall

"The food is really good. It's like eating at home town buffet everyday. I would like to see some of my hometown food though, like pupusas and some other salvadorian food.Overall is excellent."

Many on Campus, Even More Across the Street

"There are 3 on campus buffet type dining halls and a number of small dinners that offer tacos, burritos, pasta, salads, hamburgers and so much more. In the food court there is a Wendy's, Wahoo's Fish Tacos, Quizno's, Panda Express, Jamaba Jucie and the Anthill Pub & Grill. Across the Street there is a Jack-In-The-Box, Taco Bell, Lee's Sandwiches, Del Taco, and In-N-Out"

Frequently Compared Schools:

University of California - Davis
University of California - Los Angeles
University of California - San Diego
University of California - Santa Barbara

CAMPUS HOUSING

Vista Del Campo Apartments

"A little expensive, but everyone gets their own rooms. I was lucky enough to get my own bathroom. The housing office is designed just for students, complete with study rooms, a computer lab, and a lounge to take a break in."

Great Housing at UCI

"There all sorts of options for one to choose from. One can either pick to live near campus and pay less or live farther and pay more because those halls are newer. In the residence Halls provided for the freshmen are overall great because it allows the student to have the college experience, but one step at a time because we are not forced to pay individual bills or clean our hall, just our rooms. Housing at UCI are one of the best, I'd say because my experience so far has been completely great."

GUYS & GIRLS

People Are Smart

"At UCI you see plenty of different people around campus. there is mostly an Asian majority ethnicity wise, but even with this aspect there is a great majority among the types of people present. there are still definitely different styles expressed everywhere. the thing everyone seems to have in common though is that the entire campus consists of students with a desire for intelligence. They are pretty much all smart and focussed on obtaining their goals."

Geeks

"Guys and girls are mostly Asian and geeks. They are top students and they spent their time studying. Social life is minimum."

HEALTH & SAFETY

Safety

"one of the safest places in the country. dont have to worry about anything"

LOOKING FOR MORE?

Check out our full-length guide to this school at collegeprowler.com/university-of-california----irvine/.

UC Merced

5200 N. Lake Road; Merced, CA 95343
(209) 228-4400; www.ucmerced.edu

THE BASICS:

Acceptance Rate: 88%	**Student-Faculty Ratio:** 16:1
Yield: 7%	**Retention Rate:** 83%
Setting: Rural	**Graduation Rate:** —
Control: Public	**Tuition:** $34,770
Total Undergrads: 4,138	**Room & Board:** $12,801
SAT Range: 1340–1730*	**Avg. Aid Package:** —
ACT Range: 18–24	**Students With Aid:** 83%

* of 2400

Academics	B-	Greek Life	B-
Athletics	C+	Guys	B+
Campus Dining	B-	Health & Safety	B-
Campus Housing	A	Local Atmosphere	C-
Campus Strictness	B	Nightlife	C
Computers	B	Off-Campus Dining	C+
Diversity	A-	Off-Campus Housing	A-
Drug Safety	C+	Parking	B+
Facilities	B+	Transportation	C+
Girls	B+	Weather	B

CP's Student Author On...
OVERALL EXPERIENCE

There tends to be a fair amount of skepticism about UC Merced, due to its young age. Because the school is located in a fairly small town and only opened its doors a little more than six years ago, there are plenty of students who come to UCM concerned about how established the University actually is and how boring life might be on or off campus. However, students tend to be surprised at what UCM has to offer. It definitely lives up to the UC standard, providing students with research opportunities and leadership positions. Students tend to not only adjust, but eventually come to love the cozy, neighborly atmosphere of the school. Those very accustomed to the busy city lifestyle might be shocked at the smallness of the place, but the general consensus is that there is plenty to do, both on and off campus, and that it is just a matter of exploring.

Ultimately, the University is like any other college in the sense that there will be parties. However, the party scene is not so big on campus, due to its size and the fact that there are not any fraternity or sorority houses. But there is a fair share of off-campus parties.... For the rest of this editorial, visit collegeprowler.com.

Students Speak Out On...
OVERALL EXPERIENCE

Q Unique Opportunities for Involvement

"At UC Merced, I had the opportunity to be involved in any aspect of campus planning and community outreach of which I was interested. For example, I was involved with the Student Affairs Committee, Planning Advisory Committee, Ambassadors Club, Resident Housing Government, a Manager on campus, and a Research Assistant in a scientific lab. Opportunities only an innovative campus could have provided."

Q Groundbreaking Research Opps

"The facilities/labs are high end and have very top-of-the-line equipment. We have groundbreaking research opportunities, and we are small enough to have a one-on-one feel with many of the professors in various schools of studies. We are laying the groundwork for our sports teams, clubs, events, research, and much more, so come get your chance to be a part of the beginning of greatness!!!"

BEST OF UC MERCED

1. Friends and the friendly people you'll meet here
2. Great diversity
3. Helpful professors
4. Leadership opportunities
5. New, well-equipped library

Happy Students
83% of students return after their first year.

Easy Financial Aid Process
50% of students surveyed told us that the financial aid process went smoothly and they received the financial aid they needed.

WORST OF UC MERCED

1. Inflexible dining commons hours
2. Lack of athletic facilities
3. Lack of events for students over 21

Expensive
Tuition is a steep $34,770, one of the most expensive rates in the country.

Boring Place to Live
64% of students surveyed said that the local area is painfully remote.

Student Body

African American:	6%	Male Undergrads:	53%
Asian American:	33%	Female Undergrads:	47%
Hispanic:	30%	Living On Campus:	37%
International:	1%	Living Off Campus:	63%
Native American:	1%	Male Athletes:	0%
White:	24%	Female Athletes:	0%
Unknown:	5%	Fraternity Members:	4%
From Out-of-State:	1%	Sorority Members:	6%

Students Speak Out On...
EVERYTHING!

ACADEMICS

Q Teachers Are Willing to Get to Know You

"I'm recently taking an Intro to Nanotechnology course, and, off the bat, my professor took a break from her 3-hour lecture, and just started asking us what our interests were in taking the course. After getting through everyone in our 10-person class, she shared a little of her story into academia, and offered us some pointers about working in the "real world.""

Q Public School but Private Setting

"The average class sizes are 20 students and student to faculty ratio is 1 to 15. Professors are very helpful and always have office hours. Due to the small class sizes, professors are more active in a students life compared to other UCs. There is a ton of free tutoring that is available to students. A popular study area is most definitely the library which has a different noise level on each floor to supplement you study habits."

ATHLETICS

Q School Spirit

"Everybody in UC Merced is filled with tons of school spirit. They all support the different sport teams by showing up to most of the games, and by wearing the school colors. Students get involved with everything in sports."

Q Athletic Facilities

"The facilities are great, I cannot say much about the sports because I do not play any but the facilities are great."

CAMPUS DINING

Q Very Considerate of Students Wants

"The Dining Commons has a great variety of food items. They have each section of the DC dedicated to different kinds of food, from Asian to Mexican to the typical pizza or Blue Plate. The only downside is the hours of service over the weekend. But it's very convenient if you're late for class and just need to grab a snack or when you want to grab a burger and hang out with some friends."

Q UC Merced Dining Commons

"The Dinning Commons is the only place on campus to offer a complete meal. though it is small in size considering the size of the student body it makes an adequate job of feeding everyone that comes in. This dining area resembles more a cafeteria than anything else and serves to just maintain the students from just ordering food outside of the campus."

CAMPUS HOUSING

Q Brand New

"Freshman doorms are the newest on campus, and they're a great place to live. The dorms are roomier than the older UCs' dorms, and are a lot nicer. The environment is great too. The suites are even more convenient, even though they're more expensive to live in. Housing is pretty good at Merced."

GUYS & GIRLS

Q Pretty Good Variety

"There is a pretty good variety of guys and girls here. They come from all over the state of California but mostly the valley and SoCal with a few from the bay. There are a few rockers, a lot of pop fans, good group of ravers, even got a few of the hard core rap fans. Everybody is pretty chill. There are a few very good looking hotties around on campus but in general it's not too slim pickins. Someone for everyone I'd say."

HEALTH & SAFETY

Q Safety Is Outstanding

"It is extremely safe on this campus. There is no crime around and whenever something gets lost they return it to the campus police."

LOOKING FOR MORE?

Check out our full-length guide to this school at collegeprowler.com/university-of-california---merced/.

UC Riverside

900 University Ave.; Riverside, CA 92521
(951) 827-3411; www.ucr.edu

CP's Student Author On...
OVERALL EXPERIENCE

UCR grows on its students. Those who are not excited and attached to the school from the beginning usually find that they cannot help but love it once they get here. The majority of students enjoy their time at UCR. While a number of students come to UCR with the idea of transferring after their first two years, many often change their minds because they are pleasantly surprised with what a smaller campus atmosphere and community has to offer. In some ways, one could say that the positive aspects of UCR have been part of a well-kept secret that is making its way out. To the surprise of many, UCR definitely has potential to be a place where students can be extremely happy. The campus itself has an excellent and welcoming feel through both scenery and aspects of the general campus community. Although the University is growing, it still remains one of the smallest UC campuses and continues to offer a personal touch. As the school grows, an increasing number of academic programs, social clubs, and organizations are developing, providing the feel of schools within a school, which makes the University smaller for its students.... For the rest of this editorial, visit collegeprowler.com.

Students Speak Out On...
OVERALL EXPERIENCE

Q Never-Ending Opportunities

"I started out as a Neuroscience Major and lived a really unforgettable experience with one of my professors by volunteering in his lab and helping out with his research. As a volunteer I got to be involved in something amazing without having to be completely tied down to the lab. There is an incredible amount of on campus clubs, or you can even start your own, either way there are many opportunities to get involved with the community there or just network."

Q University of California Riverside

"I have enjoyed my time at college a lot more than i lot i was going to. I have many tons of new friends, have been involved in several different activities and have enjoyed myself here immensely."

Q College Experience

"My experience overall has been quite good. The staff and faculty are more than helpful. There is a lot of promotion for good health and wellness. As long as one can balance their studies and social life, all is well."

BEST OF UC RIVERSIDE

1. Almost all the buildings and classrooms are new
2. It's a small campus for UC
3. Biomedical sciences accelerated program
4. The only UC to offer a creative writing major
5. One of the most diverse schools in the nation

Happy Students
87% of students return after their first year.

Easy Financial Aid Process
59% of students surveyed told us that the financial aid process went smoothly and they received the financial aid they needed.

WORST OF UC RIVERSIDE

1. Homeless people
2. Lack of nightlife
3. Unpredictable weather
4. On-campus dining
5. Too close to local casinos
6. Tuition increases
7. Parking
8. Very bureaucratic system

Expensive
Tuition is a steep $28,183, one of the most expensive rates in the country.

Student Body

African American:	8%	Male Undergrads:	49%
Asian American:	40%	Female Undergrads:	51%
Hispanic:	27%	Living On Campus:	30%
International:	2%	Living Off Campus:	70%
Native American:	0%	Male Athletes:	2%
White:	17%	Female Athletes:	3%
Unknown:	5%	Fraternity Members:	6%
From Out-of-State:	1%	Sorority Members:	6%

Frequently Compared Schools:

University of California - Irvine
University of California - San Diego
University of California - Santa Barbara
University of California - Santa Cruz

Students Speak Out On...
EVERYTHING!

ACADEMICS

Very Proud UCR Biz Student

"I love my major! It gives me a great chance to succeed. There is not too much work, professors are helpful, and the internship opportunities are enormous! I want everyone to come here!"

Helpful Learning Center

"Here at UCR, the faculty tries their very best to provide a good learning environment for each and every student. Especially in the Biochemistry department, there are learning communities provided for first year students to join. There is also what is called the Learning Center where there are upper classmen and TA's willing to tutor students. The faculty makes sure that students are aware of these Supplemental Instruction in case they need help in class."

ATHLETICS

Very Spirited

"Students who attend the campus love it. They provide great support for our athletes."

Athletes

"the school has many sports available and most of them are fun to watch and play."

CAMPUS DINING

The HUB

"The central dining place in UC Riverside is always bustling with activity on the inside. You are always bound to run into a friend while getting food between classes. Everything is always fresh and delicious coming from our dining area. Italian, Japanese, Panda Express, and Mexican food is all offered in the HUB. Outside, there are tables shaded by umbrellas, where you can sit and enjoy your lunch in the sunny southern California weather. I have no complaints."

There's Something for Everyone!

"The food choices at the UCR cafeteria change throughout the day, only certain places are open early. It takes time to get to know all the places available to eat, and one of the best is almost a secret, and it's very easy to run into your TA or

professor there! I love the variety and the fact that you can find something to eat or snack on pretty much anywhere around campus..."

CAMPUS HOUSING

Did Not Live on Campus

"But many of my friends did, and they loved the experience, wouldnt trade it for the world."

Fun

"Although the Coed dorms can be crowded, they offer a great atmosphere socially and academically because students tend to help each other while studying and they also provide a good place to have fun."

GUYS & GIRLS

A Very Diverse Campus

"There is many cultures on campus and with that a lot of hot guys. You can find all sorts of types from the hippies that sit around playing music to the skater boys skating around the bell-tower. The christian club singing their gospel music to the break dancing club competing against people around campus who can dance. You can also find all the Frats and Sorority's camping out during the day and showing off what their fraternity and sorority has to offer."

Better than average

"Better than average with a good number of good-looking people."

HEALTH & SAFETY

Safe to Anyone

"I have never felt unsafe on UC Riverside's campus. It is a small, beautiful, safe place to be. Keep your doors locked to avoid petty theft or late-night pranks. And be warned that Campus Security isn't too happy 'bout drinking games, so keep your Beirut games under control."

LOOKING FOR MORE?

Check out our full-length guide to this school at collegeprowler.com/university-of-california---riverside/.

UC San Diego

9500 Gilman Drive; La Jolla, CA 92093
(858) 534-2230; www.ucsd.edu

THE BASICS:

Acceptance Rate: 40%	**Student-Faculty Ratio:** 19:1
Yield: 23%	**Retention Rate:** 95%
Setting: Large city	**Graduation Rate:** 85%
Control: Public	**Tuition:** $31,461
Total Undergrads: 24,217	**Room & Board:** $11,057
SAT Range: 1700–2040*	**Avg. Aid Package:** $14,961
ACT Range: 24–30	**Students With Aid:** 68%

* of 2400

Academics	B+	Greek Life	C+
Athletics	C	Guys	B
Campus Dining	B+	Health & Safety	C+
Campus Housing	C	Local Atmosphere	A-
Campus Strictness	B-	Nightlife	B
Computers	B	Off-Campus Dining	B+
Diversity	B-	Off-Campus Housing	B+
Drug Safety	C+	Parking	C
Facilities	B+	Transportation	A
Girls	C-	Weather	A

CP's Student Author On... OVERALL EXPERIENCE

When students contemplate their overall experience at UCSD, they usually base their opinions around the friends they have made and the good memories they have. Although academics at UCSD are world-class, they are not always the most important factor in the overall experience. Social life at UCSD is known to be a little boring. Many students wish they had a more active social life, but most still manage to find friends with whom they create lasting memories.

After adjusting to life at a large university, students say they enjoyed their time at UCSD and could not imagine going anywhere else. They especially like living in such a beautiful area and attending a challenging research university. Living on your own in college is an invaluable experience and teaches many students just as much as lectures and labs. Most of all, students are appreciative of their friends, and the people they meet have the biggest impact on their overall experience.

Students Speak Out On... OVERALL EXPERIENCE

Q A University That Caters to All.

"Compared to Hogwarts, UCSD's six different colleges give a unique blend to a prestigious university. Research is cutting-edge and half of our school or more is on their way to becoming future doctors and nobel prize winners. As long as you don't get too lost on our rolling lawns, you'll probably become the next big thing."

Q Would Choose UCSD Again!

"I loved the organizations at UCSD. I got involved and really enjoyed my time at UCSD. I was able to balance academics with my social life and it was just a great experience. the only thing i regret is not learning how to surf...we are RIGHT by the beach!"

Q Triton Pride

"UCSD is a great college. There isn't much social life, but college is what you make it. Overall, a beautiful campus."

BEST OF UC SAN DIEGO

1. The beach
2. The Sun God Festival
3. Lots of diverse and intelligent people
4. The Eucalyptus forest and talking trees
5. Proximity to Mexico

Happy Students
95% of students return after their first year.

Proven Success
85% of students will complete their education and graduate with a degree.

WORST OF UC SAN DIEGO

1. Too much studying
2. Having midterms and finals three times a year because of the quarter system
3. Parking
4. Overcrowded
5. Not located in a college town

Expensive
Tuition is a steep $31,461, one of the most expensive rates in the country.

Lost in the Crowd
Expect to take at least a few classes in a lecture hall—30% of classes have more than 50 students.

Student Body

African American:	2%	Male Undergrads:	48%
Asian American:	47%	Female Undergrads:	52%
Hispanic:	12%	Living On Campus:	33%
International:	3%	Living Off Campus:	67%
Native American:	0%	Male Athletes:	3%
White:	27%	Female Athletes:	3%
Unknown:	8%	Fraternity Members:	10%
From Out-of-State:	4%	Sorority Members:	10%

Frequently Compared Schools:

University of California - Berkeley
University of California - Davis
University of California - Los Angeles
University of California - Santa Barbara

Students Speak Out On... EVERYTHING!

ACADEMICS

Q Greatest school ever

"Whats harvard? below UCSD. This school is honestly not expensive, and if you complain about that stuff because what you get out of this school education wise for the price you pay is better than every other school in the country, except Berkley."

Q Biological Sciences

"The major is impacted and has a very rigorous structure. If you want to go bio, go general. You have much more choice within courses you can take that apply to your major."

ATHLETICS

Q Sport in San Diego

"Sport in San Diego are average, but surfing is really popular in San Diego"

Q Some Teams Have a Good Reputation and Perform Well but the Student Spirit Is Lacking.

"We have to constantly bribe students to come to our games instead of them wanting to go out and cheer for us. Again the athletic facilities are not well taken care of constantly and the only fans that are there every week are the athlete's families and other athletes. Our school is very into academics and not into the social life scene and athletics."

CAMPUS DINING

Q Lots of Food Choices

"there are 6 different cafeterias, one for each college. at the student center there are also a handful of fast food places, some of which are open 24 hours. as a result, there are always food options available at any time of the day. i think the cafeteria food is pretty good and the menu changes every day."

Q More Variety Coming

"There is a good variety of places to eat, such as cafeterias/ dining halls, and fast food and sit-down places, and sports bars. My favorite place is Yogurt World! It's a cute building with really good frozen yogurt and condiments."

CAMPUS HOUSING

Q Dorms- Sixth College

"I loved Camp Snoopy- as the brown summer camp cabins are fondly termed. They are cozy, and quickly became home to me. The portal through the bathroom led to the magical world of the Girls' Dorms part Deux, and we had plenty of house activities led by our RA to bring everyone together. I can't speak for the rest of the five colleges, but my dorm experience was the best. The way they're situated and built, you end up with at least thirteen new friends without doing anything but existing."

Q Great Living Experience.

"I am only a freshman living at the reshall dorms, but I really enjoy everything there is around to do. There are so many events to participate in and get to know more people."

GUYS & GIRLS

Q Yellow Fever

"If you're into Asian girls this is the place to be. The girls are incredibly hot here."

Q Triton Eye?

"some people say we have the ugliest students, but that's not true- engineers are hot."

HEALTH & SAFETY

Q Extremely Safe

"Unlike many of the other UC campuses, there are no riots or anything keeping us from getting to class or anyone threatening to harm us. We are also in La Jolla, which is extremely wealthy and safe, so walking around campus even at night isn't something to be afraid of."

LOOKING FOR MORE?

Check out our full-length guide to this school at collegeprowler.com/university-of-california---san-diego/.

UC Santa Barbara

552 University Road; Santa Barbara, CA 93106
(805) 893-8000; www.ucsb.edu

THE BASICS:

Acceptance Rate: 49%
Yield: 19%
Setting: Suburban
Control: Public
Total Undergrads: 19,805
SAT Range: 1590–1950*
ACT Range: 23–29

Student-Faculty Ratio: 17:1
Retention Rate: 91%
Graduation Rate: 81%
Tuition: $31,746
Room & Board: $12,765
Avg. Aid Package: $14,216
Students With Aid: 64%

of 2400

Academics	B+	Greek Life	B-
Athletics	B-	Guys	A
Campus Dining	B	Health & Safety	C+
Campus Housing	B	Local Atmosphere	B
Campus Strictness	B	Nightlife	A-
Computers	C+	Off-Campus Dining	B
Diversity	B-	Off-Campus Housing	C+
Drug Safety	C-	Parking	B
Facilities	B	Transportation	A-
Girls	A	Weather	A+

CP's Student Author On...
OVERALL EXPERIENCE

UCSB students can't say enough good things about this place, and most never want to leave. Whether it's the academics, the weather, the social scene, or the laid-back atmosphere, practically all students fall in love with something here. And, if you do get the urge to leave, LA is an hour and a half south, the wine country is a half-hour inland, San Francisco is five hours north, and San Diego is four hours south. Or you can spend your entire four years exploring Isla Vista and Santa Barbara. Tourists pay money to hang out here for a vacation, and UCSB students get to live here full time!

Give yourself a chance to get to know the school and the town. It can take a year to find your type of friends, your major, or your favorite club, but if you are actively searching, you will be able to find what you are looking for at UCSB. The students who excel at UCSB are independent and able to take care of themselves.... For the rest of this editorial, visit collegeprowler.com.

Students Speak Out On...
OVERALL EXPERIENCE

Q Party School, but Nerds Are Just as Cool

"There's a niche for every social piece of the fabric. The athletic kids, the computer kids, the engineering/science kids, the humanities kids, and the party-crashers. Plus all of the scenes want nothing more than to include people from the other niches, so it makes it that more enjoyable to pass your free time (if you ever have any)."

Q Paradise

"Fun and classes are intersting and not to challenging."

Q Fantastic, Opportunistic, Unique

"Because of the location of campus and the social life that Isla Vista offers, experiencing UCSB is wonderful. Not only are the academics great and challenging, I have been able to make wonderful friends in the perfect social environment that offers fun on all accounts. The beach is in walking distance as well as other activities. Fifteen minutes away is the beautiful downtown area of Santa Barbara which offers a multitude of bars, restaurants, beaches, and other activities."

BEST OF UC SANTA BARBARA

1. The laid-back beach atmosphere.
2. Lots of opportunities to get involved in different things.

Happy Students
91% of students return after their first year.

Proven Success
81% of students will complete their education and graduate with a degree.

WORST OF UC SANTA BARBARA

1. There is no football team.

Expensive
Tuition is a steep $31,746, one of the most expensive rates in the country.

Expensive to Just Get By
65% of students surveyed felt that the amount it costs to live while at school was worse than average.

Student Body

African American:	3%	Male Undergrads:	46%
Asian American:	17%	Female Undergrads:	54%
Hispanic:	21%	Living On Campus:	31%
International:	1%	Living Off Campus:	69%
Native American:	1%	Male Athletes:	3%
White:	51%	Female Athletes:	3%
Unknown:	7%	Fraternity Members:	4%
From Out-of-State:	4%	Sorority Members:	4%

Frequently Compared Schools:

University of California - Davis
University of California - Los Angeles
University of California - San Diego
University of California - Santa Cruz

Students Speak Out On...
EVERYTHING!

ACADEMICS

Q Availablity of Information

"UCSB has almost anything you need regarding academic information. Whether you're doing a research or working on a class project, all the information you need is at the tip of your fingers"

Q Professors

"The top professors from all over the country (and even, sometime, the world) come to UCSB because of its great location: right on the beach. Thankfully, the prestige of the UC system and the beachside campus attract fantastic professors, who have left their indelible mark on me now...and for many years to come."

Q Underrated

"Everyone thinks UCSB is just a party school. It is a party school, but the academic program is also very rigorous. Being a physics major is tough!"

ATHLETICS

Q Soccer!!!

"our Soccer team is one of the best in the states. We beat UCLA to win the championship on 2007!!"

Q Soccer!

"UCSB has a fantastic soccer team, it is definitely the most popular sport on campus. UCSB does NOT have a football team, so if you are looking for football culture, look elsewhere. Soccer games are extremely fun and UCSB has broken multiple records for attendance. UCSB is also the birthplace of ultimate frisbee. Many students participate in intramural sports, of which there are a variety."

CAMPUS DINING

Q DLG

"Very eco concious and always ahs something to eat that is tasty. Options are varied and never boring."

Q Great

"The campus dining halls are the best I've seen at any college. Buffet-style. You buy a certain number of meals per week."

CAMPUS HOUSING

Q Dorms

"The dorms are absolutely amazing. Some of the best views in the world. Beautiful"

Q Upperclasman Dorm Are Awsome

"Manzanita rocks. People are respctful. Check it out."

GUYS & GIRLS

Q Friendly

"UCSB has diverse student so you're bound to meet people from every walks of life. in addition, everyone seems nice friendly all the time; how can you not be when surrounded by all that beauty to take all your stresses away"

Q Girls Are Fine

"In general, people are friendly and laid back.....girls are well dressed and easy on the eyes"

HEALTH & SAFETY

Q Really Safe Environment

"There has never been a time when I've felt truly unsafe on campus, even at night by myself. The residence halls have fairly low crime rates; my roommate and I rarely lock the door (but I would lock the door living in Isla Vista!). Even if you do feel uncomfortable, you can call a Community Service Officer at any time and they will walk or bike with you to your destination."

Q Totally Safe

"i have never felt unsafe on UCSB's campus. I remembered one day there was a guy with a gun on the campus, and UC police caught him in an hour, great job!"

LOOKING FOR MORE?

Check out our full-length guide to this school at collegeprowler.com/university-of-california----santa-barbara/.

UC Santa Cruz

1156 High St.; Santa Cruz, CA 95064
(831) 459-0111; www.ucsc.edu

THE BASICS:

Acceptance Rate: 72%
Yield: 20%
Setting: Small city
Control: Public
Total Undergrads: 15,550
SAT Range: 1540–1890*
ACT Range: 22–27

Student-Faculty Ratio: 18:1
Retention Rate: 89%
Graduation Rate: 72%
Tuition: $31,531
Room & Board: $13,641
Avg. Aid Package: $14,422
Students With Aid: 61%

* of 2400

Academics	B+	Greek Life	C
Athletics	D+	Guys	A
Campus Dining	A	Health & Safety	B-
Campus Housing	B	Local Atmosphere	B
Campus Strictness	B+	Nightlife	B
Computers	C+	Off-Campus Dining	A
Diversity	B	Off-Campus Housing	B
Drug Safety	D+	Parking	B-
Facilities	B	Transportation	A-
Girls	A-	Weather	A-

CP's Student Author On...
OVERALL EXPERIENCE

Most students seem pretty happy at UCSC, although many indicate that it took some time to adjust to the school and its surroundings. Many say UCSC takes some getting used to, but once you find your niche, it is a cool place to be socially and politically active and also to receive a good education. Students are particularly fond of the overall beauty of the area, the laid-back atmosphere, the happening town, and the liberal academic setting. If these things are not your style or are not really important in regards to your college search, maybe you would not be as happy in Santa Cruz as other students. The most problematic things students mention about UCSC are the lack of school spirit, the overall resentment of Greek life, the student body's apathy for athletics, and, in some few cases, the professors.

The town of Santa Cruz is small, but the University is pretty big, so it is easy to hang out with different groups of people throughout your college years. Some people get sick of the town, but fortunately the school offers chances to get away. There is an Education Abroad Program, and programs to study in Washington DC and the Sierra Institute, as well.... For the rest of this editorial, visit collegeprowler.com.

Students Speak Out On...
OVERALL EXPERIENCE

Q A Wonderful University

"It is the university where undergraduates receive a lot of help, and the university provides almost every occupation major for all students of UCSC!BANANA Slugs FTW"

Q Too Late Now

"In my future I may look to more competitive schools, or once I know exactly what I want I'll find a school that really specializes in that field. But for now, in the first two to four years of college, I couldn't be happier. Sure, Berkeley would've been nice, but Santa Cruz offers a quality education, a beautiful learning environment, and good people."

Q Life at Ucsc

"Santa Cruz is a great school that makes you feel like you are on vacation. It i very relaxing and fool of nature. It as good professors and people mind their own business"

BEST OF UC SANTA CRUZ

1. The beautiful campus
2. The friendly deer
3. Convenient public transportation
4. Great facilities
5. Approachable people
6. Activists
7. Fun downtown area

Happy Students
89% of students return after their first year.

Proven Success
72% of students will complete their education and graduate with a degree.

WORST OF UC SANTA CRUZ

1. Lack of parking
2. Lack of school spirit
3. The spread-out campus
4. It can be quiet on the weekends
5. Lack of sports teams
6. Lame parties
7. No Greek Life

Expensive
Tuition is a steep $31,531, one of the most expensive rates in the country.

Expensive to Just Get By
55% of students surveyed felt that the amount it costs to live while at school was worse than average.

Student Body

African American:	3%	Male Undergrads:	47%
Asian American:	21%	Female Undergrads:	53%
Hispanic:	17%	Living On Campus:	47%
International:	1%	Living Off Campus:	53%
Native American:	1%	Male Athletes:	2%
White:	50%	Female Athletes:	2%
Unknown:	8%	Fraternity Members:	1%
From Out-of-State:	3%	Sorority Members:	1%

Students Speak Out On... EVERYTHING!

ACADEMICS

Q Nice Campus!

"the professors look professional. Its a very competitive process, but if you do what you have to do to get accepted just like any other schools you will be accepted. The view aroun campus is amazing, half is woods and nature, the other half you get a beatiful view of the beach/ocean."

Q Excellent Resources

"The professors are great resources for improving your necessary job skills. Additionally, they are always available for consultation and are extremely accessible to assist students."

ATHLETICS

Q None!

"The mascot for the school is a banana slug. Says something, don't it? Yet, the lack of school jingoism is really calming. Nobody pushes school colors and there aren't any rivalries."

Q All the Rush Even Without a Football Team

"It's a bummer that the school doesn't have a football team, but this doesn't stop everyone on campus from being active and supportive of the sporting teams we do have on campus. Everyone on campus is very fit and there are many opportunities for students to get together and work out together, or play sports, and things of that nature. UCSC is truly unique in more ways than one."

CAMPUS DINING

Q Oakes Cafe

"Awesome food from burgers to Chinese cuisine and at a low great price. Although its far on the west side of campus its worth the trip."

Q Good, Fresh Menu

"Overall good food. You will get sick of it after a while. But the dining hall always has organic and vegetarian options. Also a fresh salad bar that is amazing!! Always a sandwich bar, desserts and a few entrees available."

Frequently Compared Schools:

University of California - Davis
University of California - Los Angeles
University of California - San Diego
University of California - Santa Barbara

CAMPUS HOUSING

Q Plenty of Variety

"UC Santa Cruz is divided into ten colleges. As an incoming frosh, your first major decision is choosing which college you will belong to. Each college has its own dorms, frosh core course, unique aesthetic value, library and staff. This makes the college experience more intimate and helps students find the living situation that will work best for them."

Q Scenic View

"Wow, I have a fabulous view of the Pacific Ocean from Cowell College. It's like a resort."

GUYS & GIRLS

Q Consistent With the UCSC Culture

"There is no doubt that a great number of students are drawn to UCSC because they have prior knowledge of it's unique culture. The tolerant attitude for differences is the hallmark of student life at the Santa Cruz campus. Consequently, the manner in which people dress, the lifestyle choices and their social interests is of little consequence when forming relationships, joining clubs are general acceptance by others."

Q Student Social Behavior

"both guys and girls overall are friendly and down to earth. dress is very casual"

HEALTH & SAFETY

Q Safety

"I always feel safe at my campus. It is nice and lush and the environment sparks my creativity bulbs."

Q Health Care Center

"Everyone at the health care center is extremely nice and most important of all helpful."

LOOKING FOR MORE?

Check out our full-length guide to this school at collegeprowler.com/university-of-california----santa-cruz/.

UCLA

405 Hilgard Ave.; Los Angeles, CA 90095
(310) 825-4321; www.ucla.edu

THE BASICS:

Acceptance Rate: 23%
Yield: 37%
Setting: Large city
Control: Public
Total Undergrads: 26,556
SAT Range: 1730–2100*
ACT Range: 24–31

Student-Faculty Ratio: 17:1
Retention Rate: 97%
Graduation Rate: 89%
Tuition: $30,935
Room & Board: $13,310
Avg. Aid Package: $15,646
Students With Aid: 67%

* of 2400

Academics	A-	Greek Life	A-
Athletics	A	Guys	A-
Campus Dining	A+	Health & Safety	B
Campus Housing	B	Local Atmosphere	A-
Campus Strictness	B+	Nightlife	A-
Computers	B+	Off-Campus Dining	A
Diversity	A-	Off-Campus Housing	B
Drug Safety	C-	Parking	C
Facilities	A-	Transportation	B+
Girls	A-	Weather	A

CP's Student Author On...
OVERALL EXPERIENCE

Smack dab in the middle of Los Angeles and on the list of America's top colleges, UCLA is a school for those who want to have a blast while focusing on schoolwork. Although course registration is a battle, classes are crowded, and the registrar is impersonal, students praise the wisdom of their professors and feel that a UCLA degree will open major doors in the job market. The quarter system moves fast and tests tend to sneak up stealthily, but this allows for more experimentation when choosing courses and far less boredom. With more than 100 majors to choose from, the campus is bustling with students of all ideologies, races, and academic interests, making rousing discussions an everyday experience.

One of the nation's few top-notch universities that isn't private, UCLA is a place for those who want to learn more than a textbook contains. There's pressure to shine socially and academically among the approximately 25,000 high-achieving Bruin undergrads, but there are plenty of campus organizations that give students a go-to friend group in the midst of the giant student body.... For the rest of this editorial, visit collegeprowler.com.

Students Speak Out On...
OVERALL EXPERIENCE

Q Awesomeness

"UCLA is the best school ever. I love it here. There's a great balance of social and academic life. I'm so glad I chose to come here—it's made my college experience memorable."

Q Best Choice I Ever Made

"Going to UCLA was the best choice I ever made! It is a great party school, with outstanding academics. If you can juggle it all, then it's great!"

Q It's Been a Great Year of Life

"I am learning so much that I am just in love with school. You can find everything you dream of."

Q Experience

"UCLA is overall an excellent school, with fantastic athletics, academics, and overall experience."

BEST OF UCLA

1. Awesome food in dining halls and off campus
2. Location in LA and its close proximity to beaches
3. 60-degree winters
4. Movie premieres in Westwood and seeing actors on campus

Happy Students
97% of students return after their first year.

Proven Success
89% of students will complete their education and graduate with a degree.

WORST OF UCLA

1. No parking!
2. Traffic
3. Smog
4. Stupid school politics
5. Student body size
6. High-priced Westwood apartments

Expensive
Tuition is a steep $30,935, one of the most expensive rates in the country.

Expensive to Just Get By
57% of students surveyed felt that the amount it costs to live while at school was worse than average.

Student Body

African American:	4%	Male Undergrads:	45%
Asian American:	38%	Female Undergrads:	55%
Hispanic:	15%	Living On Campus:	36%
International:	5%	Living Off Campus:	64%
Native American:	0%	Male Athletes:	4%
White:	34%	Female Athletes:	3%
Unknown:	5%	Fraternity Members:	13%
From Out-of-State:	10%	Sorority Members:	13%

Frequently Compared Schools:

University of California - Berkeley
University of California - San Diego
University of California - Santa Barbara
University of Southern California

Students Speak Out On... EVERYTHING!

ACADEMICS

Psychology Is the Biggest Department on Campus, and for Good Reason

"Though many students are put off by the application process for psychology, this department has some of the most interesting classes and professors at UCLA. There are also plenty of research opportunities for undergrads, and professors are usually more than happy to interact with students on a personal level."

Great School

"UCLA offers an amazing array of knowledgeable professors that catered to their student's needs."

ATHLETICS

Best Athletics!

"We have the best teams!"

School Spirit

"UCLA students have a lot of school spirit!"

CAMPUS DINING

UCLA Dining

"UCLA offers a wide variety of food options to its students. Each of the four dormitory dining halls offers a fresh and diverse menu that is open to both students and non-students. Along with the dining halls, several eateries are scattered around the dorms, as well as all over campus, and provide anything from quick burgers to Asian to loaded gourmet salad bars. The student union, known as Ackerman, is a wonderful location that houses a small market along with the fast food/snack stations."

Excellent Dining Quality and Options

"There is tons of variety. We have multiple ethnic foods ranging from Mexican burritos and quesadillas; Chinese orange chicken and varieties of fried rice; Thai and Indian curry; Italian-style pizzas, pastas, and paninis; and your standard hamburgers, sandwiches, and wraps."

CAMPUS HOUSING

Love My Roomies!

"When applying for campus housing, the coordinators take into consideration the similarities and interests of the roommates. I have made lifelong friends with my college roommates simply because of the superb matching of interests."

UCLA Living

"Despite the cost of living in the dorms at UCLA, it is definitely an experience worth having. The accommodations that UCLA has to offer are not only state-of-the-art, but they are essential to the UCLA experience. With the opportunity to socialize and bond with your fellow Bruins in a comfortable and secure place, the UCLA students thrives in such a community."

GUYS & GIRLS

Diverse

"The relationships are so diverse here. Everyone is different and everyone dresses different, yet we all interact, accept, and love our differences."

UCLA Girls

"UCLA girls are very attractive. Guys, I would say, are attractive, too. Overall, it's a great school to meet people, and the weather allows for everyone to show off a little skin."

HEALTH & SAFETY

Personal Safety

"Being a former fan of USC, the differences in safety are day and night. I do not have to be afraid simply walking to class or being less than 10 feet off campus!"

Safety

"UCLA is a very safe university. We have our own police department. In addition, we have our very own UCLA EMS service. The campus is extremely well lit, and there are always students on campus. We even have a number you can call to have a UCLA safety van pick you up from anywhere on campus late at night."

LOOKING FOR MORE?

Check out our full-length guide to this school at collegeprowler.com/university-of-california----los-angeles/.

Union College

807 Union St.; Schenectady, NY 12308
(518) 388-6000; www.union.edu

THE BASICS:

Acceptance Rate: 41%
Yield: 26%
Setting: Small city
Control: Private Non-Profit
Total Undergrads: 2,194
SAT Range: 1700–1990*
ACT Range: 24–29

Student-Faculty Ratio: 10:1
Retention Rate: 91%
Graduation Rate: 85%
Tuition: $48,552
Room & Board: $0
Avg. Aid Package: $23,600
Students With Aid: 68%

* of 2400

Academics	B	Greek Life	A
Athletics	B	Guys	A-
Campus Dining	B	Health & Safety	B+
Campus Housing	B+	Local Atmosphere	C+
Campus Strictness	B	Nightlife	B
Computers	B	Off-Campus Dining	B-
Diversity	C-	Off-Campus Housing	C-
Drug Safety	C+	Parking	C
Facilities	B	Transportation	C+
Girls	B+	Weather	D

CP's Student Author On...
OVERALL EXPERIENCE

Sure, Schenectady isn't what you would call an "ideal college town," but that doesn't seem to affect the students' overall experience here at Union. Sure, the food gets old after awhile, but that seems to happen at every school. And students party hard at Union, too. So, what makes Union different? Three things: 1) Incredible academics. There are very small class sizes and incredibly devoted professors with long office hours. Furthermore, it's easy to have an interdisciplinary major or to design your own major. 2) Funding. Although students are into doing their "own thing," funding is available for just about anything. Want to start a club? Get 10 people and write a budget. Want to organize a protest in DC? Get an IEG (Intellectual Enrichment Grant) and/or a SEG (Social Enrichment Grant) or find funding from a particular department. 3) The Minerva System. No one knows where exactly the house system will take Union (the fraternities aren't quite in love with the fact that they've lost their housing), but it has the potential to add a lot to the campus.... For the rest of this editorial, visit collegeprowler.com.

Students Speak Out On...
OVERALL EXPERIENCE

Q Wow

"Union is an awesome school. If you are looking for a small liberal arts college, your search should end here."

Q Awesome

"Union is a beautiful, small, selective, and very good school. Amazing academics, intelligent teachers, and great teaching facilities. Gorgeous campus and buildings. Lots of new, spacious housing options. Lots of options and assistance and planning for future. Liberal arts with engineering."

Q Overall Experience

"Union is fantastic. There truly is something for everyone, which is hard to believe considering its size. I am so glad I chose to attend school here, and look forward to the next four years."

BEST OF UNION

1. Spring in Schenectady
2. The professors
3. Trimester system
4. Small class size
5. Beautiful campus
6. The parties
7. The Minerva Houses

Happy Students
91% of students return after their first year.

Commitment to Teaching
There are 10 students for every member of faculty on campus.

WORST OF UNION

1. Schenectady
2. Winter in Schenectady
3. The cost of tuition
4. Lack of diversity
5. Somewhat sheltered social scene
6. Small school
7. School lets out in June

Expensive
Tuition is a steep $48,552, one of the most expensive rates in the country.

Student Body

African American:	4%	Male Undergrads:	51%
Asian American:	6%	Female Undergrads:	49%
Hispanic:	4%	Living On Campus:	88%
International:	4%	Living Off Campus:	12%
Native American:	0%	Male Athletes:	32%
White:	81%	Female Athletes:	26%
Unknown:	1%	Fraternity Members:	29%
From Out-of-State:	59%	Sorority Members:	22%

Frequently Compared Schools:
Bucknell University
Lafayette College
Skidmore College
Trinity College

Students Speak Out On...
EVERYTHING!

ACADEMICS

Political Science

"Great major - amazing professors, great opportunities as well as alumni network. Abroad programs for this major are also incredibly fulfilling. It is a difficult major, but rewarding and valuable."

"The majority of professors at Union are very willing to help and to encourage you. However, it is also generally understood that this initiative will come from the student. The class highly depends on the professor and the willingness of the students to participate, which is often lacking. My classes have been very interesting. If you like to learn, you'll have no problem. I made my classes interesting, even when class itself was boring."

ATHLETICS

Hockey

"our D1 hockey team is great. students thoroughly enjoy the sport and its where most of our school spirit is invested."

Dutchmen

"Everyone supports Union athletics but that doesn't mean everyone cares or goes to the games. If your team is good, people will go. If you are not, no one will go but thats really no different from any other college. Students often go to hockey games as they are having a great season."

CAMPUS DINING

Great Staff

"The staff puts hard work into every meal of every day. The food is prepared with love and care. And the staff is very friendly and open to any ideas you have."

Not Bad

"The food and dining options at Union are not bad. Except for freshman year when you dont have the option of eating at upper, the food isn't that bad. Having Dutch and Rathskellar helps give the campus a diverse menue for when you want to fill up your stomach. You can also enjoy a nice organic meal at the organic stop we have at Reamer."

CAMPUS HOUSING

Minerva Program

"The Minerva program is unique to Union College. It is an inclusive social house system. There are seven Minervas on campus and they are controlled by students. All students are randomly placed in a house upon matriculation to Union College. Each Minerva has a budget of close to $30,000. This budget is allocated by the student leadership in each Minerva. Every house has rooms upstairs for upperclass students and they are very plush and large."

Dorms

"They're very comfortable and they allow you to be closer to campus and be more involve."

GUYS & GIRLS

So Classy

"Everyone at Union takes care of themselves. The majority of students are at least average looking and I honestly think there are like ten fat people at Union. Students dress very well and do not leave their residence halls without looking their best. Polos, khakis, and boat shoes are the norm. Designer brands are a must."

HEALTH & SAFETY

Health and Safety

"I feel very safe on campus. There is always the blue light system around that if something were to happen to me I could easily get to them and get help right away. Campus security is also always available. If you need an escort at night back to your dorm, you just give them a call and they will be right there to get you. I feel like the campus is always very safe and that there's always someone looking out for someone else."

LOOKING FOR MORE?
Check out our full-length guide to this school at collegeprowler.com/union-college/.

University at Albany

1400 Washington Ave.; Albany, NY 12222
(518) 442-3300; www.albany.edu

THE BASICS:

Acceptance Rate: 50%
Yield: 22%
Setting: Small city
Control: Public
Total Undergrads: 13,151
SAT Range: 1010–1190*
ACT Range: 22–26

Student-Faculty Ratio: 19:1
Retention Rate: 85%
Graduation Rate: 64%
Tuition: $14,648
Room & Board: $10,238
Avg. Aid Package: $8,228
Students With Aid: 80%

* of 1600

Academics	B-	Greek Life	C-
Athletics	C	Guys	B
Campus Dining	B	Health & Safety	B+
Campus Housing	B-	Local Atmosphere	B
Campus Strictness	B	Nightlife	B+
Computers	B-	Off-Campus Dining	B
Diversity	C	Off-Campus Housing	B-
Drug Safety	C-	Parking	C
Facilities	C+	Transportation	B-
Girls	B	Weather	D

CP's Student Author On...
OVERALL EXPERIENCE

Students at the University at Albany generally tend to enjoy the overall experience the school offers. They are pleased with not only the excellent education they receive, but also with their social standing and the life-long friends they meet. When students first begin at the University, they do not realize the opportunities available to them. From internships and community service to study abroad programs and hundreds of different clubs and organizations, the school offers something for everyone. Despite the bad weather, frustrating parking situation, and crazy party scene, most students are genuinely content with their college choice.

The University is not only diverse in the students who attended the institution, but also in the school's ability to give a well-rounded education and experience to every student. Any college experience is what you make of it, and Albany is a great place to make something great out of what could be the four best years of your life.

Students Speak Out On...
OVERALL EXPERIENCE

Q I Love It

"my school is really diverse and i don't feel like i'm left out. there is always something fun going on in and around campus. there are a lot of resources that help students in achieving there goals it couldn't be any better for me and i'm blessed."

Q I Love It

"School has been great so far and exactly what I expected it to be. The classes aren't too tough and I have plenty of friends and there is always something to do."

Q Diversity and Experience

"The University at Albany is diverse in every way. Including the food, the people, and the available courses. There's always someone new to talk to or something new to do or try. I love Albany because I never get bored here. The partying scene does gets insane though. It's best not to get too wrapped up in that aspect of the school."

Q Not Bad

"This school is largely a party school and personally, I am not a partier. I find that there are many opportunities to get involved with clubs and sports. I enjoy the city-like environment."

BEST OF ALBANY

1. Fountain Day
2. Bars, bars, bars everywhere
3. Crossgates Mall
4. Diversity
5. Concerts at the RACC
6. Big Purple Growl
7. Empire Commons

Happy Students
85% of students return after their first year.

Genders Equally Represented
A male-to-female ratio of 51/49 means there's a pretty even balance of students on campus.

WORST OF ALBANY

1. The student ghetto
2. Parking
3. Dining halls
4. Professors with thick accents
5. The winter
6. Too much cement
7. Athletics

Expensive Dorms
Living on campus doesn't come cheap, with an average housing price tag of $6,324.

Want a Job? On Your Own
There aren't any placement services for graduates.

Student Body

African American:	9%	Male Undergrads:	51%
Asian American:	6%	Female Undergrads:	49%
Hispanic:	8%	Living On Campus:	57%
International:	3%	Living Off Campus:	43%
Native American:	0%	Male Athletes:	5%
White:	55%	Female Athletes:	4%
Unknown:	19%	Fraternity Members:	3%
From Out-of-State:	10%	Sorority Members:	6%

Students Speak Out On... EVERYTHING!

ACADEMICS

Q Ivy League Academics

"UAlbany's Nano College was ranked #1 in the WORLD. Harvard, MIT nor Georgia Tech can boast that. UAlbany can make that boast according to "Small Times" Magazine, which is the Nano Tech business publication. Let's add on to that with a dozen top 10 programs according to US News. Why stop there? Lets add on $400M in R&D last year. Binghamton by comparison was around $50M. Do you want to do research or read about it?"

Q More Than You Think

"I came to Albany expecting a very easy workload however the academics are no walk in the park. The difficulty varies from major to major. For example Communications is known to be an easy major but Political Science is a harder one. Quality of Professors vary as well."

ATHLETICS

Q Groups

"there are a lot of different groups on campus that can help student to get involve in different activities . i'm part of the ASA,MSA,NAACP and these orgonazation are the best ways to meet new people and learn new things as well."

Q Sports Are Superb!

"At least I can talk about sports which are very well developed at Albany, you can see sports an anywhere around albany that too in good spirits."

CAMPUS DINING

Q Dining Halls

"Sometimes the food is really good, and sometimes it's okay. They have a lot of options though from kosher to vegetarian and during Lent they offer fish on Fridays. There are five dining halls on campus, all of them different from the last, and the employees are good people, I would know because I work at one of the dining halls on campus."

Frequently Compared Schools:

Binghamton University
Stony Brook University
Syracuse University
University at Buffalo

Q Dining Halls

"Not terrible, but I wouldn't say that it's good either. I enjoy eating healthy and the dining halls have a fairly healthy selection so I don't complain usually, but it's certainly nothing to write home about. There are wrap stations, which are pretty good; as well as fast food, hot stations (grilled chicken, fish etc.)."

CAMPUS HOUSING

Q Good but Not Diverse

"The quads all have similar set-ups, with good dorms, especially in the housing towers. The off-campus housing options, such as the apartments are nice, but it can sometimes be hard to get back to campus. The atmosphere can sometimes be cramped and hectic, but is altogether friendly."

Q Dorms Are Too Small

"They tend to squeeze too many people into the on-campus dorms. Off campus (freedom quad & empire) are nicer-apartment style living with suitemates, and roommates. Just sucks because its farther from classes and scheduling your time around the shuttle bus is a pain sometimes."

GUYS & GIRLS

Q Diverse, Available

"Diverse student body means everyone's tastes can be met. The student body size is great too, a lot of opportunity."

HEALTH & SAFETY

Q Very Safe

"I have never felt unsafe on the University at Albany's campus. The size of the campus is pretty big but overall there is thorough campus security. I always see patrol cars any time of the day or night. The members of the University Police Department are also very friendly."

LOOKING FOR MORE?

Check out our full-length guide to this school at collegeprowler.com/university-at-albany/.

University at Buffalo

12 Capen Hall; Buffalo, NY 14260
(716) 645-2000; www.buffalo.edu

THE BASICS:

Acceptance Rate: 52%	Student-Faculty Ratio: 16:1
Yield: 31%	Retention Rate: 89%
Setting: Large city	Graduation Rate: 62%
Control: Public	Tuition: $13,380
Total Undergrads: 19,368	Room & Board: $10,442
SAT Range: 1060–1250*	Avg. Aid Package: $7,368
ACT Range: 23–28	Students With Aid: 74%

* of 1600

Academics	B	Greek Life	C
Athletics	C	Guys	B+
Campus Dining	B-	Health & Safety	C-
Campus Housing	B-	Local Atmosphere	B
Campus Strictness	B+	Nightlife	B+
Computers	A	Off-Campus Dining	B
Diversity	B+	Off-Campus Housing	A-
Drug Safety	C-	Parking	A-
Facilities	B	Transportation	A-
Girls	B-	Weather	B-

CP's Student Author On...
OVERALL EXPERIENCE

From the overwhelmingly diverse campus culture to the odd architecture, UB takes some getting used to. But nearly all students say they've gotten a lot out of their four (or five, or six) years here, and many simply love the place. There are some institutional problems that get people down: administrative hassles, bland campus food, and rotten parking. The decentralized campus can lead to a diminished feeling of community. And the weather is a challenge to the spirit. But UB's modern facilities and world-class computer network get high marks, and most UB students grow to appreciate the great academics, the friendly people, and Buffalo's high quality of life.

UB has a great college experience waiting, but instead of gently offering it to you, it challenges you to "come and get it." If you're not intimidated by the diversity and the sprawling campus and if you get involved, you'll have an eclectic and inspirational experience. Students say UB is no utopia, but it's a lot of fun. And when it's over, nearly everyone remembers it fondly.

Students Speak Out On...
OVERALL EXPERIENCE

Q UB Experience

"great school,most teacher are very helpful, i have made many good friends here. After visiting UB, my sister even transfer to this school."

Q Love It!

"I love the great people I've met, and the awesome professors I've been taught by. My first year in college had its ups and downs but overall I had the best time. I was a bit homesick at first but soon enough I made lots of friends and got to really connect with them. I also didn't find it hard to find friends to study with or go to parties with. I studied hard and played hard!"

Q Love It!

"I am in love with this school. It was very intimidating at first since it is so huge, but it's so easy to get around! Everything is connected for the most part. I also love my intended major... after changing majors and schools multiple times, I think I found my spot here at UB!!!"

BEST OF BUFFALO

1. Academics that range from good to extraordinary
2. The genuine, unpretentious, laid-back friendliness of everyone you meet

Happy Students
89% of students return after their first year.

Easy Financial Aid Process
55% of students surveyed told us that the financial aid process went smoothly and they received the financial aid they needed.

WORST OF BUFFALO

1. Parking in Siberia
2. North Campus's dreary isolation and Stalinist architecture (to continue the Russia metaphor)
3. The football team reaching the top of ESPN's "Bottom 10"

Lowest Grades
Drug Safety: C-
Health & Safety: C-
Greek Life: C

Student Body

African American:	7%	Male Undergrads:	54%
Asian American:	9%	Female Undergrads:	46%
Hispanic:	3%	Living On Campus:	35%
International:	12%	Living Off Campus:	30%
Native American:	0%	Male Athletes:	3%
White:	57%	Female Athletes:	3%
Unknown:	11%	Fraternity Members:	3%
From Out-of-State:	19%	Sorority Members:	4%

Students Speak Out On... EVERYTHING!

ACADEMICS

Q Advisors and Dept Chairperson Teach, Too

"I'm an Interdisciplinary Sciences major with a concentration in Early Childhood, and when I signed up for my classes, the instructor name wasn't available at the time. When I got to class on the first day of school, one of my teachers was the Department Chair for Interdisciplinary Sciences. It's good to know that those who are in higher positions still teach and work one on one with students."

Q Education

"There are many courses offered in multiple time and the professors are there to really help"

ATHLETICS

Q UB Athletics

"The school makes sure that students know when there are important sporting events going on. They will write it on the boards, hand out flyers and also having special events at the sporting events."

Q Go Bulls!!!

"The team spirit is awesome. The entire school will be eager about the Bulls playing a game and a lot of students come and show their support during the matches. The True Blue Spirit is almost undeniable."

CAMPUS DINING

Q They listen and plans are flexible

"The dining people really listen and have made a lot of improvements in the past year. Meal plans can be used at almost every location and the exchange program is generous. In Fall 2010 the plans are even more flexible. They really believe in sustainability and being green too."

Q Great Variety

"Not only are there the campus dining halls but there are also fast food places like Moe's,Burger King, Subway, Starbucks, Tim Hortons, etc. So there is a variety of places to eat ontop of the dining halls."

Frequently Compared Schools:

Binghamton University
Stony Brook University
Syracuse University
University at Albany

CAMPUS HOUSING

Q Go With Goodyear

"For freshmen, the best dorm is Goodyear. Although it's on south campus and you often hear that 'south campus isn't safe', I argue that's not true. The area around south is the dangerous part, but on campus it's perfectly safe. I have never met anyone who did not like Goodyear- it is a fun, crazy atmosphere and you make amazing friends there. Plus, you get your own bathroom!"

Q The Dorming Life at SUNY Buffalo

"Living on campus is a very nice experience more so because all the students are somewhat interconnected and there is always an opportunity to meet new people. We have a great transportation system that allows us to go from the dorms to the academic spine quite frequently."

GUYS & GIRLS

Q Do You Want Looks or Brains?

"UB has a really diverse population. You'll find city boys, punks, rednecks, all of them. The same applies to the girls. Here's the thing, though: not everyone is gorgeous, and not all the greek gods/goddesses are intelligent. You'll find those who have looks and brains, but most have just one. Either way, most people here I know are pretty witty, so if you like mental exercises, UB is where you should be."

Q Guys Vs. Girls

"I would say that the students always come well dressed for the weather both warm and cold however I feel like there is somewhat of an unconscionable segregation in which people just automatically drift to their own races. However there is still mingling so as much as one makes an active effort to assert themselves. And the girls are very hot on warm days."

HEALTH & SAFETY

Q Safe but Scary

"There have been reports of rapes on campus but I've walked alone through both campuses at night for 4 years and nothing has ever happened to me or during the times I've been out."

LOOKING FOR MORE?

Check out our full-length guide to this school at collegeprowler.com/university-at-buffalo/.

University of Alabama

739 University Blvd.; Tuscaloosa, AL 35487
(205) 348-6010; www.ua.edu

THE BASICS:

Acceptance Rate: 59%
Yield: 46%
Setting: Small city
Control: Public
Total Undergrads: 23,700
SAT Range: 990–1240*
ACT Range: 21–28

Student-Faculty Ratio: 20:1
Retention Rate: 83%
Graduation Rate: 64%
Tuition: $19,200
Room & Board: $10,400
Avg. Aid Package: $10,589
Students With Aid: 66%

of 1600

Academics	B	Greek Life	A-
Athletics	A+	Guys	A+
Campus Dining	A-	Health & Safety	B+
Campus Housing	A-	Local Atmosphere	A-
Campus Strictness	B-	Nightlife	A+
Computers	B+	Off-Campus Dining	B
Diversity	C+	Off-Campus Housing	A
Drug Safety	D+	Parking	B
Facilities	A	Transportation	B
Girls	A+	Weather	B

CP's Student Author On...
OVERALL EXPERIENCE

University of Alabama students constantly brag about their school's traditions and spirit, and their pride is shown throughout the town. Some say it's the incredible education that drew them here, and others say it's Bama football that brought them to this Southern school. But no matter what reason these students choose to come to UA, most believe it was the best choice they could have made.

After graduation, some students get a job, some further their education by going to UA's grad school, and some even go to UA's law school. No matter what the students decide to do with their future, they believe Bama has prepared them for it. Students advise upcoming freshmen to walk around the Quad, visit the Strip, or watch a football game to understand why so many love UA.

Students Speak Out On...
OVERALL EXPERIENCE

Q Favorite Experience

"My favorite experience was the day that I moved onto campus. I was struggling, trying to get my things onto the elevator when 3 guys came up and introduced themselves and welcomed me to the dorm. They then asked what floor I was on and carried all of my things to my room. 2 of them went to grab the rest of my stuff while the other guy helped me unpack and place my things."

Q Great School!

"The university here is great. Help is everywhere when needed and most students are friendly. There are activities all the time and lots of student orginizations to become involved in. Support in any way you may need is easily available. The school is great and the campus is beautiful."

Q Could Not Be Better

"I am having the time of my life while at the same time knowing that our strong alumni network is going to help me get the job i want in the city i want to live in. This place better than a dream"

BEST OF ALABAMA

1. Football season
2. The student's Southern hospitality
3. The Rec's new pool and water slides
4. The Strip that is located so close to campus
5. The free movie channel on campus

Happy Students
83% of students return after their first year.

Knowledgeable Professors
92% of students surveyed rated the general knowledge of professors as above average.

WORST OF ALABAMA

1. The computer labs
2. The +/- grading system
3. Parking
4. Random weather
5. The old dorms
6. Teachers that don't speak English well

Lowest Grades
Drug Safety: D+
Diversity: C+
Campus Strictness: B-

Student Body

African American:	12%	Male Undergrads:	48%
Asian American:	1%	Female Undergrads:	52%
Hispanic:	2%	Living On Campus:	30%
International:	2%	Living Off Campus:	70%
Native American:	1%	Male Athletes:	3%
White:	82%	Female Athletes:	3%
Unknown:	0%	Fraternity Members:	22%
From Out-of-State:	39%	Sorority Members:	29%

Frequently Compared Schools:

Auburn University
University of Georgia
University of Mississippi
University of South Carolina

Students Speak Out On... EVERYTHING!

ACADEMICS

Professors

"The professors seem to really care about your progress. There were many times that I had concerns about classwork and wanted to just drop a class but after talking to a professor I stayed and excelled in the classes."

Political Science

"I was lucky, and always knew exactly what I wanted to go to college for. The University of Alabama has, hands down, one of the best political science programs in the country. The professors are excellent; not only are they great instructors, but they remain objective so you can form your own opinions. In this program, the opportunities you receive are astronomical."

ATHLETICS

Great Athletics

"The athletics at the University of Alabama are very good, especially our football team."

Football Players Are UA Royalty

"Sports in general are a major part of life here at the Capstone- and we couldn't be prouder of it. Obviously by taking the National Championship title in football this year we've become even more well-known, but then, Bama has always been renowned for the football program. However, we also have a nationally ranked gymnastics team, and every sport here tends to be on top of the game."

CAMPUS DINING

Meal Plan/Flex Dollars

"I enjoy our many dining halls, however having an option of eating at other places is really great. It makes it so convenient when they accept your meal plan card."

YUMM:)

"A little bit of something for everyone and there are some great local resteraunts. Though if your a vegeterian like me, rememeber this is the south."

CAMPUS HOUSING

Obviously, no one from Prowler has visited Bama housing lately

"Bama's housing is A+Bama now has over 4000 Super Suites Housing beds. Each student has his own room in a 4 bedroom Super Suite that has a living room, kitchenette, and 2 bathrooms.These Super Suites are in 9 newish Residence Halls. Riverside North, East, West; Lakeside East & West, Ridgecrest East, West, and 2 buildings for South.Prowler should know this by now. About half of these Super Suites were built more than 5 years ago."

Each Year More Dorms Are Being Built.

"Due to the larger enrollment The University of Alabama have been building new dorms on a first call first come serve. However, I like to avoid even the idea of living in a dorm."

GUYS & GIRLS

Friendly People

"The guys at Alabama come in many different varieties; fraternity look(you know, croakies, guy harvey and costas), nerdy, country boys, ravers, jocks and many others. The girls are very pretty, although we (and I mean all) wear nike shorts and oversized t-shirts during warm weather. The social life is very exciting and there is always something going on at night. Many go to the pool or quad during the day."

Fine Women

"The vast majority of the girls that I've seen in my two years at the University of Alabama have been incredibly attractive. This is especially true in the warmer months, when booty shorts rule the campus."

HEALTH & SAFETY

Police and Safety Services

"I feel really good about campus security. They try to get to know you and even go so far as to act as a father figure to you."

University of Arizona

1401 E. University Blvd.; Tucson, AZ 85721
(520) 621-2211; www.arizona.edu

THE BASICS:

Acceptance Rate: 78%
Yield: 36%
Setting: Large city
Control: Public
Total Undergrads: 30,346
SAT Range: 970–1220*
ACT Range: 21–27

Student-Faculty Ratio: 20:1
Retention Rate: 78%
Graduation Rate: 57%
Tuition: $22,264
Room & Board: $8,614
Avg. Aid Package: $6,478
Students With Aid: 80%

* of 1600

Academics	B	Greek Life	B+
Athletics	A	Guys	B
Campus Dining	B+	Health & Safety	B
Campus Housing	B-	Local Atmosphere	B
Campus Strictness	B-	Nightlife	A-
Computers	B	Off-Campus Dining	B
Diversity	B	Off-Campus Housing	B-
Drug Safety	C-	Parking	B-
Facilities	A-	Transportation	B
Girls	B+	Weather	A-

CP's Student Author On...
OVERALL EXPERIENCE

UA is a great school in a chill city that has nice weather and beautiful, beautiful people. You will become attached to it. Maybe it will be the way cars splash dirty street water into your face every time it rains, since there are practically no drainage systems in Tucson, and water just sits in dangerously deep pools along the sides of the road. Maybe it will be all the construction that will make you walk miles out of you way to get to early-morning classes. Or, perhaps it will be vying for couches to sleep on during class breaks. But, despite all of the hard times, the UA will become an endearing place that you'll always remember.

You will probably eat so many meals in the Student Union Memorial that you will see them in your dreams. You will walk the same sidewalks over and over in both the sunshine and in the rain. You'll have long talks with friends in parking lots. You may read John Updike for the first time here, rediscover Faulkner in the Modern Languages Building, or pull an all-nighter in the library. Some stumble through Calculus with a teacher who hardly spoke English.... For the rest of this editorial, visit collegeprowler.com.

Students Speak Out On...
OVERALL EXPERIENCE

Q Amazing

"I loved my experience at u of a. It can be kind of annoying in the dorms but you meet good friends there. Once your living on campus the party scene gets ridiculous! and once your 21 the bar scene gets really fun."

Q It's So Great

"I really enjoy being on the U of A campus. It's such a good feeling to walk around campus. I really like how Tucson is such a college town, everyone is so involved with the U of A. It's nice to have a little family here."

Q Great School

"Goos academics, Hot girls, Good food and amazing weather - whats not to love."

Q Is a Little Town

"University Of Arizona is the best little town school ever. I love it here, it's so quiet and peaceful. I love that we get to choose what, when, and where our classes are. I also like that we have a lot of clubs to choose form and we are different from other schools. I would not change where I am right now."

BEST OF ARIZONA

1. The beautiful people
2. The weather
3. The outdoor activities
4. Our sports teams
5. The fact that President Peter Likins is short
6. The diversity

Knowledgeable Professors
78% of students surveyed rated the general knowledge of professors as above average.

Low-Stress Course Load
81% of students surveyed rated the manageability of work as above average.

WORST OF ARIZONA

1. Rock gardens/dirt front yards/dirt back yards
2. Heatstroke
3. Dehydration
4. Inability to look sexy when your body sweats a lot
5. Inability to wear cool, trendy winter clothes

Don't Move Off Campus
Average off-campus housing is a steep $11,234.

Student Body

African American:	3%	Male Undergrads:	48%
Asian American:	5%	Female Undergrads:	52%
Hispanic:	18%	Living On Campus:	20%
International:	3%	Living Off Campus:	80%
Native American:	2%	Male Athletes:	2%
White:	63%	Female Athletes:	2%
Unknown:	3%	Fraternity Members:	10%
From Out-of-State:	40%	Sorority Members:	11%

Students Speak Out On... EVERYTHING!

ACADEMICS

Q My Experience

"Taking classes during the summer has given me pre insight about the school's academics. I was well pleased with the professors and the tutors. They were always there to help me out. I always knew I would enjoy the University of Arizona."

Q Getting Help

"Professors try their best to aid students. With programs such as Think Thank it is easy to seek out help."

Q University of Arizona Wildcats!

"The University of Arizona has a great business school. I have only had classes taught by the pre-business professors, and I have learned a lot. The workload has been a lot and made me study many hours a day to receive the grades I strived for. The campus is beautiful for Tucson, and makes everyone feel welcome. The athletics at UA are amazing; whether its the tailgates before, the games, the half time performances, its always a lot of spirit shown by the crowd! I love it."

ATHLETICS

Q Sports

"The sports events are so much fun to go to. Everyone gets really into the games and shows amazing school spirit!"

Q Amazing Sports Teams

"We had an amazing football team this previous year and we made it to the Hollywood Bowl...at least. Our basketball team was pretty dominant in the the Pac 10 as well."

CAMPUS DINING

Q Love

"I just love it! You have so many oppurtonities and there is always a variety! It is also very good!"

Q Great

"There is quite a variety on campus/surrounding campus. There are little shops near campus too which has different varities. All the dining places are close to campus which is convinent and most place have very reasonable prices."

CAMPUS HOUSING

Q Campus Life

"My experience on campus was great. All the activities held were informational and fun at the same time. The rooms are not small at all which I thought they would be. I believe I will live in on campus housing while I am an undergraduate student."

Q Lots of Fun

"Definitely recommend living on campus as a freshman."

GUYS & GIRLS

Q Guys & Girls

"What an array....and everyone is tanned and smiling in the abundance of sunshine. All types - sports minded to the classic nerd - everyone is smiling at University of Arizona."

Q Girls are banging

"Seriously, we get the best from all over the US. Especially California. It's amazing"

HEALTH & SAFETY

Q Safety at the University of Arizona

"It is very safe here at the University of Arizona, I always feel safe even after walking back to the dorms when my 10 pm chemistry lab is finished. There are emergency phones pretty much everywhere and campus security is helpful and quick to act."

Q Feel Safe

"With UAPD right down the road and Safe Ride available to pick you up late at night, I feel safe almost all the time while on campus."

LOOKING FOR MORE?
Check out our full-length guide to this school at collegeprowler.com/university-of-arizona/.

University of Arkansas

471 N. Garland Ave.; Fayetteville, AR 72701
(479) 575-2000; www.uark.edu

THE BASICS:

Acceptance Rate: 56%
Yield: 43%
Setting: Small city
Control: Public
Total Undergrads: 15,835
SAT Range: 1020–1260*
ACT Range: 23–29

Student-Faculty Ratio: 18:1
Retention Rate: 83%
Graduation Rate: 58%
Tuition: $15,336
Room & Board: $7,732
Avg. Aid Package: $9,030
Students With Aid: 69%

* of 1600

Academics	B	Greek Life	A
Athletics	A	Guys	B+
Campus Dining	B	Health & Safety	B-
Campus Housing	B	Local Atmosphere	B
Campus Strictness	C+	Nightlife	A
Computers	B+	Off-Campus Dining	A-
Diversity	C+	Off-Campus Housing	A
Drug Safety	B-	Parking	C
Facilities	B	Transportation	A
Girls	B	Weather	B-

CP's Student Author On...
OVERALL EXPERIENCE

Sometimes, the first-year experience in the dorm can really depend on the roommate. Roommates can end up in each other's weddings or end up as gossip fodder for friends and classmates. Freshman year can be a little overwhelming. The best thing to do is keep an open mind and remember that everyone else is in the same boat. Students are the master of their own college experience, so they shouldn't just sit in their dorm rooms playing Call of Duty. Joining a fraternity or sorority is one way to meet people. In addition, there are more than 350 registered student organizations on campus; there should be something for everybody, and if not, students can always start their own club. It's easy!

Arkansas will prepare students for whatever major they choose, but once again, this is college. Students are not living in their parents' house anymore; they have to do their own laundry and force themselves to go to class. "Ninety percent of success is showing up," as Woody Allen once said, and this saying applies with going to class. Some teachers keep attendance, but most don't.... For the rest of this editorial, visit collegeprowler.com.

Students Speak Out On...
OVERALL EXPERIENCE

Q Best Years of My Life

"I almost did not attend U of A, but I am so glad I did. Joining a Fraternity was one of the best decisions I had made"

Q LOVE It!

"The University of Arkansas is so amazing! It was my first choice and I'm so glad I'm here. My social life is wonderful and my academic life is just as amazing! Couldn't have picked a better college."

Q Everything I Hoped for, and More

"Truly a beautiful campus, with a unique feel. Students can find their niche where ever, and the school spirit and academics is superb. Very laid back feeling, with still a great atmosphere to study. The area is gorgeous and offers lots of activities to do, especially if you are outdoorsy, but even if your not, it is a big enough town where you have plenty of things to choose from."

Q Greek Life

"The Greek community is very active and I would recommend everyone to try it out, more people fit in than you would imagine."

BEST OF ARKANSAS

1. A small fee is added (per credit hour) to every student to bring in one large artist a year for a free concert. Some of the artists in the past have included O.A.R, Dierks Bentley, Third Eye Blind, and T.I.

Happy Students
83% of students return after their first year.

Knowledgeable Professors
83% of students surveyed rated the general knowledge of professors as above average.

WORST OF ARKANSAS

1. The parking
2. The hilly campus
3. The weather can be unpredictable.
4. No Jack in the Box
5. Twenty minutes away from the nearest regional airport

Lowest Grades
Parking: C
Diversity: C+
Campus Strictness: C+

Student Body

African American:	5%	Male Undergrads:	51%
Asian American:	3%	Female Undergrads:	49%
Hispanic:	4%	Living On Campus:	33%
International:	3%	Living Off Campus:	71%
Native American:	2%	Male Athletes:	5%
White:	82%	Female Athletes:	4%
Unknown:	1%	Fraternity Members:	17%
From Out-of-State:	37%	Sorority Members:	23%

Frequently Compared Schools:

Louisiana State University
University of Alabama
University of Mississippi
University of Oklahoma

Students Speak Out On... EVERYTHING!

ACADEMICS

A Great First Year

"I have always wanted to come to the University of Arkansas, and I couldn't be happier that I did. All of my teachers truly care about seeing my succeed. The class discussions are diverse and interesting, and all my teachers are willing to hear each opinion."

Walton College of Business

"Very engaged Professors. The environment is very competitive."

ATHLETICS

Razorback Student Involvement Is Overwhelming

"There is always students cheering on the Razorbacks for their next big win"

Uofa Athletics

"Sports at Arkansas are probably the biggest part of campus! We have great coaches and even better players. We love our hog football! Greatest stadium and facilities too."

CAMPUS DINING

Food on Campus

"Delicous! tons of options. I don't' really use my flex dollars."

OK

"The dining halls on the University of Arkansas campus are great at first. Over time the food can become repetitive. The make your own pasta is always the best section of the dining halls. After time though the sandwiches and pasta gets old. Freshmans should buy a meal plan though that will feed them three times a day. Breakfast is a must and is great at the dining halls! Also eating "Late Night" at the Union is always a great place to get fast food and snacks!!!"

CAMPUS HOUSING

Off-Campus

"I live close to campus in an apartment and I love it. The on-campus apartments are over-priced, but living close is just as easy and much more affordable. I love having my own kitchen and enough room for a huge bed. My complex also offers lots of amenities that I get in addition to the on campus amenities."

Home Away from Home

"There are many different choices for campus living, from all girls to co-ed to international students, the University of Arkansas has it all."

GUYS & GIRLS

Gorgeous All Around!

"Most people are very good looking at the University of Arkansas. The men (especially Greek) are handsome southern gentlemen who will wait to hold the door open or carry something for a lady. The girls are stunning as well."

A Lot of Diversity

"You can find every type at the U of A. The student population is made up of a little of everything, so take your pick!"

HEALTH & SAFETY

Fayetteville Is Safe

"There is very little crime in the city. Besides the minor crimes that are bound to happen when you gather 10,000 people in one location, Fayetteville is very safe. There are plenty of police and surveillance, especially around campus."

It Feels Like Home

"I have never in my college life felt unsafe on this campus. We have security post and lots of lighting at night. There are always security or cops walking around campus at night and we have razorback patrol that will pick you up anywhere on campus and take you anywhere on campus at night so you do not have to wlak alone in the dark. I love this place and feel completly safe and secure."

LOOKING FOR MORE?

Check out our full-length guide to this school at collegeprowler.com/university-of-arkansas/.

University of Arkansas at Little Rock

2801 S. University Ave.; Little Rock, AR 72204
(501) 569-3000; www.ualr.edu

THE BASICS:

Acceptance Rate: Open	Student-Faculty Ratio: 11:1
Yield: 95%	Retention Rate: 65%
Setting: Mid-sized city	Graduation Rate: 21%
Control: Public	Tuition: $14,798
Total Undergrads: 9,852	Room & Board: $3,198
SAT Range: —	Avg. Aid Package: $7,470
ACT Range: 17–25	Students With Aid: 86%

This School Isn't Graded Yet!

College Prowler grades are calculated using tons of criteria, including survey responses that come from students at this school.

Unfortunately, we haven't gathered enough student surveys yet for this school to be able to calculate the grades for each section. Stay tuned to *CollegeProwler.com* for grade updates and more!

CP's Student Author On...
OVERALL EXPERIENCE

Even though everyone here is attending the same school, each student at the University of Arkansas at Little Rock can have a unique experience. There are many opportunities offered here, and it's up to each student to take advantage of them—students have the power to determine what their time here will be like. Not only do the students get a traditional education in the classroom, but they're also able to learn things outside of the classes, as well. Students can learn about teamwork, responsibility, self-motivation, and adaptability in the classroom, as well as through extracurricular activities or internships. Also, the student body is made up of so many different types of people, that students learn a lot just by interacting with one another.

The UALR faculty genuinely wants to see the students succeed, and most of the professors and instructors are professionals in their field. For example, many criminal justice professors are lawyers, and some psychology professors work in clinics that deal with mental conditions.... For the rest of this editorial, visit collegeprowler.com.

Students Speak Out On...
OVERALL EXPERIENCE

Q Overall Campus Experience.

"Over the short period of time I have been on the UALR campus, I have obtained a high view and standards for the school. The school is very unique and is great for learning."

Q Why I Would Choose to Attend U of a at Little Rock Again

"I would choose to attend the U of A at Little Rock again because it is convenient. The college is in the heart of the city and is very accessible to everyone in town. I would also choose this school again because it offers a variety of degree options, and the instructors are helpful."

Q Wouldn't Choose Another School

"If I had to choose schools over again I would still choose UALR. For me UALR isn't far from my hometown and their are plenty of people there to get to know. UALR is a type of school where you can easily make time for both you social life and academic life. The professors at UALR care about you and what you want to make out of your future."

BEST OF ARKANSAS LITTLE ROCK

1. Faculty
2. Good atmosphere
3. On-campus housing
4. Degree plans and options
5. Basketball team
6. Convenient location
7. Fitness center
8. Shool spirit

Easy Financial Aid Process
50% of students surveyed told us that the financial aid process went smoothly and they received the financial aid they needed.

WORST OF ARKANSAS LITTLE ROCK

1. The wait time in the Financial Aid office
2. Only a smaller percentage of students live on campus, so it can get a little boring
3. Food can be a bit pricey

Not Everyone Graduates
21% of students do not complete their education or graduate with a degree.

Student Body

African American:	9%	Male Undergrads:	40%
Asian American:	21%	Female Undergrads:	60%
Hispanic:	2%	Living On Campus:	6%
International:	1%	Living Off Campus:	94%
Native American:	1%	Male Athletes:	4%
White:	64%	Female Athletes:	3%
Unknown:	1%	Fraternity Members:	2%
From Out-of-State:	5%	Sorority Members:	2%

Frequently Compared Schools:
Arkansas State University
University of Arkansas
University of Central Arkansas
University of Memphis

Students Speak Out On...
EVERYTHING!

ACADEMICS

Chemistry Department
"I am going to UALR to acquire my major in chemistry before attending pharmacy school. The professors in the chemistry department are amazing. They are always available for help and encourage students to get involved, whether it is sitting in the student lounge in the chemistry building or becoming involved in research with one of the professors!"

Ready for the Real World
"The primary professor of my major has many years of experience in the profession. His insight and contacts are invaluable so his lectures are not all academic theory. The curriculum is reasonably current, good facilities and internships are required for my major."

ATHLETICS

Team Players
"All the "Team Players" at UALR are superb, and they strive for nothing but excellence. The Team Players consist of the athletes, fans, and faculty. The fans and spirit that they support is contagious, and our athletic teams always achieve the the fullest in every sport they do. I am proud to say that after not being in school for almost 20 years and being the second person in my family to attend college, I am proud to take a stand and expand myself as a "Team Player.""

Athletic Facilities
"The athletics facilities at the University of Arkansas at Little Rock are far superior to other colleges in the Little Rock area. The facilities offer various programs to accommodate a trainer's need to enhance a student's physical strength, endurance, stamina, and speed."

CAMPUS DINING

Dining at Ualr
"Dining at ualr isnt all that great because the prices are high but u dont get that much food. If you are new to the school there are going to be a lot of choices but if you use your meal plan everyday the new will become old very soon. I like the c store the best because there are more options than allthe other food place on campus."

Many Options
"UALR offers many small convenient stores on campus to grab a snack or even grab lunch. There is also a cafeteria that offers pizza, Chinese cuisine, Southern-style food, and many other options. There is also a Starbucks, Taco Bell, and Quiznos."

CAMPUS HOUSING

Housing Is Nice
"Private bathrooms! That is a very nice perk, considering most colleges have public bathrooms for the whole floor. Dorms are only about 10 years old at most, so they look very nice, and new ones are being built and are scheduled to open in fall 2011. Rooms are clean and decently spacious. No stoves though."

GUYS & GIRLS

Guys and Girls at UALR
"At the University, there are many diverse types of people. There are some who come from other backgrounds and some from right here in Little Rock. There aren't "typical" looks, interests, dress, social lives, or relationships because everyone at UALR is very different. Some dress professionally, and some dress just in sweats and a T-shirt. Everyone is nice!"

Friends
"There is a wide variety of people at UALR. If you attend you will always find someone in common with you. Everyone at UALR is friendly and is willing to make and get to know new friends."

HEALTH & SAFETY

Very Safe
"I have always felt safe while on campus. There is always security presence"

Health and Safety
"I've always felt safe on campus."

LOOKING FOR MORE?
Check out our full-length guide to this school at collegeprowler.com/university-of-arkansas-at-little-rock/.

University of Baltimore

1420 N. Charles St.; Baltimore, MD 21201
(410) 837-4200; www.ubalt.edu

THE BASICS:

Acceptance Rate: 65%
Yield: 42%
Setting: Large city
Control: Public
Total Undergrads: 3,004
SAT Range: 1250–1600*
ACT Range: 15–21

Student-Faculty Ratio: 18:1
Retention Rate: 82%
Graduation Rate: —
Tuition: $20,677
Room & Board: —
Avg. Aid Package: $7,941
Students With Aid: 98%

* of 2400

This School Isn't Graded Yet!

College Prowler grades are calculated using tons of criteria, including survey responses that come from students at this school.

Unfortunately, we haven't gathered enough student surveys yet for this school to be able to calculate the grades for each section. Stay tuned to *CollegeProwler.com* for grade updates and more!

CP's Student Author On...
OVERALL EXPERIENCE

There are many reasons why attending UB is a great experience for students. One, the student-to-teacher ratio is 18 to 1, which is commendable because students can receive feedback and more one-on-one time with professors. The majors and classes are eye-opening and interesting, as well. Another great facet of UB is that it's diverse and transfer friendly. Once students are ready to move on from UB, the Career Center helps students find the right career path to help them land their dream job. Students from all over Maryland and the United States can enroll at UB and have a good academic and social experience.

While the University doesn't have residence life, nor does it have traditional dining halls, the apartments offered in the area are great, and the restaurants are close and feature delicious food. Because there aren't any dorms, students and parents save money because the tuition does not include room and board, meal plans, and other extra fees and expenses associated with traditional schools. Moreover, the tuition is cheaper compared to other Maryland schools, both private and public.

Students Speak Out On...
OVERALL EXPERIENCE

Q I Love This School!

"UB is a very good school. When I left here with my first degree, I was ready for he workforce. The group assignments (that I hated) offered team building experience that is valuable in the workforce."

Q TRANSFER FRIENDLY

"My overall experience at UB is a great one, especially being a transfer student."

Q Thus Far Boring

"I have sworn a vow to first improve my mind, and the socializing can wait, while i become my destined self."

BEST OF BALTIMORE

1. Academic/career options
2. Career center/professors that assist you with finding jobs and internships
3. Cost
4. Fairly easy to get admitted
5. Great professors

Happy Students
82% of students return after their first year.

Easy Financial Aid Process
71% of students surveyed told us that the financial aid process went smoothly and they received the financial aid they needed.

WORST OF BALTIMORE

1. There isn't any Greek life.
2. Class scheduling
3. Construction
4. Not enough daytime classes during the summer
5. On-campus food (or lack thereof)

Don't Move Off Campus
Average off-campus housing is a steep $13,100.

Student Body

African American:	34%	Male Undergrads:	43%
Asian American:	4%	Female Undergrads:	57%
Hispanic:	2%	Living On Campus:	0%
International:	1%	Living Off Campus:	100%
Native American:	0%	Male Athletes:	—
White:	36%	Female Athletes:	—
Unknown:	22%	Fraternity Members:	0%
From Out-of-State:	3%	Sorority Members:	0%

Frequently Compared Schools:

Towson University
University at Buffalo
University of Maryland
University of Maryland - Baltimore County

Students Speak Out On... EVERYTHING!

ACADEMICS

Q U Balt

"University of baltimore is a very student friendly school. The past few years here have been a truley great experience. I have enjoyed getting to know my classmates as well as my teachers"

Q Positive Energy Inspires the Writing Process

"There is a positive "can-do" attitude within the English Department at BU. The diversity found within the student body creates a teaching challenge which is met with equanimity by all professors. Every student grasps his or her possibility as a creator of excellent writing by gradually growing into the truth of his or her own unique voice."

Q Academic Ratings

"I have not begun to attend, but UB is rated very highly as aLaw and Business school"

ATHLETICS

Q Sports Abound!

"UB offers regular and intramural sports, boot camp for weight loss, and a campus wellness center. If you have the time, there is definitely something you can get involved in."

Q Athletic Description

"Sports are always being advertised but I don't hear much about them. At this school it is a means to a balanced life versus trying to be a professional athlete one day"

CAMPUS DINING

Q A Variety of Choices and Great Food

"As a commuter school, there were many restaurants in the area that appealed to students. One particular restaurant sold sushi and really great tasting sandwiches."

Q There's Food Everywhere

"UB has plenty of locations in and around the campus to grab a meal or snack before classes. The staff works pretty fast to get you in and out because the time between class is short. I'm an evening student and the meal choices for the restaurants nearby are affordable. UB is located in the heart of the city so there's always an abundance of places to chow down."

CAMPUS HOUSING

Q Mt. Vernon

"I live at the copycat building and go to UB part time so my case is unique. I live amongst MICA students and other artistic types and it is truly a great place to live. In my 10 years of living in Baltimore City, never have I felt such a sense of community and inspiration. A community of inspiration is the most important thing to a college, I believe."

Q We Don't Have Dorms

"But that's ok. I rather live in an apartment in the city of Baltimore!"

GUYS & GIRLS

Q Everyone Is Cool

"this is a very diverse college. The boys and girls here are on a mission to get their degrees and land the job of their dreams. Just like myself, motivation is the key here at UB. #truestory"

Q Boys and Girls, Women and Men

"This is college and everyone is different in their own way. Students' looks are not of interest. I come here to learn and I am glad that UB does not have some sory of popularity contest. Social life is ok, but everyone stay out of others personal relationships."

HEALTH & SAFETY

Q Totally Safe

"I've been a student at UB since 2001. I have never had a problem with crime nor do I know anyone personally affected by crime. When ever I took night classes, I simply had security escort me to my car."

Q UB Has Good Safety

"There are campus police around to make sure the safety of the students are the primary focus."

LOOKING FOR MORE?

Check out our full-length guide to this school at collegeprowler.com/university-of-baltimore/.

University of Central Florida

4000 Central Florida Blvd.; Orlando, FL 32816
(407) 823-2000; www.ucf.edu

THE BASICS:

Acceptance Rate: 47%	Student-Faculty Ratio: 31:1
Yield: 42%	Retention Rate: 87%
Setting: Suburban	Graduation Rate: 63%
Control: Public	Tuition: $20,005
Total Undergrads: 45,255	Room & Board: $8,574
SAT Range: 1600–1870*	Avg. Aid Package: $5,903
ACT Range: 23–28	Students With Aid: 97%

of 2400

Academics	B	Greek Life	B-
Athletics	B-	Guys	A-
Campus Dining	B+	Health & Safety	B
Campus Housing	B+	Local Atmosphere	A-
Campus Strictness	B-	Nightlife	A-
Computers	B	Off-Campus Dining	A-
Diversity	B	Off-Campus Housing	B+
Drug Safety	C	Parking	B-
Facilities	A-	Transportation	A-
Girls	B+	Weather	A-

CP's Student Author On...
OVERALL EXPERIENCE

UCF is growing by leaps and bounds. The students love to hang out, and they all know how to have a good time. There's so much to do and there's something for everyone. Do you really need any more reasons to go to college in Florida?

Orlando is an exciting city with tons of attractions and activities available to all. In many ways, going to school at UCF resembles a four-year vacation (Disney on Sunday, classes on Monday!). Downtown Orlando on a Friday night can, at times, seem like Mardi Gras, and City Walk on a Saturday night isn't to be missed. Also, Floridians are welcoming and friendly and most students at UCF make friends quickly and easily. Friendly faces and sunny skies, what more could a college student ask for? The stellar academics, up-and-coming sports teams, and state-of-the-art facilities are reason enough to spend the next four years of your life at UCF; the city of Orlando is just one big fringe benefit. Come join us!

Students Speak Out On...
OVERALL EXPERIENCE

Q Amazing
"All the people are friendly and the campus feels very safe and secure"

Q Enjoyable
"My experience at school has been wonderful, whaat makes it unique is the staff is the best. Teachers are there to answer any question and a very helpful an friendly."

Q UCF
"This school is amazing, I've gone here for three years and every year has been more fun than the last. I strongly encourage everyone to, at the very least, visit the UCF campus."

Q Fantastic.
"UCF has be an unbelievable experience thus far and has allowed for me to grow and expand my interests. The diversity of students and vast choices for student organizations has added to making my time at UCF very enjoyable and enlightening."

BEST OF CENTRAL FLORIDA

1. The state-of-the-art athletic center!
2. Spirit Week
3. Wackadoo's
4. Wireless Internet
5. Shuttles to and from campus

Happy Students
87% of students return after their first year.

Knowledgeable Professors
96% of students surveyed rated the general knowledge of professors as above average.

WORST OF CENTRAL FLORIDA

1. No parking! Anywhere!
2. Too many apathetic students
3. Rainstorms in the summer
4. Walking in the heat to class
5. Advisors are not always helpful

Overextended Faculty
There are 31 students for every faculty member on campus.

Student Body

African American:	9%	Male Undergrads:	45%
Asian American:	5%	Female Undergrads:	55%
Hispanic:	14%	Living On Campus:	21%
International:	1%	Living Off Campus:	79%
Native American:	0%	Male Athletes:	1%
White:	66%	Female Athletes:	1%
Unknown:	3%	Fraternity Members:	11%
From Out-of-State:	10%	Sorority Members:	9%

Frequently Compared Schools:

Florida State University
University of Florida
University of Miami
University of South Florida

Students Speak Out On... EVERYTHING!

ACADEMICS

Q JOB AVAILABILITY

"I AM A HOSPITALITY MAJOR. ON A WEEKLY BASIS I RECEIVE AN E-MAIL WITH A LIST OF JOBS AVAILABLE AT NEARBY RESTURANTS AND HOTELS. THE E-MAILS ALSO CONTAIN RESUME WORKSHOP DATES AND CAREER FAIR OPORTUNITIES."

Q Professors Are Amazing!

"The academics are amazing at the University of Central Florida. The professors are always willing to help and keep true to the office hours. The curriculums that the professors have is truly educational and interesting."

Q University of Central Florida

"walking into the university i instantly felt the quick rush to learn and challange myself. the prfessors are really helpful and seem quick to respond when you ask for assistance."

ATHLETICS

Q We Love Sports

"Our school has plenty of school spirit and support for almost all it's sports teams. Our athletic facilities, especially our gym, are also top-notch."

Q Top on Espn

"Espn said they had never seen such a spirited school. Look at the football games the camras on the stadium shake from all the cheering."

CAMPUS DINING

Q Food at the Student Union

"There is a lot of variety, so you never have to eat the same thing twice... unless you want to. The area is keep very clean so you don't feel uncomfortable eating there, and there is a lot of room as well, so you always have the option of sitting in or outside."

Q Food

"There are alot of resturants on campus. There are three subways located around campus, one of which i work at. The Student union has 10 restaurants located in it and there are food any type of person. There is a salad bar for vegetarians, a halal place for those must eat blessed meat and every thing in between."

CAMPUS HOUSING

Q Living on Campus at UCF

"UCF has the nicest living conditions of any other Florida State school. The "Towers" dorms compete with top-of-the-line apartment living."

Q Little City

"They have everything on campus. It's like a mini town."

GUYS & GIRLS

Q Girls

"not to be biased but with over 50000 floridian students... come on..statistically there are tons of beautiful girls. just beware"

Q Holy Cow.

"There are lots of attractive females at UCF, and lots of jerky dudes. If you're into the trendy indie culture, I'd suggest attending UCF. If you're into Greek life, it's alright as well."

HEALTH & SAFETY

Q Totally Safe

"I have never felt unsafe nor have ever had any problems when it comes to Health and Safety at the University of Central Florida."

Q Extremely Safe

"The University of Central Florida is practically the safest place that I ever been to. The Campus security and staff are the best in terms of making sure that everything are safe."

LOOKING FOR MORE?

Check out our full-length guide to this school at collegeprowler.com/university-of-central-florida/.

University of Central Oklahoma

100 N. University Dr.; Edmond, OK 73034
(405) 974-2000; www.ucok.edu

THE BASICS:

Acceptance Rate: 75%	Student-Faculty Ratio: 21:1
Yield: 57%	Retention Rate: 65%
Setting: Suburban	Graduation Rate: 36%
Control: Public	Tuition: $10,652
Total Undergrads: 14,413	Room & Board: $7,776
SAT Range: —	Avg. Aid Package: $7,249
ACT Range: 19–24	Students With Aid: 67%

Academics	C+	Greek Life	B
Athletics	B-	Guys	A-
Campus Dining	B-	Health & Safety	B-
Campus Housing	C	Local Atmosphere	B
Campus Strictness	C	Nightlife	B-
Computers	B-	Off-Campus Dining	B-
Diversity	B	Off-Campus Housing	B-
Drug Safety	B	Parking	C+
Facilities	B+	Transportation	C
Girls	B-	Weather	C+

CP's Student Author On...
OVERALL EXPERIENCE

UCO is an amazing university for students of all walks of life to grow and excel to the best of their ability. There are tons of opportunities available to help students reach their potential in every aspect of college life both on and off campus. Campus courses, activities, events, housing, and student organizations are all designed to assist students in becoming more familiar with and preparing for real-life experiences they may not have been able to encounter otherwise. What makes UCO unique is its overwelming amount of community participation and its will to help students build successful lives and careers. There is always someone or some office willing to help with questions or concerns or opportunities to meet new people, and students become a part of something bigger than they can imagine. UCO also exercises its convenience to students with flexible classes, extended hours of facility use such as the campus library, or use of community designated resources. If you are looking forward to building new relationships, learning new concepts, expanding your networking skills, or just looking to experience authentic college life, UCO is the university for you.

Students Speak Out On...
OVERALL EXPERIENCE

Q Overall Experience
"I love UCO! It sometimes gets a bad wrap because we are not as big as OU and OSU. However, UCO's nursing school is better than OU's so I dont mind defending my school! I have never lived on campus because it is kind of expensive. UCO is a very diverse school. There are many different ethnicites here and getting to be apart of those experienes is really amazing!"

Q Only Program in the State
"They have the only Forensic Science program in the state."

Q It's a Good School
"It's a very good school. I'm currently a Forensic Science and Criminal Justice major, and this is the best school in the country to be at for that major. It's a fairly easy campus to navigate once you get used to it, although parking is somewhat of a pain."

Q Average
"there are several things about UCO I can't stand. 1) Parking 2) they hate helping transfer students with questions about enrollment. 3) Teachers are not very helpful when you ask questions about grades"

BEST OF CENTRAL OKLAHOMA

1. Awesome community life
2. The beautiful campus
3. Broncho Lake
4. Campus involvement within the community
5. Forensic science program
6. Great academics

Affordable
Tuition is only $10,652, one of the most affordable rates in the country.

Big Dorms
57% of students surveyed felt that dorms were more spacious than average.

WORST OF CENTRAL OKLAHOMA

1. The attendance policy
2. Certain classes are only offered in the spring every other year.
3. Because some classes are not offered regularly, it can take longer to graduate.
4. Construction

Not Everyone Graduates
36% of students do not complete their education or graduate with a degree.

Life is NOT a Party
50% of students surveyed said it's almost impossible to find a good party.

Student Body

African American:	9%	Male Undergrads:	43%
Asian American:	3%	Female Undergrads:	57%
Hispanic:	4%	Living On Campus:	11%
International:	6%	Living Off Campus:	89%
Native American:	5%	Male Athletes:	5%
White:	62%	Female Athletes:	3%
Unknown:	11%	Fraternity Members:	5%
From Out-of-State:	5%	Sorority Members:	3%

Students Speak Out On...
EVERYTHING!

ACADEMICS

Q Psychology Program

"The Psychology program is one of the best in Oklahoma. It is uniquely structured to build on itself so that a student has several opportunities to utilize the information in a comprehensive manner. The professors go above and beyond to ensure the the students grasp information necessary to prepare them for the next course in the curriculum. I highly recommend UCO as a reputable institution known for its psychology program."

Q Willing to Work With Students

"Found an acounting instuctor who was willing to work with me when I gone behind in my course."

ATHLETICS

Q Athletics

"UCO has many college sports - but more important to most people are the intra-mural sports. There is something for everyone! And - UCO has a fantastic wellness center!"

Q University of Central Oklahoma

"At UCO sports are not as big of a deal since we are so close to OU and OSU however many students still go to football games and baseball games because it is cheap and a lot of fun. Most of the people at school have school spirit and decorate the school just about every week for whatever sport events are happening that week, Overall even though our teams are not the most popular in Oklahoma they still do a great job of getting people at the school to have school spirit and be involved."

CAMPUS DINING

Q Dining

"There are many places to go to eat around campus. You can go to Buddy's and use your meal plan. The food court is available and you can use either cash or your flex dollars. Also, meal exchanges are available for certain places on campus. The food is not bad, but can get a little old after a while."

Frequently Compared Schools:

Oklahoma City University
Oklahoma State University
University of Arkansas
University of Oklahoma

Q Dining Options

"I am not very familiar with all of the dining options available on campus since I am a commuter student, but the on campus restaurants and the fact that it's not far from major restaurants or other fast food locations definitely helps."

CAMPUS HOUSING

Q Broncho Housing

"Several choices. All are nice, but Commons and Suites are new and very nice."

Q Housing

"Our housing is actually pretty good. It is smaller than others because we are a commuter school. But if you do live on campus its awesome! The hall directors and RA's work hard to keep a community when it comes to housing, so it makes a comfortable place for new college students, and students from far away to live"

GUYS & GIRLS

Q Lots of International Students

"University of Central Oklahoma is a great university. Here are a lot of international students. It is awesome. There are different cultures, nationalities, races. Everybody is interested at a sport and a good education. People are free, polite, and very open-mined."

Q A Multicultural Mix

"There are tons of different students at UCO. We get a lot of transfer students. I have already met some from China, Russia, Germany, and France."

HEALTH & SAFETY

Q Safety on Campus

"Overall it has a great atmosphere and is really low on crime, etc."

LOOKING FOR MORE?

Check out our full-length guide to this school at collegeprowler.com/university-of-central-oklahoma/.

University of Chicago

5801 S. Ellis Ave.; Chicago, IL 60637
(773) 702-1234; www.uchicago.edu

THE BASICS:

Acceptance Rate: 27%
Yield: 36%
Setting: Large city
Control: Private Non-Profit
Total Undergrads: 5,157
SAT Range: 1370–1560*
ACT Range: 28–33

Student-Faculty Ratio: 6:1
Retention Rate: 98%
Graduation Rate: 92%
Tuition: $39,381
Room & Board: $11,697
Avg. Aid Package: $33,441
Students With Aid: 72%

* of 1600

Academics	A+	Greek Life	C
Athletics	C+	Guys	B-
Campus Dining	B+	Health & Safety	B-
Campus Housing	B	Local Atmosphere	A
Campus Strictness	A+	Nightlife	B+
Computers	A-	Off-Campus Dining	A+
Diversity	A-	Off-Campus Housing	B-
Drug Safety	A-	Parking	D
Facilities	B+	Transportation	A
Girls	C+	Weather	D

CP's Student Author On...
OVERALL EXPERIENCE

Everything at Chicago centers around providing students an ideal education. Not only the Core Curriculum with its balanced approach to the disciplines and rigorous opposition to mediocrity, but also the House System, the campus design, the athletic structure, and the graduate-undergraduate dynamics all contribute to Chicago's continuing pursuit of the perfect academic experience. This aids the U of C student in their search for truth. This approach, however, has its own shortcomings. The College's dismissal of the vocational puts U of C students at an initial disadvantage in the workplace. Recruiters often say (sometimes improperly) U of C students lack any marketable skills. This is an important criticism, though the University has done much to give students the tools they need to survive in the job market: placement services for history and English concentrators (typically the two highest unemployed concentrations), seminars on preparing resumes, and marketing a U of C education, all are part of a suite of services the University has rolled out to help its students make it in real life.... For the rest of this editorial, visit collegeprowler.com.

Students Speak Out On...
OVERALL EXPERIENCE

Q **Awesome**
"You're not here for prestige, you're here for an education - you'll get it."

Q "I'm very glad I'm here; what I wanted most out of college was intense intellectual activity, and at the University of Chicago, I got exactly that. This is not the place for either partying or pre-professionalism. It's the place where every idea you have will be questioned, analyzed, and ripped apart to shreds, leaving you a wiser person in the end. If you like hard work, come here. It's worth it."

Q "The social atmosphere here is a bit lacking, and the academic pressure is immense. Aside from that, I guess this is a great school to be at. I think that if I had it all to do over again, I might be somewhere else. This school takes a lot out of me. I think we have the highest transfer rate of any 'top 50' school, and I may just add to that."

BEST OF CHICAGO

1. The Core
2. O-Week
3. The House System
4. Scav Hunt
5. Scoffing at Ivy League grade inflation with friends over bubble tea in Chinatown

Happy Students
98% of students return after their first year.

Commitment to Teaching
There are 6 students for every member of faculty on campus.

WORST OF CHICAGO

1. The Core
2. The weather
3. The Reg
4. The walk to Shoreland in the winter
5. The swim test
6. Overpriced meal plan
7. Nerdy social life

Expensive
Tuition is a steep $39,381, one of the most expensive rates in the country.

Student Body

African American:	6%	Male Undergrads:	50%
Asian American:	14%	Female Undergrads:	50%
Hispanic:	8%	Living On Campus:	60%
International:	9%	Living Off Campus:	40%
Native American:	0%	Male Athletes:	10%
White:	45%	Female Athletes:	7%
Unknown:	19%	Fraternity Members:	15%
From Out-of-State:	81%	Sorority Members:	15%

Students Speak Out On... EVERYTHING!

ACADEMICS

Amazing
"Definitely deserves its ranking as one of the top schools in the world!"

Economics
"Fantastic teachers, top-niche curriculum, heavy workload"

Academics
"The teachers here clearly know what they are doing, even if some of the intro level classes are taught by graduate students. The classes themselves can be very tough and challenging, it strives the students to do their best. Our core curriculum is set for the students to explore wide range of areas including humanities, social science, physical science, biological science, and music/art/drama. I think this is a great school to spend the 4 years in college."

ATHLETICS

Good Athletics and Facilities, but Nobody Really Cares
"Although our team do well in their division, and all our gyms and fields are either new or recently remodeled, the school spirit of UChicago does not rest at all in athletics. There's significant participation in intramural sports, but even that fails to fuel any flames of inter-house rivalry. Sports occupy the last page of the student newspaper, enough said."

At the Lower Division
"Although sports were big time at the university,Chicago places no emphasis on sports now.The University of Chicago once belonged to the Big Ten and had the first Heisman Trophy winner. Now they play in a lower division."

CAMPUS DINING

Good Food, Repetitive
"the food at the dining halls is, on most days, extremely good. they have kosher, vegan and halal options. Sometimes a few meals are however below average. Meal plan is $$$,but worth it if you dont enjoy cooking. If you like cooking, don't take the meal plan after your first yr."

Frequently Compared Schools:
Brown University
Columbia University
Northwestern University
University of Pennsylvania

Better Than Expected
"Some complain, and it's not amazing, but I don't mind it"

CAMPUS HOUSING

Good
"Some people complain about the conditions, but I love it"

"All types of living conditions are available: suites, apartments, singles, and doubles—whatever you want."

GUYS & GIRLS

"There are more attractive girls here than guys. Most attractive guys have significant others, usually from back home. Otherwise, they are going out with the attractive girls. The dating scene can be kind of depressing for everyone else."

"There is a lack of hot guys here! It's really sad and upsetting, but oh well. Actually, though, I don't go for younger boys, but the incoming freshman class this year wasn't too bad. I think things are getting better."

HEALTH & SAFETY

Safest Campus I've Been on
"I've never felt unsafe at U of C. For as big of a city as it is, the campus is very safe. I've taken the train home several dozen times at 3 am and have NEVER had any problems even though I live further into the southside. Also, the campus police are amazing. One of my friends was wandering outside drunk at 4 am after a frat party. The police got him home safely in spite of his drunken stupidity."

A Very Safe Place, but Be Careful
"The university's neighborhood of Hyde Park is one of the top 5 safest neighborhoods in Chicago. Additionally UChicago has the second largest private police force in the world, which patrols not only campus, but the surrounding area, including places frequented by students. In spite of this, there are places off campus that should be avoided when alone at night."

LOOKING FOR MORE?
Check out our full-length guide to this school at collegeprowler.com/university-of-chicago/.

University of Cincinnati

2624 Clifton Ave.; Cincinnati, OH 45221
(513) 556-6000; www.uc.edu

THE BASICS:

Acceptance Rate: 61%
Yield: 36%
Setting: Large city
Control: Public
Total Undergrads: 21,884
SAT Range: 1510–1850*
ACT Range: 22–27

Student-Faculty Ratio: 16:1
Retention Rate: 85%
Graduation Rate: 46%
Tuition: $23,922
Room & Board: $9,702
Avg. Aid Package: $5,357
Students With Aid: 81%

* of 2400

Academics	B-	Greek Life	A
Athletics	A-	Guys	A-
Campus Dining	B	Health & Safety	C
Campus Housing	C+	Local Atmosphere	A-
Campus Strictness	B	Nightlife	B+
Computers	B+	Off-Campus Dining	B+
Diversity	B-	Off-Campus Housing	B-
Drug Safety	C-	Parking	B-
Facilities	B	Transportation	A-
Girls	B+	Weather	C

CP's Student Author On...
OVERALL EXPERIENCE

The University of Cincinnati is ideal for anyone looking to graduate with a solid education and experiences of a lifetime. At UC, there is something for everyone, no matter what background you come from and no matter what your goals are. The faculty and staff are helpful and passionate about helping students learn, so whatever program you choose, you'll get a good education. Plus, the University is always expanding the curriculum, so students have more and more options of what they can study.

The campus itself is as diverse at the curriculum, so students will be learning something new even if they aren't in the classroom. UC brings in a variety of speakers, events, and exhibits that promote different ways of thinking and cultures. The majority is not the only group that gets its voice heard. You may not get that experience at another college, so take advantage of the openness that UC provides. Cincinnati is also becoming a more diverse city, so students who are open to going off campus can experience even more.... For the rest of this editorial, visit collegeprowler.com.

Students Speak Out On...
OVERALL EXPERIENCE

Q Love It

"I Love cincinnati, the design school is by far the best, and its really tough work. Ironically if you are in either the Art&Design or the Music college you will be worked harder than any other academic major."

Q Great Facilities and Technology

"The University of cincinnati has extremely good facilities, which are many computer labs, availability of computers, many restrooms, many work spots, fast students services, offering of tremendous amount of majors, minors, and certificates, and cultural programs."

Q I Live a Very Busy Life.

"The College of Design Architecture Art and Planning at the University of Cincinnati keeps me on my toes. The amount of homework and quality of the work expected from the students is top notch. It does not leave much room for free time. Despite the intensity of my program, I know this is where I want to be. I have never before been challenged like this and I love it. I know that in the end, the University of Cincinnati will give me the best chances at being able to succeed."

BEST OF CINCINNATI

1. Accessibility of professors, advisors, and other faculty
2. Internship and job opportunities
3. Co-op programs
4. Facilities are modern and clean

Happy Students
85% of students return after their first year.

Knowledgeable Professors
69% of students surveyed rated the general knowledge of professors as above average.

WORST OF CINCINNATI

1. Parking—availability and cost
2. Off-campus crime
3. It's not a 24-hour campus
4. Cincinnati weather
5. There's very little variety with on-campus dining

Lowest Grades
Drug Safety: C-
Weather: C
Health & Safety: C

Student Body

African American:	12%	Male Undergrads:	48%
Asian American:	3%	Female Undergrads:	52%
Hispanic:	2%	Living On Campus:	20%
International:	2%	Living Off Campus:	80%
Native American:	0%	Male Athletes:	3%
White:	76%	Female Athletes:	3%
Unknown:	6%	Fraternity Members:	75%
From Out-of-State:	9%	Sorority Members:	86%

Frequently Compared Schools:

Miami University
Ohio State University
Ohio University
University of Michigan

Students Speak Out On...
EVERYTHING!

ACADEMICS

ℚ Learning Community

"A group of about 20 people all in the same major can work together to help each other succeed. We are all in the same classes."

ℚ Chemical Engineering

"We have a harder work load than most majors, but UC prepares us well for it. I chose this school because of its amazing co-op program within my field. Our curriculum coincides with our job routines and strengthens our skills."

ATHLETICS

ℚ Sports Are a Large Part of Student Life.

"The athletic scene at the University of Cincinnati is very popular. Almost everyone has team spirit, and rightfully so. Our school seems to excel in the sports that we participate in. The Recreation Center at UC is spectacular with many different events and machines available for use. Consequently, athletics at the University of Cincinnati are very important."

ℚ Sports

"Our athletic department is involved and with campus and campus is involved with our athletic department."

CAMPUS DINING

ℚ So Many Options

"The University of Cincinnati has three halls with all different options. All of them are buffet style and have change some stations but some are for regulars. The food is cooked by professionals. The service people can be rude sometimes but understandable because college kids can be hard to work with or for."

ℚ Food Court

"The food is good, but it is very expensive to eat. Also the food isnt that healthy, and is very easy to gain the freshman 15."

CAMPUS HOUSING

ℚ Lets Be Reasonable

"The housing for upperclassmen is great but the windows are very, very, small. The high capacity dorms are right on the street and walking back alone at night is very unsafe. The newest dorm is the best for freshmen, althoug it is a bit pricey."

ℚ Housing Needs an Update

"My dorm year was spent in Daniels Hall - filled with quads and doubles. The spaces were pretty cramped, much more so than other dorms on campus, so my experience was pretty biased. Overall, the dorms are just okay - they are well heated and we had internet in our room. The elevators were kind of janky, though."

GUYS & GIRLS

ℚ Lots of Guys

"There are a ton of good looking guys on campus. If I were more outgoing I would attempt to talk to all of the hot guys, but I'm way too shy to do that. Nevertheless, it's still fun people watching and looking at all the hot guys UC has to offer."

ℚ Diversity

"What I love about UC is the range of people it draws. There are about 30,000 students, and you see all sorts - the drama kids, the hipsters, the goths, the christians, the jocks - you can find pockets of more concentrated steriotypes if you are in one of the more specific colleges sometimes - like the school of art, or the music conservatory, but for the most part, you meet a wide range of people in classes."

HEALTH & SAFETY

ℚ Security at the University of Cincinnati

"I feel safe attending school at UC because I live off campus and I am only there during the daylight hours. Therefore, I cannot give the best answer to this question because I am not around campus during the nighttime when most of the crimes in the city occur."

LOOKING FOR MORE?

Check out our full-length guide to this school at collegeprowler.com/university-of-cincinnati/.

University of Colorado

1 Regent Drive; Boulder, CO 80309
(303) 492-1411; www.colorado.edu

THE BASICS:

Acceptance Rate: 84%
Yield: 34%
Setting: Small city
Control: Public
Total Undergrads: 27,069
SAT Range: 1080–1280*
ACT Range: 24–29

Student-Faculty Ratio: 21:1
Retention Rate: 83%
Graduation Rate: 67%
Tuition: $28,186
Room & Board: $10,378
Avg. Aid Package: $13,605
Students With Aid: 52%

* of 1600

Academics	B-	Greek Life	B-
Athletics	B+	Guys	B
Campus Dining	B+	Health & Safety	B
Campus Housing	B+	Local Atmosphere	B+
Campus Strictness	B-	Nightlife	B+
Computers	B	Off-Campus Dining	A-
Diversity	C+	Off-Campus Housing	B
Drug Safety	D+	Parking	B
Facilities	B+	Transportation	A+
Girls	B-	Weather	B+

CP's Student Author On...
OVERALL EXPERIENCE

There will be many times throughout the college experience when a student will question his decision and dwell on other possibilities. The University of Colorado-Boulder is a significantly large school where an incoming freshman will undoubtedly feel lost on the long and lonely walk to class. You will find yourself contemplating the benefits that a smaller school could have offered and wonder whether you made the right choice. But it isn't hard to lose that in the amazing beauty of the campus and the kind, openness of the students, which makes it easy to find your place. As the years progress, you will notice more the value in choosing Boulder with the pure intention of skiing as many days as possible. Throughout your time spent at CU, you will ask if you have surrounded yourself with the right people. Later, when you are confronted with choosing a profession, serious criticism may be cast onto your once prized major.

Such questions will plague several students attending a number of universities, yet not all of them will find solace in knowing they spent four years studying in one of the most stimulating cities in the country.... For the rest of this editorial, visit collegeprowler.com.

Students Speak Out On...
OVERALL EXPERIENCE

Q The Best!

"I absolutely love it here! It is affordable and its nice to go somewhere that isn't too big. They are really great about financial aid too!"

Q Best Place on Earth

"With 300 days of sunshine a year, great teachers, fantastic friends, and unbelievably awesome public transportation, you can't go wrong with CU Boulder. Go Buffs!"

Q Great

"College is what you make it first and foremost. people are friendly...easy to meet other students if you are open to it... Rember you are here to study, grades CAN drop if you do not stay on top of your school work, no one is here to tell you to do stuff...most grades based on only tests...hot or miss concept. Great atmosphere and college town!"

BEST OF CU-BOULDER

1. Campus
2. Boulder
3. Ski season
4. Quality of life
5. Variety of courses
6. The Hill
7. The bars
8. Gorgeous weather

Happy Students
83% of students return after their first year.

Knowledgeable Professors
93% of students surveyed rated the general knowledge of professors as above average.

WORST OF CU-BOULDER

1. Boulder police
2. High cost of living
3. Core requirements
4. Lack of diversity
5. Rich kids
6. Parking and traffic
7. Icy and snowy days
8. TAs (Teaching Assistants)

Expensive
Tuition is a steep $28,186, one of the most expensive rates in the country.

Expensive to Just Get By
67% of students surveyed felt that the amount it costs to live while at school was worse than average.

Student Body

African American:	2%	Male Undergrads:	53%
Asian American:	6%	Female Undergrads:	47%
Hispanic:	6%	Living On Campus:	25%
International:	2%	Living Off Campus:	75%
Native American:	1%	Male Athletes:	2%
White:	77%	Female Athletes:	2%
Unknown:	6%	Fraternity Members:	8%
From Out-of-State:	41%	Sorority Members:	13%

Frequently Compared Schools:

University of Arizona
University of Denver
University of Oregon
University of Washington

Students Speak Out On... EVERYTHING!

ACADEMICS

Q Architecture Student

"I am very satisfied with the program I am in. The teachers are there for you at all times, and willing to succeed 100%. They want you to understand everything before you leave their class for the day. The Advisers are always there to lead you in the right direction when you feel lost. I am very confident that this school will prepare me for the real world and help me become a Successful Architect."

Q Love It

"I came to University of Colorado because of it's school of journalism, the campus is amazing, and most of the professors I have had have been very inspiring, as well as the advisors. They are available for any needed help, and are really encouraging."

ATHLETICS

Q Sports Are Big

"Everybody here has some sort of athletic activity they love to do. Some play varsity, club and IM sports, others are addicted to tossing the frisbee, playing catch, running, swimming, hiking, or working out. If you refuse to do any sports buy a bike."

Q School Spirit

"Students are always cheering on the home teams and going to all of the games. There are even pranks pulled between students of rival campuses and ourselves."

CAMPUS DINING

Q CU Boulder Housing and Dining

"On campus, Housing and Dining services work hard to keep their clients (the students) happy. The vegan options are surprisingly varied, which makes the lifestyle change much easier."

Q Lots of Options

"This year the University of Colorado opened a brand new facility. The main feature is a dining hall that handles a thousand students at a time with food choices of Chinese, Persian, Italian, Kosher, a grill, salad bar, deli station with panini makers, burrito station, sushi, and a desert station with an ice cream bar. Our other dining centers are also pretty nice but lack the options. We also have some nice grab n gos with lots of good food to go including made to order hamburgers."

CAMPUS HOUSING

Q Student Transportation

"If you don't have a car, you don't feel stranded. There are buses that run everywhere in Boulder, allowing you the freedom of having a car without worrying about maintenance, tickets or parking."

Q Dorms Convenient and Great!

"I had virtually no complaints living my freshman year on campus. I loved the Engineering Quad and the free tutoring and experiences offered are fantastic. The roommate selection process worked great and I've been living with my selected roommate for four years and counting. The dorms seem to be renovated when needed and even the older ones are clean for their age."

GUYS & GIRLS

Q Endless Choices of Gorgeous

"It really doesn't matter if you're into guys, girls, hipsters, hippies, prudes or sexual diviants; you'll find a multitude of sexy people to look at and enjoy. Just take a glance at Farrand Field on a sunny day and you'll get the picture."

HEALTH & SAFETY

Q The Boulder and University of Boulder Police

"i must say, i feel safest when i am in boulder or within campus, apart from the boulder police, university of colorado has a a well structured independent police group right inside campus. you can see them patroling in their cars(cu police) 24hours in a day. every incident that occur is taken serious nd investigations begin almost immediately, crime isnt tolerated in the boulder campus and i really havent witnessed any yet.apart from the police force, the hostels have a form of security too."

LOOKING FOR MORE?

Check out our full-length guide to this school at collegeprowler.com/university-of-colorado/.

University of Connecticut

2131 Hillside Road; Storrs, CT 06269
(860) 486-2000; www.uconn.edu

THE BASICS:

Acceptance Rate: 50%
Yield: 29%
Setting: Town
Control: Public
Total Undergrads: 17,008
SAT Range: 1670–1960*
ACT Range: 24–29

Student-Faculty Ratio: 18:1
Retention Rate: 92%
Graduation Rate: 76%
Tuition: $25,486
Room & Board: $10,120
Avg. Aid Package: $11,459
Students With Aid: 78%

* of 2400

Academics	B+	Greek Life	B+
Athletics	A	Guys	B+
Campus Dining	B+	Health & Safety	C+
Campus Housing	B	Local Atmosphere	C+
Campus Strictness	B	Nightlife	B+
Computers	B-	Off-Campus Dining	B-
Diversity	B-	Off-Campus Housing	B
Drug Safety	C-	Parking	B-
Facilities	B+	Transportation	B+
Girls	B	Weather	C-

CP's Student Author On...
OVERALL EXPERIENCE

For many students, the University of Connecticut wasn't a first choice, but after discovering all it had to offer, few students can imagine themselves anywhere else. UConn is a very large school, and with more than 15,000 undergraduates, you will not have your opportunities handed to you. For example, in high school and smaller colleges, it's common for a music teacher to do some recruiting, and if you're a great musician, you'll be recruited one way or another into the band. At the University of Connecticut, you could be Miles Davis and never become discovered, and this applies to every aspect of campus life. It seems if you don't go out and get what you want, you'll sit idly in your dorm room doing little more than classwork and meeting a few people other than those on your floor. At UConn, motivation is either a most fervent asset or your most cankerous liability. No one will make your college experience for you, and you are guaranteed to get out only as much as you put in.... For the rest of this editorial, visit collegeprowler.com.

Students Speak Out On...
OVERALL EXPERIENCE

Q Personalized Experiences

"The great thing about UConn is the variety of activities available. Whether you're into sports (as an athlete or a spectator), have a passion in language and the arts, or are looking to join a club based on your interests, there is guaranteed to be a group of people ready and willing to experience it with you. The large campus and student body make everything really accessible and obtainable, and I wouldn't want to be anywhere else for my undergraduate years."

Q Pharmacy College

"I am a first year pharmacy college student and my experience so far is very good. We are a small group on a very large campus which makes us unique and close-knit. Networking will one of the keys to success."

BEST OF CONNECTICUT

1. Basketball
2. Spring Weekend
3. Football at the new stadium
4. There's an even ratio of guys to girls
5. Academic and technology support

Happy Students
92% of students return after their first year.

Proven Success
76% of students will complete their education and graduate with a degree.

WORST OF CONNECTICUT

1. Parking
2. Math teachers
3. Construction
4. The "Wind Tunnel Effect"
5. New England weather in general

Boring Place to Live
54% of students surveyed said that the local area is painfully remote.

Student Body

African American:	6%	Male Undergrads:	50%
Asian American:	8%	Female Undergrads:	50%
Hispanic:	6%	Living On Campus:	68%
International:	1%	Living Off Campus:	32%
Native American:	0%	Male Athletes:	5%
White:	63%	Female Athletes:	4%
Unknown:	16%	Fraternity Members:	6%
From Out-of-State:	32%	Sorority Members:	8%

Students Speak Out On... EVERYTHING!

ACADEMICS

Q Popular Study Areas

"I came to the University of Connecticut because it was a large school that has the ability of offer a wide variety of majors and course possibilities. Often, advisors are willing to help explore different career possibilities as well as help find internships for your major."

Q Good Teachers

"Although I have been at the University of Connecticut for a relatively short time, so far, I would say that all my teachers are very good. All the ones I have met are passionate about their subjects. I feel I can always find help from a professor or a TA if I have a problem, although I might have to take the initiative and look for it. Classes vary in difficulty. Some teachers are harder than others."

ATHLETICS

Q Go Huskies!

"Isn't it obvious by our basketball wins that we have the best teams in the country? Our sports are awesome, and our club sports are great too if a person didn't make UConn's team, or just like playing for fun. UConn life revolves around our sports and we're very proud huskies."

Q Athletes Are Awesome

"The athletes at UConn are incredibly nice and cool. The teams are really good and top-rated."

CAMPUS DINING

Q Wide Variety and Great Quality

"There are a number of cafes where anyone with "Points" (given in 2 out of the 3 meal plans), cash, or a credit/debit card can go to get either a snack, yogurt, coffee, sandwiches, etc. There are 8 different dining halls on campus, that let all people with a meal plan swipe in an unlimited amount of times. The dining halls have a wide range of foods including Kosher items and Halal food. The quality of the food is awesome."

Frequently Compared Schools:

Northeastern University
Penn State
University of Delaware
University of Massachusetts

Q Food and Options Great at All Dining Units

"I have to disagree with the review that Buckley and North are less desirable places to eat. Each of the dining units has a unique flair, but they all share a quality menu and a lot of options. Buckley for example has a great atmosphere that a lot of arts and music students really enjoy. Overall, I've enjoyed my time at UConn and have always boasted that we have the best food options out of any college I've visited."

CAMPUS HOUSING

Q Campus Housing

"The dorms are a perfect way to seperate from the family and live on our own. Builds maturity and character. The atmosphere is friendly and very adaptable. The cost is fair compared to all the activites that go on."

Q The Dorms Are Really Nice Here

"The freshman dorms are just average, but the upperclassmen housing is really nice."

GUYS & GIRLS

Q Lots of Diversity

"Girls always look cute and put together. Most guys look like the typical college athlete or frat boy. However there are many cultural centers on campus so there is a wide range of activities and social life. There are punk guys and girls as well as the frat boys and sorority girls."

HEALTH & SAFETY

Q Safe...For Me at Least

"Overall the security system works very well. There are blue light posts where a person can press a button if they feel they are in danger, and the cops will get to them. You can see one blue light post from another. Aside from a stabbing last semester, there have been no other major crimes that I know about."

LOOKING FOR MORE?

Check out our full-length guide to this school at collegeprowler.com/university-of-connecticut/.

University of Delaware

116 Hullihen Hall; Newark, DE 19716
(302) 831-2000; www.udel.edu

THE BASICS:

Acceptance Rate: 57%
Yield: 30%
Setting: Suburban
Control: Public
Total Undergrads: 17,504
SAT Range: 1580–1920*
ACT Range: 24–28

Student-Faculty Ratio: 13:1
Retention Rate: 89%
Graduation Rate: 73%
Tuition: $23,186
Room & Board: $9,308
Avg. Aid Package: $10,798
Students With Aid: 71%

* of 2400

Academics	B+	Greek Life	B-
Athletics	B-	Guys	A
Campus Dining	B+	Health & Safety	B-
Campus Housing	B	Local Atmosphere	B
Campus Strictness	B+	Nightlife	A-
Computers	B-	Off-Campus Dining	A-
Diversity	C+	Off-Campus Housing	B+
Drug Safety	C+	Parking	B
Facilities	B-	Transportation	B+
Girls	B+	Weather	B-

CP's Student Author On...
OVERALL EXPERIENCE

By the end of their years here, most students look back and are happy with their choice. They've received a good education and generally met some people who they will keep in touch with far into their 'real' lives. This love of the school comes about gradually for many students. While some students love it automatically and fit in easily with the relatively homogenous campus, others take longer to find their place and truly start to enjoy themselves.

While many students have a slow start here at Delaware, they all report that once they decided to give it a chance, they found their experience rewarding, not only academically but socially. This University tends to provide a nice balance between a social life and an academic one. There is always plenty of time to hang out and get your work done, so no matter what you are interested in, you have a chance to get it all done. This is the major benefit of attending the University of Delaware.

Students Speak Out On...
OVERALL EXPERIENCE

Q Great Time

"I've had a great time at UD. Many fond memories have been made here, and I will always look back on it as some of the best times of my life."

Q Overall Experience

"I think Delaware is an amazing school. It offers so many opportunities for its students and most of my professors have been nothing but helpful in my past two years there. I think my school caters to the students needs/wants a LOT. I wouldn't choose another school if I could do it all over again. The academic challenge perfectly meets my capabilities."

Q Having a Blast!

"I have loved my time so far at delaware. It is a weird transition from high school but it is so much fun."

Q Amazing

"I love Delaware, it has the perfect balance of work hard and party hard. You are never out of things to do and everyone is really friendly. A great place to spend four years."

BEST OF DELAWARE

1. Internet access
2. Academics
3. Student access to fitness centers
4. Theater groups and productions
5. Cheap movies
6. Professors

Happy Students
89% of students return after their first year.

Proven Success
73% of students will complete their education and graduate with a degree.

WORST OF DELAWARE

1. Parking
2. Poor food quality
3. Diversity
4. Excessive drinking and partying
5. Too many girls to guys
6. Lack of air-conditioning in most dorms

Lowest Grades
Drug Safety: C+
Diversity: C+
Weather: B-

Student Body

African American:	6%	Male Undergrads:	42%
Asian American:	5%	Female Undergrads:	58%
Hispanic:	5%	Living On Campus:	46%
International:	2%	Living Off Campus:	54%
Native American:	0%	Male Athletes:	6%
White:	78%	Female Athletes:	4%
Unknown:	4%	Fraternity Members:	10%
From Out-of-State:	62%	Sorority Members:	14%

Students Speak Out On...
EVERYTHING!

ACADEMICS

Great Teaching

"I came to University of Delaware for the Chemical Engineering program and it is absolutely great. I feel like the way I think has changed for the better after just one year and can't wait for the next ones. The teachers are extremely interesting in helping and have given me research opportunities and contacts for internships next summer before I even entered my sophomore year."

Fashion Merchandising

"The faculty are great and always available for help. Also, they give you a four year plan for your years there so you can easily create your schedule. As well, they offer a great study abroad trip to Paris!"

ATHLETICS

UD Athletics

"Not all sports at UD are really intense. The best we have are definitely football, lacrosse and girls volleyball. Fans are really supportive and school spirit is huge here. Blue Hens are very proud!"

Fun!

"Varsity School athletic events are a great place to show school pride and socialize. IM sports are also very popular and easy to get involved in."

CAMPUS DINING

FOOD

"There is a variety of food places all around the campus that offer good food. Its a little pricey but satisfying."

Nothing Special

"I do love the occasional premium dessert nights and desserts but other than that the food is not bad but also nothing to rave about. It is convenient because there are a few dining halls and the food is alright. It does get very repetitive and I wish there was a smaller dining plan than 125 meals because I do not eat each meal and would rather more points."

CAMPUS HOUSING

Dorms

"Russell Hall rooms are large and laid out well. A bit hot in fall and spring, bring a fan. My hall was just redone and the furniture is all new. Definitely need rugs in winter. I met lots of people and made some good friends. Other than some odd rules, I liked it."

Housing Varies

"Honors Housing is quite nice. There are a variety of housing options depending on your living preferences (suite style vs typical dorm, proximity to campus, etc.) and overall each is pretty nice. The lottery system worked out for me (but may be a result of being a good student)."

GUYS & GIRLS

Girls: A+   Guys: B

"I've definitely noticed there is an uneven amount of pretty girls to guys. We constantly hear from visiting friends about how many hot girls are around campus, and it's no lie. There are your classic stuck up, done-up girls... or your down-to-earth, minimal make-up, genuinely gorgeous ones. Either way, they're everywhere. On the other hand, the guys are just average."

Trendy

"Both guys and girls are very good-looking. Overall, students dress fairly preppy and trendy and everyone seems to care a lot about how they look."

HEALTH & SAFETY

Safe Town

"There are always police officers and public safety around and there is little crime in newark."

LOOKING FOR MORE?

Check out our full-length guide to this school at collegeprowler.com/university-of-delaware/.

University of Denver

2199 S. University Blvd; Denver, CO 80208
(303) 871-2000; www.du.edu

THE BASICS:

Acceptance Rate: 70%
Yield: 20%
Setting: Large city
Control: Private Non-Profit
Total Undergrads: 5,376
SAT Range: 1610–1910*
ACT Range: 24–29

Student-Faculty Ratio: 12:1
Retention Rate: 86%
Graduation Rate: 74%
Tuition: $35,481
Room & Board: $9,495
Avg. Aid Package: $22,017
Students With Aid: 81%

* of 2400

Academics	B+	Greek Life	B
Athletics	B	Guys	B+
Campus Dining	B-	Health & Safety	B
Campus Housing	B	Local Atmosphere	A
Campus Strictness	B	Nightlife	A
Computers	B	Off-Campus Dining	A-
Diversity	B-	Off-Campus Housing	B+
Drug Safety	C-	Parking	B-
Facilities	A-	Transportation	A-
Girls	B	Weather	B+

CP's Student Author On...
OVERALL EXPERIENCE

Students generally enjoy their time at DU and are content staying for four years. Classes are interesting, professors are friendly, and the campus is in the middle of a growing, energetic city. Social life at DU is varied and engaging, and students often say the best part of their time at DU has been the memories and friends they've made.

Some students complain that DU lacks diversity, and they say that the campus is too small, there's not enough school spirit, and it's too expensive. Some can't wait to get away on the weekends to go party or attend football games at CU Boulder or CSU. Others are looking for more of an academic challenge in their college careers. DU offers a nice balance of academia and partying. If you're looking to dedicate your college years solely to developing your career and learning as much as you can, DU probably isn't the place for you. If you want to learn, but also want to have some fun in the process, DU might be the perfect fit.

Students Speak Out On...
OVERALL EXPERIENCE

Q Overall Experience at DU
"A great education at a reputable school in a wonderful city."

Q Balance
"My school is one large community. Everyone encourages each other to be a better person without being pushy. I have had an incredible first quarter. There is a great balance between social and academic life."

Q I Love DU
"The University of Denver is fabulous! I love going to school here and I feel like I am getting a great education. The classes are small and the professors are personable. It's a great university overall, plus our hockey team is great."

Q Having Fun
"I enjoy attending DU"

BEST OF DENVER

1. Denver!
2. The 10-week quarter system
3. May Daze
4. Small campus size
5. Greek bar parties
6. The Border

Happy Students
86% of students return after their first year.

Proven Success
74% of students will complete their education and graduate with a degree.

WORST OF DENVER

1. Next-to no diversity
2. Kind of feels like high school
3. Expensive
4. Horrible parking
5. Centennial Halls and Towers

Expensive
Tuition is a steep $35,481, one of the most expensive rates in the country.

Student Body

African American:	3%	Male Undergrads:	44%
Asian American:	4%	Female Undergrads:	56%
Hispanic:	6%	Living On Campus:	41%
International:	6%	Living Off Campus:	59%
Native American:	1%	Male Athletes:	7%
White:	60%	Female Athletes:	6%
Unknown:	20%	Fraternity Members:	20%
From Out-of-State:	56%	Sorority Members:	11%

Frequently Compared Schools:

Colorado College
University of Colorado
University of Oregon
University of Southern California

Students Speak Out On...
EVERYTHING!

ACADEMICS

Q Great Academics

"I love the academics at the University of Denver. The classes are really small and all my teachers have been awesome."

Q Academics Are Only as Easy as You Make Them

"The professors are extremely helpful if you're willing to put forth the effort to get help. The professors will even give you their cell phone numbers if you REALLY need help. Most of the classes are challenging, but they are not impossible by any means. They are not as challenging as they could be though. If you read everything, you can get an A in the class."

ATHLETICS

Q Awesome Athletics &Amp; Facilities

"Athletics are great here at DU. The hockey team is really good, and the games are a lot of fun. The athletic facilities are amazing! The Coors Fitness Center is really nice, and they offer free ahtletic classes to students such as yoga, pilates, zumba, ab classes... they're great to take advantage of. Overall, DU is a really fit campus with lots of ways to get involved in sports and athletics."

Q Hockey Hockey Hockey

"Hockey is the big sport at Denver, its like football to the south. The games are great and very exciting! Thats where you will find a great majority of students at the beginning of the weekend, cheering on our Pios! We also have the best ski team in the nation 3 years running. Our other sports do not bring a big crowd but are still fun to attend"

CAMPUS DINING

Q Flex Plan

"I have only eaten at the new Nagel Hall facility and the food is made from scratch and delicious. A wide variety of foods, Italian, Salads, Breakfast, etc."

Q The Dining Halls Can Get a Little Repetitive, but...

"The dining halls can get a little repetetive, but there are other great places on campus where you can spend your meal plan cash."

CAMPUS HOUSING

Q Great Recent Improvements

"I loved the dorms at DU. When I lived in them there wasn't wireless internet, but now this year there is. This is a great improvement."

Q Dorms in DU Campus

"I have not had the experience to live on campus. But for what I've heard from friends, it's convenient to the student's daily life. Students really enjoy to have an easy access to the restaurant, gym, and variety of activities."

GUYS & GIRLS

Q HOT

"You will find all sorts of guys at DU - and most of them are really attractive! The girls are pretty, too. Most girls will get all dolled up even if their first class is at 8am."

Q Diverse

"There are many different guys and girls at my school ranging from hippies to big city girls to redneck girls and country boys to big city boys."

HEALTH & SAFETY

Q Campus Safety

"DU has an excellent notification system, and actively notifies students of any incidents."

Q I Have Never Felt Unsafe.

"Even walking across campus at night, I have always felt safe. The area is well-lit and there are always others walking nearby. They have blue light security phones available in case of an emergency. To be honest, I feel a lot more threatened when I walk off campus because the (majority) middle eastern minorities that live around campus catcall women and honk."

LOOKING FOR MORE?

Check out our full-length guide to this school at collegeprowler.com/university-of-denver/.

University of Florida

355 Tigert Hall; Gainesville, FL 32611
(352) 392-3261; www.ufl.edu

THE BASICS:

Acceptance Rate: 43%
Yield: 57%
Setting: Mid-sized city
Control: Public
Total Undergrads: 33,628
SAT Range: 1140–1360*
ACT Range: 25–29

Student-Faculty Ratio: 20:1
Retention Rate: 96%
Graduation Rate: 82%
Tuition: $23,744
Room & Board: $7,500
Avg. Aid Package: $11,106
Students With Aid: 99%

* of 1600

Academics	B+	Greek Life	A
Athletics	A+	Guys	A+
Campus Dining	A-	Health & Safety	B-
Campus Housing	B	Local Atmosphere	B+
Campus Strictness	B-	Nightlife	A
Computers	B+	Off-Campus Dining	A
Diversity	B	Off-Campus Housing	A-
Drug Safety	C	Parking	C+
Facilities	B+	Transportation	A-
Girls	A	Weather	B

CP's Student Author On...
OVERALL EXPERIENCE

Some schools have certain advantages over one another: small schools give a feeling of community, large schools have lots of resources, private schools are ripe for close academic relationships with faculty, state schools offer a good value, and so on. Well, UF is not your typical state school, and Gainesville is certainly not your stereotypical small town. Because this place is so big, we have all the libraries, dorms, athletics, courses, clubs, and services you could want at a good price, but if you put out just a little effort, you'll find that we also have more compassionate, down-to-earth professors, locals, and students that any small, private school could ever dream of having.

For an incoming student coming from a small town, however, this may all seem a little overwhelming at first. There are so many people here that sometimes things take a little time. For instance, you can't just waltz into your college dean's office and expect to see him instantly, like you could expect to see a high school principal. Just realize that at UF—or anywhere else you decide to go—there will be hard times.... For the rest of this editorial, visit collegeprowler.com.

Students Speak Out On...
OVERALL EXPERIENCE

Q Unique
"I think that the University of Florida is very unique. Many people want and dream of being able to enter this university and for some it is a pleasure to be here. I think our campus is very big and very diverse. I wouldn't want to go to any other school other than UF."

Q The Greatest
"UF is the best school! We have a strong emphasis on academics, an awesome athletic program, and the best school spirit!"

Q No Regrets
"The overall experience here is awesome. I applied early decision, was accepted and never looked back. The University of Florida has academic programs that are arguably among the best in Florida. The sports atmosphere is amazing despite not being close to any professional team arenas. The bars/clubs are always having specials so it's not too expensive depending on where you go and a few places are 18+. The bars vary in atmospheres so anybody can find a favorite."

BEST OF FLORIDA

1. Saturdays during football season.
2. Gainesville is a quintessential college town.
3. Professors are usually cool.
4. You can change majors without changing schools.

Happy Students
96% of students return after their first year.

Proven Success
82% of students will complete their education and graduate with a degree.

WORST OF FLORIDA

1. Parking is dismal.
2. Get used to walking. Everywhere.
3. Gas is expensive.
4. Frequent fire drills at the most inopportune times.
5. You can't always get a spot in a class you really want.

Lowest Grades
Drug Safety: C
Parking: C+
Health & Safety: B-

Student Body

African American:	10%	Male Undergrads:	46%
Asian American:	8%	Female Undergrads:	54%
Hispanic:	14%	Living On Campus:	22%
International:	2%	Living Off Campus:	78%
Native American:	1%	Male Athletes:	2%
White:	63%	Female Athletes:	1%
Unknown:	3%	Fraternity Members:	14%
From Out-of-State:	9%	Sorority Members:	20%

Frequently Compared Schools:

Florida State University
University of Central Florida
University of Georgia
University of Miami

Students Speak Out On... EVERYTHING!

ACADEMICS

Q UF: up for the Challenge

"Being a Health Science major is awesome, although classes and workloads can be difficult and require a lot of critical thinking. However, challenges are only presented to students to help them better prepare for their respective careers and be on top in any chosen field. UF's facilities are high tech and advanced; also a neat, clean atmosphere perfectly describes the campus, as a whole."

Q Best Academics in the State

"The University of Florida is the top university in the state of Florida. It is a top research university with professors that are experts in their respective fields."

ATHLETICS

Q GATORS RULE

"Our school is definitely supportive of our variety of sports' teams. Sometimes too much...they seem to put more focus on sports than academics at times, which I don't always like. However, I do enjoy the energy and school pride on campus."

Q Its Great to Be a Florida Gator!

"The athletic experience at the University of Florida is truly none like any other. There is a great deal of fan support, school spirit and athletic facilities. Everyone is constantly in gator apparel and always talking about how great it is to be a Florida Gator. Game day experiences are beyond what most folks imagine; you truly have to see it to believe it."

CAMPUS DINING

Q It Is Great.

"There are a lot of different options to choose from on campus."

Q Variety

"There is many different places to eat on campus and if you aren't in the mood for any of them then there are great place within walking distance of campus."

CAMPUS HOUSING

Q Best and Worst Dorms

"The most social dorms to live in (and in my opinion the best) are Rawlings, Jennings, and Broward, in that order. The most luxurious are the suites: Lakeside, Springs, and Beaty Towers. The least expensive dorm is Thomas, because it has no air conditioning. Do not live there in the summer semesters."

Q Freshmen Experience

"Living on campus has been pretty convienent for me. I have a dining hall less than a block away and the amentities such as laundry, electricity, a/c are all pretty nice. Then again, I reside in newly renovated dorm. Go Gators!"

GUYS & GIRLS

Q Diversity

"At the University of Florida, you'll be able to find all sorts of guys and girls. Most students are focus on their study habits, nonetheless, they all find time to socialize and attend many social events."

Q Clothes

"Because we are such a diverse group of students, the look goes from one extreme to the other. It's really not just one look. You wear what you want to and other people don't really care. They even except you for who you are and what you choose to wear."

HEALTH & SAFETY

Q Extremely Safe

"I have never felt unsafe at the University of Florida. Special security measures are under effect, for example in case of an emergency all the students (who have signed up) will recieve a text message."

LOOKING FOR MORE?

Check out our full-length guide to this school at collegeprowler.com/university-of-florida/.

University of Georgia

212 Terrell Hall; Athens, GA 30602
(706) 542-3000; www.uga.edu

THE BASICS:

Acceptance Rate: 56%
Yield: 51%
Setting: Mid-sized city
Control: Public
Total Undergrads: 26,145
SAT Range: 1690–1980*
ACT Range: 24–29

Student-Faculty Ratio: 18:1
Retention Rate: 94%
Graduation Rate: 79%
Tuition: $25,740
Room & Board: $8,046
Avg. Aid Package: $8,170
Students With Aid: 93%

of 2400

Academics	B+	Greek Life	B
Athletics	A+	Guys	A-
Campus Dining	A+	Health & Safety	B
Campus Housing	B	Local Atmosphere	A-
Campus Strictness	B-	Nightlife	A
Computers	B+	Off-Campus Dining	B+
Diversity	C+	Off-Campus Housing	A
Drug Safety	C-	Parking	B
Facilities	A+	Transportation	A-
Girls	B+	Weather	B

CP's Student Author On...
OVERALL EXPERIENCE

One of the most amazing things about students at UGA is that I have never heard one person say they don't like being here. UGA and Athens have so much to offer in so many different categories, that there really is something for everyone. The positive energy of 30,000 people who are happy to be here is captivating, and something you will instantly want to be a part of. It will not take long before you regard Athens as your second home, and after about a week, most students forget how big a school it is.

It's exciting to be in Athens because there is always something going on, whether it is entertainment, a demonstration, job fairs, or just a chance to hang out with people you just met who are now your best friends. Students are encouraged to explore their talents and make the most of their four years here, and most students are able to achieve their ultimate "college experience." Sometimes, it seems like we are all characters in some cheesy teen movie because college life in Athens is so classic, but academically, socially, and personally, this school seems to have changed most of us for the better.

Students Speak Out On...
OVERALL EXPERIENCE

Q Happy I Chose Here

"UGA is an awesome school. I love it here. I have fun and i know that i'm getting a well respected education. It's the best of both worlds!"

Q It's AMAZING Here

"UGA has got to be the best school on earth. Every aspect of the school is wonderful. We have the best sports fans on the planet and they really know how to cheer on their DAWGS!!"

Q University of Georgia

"I love that it's far enough away from home that I'm forced to be independent, but at the same time it's close enough that if things get really bad home is an hour away. I'm doing really well balancing school and work, and I'm really enjoying my time here at the University of Georgia!"

BEST OF GEORGIA

1. The people
2. Football season
3. Downtown
4. The weather
5. Uga
6. The music scene
7. Proximity to Atlanta
8. The food

Happy Students
94% of students return after their first year.

Proven Success
79% of students will complete their education and graduate with a degree.

WORST OF GEORGIA

1. Constant construction
2. Competition for majors
3. Humidity
4. Diversity
5. Greedy and/or stupid athletes and coaches
6. Parking

Expensive
Tuition is a steep $25,740, one of the most expensive rates in the country.

Student Body

African American:	7%	Male Undergrads:	42%
Asian American:	7%	Female Undergrads:	58%
Hispanic:	2%	Living On Campus:	27%
International:	1%	Living Off Campus:	73%
Native American:	0%	Male Athletes:	3%
White:	81%	Female Athletes:	2%
Unknown:	2%	Fraternity Members:	20%
From Out-of-State:	12%	Sorority Members:	25%

Frequently Compared Schools:

University of Alabama
University of Florida
University of North Carolina
University of South Carolina

Students Speak Out On...
EVERYTHING!

ACADEMICS

Q A Top School That Offers a Top Experience

"UGA is a great school. It is highly ranked and for a good reason. The classes are tough but that is what it is known for, for being a school that produces graduates that are prepared for success. The Professors are highly qualified, so you know that the education you are paying for is of a good quality. The Campus life though makes up for the hard work you put into classes. There facilities are top, and its just an all around great place to go to school."

Q Top Ranking University

"The application process was simply great and easy. The counselors were a big help throughout. I will be starting UGA in Spring 2011 and feel great about it. It is one of the best universities in the state and the nation as well."

ATHLETICS

Q Very Good Sports

"UGA has always been ranked in the SEC in football. Has won almost every year in gymnastics. Has an awesome basketball team."

Q School Spirit

"I think that there is so much school spirit at athletic events. It's so much fun and so awesome!!!"

CAMPUS DINING

Q UGA Dining Halls

"UGA has the best meal plan because it allows a student to go to the dining hall as many times as you want and get as much food as you want. There are a multitude of options of styles of foods for vegetarians and nonvegetarians."

Q Award Winning Dining Halls

"the dining halls are ridiculously good. there's a 24 hour dining hall and one that even offers hibachi and sushi. and there are so many amazing restaurants to choose from outside of school if you don't have a meal plan."

CAMPUS HOUSING

Q Social Atmosphere

"Everyone is friendly on campus. You can meet new people going to and from class."

Q Home Away from Home

"The on-campus apartments are amazing. They feel like home and it is still convienient to dining halls and classes. Meal plan is the best because you get unlimited meals. Social atmosphere is very relaxed. Night life is only exciting if you are 21 (old enough to drink). Cost is highly affordable. UGA barely has any complications with anything."

GUYS & GIRLS

Q Social Life of Girls and Guys

"The University of Georgia offers many different activities that both boys and girls can participate in."

Q People Make This Place

"Athens is full of the most diversified people. Everyone is into something different. The music and art crowd, the athletes, the outdoorsy crowd, the strong Christians, the Greeks, .. The list goes on forever. The people are all beautiful inside and out. Everyone is extremely welcoming and so much potential for romance."

HEALTH & SAFETY

Q Safety Overkill

"Police are everywhere, and our Health Center is unmatched. Crosswalks have flashing lights and "State Law: STOP for pedestrians in crosswalk" signs are clearly posted. On top of it all, there is an emergency communication system in place called UGA Alert that sends an email, a TXT message, and a phone call to everyone affiliated with the university any time a danger arises on/near campus."

Q UGA Is a Very Safe Campus

"You will get alerts straight to your phone by text and phone calls. Campus security can be reached very easily."

LOOKING FOR MORE?

Check out our full-length guide to this school at collegeprowler.com/university-of-georgia/.

University of Hartford

200 Bloomfield Ave.; West Hartford, CT 06117
(860) 768-4100; www.hartford.edu

THE BASICS:

Acceptance Rate: 67%
Yield: 15%
Setting: Small city
Control: Private Non-Profit
Total Undergrads: 5,516
SAT Range: 900–1120*
ACT Range: 19–24

Student-Faculty Ratio: 12:1
Retention Rate: 72%
Graduation Rate: 54%
Tuition: $28,980
Room & Board: $11,238
Avg. Aid Package: $23,574
Students With Aid: 82%

* of 1600

Academics	B-	Greek Life	B-
Athletics	C	Guys	A-
Campus Dining	C+	Health & Safety	C+
Campus Housing	C	Local Atmosphere	C+
Campus Strictness	B	Nightlife	B+
Computers	B	Off-Campus Dining	B-
Diversity	B	Off-Campus Housing	B-
Drug Safety	C+	Parking	B
Facilities	B-	Transportation	B+
Girls	B	Weather	C-

CP's Student Author On...
OVERALL EXPERIENCE

Different students will have different opinions about their experience at the University of Hartford. Some will say they hate, and some will say they love it, but the overall experience is really what you make it. In general, it seems like students who are involved on campus are more likely to have a better overall experience than those who are not. Participating in activities and keeping busy on campus means you will meet more people and share enjoyable times with them. You will likely have the strongest bonds with people you meet in clubs and organizations, but students in the same major are bound to have almost every class together, and friendship will form from that, as well. Suitemates and roommates also become great friends while at the University.... For the rest of this editorial, visit collegeprowler.com.

Students Speak Out On...
OVERALL EXPERIENCE

Q I Love My School

"I love my school. I'm sad that I only have a year left. I went to visit and walked around the campus and knew it was the place I wanted to be. It has an education major for teaching children birth through kindergarten, which is exactly what I want. Its a relatively flat campus that does not set off my excersized induced asthma. Its easy to get off campus with a car but I can find everything I need for everyday living on campus including school supplies, groceries, and entertainment."

Q Looks or No Looks

"A unique school is not all about the beauty or the looks of it—it may be ugly on the outside, but inside, the school can actually look nice and have very respectable students ready to learn. On the flip side, a school may look nice on the outside, but inside, the student are very unpleasant. School is about your learning ability, not about looks."

BEST OF HARTFORD

1. Social community
2. Red Caps (student orientation leaders)
3. Greek life
4. Easy to make friends
5. Everyone is nice.
6. Helpful teachers

Easy Financial Aid Process
50% of students surveyed told us that the financial aid process went smoothly and they received the financial aid they needed.

WORST OF HARTFORD

1. Tuition
2. Weather
3. Meal plans
4. Small school means gossip spreads quickly
5. The food

Expensive
Tuition is a steep $28,980, one of the most expensive rates in the country.

Expensive Dorms
Living on campus doesn't come cheap, with an average housing price tag of $6,908.

Students Speak Out On... EVERYGTHING!

ACADEMICS

Uoh Excellant

"i find the professors quite good. they are on top of their game workload freshman year was tollerable. amazing speical study options, they are tops in theor area. they address each college program within the univeristy"

Biology

"Great Professors. They Know who You are personally and always have time to help you outside of class."

Plenty of Faculty!

"Even though the student body is rather large, the student/faculty ratio is quite low and the quality of professors is very good. Of course, there are always a few that leave a lot to be desired."

ATHLETICS

School Spirit Is Awesome

"Lots of different sports are offered at University of Hartford. They even have intramural sports for students who just like playing on the side, or who didn't have a chance to get on a school team. A lot of people come and show the support to all the games, which creates great atmosphere."

Gym

"Basketball is the biggest sport. The gym is a great resource for all students. It is free but closes for the hours around and during basketball games, which is very frustrating."

Lots of Machines

"We seem to have a lot of teams and sporting events, though I do not attend them. I do however, use the gym and pool at the school and I would say that the gym facilities are great. They have lots of machines and its never too crowded to get on one."

CAMPUS DINING

Food is fine

"Food is just fine. I don't mind it at all!"

High Food Prices

"Prices of food and drinks are way too high, so I have to bring food from home."

CAMPUS HOUSING

Living on Campus

"It depends where you live when you are a freshman. I live in Hawk Hall, and I absolutely love it. It is a new building, air-conditioned, and cleaned every night. The people who live in Hawk Hall tend to be closer and like family compared to the other freshman housing."

Good Variety

"There are many places to live. From party dorms to quite dorms, there are many choices. Some of the dorms are old and some are new. Some have kitchens, some do not. All are relatively close to classes."

GUYS & GIRLS

Fun

"Most people are from New England. Variety of intrests and styles. People like to hang out."

Interesting...

"The guys are of all varieties. Most of the girls are rather, well, slutty, but very good-looking."

HEALTH & SAFETY

Safety

"While it's not 100% safe, the school is pretty close to it. There are only two entrances to the campus and one is closed at night. As such, the crime rate is really low, though that doesn't mean you can just leave your doors unlocked."

Not Bad at All

"Campus security is often driving around the campus. IDs are used to get into the dorms."

University of Illinois

601 E. John St.; Champaign, IL 61820
(217) 333-1000; illinois.edu

THE BASICS:

Acceptance Rate: 65%	**Student-Faculty Ratio:** 19:1
Yield: 41%	**Retention Rate:** 93%
Setting: Small city	**Graduation Rate:** 82%
Control: Public	**Tuition:** $26,670
Total Undergrads: 31,473	**Room & Board:** $9,284
SAT Range: 1200–1430*	**Avg. Aid Package:** $10,288
ACT Range: 26–31	**Students With Aid:** 68%

* of 1600

Academics	A-	Greek Life	A+
Athletics	A-	Guys	A+
Campus Dining	A-	Health & Safety	C-
Campus Housing	B-	Local Atmosphere	B
Campus Strictness	B	Nightlife	A
Computers	B+	Off-Campus Dining	B
Diversity	B	Off-Campus Housing	B+
Drug Safety	C-	Parking	C+
Facilities	B+	Transportation	A-
Girls	A	Weather	C+

CP's Student Author On...
OVERALL EXPERIENCE

One might expect some tentative and even negative opinions about any school, but this is truly not the case here at U of I. Students are proud of U of I's history, proud of is academic accomplishments, proud of the social opportunities it offers, and, most of all, they are proud to be alumni. For so many students to view their choice to come here as an unequivocally good one is a fantastic testament to the University's strength.

Of course students here have plenty to complain about—the weather, the parking, the Greek social scene, the rural location. But all things considered, the positive points of the U of I experience tipped the scale—the University's academic excellency, the safety, the social atmosphere, the athletic tradition, the city's excellent transportation system. Some students admitted that they had a hard time adjusting, that they occasionally wished they had made another decision—but in the end, they were all happy to be here.... For the rest of this editorial, visit collegeprowler. com.

Students Speak Out On...
OVERALL EXPERIENCE

Q Awesom!

"I love this school! Didn't really want to get away from home, so glad I did. The U of I is the best school ever! I have so much fun with friends! and the education that I am getting is awesome!"

Q Phenomenal Thus Far

"I believe my college experience thus far has been a phenomenal one. My friends contribute to my happiness on this campus. Theres never a day when i can say im just bored or unsatisfied with this campus. I LOVE MY SCHOOL"

Q A Community

"My experience here at The University has so far been the BEST! i have met many good friend and have been presented with wonderful oppertunities. My favorite thing about attending the University would have to be Homecoming. its a real enjoyment to see all the differents race groups come together and enjoy eachother."

BEST OF ILLINOIS

1. Meeting new people every day
2. Staying up 'til 4 a.m. eating Gumby's with friends
3. Just a short drive from home for most people

Happy Students
93% of students return after their first year.

Proven Success
82% of students will complete their education and graduate with a degree.

WORST OF ILLINOIS

1. Feeling like a number
2. The dining halls
3. Administrative hurdles and red tape
4. Likelihood that discussions will be led by TAs
5. Required classes that are useless

Expensive
Tuition is a steep $26,670, one of the most expensive rates in the country.

Student Body

African American:	7%	Male Undergrads:	54%
Asian American:	13%	Female Undergrads:	46%
Hispanic:	7%	Living On Campus:	50%
International:	8%	Living Off Campus:	50%
Native American:	0%	Male Athletes:	2%
White:	63%	Female Athletes:	2%
Unknown:	2%	Fraternity Members:	22%
From Out-of-State:	16%	Sorority Members:	23%

Frequently Compared Schools:

Northwestern University
Purdue University
University of Michigan
University of Wisconsin

Students Speak Out On... EVERYTHING!

ACADEMICS

Q Learning to Teach

"I've only been at the University of Illinois for two semesters and only one of those semesters was spent within the college of Education. However, in that one semester, I've found that there are all sorts of opportunities to do tutoring ad teachers aide work in schools around the University and I'm really happy that I have so many of these opportunities to see what it's like to teach, and I've already volunteered quite a bit."

Q Human Osteology

"Human Osteology is a great course for those who are interested in the human skeleton, like I am. The professor who teaches it is great."

ATHLETICS

Q AWESOME!

"There are any and every sport at UIUC! The football games, basketball games, volleyball games, soccer games, women's basketball games, etc. All the games are just extremely fun and energetic. There's never a dull moment at any games. IM sports are also huge and get pretty intense. I can't wait until IM comes up again for basketball. UIUC has it all!"

Q Football

"We have a big ten football team. That means the pre-gaming, and games are incredible. The stadium is always packed, and the games are thrilling to watch. The football stadium is big and always fun to walk around. Our team has a very rich history and I am proud to be part of it."

CAMPUS DINING

Q Great, Lots of Variety!

"There are many of options offered to students looking to dine out. There are food places all over campus, so students are never far from being hungry!"

Q Good Quality but Repetitive

"There are dining halls in every residence hall, and their menus are different from one another, but the main meals become repetitive after eating there for a few weeks. I recommend getting cafe credits, which allow you both to eat in the dining halls and to shop at convenience store type places on campus for some different food."

CAMPUS HOUSING

Q Housing

"The dorms are great for freshman and sophomores and a wonderful way to meet people. They are however expensive. There is the option of private or public. Private dorms such as Newman and Bromley are very nice. The Six-Pack which is public was recently renovated and very nice also. Most of the dorms are located close to classes and have bus systems. I would not recommend living in PAR or FAR. They are a long way from classes and the social areas."

Q Freshmen Should Live in Dorms

"Freshmen should definitely live in dorms. They meet people more easily and make friends that are just as eager to meet them."

GUYS & GIRLS

Q Social Scene on Campus

"There are lots of activities that guys and girls can get into, from sororities to skydiving clubs. Many people are from the Chicago area, dress well, and put on tons of events on campus."

Q Easy on the Eyes and Love to Party

"The boys on this campus are definitely nice to look at. There's always someone around who's willing and ready to go out and have fun."

HEALTH & SAFETY

Q Illinois Safety

"I always feel safe when I am around the main part of campus. The outer limits can be creepy though and there is some crime in the surrounding city. Just dont walk alone at night and you're fine."

LOOKING FOR MORE?

Check out our full-length guide to this school at collegeprowler.com/university-of-illinois/.

University of Illinois at Chicago

601 S. Morgan St.; Chicago, IL 60607
(312) 996-7000; www.uic.edu

THE BASICS:

Acceptance Rate: 63%	**Student-Faculty Ratio:** 18:1
Yield: 34%	**Retention Rate:** 81%
Setting: Large city	**Graduation Rate:** 48%
Control: Public	**Tuition:** $24,424
Total Undergrads: 15,972	**Room & Board:** $9,435
SAT Range: 1460–1920*	**Avg. Aid Package:** $12,497
ACT Range: 21–26	**Students With Aid:** 79%

* of 2400

Academics	B-	Greek Life	C
Athletics	C	Guys	B+
Campus Dining	B	Health & Safety	B-
Campus Housing	C+	Local Atmosphere	B+
Campus Strictness	C+	Nightlife	B
Computers	B	Off-Campus Dining	A-
Diversity	A-	Off-Campus Housing	B+
Drug Safety	C+	Parking	B-
Facilities	B-	Transportation	A-
Girls	B-	Weather	C

CP's Student Author On...
OVERALL EXPERIENCE

The academic curriculum, the opportunities for research and international collaboration, and the cultural richness of the city are all things students come to love over the course of their experience at the University of Illinois at Chicago. From artists such as Ed Uhlir (who designed Millennium Park in Chicago) to professors conducting research in technologies that have come to affect people's everyday lives, UIC has and continues to produce many leaders in numerous areas of study. And although it has its flaws, UIC is always seeking to grow economically and academically.

Apart from its Research I Institution status, rigorous academic programs, and numerous internship and job opportunities, what further makes UIC unique is its ample diversity. Diversity in the student body and faculty, coupled with programs such as study abroad and student exchange, continue to propel UIC into becoming a world leader in technology, business, and politics, as well as in humanitarian and cultural affairs.... For the rest of this editorial, visit collegeprowler.com.

Students Speak Out On...
OVERALL EXPERIENCE

Q Great City School

"If you love the city, Then you cant get any better than UIC. Great school, awesome location and near the Downtown area, and fairly cheap costs compared to other local schools"

Q Awesome

"Great campus, with a wide selection of interesting classes. There are also good teachers, plenty of food options, and a reasonable tuition rate."

Q 3Rd College Year

"I love it here. I am glad I chose to attend UIC. I have met and established long lasting relationships with people from various ethnic and religious backgrounds. I have learned a lot about the school. The urban experience at UIC has proved to be spectacular as well."

Q It's All up to You

"It's a really good place. If you use you time and resources wisely, you will be successful."

BEST OF ILLINOIS AT CHICAGO

1. Affordable off-campus housing
2. Amazing and exciting city
3. Ample supply of assorted restaurants
4. Challenging academic programs for a well-rounded education
5. Diversity

Happy Students
81% of students return after their first year.

Knowledgeable Professors
73% of students surveyed rated the general knowledge of professors as above average.

WORST OF ILLINOIS AT CHICAGO

1. Budget constraints
2. Classes go on regardless of inclement weather.
3. Confusing buildings
4. Expensive parking
5. Few nationally recognized sports teams

Expensive Dorms
Living on campus doesn't come cheap, with an average housing price tag of $6,650.

Don't Move Off Campus
Average off-campus housing is a steep $10,480.

Student Body

African American:	9%	Male Undergrads:	48%
Asian American:	22%	Female Undergrads:	52%
Hispanic:	17%	Living On Campus:	21%
International:	2%	Living Off Campus:	79%
Native American:	0%	Male Athletes:	4%
White:	45%	Female Athletes:	2%
Unknown:	5%	Fraternity Members:	5%
From Out-of-State:	3%	Sorority Members:	3%

Students Speak Out On...
EVERYTHING!

ACADEMICS

Q Courses at UIC

"I can safely say that UIC has a wonderful variety of classes to take. They have many different time slots open so a class can fit into almost anybody's schedule. The workload at UIC I would say is normal. I have attended community college before and would say that the coursework at UIC takes just about an extra 3 hours (for all classes) or so to complete. It's not too easy and not too challenging so it's a really good balance."

Q Econ for Pre-Law

"Since my university does not have a pre-law major, econ was a good major to pick. Once you get to the 300 level courses there will be a lot of overlap for Law."

ATHLETICS

Q Good Sports

"I am currently not involved in any sports, but we do have good teams. The school takes great pride in its sports. Go Flames!"

Q UIC Athletics and Sports Programs

"I can say that the athletic programs at University of Illinois at Chicago are great. It may only be a AA Division but the student invovlement, school spirit and fan support are that of any Big Name School"

CAMPUS DINING

Q OK but Repetitive

"I think I can eat a lot of food and I can choose different kinds. But I can see similar foods whenever I go there. In other words, all foods are fixed."

Q Food Is Pretty Good

"The places around the campus have pretty decent food but you could easily get tired of the food. There isn't much flare to it, and after a while most of the student body starts eating out."

Frequently Compared Schools:

DePaul University
Loyola University Chicago
Northwestern University
University of Illinois

CAMPUS HOUSING

Q On Campus Living

"Living on campus has been the best college experience yet! I really enjoy living here and the activities that are offered for residents, including ice cream socials, snack nights, movie nights, game nights, etc. It is also very affordable for me with the finances I currently receive. The location to campus is awesome as well because I can leave for class about fifteen before it starts and get there on time. I love living on campus and it means a lot to actually live near school."

Q Educated Living

"The campus has an air of security; those enrolled in Elgin Community College are a diverse bunch and it is wonderful to see so many walks of life converging towards a common goal. Parking may possibly be the worst aspect of the college, but once settled the environment and scenery of campus grounds will take your mind off of it."

GUYS & GIRLS

Q Diversity on Campus

"UIC is very diverse and as such the people look and act very differently. UIC has many students who are international from Asian to Middle Eastern and European. If you come from an area with little diversity, UIC is a culture shock and you become familiar with many different attitudes and looks."

Q Social Life

"Its great, different kinds of people around the school. Everyone is friendly"

HEALTH & SAFETY

Q UIC Police Department

"UIC has a vary active police department that patrols the campus day and night. The UIC police work closely with the Chicago police to investigate crimes that may happen to students on or off campus. The department offers several security tips for students, faculty, and staff when on campus during the late hours of the day. UIC is a very place for anyone to be."

LOOKING FOR MORE?

Check out our full-length guide to this school at collegeprowler.com/university-of-illinois-at-chicago/.

University of Iowa

101 Jessup Hall; Iowa City, IA 52242
(319) 335-3500; www.uiowa.edu

THE BASICS:

Acceptance Rate: 83%	Student-Faculty Ratio: 15:1
Yield: 32%	Retention Rate: 83%
Setting: Small city	Graduation Rate: 66%
Control: Public	Tuition: $22,198
Total Undergrads: 20,574	Room & Board: $8,004
SAT Range: 1060–1330*	Avg. Aid Package: $7,445
ACT Range: 23–28	Students With Aid: 76%

of 1600

Academics	B	Greek Life	C+
Athletics	A	Guys	A-
Campus Dining	A-	Health & Safety	B-
Campus Housing	B-	Local Atmosphere	B+
Campus Strictness	C	Nightlife	A
Computers	B+	Off-Campus Dining	B+
Diversity	C	Off-Campus Housing	A-
Drug Safety	C-	Parking	C+
Facilities	B+	Transportation	B+
Girls	B	Weather	B-

CP's Student Author On...
OVERALL EXPERIENCE

Most students who come to the University of Iowa are happy with what they've found, and few are willing to trade their experiences for anything else. With a combination of solid academics and a college town atmosphere that caters to the social scene, UI students find themselves in a well-balanced environment. Iowa isn't an Ivy League school, but it does provide a strong education with a focus on career choices. Iowa is not a party school, but its students know how to relax and have fun while keeping up with their workload.

Since it is such a large institution, UI can seem faceless and intimidating at first, but this quickly dissolves as the tight-knit social scene among college students presents itself. With a huge variety of clubs, sports, and other activities on and around campus, plus Iowa City's bars and downtown area, there are as many ways to meet people and make friends as there are people to meet. Students who have the worst experience at Iowa—or at college in general—are the ones who don't become involved with things that are going on around them.... For the rest of this editorial, visit collegeprowler.com.

Students Speak Out On...
OVERALL EXPERIENCE

Q **Love IC**
"I love Iowa City and the University. It broke me out of my comfort zone and exposed me to new things."

Q **Really Nice Place to Be**
"Everything's close, it's a safe area, and there's a lot of things to do."

Q **LOVE IT!**
"I love the UofI. Foot ball season is awesome and you meet a ridiculous number of fun people. Campus has everything you need to have fun and function and is beautiful most of the time. Weather in the winter sucks but this is Iowa so that is expected."

Q **I Like Art.**
"Atmosphere of literature is good here. And I can play pianoes everywhere I can find it."

BEST OF IOWA

1. The friends you'll make
2. Getting a well-rounded education
3. Early morning tailgating for football games
4. Downtown Iowa City
5. Being able to walk anywhere you need to go

Happy Students
83% of students return after their first year.

Big Dorms
59% of students surveyed felt that dorms were more spacious than average.

WORST OF IOWA

1. No parking!
2. Large gen ed class sizes
3. When the cops come to the bars
4. Budget cuts
5. Dining hall food gets old fast

Lowest Grades
Drug Safety: C-
Diversity: C
Campus Strictness: C

Student Body

African American:	2%	Male Undergrads:	48%
Asian American:	4%	Female Undergrads:	52%
Hispanic:	3%	Living On Campus:	30%
International:	4%	Living Off Campus:	70%
Native American:	0%	Male Athletes:	5%
White:	82%	Female Athletes:	4%
Unknown:	5%	Fraternity Members:	8%
From Out-of-State:	50%	Sorority Members:	12%

Frequently Compared Schools:

Indiana University
University of Illinois
University of Minnesota
University of Wisconsin

Students Speak Out On... EVERYTHING!

ACADEMICS

Q Psychology at the University of Iowa

"As a Pyschology Major at the University of Iowa I feel that I have access to some great resources and have the privillage to have caring and intelligent professors in the Pyschology field."

Q Student Life

"I came to the University of Iowa to pursue a degree in pharmacy and I really enjoy all of my classmates and also the new recreation facility. It is a great place to work out and also hang out with my friends."

ATHLETICS

Q Iowa Has So Many Fans!

"When I went to see an Iowa football game it was insane. It was amazing to see not only how many students went to support their school but also there were hundreds of alumni who came back to support their school as well. It was great to see the tradition in their sports."

Q Everyone Is Into the Sports

"Varsity sports at the University of Iowa are huge, especially when we're playing a rival. Fan support and school spirit are big too, everyone gets into it. Whether youre attending the games or not, you are expected to be wearing the gold and black on game day."

CAMPUS DINING

Q Great, Lots of Options!

"The cafeterias both offer a lot of variety in their culture of food and optional add-ons. The food is always fresh and abundant and staff is nice. There are also what we call "c stores," it stands for corner store in some of the dorms. It's like a little gas station store, but offers warm pizzas and other things you wouldnt find at a gas station. Here you can use flex dollars."

Q The River Room

"The River Room is located in the IMU on campus. If you are sick of eating at Burge and Hillcrest, The River Room is the BEST alternative. The food is amazing, large portions, and the best part is that you can use flex and U-Bill to pay for it! This is a great alternative to mix up your meals without spending money."

CAMPUS HOUSING

Q Daum Dorm

"I lived in this dorm 2 years and loved it. It's the honors dorm and as such is very quiet, clean, and academically focused. The people living there get it when you say you need to study and will often help/study with you. Facilities managment and custodian staff do an amazing job keeping things clean and functioning and there has been remodeling going on the past two years."

Q Living-Learning Communities a Good Choice

"The University of Iowa has a good system of Living and Learning communities that freshmen (and others, in some cases) can choose to live in. I was part of a Learning Living community, and it definitely contributed to my social and academic success during my first year. Living with people of a similar interest made the first year transition very easy, and I have made a very strong group of friends from that floor, whom I am positive I will be friends with for the rest of my life."

GUYS & GIRLS

Q Guys and Girls

"Well, just like any school some of the people are super hot, while some are just average. As for how people dress, its pretty much anything goes. You can get people who dress up everyday to sweatpants and sweatshirts. A lot of the attire is black and gold to support the school colors."

HEALTH & SAFETY

Q The Iowa Police System

"The Iowa Police system is devised into 2 categories. There are the college police officers and the town police officers, both sets of officers go around the campus to ensure a good security level."

LOOKING FOR MORE?

Check out our full-length guide to this school at collegeprowler.com/university-of-iowa/.

University of Kansas

1502 Iowa St.; Lawrence, KS 66045
(785) 864-2700; www.ku.edu

THE BASICS:

Acceptance Rate: 92%	Student-Faculty Ratio: 20:1
Yield: 45%	Retention Rate: 78%
Setting: Small city	Graduation Rate: 60%
Control: Public	Tuition: $20,175
Total Undergrads: 21,066	Room & Board: $6,802
SAT Range: —	Avg. Aid Package: $9,358
ACT Range: 22–27	Students With Aid: 62%

Academics	B	Greek Life	B-
Athletics	A	Guys	A
Campus Dining	B+	Health & Safety	B
Campus Housing	B+	Local Atmosphere	A-
Campus Strictness	B	Nightlife	A
Computers	B+	Off-Campus Dining	A+
Diversity	B-	Off-Campus Housing	A
Drug Safety	C+	Parking	B
Facilities	B+	Transportation	A-
Girls	A+	Weather	B-

CP's Student Author On...
OVERALL EXPERIENCE

The majority of students at the University of Kansas only have positive things to say about the college. Students have the opportunity to get a quality education at a fairly cheap price, which is something that not a lot of schools can boast. The community around Lawrence offers all of the important features of a great college town. There is entertainment, nightlife, and fine dining seemingly around every corner. You'll have no problem finding everything you'll need for four years of good living. Aside from some minor complaints, it's safe to say that many students would be in favor of spending four more years at KU.

The combination of receiving a quality education and experiencing the freedom and exhiliration of college life makes students feel happy, and more importantly, at home at KU. The University also has a long-standing tradition that dates back to the 1860s, which makes you feel like you're a part of something bigger than just your own educational advancement. Lawrence is a tight-knit community, and you'll experience many Midwestern personalities on a daily basis, which can have its good and bad sides.... For the rest of this editorial, visit collegeprowler.com.

Students Speak Out On...
OVERALL EXPERIENCE

Q **Born and Raised a Jayhawk**

"Growing up in Kansas, I had no desire to attend anywhere else and after being here, I know why. KU has a great student atmosphere, incredible academic resources and support and a basketball team that wins championships!"

Q **Amazing**

"KU is the perfect balance of fun and seriousness. There is a ton of nightlife here, but theres also a lot of people in the libraries at all times. So many groups to join. Tons of activities and friends to meet."

Q **Great School to Attend**

"The school is a very welcoming and easy to attend and to feel comfortable, I am very shyu and have truely enjoyed the classes the the other students I have met. This university lets every one feel at home and welcome."

Q **Its Great to Be a Jayhawk**

"I mostly chose KU out of convenience, but I would do it again in a heartbeat. Everyone is so excited to be a Jayhawk."

BEST OF KANSAS

1. The traditions
2. KU athletics
3. Downtown Lawrence
4. The beautiful campus
5. The restaurants and bars
6. The Recreation Center
7. The local atmosphere

Big Dorms
61% of students surveyed felt that dorms were more spacious than average.

WORST OF KANSAS

1. Parking
2. The unpredictable weather
3. University construction
4. Packed libraries during midterms and finals
5. Communal dorm showers

Lowest Grades
Drug Safety: C+
Greek Life: B-
Diversity: B-

Student Body

African American:	4%	Male Undergrads:	50%
Asian American:	4%	Female Undergrads:	50%
Hispanic:	4%	Living On Campus:	23%
International:	4%	Living Off Campus:	77%
Native American:	1%	Male Athletes:	3%
White:	80%	Female Athletes:	4%
Unknown:	3%	Fraternity Members:	12%
From Out-of-State:	30%	Sorority Members:	17%

Students Speak Out On... EVERYTHING!

ACADEMICS

Extremely Diverse Department

"The English department is absolutely filled with highly intelligent, skilled, and published professors. The workload as an English major is as expected, quite a bit of reading and writing. It is all worth it though, the things you learn from the staff at the University of Kansas are invaluable. The entire department is quick to help when a student is in need of an internship, reference, scholarship, or any other personal matter. If you work hard for them, they will return the favor."

Competitive

"This course load is very competitive and prestigeous. Workload is tough at times, but I Love not having to share my studio desk with others and the environment"

ATHLETICS

Basketball, Basketball, Basketball

"Everyone follows KU Basketball. There have a really great team. However, there isn't much of a focus on the other sports and the overall sports attitude isn't very inclusive."

Is This a Serious Question?

"KU athletics. Have you heard of them? If you haven't, you must be a hermit. KU basketball number one in the country!!!!"

CAMPUS DINING

Food

"The University of Kansas offers a lot of places to dine while on campus. Students can eat at the dorm or they have the option to eat on campus at some restaurants such as Pizza Hut and Chick Fil A."

Mrs. E's

"Mrs. E's is the biggest campus dining facility on campus, and the one that I visited daily. It has lots of options, and even when nothing looks good, there is always something to eat. They have special events that are very cool and probably took a lot of time. Mrs. E's is also a really good place for an on-campus job, they hire tons of students."

Frequently Compared Schools:

Kansas State University
University of Missouri
University of Oklahoma
University of Texas

CAMPUS HOUSING

Campus Life

"The dorms are fun and it is a great experience with a lot of diversity"

Campus Living

"Living on the University of Kansas is relaxing none the less. It's atmosphere provides for fun times but also allows for the times when students need to begin studying in a relaxing setting. Life on KU's campus is refreshing and is set out to make the college experience worthwhile."

GUYS & GIRLS

Diverse

"We have everything. I was surprised at the racial, ethnic, social, and visual diversity of students that I see everyday."

Ugly to Sexy

"You will find all kinds of people at KU, some you don't even want to look at other you don't wanna stop looking at."

HEALTH & SAFETY

Safe as Can Be!

"The quality of public safety that I've experienced at the University of Kansas is a bit above average for a public school. I keep my doors locked when I leave and I keep the valuables in my car (i.e., ipod, phone charger, change) hidden when I exit my vehicle."

Pretty Safe and Secure

"There are campus police driving around at night so if you're on campus at night you're safe. There have been a few thefts in the art department, but they're working on that. There have also been a few incidents that there could have been more security."

LOOKING FOR MORE?

Check out our full-length guide to this school at collegeprowler.com/university-of-kansas/.

University of Kentucky

410 Administration Drive; Lexington, KY 40506
(859) 257-9000; www.uky.edu

THE BASICS:

Acceptance Rate: 79%
Yield: 47%
Setting: Large city
Control: Public
Total Undergrads: 19,187
SAT Range: 1470–1840*
ACT Range: 22–27

Student-Faculty Ratio: 18:1
Retention Rate: 80%
Graduation Rate: 58%
Tuition: $16,678
Room & Board: $9,100
Avg. Aid Package: $4,950
Students With Aid: 92%

* of 2400

Academics	B-	Greek Life	A-
Athletics	A+	Guys	A+
Campus Dining	A-	Health & Safety	B-
Campus Housing	B	Local Atmosphere	B+
Campus Strictness	C	Nightlife	A
Computers	A-	Off-Campus Dining	B+
Diversity	C+	Off-Campus Housing	B
Drug Safety	C	Parking	C
Facilities	A-	Transportation	B+
Girls	A-	Weather	B-

CP's Student Author On...
OVERALL EXPERIENCE

Kentucky students bleed blue and take any chance they have to display their spirit. Some students can feel overwhelmed when they first come to campus by all the organizations and people. It takes about a year to really settle in and find a group or niche on campus that makes you feel like you belong.

Kentucky offers a well-rounded education and opportunity for networking and making friends while staying in a mid-sized city with traditional values. With the exception of the parking problem, lack of diversity, and sometimes annoying Greek population, Kentucky can provide a student with a great education, both in and out of the classroom.

Students Speak Out On...
OVERALL EXPERIENCE

Q Kentucky Basketball
"kentucky basketball is a rich tradition. almost all of kentucky are die hard UK fans, which makes a very fun atmosphere during basketball season"

Q Hospitality
"Everyone is so nice and social, people are happy to be here which creates a great vibe across campus."

Q Awesome
"awesome in every way"

Q It Is an Awesome College
"So many great educational choices here and very cultrally diverse."

Q It Is Great
"the university of kentucky allows you to fully experience college life and to get a great education. if you choose to go to the university of kentucky i can garuntee you you wil.l not regret it"

BEST OF KENTUCKY

1. School spirit
2. Southern hospitality
3. Basketball season
4. Great workout facility
5. Friendly student body
6. The only daily student newspaper in the state (award- winning)

Happy Students
80% of students return after their first year.

Knowledgeable Professors
70% of students surveyed rated the general knowledge of professors as above average.

WORST OF KENTUCKY

1. Parking spaces are impossible to find
2. Construction that never seems to end
3. Limited class availability
4. Dorms are old and overcrowded (they are building a few new ones)
5. Large class sizes

Not Much Diversity
One of the least racially diverse campuses—only 14% of students are minorities.

Student Body

African American:	6%	Male Undergrads:	49%
Asian American:	2%	Female Undergrads:	51%
Hispanic:	1%	Living On Campus:	29%
International:	1%	Living Off Campus:	71%
Native American:	0%	Male Athletes:	5%
White:	86%	Female Athletes:	3%
Unknown:	3%	Fraternity Members:	9%
From Out-of-State:	22%	Sorority Members:	12%

Frequently Compared Schools:

Ohio State University
University of Alabama
University of Louisville
University of Tennessee

Students Speak Out On...
EVERYTHING!

ACADEMICS

Q Filled With Efficiency

"The University of Kentucky is loaded with resources available to help an prospective, incoming and current studies make necessary adjustments to college life and to assist in academic success. This was essential to the progress needed to maintain the confidence of success in continuing higher education."

Q Study Facilites

"They have the best library and most helpful resources I have seen on a college campus. It gives you the full opportunity you need to succeed."

ATHLETICS

Q School Athletics Are Above the Rest

"School athletics are to most students the main focus at the Universtiy of Kentucky. I mean huge! Sometime resulting in camping out for tickets to the next big game, or possibly waiting in lines for hours just for a chance in the lottery to get tickets. Most focus is on our football and basketball teams, but all sports at the Universtiy do well. With the top notch facilities on campus, you can't get any better than the amentities seen here at the universtiy."

Q Fan Support and Spirit Some of the Best in the Country

"Any athletic team at the University of Kentuck whether the most popular basketball team or a not so well known baseball team, we have awesome school spirit and fan support. Not only to the players but to the coaches as well. There is not a day that goes by that you don't see someday in blue and white."

CAMPUS DINING

Q Food Pretty Good but Sometimes Too Similar

"There are many places to eat across campus, including dining halls and cafes. While the school tries to keep variety in the food, at the end of the semester the food becomes somewhat the same. The overall taste and quality of the food available is good."

Q Amazing Mac and Cheese

"I lived on North Campus, so I'm a big fan of Blazer Cafe. They have THE best mac and cheese, hands down. That's the only thing I miss about living on campus; the food! Also, check out Ovid's at W.T. Young Library. The spicy beef wrap is the best meal in Lexington, no doubt.Only downside? The food can get repetitive, and some places aren't so good (cough cough K-Lair)."

CAMPUS HOUSING

Q Being a Social Butterfly

"At the University of Kentucky it is so easy to meet people and keep in touch with them. There are numerous activities going on any given day of the week that the Student Activities Board organizes. Because Lexington is not a large city everyone is relatively close and it there really is a sense of community."

Q Wonderful

"Living on campus has been an amazing experience. The dorms are always clean and if there are any problems someone can come and fix it."

GUYS & GIRLS

Q University of Kentucky Women

"There are many more women at the University of Kentucky compared to men. Most women at UK are very social and love the Lexington nightlife. The majority of the women at Kentucky are very attractive."

HEALTH & SAFETY

Q University of Kentucky Healthcare

"The University of Kentucky has excellent health care resources. Hospitals are located all around campus (about five in all) since UK is known for its tough nursing and doctor programs. Also, the student clinic allows for safe travel and good care, the nurses take care of all your needs."

LOOKING FOR MORE?

Check out our full-length guide to this school at collegeprowler.com/university-of-kentucky/.

University of Louisville

2301 S. Third St.; Louisville, KY 40292
(502) 852-5555; www.louisville.edu

THE BASICS:

Acceptance Rate: 70%
Yield: 48%
Setting: Large city
Control: Public
Total Undergrads: 15,329
SAT Range: 1010–1260*
ACT Range: 21–27

Student-Faculty Ratio: 19:1
Retention Rate: 79%
Graduation Rate: 46%
Tuition: $19,272
Room & Board: $6,602
Avg. Aid Package: $10,170
Students With Aid: 96%

of 1600

Academics	B-	Greek Life	B
Athletics	A	Guys	B+
Campus Dining	C	Health & Safety	C-
Campus Housing	C+	Local Atmosphere	B+
Campus Strictness	C+	Nightlife	B+
Computers	C+	Off-Campus Dining	B-
Diversity	B-	Off-Campus Housing	B
Drug Safety	C+	Parking	C+
Facilities	B-	Transportation	A-
Girls	B	Weather	B-

CP's Student Author On...
OVERALL EXPERIENCE

The University of Louisville isn't perfect, but to those who love it, the flaws only add to the experience. Not everyone likes going to such a large university—it can be very intimidating, especially if you come from a smaller high school. However, the crowds offer an opportunity to improve your social skills and make as many new friends as you want. And even with a huge student body, most people find a tight group of friends that they stick with throughout their time at U of L. Most students make friends with other residents in their dorm hall or by joining clubs or Greek organizations.

The professors and other University staff are so friendly and offer lots of personal attention. You wouldn't normally expect this at such a big school, but that's one thing that makes U of L special. Another thing the University provides is an almost endless list of opportunities for students. They may have to go looking in the right places, but there are so many things for U of L student to try out and experience.... For the rest of this editorial, visit collegeprowler.com.

Students Speak Out On...
OVERALL EXPERIENCE

Q Campus Experience

"I LOVE the University of Louisville. I am a commuter student, and my parents over protect me a little. Therefore, that school is a scape. That's the place where I can go without my parents checking at everything I do, It's the place where I go for lunch with the girls, and friends. It's the place I experienced love for the first time. That place is a refuge for a lot of students and I am glad of belong to it."

Q First Year Experience

"My first year at the University of Louisville has been one of the best years I have experienced so far. There are so many ways to get involved and meet people on campus. I've met so many new friends in my first year. If I could repeat this year all over, I would because there were many different opportunities that I got to take advantage of."

Q Its a Great School

"U of L is a great school. The people are friendly, the teachers are helpful, and there are definitely plenty of opportunities to have fun."

BEST OF LOUISVILLE

1. The athletics are great, especially football and men's basketball.
2. Proximity to downtown Louisville
3. Advisers
4. The students have a relaxed, friendly attitude.

Easy Financial Aid Process
52% of students surveyed told us that the financial aid process went smoothly and they received the financial aid they needed.

WORST OF LOUISVILLE

1. There aren't enough computers on campus for everyone.
2. A meal plan is required, even for students who live off campus.
3. Parking is limited and expensive.

Lowest Grades
Health & Safety: C-
Campus Dining: C
Computers: C+

Student Body

African American:	13%	Male Undergrads:	48%
Asian American:	3%	Female Undergrads:	52%
Hispanic:	2%	Living On Campus:	17%
International:	2%	Living Off Campus:	83%
Native American:	0%	Male Athletes:	5%
White:	79%	Female Athletes:	6%
Unknown:	2%	Fraternity Members:	15%
From Out-of-State:	17%	Sorority Members:	9%

Frequently Compared Schools:

University of Alabama
University of Cincinnati
University of Kentucky
University of Tennessee

Students Speak Out On... EVERYTHING!

ACADEMICS

Q My Experience in Uofl

"I think that the University of Louisville is the best school of the United States. The first time I got there it was amazing, everybody was smiling at me. My major right now is Education. What I like about my program is that I get take some courses that will help me in my future career. I love the University of Louisville."

Q Helpful

"My professors at the University of Louisville are helpful and always offer resources for research and extra study material. Classes are fun and entertaining"

ATHLETICS

Q U of L Athletics Rock!

"I love being a U of L Cardinal! Overall, our sports teams are the best, everyone on campus is usually pretty psyched when U of L is playing! The student involvement and school spirit at U of L is amazing!!"

Q Great Athletics

"Athletics are great. We have a lot of amazing teams in all of the sports. There are many areas for even non-athletes to work out and play intermurals. Overall I would rate team performance, fan support, school spirit, and athletic facilities excellent!"

CAMPUS DINING

Q Why Even Leave Campus to Eat!

"UofL's campus has cafes, restaurants and even mini grocery stores. Fast food places include Wendys! Subway! Papa Johns! Chick- Fila! You can't throw a penny without hitting a coffee shop! The main cafeteria is huge! It can fit about 1500 people in it and serves as a student activity center as well. Tons of Options! I 'm hungry now!"

Q Dining

"You can go to the SAC and have subway and wendys and a variety of different food.While at westside you get an all you can eat wheather its lunch breakfast or dinner"

CAMPUS HOUSING

Q Betty Johnson

"I lived at Betty Johnson student apartments my freshman year of college. I loved the location and how easy it was to get to class in the mornings. The cost of living here was more than what it was worth. The apartments themselves had a great deal of amenities. There was a pool during summer times as well as mini fitness center."

Q ULP

"The University of Louisville dorms are for the most part very well kept, modern, and comfortable living spaces for students. Bettie Johnson could use a little more work in refurnishing the rooms, but Community Park and Kurz Hall are brand new and ideal fro underclassman and upperclassman alike."

GUYS & GIRLS

Q Best guys and girls are in Greek life

"The guys at University of Louisville are hot and like to have fun. Most of the friendly guys are in fraternities. The girls are sweet, and some are a little more shy than others. Most girls that you might want to consider are in sororities."

Q There's a Lot of Diversity on U of L's Campus.

"A lot of people are nervous that when attending college they'll be surrounded by stuck-up snobs or people they just don't get along with. Lucky for us, the student population is very diverse. I don't mean in like a clique way, but there are students who enjoy such a broad range of things that you're bound to find someone who's interested in the same things you are. So if you are worried about making new friends, don't be."

HEALTH & SAFETY

Q It's the Rumor Mill That Scares People

"If it weren't for the stories, I wouldn't know that anything ever happened. I understand the necessity of having campus alerts, but they scare people."

LOOKING FOR MORE?

Check out our full-length guide to this school at collegeprowler.com/university-of-louisville/.

University of Maine

Chadbourne Hall; Orono, ME 04469
(207) 581-1110; www.umaine.edu

THE BASICS:

Acceptance Rate: 77%	Student-Faculty Ratio: 12:1
Yield: 36%	Retention Rate: 79%
Setting: Suburban	Graduation Rate: 59%
Control: Public	Tuition: $24,776
Total Undergrads: 9,575	Room & Board: $8,348
SAT Range: 1440–1760*	Avg. Aid Package: $12,004
ACT Range: 21–26	Students With Aid: 87%

of 2400

Academics	B	Greek Life	B+
Athletics	B-	Guys	A-
Campus Dining	C+	Health & Safety	B+
Campus Housing	C+	Local Atmosphere	C+
Campus Strictness	B	Nightlife	B
Computers	B	Off-Campus Dining	B+
Diversity	C	Off-Campus Housing	B+
Drug Safety	C	Parking	B-
Facilities	B	Transportation	A-
Girls	B+	Weather	C+

CP's Student Author On...
OVERALL EXPERIENCE

The students who offered responses regarding their overall experience at UMaine have overwhelmingly praised the University for its affect on the students who attend it. Many of the students make Maine their home, even after graduation. More in-state students remain in Maine, while more out-of-state students tend to move on to other areas, or back to their indigenous locations. The University has an abundance of assets of immeasurable value to offer to its students. There are activities and clubs for nearly every student interest. There is some organization that fits well into their majors, providing real experience within their fields to build resumes and get careers off to a head start, while tying them into a new circle of friends. The Career Center services for job placement after graduation are not only a help for current students, but they are available to students for one year at no charge after graduation.

The University of Maine prides itself on its reputation most importantly among its students, but also with its alumni. UMaine is a welcoming trip home during alumni functions and special events.... For the rest of this editorial, visit collegeprowler.com.

Students Speak Out On...
OVERALL EXPERIENCE

Q It's Perfect for Me

"I couldn't imagine being at any other school. Orono is such a close-knit little town, with a big city vibe. The businesses cater to students a lot and everyone is so friendly. My other option was Boston, but I'm glad I picked Orono. I love having everything so close by - most times, students don't even need to have a car!"

Q The Best!

"I can't imagine being anywhere better than UMaine. It's seriously great. My favorite thing was how every single person on my floor got to know and enjoy hanging out with each other. We were all really close. My roommate ended up being great even though I didn't know her at first. The food is excellent. My classes are interesting. The school is unique because it's like a big group of 20,000 something people who get along well. I'd do UMaine over a million times."

Q Just the Right Size

"UMaine is just the right size and offers a variety of entertainment."

BEST OF UMAINE

1. Small campus life with large student population
2. Abundance of extracurricular activities
3. Excellent resources for career exploration
4. First-year students may bring automobiles
5. Flexible class scheduling

Highly Satisfied Students
80% of students surveyed would make the same school choice if they could do it all over again.

WORST OF UMAINE

1. Lack of diversity in faculty and student population
2. Inadequate parking
3. Telephone and Internet registration systems crash
4. Bursar's Office
5. Parking ticket appeals process

Lowest Grades
Diversity: C
Drug Safety: C
Local Atmosphere: C+

Student Body

African American:	1%	Male Undergrads:	49%
Asian American:	1%	Female Undergrads:	51%
Hispanic:	1%	Living On Campus:	42%
International:	2%	Living Off Campus:	58%
Native American:	2%	Male Athletes:	7%
White:	75%	Female Athletes:	7%
Unknown:	18%	Fraternity Members:	—
From Out-of-State:	19%	Sorority Members:	—

Frequently Compared Schools:

University of Massachusetts
University of New Hampshire
University of Rhode Island
University of Vermont

Students Speak Out On... EVERYTHING!

ACADEMICS

Q Close Family in Music

"In my major, all of the teachers are on a first name basis. They care abou twhat we are doing and how well we are doing it. The classes are the perfect size and they cover what we need in order to be successful."

Q Elementary Education

"The advisors in the department are extremely helpful and very nice. If you pursue them they are more than willing to answer any of your questions. The workload is not very much, but I was also in my freshman year and taking mostly Gen.Ed.s so I haven't been taking all Education courses yet. By the looks of the curriculum though, it doesn't seem too difficult. I'm looking forward to the upcoming years and to find what job opportunities/internships that may become available."

ATHLETICS

Q Hockey games are the best

"We have some very good athletic teams at UMaine. Some of the best games to go to are the hockey games. Tickets for students are free, so there is no reason not to go."

Q Hockey

"Going to D-1 school, you know that you're in for a treat when you attend games. Hockey clearly being the big one up here. Students wait outside in the wonderful, winter Maine weather all afternoon just to try and get a seat in the student section."

CAMPUS DINING

Q Good Food, Great Place.

"The dining halls at UMaine are great. There is a wide variety of food available. The food itself is well prepared and and sometimes made to order."

Q Variety Quantity Value

"York dining offers all you can eat. Also dining at Oxford or at the Union."

CAMPUS HOUSING

Q I Am Not Familiar Enough With the Dorms at Umaine.

"I had no problems with Gannett Hall (A Freshman dorm) last year and I hope that Hart Hall is everything I've hoped for and more for the semester to come. I have heard it's the bees knees."

Q I Own a Home Off Campus

"But, from my conversations with students and public safety I feel that I would be comfortable living in any dorm especially since UMO will be a smoke free campus as of January 1, 2011 and there is a strong connection of RA's and campus security."

GUYS & GIRLS

Q Diversity

"Everyone is different, the style is nothing specific and everyone gives me different ideas of new experiences everyday, whether it be a new setting, study group or clothing. The people come from many backgrounds and the boys are all different."

Q Guys

"There are a wide variety of guys to choose from. There are the Greeks who are HOT! And the football players, hockey players. Even the geeks are good lookin! But I am partial to Geeks."

HEALTH & SAFETY

Q The Emergency Text System Is Great.

"I feel completely safe on campus with all of the safety buttons to push if bothered while walking, police around every corner, and the emergency text/message system you sign up for."

LOOKING FOR MORE?

Check out our full-length guide to this school at collegeprowler.com/university-of-maine/.

University of Maryland

Mitchell Building; College Park, MD 20742
(301) 314-8385; www.umd.edu

THE BASICS:

Acceptance Rate: 45%	**Student-Faculty Ratio:** 18:1
Yield: 34%	**Retention Rate:** 93%
Setting: Suburban	**Graduation Rate:** 82%
Control: Public	**Tuition:** $24,831
Total Undergrads: 26,922	**Room & Board:** $9,599
SAT Range: 1750–2060*	**Avg. Aid Package:** $9,219
ACT Range: —	**Students With Aid:** 74%

* of 2400

Academics	B+	Greek Life	B-
Athletics	A	Guys	B+
Campus Dining	B-	Health & Safety	C-
Campus Housing	C+	Local Atmosphere	C+
Campus Strictness	B	Nightlife	B+
Computers	B	Off-Campus Dining	B-
Diversity	B	Off-Campus Housing	C+
Drug Safety	C	Parking	C+
Facilities	A-	Transportation	B+
Girls	B	Weather	B-

CP's Student Author On... OVERALL EXPERIENCE

The University of Maryland, College Park is paradise compared to some schools and locations across America. Most students who join the campus community stay awhile, and some don't want to leave, even after being there for four or even five years. It's universities like this that have contributed to the popular expression of college being four of the best years of your life. From students' first year on campus to their final days leading up to graduation, students' academic, personal, physical, professional, and social lives come together to prepare them for the real world. Once entering such a world, many alumni look back and agree that, even if they could, they wouldn't change a thing about their overall experience at UMCP.

There are also students who can't wait to get out of here by the time graduation rolls around.... For the rest of this editorial, visit collegeprowler.com.

Students Speak Out On... OVERALL EXPERIENCE

Q There's a Reason to Fear the Turtle

"Maryland is great. I've visited other schools and they are either too spread out and you can't really figure out where campus is, or no one is on campus unless they're in class. At Maryland there is so much to do, and no matter where you are or what your doing someone will have some type of Terps gear on."

Q My Experience

"If I could, I would choose UMCP all over again. I'm so happy with my choice. At first I wanted to go to a school far away from home, but I'm glad I didn't. This school combines challenge and fun. We go by the work hard, play hard mantra and that was exactly the type of environment I was looking for. Plus it is an extremely diverse school without the cutthroat mentality of the elite schools."

BEST OF MARYLAND

1. The overall UMCP college experience
2. Location, location, location
3. Academics
4. Gorgeous campus
5. Athletics

Happy Students
93% of students return after their first year.

Proven Success
82% of students will complete their education and graduate with a degree.

WORST OF MARYLAND

1. College Park as a town
2. The on-campus housing process
3. The omnipresent construction
4. The lack of variety in nightlife
5. Too much brick

Lowest Grades
Health & Safety: C-
Drug Safety: C
Local Atmosphere: C+

Student Body

African American:	14%	Male Undergrads:	52%
Asian American:	14%	Female Undergrads:	48%
Hispanic:	6%	Living On Campus:	41%
International:	2%	Living Off Campus:	59%
Native American:	0%	Male Athletes:	3%
White:	56%	Female Athletes:	3%
Unknown:	7%	Fraternity Members:	13%
From Out-of-State:	36%	Sorority Members:	10%

Frequently Compared Schools:

Penn State
University of Delaware
University of Pittsburgh
University of Virginia

**Students Speak Out On...
EVERYTHING!**

ACADEMICS

Q WIDE Variety

"There are a TON of classes and majors to explore. From History to Rock to Basketball (Yep, as a class!) you're definitely going to find something you love to do. Registration is SO simple, it's all done online on your own time. There are tons of accelerated an honors study options such as College Park Scholars, Gemstone, Living/Learning Programs, Fellowship, etc. Study Abroad is a MUST!"

Q Architecture

"My intended major is architecture, but I can't apply to the program until spring semester sophomore year. With this being the case, I am still an Undecided (Letters & Sciences) Major and my workload hasn't been too difficult. I was a pretty good student at my all girls Catholic college prep high school (I had a 3.5). I just got a letter from Maryland saying that I made the Dean's List! So draw your own conclusions from that hahah"

ATHLETICS

Q Sports

"Athletics are a huge part of campus life. Our basketball team wins championships almost every year, and football games are always crowded. We also have tons of variety: lacrosse, soccer, even a fencing team! And, there are club teams if varsity isn't right for you."

Q Sporty Spice

"AMAZING D1 sports teams, clubs are also pretty intense! Intramurals are all over, a ton of people play!"

CAMPUS DINING

Q Good Food

"I love the campus dining. There are a lot of great places to eat in the area."

Q Dining at Maryland Is Good but Not Very Healthy

"The dining hall has a lot of options most of which tastes great, but aren't exactly low calorie. Once your cooking for yourself you start to miss the convenience of the dining hall."

CAMPUS HOUSING

Q Living on Campus Is Amazing and Its Gets Better Every Year.

"Living on campus is amazing. Freshman year it can be sort of hot without AC. But its the most social and fun living situation for freshman because everybody lives together in huge high risers. As you get older, you get more space and live in more secluded suites and apartments with your friends. By the time your a junior most students live in 4 single bedroom apartments with 2 bathrooms, full kitchen and living room."

Q Housing at Maryland

"Living on campus at the University of Maryland is an exciting experience. The freshman dorms are a bit old and, therefore, have no air conditioning but the upperclassmen dorms are awesome. All residents are friendly and sociable, there is no way you can live on campus and not make friends. There are usually lounges on every floor where students can cook food and study quietly. Bathrooms are always clean. Laundry rooms are located in every dorm for convenience."

GUYS & GIRLS

Q So Many People

"there are so many people at umd that you are bound to find someone you are interested in. there are an array of people from all walks of life."

HEALTH & SAFETY

Q Crime Alerts

"UMD texts and emails students when a crime occurs immediatly. There are emergency blue lights on just about every street and by every dorm with a button that will automatically contact police. These devices make me feel safe and protected around campus plus student auxiliary and campus police are everywhere."

LOOKING FOR MORE?

Check out our full-length guide to this school at collegeprowler.com/university-of-maryland/.

University of Maryland Baltimore County

1000 Hilltop Circle; Baltimore, MD 21250
(410) 455-1000; www.umbc.edu

THE BASICS:

Acceptance Rate: 69%
Yield: 37%
Setting: Suburban
Control: Public
Total Undergrads: 13,161
SAT Range: 1610–1920*
ACT Range: 22–29

Student-Faculty Ratio: 19:1
Retention Rate: 85%
Graduation Rate: 59%
Tuition: $18,791
Room & Board: $9,620
Avg. Aid Package: $11,409
Students With Aid: 75%

of 2400

Academics	B	Greek Life	C
Athletics	C-	Guys	A-
Campus Dining	B	Health & Safety	B-
Campus Housing	B+	Local Atmosphere	C+
Campus Strictness	B-	Nightlife	B-
Computers	B-	Off-Campus Dining	C-
Diversity	A	Off-Campus Housing	B
Drug Safety	B-	Parking	B+
Facilities	B	Transportation	B-
Girls	B+	Weather	B-

CP's Student Author On...
OVERALL EXPERIENCE

UMBC is a great university. Its diversity, high-quality education, and leadership opportunities make it a place where everyone can shine. UMBC's is small enough so students won't feel like just a face in the crowd, but it is big enough for all students to find something they may be interested in. You can mingle with students from 120 different countries, and do everything from attend Bhangra classes to Shabbat dinners. Education is top-notch here, and classes are taught by experienced professors who also dedicate a lot of time to research. The curriculum is always up-to-date and interesting, and UMBC has excellent programs, especially for students looking to major in the arts, sciences, or engineering.

The numerous leadership opportunities available in student government, clubs, and the Shriver Center help prepare students for their future careers, and the University often has programs to help promote leadership among students, such as retreats for current leaders or anyone looking to gain leadership skills.... For the rest of this editorial, visit collegeprowler.com.

Students Speak Out On...
OVERALL EXPERIENCE

Q Bout the College

"The school is perfect especially in the biological sciences. It has students from over 120 countries,very diverse institution. UMBC is proud to be recognized as a national leader in higher education by the U.S. News & World Report America's Best Colleges Guide."

Q An Overall Experience at UMBC

"Overall, I loved the professors and the knowledge they offered. Our school is unique in that we have some of the top notch professors and one of the best university Presidents. The staff are always willing to help you even if they weren't currently your professor. I would change my school experience by being more social with regard to night life."

Q The Best!!

"UMBC is definitely a school that gives the students many opportunities and options to learn about different things. The school is very diverse which makes school life all the more interesting. Everyone at UMBC is focused and the teachers are highly intelligent and humorous. I definitely wouldn't choose any other!"

BEST OF MARYLAND BALTIMORE CO

1. Friendly and welcoming students
2. Diversity
3. Concerts
4. Approachable staff and faculty
5. Undergraduate research opportunities

Happy Students
85% of students return after their first year.

Knowledgeable Professors
88% of students surveyed rated the general knowledge of professors as above average.

WORST OF MARYLAND BALTIMORE CO

1. Having to park in the satellite lot if you are a freshman
2. Limited nightlife in the immediate area near campus
3. No football team
4. Campus is empty on some weekends

Don't Move Off Campus
Average off-campus housing is a steep $11,290.

Student Body

African American:	16%	Male Undergrads:	53%
Asian American:	20%	Female Undergrads:	47%
Hispanic:	4%	Living On Campus:	37%
International:	5%	Living Off Campus:	63%
Native American:	0%	Male Athletes:	5%
White:	52%	Female Athletes:	5%
Unknown:	3%	Fraternity Members:	3%
From Out-of-State:	13%	Sorority Members:	3%

Frequently Compared Schools:
Penn State
Towson University
University of Delaware
University of Maryland

Students Speak Out On... EVERYTHING!

ACADEMICS

Q Academics

"The professors are helpful. Registration process is easy. The curriculum in ok. Workload to me is good provided you manage your time wisely."

Q Visual Arts

"The visual arts program is quite amazing, though UMBC is known for sciences. The visual arts program actually has a good reputation in the workforce. I have very good instructors and have felt that I have learned so much and feel much more confident in what I am producing."

Q Amazing

"The academics are simply amazing here."

ATHLETICS

Q School Spirit

"I am not a huge fan of sports, but I did attend the basketball games during fall semester at the RAC. There was always a one last, end of the season game, at which they handed out T-shirts to all the students and this was usually everyone's favorite one to attend. There was lots of school spirit seen during this time of the year."

Q UMBC Athletics

"Our school had an enormous amount of pride in the track and the lacrosse team, although we lacked a football team."

CAMPUS DINING

Q Very Accommodating

"Very accommodating. It offers many different dining and cuisine options at all meals. Vegan and halal/kosher are available, which is amazing."

Q Quality has improved a lot

"Food is pretty good. A new food service company "took&" over about a year ago, and the food quality went up a lot. The d-hall has been revamped and is a nice change. The Commons has good places, not to mention Chick-fil-A, Starbucks, and that amazing little shop in the administration building!"

CAMPUS HOUSING

Q Great Dorms

"The dorms here are great. The percentage of people that house on campus is increasing, and the proportion is as big as UMCP's. UMBC was once known as a commuter school years ago, and these years ago are long gone. I recommend that anyone house here for the first three years of their college career."

Q Dorms Are Quite Nice

"UMBC's dorms are really much, much better than at most other colleges. We get private bathrooms and pretty large bedrooms, and every dorm building has a community feel to it, and the Residential Assistants (RAs) host activities and social events throughout the semester. Many of our dorms even have suites with living rooms and beautiful, large windows. My room has an awesome view of campus buildings and the sports field. I love living on campus!"

GUYS & GIRLS

Q Academic Life

"Most people care a great deal about their school work and dedicate a lot to it."

Q THE BEST Girls and Guys Go to UMBC!

"The girls and guys here are really good looking and put together, yet carry really nice and open attitudes. It's truly a singular school in this regard."

HEALTH & SAFETY

Q Safe School

"our school is extremely safe, such that little crime ever happens. the police notify all students and faculty if and event occurs be it health or crime. usually the issue is solved within a day to two days. i feel very safe knowing that the police is 1 min away"

Q Great Security

"I feel safer here then I do in the comfort of my own home."

LOOKING FOR MORE?
Check out our full-length guide to this school at collegeprowler.com/university-of-maryland----baltimore-county/.

University of Maryland Eastern Shore

J.T. Williams Hall; Princess Anne, MD 21853
(410) 651-2200; www.umes.edu

THE BASICS:

Acceptance Rate: 53%
Yield: 40%
Setting: Town
Control: Public
Total Undergrads: 3,922
SAT Range: 1130–1390*
ACT Range: 15–18

Student-Faculty Ratio: 18:1
Retention Rate: 70%
Graduation Rate: 38%
Tuition: $13,306
Room & Board: $7,230
Avg. Aid Package: $13,352
Students With Aid: 99%

* of 2400

Academics	C-	Greek Life	B
Athletics	C	Guys	B+
Campus Dining	B-	Health & Safety	C+
Campus Housing	C+	Local Atmosphere	C
Campus Strictness	D+	Nightlife	C
Computers	C	Off-Campus Dining	C-
Diversity	B-	Off-Campus Housing	B
Drug Safety	C	Parking	B-
Facilities	B-	Transportation	C-
Girls	B-	Weather	B-

CP's Student Author On...
OVERALL EXPERIENCE

The University of Maryland Eastern Shore is a great school because it's not far from home for the many students who come from the DC, Maryland, and Virginia area and tuition is not extremely expensive. Another plus is that the campus is large but the student body is not. This allows students and teachers to make and maintain great relationships. The availability of classes and other resources is another plus here.

And the University is only on the rise. Buildings have been added and the campus is expanding, which has allowed for the number of students, faculty, and programs on campus to grow, as well. Recent programs that have become available at UMES include aviation and pharmacy, which have brought good media attention to the campus, and in turn, brings even more students to the University. These great programs and others make it nearly impossible for a student not to find a job or go on to grad school after graduating with a bachelor's from UMES. The University's uniqueness is what brings students to the campus.... For the rest of this editorial, visit collegeprowler.com.

Students Speak Out On...
OVERALL EXPERIENCE

Q I Love UMES
"I love my school, which is why I chose to come back."

Q Growth in Retrospect
"I honestly love being at UMES. Since I came to the university I have grown on so many different levels: spiritually, socially, intellectually. This university has helped me to grow as a individual, student, and future professional. I praise God for this experience at the University of Maryland Eastern Shore."

Q Teachers
"The professors at UMES are the best. I've learned so much and enjoyed the lectures of those that have taught me."

Q I Love UMES
"My overall experience at UMES has been very fun. There is a lot of diversity and a lot of activities. There's something to do just about every night. As far as academics, most of my teachers have been very helpful. They care about your success."

BEST OF MARYLAND EASTERN SHORE

1. Teacher and student relationships
2. Quality of programs
3. Parties
4. Ocean City is nearby.
5. There of lots of tutors, and everyone is willing to help.

Easy to Get By on a Student's Budget
54% of students surveyed felt that the amount it costs to live while at school was better than average.

WORST OF MARYLAND EASTERN SHORE

1. Campus security
2. Math classes
3. Rural setting
4. Small area
5. Lack of under-21 areas to go
6. Campus can get boring at times.

Not Everyone Graduates
38% of students do not complete their education or graduate with a degree.

Disappointed Students
27% of students surveyed would not choose to attend this school if they could do it all over again.

Student Body

African American:	78%	Male Undergrads:	40%
Asian American:	1%	Female Undergrads:	60%
Hispanic:	1%	Living On Campus:	54%
International:	4%	Living Off Campus:	46%
Native American:	0%	Male Athletes:	4%
White:	10%	Female Athletes:	4%
Unknown:	5%	Fraternity Members:	25%
From Out-of-State:	29%	Sorority Members:	30%

Students Speak Out On... EVERYTHING!

ACADEMICS

Q Tutors

"UMES has a lot of different tutoring services and different ways to get help with assignments, such as online services, learning lab, math department, writing lab, math lab, and the Center for Access and Academic Success."

Q Always Available

"My parents convinced me to go to the University of Maryland Eastern Shore and I am glad. The professors are always helpful, and everyone is friendly and they have a Doctor of Physical Therapy program, which will give me a doctoral degree in 5 years."

Q Telecommunication

"Telecommunications is a very good major. Many people leave my school with nice jobs but they don't really offer a wide range of information or classes for that major. It isn't even a full major, it has to be taken as a minor."

ATHLETICS

Q Sports Are Great

"The school currently doesn't have a football team but they are working on it. The women's bowling team has won some national titles. The basketball teams and track and field are pretty good also. This school has a lot of team spirit with fans, and they have new facilities for the basketball team."

Q Athletics at UMES

"They have a really good basketball team and are now getting a football team together."

CAMPUS DINING

Q Ok

"The food in the Hawks Nest is the best. The cafeteria food is not bad either, it just can be the same thing over and over again. If you are trying to gain weight, the caf is the place to go."

Frequently Compared Schools:

East Carolina University
Howard University
Towson University
University of Maryland

Q The College Meal

"I would say that, overall, the food isn't bad. There is usually a variety. There are a couple of different places you can go. The prices are very reasonable. There is one particular restaurant that is frequented by the public. You can choose to be on a meal plan or not. If you aren't satisfied with the choices available to you, there are restaurants close by."

CAMPUS HOUSING

Q Living on UMES Campus

"It is a new experience to live on the UMES campus. The campus is beautiful and easy to get around because I can walk to my classes. I live three hours away from the school, so it is necessary for me to live on campus. Sometimes it stinks because of the farm close by, but I still love living on campus. It is not very expensive and a convenience to attending the school."

Q Acceptable

"It's acceptable but has some unnecessary rules."

GUYS & GIRLS

Q Guys and Girls

"Everyone is very diverse."

Q Girls Vs Guys

"Now, all schools usually have girls trampling over guys in the petcentages, but actually at UMES, it's pretty even. I can't give our actual numbers but it's split in the middle I think."

HEALTH & SAFETY

Q Security Is Fine

"I have no problems. Security is always around. I feel safe going to classes in the evening, and if I need a security guard for escort I can call them anytime."

Q Always Safe on Campus

"I always feel safe at the University of Maryland Eastern Shore. All the students try to look out for each other, and the security is always present."

LOOKING FOR MORE?

Check out our full-length guide to this school at collegeprowler.com/university-of-maryland-eastern-shore/.

University of Massachusetts

181 President's Dr.; Amherst, MA 01003
(413) 545-0111; www.umass.edu

THE BASICS:

Acceptance Rate: 67%	**Student-Faculty Ratio:** 18:1
Yield: 21%	**Retention Rate:** 87%
Setting: Town	**Graduation Rate:** 68%
Control: Public	**Tuition:** $23,414
Total Undergrads: 20,873	**Room & Board:** $8,276
SAT Range: 1060–1280*	**Avg. Aid Package:** $13,314
ACT Range: 23–28	**Students With Aid:** 84%

* of 1600

Academics	B	Greek Life	B-
Athletics	B-	Guys	B+
Campus Dining	A	Health & Safety	C+
Campus Housing	C+	Local Atmosphere	B
Campus Strictness	B	Nightlife	B+
Computers	B	Off-Campus Dining	A
Diversity	B-	Off-Campus Housing	B
Drug Safety	D+	Parking	C+
Facilities	B-	Transportation	A
Girls	B	Weather	C

CP's Student Author On...
OVERALL EXPERIENCE

Despite the bad parking and unpredictable weather here, it's still hard to find someone who genuinely hates UMass. The University's large size provides its students with more resources and options than smaller schools, so take advantage of this. If you work hard and don't let yourself get too distracted by all the parties, you will be able to avoid some of the pitfalls that plague students who are fresh out of high school and aren't used to such responsibility.

A lot of students are concerned with the recent budget cuts, but UMass's financial situation will improve over time and may not even affect future incoming classes. Regardless, going to UMass and experiencing such a multifaceted institution will open doors for you. And, judging from the comments students have made about the University, coming to UMass has truly enriched their lives, academically and socially, and it can do the same for yours!

Students Speak Out On...
OVERALL EXPERIENCE

Q Awesome Practise for the Real World

"In my opinion college bound high schoolers should either go to ivy league schools or Umass Amherst. There is every type of person here from academic geniuses at the honors college who couldn't afford ivy league schools to students where academics are definitely second to having fun. Umass is what you make of it and the students who balance academics and socializing with friends leave with an underestimated degree and an amazing ability to function in the real world."

Q Love It!

"It's awesome, but not good for everyone."

Q Excellent School

"Excellent school. There are so many activities and things to do. The professors are great. The campus is beautiful. It's the best school in the country."

BEST OF UMASS

1. Parties
2. Great teachers and a variety of majors
3. Low tuition
4. The library
5. Career Services
6. Location
7. Student resources

Happy Students
87% of students return after their first year.

Knowledgeable Professors
84% of students surveyed rated the general knowledge of professors as above average.

WORST OF UMASS

1. Budget cuts
2. Parking
3. Office of Information Technology
4. Decreased school spirit
5. Campus dining

Students Can't Wait to Get Out of Town
50% of students surveyed said that there's no way they would live here after graduation.

Student Body

African American:	5%	Male Undergrads:	50%
Asian American:	8%	Female Undergrads:	50%
Hispanic:	4%	Living On Campus:	63%
International:	1%	Living Off Campus:	37%
Native American:	0%	Male Athletes:	4%
White:	68%	Female Athletes:	4%
Unknown:	14%	Fraternity Members:	5%
From Out-of-State:	22%	Sorority Members:	5%

Frequently Compared Schools:

Boston University
Northeastern University
University of Connecticut
University of Vermont

Students Speak Out On... EVERYTHING!

ACADEMICS

Business - Operations Management

"I came to UMass for Isenberg, the School of Management. This is the type of place where dreams come true and students are given every opportunity to realize them. At how many other schools can the head of a major say, "Stop worrying, you're all going to get internships"? Please, for all the other benefits I get from being a part of the UMass community as a whole, there are few, if any, places I'd rather be."

SOM is awesome

"Being in the Isenberg School of Management is awesome because I feel like it gives me an advantage over a lot of other students. The classes can be hard, but teachers are almost always willing to help, especially in big classes, where TAs can help, too. The Chase Career Center is especially helpful for SOM students, and it helps a lot of kids find great jobs and internships with companies like Target or TJX."

ATHLETICS

UMass Games Are a Good Time

"Everyone loves going to the football, basketball, and hockey games. They are also a lot of fun."

UMass Sports

"I haven't been to many sporting events here on campus, just a couple of hockey games and football games. From what I have experienced, everything seems great."

CAMPUS DINING

Pita Pit good for late-night food

"The Pita Pit is an awesome stop for late-night food after the dining commons close. They offer a variety of pitas and sandwiches, from buffalo chicken to chicken caesar to philly steak. The pitas are healthy, made with lean meats only. The combination YCMP (your campus meal plan swipes) include a pita, a bag of chips or a baked item, and a fountain drink or water. It is fulfilling, delicious, and different from what is offered in the dining halls."

Food Is Amazing

"The food is way better than my mother's. Name one other university dining system that has steak, lobster, and sushi on a regular basis."

CAMPUS HOUSING

I Heart Umass

"I pretty much love it here."

Cost

"UMass is a great university to live at cost-wise."

GUYS & GIRLS

There Is No Typical Student.

"There are all kinds—it all depends on what group you're in and what part of campus you're in. There are the crazy, done-up partiers, the hippies, the artsy folks, the outdoorsy people, the nerd burgers, and everything in between."

Mix of Everything

"There are so many students in Amherst and from neighboring schools that there is somebody for everybody here. There are lots of attractive and considerate people here!"

HEALTH & SAFETY

They keep us safe

"The campus police and general security do exactly what their jobs are: keep us safe."

Never Felt in Danger...

"I know that UMass used to have a reputation of being dangerous but really I have never felt in danger. There is campus security and phones to reach them all around. The campus is lit up enough that I feel comfortable walking alone at any hour around the campus. I have spend many late nights in the library and I have walked home late and felt totally fine. I have never encountered, personally, any campus crime or anything. The police and safety are great and quick when needed. I feel very safe."

LOOKING FOR MORE?

Check out our full-length guide to this school at collegeprowler.com/university-of-massachusetts/.

University of Miami

1252 Memorial Drive; Coral Gables, FL 33124
(305) 284-2211; www.miami.edu

THE BASICS:

Acceptance Rate: 44%
Yield: 21%
Setting: Suburban
Control: Private Non-Profit
Total Undergrads: 10,370
SAT Range: 1740–2050*
ACT Range: 27–31

Student-Faculty Ratio: 11:1
Retention Rate: 90%
Graduation Rate: 77%
Tuition: $36,188
Room & Board: $10,800
Avg. Aid Package: $29,170
Students With Aid: 80%

* of 2400

Academics	B+	Greek Life	B-
Athletics	A	Guys	A
Campus Dining	B+	Health & Safety	B-
Campus Housing	B+	Local Atmosphere	A-
Campus Strictness	B	Nightlife	B+
Computers	B+	Off-Campus Dining	B+
Diversity	A	Off-Campus Housing	B+
Drug Safety	C+	Parking	B-
Facilities	A-	Transportation	B+
Girls	A-	Weather	A+

CP's Student Author On... OVERALL EXPERIENCE

Despite daily griping about tuition costs, parking, thunderstorms, and hard classes, most students really seem to enjoy UM. Excellent attributes like the nightlife, weather, and culture seem to cancel out some of the bad things about being in Miami. For some students, these bad things include the unapproachable "hot" girls and guys on campus, while others find life in the dorms to be a challenge. The complaints about college are basically what you'd expect to hear anywhere. It appears that the bad things at UM really aren't that bad, but the good things are very good. Miami is one of the coolest cities in the world for a college student, and that goes deeper than just the superficial bar and club scene.

Students who are unhappy generally figure it out within a semester and transfer out of UM, usually to somewhere closer to home. College is tough, especially the first couple weeks if you come without knowing anyone. Making a whole new group of friends for the first time since kindergarten is one of the hardest and most stressful things you may ever have to do.... For the rest of this editorial, visit collegeprowler.com.

Students Speak Out On... OVERALL EXPERIENCE

Q Student Opportunities

"The University of Miami is high cost academic institution, but the sacrifice pays off incredibly. That money that students is received back tenfold in value if you take advantage of the events and activities availables to students. The school budgets provides so many leadership, social, cultural, and volunteer opportunites, with free transportation included."

Q Awesome School

"The social scene, and the campus involvement at this school is amazing. There is a place for everyone. Also, classes are small and students receive a lot of attention."

Q Best Choice

"This was the best decision I have ever made. Coming to UM is like a dream come true. You do not have to be rich, drunk, or high all the time to fit in. There is so much diversity on campus that you will find your niche. Whether it is a club, sport, or greek organization there is bound to be something for you. Yeah there are parties and stuff but majority of the people here work hard everyday and it shows, that is why we are #50!"

BEST OF UNIVERSITY OF MIAMI

1. Sports teams
2. Hot guys and girls
3. Local clubs and bars - Miami has great nightlife, and some bars and clubs don't close until 4 a.m.
4. Walking around in December in sandals

Happy Students
90% of students return after their first year.

Proven Success
77% of students will complete their education and graduate with a degree.

WORST OF UNIVERSITY OF MIAMI

1. The traffic everywhere in Miami
2. When tropical storms and hurricanes cause several straight days of rain
3. Parking availability close to the dorms
4. Dining halls

Expensive
Tuition is a steep $36,188, one of the most expensive rates in the country.

Expensive to Just Get By
62% of students surveyed felt that the amount it costs to live while at school was worse than average.

Student Body

African American:	8%	Male Undergrads:	47%
Asian American:	5%	Female Undergrads:	53%
Hispanic:	23%	Living On Campus:	44%
International:	9%	Living Off Campus:	56%
Native American:	0%	Male Athletes:	5%
White:	43%	Female Athletes:	6%
Unknown:	12%	Fraternity Members:	14%
From Out-of-State:	60%	Sorority Members:	14%

Students Speak Out On... EVERYTHING!

ACADEMICS

Q Professors Are Approachaple, Helpful and It Is Easy to Get Individual Attention

"One of the best things about UM is the academic life. Despite its reputation, University of Miami students care about their academics and there are always interesting classes to take. Seniors get priority during course registration but there are never any problems getting into classes you need to take for your major. Most classes are smaller than about 25 students, and all of my professors know me by name."

Q Professors

"The professors at UM are generally very good compared to other schools. Additionally, because of the (generally) small class sizes, they get to know you on a personal level, and are very willing to work with you."

Q Challenging

"Registration process is simple, workload is challenging, tutoring always available, library is a great resource."

ATHLETICS

Q Cane Football

"Football at the you is just like takeing a breath,without you would survive. everyonr supports the team on good and bad days,just dont see hoe i could go wrong by not participating."

Q The U Invented Swagger

"The teams aren't always the best, but we have swagger"

CAMPUS DINING

Q Very Good

"Dining options are very good, there is a good amount of things to choose from."

Q Food Court

"I am a commuter so only eat at the food court not at the dining hall and there is a lot of variety there."

CAMPUS HOUSING

Q Hecht - the True Freshman Experience

"If you are really looking for a freshman experience to the T, live in Hecht your first year. Yeah, Stanford is way more chill and the people are nicer, but Hecht has the comradorie that Stanford doesn't. People in Hecht are much hyper and there is always something fun to do. It cna get annoying after a while but as long as you have friends on your floor/tower, then you are set."

Q Upperclassmen Apartments

"The University Village Apartments at the University of Miami are great because they have spacious rooms and a good sized kitchen and living area."

GUYS & GIRLS

Q EXTREMELY Attractive Student Body

"The students at UM are, what can I say - very attractive. As a result, there are a lot of "dude bros" and skanky girls. However, there is no shortage of beautiful, down to earth guys and girls here. You just have to make friends according to your taste. Since there is so much diversity, there are tons of different kinds of people with different interest that are bound to match your own."

Q Campus Life

"The students at UA are from all over the country. Easy to mingle. Great football team and special events."

HEALTH & SAFETY

Q It's Safe on Campus

"There are always patrols on campus so if you are at UM there is no need to worry. But if you are out of campus, you have to be careful."

Q Police and Safety Services

"I feel like the cops really care about the students"

University of Michigan

503 Thompson St.; Ann Arbor, MI 48109
(734) 764-1817; www.umich.edu

THE BASICS:

Acceptance Rate: 50%
Yield: 41%
Setting: Mid-sized city
Control: Public
Total Undergrads: 26,208
SAT Range: 1230–1430*
ACT Range: 27–31

Student-Faculty Ratio: 12:1
Retention Rate: 96%
Graduation Rate: 88%
Tuition: $34,937
Room & Board: $8,924
Avg. Aid Package: $11,174
Students With Aid: 79%

* of 1600

Academics	A-	Greek Life	A
Athletics	A	Guys	A-
Campus Dining	B	Health & Safety	B-
Campus Housing	B	Local Atmosphere	B+
Campus Strictness	B	Nightlife	A
Computers	B+	Off-Campus Dining	A
Diversity	B	Off-Campus Housing	A-
Drug Safety	C+	Parking	C+
Facilities	A-	Transportation	A
Girls	B+	Weather	C+

CP's Student Author On...
OVERALL EXPERIENCE

Although many students gripe about the weather, the cost of living, and the calculus GSIs with incoherent accents, one thing holds true: the Michigan experience is one to be envied by all. Students here love their school, and they're not ashamed to say so. Few schools have a greater academic reputation, better sports, and more opportunities for extracurricular involvement There are 900 student organizations from which to choose.

Picking a school is a tough decision, and no one expects you to know exactly what you want to do with your life before you've even graduated high school. Fortunately, a school like Michigan can help you find yourself by giving you the chance to try everything under the sun. Nearly every academic area is in the top 10, the sports teams warrant immediate respect, the social life is right with the times, and there are so many ways in which to become involved (it's almost impossible to become a couch potato here). As a Michigan graduate, your degree will be one of the most highly respected in the nation.... For the rest of this editorial, visit collegeprowler.com.

Students Speak Out On...
OVERALL EXPERIENCE

Q Leaders and Best!

"Michigan is the finest institution in all the land. Nowhere has a better mixture of academics, sports, and social and cultural opportunities!"

Q Town to Campus Ratio

"The thing I love about Ann Arbor is that you don't feel stuck in a campus town. Ann Arbor has a thriving arts community and is intertwined with the university campus. We are never at a loss for something to do and everything is in walking distance!"

Q Great!

"I would choose U of M again in a heartbeat. You get a superb education and the campus is gorgeous."

Q The Leaders and Best

"This school is amazing and I would not want to enroll anywhere else. It is a very prestigious university and I also feel like it has the best social scene out of all schools in Michigan. There are hundreds of university clubs, groups, and Greek life. I can guarantee that any person that enrolls in this university will find a group of peers that they can fully relate too."

BEST OF MICHIGAN

1. Football Saturdays
2. Lovely Ann Arbor
3. Stellar academics
4. Great social life
5. 900 student organizations
6. School spirit
7. Proud reputation
8. Research opportunities

Happy Students
96% of students return after their first year.

Proven Success
88% of students will complete their education and graduate with a degree.

WORST OF MICHIGAN

1. Long and cold winters
2. Overly eccentric GSIs
3. Poor dorm food
4. Outdated residence halls
5. No parking, anywhere!
6. Tuition (most expensive public school)
7. Cost of living

Expensive
Tuition is a steep $34,937, one of the most expensive rates in the country.

Student Body

African American:	6%	Male Undergrads:	50%
Asian American:	12%	Female Undergrads:	50%
Hispanic:	4%	Living On Campus:	63%
International:	5%	Living Off Campus:	37%
Native American:	1%	Male Athletes:	3%
White:	63%	Female Athletes:	3%
Unknown:	8%	Fraternity Members:	15%
From Out-of-State:	35%	Sorority Members:	17%

Students Speak Out On... EVERYTHING!

ACADEMICS

Excellent Place to Grow

"Michigan is one of the best places to come if you want to get an education in Engineering. It consistently has one of the top three programs in the country for Aerospace Engineering. The professors are always available to answer questions and help guide students when they are having trouble. The varying personalities of the professors keep the classes interesting and thats why i attend every lecture."

Great

"I came to the university to study political science, and have not only gotten an education in that area that exceeded my expectations but I also am very prepared for careers in a variety of fields based on the attention to skill building in the school of Literature, Science, and the Arts."

ATHLETICS

Maize and Blue Faithful

"U of M sports are top notch. I actually just read that we won the Mens Gymnastic National Championship. No other school can compare to the tradition of the maize and blue. No football stadium can compare to the Big House. Also I am a referee for IM basketball and football and it is very fun and competitive. I also play 4 IM sports along with refereeing. I love the athletic scene overall."

Sports Are Huge

"Saturdays in the fall are devoted to football. It's an all-day event, with people partying before, after, and during games. Plus we have the Big House, the third biggest stadium in the world."

CAMPUS DINING

Fantastic Eats in Ann Arbor

"Plenty of variety on campus and with my BlueBucks it is so convenient to grab snacks or a meal between classes.n"

Great

"Ann Arbor's cuisine is amazing. I am not familiar with the campus dining halls or menu plans, but I really don't need to be. If I want good food at a fairly low cost, it is available, and usually within a short distance walk."

CAMPUS HOUSING

Social

"You will be able to find someone to hang out with guaranteed. With countless clubs and social engagements on campus, you will find a spot in the social life at the University of Michigan."

Extremely Convienient but Pricy.

"Living in the dorm is great but few students choose to live there for more than 2 years. Very few freshman are not in dorms and it is a great way to meet new people. The bathrooms and lounges are kept very clean and the computer labs are nice to work in. The dining halls are very convenient also. Unfortunately no Ann Arbor housing is cheap but dorms are pricy too."

GUYS & GIRLS

Many Fish in This Sea

"With this many undergrads and the current admission standards, there are definitely a good mix of students here."

Girls Are Hot

"You will find people from all over the world a the University of Michigan. People are fun, hardworking, the girls are very hot always working out."

HEALTH & SAFETY

Safe

"Ann Arbor is a peace small town and UM is definitely a quiet place for living."

LOOKING FOR MORE?

Check out our full-length guide to this school at collegeprowler.com/university-of-michigan/.

University of Minnesota

100 Church St. SE; Minneapolis, MN 55455
(612) 625-5000; www1.umn.edu/twincities

THE BASICS:

Acceptance Rate: 50%
Yield: 32%
Setting: Large city
Control: Public
Total Undergrads: 33,236
SAT Range: 1650–2030*
ACT Range: 24–29

Student-Faculty Ratio: 21:1
Retention Rate: 90%
Graduation Rate: 66%
Tuition: $15,466
Room & Board: $7,392
Avg. Aid Package: $6,936
Students With Aid: 83%

of 2400

Academics	B+	Greek Life	B-
Athletics	A	Guys	A-
Campus Dining	B	Health & Safety	B-
Campus Housing	B	Local Atmosphere	A
Campus Strictness	B	Nightlife	A-
Computers	B+	Off-Campus Dining	B+
Diversity	B-	Off-Campus Housing	B-
Drug Safety	C	Parking	C+
Facilities	B+	Transportation	A
Girls	A-	Weather	C+

CP's Student Author On...
OVERALL EXPERIENCE

The University of Minnesota, Twin Cities provides admirable academic opportunities, an environment that facilitates those opportunities, and a surrounding in which students are able to construct their own unique opportunities and experiences. Get out to the theater once in a while, walk around one of the many lakes, get involved in a student organization, bike along the river, visit an art exhibit, participate in a school function, shop for a friend, take an extra class just because it sounds interesting, go to a concert, create your own projects, and experience all that you can.

College really is a uniquely rewarding experience. Being centered in a large metro area adds to this experience by exposing students to a wide range of people, ideas, and opportunities. By committing yourself to University life, your academic aptitude will grow, you will build strong interpersonal skills, and you will learn about the meaning of dedication and responsibility.... For the rest of this editorial, visit collegeprowler.com.

Students Speak Out On...
OVERALL EXPERIENCE

Q I Was a Transfer Student and I Was Made to Feel at Home

"I transferred to the U of MN two semesters ago, but I have never felt like an outsider at school. There were many events to help transfer students learn about the school and the clubs that I joined were welcoming and made coming to the U of MN worth the change."

Q Diversity and Opportunity

"The University of Minnesota is teaming with a diverse student body. Gender integration is very high. The engagement of my professors is top notch as are the backgrounds and credentials. For a state school I have access to professors who have experienced Ivy League educations and experiences in their fields of expertise that reflect global travels and professionalism."

BEST OF MINNESOTA

1. Research programs
2. Internship and job opportunities
3. The Twin Cities nightlife
4. Cleanliness of campus
5. Athletics
6. Great professors
7. The vibrant social scene

Happy Students
90% of students return after their first year.

Knowledgeable Professors
89% of students surveyed rated the general knowledge of professors as above average.

WORST OF MINNESOTA

1. Winter weather
2. Parking
3. Cost of off-campus housing
4. Dorm food
5. Tuition
6. Lack of large campus events

Lowest Grades
Drug Safety: C
Weather: C+
Parking: C+

Student Body

African American:	5%	Male Undergrads:	46%
Asian American:	9%	Female Undergrads:	54%
Hispanic:	2%	Living On Campus:	22%
International:	3%	Living Off Campus:	78%
Native American:	1%	Male Athletes:	4%
White:	71%	Female Athletes:	4%
Unknown:	8%	Fraternity Members:	3%
From Out-of-State:	35%	Sorority Members:	3%

Students Speak Out On... EVERYTHING!

ACADEMICS

Q Bachelor of Science in Health Sciencs (Rochester Campus)

"This program is great for anyone interested in health sciences. It gives you the freedom to explore different careers without wasting your time or money. The faculty are extremely supportive and really want you to succeed. I highly recommend the BSHS program."

Q Amazing

"So many classes and majors to choose from! What I love about the U of Minnesota is that not only are there so many options but also the classes are extremely thorough and the requirements make students look at all areas of study."

ATHLETICS

Q The U Is a Great Place for Sports

"New stadium for football, tons of gopher pride, teams could be better - but we bleed maroon and gold!"

Q U of MN Gophers

"The U of Mn Twin Cities are very proud of the Golden Gophers! We have had many spectacular games here on campus in football and hockey."

CAMPUS DINING

Q The Usual

"The on-campus dining halls in the dorms are good. As in any dorms the food gets old fast, but I'd say there are plenty of options. The menu usually includes a main meal, salad bar, other bar, dessert bar, drink options, and cereal is always an option. As far as off-campus dining goes, the Twin Cities is where its at! There are awesome restaurants that are very easily bus-able, and every type of food you can imagine!"

Q Decent

"Its a decent dining hall if about 15 different dinning halls to choose from. Different menu with Vegan and Vegetarian options with also Late night meals for those that have night classes and want some food at that time, the late night meals are open from 7pm till 12am"

Frequently Compared Schools:

University of Illinois
University of Iowa
University of Michigan
University of Wisconsin

CAMPUS HOUSING

Q Dorms on Campus

"The dorms are nice to live in and are close to campus but are overly expensive, as are the meal plans. The best dorm to be in is Territorial Hall since most of its ammenities are new and their is a tunnel that leads to the dining hall."

Q Standford Hall

"This is the best dorm on campus. The food is excellent for dorm food, the building is nice, and it's in a good location."

GUYS & GIRLS

Q Good-looking guys/girls

"There are some very good looking men and women at my school."

Q Guys and Girls

"The social life on campus is really fun. I especially like hanging out with the boys in the Greek Community. There are so many students with so many interests that anyone can fit in."

HEALTH & SAFETY

Q Campus Crime and Safety Services

"There aren't many campus crime here at the Univ but I have heard a few..but I like how they handle it..they shoot out e-mails to students and staff about the incident and warn them to stay safe and alert. They also have securities available through out the day until late in the evening and so if students don't feel safe in the evenings they can call in to the securities hotline and request someone to take you to your car or your dorm room, which is really nice."

Q Health and Safety

"I usually am not out past 8 o'clock, because I don't want to be put in a conflicted situation, but when I have been out later, I always feel safe. I stay close to the bus stops, which are always well lit and have emergency lights at all of them. I always see campus security walking around or driving around as well. I would say that campus safety is excellent on my campus."

LOOKING FOR MORE?

Check out our full-length guide to this school at collegeprowler.com/university-of-minnesota/.

University of Mississippi

1848 University Circle; University, MS 38677
(662) 915-7211; www.olemiss.edu

CP's Student Author On... OVERALL EXPERIENCE

Overall, students don't want to leave Ole Miss or Oxford, even after they graduate. There are many students who choose to get additional degrees just so they don't have to leave. The University provides almost everything one could want in a college experience. There are great sporting events that are heavily attended by the student body. There's a hopping nightlife. There are many religions and church denominations. There's a supportive faculty, a beautiful campus, and interesting classes. The job rate for recent graduates is very high and offers salaries that are competitive with other SEC schools.

If there's something students say they would change about their Ole Miss experience, it's typically that Oxford doesn't have some of the conveniences, such as a mall, which other campuses in larger cities have. For most, this minor inconvenience is counteracted by Memphis, Tupelo, and Jackson being so close to Oxford. Many students credit Ole Miss with making them who they are and say they have fond memories that will last a lifetime from a place that remain with them forever.

Students Speak Out On... OVERALL EXPERIENCE

Q Could Not Have Asked for Anything Better

"From the academic experience to the nightlife this school could not be better for me. i wish everyone could see how amazing this place is, but then it just wouldnt be ole miss. This school has more pride and tradition then any other school in the country, i truly love this place HOTTY TODDY"

Q Welcome to the Best Four Years of Your Life- Ole Miss

"Ole miss is one of the coolest places on earth. I love Ole Miss and couldn't imagine not being at school here. Naturally, Ole Miss is known for parties, but it is so much more than that. I feel as though Ole Miss is one big family. The southern hospitality is something that I have never experienced before. The students and professors share this bond coming from this great school, and that is what makes the Ole Miss family so special to me. I love this place."

Q Two Words: LOVE IT!!

"Ole Miss is awesome. You have a great academic experience, meet lots of different new people and create lasting memories"

BEST OF OLE MISS

1. Traditions, especially groving on football weekends
2. Great work experience that's available in your field of study before you graduate

Affordable
Tuition is only $13,050, one of the most affordable rates in the country.

Happy Students
81% of students return after their first year.

WORST OF OLE MISS

1. Parking
2. Constant construction on buildings, even though it will pay off in the end
3. The stereotypes that others have about Ole Miss
4. The communal bathrooms in the dorms

Lowest Grades
Drug Safety: D+
Diversity: D+
Parking: B-

Student Body

African American:	14%	Male Undergrads:	47%
Asian American:	1%	Female Undergrads:	53%
Hispanic:	1%	Living On Campus:	28%
International:	3%	Living Off Campus:	72%
Native American:	0%	Male Athletes:	4%
White:	76%	Female Athletes:	2%
Unknown:	4%	Fraternity Members:	32%
From Out-of-State:	46%	Sorority Members:	34%

Frequently Compared Schools:

Auburn University
Louisiana State University
University of Alabama
University of Georgia

Students Speak Out On... EVERYTHING!

ACADEMICS

Q Attending Ole Miss Has Been a Life Long Dream of Mine.

"I had always wanted to attend the University of Mississippi ever since I was a little boy. The campus is awesome. I love Ole Miss football, and campus life is amazing."

Q Medicine and Law

"I would say this university has pretty on par sciences and law departments. Many successful doctors and lawyers have come out of this school."

Q Ole Miss Art Department

"The Ole Miss Art department has many great artists. The workload tends to vary based on who you have as a teacher. Like in printmaking, I have already made 30 prints in two weeks, but then in my 3-d design class we did only 4 projects. It has been a great experience."

ATHLETICS

Q Track and Field

"I feel students attending the University should be able to try-out for any sport available."

Q SEC SEC SEC

"football is a religion here and baseball is huge as well. Tailgating for football games here is the best there is. SI rates it the #1 taigate spot in the country every year"

CAMPUS DINING

Q Food at Ole Miss Is Awesome

"There are some many different dining facilities that I never have to leave campus to get my favorite foods such as pizza and sushi."

Q Ole Miss

"Ole Miss has a great variety of foods from subway to pizza to sushi. It's also a very easy process to pay. Johnson Common is also a great place on campus, total buffet! Ole Miss also has a great flex plan that is $200. You can use it in the Union, the JC, or any of the vending machines, and what you don't use, rolls over to the next semester!"

CAMPUS HOUSING

Q Residential College

"The Residential College at Ole Miss is a state of the art dorm that allows for the betterment of its inhabitants. Living in this dorm has been really nice. Here we have our own cafe, fitness area, library, study groups, computer lab, and much more. It is definately a privilege to have been chosen to live here."

Q Dorm Life Is Exellent

"you meet a lot of your best friends through the dorms and its great for your social life. I just wish they were co-ed..."

GUYS & GIRLS

Q Variety

"At Ole Miss you will see very different types of personalities. You will also fall in love at first sight many times a day walking to class."

Q OH the Girls

"The girls here are somthing else. I honestly believe that a fairy comes to all the hottest girls in the south and tells them they need to go to ole miss, there's no other explaation"

HEALTH & SAFETY

Q The Best

"Ole miss is the safest campus i have ever seen. Oxford is the kind of town where you can leave your doors and windows unlocked and not have to worry about a thing"

Q Nice :)

"The safety and security on campus is very good. In fact, it was one of the deciding factors in my decision to attend Ole Miss, my mom was just overjoyed by all the Emergency Booths located all around. It's great!"

LOOKING FOR MORE?

Check out our full-length guide to this school at collegeprowler.com/university-of-mississippi/.

University of Missouri

105 Jesse Hall; Columbia, MO 65211
(573) 882-2121; www.missouri.edu

THE BASICS:

Acceptance Rate: 83%
Yield: 41%
Setting: Mid-sized city
Control: Public
Total Undergrads: 23,799
SAT Range: 1060–1300*
ACT Range: 23–28

Student-Faculty Ratio: 19:1
Retention Rate: 85%
Graduation Rate: 69%
Tuition: $19,592
Room & Board: $8,170
Avg. Aid Package: $12,757
Students With Aid: 80%

* of 1600

Academics	B+	Greek Life	A-
Athletics	A+	Guys	A-
Campus Dining	B+	Health & Safety	B
Campus Housing	B	Local Atmosphere	A-
Campus Strictness	C+	Nightlife	A-
Computers	B+	Off-Campus Dining	A-
Diversity	C+	Off-Campus Housing	A
Drug Safety	C+	Parking	C+
Facilities	A-	Transportation	B
Girls	A	Weather	C+

CP's Student Author On...
OVERALL EXPERIENCE

Mizzou is not the best college in the country. It's not even the best college in the Big 12 (that honor belongs to Texas). But, beyond its simple exterior, the University of Missouri is truly a complex, sociable, and at times, incredibly fun place to be. There are always down times when you're not doing a whole lot, and sometimes, that can be a little unnerving. But, there are also periods where it will seem like the fun will never end.

Mizzou is not, however, an immaculate institution. Diversity is certainly lacking, some of the dorm food is sub-par, and parking is difficult. Plus, it seems to be going through some difficult budgetary times, which is causing our tuition to skyrocket. But all of those drawbacks are compensated for by the thrill of screaming "screw KU" at the top of your lungs, gyrating with the apple of your eye in a crowded dance club, or participating in a meaningful club or organization. It's those things that make Mizzou worth going to.

Students Speak Out On...
OVERALL EXPERIENCE

Q **Experience**
"I've met a lot of people, and been to a lot of fun parties. Facilities are great, sports are competetive. Its all great!"

Q **Homecoming**
"Homecoming was a blast, the spirit around Mizzou is amazing!"

Q **Gameday 2010**
"Rushing the field after the OU game win was by far the most memorable expierence of my LIFE thus far. So amazing, being on the field with thousands of my fellow students. Such a rush! Much of Mizzou is based on sporting events which I never understood until that experience."

BEST OF MIZZOU

1. The MU-KU basketball game
2. The columns
3. STRIPES
4. Football games vs. quality opponents
5. Stankowski Field
6. Quinn Schneider's hair

Happy Students
85% of students return after their first year.

Knowledgeable Professors
100% of students surveyed rated the general knowledge of professors as above average.

WORST OF MIZZOU

1. Extremely cold weather
2. Pervasive Greek life
3. Getting blown out by Kansas State year after year
4. Parking
5. Overcrowded general education classes

Not Much Diversity
One of the least racially diverse campuses—only 16% of students are minorities.

Student Body

African American:	6%	Male Undergrads:	48%
Asian American:	3%	Female Undergrads:	52%
Hispanic:	2%	Living On Campus:	32%
International:	2%	Living Off Campus:	68%
Native American:	1%	Male Athletes:	3%
White:	84%	Female Athletes:	2%
Unknown:	3%	Fraternity Members:	24%
From Out-of-State:	28%	Sorority Members:	18%

Frequently Compared Schools:

Indiana University
University of Illinois
University of Iowa
University of Kansas

Students Speak Out On... EVERYTHING!

ACADEMICS

Missouri's Agriculture Program

"The University of Missouri is known for having one of the best agriculture programs in the country. It is a privilege to be able to attend the school and I know I will be able to find a great job after graduation."

Nothing Beats a Tiger

"Mizzou has some of the best professors you could ask for. They're experienced and used to dealing with many students at once, so they can answer even the most strange of questions. And, after getting the always available help that's needed, you can feel free to head to Ellis or the Shack or anywhere in between."

ATHLETICS

Sports Are Direct Tie to MU Pride

"School spirit is HUGE here. Football games in the fall and basketball games in the spring rule students' schedules and social lives. Professors do the M-I-Z, Z-O-U cheers prior to class. MASSIVE new student recreation center is award winning. SPORTS ARE A BIG DEAL at MU--a VERY big deal."

MIZ-ZOU!

"Missouri athletics are amazing! Student spirit is high and i vital part to our teams success."

CAMPUS DINING

Mu Food

"I work in the dining halls so I have a first hand look at the food served at mizzou. the dining halls are extremely diverse aswell as clean. the health standars mizzou dining services requires is matched by no one. the value is amazing every hall is all you can eat. If you do not finish your meal plan, or go out of town you are able to buy grocieris with your extra points"

FOOD!! Is Great.

"The dining options at mizzou are pretty great. There's like 5 or 6 dining halls and I'd say the food there is really good especially compared to other schools. There's lots of options especially healthy ones. In addition to that there are at least

15 other places for you to use your E.Z. charge including restaurants, 3 markets to buy stuff like groceries, snacks and its pretty good. There's something for everyone and it's all within walking distance."

CAMPUS HOUSING

Housing Options

"As a first year student you are required to live in some kind of University housing, they have many options for you to chose from including double to single room in dorms or even apartment style living off campus. There are many new dorm buildings and most of the buildings are being renovated as well for nicer cleaner living areas."

It's a College Town..

"It is definitely a small town vibe, with not much way of getting around without a cab or bus service. I'd bring a car if I could by my second semester of freshman year. The dining facilities are great, and the food is great. The Rec facilities are great as well. Most of the dorms are renovated and nice. There is always something to do, and there are good minority scholarships, other than thought it can be a costly school if you're an out-of-state student."

GUYS & GIRLS

Attractive People of All Types

"A typical student at Mizzou ranges. There are the typical sorority girls and frat boys but there are also a lot of down to earth students, religious students, country boys/girls, and bohemian looking people. There are attractive people of all types on Mizzou's campus. The people at Mizzou don't really have an accent."

HEALTH & SAFETY

MU Safety

"The safety here is excellent. I haven't felt unsafe since i been here. There is construction going on but those places are kept blocked off to ensure safety."

LOOKING FOR MORE?

Check out our full-length guide to this school at collegeprowler.com/university-of-missouri/.

University of Montana

32 Campus Drive; Missoula, MT 59812
(406) 243-0211; www.umt.edu

THE BASICS:

Acceptance Rate: 95%
Yield: 42%
Setting: Rural
Control: Public
Total Undergrads: 13,072
SAT Range: 1440–1780*
ACT Range: 20–26

Student-Faculty Ratio: 19:1
Retention Rate: 73%
Graduation Rate: 41%
Tuition: $17,764
Room & Board: $6,611
Avg. Aid Package: $8,638
Students With Aid: 80%

* of 2400

Academics	B-	Greek Life	C+
Athletics	B	Guys	A-
Campus Dining	B	Health & Safety	B+
Campus Housing	B	Local Atmosphere	B+
Campus Strictness	B	Nightlife	B+
Computers	C+	Off-Campus Dining	B
Diversity	C	Off-Campus Housing	B
Drug Safety	D+	Parking	C+
Facilities	B	Transportation	A-
Girls	B	Weather	B-

CP's Student Author On...
OVERALL EXPERIENCE

The University of Montana does not provide an escape from "the real world" the same way that private liberal arts colleges and Ivy Leagues do. UM provides a diverse mix of diligent and lazy, smart and dumb, rich and poor—not a selective group of wealthy nerds with a love of learning and high SAT scores. Since the University of Montana admits 70 percent of its applicants, UM students work with all types of people with different levels of drive, intelligence, and economic class.

Life is what you make of it at UM. If UM students form relationships with professors, get involved, utilize resources and opportunities, and don't assume that a mere college degree guarantees a job, then they will get back what they put into the University. UM does not coddle or compliment its students, unless those students have the initiative to make themselves known within the community. It's not an isolated bubble, and students have to eke out their own jobs, opportunities, and attention in order to succeed. The campus itself looks Edenic, untouched, and beautiful.... For the rest of this editorial, visit collegeprowler.com.

Students Speak Out On...
OVERALL EXPERIENCE

Q I love this school

"I love this school. The people, the scenery, the fresh air, the great teachers. Everything about my experience so far is exactly what I would expect for the ultimate college experience."

Q I've had so much fun

"In an instant I would do it again. I've had so much fun. My favorite part of this town is the mountains and all the outdoor activities. I live outdoors here because there is something to do in every season. Raft in the summer, snowboard in the winter, hike in the spring, and camp in the fall. It's all in one place, the great town of Missoula."

Q I love this town and UM

"I grew up here knowing that I would go to the UM. I love this town and will probably stay here to have a family. It's the perfect balance between a college town and a family town. There is something to do for every type and every age person. Besides being beautiful here, the people are spectacular and will give you an experience you will never forget."

BEST OF MONTANA

1. Beautiful campus
2. Overall atmosphere of Missoula and UM
3. Large community of writers and artists
4. Good compromise between a city and a small town

Knowledgeable Professors
100% of students surveyed rated the general knowledge of professors as above average.

Low-Stress Course Load
85% of students surveyed rated the manageability of work as above average.

WORST OF MONTANA

1. Cold weather winters
2. Low funding for liberal arts as opposed to athletics
3. Expensive on-campus food
4. Parking
5. The Financial Aid Office's lack of communication

Lowest Grades
Drug Safety: D+
Diversity: C
Computers: C+

Student Body

African American:	1%	Male Undergrads:	47%
Asian American:	2%	Female Undergrads:	53%
Hispanic:	2%	Living On Campus:	29%
International:	1%	Living Off Campus:	75%
Native American:	4%	Male Athletes:	6%
White:	82%	Female Athletes:	3%
Unknown:	8%	Fraternity Members:	6%
From Out-of-State:	27%	Sorority Members:	6%

Frequently Compared Schools:

Montana State University
University of Colorado
University of Oregon
University of Washington

Students Speak Out On...
EVERYTHING!

ACADEMICS

Q Great Biology Program

"The Biology program has fantastic instructors who strive to provide students with relevant and current information. The department provides numerous opportunities for students such as undergraduate research opportunities that are invaluable experiences for students. The advising and opportunities help students understand all possible career opportunities and how best to prepare for those careers."

Q Great!

"I haven't yet started the Education program, but so far, Jayna Lutz has made the transition SUPER easy from Business Management to Education"

Q My education here is worth every penny

"I know I will walk out of this school knowing my stuff. Professors have gone out of their way to help me to understand hard concepts. My education here is worth every penny."

ATHLETICS

Q We have a great athletic program

"Football is huge at UM. We have a great athletic program. Athletes have their own facilities, personal trainers, nutritionist, and training. UM takes care of their athletes."

Q So much school spirit here

"There is so much school spirit here. People paint their whole bodies maroon and silver. There is not a day that goes by that I don't see at least 50 people wearing Griz sweatshirts. There is even this one guy that wears a shirt that looks like it was attacked by a grizzly. UM is all about Football spirit."

CAMPUS DINING

Q I have a job in Dining Services

"I've got a job in Dining Services. It's great! For each shift you work, you get a stipend for a free meal and they work around your class schedule."

Q Award-winning

"The University of Montana has won awards for its exceptional on-campus dining."

CAMPUS HOUSING

Q College Living

"Campus is small but big enough to run into new people. On a warm day, the Oval is buzzing and there's always lots to do. Including some great music."

Q Life on Campus

"During my four years at UM, I lived in the dorms. They were nice dorms with great people and it was wonderful to live in the midst of UM's campus life. Everything I needed was a simple walk away and if anything fun was going on, and there usually was, I didn't have to go very far."

GUYS & GIRLS

Q Every kind of person on campus

"There is every kind of person that I can think of on this campus. There are the hippies that smoke openly, there are the business students that look all proper but spent the weekend the drunkest at the party, there are the artsy people who are always looking for an abstract answer to an easy problem. UM is an open-minded place with really cool people."

Q Hella cool

"People here are hella cool."

HEALTH & SAFETY

Q I feel totally safe here

"I feel totally safe here, even walking alone at night."

Q Leave Your Car Unlocked

"I've never felt scared here. Maybe I'm naive, but I leave my car unlocked and even feel comfortable hiking the M at night."

LOOKING FOR MORE?

Check out our full-length guide to this school at collegeprowler.com/university-of-montana/.

University of Mount Union

1972 Clark Ave.; Alliance, OH 44601
(800) 992-6682; www.muc.edu

THE BASICS:

Acceptance Rate: 75%
Yield: 33%
Setting: Town
Control: Private Non-Profit
Total Undergrads: 2,193
SAT Range: 870–1130*
ACT Range: 19–25

Student-Faculty Ratio: 14:1
Retention Rate: 78%
Graduation Rate: 65%
Tuition: $23,880
Room & Board: $7,420
Avg. Aid Package: $19,081
Students With Aid: 100%

* of 1600

Academics	B-	Greek Life	B+
Athletics	B-	Guys	B+
Campus Dining	B-	Health & Safety	C+
Campus Housing	B	Local Atmosphere	C-
Campus Strictness	C+	Nightlife	C+
Computers	B	Off-Campus Dining	C+
Diversity	C	Off-Campus Housing	B-
Drug Safety	C	Parking	B+
Facilities	B+	Transportation	C
Girls	B-	Weather	C-

CP's Student Author On...
OVERALL EXPERIENCE

It may be cliché, but it's true: At Mount Union, you really are a name and not a number. The small size of campus makes it easy to meet people—professors, staff members, and other students—and to really find your niche. Students love the small class sizes, individual attention from professors, and the close-knit feel of campus. If you take advantage of opportunities like student organizations, study abroad, athletics, Greek life, and whatever else interests you, it won't be long before Mount ceases to be just a school and becomes a home. Like its students, the University is constantly striving to expand its own horizons, with new facilities, programs, and opportunities for growth that you won't find at other schools of its size. Mount Union graduates leave with great friends, amazing life experiences, and a strong education, and most go on to become successful and fiercely loyal alumni.

There are a handful of things Mount Union students would change about their college, but when it comes down to it, most of them would still choose Mount if they had to do it all over again.... For the rest of this editorial, visit collegeprowler.com.

Students Speak Out On...
OVERALL EXPERIENCE

Q It's Great

"Mount Union is overall a great school. I don't really have too many complaints. School work is the most important thing here and it really shows with the student's grades and graduation rates."

Q Mount Union College :)

"My four years at Mount Union College meant the world to me. I could not have asked for a better college experience. There are plenty of opportunities to grow both academically and socially at Mount."

Q No Problem

"At Mount Union, all of the people are fun and easy to get along with. It's small, so you see a lot of the same people from day to day and that makes it easier to get to know people. The small size also contributes to small class sizes, which are helpful in getting to know the professors on a more personal level—you are known by your name and not just a number."

Q Overall Experience

"I love Mount Union. Going to school there has been a great and exciting experience so far."

BEST OF MOUNT UNION

1. Amazing professors!
2. Excellent athletics
3. Football, football, football!
4. Plenty of opportunities to get involved
5. Strong academics
6. The beautiful campus

Easy Financial Aid Process
53% of students surveyed told us that the financial aid process went smoothly and they received the financial aid they needed.

WORST OF MOUNT UNION

1. The cafeteria food
2. The shortage of campus housing
3. There aren't enough things to do in the area.
4. The lack of parking
5. The small size
6. The price of tuition

Students Can't Wait to Get Out of Town
52% of students surveyed said that there's no way they would live here after graduation.

Student Body

African American:	4%	Male Undergrads:	50%
Asian American:	1%	Female Undergrads:	50%
Hispanic:	1%	Living On Campus:	70%
International:	3%	Living Off Campus:	30%
Native American:	0%	Male Athletes:	52%
White:	86%	Female Athletes:	22%
Unknown:	3%	Fraternity Members:	15%
From Out-of-State:	16%	Sorority Members:	28%

Frequently Compared Schools:

Baldwin - Wallace College
College of Wooster
Kent State University
Ohio State University

Students Speak Out On... EVERYTHING!

ACADEMICS

Internships/Department

"I love the psychology department. I love the professors and the material. I love my adviser. Everything about the department is amazing. I just wish Psi Chi was better."

Great Preparation

"I am a communications major and the curriculum offered at the University of Mount Union is very good. The institution is on the rise....big time! It offers state-of-the-art facilities and allows students every possible opportunity to be successful men and women."

ATHLETICS

Football

"Football is huge at Mount Union College. They win almost every game and have gone to the national championship the past few years in a row. There are so many fans at the games and they are well-supported."

Timken

"Timken has a pool, weight training areas, treadmills, track, and basketball court."

CAMPUS DINING

What Menu

"While the food is pretty good, the menu is so boring and repetitive. When you're starving or need a snake between classes it's a nice place to come get whatever food you need, but don't expect too many different options from day to day."

Variety of Food

"The food is good in general, but there doesn't seem to be a lot of variety. The times that hot food is served are convenient when you are not in class."

CAMPUS HOUSING

Campus

"The campus options to pick from are all very similar your first year but the entire grounds of the campus is incredibly well kept. It is always spotless and clean like a hospital. The people are all friendly and really seem like they want to be there and get involved, not just show up."

Living in a Theme House Is the Best

"All the dorms are well taken care of on campus. They are dorms, so they are small, but they get bigger as you become an upperclassman. The housing options are wonderful as well. There are plenty of Greek houses to chose from, as well as theme housing. I prefer the theme housing the best because you can chose who you'd like to live with; it becomes a family."

GUYS & GIRLS

Woooowww!

"There are all different types of guys on campus! For the most part, they are very friendly and some just stick to their groups. The women are just so beautiful—so many fine ladies all over campus. Intelligent, funny, and just awesome!"

Very Casual Dressing

"The students dress casually or in sweats; dressier clothes depend on the day and class requirements. The social life is fantastic. The students and staff make you feel just like you're at home. They all talk to you. Relationships at the school are very good. Professors are always saying if you need help, just ask—that is what we are here for."

HEALTH & SAFETY

Safety

"Mount Union is very safe. I have never felt that I was in danger while on campus, and I don't know of any major crimes on campus. Campus Security is always 5 minutes away at most and will come to you, regardless of time of day."

LOOKING FOR MORE?
Check out our full-length guide to this school at collegeprowler.com/university-of-mount-union/.

University of Nebraska

1400 R St.; Lincoln, NE 68588
(402) 472-7211; www.unl.edu

THE BASICS:

Acceptance Rate: 63%
Yield: 67%
Setting: Large city
Control: Public
Total Undergrads: 18,955
SAT Range: 1040–1350*
ACT Range: 22–29

Student-Faculty Ratio: 17:1
Retention Rate: 84%
Graduation Rate: 64%
Tuition: $17,897
Room & Board: $7,260
Avg. Aid Package: $10,356
Students With Aid: 77%

* of 1600

Academics	B+	Greek Life	B
Athletics	A	Guys	B+
Campus Dining	B+	Health & Safety	B+
Campus Housing	B-	Local Atmosphere	B
Campus Strictness	C	Nightlife	B+
Computers	A-	Off-Campus Dining	A-
Diversity	C+	Off-Campus Housing	A-
Drug Safety	C+	Parking	B
Facilities	B+	Transportation	B+
Girls	A-	Weather	B-

CP's Student Author On...
OVERALL EXPERIENCE

Although it has its blemishes, most students just can't say enough about the University of Nebraska. They love the atmosphere, they love the activities, and, most of all, they love the people they have met here. Students here believe that almost any college can provide a great experience if you come to school with the right attitude and work ethic, and they agree that UNL is no different.

All in all, it is quite common for prospective students to put UNL on the back burner and place the more glamorous private schools first on their agendas. But, students eventually learn that Nebraska's academics and culture are almost the same as any other place. When it comes to good people and high spirits, there's really no other place like it.

Students Speak Out On...
OVERALL EXPERIENCE

Q Excellent University

"UNL is the place to be. There are a lot of things to do as well as great opportunities to watch some of the best college sports teams in America as well as experience top-notch fine arts and campus faciities. Even though UNL is a very large public university it is cozy enough that you won't get lost and you'll know a lot of people."

Q UNL

"It is a good school. Good classes, good teachers, and good students. Not a big party school, but one that is very prideful."

Q There is no place like Nebraska

"I love UNL. It's a great campus and the people I've met are incredible."

Q I Love It Here.

"I visited tons of schools before deciding on UNL. It has the best parts of big schools and little schools at one perfect sized University. Walking around campus is easy and convenient and everyone is friendly. I just wish that we didn't have winter, although snow doesn't stay on the ground very long here."

BEST OF NEBRASKA

1. Husker Football
2. School spirit
3. Beautiful campus
4. Friendly people
5. Safety
6. Internships opportunities
7. Openness to others

Happy Students
84% of students return after their first year.

Knowledgeable Professors
91% of students surveyed rated the general knowledge of professors as above average.

WORST OF NEBRASKA

1. The weather
2. Crazy cats
3. Lack of diversity
4. Parking
5. Freaky squirrels
6. The dorm food after about six months
7. Small dorms rooms

Lowest Grades
Campus Strictness: C
Diversity: C+
Drug Safety: C+

Student Body

African American:	3%	Male Undergrads:	54%
Asian American:	3%	Female Undergrads:	46%
Hispanic:	4%	Living On Campus:	41%
International:	3%	Living Off Campus:	59%
Native American:	1%	Male Athletes:	5%
White:	82%	Female Athletes:	4%
Unknown:	5%	Fraternity Members:	14%
From Out-of-State:	19%	Sorority Members:	18%

Frequently Compared Schools:

Kansas State University
University of Kansas
University of Missouri
University of Oklahoma

Students Speak Out On... EVERYTHING!

ACADEMICS

Q Great

"Everything academically about UNL is great. I'm going through nursing, and everything gets an A+."

Q Lots of Possibilities

"There are a million majors- lots that I had never heard of before I came to UNL. If I ever want to change my major, UNL is a school where that is a possibility. The professors are very helpful and the classes are awesome. Classes vary in size- I have less than 20 people in my French class!"

Q Great Classes

"All of the classes offered here are wonderful! They are offered at convenient times and don't drag on. The teachers are so nice and always available for help. The academics are one of the main reasons I came to Nebraska"

ATHLETICS

Q Husker Spirit

"Need I say more? Through thick and thin, student involvement, fan support, and school spirit all go hand-in-hand. There's nothing like being a part of the tradition behind Husker athletics or being a part of the Sea of Red."

Q Football Is King!

"At the University of Nebraska, football season is celebrated August-July. On game days, Memorial Stadium is quite literally the third largest "city" in the state! The Huskers seem to unify everyone in the state, and that kind of school spirit is pretty powerful to experience."

CAMPUS DINING

Q Awesome

"The food is prepared fresh right in front of you, workers are helpful and nice. UNL has great food."

Q Dining Halls at Nebraska

"The dinging halls at Nebraska are convenient. A meal plan is a must if you are living on campus. At times the food that is avaliable can seem to be repetitive. That being said, going from a meal plan to now not having a meal plan, I really miss eating at the dining halls. Unless you are a great cook you really can't make food that will compare. Only buy a meal plan if you live on campus. If you live off campus it might be hard to get your moneys worth because they are pricey."

CAMPUS HOUSING

Q Good Experience

"Fun exeperience. Socially worth it. Little expensive, but not bad compared to other schools."

Q Convenience

"the convenience of everything in lincoln is fantastic. Almost anything that one would want to do academically or otherwise is within a couple miles of campus"

GUYS & GIRLS

Q Nice!

"The kids at UNL are all very friendly! You really get to know everyone in your dorm and on your floor."

Q Social Life

"Wide range of social activities for all class levels. Fraterities and Sororities are well regulated and interact socially. University Program Council which promotes social activities for students is student run and funded by the University."

HEALTH & SAFETY

Q Safe

"UNL has a great security system, it has emergency phones set up around campus and a great campus police force. In addition, the crime rate is low."

Q University of Nebraska

"I have always felt very welcome and everyone is very friendly. Most seem to have their primary goal in mind... graduating, and this makes UNL a wonderful campus. There is not very much campus crime and the police on campus definately seem to be doing their job well!"

LOOKING FOR MORE?

Check out our full-length guide to this school at collegeprowler.com/university-of-nebraska/.

University of New Hampshire

105 Main St.; Durham, NH 03824
(603) 862-1234; www.unh.edu

THE BASICS:

Acceptance Rate: 72%
Yield: 26%
Setting: Suburban
Control: Public
Total Undergrads: 12,591
SAT Range: 1030–1240*
ACT Range: 21–26

Student-Faculty Ratio: 19:1
Retention Rate: 87%
Graduation Rate: 71%
Tuition: $26,713
Room & Board: $8,874
Avg. Aid Package: $16,852
Students With Aid: 75%

of 1600

Academics	B+	Greek Life	B
Athletics	B-	Guys	A-
Campus Dining	A-	Health & Safety	B-
Campus Housing	B	Local Atmosphere	B
Campus Strictness	C+	Nightlife	A-
Computers	B	Off-Campus Dining	B+
Diversity	C	Off-Campus Housing	B+
Drug Safety	C+	Parking	C+
Facilities	A-	Transportation	A
Girls	B+	Weather	D+

CP's Student Author On...
OVERALL EXPERIENCE

For most students, UNH was not their first choice. However, many of these same students will tell you that they learned to appreciate UNH and its well-rounded course curriculum, spectacular seasons, local "college town" atmosphere, and myriad of activities for students of all ages. It's safe to say that UNH is a school that caters to the needs of many different personalities. The campus also encourages students to explore all that they have to offer through many different organizations including the American Students Association, several fraternities and sororities, and the National Society of Minorities in Hospitality. Although the campus has its shortcomings in some areas, the effort of the administration is greatly evident through renovations of several dormitories and on-campus facilities. This open and accepting environment seems to carry over to the non-student residents of Durham, as well, which is obvious, due to the amount of specials by local businesses geared toward UNH students.

The town of Durham revolves around the students and vice versa.... For the rest of this editorial, visit collegeprowler.com.

Students Speak Out On...
OVERALL EXPERIENCE

Q A+ Overall

"I am glad i picked UNH, it is the best place for me to gain knowledge and join in organizations and activities that are deemed 'college-like' with out pressure. You need to study, UNh has a strict 2.0+ requiremnt or the school may ask the student to take a break to recoop. This is for the best- UNH shows you to time manage!"

Q Best Decision. . .

"UNH is the best decision I have ever made. Period."

Q My Last Choice

"Though UNH was my safety school, the right choice was made for me when all other school rejected my applications. This is where I belong. I have learned and so much I may not have otherwise. This university has great opportunities and offers something for everyone."

BEST OF NEW HAMPSHIRE

1. The men's hockey team
2. Outdoor barbeques
3. The country scenery
4. The ocean beaches
5. $1 pizza
6. Thompson Hall lawn on a warm spring day
7. Broomball competitions

Happy Students
87% of students return after their first year.

Proven Success
71% of students will complete their education and graduate with a degree.

WORST OF NEW HAMPSHIRE

1. The bell tower that rings every 30 minutes
2. Parking
3. The lack of holidays
4. Mud season
5. The wind
6. Traffic on Main Street

Expensive
Tuition is a steep $26,713, one of the most expensive rates in the country.

Student Body

African American:	1%	Male Undergrads:	44%
Asian American:	3%	Female Undergrads:	56%
Hispanic:	2%	Living On Campus:	55%
International:	1%	Living Off Campus:	45%
Native American:	0%	Male Athletes:	7%
White:	80%	Female Athletes:	6%
Unknown:	13%	Fraternity Members:	2%
From Out-of-State:	46%	Sorority Members:	7%

Students Speak Out On...
EVERYTHING!

ACADEMICS

Q Engineering and Business

"Definitely one of the Best Engineering Schools and Facilities I have seen in the New England area. Brand new WSBE school coming soon"

Q Zoology Excellent Program

"I feel that the science program is very well developed.   As a Zoology major, I have many opportunities within the field and with the many devoted professors. I was able to work in the lab with my Zoology professor first semester for credit, however, the experience was worth more than the credit."

ATHLETICS

Q Go Wildcats!

"The team spirit here for the hockey team is amazing. Everyone on campus is a fan and it is a rat race the moment the tickets go on sale."

Q D-1 Wahoo

"UNH is a D1 school so the athletics on campus are great! Hockey is by far the school's biggest sport, with a multi-million dollar hockey rink! The fans really get into all of the games making it a really fun environment!"

CAMPUS DINING

Q Get Fat

"The Dining Hall food is not considered dining hall food. It is so good, they will keep you coming back for more. Whether it be stir-fry, omelettes, or the European stations, you can't just have one plate."

Q Amazing!

"The UNH dining is great! We have plenty of dining halls, and cafés around campus. We even have little stores open until 4 am on Thur-Sat. We also have a lot of special food nights. Compared to what my friends at other colleges say about their food, I'm very lucky at UNH."

Frequently Compared Schools:

University of Connecticut
University of Massachusetts
University of Rhode Island
University of Vermont

CAMPUS HOUSING

Q Hubbard Is Awesome!

"I live in Hubbard which is the Honors dorm and is open to upper and under classmen.   It offers a helpful environment and social community where you can both have fun and keep your grades up. It also has an amazing study lounge."

Q Freshman Living. . .

"I would definitely recommend to the incoming Freshman one of the two Freshman dorms: Williamson & Christiansen. Although they are out of the way and a long walk to some of campus, the amount of people you meet and friends that you make is well worth it. Plus, Philbrook dining hall is a 2-second walk. They are always open late for whenever you want a late-night snack or PANCAKES!!!"

GUYS & GIRLS

Q Guys Are Sweet

"You'll find all sorts of guys at UNH. They are all sweet and fun to hang out with. There are all different types of guys; rednecks, jocks, preps, nerds, you name it."

Q Little Bit of Everything

"It's a big school, and what we lack in ethnic diversity, we make up for with personality diversity."

HEALTH & SAFETY

Q Wonderful Safety Programs

"I always feel safe on campus. We have the blue lights in case of emergencies, like a lot of college campuses today, and police cars are always circling. There have been a few campus alerts of theft or assault on campus, but they've never affected me."

Q Fine by Me

"There are blue lights all over the place, tons of hot lines, and cops around at night."

LOOKING FOR MORE?

Check out our full-length guide to this school at collegeprowler.com/university-of-new-hampshire/.

University of North Carolina

200 E. Cameron Ave.; Chapel Hill, NC 27599
(919) 962-2211; www.unc.edu

THE BASICS:

Acceptance Rate: 34%	**Student-Faculty Ratio:** 14:1
Yield: 53%	**Retention Rate:** 96%
Setting: Small city	**Graduation Rate:** 86%
Control: Public	**Tuition:** $23,513
Total Undergrads: 17,905	**Room & Board:** $8,670
SAT Range: 1800–2080*	**Avg. Aid Package:** $11,881
ACT Range: 28–31	**Students With Aid:** 51%

* of 2400

Academics	A-	Greek Life	B
Athletics	A	Guys	A
Campus Dining	B	Health & Safety	B-
Campus Housing	B-	Local Atmosphere	B+
Campus Strictness	B	Nightlife	B+
Computers	B+	Off-Campus Dining	B+
Diversity	B-	Off-Campus Housing	B-
Drug Safety	C+	Parking	C-
Facilities	A	Transportation	B+
Girls	A-	Weather	B-

CP's Student Author On...
OVERALL EXPERIENCE

Students who attend Carolina are often happy with their choice—even if it wasn't their first. UNC is surrounded by a great college town, is one of the most prestigious public schools in the nation, and is one of the most diverse schools in the nation. The list goes on and on. What more could a college student ask for? At times, yes, Carolina can seem a little redundant and repetitious, but so can any other school. However, if you find a good group of friends and find your niche at Carolina, you'll always find something new around the corner.

This book is proof that your good experiences will outweigh your negative experiences by a ton at Carolina. Yes, there will be run-ins with teachers, failed midterms, pop-quizzes, parking catastrophes, shallow people, and messy, annoying roommates. However, that's a part of college life at any school. It doesn't take long to adjust to Carolina. It's mainly common sense—hang out with old friends, make new friends, party, take a weekend trip or two (but don't forget to bring along your books). Students who attend UNC realize that they are receiving a great college education and an even better college experience.

Students Speak Out On...
OVERALL EXPERIENCE

I Love Being a Tar Heel
"Being part of the tar heel family is great. My school is amazing and I wouldn't want to be any where else. Basketball games are so much fun and going to UNC is the best. Not only do we pride ourselves in a strong history of academics, but sports as well. GO HEELS!"

Atmosphere on Campus Is Great
"When walking around campus during the normal class hours, the whole school seems to walk by one area at least once a day. You can sit in one spot all day and see almost every student enrolled here. I love seeing my fellow students enjoying our beautiful campus every day."

The Best.
"Carolina = the "college experience."Amazing sports teams, an enthusiastic student population, a FANTSTIC college town, great professors, prestige. Could you want more in a university? UNC has everything. I loved my four years there."

BEST OF NORTH CAROLINA

1. UNC athletics
2. The diverse people you'll meet
3. Rushing Frankling Street/ Halloween on Franklin
4. Wireless Internet virtually everywhere
5. The Pit

Happy Students
96% of students return after their first year.

Proven Success
86% of students will complete their education and graduate with a degree.

WORST OF NORTH CAROLINA

1. Lack of parking
2. Move-in day
3. The ratio of guys to girls (for girls)
4. Registering for classes when the system shuts down
5. Unexpected snow or ice storms

Lowest Grades
Parking: C-
Drug Safety: C+
Diversity: B-

Student Body

African American:	11%	Male Undergrads:	42%
Asian American:	7%	Female Undergrads:	58%
Hispanic:	5%	Living On Campus:	45%
International:	1%	Living Off Campus:	55%
Native American:	1%	Male Athletes:	7%
White:	70%	Female Athletes:	4%
Unknown:	4%	Fraternity Members:	15%
From Out-of-State:	18%	Sorority Members:	17%

Frequently Compared Schools:

Duke University
University of Virginia
Vanderbilt University
Wake Forest University

Students Speak Out On... EVERYTHING!

ACADEMICS

Q Great Research Opportunities

"They are always looking for student interested in research or hands on work alongside professors. Great internships."

Q English Major- Freshman Experience

"Since I'm just ending my freshman year, I haven't experienced too much of the program so far. However, what I have seen is a diverse English curriculum offered, and have already received many mass-emails to English majors about internship/job opportunities, workshops, and writing contests. It seems as though there is a lot of opportunity within the English department, both academically and in assistance with job placement."

ATHLETICS

Q Great Sports

"Every sport has competitive athletes. I haven't been to any sporting event in which we just got trashed on."

Q True Blue; Carolina!

"Home of National Champs! Every sport is a big deal at Carolina! School spirit turns the campus blue every day and everyone is proud to say they're a Carolina _____ (insert sport here) fan!"

CAMPUS DINING

Q Two Cafeterias!

"UNC has two places to dine. One is on north campus and the other is on south campus. Both places serves variety of food. Even have international dishes and theme days. Sometimes you may see the same food at dinner that you saw at lunch."

Q Dining Is Not Too Shabby

"There are two dining halls on campus, one for north and one for south campus. The food changes with some standbys that you can always get (pizza, burgers, etc) as well as a salad bar and vegetarian/vegan options."

CAMPUS HOUSING

Q Campus Housing

"Living on campus is definitely a plus. Unfortunately, it is very costly and if you get south campus, it is a rather long walk to where classes are. However, I would much rather have campus housing than live at home.If you like to party and go out at night, you'll definitely love Chapel Hill. There's always something going on and there are plenty of options."

Q Convenience

"Living on campus has a lot of perks. If you forget something in your room or want to take a nap before your next class, it's only a 5-10 minute walk from the heart of campus. Most freshmen live on south campus and while it is further away from classes and libraries, there are some good things about it. You're close to the Dean Dome, SASB (Student Academic Services Building) and Rams Head (Dining Hall, Recreation Center and Market). North campus is really close to most classes."

GUYS & GIRLS

Q There Is an Extreme Diversity Between the Two Sexes.

"At Carolina, you are not going to find more of one type of sex or even ethinicity. There is a wide range of people and the guys and girls are about the same amount. they are also very intelligent and very good lokking people."

Q Cute Guys!

"The guys at my school are so cute and are mostly athletes. Since its in the south, most of the population is lumbee and dey have a different accent."

HEALTH & SAFETY

Q Feel Comfortable Walking Around at Any Time

"UNC has made large strides to ensure that its students are safe. These include emergency poles every few hundred feet and safe walkers at night. I've never felt uncomfortable walking anywhere at UNC."

LOOKING FOR MORE?

Check out our full-length guide to this school at collegeprowler.com/university-of-north-carolina/.

University of North Carolina - Greensboro

1000 Spring Garden St.; Greensboro, NC 27402
(336) 334-5000; www.uncg.edu

THE BASICS:

Acceptance Rate: 72%
Yield: 38%
Setting: Large city
Control: Public
Total Undergrads: 17,445
SAT Range: 1380–1680*
ACT Range: 19–24

Student-Faculty Ratio: 18:1
Retention Rate: 77%
Graduation Rate: 53%
Tuition: $15,995
Room & Board: $6,697
Avg. Aid Package: $9,204
Students With Aid: 73%

* of 2400

Academics	B-	Greek Life	C
Athletics	C	Guys	B+
Campus Dining	C+	Health & Safety	B
Campus Housing	C+	Local Atmosphere	B+
Campus Strictness	B	Nightlife	B+
Computers	B	Off-Campus Dining	B-
Diversity	B	Off-Campus Housing	B-
Drug Safety	B-	Parking	C
Facilities	B-	Transportation	B+
Girls	B-	Weather	B

CP's Student Author On...
OVERALL EXPERIENCE

While there are always a few students who are critical of the University, you will find that most students are very happy with their experience at UNCG. After all, it isn't like high school—students actually pay to be here. They wouldn't stay at UNCG if they didn't think it was the best place to spend their money and the next four years of their lives.

In the end, that's really what a college experience is all about: life. Sure, you're paying thousands of dollars to further your education, but you will actually end up getting a lot more out of it than that. Living and learning in the UNCG community will enrich your life. You will make friends that will feel like family, and you will keep in touch with them for years to come. You will learn to love Greensboro and all that it offers. Your mind will be broadened, both with things you learn in and outside of class. You will listen to inspiring speakers, watch amazing stage productions, attend awesome parties, and discover more about yourself and the person you want to be. Students love UNCG because it encourages and enables them to have the time of their lives.

Students Speak Out On...
OVERALL EXPERIENCE

Q CAB and OLSL

"The campus activities board has made my time here enjoyable. Every week they provide activities for everyone. This includes bowling, video game contests and giveaways, comedy shows. They make you want to get involved and come out. The office of leadership and service learning is also one of my favorites because I love to do community service. They provide a variety of opportunites inside the city, and in other areas of the country"

Q Why UNCG Is Awesome

"UNCG can offer what most North Carolina schools can't; the big campus life with a small campus student population. You have the opportunity to be in a huge lecture class or a small discussion class. There are plenty of on campus organizations to get students involved and campus is only a 3 minutes from downtown Greensboro. There is always something to do on the weekends. On top of the location of campus it's beautiful."

BEST OF UNC GREENSBORO

1. Diversity
2. Strong reputation for academic programs
3. The city of Greensboro
4. Campus-wide wireless Internet access
5. Study abroad programs
6. The EUC

Big Dorms
54% of students surveyed felt that dorms were more spacious than average.

WORST OF UNC GREENSBORO

1. Parking
2. No air conditioning in the Quad
3. Caf food
4. Financial aid
5. Parking (yes, again!)
6. Strictly enforced rules in dorms

Lowest Grades
Greek Life: C
Athletics: C
Parking: C

Students Speak Out On... EVERYTHING!

ACADEMICS

Grad Students

"The teachers at UNCG are, for the most part, very willing to help you—but the grad students who are teaching are the best teachers to have. They have taught me the most by far and have been the most responsive and easiest to relate to."

Religious Studies

"Teachers, at least in the humanities, are generally well educated and patient. They understand that many students are commuters and adults returning to school and adjust their styles and workload accordingly. UNCG is known, among those in the field, for their Religious Studies department, which has teachers from Harvard, Yale, and the bulk coming from Princeton and Chicago."

ATHLETICS

Big Sports

"The varsity sports on campus are big. The biggest sport on campus is by far soccer. We won a championship of some sort a few years back. The sports clubs on campus, such as football, rugby, other soccer leagues, and basketball leagues are very big for students. It gives everyone a chance to play a sport, even if they don't make the school's cut."

Tennis

"I love the tennis courts. My dorm is on the Quad, so it's really simple for me to just walk over and knock a few balls around with my best friend. I think UNCG really understands the athletic needs of its students, because the fields and other facilities are really awesome."

CAMPUS DINING

Food....Pretty Good

"You have the 3 to 4 fast food in the EUC and then if you want you can eat in the cafe and below the cafe there are a few different fast food options!"

Meal Cards

"The food is pretty good. If you live on campus, you have to have a meal card which allows you access into the Caf whenever you are hungry. Spencer's Cafe is the fanciest place to eat on campus, and it's really good."

CAMPUS HOUSING

Spring Garden Apartments

"The Spring Garden Apartments are amazing! My favorite part is the bigger bed because now my girlfriend can comfortably spend the night without the two of us having to make do with a twin-sized mattress."

Dorm Renovations

"I was lucky enough to only have to stay in a dorm for one year, but the dorm that I did stay in—Ragsdale-Mendenhall—was the nicest one, in my opinion, especially for the freshmen. Mendenhall had just had the bathrooms redone and the rooms were bigger than the ones in the other dorms."

GUYS & GIRLS

Dating Around

"I dated around until I found the person of my dreams. I know that's probably not a common story here at UNCG, but I'm proof that it can happen!"

Couples

"You hear people complain about how it's hard to find a great guy or a great girl, but I always see couples walking around holding hands. I've got friends who have been in long-term relationships with people they've met here, so clearly it isn't impossible to find someone."

HEALTH & SAFETY

Safety

"At anytime a student feels unsafe they can be escorted by a campus policeman. It is a great feeling knowing there are options for you about campus security at anytime."

University of Notre Dame

112 N. Notre Dame Ave.; South Bend, IN 46556
(574) 631-5000; www.nd.edu

THE BASICS:

Acceptance Rate: 29%
Yield: 50%
Setting: Suburban
Control: Private Non-Profit
Total Undergrads: 8,372
SAT Range: 1970–2240*
ACT Range: 31–34

Student-Faculty Ratio: 10:1
Retention Rate: 98%
Graduation Rate: 96%
Tuition: $38,477
Room & Board: $10,368
Avg. Aid Package: $30,780
Students With Aid: 79%

* of 2400

Academics	A	Greek Life	N/A
Athletics	A-	Guys	A+
Campus Dining	A	Health & Safety	B+
Campus Housing	A-	Local Atmosphere	C
Campus Strictness	B-	Nightlife	B+
Computers	A-	Off-Campus Dining	B+
Diversity	C	Off-Campus Housing	A
Drug Safety	C+	Parking	A-
Facilities	A+	Transportation	B+
Girls	B	Weather	C+

CP's Student Author On...
OVERALL EXPERIENCE

"Wonderful," "amazing," "special," "family"—these are the most common words that students use to describe their times at Notre Dame. The University has a unique atmosphere that is embraced by many; the campus is basically self-contained, the dorms are all very close-knit, and there are truly strong connections between students. While the weather may test your survival skills and the administration may try your patience, the Notre Dame experience is unlike any other you'll ever have. The school's tradition and history create an environment where you'll feel welcomed the moment you step foot on campus.

Notre Dame is not an easy school, and it's important to remember that academics are huge. Above all else, you need to be willing to study and focus, or you're not going to make it through the University's workload. Students here are universally dedicated to their studies, and campus life reflects it. This is not a party school. Students may find themselves frustrated by the value system or the lack of outside activities. The best recommendation for Notre Dame is to visit and check out campus life firsthand.... For the rest of this editorial, visit collegeprowler.com.

Students Speak Out On...
OVERALL EXPERIENCE

Q It's Not All About the Football

"okay, so the football team here is pretty well known. Games are something else, extremely spirited, but they aren't the focus of the university. classes are extremely rigorous, so if you focus on your social life you are going to fall behind pretty quickly. thats why partying happens on weekends"

Q People Are Great

"I feel so lucky to attend school here. Not only have the academics challenged me and helped me to grow and learn, I have also become more responsible and motivated. Most importantly, the people here are genuine. They are generally confident in themselves, and do not feel a need to prove themselves to others. The professors bend over backwards to help, and the students are a support system for one another."

Q Great School

"I love it here. Greatest place on earth to be on a football saturday."

BEST OF NOTRE DAME

1. The friends you make
2. Irish football
3. The classroom experience
4. Awesome facilities
5. Dorm life
6. Road trips to away games
7. Bookstore sales

Happy Students
98% of students return after their first year.

Commitment to Teaching
There are 10 students for every member of faculty on campus.

WORST OF NOTRE DAME

1. The weather
2. Parietals
3. The lack of diversity
4. CORE
5. All-nighters (studying)

Expensive
Tuition is a steep $38,477, one of the most expensive rates in the country.

Frequently Compared Schools:

Boston College
Cornell University
Duke University
Northwestern University

Students Speak Out On...
EVERYTHING!

ACADEMICS

Q Outstanding Academics.

"ND is THE place to learn. Courses are challenging, and the teachers really know how to teach."

Q Economics Department Is Rapidly Improving

"As an econ major over the past few years I have had to suffer through a fair share of boring classes, but the professors that have recently been hired are top notch. They really seem to care about how well the students are doing and are very accomplished compared to other schools. Also, none of the economics majors I knew had any trouble getting a very good job coming out of school."

ATHLETICS

Q You Don't Have to Be Varsity

"One of the Great features at Notre Dame is the intramural sports program. Played between different dorms, it covers almost every major sport and then some. The overall winners get a trophy and bragging rights as Interhall Sports Champions. If you want to play with friends from other dorms, the CoRec league facilitates that and offers almost just as many sports."

Q Football Football Football Football Football!!!

"Notre Dame athletics is basically football. But the football games are absolutely amazing. One football game spreads out over the entire weekend, and almost all students attend games."

CAMPUS DINING

Q Dining Halls ROCK

"Notre Dame's dining hall food is simply incredible- they have nearly every variety of any kind of food you could like. With two dining halls located on campus and a variety of small snack places, who could ask for more?"

Q The Best

"Not only do the two dining hall provide Notre Dame students with a variety of food, student's FlexPoints can be at several different cafes around campus, as well as in the LaFortune

student Canter. The dining hall is only repetitive if YOU make it repetitive; try out another cafe or a different dining hall that would offer something else."

CAMPUS HOUSING

Q Random Placement

"You are randomly placed in a dorm so there is no stress over picking dorms before your freshman year. All of the dorms are good with some locations being better then others."

Q Pretty good

"The dorm staffs are great from what I've seen. Overall there's little to complain about with the housing itself; the only problem are cretin residents who vandalize the place and don't know how to flush a toilet."

GUYS & GIRLS

Q Great

"Everyone on campus is extremely oriented towards community and making the University the great place that it is."

Q Girls

"People always complain about the girls at notre dame, but honestly there are plenty of attractive girls on campus. And, not only are they attractive, they're smart and funny, and most of them played sports in high school."

HEALTH & SAFETY

Q Safe Campus

"Notre Dame's campus is always safe and I never feel in danger. All the students are considerate of each other so there;s no worry about disputes or anything."

Q Safest University EVER.

"I feel comfortable walking around campus at 3 a.m. by myself."

University of Oklahoma

660 Parrington Oval; Norman, OK 73019
(405) 325-0311; www.ou.edu

THE BASICS:

Acceptance Rate: 78%	**Student-Faculty Ratio:** 17:1
Yield: 45%	**Retention Rate:** 82%
Setting: Suburban	**Graduation Rate:** 62%
Control: Public	**Tuition:** $17,464
Total Undergrads: 19,856	**Room & Board:** $7,598
SAT Range: 1040–1300*	**Avg. Aid Package:** $9,811
ACT Range: 23–29	**Students With Aid:** 82%

* of 1600

Academics	B	Greek Life	A-
Athletics	A	Guys	A
Campus Dining	A-	Health & Safety	B
Campus Housing	B	Local Atmosphere	B
Campus Strictness	C+	Nightlife	A-
Computers	B+	Off-Campus Dining	B+
Diversity	B-	Off-Campus Housing	B+
Drug Safety	B-	Parking	C
Facilities	A	Transportation	B
Girls	A-	Weather	B

CP's Student Author On...
OVERALL EXPERIENCE

The majority of students were very satisfied with their time spent at OU. They feel that the small town of Norman offers a true college experience, along with the ability to give back to the community. Most feel that people in Norman are genuinely friendly and, for the most part, down to earth. The academics at OU are strong, and, generally speaking, the professors are understanding and qualified.

Although there are some aspects that could use improvement, like parking, OU offers many great perks that make up for the minor inconveniences. OU has a strong athletic tradition, and the facilities available to students and athletes alike are top-of-the-line. There are numerous things to do, depending on what or with whom you care to do them with. Ultimately, what makes OU such a great place was different for every student, which only proves that OU truly does have something for everybody.

Students Speak Out On...
OVERALL EXPERIENCE

Q Overall

"Overall I have had a great experience at OU. The atmosphere is academic and exciting. We have plenty of organizations to join and churches of all kinds. There are concerts, plays, and guest speakers. We have two museums on campus that are free for OU students. I have had really good relationships with my professors and have made lots of friends along the way. OU is great about offering a wide variety of student jobs with flexible schedules."

Q It Is Amazing

"The atmosphere is awesome and all of the students and faculty are friendly and willing to help."

Q Great University

"OU is a great place to go to school. There is ALWAYS plenty to do, but if you feel like staying in thats an option also. The classes are great and our University president has done so much for our school. OU has so much to offer and I love going to this school."

BEST OF OKLAHOMA

1. The people
2. The beautiful campus
3. Motivated and qualified professors
4. School spirit
5. Facilities
6. Opportunities (study abroad, leadership)

Happy Students
82% of students return after their first year.

Knowledgeable Professors
93% of students surveyed rated the general knowledge of professors as above average.

WORST OF OKLAHOMA

1. Fraternity boys and sorority girls
2. Parking
3. Weather (cold in winter, flooding)
4. Traffic
5. Wasteful ways with student tuition

Lowest Grades
Parking: C
Campus Strictness: C+
Diversity: B-

Student Body

African American:	6%	Male Undergrads:	50%	
Asian American:	5%	Female Undergrads:	50%	
Hispanic:	4%	Living On Campus:	29%	
International:	3%	Living Off Campus:	71%	
Native American:	7%	Male Athletes:	4%	
White:	75%	Female Athletes:	4%	
Unknown:	0%	Fraternity Members:	19%	
From Out-of-State:	37%	Sorority Members:	26%	

Frequently Compared Schools:

Texas A&M University
Texas Tech University
University of Kansas
University of Texas

Students Speak Out On... EVERYTHING!

ACADEMICS

Technology Center

"Im in different activities to help my future career take off. Im focused on making it more and more easier to make something of my self."

BEST SCHOOL EVER

"Prof are very well know in their field. They hold everyone with high standards, and it is not a very easy school. If you are just looking for an easy A do not go to OU. Everyone hear takes pride in our school."

ATHLETICS

Collegiate Athletics Is a Big Deal

"Going to a Big 12 school implies that athletics are widely cared about and followed by fans and students. Facilities are great, spirit is great, performance has its ups and downs."

BOOMER SOONER!

"Our school is really involved in sports. Our university one of the top ranked football and basketball teams and school spirit remains at a high because of our rivalry with UT. I am really looking forward to trying to get season tickets this year. Boomer Sooner all the way!"

CAMPUS DINING

Pretty Good Food

"OU has lots of dining options, from sushi to hamburgers, pitas, greek and barbeque. The main dining hall gets pretty boring after a while, but there is always Cate Center restaurants, Crossroads, and Lots of restaurants in the union. In the union, there is a pizza place, a chick-fil-a, a quiznos, a chinese place, and the laughing tomato. Another option you have is all of the restaurants that are on Campus Corner, only a 20 minute walk from the dorms."

Campus Has a Great Variety of Food to Offer Students

"The many restaurants around campus do a great job of appealing to a variety of preferences. All restaurants accept points and a times meal plans."

CAMPUS HOUSING

A New Experience

"Living in the doors on campus was by far one of the best experiences I've ever had in my life. I grew so close to the girls that I lived in the same hall with. The convience of making friends, having a variety of cheap places to eat at any time of the day, and how close it was to classrooms was really great. The three main dorm buildings were very close and it was nice to be surrounded with people going through the same things I was."

Walker Tower Is the Best

"Walker is the best dorm to live in because it has Excetera and the living areas of the dorms are nicer. It is also closest to the Huff and campus. It doesn't smell like food like Couch and Adams do. Housing is strict and rooms are small but it is awesome and I would live in the dorms again."

GUYS & GIRLS

Looks

"The looks are so diverse, and I love it. You can walk from one end of the campus and see a bunch of frat guys with their lacoste wear, or someone in all middle eastern wear, to the hipsters that ride their long boards everywhere."

Great Diverse Choice

"The guys and girls at the University of Oklahoma are very diverse. This is great so that everyone can find someone who is just like them!"

HEALTH & SAFETY

Safe

"I've always felt safe on campus, anytime day or night, alone or with friends. Going off campus is another story."

Police and Safety Services

"There are always bicycle police riding around campus to make sure everything is running smoothly."

LOOKING FOR MORE?

Check out our full-length guide to this school at collegeprowler.com/university-of-oklahoma/.

University of Oregon

1585 E. 13th Ave.; Eugene, OR 97403
(541) 346-1000; www.uoregon.edu

THE BASICS:

Acceptance Rate: 85%	**Student-Faculty Ratio:** 24:1
Yield: 33%	**Retention Rate:** 84%
Setting: Mid-sized city	**Graduation Rate:** 66%
Control: Public	**Tuition:** $23,720
Total Undergrads: 18,502	**Room & Board:** $8,939
SAT Range: 990–1230*	**Avg. Aid Package:** $4,756
ACT Range: 21–27	**Students With Aid:** 68%

* of 1600

Academics	B	Greek Life	B
Athletics	A	Guys	B
Campus Dining	A-	Health & Safety	C+
Campus Housing	B-	Local Atmosphere	B+
Campus Strictness	B+	Nightlife	B+
Computers	C+	Off-Campus Dining	A-
Diversity	B-	Off-Campus Housing	B
Drug Safety	C	Parking	C+
Facilities	B+	Transportation	A-
Girls	B+	Weather	C+

CP's Student Author On...
OVERALL EXPERIENCE

The University of Oregon is a big school in a small town. Eugene is more liberal than many college towns, however, and offers a lot of atmosphere for its size. Tolerance and acceptance are strong values in the area, and many students like the feeling of community that comes from living in a town this close-knit. UO has something for every style and mindset, along with a wealth of opportunities and experiences to prepare you for the world outside college. At the UO, you'll find a school that is strong in both athletics and academics, as well as a campus surrounded by the perfect area for outdoor activities. With a beautiful campus and laid-back atmosphere, Oregon definitely stands apart from similar schools. Although ethnic diversity is lacking, there is a wealth of lifestyles and ideas to be found on and off campus. The weakest elements of the UO are more trivial things, such as parking and weather. While the academics may not be Harvard-level, most students feel that they're being prepared for a competitive world both in the classroom and outside of it.... For the rest of this editorial, visit collegeprowler.com.

Students Speak Out On...
OVERALL EXPERIENCE

Q The Best
"met many people and enjoy the learning environment"

Q I Love Being a Duck!
"Eugene is amazing, I am so glad that I picked the University of Oregon as my school. Everything that happens on campus is fun and the academics are incredible. We are known for our great football team and our amazing architecture program as well. The positives of the campus are so diverse, I couldn't imagine being anywhere else."

Q Oregon
"I absolutely love the school. It is gorgeous. There is green everywhere and the air and water are so clean. I have never felt so at home at a school in my life. There is no place better. The education I am recieving is also phenomenal. It is very focused and in depth."

Q We Have Autzen.
"Enough said. Oe of the best experiences on campus is going to a game at Autzen"

BEST OF OREGON

1. The beautiful location
2. Top rankings in athletics
3. State-of-the-art recreation center
4. Coffee that flows like a river
5. The liberal, tolerant climate of Eugene

Happy Students
84% of students return after their first year.

Knowledgeable Professors
100% of students surveyed rated the general knowledge of professors as above average.

WORST OF OREGON

1. It rains . . . a lot.
2. The school can be far too liberal
3. The occasional campus riot
4. A Greek system gone dry
5. Campus becoming more corporate-oriented

Overextended Faculty
There are 24 students for every faculty member on campus.

Student Body

African American:	2%	Male Undergrads:	49%
Asian American:	6%	Female Undergrads:	51%
Hispanic:	4%	Living On Campus:	21%
International:	6%	Living Off Campus:	79%
Native American:	1%	Male Athletes:	3%
White:	73%	Female Athletes:	2%
Unknown:	8%	Fraternity Members:	8%
From Out-of-State:	43%	Sorority Members:	10%

Frequently Compared Schools:

University of Arizona
University of Colorado
University of Southern California
University of Washington

Students Speak Out On... EVERYTHING!

ACADEMICS

The Professors

"The professors are incredibly invested in making learning a top priority. My experience has been absolutely wonderful regarding one on one tutoring, mentoring, and the overall sharing of knowledge. I feel fortunate to be able to attend such a dynamic University."

International Studies Department Is Amazing

"The Professor's here are all passionate about their chosen field. They definitely were a factor in my choice of the International Studies major. Best advice I have for anyone is go talk to your professors. Period."

Smart Ducks

"School is tough here but if you study you can get A's!!"

ATHLETICS

I Love My Ducks

"We made it to state last year in football and we have Hawyard field where the track olympic trials are held...enough said."

GO DUCKS

"The University of Oregon is an athletically driven school. Seeing as how Eugene is track town USA and the U of O is the home of the famous Hayward track naturally Cross Country and Track and field are two very prominent sports. The U of O's infamous track members are ranked nationally and world wide. The other main sport at U of O is Football. Almost every student follows the team passionately."

CAMPUS DINING

On Campus and Around Campus Dining

"In my experience the places around and on the University of Oregon campus are very good and also very diversified. There something for everyone. In general the preferred "Hot spots" tend to be health food restaurants and quaint coffee shops. In addition to these places offering excellent food and atmosphere they also tend to be excellent places to study and/or meet new people."

Food?

"Good h ealthy options all the time. Pretty sweet deals if you are on the food plan."

CAMPUS HOUSING

Great Dorms!

"Smallest dorm is Bean. I lived in Carson and loved it. It is in the heart of the UO campus! My friend's lived in the LLC which are the newest dorms. Big and spacious!!"

Living on Campus

"Living on campus puts you right in the middle of everything. Food is super close and convenient. There are always a lot of different activities that the Housing Department puts on like karaoke, movies, cookie decorating and dance parties."

GUYS & GIRLS

Melting Pot

"There is every type of person here. If you're looking for friends, you'll find someone you like."

All Sorts of People!

"Girls & guys here pretty much are split 50/50. There are so many beautiful girls walking this campus it is almost unreal at times. You have a bunch of pretty girls coming for California and you get your typical geeky girls as well. Guys here could be described as jocks,emo,boys next door, and nerds."

HEALTH & SAFETY

Very Satifactory

"The safety units were on site constantly and willing to help"

Oregon

"A safe and welcoming community with a variety of entertainment."

LOOKING FOR MORE?

Check out our full-length guide to this school at collegeprowler.com/university-of-oregon/.

University of Pennsylvania

3451 Walnut St.; Philadelphia, PA 19104
(215) 898-5000; www.upenn.edu

THE BASICS:

Acceptance Rate: 18%	**Student-Faculty Ratio:** 6:1
Yield: 61%	**Retention Rate:** 98%
Setting: Large city	**Graduation Rate:** 95%
Control: Private Non-Profit	**Tuition:** $38,970
Total Undergrads: 12,010	**Room & Board:** $11,016
SAT Range: 2020–2290*	**Avg. Aid Package:** $29,672
ACT Range: 30–34	**Students With Aid:** 61%

* of 2400

Academics	A	Greek Life	A
Athletics	B+	Guys	B
Campus Dining	C+	Health & Safety	B-
Campus Housing	B-	Local Atmosphere	A
Campus Strictness	A	Nightlife	A
Computers	A-	Off-Campus Dining	A
Diversity	A-	Off-Campus Housing	C+
Drug Safety	B	Parking	C-
Facilities	B+	Transportation	A-
Girls	B-	Weather	B-

CP's Student Author On...
OVERALL EXPERIENCE

Students seem to be extremely content and do not regret their decision to come to Penn, even though the school definitely has a pre-professional feel. Despite this fact, it is extremely common to find yourself in an intellectual conversation, and the students really do work hard, while remembering that college is about fun as well. The opportunities provided at Penn are astounding; in fact there is almost too much to do. Most students base the reasons for their happiness around the people, the academics, the urban environment, and the endless opportunities. People who enjoy their experience at Penn tend to appreciate city life, socializing, and a busy schedule. Usually, students do not hesitate to endorse Penn, and many feel that everyone should love the school as much as they do.

Many adults call their years as an undergraduate the best four years of their lives. Penn students certainly can not make that prediction so soon, but most would agree that their time at Penn has been the best years of their life so far.... For the rest of this editorial, visit collegeprowler.com.

Students Speak Out On...
OVERALL EXPERIENCE

Q Fantastic Facilities and Faculty

"I was impressed with the levels of dedication of everyone involved. A serious campus, and somewhat underrated."

Q Penn Is Amazing!

"Penn is amazing. I absolutely love college life. Classes are stimulating and challenging, but it doesn't effect one's social life. Penn students like to work hard and party harder."

Q Best 4 Years Ever!

"I had a fabulous time at UPenn! I was very happy with the academics, research opportunities, extra-curricular activities, and student life in general. The administration really listens to students and responds to their wants and needs. I was able to find my niche in the performing arts community (theater and dance), but felt at home in professional student groups and just hanging out around campus. I'd choose it again in a heartbeat!"

Q I Love It!

"I love Penn. It really is great all around, and is what you make of it. There is definitely something for everyone- athletics, greek life, academics, etc."

BEST OF PENN

1. Spring Fling
2. Penn Relays
3. Fast-speed Internet
4. The Quad
5. The Libraries (over 5 million volumes)
6. Philly
7. Cheesesteaks

Happy Students
98% of students return after their first year.

Commitment to Teaching
There are 6 students for every member of faculty on campus.

WORST OF PENN

1. Parking
2. Inconvenient hours at the dining halls
3. Cold winters
4. Teachers with indecipherable accents
5. Stereotypical Ivy-league students

Expensive
Tuition is a steep $38,970, one of the most expensive rates in the country.

Expensive to Just Get By
50% of students surveyed felt that the amount it costs to live while at school was worse than average.

Student Body

African American:	7%	Male Undergrads:	49%
Asian American:	15%	Female Undergrads:	51%
Hispanic:	5%	Living On Campus:	64%
International:	8%	Living Off Campus:	36%
Native American:	0%	Male Athletes:	13%
White:	39%	Female Athletes:	8%
Unknown:	25%	Fraternity Members:	30%
From Out-of-State:	84%	Sorority Members:	26%

Frequently Compared Schools:
Brown University
Cornell University
Harvard University
Yale University

Students Speak Out On... EVERYTHING!

ACADEMICS

Dream College
"Located in busy West Philadelphia, my college is alive with abundant opportunities for challenge and diversity."

There Are So Many Resources Available to the Students
"I am in the Wharton School of Business. At an Ivy League institution alone, one expects everything to be top-notch. However, this school far exceeded my expectations. The professors are great, the food is great and there are so many resources available to the students. There is really no reason why any person would not succeed in a great place like Penn!"

ATHLETICS

Sports Are Fun but Not Central
"There is a good amount of support for sports teams, and there are lots of great traditions."

Sports at Upenn
"Football is the biggest sport at Penn; the homecoming game is always anticipated. Outside of that, however, I feel that many students aren't really into the sports scene. But we do host the Penn Relays every spring, and that receives a lot of spectators. The facilities are great, with Franklin Field and Pottruck gym (free for students)."

CAMPUS DINING

On-Campus Sucks, So Go Off-Campus!
"The dining halls on campus are truly terrible. Luckily, there are great restaurants in University City and downtown."

Not a Great Selection
"There are some decent foods in the dining hall, but the selection is lacking. Since Penn is around decent restaurants, it seems to not have as many foods to choose from within the dining hall. This aspect keeps me from eating in the dining hall on most days. Luckily, there are other food choices surrounding the campus!!"

CAMPUS HOUSING

The Quad Isn't Everything
"As a freshmen, everyone wants to live in one of the three dorms in the Quad. I must say the Quad is really oretty and does have a lot of things to do, but if you don't live there freshmen year its no big deal. I would personally reccommend Hill because it tends to be a bit friendlier. If you live in the quad you may find a lot of cliques develop which is something that should be left in high school."

Housing Is Not Guaranteed
"Many students are unable to get on campus housing, and need to go off campus. Often these houses are very nice, but having a whole year lease is a pain."

GUYS & GIRLS

Lots of Interesting People
"A very interesting mix of people. Many beautiful girls. A roughly 25% Jewish population. Lots of intellectual types. Pretty much all cultural sterotypes are represented here."

guys are geeky, but lots of options
"A lot of the guys here are very nerdy, but then again, there are the hot guys. Some frat guys seem pretty sleazy, but overall most seem to be good, interesting people. Drexel students tend to crash our parties, which can be a good thing or a bad thing depending on your perspective (it does add variety)."

HEALTH & SAFETY

Pretty Safe
"Even though the campus is located in West Philadelphia, I have always felt safe thanks to the many PENN security guards."

LOOKING FOR MORE?
Check out our full-length guide to this school at collegeprowler.com/university-of-pennsylvania/.

University of Pittsburgh

4200 Fifth Ave.; Pittsburgh, PA 15260
(412) 624-4141; www.pitt.edu

THE BASICS:

Acceptance Rate: 55%	Student-Faculty Ratio: 15:1
Yield: 30%	Retention Rate: 93%
Setting: Large city	Graduation Rate: 76%
Control: Public	Tuition: $23,852
Total Undergrads: 18,031	Room & Board: $8,900
SAT Range: 1160–1360*	Avg. Aid Package: $10,197
ACT Range: 25–30	Students With Aid: 71%

of 1600

Academics	B	Greek Life	B-
Athletics	A-	Guys	B+
Campus Dining	B	Health & Safety	C
Campus Housing	B	Local Atmosphere	A-
Campus Strictness	B	Nightlife	A-
Computers	B+	Off-Campus Dining	B+
Diversity	C+	Off-Campus Housing	B-
Drug Safety	C-	Parking	C
Facilities	B	Transportation	A+
Girls	B	Weather	C

CP's Student Author On...
OVERALL EXPERIENCE

Overall, students agree that they wouldn't trade their Pitt experience for anything. As with most decisions, there are a lot of things to consider. If you don't like living in a city environment, Pittsburgh may not be the place for you. While it doesn't have the feel of New York of Philadelphia, the area is definitely urban. Also, Pitt is a large school—you're in for some big lecture classes and a somewhat overwhelming campus during the first year or so. Everything will seem to get smaller after you've been around awhile, though. Weather can be a concern if you're used to a warmer climate—snow, rain, and wind rule Pittsburgh winters. This is something that you can easily get used to though, unless you're a diehard warm weather fan.

What Pitt does offer is high-caliber academics, plenty of student organizations, and countless opportunities, such as study abroad, cultural activities, and sports. If you're willing to become active on campus, there's a lot more to Pitt than meets the eye.... For the rest of this editorial, visit collegeprowler.com.

Students Speak Out On...
OVERALL EXPERIENCE

Pitt Is It.

"My freshman year at Pitt is coming to an end with finals about three weeks away. I made the two best decisions possible, with coming to Pitt and joining the Pitt Varsity Matching Band. College like anything else is what you make of it, and Pitt is full of wonderful oppurtunities, they are here waiting for students to take them."

AWESOME

"I love it here and I wouldn't go anywhere else. Great classes, teachers who are the best in their field, good cultural diversity, a present Greek system, Nationally ranked NCAA sports (football, basketball, and baseball), nice people, and awesome social scene."

Apply Now!

"Pitt has been a great experience. I have spent most of my college experience here. I was a transfer student, however, I wish I had applied as a freshman. It is great to be around other schools such as CMU and to experience living in a small but up and coming city. It was life changing to be in Pittsburgh around the time of G20."

BEST OF PITT

1. Going out on Thursday nights
2. Not having class on Fridays
3. Nationally ranked football and basketball teams
4. Events with free food

Happy Students
93% of students return after their first year.

Proven Success
76% of students will complete their education and graduate with a degree.

WORST OF PITT

1. On-campus meals
2. Parking (or lack thereof)
3. Hiking up "Cardiac Hill"
4. Waiting for shuttles and buses
5. Bureaucracy
6. Large introductory lectures

Lowest Grades
Drug Safety: C-
Health & Safety: C
Parking: C

Student Body

African American:	7%	Male Undergrads:	49%
Asian American:	5%	Female Undergrads:	51%
Hispanic:	1%	Living On Campus:	44%
International:	1%	Living Off Campus:	55%
Native American:	0%	Male Athletes:	4%
White:	81%	Female Athletes:	4%
Unknown:	4%	Fraternity Members:	8%
From Out-of-State:	30%	Sorority Members:	8%

Frequently Compared Schools:

Penn State
University of Delaware
University of Maryland
University of Michigan

Students Speak Out On...
EVERYTHING!

ACADEMICS

Neuroscience

"My academic area of interest is in the rapidly expanding field of neuroscience. Providing students with a pre-med and science background, a neuroscience major is an enriching and popular field of study at the University of Pittsburgh."

The Statistics Major

"This department is a relatively small one, with about only 20 undergraduate students, but plenty of dedicated staff. The head of undergraduate statistics is the statistics counselor and also teaches at least two classes a semester. Everyone is friendly and very approachable. Even with very few students, many classes are available each term with dedicated professors. I couldn't chose a better school for this major."

ATHLETICS

Athletics

"Everything about the Pitt athletics program is great! Every sport has a great number of close followers, and every student has a good time. Tickets are very available and all have good student pricing."

Varsity Sports Are a Staple of Student Life

"The varsity football and basketball teams at Pitt are generally gppd, and have recently been improving further. The students are generally very supportive fans, the campus runs with school spirit on game days, the Oakland Zoo has made the Pete one of the most intimidating places to play basketball. Work out facilities which are open to all students as well are superb and accesible."

CAMPUS DINING

Pretty Good

"As a freshman, you eat on campus a lot, but there are plenty of options. At first Market Central is awesome- until you go there twice a day every day. Off campus, there is so much variety. There are the typical fast food places like McDonalds, but you also get awesome places like Dave and Andy's ice cream, Fuel and Fuddle, and Rita's italian ice. My favorite on-campus place to eat is in the basement of the cathedral. They have a chick-fil-a and awesome sandwiches and sweet potato chips."

Good Variety

"I think Pitt offers a good variety of places to eat around campus. The main dining hall can get a little repetitive, but the stir fry and vegetarian options are delicious. Pitt also offers Taco Bell and Chick-fil-a as alternatives to the dining halls, bagel shops, and coffee carts all over campus. I wouldn't buy an enormous amount MEAL PLAN freshmen year, but rather stick to dining dollars and panther funds for more flexibility."

CAMPUS HOUSING

Top of the Hill

"though a bit expensive, and out of the way. It is totally worth it"

GUYS & GIRLS

Eclectic

"I find that many of the girls/guys at University of Pittsburgh's campus march to their own drum. Many people are interested in an array of unusual things, but you can also find many people who watch the typical tv shows, etc."

HEALTH & SAFETY

Extremely Safe

"Being so close to the city, the campus not only has a set of full time campus police but a strong force of city police as well. If there is ever a medical emergency it is not worried about because UMPC is located right on campus and is one of the bet hospitals around. Campus police are there to make sure everyone is ok and safe, but definitely not there to spoil a good party or ruin a good time."

LOOKING FOR MORE?

Check out our full-length guide to this school at collegeprowler.com/university-of-pittsburgh/.

University of Puget Sound

1500 N. Warner St.; Tacoma, WA 98416
(253) 879-3100; www.ups.edu

THE BASICS:

Acceptance Rate: 63%
Yield: 20%
Setting: Mid-sized city
Control: Private Non-Profit
Total Undergrads: 2,595
SAT Range: 1680–2003*
ACT Range: 25–30

Student-Faculty Ratio: 12:1
Retention Rate: 86%
Graduation Rate: 76%
Tuition: $35,635
Room & Board: $9,190
Avg. Aid Package: $20,688
Students With Aid: 86%

* of 2400

Academics	B	Greek Life	B
Athletics	C+	Guys	C+
Campus Dining	A-	Health & Safety	A-
Campus Housing	A-	Local Atmosphere	B-
Campus Strictness	B+	Nightlife	C
Computers	B+	Off-Campus Dining	C+
Diversity	C-	Off-Campus Housing	C+
Drug Safety	B	Parking	B+
Facilities	B	Transportation	B+
Girls	B-	Weather	C-

CP's Student Author On...
OVERALL EXPERIENCE

Overall, students are very happy at UPS and satisfied with their decision to stay at the University. Several students found their niche here early on during the well-crafted orientation program, "Prelude, Passages, and Perspectives," which gives freshmen a taste of the Northwest and the college lifestyle through academic sessions and community service. The vast majority of students find the extracurricular activities, clubs, and community that UPS offers to be equally as valuable as the time spent in the classroom. While every student will complain from time to time about the high workload, the rain, or a host of other issues, people here are proud to be a part of the Puget Sound Community. Everyone in the Puget Sound community contributes to everyone else's learning experience; meeting and building friendships with other students from different walks of life is one of the greatest teaching tools you will find. Puget Sound is a community that works together, plays together, and encourages each other to strive to reach his or her fullest potential.... For the rest of this editorial, visit collegeprowler.com.

Students Speak Out On...
OVERALL EXPERIENCE

Q Great School Love It.

"I wish it was cheaper. But otherwise it rocks. Living in Schiff freshman year was one of the best things that could've happened. Especially if you like outdoor stuff and chill people. Get ready to write some papers, but don't worry too much. Professors are really helpful (usually). Get to know them. Have coffee with them sometime. Be interested. It's great fun."

Q Best School in the Northwest.

"Pretty much the only thing that would have persuaded me from going somewhere other than UPS would be along the lines a full ride to an ivy league school. Since that isn't in the realm of possibility for me, UPS is a perfect fit. People are excited to be here, are excited to learn, and are happy to be part of the Puget Sound community."

Q "The overall experience is great here. I find that I am learning everyday through the fantastic people I meet. Puget Sound provides an excellent education and the community helps it grow."

BEST OF PUGET SOUND

1. Small, discussion-based classes
2. The beautiful campus
3. Great campus food
4. Nice, spacious dorms
5. Prelude, Passages, and Perspectives orientation

Happy Students
86% of students return after their first year.

Proven Success
76% of students will complete their education and graduate with a degree.

WORST OF PUGET SOUND

1. The heavy workload
2. Rain, rain, and more frickin' rain
3. Not much of an athletic scene
4. Not much of a nightlife scene
5. Girl to guy ratio (If you're a girl)

Expensive
Tuition is a steep $35,635, one of the most expensive rates in the country.

Students Speak Out On...
EVERYTHING!

ACADEMICS

Professors

"Lisa Johnson is an amazing professor. The French department is also fantastic. Professors are VERY accessible and it is in your best interest to use them."

The Best Part of UPS

"The academics at UPS are hands down the best part of the school. Many departments are very strong, and professors will push you. I have found most profs to be exceptional teachers. However, if you come across a visiting prof, RUN! Ask your peers about the best teachers and you won't be disappointed. Solid A for academics!"

ATHLETICS

Fairly Average Quality, Strong Community

"Overall, Puget Sound's athletics are decent when it comes to competition, but excellent in terms of the community it offers. It's a welcoming community that works very hard and pushes students' limits, but it's not like we're dominating every regional championship possible. Of note is the Men and Womens Crew teams -varsity and novice are stellar competitors and wonderful people."

We Have Athletics?

"I've been to one sports event, a soccer game, at UPS and we played the San Diego "Banana Slugs" or something weird like that. Athletics are not a big deal, our teams aren't great, and our stands are usually pretty empty. The Ultimate Frizbee team gets more attention than any other team."

CAMPUS DINING

Food on Campus

"There is a great sandwhich bar and vegetarian and vegan options, along with all the typical college food. The cafeteria brings in a lot of local and organic food, as well."

Good Food, Repetitive

"The food is good (not great, usually) but gets repetitive. The full fare switches it up every now and then but for the most part things seem to stay the same. The pasta could use serious improvement, currently tastes like vomit."

CAMPUS HOUSING

Campus Housing

"All dorms are very conveniently located. Todd Phibbs offers the smallest dorms. Schiff is known as the "outdoorsy" dorm. You have to fill out an application to live there, but its worth it if you're an athletic and outdoorsy person that wants to meet likeminded people. The theme houses also make Puget Sound awesome. With a group of friends, you can fill out an application to move into one. The university gives you money to put on wholesome parties/activities pertaining to your theme."

GUYS & GIRLS

Average Oregon-Washington Students

"People at the University of Puget Sound always look happy and are your average West coast kids (minus Cali). The students dress nice but very comfortably. Don't forget your Northface jacket!"

HEALTH & SAFETY

Moderate to High Safety

"The campus is pretty safe. Occasionally there are break-ins to the dorms, bikes get stolen, etc. There has never been violent crime on campus that I know of while I have been a student there. Areas surrounding campus are slightly more dangerous in terms of theft, mugging, etc - although still not very common, and I have never experienced crime myself."

University of Rhode Island

45 Upper College Road; Kingston, RI 02881
(401) 874-1000; www.uri.edu

THE BASICS:

Acceptance Rate: 84%
Yield: 22%
Setting: Suburban
Control: Public
Total Undergrads: 13,277
SAT Range: 950–1140*
ACT Range: 21–25

Student-Faculty Ratio: 16:1
Retention Rate: 79%
Graduation Rate: 58%
Tuition: $26,026
Room & Board: $10,334
Avg. Aid Package: $12,654
Students With Aid: 89%

* of 1600

Academics	B	Greek Life	N/A
Athletics	C+	Guys	A-
Campus Dining	B-	Health & Safety	B-
Campus Housing	B-	Local Atmosphere	B-
Campus Strictness	B	Nightlife	B-
Computers	C+	Off-Campus Dining	B
Diversity	C+	Off-Campus Housing	B
Drug Safety	D+	Parking	C-
Facilities	B	Transportation	B
Girls	A-	Weather	C+

CP's Student Author On...
OVERALL EXPERIENCE

URI is a school with two identities: It is a place to learn and a place to party. The University offers students many options in the classroom, which leads to many options in life. Students here know the importance of being motivated and focused and are dedicated to getting the best out of their four (or more) years of college. At URI, you will find an atmosphere that is extremely well balanced when it comes to work and play. If URI students learn two things while they are here, they learn how to succeed and how to have a good time. Most students are happy with their choice of making URI their home for higher education.

Students agree that there is an equal balance of academics and social life, and they are expected to do well and are given many opportunities to succeed. The biggest part of college is learning to adjust and knowing what is out there. URI is a friendly environment, and most students are happy here. Academics are the biggest challenge, and getting into the right classes is often an obstacle. There are a lot of organizations and events that engage students throughout the year. Overall, students have a positive experience at URI, and there's definitely something for everyone to enjoy.

Students Speak Out On...
OVERALL EXPERIENCE

Q There's a Big Party Scene, but Also a Big Emphasis on Academics

"I have really enjoyed my experience at URI. I think there is a good balance between the social like and the academic life. There is always something going on, which I really like. There are always different shows or concerts, it's great!"

Q Its Great

"Like all places, if you let your social life out weigh your responsibilities you could fall behind and make it a bit stressful for yourself. however, if you mmanage your time and responsibilities you will see just how great this college is"

Q Pretty Good

"You have the experience of a big school atmosphere, in a small town environment. The academics are good as long as you put time in. The school sports, with the exception of basketball, are not very good. Social scene is a little above average, and the school pride/spirit is excellent."

BEST OF RHODE ISLAND

1. Being by the beach
2. Parties
3. All the people you meet
4. Off-campus housing
5. Being in the middle of nowhere but having lots to do

Learn from the Best
89% of faculty have earned the highest degree in their field.

Help to Succeed
The school has academic and career counseling available to help you when you need it.

WORST OF RHODE ISLAND

1. Parking
2. Registering for classes/ Not getting the classes you need
3. Campus is dry
4. Walking up one big hill
5. Overcrowded shuttles

Expensive
Tuition is a steep $26,026, one of the most expensive rates in the country.

Expensive Dorms
Living on campus doesn't come cheap, with an average housing price tag of $6,624.

Student Body

African American:	5%	Male Undergrads:	44%
Asian American:	3%	Female Undergrads:	56%
Hispanic:	6%	Living On Campus:	45%
International:	0%	Living Off Campus:	55%
Native American:	0%	Male Athletes:	6%
White:	70%	Female Athletes:	5%
Unknown:	15%	Fraternity Members:	0%
From Out-of-State:	49%	Sorority Members:	0%

Frequently Compared Schools:

University of Connecticut
University of Massachusetts
University of New Hampshire
University of Vermont

Students Speak Out On... EVERYTHING!

ACADEMICS

Professors

"Most of my professors are very good. They know about the subject they are teaching and get excited about it. They are also available for students to ask for help."

Love the Program

"This program is amazing. You get hands on experience and have great professors!"

Great University.

"I decided to go to University of Rhode Island because their Nutrition Program was known as a good program for college students looking to be a Nutritionist or a Registered Dietitian. I feel that this school is always helpful and encourages you to ask questions. The curriculum and special study options are great."

ATHLETICS

Athletic Facilities Are Awesome

"Although I am not a college athlete, I participated on the Track & Field team for three yeas at my high school. I did not want that dreaded "freshman fifteen" to come live in my dorm. One of my dorm mates(who I attended high school with and also ran Track) and I made a pact to keep the bodies we honed in high school. The gym provides us with everything we needed to keep in shape. We also use the nicely surfaced tennis courts to have fun!"

Sports at URI

"The University of Rhode Island offers a strong NCAA sports presence that is easily overlooked."

CAMPUS DINING

Always Hungry Never Starved

"dininghalls great,variety anything you want, panera bread dnkin donuts narraganset beach restraunts on campus pizza sandwiches etc great atmosphere wonderful people"

Dining Halls

"Two dining halls and many on campus places to buy food. The dining halls are on your meal plan and the others are ones you have to buy if you want it. Also, won't accept credit or debit cards. Money or ram card."

CAMPUS HOUSING

Burger Shack

"Off-Campus dining needs to accept dining dollars more. Overall the I-Zones are really great and Burger shack is definitely the best place to have an awesome burger between classes, cheap too."

Freshman Dorm

"I live in the biggest freshman dorm on campus and i like it. as for the upper class-man dorms they tend to not be attractable which sometimes make people aim for a particular dorm but sometimes cant get in due to first picks by the seniors or juniors"

GUYS & GIRLS

Interesting

"I usually pay most of my attention to the girls on campus. There are a lot of women; women from all backgrouds. I guess there are an equal amount of diverse guys, but my attention is more focused on females."

Plenty of options

"It doesn't matter what your type is, they go to URI."

HEALTH & SAFETY

Totally Safe

"I have never felt unsafe on the URI campus. There is security everywhere and the blue lights with phones to call. The campus is medium sized and cozy as well as well-lit. It is a dry campus so people are more discreet about drinking around campus and security is very tough on drinking."

Safe

"It's a little scary being alone but overall I always feel safe."

LOOKING FOR MORE?

Check out our full-length guide to this school at collegeprowler.com/university-of-rhode-island/.

University of Richmond

28 Westhampton Way; Richmond, VA 23173
(804) 289-8000; www.richmond.edu

THE BASICS:

Acceptance Rate: 39%
Yield: 30%
Setting: Mid-sized city
Control: Private Non-Profit
Total Undergrads: 3,387
SAT Range: 1750–2040*
ACT Range: 26–30

Student-Faculty Ratio: 8:1
Retention Rate: 92%
Graduation Rate: 87%
Tuition: $40,010
Room & Board: $8,480
Avg. Aid Package: $30,646
Students With Aid: 64%

* of 2400

Academics	B+	Greek Life	A+
Athletics	B+	Guys	A-
Campus Dining	B-	Health & Safety	A-
Campus Housing	B+	Local Atmosphere	B
Campus Strictness	C+	Nightlife	A-
Computers	B	Off-Campus Dining	B
Diversity	C	Off-Campus Housing	C
Drug Safety	C+	Parking	B-
Facilities	B	Transportation	B-
Girls	A-	Weather	B

CP's Student Author On...
OVERALL EXPERIENCE

Students really seem to enjoy UR and its retention rate, 92 percent, seems to reflect that. Those people who just don't feel like they fit in transfer out after freshman year, so by the time senior year comes around, everyone in your class likes the school and knows one another, for the most part. There is also an influx of students who transfer into the school at the beginning of sophomore year. The best part about UR is the intimate atmosphere that it has, being a somewhat small, private university. It is a comfortable atmosphere that allows them to study in peace and relax when they need to. You get to know a lot of people and develop close friendships with many of them. The campus is gorgeous and so are the people.

Students at UR rarely have much to complain about and few could see themselves at any other school. They realize how lucky they are to be here and try to make the most of their opportunity by taking advantage of the great education, strong alumni network, and career preparation activities that the school provides.... For the rest of this editorial, visit collegeprowler.com.

Students Speak Out On...
OVERALL EXPERIENCE

Q **Love It**

"I wouldnt want to be anywhere else. It was everything I wanted and more."

Q **Experience**

"So far Richmond has been a wonderful place. If you're coming from a big city it might be a shock and take a while to adapt but you'll find your place in Richmond. It's very small so you know everyone from the athletes to the dancer to the musician to the average student. Professors are extremely helpful. Although the night scene isn't ideal you still have lots of fun."

Q "I couldn't be happier. I've never regretted coming here, and I can't picture myself anywhere else."

Q "I've had a great experience at UR, and am very happy that I chose to go here. Other than sometimes wishing we had better sports teams or larger parties like at a bigger school, I've never wished I was somewhere else."

BEST OF RICHMOND

1. Beautiful, park-like campus
2. Pig Roast
3. Beach Week
4. National A-10 Football Champions
5. Beautiful people
6. Great alumni network

Happy Students
92% of students return after their first year.

Commitment to Teaching
There are 8 students for every member of faculty on campus.

WORST OF RICHMOND

1. Parking
2. Lack of alcohol-free parties
3. Lack of on-campus dining options
4. Too few concerts on campus
5. Lack of school spirit

Expensive
Tuition is a steep $40,010, one of the most expensive rates in the country.

Student Body

African American:	8%	Male Undergrads:	46%
Asian American:	3%	Female Undergrads:	54%
Hispanic:	3%	Living On Campus:	92%
International:	6%	Living Off Campus:	8%
Native American:	0%	Male Athletes:	17%
White:	70%	Female Athletes:	17%
Unknown:	10%	Fraternity Members:	31%
From Out-of-State:	79%	Sorority Members:	44%

Frequently Compared Schools:

Elon University
University of Virginia
Vanderbilt University
Wake Forest University

Students Speak Out On...
EVERYTHING!

ACADEMICS

Small Class Sizes Ensure Thorough Learning

"Most class sizes are small (about under 25 people) and none of them are taught by TAs, which means you feel up close and personal with the professors. Most of them are brilliant yet very demanding. Class discussions are common and the professors encourage visitations and group study outside of class. Richmond specializes in the liberal arts, so it's guaranteed that you'll be free to explore many interdisciplinary studies."

"There isn't a well-developed teaching program here. Although you can be certified, there isn't an education major, and I'm not sure that my classes are going to prepare me well enough for a teaching job. The required semester of student teaching was a good experience, however."

ATHLETICS

Solid

"We just got a new football stadium on campus and the basketball team consistently delivers during March madness. Lots of club sports too."

Low School Spirit

"Football i guess is the biggest sport here. We used to be more popular when we were national champions. We'll see how it goes this year. No one really goes to basketball games so they bribe you to go with free pizza and shot glasses. People arent really school spirited here they just go for social engagement. Blah"

CAMPUS DINING

Good Quality, Ok Variety

"Food here is pretty good! They have a wide variety of foods in d-hall and they try to mix it up as much as possible but overall the quality of food is always above average"

"The campus food is surprisingly good. The Heilman Dining Hall (aka "D-Hall") was remodeled only a few years ago, and the food is top-notch quality. Even if you have very specific dietary requirements, you will be fine because you can have the dining center buy and prepare specific food for you if you absolutely need it. It can get boring to eat at D-hall all the time, but there is also Tyler's Grill, Freshens, E.T.C., and the Dean's Den."

CAMPUS HOUSING

Campus Housing Quality

"After hearing from various friends at other colleges, one thing that I cannot complain about at the University of Richmond is the housing quality. Dorms are generally clean, on the larger side, and well taken care of. The large number of alcoholics and uneducated individuals that destroy the dorm throughout the year are an entirely different story and often make residential life irritating and and expensive (dorm damage is divided up and paid by the entire dormitory.)"

Freshman

"As a freshman you are assigned possibly the worst places to live. Everything is dorm style ie communal bathroom, laundry, no kitchens. The dorms are kept clean as are the bathrooms. Best freshman girl dorms are Lora Robins. Best dorms overall is Lakeview and the Forest Apartments."

GUYS & GIRLS

Preppy Is Perfection

"UR has a good looking student population, filled with physically fit and fashionable guys and girls. Imagine guys in pink shrots and girls in sundresses.Partying is pretty much the only social activity, although for such a small school UR knows how to throw a good party. People seem snobby but away from their group everyone is nice."

HEALTH & SAFETY

Extremely Safe!

"The University of Richmond has its own police. I have never felt unsafe walking back to my dorm in the middle of the night. Tons of emergency telephones on campus and a safety shuttle for women. Only crime on campus is underage drinking"

LOOKING FOR MORE?

Check out our full-length guide to this school at collegeprowler.com/university-of-richmond/.

University of Rochester

300 Wilson Blvd.; Rochester, NY 14627
(585) 275-8063; www.rochester.edu

THE BASICS:

Acceptance Rate: 39%
Yield: 23%
Setting: Mid-sized city
Control: Private Non-Profit
Total Undergrads: 5,432
SAT Range: 1820–2100*
ACT Range: 28–33

Student-Faculty Ratio: 11:1
Retention Rate: 96%
Graduation Rate: 84%
Tuition: $38,690
Room & Board: $11,200
Avg. Aid Package: $15,878
Students With Aid: 96%

of 2400

Academics	A-	Greek Life	A-
Athletics	B-	Guys	A-
Campus Dining	C+	Health & Safety	B-
Campus Housing	B	Local Atmosphere	B-
Campus Strictness	B	Nightlife	B+
Computers	B-	Off-Campus Dining	A-
Diversity	B+	Off-Campus Housing	B+
Drug Safety	C+	Parking	C
Facilities	B+	Transportation	A-
Girls	A-	Weather	C+

CP's Student Author On...
OVERALL EXPERIENCE

Students are enamored with the school and overlook its faults—they are faults common to many universities and are easily balanced out by its many excellent qualities. The strong suits of academics and atmosphere make UR a perfect fit for a lot of people. Some stumble into the school by chance and end up loving it, never imagining themselves anywhere else. Others, especially locals, know of UR's reputation and fully planned on enrolling. All agree, though, that the environment and the people are all one could ask for in a college.

Even if it takes a while to adjust and find your niche, once you do, you will easily fall in love with the school. Beyond the food and small inconveniences, UR comes out ahead for student approval. The student body as a whole is intelligent and ambitious, and the faculty are talented and welcoming. You will not find acts of sabotage or students scratching at each other's throats to get a better grade than someone else. UR students are independent and capable; the only competition is against yourself. You will learn things and make friendships that will last a lifetime.... For the rest of this editorial, visit collegeprowler.com.

Students Speak Out On...
OVERALL EXPERIENCE

Q I Love U-Roch

"The classes at U of R are tough, but rewarding. There are classes in every category, from Rock and Roll History to Molecular Biology. The faculty and other students around campus make everything you do exciting and engaging. It's hard to be anti-social here, and that's a good thing."

Q Great Experience

"So far my experience at U of R has been fantastic. I really love the people and feel as if this is my home. I would 100% chose to go here again if i had the choice."

Q Freedom to Choose Classes

"There are very few required classes at Rochester, which is great! The open curriculum allows for a lot more time to focus on your major, or figure things out. Pre-Major Advisors are hit-or-miss...it's best to just ask around; talk to enough people and you'll get the answers you need. Make sure you keep meeting with your advisor though! They can be a good resource down the road if you need a recommendation."

BEST OF ROCHESTER

1. The Rochester curriculum
2. Tight relationship with the Eastman School of Music
3. Academics
4. Friendly people
5. Proximity to Rochester
6. Weather in the summer
7. The snow

Happy Students
96% of students return after their first year.

Proven Success
84% of students will complete their education and graduate with a degree.

WORST OF ROCHESTER

1. The weather for most of the year
2. Campus food
3. Workload
4. No support for sports teams
5. Poor parking

Expensive
Tuition is a steep $38,690, one of the most expensive rates in the country.

Expensive Dorms
Living on campus doesn't come cheap, with an average housing price tag of $6,750.

Students Speak Out On...
EVERYTHING!

ACADEMICS

Come Prepared to Work

"The workload, known to students as the "Rochester Workload" is all but easy. Depending on their major, each student knows how much time per day they must put in to succeed. Homework is abundant and exams are frequent, meaning anybody who slacks off WILL be left behind in the dust. However, there is a lot of help offered. Professors, teaching assistants, and tutors are readily available at your convenience. The professor quality varies, but the majority of them are excellent."

Challenging, Time-Consuming, Fun!

"The Japanese department could be more rigorous, but the Russian department is fantastic."

ATHLETICS

Division 3

"This school definitely has some great athletes and the teams do pretty well, but school comes first here. However, that makes it all the more manageable to play a sport in college, and even play more than one! It's a great way to meet new people and become part of a group, but you also have to be very committed and able to juggle schoolwork and athletics."

Pros and Cons

"the sports teams themselves are very segregated, they stay in their own communities and basically act as their own fraternities and sororities. the campus has very low spirit for the teams which is sad, because so many of them are actually very good and win conference and tournament titles regularly."

CAMPUS DINING

Great Variety

"There are three main dining halls, the Pit, Danforth, and Douglass and each of them serve very different meals. You have the choice of so many different types of foods, from pizza to subs, quesadillas to pasta, pulled pork wraps to steak and cheese sandwiches off the grill. The only thing is that like every college campus, by the end of the semester you still want

something different. But currently they are changing up are meal options for the better and I can't wait for that!"

Not Too Bad...

"There are a few options for dining halls. Sometimes it gets old, but Douglass is one of the better places on campus. There's always the Mel too. It's always nice we have Starbucks and we can use declining. Freshmen always have to work hard to use up their clubs AND their declining. Be prepared to buy a lot of nothing, just so you can use it up."

CAMPUS HOUSING

Nice Housing

"Residential quad dorms and Greek houses are the most conveniently located on campus. Both options are quite nice and spacious. Upperclassman housing is a little further, but it is all within walking distance of the campus center. There is active transportation to Southside which is the furthest housing available. Almost all students live on campus (counting Riverside)."

GUYS & GIRLS

Pretty Diverse

"This campus is extremely diverse, mostly due to the number of international students that come here. Essentially, there is definitely a type of person here to suit your fancy, and a major plus? They're all really intelligent!"

HEALTH & SAFETY

Safety & Security

"I've never really felt unsafe while being on campus. There are many blue boxes (which are directly connected to Campus Security) around campus and quite a few security officers walk around campus during the day and night to make sure everything is as it should be. Overall I feel very safe."

LOOKING FOR MORE?

Check out our full-length guide to this school at collegeprowler.com/university-of-rochester/.

University of San Diego

5998 Alcala Park; San Diego, CA 92110
(619) 260-4600; www.sandiego.edu

THE BASICS:

Acceptance Rate: 49%	**Student-Faculty Ratio:** 15:1
Yield: 20%	**Retention Rate:** 85%
Setting: Large city	**Graduation Rate:** 75%
Control: Private Non-Profit	**Tuition:** $36,292
Total Undergrads: 5,111	**Room & Board:** $12,602
SAT Range: 1665–1950*	**Avg. Aid Package:** $28,993
ACT Range: 25–29	**Students With Aid:** 71%

* of 2400

Academics	B+	Greek Life	B
Athletics	C	Guys	A-
Campus Dining	A-	Health & Safety	B+
Campus Housing	A	Local Atmosphere	A
Campus Strictness	C	Nightlife	B+
Computers	B	Off-Campus Dining	A-
Diversity	C+	Off-Campus Housing	B+
Drug Safety	C	Parking	B
Facilities	B+	Transportation	B-
Girls	B+	Weather	A+

CP's Student Author On...
OVERALL EXPERIENCE

Four years at USD will fly by quickly, and toward the end, many students find themselves dreading leaving the leisurely world of USD to go out into the "real world." All universities have their ups and downs, but USD definitely has more ups. When you ask USD students, most will say they love almost everything about the University, except for a few minor things, like strictness. Professors here go out of their way to help students succeed, and the small campus makes networking and forming relationships easier—by the time you graduate, you will have close relationships with faculty and other students. Many look back on their years at USD and feel nostalgic for the laid-back lifestyle they once had, and when reality hits, it's easy to wish you were back at USD, spending every weekend at the beach.

Life in San Diego is unlike living in other cities, and some freshmen may have a hard time adjusting at first. Everything is slower and more laid-back here, and you need to be able to balance serious schoolwork with the fun aspects of the city.... For the rest of this editorial, visit collegeprowler.com.

Students Speak Out On...
OVERALL EXPERIENCE

Q I Love It Here
"It's hard not to be happy at a school so beautiful. Most students are down to earth and really nice. The classes are small, so you get a lot of attention, and professors are always willing to help you."

Q No Better Choice
"The University of San Diego is the best decision I made. A smaller-sized school with a big atmosphere makes for a great experience. The wonders of San Diego are all around, and there's never a dull moment. Teachers are accessible and classes are small enough to build rapport with professors. Once the weekend hits, everyone's ready to have fun!"

Q Perfect!
"USD is the place to attend school. The location, the people, the environment is all perfect! After attending Sonoma State for 2 years and then transfering to USD, USD has blown Sonoma State out of the water based on academics, social events, location, etc. USD is the place to be!"

BEST OF SAN DIEGO

1. The city of San Diego and the nearby beaches
2. Small class sizes
3. Academics and business school
4. Beautiful campus
5. The weather
6. Dorm life

Happy Students
85% of students return after their first year.

Proven Success
75% of students will complete their education and graduate with a degree.

WORST OF SAN DIEGO

1. Classes with mandatory attendance
2. Parking
3. San Diego traffic
4. Some people can be stuck up.
5. Everyone knows everything about everyone else.

Expensive
Tuition is a steep $36,292, one of the most expensive rates in the country.

Student Body

African American:	2%	Male Undergrads:	42%
Asian American:	10%	Female Undergrads:	58%
Hispanic:	14%	Living On Campus:	48%
International:	4%	Living Off Campus:	52%
Native American:	1%	Male Athletes:	11%
White:	63%	Female Athletes:	9%
Unknown:	6%	Fraternity Members:	19%
From Out-of-State:	48%	Sorority Members:	26%

Frequently Compared Schools:

Loyola Marymount University
Santa Clara University
University of California - Santa Barbara
University of Southern California

Students Speak Out On...
EVERYTHING!

ACADEMICS

Always Available for Help

"One of the greatest things about academics at USD are the small class sizes and the availability of the professors. My professors all know me by my first name and are willing to help me understand the material outside of class time. They are always available for office hours. Overall, my teachers at USD have been very knowledgeable and organized, and I have learned a lot from my classes."

Help With English

"I am a freshman and will declare my major for English soon. There are greek life clubs that will help me with my english major, as well as classes and workshops dedicated to helping me become a better writer."

ATHLETICS

Athletics are Awesome

"The athletics here are awesome, and the school spirit is great! Each team does very well. The trainers here are excellent, and they are able to help all of us student athletes a ton!"

Lots of Sports Options, but Not Necessary to Care About Them

"Athletics are not as big as at other colleges, but they're important. Many people play a sport, whether they on a team or recreationally. Students are often highly encouraged to attend games, and they are a great place to hang out. Our big sports are basketball and soccer—do not expect to get much out of a football game. You can make the sports as important or as unimportant as you want them to be."

CAMPUS DINING

So Many Choice

"You just have everything: a new cafeteria where you can eat all you want at night (with a grill, Chinese food, Mexican food, European food, healthy food, etc.), a fancy restaurant, and three bistros."

High-End Gourmet

"USD just opened a brand new, state-of-the-art dining hall in the Student Life Pavilion. The food is pretty good, and throughout the campus you can find some good food that you can have either on the go or enjoy sitting down. USD is very focused on providing healthy options for students, so there are a lot of gourmet items to choose from; however, it can get pretty pricey. There is also a five-start restaurant on campus that serves awesome food."

CAMPUS HOUSING

Campus!

"Campus life is very fun and exciting. I love it."

GUYS & GIRLS

Beautiful People

"USD is known for its incredibly good-looking and attractive student body. The girls are absolutely gorgeous, and the guys aren't too shabby themselves. Since a lot of students live on the beach in Mission Beach, many sport amazing tans as they enjoy sunbathing and surfing. The campus is not that diverse, with many students fitting the perfect California model mold. The bottom line: a campus does not get more attractive then USD."

HEALTH & SAFETY

Complete Saftey

"There are never any problems with safety. It's so safe that you don't even have to worry about walking around at night alone."

LOOKING FOR MORE?

Check out our full-length guide to this school at collegeprowler.com/university-of-san-diego/.

University of San Francisco

2130 Fulton St.; San Francisco, CA 94117
(415) 422-5555; www.usfca.edu

THE BASICS:

Acceptance Rate: 67%
Yield: 19%
Setting: Large city
Control: Private Non-Profit
Total Undergrads: 5,327
SAT Range: 1520–1840*
ACT Range: 22–27

Student-Faculty Ratio: 15:1
Retention Rate: 82%
Graduation Rate: 67%
Tuition: $36,000
Room & Board: $11,990
Avg. Aid Package: $9,184
Students With Aid: 68%

of 2400

Academics	B+	Greek Life	C-
Athletics	C	Guys	B
Campus Dining	B+	Health & Safety	C+
Campus Housing	B+	Local Atmosphere	A+
Campus Strictness	B	Nightlife	B+
Computers	A-	Off-Campus Dining	A+
Diversity	A-	Off-Campus Housing	B-
Drug Safety	C-	Parking	B+
Facilities	B+	Transportation	A+
Girls	B	Weather	B+

CP's Student Author On...
OVERALL EXPERIENCE

Most students will tell you that the best thing about USF is the city of San Francisco. Granted, the city provides an amazing backdrop, but the school itself is also very fascinating and, in some ways, reflective of the city. Like San Francisco, USF is quite old with a rich history and a positive outlook on the future. Buildings are being renovated in order to keep up with the times and the demands of the students. Here, you will find students with strong morals, dedicated to service and justice, and most importantly, a university that supports them. Also, like the city it resides in, USF is incredibly diverse and tolerant. Coming here, you will meet people from all over the world, all ethnicities, religions, and cultures. By exposing students to the culture of San Francisco, USF can mold any student into a conscious, cultured, and well-grounded individual.

USF gives its students the opportunity to enjoy both the intimacy of a small college experience and life in the big city. When the campus feels too consuming or school work becomes too demanding, San Francisco provides an amazing release.... For the rest of this editorial, visit collegeprowler. com.

Students Speak Out On...
OVERALL EXPERIENCE

Q **Gets It Done.**

"The University of San Francisco allows me to get my education done. It it a very challenging school with instructors who are very well qualified and very personable. I love the school's electronic web page and my acedemic advisor because they are easy to use and there to help me. I am already considering pursuing my master's degree at this school. Great experience!!!"

Q **Small School Is the Way to Go.**

"USF is great because it is small and you really get to know your professors. There are a lot of ways to get involved, and I love the small/intimate school experience. I would definitely pick it over again."

Q **Happy**

"Definitely Happy I transferred here. Now if only they'd give more money to students who needed it."

BEST OF USF

1. The city of San Francisco
2. The size of the school and its population
3. The aesthetics of the campus
4. Diversity
5. Quality of teaching
6. Accessibility of professors

Happy Students
82% of students return after their first year.

Easy Financial Aid Process
55% of students surveyed told us that the financial aid process went smoothly and they received the financial aid they needed.

WORST OF USF

1. Cost of tuition
2. Parking
3. Lack of school spirit
4. Lack of weekend events and parties on campus
5. Four-unit system
6. Freshman and sophomore dorms

Expensive
Tuition is a steep $36,000, one of the most expensive rates in the country.

Expensive Dorms
Living on campus doesn't come cheap, with an average housing price tag of $7,730.

Student Body

African American:	5%	Male Undergrads:	39%
Asian American:	20%	Female Undergrads:	61%
Hispanic:	13%	Living On Campus:	41%
International:	10%	Living Off Campus:	59%
Native American:	1%	Male Athletes:	7%
White:	37%	Female Athletes:	3%
Unknown:	15%	Fraternity Members:	2%
From Out-of-State:	37%	Sorority Members:	2%

Students Speak Out On... EVERYTHING!

ACADEMICS

Academics

"The academics here is wonderful! the professors are amazing and they are absolutely genuinely nice and actually care about you. They make sure you pass all your classes and help you get through them! I have learned alot coming here in USF the education is really good quality and worth the money that we pay for!"

Profs Constantly Encourage Team Projects

"I'm in University of San Francisco, and I've been extremely satisfied with my education since i transferred in Fall 2010. I'm a Business major-Accounting- with a minor in Legal Studies. All the teachers i had so far promote team projects by dedicating a huge percentage of our grade doing group research and projects. i get to work with other students and it helps creating new ideas every time we meet."

ATHLETICS

Go Dons!

"Although school spirit isnt in full force on most days, it shine though in student activites and sporting events. If you really want to see and experience Don Spirit, get involved and join a club and go to the soccer, basketball and baseball games. Theres nothing like bleeding green and gold on a friday night."

GO DONS

"Our athletics are fairly good and alot of people attend the games to support our teams! when students really get into the games they really cheer and support our teams! go dons!"

CAMPUS DINING

Diverse

"One main dining hall, but 2-3 options for snacks and/or food for apartment based living"

Ok

"Food is alright. I don't go to the dining hall to frequently."

CAMPUS HOUSING

Housing

"I lived on Gillson Hall my freshman year and it has been great. Ofcourse upperclassmen housing are much better but for a freshman housing everything is clean and kept in order. There are great views of the San Francisco city and it really felt like a home while I stayed here."

Great View With Lots of Walking Stairs

"University of San Francisco is located on the steepest hill of San Francisco called Lone Mountain which means we have to walk up 180 steps to get to some of our classes. On the bright side, you get to see the beautiful and busy view of San Francisco"

GUYS & GIRLS

Trendy kids

"USF kids are pretty trendy and they have nice style. Most of their style is definitely san francisco. The style of USF students are up to par and everyone wears classy appropriate clothing around campus."

Engaged

"More girls than boys on campus. Not as much diversity on campus as I was lead to believe, but people really nice."

HEALTH & SAFETY

Safe

"There were a few incidents but I always felt very safe in the city and on campus."

The Different Forms of Safety and Crime Prevention

"The school does not only educate the students about staying safe but encourage the students to call or contact the campuses Public Safety. The Department of Public Safety also has installed a series of emergency phones on campus. There are 168 emergency phones located throughout the campus as in on main campus, Lone Mountain campuses, inside campus buildings, including all elevators. The campus has other crime prevention help and information from harassment to theft."

University of South Carolina

700 Sumter St.; Columbia, SC 29208
(803) 777-7000; www.sc.edu

THE BASICS:

Acceptance Rate: 58%
Yield: 40%
Setting: Mid-sized city
Control: Public
Total Undergrads: 20,453
SAT Range: 1090–1280*
ACT Range: 24–28

Student-Faculty Ratio: 18:1
Retention Rate: 87%
Graduation Rate: 67%
Tuition: $23,732
Room & Board: $7,328
Avg. Aid Package: $10,558
Students With Aid: 91%

* of 1600

Academics	B	Greek Life	B+
Athletics	A	Guys	A-
Campus Dining	B+	Health & Safety	B-
Campus Housing	B+	Local Atmosphere	B+
Campus Strictness	C+	Nightlife	A+
Computers	B+	Off-Campus Dining	B+
Diversity	B-	Off-Campus Housing	A
Drug Safety	C-	Parking	B-
Facilities	A-	Transportation	B+
Girls	A-	Weather	B-

CP's Student Author On...
OVERALL EXPERIENCE

If there is one word to describe the experiences you will have at USC, it would have to be "unforgettable." Being away from home for the first time at USC is both exciting and scary at times, but the freedom you get when you come here feels natural. It makes you wonder why they don't send people to college sooner! Academically, there are courses and professors who can make you look at things in ways you never considered before. Facts and figures will be thrown at you, but some of the professors (and your peers) can teach you a lot about life as well. It's also a very cool thing to see laid-back professors who will sometimes move their classes out onto the Horseshoe lawn.

On top of this, with such a large student population, you will inevitably form new relationships that will last a lifetime. As at any college, the quality of the experience depends on what you put into it. There are thousands of new people to meet, tons of activities going on, and things to learn both in and out of class. Those who don't take advantage of these opportunities will not get a lot out of their experience here.... For the rest of this editorial, visit collegeprowler. com.

Students Speak Out On...
OVERALL EXPERIENCE

Life Altering

"USC is such an amazing place to go to school. The campus is one block away from the State House, two from the SC Supreme Court, and surrounded by the very cute city of Columbia. Students are friendly, academics are intellectually challenging, athletics are exciting, facilities are top-notch, and the bounty of resources for students is unparalleled. I am so glad I chose to attend USC."

Everything I Wanted and More

"I could have never picked a greater school than USC. I have so much pride in my school and when my family comes to visit I always have something new to show or tell them about. There will always be downsides to college campuses, but I try to focus on the positive. The helpful professors outweigh the bad, and the friends I have made outweigh the bad experiences I have had with others. I feel so much at home at the University of South Carolina and I wouldn't trade my school for anything."

BEST OF SOUTH CAROLINA

1. Football games
2. Cocky the mascot and Cocks paraphernalia
3. International Business School
4. Honors College
5. Strom Thurmond Fitness and Wellness Center

Happy Students
87% of students return after their first year.

Knowledgeable Professors
80% of students surveyed rated the general knowledge of professors as above average.

WORST OF SOUTH CAROLINA

1. Parking
2. Tuition increases
3. Under-21 nightlife scene
4. Hot summers
5. Incompetent advisors
6. Diversity (or lack thereof)
7. Did I mention parking?
8. Campus strictness

Lowest Grades
Drug Safety: C-
Campus Strictness: C+
Diversity: B-

Student Body

African American:	12%	Male Undergrads:	46%
Asian American:	3%	Female Undergrads:	54%
Hispanic:	2%	Living On Campus:	40%
International:	2%	Living Off Campus:	60%
Native American:	0%	Male Athletes:	4%
White:	72%	Female Athletes:	3%
Unknown:	9%	Fraternity Members:	14%
From Out-of-State:	43%	Sorority Members:	15%

Frequently Compared Schools:

Clemson University
College of Charleston
University of Georgia
University of North Carolina

Students Speak Out On... EVERYTHING!

ACADEMICS

Apply early

"It is getting tougher each year to be accepted. This has become a popular school for Northerners. SEC football and great weather are hard to beat. The academic programs like international business, prelaw, premed,marine science and pharmacy are all first rate."

Great programs

"The academic reputation of USC is growing. The top ranked international business has helped make a name for the school. The school of public health and pharmacy are top notched as well."

International Business & Marketing

"The curriculum and work load is intensive, but the benefits pay off well. The classroom and real life training prepares you for upcoming internships and opportunities. It is very competitive, but you are among peers that work hard and are dedicated just as you are :)"

ATHLETICS

Athletics

"Very good football and baseball teams...Games are very fun!!"

Athletic Facilities

"The athletic facilicits at usc are in my opinion some of the best. It is clear a lot of money and time were spent on them. The university definitely treats the atheletes well."

CAMPUS DINING

Good Variety

"You can get whY you want on campus,but if you want variety there's plenty around. Insomnia cookies are amazing late at night."

Russell House

"Hours and food are great. You can get whatever you want at Russell house."

CAMPUS HOUSING

Good Houaing

"Good housing with a lot of choices. Capstone is new and huge, lots of choices in other dorms. Greek Village is in a class by itself, look at pictures to see.."

Dorms

"The dorms are a lot better then I have seen at other campuses. Scholars and capstone are amazing. A lot of different options available"

GUYS & GIRLS

People at USC

"There are many different types of people at USC. There are many attractive people, and the social life is great."

Diversity

"Our university has 20,000 undergraduate students. We have people from 50 different states and over 100 countries. My school is one of the most diverse places that you can view. There is always preppy, emo, the jocks and of course the typical black vs. white. Everyone is so different here but everyone also fits in because we are all part of the Gamecock family."

HEALTH & SAFETY

Safety Come First

"I have never had a problem on campus where I felt unsafe. They school is monitored with over 150 security cameras and security is always walking around campus. Unlike some colleges and universities who have security cops, my campus has certified state and county officers on duty."

City living

"Even though it's a small city and the Capitol you need to smart when you go out."

LOOKING FOR MORE?

Check out our full-length guide to this school at collegeprowler.com/university-of-south-carolina/.

University of South Dakota

414 E. Clark St.; Vermillion, SD 57069
(605) 677-5301; www.usd.edu

THE BASICS:

Acceptance Rate: 87%
Yield: 41%
Setting: Town
Control: Public
Total Undergrads: 7,098
SAT Range: 1400–1900*
ACT Range: 20–25

Student-Faculty Ratio: 15:1
Retention Rate: 73%
Graduation Rate: 48%
Tuition: $7,841
Room & Board: $5,442
Avg. Aid Package: $5,545
Students With Aid: 94%

* of 2400

Academics	B-	Greek Life	B+
Athletics	B	Guys	B
Campus Dining	C+	Health & Safety	A
Campus Housing	C	Local Atmosphere	B
Campus Strictness	B	Nightlife	B
Computers	B+	Off-Campus Dining	B-
Diversity	D-	Off-Campus Housing	A
Drug Safety	C+	Parking	C+
Facilities	B-	Transportation	D+
Girls	B-	Weather	B-

CP's Student Author On...
OVERALL EXPERIENCE

USD may not be well-known nationally, but the Midwest ranks many of the University's departments as some of the top ones in the area, and most of the students say they wouldn't wish to be anywhere else. Students unhappy with USD are usually those that are unhappy with the locale and the expected degree of work. After all, there's nothing wrong with small-town South Dakota. In fact, when it comes to a friendly atmosphere, USD couldn't get much better. Whether you're in class or just hanging out chatting on one of Vermillion's green lawns, students and faculty on campus are polite, conversational, and generally happy. And with all the tutorial opportunities and student advisors, leaders, and philanthropists, USD students, for the most part, are always willing to meet a new face and began a new friendship.

USD may lack transportation and have students who speak with a Midwestern accent, but there definitely is a huge variety of student interests, considering the school attracts not only city kids and future doctors but also farm-raised tomboys and top ACT rankers.... For the rest of this editorial, visit collegeprowler.com.

Students Speak Out On...
OVERALL EXPERIENCE

Q Great but Work
"USD may be the state party school but you can't party your life away here. It's a serious school that expects you to work hard for your degree. It is pretty fun though and the people here are great. All and all this place is great for a small school."

Q "My experiences at USD have been great because of great friends. Otherwise, I would have ditched this prairie dump."

Q "Sometimes I wish I went elsewhere, but I love my friends here, and I've kind of made it home."

Q "If I had to choose all over, I would go here again."

Q "I love USD. I think a lot of it has to do with the major I picked. I don't know a lot about the other departments on campus, so I am not sure if the faculty I have worked with is exceptional or the standard for the school, but my teachers have been unbelievable. I am really glad that I came here."

BEST OF SOUTH DAKOTA

1. The short walk between classes
2. The remodeled DakotaDome
3. Professors' accessibility
4. Medical school
5. Al Neuharth Media Center

Affordable
Tuition is only $7,841, one of the most affordable rates in the country.

Personal Attention
You can expect personal attention with 54% of classes having less than 20 students.

WORST OF SOUTH DAKOTA

1. Parking
2. Parking tickets
3. Overpriced campus food
4. Tiny dorm rooms
5. Some bad advisors
6. The Bump's hours
7. Pool tables in the CSC

Not Much Diversity
One of the least racially diverse campuses—only 15% of students are minorities.

Student Body

African American:	2%	Male Undergrads:	36%
Asian American:	1%	Female Undergrads:	64%
Hispanic:	1%	Living On Campus:	31%
International:	0%	Living Off Campus:	69%
Native American:	3%	Male Athletes:	12%
White:	85%	Female Athletes:	9%
Unknown:	8%	Fraternity Members:	9%
From Out-of-State:	29%	Sorority Members:	8%

Students Speak Out On... EVERYTHING!

ACADEMICS

Q University Excels in Academics

"The University of South Dakota prioritizes academic success in their students. Most classes are small in size and teachers are willing to meet at times outside of class hours. For larger lecture classes, study sessions, help tables, and supplemental information sessions are provided to give students additional support. Professors encourage office visits and emails and have a genuine interest in the student's learning and progess."

Q Art Program at USD

"The Art Department here is great. I really like all of my professors. They have a lot of knowledge and are impressive instructors. I am busy but not overwhelmed with the courses. The facilities are good and very comfortable. They are very willing to help you find jobs and internships.."

ATHLETICS

Q Sporting Events

"Student involvement in the sporting events is very poor. Coming from Madison, Wisconsin to Vermillion, South Dakota really is different. Here barely anyone goes to sporting events, they don't have chants or songs they are known for. It could use some work on that aspect. But the dome is amazing I love going to football games there."

Q We Have Sports at USD?

"Hardly any school spirit transcends in the community or within the students, except for our homecoming which is a big drink and sex fest."

CAMPUS DINING

Q MUC Is Best!

"The MUC is by far the best place to go grab a bite to eat. The Commons in North Complex is not all that bad, but it does get repetitive when you eat there every day. If you want variety, definitely head to the MUC where you can find yourself some great coffee and a great little complex of different areas to eat."

Frequently Compared Schools:

Creighton University
South Dakota State University
Truman State University
University of Nebraska

Q Good but Not Stellar

"The fact that freshman have to buy such a huge meal plan is ridiculous. It would be better if they could have more flex."

CAMPUS HOUSING

Q Not your typical "dorm"

"I can't wait for next fall. I'm going to be one of the first residents of Coyote Village. I have a 2 bedroom apartment with a stove/oven and full size fridge. I get my own bedroom an don't have to stare at toothpaste my roommate left in the sink because I get my own bathroom sink too!"

Q

"I think they are smelly, crowded, and dirty. I recommend keeping out. But since you don't have a choice, head for any of the rooms that have been remodeled."

GUYS & GIRLS

Q Surprising Variety

"I've lived in South Dakota my whole life and assumed that USD would have the same homogeneous typical white people like myself. However, there is a very surprising amount of variety in culture and ethnicity that I think is really refreshing."

Q Guys and Girls

"The guys and girls on campus seem to be pretty average."

HEALTH & SAFETY

Q Helpful Information

"It is nice that USD sends out text messages and emails about possible threats to their students."

Q Not a Worry

"On the University of South Dakota campus in the small town of Vermillion, South Dakota, I have never felt that I could not walk anywhere alone. The campus is fairly small with each building not far from another. There are call buttons on various sidewalks around the campus should any emergency come up. There are always campus policeman walking and driving around, open to answer any questions or there for any reason."

LOOKING FOR MORE?

Check out our full-length guide to this school at collegeprowler.com/university-of-south-dakota/.

University of South Florida

4202 E. Fowler Ave.; Tampa, FL 33620
(813) 974-2011; www.usf.edu

THE BASICS:

Acceptance Rate: 42%
Yield: 33%
Setting: Large city
Control: Public
Total Undergrads: 30,559
SAT Range: 1550–1860*
ACT Range: 22–28

Student-Faculty Ratio: 27:1
Retention Rate: 86%
Graduation Rate: 48%
Tuition: $15,386
Room & Board: $8,750
Avg. Aid Package: $9,849
Students With Aid: 96%

* of 2400

Academics	B	Greek Life	B
Athletics	A	Guys	A-
Campus Dining	B+	Health & Safety	B
Campus Housing	B-	Local Atmosphere	A-
Campus Strictness	B-	Nightlife	B+
Computers	B+	Off-Campus Dining	A-
Diversity	B+	Off-Campus Housing	A
Drug Safety	C+	Parking	B-
Facilities	B+	Transportation	A-
Girls	B	Weather	A-

CP's Student Author On...
OVERALL EXPERIENCE

Most students sincerely enjoy USF. Students can look forward to meeting many people from diverse backgrounds, and the teachers here are strong role models for students. While classes are sometimes stressful and unbearable, the lessons taught outside of school are invaluable. Sometimes classes can be difficult, but the school offers students numerous ways to relieve their anxieties and stress. With the various top-notch facilities on campus, nighttime activities, dining out, or just laying around in the sun, USF has much more to offer than rock-solid academics. Even shy students who find venturing to a new school hard on them grow fond of USF quickly.

Of course, college is what you make of it. Students who spend their time in their dorm rooms miss out on opportunities to make friends and grow as individuals. Those who get involved in student activities seem to enjoy their college experience much more than those who choose not to get involved. That's why it is important to take advantage of the opportunities that USF presents to its students.... For the rest of this editorial, visit collegeprowler. com.

Students Speak Out On...
OVERALL EXPERIENCE

Q Best School Ever
"Wonderful, love all the people I have met and the professors are great."

Q FRESHMAN
"So far as a freshman at USF, I have really enjoyed myself. As soon as you step foot on campus the people here make you feel so welcome. I have been to organization informals, parties, cook-outs, and more. I am having a pretty good college experience for my first year."

Q Overall Experience
"I love USF. I am glad that i decided to go here and i really wouldn't prefer to be any where else. I've had tons of great experiences at games and other fun events all over campus and i really feel like this is where i belong."

Q USF Experience
"I have had a wonderful time while attending USF. I went here for my undergraduate and now my masters. The professors are very welcoming and encouraging. The seem to really care and want their students to succeed."

BEST OF SOUTH FLORIDA

1. Hot girls/cute guys
2. Wild parties
3. The Greenery Pub
4. Rocky the Bull
5. Great football team!
6. Free food all the time
7. Bull Market
8. Homecoming Weekend

Happy Students
86% of students return after their first year.

Knowledgeable Professors
91% of students surveyed rated the general knowledge of professors as above average.

WORST OF SOUTH FLORIDA

1. No parking
2. No 24-hour dining on campus
3. Public transportation in Tampa is not very good.
4. Obnoxious, drunken students at parties
5. Parking spot vultures

Overextended Faculty
There are 27 students for every faculty member on campus.

Student Body

African American:	13%	Male Undergrads:	43%
Asian American:	7%	Female Undergrads:	57%
Hispanic:	15%	Living On Campus:	13%
International:	2%	Living Off Campus:	87%
Native American:	1%	Male Athletes:	3%
White:	62%	Female Athletes:	3%
Unknown:	2%	Fraternity Members:	8%
From Out-of-State:	9%	Sorority Members:	6%

Students Speak Out On...
EVERYTHING!

ACADEMICS

Q Positive Outlook

"From what I have researched, the University of Florida has wonderful academics and is among the top research schools in the state. One benefit to my major, Nursing, is that students get to work with robots created right there on campus by other intelligent students. I am looking forward to working in such a knowledgeable community toward achieving my goal in Nursing field with such an elite program of study."

Q ABOUT ME

"IM CURRENTLY ENROLLED AT UNIVERSITY OF SOUTH FLORIDA MY MAJOR IS PHILOSHPY IM CURRENTLY TRYING TO TEST MY SKILLS ON DIFFRENT EDUCATIONAL SKILLS WHAT I INTEND ON DOING AFTER COLLEGE DOESN'T HAVE ANYTHING TOO DO WITH MY EDUCATIONAL SKILLS"

ATHLETICS

Q Sports Are Top-Notch!!!

"Varsity sports at University are pretty huge, especially the way campus treats us. We have wonderful training and workout facilities, including our own trainers, psychologists, and academic advisers. IM sports are pretty huge, too, because anyone can play. We have some pretty diverse ones, too."

Q Go Bulls!

"The Athletics at USF are awesome! It is always nice to see, such a big school with that much school spirit, every sport whether its soccor, football, baseball or basketball the stands are full! I love going to the different games!"

CAMPUS DINING

Q Great Dining

"I have tried a few of the eating facilities on campus, I found them all excellent in freshness, taste, and service.The meal plan gives me the freedom to pick and choose any of the restaurants and at all times of day.The Bulls Bucks really make it easy to stay on campus and have from Starbucks to covinience foods.My parents and i are very happy with all the perks that come with this campus food facilities."

Frequently Compared Schools:

Florida State University
University of Central Florida
University of Florida
University of Miami

Q Our Cafe

"I love eating on campus. Sometimes i would leave my house early so taht i may have something to eat before class because, they food on campus was always great and not expensive."

CAMPUS HOUSING

Q USF on Campus Housing

"The best dorms are Juniper and Poplar Hall. They are huge! They have their own maid service and flat screen tv's on each floor. There is also a dining hall on the first floor. next to the dining hall, USF's red box equivalent is frequented by many students who want to rent movies. A convenience store is also located in the building."

Q Always Improving

"University of South Florida just built a new Residence hall that helps the campus to hold all freshman students as it is mandatory for all freshman to experience campus life their freshman year. It is a great way for students to interact with each other as well as help them with their academics. The cost of living on campus is competitive to places off-campus."

GUYS & GIRLS

Q Extreme Diversity

"USF has one of the most diverse student populations in the country in every sense, and there are a huge number of students here--plenty of fish in the sea."

Q USF Girls and Guys

"Diversity in the USF student body describes the girls and guys that attend this school. You can spot fraternity brothers and sorority girls as well as latin, asian, middle eastern, african, etc. roaming the campus. USF allows you to be yourself and find your own niche in college."

HEALTH & SAFETY

Q Very Safe

"I've never had a safety or security issue and feel very safe at USF."

LOOKING FOR MORE?

Check out our full-length guide to this school at collegeprowler.com/university-of-south-florida/.

University of Southern California

3650 Watt Way; Los Angeles, CA 90089
(213) 740-2311; www.usc.edu

THE BASICS:

Acceptance Rate: 24%	**Student-Faculty Ratio:** 9:1
Yield: 33%	**Retention Rate:** 96%
Setting: Large city	**Graduation Rate:** 88%
Control: Private Non-Profit	**Tuition:** $39,183
Total Undergrads: 16,751	**Room & Board:** $11,458
SAT Range: 1910–2180*	**Avg. Aid Package:** $31,212
ACT Range: 29–32	**Students With Aid:** 76%

* of 2400

Academics	A	Greek Life	A-
Athletics	A	Guys	A+
Campus Dining	B+	Health & Safety	B-
Campus Housing	B+	Local Atmosphere	B
Campus Strictness	B+	Nightlife	A-
Computers	B+	Off-Campus Dining	C+
Diversity	A-	Off-Campus Housing	B
Drug Safety	C	Parking	B-
Facilities	A	Transportation	A-
Girls	A-	Weather	A

CP's Student Author On...
OVERALL EXPERIENCE

Students from Southern California usually love USC from the beginning and strengthen their bonds with the school as time passes. Students who travel to USC from longer distances tend to adapt more slowly, dealing at first with the culture shock that inevitably comes with a first impression of LA. Universally, those who can survive the transition into the USC way of life fall in love with the school after first semester. Typically, students entering school with a skeptical mind-set ends up getting the most pride out of being a Trojan. At the very least, they come away with a new affinity toward college football.

The opportunities on campus are plentiful, and in LA, opportunities are endless. Time flies for everyone at USC, and changes in living conditions, academic standards, and career goals come quicker than newcomers might expect. USC graduates are sure to look back on a college experience that could not have been offered anywhere else. Basically, the more that students are willing to explore the opportunities available to them, the more they endorse the idea that USC is the perfect school for its time and place.

Students Speak Out On...
OVERALL EXPERIENCE

Q I Love It
"I have only been at USC for one semester but I enjoyed the experience extremely! The classes were challenging but taught me so much. The people just have an abundance of school spirit, supporting all things related to the school. I also made many great friends who make my experience even better!"

Q Love It
"Great School. Great people. Great city. There's not much to say but if you like the big city scene you will love it here. Great academics and programs."

Q Best Choice I Ever Made
"Academics are challenging but rewarding, social life is great, and you have the LA weather/experience... what is there not to love?"

BEST OF SOUTHERN CALIFORNIA

1. The campus
2. The film school
3. Football games at the coliseum
4. The marching band
5. The weather
6. Los Angeles nightlife

Happy Students
96% of students return after their first year.

Commitment to Teaching
There are 9 students for every member of faculty on campus.

WORST OF SOUTHERN CALIFORNIA

1. Proximity to some of LA's toughest neighborhoods
2. No In-N-Out Burger
3. No men's soccer team
4. Everything is expensive
5. Needing a car to get anywhere
6. Traffic in Los Angeles

Expensive
Tuition is a steep $39,183, one of the most expensive rates in the country.

Expensive to Just Get By
52% of students surveyed felt that the amount it costs to live while at school was worse than average.

Student Body

African American:	5%	Male Undergrads:	50%
Asian American:	22%	Female Undergrads:	50%
Hispanic:	13%	Living On Campus:	39%
International:	9%	Living Off Campus:	61%
Native American:	1%	Male Athletes:	5%
White:	45%	Female Athletes:	5%
Unknown:	4%	Fraternity Members:	18%
From Out-of-State:	42%	Sorority Members:	21%

Frequently Compared Schools:

New York University
University of California - Berkeley
University of California - Los Angeles
University of Pennsylvania

Students Speak Out On... EVERYTHING!

ACADEMICS

Roski School of Fine Art

"The Roski School of Fine Art has a state of the art facility that caters to the needs of aspiring artists and designers. The class rooms and studios act as playgrounds- allowing the minds of the students to go wild and express themselves."

Opportunities Everywhere

"Being a Business Major at the University of Southern California provides you with opportunities like no other college. Marshall Alumni are known for their preference for graduates of their Alma Mater, and the Trojan Network is extensive. The workload isn't too overwhelming, and you can easily pick up a minor or two. There are tons of internship opportunities, and the professors are willing to pull strings for you if you get to know them."

ATHLETICS

The One Thing That Brings the WHOLE Student Body Together

"USC Football --> enough said.No matter how good/not so good we are each season, all of Los Angeles supports our team. Spirit couldn't be any bigger.Even outside of football, athletes get pretty great treatment. There is a special dining hall strictly for athletes, and certain sports even get special living arrangements. Teachers are more helpful too, from what I hear."

Great Football Team!

"The USC Trojans are awesome and the other sports are very nice too."

CAMPUS DINING

I Eat Anything

"I personally love all the dining halls, especially Everybody's Kitchen (EVK)"

Eating at SC

"USC offers everything you could possibly wish to consume. Every food from high end Lemonade to fast food Carl's Jr. to delicious California Pizza Kitchen is available at USC. The sole drawback to the eating experience at USC is the freshman meal plans. Meal plans are required the first year and are less than perfect. While one of the dining halls offers excellent food such as Mahi Mahi, ice cream, and tri-tip, the other more conveniently located hall is less than desirable."

CAMPUS HOUSING

Gotta Live on Campus!

"There are very different on campus living experiences. Some of the dorm are more for partying where others are quieter. The whole social spectrum is covered. Every living space has food nearby, and most have treadmills, which is convenient. I love dorm life"

School Environment

"Campus life is great. Student organizations really encourage/ promote school involvement. There are a lot of resources to ensure your success in school. Everyone has been helpful and dorm life is a great way to transition to a new school and make friends."

GUYS & GIRLS

Good-Looking & Diverse

"Students are very good-looking for the most part as well as diverse. It is easy to find several groups of people that you get along with and have similar interests, making social life at USC great."

HEALTH & SAFETY

A Secure Enviornment

"I personally know a lot of security members on USC Campus. While there are many students who casually break rules and regulations, such as traffic and pedestrian laws, there are not too many instances where anyone is in strict danger. The security is top notch and spread throughout campus, constantly nailing the many ignorant and lazy students on campus. The only threat is that you personally ignore the law."

LOOKING FOR MORE?

Check out our full-length guide to this school at collegeprowler.com/university-of-southern-california/.

University of St Thomas - Texas

3800 Montrose Blvd.; Houston, TX 77006
(713) 522-7911; www.stthom.edu

THE BASICS:

Acceptance Rate: 80%
Yield: 41%
Setting: Large city
Control: Private Non-Profit
Total Undergrads: 1,792
SAT Range: 1620–1850*
ACT Range: 23–27

Student-Faculty Ratio: 12:1
Retention Rate: 70%
Graduation Rate: 47%
Tuition: $21,830
Room & Board: $7,700
Avg. Aid Package: $15,107
Students With Aid: 87%

* of 2400

This School Isn't Graded Yet!

College Prowler grades are calculated using tons of criteria, including survey responses that come from students at this school.

Unfortunately, we haven't gathered enough student surveys yet for this school to be able to calculate the grades for each section. Stay tuned to *CollegeProwler.com* for grade updates and more!

CP's Student Author On...
OVERALL EXPERIENCE

The University of St. Thomas is not for everyone. It's not a party school with Greek life, thousands of students to meet, wild fans at huge sporting events, or Ivy League admissions standards. But for those who decide to attend UST, there are great opportunities to flourish here. The small community provides students a comfortable environment in a large city. Students are well prepared for careers, and many departments help students find internship, research, and networking opportunities to help better the chances of students landing a dream job. As a Catholic institution, there are convenient Mass times, and friendly priests and nuns who provide moral support for students, regardless of their religion. Catholic students can get involved with religious activities to deepen their faith and meet other people who share the same values.

There are so many ways to become a big fish in a small pond here, with students encouraged to become leaders on campus. The small population allows most students to become familiar faces. Even the shyest people make long-lasting friendships.... For the rest of this editorial, visit collegeprowler.com.

Students Speak Out On...
OVERALL EXPERIENCE

Q Charming Atmosphere

"I love coming here. It contains a lot of old houses that were refurbished as classrooms, its small, the classes are small and more personable, everyone is helpful."

Q Overall Good Experience

"Rigorous academics, caring professors with small classes and one on one interaction, close campus community with opportunities to get involved. Definately not a party school, but the Catholic foundation does not preclude one from having a good time. As at any campus, you have to find your niche, make friends and get involved."

Q Great Atypical College Experience

"UST provides a great environment conducive to studying and socializing simultaneously. The small student-teacher ratio ensures that professors usually know their students really well, and can provide the best help with assignments. Facilities are good. Students and staff are easy to get along with, and the Catholic background and focus of the university is accomodating to people of all races and religions."

BEST OF ST. THOMAS TEXAS

1. The bars, clubs, restaurants, and shops in the trendy Montrose area
2. Catholic tradition
3. Diversity
4. Houston nightlife
5. A lot of great academic programs

Learn from the Best
92% of faculty have earned the highest degree in their field.

Personal Attention
You can expect personal attention with 61% of classes having less than 20 students.

WORST OF ST. THOMAS TEXAS

1. The food—not a lot of options and it's rather expensive.
2. Freezing cold classrooms
3. High cost of tuition
4. Hot and humid Houston weather
5. Lack of funding for a lot of clubs and sports

Student Body

African American:	5%	Male Undergrads:	41%
Asian American:	11%	Female Undergrads:	59%
Hispanic:	32%	Living On Campus:	18%
International:	5%	Living Off Campus:	82%
Native American:	1%	Male Athletes:	6%
White:	35%	Female Athletes:	1%
Unknown:	11%	Fraternity Members:	0%
From Out-of-State:	9%	Sorority Members:	0%

Frequently Compared Schools:

Houston Community College System
Rice University
University of Houston
University of Texas

Students Speak Out On... EVERYTHING!

ACADEMICS

Q Very Comfortable Work Environment; Good Professors

"Many different programs are available from st. Thomas including pre-law, pre-med, education, science, math, and engineering. The professors are usually available if you have any questions and there are many places to study too."

Q Music Major

"I love the music program. it is very personable. We are all like a family. The classes are very challenging but it pays off. I would definitely suggest this music program to other serious musicians."

Q Zzzzz

"Profs in this department are either incredibly boring or rather disturbing. I had better instructors in high school."

ATHLETICS

Q Sports

"The athletics program at the University of St. Thomas is a three year program growing year by year. The school spirit and fan support is growing along with it. The three sports are soccer, basketball, and volleyball. I am involved with the soccer team. The year coming up, we will be getting new facilities which is very exciting for all."

Q High School Much?

"High school sports are more competitive then St Thomas. People try to get stuff going but nothing really works out. The only positive sport that st thomas has the only chance left is with soccer. Without soccer st thomas wouldn't have anything left besides basketball."

Q Sports Aren't Too Big Here

"The university does not take sports seriously. The administration just want sports to increase admissions, but they don't take it all the way. There is not a whole lot of school spirit"

CAMPUS DINING

Q GET HEALTHY!

"Not enough healthy options in the cafeteria, but overall good."

Q Campus Food

"The food doesn't have any variety, and its not very healthy."

Q Rip Off

"Food is both overpriced and bad. Best choice is Quiznos. Hope you like sandwichs, sandwichs, sandwichs."

CAMPUS HOUSING

Q Emphasis on Resident Life, Not Dorm Life.

"Plenty of activities scheduled throughout the week, and staff are usually supportive and encouraging. Visitors are strictly held to rules, and so there is always an environment of safety in resident hall. The courtyard is pretty, although sometimes noisy neighbors can be heard easily through the walls. To deal with this, however, there are designated respectful quiet times for studying and sleeping."

GUYS & GIRLS

Q Welcoming of Differences, but Overall Pretty Tame

"I tend to only encounter the most high achieving undergraduates, graduate students are diverse professionals. Students tend to dress and act relatively conservatively. I am not aware of too many wild parties or behavioral problems, so it seems the students are pretty mature and well behaved. I'll say this, it's a lot more tame around here than it was at my undergraduate university."

HEALTH & SAFETY

Q Safet on Campus

"I feel completely safe on campus because there are always police patrolling and walking near by all day and night."

Q Safe

"area is not so safe, but the campus is safe and there is security guards around campus"

LOOKING FOR MORE?

Check out our full-length guide to this school at collegeprowler.com/university-of-st-thomas---texas/.

University of Tampa

401 W. Kennedy Blvd.; Tampa, FL 33606
(813) 253-3333; www.ut.edu

THE BASICS:

Acceptance Rate: 60%	Student-Faculty Ratio: 17:1
Yield: 23%	Retention Rate: 74%
Setting: Large city	Graduation Rate: 58%
Control: Private Non-Profit	Tuition: $22,482
Total Undergrads: 5,559	Room & Board: $8,296
SAT Range: 1450–1720*	Avg. Aid Package: $16,003
ACT Range: 21–25	Students With Aid: 94%

of 2400

Academics	B	Greek Life	B-
Athletics	B-	Guys	A
Campus Dining	B+	Health & Safety	C-
Campus Housing	A	Local Atmosphere	B+
Campus Strictness	C+	Nightlife	A
Computers	B	Off-Campus Dining	C+
Diversity	B+	Off-Campus Housing	A
Drug Safety	C-	Parking	B
Facilities	B-	Transportation	C
Girls	A+	Weather	A

CP's Student Author On...
OVERALL EXPERIENCE

Of the many colleges and universities in Florida, the University of Tampa is one of the best places to study and enjoy college life. Not only is UT known for being a great place with high academic standards, but also the diversity and different cultures that are found here make the campus an enjoyable place to be. The amazing weather and location also help—thanks to the fact that Tampa is on the West coast of Florida. There is a wide variety of beaches within minutes of the campus. Also, the nightlife makes the University of Tampa a pretty attractive place for kids who are used to the city style of living.

The school spirit can be felt everywhere, and there is always something to do or an event to attend. Overall, the University of Tampa is a wonderful place to study and also to relax in between coursework. Once you're here, you'll feel like you're home.

Students Speak Out On...
OVERALL EXPERIENCE

Q **Best Place Ever**
"The University of Tampa is a excellent place to come study and chill out. Everyone here is extremely nice, and don't forget about the weather. We are in the Sunshine State!!"

Q **The School Has Provided Me a Unique Experience Unlike Anywhere Else!**
"My college experience has literally gone by so quick, with a lot of partying but with just as much studying i'm glad i chose the University of tampa as my college decision and i recommend anyone to do the same."

Q **I Would Chose UT Over and Over Again**
"As soon as I visited UT i knew it was made for me. I felt in love with the campus, people are very friendly, staff is amazing, very helpful, same as most professors. Campus is small which could be an advantage (or a disadvantage depending the situation) it is very well located, transportation is always available, there are many things to do in tampa, from dining, recreation to clubbing and bars. Close to orlando, the beach, it has it all!"

BEST OF TAMPA

1. Excellent academics
2. Great diversity
3. Beautiful campus
4. Excellent athletic programs
5. Sunny Florida weather

Big Dorms
67% of students surveyed felt that dorms were more spacious than average.

WORST OF TAMPA

1. Safety

Lowest Grades
Health & Safety: C-
Drug Safety: C-
Transportation: C

Student Body

African American:	6%	Male Undergrads:	41%
Asian American:	2%	Female Undergrads:	59%
Hispanic:	10%	Living On Campus:	60%
International:	9%	Living Off Campus:	40%
Native American:	0%	Male Athletes:	7%
White:	62%	Female Athletes:	5%
Unknown:	9%	Fraternity Members:	12%
From Out-of-State:	70%	Sorority Members:	11%

Frequently Compared Schools:

Florida State University
University of Central Florida
University of Miami
University of South Florida

Students Speak Out On... EVERYTHING!

ACADEMICS

Business School

"The Business school is highly regarded nationwide. It is by far one of the best business schools there is. The opportunities are vast and self-application is that is required to excel here at UT. The resources are available. It's just a great door opener to the real world especially if you are a business major."

Great Business School

"The college of Business at UT is phenomenal. Great professors and classes. Very laid back at times and professionally intense at other times."

ATHLETICS

Home of the Top-Ranked Spartans!

"The athletics department at UT is one of the top-seeded in the nation. Even though UT is a 2nd Division school, The University of Tampa has been recognized in the past years as one of the most competitive colleges in athletics. Baseball, Volleyball, Basketball, Soccer you name it! UT has excelled in many sports, clinching National Titles in the past few years."

Awesome

"The sports teams at UT pride themselves on excellence. Most noticeably the women's volleyball team. They are a cut above the rest and a true example of what Spartan pride is all about. The competition is tough though as there is such a diverse range of students with varying talents. Nevertheless, the sports here at UT are great!"

CAMPUS DINING

Delicious! It Literally Never Gets Old!

"Although like any place one might need more variety. The On - Campus establishments provide a new fresh menu nearly every day. Most students will agree that the food on campus is exceptional. And you tend to get rather close to the chefs that make it, even if most due believe their ex convicts."

Many Choices

"There are a lot of choices to eat. I do not live on campus so I do not eat there everyday, but when I do eat there I can choose anything I want to eat and it is good."

CAMPUS HOUSING

Overall the Dorms Here on Campus Are the Best.

"Majority of the dorms have been newly renovated on campus, each dorm you enter is nearly brand new. And each are extremely spacious and overall very accommodating. The only ones that are considered "bad" would be Mckay and Smiley but as a previous resident of Smiley, one can find the open residents to make this dorm one of the most closely knit among campus."

Great Housing for Everyone!!!

"It doesn't matter if you just enter UT or if you're an upperclassmen, housing at UT is great! It is well organized and everywhere you go people are friendly and no matter where you may live you will always have great neighbors."

GUYS & GIRLS

Both Sides Can Be Found Extremely Hot.

"It's the south, it seems as though everyone has an in shape body. Most of the campus looks as though they have walked out of a fashion catalogue, and with the ratio being 3:1 (girls/guys) majority of men can agree that this campus has a lot to choose from."

Most are HOT

"It seem like the girl-to-guy ratio is 7:1. Most are very hot! It's easier to hook up with the prettiest girls than to find guys to play football. Tampa is a party city, and and Ybor City is just as cool."

HEALTH & SAFETY

Lucky the Safety Guide

"The campus is very safe. Security is constantly on patrol. During late hours you can be transported from one side of the small campus to the next by golf cart."

LOOKING FOR MORE?

Check out our full-length guide to this school at collegeprowler.com/university-of-tampa/.

University of Tennessee

527 Andy Holt Tower; Knoxville, TN 37996
(865) 974-1000; www.tennessee.edu

THE BASICS:

Acceptance Rate: 73%
Yield: 42%
Setting: Mid-sized city
Control: Public
Total Undergrads: 21,183
SAT Range: 1040–1290*
ACT Range: 24–29

Student-Faculty Ratio: 19:1
Retention Rate: 84%
Graduation Rate: 60%
Tuition: $22,168
Room & Board: $7,200
Avg. Aid Package: $9,611
Students With Aid: 93%

* of 2400

Academics	B	Greek Life	B
Athletics	A	Guys	A-
Campus Dining	C+	Health & Safety	C
Campus Housing	B-	Local Atmosphere	B
Campus Strictness	C+	Nightlife	A-
Computers	B+	Off-Campus Dining	B
Diversity	C	Off-Campus Housing	A-
Drug Safety	C	Parking	C
Facilities	B	Transportation	B+
Girls	B	Weather	B-

CP's Student Author On...
OVERALL EXPERIENCE

UT draws students from all over, and it is little wonder why. UT has a personality all its own. The level of pride and tradition here is among the strongest in the country, and the amount of support Knoxville has for UT is amazing, especially with sports. You will love the laid-back Southern style UT has to offer, and you will enjoy spending time with the people you meet here. Ask any UT alumni about their most positive life experiences, and I guarantee you that most of those experiences will have occurred at UT.

It is understandable to see how UT can appear intimidating on paper, especially to those coming from a small town. There are many different activities to become involved in, and they are yours for the taking if you are willing to make the effort and work hard. The key to success at UT, as well as any college, is to learn to manage your time properly. As long as you remember that education is the main reason for coming to UT and prioritize accordingly, you will be very happy during your college days.

Students Speak Out On...
OVERALL EXPERIENCE

Q It's Great

"I have really enjoyed my time at UT Knox. I can't wait to return in the Fall. I would refer all my younger friends to take a look at UT when they are searching for colleges."

Q My Favorite Experience

"My favorite experience here at The University of Tennessee, would probably be the Volunteer Football game on Saturdays. The games are great way to have safe fun."

Q Sports

"My overall experience at UT has been great. There's nothing better than seeing all the visitors and alumni visit to see a football, basketball, soccer game or some other event. The overall campus is beautiful and full of excitement."

BEST OF UT KNOXVILLE

1. The rowdy and raucous Neyland Stadium
2. Caring and compassionate professors
3. A wide variety of Greek organizations to choose from
4. Old City
5. The free downtown trolly

Happy Students
84% of students return after their first year.

Knowledgeable Professors
92% of students surveyed rated the general knowledge of professors as above average.

WORST OF UT KNOXVILLE

1. Large class sizes (especially for general courses)
2. The recent crackdown by campus security
3. No parking
4. The unpredictable (and often way too humid) weather

Want a Job? On Your Own
There aren't any placement services for graduates.

Not Much Diversity
One of the least racially diverse campuses—only 16% of students are minorities.

Student Body

African American:	8%	Male Undergrads:	50%
Asian American:	3%	Female Undergrads:	50%
Hispanic:	2%	Living On Campus:	26%
International:	1%	Living Off Campus:	74%
Native American:	0%	Male Athletes:	3%
White:	84%	Female Athletes:	2%
Unknown:	1%	Fraternity Members:	14%
From Out-of-State:	11%	Sorority Members:	14%

Frequently Compared Schools:

Auburn University
University of Alabama
University of Georgia
University of South Carolina

Students Speak Out On...
EVERYTHING!

ACADEMICS

Civil Engineering

"The Engineering program at Chatt is very superb. They just built an engineering mathematics and computer science building especially for the major.New car factories in the area are offering great internship opportunities that will help jump-start any engineering career. The work load is the same as any engineering student. It requires a lot of hard dedicated work, but there is always someone there to help."

Unlimited Resourses

"I chose to attend University of Tennessee at Knoxville mainly because I loved the social environment there. Once I got in the classrooms and started doing the work, the resources that were available to me seemed endless. I could get free tutoring in whatever class I needed, there was a 24 hour library with staff available to help me, and the internet database was stocked with information. It was practically impossible to fail."

ATHLETICS

Go Vols!

"Football and basketball is very popular at the home of the VOLS. I love going to the games with my friends. The only change I wish they would make would be to lower football tickets. We can attend basketball games for free. We already pay so much for tuition, books, and other fees so I really think they should take this into consideration; plus, the students ARE the BIGGEST fans!"

UT Athletics Are the Best!!

"Athletics at UT is a huge deal, especially around football season. People from all over come to the Neyland Stadium to see the VOLS play. Our fan support is outrageous! At every football game, we seat roughly 120,000 people in the stadium! We have a great basketball and football team, there is so much school spirit (EVERYONE BLEEDS ORANGE!!)"

CAMPUS DINING

Campus Dining

"The amount of dining UT has to offer is great for the student body. There are fast food restaurants located around camp to help give that variety just in case the cafeteria food may get tiring. The quality of food has been very good and I have yet to be disappointed."

Dining Halls

"I think they have great facilities for food service for the students here. You get what you pay for. And everything is delicious!"

CAMPUS HOUSING

Very Good

"Very good experience. Lived in housing an really liked it. I was part of a Learning community for Engineers and it really helped me with my classes"

Dorm Life

"The freshman dorms are some of the best on campus. Most of the dorms are being redone so in the Fall, the new students will feel more comfortable."

GUYS & GIRLS

Large Variety

"Another plus of a big university is the variety of students. I love meeting new people and at UT Knoxville, there are a ton of great guys and girls. Of course you have those that are not the most fun to hang out with, like some of the stuck-up frat guys or really spoiled rich girls. However, in my 3 years at this university I have almost always had a positive experience meeting new people. I know athletes, honor students, people from church, partiers, etc."

HEALTH & SAFETY

Very Safe

"The campus isn't crawling with police but you know they're there if you need them. We have safety stations set up all around campus and you can push the button and police will be there within seconds."

LOOKING FOR MORE?

Check out our full-length guide to this school at collegeprowler.com/university-of-tennessee/.

University of Tennessee at Chattanooga

615 McCallie Ave.; Chattanooga, TN 37403
(423) 425-4111; www.utc.edu

THE BASICS:

Acceptance Rate: 79%	Student-Faculty Ratio: 18:1
Yield: 42%	Retention Rate: 67%
Setting: Mid-sized city	Graduation Rate: 40%
Control: Public	Tuition: $16,954
Total Undergrads: 9,039	Room & Board: $8,190
SAT Range: 940–1180*	Avg. Aid Package: $9,853
ACT Range: 21–25	Students With Aid: 94%

of 1600

Academics	C-	Greek Life	C+
Athletics	C+	Guys	B
Campus Dining	B	Health & Safety	C+
Campus Housing	B	Local Atmosphere	B+
Campus Strictness	C	Nightlife	B+
Computers	B-	Off-Campus Dining	B+
Diversity	B-	Off-Campus Housing	B
Drug Safety	C	Parking	B-
Facilities	B+	Transportation	A-
Girls	B-	Weather	B

CP's Student Author On...
OVERALL EXPERIENCE

Most students agree that UTC is a diverse school that has introduced them to a great college experience. The city of Chattanooga has a great impact on students with the many outdoors activities available and the breathtaking scenery. Chattanooga is a like a large southern city and smaller suburbs rolled into one place. The only negatives from students are the city can get boring and you have to try to meet new people to have a great experience. UTC is a great change for students who are used to bustling city life and no outdoor activities.

The campus is small enough to see the same people throughout the day but large enough to always find something to do. The wide selection of organizations to join influenced many students to stay. Greek life is popular among students and is a great way to get to know more people. The key to loving UTC is to be involved. Try everything you can do. If you don't like it, try something new. Come with an open mind and you will love the school.

Students Speak Out On...
OVERALL EXPERIENCE

Q LOVE IT!
"UTC IS A GREAT SCHOOL I WOULD RECOMMEND ANYONE WHO WANTS TO ATTEND A UNIVERSITY WHERE YOU FEEL AT HOME AND ACCEPTED YOU SHOULD ENROLL HERE. THERE ARE ALWAYS SOME THINGS YOU DISLIKE ABOUT YOUR SCHOOL BUT AS A WHOLE I DO NOT HAVE MANY BAD THINGS TO SAY ABOUT UTC."

Q Convenient but Nice
"The biggest reason I am currently at this school is that it is in my home town where I was raised. I get to live at home for free and eat relatively free. This saves me a lot of money, which is fantastic. I do like the campus though. It's quite nice. An excellent setting for my college experience."

Q Enjoyable
"great experience. i love it. it has the charm of a medium sized city but with a cheap price tag and not overloads of kids"

Q I'd Choose UTC Again
"I like UT Chatt. It's a great place to attend school. The scenery is beautiful, surrounded by the mountains. The people are friendly, and the activities on campus are entertaining."

BEST OF UT CHATTANOOGA

1. Smaller campus, which means less walking and the chance to get to know people
2. Being close to many outdoor activities
3. Apartment-style dorms
4. Subway is open until midnight.

Big Dorms
86% of students surveyed felt that dorms were more spacious than average.

WORST OF UT CHATTANOOGA

1. It rains a lot.
2. Cardiac Hill can leave you breathless.
3. You tend to see the same people all the time.
4. Limited food options
5. Not enough parking
6. The cliquey student body

Lowest Grades
Academics: C-
Drug Safety: C
Campus Strictness: C

Student Body

African American:	17%	Male Undergrads:	44%
Asian American:	2%	Female Undergrads:	56%
Hispanic:	2%	Living On Campus:	34%
International:	2%	Living Off Campus:	66%
Native American:	0%	Male Athletes:	7%
White:	77%	Female Athletes:	3%
Unknown:	0%	Fraternity Members:	6%
From Out-of-State:	6%	Sorority Members:	8%

Students Speak Out On... EVERYTHING!

ACADEMICS

Q Science

"All science class are tough. There are hardly ever enough prof. for Biology class. However, once you get into a calss you will enjoy it and learn a lot."

Q Academics Is Key

"The academics at my school is about average. The professors for the most part are willing to help you and keep your grades up . However the workload at some times can get a little overwhelming because some of the professors take it a little over board. The registration process is awful, it takes you for ever to register for classes because as soon as the registration will open the system will shut down."

ATHLETICS

Q Great Sport Programs

"From the Varsity to the intramural, the sports here in Chattanooga are great. The games are a blast to watch and the environment is wonderful."

Q Sports Are Not My Thing but....

"I have never been into sports but I attend the football/ basketball games mostly everyone shows up! I guess our athletics are very good, we aren't the best but I am proud of how we perform. At the games the school spirit is always there. You would see some people dressed in our schools colors and some people without shirts and UTC painted on their chest. it's always fun to watch. Even though I'm not a sport fanatic, i do support them!"

CAMPUS DINING

Q Food Choices

"The food court offers a gread variety to choose from. Although, it is nice to go out once in a while, it is great food and convenient and centrally located on campus."

Q Variety of Food on UTC Campus

"There are many things to choose from when eating on campus. Everything taste good and is prepared fresh."

Frequently Compared Schools:

Belmont University
Middle Tennessee State University
Tennessee State University
University of Tennessee

CAMPUS HOUSING

Q Campus Life

"Campus life is great at UTC. It is apartment only housing with great amenities & social atmosphere. With full kitchen & community rooms it makes the apartments great to live in. The cost is very affordable as the apartments can be as cheap as $2000 a semester. It is convenient as most of living areas are right in the area of classrooms & campus sites. The housing process as a whole is quite easy as UTC takes great care in helping all students get the perfect apartment for them."

Q South Campus Dorms Are Great for Their Prices

"The Entire South Campus at the University of Tennessee at Chattanooga are fantastic! By far the greatest atmosphere you could ask for. The cost of living for these dorms are more upscale than the rest of campus, but it is worth it. As far as convenience, they are the farthest from campus but the living atmosphere and items that the room and dorm offer make it worth it."

GUYS & GIRLS

Q Girls Lookin Good

"All are great looking with interests in campus life. All dress nice & make campus life fun."

Q Boys, Boys ,Boys,

"you see all kinds of different types of people at UTC. greek life is pretty big on campus, there are lot of sororities and frats everywhere you turn."

HEALTH & SAFETY

Q Safe or Sorry

"At UTC there is always people around. I have never felt unsafe because if i don't see an officer, there is the little blue light system they have. No matter where you are on campus you can always see at least two of them."

LOOKING FOR MORE?

Check out our full-length guide to this school at collegeprowler.com/university-of-tennessee-at-chattanooga/.

University of Texas

1 University Station; Austin, TX 78712
(512) 471-3434; www.utexas.edu

CP's Student Author On...
OVERALL EXPERIENCE

Most students agree that they have loved their time here at UT, and they wouldn't want to be anywhere else. College is the best time of your life, and I can't think of a better place to spend it than at the University of Texas. Students get a great education while having an awesome college town with everything at their disposal. Don't try to graduate early. Enjoy your time at UT—go cheer on the Longhorns at all the home games for all sports: football, basketball, baseball, intramurals. See the amenities that the Forty Acres has to offer—the Harry Ransom Center, go to our libraries and see our more than eight million volumes. Go to Gregory Gym and the Rec Center—you have a free gym membership for four years or more—use it.

I came to UT convinced that I was going to transfer to a school in California in the spring. I spent two days here before school started and I never wanted to leave, even to go home and visit my parents and high school friends! I couldn't leave because I was always afraid that I would miss something because there was always something exciting going on.... For the rest of this editorial, visit collegeprowler.com.

Students Speak Out On...
OVERALL EXPERIENCE

Q I Would Not Choose Any Other College

"UT Austin is the college for me. The professors are great. The staff is very friendly. It is a beautiful and history-filled campus."

Q Best School Ever

"i absolutely love my school. the social life is amazing. it is also one of the top schools in the nation. it's a great balance. i think anyone would have an awesome experience at UT"

Q Why Wouldn't You Come Here?

"It's one of the top partying schools in the nation. Academics are also at the top of the nation. Our sports teams are also at the top. Over here we study hard and party hard, as well. There's always something going on anywhere on campus. It could be organization events, sports events, and class, of course. The environment is very friendly, and there's nice weather throughout the year."

Q Great

"There is a great atmosphere on UT's campus, let alone it's a beautiful campus. I would definitely choose to go to UT again if I'd do it all over again."

BEST OF TEXAS

1. Longhorn football
2. Wearing shorts and flip-flops all year
3. Good academics at a quality price
4. 6th St. when you are 21+
5. Great alumni
6. Greek system

Happy Students
92% of students return after their first year.

Proven Success
78% of students will complete their education and graduate with a degree.

WORST OF TEXAS

1. No parking
2. Heavy traffic
3. Cost of living
4. 6th St. until you are 21
5. Drag rats
6. Foreign professors that you can't understand
7. Jester

Expensive
Tuition is a steep $30,006, one of the most expensive rates in the country.

Student Body

African American:	5%	Male Undergrads:	48%
Asian American:	17%	Female Undergrads:	52%
Hispanic:	18%	Living On Campus:	20%
International:	4%	Living Off Campus:	80%
Native American:	0%	Male Athletes:	2%
White:	55%	Female Athletes:	2%
Unknown:	0%	Fraternity Members:	9%
From Out-of-State:	7%	Sorority Members:	12%

Frequently Compared Schools:

Duke University
Texas A&M University
University of California - Los Angeles
University of Southern California

Students Speak Out On... EVERYTHING!

ACADEMICS

Top Notch

"It's like an educational wonderland. The professors are top notch and the classes are interesting and awesome."

Business Program Support

"The McCombs School of Business provides great informational sessions on coursework and its relevance to career opportunities from UT grads who are now leaders in their industry."

ATHLETICS

Sports at Their Best

"The workout facilities are wonderful and always in use. Intramural sports are a big part of campus life."

Great School Spirit

"Texas football!!! what more can i say?? I love it.Especially football season...probably the best time during the whole school year.Also Texas relays"

CAMPUS DINING

You Want It, You Got It.

"The local food joints have teamed up with the university to allow your flex dollars to be spent at places outside the university facilities. UT has 2 large dining halls, each on opposite sides of campus and several cafes and markets. The Union has chain restaurants and across the street on 'The Drag', students can find all sorts of food, from a 'Phat' sandwich to ethnic cuisine."

Yum

"The food is pretty good. Lots to choose from. Meal plan is required for those who live in dorms. Flexible use of money though."

CAMPUS HOUSING

Dorms Are Great

"love the location of jester. super convenient and right next to gregory gym. jester is older, but newer dorms are really nice looking."

It's as Diverse as Any School Can Get

"This campus is extremely diverse. Any student can find their place here. It is an extremely friendly environment and the night life in Austin is the best."

GUYS & GIRLS

They Say Texas Has the World's Most Beautiful Women, and They're Right

"It doesn't matter what you're into, you'll find it here among one of the most diverse (and largest) student bodies in the country. Asian and middle eastern nations are well represented, as are almost all US states. Texans make up a slight majority, though you won't find any reason to complain there. Whether you want studious companions or stoners, partiers, patricians, or pizza delivery drivers, you can get it pretty easily."

Lots of Different Styles - Every Type of Student You Can Imagine

"Because this campus is so large, you'll find every kind of student you can imagine. There are many different organizations to join including cultural orgs, fraternal orgs, volunteer services, etc. You hardly ever need to dress up, most people wear whatever they feel like when going to class."

HEALTH & SAFETY

Campus Safety Is a Priority

"Security personnel is very visible and the 911 call boxes are easily accessible."

Fairly Safe

"Although The University of Texas at Austin is relatively safe during the day, it's not safe to walk around campus during the night. The university is right in the middle of downtown Austin, so there are a lot of weirdos walking around. (Keep Austin weird)! Also, there recently was a shooting near the tower, but that's not a usual occurance. Austin is a great place to party!"

LOOKING FOR MORE?

Check out our full-length guide to this school at collegeprowler.com/university-of-texas/.

University of Texas - El Paso

500 W. University Ave.; El Paso, TX 79968
(915) 747-5000; www.utep.edu

THE BASICS:

Acceptance Rate: 99%
Yield: 47%
Setting: Large city
Control: Public
Total Undergrads: 17,205
SAT Range: 790–1020*
ACT Range: 15–20

Student-Faculty Ratio: 20:1
Retention Rate: 71%
Graduation Rate: 31%
Tuition: $14,583
Room & Board: $4,203
Avg. Aid Package: $12,159
Students With Aid: 78%

* of 1600

This School Isn't Graded Yet!

College Prowler grades are calculated using tons of criteria, including survey responses that come from students at this school.

Unfortunately, we haven't gathered enough student surveys yet for this school to be able to calculate the grades for each section. Stay tuned to *CollegeProwler.com* for grade updates and more!

CP's Student Author On...
OVERALL EXPERIENCE

The University of Texas at E! Paso provides students with a period of time that they can look back on fondly, like shuffling through an album of memories. By the end of their stay, students think of the school as a part of their family. Resources are available in droves to keep students on their feet and motivated. As far as events, UTEP promotes itself very efficiently. Minerpalooza is an event hosted on campus to promote the season-opener game for the football season. This event is similar to a fair, and many students and residents of the city attend every year.

As far as preparing students for achieving their goals, UTEP opens doors. Internships are available through school programs or advertised to give students a broader view. Opportunities are presented for programs outside of El Paso, giving students the chance to step outside the front door. The University prepares students to be first-rate versions of themselves, with a staff dedicated to the school's vision of growing and changing for the best. The students may be diverse, but everyone seems to smile and be very approachable.

Students Speak Out On...
OVERALL EXPERIENCE

Q UTEP Has a Great Learning Environment
"There are lots of organizations here to get you through the stress of your studies. plus live music every Wednesday to relax."

Q My Experiences
"I have very good experiences in my school. I have taken courses that are reqiered and some that are not. I loved all my physical education classes and french course. People there is very nice, and I feel very good on that school becuase there is many Mexican people, and I love being around my culture. Most of my teacher are very strict but at the end the one is the one that gets benefited."

Q It's an Experience, I Wouldn't Change It for the World
"I enjoy attending UTEP overall. The organizations are great and the football season celebrations always make the best of the Fall semester."

BEST OF UT EL PASO

1. Affordable cost of living
2. El Paso has friendly residents.
3. Good education at a good price

Big Dorms
70% of students surveyed felt that dorms were more spacious than average.

WORST OF UT EL PASO

1. Construction on campus
2. Parking

Not Everyone Graduates
31% of students do not complete their education or graduate with a degree.

Don't Move Off Campus
Average off-campus housing is a steep $10,504.

Student Body

African American:	3%	Male Undergrads:	45%
Asian American:	1%	Female Undergrads:	55%
Hispanic:	78%	Living On Campus:	—
International:	8%	Living Off Campus:	—
Native American:	0%	Male Athletes:	4%
White:	9%	Female Athletes:	3%
Unknown:	1%	Fraternity Members:	—
From Out-of-State:	8%	Sorority Members:	—

Frequently Compared Schools:

Texas Tech University
University of Houston
University of North Texas
University of Texas

Students Speak Out On...
EVERYTHING!

ACADEMICS

New Degree Plans

"The University of Texas at El Paso is a constantly growing campus. There have been many modifications and improvements such as a new building for Engineering, Biology, and Health Sciences. This improvements have made possible the establishment of new degree plans that can help you get a double major or even allow you to get both your Bachelor and Masters at the same time."

Theatre

"Being a theatre major at UTEP has been very fulfilling and rewarding. Everyone becomes a family and everyone in the department knows one another. Just about every student has the opportunity to work on their craft each semester and have an audience. Workload is challenging but never beyond possible as long as priorities are set. Many of our students also participate in various internships around the states."

ATHLETICS

A Little of Everything

"UTEP has the fame of having the first all american black male team to win the NCAA basketball tournament. For this a movie with the name of Glory Road came out to remember this historical achievement. Plus UTEP has good basketball, and football program"

Basketball

"in the last few years the basketball team hs been more successful."

CAMPUS DINING

Food

"There is many food places inside the school, the one thing that I have noticed is that the school does not have a cafeteria which would be really good for those who have the meal plans in the school. I however did not have the meal plan and would have to buy food there which was expensive and that is basically where all my money went to."

CAMPUS HOUSING

Great!

"I do not live in on-campus housing but I believe it is very good."

Dorms Should Be an Experience to Take

"The dorms are a place that should be lived at least once in the 4 years you are at school. I enjoyed my time staying all day at school to go to activities, events, studying with friends and having a fun time with fellow peeps"

GUYS & GIRLS

How Students Are in My School

"most of the students here dress nice, but there are some that just don't know what to do to bring attention to themselves. Most of them are social, but there are some who just like to befriend themselves."

Mostly Average Guys and Girls

"most guys dress casual. most girls dress casual. Everywhere you look you can see all the groups that have formed around campus looking for fun activities to do. Most of the interests around campus are electronics, everyone has something new to show."

HEALTH & SAFETY

Safety

"The safety and security on my campus is wonderful. I know if I ever had a problem with something the campus security will be there fast. Also I like how the campus will alert us on our cell phones if something major is happening at our school just to let us know what to watch out for."

Safe

"I feel safe at UTEP's campus. There is always security in campus. It is not too big, and people are friendly. I have never experienced nor know about any robbery or assaults in UTEP."

LOOKING FOR MORE?

Check out our full-length guide to this school at collegeprowler.com/university-of-texas----el-paso/.

University of the District of Columbia

4200 Connecticut Ave. NW; Washington, DC 20008
(202) 274-5012; www.udc.edu

THE BASICS:

Acceptance Rate: Open
Yield: 33%
Setting: Large city
Control: Public
Total Undergrads: 4,770
SAT Range: —
ACT Range: —

Student-Faculty Ratio: 13:1
Retention Rate: 57%
Graduation Rate: 8%
Tuition: $14,000
Room & Board: $13,200
Avg. Aid Package: $2,904
Students With Aid: 63%

This School Isn't Graded Yet!

College Prowler grades are calculated using tons of criteria, including survey responses that come from students at this school.

Unfortunately, we haven't gathered enough student surveys yet for this school to be able to calculate the grades for each section. Stay tuned to *CollegeProwler.com* for grade updates and more!

CP's Student Author On...
OVERALL EXPERIENCE

The teachers at UDC are wonderful for the most part, and the assistant professors and others who have been working and teaching for years are sincerely interested in seeing their students do well. The University of the District of Columbia may not be the most popular school in the district, but some of the professors here also teach at other great universities in D.C.

The University is the only public institute of higher education in Washington, D.C. This means it relies on district funding, and due to budget constraints, UDC doesn't offer some of the things that can be found at the local private universities. However, the University is undergoing construction projects and is growing, and tuition is a lot more affordable than the private institutions here. Overall, the price and location of UDC is wonderful and provides a great learning experience. As long as you stay aware of what and who is around you, your experience here should be good.

Students Speak Out On...
OVERALL EXPERIENCE

Q UDC: Best-Kept Secret

"UDC does not have a hot reputation, but it should. The law school is consistently ranked well, and the teaching staff is top-notch. MANY profS come from other area schools, like Georgetown, American University, Catholic University, George Washington University and Howard. The UDC campus is nothing to write home about (it has no dorms), but that is rapidly changing as the school re-vamps itself to compete with all the city schools."

BEST OF DISTRICT OF COLUMBIA

1. The school is changing for the better.
2. Focused students
3. Good, experienced teachers
4. Location of campus

Help to Succeed
The school has academic and career counseling available to help you when you need it.

WORST OF DISTRICT OF COLUMBIA

1. The high school mentality of some students who go to UDC

Not Everyone Graduates
8% of students do not complete their education or graduate with a degree.

Don't Move Off Campus
Average off-campus housing is a steep $11,100.

Student Body

African American:	72%	Male Undergrads:	41%
Asian American:	4%	Female Undergrads:	59%
Hispanic:	6%	Living On Campus:	0%
International:	0%	Living Off Campus:	100%
Native American:	0%	Male Athletes:	3%
White:	6%	Female Athletes:	4%
Unknown:	11%	Fraternity Members:	4%
From Out-of-State:	39%	Sorority Members:	6%

Frequently Compared Schools:
Hampton University
Howard University
Stony Brook University
University of Hartford

Students Speak Out On...
EVERYTHING!

ACADEMICS

School of Business Is Tough

"The School of Business courses are very tough. The Accounting professors will give you great CPA training."

Good, Not Amazing

"I came to UDC because it was a local school, and I wanted to remain part of the city. My professors so far have been decent, but I would only describe one of them as very good. The campus is small, but it is nice. The school's list of programs is growing."

ATHLETICS

Needs Improvement

"I believe that the most popular sport, or one I am interested in, would be basketball. I have worked during halftime at the games and most of the support comes from family members and friends. There really is no school spirit or interest in sports. There are other sports such as tennis, track and field, boys soccer, and girls volleyball."

Shouting: More Sports!!!!

"Athletics should be an important part of any school. Unfortunately, athletics does not play a very huge part in this school. There are very few sports teams and that needs to change soon."

CAMPUS DINING

Dining at the University of D.C

"Well, my dining experience has been very average at the campus dining hall. The food is okay, but it is very expense to eat at the dining hall. I can walk up the street to McDonald's and buy a value meal and still have money in my packet, but if I was to dine in the dining hall here at UDC, I will leave here penny-pinching."

CAMPUS HOUSING

Housing

"They just started offering a housing option, but it is limited to athletes or their "valuable" citizens. Even so, the housing isn't top-notch."

Its Not Too Bad

"it could be a lot better than it is. everything doesnt work like it should. tution is rising each year making college very expensive"

New

"I don't really know too much about the housing except the cost and location. This is the first semester that apartments are being provided to students who are not athletes, which is good. I do think the price is too expensive but the cost of living in DC is high, and I don't know how they look inside. The location of the dorms are convenient since they are right across the street."

GUYS & GIRLS

Lots of Variety

"There are girls from every part of the world."

Remnants of University Students

"Students at this overwhelmingly mediocre university are mostly DC public school students who, if you ask me, couldn't get into or didn't try to get into other schools. The school is cheap, and it feels cheap because of its makeup of students. A lot are just scraping by, and as a whole, make the school feel like a high school sometimes instead of an actual university."

HEALTH & SAFETY

It's a Good Community College

"UDC is a good community college but it is just for people who are trying to get their grades up to par or who don't have the money. That is its sole purpose,. If it offers other things, that is not what I am looking for. I would like to go to a four-year university."

LOOKING FOR MORE?
Check out our full-length guide to this school at collegeprowler.com/university-of-the-district-of-columbia/.

University of the Incarnate Word

4301 Broadway St.; San Antonio, TX 78209
(210) 829-6000; www.uiw.edu

THE BASICS:

Acceptance Rate: 96%
Yield: 38%
Setting: Large city
Control: Private Non-Profit
Total Undergrads: 5,464
SAT Range: 1380–1590*
ACT Range: 18–23

Student-Faculty Ratio: 14:1
Retention Rate: 67%
Graduation Rate: 42%
Tuition: $21,890
Room & Board: $9,220
Avg. Aid Package: $17,171
Students With Aid: 90%

* of 2400

Academics	C+	Greek Life	B
Athletics	C	Guys	B+
Campus Dining	B-	Health & Safety	A-
Campus Housing	B+	Local Atmosphere	A-
Campus Strictness	C-	Nightlife	B
Computers	C+	Off-Campus Dining	B
Diversity	B	Off-Campus Housing	C+
Drug Safety	B+	Parking	B-
Facilities	B	Transportation	B+
Girls	B	Weather	B+

CP's Student Author On...
OVERALL EXPERIENCE

The University of the Incarnate Word has so much to offer. From the academics and excellent professors to the life-long friendships, you will not look back and regret coming to UIW. Most of the students really enjoy their experience at UIW. The friendships formed here usually last through college and beyond. There are also more genuine friendships since UIW is a small school, and keeping in contact with fellow classmates is very easy because you see the same people almost daily. UIW is a very diverse school, so it is like a "small world." The memories formed at UIW are endless.

The education is top-of-the-line, as it thoroughly prepares each student to excel in his or her desired field of study. The smaller atmosphere allows for more personal attention for each student. The relationships between students and teachers is very strong, and professors know students by their names because of the low student-to-teacher ratio. Sure, you will hear complaints here and there, whether it be about residence life or the cafeteria food, but keep in mind that everyone has different tastes, and nothing is perfect.... For the rest of this editorial, visit collegeprowler.com.

Students Speak Out On...
OVERALL EXPERIENCE

Q Love everything

"I love it! And the things I want to change I'm working toward, so it's fun and I get to learn about what I want."

Q Excellent Staff & Programs

"The Adcap, (adult continuing education), program is outstanding for those of us picking it up again while working, and with family committments. Outstanding teaching and support staff, very relevant and intense courses. I love it!"

Q I Love It

"incarnate word is a small private university and what i like the most is that the student to teacher ratio is very small. you get to learn on a closer relationship with the teacher. BUT..IT IS EXPENSIVE"

Q My Experience

"my experience here at uiw has been good classes have been relevant to my field of study and teachers have been great. my only bad experience has been with my housing. i had a very bad roomate experience las ssemester thankfully it all cleared up this semester."

BEST OF INCARNATE WORD

1. Small campus
2. Low student-to-teacher ratio
3. Beautiful scenery
4. Diversity
5. Helpful faculty
6. Education
7. Availability of teachers

Highly Satisfied Students
90% of students surveyed would make the same school choice if they could do it all over again.

WORST OF INCARNATE WORD

1. Parking
2. Expensive dorms
3. Cafeteria food
4. Expensive bookstore
5. Really old school
6. Students who are too sheltered
7. Policies

Lowest Grades
Campus Strictness: C-
Athletics: C
Computers: C+

Frequently Compared Schools:

Texas State University - San Marcos
University of Texas at San Antonio
University of Texas at Tyler
University of Texas of the Permian Basin

Students Speak Out On...
EVERYTHING!

ACADEMICS

UIW has great teachers

"I love UIW. It has the two majors I want, music industry and religious studies, and tremendous teachers in both categories."

Computer Graphics Art 3D Animation

"I've been very satisfied that i'm entering a private college everyone is willing to help students with there needs."

Biology Major

"I've enjoyed attending UIW because everyone is helpful, the advisors and counselors stand by you and help you accomplish your semester goals. The professors are understanding and help you if you need tutoring."

ATHLETICS

New Football Team and Stadium Are Wonderful

"UIW recently started a football program and our new Benson Stadium is very nice. The training and workout facilities are up to date and also more user friendly. All of our football boys are looked up at on campus and even off campus. We are very proud of our new football team!"

Go Team!

"The University of the Incarnate Word has several altlhetic teams. So there is someting going on at any time of the year."

CAMPUS DINING

Yummy

"The University of The Incarnated word has a variety of places to eat such as, chick fa la and Java on the hill. These places are great for when you are in a hurry and want to grab your food on the go."

Dining

"The main dining hall Marian, has a buffet style food. This includes two hot meals, a grill, pizza, salads, and sandwiches. Hortencia's serves Chick-Fil-A daily along with fresh mad sandwiches, smoothies, and snacks. Finnegan's serves

Starbucks coffee and sweets. Java on the Hill serves hot sandwiches, pizza, burgers, and sandwiches."

CAMPUS HOUSING

Graduate Professors

"The staff and faculty are very professional and amicable."

Freshmen Dorms

"As a frieshmen I was afraid about meeting people. but thankfully freshmen dorms are right in the middle of main campus, so it makes it easy to socialize."

GUYS & GIRLS

We Have...

"A little bit of everything. We have the Greeks, the jocks, the stuck-up, the sweethearts, the lovers, the drama kids, the music kids and of course the religious kids!"

Diverse

"The university has a diverse group of people. There are all types of students, ranging from international to native Texans. All the students are interested in a multitude of things from our new football team to weekly Bible studies. We are an eclectic group and do many things to get help the community."

HEALTH & SAFETY

Health and Safety

"The safety on the campus is excellent. There campus police and I have yet to hear about any campus crimes. They have their own health services area and even provide their own insurance for the kids enrolled. I feel no threats when on this campus, everything seems safe. Even at the dorms they have strict rules that the residents must follow to ensure safety."

Great Campus

"The campus is very safe, people are always friendly, and I have never felt unsafe."

LOOKING FOR MORE?

Check out our full-length guide to this school at collegeprowler.com/university-of-the-incarnate-word/.

University of Utah

201 Presidents Circle; Salt Lake City, UT 84112
(801) 581-7200; www.utah.edu

THE BASICS:

Acceptance Rate: 80%	Student-Faculty Ratio: 15:1
Yield: 59%	Retention Rate: 85%
Setting: Mid-sized city	Graduation Rate: 51%
Control: Public	Tuition: $18,136
Total Undergrads: 22,149	Room & Board: $6,743
SAT Range: 1470–1860*	Avg. Aid Package: $7,719
ACT Range: 21–27	Students With Aid: 55%

* of 2400

Academics	B	Greek Life	B
Athletics	B	Guys	B+
Campus Dining	B	Health & Safety	B
Campus Housing	B-	Local Atmosphere	A-
Campus Strictness	B	Nightlife	B
Computers	A-	Off-Campus Dining	B-
Diversity	B-	Off-Campus Housing	B
Drug Safety	B-	Parking	C+
Facilities	B+	Transportation	A+
Girls	B	Weather	B-

CP's Student Author On...
OVERALL EXPERIENCE

The University of Utah is a campus of contrasts. On the one hand, it's cold, bureaucratic, and impersonal, but on the other hand, because it's so large, there's no shortage of opportunities in which to distinguish yourself, groups to join, or people to meet. On the one hand, it's a bleak commuter campus, but on the other hand, you have arguably the finest on-campus housing in the United States. You have the LDS Institute of Religion on the South Side of campus and Greek Row on the North Side of campus. You have a magnificent light rail system to get to school, and you have a harsh, brutal parking system if you drive.

The trick to having a rich experience at the U is to get involved. If you live off campus and only come to school to "go to school," then your good old college days will be very bland, indeed. There is no campus community; there simply isn't. But there are dozens and dozens of sub-communities on campus to find and become a part of. People who enjoy the U are those who take ownership of their education and college experience.... For the rest of this editorial, visit collegeprowler.com.

Students Speak Out On...
OVERALL EXPERIENCE

Q MOUNTAINS

"If you love the great outdoors, come to University of Utah. The snow is amazing, lots of great rock climbing spots, mountain biking, hikes, the possibilities are endless. If I could do it all over, I would definitely choose this school."

Q U of U Is Great

"Great school, great people, great sports, great community. Lots to do outside of school"

Q Very Good

"Campus is big, nice environment, some worn down building (but they are getting the renew)"

Q Housing

"I was able to find off-campus housing close to the university. It is great avoiding the mystery-roommate situation and having so many conveniences near by."

Q School Experience Is Great

"I like it a lot. It is awesome and the people are very cool. There are many things to do and many people to meet as well as school parties to go to."

BEST OF UTAH

1. Ample green space
2. The ASUU "hookup card"
3. B&D's dollar burger Tuesdays
4. The Daily Utah Chronicle
5. Easy access to the breathtaking Wasatch Mountains

Happy Students
85% of students return after their first year.

Knowledgeable Professors
85% of students surveyed rated the general knowledge of professors as above average.

WORST OF UTAH

1. Battles with the state legislature
2. Commuting around the non-stop nightmare of construction
3. Foreign teachers with poor English skills

Lowest Grades
Parking: C+
Off-Campus Dining: B-
Drug Safety: B-

Students Speak Out On...
EVERYTHING!

ACADEMICS

Great School

"I loved the University of Utah. It's a commuter school, so there isn't a huge campus life apart from the Greek scene, but I was there to study, not socialize. My teachers and fellow students are amazing, very intelligent and energetic. The political science department is incredible, especially the Hinckley Institute of Politics. Highly recommended."

Criminology Certificate Program Is Excellent

"The University of Utah offers a Criminology Certificate through their Sociology Department. I am interested in criminal behavior and finding out why some people go onto commit acts of violence and crime and why others, who may have the thought chose not behave as such. Is this a matter of free will, or are actions that go against societal norms based on innate human nature of violence, as depicted throughout history? I am also interested in the rehabilitation of low risk offenders."

ATHLETICS

Awesome football, basketball, soccer, and ski teams

"School spirit is nonexistent outside of the MUSS (Mighty Utah Student Section), but our athletics are amazing. We have world-class football, basketball, soccer, and ski teams, plus students get free tickets."

Go Utes!

"U of U football are THE BCS BUSTERS! Fans are awesome, tons of local support."

CAMPUS DINING

Large Variety

"for the most part food is pretty average as far as cost but if you are looking for variety you would be very satisfied"

A Variety of Foods

"The meals that are provided in the campus dining halls are both delicious and healthy. Furthermore, much variety exists on the menus, which will satisfy vegetarians and the pickiest of eaters."

CAMPUS HOUSING

Its a Must

"Living on campus at the University of Utah is a must! Literally! It is required that all freshman lives on campus in the provided dorms. Just like any other living quarters options, it can be as bad as you make it or as great as you make it! Its all about interaction, socializing, and engaging in the college life around you!"

Nice Location

"I like mostly the location of the campus, it's really a nice area. The only thing i would like to improve is the transportation from there to the city."

GUYS & GIRLS

My Experience

"The types of guys and girls at the University of Utah is diverse. A lot of the students are neatly-dressed. They are approachable if you ever have any questions while walking around campus."

Football Fans

"The Utah Utes football games have the loudest most supportive MUSS fan section! Super rowdy, fun, awesome people!"

HEALTH & SAFETY

I Feel Safe

"I have never felt unsafe at the U of U, but you never know when bad stuff can happen. Just like at any college, you want to be safe. I have never heard of anything bad happening at the U of U. But sometimes I am at the Campus late at night and when I go home I am careful to look and watch for any strange people. The U of U is safe overall. It is a large campus, but beautiful."

Great Campus

"I have nere felt unsafe here at college. The only time I have ever worried was walking through the graveyard. I wasn't fraid o students though, I was more afraid of zombies."

University of Vermont

85 S. Prospect St.; Burlington, VT 05405
(802) 656-3131; www.uvm.edu

THE BASICS:

Acceptance Rate: 71%	Student-Faculty Ratio: 17:1
Yield: 17%	Retention Rate: 85%
Setting: Small city	Graduation Rate: 71%
Control: Public	Tuition: $31,410
Total Undergrads: 11,382	Room & Board: $8,996
SAT Range: 1630–1920*	Avg. Aid Package: $15,878
ACT Range: 24–28	Students With Aid: 93%

of 2400

Academics	B+	Greek Life	B
Athletics	B-	Guys	A-
Campus Dining	B	Health & Safety	B+
Campus Housing	B	Local Atmosphere	B+
Campus Strictness	B	Nightlife	B+
Computers	B	Off-Campus Dining	A
Diversity	C	Off-Campus Housing	B+
Drug Safety	C-	Parking	B-
Facilities	B	Transportation	A+
Girls	A	Weather	C-

CP's Student Author On...
OVERALL EXPERIENCE

Students are in agreement that the University of Vermont is a remarkable place to go to school. The refreshing environment and lovely surroundings meld well with the progressive, laid-back city of Burlington. One particular area students wish to see change is an increase in the amount of racial diversity. Perhaps the coming years will bring a more diverse application pool, allowing students to learn in a varied and culturally aware environment. And while less consequential factors, such as parking or Greek life, were neither praised nor abhorred, the most important aspects of college—academics, atmosphere, and housing—consistently achieved superior rankings according to the students.

Compared with most other state universities, the University of Vermont offers a very competitive educational experience in an unbeatable setting. UVM is like an epicenter—it's within a day's drive of New York, Boston, the Atlantic Ocean, and Canada. The University of Vermont houses provocative and diverse thoughts, mixed with a dedicated student body and the additional flair of Burlington.... For the rest of this editorial, visit collegeprowler.com.

Students Speak Out On...
OVERALL EXPERIENCE

I Love UVM
"I absolutely love it here. The people are so laid back and everyone seems to have the same mindset- live up the college experience! Vermont is a very unique place. Even though I have lived in Vermont for my whole life, UVM feels like an entirely new world."

Long Winter but Beautiful Spring!
"What I like least about Vermont is the long gloomy dark winters. It's very hard to take the 10 minute walk to class in -10 degree weather. However, spring comes early in Burlington and most students can be found at North Beach on beautiful Lake Champlain right down the hill on warm April days."

Great
"I love going to school here, but the social life could use a revamping. I'm not into parties and that seems to be the main and only attraction here as far as social life goes. But other than that it's great!"

BEST OF VERMONT

1. The weather (If you are a skier or outdoors person)
2. Spectacular scenery
3. Laid-back people
4. Outstanding professors
5. Progressive student body
6. Safe and thriving city locale

Happy Students
85% of students return after their first year.

Proven Success
71% of students will complete their education and graduate with a degree.

WORST OF VERMONT

1. The weather (cold winters and unpredictability)
2. Parking (or lack thereof)
3. Strict policies
4. 6 a.m. registration
5. Few on-campus housing alternatives to dorm rooms

Expensive
Tuition is a steep $31,410, one of the most expensive rates in the country.

Expensive Dorms
Living on campus doesn't come cheap, with an average housing price tag of $5,964.

Frequently Compared Schools:

Boston University
Northeastern University
University of Massachusetts
University of New Hampshire

Students Speak Out On...
EVERYTHING!

ACADEMICS

Q UVM's Academics Are Underrated

"As a science major and member of UVM's Honors College, I have found many UVM courses to be academically stimulating. Most professors are truly passionate about the material they teach and are willing to share their wealth of knowledge with students. From chemistry to political science, UVM is host to some brilliant, experienced professors who are very well-regarded in their fields."

Q Accesible Profesors

"Most professors are easily accesible and are enthusiastic to help students if asked. There are big lecture classes, but there are also small classes as well."

ATHLETICS

Q Club Sports Is the Way to Go

"UVM is not known for its varsity athletics outside of ice hockey. Our school is a supporter of our men's hockey team, last year they competed in the frozen four. However, UVM does carry a lot of pride in their club sports. We have everything you could imagine from rugby (number 1 in the country), field hockey (number 6 in the nation) to hollahooping club and juggling club."

Q Sports Are Important

"Everyone in the school loves the sports teams, especially hockey and basketball. We have nice facilites available through out campus and the sports teams are treated very good."

CAMPUS DINING

Q Everything You Need

"places around campus are a little expensive, but there is every kind of food within a 10-minute radius, most of it is really good. i wouldn't go with a meal plan though because the school cafeterias are not great."

Q Food @ UVM

"Overall the food at UVM isn't bad, as long as you know where to look, and that you're willing to wait for good food to be prepared for you, so it's fresh and ready for you to eat. I believe there are some things that aren't always great here, but that's true for most big institutions. Again, being open minded, and willing to try new foods, and learning about local food places is always a must when you're at the university!"

CAMPUS HOUSING

Q Dorms

"Dorms aren't bad at all Redstone campus and athletic campus have the nicest dorms, can get over crowded but with the addition of new dorms to trinity campus the situation is better. Honors dorms are the best! Available to upper classmen and students involved with Green living and other programs."

Q Off-Campus Student!

"As an off-campus student and infrequent visitor to dorms, I've noticed that many of the outlying dorms lack many facilities, where as the more centrally located ones are well-equipped with fitness centers and places to eat."

GUYS & GIRLS

Q Steezy Snowboarders and Hippies

"UVM's proximity to some of the best skiing and snowboarding on the east coast, guarantees a huge population of cute snow/skate boarders and snowbunnies. Some girls ride hard some are there for the boys regardless everyone has a good time the Ski and Snowboard Club is the biggest club on campus offering free rides to the mountains and awesome weekend trips. Being in green Vermont also pulls the countries hippies in, dreads, longboards and yoga dominate."

HEALTH & SAFETY

Q Walking Alone at Night

"There are special blue lights positioned within visible range all over campus, so if you ever feel uncomfortable walking or there is an emergency you can press a button and police services will come within minutes."

LOOKING FOR MORE?

Check out our full-length guide to this school at collegeprowler.com/university-of-vermont/.

University of Virginia

1740 University Ave.; Charlottesville, VA 22904
(434) 924-0311; www.virginia.edu

THE BASICS:

Acceptance Rate: 32%
Yield: 48%
Setting: Suburban
Control: Public
Total Undergrads: 15,550
SAT Range: 1840–2150*
ACT Range: 27–32

Student-Faculty Ratio: 18:1
Retention Rate: 97%
Graduation Rate: 93%
Tuition: $31,872
Room & Board: $8,220
Avg. Aid Package: $18,564
Students With Aid: 55%

* of 2400

Academics	A-	Greek Life	B+
Athletics	A	Guys	A
Campus Dining	C+	Health & Safety	C+
Campus Housing	A-	Local Atmosphere	B
Campus Strictness	A-	Nightlife	A-
Computers	B	Off-Campus Dining	A
Diversity	B-	Off-Campus Housing	A-
Drug Safety	C	Parking	C+
Facilities	B+	Transportation	A-
Girls	A	Weather	B+

CP's Student Author On...
OVERALL EXPERIENCE

Most students talk about the wonderful experiences and positive feelings they associate with UVA. The University has some of the most devoted alumni in the country. Of course, there are those who wished they had gone somewhere else and those who were turned off by things such as the lack of diversity, the prominence of Greek life, student naïvety, or the pretentiousness that is, in fact, present on campus. Those who really like UVA appreciate its traditions, the friendly and outgoing atmosphere, the beautiful setting, and the outstanding academic environment. Students definitely have their share of rough, sad, or aggravating moments at UVA, but when all is said and done, many claim that they couldn't imagine being anywhere else.... For the rest of this editorial, visit collegeprowler.com.

Students Speak Out On...
OVERALL EXPERIENCE

Q Great Experience!!!!

"I love UVa. It's a different type of school than the rest. If you learn to balance academics and social life...im sure you will have a great Experience!"

Q Tradition and Uptight Students

"Uva is definitely a fantastic experience. The academics are rigorous but the social scene is great too. There are fraternities/sororities to join but don't have to dominate party life. Sports are an important part of life but not an obsessive cult. UVA manages to mix modern ingenuity along with a long lasting history of tradition. Modern facilities mixed with traditions revolving around Thomas Jefferson, our architecture, sports, etc."

Q UVA-An Unforgettable Experience

"As a prospective UVA student, I have become familiar with its ammenities, the people and the gorgeous weather. This is my ideal school because not only is the atmosphere just right, but I feel it compliments my individuality and warm and enthusiastic personality. UVA is the perfect fit for me."

BEST OF VIRGINIA

1. Beautiful surroundings!
2. Amazing professors and classes
3. Vibrant, outgoing people
4. Fun social scene
5. Excellent athletic facilities
6. Incredibly low in-state tuition

Happy Students
97% of students return after their first year.

Proven Success
93% of students will complete their education and graduate with a degree.

WORST OF VIRGINIA

1. The level of competition among students both in the classroom and in extracurriculars
2. The advising system, or lack thereof
3. Parking, or lack thereof
4. Diversity problems such as self-segregation

Expensive
Tuition is a steep $31,872, one of the most expensive rates in the country.

Student Body

African American:	8%	Male Undergrads:	44%
Asian American:	10%	Female Undergrads:	56%
Hispanic:	4%	Living On Campus:	43%
International:	5%	Living Off Campus:	57%
Native American:	0%	Male Athletes:	7%
White:	63%	Female Athletes:	5%
Unknown:	10%	Fraternity Members:	30%
From Out-of-State:	31%	Sorority Members:	30%

Frequently Compared Schools:

Duke University
University of North Carolina
University of Pennsylvania
Vanderbilt University

Students Speak Out On...
EVERYTHING!

ACADEMICS

Q Yes

"I love everything about it, albeit there were a couple T.A.s in introductory courses."

Q Rigorous Courses

"I came to the University of Virginia because overall education is rigorous. The courses are no joke. Professors take their job seriously, as well as the students. Everyone seems to want to do well, which helps everyone else strive to do their best."

ATHLETICS

Q Great Sports Programs

"The hype around our football and basketball teams overshadow the talent and successes of the other sports teams. We have Hoo Crew, which fosters school spirit and support (you get a free t-shirt). Games are always fun, whether we win or lose."

Q Fun Sports Experience

"Every sport, even ones you wouldn't expect, is excelling in a big way! The football team is the only exception, but games are still very fun to go to with friends (and free for students!). The "Hoo Crew" helps you get free student tickets for every sport. The AFC (Aquatic and fitness center) is a beautiful place to work out and very close to first year dorms."

CAMPUS DINING

Q UVA DINING

"UVA dining is excellent! There is a wide selection of food at every dining hall and the people working there are very nice. The food is great and the theme meals only make it better!!!"

Q I love my meal plan!

"UVa Dining offers 3 main dining halls and several on-grounds spots to grab a quick lunch, dinner, or snack. There are a variety of meal plans that allow every student to eat in a way that best meets their needs. Plus Dollars on most meal plans can be used at the smaller dining locations, such as the recently added Starbucks. Although, the prices are a bit higher.

I definitely eat healthier in the dining halls than I would be able to do on my own. The staff is great and always friendly!"

CAMPUS HOUSING

Q Gooch/ Dillard

"Upper-class Housing is very spacious. Suite style. 6 single bedrooms large common-room and bathroom. Individual rooms actually have a good amount of space and storage. Close to bus stops, the AFC and Scott Stadium. Right next to Runk and down the road from O'Hill. Not an anti-social dorm complex as everyone says. Area Council does alot to bring people out and together."

Q Kellogg Dorm

"Would get an A+ but it is a bit far away from everything. Facilities are great, and when the A/C is on it's awesome."

GUYS & GIRLS

Q Friendly

"Most of the students are very outgoing and have different groups. However, everyone gets along with the grade gets together as a whole."

Q Guys in Ties, Girls in Pearls

"A lot of people act like typical college students. There are a handful of "snobby" people, but there are lots more of really nice people. Almost everyone I've met at UVA has found people who share their interests and created a solid group of friends."

HEALTH & SAFETY

Q There's Danger?

"There's very little crime, except in recent news about that unfortunate girl. The grounds have blue lights all in seeing distance from eachother. There are police, and they care about your safety; they aren't there to bust you for alcohol, but rather help you get home with no questions asked. There's a Safe Ride program to get you home safely, and a taxi cab service that doesn't ask to be paid on the spot."

LOOKING FOR MORE?

Check out our full-length guide to this school at collegeprowler.com/university-of-virginia/.

University of Washington

1400 NE Campus Parkway; Seattle, WA 98195
(206) 543-2100; www.washington.edu

THE BASICS:

Acceptance Rate: 61%	Student-Faculty Ratio: 11:1
Yield: 45%	Retention Rate: 93%
Setting: Large city	Graduation Rate: 77%
Control: Public	Tuition: $24,367
Total Undergrads: 28,575	Room & Board: $8,949
SAT Range: 1630–1970*	Avg. Aid Package: $11,552
ACT Range: 24–29	Students With Aid: 57%

* of 2400

Academics	B	Greek Life	B-
Athletics	A	Guys	B
Campus Dining	B	Health & Safety	C
Campus Housing	B-	Local Atmosphere	A
Campus Strictness	B	Nightlife	A
Computers	B	Off-Campus Dining	A-
Diversity	B+	Off-Campus Housing	B
Drug Safety	C	Parking	C+
Facilities	B+	Transportation	B
Girls	B-	Weather	B-

CP's Student Author On...
OVERALL EXPERIENCE

Similar to the academic experience at the UW, the University is so huge that it's virtually impossible to predict what a student will think of the school. As the quotations attest, some people fall in love from day one and have to tear themselves away on graduation day, while others drag themselves through school as a chore and can't wait to get out into the post-college world, but it seems, like most things at this school, that it truly is what you make of it. Perhaps for a less socially-motivated person, UW isn't the ideal school. In a bigger environment, maybe it helps to be a little more outgoing—introduce yourself to people in class, meet some people at parties; you sort of have to put yourself out there in order to get anything back.

In all, if a student is determined to make his or her time at UW a positive social experience, it's definitely within the realm of possibilities to do so. There are so many groups to join, parties to go to, and people to meet that there's basically an endless list of social opportunities. There are always more people to meet, so if you don't want to get pigeonholed in a certain crowd, you can move on to a new one.... For the rest of this editorial, visit collegeprowler.com.

Students Speak Out On...
OVERALL EXPERIENCE

Q Love It.
"My Experience has been great since being here at school"

Q Active to an a!
"University of Washington is a school where you make of it what you want to make of it. There are thousands of opportunities, and if you access them, then the school is amazing. Absolutely, 100% pure awesomeness."

Q I Love It
"Regardless of the problems at UW, the atmosphere and classes are fantastic. I could rave for hours about it, and the party scene doesn't interfere with academics! I love it so much! Not to mention going to college in Seattle is like a dream!"

Q Its a Great Experience!
"I love the University of Washington! Its a great university and I enjoy going to school everyday and meeting new people all the time."

BEST OF WASHINGTON

1. The Quad on a spring day when the cherry trees are in bloom
2. The view of Mt. Rainier on clear days
3. The Husky Den
4. The IMA
5. Diverse course offerings

Happy Students
93% of students return after their first year.

Proven Success
77% of students will complete their education and graduate with a degree.

WORST OF WASHINGTON

1. Feeling lost in the crowd
2. Segregation between Greeks and non-Greeks
3. Parking
4. Rain (unless you like it)
5. Large class sizes
6. Professors with heavy accents

Don't Move Off Campus
Average off-campus housing is a steep $12,876.

Student Body

African American:	3%	Male Undergrads:	48%
Asian American:	25%	Female Undergrads:	52%
Hispanic:	5%	Living On Campus:	23%
International:	4%	Living Off Campus:	77%
Native American:	1%	Male Athletes:	4%
White:	50%	Female Athletes:	3%
Unknown:	11%	Fraternity Members:	2%
From Out-of-State:	18%	Sorority Members:	2%

Frequently Compared Schools:

University of California - Berkeley
University of Oregon
University of Southern California
University of Texas

Students Speak Out On...
EVERYTHING!

ACADEMICS

Interdisciplinary - Public Health

"Great mixture of social and hard sciences to build a strong understanding of health on a scale larger than clinical practice. Although an MPH is really required to work in the field, UW's undergraduate Public Health curriculum has a lot of direction for students headed towards medical and public health careers in the future. Lots of the curriculum comes from a large list of approved courses, allowing students to focus their degree to their particular interests within the field."

Cascadia CC

"Most of the teachers I've had were really great. I love that most of them have been to at least a couple other countries around the world and always have some cool things to share with the class. Even some of the online classes were pretty decent considering you have limited interaction with the rest of the people. The library is awesome. There are a bunch of computers to use and many study rooms, and the library staff is always ready and helpful. Food...eh."

ATHLETICS

School Spirit

"Atheletes get a lot of support from students and other people. They come dress up in school colors and sit in any type of weather. Seats are hard to get during the season."

School Spirit

"University of Washington has great school spirit no matter how bad our teams are doing."

CAMPUS DINING

Improving Campus

"gym, student center - state of art, aesthetics best in country, rest is above average, renovation/improvments occur when needed."

UW Campus Dining

"the dining options aren't huge but they provide options. food is generally good. sometimes try and be fancy and its not so good."

CAMPUS HOUSING

It's All About the Ave

"Everything you could ever want to eat is available on what we call "the ave," which to be perfectly honest is really just University Way. They have lots of different restaurant options including Thai, Korean, Japanese, Mexican, hamburgers, hotdogs, pizza, cafés, grills, pubs, and a deli! Close by there are more chain restaurants and a vegetarian spot as well. Even if you don't want to go to the ave for food, there is also a lot of good shopping!"

Get Past the Rumors

"The dorms at UW are very acceptable. Once you get settled in and used to everything it can be a very enjoyable time. Despite all the rumors of foot fungus in the showers and how dreadful a triple dorm can be everything turns out to be okay!!"

GUYS & GIRLS

A Melting Pot of Style

"The people in Seattle are colorful, daring, edgy, sporty, relaxed, unique, and individualistic. The University of Washington has people of all different walks of life that are all very accepting of one another. People create and eminate every kind of personality-they are true to themselves, whatever that may be. It is an incredibly diverse campus of people from all over the world which creates a culture that is very unique and educational."

Pretty Serious Students

"there is not like in high school or other colleges where students think more about personal life than school. Students tend to be very serious about school at school..."

HEALTH & SAFETY

Safety and Security

"University of Washington does a great job on safety and security of its' students. It has e-mail notification system, Night walkes, night taxi, great campus"

LOOKING FOR MORE?

Check out our full-length guide to this school at collegeprowler.com/university-of-washington/.

University of Western Ontario

1151 Richmond St.; London, ON
(519) 661-2111; www.uwo.ca

THE BASICS:

Acceptance Rate: 31%	Student-Faculty Ratio: —
Yield: —	Retention Rate: 91%
Setting: Suburban	Graduation Rate: —
Control: Public	Tuition: $14,100
Total Undergrads: 23,052	Room & Board: $9,645
SAT Range: —	Avg. Aid Package: —
ACT Range: —	Students With Aid: —

Academics	B	Greek Life	B-
Athletics	B	Guys	A+
Campus Dining	B+	Health & Safety	B
Campus Housing	B+	Local Atmosphere	B+
Campus Strictness	B	Nightlife	A
Computers	B	Off-Campus Dining	A
Diversity	C+	Off-Campus Housing	A+
Drug Safety	C+	Parking	B-
Facilities	B	Transportation	A-
Girls	A	Weather	B-

CP's Student Author On...
OVERALL EXPERIENCE

One thing is certain: Western students love their University. Known for its beautiful campus and steadfast school pride, Western offers an "all-American" experience in a Canadian school. The campus is large, but it's easy to see a familiar face wherever you go. London is a fantastic city for the University, and the students truly run the town. Over time, the city may seem small for the more cosmopolitan students, but Western's school spirit for Homecoming and other rowdy days is irreplaceable. Academically, Western is renowned for its role as a research university and subsequently for its reputable professors. The staff genuinely cares for students, which is unexpected for such a large school. For certain programs and courses, Western isn't difficult in terms of its academics; as long as you do your work, you will succeed.

In the Canadian workforce, the University of Western Ontario has a stellar reputation. However, aside from the Richard Ivey School of Business, companies in the States might not recognize the University.... For the rest of this editorial, visit collegeprowler.com.

Students Speak Out On...
OVERALL EXPERIENCE

Q I would definitely choose Western...
"I would definitely choose Western if I had to do it all over again. Western has a great Greek Scene and I'm so honored to be apart of it. The students here know how to party and have a good time but they also know when to study and buckle down, which makes it a really easy going atmosphere. I've met my best friends for life here and I owe it all to Western!"

Q Western is unreal...
"Western is unreal! It's definitely the best student experience at a research intensive university."

Q The school atmosphere is...
"The school atmosphere is incredible. It's a party school, but it's a smart party school. Be sure to balance it all. Also, purple looks good on everyone"

Q Western has a ton of spirit...
"Western has a ton of spirit and a great Science program. I love Western! Greek life is fun and everyone is really involved. No matter which activities you become involved in, Western offers students a great social life and the best student experience in Canada."

BEST OF WESTERN

1. Western is known to provide the best student experience in Canada among research-intensive universities.

Happy Students
91% of students return after their first year.

Knowledgeable Professors
92% of students surveyed rated the general knowledge of professors as above average.

WORST OF WESTERN

1. Food on campus is expensive, and it's easy to spend more than $7 on a meal.

2. Campus is especially cramped during exam periods, and it's difficult to claim a study spot.

Students Can't Wait to Get Out of Town
64% of students surveyed said that there's no way they would live here after graduation.

Student Body

African American:	—	Male Undergrads:	45%
Asian American:	—	Female Undergrads:	55%
Hispanic:	—	Living On Campus:	20%
International:	—	Living Off Campus:	80%
Native American:	—	Male Athletes:	—
White:	—	Female Athletes:	—
Unknown:	—	Fraternity Members:	—
From Out-of-State:	—	Sorority Members:	—

Frequently Compared Schools:

McGill University
University of British Columbia
University of Toronto
Yale University

Students Speak Out On... EVERYTHING!

ACADEMICS

English Literature at Western...

"English Literature at Western is a great program. The professors are intelligent, and there is a close interaction with faculty due to small class sizes. The workload is challenging, but worth it. It's a program that breeds intelligent, aware, and tolerant individuals. The professors are absolute gems."

I came to Western's Huron College...

"I came to Western's Huron College because I wanted smaller classes on a big campus for a greater student atmosphere. The profs at Huron (especially for philosophy) are engaging. They offer interesting courses that are a thrill to partake in. Smaller classes allow you to create a close connection with your professors and class peers."

ATHLETICS

The campus has a reaaally nice...

"The campus has a reaaally nice recreational center, that you get free gym membership to. It's definitely worth it -- there's so much there!"

I'm not involved in athletics, but...

"I'm not involved in athletics, but I get really excited about sporting events. Everyone at UWO has a very strong sense of pride for our athletic teams. Intramural sports are also incredibly popular for students."

CAMPUS DINING

The food is good with...

"The food is good with a lot of selection, but it is expensive."

The salad bars in residence are...

"The salad bars in residence are good for the most part. Food isn't cheap enough for a student budget, but there are lots of choices for variety. Western also boasts vegetarian options. Our campus-run restaurants (the Spoke and the Wave) are popular among students."

CAMPUS HOUSING

Some of the dorms...

"Some of the dorms on campus are quite old, but they are still well-maintained. The newer residences are well built and very clean. Living on campus during freshman year is quite expensive, but absolutely worth the cost."

There are nearly ten residences...

"There are nearly ten residences, all of which students who live in them fall in love. No matter which residence, you will meet friends, and learn to enjoy first year."

GUYS & GIRLS

Everyone is beautiful...

"Everyone is beautiful here. No word of a lie. Perfectly dressed, perfectly polished. A lot of hook ups..."

Western students are very...

"Western students are very fashionable and good looking. You will not find students on campus in pajama pants, and not very often do you even see students is sweatpants. There is a vibrant social social for Western students. It is a large school so it is easy to find a niche and go with it."

HEALTH & SAFETY

There has never been a...

"There has never been a moment where I have felt unsafe at Western. Although I wouldn't recommend this risk, I've left my laptop completely unattended and it has never been stolen."

I always feel safe...

"I always feel safe on campus. Foot Patrol services are offered for anyone needing an escort at night. There's surveillance in almost every computer lab, as well as security guards in buildings that are open overnight. Make sure not to leave any valuables unattended. There have been numerous cases of students having their laptops stolen, but this is 100% preventable if you are careful!"

LOOKING FOR MORE?

Check out our full-length guide to this school at collegeprowler.com/university-of-western-ontario/.

University of Wisconsin

500 Lincoln Drive; Madison, WI 53706
(608) 262-1234; www.wisc.edu

THE BASICS:

Acceptance Rate: 59%
Yield: 43%
Setting: Mid-sized city
Control: Public
Total Undergrads: 29,922
SAT Range: 1740–2070*
ACT Range: 26–30

Student-Faculty Ratio: 22:1
Retention Rate: 94%
Graduation Rate: 81%
Tuition: $23,059
Room & Board: $7,157
Avg. Aid Package: $9,948
Students With Aid: 68%

of 2400

Academics	B	Greek Life	B
Athletics	A	Guys	A
Campus Dining	A-	Health & Safety	B+
Campus Housing	B-	Local Atmosphere	A
Campus Strictness	B+	Nightlife	A
Computers	B+	Off-Campus Dining	A
Diversity	B-	Off-Campus Housing	B+
Drug Safety	C-	Parking	C+
Facilities	B+	Transportation	A-
Girls	B+	Weather	C

CP's Student Author On...
OVERALL EXPERIENCE

Students put a lot of time and energy into their undergraduate education. Luckily for those at UW, many feel it has been a positive experience. The college atmosphere, expansive campus, and intense academics are only some of the reasons students enjoy UW so much. Students feel they are able to form relationships with other students, as well as their professors. Furthermore, UW leaves them prepared for their future.

An individual's undergraduate experience is one of the most exciting times in their lives. It is often the first time they are away from parents and making serious decisions about their future. Therefore, it is essential to pick the best university to spend these busy years at. UW offers amazing academics, an inviting atmosphere, and energetic student body. Its location geographically makes it comfortable as well as gorgeous. The facilities are very accommodating, as is the transportation system. Though like any school, there are things that can be improved upon or changed. Parking remains a prevalent issue, for instance.... For the rest of this editorial, visit collegeprowler.com.

Students Speak Out On...
OVERALL EXPERIENCE

Q **The Best College Experience, Period.**
"There is absolutely no other place on earth that gives a college student the type of experience they receive at UW-Madison. Beautiful campus catered to student's needs, large city, campus life is abundant and lively. You have everything you need here, and every experience is positive. The academics are hard but great and worth it, and the student life is enviable and great."

Q **Madison Is Where It Is at!**
"I love it at Madison. Because campus is so big there are activities for everyone. Plus, the sporting events have an atmosphere like no other. When I was thinking about where to go I feared that Madison might be too much for me but I quickly found my place here and now I cannot imagine being happy anyplace else."

Q **UW Is Unique**
"My overall experience at UW Madison has been great. You actually learn a lot in school and there is always something to do. There are sporting events, shows, extracurricular activities and great entertainment venues."

BEST OF WISCONSIN

1. The number and variety of people
2. Expansive academic programs and resources
3. The atmosphere
4. Summertime and the lakes
5. Opportunities to socialize

Happy Students
94% of students return after their first year.

Proven Success
81% of students will complete their education and graduate with a degree.

WORST OF WISCONSIN

1. Walking up Bascom hill during the winter
2. The distance between some academic buildings
3. Bar crowds
4. Lack of parking
5. Winter
6. Dorm sizes

Lowest Grades
Drug Safety: C-
Weather: C
Parking: C+

Student Body

African American:	3%	Male Undergrads:	47%
Asian American:	5%	Female Undergrads:	53%
Hispanic:	3%	Living On Campus:	24%
International:	6%	Living Off Campus:	76%
Native American:	1%	Male Athletes:	3%
White:	82%	Female Athletes:	3%
Unknown:	0%	Fraternity Members:	9%
From Out-of-State:	39%	Sorority Members:	8%

Frequently Compared Schools:

Indiana University
University of Illinois
University of Michigan
University of Minnesota

Students Speak Out On... EVERYTHING!

ACADEMICS

Awesome Advisors!

"I came into this university with absolutely no idea what I wanted to major in - well, that's not exactly true, I just wanted to major in everything. The cross-college advising staff was excellent. They really helped me narrow down the fields that I wanted to go into while still managing to get general education credits out of the way. Now, with two declared majors, I feel ready to tackle my last two years here!"

PT Is Very Competitive

"Physical Therapy is a very competitive field. There are a lot of classes you must take, and it is all together a 7 year doctorate program (including undergraduate). The best thing about PT is you can have any undergraduate major you want as long as you have the requirements to get into the PT doctorate program. For example, I am planning on majoring in Spanish."

ATHLETICS

Wisconsin Athletics Are GREAT

"Everyone gets really into athletics at Madison, especially football. There are die-hard fans of every sport, but everyone gets excited about football. Game days are obvious because the entire city wears red, there's huge fan support and school spirit. And the teams are all usually pretty good too, so they're worth cheering for. There are also lots of inturmurals for people who want to play just for fun."

Awesome Badger Athletics

"As a big ten team, UW Madison has wonderful fans and an excellent football team. Go Badgers!"

CAMPUS DINING

Good Food, Lots of Choices

"Eat anytime, lots of places... good choices for fast eating."

Campus Dining

"State Street is arguably the best venue for anything and everything in Madison. It has the best restaurants around with the biggest variety you could imagine."

CAMPUS HOUSING

House, Apt, Dorms?

"While most incoming freshman stay in Dorms there are many more options. Just like many large schools off-campus housing is available. After being a year at home a person can really try to feel comfortable knowing where to live the following year."

So Many Choices

"I don't live on campus yet, but I move in in August. From choosing a dorm, I learned that there is the perfect dorm for everyone. From learning communities to smaller dorms, there's something for every single person."

GUYS & GIRLS

Girls Are Hot but...

"In the party scene there can be found a large amount of extremely attractive females but at the same time a large amount of these girls do not appear to be "dateable"."

Wide Variey

"On campus you can find any type of person you could imagine. There is no shortage of attractive guys and girls which is kind of amazing when you think of all the different ways that people are attracted to one another. Anyone can find someone here, be it the hot athlete or the cute geek next door, the high maintenance girls to the low-key hippies."

HEALTH & SAFETY

Campus Is Very Safe--Don't Need to Worry About Much

"It's very safe here; you can leave your stuff alone for a while and go do tasks, and then come back and your things will still be there."

Low Crime and Safe Proof

"When cruising through campus there is nothing to be afraid of. People are friendly and always willing to help. Last but not least, always fight for a parking spot!"

LOOKING FOR MORE?

Check out our full-length guide to this school at collegeprowler.com/university-of-wisconsin/.

University of Wisconsin - Stout

1 Clock Tower Plaza; Menomonie, WI 54751
(715) 232-1431; www.uwstout.edu

THE BASICS:

Acceptance Rate: 91%	**Student-Faculty Ratio:** 21:1
Yield: 52%	**Retention Rate:** 71%
Setting: Town	**Graduation Rate:** 53%
Control: Public	**Tuition:** $15,566
Total Undergrads: 7,931	**Room & Board:** $5,336
SAT Range: —	**Avg. Aid Package:** $9,291
ACT Range: 19–23	**Students With Aid:** 79%

Academics	B	Greek Life	C-
Athletics	B-	Guys	B
Campus Dining	B+	Health & Safety	B+
Campus Housing	B	Local Atmosphere	B-
Campus Strictness	B-	Nightlife	B
Computers	A	Off-Campus Dining	B+
Diversity	D-	Off-Campus Housing	A-
Drug Safety	B-	Parking	A-
Facilities	B	Transportation	C
Girls	B	Weather	C

CP's Student Author On...
OVERALL EXPERIENCE

When Stout students walk across the stage during their commencement ceremony, they are filled with emotions and memories, feelings of excitement about the future and sadness for a journey coming to an end. More than anything, UW-Stout provides opportunity and community. Once you set your roots at Stout, you'll never want to leave. The perfect size of the student body allows students to build a community of friends that last a lifetime. Community is built in many different ways and venues—the classroom between a class and the instructor, in the residence halls between residents, at an on-campus job between coworkers, and between teammates on an intramural team. These are just a few ways that students make connections with each other, as well as with people within the Menomonie community.

Stout provides a world of opportunity in and out of the classroom.... For the rest of this editorial, visit collegeprowler.com.

Students Speak Out On...
OVERALL EXPERIENCE

Q **Its a Great Place**
"i do love stout its a great campus and the academics are good and the teachers and administrative people are really cooperative and understanding. its just not the place for me."

Q "I really don't like it and I am going to a different University next fall. I wouldn't come here again."

Q "Favorite parts were hanging out with my friends and working at Stout Adventures. Being involved with campus organizations/clubs was well worth it."

Q "I like it a lot. The location is great with being only an hour away from the Twin Cities and 30 min form Eau Claire."

Q "I loved college. If I could go back, I would in a heartbeat. My favorite parts were spending time with friends on a Saturday or Sunday afternoon grilling out and having a good time."

Q "Your college years are what you make of it."

Q "Stout has exceeded all my expectations and then some."

BEST OF WISCONSIN STOUT

1. Individual attention received by students from professors and staff
2. Hands-on learning
3. 120-plus student organizations
4. Awesome employment rate
5. Blue Devil Productions

Genders Equally Represented
A male-to-female ratio of 49/51 means there's a pretty even balance of students on campus.

WORST OF WISCONSIN STOUT

1. Lake Menomin turns green.
2. Diversity
3. Nonexistent public transportation
4. Lack of quality shopping in town
5. Old grocery store eyesore

Not Much Diversity
One of the least racially diverse campuses—only 7% of students are minorities.

Student Body

African American:	1%	Male Undergrads:	52%
Asian American:	3%	Female Undergrads:	48%
Hispanic:	1%	Living On Campus:	40%
International:	1%	Living Off Campus:	60%
Native American:	1%	Male Athletes:	8%
White:	93%	Female Athletes:	6%
Unknown:	0%	Fraternity Members:	2%
From Out-of-State:	35%	Sorority Members:	3%

Frequently Compared Schools:

University of Minnesota
University of Wisconsin
University of Wisconsin - Eau Claire
Winona State University

Students Speak Out On... EVERYTHING!

ACADEMICS

Q Knowledgable Professors

"Almost every professor I have had, I have liked. In my major of Hotel Management, every professor has a tremendous amount of information and knowledge to share."

Q Long-Term Relationships

"I found that most of my professors are the type to carry me through not just for that semester, but for my college career. I can still get a hold of many of them if I need their assistance four semesters after I had them as a teacher."

ATHLETICS

Q Sports Are Nice, and Not the Main Focus on Campus, Which Is Great

"The sports at Stout aren't treated like the main focus of campus, which is really great for non-sports fans like myself, though there is enough on campus for sports fans to get involved."

Q Games

"There are always games to go to!"

CAMPUS DINING

Q No Problem

"I never had a problem with the food. There is such a variety of things to have you should always find something to eat. The dining halls are large and clean."

Q All You Can Eat

"There are tons of places to eat on campus- great sit down being the heritage cafe, the terrace being like a food court, and then the convenience of the Pawn- they deliver to dorm rooms! The commons was better than high school and gave you the freedom of tons of options for every meal- and best of all it is mostly all you can eat for cheap."

CAMPUS HOUSING

Q Missing On-Campus Living

"I loved living in the dorms. Each dorm offers a unique experience. It is a great way to meet people and to get involved. I now live off campus and I miss the way that I could walk out my door and run into people to hang out with without even trying."

Q Renting Supplies

"University Housing at Stout works really hard to provide as many services to their students as possible. Most of the Residence Halls offer very similar features and rooms. My favorite part of the res halls was the front desk features. Residents can check out a variety of items for free including hundreds and hundreds of DVD's, kitchen equipment, board games, recreational equipment and tools."

GUYS & GIRLS

Q Trend Setters

"Apparel Design students are always trying to set new trends even though it never catches on. Art students try to style their hair and clothes in a "different" way. Construction Management students all wear Carharts and beer/camo baseball caps. Business majors mostly wear jeans and t-shirts. Early Childhood Development majors look like moms and dads (clean cut). Everyone is beautiful on the inside. Small campus = community."

Q Something for Everbody

"College is college. You sleep, go to class and study, eat and party. There is going to be something for everybody. In my past, I came from a small town so most guys I saw were the worker type that I enjoy."

HEALTH & SAFETY

Q Safe Campus

"I personally do not think Stout has much crime going on. It's a pretty safe campus. Sometimes I have to walk by myself to the gym or a friend's dorm but I always feel safe. However you should always try and find someone to walk with, just in case."

LOOKING FOR MORE?

Check out our full-length guide to this school at collegeprowler.com/university-of-wisconsin----stout/.

UNLV

4505 S. Maryland Parkway; Las Vegas, NV 89154
(702) 895-3011; www.unlv.edu

THE BASICS:

Acceptance Rate: 78%
Yield: 53%
Setting: Mid-sized city
Control: Public
Total Undergrads: 22,708
SAT Range: 890–1140*
ACT Range: 19–24

Student-Faculty Ratio: 21:1
Retention Rate: 73%
Graduation Rate: 41%
Tuition: $17,437
Room & Board: $10,456
Avg. Aid Package: $6,037
Students With Aid: 82%

* of 1600

Academics	C+	Greek Life	B-
Athletics	C+	Guys	B-
Campus Dining	B	Health & Safety	B-
Campus Housing	B-	Local Atmosphere	B+
Campus Strictness	B+	Nightlife	A
Computers	B+	Off-Campus Dining	B+
Diversity	B+	Off-Campus Housing	B-
Drug Safety	B-	Parking	B-
Facilities	B+	Transportation	B-
Girls	B-	Weather	B+

CP's Student Author On...
OVERALL EXPERIENCE

UNLV is an up-and-coming school. In the past few years alone, the University has made great strides with its academics and facilities. The Boyd School of Law ranks high nationally, even though only having been in existence ten years. UNLV just opened its doors in Singapore where students from the William F. Harrah College of Hotel Administration can attend for a year of study abroad. In the Entertainment Capital of the World, UNLV offers the Entertainment Engineering and Design Program where disciplines in engineering and the fine arts are interwoven to help create the spectacular shows on the Strip. The College of Business is one of the 6 percent of business colleges in the world to be accredited by the Association of the Advance Collegiate Schools Business, representing the highest standard of achievement for business schools and management education. It's also one of the select few business schools to receive the dual accreditation for both the college and accounting program.... For the rest of this editorial, visit collegeprowler.com.

Students Speak Out On...
OVERALL EXPERIENCE

Q Very Helpful
"My first day on campus I did not know where I was going. I just walked into a random building and asked people who worked in that building if they knew where I should go and they made sure I knew how to get there."

Q I Love College
"I have learned to have a great and fulfilled academic and social life here at UNLV. It is a great school. You just have to have to apply yourself."

Q Student Union Is Amazing
"It's a great place to hang out and eat. Even though there are tons of people in the student union, it's always welcoming."

Q Not Yet Attended
"UNLV is located in a great city. There is always something to do here anytime of day."

BEST OF UNLV

1. Lied Library.
2. The variety and amount of activities available around campus.
3. The Recreation and Wellness Center.
4. Rebel Recycling, and the school's efforts to be eco-friendly.

Knowledgeable Professors
79% of students surveyed rated the general knowledge of professors as above average.

Low-Stress Course Load
50% of students surveyed rated the manageability of work as above average.

WORST OF UNLV

1. The Las Vegas heat.
2. The lack of parking, especially when the rodeo is in town.
3. The long walk between classes.
4. Camaraderie and school spirit is low.

Expensive Dorms
Living on campus doesn't come cheap, with an average housing price tag of $6,546.

Don't Move Off Campus
Average off-campus housing is a steep $10,100.

Student Body

African American:	8%	Male Undergrads:	44%
Asian American:	17%	Female Undergrads:	56%
Hispanic:	15%	Living On Campus:	10%
International:	4%	Living Off Campus:	90%
Native American:	1%	Male Athletes:	3%
White:	47%	Female Athletes:	3%
Unknown:	5%	Fraternity Members:	5%
From Out-of-State:	18%	Sorority Members:	3%

Frequently Compared Schools:
Arizona State University
San Diego State University
University of Arizona
University of Nevada - Reno

Students Speak Out On... EVERYTHING!

ACADEMICS

Academics Are Great
"I have enjoyed each of my teachers and classes. I have learned alot these past 2 years and look forward to the new semester starting."

Professors and Life
"At UNLV, I have been verry happy with the level of experience that each professor brings to the class. Each of my major teachers are or have been in the field to great lengths and bring a wealth of knowledge to the class room. Each teacher seems to offer real life experiences as lesson subjects involving the text and life. The connections they have are amazing and finding your groove is much easier with their advice."

Casino Gaming
"This major gives you the basic fundamentals of gaming management. This major is different and offers many employment oppertunities. I find this major particularly interesting because of their hands on approach by introducing you to the actual field. The proffesors are actual represebntatives of the gaming business and offers many internship oppertunities."

ATHLETICS

Over Hyped
"Most of the sports team are over hyped. Football tema sucks and volleyball is avergae. They only receive an A+ because of the great basketball team."

Sports
"Tailgates and football games are a ton of fun. Your team hasn't been the best but with a new coach the games should be good! Basketball is our sport and the whole school waits around for basketball season, you can just fell the love and support around school on game days."

CAMPUS DINING

Dining at UNLV Is Great!
"I love the dining at UNLV. The Dining Commons has quality food. he food court at the Student Union has variety, and the number of location off campus that give student discounts are phenomenal! I love it!"

Pretty Good
"There are plenty of options for students, no matter what you like to eat or what you are craving that day."

CAMPUS HOUSING

Good
"They recently buid a brand new building of new dorms"

Hello, Life
"great environment to meet people of different status"

GUYS & GIRLS

Fun
"The guys and girls at UNLV are all very friendly. They all are welcoming and at UNLV to get a good education."

Las Vegas Partyers
"Every one in Las Vegas pretty much knows everyone, it is a small city. But you will either be in the in crowed or not known at all. Girls are pretty snobby and guys always think they are hot stuff, but thats the Vegas life and i love it!"

HEALTH & SAFETY

Personal Safety
"As a student at the University of Nevada Las Vegas, I feel extremely safe. I constantly see security on bicycles roaming around to make sure students are safe. The campus always stays well lit and security is always watching."

Very Healthy and Very Safe
"Safety is very important to UNLV. There are police emergency buttons posted on all of the paths across campus. Health is also very important, there is a free clinic that is on campus, where I go often with health concerns. The recreation center at UNLV is also spectacular with many classes and incredible hours to offer complete health."

Urbana University

579 College Way; Urbana, OH 43078
(937) 484-1301; www.urbana.edu

THE BASICS:

Acceptance Rate: 74%
Yield: 43%
Setting: Town
Control: Private Non-Profit
Total Undergrads: 1,449
SAT Range: 820–1050*
ACT Range: 17–21

Student-Faculty Ratio: 18:1
Retention Rate: 44%
Graduation Rate: 27%
Tuition: $20,130
Room & Board: $7,990
Avg. Aid Package: $13,460
Students With Aid: 81%

* of 1600

This School Isn't Graded Yet!

College Prowler grades are calculated using tons of criteria, including survey responses that come from students at this school.

Unfortunately, we haven't gathered enough student surveys yet for this school to be able to calculate the grades for each section. Stay tuned to *CollegeProwler.com* for grade updates and more!

CP's Student Author On...
OVERALL EXPERIENCE

Most students have a great time at Urbana University and consider the people and professors here a part of their extended families. You might hear some people say "This place sucks!" every day, but they probably only feel that way because they're not active in anything. If you get involved in clubs and other organizations on campus, you'll never be bored. You get out of it what you put into it, and that's true anywhere. Whine all you want about how there's nothing to do, but until you get out of your room or your select clique of friends and make an effort, you won't be having any fun.

At larger state schools, you could find yourself feeling like more of a number instead of a person as you sit in giant lectures, whereas at UU, your largest class will probably have about 25 people. You might even end up in a class with fewer than 10 students! The people and the professors really want you to succeed, and they care about you, and that's what helps to set Urbana apart from a lot of other universities and makes it a great choice.

Students Speak Out On...
OVERALL EXPERIENCE

Q Fun, Exciting and Enjoyable

"there are plenty of things to do on campus. every week there seems to be something new to do. events are exciting to participate in which o get to meet new people and get to know them."

Q UU Was Home!

"I really enjoyed my time at the UU. I got a decent education, made some life-long friends, and learned a great deal about myself. The classes are not too academically challenging, but I think that what you bring to the classroom, in terms of effort and preparation, you will get out of the classroom! I can also say that I really enjoyed the faculty at UU, and consider a couple of them friends since my graduation."

Q It's a Nice College!

"Urbana is a great small town college. It is a lot like high school where everyone knows everybody and everybody's busniess, but it is really friendly. It is a great place to make lasting friendships and in my 5 years there I have not regreted my decision to obtain my degree here!"

BEST OF URBANA

1. All the activities and chances to win free stuff and cash!
2. A chance to continue with athletics
3. The opportunity to continue playing a musical instrument without having to major in music

Help to Succeed
The school has academic and career counseling available to help you when you need it.

WORST OF URBANA

1. The facilities aren't as up-to-date as they probably should be.
2. If you're from a big town and like having that kind of environment, the smallness of Urbana can be painful.

Not Everyone Graduates
27% of students do not complete their education or graduate with a degree.

Students Speak Out On...
EVERYTHING!

ACADEMICS

Great
"Professors are good about helping you out. They challange you but at the same help students to understand the material at hand. They try not to leave someone behind"

Academic programs are good
"The academic programs are good. The social seen is whatever the studetns decide to do. The student activities comittee brings in acts but not too many people attend ased on the demographics of the campus. The dorms are decent and the food is improving."

ATHLETICS

Athletics
"Athletics is a very important part of Urbana University. Most students attend sporting events and the school spirit is good. The athletic facility (the gym) is horrible. It is not a division 2 gym and should be updated."

School Spirit
"Athletes and teachers get excited about althetics, but those of us who don't participate don't even know where to get the game schedules. It is hard to cheer on your team when you don't know when or where to do it."

CAMPUS DINING

Good
"Hard for me to rate, i eat everything in front of me"

The Commons
"The amount we pay for a meal doesn't come close to the quality of the food we receive. First, we only have one dining hall with horrible hours, I always seem to be missing a meal. The variety is very limited I seem to be choosing between the same selection everyday. We have the White Family Grill which has great food, but it is rarely ever open on the weekends."

CAMPUS HOUSING

Dorms are basic
"The dorms at UU are basic. They don't have anything really special about them. Hazard and Sycamore aren't great to live in but McConnell is nice."

It All Depends on Where You're at
"At this point I've lived in both the Freshman men's dorm and the upperclassmen dorm. The Freshman guy's dorm itself isn't too bad, although you will be surrounded by nothing but Freshman guys, so expect it to be loud and messy. The upperclassmen's dorm is much quieter for the most part, and is also newer, so I personally enjoy it more. The only problem is that the showers aren't made for tall people, so if you're 6'6" or taller, be prepared to git your head a lot in there."

GUYS & GIRLS

Guys and Girls
"Urbana as a whole is kinda of like a salad bowl. All three types of living conditions can be observed at Urbana. We have a multitude of Rural students because we are based in Urbana. Overall, our closer suburb students come from around Springfield, Hilliard, and Grove City areas. Lastly, there are a ton of students from the urban areas such as Columbus, Toledo, and Cleveland. This can all be attributed to the growing athletic program at Urbana."

HEALTH & SAFETY

There Is Very Little to Worry About
"In my time here, there haven't been any fights or riots or anything. Campus safety is usually on the ball, and the only thing we really have a problem with it theft. All the recent incidents have taken place in the Freshman guy's dorm. I personally had a text book stolen, so as long as you and your roommate keep your door locked you shouldn't have a problem."

Ursinus College

601 E. Main St.; Collegeville, PA 19426
(610) 409-3000; www.ursinus.edu

THE BASICS:

Acceptance Rate: 57%
Yield: 15%
Setting: Suburban
Control: Private Non-Profit
Total Undergrads: 1,742
SAT Range: 1700–2010*
ACT Range: 24–29

Student-Faculty Ratio: 12:1
Retention Rate: 89%
Graduation Rate: 76%
Tuition: $38,670
Room & Board: $9,250
Avg. Aid Package: $23,300
Students With Aid: 90%

* of 2400

Academics	B+	Greek Life	A
Athletics	B-	Guys	B+
Campus Dining	C+	Health & Safety	B
Campus Housing	B	Local Atmosphere	B-
Campus Strictness	B+	Nightlife	B
Computers	A-	Off-Campus Dining	B
Diversity	C	Off-Campus Housing	D-
Drug Safety	B	Parking	B
Facilities	B+	Transportation	B-
Girls	B+	Weather	B-

CP's Student Author On...
OVERALL EXPERIENCE

Students love this school, despite its drawbacks. It is not big or in a nice cultural area, the town offers little to do, and the food on campus definitely could use improvement. But Ursinus' strength lies in its excellent academic program, and the students and professors are a tight-knit group. There are no graduate students that teach classes here. Instead, almost all courses are taught by someone with a doctorate or the highest degree in their field. The professors have a passion for what they teach, and this bleeds into the passion students get when they learn new material. Of course, this doesn't mean that the professors are perfect. Some hold themselves in very high regard because of their degree, others forget that students aren't quite at their level, and several assign insane amounts of work with brutal deadlines. But, that's college—students are forced to manage their time and push themselves academically to new levels, and professors do their best to ensure that students successfully make the leap from high school to college.

The town of Collegeville is picturesque in parts, but it doesn't have much for college students to do.... For the rest of this editorial, visit collegeprowler.com.

Students Speak Out On...
OVERALL EXPERIENCE

Q Best Decision I Ever Made

"Choosing to attend Ursinus was the best decision I ever made. I love the faculty, students, and academic opportunities at this school."

Q Small Schools for the WIN

"I've always been in big schools, so I found Ursinus to be refreshing because of its size. The quality of the education and the quality of the faculty is certainly top notch, at least they are are the professors in my field. I love the small class room settings and I love the intimacy between professor and students when it comes down to teaching and understanding materials and even down to the interaction."

Q "I've had an excellent experience. I have taken classes elsewhere over the summer and attended conferences at other schools, and I am very happy with my decision to come here."

BEST OF URSINUS

1. Free laptops
2. Wireless Internet
3. Jazzman's
4. Awesome professors
5. Campus scenery
6. Study abroad program
7. Women's rugby

Happy Students
89% of students return after their first year.

Proven Success
76% of students will complete their education and graduate with a degree.

WORST OF URSINUS

1. Campus food
2. Bias toward the sciences
3. Lack of things to do in Collegeville
4. Certain dorms aren't great
5. Sometimes students stay in their dorm rooms too long

Expensive
Tuition is a steep $38,670, one of the most expensive rates in the country.

Student Body

African American:	6%	Male Undergrads:	45%
Asian American:	4%	Female Undergrads:	55%
Hispanic:	3%	Living On Campus:	95%
International:	1%	Living Off Campus:	5%
Native American:	0%	Male Athletes:	50%
White:	72%	Female Athletes:	29%
Unknown:	14%	Fraternity Members:	18%
From Out-of-State:	55%	Sorority Members:	28%

Frequently Compared Schools:

Dickinson College
Franklin & Marshall College
Muhlenberg College
Villanova University

Students Speak Out On...
EVERYTHING!

ACADEMICS

Ursinus Academic Pride

"The best program offered here is the biology/pre-med program. My school is excellent in the sciences, although it is a liberal arts school. The professors all have their doctorates or higher, and are highly qualified in their fields."

"The faculty and staff at Ursinus College are, for the most part, extremely friendly and helpful. This is largely due to the intimate atmosphere and small student-to-faculty ratio, both of which help contribute to a sense of being part of a community."

"The teachers are so much more than teachers—they are mentors. I respect and look up to them. They always invite students into their offices for extra help or just to chat, and they even invite you to their homes for meals."

ATHLETICS

UC Sports

"Sports at Ursinus receive a pretty good following because you usually know at least one person on the team. The facilities are really nice and are never limited to just athletes. We are D3, so academics always come first. We aren't always the best at sports, but we try hard."

"Ursinus is a very involved campus, and there are loads of student athletes here. Students are always offering amazing support by watching important games, matches, and meets."

"Some varsity sports, such as basketball, are big, but IM sports are huge—many people play."

CAMPUS DINING

Campus Dining

"Although campus dining at Ursinus has improved significantly over the past couple of years, there is still not enough variety of healthy food options."

"The food is still cafeteria food, so it is nothing spectacular. The upside is that they try to offer a large variety of food so that you will hopefully find at least one thing you'd enjoy eating."

CAMPUS HOUSING

Campus Housing Is Decent

"Fortunately, there are plenty of housing options at Ursinus, but not all students have access to the finest houses or dormitories."

"Any college kid will complain about the dorms. However, compared to other schools, I'd say we have great ones. The fact that more than 90 percent of students live on campus says that the dorms must be fine."

GUYS & GIRLS

General Student Body

"The girls and guys at this school are very wealthy. Everyone is very nice and seems to take very good care of themselves. I would say that people are not snobby at all. The students are very open when getting to know new students."

"The boys are pigs, and the girls are drunken idiots. Welcome to college."

HEALTH & SAFETY

What You See Is What You Get

"Since Ursinus is such a small school, you can't really expect much from the safety office there. Though I do appreciate that the office is open 24 hours a day, seven days a week, I really don't see officers walking around to make sure students are safe that often, unless you live in one of the big dorms. However, I have never had an issue with feeling unsafe on campus."

"It is a very safe campus. If you don't feel safe walking at night, a campus safety officer will give you a ride."

LOOKING FOR MORE?

Check out our full-length guide to this school at collegeprowler.com/ursinus-college/.

Valparaiso University

1700 Chapel Dr.; Valparaiso, IN 46383
(219) 464-5000; www.valpo.edu

THE BASICS:

Acceptance Rate: 91%	**Student-Faculty Ratio:** 14:1
Yield: 25%	**Retention Rate:** 83%
Setting: Suburban	**Graduation Rate:** 75%
Control: Private Non-Profit	**Tuition:** $28,320
Total Undergrads: 2,888	**Room & Board:** $7,960
SAT Range: 1460–1860*	**Avg. Aid Package:** $24,061
ACT Range: 22–29	**Students With Aid:** 99%

* of 2400

Academics	B-	Greek Life	B
Athletics	C+	Guys	B
Campus Dining	B	Health & Safety	B
Campus Housing	C+	Local Atmosphere	C
Campus Strictness	C-	Nightlife	B
Computers	B	Off-Campus Dining	B-
Diversity	C	Off-Campus Housing	B
Drug Safety	C+	Parking	B+
Facilities	B	Transportation	B-
Girls	C+	Weather	C

CP's Student Author On...
OVERALL EXPERIENCE

When trying to determine the best part about their VU experience, most students recount the great friends and the encouraging atmosphere the professors work hard to create. A great advantage to the students at Valpo is the willingness of professors to speak with you, even if you aren't in their class or even their department. If a change of majors might sound good, any professor from any department is willing to take time out of his/her schedule and talk about the department and its programs. The education and chances to learn from professors, who are there to teach first and research/publish second, is by far the best aspect of Valpo. It feels like a lot of work at the beginning because the classes are designed to make thought and discussion happen on a daily basis, but the work definitely pays off at graduation when you realize how much you've learned.

Students consistently comment that they have left Valpo with lasting friendships and a deep appreciation for learning. Valpo is a one-of-a-kind place that just seems to draw you in.... For the rest of this editorial, visit collegeprowler.com.

Students Speak Out On...
OVERALL EXPERIENCE

Q Valparaiso University Is a Great School!

"Between the variety of majors, clubs, religious life, and academic opportunities, Valpo is great. Even though it is small, it has big opportunities. The academic programs at Valpo are generally highly regarded, and many Valpo grads go on to be very successful in life. Although it is affiliated with Lutheranism, you do not have to be Lutheran or Christian at all to enjoy your experience at Valpo. The diversity of people is also great as Valpo attracts students from all over the world."

Q Go VU!

"I am so glad I came to Valpo. I have found some of the best friends in the world, and the professors really care about students. If you are committed to working (and playing) hard, it will totally pay off in the end."

BEST OF VALPARAISO

1. Basketball
2. Free movies from Union Board
3. On-campus concerts
4. The library
5. Awesome academic programs
6. Great local restaurants

Happy Students
83% of students return after their first year.

Proven Success
75% of students will complete their education and graduate with a degree.

WORST OF VALPARAISO

1. Snow over two feet deep in the winter
2. Community bathrooms
3. VUPD
4. Rain and clouds—a lot of the time
5. Dining hall food

Expensive
Tuition is a steep $28,320, one of the most expensive rates in the country.

Student Body

African American:	5%	Male Undergrads:	47%
Asian American:	2%	Female Undergrads:	53%
Hispanic:	4%	Living On Campus:	66%
International:	4%	Living Off Campus:	32%
Native American:	1%	Male Athletes:	21%
White:	81%	Female Athletes:	10%
Unknown:	4%	Fraternity Members:	24%
From Out-of-State:	64%	Sorority Members:	20%

Frequently Compared Schools:

Loyola University Chicago
Northwestern University
Purdue University
Wheaton College - Illinois

Students Speak Out On... EVERYTHING!

ACADEMICS

Political Science Opportunities Readily Available

"Our political science department is diverse and has a number of different fields to go into. We have a study abroad opportunity in which you can go to the American University in Washington D.C. We also have internship opportunities in D.C. through the Lutheran Consortium Program."

Extra Help - Willing to Work With You

"One thing I found out about Valparaiso is all the professors are more than willing to work with you to give you extra help. They also are extremely understanding of your busy lives and if you need it they are usually willing to give you an extension on a project. I've found most of my professors to be personable, and all around fun to talk to!"

ATHLETICS

A First Year

"This year Valparaiso started a women's bowling team. With it only being their first year, they are already ranked 10th in the nation according to the NCAA. The girls are very hard-working and practice 3 days a week, working out everyday. The team has high hopes for next year and plan on attending the NCAA national championships."

VU BBALL

"Basketball is really the only big sport here. Volleyball is pretty popular as well. Football is a complete joke; the whole team is still cocky even though they've lost 20+games in a row. The soccer teams are usually fairly good and their games can be fun to attend. Basketball games versus big schools like Purdue, ND, Kansas, MSU, and the all-too-famous Butler are exciting and fun."

CAMPUS DINING

Adult Scholar

"As an adult scholar I don't get to utilize dining services too much. However the new Union has is the main gathering place for meals. Besides the beauty of this new building thge menus are pretty good offering brick oven pizza, a fresh deli sandwich section, a hot meal section topped off with a great salad and desert bar. There are great salads and sandwiches pre-packed along with a great variety of fresh fruit, soy products and soda"

Meal Options on Campus in Two Places

"There's only two main places to grab food on campus, but they do have a variety of options. There's an executive chef now that makes something new every day... although the schedule does rotate. Every once in a while there will be a day dedicated to a food like corn and everything will have it in it. There are no fast food choices or highly known brand names on campus."

CAMPUS HOUSING

Campus Housing

"The housing at Valpo is amazing. The rooms are spacious and classy."

Freshman Dorms Are Fun, but Upperclassmen Dorms Are Quiet

"Freshman dorms do not have air conditioning, and the furniture is stationary. The rooms are a little on the small side. Guild/Memorial is my top pick. The rooms are air conditioned with a thermostat, all the furniture is movable, good sized rooms, and its quite. All dorms on campus have sinks in them, except for in warrenberg."

GUYS & GIRLS

Good, Everyone Is Friendly

"I really like the people at Valpo. There's a general good quality to the student population. The small school atmosphere allows you to be friends with a good portion of the school, if you be social and go to parties and stuff."

HEALTH & SAFETY

Campus Is Very Safe

"Crime is very low on campus. One rarely hears of any sort of crime. Cops have a strong presence in and around campus. They are on constant patrol."

LOOKING FOR MORE?

Check out our full-length guide to this school at collegeprowler.com/valparaiso-university/.

Vanderbilt University

2101 West End Ave.; Nashville, TN 37240
(615) 322-7311; www.vanderbilt.edu

THE BASICS:

Acceptance Rate: 20%
Yield: 41%
Setting: Large city
Control: Private Non-Profit
Total Undergrads: 6,794
SAT Range: 2010–2270*
ACT Range: 30–34

Student-Faculty Ratio: 8:1
Retention Rate: 96%
Graduation Rate: 89%
Tuition: $38,578
Room & Board: $12,650
Avg. Aid Package: $37,553
Students With Aid: 62%

* of 2400

Academics	A	Greek Life	A+
Athletics	A-	Guys	A
Campus Dining	B	Health & Safety	B+
Campus Housing	B	Local Atmosphere	A-
Campus Strictness	A-	Nightlife	A-
Computers	A	Off-Campus Dining	A-
Diversity	B-	Off-Campus Housing	B
Drug Safety	C-	Parking	C+
Facilities	B	Transportation	B
Girls	A+	Weather	B

CP's Student Author On...
OVERALL EXPERIENCE

Any student beginning a college career will pass through the phase of questioning his or her decision. For Vanderbilt students, this phase is a short one. The beauty and excitement of campus quickly pushes away any negative thoughts. Southern hospitality is alive and strong around Vanderbilt, and for those out-of-towners, it's usually a welcome surprise. Taking the time to meet new people, whether they are Southern natives or people from across the country, will make the transition from high school to college a lot smoother. Finding your niche at any college is the most important thing to having a successful four years. Vanderbilt is big enough to accommodate almost anyone's desires and small enough to make this campus feel like home for the years you spend here.

While Vanderbilt has a lot of positive qualities, it isn't the best choice for everyone. Choosing Vanderbilt means choosing to be in a situation where name-brand clothes and high-end cars have a certain amount of importance.... For the rest of this editorial, visit collegeprowler.com.

Students Speak Out On...
OVERALL EXPERIENCE

Q Fantastic

"You have to make sure to do your work—going to class helps—but it would be a crime if you didn't party and experience all the great things that Vanderbilt offers every day. I've been five feet from the stage at the Jay-Z concert, which I paid $40 for, but I've also been just as content at a frat party where they bring in bands, as well. The school is bustling with activity. Balance is the word that you must remember, though."

Q Vandy Is a Great Place to Go to School

"Greek life dominates the social structure, and in general, the students are pretty homogenous. The culture is snobby and immature at times but once you get used to it its not bad."

Q "Even though a few friends are like family to me now, I think I would've enjoyed my college years more if I had transferred that first year or taken a more active interest in my college search. I needed somewhere more liberal, less preppy, and less Greek. However, I excelled in my classes and graduated with honors, and even spent time abroad, so maybe it all worked out in the end."

BEST OF VANDERBILT

1. Strong academics
2. Beautiful campus
3. Urban environment
4. Party scene
5. Southern culture
6. Excellent faculty
7. Big research university with a small-school feel

Happy Students
96% of students return after their first year.

Commitment to Teaching
There are 8 students for every member of faculty on campus.

WORST OF VANDERBILT

1. Upperclassmen housing
2. Traffic and parking
3. Lack of diversity (economic, racial, and social)
4. Domination of Greek life
5. Expensive

Expensive
Tuition is a steep $38,578, one of the most expensive rates in the country.

Expensive Dorms
Living on campus doesn't come cheap, with an average housing price tag of $8,200.

Student Body

African American:	9%	Male Undergrads:	48%
Asian American:	7%	Female Undergrads:	52%
Hispanic:	6%	Living On Campus:	90%
International:	3%	Living Off Campus:	11%
Native American:	0%	Male Athletes:	6%
White:	59%	Female Athletes:	4%
Unknown:	16%	Fraternity Members:	35%
From Out-of-State:	87%	Sorority Members:	50%

Frequently Compared Schools:
Duke University
University of Pennsylvania
University of Virginia
Wake Forest University

Students Speak Out On... EVERYTHING!

ACADEMICS

Professors

"Students will definitely tell you it depends on your major but these professors are some of the best in their field for a reason. Intelligent, challenging, and most importantly to me, helpful and personable. Most of my classes, I actually enjoy learning and professors emphasize learning over grades."

Great Professors

"Great professors; challenging academics; opportunities for out-of-class intellectual engagement. Workload depends on your field of study, but even the pre-med students are active on campus."

ATHLETICS

Vanderbilt Athletics

"Hmm... we are in the SEC which is a pretty competitive conference, but Vandy athletics go from mediocre to stellar depending on the sport. Football: mediocre, but school spirit makes the games a blast with tailgates, girls in sundresses and boys in khakis and button downs. Then we have Memorial Madness with our Commodore basketball which is amazing! It really just depends, but lots of school spirit regardless."

It's Great to Watch Other Good Teams

"Vandy is in the SEC, which means we get to watch really good teams play, just rarely is Vandy that "good team." Men's football and basketball programs are consistently promising, then largely disappointing. But hey, if you're into Women's Bowling, then Vandy may be the place for you. Students love their Commodores, but when push comes to shove, school spirit is seemingly lacking."

CAMPUS DINING

Good, Not Great

"The food on campus is decent, but the first year students are spoiled. They get the best dining center, etc. On main campus, it can be really crowded at meal times and can cause long waits. Vandy takes initiatives to give the students off-campus options though, which is helpful."

Good....If Open

"The food isn't bad, especially compared to the food at my friends' schools. However, a lot of places aren't open on campus for a large percentage of the time, which is rough when you're hungry past, say, 7:30 at night, or at all on the weekends."

CAMPUS HOUSING

Living on the Commons

"The dorms where most sophomores get stuck are all singles, small, and in an awful location. However, the freshman, who all live on the commons, have excellent dorms with their own dining hall and workout facility."

Commons

"Freshmen... welcome to Hogwarts! You will be pampered living on the Commons, getting to your classmates as you work, study, sleep, eat, and party together for a fantastic year on an eco-friendly and glitteringly green campus."

GUYS & GIRLS

Southern Blond Girls

"A bit homogeneous, but there are pretty attractive girls all around campus. Better than most other schools I have been to."

Girls a Little Hotter Than They Think

"Sure the girls at Vanderbilt are hot. But in their minds they are all Jessica Simpson. Guys are a mix of a majority of southern boys and a minority of northern city boys."

HEALTH & SAFETY

Vanderbilt Safety

"There are many services available to protect student safety and welfare on campus, such as VUPD, Vandy Vans for nighttime cross-campus travel, blue emergency lights, and much more. Even Greek row is monitored by campus police during parties and they are always ready to help anyone. I always feel safe on campus!"

LOOKING FOR MORE?
Check out our full-length guide to this school at collegeprowler.com/vanderbilt-university/.

Vassar College

124 Raymond Ave.; Poughkeepsie, NY 12604
(845) 437-7300; www.vassar.edu

THE BASICS:

Acceptance Rate: 24%
Yield: 36%
Setting: Small city
Control: Private Non-Profit
Total Undergrads: 2,500
SAT Range: 1960–2220*
ACT Range: 29–33

Student-Faculty Ratio: 8:1
Retention Rate: 96%
Graduation Rate: 92%
Tuition: $42,560
Room & Board: $10,080
Avg. Aid Package: $25,222
Students With Aid: 70%

* of 2400

Academics	A	Greek Life	N/A
Athletics	C+	Guys	B
Campus Dining	C+	Health & Safety	B+
Campus Housing	A-	Local Atmosphere	B-
Campus Strictness	A-	Nightlife	C-
Computers	A-	Off-Campus Dining	B-
Diversity	B-	Off-Campus Housing	D
Drug Safety	C-	Parking	B-
Facilities	A-	Transportation	C-
Girls	B+	Weather	C-

CP's Student Author On...
OVERALL EXPERIENCE

Perhaps it's all the marijuana on campus, but Vassar students, for the most part, seem happy. As a matter of fact, Vassar students were ranked the second happiest student body in the country in 2002. And what's not to be happy about? Vassar students are spoiled with brilliant professors who spend most waking hours teaching and mentoring their students. Among breathtaking campus facilities and endless acres of greenery to play on, you'll find academic freedom and a highly-intellectual and interesting student body. There are an infinite number of activities with which to busy yourself, and a social environment as open as a Colorado sky.

Probably the biggest complaint among students is the small size and "bubble-like" quality of Vassar living, which at times can be limiting. But few schools have a community this small and as liberating and far from the social hierarchies of high school as Vassar's. At Vassar, it's not about fitting in; it's not even about fitting.... For the rest of this editorial, visit collegeprowler.com.

Students Speak Out On...
OVERALL EXPERIENCE

Q **I Love Vassar.**
"I've never been happier anywhere. The people are so friendly and it's, for the most part, an extremely accepting environment. People that aren't happy here are people who:a) get easily offended (there are a lot of these people at Vassar. They're so liberal that they take offense to everything and make everyone else unhappy.b) you are anti-socialc) you're a homophobe, racist, or radical Christian."

Q **I'd Go Back in a Heartbeat**
"The amount of fun I had, the things I learned, the ways that I grew at Vassar ... it's indescribable. I would do it all over again, and again and again if I could."

Q **Vassar Is Diverse**
"Vassar is a very diverse place filled with all sorts of people. If you are not comfortable with variety and outre and even outrageous ideas, personalities, and lifestyles then Vassar is probably not the place for you."

BEST OF VASSAR

1. Open-mindedness
2. Academic freedom with good professors
3. Vassar Farm
4. Easy access to New York City
5. The dorms and the people

Happy Students
96% of students return after their first year.

Commitment to Teaching
There are 8 students for every member of faculty on campus.

WORST OF VASSAR

1. Poughkeepsie
2. 60/40 sex split
3. Small size
4. The Vassar bubble
5. Lack of diversity
6. Housing process
7. Limited eating options
8. The brutal winters

Expensive
Tuition is a steep $42,560, one of the most expensive rates in the country.

Student Body

African American:	5%	Male Undergrads:	41%
Asian American:	10%	Female Undergrads:	59%
Hispanic:	7%	Living On Campus:	98%
International:	6%	Living Off Campus:	2%
Native American:	0%	Male Athletes:	24%
White:	72%	Female Athletes:	16%
Unknown:	0%	Fraternity Members:	0%
From Out-of-State:	74%	Sorority Members:	0%

Frequently Compared Schools:

Brown University
Middlebury College
Tufts University
Wesleyan University

Students Speak Out On... EVERYTHING!

ACADEMICS

Rigorous But Doable

"Coming from a somewhat crappy high school, I have found the academics amazing. It is great to be around teachers from the best universities in the country who know what they are teaching and love what they are teaching. Expect to work a decent amount if you're doing a difficult major."

Freshman

"The teachers are amazing, whatever the field, and course requirements are non-existent. Other than a Quantitative and Writing Seminar, you have free reign to take whatever courses you choose. Even after declaring a major, the curriculum is set up to encourage exploration of new fields."

ATHLETICS

Athletics

"Although Vassar doesn't always win, the amount of school spirit is huge; and sports aren't a job; they're still meant for fun."

I Don't Know

"I don't know too much about the athletics at Vassar because they aren't a huge part of campus life. Our facilities are pretty nice and when teams get far we generally become more aware and gain a high amount of spirit. The school recently cut the crew team which was a really unfortunate decision and makes me somewhat negative toward athletics here in general."

CAMPUS DINING

Good but Gets Old

"The food is good, but after eating nothing else all year you'll get sick of it. Good vegetarian options though."

Okay

"There are few on campus dining centers. The food can get reasonably repetitive and the workers can get really unmotivated causing the food choices to be very slim certain nights. It's not horrible but it's not good either."

CAMPUS HOUSING

Overall Good

"When I first moved into my dorm room, I thought it was a piece of crap. But as you live in it, it becomes more and more of a home. Even though most of the dorms are old and seem dilapidated, it is something that you grow to love. Each of the dorms has its own personality and type of student who lives there and it is very Harry Potter-esque. After you are a freshman you can move out of the tiny doubles which makes housing even better."

Uneven but Charming

"On Campus housing varies wildly from dorm to dorm and room to room, which is great if you land that two-room double in Cushing with its own private bathroom or if you nag the stain-glassed bejewled suites in Joss, but terrible if you live in a musty closet of a room on the 5th floor of Raymond. Dorm communities can be fun and homey but also obnoxious."

GUYS & GIRLS

Lust Is in the Air.

"Lust is definitely in the air here. There is a reason Vassar is on the top ten sexiest schools in the country. Everyone does their best to look good and there is definitely a vibe of sexuality in the air. Guys are generally more well put together than they are in the rest of society, but this could be due to the high gay population. Girls are also hot and have great style."

HEALTH & SAFETY

The Safest Place in the Area

"The "Vassar Bubble" as they call it is honestly the safest place I have ever lived/been. There are occasional thefts, but if you lock your door you should have no problems. Security is not there to get students into trouble; they just want to keep students safe, which is, if you ask me, the way it should be. Don't be too loud too late at night and have a little bit of tact when it comes to your partying and you'll be absolutely fine."

LOOKING FOR MORE?

Check out our full-length guide to this school at collegeprowler.com/vassar-college/.

Villanova University

800 Lancaster Ave.; Villanova, PA 19085
(610) 519-4500; www.villanova.edu

THE BASICS:

Acceptance Rate: 46%
Yield: 27%
Setting: Suburban
Control: Private Non-Profit
Total Undergrads: 7,201
SAT Range: 1790–2080*
ACT Range: 30–33

Student-Faculty Ratio: 11:1
Retention Rate: 94%
Graduation Rate: 89%
Tuition: $38,820
Room & Board: $10,340
Avg. Aid Package: $25,258
Students With Aid: 62%

of 2400

Academics	B+	Greek Life	B
Athletics	A	Guys	A-
Campus Dining	B+	Health & Safety	A-
Campus Housing	B+	Local Atmosphere	B
Campus Strictness	C-	Nightlife	B
Computers	B+	Off-Campus Dining	A-
Diversity	C	Off-Campus Housing	C+
Drug Safety	B-	Parking	C
Facilities	B	Transportation	B
Girls	A	Weather	B-

CP's Student Author On...
OVERALL EXPERIENCE

Villanova is a school that grows on you—for some it takes only until the end of orientation, for others it takes two semesters or more. Whatever the case, students get caught up in what it means to be a Villanovan and to be from the 'Nova nation. Villanova provides students with an excellent education, well enough to confidently put alumni head-to-head with Ivy grads and be successful. Outside of its rich academic tradition, the students at Villanova come to know and appreciate their fellow students, professors, and surrounding community.

Going to Villanova gives students a unique perspective on college life. Even with a lack of diversity and a party scene that doesn't start to pick up until you are a junior, Villanova is a fun place to be. Villanova will not give you the typical college life of a wild youth, but regardless, it is a school that is exciting and full of good times. While that might not be what you are looking for, the students who do attend Villanova end up loving the school for everything it offers, from its basketball games and rich traditions, to its Catholic heritage and the full load of academics.... For the rest of this editorial, visit collegeprowler.com.

Students Speak Out On...
OVERALL EXPERIENCE

Life Is Good at Villanova

"Most students are very happy here, there are a lot of neighboring schools, great professors, nice students, and a good social life. Basketball season is definitely one of the best aspects of Villanova and almost everyone gets involved. NOVA NATION! The parties are a lot of fun if you have good connections (which are easy to get) but hard to get to. If you want diversity, do not come here, there is minimal diversity."

What You Make of It

"I love it here, the people are amazing and I am so happy I go here. That being said, you just have to remind yourself that it is not a party school, but there are always parties and fun like any other school- you just have to make the effort. Get to know people, branch out, have fun. Don't write it off"

BEST OF VILLANOVA

1. Villanova basketball
2. Class sizes
3. School spirit
4. Location, location, location
5. Philadelphia
6. The Suburban Main Line

Happy Students
94% of students return after their first year.

Proven Success
89% of students will complete their education and graduate with a degree.

WORST OF VILLANOVA

1. It can be relatively quiet some weekends
2. Main Line is better accessible with a car
3. Work load can be intense
4. When Villanova basketball loses
5. Older buildings

Expensive
Tuition is a steep $38,820, one of the most expensive rates in the country.

Don't Move Off Campus
Average off-campus housing is a steep $10,340.

Student Body

African American:	5%	Male Undergrads:	49%
Asian American:	6%	Female Undergrads:	51%
Hispanic:	6%	Living On Campus:	70%
International:	3%	Living Off Campus:	30%
Native American:	0%	Male Athletes:	11%
White:	75%	Female Athletes:	9%
Unknown:	4%	Fraternity Members:	14%
From Out-of-State:	81%	Sorority Members:	28%

Frequently Compared Schools:

Boston College
Lehigh University
University of Virginia
Wake Forest University

Students Speak Out On... EVERYTHING!

ACADEMICS

Good Education

"Regardless of your major, the workload at Villanova can be really hard and heavy at times but the professors are usually good and are willing to help outside of class. They are many spots to study on campus, and as long as you can stay focused and get you work done, you should be fine. You will also graduate confident that you had a good college education."

Awesome

"The math program is great. The professors are very helpful and enthusiastic about the subject."

ATHLETICS

Athletics Play a Big Role

"Athletics play a big role at Nova, especially the basketball team - the members are like celebrities on campus."

Big East Frenzy

"Villanova is a member of the Big East conference. The basketball team is a pretty huge deal on campus, making it to the Final Four in 2009. The facilities are pretty nice. The football team is looking to move to the Big East too, which could make for some great games and tailgating. Intarmurals and club sports are both great way for non-student athletes to stay involved in sports they played in high school, or pick up something new"

CAMPUS DINING

Great Food, Lots of Variety, Lots of Loctions.

"i thought college food would get boring but with all the different places to eat on campus, along with a couple hidden gems the food is always desired. meal plans vary adn there is definately one that fits every need."

Lots of Options

"Villanova has three dining halls and numerous other dining places on campus. While the food can get kind of repetitive if you continually go to the same places to eat, Villanova is nice because there are tons of options for dining. Also, if you get tired of campus food there are lots of restaurants really close

to campus that you can go to or if you prefer to stay in the dorm, there are a lot of places that deliver."

CAMPUS HOUSING

A Good Mixed Bag

"Most dorms on campus are great. Obviosuly, some are better than others but what they lack in amenities, they make up for in local (i.e. the quad). There is a LEED certified dorm, Fedigan, and many leaning communities houses as well. They can be pretty strict about vistors though."

"I have to say that I'm spoiled after living in St. Mary's since the rooms are very big, and they have their own sinks. Although, I don't think that there are any really bad dorms on campus to live in."

GUYS & GIRLS

Everyone Is Beautiful

"The guys and girls at Villanova are among the most beautiful people you will see anywhere. You will see very few ugly or even mildly unattractive people walking around campus."

Lots of Pretty Girls, Some Are Superficial

"Girls get A+ for their looks, no doubt about that. However, not all of them have charming personalities. There are some who are trying too hard to be popular and think they are too cool. Bottom line, you can find every type of girl you are looking for here."

HEALTH & SAFETY

Safety at Villanova

"I have never felt unsafe at school. I've never heard of theft and there are constantly public safety officers driving and walking around campus. All students have public safety's emergency and non-emergency phone numbers in their phones. It's a great school."

LOOKING FOR MORE?

Check out our full-length guide to this school at collegeprowler.com/villanova-university/.

Virginia Commonwealth University

910 W. Franklin St.; Richmond, VA 23284
(804) 828-0100; www.vcu.edu

THE BASICS:

Acceptance Rate: 70%	**Student-Faculty Ratio:** 18:1
Yield: 36%	**Retention Rate:** 83%
Setting: Mid-sized city	**Graduation Rate:** 49%
Control: Public	**Tuition:** $20,751
Total Undergrads: 23,378	**Room & Board:** $10,960
SAT Range: 1460–1770*	**Avg. Aid Package:** $13,806
ACT Range: 20–25	**Students With Aid:** 71%

of 2400

Academics	B	Greek Life	B-
Athletics	B-	Guys	A+
Campus Dining	A-	Health & Safety	B-
Campus Housing	C	Local Atmosphere	B+
Campus Strictness	B-	Nightlife	A
Computers	B	Off-Campus Dining	A-
Diversity	A	Off-Campus Housing	B+
Drug Safety	C	Parking	B
Facilities	B-	Transportation	A-
Girls	B+	Weather	B-

CP's Student Author On...
OVERALL EXPERIENCE

Students who attend VCU either love it or hate it. If they hate it, they most likely transfer or don't stay around campus on the weekends to find out everything the city has to offer. VCU has several nationally ranked academic programs and is continuing to grow and expand the classes offered to students. There are so many different fields that a student can major in that there's no need to decide right way if you are unsure of your major. More and more students are enrolling at VCU, and instead of being a backup school, it's becoming the first choice for a majority of the incoming freshman. While outsiders may consider it an art school, VCU students know that it is too diverse to label as any one type of school. Although VCU is in a city and some consider that a danger, the VCU security and police systems are arguably some of the best in the state.

VCU offers several opportunities for students to join clubs, fraternities, and sororities and even to travel abroad for a semester.... For the rest of this editorial, visit collegeprowler.com.

Students Speak Out On...
OVERALL EXPERIENCE

Q Experience

"Virginia Commonwealth is a very diverse school, there are many enthic groups and its ok. Its like a big family here, everyone I've met from all backgrounds greet each other with respect. I'm proud to be a ram, there are also varies activities that go on around campus where everyone can participate in. I definitely would not change schools because I am content where I'm at, I have yet to find a school that feels like home away from home. I've done my research and thats why I chose VCU"

Q I Want to Stay at VCU Forever

"VCU and Richmond are pretty much co-dependent, so everywhere you go in the city, you see a VCU element somewhere. There are endless ways to get involved in the school community besides just being a student. The VCU life is hard if you don't apply yourself, but it's still a blast."

Q Excellent

"I love my school, excellent quality classes, stimulatin atmosphere"

BEST OF VIRGINIA COMMONWEALTH

1. Students and faculty are both incredibly diverse.
2. The internship possibilities are endless with all of the companies downtown, including seven Fortune 500 businesses.

Happy Students
83% of students return after their first year.

Knowledgeable Professors
100% of students surveyed rated the general knowledge of professors as above average.

WORST OF VIRGINIA COMMONWEALTH

1. Thirsty? Drinks from vending machines on campus cost $1.25. It may not be faster, but it's definitely cheaper to get a drink from the cart vendor on the side of the road.

Don't Move Off Campus
Average off-campus housing is a steep $10,960.

Student Body

African American:	19%	Male Undergrads:	44%
Asian American:	10%	Female Undergrads:	56%
Hispanic:	4%	Living On Campus:	20%
International:	5%	Living Off Campus:	80%
Native American:	1%	Male Athletes:	2%
White:	51%	Female Athletes:	1%
Unknown:	11%	Fraternity Members:	6%
From Out-of-State:	8%	Sorority Members:	4%

Students Speak Out On...
EVERYTHING!

ACADEMICS

The Music Department Here Is Amazing.

"The music staff members here are really top-notch. We are taught by world-renowned performers, composers, and educators."

By Far the Most Willing and Helping Faculty I've Ever Come Across

"At Virginia Commonwealth University academics are both challenging and inspirational. Faculty expects the best from students, and students expect the best from faculty. Speaking from my point of view, our biology and chemistry department is fantastic. There is always a way to get help anytime you may be in need. From extra study sessions, to supplemental instruction, to teachers office hours, where they beg you to come talk to them!"

Solid

"I came to VCU because their School of Education was ranked very high by U.S. News. Once I started my classes, I understand why they had such a terrific reputation. The professors have been very helpful. VCU is a big school, but all of the classes have been small, which creates more opportunities for discussion."

ATHLETICS

Fun Fun Fun

"There is a lot of school spirit here. I wish there was a football team though."

VCU Athletics Are Cream of the Crop

"At Virginia Commonwealth University, athletics are kind of a big deal. We have exceptional sports teams, a great fan base, huge school spirit, and amazing facilities."

CAMPUS DINING

Food Is Great

"The food is wonderful and there are many options available for everyone's taste buds"

Frequently Compared Schools:

James Madison University
Old Dominion University
University of Virginia
Virginia Tech

Variety

"chinese, korean, mexican, ethiopian, american, italian, jamaican, southern"

CAMPUS HOUSING

Don't Bother After Freshman Year

"The dorms are decent, but they aren't popular for anyone but Freshman. Dorms are for the sole purpose of making a bunch of friends in a very close proximity, but after your first year everyone moves off campus."

Not Bad, Just Not Enough

"There needs to be more options for Upperclassman housing."

GUYS & GIRLS

The VCU Scene

"There are so many people in skinny jeans, you wonder if the guys actually have balls or not. Lots of artsy people with grandpa glasses, cut-offs, and Chuck Taylors. They definitely outnumber the popped collar crowd."

VCU Guys and Girls Are Diverse

"Many of the students at VCU are quite artistic, so VCU is a very diverse school where you can find a little bit of everything. It it is wonderful. You can find everything that you need and could every want at VCU."

HEALTH & SAFETY

Information Gotten Form School

"From the information that I got from my orientation, the school and its surrounding is very secure and safe."

Generally Safe

"VCU has its share of robberies and things, like any other university in the nation, but it's generally safe. There are many safety services as well, like police shuttles and phones on almost every corner."

LOOKING FOR MORE?

Check out our full-length guide to this school at collegeprowler.com/virginia-commonwealth-university/.

Virginia Tech

201 Burruss Hall; Blacksburg, VA 24061
(540) 231-6000; www.vt.edu

THE BASICS:

Acceptance Rate: 67%
Yield: 36%
Setting: Small city
Control: Public
Total Undergrads: 23,558
SAT Range: 1660–1950*
ACT Range: 25–29

Student-Faculty Ratio: 16:1
Retention Rate: 91%
Graduation Rate: 78%
Tuition: $21,878
Room & Board: $6,580
Avg. Aid Package: $10,517
Students With Aid: 73%

* of 2400

Academics	B+	Greek Life	B+
Athletics	A	Guys	A+
Campus Dining	A+	Health & Safety	B-
Campus Housing	B	Local Atmosphere	B+
Campus Strictness	B	Nightlife	A-
Computers	B+	Off-Campus Dining	B+
Diversity	C+	Off-Campus Housing	A-
Drug Safety	C	Parking	C+
Facilities	A-	Transportation	A-
Girls	A	Weather	C

CP's Student Author On...
OVERALL EXPERIENCE

Virginia Tech students have strong school spirit and value the education their university provides. In fact, many Tech students have such a great time as undergraduates that they stay at Tech for graduate work. Tech's academics have been improving each year, and admissions into the University is becoming more selective. Each freshman class has come in with higher high school GPAs and SAT scores. The rural setting of Blacksburg, Virginia is enjoyable for some students and frustrating for others. Even though Tech is home to more than 20,000 undergraduates, Blacksburg is still a small town. The area surrounding the town provides all kinds of outdoor activities. Even the drive to Virginia Tech down Route 81 is enjoyable. For students who come from more urban settings, Virginia Tech's small downtown and limited number of restaurants can be exasperating. However, even city students can appreciate how easy it is to walk from campus to town and how safe the town is. It is a friendly town and school, and that makes it easy to meet people.... For the rest of this editorial, visit collegeprowler.com.

Students Speak Out On...
OVERALL EXPERIENCE

Q Never Realized I Could Love It This Much
"I was hesitant about coming here but now that I'm here, I really cannot imagine any other place on earth. This school's got the best school spirit and we support each and every person. The people here are extremely friendly and there is a good amount of southern hospitality present. The respect shown by every Hokie resonates far beyond the campus. I'm a part of something that is huge. I am proud to say I chose this school and this is where I know I belong."

Q Great
"I really love the school, the people there are very nice, very nice. They also make you feel very welcome."

Q Great Experience
"Virginia Tech has shown me a great experience. The faculty have been very kind and helpful. Just work hard when you get here and learn how to manage your time and I guarantee a great and memorable college experience."

Q Hokies
"I love the environment at Virginia Tech. It is a large school with a small school feel. Everyone is nice to each other."

BEST OF VIRGINIA TECH

1. Hokie football is a fever that you need to catch. The students at Tech bleed orange and maroon, and spirit is incredibly high.

Happy Students
91% of students return after their first year.

Proven Success
78% of students will complete their education and graduate with a degree.

WORST OF VIRGINIA TECH

1. Honk, honk, honk. There is no parking to be found anywhere. The University gives out way too many parking passes.

2. The wind, not to mention the weather in general, is unpredictable.

Lowest Grades
Drug Safety: C
Weather: C
Diversity: C+

Student Body

African American:	4%	Male Undergrads:	58%
Asian American:	8%	Female Undergrads:	42%
Hispanic:	3%	Living On Campus:	39%
International:	2%	Living Off Campus:	61%
Native American:	0%	Male Athletes:	3%
White:	73%	Female Athletes:	2%
Unknown:	10%	Fraternity Members:	13%
From Out-of-State:	28%	Sorority Members:	15%

Students Speak Out On...
EVERYTHING!

ACADEMICS

Q Engineering

"It is amazing to be studying Civil Engineering at Virginia Tech. Our college is in the Top 10 in the nation, which represents how challenging and effective the curriculum is. The facilities integrate the newest technologies, which makes Virginia Tech one of the best Colleges of Engineering in the nation."

Q What I Like About School

"Im an agriculture student and live on campus. School at tech has been grate everyone said i would like such a large campus but theres lots to do and great places to eat. The teachers are also great they help you as long as you make time to ask and learn."

ATHLETICS

Q Football Is a Blast

"Football is a huge part of Virginia Tech and is so much fun. People always get together to tailgate and the after-parties are great. Our football team is great and the program is well organized. Student tickets can be difficult to come by but if there is always a lottery for free student tickets."

Q HOKIES!!!

"School spirt is amazing. Football games are the most amazing thing at school. Intramural sports are a great way to meet people too."

CAMPUS DINING

Q 5 Star Dining

"There are 3 of the 9 places to eat on campus are major dining halls (2 a-la-carte, 1 all you an eat) and the quality and selection at any time of the day is incredible. You can eat steak cooked to order, fresh Maine lobster, Philly Cheese Steaks, burritos, sandwiches, salads, wraps, gourmet burgers, pastas, pizza, authentic Appalachian bar-b-que etc. Definitely buy a large meal plan."

Q Delicious!

"Lots of variety, very yummy. Just about anything to suit your mood."

Frequently Compared Schools:
Clemson University
James Madison University
Penn State
University of Virginia

CAMPUS HOUSING

Q Freshman Year Can't Be Touched!

"I only lived on campus my freshman year and I lived on a hall that took a "welcome to college" type class together. IT WAS THE BEST! Our hall was incredibly diverse and everyone got along incredibly well. I couldn't have possibly imagined a better living experience. Sometimes it was hot without Air Conditioning in my building but that just meant our winters were perfect. Loved the hall and had everything I ever needed."

Q Lots of Chill People

"The dorms are great, with sinks and everything. Pregaming in your room isn't hard, just don't smoke, because police can smell it if they walk by."

GUYS & GIRLS

Q Everyone Is Helpful

"Almost anyone you meet will be helpful. There are a lot of people on campus that will point you in the right direction to find your way and there are a lot of tutors and mentors to get you on the right track academic wise."

Q Class Is Casual, and It Is Your Choice on Weekends!

"In the classroom students are usually comfortable and casual. Virginia Tech is a big campus, seeing someone trekking across in uncomfortable shoes is unusual. On nights and weekends it is easy to find a great crowd to interact with, no matter what the attire. No one is out of place, be it in jeans or a cool party dress."

HEALTH & SAFETY

Q Very Safe

"The campus is very safe."

Q Cops Everywhere

"Blacksburg is a very safe town, there are tons of cops everywhere to keep everyone safe"

LOOKING FOR MORE?
Check out our full-length guide to this school at collegeprowler.com/virginia-tech/.

Wagner College

1 Campus Road; Staten Island, NY 10301
(718) 390-3100; www.wagner.edu

THE BASICS:

Acceptance Rate: 66%
Yield: 28%
Setting: Large city
Control: Private Non-Profit
Total Undergrads: 1,857
SAT Range: 1570–1930*
ACT Range: 23–28

Student-Faculty Ratio: 14:1
Retention Rate: 73%
Graduation Rate: 69%
Tuition: $32,580
Room & Board: $9,700
Avg. Aid Package: $20,457
Students With Aid: 96%

* of 2400

Academics	B-	Greek Life	B
Athletics	C+	Guys	B+
Campus Dining	D+	Health & Safety	B+
Campus Housing	C	Local Atmosphere	B
Campus Strictness	B+	Nightlife	B
Computers	C	Off-Campus Dining	C-
Diversity	C	Off-Campus Housing	C-
Drug Safety	C-	Parking	A-
Facilities	C	Transportation	B+
Girls	B+	Weather	B+

CP's Student Author On...
OVERALL EXPERIENCE

College is what you make of it, and Wagner isn't any different—you can either have a terrible experience or a fantastic one. If you come here looking to make some great friends, grow as a person, become an adult, and learn about the things you're interested in, then you will. If you have an idea of the person you want to be but don't put yourself out there, then your path will be much more difficult. During orientation, you'll meet a lot of new people, and some of them will become your friends. You'll learn how to party, if that's what you want to do, and you'll learn how to have a good time without partying, if that's more your speed. If you've never shared a room before, now's your chance. If you've never been to New York City, you'll experience it for the first time, and if you've been here before, you'll see it with new eyes. The whole world is yours, like it's never been before. You'll make your first adult mistakes, and you'll leave high school behind.

Wagner has something to offer everyone, but you may just have to go looking for it at times.... For the rest of this editorial, visit collegeprowler.com.

Students Speak Out On...
OVERALL EXPERIENCE

Q I Love It Here!!!!

"Wagner College was everything I could have imagined it to be. The program I am in is perfect. I will be able to get my MBA in Accounting and then sit for the CPA exam. I am challenged by my professors and my classes. I loved the Learning Community that I was part of. I love the proximity to NYC and the ease with which I can get there. Although Wagner is expensive, I think they do what they can to help students financially."

Q Wagner Is Great

"My experience has been wonderful so far at Wagner College, and I do not regret my decision four years ago."

Q It's What You Make of It

"I love it at Wagner. There are always going to be people who complain about it, but those are the people who will never be happy anywhere. I knew a girl who transferred, but she ended up hating the school she went to even more. Like anything else in life, it is what you make it. Being involved in campus activities was the best thing I chose to do and made me like the school even more."

BEST OF WAGNER

1. The low student-to-faculty ratio allows the professors to get to know each student individually, and it allows the students to meet with the professors on a one-to-one basis.

Knowledgeable Professors
80% of students surveyed rated the general knowledge of professors as above average.

Low-Stress Course Load
70% of students surveyed rated the manageability of work as above average.

WORST OF WAGNER

1. Dining hall hours (you can't get food on campus after nine unless you want cereal)

2. The gym can get a little crowded sometimes, especially if a sports team is working out.

Expensive
Tuition is a steep $32,580, one of the most expensive rates in the country.

Good Luck Finding a Part-Time Job
Employment services are not available for students.

Student Body

African American:	5%	Male Undergrads:	38%
Asian American:	2%	Female Undergrads:	62%
Hispanic:	6%	Living On Campus:	68%
International:	1%	Living Off Campus:	32%
Native American:	0%	Male Athletes:	43%
White:	83%	Female Athletes:	17%
Unknown:	1%	Fraternity Members:	9%
From Out-of-State:	61%	Sorority Members:	13%

Students Speak Out On...
EVERYTHING!

ACADEMICS

Q Academics are Fantastic

"The academics are fantastic! Wagner College offers many great programs that truly have the ability to create great professionals in the workforce, as well as respectable individuals."

Q Major

"Wagner College is primarily an arts college, but the Accounting major is challenging and with the option of a 5 year masters program and being able to sit for the CPA it is a great program."

ATHLETICS

Q Involvement

"Athletics are huge at this school. Almost everybody plays a sport, and those who do not are in theatre. There are not too many people who are involved in neither, and those who aren't involved usually get involved in Greek life. There is a lot of spirit for the teams, even though they do not win a lot. Almost the entire school goes out to support football, basketball, and lacrosse. They definitely make Wagner a better place."

Q Very Exciting

"although I played sports in high school, Wagner College didn't offer my sport, field hockey. The sports at Wagner are very exciting and it is a lot of fun to go with friends to the games."

CAMPUS DINING

Q Dog Food

"The dining places around school are ridiculous and expensive. We are college students for crying out loud—"it's hard out here!!" They neglect the fact that all students do not come from privilege, and it would be nice if once in a while I could afford to treat myself to something other than the dog food we have to eat in the meal plan."

Frequently Compared Schools:

Fordham University
New York University
Rutgers University
Seton Hall University

Q There Is Little Variety but a Lot of Availability

"The only real options are the general cafeteria, pizza/pasta shop, a grill with burger and fries, and a couple cafes with coffee and cereal, but the good thing is there is almost always something open from 7:30 a.m. to 12 a.m."

CAMPUS HOUSING

Q Dorm Life

"Dorm LIfe.... It is what it is. I have a good roommate and we get along very well. The only downside to dorm life is that not all students take their education as seriously as I do and they spend the entire weekend and some week nights partying. I like to have a good time, but I am at Wagner to get an education."

Q Dorm Life

"Most dorm rooms are relatively small. There are a few suites in Towers and all of Foundation Hall has nice rooms. Upperclassmen definitely have better options. All of the dorms are fairly large, so they are very social and there is always something going on. Living on campus is nice because nothing is more than a 5- or 10-minute walk. Not to mention some of the best New York City views anywhere."

GUYS & GIRLS

Q If You Are Not Into Fashion You Will Be by the Time You Graduate

"The fashion at this school is awesome because of the proximity to NYC. You can dress however you want but know you will definitely be more conscious of what is "in" by the time you graduate. You may even find that you really enjoy it!"

HEALTH & SAFETY

Q AMAZING

"It's very safe, the safest!"

LOOKING FOR MORE?

Check out our full-length guide to this school at collegeprowler.com/wagner-college/.

Wake Forest University

1834 Wake Forest Road; Winston Salem, NC 27106
(336) 758-5000; www.wfu.edu

THE BASICS:

Acceptance Rate: 38%
Yield: 30%
Setting: Mid-sized city
Control: Private Non-Profit
Total Undergrads: 4,566
SAT Range: 1180–1390*
ACT Range: 27–31

Student-Faculty Ratio: 11:1
Retention Rate: 95%
Graduation Rate: 88%
Tuition: $38,622
Room & Board: $10,410
Avg. Aid Package: $33,285
Students With Aid: 79%

* of 1600

Academics	A-	Greek Life	A-
Athletics	B+	Guys	A+
Campus Dining	C	Health & Safety	B+
Campus Housing	B+	Local Atmosphere	C
Campus Strictness	B-	Nightlife	B+
Computers	A+	Off-Campus Dining	B
Diversity	C	Off-Campus Housing	B+
Drug Safety	C	Parking	C+
Facilities	B+	Transportation	C
Girls	A-	Weather	B+

CP's Student Author On...
OVERALL EXPERIENCE

Students overwhelmingly agree that their experience at Wake Forest was a very special one. Despite the "Work Forest" reputation (and reality), the challenging liberal arts coursework of Wake Forest prepares students to be successful leaders in the world. Students are often very well-rounded and take part in a variety of activities, including athletics, Greek life, and clubs. ACC Athletics and supporting the Demon Deacon sports teams are an important part of Wake Forest's identity. As one of the smallest Division I schools, Wake Forest offers sporting events of the caliber of a much larger institution. Despite the intimate campus community, Wake Forest encourages students to engage the wider world, from Winston-Salem to Vietnam and everywhere in between. As a true "liberal arts university," Wake Forest gives students access to the research resources of a much larger university. In particular, Wake Forest Baptist Medical Center is a nationwide leader in medical research. In short, for many alumni, graduation day was a very sad one indeed. Nonetheless, students do not pretend that Wake Forest is an absolutely perfect place.... For the rest of this editorial, visit collegeprowler. com.

Students Speak Out On...
OVERALL EXPERIENCE

Q Overall Experience

"I love Wake Forest. It is an incredibly wonderful place to live and learn. My favorite experiences have involved taking part in the intramural and club sports offered. I would choose Wake again because it is my home. My friends are all here as well as a phenomenal education. I give it an A+, even if Wake doesn't!"

Q Faculty

"From my own experience the faculty of Wake Forest are extremely knowledgeable is their given areas of expertise."

Q My Experience at Wake

"I had a great time at Wake Forest. I learned a lot and had some amazing professors (individuals who excelled at both teaching and their personal research) and had an awesome time! I made friends from all over the U.S., and the world, and got to experience a little bit of life in the South."

BEST OF WAKE FOREST

1. Amazing faculty
2. Gorgeous campus
3. Demon Deacon basketball
4. Demon Deacon football
5. Excellent professor-student interaction
6. Greek life

Happy Students
95% of students return after their first year.

Proven Success
88% of students will complete their education and graduate with a degree.

WORST OF WAKE FOREST

1. Parking
2. Grade deflation
3. Homogenity
4. Greek life is big.
5. Lack of on-campus parking
6. The reputation of "Work Forest"

Expensive
Tuition is a steep $38,622, one of the most expensive rates in the country.

Expensive Dorms
Living on campus doesn't come cheap, with an average housing price tag of $6,550.

Student Body

African American:	8%	Male Undergrads:	49%
Asian American:	5%	Female Undergrads:	51%
Hispanic:	3%	Living On Campus:	70%
International:	2%	Living Off Campus:	30%
Native American:	1%	Male Athletes:	12%
White:	80%	Female Athletes:	6%
Unknown:	2%	Fraternity Members:	35%
From Out-of-State:	74%	Sorority Members:	50%

Frequently Compared Schools:

University of North Carolina
University of Richmond
University of Virginia
Vanderbilt University

Students Speak Out On...
EVERYTHING!

ACADEMICS

Q Economics Major

"I learned more taking economics classes while I was abroad in Cambridge. I always had incredibly smart professors but usually they were not so good at actually teaching. I also did not get a whole lot of direction or information about what it means to be an econ major, meanwhile my friends had advisors in other departments were extremely helpful. However, when I tell people I am an econ major from Wake Forest they are always impressed."

Q Good, but Too Easy

"I've generally liked my academic experience here. Professors are very accessible and friendly, and their courses are interesting. That said, though, classes here are really easy and kind of go slowly. I haven't felt challenged at all."

ATHLETICS

Q How About Them DEACS!!!

"Sports play a huge roll at Wake Forest but Men's Football and Basketball take the center stage. We are often encouraged to go to low attendance athletic events, like soccer and women's athletic events, with things like dorm attendance competitions and charity events. There is a lot of school spirit when it comes to our teams and even those who can't make it to games keep up with the scores and achievements."

Q Atheltics

"Even though our sports teams are not always very good, the Athletics programs are great in itself though. There is tons of student involvement in all sports, maybe more so in male sports than female sports though. School spirit is good. The gym could be updated though."

CAMPUS DINING

Q Dining

"The pit (cafeteria on campus) is great the majority of the time. There is a wide selection of food options, a lot of healthy alternatives, as well as good to-do options. However there are days when the food is cold all day, and nearly inedible. With Wake's cafeteria, they're either on or you better have a stash of food in your fridge."

Q Could Be Worse

"The dining options on campus really aren't that terrible. The pit has a lot of options, but it does get old after a while. At least it's not as bad as the dining on some other campuses."

CAMPUS HOUSING

Q DIVERSE

"Campus life is very interesting, and there are many activities to be involved in."

Q Freshmen Have It Made

"The freshman dorms are all newer (including South Hall, the newest dorm which resembles a hotel more than a typical residence hall) but they are a three minute walk away from the cafeteria and classrooms compared to the one minute walk from upperclassmen dorms. Upperclassmen dorms are older and smaller, but when you are part of a Greek Organization, it is nice to live on the halls above the lounge."

GUYS & GIRLS

Q Beautiful People

"Everyone on this campus is beautiful...it's rare to see an overweight person as well. The typical student is the typical overachiever who is completely stressed during the week but then everyone cuts loose on Wake Wednesdays and the weekend which makes up for the high pressure academically. There is a mix of Southern and Northern brands but definitely buy cowboy boots and bring sundresses/buttondowns and ties for tailgates!"

HEALTH & SAFETY

Q Trusted and Reliable

"Should there be a problem, I feel confident that security will be there to assist."

LOOKING FOR MORE?

Check out our full-length guide to this school at collegeprowler.com/wake-forest-university/.

Warren Wilson College

701 Warren Wilson Road; Swannanoa, NC 28778
(828) 771-2000; www.warren-wilson.edu

THE BASICS:

Acceptance Rate: 76%	**Student-Faculty Ratio:** 12:1
Yield: 30%	**Retention Rate:** 70%
Setting: Suburban	**Graduation Rate:** 46%
Control: Private Non-Profit	**Tuition:** $24,196
Total Undergrads: 956	**Room & Board:** $7,700
SAT Range: 1560–1910*	**Avg. Aid Package:** $14,890
ACT Range: 23–27	**Students With Aid:** 79%

* of 2400

Academics	B	Greek Life	N/A
Athletics	B-	Guys	B
Campus Dining	C+	Health & Safety	A-
Campus Housing	C+	Local Atmosphere	C+
Campus Strictness	B+	Nightlife	C
Computers	C	Off-Campus Dining	B+
Diversity	D+	Off-Campus Housing	D+
Drug Safety	C+	Parking	A-
Facilities	B-	Transportation	C+
Girls	B+	Weather	B+

CP's Student Author On...
OVERALL EXPERIENCE

Warren Wilson is a wonderfully unique college. It tends to be described as something more than a college—students are not attracted here exclusively for the academic program, or even the work and service components. It is an experience more than an education, and what students learn here goes beyond any of their expectations. Because of this special "other" aspect, Wilson can't be described properly in words, especially in the same categories as other schools.

When students visit, they tend to feel either an overwhelming attraction or a sincere repulsion, and we understand and respect both reactions. When it is right for someone to be here, they find a way to be here and help our community become as supportive and joyous as it can be. It certainly is not the right college for everyone, but the people who become Warren Wilson students hold this special place close to our hearts our entire lives, and are always thankful for the lessons learned and the people met in our little corner of Appalachia.

Students Speak Out On...
OVERALL EXPERIENCE

Q :)
"Warren Wilson admits it's not for everyone. If you are open to things you never encountered before and to ideas you've never dreamed of existing, then you will find an open community. Though many people here have opinions varying quite considerably from the norm, everyone is respected. At Warren Wilson you will work and learn and have fun doing it."

Q Overall...
"My experience at WWC has been okay. However, I am transferring after one semester. I realized that I was not a hippie, and that I wanted to be in a place where people challenged themselves academically and cared about their surroundings and personal hygiene. Come here if you want to learn an outdoor skill, to learn how to get away with not showering, to learn how to do tons of drugs, and become an environmental science major. Otherwise, it's not the place for you."

BEST OF WARREN WILSON

1. The view of the mountains
2. The professors
3. The Farm
4. The people—students, faculty, and staff
5. Work crews
6. Cow Pie vegetarian café
7. Dogwood pasture

Learn from the Best
95% of faculty have earned the highest degree in their field.

Personal Attention
You can expect personal attention with 90% of classes having less than 20 students.

WORST OF WARREN WILSON

1. Cost of tuition
2. Getting trapped in the Wilson bubble
3. Cigarettes
4. Small academic departments
5. Carrot loaf

Not Much Diversity
One of the least racially diverse campuses—only 11% of students are minorities.

Student Body

African American:	1%	Male Undergrads:	41%
Asian American:	1%	Female Undergrads:	59%
Hispanic:	2%	Living On Campus:	90%
International:	3%	Living Off Campus:	10%
Native American:	1%	Male Athletes:	17%
White:	89%	Female Athletes:	11%
Unknown:	2%	Fraternity Members:	0%
From Out-of-State:	82%	Sorority Members:	0%

Frequently Compared Schools:

Guilford College
Wake Forest University
Wesleyan University
Whitman College

Students Speak Out On... EVERYTHING!

ACADEMICS

Tutoring

"I am a Biochemistry major at Warren Wilson College. The tutoring hours for students available are extremely helpful and important. It has helped me succeed a lot."

Psychology

"I've only started here as a freshman, but I am deeply impressed with our psychology department."

ATHLETICS

A Lot of Heart

"There is no football team, which may seem like a drawback to some. Athletics at Wilson are more about having fun and building camaraderie than actual competition. That being said, our mountain biking team consistently places well in collegiate national competitions."

Not Too Competitive

"Athletics are not really a big deal at Warren Wilson. Not many students go to games with any regularity. The teams aren't often competitive. If you're looking to go pro, this probably isn't the school for you. However, students on teams do tend to form close bonds and have a good time, which is what sports are supposed to be about."

CAMPUS DINING

Dual Dining

"We have two dining areas. The larger Gladfelter which is on a 3 week rotation more or less. The food includes those purchased through Sodexo as well as food grown on the campus and animals raised on our farm. We also have Cowpie which is a vegan cafeteria. All the food there is organic and they have a speaker system. People generally skip breakfast and eat out weekends so you don't need the largest meal plan."

Something for Everyone...

"While Gladfelter and Cowpie generally aren't that clean, their food is pretty okay most nights. Vegetarians and vegans will find no problems in their search for healthy, meatless, or dairy-free foods. However, when meals aren't happening, there isn't a place that will sell you food on campus. It's an issue."

CAMPUS HOUSING

Spacious Rooms and Small Residences

"The housing for sophomores and above is great at Warren Wilson. The Ecodorm is LEED Platinum certified, and all of the upperclassmen housing has less than 100 students per residence - most have under fifty. The rooms are more spacious than many other schools I've visited, and the accommodations are more than adequate."

If You Like It Dirty...

"If you like campus housing that looks nice from afar and is filthy close-up, then WWC is the place for you. The buildings are generally all right, but really, they don't get cleaned as thoroughly or as often as they should. Also, upperclassmen housing is a bit of a hike."

GUYS & GIRLS

Same Difference

"Most people here think they are different and try to stand out. We have the classic hippies who go shirtless and barefoot with their dreads. A lot of guys are in pretty good shape and many girls are stunning. It all depends on your perspective."

HEALTH & SAFETY

A Friend in Need..

"When it comes to it WWC and it community is very understanding and heartfelt. The schools makes it so that every student is very well informed about the happenings of Wilson. The consolers here at this school are very professional and will do everything in their power to help out person in need. the students and staff are the same way always there to help each other."

LOOKING FOR MORE?

Check out our full-length guide to this school at collegeprowler.com/warren-wilson-college/.

Washington & Jefferson College

60 S. Lincoln St.; Washington, PA 15301
(724) 503-1001; www.washjeff.edu

THE BASICS:

Acceptance Rate: 42%
Yield: 14%
Setting: Suburban
Control: Private Non-Profit
Total Undergrads: 1,514
SAT Range: 1030–1230*
ACT Range: 22–28

Student-Faculty Ratio: 12:1
Retention Rate: 86%
Graduation Rate: 73%
Tuition: $32,895
Room & Board: $8,925
Avg. Aid Package: $21,882
Students With Aid: 99%

* of 1600

Academics	B	Greek Life	A-
Athletics	B+	Guys	B-
Campus Dining	C+	Health & Safety	A-
Campus Housing	B+	Local Atmosphere	C+
Campus Strictness	A	Nightlife	C+
Computers	B	Off-Campus Dining	B
Diversity	D-	Off-Campus Housing	C-
Drug Safety	C+	Parking	A-
Facilities	B	Transportation	C
Girls	C	Weather	C+

CP's Student Author On... OVERALL EXPERIENCE

Not many students walk out of W&J with feelings that it was "alright" or "so-so." Most shoot off to either extreme of loving it or despising its very existence. Come to think of it, many are a complicated mix of both. Regardless of where their loyalties lie at graduation, students seem to share a strikingly common belief that succeeding at W&J makes the rest of the challenges still to come comparably easier. Grads leave here with feelings of tremendous relief that they passed their classes and they know that the education they received has helped get them one step closer to the next phase of their lives. Even though many are racked with doubt about exactly what that phase is, the general attitude is positive and optimistic. It's difficult to write a summary about students' overall experience here because, to put it bluntly, it's so varied and complex that one person simply cannot capture it all. I consider it safe to say that no one leaves W&J just how they expected they would be when they came here as freshmen. Four years at W&J has burned some students out and made some wish they had considered going somewhere less rigorous, but it has given others boundless confidence in their academic abilities.... For the rest of this editorial, visit collegeprowler.com.

Students Speak Out On... OVERALL EXPERIENCE

Q Earnest

"If I could describe a dub jay student in one word it would be earnest. They are super hard-working and real people. The professors want you to succeed at life and the lunch ladies know your favorite food and your birthday. Its a community built not around buildings, but people who genuinely care... you can chose to hate it, or love it, but either way it changes your life."

Q Great Education

"Overall, W&J provides the best education. The academic life is superb and professors go out of their way to help you. I have even had a professor that freely gives out his home phone number. Of course, there are those that don't care at all, but they are few in number. You will be challenged, you will grow, and you will get a great job."

Q "(In a quiet voice) Never . . . again . . . never . . . again."

BEST OF WASHINGTON & JEFFERSON

1. The professors
2. Traveling abroad for Intersession
3. Crazy partying for those who stay here for Intersession
4. Self-designed majors

Happy Students
86% of students return after their first year.

Proven Success
73% of students will complete their education and graduate with a degree.

WORST OF WASHINGTON & JEFFERSON

1. Spending four of your best years in Washington, PA
2. Confusing meal plans
3. Buildings in dire need of repair
4. Occasionally unmanageable workloads
5. The prevalence of gossip

Expensive
Tuition is a steep $32,895, one of the most expensive rates in the country.

Not Much Diversity
One of the least racially diverse campuses—only 16% of students are minorities.

Student Body

African American:	3%	Male Undergrads:	54%
Asian American:	1%	Female Undergrads:	46%
Hispanic:	1%	Living On Campus:	82%
International:	0%	Living Off Campus:	18%
Native American:	0%	Male Athletes:	46%
White:	84%	Female Athletes:	29%
Unknown:	10%	Fraternity Members:	43%
From Out-of-State:	30%	Sorority Members:	37%

Students Speak Out On...
EVERYTHING!

ACADEMICS

Q Liberal Arts

"If you don't know what a liberal arts degree is now, by the end of your time at dub jay they will have it drilled into your head why everyone should go to a liberal arts college."

Q Quality Academics

"Washington and Jefferson is a prestigious college with renown academics. The professors, at least the ones I have had, are always willing to go above and beyond to help. The workload can be quite a bit, but it will all be worth it."

ATHLETICS

Q Not Bad

"Lots of students are involved in a sport and there are very nice facilities on campus. However, the fan support is really low and there is very little school spirit. A lot of the athletes at W & J are immature and at times it seems like an extension of high school. A nice variety of intramural sports gives everyone an opportunity to compete."

Q 2 Year Limit

"I feel like lots of people play sports at dub jay, but there seems to be a 2 year limit to liking it. Either they like it the first 2 years and hate it the second 2 years or vice versa. Some people quit playing because they get fed up others trudge on, but for some reason few actually enjoy playing all 4 years."

CAMPUS DINING

Q Not Too Many Options

"Washington and Jefferson does not offer a variety of meal plans, nor are their many places to choose from. This is understandable though when taking in account the size of the school, no more than 1500 students. It would be nice though if other plans were offered."

Q "The food on campus is terrible! The only viable places to eat are the Commons and George and Tom's, and neither of them are any good."

Frequently Compared Schools:

Allegheny College
Dickinson College
Penn State
University of Pittsburgh

CAMPUS HOUSING

Q Life on Campus

"I've heard Washington and Jefferson compared to a "mullet," business in the front and a party in the back. Hard work during the week and parties on the weekends. The dorms are not the best, but I find them enjoyable."

Q Dorm Life in Comparison to Cost

"The Washington and Jefferson campus is state-of-the-art but the dorms look like they are from the early 1900's. They have just built a new science building and from the looks of it, it cost a bundle but they could spruce up the dorm rooms. For a learning experience like none other, go to Washington and Jefferson but stay at home."

GUYS & GIRLS

Q There's a Little Bit of Everything.

"I think that the reason Washington and Jefferson has such a great student body is because of the fact that everyone is so diverse. We have people interested in Theatre, and people into community service. There are people into Woman's rights and people into Anime. All the guys that go are pretty different and the same goes for the girls. However, these differences work because they make the campus stronger. A person can find any type of person here."

Q Lots of Variety

"There are tons of different types of people you can definitely find a group to fit into or mix things up. There's people from the country, from cities, international students, etc. Everybody is pretty nice and everybody wants to make friends."

HEALTH & SAFETY

Q Very Safe Campus

"Campus is totally safe. Very little crime on campus. Small campus, you can almost always see a security guard no matter where you are. Off campus in certain directions is not a great place to venture off to but walking to the main stretch of businesses is not a hassle at all."

LOOKING FOR MORE?

Check out our full-length guide to this school at collegeprowler.com/washington--and--jefferson-college/.

Washington & Lee University

204 W. Washington St.; Lexington, VA 24450
(540) 458-8400; www.wlu.edu

THE BASICS:

Acceptance Rate: 19%	**Student-Faculty Ratio:** 7:1
Yield: 40%	**Retention Rate:** 94%
Setting: Town	**Graduation Rate:** 89%
Control: Private Non-Profit	**Tuition:** $38,877
Total Undergrads: 1,762	**Room & Board:** $8,755
SAT Range: 1970–2200*	**Avg. Aid Package:** $30,933
ACT Range: 29–32	**Students With Aid:** 60%

* of 2400

Academics	A	Greek Life	A+
Athletics	C+	Guys	B
Campus Dining	B	Health & Safety	A
Campus Housing	B	Local Atmosphere	C-
Campus Strictness	C	Nightlife	C-
Computers	A-	Off-Campus Dining	B+
Diversity	D	Off-Campus Housing	A-
Drug Safety	B	Parking	C
Facilities	B+	Transportation	C+
Girls	B+	Weather	C+

CP's Student Author On...
OVERALL EXPERIENCE

Year after year, Washington and Lee has been remarkably successful at producing happy students. Freshmen usually come in starry-eyed, and leave four years later, content, happy, grateful for an awesome experience, and nostalgic for all the good times gone by. The demanding expectations of faculty don't seem to put a serious damper on the general feeling of good cheer. One objective gauge of this is W&L's remarkably active and supportive alumni network, which supports the University, stays in touch to get jobs for students, and most recently, chipped in cash to the tune of $240 million for massive modernization projects.

Students give high marks to the educational quality here, as well as to the natural setting and the sense of community and respect engendered by the Honor System and a tradition of gentility. But as their comments have shown, some students are put off by the small-town environment and the dominance of Greek life on campus, as well as by recent friction between students and the administration over alcohol policies and changes to their beloved Spring term.... For the rest of this editorial, visit collegeprowler. com.

Students Speak Out On...
OVERALL EXPERIENCE

Q It's So Much Fun

"I've had the best year of my life here. The parties are great, but I've still learned a lot. When I talk to all my high school friends, it's obvious I've had the best college experience, and I'm really happy here. There are definitely times (like winter term) when you can feel claustrophobic and homesick, but come Spring Term I'm not ready to go home."

Q "I knew that I wanted to come to W&L from the second I drove up, and it's met every single expectation that I had. The Honor Code is everything I expected, and the profs were more challenging—and yet more genuine—than I expected."

Q "W&L is not for everybody. I've ended up really liking it because I've found people who share my interests. But then there's some people that the school's just not suited for. Make sure you look into the school extensively—spend the night if you can. Know that it's almost exclusively Greek—you have to be a really independent person to thrive here and enjoy it if you're not going to get involved in the Greek system."

BEST OF WASHINGTON & LEE

1. Academic excellence
2. Friendly, trusting, close-knit community
3. The Honor Code and being able to trust your classmates
4. Greek madness and the fun social scene

Happy Students
94% of students return after their first year.

Commitment to Teaching
There are 7 students for every member of faculty on campus.

WORST OF WASHINGTON & LEE

1. Waking up in a trashed and disgusting residence after a big party weekend
2. A sometimes tone-deaf administration
3. Lack of alternatives to Greek activities and partying

Expensive
Tuition is a steep $38,877, one of the most expensive rates in the country.

Good Luck Finding a Part-Time Job
Employment services are not available for students.

Student Body

African American:	3%	Male Undergrads:	50%
Asian American:	3%	Female Undergrads:	50%
Hispanic:	3%	Living On Campus:	43%
International:	5%	Living Off Campus:	57%
Native American:	0%	Male Athletes:	39%
White:	85%	Female Athletes:	26%
Unknown:	0%	Fraternity Members:	79%
From Out-of-State:	86%	Sorority Members:	76%

Frequently Compared Schools:

Vanderbilt University
Wake Forest University
Washington University in St. Louis
Yale University

Students Speak Out On... EVERYTHING!

ACADEMICS

Q Availability :

"Washington and Lee professors are always available for students. There is practically no need to schedule an appointment to meet them, and they are all more than delighted to meet with the students even outside their office hours."

Q "Every teacher I've had (and I'm a senior) has been

extremely accessible. All have set office hours, but they also have no problem if you drop in on them unannounced to ask a question or just chat."

ATHLETICS

Q There's Something for Everybody

"Like any town in America, you have your good and your bad. For the most part, off-campus housing is easy to find and relatively nice (unless you live in one of the Greek associated houses). Safety is definitely not a problem overall. Most people leave their house/apartment unlocked."

Q "School spirit with regards to sports is unfortunately low.

At a school based around tradition, it's sad that more people don't go to games and support their classmates."

CAMPUS DINING

Q Not Too Bad

"The Marketplace (our dining hall) has good food but it's too repetitive for me. However, once a month it organizes a themed dinner and the food is different. One can also get food from the Co-Op, but it is mostly the same as the food in the Marketplace. At any rate, one can try finding more things in Lexington"

Q "I think the food is okay; people just complain because

they feel the need to complain about something."

CAMPUS HOUSING

Q Freshman Dorms Are a Necessary Evil

"Freshman dorms are not really great, but they are

relatively big compared to the other colleges I have visited. Upperclassman dorms on the other hand are great, and I can't wait for next year to move into one of them!"

Q "No one lives in Gaines or Woods Creek unless they have

to (the perks of being an RA). Living on campus sucks. You can't drink, you can't be loud if you want to, and, in general, the living arrangements are just kind of depressing."

GUYS & GIRLS

Q "There aren't any set visiting hours for members of the

opposite sex in the dorms. Individual freshmen halls or suites can set policies if they want to do so, but everyone tends just to operate under the general rules of common courtesy."

Q "While there might be consequences for being caught

fooling around in, say, Lee Chapel, outside of that, the worst penalty you would pay for being caught in an intimate moment in your dorm room would be some mockery from your hallmates (or congratulations, as the case may be)."

HEALTH & SAFETY

Q Completely Safe

"In W&L you can leave your things unattended basically anywhere and you will find them when you get back there. If not, they are at the information desk for the lost and found items. Thanks to the Honor Code, students respect each other's possessions and everybody always feels safe about leaving their doors unlocked or just walking around campus at any time."

Q As Safe as It Gets

"The honor system assures complete campus safety. Thefts and petty crime rarely occur on campus and even in town. People always leave their doors unlocked - and even open - and their valuables lying around without fear. You can walk around at any time and will not have to call for an escort or friend to go with you."

LOOKING FOR MORE?

Check out our full-length guide to this school at collegeprowler.com/washington--and--lee-university/.

Washington University in St. Louis

1 Brookings Drive; Saint Louis, MO 63130
(314) 935-5000; www.wustl.edu

THE BASICS:

Acceptance Rate: 22%
Yield: 30%
Setting: Suburban
Control: Private Non-Profit
Total Undergrads: 7,129
SAT Range: 1390–1530*
ACT Range: 32–34

Student-Faculty Ratio: 7:1
Retention Rate: 97%
Graduation Rate: 94%
Tuition: $38,728
Room & Board: $12,465
Avg. Aid Package: $29,491
Students With Aid: 66%

* of 1600

Academics	A+	Greek Life	A+
Athletics	C	Guys	B+
Campus Dining	A+	Health & Safety	C+
Campus Housing	A+	Local Atmosphere	B+
Campus Strictness	A	Nightlife	B
Computers	B	Off-Campus Dining	A
Diversity	B-	Off-Campus Housing	A-
Drug Safety	C	Parking	B+
Facilities	A	Transportation	B+
Girls	C+	Weather	C+

CP's Student Author On... OVERALL EXPERIENCE

Beyond the initial enthusiasm that so many students express for their overall experience at Wash U, a common subject of praise relates to the freedom that characterizes student life. In the academic sense, this translates into an ability to bend the rules, an encouragement to build things if they aren't already available, and support from the University for students who propose new and well-thought-out initiatives. Wash U is a young school, and the University is very much interested in channeling the energy and enterprises of its students into new traditions and organizations that can help shape its identity.

Still, not everybody likes Wash U from the outset. St. Louis can get dull, the academic life can become overwhelming, and the social scene will eventually feel a bit claustrophobic. But the quality of the faculty, the ease and relative affordability of life in St. Louis, and the receptiveness of the administration to student projects makes it a place where a motivated student can do anything he or she wants.... For the rest of this editorial, visit collegeprowler.com.

Students Speak Out On... OVERALL EXPERIENCE

Q I Couldn't Be Happier

"This campus is very academically driven. The kids are smart and work very hard. At the same time, everyone likes to have fun. The party culture fits my social and academic needs, and any day of the week where I want to go out I am able to do, but it's never a "social requirement" unless it's the weekend. The kids are friendly, the professors and academics are great, and the facilities on campus could not be nicer."

Q I Wouldn't Want to Be Anywhere Else

"I love it here. The people are driven, approachable, friendly, and the most wonderful assortment of people I could ever imagine. Classes and teachers are great. The food is fantastic (I miss it when I'm home) and dorms are luxurious. The administration cares about the students. Social life is vibrant and fun but not overwhelming."

Q Great!

"Campus life is great. No major problems. Treated really well but then again we are paying for it."

BEST OF WASH U

1. WILD
2. Your freshman floor
3. Residential College Olympics
4. Frisbee in the Swamp
5. Study abroad
6. Chancellor Wrighton's good eye

Happy Students
97% of students return after their first year.

Commitment to Teaching
There are 7 students for every member of faculty on campus.

WORST OF WASH U

1. The price of tuition ($$$)
2. Snobby rich kids
3. The weather
4. Chancellor Wrighton's lazy eye
5. Graduation requirements
6. Teachers with heavy accents

Expensive
Tuition is a steep $38,728, one of the most expensive rates in the country.

Expensive Dorms
Living on campus doesn't come cheap, with an average housing price tag of $8,061.

Student Body

African American:	7%	Male Undergrads:	47%
Asian American:	12%	Female Undergrads:	53%
Hispanic:	3%	Living On Campus:	73%
International:	5%	Living Off Campus:	27%
Native American:	0%	Male Athletes:	12%
White:	58%	Female Athletes:	7%
Unknown:	14%	Fraternity Members:	23%
From Out-of-State:	92%	Sorority Members:	23%

Frequently Compared Schools:

Northwestern University
University of Pennsylvania
Vanderbilt University
Yale University

Students Speak Out On... EVERYTHING!

ACADEMICS

Curriculum

"the curriculum offered at Washington Uniersity in St. Louis is outstanding."

World Class Faculty That's Actually Approachable

"Academics are one of the universities greatest strengths. Nobel Prize winning professors are numerous. Teachers want to get to know you. Classes are difficult but stimulating, and peers are engaged but not stuck-up."

ATHLETICS

Varsity Athletics Are Strong

"The athletics are really strong here, but most athletes don't get much credit. The men's basketball team and the women's volleyball team probably get the most fan support. The football team is terrible and I don't think anyone really goes to the games."

Wonderful, but

"Wash. U.'s athletics are spectacular, regularly ranked overall in the top three schools in Division 3, and the basketball and volleyball teams are national title holders. Unfortunately, the average Wash. U. student seems to discount the athletic teams in general, and the administration is stingy with money for facilities."

CAMPUS DINING

Amazing and Sourced Responsibly

"WashU has extremely green dining practices. The food could not taste better and much of it is sourced locally and with cruelty free/ fair trade practices."

Food Is Great!

"I'm a vegetarian, and I've never had problems with finding options or variety in food. There's something for everyone and every kind of diet -- including vegan and kosher. The options can sometimes get repetitive, but it's awesome quality, and there are a lot of healthy options available to help avoid the freshmen 15."

CAMPUS HOUSING

Dorms Like Palaces

"Dorms are wonderful. Rooms are huge, for both modern and traditional housing. Most rooms have temperapeutic mattresses. Modern suites have four people sharing a bathroom, and housekeeping twice a week for the bathroom. Each floor has a kitchen, and each dorm has a laundry room and a computer lab. Substance-free housing available. Costly."

Housing is great!

"Wash U spoils most underclassmen with housing. The modern dorms are very, very nice, and all of the traditional dorms receive tempurpedic mattresses as a consolation for not being in modern. Traditionals are still very nice though too. The halls are big enough in all of the dorms to have a fun, social atmosphere."

GUYS & GIRLS

Nice People and Wide Variety

"The people at wash U are amazing, fun, and very tolerable. People are nice to each other and respect each other very well."

Relationships

"Relationships between guys and girls at WashU are really strong. Many students are in long-term romantic relationships and most groups of friends are well mixed between guys and girls. Overall, there are many opportunities for positive opposite sex interactions."

HEALTH & SAFETY

I have never felt unsafe

"I have never felt unsafe on this campus in any way. The campus police are located right in one of the dorms, so I always feel that if there ever was any problem, I would have help in a matter of moments. I never see strangers on campus, but students and staff, and have never felt uncomfortable or unsafe in any way. I keep my bedroom door open all day, and the suite door open when I am around."

LOOKING FOR MORE?

Check out our full-length guide to this school at collegeprowler.com/washington-university-in-st.-louis/.

Wayne State University

656 W. Kirby St.; Detroit, MI 48202
(313) 577-2424; www.wayne.edu

THE BASICS:

Acceptance Rate: 79%
Yield: 38%
Setting: Large city
Control: Public
Total Undergrads: 20,765
SAT Range: —
ACT Range: 17–23

Student-Faculty Ratio: 16:1
Retention Rate: 76%
Graduation Rate: 34%
Tuition: $18,412
Room & Board: $7,659
Avg. Aid Package: $12,125
Students With Aid: 83%

Academics	B-	Greek Life	C
Athletics	C	Guys	B+
Campus Dining	B-	Health & Safety	B
Campus Housing	B-	Local Atmosphere	B-
Campus Strictness	B-	Nightlife	B+
Computers	B	Off-Campus Dining	B
Diversity	A-	Off-Campus Housing	B-
Drug Safety	B-	Parking	B-
Facilities	B	Transportation	C+
Girls	B-	Weather	C+

CP's Student Author On...
OVERALL EXPERIENCE

Wayne State University is big but still small enough where all the classes are located relatively close together and you are able to form bonds with your professors and many other students. In general, the people on campus are friendly and willing help you out. Professors, staff, RAs, and peer mentors are available to talk to if you ever need help with anything, whether it is homesick or problems in a class. The University offers free tutoring and Supplemental Instruction (SI) to help if you're having academic trouble. SI is basiclaly a study group led by a student who already took the class and received an A. The SI leader tries to explain the material in an easier method of understanding and will make up practice tests to help students prepare for real tests. Some professors even use examples from the practice tests in the class exams, so it's beneficial to go to SI. It is purely optional, but students have found that it raises their grades, on average, by half a grade.

There are so many opportunities available on campus, and you can get involved as much as you want.... For the rest of this editorial, visit collegeprowler.com.

Students Speak Out On...
OVERALL EXPERIENCE

Q So much to do here

"Wayne State has a lot to offer, it's just expensive. But, I wouldn't go anywhere else because there's so much to do here."

Q Good Times With Great Friends

"After my first year at Wayne State University I have come to see that the student body is culturally diverse. So far the best experiences that I have had were with my friends from high school that also go to school here. If I were to go back in time a year, I think I would actually go somewhere else just so I could get the "full college experience" and go somewhere that I would have to live on campus to attend."

BEST OF WAYNE STATE

1. Faculty/staff members are amazing and very willing to help students
2. Range of diversity
3. Private bathrooms in the dorms
4. The dining hall actually has good food.

Knowledgeable Professors
82% of students surveyed rated the general knowledge of professors as above average.

Big Dorms
60% of students surveyed felt that dorms were more spacious than average.

WORST OF WAYNE STATE

1. Weather has a mind of its own.
2. Parking is terrible without a pass.
3. Homeless sometimes gather around the student center when the police are not watching.

Not Everyone Graduates
34% of students do not complete their education or graduate with a degree.

Frequently Compared Schools:

Michigan State University
Oakland University
University of Michigan
Western Michigan University

Students Speak Out On... EVERYTHING!

ACADEMICS

Wayne State Theatre Majors

"I attend Wayne State University, and I am a Theatre major specializing in performance. The curriculum provided is very rigorous and similar to the professional world of theatre. The professors in the department are very nurturing and dedicated to your development in the arts."

Journalism

"The journalism department at Wayne State University is great. The majority of teachers and faculty in this department have loads of journalism experience, which they teach students from. We have world-class studios for recording that are specifically for broadcast journalist majors. There are a lot of opportunities on campus for journalism majors to get involved with, i.e. The South End newspaper and WDET, the radio station."

ATHLETICS

Great

"All so fun and great."

Team Work

"We have one of the greatest athletics department because of commitment."

CAMPUS DINING

Campus Dining

"The Student Center is equipped with the healthiest fast food restaurants in the country. The dining halls are buffet-style and all-you-can-eat. They provide fresh fruits and vegetables, and food is cooked fresh daily."

Wayne State

"I love all of the options available at Wayne State, and there are vending machines all over the place. I just wish there were more places that weren't as fattening."

CAMPUS HOUSING

Apartments

"I live in on-campus housing, and i love it. It's right across from campus."

Housing on Campus

"I personally do not live on campus, do to the fact that I only live 15min away from the university. I have many friends that live on campus and by their experience, they absolutely love it. Everyone is together, always having a great time and its right smack down in the middle of campus. The costs are not that bad, I would definitely want live on campus, but in my situation that would be a waste of money."

GUYS & GIRLS

The WSU Students

"A lot of my friends attend Wayne State with me and we love all the activities. From hanging at the food court to playing sports to partying it up. Everyone knows how to have fun at this campus."

The Guys and Girls and Wayne State University

"The unique aspect about Wayne State University is that it is a commuter school and the guys and girls come from all walks of life and cultures. Wayne State University has a mixture of students that are preppy, artistic, athletic, trendy, a little wild and those that are very conservative and they dress, act and look accordingly. There are some very attractive guys on campus who are mostly in a fraternity or are into body building."

HEALTH & SAFETY

Just Like National Security.

"Wayne State Police are like SWAT and the FBI. All it takes is one call."

Wellesley College

106 Central St.; Wellesley, MA 02481
(781) 283-1000; www.wellesley.edu

THE BASICS:

Acceptance Rate: 35%
Yield: 40%
Setting: Suburban
Control: Private Non-Profit
Total Undergrads: 2,324
SAT Range: 1930–2210*
ACT Range: 29–32

Student-Faculty Ratio: 8:1
Retention Rate: 94%
Graduation Rate: 91%
Tuition: $38,062
Room & Board: $11,786
Avg. Aid Package: $33,843
Students With Aid: 66%

* of 2400

Academics	A	Greek Life	D
Athletics	C+	Guys	N/A
Campus Dining	B	Health & Safety	B+
Campus Housing	B	Local Atmosphere	B
Campus Strictness	D-	Nightlife	B
Computers	B	Off-Campus Dining	B+
Diversity	A	Off-Campus Housing	D-
Drug Safety	A	Parking	C+
Facilities	A-	Transportation	C+
Girls	B	Weather	C-

CP's Student Author On...
OVERALL EXPERIENCE

The nightlife stinks, it's too darn strict, and students constantly battle the fear of four years of celibacy. Hold on, why do Wellesley students love this place again? Oh, right—the academics rock, it's possible to make shockingly amazing friends, the campus is gorgeous, and graduates wind up with a prestigious name on their diplomas. Some students might feel they're missing out by coming to Wellesley, while others say they're gaining incredible resources of support, critical thinking, and endurance. Whether or not they're happy about it, this latter group is right.

A community like Wellesley College would be difficult to achieve in a coed environment because living at Wellesley is like living with 2,300 sisters—you complain, you fight, and you talk about sex in ridiculously frank ways. You hate and love each other at the same time. Wellesley is intense and bizarre, both restrictive and liberating. Students learn to adapt, or they learn to overcome.

Students Speak Out On...
OVERALL EXPERIENCE

Q Great Academics, Lacking Party Scene
"Wellesley is known for its stellar academics and great access to professors. However, if one is looking for a party scene, they will not be finding it at Wellesley. Even so, Boston and Cambridge are just 40-minute bus rides away, where there is an abundance of activities to do. Parties at MIT and Harvard are relatively easy to find and attend."

Q "Sometimes I wonder what I'm missing out by going to an all-women's school. I often have thoughts of transferring, but I don't think I will ever act upon them."

Q "The term 'the Wellesley bubble' is tossed around among Wellesley women so much, and unfortunately, the so-called bubble is a truth: we are indeed cut off from the 'real world' and insulated from men and from all reality. My experience has been that after my first year here, I'm not stronger, but more scared to challenge men. Perhaps the change hasn't come yet. I feel very isolated from everything else, and almost suffocated in this kind of atmosphere."

BEST OF WELLESLEY

1. Gorgeous campus and buildings
2. Excellent professors and small class sizes
3. All on-campus activities are free
4. FirstClass, which facilitates academics and social life
5. The all-women thing

Happy Students
94% of students return after their first year.

Commitment to Teaching
There are 8 students for every member of faculty on campus.

WORST OF WELLESLEY

1. Stress
2. The weather
3. The all-women thing
4. Limited nightlife
5. Location
6. Few independent living options

Expensive
Tuition is a steep $38,062, one of the most expensive rates in the country.

Expensive Dorms
Living on campus doesn't come cheap, with an average housing price tag of $5,980.

Student Body

African American:	6%	Male Undergrads:	4%
Asian American:	25%	Female Undergrads:	96%
Hispanic:	7%	Living On Campus:	98%
International:	0%	Living Off Campus:	2%
Native American:	1%	Male Athletes:	0%
White:	43%	Female Athletes:	8%
Unknown:	19%	Fraternity Members:	0%
From Out-of-State:	88%	Sorority Members:	0%

Students Speak Out On... EVERYTHING!

ACADEMICS

Rigorous, Yet Do-Able

"I find most classes to be quite challenging and there to be a significant workload, yet professors and upperclasswomen frequently go out of their way to help you succeed academically. Some math and science classes have Supplemental Instruction taught by upperclasswomen and many subjects have help rooms for students to bring specific questions, both of which are extremely useful."

Qualified Professors

"I'm a Psychology major at Wellesley, and it's amazing. The professors here have so much experience in their field, and are genuinely interested in their classes. Also, with no graduate students, the undergrads get to help the professors with their research, which gives students good experience in their field of interest."

ATHLETICS

Sports Are Awesome

"Wellesley Women breathe commitment. We are committed in every aspect of our lives, including sports, and it shows."

School Spirit- What's That?

"There is zero school spirit. As a former athlete, I attest that athletics are very far from the focus of our college. Granted, we're all women and we don't have the bigger male sports like football, but our games go unattended.Plus, we don't even have a real mascot- our mascot is "blue"."

CAMPUS DINING

Dining Halls Everywhere

"Every dorm complex has a dining hall, so getting food is very convenient. We do not use a point system, so food is always all-you-can-eat. The quality of food has gone down with the use of a new food system this year, but there is generally still a lot of variety and great food."

Frequently Compared Schools:

Bryn Mawr College
Mount Holyoke College
Smith College
Wesleyan University

Unlimited Food!

"Free food! Everyone has the same meal plan, so everyone can eat in any dining hall, and can get an unlimited amount of food. Sure, the food is a little "cafeteria-ish", but we're usually allowed to take things like milk, fruit, cereal, and bread up to our rooms to save."

CAMPUS HOUSING

Everyone Lives in the Dorms

"Dorms are fun and campus life centers around them. Sometimes it gets annoying to live in a dorm year after year and not be able to have your own place, kitchen, etc, but you deal. Your room size/niceness will vary from building to building, but juniors and seniors usually live in singles and nothing on campus is more than 10 minutes away from anything else."

GUYS & GIRLS

All Women

"If ladies are your thing, there are some very beautiful and smart women. If guys are your thing, Wellesley is very close to MIT and Harvard, where guys are pretty cute. If you're worried about Wellesley being all women, don't. You see men, often. At parties, in the city, or even on campus taking advantage of the pretty landscape."

HEALTH & SAFETY

The Police Are Your Parents

"have never felt unsafe at Wellesley. It is a small, beautiful, safe place to be. Our honor code allows people to feel safe with their doors unlocked and their bikes unchained. Our campus police are looking out for our well-being 100% of the time."

LOOKING FOR MORE?

Check out our full-length guide to this school at collegeprowler.com/wellesley-college/.

Wesleyan University

237 High St.; Middletown, CT 06459
(860) 685-2000; www.wesleyan.edu

THE BASICS:

Acceptance Rate: 27%
Yield: 32%
Setting: Small city
Control: Private Non-Profit
Total Undergrads: 2,787
SAT Range: 1940–2220*
ACT Range: 30–32

Student-Faculty Ratio: 9:1
Retention Rate: 95%
Graduation Rate: 93%
Tuition: $40,092
Room & Board: $11,040
Avg. Aid Package: $30,543
Students With Aid: 52%

* of 2400

Academics	A-	Greek Life	C-
Athletics	C	Guys	C+
Campus Dining	B	Health & Safety	C+
Campus Housing	B	Local Atmosphere	C-
Campus Strictness	B	Nightlife	C-
Computers	B+	Off-Campus Dining	B-
Diversity	A-	Off-Campus Housing	D+
Drug Safety	C+	Parking	B
Facilities	B+	Transportation	C-
Girls	C+	Weather	C+

CP's Student Author On...
OVERALL EXPERIENCE

What can one say about Wesleyan except that it's an all-around great college? Make no mistake about it, though, when you move into your dorm the first day of freshman year, you'll be petrified. You may very well be freaked out by the strange attire of your classmates or about the angry protesters on Foss Hill. Plunging into a bizarre world of drugs, hippie-paranoia, and ultra-left-wing weirdness may, at first, seem imminent. You might even lock yourself in your room and refuse to come out, worried that those tree-hugging granola heads on campus might sacrifice you to their hemp god. These fears, of course, are unfounded, ridiculous, and are all part of becoming a college student (except maybe the part about the tree-hugging granola heads).

Wesleyan has a lot of reputations, and it lives up to some of them. It's often called "Diversity University," and has been portrayed as being extremely politically-correct in the movies (PCU), and has been depicted in papers like the New York Times as being "naively liberal.... For the rest of this editorial, visit collegeprowler.com.

Students Speak Out On...
OVERALL EXPERIENCE

Q "I wasn't wild about Wesleyan at first. Everyone I met was so eccentric and over-the-top, I thought it couldn't be real. There are some fakers out there, but for the most part, Wesleyan is filled with some really wonderful people."

Q "I'm really happy here. I'm only going into my sophomore year, and I already have made many exceptional friends. We're never bored because the school (and the students) provide so much to do."

Q "I only wish the the lackluster atmosphere and sports teams at Wesleyan matched the school's academic intensity. Many times I felt myself longing for that 'big-school' feel."

Q "Let's get one thing straight—Middletown is not your average college town. It's not really the safest town either. Some students choose to transfer on that account alone."

Q "Wesleyan is not for everybody. It's not a 'typical college,' if there is such a thing. It's very eccentric and very artsy. It's a place for creative people, a place where they can grow and flourish. It's for open-minded people, people with a sense of humor. It's not for the faint of heart."

BEST OF WESLEYAN

1. The amazing and unique student body
2. The beautiful campus
3. The exposure to all sorts of different ideas
4. The professors
5. The freedom to choose your own academic course

Happy Students
95% of students return after their first year.

Commitment to Teaching
There are 9 students for every member of faculty on campus.

WORST OF WESLEYAN

1. Pretentious artists and writers
2. The drug scene
3. The occasionally emotionless administration
4. The chaotic course and housing selection process
5. Mediocre campus security

Expensive
Tuition is a steep $40,092, one of the most expensive rates in the country.

Student Body

African American:	7%	Male Undergrads:	50%	
Asian American:	10%	Female Undergrads:	50%	
Hispanic:	8%	Living On Campus:	99%	
International:	7%	Living Off Campus:	1%	
Native American:	0%	Male Athletes:	31%	
White:	59%	Female Athletes:	20%	
Unknown:	8%	Fraternity Members:	2%	
From Out-of-State:	94%	Sorority Members:	1%	

Frequently Compared Schools:

Tufts University
Vassar College
Williams College
Yale University

Students Speak Out On... EVERYTHING!

ACADEMICS

The Wesleyan Education

"One of the best in the country, in my opinion. Grades are important, but one should not obsess about them. It's what you get out of the course that matters, and here you get a lot"

Academics Come First

"I decided to attend Wesleyan University for many different reasons, but one aspect Wesleyan that never has failed to surprise me is the student and faculty commitment to learn from each other. Classes are both challenging and fun, and professors are always available to meet with for extra help or discussion."

ATHLETICS

I Don't Really Know

"not everyone goes to sports stuff, but i know our football team sucks"

"You can find a good intramural team if you'd like and take it as seriously as you want. As for varsity sports, I never see the football team, except on homecoming."

CAMPUS DINING

Pretty Good Comparatively Speaking

"i've seen other college's dining halls and in comparison Usdan is pretty darn great.... but summerfields is pretty much "bummerfields"... not so awesome. And points go fast fast fast..."

Satisfactory

"The campus dining options are not too diverse, and so it tends to become repetitive."

CAMPUS HOUSING

Amazing

"Many of the dorms have Balconies! It is so amazing to socialize and have parties or events in your dorm with an open balcony. The lounges are cozy, many of the bathrooms are co-ed, which I love, and the RA's I have had have been understanding and awesome. Dorm life is exactly what I hoped for in every way."

"Try not to live in Hewitt, because a lot of it is either sub-free or single-sex housing, so I know a lot of people didn't really like it there. Although I know a lot of lovely people who were there, so it's really fine."

GUYS & GIRLS

The Pot Head Atheists

"wesleyan has a big hipster scene. there are a lot of scraggly-looking ppl and metro lookin ppl with vnecks and large glasses and plad shirts and tight shorts. A lot of nerd-looking ppl and a few jocks"

Guys and girls are decent

"The guys and girls here at Wesleyan are not too shabby at all. The guys can be hot and many times well dressed. The girls tend to be well dressed and slim. Wesleyan's student body definitely leans toward slender but not necessarily so much muscular, though it is heading towards attracting more athletes."

HEALTH & SAFETY

Safe

"Crime is relatively uncommon. There is the occasional theft or petty crime, however due the school's location, most students generally don't worry too much about crime."

Walk With a Buddy

"Middletown has been the site of a few shootings in recent years, and I wouldn't go there alone at night -- girls are also at risk of being catcalled. On campus, two students were beaten up this past year by nonstudents, but generally I feel safe walking around alone, even at night. You can always (24/7) call for a campus-safety escort, or often a student escort if you prefer, and "the Ride" is a van you can hop on that travels campus in circuits after 7pm."

LOOKING FOR MORE?

Check out our full-length guide to this school at collegeprowler.com/wesleyan-university/.

West Point Military Academy

646 Swift Road; West Point, NY 10996
(845) 938-4011; www.usma.edu

THE BASICS:

Acceptance Rate: 14%
Yield: 80%
Setting: Suburban
Control: Public
Total Undergrads: 4,621
SAT Range: 1680–1970*
ACT Range: 25–29

Student-Faculty Ratio: 7:1
Retention Rate: 92%
Graduation Rate: 79%
Tuition: $0
Room & Board: $0
Avg. Aid Package: $0
Students With Aid: 0%

* of 2400

Academics	B+	Greek Life	N/A
Athletics	B+	Guys	B+
Campus Dining	C-	Health & Safety	A
Campus Housing	D	Local Atmosphere	C+
Campus Strictness	F	Nightlife	C-
Computers	B+	Off-Campus Dining	C-
Diversity	C+	Off-Campus Housing	N/A
Drug Safety	A+	Parking	C
Facilities	B+	Transportation	B-
Girls	C-	Weather	C+

CP's Student Author On...
OVERALL EXPERIENCE

West Point takes pride in attracting the top talent from across the nation. The extensive application process is one of the many indicators as to the type of student who applies to West Point. Applying to West Point is best described as a process of attrition. Each year, over 10,000 prospective high school juniors and seniors submit requests for information on West Point. Applicants are assessed, and approximately 2,000 are qualified through West Point's academic, physical, and medical criteria. Of this number, West Point admits between 1,150–1,200 young men and women each year. Candidates are evaluated for admission on the basis of academic performance (high school record and SAT or ACT scores, as well as SAT II subject test scores), demonstrated leadership potential, physical aptitude, and medical qualification. Each candidate must also obtain a nomination from a member of Congress or from the Department of the Army. West Point seeks a class composition of top scholars, leaders, athletes, women, and minorities to maintain a diverse collegiate environment and student body. As you can see, the application process is quite extensive.... For the rest of this editorial, visit collegeprowler.com.

Students Speak Out On...
OVERALL EXPERIENCE

Q Life at USMA
"Duty, Honor, Country. Those hallowed words are the values that are instilled in every single West Point cadet. Cadets learn how things are in the real world and step up and take real world responsibilities and leadership roles."

Q "Life is definitely more concentrated here. A famous saying is that we experience more in a day than most college students experience in a week."

Q "You have to compete with everybody at everything. But, competition does not override the need for teamwork. 'Cooperate and graduate' is one of the most popular sayings at West Point, because this is a tough place to get through all on your own."

Q "Many colleges look for high school students with good grades, but West Point looks for young men and women who will make good Army officers. You should be intelligent, have good athletic skills, and get along with people. You should also demonstrate your leadership ability. They call it the 'whole person' concept here."

BEST OF WEST POINT

1. Every so often, they will let you sleep. And when they do, it is the best sleep you have ever had. There's nothing like falling asleep after a full day of work, both mentally and physically.

Affordable
Tuition is only $0, one of the most affordable rates in the country.

Happy Students
92% of students return after their first year.

WORST OF WEST POINT

1. You will miss all of the sleep you used to take for granted.

2. Drill is a hard thing for civilians to get used to.

3. Sometimes the fun is "mandatory fun," and that isn't very fun at all.

Unbalanced Student Population
It might be hard for some students to find a date with a male-to-female ratio of 86/14.

Student Body

African American:	6%	Male Undergrads:	85%
Asian American:	6%	Female Undergrads:	15%
Hispanic:	8%	Living On Campus:	100%
International:	1%	Living Off Campus:	0%
Native American:	1%	Male Athletes:	30%
White:	72%	Female Athletes:	30%
Unknown:	1%	Fraternity Members:	0%
From Out-of-State:	94%	Sorority Members:	0%

Students Speak Out On...
EVERYTHING!

ACADEMICS

"At West Point, you take a lot of classes and receive a very broad education, but you don't really study anything in depth. It is like they want to develop every little corner of your brain or something."

"Every instructor seems to think that their subject is more important than any other. It is like if you don't know astrophysics and can't make at least a C in my class, then you are not going to be a good officer. It gets real annoying, fast."

ATHLETICS

"One of the great things about West Point is that you can, at almost anytime of the day, get involved in a pickup game. Over at Arvin, there are always basketball, racquetball, volleyball, and other games going on."

"Everyone here is an athlete. There are so many different opportunities to try something new. Every year they have a club night, where the different clubs all set up stands and hand out information. There are so many different athletic clubs on post. What is great about the majority of them is that you don't have to have any prior experience."

CAMPUS DINING

Cadet Mess Hall

"The food is really very good. The buffets are all you can eat or carry out, and everything is free. Really diverse food, steak is served usually 1x/wk, different "culture" nights every Tuesday, lots of banquets w/great menus. Great lunch meals. Breakfast needs work but overall good."

Synonyms for Amazing for $1000 Please

"The food is simply amazing. One could get tired of eating at the dining hall, but you are squeezed into a huge ancient building along with every other person on campus and feed in less than 30 minutes. It is a nearly impossible feat. There is also a snack place if you need something late at night. And the only McDonalds that delievers is right off of the base."

Frequently Compared Schools:

Harvard University
United States Naval Academy
University of Pennsylvania
Yale University

CAMPUS HOUSING

Housing Process

"Everyone lives on campus so it is easy to contact people and go to classes. Everything is nearby so you don't ahve to walk far."

"The barracks are okay. You have two sinks and what amounts to bunk beds. You also have two sets of drawers and closets. Overall, they are pretty small. What really sucks is when you have three cadets living in a one-person room. For some cadets, it is like prison. And four years in prison is a pretty long time."

GUYS & GIRLS

"A large percentage of the girls here are fairly attractive, but you are not even cognizant of the fact that they are girls when you see them in a military environment. It's really not until you see them wearing civilian clothes that you realize that they are almost cute."

"The guys here are all studs. Take me for example: I am 145 pounds of raw steel and sex appeal. West Point definitely has the studliest guys on the face of the planet. And the studliest guys at West Point are found right here, in Pershing Barracks, baby."

HEALTH & SAFETY

Safest

"Military Police and local safety ensure WP is one of the safest places to be."

"A lot of people are worried about the possibility of their being a terrorist attack in the near future at West Point. If you stop and think about it, West Point is a perfect place for a terrorist strike. There is so much senior military brass around here, and the cadets are the future of the military. West Point is also very symbolic."

LOOKING FOR MORE?

Check out our full-length guide to this school at collegeprowler.com/west-point-military-academy/.

West Virginia University

University Avenue; Morgantown, WV 26506
(304) 293-0111; www.wvu.edu

THE BASICS:

Acceptance Rate: 79%
Yield: 39%
Setting: Small city
Control: Public
Total Undergrads: 22,303
SAT Range: 950–1140*
ACT Range: 21–26

Student-Faculty Ratio: 23:1
Retention Rate: 80%
Graduation Rate: 56%
Tuition: $17,002
Room & Board: $7,868
Avg. Aid Package: $4,262
Students With Aid: 84%

* of 1600

Academics	B-	Greek Life	B
Athletics	A	Guys	A+
Campus Dining	B+	Health & Safety	C
Campus Housing	B	Local Atmosphere	B+
Campus Strictness	B	Nightlife	A+
Computers	A-	Off-Campus Dining	A-
Diversity	C+	Off-Campus Housing	B
Drug Safety	C	Parking	C
Facilities	B+	Transportation	A-
Girls	A	Weather	B-

CP's Student Author On...
OVERALL EXPERIENCE

Overall, students have made it pretty clear that they are really enjoying their time at WVU. Looking back through this book, it can be seen that WVU has garnered many high grades for subjects such as social scene, academics, and athletics. It is clear that there are many things the school excels in. The aforementioned are huge parts of campus life at WVU, and the students have said nothing but good things about them. While there were many high grades, there were a few grades that show the University could still improve in certain areas. It is clear that the campus dining services are not doing a great job pleasing the students, nor is the parking situation on campus. Considering these are two pretty important things on a college campus, the University should quickly take the right steps to move those two issues into a positive direction.

The attitude at WVU seems pretty split between academics and social events. While most students attend WVU with the expectation of a great education, there are a select few who come to WVU because of the potential party scene. Either way, WVU offers something for each side.... For the rest of this editorial, visit collegeprowler.com.

Students Speak Out On...
OVERALL EXPERIENCE

Q WVU is my home

"I've only been here for 4 weeks now, and I can already say that I know these next four years are going to be best thing that's ever happened to me. I feel right at home here and coming from the northeast, the people are very friendly. The food variety is amazing and it really is impossible to gain the Freshman Fifteen with all the hills and stairs here. Our rec center is one of the best with an amazing fitness facility and swimming pool."

Q Love Being a Mountaineer

"Never expected to enjoy a place as much as I have at West Virginia University. Did my undergraduate work here and now enrolled in their DPT program so I will have three more years at West Virginia University. Can't imagine being anywhere else."

BEST OF WEST VIRGINIA

1. Party scene
2. Mountaineer football games
3. People/friends
4. Rec Center
5. Up All Night
6. Christmas lights on Woodburn Hall

Happy Students
80% of students return after their first year.

Knowledgeable Professors
90% of students surveyed rated the general knowledge of professors as above average.

WORST OF WEST VIRGINIA

1. Traffic
2. Hills
3. PRT always breaking down
4. Dining hall food
5. Parking
6. Cold weather
7. Sorority girls

Not Much Diversity
One of the least racially diverse campuses—only 11% of students are minorities.

Student Body

African American:	3%	Male Undergrads:	55%
Asian American:	2%	Female Undergrads:	45%
Hispanic:	2%	Living On Campus:	26%
International:	2%	Living Off Campus:	74%
Native American:	0%	Male Athletes:	3%
White:	89%	Female Athletes:	3%
Unknown:	1%	Fraternity Members:	7%
From Out-of-State:	52%	Sorority Members:	8%

Frequently Compared Schools:

James Madison University
Penn State
University of Pittsburgh
Virginia Tech

Students Speak Out On...
EVERYTHING!

ACADEMICS

The Ease of Learning About My Major

"I haven't attended any classes yet at West Virginia University, but it was so easy to find information about my intended major. I know the extent of the education I can receive in my specific area of study, and I know exactly where I will be attending classes. I found all this information by using the very extensive and easily navigable website, http://www.wvu.edu."

Professors

"Professors at West Virginia University are very interested in the grades that each of theirs students recieve. They ask for our feedback and are always sure to tell us when their office hours are. They are more than happy to help students and if a student can not make it to a professors designated office hours they are more than happy to schedule an appoint me with the students to go the extra mile and make sure we are learning the material."

ATHLETICS

The Best

"BCS champions in FootballCurrently in final 4 in NCAA basketball - GO MOUNTAINEERS!!"

The Mountaineers

"West Virginia University is known for its athletics! It speaks for itself for team performance, but the fan support and student involvement is always overwhelming and touching. To know we can all come together to support the same cause, our school's team, is more than wonderful. All of the students work hard to have a good time, whether we win or lose."

CAMPUS DINING

Good Food!

"As a vegetarian, I have many selections as to where I can dine with my omnivorous friends! On any of the campuses at West Virginia University, there is always a place everyone can agree to go. Plus, the dining hall food is full of selection and finger-licking entrees!"

MEALS AND DEALS

"There are several places to choose from to eat at and the flex dollars are welcomed at them all. There are pizza places, chicken places, the cafeteria, coffee shops, juice bars and smoothies and what is nice, there are always tables available to sit at."

CAMPUS HOUSING

Great

"Never had a problem while On-campus. They only let you stay 1 year."

Great Way to Meet People

"For freshmen, the housing is a great way to meet people. If wanting to stay on the Evansdale campus, Towers is the place to be. All four residential towers are connected, making it easy to interact and meet others, even if they are staying in another tower. Aside from living on campus, there is no shortage of off-campus housing, and there are some campus buildings in the downtown area of Morgantown. The quality of the dorms is just average, but the ease of being with others makes up for it."

GUYS & GIRLS

Guys Are Picky

"The guys at WVU are pretty hot for the majority of them. Most of them are the typical frat boys, stuck up, nice bodies and looking for one thing. BUT you can come across a few sexy sweethearts, just have to look in the right place!"

Community

"There is a lots of diversity at the college. People who come from all over the United States and even foreign countries. The dress is as anywhere, some dress casual, some dress fancier, but every one has manners and are kind and thoughtful."

HEALTH & SAFETY

Security

"I always feel safe on campus. Security presence is visible."

LOOKING FOR MORE?

Check out our full-length guide to this school at collegeprowler.com/west-virginia-university/.

Western Illinois University

1 University Circle; Macomb, IL 61455
(309) 298-1414; www.wiu.edu

THE BASICS:

Acceptance Rate: 65%
Yield: 21%
Setting: Town
Control: Public
Total Undergrads: 11,439
SAT Range: —
ACT Range: 19–23

Student-Faculty Ratio: 16:1
Retention Rate: 74%
Graduation Rate: 55%
Tuition: $10,829
Room & Board: $8,138
Avg. Aid Package: $9,423
Students With Aid: 78%

Academics	B-	Greek Life	B-
Athletics	C	Guys	B
Campus Dining	C+	Health & Safety	C+
Campus Housing	C	Local Atmosphere	D+
Campus Strictness	B	Nightlife	A-
Computers	C	Off-Campus Dining	C
Diversity	C+	Off-Campus Housing	B
Drug Safety	C-	Parking	B+
Facilities	B-	Transportation	A
Girls	B-	Weather	C

CP's Student Author On...
OVERALL EXPERIENCE

Overall, the majority of students say they had a great experience at Western Illinois University and that they learned so much about themselves during their time here. Of course, it's not all smooth sailing. Students might struggle with their academics at times or may have trouble getting involved in student activities at first, but they learn that it is important to find the resources that will help them in the long run—and there are many resources on campus, so use them!

Students at Western Illinois University are able to learn and grow from their mistakes. For example, students quickly learn that it is important to ask their professors questions if they don't understand something; otherwise, if they say nothing, their grades could suffer. Students also learn about friendships and who to hang with. A big part of college is networking and finding the right people to hang out with.

Students Speak Out On...
OVERALL EXPERIENCE

Q I'm Loving It
"Having a really good time here. I'm loving this school year!!!"

Q Western Illinois University.
"So far i love my school and can not picture myself going anywhere else. The one issue i have had with the school is some of the members of the athletic department particularly in the swimming and diving program."

Q Overall Experience
"My overall experience at this school has been a positive one. I have had many mentors and people helping me achieve my goal. If I could do this all over again, I would have come here right after high school. That way I would have had more friends and greater chances at other items in life."

Q Unique
"There's a lot of diversity and people who are nice and willing to help at any time."

BEST OF WESTERN ILLINOIS

1. Student activities around campus
2. Homecoming
3. Rec center
4. Sense of community
5. Personal classes
6. Top-notch programs, especially LEJA and music

Affordable
Tuition is only $10,829, one of the most affordable rates in the country.

Knowledgeable Professors
92% of students surveyed rated the general knowledge of professors as above average.

WORST OF WESTERN ILLINOIS

1. Sports teams are very inconsistent.
2. The food
3. In the middle of nowhere
4. Not much to do off campus
5. The weather
6. Low school spirit

Students Can't Wait to Get Out of Town
69% of students surveyed said that there's no way they would live here after graduation.

Student Body

African American:	8%	Male Undergrads:	54%
Asian American:	1%	Female Undergrads:	46%
Hispanic:	5%	Living On Campus:	45%
International:	2%	Living Off Campus:	55%
Native American:	1%	Male Athletes:	6%
White:	77%	Female Athletes:	4%
Unknown:	6%	Fraternity Members:	9%
From Out-of-State:	5%	Sorority Members:	9%

Students Speak Out On... EVERYTHING!

ACADEMICS

Computer Programming
"This school is the best fit for me and offers me the most chances in the field I want to major in, which is computer science."

Professors
"They're very helpful and understanding and personable."

Really World Experience/In the Classroom Workshops
"The program has some instructors who have worked in the sector adn the program has an emphasis on the hotel/restaurant industry really opening the door for the job search."

ATHLETICS

Softball
"The girls are really good at playing softball. They make people want to come to their games. The girls treat one another like family."

Western Athletics
"I enjoyed going to all the home football games this past season, but it dosen't seem that for ohter sports like basketball, soccer, or volleyball are as heaviy advertised so it seems that people miss out on those. I think there should be more things about athletic events posted around campus."

Sports
"The football team is pretty good but no one goes to the games at all which makes it makes it less appealing"

CAMPUS DINING

Thompson Dining
"Has a lot of space to eat. There are many food options to eat. The people are really friendly."

Food
"The food is average."

Food
"It's the same thing all day every day and it doesn't get better... it's good for about the first 2 weeks."

CAMPUS HOUSING

WIU Residence Halls
"The dormitories at Western Illinois University aren't the best, but they're convenient with snack stores, computer labs and a large lounge for social events."

Dorms Are Ok
"The freshmen only have a choice of two dorms at Western Illinois University, so you either get the one closer to classes or away from them. The upperclassmen have far more places to choose from, but still, the dorms need to renovated and brought up to date because they are old and falling apart."

Dorms
"The rooms are small, but all dorm rooms are. It is ok living in them, nothing special, but nothing too horrible."

GUYS & GIRLS

Lots of Guys
"There's a lot of different types of guys at Western; rednecks, country boys, potheads, city boys, jocks, preps. Girls are generally into the party scene and drinking, but there's a lot of diversity with them. Most people seem to be single or just casually dating."

Very Diverse
"You'll find an eclectic group of people. Tons of people interested in agriculture, law enforcement, and of course, partying."

HEALTH & SAFETY

Never Had a Problem
"Never felt like I was in a position where I was threatened or in danger."

Police
"The security at Western Illinois is very good. They take appropriate measures such as the blue-light callboxes around campus. Also there's a ton of police driving around and even the campus police do their job well."

Western Kentucky University

1906 College Heights Blvd.; Bowling Green, KY 42101
(270) 745-0111; www.wku.edu

THE BASICS:

Acceptance Rate: 94%	Student-Faculty Ratio: 19:1
Yield: 47%	Retention Rate: 74%
Setting: Small city	Graduation Rate: 42%
Control: Public	Tuition: $17,784
Total Undergrads: 17,648	Room & Board: $6,351
SAT Range: 860–1110*	Avg. Aid Package: $11,854
ACT Range: 18–24	Students With Aid: 95%

* of 1600

Academics	C+	Greek Life	B-
Athletics	C+	Guys	B+
Campus Dining	B+	Health & Safety	B-
Campus Housing	C+	Local Atmosphere	B-
Campus Strictness	C-	Nightlife	B
Computers	A-	Off-Campus Dining	B-
Diversity	B-	Off-Campus Housing	B+
Drug Safety	C	Parking	B
Facilities	B+	Transportation	B+
Girls	B	Weather	B-

CP's Student Author On...
OVERALL EXPERIENCE

Though most people don't choose WKU as their dream school, most students are still satisfied with their choice to attend. The University may have its problems with little things around campus (like parking), but as far as universities go, students know that overall they have it pretty good.

When asked whether they would do it all over again, many say that they would still choose Western. WKU really becomes home to many students over the course of their time spent in Bowling Green, and there are tons of opportunities to do anything they choose. The atmosphere—featuring lots of experiences to get involved with infused with a sense of belonging—is really what makes Western unique.

Students Speak Out On...
OVERALL EXPERIENCE

Q Love It!

"I love the friendliness and sociability of this campus. It is within walking distance of a variety of places, and the campus is not too big. There is only one big hill on campus, so walking clear across campus is not overwhelming. The students are very sociable and friendly which eases college experience even if you do not live on campus."

Q LOOOOOVE IT!

"Western is a great universtity to start out at, it is all real close where you don't have to walk forever to get to class. It is a beautiful campus, for the most part everyone is real nice. The teachers are mostly willing to help you out when you need it instead of making you stress about it."

Q WKU Is Awesome!!

"I once thought I wanted to go somewhere else for school, but choosing WKU was the best decision of my life!!"

BEST OF WESTERN KENTUCKY

1. Beautiful campus
2. Diversity on campus
3. Friendly environment
4. Lots of opportunities
5. Variety of majors/minors
6. Great professors
7. Conveniently close to shopping, eating, etc.

Knowledgeable Professors
90% of students surveyed rated the general knowledge of professors as above average.

Low-Stress Course Load
90% of students surveyed rated the manageability of work as above average.

WORST OF WESTERN KENTUCKY

1. Calendar
2. Construction
3. Parking
4. Old facilities
5. Housing bureaucracy
6. Not much to do in Bowling Green

Lowest Grades
Campus Strictness: C-
Drug Safety: C
Academics: C+

Student Body

African American:	10%	Male Undergrads:	42%
Asian American:	1%	Female Undergrads:	58%
Hispanic:	2%	Living On Campus:	29%
International:	2%	Living Off Campus:	71%
Native American:	0%	Male Athletes:	5%
White:	83%	Female Athletes:	2%
Unknown:	2%	Fraternity Members:	9%
From Out-of-State:	18%	Sorority Members:	9%

Frequently Compared Schools:

Belmont University
Middle Tennessee State University
University of Kentucky
University of Louisville

Students Speak Out On...
EVERYTHING!

ACADEMICS

Ag Is Important

"This is one of the major agricultural school in Kentucky so obviously my major is very important to many prople here. I am an animal science major, while the workload is very intense due to all the science classes you have to take there is always a teacher or classmate there to help you out when you need it. With this school you have the oppurtunity to live and work on a farm and get hands on with your major."

Honors College Professor

"I am apart of the WKU Honors College and I love every single Honors teacher that I have had. They really go beyond a normal professor. The classes are so interactive and have room for discussions and questions. They really have provided a lot of help to me in my Honors classes. It makes classes a lot more enjoyable to be able to interact in the classroom."

ATHLETICS

Awesome Athletics

"we have an awesome fan base made up of faculty,students and the community. The seats are always pretty full at games. The teams are awesome especially our basketball teams! They have broke several records. We have athletic facilities where you can really get a good workout or just have fun shooting baskets or playing raquetball. The bike and running machines even have TVs on them with free cable! It is excellent."

Spirit

"The football team at my school just went up a division, so they recently lost every game they played last year. I guess you would expect one win, but not even that. Every year though, despite the losses, our team plays with a lot of heart and never gives up. Even when they lose, they step on the court and field every time expecting to do their best."

CAMPUS DINING

Always Full

"Almost every place on campus you can use your meal plans, they have a variety of choices, from a taco place, a burger place, some chicken places, and a buffet place, where you use one meal plan and can eat all you want until you leave. I am always full when I leave a place after eating."

Food Is Great

"Western offers a variety of meal plans for students and there are many different places to eat on campus. The food court has a typical dining hall as well as several fast food chain restaurants. There is even a school run sit down and eat "fine dining" restaurant."

CAMPUS HOUSING

On Campus Housing

"All of the dorms have been recently renovated and are nice to live in. There are options of co-ed, greek, and suite style dorms. Rooms are highly custumizable, and bathrooms and halls are kept very clean. All dorms are quiet close to parking, food, and classes."

Dorms

"WKU has beautiful and clean dorms.The rooms are well furnished, and they are safe. The school provides a system where you can choose your room, and your roommate."

GUYS & GIRLS

WKU Students

"WKU students are an involved community. With the majority of the student population being in a Greek organization, there are plenty of ways to meet new people and expand your social circle. If the Greek life isn't for you, you can always join a student orgainzation such as SIFE (Student in Free Enterprise), intramural team or special interest group."

HEALTH & SAFETY

Never Felt Unsafe

"I've never felt unsafe on campus, but I probably would if I spent a lot of time walking around at 4 a.m., and I get freaked out if my roommate randomly decides to go for a run in the early morning. But, overall, I think campus is really safe and those emergency station things must be pretty good because I want to push the button every single time I walk by one."

LOOKING FOR MORE?

Check out our full-length guide to this school at collegeprowler.com/western-kentucky-university/.

Wheaton College - Illinois

501 College Ave.; Wheaton, IL 60187
(630) 752-5000; www.wheaton.edu

THE BASICS:

Acceptance Rate: 71%	**Student-Faculty Ratio:** 11:1
Yield: 46%	**Retention Rate:** 96%
Setting: Suburban	**Graduation Rate:** 86%
Control: Private Non-Profit	**Tuition:** $26,520
Total Undergrads: 2,399	**Room & Board:** $7,770
SAT Range: 1790–2110*	**Avg. Aid Package:** $14,490
ACT Range: 27–31	**Students With Aid:** 76%

of 2400

Academics	A-	Greek Life	N/A
Athletics	B-	Guys	A-
Campus Dining	A	Health & Safety	A+
Campus Housing	A+	Local Atmosphere	B+
Campus Strictness	C	Nightlife	C
Computers	C+	Off-Campus Dining	B+
Diversity	C-	Off-Campus Housing	A-
Drug Safety	A+	Parking	A
Facilities	A-	Transportation	B+
Girls	A	Weather	C+

CP's Student Author On...
OVERALL EXPERIENCE

The words "For Christ and His Kingdom" resound through the air of Wheaton's campus, defining Wheaton students and guiding the faculty. Statistically, Wheaton students are some of the most contented in the nation. Why? The main reason given for this love of Wheaton is, simply, the fellow students. Nowhere else will you find so many talented, passionate, genuine, and Christ-centered students gathered in one place. The people you find at Wheaton will inspire you. They will challenge you, teach you, and change your life for the better. Likewise, the professors at Wheaton are dedicated to educating the whole person. Yes, you will have to study at Wheaton. That's a fact. But you will also be given the tools necessary to use your hard-earned knowledge to make a difference in the world. The few students that express discontent generally are not at Wheaton by their own choice and are upset about the restrictions placed upon them.

The Wheaton College experience is completely unique.... For the rest of this editorial, visit collegeprowler.com.

Students Speak Out On...
OVERALL EXPERIENCE

Q It's Been Great
"Wheaton is a good place. It's really seeks to mix faith and learning. And there are a lot of good people."

Q Phenomenal
"If you care about your academics and want to be trained to make a massive difference in the future, you have to be at Wheaton College. The quality of people, the fun events, and the unbelievable Jesus-centered atmosphere are unprecedented for the Christian student."

Q An Awesome, Enriched College Experience
"Wheaton College has been the best decision of my life. Great Profs, great students, great values."

Q It Depends Who You Are, Obviously
"Rest assured, Wheaton is extremely difficult academically. There's certainly no party life, so that's a reason people go there. So, if you do go there, expect to study. Want to study, even. If you consider yourself liberal, be careful. You must be strong, especially for the first couple semesters. People will try to convince you that you're not really a Christian if you're for gay marriage."

BEST OF WHEATON IL

1. The aesthetic beauty of the campus
2. Brother-sister floors
3. Chicago is only a train ride away.
4. Challenging academics
5. Cafeteria food—some of the very best campus food in the nation!

Happy Students
96% of students return after their first year.

Proven Success
86% of students will complete their education and graduate with a degree.

WORST OF WHEATON IL

1. Winter weather
2. Only one cafeteria
3. Mandatory chapel three times a week
4. Not enough parking available on campus
5. Not much to do at night in Wheaton

Expensive
Tuition is a steep $26,520, one of the most expensive rates in the country.

Life is NOT a Party
79% of students surveyed said it's almost impossible to find a good party.

Student Body

African American:	3%	Male Undergrads:	50%
Asian American:	7%	Female Undergrads:	50%
Hispanic:	4%	Living On Campus:	90%
International:	2%	Living Off Campus:	10%
Native American:	0%	Male Athletes:	29%
White:	82%	Female Athletes:	19%
Unknown:	2%	Fraternity Members:	0%
From Out-of-State:	78%	Sorority Members:	0%

Frequently Compared Schools:

Grove City College
Loyola University Chicago
Northwestern University
University of Chicago

Students Speak Out On...
EVERYTHING!

ACADEMICS

Q It's Really Good.

"The classes in Chemistry, my major, though challenging, are very awesome. The profs are great, there are plenty of jobs available in the department, and lots of opportunities to do summer research. The workload can be heavy, but that's the sciences."

Q Solid Christian Academics

"At Wheaton, I am so glad to have found professors who are knowledgeable, personable, and engaging. Wheaton is committed to integrating a Christian perspective into each class, and the students are committed to learning. All in all, the academics here are solid."

ATHLETICS

Q Sports Are Simple to Be Involved in

"Participating in sporting events is simple at Wheaton College. Students and faculty love to support the numerous varsity as well as club sports offered. Even not-so-athletic people can get involved with IM sports. There are many to choose from, and if the one you want isn't already established, getting it started is no problem!"

Q My XC Experience

"Upon coming to Wheaton, I didn't expect much from the sports programs. However, after one year of running XC and track on the team, I am proud to say that the men, women, and coaches on the team are some of the most encouraging, supportive, and awesome people that I have ever met! Besides that, they are competitive athletes and they train hard. I couldn't have asked for a better first year."

CAMPUS DINING

Q SAGA

"A few years ago the food here was rated the best in the nation for a college. It hasn't gotten any worse since then."

Q Ice Cream Everyday?!?

"Wheaton's dining is awesome--they have great food, solid variety, and of course, soft serve ice cream! For meals, you can either eat at the main cafeteria or the student grill (The Stupe), which are both delicious and healthy (if you skip the ice cream)."

CAMPUS HOUSING

Q Livin' It up

"The dorms at Wheaton are close to campus, classy, and completely outfitted. There's nothing to complain about here!"

Q Dorm Living Isn't Lacking

"Living in the dorms is convenient and fun. The freshman dorms at Wheaton College are community centered and a fantastic place to spend the first year away from home!"

GUYS & GIRLS

Q Honest Friendships at Wheaton

"Ok, I think one of my favorite parts of Wheaton was getting to know the girls on my sister floor--not only are they outgoing and friendly, but they are also solid Christians and pretty smart as well."

Q A Treasure

"I don't like to rate people, but the people at you'll meet at Wheaton, for the most part, are fantastic. Many, many talented people, whether in the arts or athletics. Beautiful people, inside and out. There are a variety of people too. You'll find friends for sure."

HEALTH & SAFETY

Q Not an Issue

"I've never seen or heard of an issue with campus security at Wheaton. Everyone feels totally safe walking around, even in the middle of the night."

LOOKING FOR MORE?

Check out our full-length guide to this school at collegeprowler.com/wheaton-college----illinois/.

Wheaton College - Massachusetts

26 E. Main St.; Norton, MA 02766
(508) 285-7722; www.wheatoncollege.edu

THE BASICS:

Acceptance Rate: 59%	**Student-Faculty Ratio:** 11:1
Yield: 22%	**Retention Rate:** 88%
Setting: Suburban	**Graduation Rate:** 81%
Control: Private Non-Profit	**Tuition:** $39,850
Total Undergrads: 1,642	**Room & Board:** $9,590
SAT Range: 1160–1350*	**Avg. Aid Package:** $25,522
ACT Range: 26–29	**Students With Aid:** 70%

* of 1600

Academics	B+	Greek Life	N/A
Athletics	B	Guys	C+
Campus Dining	A-	Health & Safety	B
Campus Housing	B	Local Atmosphere	C+
Campus Strictness	D	Nightlife	C+
Computers	B	Off-Campus Dining	B
Diversity	C	Off-Campus Housing	D
Drug Safety	B	Parking	B
Facilities	B+	Transportation	B-
Girls	B+	Weather	C-

CP's Student Author On...
OVERALL EXPERIENCE

Students sometimes wonder what course their lives would have taken had they attended a different school—perhaps a larger one in a city. And then the majority usually realizes it probably couldn't have turned out any better than it was at Wheaton. In the course of four years, Wheaton allows students to discover who they are and what they love in life, and that is far more valuable to them than being super competitive with classmates and always worrying about grades.

Don't get the wrong idea: Wheaton is competitive, but there is an overall sense that there is more to life here than just people passing through to get a job. The school's motto is, "That they may have life and have it abundantly," and many think that it truly does fit the school's character. Students aren't a number on a sheet here—they are individuals who are looking for a path in life that will let them continue to learn, live, and love what they do. Many wouldn't trade an outlook like that for anything.

Students Speak Out On...
OVERALL EXPERIENCE

Q "I wish this place was more urban, otherwise it's 'aight."

Q "Freshman year, I wanted to transfer, but once I took some classes I enjoyed and made some good friends, I loved it here. At first, the small campus was a negative thing, but I learned to love it, and knowing most people on campus is really nice."

Q "The classes and teachers are interesting, and the campus is beautiful. It can get boring during weekends, but the weeks are busy with lots of events (movies, vendors, fairs). Drinking and vandalism are problems, but I never feel unsafe. I'm glad I chose Wheaton."

Q "Overall, I've enjoyed my experience at Wheaton, the learning environment is awesome and the social scene is alright. I'm happy here and don't really want to be anywhere else."

BEST OF WHEATON MA

1. Professors
2. Class size
3. Opportunity for research
4. The Dimple
5. Upper campus
6. Watson Fine Arts Center
7. 10-minute play festival
8. Spring Weekend

Happy Students
88% of students return after their first year.

Proven Success
81% of students will complete their education and graduate with a degree.

WORST OF WHEATON MA

1. Girl/boy ratio (for girls)
2. High tuition
3. The town of Norton
4. Lack of diversity
5. Peacock Pond's unpleasant scent on warm, muggy days
6. Dining hall food

Expensive
Tuition is a steep $39,850, one of the most expensive rates in the country.

Frequently Compared Schools:

Clark University
Connecticut College
Skidmore College
Trinity College

Students Speak Out On...
EVERYTHING!

ACADEMICS

Readily Available

"I am currently attending Wheaton College, and one of my favorite things about the school is how readily available the professors are. Because the student body is small, the teacher to student ratio is small, therefore making teachers more available to communicate and assist. For example, my adviser and seminar professor will come back to campus if, for whatever reason, a student is unable to make his specific office hours. Truly wonderful!"

"They prepare you well for exams, teach interesting material, and don't expect you to do impossible amounts of work."

"The teachers are generally very helpful through office hours and help sessions. There are the occasional teachers who appear to have no interest in their students or being here, but these types are everywhere."

ATHLETICS

"The sports we have are moderately big. We have basketball, lacrosse, rugby, soccer, baseball, swimming, and others. I try not to follow sports, but despite my efforts, news of a big victory seems to reach me. We're proud of our athletes, but it's not like high school in that way."

"Wheaton is very good in men's and women's soccer, and it is also known for synchronized swimming. There are intramural sports, but I don't know much about those."

"They are a sizable deal, but they don't consume the campus."

CAMPUS DINING

Dining Is All You Can Eat.

"Wheaton has only one meal plan and it is all you can eat. Dining halls are open from 8am to midnight every day. The food is nothing special and can get old towards the end of the year."

"You have to be creative, and make your own food when you go into Emerson or Chase."

CAMPUS HOUSING

"They're all pretty good, clean, and decent. There are different themes for different personalities."

"All of the dorms are pretty nice, but it depends on what you're looking for in a living environment. Besides, the home away from home is what you make it, and the people you live with have a big impact on whether it's a pleasant living environment or not."

GUYS & GIRLS

Student's Looks

"Most students wear sweat pants and the school's sweater, jeans, sneakers and there are some people that dress fancy."

Guys at School

"They are not attractive at all. None of them grab my attention."

HEALTH & SAFETY

Totally Safe

"I have never felt unsafe at Wheaton. Public safety offers safe-rides from the further parking lots to ensure safety and on the weekends there is a "drunk cab" that you can call to get a ride back to campus from neighboring parties. Safety policies, including response to sexual assault and drinking, need to be reviewed but I am positive that the future SGA will be able to implement effective policy to improve safety on campus."

"There is very little crime on campus. Someone stole the power cable to my laptop once when I left it in library, but I never hear of anything violent happening and always feel safe."

LOOKING FOR MORE?

Check out our full-length guide to this school at collegeprowler.com/wheaton-college----massachusetts/.

Whitman College

345 Boyer Ave.; Walla Walla, WA 99362
(509) 527-5111; www.whitman.edu

THE BASICS:

Acceptance Rate: 42%	Student-Faculty Ratio: 10:1
Yield: 28%	Retention Rate: 93%
Setting: Town	Graduation Rate: 92%
Control: Private Non-Profit	Tuition: $36,940
Total Undergrads: 1,515	Room & Board: $9,260
SAT Range: 1850–2140*	Avg. Aid Package: $23,463
ACT Range: 28–33	Students With Aid: 81%

of 2400

Academics	B+	Greek Life	B
Athletics	C+	Guys	B
Campus Dining	B+	Health & Safety	A
Campus Housing	B	Local Atmosphere	C+
Campus Strictness	A-	Nightlife	C
Computers	A-	Off-Campus Dining	C+
Diversity	C+	Off-Campus Housing	B-
Drug Safety	B+	Parking	A-
Facilities	B	Transportation	C-
Girls	B+	Weather	C

CP's Student Author On...
OVERALL EXPERIENCE

Though Whitman has had its ups and downs, overall, most students have absolutely loved it and feel there is no possible college better for them. Many warn that it does take some adjusting (especially with Walla Walla being less metropolitan than what some are used to), but of course, that's a large part of what college itself is, no matter where you are. At Whitman, it's challenging to adjust to the environment; if you find something drastically contrasting to what you're accustomed to before college, perhaps more so than it would be at other schools closer to larger cities. In general, most students have found they need to make a larger adjustment of some kind to Whitman's environment, but most have loved their experiences once they found a comfortable niche.

Many seniors find it difficult to leave Whitman because of the bonds they create with people there, be it with students or professors. Whitman also has a very strong and supportive network of alumni, which is indicative of the bond many people have with Whitman.... For the rest of this editorial, visit collegeprowler.com.

Students Speak Out On...
OVERALL EXPERIENCE

Q Still Loving It

"Though the big price tag and difficult academics can get you down, the Whitman Community is really a joy to be a part of. We all complain about the food and registration, but when I and my friends consider how little time left we have here, we get really sad."

Q
"The first few months were rough—getting used to such an open, liberal environment was challenging coming from my hometown and background, but I wouldn't change the experience for anything. I learned an equal amount from the living experiences and personal interactions at Whitman as I did in the classroom."

Q
"My experience at Whitman improved each successive year I attended. I loved Whitman and wish graduation hadn't come so soon."

Q
"Overall, my experience has been very educational and growthful; it has been rocky at times, but overall, very, very good. Sometimes, I wish I were somewhere else, but when it comes down to it, I really love Whitman and appreciate it for what it is."

BEST OF WHITMAN

1. The friendly, laid-back student body
2. Great, caring, intelligent professors
3. Availability and range of campus events
4. 24-hour libraries and health center
5. Core

Happy Students
93% of students return after their first year.

Commitment to Teaching
There are 10 students for every member of faculty on campus.

WORST OF WHITMAN

1. Small-school gossip and students' ignorance about the real world
2. Students' hatred of Walla Walla, and the subsequent town-gown tension
3. Greek vs. indie debate
4. Excessive alcohol use

Expensive
Tuition is a steep $36,940, one of the most expensive rates in the country.

Want a Job? On Your Own
There aren't any placement services for graduates.

Student Body

African American:	2%	Male Undergrads:	44%
Asian American:	10%	Female Undergrads:	56%
Hispanic:	6%	Living On Campus:	62%
International:	3%	Living Off Campus:	38%
Native American:	1%	Male Athletes:	20%
White:	65%	Female Athletes:	14%
Unknown:	12%	Fraternity Members:	34%
From Out-of-State:	61%	Sorority Members:	29%

Students Speak Out On... EVERYTHING!

ACADEMICS

Challenging, Beneficial, Interesting, Intense, Serious

"My classes force me to use my mind in creative and thoughtful ways. The professors expect a lot from their students so naturally the students respond with many hours of studying, essay writing, lab work, and more. I feel as if my education has given me not just knowledge, but the ability to learn."

"Classes are often enjoyable and unexpected because they constantly force students to look at the world in different ways and to challenge and consider their own views."

ATHLETICS

"Definitely play an IM or club sport! It was really nice after a long day of classes to let loose some stress and have fun with friends. Plus, people are accepting in most IM sports, and they recognize that students have all kinds of athletic abilities, despite the fact that many IM sports are pretty intense and serious."

"Generally speaking, Whitman's varsity teams are not very good. Our ski and snowboard teams have won national awards, and though not usually successful in their league, the basketball team really rallies to get people to come to its games."

CAMPUS DINING

Bon App

"There are so many options on campus where you want to eat, when you want to eat, and how you want to eat. The college does a great job getting vegan and vegetarian views into the menu. The only thing I have a hard time with are the hours of operation for dining halls. They don't stay open for student athletes after practices."

Great, Could Have More Options

"The cooking here at whitman has spoiled me and I I dread the day I have to start cooking for myself."

Frequently Compared Schools:

Lewis & Clark College
Reed College
University of Puget Sound
University of Washington

CAMPUS HOUSING

I Love Where I Live

"Whitman does an awesome job both providing excellent living spaces and selecting roommates. The survey I filled out was akin to a dating profile, they really try to put you in the right spot, with the right person. And the facilities are great; large rooms, plenty of storage, great location literally steps from class."

Ok.

"I moved out of the dorms after a few weeks of living there. Compared to other schools, the rooms are huge and well furnished, but the cleanliness of common areas and bathrooms left something to be desired. Also the lack of air conditioning was unbearable. Walla Walla had 100+ summers."

GUYS & GIRLS

AWESOME

"Everyone's down to earth and ready to chill. A lot of the campus is Greek, including myself, which is really fun!"

"Most guys at Whitman were pretty attractive, especially if you like the more rugged-looking guys. A lot of them are like scruffier Greek gods, and it's great in spring when they all walk around without their shirts."

HEALTH & SAFETY

Easy

"The student health center is fantastic and the campus is completely safe. Whitman really cares about its students and it shows in this area"

Over All Safety

"I have never felt unsafe on whitman's campus. There are only 1,400 students which creates a great environment. Every one respects each other, and the people that attend school generally look out for each other. We have a green dot program which emphasizes student responsibility when seeing potentially unsafe behavior between two other students."

LOOKING FOR MORE?

Check out our full-length guide to this school at collegeprowler.com/whitman-college/.

Wilkes University

84 W. South St.; Wilkes-Barre, PA 18766
(570) 408-5000; www.wilkes.edu

THE BASICS:

Acceptance Rate: 75%
Yield: 27%
Setting: Small city
Control: Private Non-Profit
Total Undergrads: 2,246
SAT Range: 1370–1730*
ACT Range: —

Student-Faculty Ratio: 15:1
Retention Rate: 80%
Graduation Rate: 58%
Tuition: $26,010
Room & Board: $11,100
Avg. Aid Package: $18,718
Students With Aid: 97%

of 2400

Academics	B-	Greek Life	N/A
Athletics	B	Guys	B
Campus Dining	B+	Health & Safety	B
Campus Housing	A	Local Atmosphere	C-
Campus Strictness	C+	Nightlife	C+
Computers	B-	Off-Campus Dining	B-
Diversity	D-	Off-Campus Housing	B+
Drug Safety	C+	Parking	C+
Facilities	B	Transportation	C+
Girls	B	Weather	C

CP's Student Author On...
OVERALL EXPERIENCE

The overall experience reported by most Wilkes students is overwhelmingly positive. The outstanding mentoring environment, caring faculty, wide array of student activities, and some darn good academics overshadow the occasional blizzard and unfavorable happening on campus. The positive experiences had by students are backed up by Wilkes's positive retention rate, the percentage of people who start and finish at Wilkes. This means that people like the campus enough to hang around, rather than transfer out. Homecomings are bigger and better than ever, proving that the Wilkes experience was so positive, alumni love coming back to visit—and donating to the school. Finally, many Wilkes graduates return for a second Wilkes experience through the acclaimed MBA program or one of the other fine master's programs.

Hands-down, Wilkes is truly a school where undergrads get the full college experience. The campus is a beautiful place to be, a very green campus for an urban institution.... For the rest of this editorial, visit collegeprowler.com.

Students Speak Out On...
OVERALL EXPERIENCE

Q **Great School**
"As a nontraditional aged student, I highly recommend Wilkes. From day 1 every member of the staff from the coffee lady to the head of the department have been incredibly supportive and accomodating. For this reason alone, I would recommend Wilkes to anyone looking for a good education in a small city setting."

Q "I would not come to this school again. While it was a great experience, I would prefer something larger."

Q "Yeah, I would come here again. The people I have met and the relationships I have established with my teachers because of the small size of the University have made this an enjoyable place to go to school."

Q "Overall, Wilkes is a decent school. I personally went to it to save money dorming elsewhere. If I did college over again, I'd probably make the same decision because the communications department is really good with all the extra curricular activities to get involved with."

BEST OF WILKES

1. Mentoring
2. Downtown revitalization means more active college town
3. Old mansions as dorms
4. The Greenway and other scenic landscaping
5. Interdisciplinary learning

Happy Students
80% of students return after their first year.

Genders Equally Represented
A male-to-female ratio of 48/52 means there's a pretty even balance of students on campus.

WORST OF WILKES

1. On-campus parking limited
2. Problem landlords abound off-campus
3. Downtown crime close to campus

Expensive
Tuition is a steep $26,010, one of the most expensive rates in the country.

Expensive Dorms
Living on campus doesn't come cheap, with an average housing price tag of $6,680.

Students Speak Out On...
EVERYTHING!

ACADEMICS

Academics at Wilkes University

"I recently graduated from Wilkes University with an MSEd degree because I was thrilled with the course offerings available to me as an adult learner. The entire course was online and the focus was on flexibility, allowing me to complete work at my own pace. I am not in the process of enrolling in a Doctoral level program at Wilkes University as I know I will receive the attention I desire and knowledge that I thirst for."

"The teachers are personable, and most of them try to get to know the students. The general workload is very reasonable; students in the pharmacy program have the greatest workload."

"So far, the teachers that I have encountered have been great! The workload can be very stressful at times, but in the end, it is all worth it."

ATHLETICS

Sports aren't a big deal

"We are a small university so I don't think sports are as big a deal here as in larger universities. There is a fairly good fan base though."

"The most well known varsity sports are football, men's and women's lacrosse, men's and women's basketball, wrestling, and tennis. There is also a cheerleading team for football and basketball, as well as intramural basketball in the spring."

CAMPUS DINING

Dining at Wilkes

"Dining at Wilkes University I think has been very good! A tremendous amount of variety is available. From soups, salads, classic meals to international, sandwiches and pizza. The cafe is a great place to go and be with your friends and eat a meal. Sometimes there may be days that you won't really want what they have, but that's why there is always something you can resort to like a salad or just pizza."

"I like the food, but this question is really not applicable to me because I eat the exact same thing every day."

CAMPUS HOUSING

Overpriced

"Housing on campus is overpriced and not worth it, especially in University Towers. For 2 people to rent and apt there before it was owned by the school, it cost about $1,000 with all bills included for heat, phone, internet, and cable. Now, the school charges $10,000 a person to live there for 7 months and crams 3 people in an apartment meant for 2. Can you say rip off?! They have not maintained their properties and the buildings are in poor condition."

"There are a lot of mansions on campus that have been converted into dorms. The only 'real' dorm we have is Evans."

GUYS & GIRLS

"There are some beautiful girls, and not the typical stuck-up ones, either. The guys vary a lot. Typical student? No such thing. Students vary, and they are kind of in their own little cliques."

"Most guys are hot, and girls are beautiful. The girls I find to be most attractive because their personalities tend to be cooler, more open-minded, and more chill than the guys."

HEALTH & SAFETY

"The campus is very secure and safe—it's just rough going if you travel three blocks from campus in any direction."

"Security is really tight. You have to have keys to get into the dorms and swipe cards to get into the buildings. If it is late and you want to get across campus, all you have to do is call campus security and they will walk or drive you, depending on the weather."

LOOKING FOR MORE?

Check out our full-length guide to this school at collegeprowler.com/wilkes-university/.

Willamette University

900 State St.; Salem, OR 97301
(503) 370-6300; www.willamette.edu

THE BASICS:

Acceptance Rate: 60%	**Student-Faculty Ratio:** 10:1
Yield: 16%	**Retention Rate:** 88%
Setting: Mid-sized city	**Graduation Rate:** 71%
Control: Private Non-Profit	**Tuition:** $37,150
Total Undergrads: 1,940	**Room & Board:** $8,900
SAT Range: 1660–1970*	**Avg. Aid Package:** $27,974
ACT Range: 25–30	**Students With Aid:** 97%

* of 2400

Academics	B+	Greek Life	B+
Athletics	C+	Guys	B
Campus Dining	B+	Health & Safety	A-
Campus Housing	B+	Local Atmosphere	C
Campus Strictness	C	Nightlife	C
Computers	B+	Off-Campus Dining	B-
Diversity	C+	Off-Campus Housing	B+
Drug Safety	B-	Parking	B-
Facilities	B	Transportation	B-
Girls	B+	Weather	B-

CP's Student Author On...
OVERALL EXPERIENCE

Students love Willamette because it has the potential to be the perfect school. It has a small-town location, offers an incredible amount of financial aid, has an even balance of social life and academics, the class sizes are small and ideal for one-on-one learning, and students can get the top-rate education for which they are paying. With all the smiling, happy people walking around, it is no wonder why students fall in love with Willamette. The downside of the University is that it is like a buffet: It offers a little bit of many subjects and activities, but students are required to take only small bits of everything and cannot fill up on one specific thing. This idea makes it difficult for students who want an in-depth focus on one subject. Willamette students do not learn how to do things, they learn about things, which is what sets a liberal arts education apart from more-technical ways of study. Students who know exactly want they want to study and have a set career path in high school should not attend Willamette. It is a college for students who are still trying to find their passions in life. Hopefully, by the end of four years they will have found it and can get a master's degree in whatever subject they want to pursue.... For the rest of this editorial, visit collegeprowler.com.

Students Speak Out On...
OVERALL EXPERIENCE

Q The Excellent Atmosphere
"I love Willamette. The atmosphere is close and homey. The real downside to the community type feeling is that everyone knows everyone's business and gossip is hugely prevalent. It's definitely a small town atmosphere, so if you prefer anonymity you might want to look elsewhere."

Q "Whatever you want Willamette to be, it will be. If you want a crazy, party, drunkfest every weekend, you can have it, but your grades will suffer. If you want to graduate magna cum laude with an acceptance letter to Harvard Law, that can happen, too. There are so many opportunities that Willamette will present, and if you make the most of these opportunities you will find your college career very fulfilling."

Q "I still have two years until I graduate, but just looking back on the past two years, I know I have grown as a person and expanded my interests. I'm looking forward to studying abroad next year because I know it will be a once-in-a-lifetime experience, just like Willamette has been."

BEST OF WILLAMETTE

1. Welcoming and friendly environment
2. The wide variety of extracurricular activities
3. One-on-one relationships with the professors
4. Beautiful landscaping and architecture on campus

Happy Students
88% of students return after their first year.

Commitment to Teaching
There are 10 students for every member of faculty on campus.

WORST OF WILLAMETTE

1. Parking
2. Gossip
3. High tuition
4. Lack of school spirit
5. The city of Salem
6. The dating/social scene
7. Varsity athletics

Expensive
Tuition is a steep $37,150, one of the most expensive rates in the country.

Students Speak Out On...
EVERYTHING!

ACADEMICS

Willamette Faculty Care

"More than any other school I've seen, the Professors and staff at Willamette University care about their students. Faculty here are more of a presence on campus as well; they often take part in activities and can be regularly seen at the university cafe or the library."

"I definitely think Willamette is in the top tier of liberal arts schools in terms of academics. I'm constantly being challenged in my courses to think outside the box and push myself."

"The best place to study is locked up in a classroom with your cell phone on silent. If you go to the library, especially during finals week, it is loud and crowded because everyone and their roommate is there trying to cram a semester's worth of information into one night of studying. It's not the most productive environment."

ATHLETICS

Much to Do

"From Intramural programs to club sports and varsity athletics everyone can get involved. There are recreation leagues just for fun and competitive leagues where individuals can really shine. Beyond that the club sports such as rugby and lacrosse travel like any varsity team and build some great relationships."

Personally Not Involved

"Athletics are a moderate part of campus life. Many students attened sporting events, although I myself do not attend them or take an interest in sporting events."

CAMPUS DINING

Hit or Miss

"Our dining hall, Goudy, makes some very good food. It also makes some food that makes you never, ever want to eat in a dining hall again. Lots of options and most of them are tasty, but it's really hit or miss as far as each individual night goes."

Decent

"There are several places on campus to catch a bite, all of them serve different types of food, the variety is pretty decent. The only problem is the dining hours, athletes often don't get the dinner that comes with the meal plan because the hours aren't flexible or cohesive with practice time. I suggest getting a moderate meal plan, the larger ones often go wasted."

CAMPUS HOUSING

Substance Free Dorms

"Baxter Hall,is generally has a friendly atmosphere. Feel safe!!"

Kaneko Commons

"Best Dorm ever! More than a dorm it's a community. Our RAs aren't even RAs, they are CMs, Community Managers. If you come here I suggest Kaneko."

GUYS & GIRLS

A Variety

"Willamette is not a party school. If you don't want to party, you absolutely can avoid it, but there are social functions set up by the Greek system as well as by the school and student organizations that you can attend. Dress is mostly casual, with some students dressing up occaionally and a few eclectic dressers."

Just Gotta Search

"The girls are often a little awkward and weird. However, the ones that are attractive can be very full of themselves which is a turnoff in and of itself. But there are those diamonds in the rough that make it worth your time to look."

HEALTH & SAFETY

I Feel Very Safe

"I feel very safe on campus, day and night. However, many bikes have been stolen this last year and it does concern me."

"It's not the Willamette students you have to worry about, it's the local Salem riffraff."

LOOKING FOR MORE?

Check out our full-length guide to this school at collegeprowler.com/willamette-university/.

Williams College

880 Main St.; Williamstown, MA 01267
(413) 597-3131; www.williams.edu

THE BASICS:

Acceptance Rate: 20%
Yield: 45%
Setting: Town
Control: Private Non-Profit
Total Undergrads: 2,064
SAT Range: 1310–1538*
ACT Range: 30–34

Student-Faculty Ratio: 7:1
Retention Rate: 98%
Graduation Rate: 96%
Tuition: $39,490
Room & Board: $10,390
Avg. Aid Package: $35,181
Students With Aid: 64%

* of 1600

Academics	A	Greek Life	N/A
Athletics	B-	Guys	C
Campus Dining	B+	Health & Safety	B+
Campus Housing	B-	Local Atmosphere	C
Campus Strictness	B+	Nightlife	D-
Computers	B-	Off-Campus Dining	C+
Diversity	B+	Off-Campus Housing	D+
Drug Safety	A-	Parking	B
Facilities	A-	Transportation	D+
Girls	C+	Weather	C-

CP's Student Author On...
OVERALL EXPERIENCE

It is very hard to get an A at Williams, so most are happy with a B+ or an A-. The same logic applies to what the school has to offer students. Williams is amazing for its incredible academic and athletic programs, and the inclusive atmosphere on campus promote and encourages personal growth. The lack of nightlife also helps the campus grow closer as people have little opportunity to go off campus and much more time to hang out with and talk to the people around them. Students acknowledge that some of the weaknesses of the school, such as location and the nature of nightlife in Williamstown, are not fixable. They also agree that Williams is working very hard on addressing other problematic issues. While the school changes with every class, every year, some positive and negative aspects of what it has to offer to the prospective student stand out. These are not only conditions that can't be changed, like the weather, but also general features of Williams that many students criticize or praise.

No matter what the admissions office tries to tell you, the Williams campus is not particularly diverse.... For the rest of this editorial, visit collegeprowler.com.

Students Speak Out On...
OVERALL EXPERIENCE

One of My Best Decisions Ever
"I love Williams. Its not perfect and there are times when aspects of the college frustrate me, but on the whole there is not much I would change. The people are interesting, the faculty are so smart and approachable and the scenic location is unbeatable. Highlights: My entry, winter study, outing club, professors, tutorials, mountain day!"

"In four years of school, you'll change a little bit. I see that I have changed other people, too, and that I have been able to stick to what matters the most to me. Professors have been great in this respect; they let you share, and they don't judge you for standing out with a different view on popular issues. Clearly, my grades were not impacted by my desire to say what I think, nor did I feel alienated, although I was always a minority."

BEST OF WILLIAMS

1. The JA System
2. Tutorials
3. Professors' love for their subject and willingness to help
4. The flexible core curriculum

Happy Students
98% of students return after their first year.

Commitment to Teaching
There are 7 students for every member of faculty on campus.

WORST OF WILLIAMS

1. The cold weather
2. Transportation to Williams (cheap but time consuming)
3. The winter

Expensive
Tuition is a steep $39,490, one of the most expensive rates in the country.

AP Credit Wasted
Any AP credits earned in high school aren't eligible for college credit.

Student Body

African American:	9%	Male Undergrads:	49%
Asian American:	11%	Female Undergrads:	51%
Hispanic:	9%	Living On Campus:	93%
International:	7%	Living Off Campus:	7%
Native American:	1%	Male Athletes:	56%
White:	63%	Female Athletes:	46%
Unknown:	0%	Fraternity Members:	0%
From Out-of-State:	87%	Sorority Members:	0%

Frequently Compared Schools:
Amherst College
Brown University
Middlebury College
Yale University

Students Speak Out On... EVERYTHING!

ACADEMICS

Williams College

"Williams College is an excellent school where the professors really care about the students inside and outside of the classroom. Students are very serious about their academics but this does not impede the social life."

"Professors are definitely one of the best things about our school. They do their jobs so well, I have thought of becoming a professor myself."

"Professors at Williams are very friendly, helpful, and knowledgeable. Most are very hard graders, though, so you will have to sweat for that A-. In the end, you know you have learned a lot to earn your grade. At Williams, there isn't much pressure to have the highest GPA, so professors are fair to their students, even though they set high standards. I know that I need some pressure in order to work hard and stay motivated, so it was good for me to be around demanding profs."

ATHLETICS

Great School Spirit

"For a small school, Williams College packs a lot of school spirit! You are sure to make plans around sports events, and lacrosse, soccer, and basketball games typically attract the entire school."

Athletics Are Big at Williams

"Almost half of students at Williams play some sort of sport and most of those who don't are still pretty active. There's a good bit of school spirit. Home games are pretty well attended and students occasionally even go out to away games to support their friends. The athletic facilities are on the whole really nice too, though some are a little warm and could use new circulation facilities."

CAMPUS DINING

Dining

"For a small student population, we have 5 dining halls. Every hall has different options, and are all vegan and gluten-free friendly."

Decent but repetitive

"The food here is decent but repetitive."

CAMPUS HOUSING

"Williams' dorms are nice. The wooden floors create a sense of warmth, and some are even carpeted. Windows are big enough to let air in. Even from the outside, most dorms look cool."

"Williams dorms have been getting better and better during my time in the school. Some of the less convenient places were renovated, especially sophomore dorms."

GUYS & GIRLS

People Are Interesting

"Everybody does so much here! You think you know somebody, and then he or she surprises you with some hidden talent or surprising area of interest. Even though Williams is small, I could never see myself becoming bored with my peers."

Hot or Not?

"There are a bunch of attractive guys here, but for the most part both guys and girls are more concerned with hookups NOT relationships. My guy friends constantly gripe about the lack of attractive girls on campus. A few of them joke about transferring to McGill just to remedy this problem."

HEALTH & SAFETY

Super Safe

"The campus is probably one of the safest places I have ever lived."

"The security officers are very nice. They help people a lot, and I really like that they offer to take you to your dorm after midnight—not that Williamstown isn't a safe place in general. It just is comforting to know that they would do that."

LOOKING FOR MORE?
Check out our full-length guide to this school at collegeprowler.com/williams-college/.

Worcester Polytechnic Institute

100 Institute Road; Worcester, MA 01609
(508) 831-5000; www.wpi.edu

THE BASICS:

Acceptance Rate: 63%	**Student-Faculty Ratio:** 14:1
Yield: 23%	**Retention Rate:** 95%
Setting: Mid-sized city	**Graduation Rate:** 79%
Control: Private Non-Profit	**Tuition:** $37,440
Total Undergrads: 3,453	**Room & Board:** $11,160
SAT Range: 1750–2040*	**Avg. Aid Package:** $25,306
ACT Range: 25–31	**Students With Aid:** 99%

* of 2400

This School Isn't Graded Yet!

College Prowler grades are calculated using tons of criteria, including survey responses that come from students at this school.

Unfortunately, we haven't gathered enough student surveys yet for this school to be able to calculate the grades for each section. Stay tuned to *CollegeProwler.com* for grade updates and more!

CP's Student Author On...
OVERALL EXPERIENCE

Most people who decide to come to WPI absolutely love the school. The small, welcoming atmosphere is wonderful. Students tend to like the campus itself, too; it's beautiful, especially in the spring. Occasionally, people dislike the workload at the school, but many people would return to WPI if they had to do it all over again.

The community at WPI is the best feature of the school; it's what keeps people there, even though the work is tough. Joining a club or a sports team is a great way to make WPI feel like "home." Even though students can be 2,500 miles from home, they can feel like they have family on campus, through involvement in sports and clubs.

Students Speak Out On...
OVERALL EXPERIENCE

Q Awesome School

"I believe most of the people who say they dont like this school is because of the work load and weather. Weather is something which one cannot avoid and weather holds a little importance in deciding a school. Yes the work load is too much sometimes but that is the reason i like this school. People who actually want to study nd make their life better come to this school."

Q Best Time of My Life

"Living and studying at WPI is a geek's dream. You'll easy find like minded people. I'd choose to do it again because you have fun while gradually learning what you need to know to be a successful adult."

Q Challenge

"WPI is not a school to slow down in. The classes are fast paced, the work is challenging, and the projects are intense. But the support from staff and students compensates. There are plenty of people that are willing to help you out. It is what I look for, a school that focuses on the major and cuts away the unnecessary classes, getting you where you want to be."

BEST OF WORCESTER POLYTECHNIC

1. A, B, C, and NR (No Record) grading scale
2. Close community
3. Computers everywhere
4. Constant on-campus activities
5. The fountain
6. Off-campus projects

Happy Students
95% of students return after their first year.

Proven Success
79% of students will complete their education and graduate with a degree.

WORST OF WORCESTER POLYTECHNIC

1. Cafeteria closes early (8 p.m.).
2. Few food options on campus
3. Harsh weather
4. Hot dorms in warm months
5. Little support for sports

Expensive
Tuition is a steep $37,440, one of the most expensive rates in the country.

Expensive Dorms
Living on campus doesn't come cheap, with an average housing price tag of $6,530.

Student Body

African American:	3%	Male Undergrads:	73%
Asian American:	6%	Female Undergrads:	27%
Hispanic:	5%	Living On Campus:	50%
International:	9%	Living Off Campus:	50%
Native American:	0%	Male Athletes:	20%
White:	76%	Female Athletes:	24%
Unknown:	1%	Fraternity Members:	30%
From Out-of-State:	51%	Sorority Members:	36%

Frequently Compared Schools:

Boston University
Northeastern University
Rensselaer Polytechnic Institute
Rochester Institute of Technology

Students Speak Out On... EVERYTHING!

ACADEMICS

Q IMGD Program

"It offers many opportunities to be real game designer, programmer, and/ or artist. The IMGD program is one of the few legitimate gaming majors currently offered."

ATHLETICS

Q Not Too Big of a Deal Here

"The teams can be very good but there are never many fans at the games and not many people follow the sport teams."

Q A Community of Shut-Ins

"This college is populated with nerds, geeks, and near-literal vampires. "Walking for Fitness" is actually a class. And because exercise is so unpopular, they had to make it required for graduation. The varsity sports are pretty good, but if you go any lower, you lose a lot of vitality."

CAMPUS DINING

Q Around Campus

"The options off campus provide students with many alternatives to the mediocre dining hall food."

Q Come Hungry, Leave Hungry.

"The dining halls on the meal plan seems nice at first, but you quickly realize at WPI the freshman 15 is the freshman 40. If you do not have a mealplan the available on campus dining options are meager and greasy, but on the plus side they are inexpensive on the whole and there are plenty of decent places to eat within walking distance, and a TON within a 5 or 10 minutes drive."

CAMPUS HOUSING

Q The Dorms Aren't Worth Their Price

"The dorms are too expensive, overcrowded, lacking amenities, inconvenience dorm specific locks, and no elevator access for the common student. Though the social atmosphere is top notch (especially because of the common rooms), and the housing process is easy."

Q Too Expensive

"Living on campus is definitely easier than being off campus in an apartment, but it is just far too expensive between housing and a meal plan. It is nice to have so many other students around you and be right on campus and close to everything, but I have found that being off campus is the way to go for me."

GUYS & GIRLS

Q Close

"The campus community is very tight. The campus is small but large enough that everyone can connect with others. The atmosphere is excellent, all the students are nice, especially the Greek Life."

HEALTH & SAFETY

Q Pretty Safe

"I can honestly say i have never had a problem on campus. But they're are certain times when you should never be alone because they're have been cases where students have run into trouble. These cases have been between the times of 2am and 5am, where its just not smart to alone at night anyway. Campus police is always round, and if anything happens the entire student body is notified within hours through the emailing system on campus."

LOOKING FOR MORE?

Check out our full-length guide to this school at collegeprowler.com/worcester-polytechnic-institute/.

Xavier University

3800 Victory Parkway; Cincinnati, OH 45207
(513) 745-3000; www.xavier.edu

THE BASICS:

Acceptance Rate: 73%
Yield: 22%
Setting: Large city
Control: Private Non-Profit
Total Undergrads: 4,228
SAT Range: 1540–1830*
ACT Range: 23–28

Student-Faculty Ratio: 13:1
Retention Rate: 84%
Graduation Rate: 79%
Tuition: $28,570
Room & Board: $9,250
Avg. Aid Package: $15,551
Students With Aid: 97%

* of 2400

Academics	B-	Greek Life	N/A
Athletics	A-	Guys	B-
Campus Dining	C+	Health & Safety	B
Campus Housing	B+	Local Atmosphere	C+
Campus Strictness	B	Nightlife	C+
Computers	B+	Off-Campus Dining	B+
Diversity	C-	Off-Campus Housing	B
Drug Safety	B+	Parking	B+
Facilities	B+	Transportation	B
Girls	B-	Weather	C+

CP's Student Author On...
OVERALL EXPERIENCE

Overall, I am definitely satisfied with my experience at Xavier so far. Adjusting to a new city, new school, and new friends was tough at first, but in retrospect, if I were somewhere else besides Xavier, it would've been a lot tougher. The combination of a small school where you can get to know everyone with a big-school atmosphere, including big-time college sports and a big city to explore, makes Xavier a fun and interesting place to be. The people at Xavier are really some of the friendliest you'll meet. (As tired as that sounds, it's absolutely true.) The reason that Xavier has such a high retention rate is that people who take an honest look at Xavier normally want to go here, and rarely are they let down. It's clear when you visit here that things are laid-back, there are no gigantic parties on a weekly basis, and everything is in general serene and comfortable. While it may differ from the typical college experience portrayed in all our favorite movies, the XU experience is enjoyable and dynamic. The beauty of X is it can be whatever you choose to make it. At another school, the pace of life is often determined by a gigantic student body, and if you don't conform, you are an outcast.... For the rest of this editorial, visit collegeprowler.com.

Students Speak Out On...
OVERALL EXPERIENCE

Q Great Experiecne!
"I have had a great experience at Xavier so far. I love that it is a small school and people can really get to know each other."

Q Go Blue
"Xavier is different from my old school because everything is scattered, but it is a beautiful with many activities."

Q A Straight B'
"So far my experience is going great. i have gotten a lot of friends and had a lot of fun. The classes are hard and sometimes the teachers teach extremely fast, but other than that it's been fairly good."

Q Experience
"Xavier is an okay place it lack excitment and that fantasy of college fun. Its A very strict place. However, I came for an education and as far as that I feel that I am getting the best of that."

Q "I sometimes wish I was somewhere else. The electronic media major is a joke if you don't want to go into television."

BEST OF XAVIER

1. Friendly and interesting people
2. The Crosstown Shootout
3. Food and housing are great
4. Gallagher Student Center
5. Extremely safe

Happy Students
84% of students return after their first year.

Proven Success
79% of students will complete their education and graduate with a degree.

WORST OF XAVIER

1. No strong sense of community in the surrounding areas
2. Very limited nightlife
3. No football
4. Not very diverse
5. Parking up on the hill

Expensive
Tuition is a steep $28,570, one of the most expensive rates in the country.

Student Body

African American:	12%	Male Undergrads:	44%
Asian American:	2%	Female Undergrads:	56%
Hispanic:	3%	Living On Campus:	46%
International:	3%	Living Off Campus:	54%
Native American:	0%	Male Athletes:	12%
White:	75%	Female Athletes:	9%
Unknown:	3%	Fraternity Members:	0%
From Out-of-State:	47%	Sorority Members:	0%

Frequently Compared Schools:

Marquette University
Miami University
University of Cincinnati
University of Dayton

Students Speak Out On... EVERYTHING!

ACADEMICS

Business School Really Prepares You for Workforce

"The core curriculum for the Williams College of Business at Xavier University really helps make you a well rounded business student. The minimum requirements are much more than the ones at other institutions. The College makes you do many things, such as simulated interviews and business meetings. They also offer help finding interships and help with increasing resources to become a more skillful worker."

Personalized Attention, Challenging Academics

"My classes sizes have remained small in the three years that I have attended Xavier, and my professors are always at the forefront of their fields."

ATHLETICS

One Word. Musketeers!!!

"Basketball is a HUGE part of Xavier. Xavier Musketeers have led us to many victories, but it wouldn't be the same without our fans! We have a student section, and we all either wear our Xavier gear, or buy a shirt dedicated to that particular game. We have chants, body pant, and everything to support our team! It's a great way to get out and have fun and support your team at the same time."

Incredible Men and Women's Basketball Team

"Fun to watch and follow, really builds a feeling of connectedness with other students who are interest, attend the games, etc."

CAMPUS DINING

Good at the Beginning . . . Bad by the End

"The food is good starting off with decent variety and pretty good taste all around. By the end of the year it is pretty bad. There is really nothing worth eating at the cafeteria. The dining outside of the cafeteria is pretty limited, but good."

Not Worth the Money.

"I have the unlimited meal plan but I wish I had gotten a smaller plan. The caf sandwiches are very good but I'm already tired of them. The other food in the caf is gross. Like highschool food. So really Subway, Ryans, Blue Gibbon, or Fresh Fusions are you options if you have either cash or enough dining dollars."

CAMPUS HOUSING

Dorms

"The dorms are great they have a kitchen on every floors and air in all the dorms rooms,no fan needed"

Fabulous

"Xavier has the best dorms out of all universities. LOVED the housing."

GUYS & GIRLS

R.E.S.P.E.C.T.

"This school definitely follows what Aretha was singing whne she song "Respect". Everyone at this school holds that view. They are very helpful so if anyone needed anything they wouldn't give them attitude and help as much as possible or send them to someone that can help them. Overall very nice people."

Guys and Girls

"They dress all kind of style you still think they in high school"

HEALTH & SAFETY

Safe and Sound

"Xavier provides a very safe community. With it being a small campus, we already quite naturally do not have to worry about much regarding safety. In the case that we do, however, precautious are always taken. Xavier Police has an easy number to remember, and they are pretty much all over campus the majority of the time. If there does happen to be any problems regarding safety, Xavier will alert us via email, blackboard, letter, or even text!"

Safety

"Xavier is very safe. The police are a constant presence on campus. it is unique that they are there to help more than punish. I feel very safe at Xavier"

LOOKING FOR MORE?

Check out our full-length guide to this school at collegeprowler.com/xavier-university/.

Yale University

500 College St.; New Haven, CT 06520
(203) 432-1333; www.yale.edu

THE BASICS:

Acceptance Rate: 9%
Yield: 68%
Setting: Mid-sized city
Control: Private Non-Profit
Total Undergrads: 5,270
SAT Range: 2100–2370*
ACT Range: 30–34

Student-Faculty Ratio: 6:1
Retention Rate: 99%
Graduation Rate: 97%
Tuition: $36,500
Room & Board: $11,000
Avg. Aid Package: $34,563
Students With Aid: 63%

* of 2400

Academics	A+	Greek Life	C+
Athletics	B-	Guys	A+
Campus Dining	A	Health & Safety	C
Campus Housing	A+	Local Atmosphere	C+
Campus Strictness	A+	Nightlife	A-
Computers	A	Off-Campus Dining	A
Diversity	A	Off-Campus Housing	B-
Drug Safety	D+	Parking	B+
Facilities	A+	Transportation	B+
Girls	A	Weather	C+

CP's Student Author On...
OVERALL EXPERIENCE

Yale is, in every sense of the word, an incredible place. Students love the faculty, the classes, and the opportunities, not only because they are among the best in the world, but because they are highly accessible and undergraduate-focused. Yale is a place where academic theory blossoms into reality and where experiences exist that can't be found anywhere else in the world. It is a great privilege for students to continually study under the most knowledgeable people in their fields, from Nobel Laureates to international statesmen. Even though the Yale experience can be rigorous and demanding, most students wouldn't trade their years here for anything.

Yale prepares its students to meet the world with energy and knowledge. Its liberal arts education teaches students to think, to analyze, to question, and to consider. Yale graduates can do nearly anything they want, from working with Goldman and Sachs to obtaining a Ph.D. in ethnomusicology. Essentially, Yale successfully prepares its students for the pursuit of their passions in any area of life.... For the rest of this editorial, visit collegeprowler.com.

Students Speak Out On...
OVERALL EXPERIENCE

Q LOVE LOVE LOVE YALE
"Academic life and student life is excellent at Yale. I could not imagine a better place to live and study."

Q Amazing
"Easily the best place on earth. It's like disney land for college students. They cater to almost any academic or social desire you could possibly want and as long as you're willing to put in the work, there is almost nothing you'll be prevented from doing. I would never in a million years trade my experience here for another one."

Q I Love It
"I love it here! It's a unique place in good and bad ways but I would do it all over again. No regrets. The people make your experience so much more wonderful-don't just study all the time, and make time for friends and events. It's so much more worth it that way."

BEST OF YALE

1. Shopping period
2. Master's Teas
3. Brilliant professors
4. Beautiful architecture
5. Study abroad programs, like Yale Summer Session or Yale in London
6. Residential college system

Happy Students
99% of students return after their first year.

Commitment to Teaching
There are 6 students for every member of faculty on campus.

WORST OF YALE

1. The weather
2. New Haven neighborhoods surrounding Yale's campus
3. Lack of time
4. Meal plan requirement
5. Distributional (Hu, Sc, So) and Skills (WR, L, QR) requirements

Expensive
Tuition is a steep $36,500, one of the most expensive rates in the country.

Expensive Dorms
Living on campus doesn't come cheap, with an average housing price tag of $6,000.

Student Body

African American:	8%	Male Undergrads:	49%
Asian American:	12%	Female Undergrads:	51%
Hispanic:	8%	Living On Campus:	88%
International:	13%	Living Off Campus:	12%
Native American:	1%	Male Athletes:	20%
White:	40%	Female Athletes:	17%
Unknown:	18%	Fraternity Members:	15%
From Out-of-State:	94%	Sorority Members:	10%

Frequently Compared Schools:
Brown University
Harvard University
Princeton University
University of Pennsylvania

Students Speak Out On... EVERYTHING!

ACADEMICS

Best Freshmen Experience

"I had always been my dream to go to yale and I finally was able to put my dreams into action and I began my freshmen year here Fall 2009. Great atmosphere, community, and the teachers really seem to care about the students. It was just everything I imagined it would be :) I did ultimately leave to attend school closer to home but I would do it all over again if I could."

None Better

"Yale really pours resources into its academics, and it shows. Professors are very available and often offer to go to coffee, have lunch, or hold office hours with students. Seminars are widely available - in three semesters, I have had mostly small seminars with awesome professors, and that was even without having declared a major. The workload at Yale is intense, and though it is not hard to get acceptable grades, doing well requires a lot of work."

ATHLETICS

Great Athletics

"Athletics is visible and just about EVERYONE participates in one or two IM sports every year. Varsity athletes probably don't receive as much attention as those in the NCAA powerhouses but most choose Yale for a Yale education and the chance to still play their sport. But there is a good deal of fan support in basketball, football and hockey."

Athletics - Varsity and Collegiate

"Athletics is good and almost everyone is involved in the residential college intramural sports. Varsity sports is big among those participate, but with the exception of the popular Yale-Harvard Football Game, fan support is pretty minimal because Yale students are all busy doing their own thing. Yale Varsity have won NCAA Championship in a couple of varsity sports in 2010."

CAMPUS DINING

15 Dining Halls, Salad Bars, Tons of Fruit, & Comfort Foods!

"There are dining halls in every college that have a similar menu (though slight differences unique to each) and also three special dining halls with other options. It creates a very family-like atmosphere at dinner time when you can walk into your college dining hall and know everyone or another dining hall and know half the people or the largest Hogwart-esque dining hall and eat like a wizard!"

Yale Dining Goes Out of Their Way to Make Our Experience Enjoyable

"The dining halls come up with innovative dishes for us to try. Sometimes, they serve all of the delicious dishes at one meal and fail to serve an appealing option at another meal. The college dining halls really feel like home and have been an important part of my Yale experience."

CAMPUS HOUSING

BEST THING EVER

"The residential college system helps foster a sense of family at Yale. It's a huge part of student life, and you've always got your residential college at your back."

Residental Colleges Are the BEST

"I literally live in a castle! Social atmosphere is very friendly, dorm rooms are beautiful, spacious, and clean. Food is awesome. It is luxurious and easy living"

GUYS & GIRLS

Beautiful People

"Love this place...Everyone is good looking, extremely interested and interesting. Student life is awesome!"

HEALTH & SAFETY

Yale Campus Is Very Safe.

"Yale cares about student safety. The campus police are visible, very friendly, helpful and communicative."

LOOKING FOR MORE?
Check out our full-length guide to this school at collegeprowler.com/yale-university/.

Youngstown State University

1 University Plaza; Youngstown, OH 44555
(877) 468-6978; www.ysu.edu

THE BASICS:

Acceptance Rate: Open
Yield: —
Setting: Small city
Control: Public
Total Undergrads: 10,739
SAT Range: 1180–1570*
ACT Range: 17–23

Student-Faculty Ratio: 18:1
Retention Rate: 70%
Graduation Rate: 34%
Tuition: $9,649
Room & Board: $7,400
Avg. Aid Package: $8,163
Students With Aid: 90%

* of 2400

Academics	C	**Greek Life**	C+
Athletics	C+	**Guys**	C+
Campus Dining	C+	**Health & Safety**	C+
Campus Housing	C+	**Local Atmosphere**	C
Campus Strictness	C+	**Nightlife**	B
Computers	C+	**Off-Campus Dining**	C
Diversity	C+	**Off-Campus Housing**	C+
Drug Safety	C-	**Parking**	B-
Facilities	C+	**Transportation**	C+
Girls	C-	**Weather**	C-

CP's Student Author On...
OVERALL EXPERIENCE

Many local high school students do not bother applying to YSU because they consider it a second-rate college that's too close to home. These students do not know what they are missing! College is only what the student makes of it, and YSU will fully satisfy students who put forth an effort into their college experience. Many current students find themselves pleasantly and unexpectedly surprised that they are actually enjoying their time on campus. As time passes, more and more people are recognizing that YSU is truly a great university.

The campus itself is pristine and gorgeous; the landscaping is well-done, and the architectural structures are being renovated to project a modern, artistic look. Walking to class on a sunny spring morning, students often find themselves stopping in wonder to gaze at the flowers and trees. A lovely atmosphere enhances the students' love for the institution and even the subject matter in classes. An important advantage for YSU's students is the high quality of their instructors and professors.... For the rest of this editorial, visit collegeprowler.com.

Students Speak Out On...
OVERALL EXPERIENCE

Q Favorite Experiences
"I love hanging out on campus with my friends. At YSU there are tons of opportunities to meet new people."

Q School
"YSU has been great to me. It has offered me many opportunities in my major that many other schools do not have, including an Emmy-nominated show to work on."

Q Love YSU
"Youngstown State University (YSU) is a great school! I am so glad I chose YSU, for a division I school the campus is small. There are a lot of people, but it's hard to get lost in the crowd. If I had to choose a college all over again I would definitely choose YSU because it makes me feel right at home! I love it!"

Q It's Peaceful
"I love Youngstown State University because it's a 10 minute drive from my house after I drop my kids off at school. I love it best in the Summer because it's so peaceful you can study anywhere. I love it in the Fall because it's new faces."

BEST OF YOUNGSTOWN STATE

1. Affordable tuition
2. Beautiful campus atmosphere
3. Compact campus
4. Helpful professors
5. Proximity to home
6. Variety of majors

Affordable
Tuition is only $9,649, one of the most affordable rates in the country.

Knowledgeable Professors
85% of students surveyed rated the general knowledge of professors as above average.

WORST OF YOUNGSTOWN STATE

1. Dining halls
2. General education requirements
3. Location
4. Not enough student life
5. Parking
6. Scheduling
7. Weather

Not Everyone Graduates
34% of students do not complete their education or graduate with a degree.

Student Body

African American:	16%	Male Undergrads:	46%
Asian American:	1%	Female Undergrads:	54%
Hispanic:	2%	Living On Campus:	10%
International:	1%	Living Off Campus:	90%
Native American:	0%	Male Athletes:	4%
White:	71%	Female Athletes:	3%
Unknown:	9%	Fraternity Members:	2%
From Out-of-State:	11%	Sorority Members:	2%

Frequently Compared Schools:

Kent State University
Ohio State University
The University of Akron
University of Toledo

Students Speak Out On...
EVERYTHING!

ACADEMICS

Q Education Major

"The education program at YSU is great! I love being able to rely on my academic advisor when I have questions. I also love that we have an education majors group on campus that actually goes out and does work in the field!"

Q Photography

"I love the classes and teachers. Fairly easy program as long as you love what you do. Wish it had classes that focused on studio photography and professional photography."

ATHLETICS

Q School Spirit

"I think that our school is very supportive of our sport teams. You walk around campus and a lot of people have YSU gear on."

Q Football

"YSU is a football school. Always has been, always will be."

CAMPUS DINING

Q Dining Halls

"The dining halls on campus are great. Many student do not know that the really good dining areas (Christman and Pete's Place) exist. The KC food court is horrible. Arby's is very good. The places around campus are great, too."

Q Good Enough Food

"I think that dining halls are actually pretty decent. There is always a variety for lunch and dinner, except for when Christman does the buffets. I also enjoy the value. I'm on a meal plan and I always have extra points so the price is good. I enjoy that we can use our points at other places too like the Candy Counter and Peaberrys."

CAMPUS HOUSING

Q Campus Life

"I do not live on campus but I have been to several of the dorms before. They are all close to the buildings on campus which gives students enough time to get to class. The ones I have had the chance of visiting are really nice. YSU is currently in the process of building new dorms for the growing number of students."

Q Cafaro House

"Cafaro House is a terrific dorm for several reasons. The students that live there are all honors students, university scholars, or international students. As such, there is a strong sense of scholarship. For the most part, it isn't loud, nor are there lingering smells. The cleaning staff are also greatly improved from last year."

GUYS & GIRLS

Q Extremely Diverse

"YSU's population has all kinds of different people. There are kids right out of high school, people in their twenties and thirties looking to restart or further their education, as well as middle-aged people who are there for a variety of reasons. Pretty much every ethnicity, socioeconomic status and sexual orientation are represented."

Q Social Diversity

"There is a wide range of social diversity on and off campus. Doesn't matter what group you claim to be in there is enough people that you wont feel like and outsider. People dress the same, you will find those who are out there and those who are very fashionable."

HEALTH & SAFETY

Q Safety and Security

"I feel that the campus is very safe. Campus security is always around. The campus is also located near two hospitals, a fire station and the police station so in the event of an emergency those services are always on the scene in minutes."

Q Daytime Safety

"I only attend school during the day and do not live on campus. From what I can tell, campus seems fairly safe. I have seen police cars on campus many times."

LOOKING FOR MORE?

Check out our full-length guide to this school at collegeprowler.com/youngstown-state-university/.

Verbal Outtakes

In the process of creating this book, we stumbled across some student quotes that were just too special to leave out. Read on for a little more of the good, the bad, and the truly insane.

"I once saw a homeless woman gathering up and eating the stray french fries on the countertops at the Lair. It made me question the security a bit, but it wasn't like an everyday occurrence."

(Loyola Marymount University Student – Safety & Security)

"The food is what it is: mass-produced, cafeteria-style goo."

(Baylor University Student – Campus Dining)

"Guys are generally gay or have a girlfriend. Girls are left being sexually frustrated, and I think that puts a crazed look in their eyes that makes them seem hotter."

(NYU Student – Guys & Girls)

"Sometimes, I think that this school and everyone in it is completely lame. Then I see something like a couch burning in the middle of the street and think, 'Wow, somebody around here is completely nuts,' and it gives me hope."

(West Virginia University Student – Overall Experience)

"They have these T-shirts: 'University of Chicago, where the squirrels are more aggressive than the guys,' and 'University of Chicago, where the squirrels are cuter than the girls.' That pretty much sums it all up."

(University of Chicago – Guys & Girls)

"Go to Bursley [Dining Hall] and get served by 'Sexy Grandpa.' He knows everyone's name and has worked there for decades. He is a campus legend!"

(University of Michigan – Campus Dining)

"Well, now you've heard it from the horses' mouths, and contrary to aphorism, feel free to look in these horses' mouths, and even to count their teeth, because they're not selling you a load of bull. Claremont just isn't cut out to be a college town. There isn't anything to do except walk around and buy overpriced doo-dads, which (i.e., the doo-dads) your grandmother might find appealing (not to cast aspersions on your grandmother's taste) but which (i.e., the doo-dads again) will likely leave you unimpressed."

(Peter Cook, Pomona College Author)

"THE GUYS ARE JERKS AND THE GIRLS ARE HOT—AND EVERY STUCK-UP, TANNED, SKINNY INCH OF THEM TELLS YOU THAT THEY KNOW IT, TOO."

(Trinity College -- Guys & Girls)

"OVERALL, THINGS HERE ARE PRETTY SAFE. I'VE NEVER HAD A PROBLEM WALKING HOME LATE AT NIGHT. THERE IS A SERIAL RAPIST ON THE LOOSE THOUGH . . ."

(University of Virginia Student – Safety & Security)

"I generally do not party on campus. I sit at home alone drinking Natural Light and reflecting on my failed life while my dogs and my cat stare at me with disgust and shame."

(Xavier Student – Nightlife)

"The dorms aren't that special. My first year in Lothrop Hall sucks. It's old, there is no air-conditioning, and right on top is a helicopter pad. Every night, the hospital helicopter takes off and lands a ton of times; it doesn't exactly help you sleep."

(University of Pittsburgh Student – Campus Housing)

"I came pretty close to getting arrested. Where? The top of Byrd Stadium. When? Some night around my junior year. Why? Cops were on a stakeout for a few students that had been throwing objects over the top of the stadium at moving vehicles and people in front of Ellicott Hall. What was I doing on top of the stadium? Well, I was throwing just about the smoothest mack-down on a pretty little girl who will remain nameless, to prevent any further embarrassment. Oh, did I tell you I had my saxophone up there? Yeah, that was 'sealing the deal' with my young lady friend. Except for the fact that the University police, after searching me, asked me to open the case very slowly and to step back, as if I had a small arsenal of dangerous and illegal objects. The cops were also on a stakeout for people smoking pot, which prompted a body search. Ah, the memories."

(University of Maryland Student – Campus Strictness)

"The best is when the vegans found out that the fries were being cooked in animal lard. Man, were they pissed."

(Bard College Student – Campus Dining)

"There's so many different kinds of people here. You'll meet people who have never even seen marijuana, and people who've snorted enough cocaine to kill a small horse! It's just like anywhere else: if you look for it, you can find it, whatever 'it' happens to be."

(University of Michigan Student – Drug Scene)

"There are all kinds here—hot, not, geek, preppy, whatever. All intelligent, though. If you're into geeky guys who think that handmade electronic teddy bears and hand-painted war game miniatures are romantic, this is definitely a good place to start. But there are plenty of more normal guys and girls out there, and plenty are interested in playing the field if you're into that sort of thing, too."

(MIT Student – Guys & Girls)

"Drive to Earhart Road and face south, then flash your headlights three times and you will see the headlights of a ghostly motorcycle appear and disappear at the curve where the rider died. Tip—remove your keys from the ignition and set them on your dashboard before you flash your lights."

(Miami of Ohio – Urban Legends)

"All undergraduates can get 12 free condoms per quarter."

(Stanford University Student – Safety & Security)

"If you ever wanted to experience what the caste system of India might be like, this is the place for you. When you step out of the 'Baylor bubble,' you can witness the plight of homeless Americans from the safety of your BMW or other equally expensive car."

(Baylor University Student – Guys & Girls)

"Varsity sports are about as popular as heat rash. No more than a few thousand students ever attend the football games (except for the season opener, which is always packed), and more people attend the cross-dressing fashion show in the Student Union than the basketball games."

(University at Buffalo Student – Athletics)

"Security once locked me into the library after doing their check to make sure the building was closed. I was studying on a couch in a public room when the lights went out . . . Our security is inadequate at best."

(Guilford Student – Safety & Security)

"The weather is freezing, miserable, and inhospitable. You sometimes feel like God wants you to die in this freezing, hellish wasteland."

(CMU Student – Weather)

"When I lived in Salley as a freshman, we couldn't decide if it was more like living in a Mexican prison cell or with the Teenage Mutant Ninja Turtles. If you like living in a shoebox complete with roaches and moldy ceiling tiles, try Kellum Hall and Smith Hall. If you like living in a shoebox with nicer furniture try Deviney and Dorman."

(Florida State Student – Campus Housing)

"One year, I got the privilege of living in a trailer —literally, a trailer. It was because Bard over-booked and ran out of places to put freshmen. Some people had to suffer in an actual building with foundations and stairs and different floors, but I was lucky enough to score something that they use to transport horses."

(Bard College Student – Campus Dining)

"The campus is very safe— Public Safety's tactics ensure that. But watch out! They have been known to run down a student or two with their Public Safety vans—I was a victim!"

(College of the Holy Cross Student – Safety & Security)

"THE GUYS HERE ARE ALL STUDS. TAKE ME FOR EXAMPLE; I AM 145 POUNDS OF RAW STEEL AND SEX APPEAL. WEST POINT DEFINITELY HAS THE STUDLIEST GUYS ON THE FACE OF THE PLANET."

(WEST POINT STUDENT – GUYS & GIRLS)

"I don't understand how you can gain the Freshman 15 if you constantly puke and poop out the food you just ate at the Fluh. Their new slogan should be, 'Weisenfluh is not just a place to eat, it's an epidemic.'"

(Slippery Rock Student– Campus Dining)

"The dorms are a great environment. The only thing they might need to change is their 'no hamster' rule; it is an inconvenience."

(Sacramento State Student – Campus Housing)

"Flip up your collar, puff out your chest, ignore your friends when you pass them on the street, develop a virgin-whore complex, complain bitterly about any and all work you're ever assigned, and buy a North Face jacket. There, you're a student at Hamilton."

(Hamilton College Student – Guys & Girls)

"Teachers range in quality from 'stunning' to 'where the hell did you graduate from? Auburn?!'"

(University of Alabama Student – Academics)

"I remember doing the 'walk of shame' a couple of times my freshman year. Those were good times."

(University of Rhode Island Student– Guys & Girls)

"ENROLLMENT AT COLBY COLLEGE IS CONTINGENT ON BEING A SEXY BEAST."

(COLBY COLLEGE – GUYS & GIRLS)

"Profs and classes. Yes, I've heard of those. Most of the time they really interfere with my sleeping schedule, but whenever I pulled myself up out of bed and went, I was glad I did. Did you know that's where all the ladies hang out during the day?"

(Wheaton College IL Student – Academics)

"The people at Willamette are just average college students. It's like if you're at the zoo and there is a cage labeled 'College Student.' Inside the cage you would see six or seven Willamette students, and they'd all be wearing sweatshirts and talking about the importance of recycling."

(Willamette University Student – Guys & Girls)

"Naked Potlucks happen usually on a Friday night. It's a bunch of girls sitting around naked trying to know their bodies in a non-sexual way. It was started by a bunch of girls who realized they only knew their bodies in a sexual context when they were with a guy. They figured that wasn't the only thing their bodies were capable of. Somebody usually brings wine, and someone else brings cheese. You get tipsy, you talk about girly things and exchange gossip. It's not erotic because it's not meant to be."

(New College of Florida Student – Nightlife)

"They are so strict. I think not smoking pot in the dorms is like one of the Ten Commandments or something. "

(Radford University Student – Campus Strictness)

"THE BEAN DIP AT LA HACIENDA IS AMAZING! I STOPPED GOING THERE FOR AWHILE BECAUSE MY FRIENDS GOT FOOD POISONING, BUT THE BEAN DIP BROUGHT ME BACK. IT'S JUST SO GOOD!"

(WILLAMETTE UNIVERSITY STUDENT – OFF-CAMPUS DINING)

"If I had to use three words to describe Kirksville, they would be 'lack of goodness.'"
(Truman State Student – Local Atmosphere)

Words to Know

Academic Probation – A suspension imposed on a student if he or she fails to keep up with the school's minimum academic requirements. Those unable to improve their grades after receiving this warning can face dismissal.

Beer Pong/Beirut – A drinking game involving cups of beer arranged in a pyramid shape on each side of a table. The goal is to get a ping pong ball into one of the opponent's cups by throwing the ball or hitting it with a paddle. If the ball lands in a cup, the opponent is required to drink the beer.

Bid – An invitation from a fraternity or sorority to 'pledge' (join) that specific house.

Blue-Light Phone – Brightly-colored phone posts with a blue light bulb on top. These phones exist for security purposes and are located at various outside locations around most campuses. In an emergency, a student can pick up one of these phones (free of charge) to connect with campus police or a security escort.

Campus Police – Police who are specifically assigned to a given institution. Campus police are typically not regular city officers; they are employed by the university in a full-time capacity.

Club Sports – A level of sports that falls somewhere between varsity and intramural. If a student is unable to commit to a varsity team but has a lot of passion for athletics, a club sport could be a better, less intense option. Even less demanding, intramural (IM) sports often involve no traveling and considerably less time.

Cocaine – An illegal drug. Also known as "coke" or "blow," cocaine often resembles a white crystalline or powdery substance. It is highly addictive and dangerous.

Common Application – An application with which students can apply to multiple schools.

Course Registration – The period of official class selection for the upcoming quarter or semester. Prior to registration, it is best to prepare several back-up courses in case a particular class becomes full. If a course is full, students can place themselves on the waitlist, although this still does not guarantee entry.

Division Athletics – Athletic classifications range from Division I to Division III. Division IA is the most competitive, while Division III is considered to be the least competitive.

Dorm – A dorm (or dormitory) is an on-campus housing facility. Dorms can provide a range of options from suite-style rooms to more communal options that include shared bathrooms. Most first-year students live in dorms. Some upperclassmen who wish to stay on campus also choose this option.

Early Action – An application option with which a student can apply to a school and receive an early acceptance response without a binding commitment. This system is becoming less and less available.

Early Decision – An application option that students should use only if they are certain they plan to attend the school in question. If a student applies using the early decision option and is admitted, he or she is required and bound to attend that university. Admission rates are usually higher among students who apply through early decision, as the student is clearly indicating that the school is his or her first choice.

Ecstasy – An illegal drug. Also known as "E" or "X," ecstasy looks like a pill and most resembles an aspirin. Considered a party drug, ecstasy is very dangerous and can be deadly.

Ethernet – An extremely fast Internet connection available in most university-owned residence halls. To use an Ethernet connection properly, a student will need a network card and cable for his or her computer.

Fake ID – A counterfeit identification card that contains false information. Most commonly, students get fake IDs with altered birthdates so that they appear to be older than 21 (and therefore of legal drinking age). Even though it is illegal, many college students have fake IDs in hopes of purchasing alcohol or getting into bars.

Frosh – Slang for "freshman" or "freshmen."

Hazing – Initiation rituals administered by some fraternities or sororities as part of the pledging process. Many universities have outlawed hazing due to its degrading and sometimes dangerous nature.

Intramurals (IMs) – A popular, and usually free, sport league in which students create teams and compete against one another. These sports vary in competitiveness and can include a range of activities— everything from billiards to water polo. IM sports are a great way to meet people with similar interests.

Keg – Officially called a half-barrel, a keg contains roughly 200 12-ounce servings of beer.

LSD – An illegal drug. Also known as acid, this hallucinogen most commonly resembles a tab of paper.

Marijuana – An illegal drug. Also known as weed or pot; along with alcohol, marijuana is one of the most commonly-found drugs on campuses across the country.

Major –The focal point of a student's college studies; a specific topic that is studied for a degree. Examples of majors include physics, English, history, computer science, economics, business, and music. Many students decide on a specific major before arriving on campus, while others are simply "undecided" until declaring a major. Those who are extremely interested in two areas can also choose to double major.

Meal Block – The equivalent of one meal. Students on a meal plan usually receive a fixed number of meals per week. Each meal, or "block," can be redeemed at the school's dining facilities in place of cash. Often, a student's weekly allotment of meal blocks will be forfeited if not used.

Minor – An additional focal point in a student's education. Often serving as a complement or addition to a student's main area of focus, a minor has fewer requirements and prerequisites to fulfill than a major. Minors are not required for graduation from most schools; however some students who want to explore many different interests choose to pursue both a major and a minor.

Mushrooms – An illegal drug. Also known as "'shrooms," this drug resembles regular mushrooms but is extremely hallucinogenic.

Off-Campus Housing – Housing from a particular landlord or rental group that is not affiliated with the university. Depending on the college, off-campus housing can range from extremely popular to non-existent. Students who choose to live off campus are typically given more freedom, but they also have to deal with possible subletting scenarios, furniture, bills, and other issues. In addition to these factors, rental prices and distance often affect a student's decision to move off campus.

Office Hours – Time that teachers set aside for students who have questions about coursework. Office hours are a good forum for students to go over any problems and to show interest in the subject material.

Pledging – The early phase of joining a fraternity or sorority, pledging takes place after a student has gone through rush and received a bid. Pledging usually lasts between one and two semesters. Once the pledging period is complete and a particular student has done everything that is required to become a member, that student is considered a brother or sister. If a fraternity or a sorority would decide to "haze" a group of students, this initiation would take place during the pledging period.

Private Institution – A school that does not use tax revenue to subsidize education costs. Private schools typically cost more than public schools and are usually smaller.

Prof – Slang for "professor."

Public Institution – A school that uses tax revenue to subsidize education costs. Public schools are often a good value for in-state residents and tend to be larger than most private colleges.

Quarter System (or Trimester System) – A type of academic calendar system. In this setup, students take classes for three academic periods. The first quarter usually starts in late September or early October and concludes right before Christmas. The second quarter usually starts around early to mid–January and finishes up around March or April. The last academic quarter, or "third quarter," usually starts in late March or early April and finishes up in late May or Mid-June. The fourth quarter is summer. The major difference between the quarter system and semester system is that students take more, less comprehensive courses under the quarter calendar.

RA (Resident Assistant) – A student leader who is assigned to a particular floor in a dormitory in order to help to the other students who live there. An RA's duties include ensuring student safety and providing assistance wherever possible.

Recitation – An extension of a specific course; a review session. Some classes, particularly large lectures, are supplemented with mandatory recitation sessions that provide a relatively personal class setting.

Rolling Admissions – A form of admissions. Most commonly found at public institutions, schools with this type of policy continue to accept students throughout the year until their class sizes are met. For example, some schools begin accepting students as early as December and will continue to do so until April or May.

Room and Board – This figure is typically the combined cost of a university-owned room and a meal plan.

Room Draw/Housing Lottery – A common way to pick on-campus room assignments for the following year. If a student decides to remain in university-owned housing, he is assigned a unique number that, along with seniority, is used to determine his housing for the next year.

Rush – The period in which students can meet the brothers and sisters of a particular chapter and find out if a given fraternity or sorority is right for them. Rushing a fraternity or a sorority is not a requirement at any school. The goal of rush is to give students who are serious about pledging a feel for what to expect.

Semester System – The most common type of academic calendar system at college campuses. This setup typically includes two semesters in a given school year. The fall semester starts around the end of August or early September and concludes before winter vacation. The spring semester usually starts in mid-January and ends in late April or May.

Student Center/Rec Center/Student Union – A common area on campus that often contains study areas, recreation facilities, and eateries. This building is often a good place to meet up with fellow students; depending on the school, the student center can have a huge role or a non-existent role in campus life.

Student ID – A university-issued photo ID that serves as a student's key to school-related functions. Some schools require students to show these cards in order to get into dorms, libraries, cafeterias, and other facilities. In addition to storing meal plan information, in some cases, a student ID can actually work as a debit card and allow students to purchase things from bookstores or local shops.

Suite – A type of dorm room. Unlike dorms that feature communal bathrooms shared by the entire floor, suites offer bathrooms shared only among the suite. Suite-style rooms can house anywhere from two to ten students.

TA (Teacher's Assistant) – An undergraduate or grad student who helps in some manner with a specific course. In some cases, a TA will teach a class, assist a professor, grade assignments, or conduct office hours.

Undergraduate – A student in the process of studying for his or her bachelor's degree.

About the Authors

Albion College

Author: Jill Hindenach

Hometown: Washington, DC

Fun Fact: This guide seemed like a daunting task at first, but Jill was happy to take part in Albion's inaugural edition.

Alfred University

Author: Chagmion Antoine

Hometown: Bronx, N.Y.

Fun Fact: Chagmion has written for publications in Connecticut, Boston, and New York and has had work featured on MSNBC.

Allegheny College

Author: Katrina Tulloch

Previous Contributor: Carolyn Keller

Alverno College

Author: Katy Kujala-Korpela

Hometown: Wisconsin

Major: History/Political Science

Fun Fact: Alverno has helped Katy become a strong, independent woman who thinks for herself and lives outside of what corporations try to make society consume.

American University

Author: Ian Hosking

Previous Contributor: Alanna Schubach

Amherst College

Author: Lem Atanga McCormick

Hometown: Chicago, IL

Major: Pre-Med (Biology and French)

Fun Fact: Lem has been to 17 different countries.

Previous Contributor: Nadav Klein

Arcadia University

Author: Stacey Wisniewski

Hometown: Schwenksville, Pa.

Major: English

Arizona State University

Author: Kaitlin Hackenberg

Hometown: Cleveland, OH

Major: Marketing

Fun Fact: Kaitlin once ate four Chipotle burritos for a very profitable bet.

Previous Contributors: Lauren Kennedy, Christopher Yen

Auburn University

Author: Jordan Luke

Hometown: Mandeville, LA

Major: Double major in English and Spanish

Fun Fact: Jordan's dream job is to be the U.S. Ambassador to Spain.

Previous Contributor: Lindsey Nolan

Austin College

Author: Natalie Taylor

Hometown: Lufkin, Texas

Major: English

Fun Fact: Natalie lived in South Africa for two years in high school. She studies to techno music and wouldn't survive in a world without green tea and chocolate.

Ave Maria University

Author: Natalia Selín

Hometown: Hialeah, FL

Major: Theology, Other

Fun Fact: Natalia plays flamenco and classical guitar and speaks English and Spanish.

Babson College

Author: Anna Klimentievna Gatker

Fun Fact: Anna lived on campus for all four years and enjoyed a well-rounded life at Babson.

Ball State University

Author: Adrian Sharp

Major: Journalism Graphics

Fun Fact: Adrian is the assistant features editor at The Ball State Daily News and the president of the Ball State chapter of the Orthodox Christian Fellowship.

Bard College

Author: Courtney Scott
Hometown: Nashville, Tenn.

Previous Contributor: Jared Killeen

Barnard College

Author: Megan Cloud

Hometown: Ft. Worth, Texas

Major: Psychology

Fun Fact: Megan says that New York was a great experience for her, and she hopes that you feel like you've gotten to know Barnard a little bit better.

Barry University

Author: Ricardo Redd

Hometown: Columbia, S.C.

Major: Professional Writing

Fun Fact: Ricardo won first place in Barry University's 2010 Sigma Tau Delta Writing Contest in the fiction category.

Baruch College

Author: Nakeisha Campbell

Hometown: Brooklyn, N.Y.

Major: Journalism

Fun Fact: Nakeisha loves to sing, and she also plays the trumpet.

Previous Contributor: Mikhail Sedov

Bates College

Author: Jessie Sawyer

Hometown: Farmington, CT

Major: English with a concentration in Creative Writing and a Spanish minor

Fun Fact: As a journalist, Jessie has interviewed two contestants on "The Bachelorette," Doug Gray (lead singer of The Marshall Tucker Band), bestselling novelist Elizabeth Strout, Pete Francis and Bradiggan of Dispatch, and actor Patrick Dempsey

Previous Contributor: Sarah Connell

Bay Path College

Author: Pamela Racine

Hometown: New Bedford

Major: Forensic Psychology

Fun Fact: I am a friend, a loyal music lover, and a dedicated student.

Baylor University

Author: Teni Odunsi

Hometown: San Antonio, TX

Major: Environmental Studies

Fun Fact: Teni was born in the U.K.

Previous Contributor: Kyra Mitchell

Belmont University

Author: Adaeze Elechi

Hometown: Nigeria

Major: Journalism

Fun Fact: Adaeze describes her perfect future as living in a nostalgic apartment in a pseudo-developing nation, writing short stories and novels until her mind can no longer form words and eating yellow mangoes on a balcony overlooking the city.

Beloit College

Author: Katie Kozak

Previous Contributor: Sarah Maehl

Bentley University

Author: Jessica Low

Major: Marketing

Fun Fact: Jessica held two different internships in public affairs and will soon be starting a career in public relations, hopefully with an agency in Boston.

Berea College

Author: Gerald Fitts

Hometown: Birmigham, Ala.

Major: Sociology and African & African American Studies

Fun Fact: Gerald loves college, is a friendly person, and loves meeting people.

Binghamton University

Author: Claire Easton
Hometown: Rutherford, NJ
Major: English
Fun Fact: Claire likes reading and chocolate.

Previous Contributor: Scott Kutscher

Birmingham-Southern College

Author: Kriti Mishra
Hometown: Hoover, Ala.

Previous Contributor: Kelli L. Hilyer

Bob Jones University

Author: So Hyeun Cho
Hometown: Seoul, South Korea
Major: Public Relations Journalism and Mass Communication
Fun Fact: I love to travel, try new food, meet new people and photograph.

Boston College

Author: Samantha Durant
Hometown: Cheshire, CT
Major: Communications with Women's Studies minor
Fun Fact: Samantha has a black belt in Shaolin Kempo.

Previous Contributor: Kelley Gossett

Boston University

Author: Stephanie Santana
Hometown: Queens, NY
Major: Anthropology/Journalism
Fun Fact: Garnering inspiration from the most famous chocolatier, Willy Wonka, Stephanie has acquired an affinity for making sweet desserts for her friends whenever she throws a party. She's always on the search for the freshest fruit to add to her latest cake creation.

Previous Contributors: Caren M. Walker, Linda Boulden

Bowdoin College

Author: Danica Loucks
Hometown: Hamilton, Mont.
Major: Probably Sociology and German
Fun Fact: Danica loves to make up new recipes, do archery, and run long distances. She enjoys celebrating the summer and winter solstices in Finland with extreme light and extreme dark. She loves learning and using languages, as well as sitting and observing human interaction. She learned how to ride a bicycle using "magic gloves" and embraces all outdoor activity. She began skiing at the ripe old age of two.

Previous Contributors: Rachel Goldman, Derrick S. Wong

Bradley University

Author: Erin Wood
Hometown: Peoria, Ill.
Fun Fact: Erin is now the proud queen of random Bradley trivia, and she loves it. Test her.

Brandeis University

Author: Shannon Ingram
Hometown: Floral Park, NY
Major: Sociology/Hispanic Studies minor
Fun Fact: Shannon enjoys rock concerts.

Previous Contributors: Emily Maskas, Andrew Katz

Brigham Young University

Author: Caitlin Bronson
Hometown: Graham, Wash.

Previous Contributor: Ashley Vance Timm

Brigham Young University - Idaho

Author: Jenica Sparks
Hometown: Olympia, Washington
Major: Communications
Fun Fact: My highest bowling score is a 201.

Brown University

Author: Justin Kim
Hometown: Austin, TX
Major: Undecided
Fun Fact: Justin ranked internationally in competitive Minesweeper.

Previous Contributor: Matthew Kittay

Bryant University

Author: Caitlin Douglas

Hometown: Poughkeepsie, N.Y.

Major: Finance

Fun Fact: Caitlin went to Germany and Greece during winter break of her sophomore year with the Bryant University Sophomore International Experience Program.

Bryn Mawr College

Author: Kaitlin Menza

Hometown: New Brunswick, NJ

Major: Sociology

Fun Fact: When Kaitlin's not updating Bryn Mawr's College Prowler guide, she's actually the school's mascot and wears owl suit for games!

Previous Contributor: Sarah Friedman

Bucknell University

Author: Jen Adams

Hometown: Washington, PA

Major: Economics/Political Science

Fun Fact: Jen can play the steel drums.

Previous Contributor: Lauren Davis

Cal Poly

Author: Sarah Parr

Hometown: Simi Valley, CA

Major: Journalism/Pre-Law

Fun Fact: Sarah is into astrology.

Previous Contributor: Nicole Biggers

Cal Poly Pomona

Author: Kyleena Harper

Hometown: Sierra Madre, CA

Major: English

Fun Fact: I'm a competitive Highland Dancer and member of Sigma Kappa sorority :)

Previous Contributor: Candyce Otis

Cal State Long Beach

Author: Arnesha Allen

Hometown: Compton, Calif.

Major: Psychology

Fun Fact: Arnesha is a Lakers fanatic, and she loves Kobe Bryant. Though she is a psychology major, she loves writing in her down time.

Cal State Monterey Bay

Author: Bennett Kogon

Hometown: Pacific Palisades, CA

Major: Film Studies

Fun Fact: Contributing Author!

Cal State Northridge

Author: Julie Ritchie

Major: English/Liberal Studies

Fun Fact: Since Julie grew up in a small, rural town, she has loved every bit of living in the city. She admits that she experienced culture shock when she moved to the Valley, but she appreciates every way it has changed her.

Cal State San Marcos

Author: Katrina Kistler

Hometown: El Segundo

Major: Literature and Writing

Fun Fact: I love to surf!

California College of the Arts

Author: Maria Vaza-Kaczynski

Hometown: Pacifica, Calif.

Major: Animation

Fun Fact: Maria is a self-described "big nerd" who loves to watch and read anime/manga, make and wear cosplay, and play video games. She has a very broad taste in music, and loves horror movies, books, and films, as well as cute things. She is in the International Order of the Rainbow for Girls, which is a Masonic youth group. She has five cats at home.

California University of Pennsylvania

Author: Alex Vucelich

Caltech

Author: Mayra Sheikh

Hometown: San Fernando Valley, Calif.

Major: Chemistry

Fun Fact: When not at school, Mayra lives with her parents and two younger sisters. She really liked Caltech overall, even though it was extremely difficult.

Carleton College

Author: Lingerr Senghor

Hometown: Unknown

Previous Contributor: Adam Zang

Carnegie Mellon University

Author: Lauren Hirata

Hometown: Palos Verdes Peninsula

Major: Creative Writing, Professional Writing

Fun Fact: It's no secret Lauren is obsessed with anything Disney.

Previous Contributor: Dan Liebermann

Case Western Reserve University

Author: Remy Olson

Hometown: Maui, Hawaii, and Glen Ellyn, Ill.

Major: Biology

Fun Fact: Remy hopes to publish more as he continues to grow as both a scientist and a writer.

Catawba College

Author: Christine Shuster

Hometown: Jackson, N.J.

Major: Music business

Fun Fact: Christine loves llamas and olives.

Catholic University of America

Author: Frankie Bustamante

Major: Politics

Fun Fact: While writing this guide, Frankie realized that there's a legitimate feeling of community (religious and secular) and belonging that really lingers throughout your time here. The people you meet and learn from really leave a mark on you that lets you forgive any mistakes or shortcomings the University may have.

Centenary College of Louisiana

Author: Ashley Moss

Hometown: Tucson, Ariz.

Fun Fact: Ashley is considering grad school and trying to figure out the best way to go about getting paid for watching movies.

Centre College

Author: Aaron Edwards

Hometown: Henderson, KY

Major: Biochemistry and Molecular Biology

Fun Fact: Aaron is addicted to coconut rum cake and calamari.

Previous Contributor: Alexandra R. Chase

Chapman University

Author: Emily Esposito

Hometown: Seattle, Wash.

Major: Public Relations/Advertising & French Language

Fun Fact: Emily eats a peanut butter and jelly sandwich almost every day!

Chatham University

Author: Samantha Greenwood

Hometown: Hamburg, N.Y.

Major: English/Secondary Education

Fun Fact: Samantha has been to Belize, Guatemala, France, England, and Italy. She now wishes to see most of Eastern Europe.

City College of New York

Author: Melissa Charles & Garri Rivkin

Hometown: New York, N.Y. & Vilnius, Lithuania

Major: International Development of Women through Arts & English Literature

Fun Fact: Garri is an avid Yankees fan.

Claflin University

Author: Claflin Prowler

Hometown: Orangeburg, S.C.

Major: Biology/Biological Sciences

Fun Fact: This author wanted to use a pen name to get students to fill out surveys. To found out who the author is, ask around at Claflin!

Claremont McKenna College

Author: Elizabeth Friede

Hometown: Philadelphia

Major: International Relations

Fun Fact: When ordering a cheesesteak, go to Pat's not Geno's.

Previous Contributor: Hayes Humphries

Clark Atlanta University

Author: Eatharon Taylor

Hometown: Arkansas

Fun Fact: Having the opportunity to write this book for prospective CAU students has been one of Eatharon's proudest accomplishments.

Clark University

Author: Angela Wu

Hometown: Bellevue, WA

Major: Undecided

Fun Fact: Angela is allergic to apples, peaches, plums, pears, and cat fur.

Previous Contributor: Mike Bertone

Clemson University

Author: Sarah Camille Hipp

Hometown: Alexandria, VA

Major: Communication Studies

Fun Fact: Orange County is Sarah's favorite movie of all time.

Previous Contributor: Andrew Coleman

Cleveland State University

Author: Ashley Ammond

Hometown: Canton, Ohio

Major: Promotional Communication, Journalism

Fun Fact: "This is I; this is my voice; this is my body; this is my life."

Coe College

Author: Manish Khadka

Hometown: Kathmandu, Nepal

Major: Accounting

Fun Fact: I am an international student from Nepal, which is in Southern Asia. I have traveled to six different countries and have also been able to collect my name in 17 different lingual scripts.

Colby College

Author: Danny Garin

Hometown: Washington, DC

Major: Government and Economics

Fun Fact: I love the city but decided to go to a rural school to see what life is like in a different setting, and I have not regretted my decision.

Previous Contributors: Lane McVey, Allyson Rudolph

Colgate University

Author: Erika Nyamé-Nséké

Hometown: Bronx, NY

Major: History- Undeclared

Fun Fact: Erika has a wicked, rapid-fire sense of humor that causes my friends to fall over from laughing too hard. Or at the very least shake their head and smile.

Previous Contributors: Desirée Abeleda, Elisa Benson

College for Creative Studies

Author: Natasha Guimond

Hometown: Massena, NY

Major: Advertising Design

Fun Fact: She wants to change the world through advertising.She was an Official Torchbearer for the 2002 Winter Olympics in Salt Lake City.She makes a killer latte - latte art and all!

College of Charleston

Author: Nancy Blayney

Previous Contributors: Robyn Burrows, Melanie Murray

College of Mount Saint Vincent

Author: Valerie Villanueva

Hometown: Floral Park, N.Y.

Major: Undecided

Fun Fact: Valerie is 19-years-old and lives in New York.

College of Notre Dame of Maryland

Author: Morgan Randall

Hometown: Randallstown, MD

Major: Communication Arts

Fun Fact: I'm an aspiring author and hope to be famous one day for my stories. I like to write poetry too, which encouraged me to start my own radio show called Poetic Pleasures. I also just like to be silly and make my friends laugh.

College of the Holy Cross

Author: Audrey Gehring
Hometown: Madison, WI
Major: English/Religious Studies
Fun Fact: Audrey enjoys riding horses in her free time.

Previous Contributor: Matthew Hayes

College of William & Mary

Author: Joe Quinn
Hometown: Fredericksburg, VA
Major: Geology/English
Fun Fact: Joe loves dogs.

Previous Contributor: Camille Thompson

College of Wooster

Author: Sarah Core
Major: English/Communication minor
Fun Fact: Sarah has been Managing Editor of the College's weekly student-run newspaper, a DJ for the College radio station, a Web master for the Babcock International Program, a member of the COW Belles (Wooster's beautiful and fabulous female a cappella group), and the cheese and hot dog girl for Circle K.

Colorado College

Author: Cobun Keegan
Hometown: Paonia, CO
Major: Psychology
Fun Fact: I was named after a creek . . .

Previous Contributors: Greg Lestikow, Jennifer Small

Colorado State University - Pueblo

Author: Brittany Ferguson
Hometown: Chandler, AZ
Major: Psychology
Fun Fact: I transferred to CSU-P as a junior, and I will be living here for the duration of my schooling.

Columbia College Chicago

Author: Whitney Fox
Hometown: Topeka, Kansas
Major: Television Writing and Producing
Fun Fact: I'm just a small-town girl living in the city and loving every minute of it.

Columbia University

Author: Alexandre Millet
Hometown: Washington D.C., Geneva
Major: Economics and Computer Science
Fun Fact: Alexandre has been to Antarctica!

Previous Contributors: Julia Green, Michelle Tompkins

Concordia College at Moorhead

Author: Matt Gantz
Hometown: Eagan, MN
Major: International Business and English Writing
Fun Fact: Matt can identify over one hundred fossils.He has seen every episode of the television show "Friends" at least twenty times.

Connecticut College

Author: Andrew Patton
Hometown: Montclair, N.J.
Major: Government and American Studies
Fun Fact: Andrew has always dreamed of owning a onesie.

Previous Contributor: Brian Sendrowski

Converse College

Author: Gwendolyn Smith
Hometown: Greenville, SC
Major: English
Fun Fact: I first tried Thai food in Dublin, Ireland.

Cornell College

Author: Erin McNeill
Hometown: Foristell, MO
Major: Sociology/Anthropology, English
Fun Fact: Born and raised in small-town Missouri, I spend most of my free time at the barn with my horse. I enjoy shopping with my sisters, devouring murder mystery novels and have a secret obsession with office supplies.

Cornell University

Author: Mandy Kain and Radhika Arora
Hometown: Hewlett, N.Y., and Ithaca, N.Y.

Previous Contributors: Maria Adelmann, Oliver Striker

Creighton University

Author: Maddy Kovarik

Hometown: Rapid City, SD

Major: Biology

Fun Fact: Maddy loves pistachio and almond ice cream. You'd never think it would work, but she says it's delicious!

Previous Contributor: Holly Morris

CUNY Lehman College

Author: Jordana Lopez-da Silva

CUNY Queens College

Author: Shira Frager

Hometown: Palo Alto, CA

Major: English

Fun Fact: Originally from California, I took a couple years off to work and travel before heading to college. I'm finding Queens to be a very friendly, comfortable atmosphere and am enjoying college life. Queens College's motto is "We learn so that we may serve" and I think this is important for students to keep in mind during our academic and social college experience.

Dartmouth College

Author: Kirk Greenwood

Hometown: Warrington, PA

Major: Comparative Literature

Fun Fact: Kirk likes to talk and listen (almost in equal measure), drink green tea and experiment, and is a lover of many things: people and Nature, innocence and wisdom, beauty, pain, happiness, experience.

Previous Contributors: Scott Glabe, Janos Marton

Davidson College

Author: Annie Maietta

Hometown: Weston, MA

Major: Undecided

Fun Fact: Annie has four siblings: one of her older sisters went to Davidson, and her younger brother aspires to.

Previous Contributor: Colin Eagan

Denison University

Author: Heather Fishel

Hometown: Unknown

Previous Contributor: Sarah Clapp

DePaul University

Author: Kristian Gist

Hometown: Cleveland, Ohio

Major: Business Management and Hospitality Leadership

Fun Fact: Kristian has never been to Disney World, her favorite food is cupcakes, she's addicted to shopping, and she loves to cook for her friends.

Previous Contributor: E. Ce Anderson

DePauw University

Author: Lynn Demos

Hometown: Unknown

Previous Contributors: Kellie Lee Hasselbeck, Meredith Siemens

Dickinson College

Author: Rachel Warzala

Hometown: Somerset, NJ

Major: English/Political Science

Fun Fact: Rachel is a campus tour guide and a member of the Orientation Committee. So if you decide to come to Dickinson, either to visit or to stay, make sure you say hi

Previous Contributor: Brooke Lewis

Dordt College

Author: Alyssa Hoogendoorn

Hometown: Rock Valley

Major: Individual Studies - Journalism

Fun Fact: My idea of a perfect morning is having a steaming cup of coffee and watching one of my favorite TV shows. My favorite kind of coffee is a café mocha. Aside from writing, I like to keep up with the latest fashion trends and take black and white photos.

Drexel University

Author: Kevin Colvin

Previous Contributor: Ryan Murphy

Duke University

Author: George Carotenuto

Hometown: East Hanover, NJ

Major: Economics

Fun Fact: Tennis player, Cameron Crazie, environmentalist, crossword enthusiast

Previous Contributor: Margaret Campbell

Duquesne University

Author: Lauren A. Hensley (pictured) and Kalifa-Afia Augustus

Hometown: Nazareth, PA (Lauren) and Petit Valley, Trinidad (Kalifa)

Major: Journalism (Lauren) and Spanish/Journalism (Kalifa)

Fun Fact: Lauren traveled across the country as a part of a documentary crew in summer 2008. Kalifa finds that the older she gets, the harder it is to dance in time with music!

Previous Contributor: Jonathan Doctorick

Earlham College

Author: Anna Benfield

Hometown: Takoma Park, Md.

Major: Women's Studies

Fun Fact: Anna enjoys cartwheeling in the rain with my housemates and procrastinating African American lit papers with boogie club extravaganzas in front of the circulation desk.

East Carolina University

Author: Samantha Mandel

Hometown: Matthews, NC

Major: Biology

Fun Fact: Samantha can make an extremely weird shape with her mouth, kind of like a "fish face," that no one else she has met is able to do.

Previous Contributor: Leanne E. Smith

Eastern Kentucky University

Author: Nakeisha Wilson

Hometown: Ferguson, KY

Major: Psychology

Fun Fact: I love to travel and recently I've been as far as China. To me, seeing different cultures and experiencing new things is what makes the best education.

Eckerd College

Author: Elise Luce

Hometown: Los Alamos, N.M./Decatur, Ga.

Major: Environmental Studies

Fun Fact: Since attending college, Elise has found the love of her life: traveling. She's learned so much about how she knows close to nothing but is optimistic that she knows introductory botany now. Elise has decided she really, really loves nature, international movies, Lolcats, Modge Podge, bubble tea, St. Petersburg, traveling gnomes, and the little swords they serve in only the classiest of drinks. Aye, aye captain!

Elizabethtown College

Author: Julie Klaski

Hometown: Hatfield

Major: English- Professional Writing

Fun Fact: I love traveling and photography and I will someday be a successful photojournalist (here's hoping for National Geographic!)

Elmhurst College

Author: Colin Ashwood

Hometown: Cedar Falls, Iowa

Major: Political Science

Fun Fact: I fell off a three-story cliff in eighth grade— unharmed!

Elmira College

Author: Sarah Burr

Hometown: Appleton, Maine

Major: Political Science, Philosophy & Religious Studies

Elon University

Author: Lauren Flood

Hometown: Ridgefield, CT

Major: Business Administration (Minor: Leadership)

Fun Fact: Lauren is excited to be studying abroad for the first time next fall in Florence, Italy!

Previous Contributor: Amy Mahon

Emerson College

Author: Vanessa Willoughby

Hometown: Waterford, CT

Major: Writing, Literature and Publishing

Fun Fact: Vanessa was her high school's Poet Laureate.

Previous Contributor: Jordan Ross

Emory University

Author: Ginny Kyuhee Chae
Hometown: Atlanta, GA
Major: English
Fun Fact: Ginny enjoys breakdancing!

Previous Contributor: Jordan Pope-Roush

Fashion Institute of Technology

Author: Heather M. DiRubba
Hometown: New York, N.Y.
Fun Fact: Heather served on the student government as vice president of communications, traveled to conferences and seminars, studied abroad in London, and completed five internships.

Ferris State University

Author: Lauren Moore
Hometown: Temperance, MI
Major: Marketing
Fun Fact: Lauren plays the violin in the Ferris State Orchestra.

Florida A&M University

Author: Angel Neal
Hometown: Tampa, Fla
Major: Journalism/Magazine Production
Fun Fact: I'm a Faces Model and secretary of Tampa Bay Area Club. I love fashion and entertainment.

Florida Atlantic University

Author: Arami Kerkian
Hometown: Bath, Ohio
Major: Communications
Fun Fact: Arami is Armenian.

Florida Southern College

Author: Erin Ferguson
Hometown: Orlando
Major: Communication
Fun Fact: I love movies, books, and chocolate. My dorm has become a second home to me and I love being so close to all my friends!

Florida State University

Author: Cheryl Justis
Hometown: Daytona Beach, Fla.

Previous Contributor: Richard Bist

Fordham University

Author: Emily Intravia
Hometown: Medford, N.Y.
Major: Playwriting/English
Fun Fact: As a playwriting major, Emily watched four of her own plays produced right in the studio theaters.

Franklin & Marshall College

Author: Danielle Glass
Hometown: New York, N.Y.

Previous Contributor: Ellen Baier

Freed-Hardeman University

Author: Meghan Beatty
Hometown: Nashville, TN
Major: Journalism
Fun Fact: I am a Marketing minor, I love photography, and I love to write!

Furman University

Author: Tenell Felder
Hometown: Columbia, SC
Major: Political Science/Communications
Fun Fact: Tenell has smelled lightning before during a very severe thunderstorm. Considering that she is terrified of thunderstorms, this was a semi-traumatic experience but also a really cool one.

Previous Contributor: Debra A. Granberry

Gannon University

Author: Courtney Lewis
Hometown: Pittsburgh, PA
Major: English
Fun Fact: Courtney can't stand the sight of a peanut butter and jelly sandwich, because she used to find them so delicious that she ate one every day for over a year.

Geneva College

Author: Kevan Gray

Hometown: Greensburg, Pa.

Major: Philosophy/Writing

Fun Fact: While in high school, Kevan was a part of the Pennsylvania Mock Trial State Champion team that went to Omaha, Nebraska to compete for a national title.

George Mason University

Author: Emily Sharrer

Hometown: Harrisonburg, Va.

Major: Communication

Fun Fact: Thrift shopping is a passion of mine, I love collecting records and cool knick-knacks to decorate my room. My reason for choosing Mason? Its proximity to dozens of concert venues where I can catch my favorite bands when they come to town.

George Washington University

Author: David Glidden

Hometown: Fuquay-Varina, NC

Major: International Affairs (Spanish minor)

Fun Fact: David thoroughly enjoys 2 a.m. trips to the national monuments!

Previous Contributor: Julie Gordon

Georgetown University

Author: Christina Malliet

Hometown: Cedarburg, WI

Major: English

Fun Fact: Christina's favorite place in the world is Walt Disney World.

Previous Contributors: Derek Richmond, Andrew Wilson

Georgia State University

Author: Megan Urry

Hometown: Franklin, New Jersey

Major: English, Journalism

Fun Fact: I'm moving to Galway, Ireland next year, and I've seen every episode of the Golden Girls post 1990. And no, the two have nothing to do with each other...

Georgia Tech

Author: Mahssa Mostajabi

Hometown: Alpharetta, GA

Major: Science, Technology, and Culture

Fun Fact: Mahssa is Iranian!

Previous Contributor: Jonathan Trousdale

Gettysburg College

Author: Steven Moxley

Hometown: Bakersfield, CA

Major: Computer Science

Fun Fact: Steven went paragliding in the Andes after driving up a mountain in a Jeep made during WWII.

Previous Contributor: Mike Howells

Gonzaga University

Author: Iain Bernhoft

Hometown: Seattle, Wash.

Major: English/Philosophy

Fun Fact: Iain spent the better part of a year studying in Florence and then at Oxford University.

Goucher College

Author: Cleo Zancope (left) and Shaine Griffin

Hometown: Amherst, MA (Cleo) and San Francisco, CA (Shaine)

Major: Communications and Media Studies (Cleo) and Psychology (Shaine)

Fun Fact: Cleo loves speaking in funny accents to get a rise out of her friends. Shaine makes surprisingly realistic sculptures of people out of sand.

Previous Contributor: Sarah Haller

Grambling State University

Author: Joseph Joseph

Hometown: Saint Lucia

Major: Computer Information Systems

Fun Fact: I am talented and love computers. I love to study and find out new facts daily. I love to party and have fun.

Grand Valley State University

Author: Kaitlin Lamphere

Hometown: Mason, Mich.

Major: English

Fun Fact: Kaitlin loves to make chainmaille in her spare time (the medieval armor kind, not the spam letter kind).

Grinnell College

Author: Lauren Standifer

Major: Physics/History

Fun Fact: Lauren was thrilled to have the chance to tell people who are trying to decide what their life is going to be like over the next four years about this little Iowan island in the sun.

Grove City College

Author: John Kloosterman

Hometown: Kalamazoo, MI

Major: English

Fun Fact: John likes to spend odd moments doodling dragons on the backs of assignments.

Previous Contributor: Jessica Prol

Guilford College

Author: Elizabeth C. Laird

Hometown: Florida

Major: English/Philosophy

Fun Fact: Elizabeth is a fourth-generation Florida native, and some of her favorite things in the world are the Cure and cats. She plans to pursue a career in writing and attend grad school for magazine journalism.

Gustavus Adolphus College

Author: Meggan Andrle

Previous Contributor: Jessica Adams

Hamilton College

Author: Sophie Vershbow

Hometown: New York City

Major: Government

Fun Fact: Sophie's favorite place to go when she's home is the Museum of Modern Art.

Previous Contributors: Catherine Johnston, Katrina Lexa

Hampshire College

Author: Tal Schechter

Hometown: Stamford, CT

Major: Health, Science, and Technology

Fun Fact: Tal loves dairy even though he's lactose intolerant

Previous Contributor: Stacy Hayashi

Hampton University

Author: Keatrice Robertson

Hometown: Queens, New York

Major: Public Relations

Fun Fact: I'm always open to new and exciting opportunities. I enjoy dancing, shopping, reading, writing and playing with my dogs. I have a vibrant personality and known to be a very down-to-earth girl. "Don't let opinions of the average man sway you. Dream and he thinks you're crazy. Succeed and he thinks your lucky."

Previous Contributor: Candace Renee' Means

Hanover College

Author: Nicole M. Smith

Major: English/Political Science minor

Fun Fact: Nicole's motto is that the more activities you do while you are at college, the more knowledge you will take with you when you leave. During her time at Hanover, she has been involved in the Student Senate, Phi Mu sorority, and the Writing and Speaking Center.

Harvard University

Author: Dominic Hood

Hometown: New Orleans, La.

Major: Psychology

Fun Fact: Dominic was excited about writing this guide because he remembered the challenge of selecting a college and wished he had found a guide like this to provide a realistic perspective on colleges, instead of relying on the admissions office propaganda.

Harvey Mudd College

Author: Yih-Jye Edward Wang

Hometown: Hacienda Heights, Calif.

Previous Contributor: Moana Evans

Hastings College

Author: Emilie Powers

Major: English/Music

Fun Fact: Emilie has participated in band, color guard, public relations council, student senate, Alpha Phi Sigma sorority, and a few honoraries and other groups. She's held offices in most of these groups, kept up with her studies, and still had plenty of time to have some crazy small town fun that would probably shock her mother.

Haverford College

Author: Kira E. Jones

Hometown: Moorestown, NJ

Major: Undecided

Fun Fact: Kira is a member of the Screen Actors Guild.

Previous Contributor: David Langlieb

Hofstra University

Author: Tayla Holman

Hometown: Boston

Major: Journalism and English

Fun Fact: Co-president of the Hofstra Association of Black Journalists (HABJ) and Undergraduate Managing Editor of NassauNewsLive.com

Previous Contributor: Brendan Fitzgerald

Hollins University

Author: Cortney Phillips

Hometown: Charlottesville, VA

Major: English/Creative Writing

Fun Fact: Cortney is one of the youngest people on record to have had a total hip replacement.

Previous Contributor: Janet Lubas

Hood College

Author: Katrina Castner

Hometown: Clarksville, Maryland

Major: Communications

Fun Fact: Katrina isn't actually a redhead! In her spare time, she enjoys writing, photography, and travelling.

Previous Contributor: Dianna Watson

Howard University

Author: Jennifer Hunter

Hometown: Detroit, MI

Major: Nutritional Science/Chemistry

Fun Fact: Jennifer enjoys everything dental. She loves dentistry!

Previous Contributor: Deborah Akinyele

Hunter College

Author: Nia Smith

Hometown: Brooklyn, N.Y.

Previous Contributor: Meredith Deliso

Idaho State University

Author: Eryn Lowe

Major: Communications/TV Broadcasting

Fun Fact: Eryn is the only girl in a family of seven. She hopes to someday be a news anchor/reporter in a big market. Her hobbies include hanging out with her roomies, hiking, running, playing tennis, reading books, and writing for the ISU student newspaper.

Illinois State University

Author: Rachel Farrer

Hometown: Chicago, IL

Major: Public Relations

Fun Fact: I dislike cheese! I love office supplies and scrapbooking.

Previous Contributor: Dana Almdale

Illinois Wesleyan University

Author: Diego Báez

Major: English Writing

Fun Fact: During his time at IWU, Diego served as editor of the campus fine arts magazine, Tributaries; as a regular contributor to the school newspaper, The Argus; and as an editor for the Park Place Economist and the Sigma Tau Delta scholarly review, The Delta. He also entertained listeners during the late hours of the evening as a DJ for the entirely student-run radio station, WESN.

Indiana University

Author: Andrew Belsky/Chelsea Demarris

Hometown: Highland Park, Ill./Unknown

Major: Public finance/Unknown

Fun Fact: Andrew is currently in an accelerated master's program at Indiana in the School of Public and Environmental Affairs, giving him an extra year in Bloomington.

Previous Contributor: Jenny Davis

Indiana University of Pennsylvania

Author: Emily Weber

Hometown: Souderton, Pennsylvania

Major: Journalism & English

Fun Fact: Emily's bookshelf contains books by Ray Bradbury, J.R.R. Tolkien, and Kurt Vonnegut.

Iowa State University

Author: Staci Harper

Major: English/Rhetorical Studies/Speech minor

Fun Fact: Staci is a leader in the Freshman Honors Program, and she performs with the drama workshop in Des Moines.

Previous Contributor: Kirstyn Miller

Ithaca College

Author: Maura Burk

Hometown: South Jersey

Major: English

Fun Fact: Maura is left handed and has webbed toes.

Previous Contributor: Sarah Hofius

IUPUI

Author: Kourtney Forrester

Hometown: Unknown

Previous Contributor: Theresa Carol Williams

Jackson State University

Author: Amy Johnson

James Madison University

Author: Rosemary Grant

Hometown: Alexandria, VA

Major: English/Media Arts & Design

Fun Fact: Rosemary's dream is to write a best-selling novel.

Previous Contributor: Sylvia Florence

John Carroll University

Author: Taylor Horen

Hometown: Toledo, OH

Major: Communications

Fun Fact: I am currently a sophomore at John Carroll University. I am a photographer for the Marketing Department as well as the award-winning campus newspaper, The Carroll News.

Johns Hopkins University

Author: Stephen Schatzman

Hometown: Manasquan, NJ

Major: Economics

Fun Fact: Stephen absolutely loves snowboarding, and before going to college, he was a sponsored snowboarder.

Previous Contributor: Christina Pommer

Juniata College

Author: Carolyn Keller

Fun Fact: Carolyn went to Mexico and Spain, two amazing, beautiful countries, with people she now calls family and places she now calls home.

Kansas State University

Author: Dan Stahl

Fun Fact: Dan Stahl is an unprincipled charlatan whose hobbies include pretending he knows more than he does and backing his father's car into fire hydrants.

Kent State University

Author: Steve Schirra

Major: English/Writing

Fun Fact: Steve plans to pursue a master's degree in publishing. Aside from his college guidebook writing duties, he also enjoys creative writing (check out his stuff on the Web) and journalism.

Kenyon College

Author: Jenny Villanueva
Hometown: Unknown

Previous Contributors: Jay Helmer, Zack Rosen

La Roche College

Author: Amy Pennington
Hometown: Zelienople, Pa.
Major: Writing/French minor
Fun Fact: Amy is a member of the Theatre Group, a public relations officer for the Italian Club, a DJ for the Web radio station, and a staff writer for the student newspaper. She also works at the college bookstore and serves as a worker in the communications, media, and technology department.

Lafayette College

Author: Elisabeth Wraase
Hometown: Bethesda, MD
Major: English with a concentration in writing
Fun Fact: Elisabeth's favorite kind of ice cream is peanut butter cookies and cream from a local ice cream store at home.

Previous Contributor: Pamela Roth

Lawrence University

Author: Alicia Bones
Hometown: Unknown

Previous Contributor: Doris Kim

Lehigh University

Author: Charlie Gimber
Hometown: Sudbury, MA
Major: English and Journalism
Fun Fact: Charlie wrote a satirical restaurant review column for Lehigh's student newspaper.

Previous Contributor: Larry Koestler

Lewis & Clark College

Author: Robin Cedar
Hometown: Seattle, WA
Major: English
Fun Fact: Robin used to collect rocks as a child.

Previous Contributor: Caitlin Fackrell

Linfield College

Author: Jennifer Mui-Chan
Hometown: San Francisco
Major: Business
Fun Fact: Enjoy Yoga, playing the Guzheng, archery, member of Phi Sigma Sigma

Louisiana College

Author: Stephanie Baer
Hometown: Monroe, LA
Major: English
Fun Fact: Stephanie is an avid advocate of the power nap. A daily 20 minute snooze right after lunch keeps her sane.

Louisiana State University

Author: Kim Moreau
Hometown: Baton Rouge, La
Major: Journalism
Fun Fact: Kim wants to thank every LSU employee, from student workers to heads of departments, who helped her get everything together she needed for the guidebook.

Loyola Marymount University

Author: Zacrie L. Scott
Hometown: Long Beach, CA
Major: English
Fun Fact: Zacrie loves writing short stories and vlogging.

Previous Contributor: Kristin Cole

Loyola University Chicago

Author: Amy Tolle

Previous Contributor: Nathan Ramin

Loyola University Maryland

Author: Kelly Hatter
Hometown: Baltimore, MD
Major: Writing
Fun Fact: Kelly has been playing the guitar for about five years now.

Previous Contributors: Victoria Lynn Bohler, Kimberly Moore

Luther College

Author: William Morris
Hometown: Wausau, WI
Major: English (with minor in Secondary Education)
Fun Fact: William sings and plays violin in the Luther ensembles

Previous Contributor: Fred Smith

Macalester College

Author: Katherine Tylevich
Major: English/Creative Writing
Fun Fact: Katherine is the features editor for the Mac Weekly.

Manhattan College

Author: Cecilio Gomez
Major: Communications/Spanish and Business minors
Fun Fact: Cecilio has plans of being a broadcaster for a sports network (radio or television), a writer for a newspaper or book company, or maybe a coach in basketball.

Manhattanville College

Author: Amanda Minck
Major: English Education

Marlboro College

Author: Seth Reeves Bowman
Fun Fact: Seth plans to continue his studies at Marlboro, focusing on television and its impact on our global society.

Marquette University

Author: Jordan Abudayyeh
Hometown: Frankfort, Illinois
Major: Broadcast and Electronic Communication
Fun Fact: I'm a sophomore at Marquette University. I plan on going into television journalism after I graduate. I am currently working on writing a book and a screenplay. I love everything pop culture, and I know way too many useless facts. I currently host two shows on MUTV an interview-based campus news show, and a satirical news show.

Previous Contributor: Jennifer Singer

Maryville University

Author: Brittney Curtis
Hometown: Camden, NJ
Major: Communications
Fun Fact: I'm 5'11. I'm a wee bit on the hyperactive side, and I'm in the process of publishing a book.

Massachusetts College of Art & Design

Author: Daria Bukesova
Hometown: Acton
Major: Architectural Design
Fun Fact: ...

McGill University

Author: Kelly Baker
Hometown: Weston, CT
Major: Sociology
Fun Fact: Kelly can moonwalk just like Michael Jackson, but she's physically incapable of doing any other dance moves.

Previous Contributor: Robin Erskine-Levinson

Mercer University

Author: Janelle Richardson
Hometown: Seattle, Wash.
Major: English
Fun Fact: I spend a lot of time having a laugh and listening to ridiculous '80s music.

Mercyhurst College

Author: Christina Mihalic
Hometown: Ohio
Major: English
Fun Fact: I love Mercyhurst College, my English major, and being involved at the College. Writing about Mercyhurst College for College Prowler has been a great opportunity that I love!

Messiah College

Author: Ashley Offenback
Hometown: Yardley, Pa.
Major: Journalism
Fun Fact: Ashley describes her trip to Germany last summer as the best time of her life. She got to stay with a host family, see the castle Neuschwanstein, and explore another culture! Her absolute favorite city is Cologne, or "Koln".

Miami University

Author: Megan Vanderslice

Previous Contributors: Nicholas Ward, Tiffany Garrett

Michigan State University

Author: Rachel McElroy
Hometown: Unknown

Previous Contributor: Amy Davis

Middle Tennessee State University

Author: Rachelle Morvant
Fun Fact: Rachelle attended MTSU for seven years in pursuit of two separate degrees.

Middlebury College

Author: Maggie Carter
Hometown: Eastford, CT
Major: International Studies
Fun Fact: Maggie was an internationally ranked, competitive trampolinist during her middle school years.

Previous Contributor: Abbie Beane

Millsaps College

Author: Bryan Dupree
Hometown: Plaquemine, LA
Major: Political Science and French
Fun Fact: Though he has never taken any theatre classes and is not a theatre major, Bryan has been cast in several leading and supporting roles in various Millsaps? productions.

Previous Contributor: John Yargo

Minnesota State University

Author: Britt Johnson
Hometown: Minnesota

Minnesota State University - Moorhead

Author: Andrew Jason
Hometown: Puposky, MN
Major: Mass Communications with an emphasis in on-line journalism and spanish minor
Fun Fact: Things I like to do:•Travel to places I've never been to.•Eat things I've never tasted.•Meet people different then me.•Try things I never thought I'd do.•Read something I've never read. •Living life without regret.•...Oh...and long walks on the beach.

Misericordia University

Author: Michele Drago
Hometown: Larksville, Pa
Major: Communications
Fun Fact: I love fashion so much, that I started my own fashion column, called "Let's Talk Fashion" in the Highlander, MU's own student newspaper. I've also been in the Style Savvy section of the local community newspaper for my stylish ways.

Missouri State University

Author: Colleen Hamilton

MIT

Author: Sun Kim
Hometown: Duluth, GA
Major: Mechanical Engineering
Fun Fact: Sun didn't know how to ride a bicycle before college, but now she's a part of the cycling club.

Previous Contributor: Susie Lee

Montana State University

Author: Erica Aytes
Hometown: Pocatello, Idaho
Major: English Literature/Spanish
Fun Fact: Erica says that writing this guide was one of the most educational experiences of her life. Not only is she now a walking dictionary of MSU facts, but she also has a better idea of which career paths she wants to pursue.

Montclair State University

Author: Catherine Winters

Hometown: Branchburg, NJ

Major: English

Fun Fact: Catherine is the chief copy editor of MSU's student paper, The Montclarion; editor in chief of the literary magazine, The Normal Review; and will be studying abroad in Paris next semester.

Mount Holyoke College

Author: Alessandra Hickson

Hometown: Philadelphia, PA

Major: Art History

Fun Fact: Alessandra loves old-school Nickelodeon cartoons, Frosted Flakes, and reading GQ, even though she's a girl.

Previous Contributor: Jennifer Lewis

Muhlenberg College

Author: Sarah Weber

Hometown: Pound Ridge, NY

Major: Theatre

Fun Fact: Sarah has been sewing since she was seven years old, and now busies herself in Muhlenberg's costume shop.

Previous Contributor: Michelle Hein

New College of Florida

Author: Joshua Rosenberg

Major: Philosophy/Psychology

Fun Fact: Josh enjoys drumming, guitar, hardcore music, and freestyle footbag.

New York University

Author: Rachel Northrop

Hometown: Plymouth, NH

Major: Secondary English Education

Fun Fact: Rachel speaks Spanish, Italian, and some Turkish!

Previous Contributor: Meredith Turley

North Carolina A&T State University

Author: Jamel Daniels

Hometown: Toledo, Ohio

Major: Family & Consumer Sciences

Fun Fact: Jamel is left-handed and has interned with Target Corporation in Minneapolis and Phillips-Van Heusen Corporation in New York City.

North Carolina State University

Author: Matthew J. Cote

Hometown: Teaneck, NJ

Major: English: Language, Writing, and Rhetoric

Fun Fact: Matthew has lived in New Jersey, Florida, North Carolina, and California -- the four poles of the United States.

Previous Contributor: Cynthia Marvin

North Central College

Author: Kyle Coia

Hometown: Lake Villa, IL

Major: Business Management/Political Science

Northeastern University

Author: Amanda Golden

Hometown: Northport, NY

Major: Sociology/Psychology

Fun Fact: Amanda has been skiing since she was three years old.

Previous Contributor: Briyah Paley

Northern Arizona University

Author: Byran LaBore

Hometown: Bismarck, ND

Major: Biology

Fun Fact: Bryan can't eat just one PopTart out of a pouch--he has to eat both!

Previous Contributor: Matt MacDonald

Northern Illinois University

Author: Alex Aguilar

Previous Contributor: Greg Feltes

Northwestern College - Saint Paul

Author: Heidi Heitzman
Hometown: Maple Grove
Major: Marketing
Fun Fact: =D

Northwestern University

Author: Kevin Echavarria
Hometown: San Antonio, Texas
Major: Journalism/Comparative Literary Studies
Fun Fact: Hi, I'm Kevin Echavarria. I'm from San Antonio, and I'm currently a freshman in Northwestern University's Medill School of Journalism.

Previous Contributor: Torea Frey

Oakwood University

Author: Angelo Deguerre
Hometown: Harlem
Major: Theology
Fun Fact: Tornadoes are commonplace at Oakwood, but there is nothing to fear, because they never touch these "holy grounds".

Oberlin College

Author: Veronica Colegrove
Hometown: Cincinnati, Ohio
Major: Latin/Computer science
Fun Fact: Veronica is an avid hip-hop head.

Previous Contributor: Sarah LeBaron von Baeyer

Occidental College

Author: William Suh

Previous Contributor: Ethan Ambabo

Oglethorpe University

Author: Marisa Manuel

Ohio State University

Author: Gilburt L. Chiang
Hometown: Marietta, Ga.
Major: Electrical engineering
Fun Fact: Gilburt created the Facebook page for the Ohio State Class of 2011.

Previous Contributors: Rolando Becerra, Adam Jardy

Ohio University

Author: Nash Bober
Hometown: Berlin Heights, Ohio
Major: Management information systems/Marketing
Fun Fact: Nash likes to play drums and work out.

Previous Contributor: Jessica Cyr

Ohio Wesleyan University

Author: Evan Matthew Reas
Major: Economics/Management concentration
Fun Fact: Evan's dream is to become one of the greatest business leaders and investors in the world.

Old Dominion University

Author: Bryoney Hayes
Hometown: The East Coast!
Major: English with a Journalism concentration
Fun Fact: Bryoney can walk on her hands!

Previous Contributor: Brandon Webb

Oral Roberts University

Author: Roman Harvey
Hometown: Kearney, Neb.
Major: Business Administration
Fun Fact: Oral Roberts University is the ideal school for any Christian college student!

Pace University

Author: Charlotte Li
Hometown: Boston, Mass.
Major: Communication studies
Fun Fact: Charlotte loves to run in the morning, especially around 5, so that she won't have to share Jamaica Pond with anyone. But normally, she's never alone; there are always at least two people in her way.

Penn State

Author: James Bunting
Hometown: Whitehall, PA
Major: Journalism
Fun Fact: James's favorite activity is traveling. He's been to Disney World three times and the Caribbean twice, and he spent three weeks in Europe.

Previous Contributors: Alyssa Fried, Tim Williams

Penn State Altoona

Author: Bridgetta Parker
Hometown: Dumfries, Va.
Major: English
Fun Fact: Bridgetta loves to travel.

Pepperdine University

Author: Jackie Fetzer
Hometown: Huntersville, NC
Major: English Writing and Rhetoric
Fun Fact: Jackie tried out for Pepperdine's water polo team without knowing how to swim first?and made it!

Previous Contributor: Steve Pinkerton

Pitzer College

Author: Melissa Armstrong
Hometown: Centerville, Ohio
Major: Organizational Studies
Fun Fact: I love everything Disney. I've lived in nine different places. In order to find the "right" college, I visited over 25 campuses across the country.

Previous Contributors: Josh Gordon, Rachel Levitan

Pomona College

Author: Peter Cook
Fun Fact: Peter envisions himself as a sort of genetically spliced version of Donald Barthelme, Ludwig Wittgenstein, and Lou Reed. Sort of like the bastard child of higher education and pop culture.

Princeton University

Author: Kristen McCarthy
Hometown: Mahwah, N.J.

Previous Contributor: Alison Fraser

Providence College

Author: Amanda Mathieu
Hometown: Groton, CT
Major: English/Business
Fun Fact: Amanda's a neat freak, to the extent that she carries a lint roller in her purse.

Previous Contributor: Kathryn Treadway

Purchase College

Author: Christie Donato
Hometown: Syracuse, NY
Major: Creative Writing and History
Fun Fact: - Played the Wicked Witch of the West my senior year of high school- Plan on visiting every state and have been to 14 already!

Purdue University

Author: Reema Siddiqui
Hometown: Unknown

Previous Contributor: Abigail Bender

Radford University

Author: Kerith Rae
Hometown: South Africa
Major: Business Management/Public Relations
Fun Fact: Kerith is very involved in campus activities at Radford, including the school newspaper, the Honors Academy, a fraternity, and a theatrical production every now and then. She is pretty much a classic over-achiever with really big dreams.

Ramapo College of New Jersey

Author: Daniel Giacobbe
Hometown: Rockaway
Major: Communication Arts
Fun Fact: My thumbs are gigantic, and I have never lost a thumb wrestling match without questionable third person intervention.

Reed College

Author: Ben DuPree
Hometown: Los Angeles, Calif.
Major: English
Fun Fact: Ben served as the editor of the school newspaper, the Reed College Quest.

Regis University

Author: Megan Vestal
Hometown: Lenexa, Kans.
Major: Biology
Fun Fact: Megan runs on the Regis cross country team.

Rensselaer Polytechnic Institute

Author: Cara Riverso

Hometown: Holmes, NY

Major: Chemical Engineering

Fun Fact: Cara is a self-professed treehugger, vegetarian, and recycling fanatic ... the whole nine yards.

Previous Contributor: Ned McTigue

Rhode Island School of Design

Author: Helen Koh

Hometown: Chicago, IL

Major: Graphic Design/Painting

Fun Fact: Helen is very good at sandwich making.

Previous Contributor: Brooke Ackerley

Rhodes College

Author: Kelly Parry

Hometown: Atlanta, GA

Major: Urban Studies

Fun Fact: Kelly loves squirrels.

Previous Contributor: Sarah Rutherford

Rice University

Author: Meenakshi Awasthi

Hometown: Arlington, TX

Major: English/Biology

Fun Fact: Meenakshi made her own dimple?by accident, of course! In Kindergarten, she fell off of the jungle gym and bruised her cheek pretty badly. Today it is a nice little dimple with a great history.

Previous Contributor: Julia Schwent

Rider University

Author: Mell Chase

Hometown: Mount Laurel, NJ

Major: Biology

Fun Fact: Mell is writing a novel, is a pre-med major, and loves to perform in theatre.

Robert Morris University

Author: Emma Venezie

Rochester Institute of Technology

Author: Alecia Crawford

Hometown: Candor, NY

Major: Advertising and Public Relations

Fun Fact: Alecia has been playing the drums and other percussion instruments for more than nine years now.

Previous Contributor: Amy Cooper

Rollins College

Author: Brittany Lee

Hometown: Connecticut

Major: English/Psychology

Fun Fact: Brittany grew up in Connecticut and came down to Florida mostly to escape the snow, but she's come to love far more about her college than the weather.

Rowan University

Author: Scott Wordsman

Hometown: Rockaway, N.J.

Major: Radio/TV/Film & Advertising

Fun Fact: Scott is a member of RTN, Honors, and club tennis.

Original Author: James R. Sanders

Previous Contributor: James Sanders

Russell Sage College

Author: Leah Foley

Hometown: Troy, New York

Major: Nutrition Science

Fun Fact: I love to go shopping and my favorite foods are pizza and wings. I am a huge Giants football and Yankees fan. I watch them every chance I get. I also hate wearing socks.

Rutgers University

Author: Jill Weiss

Hometown: Ardsley, NY

Major: English

Fun Fact: Jill went to high school with Jesse McCartney.

Previous Contributor: Taryn Sauthoff

Sacramento State

Author: Hilton Collins

Major: English

Fun Fact: Hilton plans to attend Sac State for graduate school to advance his English degree.

Saint Francis University

Author: Jillian Swisher

Hometown: Pittsburgh, PA

Major: English/literature

Fun Fact: Jillian loves kitty cats.

Saint Joseph's University

Author: Tom Acox

Hometown: Central Jersey

Major: English

Fun Fact: Tom was raised on a healthy diet of books, Springsteen, the beach, sports, and a curiosity about the world and the people in it.

Saint Leo University

Author: Colin Piacentine

Hometown: Bryn Mawr, PA

Major: Communication Management

Fun Fact: Class 2010

Saint Louis University

Author: Drew Ewing

Hometown: Columbus, Ohio

Major: Aerospace Engineering

Fun Fact: Outside of class, Drew is the arts and entertainment editor for University News, vice president of the Society of Automotive Engineers Aero Design Team, and member of the Life at SLU Television Network.

Salem College

Author: Keena Hutchens

Hometown: Yadkinvlle, N.C.

Major: Philosophy/Religion

Fun Fact: Keena wants to work at a social justice non-profit after graduation.

Salisbury University

Author: Harsh Desai

Hometown: Salisbury, MD

Major: Biology/ Pre-medicine

Fun Fact: I've lived in two other countries besides the USA and have traveled to several others. I like reading mystery novels and thrillers. I watch crime and medical shows on TV, such as CSI and Mystery Diagnosis. I am a fan of country music with Rascal Flatts being my favorite band.

Sam Houston State University

Author: Michael Silva

Hometown: Houston, Texas

Major: Broadcast journalism

Fun Fact: Michael is the sports editor of his school's newspaper. He is also an officer (web master) of SHSU's chapter of the Golden Key International Honour Society and co-president of the Sigma Delta Pi Spanish National Honors Society. He plans to pursue a career in sports journalism after graduating.

Samford University

Author: Joanna Reynolds

Hometown: Maryville, TN

Major: English

Fun Fact: I am a Christian who loves to read, watch the Indianapolis Colts dominate, ride horses, spike volleyballs, and hike in Red Rock Canyon. The quickest way to my heart is having a good sense of humor and being willing to play me in ping-pong. Even though I will beat you.

San Diego State University

Author: Brennan Wasan

Hometown: San Diego, CA

Major: Communications

Fun Fact: Life without music could never be imagined.

Previous Contributor: Brian Webb

San Francisco State University

Author: Angela Raiford

Hometown: St. Louis, Mo.

Major: Journalism

Fun Fact: Angela has a fraternal twin sister.

Santa Clara University

Author: Lauren Silk

Hometown: Bainbridge Island, WA

Major: English and French

Previous Contributor: Albert Schwartz

Sarah Lawrence College

Author: Bobby Phillips

Hometown: Chatsworth, CA

Major: Narratives

Fun Fact: Bobby can wriggle his ears.

Previous Contributor: Justin Millan

Scripps College

Author: Jenna Tico

Hometown: Santa Barbara, CA

Major: Undeclared

Fun Fact: Jenna is passionate about Brazilian music and samba dance.

Previous Contributor: Christine Tran

Seattle Pacific University

Author: Kylie Kenyon

Hometown: Paso Robles, Calif.

Major: Sociology

Fun Fact: Kylie can write backwards as easily as forward.

Seattle University

Author: Michael Lis-Sette

Hometown: Seattle, WA

Major: Journalism

Fun Fact: Michael has visited 27 states and plans to visit the other 23 (and then plans to start traveling to all the countries on various continents).

Previous Contributor: Julia Ugarte

Seton Hall University

Author: Ian Mehok

Hometown: Pittsburgh, PA

Major: Finance

Fun Fact: Ian has been on national television twice, once for an episode of a finance show, and once when he stood on the NYSE balcony to help ring the opening bell.

Previous Contributor: Rocky Rakovic

Simmons College

Author: Krista Evans

Hometown: Florence, AL

Major: Political Science/International Relations

Fun Fact: Krista brushes her teeth with a musical kiddie toothbrush that plays Hannah Montana.

Previous Contributor: Evan Kuhlman

Skidmore College

Author: Emma Beckerle

Hometown: Stony Point

Major: Business Management

Fun Fact: To overcome her fear of sharks, Emma went shark cage diving in South Africa. It didn't work.

Previous Contributors: Cara Jones, Nicolette Stewart

Slippery Rock University

Author: Liz Rekowski

Hometown: Pittsburgh, PA

Major: Communication

Fun Fact: One of Liz's favorite activities is white water rafting. She loves the rush of adrenaline she gets from it.

Previous Contributor: Ashley Hockenberger

Smith College

Author: Dara Kagan

Hometown: Croton-on-Hudson, N.Y.

Major: Government, with a minor in the Study of Women and Gender

Fun Fact: Dara absolutely loves West Wing, the New York Times, cooking shows, Capen House, Roald Dahl, and Harry Potter. She has never been happier than she is at Smith and can't imagine going to college anywhere else!

Previous Contributors: Kelly Dagan, Megan McRobert

Southern Methodist University

Author: Peter Goldschmidt
Hometown: Jefferson City, MO
Major: Financial Consulting
Fun Fact: Peter likes to run marathons.

Previous Contributor: Stacy Seebode

Southwestern University

Author: Jazz Thomas
Hometown: Houston, Texas
Major: Communication studies and Theater arts
Fun Fact: Jazz is excited to become a starving artist upon graduation!

Previous Contributor: Christiana Little

Spelman College

Author: Candace Wheeler
Hometown: Stone Mountain, GA
Major: Sociology
Fun Fact: Candace hopes to publish her own culture and lifestyle magazine upon graduation from Spelman College.

Previous Contributor: Tiffani Murray

St. Edward's University

Author: Jessica Skok

St. John's University

Author: Mark McDonald
Hometown: Mabank, TX
Major: Marketing
Fun Fact: Since moving to New York, Mark has made many people use the word y'all by accident. Southern drawl dies hard!

Previous Contributor: Antoinette Brown

St. Lawrence University

Author: Allison Talbot
Hometown: East Machias
Major: English

St. Mary's College of Maryland

Author: Jess O'Rear
Hometown: Parsippany, N.J.
Major: Gender Studies
Fun Fact: Jess has an irrational fear of sharks in places where there is no threat of a shark attack (like her bedroom).

St. Mary's University

Author: Laura O'Bar
Hometown: San Antonio, TX
Major: English-Communication Arts
Fun Fact: I spent Fall of 2008 studying and working in London, England!

St. Olaf College

Author: Nathan Hopkins
Fun Fact: Nathan had no clue what he was doing during his college search, but now that he's at St. Olaf, he can't see himself anywhere else.

Stanford University

Author: Alexandria Butler
Hometown: St. Louis, MO
Major: Communications, Spanish
Fun Fact: writing, shopping, shoes, cookie dough ice cream, Thanksgiving dinner, STANFORD, sunrises, nail polish, movies, reading, and just so much more!

Previous Contributor: Ian Spiro

Stetson University

Author: Nicholas Mrozowski
Hometown: Antioch, Calif. and Sebring, Fla.
Major: Finance/Business Law minor
Fun Fact: Nicholas wants to thank all of his friends who have helped with quotes or have let him vent to them. Thank you!

Stevenson University

Author: Christine Ivory
Hometown: Poolesville, Md.
Major: English Language and Literature
Fun Fact: Christine is a horseback riding instructor.

Stony Brook University

Author: Barbara Ross

Hometown: Hopewell Junction, NY

Major: Business Management

Fun Fact: Barbara is a diehard Yankees fan.

Previous Contributor: Douglas Swezey

SUNY Fredonia

Author: Elizabeth Christopher

SUNY New Paltz

Author: Michelle Marie Feliciano

Hometown: Bronx, N.Y.

Major: Journalism

Fun Fact: Michelle was in three runway fashion shows and even auditioned for America's Next Top Model, and she's only five feet tall!

SUNY Oswego

Author: Alma Hidalgo

Susquehanna University

Author: Jon Snyder

Hometown: Unknown

Previous Contributor: Jennifer Fox

Swarthmore College

Author: Sudarshan Gopaladesikan

Hometown: Harrisburg, Pennsylvania

Major: Math and Engineering

Fun Fact: I am a freshman at Swarthmore.

Previous Contributor: Elizabeth Collins

Syracuse University

Author: Marshal Yong

Hometown: New York City

Major: Architecture

Fun Fact: Marshal is Malaysian.

Previous Contributor: Steve Krakauer

Taylor University

Author: Kathryn Kroeker

Hometown: State College, PA

Major: Professional writing

Fun Fact: In second grade I had a story published in my local library, entitled "Julia's Magic Piano."I trained at a pre-professional ballet school for ten years, thinking that my future career role would be a ballerina.I spent three weeks as an exchange student in Germany, and I had to speak German the entire time.I have four siblings and we love doing crazy things together. We once had a wild dance party and dressed up like gangsters.I was eighteen the first time I went to Chuck-E-Cheese. My favorite candy is black licorice.

Temple University

Author: Jamira M. Burley

Hometown: West Philadelphia, PA

Major: International Business w/minors in Chinese and Management and Information Systems

Fun Fact: Jamira is one of 16 children, with 13 brothers and two little sisters.

Previous Contributor: Tiffani Joseph

Tennessee State University

Author: Stephanie Richardson

Hometown: Tuskegee, AL

Major: Art Concentration Graphic Design, Minor Communications concentration in Journalism

Fun Fact: Stephanie is obsessed with blogs and YouTube!

Previous Contributor: Raven Petty

Texas A&M International University

Author: Rudy Duran

Hometown: Laredo, Texas

Major: Political Science

Fun Fact: Rudy loves working out, is a major fan of video games, and occasionally plays guitar. (His bass is still gathering dust).

Texas A&M University

Author: Isuey Asuzena Iraheta

Hometown: Houston, Texas

Major: Psychology

Fun Fact: Isuey loves to dance, write, and read.

Previous Contributor: Ashley Marshall

Texas Christian University

Author: Marley Hutchinson
Hometown: Greenwood Village, CO
Major: Advertising
Fun Fact: Marley speaks four languages!

Previous Contributor: Jessica Fleming

Texas Lutheran University

Author: Brendan Kirkpatrick-McKee
Hometown: Converse, Texas
Major: Dramatic Media
Fun Fact: Brendan still owns, and uses, a Mighty Morphin' Power Ranger pillow (though it does need to be restuffed).

Texas State University - San Marcos

Author: Nate Stanley
Hometown: Cedar Falls, Iowa
Major: Anthropology

Texas Tech University

Author: Abby Stone
Major: Journalism
Fun Fact: Although Abby's mom assures her there is more to come, writing this guide has given her a chance to look back on what she believes were the best four years of her life.

Thomas College

Author: Shelby Gilcott
Hometown: Norridgewock, Maine
Major: Sport Management
Fun Fact: Shelby's favorite food is lobster, she is a HUGE Boston Celtics fan, and her favorite color is green.

Towson University

Author: Louise Salbego
Hometown: Baltimore, MD
Major: English Literature
Fun Fact: Louise studied French history in Paris.

Previous Contributor: Nataly Gutflais

Trinity College

Author: Rachel Clark Unkovic
Major: Creative Writing/Classical Civilization
Fun Fact: After Trinity, Rachel plans to go to graduate school to pursue an MFA. in prose fiction writing. The best advice she can give is this: Decide to have fun in college, and wherever you end up, most likely you will have a blast!

Trinity University

Author: Stephany Weaver
Hometown: Houston
Major: English
Fun Fact: I studied abroad in Dublin, Ireland during my entire junior year.

Previous Contributor: Kristin Dickson

Troy University

Author: Jessica Jackson
Hometown: Mobile, Ala.
Major: Marketing
Fun Fact: Hi! I am a sophomore at Troy university. I am the middle child of three girls. I love to shop, cook, and travel during my free time.

Truman State University

Author: Jessica Gasch
Major: French/Linguistics
Fun Fact: Between her French and linguistics degrees, Japanese courses, Detours magazine position, and editorship with the Truman State University Index, writing—in several languages—has become second nature to Jessica, and she's excited to find out where it will take her in the future.

Tufts University

Author: Chris Cote
Hometown: Ipswich, MA
Major: International Relations
Fun Fact: Chris is on the Tufts Ultimate Frisbee team.

Previous Contributor: Emily Chasan

Tulane University

Author: Lauren Toppenberg
Hometown: Knoxville, TN
Major: Spanish/Latin American Studies
Fun Fact: Lauren likes bowling competitively, sailing casually, and glass blowing frequently.

Previous Contributor: Kate Dearing

UC Berkeley

Author: Meegan Brooks
Hometown: Granite Bay, CA
Major: Political science
Fun Fact: Meegan has lived (and kind of studied) in South Africa for the past six months.

Previous Contributors: Christine Huang, Jody Leung, Tak Sato

UC Davis

Author: Korey Hlaudy
Hometown: Bakersfiled, Calif.

Previous Contributor: Tristen Chang

UC Irvine

Author: Tracey Xuan Nguyen
Hometown: Hawthorne, CA
Major: Business Economics
Fun Fact: The first time Tracey went rock climbing on a real rock she was able to climb all the way to the top, but not before scraping her whole left arm along the jagged wall and swearing like a sailor every time her foot slipped!

Previous Contributors: Jillianne Salaver, Jennifer Truong

UC Merced

Author: Harini Kompella
Hometown: Santa Clarita, California
Major: Human Biology
Fun Fact: •First Lady Michelle Obama was UCM's commencement speaker for Spring 2009 •First American research university of the 21st century•School located about an hour by driving from Yosemite National Park•Mascot: Bobcat

UC Riverside

Author: Cynthia Marie Wald

UC San Diego

Author: Juan Ramirez
Hometown: El Monte, Calif.

Previous Contributor: Shelby Gunderman

UC Santa Barbara

Author: Michael Cooper
Hometown: Danville, CA
Major: Sociology/Sports Management minor
Fun Fact: Michael was on Bob Barker's sixth-to-last Price is Right show and won a trampoline.

Previous Contributor: Kate Sandoval

UC Santa Cruz

Author: Alexandra Iorfino
Hometown: Huntington Beach, CA
Major: Politics and Psychology
Fun Fact: Alexandra has a not-so-secret obsession with squirrels.

Previous Contributor: Hadley Robinson

UCLA

Author: Suzy Strutner
Hometown: Newport Beach, Calif.
Major: Communication Studies
Fun Fact: During finals week, Suzy once consumed 12 muffins from Bruin Café.

Previous Contributor: Erik Robert Flegal

Union College

Author: Cassandra Skoufalos
Hometown: Greenwich, CT
Major: Political Science/Spanish
Fun Fact: Cassandra can speak Greek fluently.

Previous Contributors: Aaron Edelstein, Lily Gordon

University at Albany

Author: Michelle Davis
Hometown: Verona, N.J.

Previous Contributor: Jessica Joseph

University at Buffalo

Author: Christina Reisenauer

Hometown: Amherst, N.Y.

Previous Contributor: Ben R. Cady

University of Alabama

Author: Josh Morris

Hometown: Bath, Maine

Major: Public Relations

Fun Fact: Josh has lived on three separate continents.

Previous Contributor: Merrick Wiedrich

University of Arizona

Author: Kalin Mowry

Hometown: Carefree, AZ

Major: Economics/Regional Development

Fun Fact: Kalin's perfect Monday is doing the crossword puzzles, reading the Economist, and watching Gossip Girl.

Original Author: Nathan Tafoya

Previous Contributor: Nathan Tafoya

University of Arkansas

Author: Jordan Grummer

Hometown: Sherwood

Major: Print Journalism

Fun Fact: I'm a 22-year-old cook at a seafood restaurant when I'm not collecting surveys for college prowler. I'm majoring in print journalism with a minor in history. I'm a World War II nerd, and I love reading and writing.

University of Arkansas at Little Rock

Author: Harold Brown

University of Baltimore

Author: Lawanda Johnson

Hometown: Baltimore

Major: English-Creative Writing

University of Central Florida

Author: Nathalie Desdunes

Hometown: Fort Lauderdale, FL

Major: Marketing

Fun Fact: In her spare time, Nathalie loves making YouTube videos with her brothers and friends.

Previous Contributor: Lily Barrish

University of Central Oklahoma

Author: Deja Mitchell

Hometown: Oklahoma City, OK

Major: Political Science

Fun Fact: My hobbies are reading, writing, and enjoying as much as I can about college.

University of Chicago

Author: Lyss Welding

Hometown: Unknown

Previous Contributor: Joshua Steinman

University of Cincinnati

Author: Rachel Kellerman

Hometown: Cincinnati, Ohio

Major: Journalism/Spanish minor

Fun Fact: Rachel is a self-proclaimed "girly-tomboy" who loves rock and metal music, motorcycles, and cars but can still get her nails done and wear dresses, too. She is terrified of heights but loves skydiving and pretty much will try anything once. Or twice.

University of Colorado

Author: Sara K. Jordan

Hometown: Littleton, CO

Major: International Affairs

Fun Fact: Sara comes from a long line of journalists. Her grandfather was asked to be an anchorman for CBS, but he turned it down. His replacement was Walter Cronkite.

Previous Contributor: Jessica Amodeo

University of Connecticut

Author: Taylor Trudon
Hometown: Cobalt, CT
Major: Journalism/Women's Studies
Fun Fact: Taylor is a Big Sister in the Nutmeg Big Brothers Big Sisters program

Previous Contributor: Colin Megill

University of Delaware

Author: Danielle Todd
Hometown: Newark, Del.
Major: English
Fun Fact: Writing this guide helped Danielle realize that there are more good things about the University than bad, and it put a lot of things in perspective for her, including her own attitude about college.

University of Denver

Author: Anne Reiman
Hometown: Winnetka, IL
Major: English (Creative Writing)/Communications
Fun Fact: Anne is obsessed with the TV show The West Wing.

Previous Contributor: Katie Niekerk

University of Florida

Author: Jared Misner
Hometown: Clearwater, FL
Major: Public Relations
Fun Fact: Jared is a vegan.

Previous Contributor: Regine Rossi

University of Georgia

Author: Christopher Joshua Benton
Hometown: Norfolk, VA
Major: English/Magzine Print Journalism/New Media
Fun Fact: When Christopher grows up, he wants to be a forester, run through the moss on high heels.

Previous Contributor: Nicole Gross

University of Hartford

Author: Denise Morales

University of Illinois

Author: Emily Thiersch
Hometown: Wilmette, Ill.

Previous Contributor: Bridget Nicole Sharkey

University of Illinois at Chicago

Author: Tejumade Durowade
Hometown: Chicago, IL
Major: Electrical Engineering
Fun Fact: Tejumade and his family migrated to the United States when he was 11 years old.

University of Iowa

Author: Kelly McPhee
Hometown: Naperville, IL
Major: Journalism
Fun Fact: Kelly changed her major six times freshman year.

Previous Contributor: Alex Lang

University of Kansas

Author: Amanda Thompson
Hometown: Overland Park, KS
Major: Journalism/Environmental Studies
Fun Fact: Amanda likes to try adventurous things, including wakeboarding, parasailing and cliff jumping

Previous Contributor: Jonah Ballow

University of Kentucky

Author: Rachel Schilling
Hometown: Cold Spring, KY
Major: English
Fun Fact: Rachel helped bring back the girls' soccer team at her high school to win our first varsity tournament, giving the team the best record in school history.

Previous Contributor: Mandy Langston

University of Louisville

Author: Annie Muller
Hometown: LaGrange, Ky.
Major: French and English
Fun Fact: Annie has visited and loves Canada, Ireland, France, Spain, and Italy.

Previous Contributor: Lindsey Coblentz

University of Maine

Author: Justin Wozniski

Hometown: Lancaster County, Pa.

Major: Journalism

Fun Fact: Justin has a strong interest in public affairs newspaper reporting, especially with local government and politics. His interest in this type of reporting stems from his community involvement and public service in his younger years

University of Maryland

Author: Jen Memmolo

Hometown: Woodbridge, NJ

Major: Journalism

Fun Fact: Jen directed a YouTube video for an internship that has more than 5,000 hits.

Previous Contributor: Jared Meyer

University of Maryland Baltimore County

Author: Luanna Azulay

Hometown: Arlington, Va./Recife, PE, Brazil

Major: Political Science

Fun Fact: Luanna is the queen of multitasking. She particularly loves world music, dislikes going to concerts in places that fit more than 1,000 people, and enjoys walks on the beach or pretty much anywhere.

University of Maryland Eastern Shore

Author: Kennice Evans

Hometown: Eastern Shore, Md.

Major: English

Fun Fact: I love to write!

University of Massachusetts

Author: Danielle Muise

Hometown: Medway, Mass.

Major: Marketing and Communication Disorders

Fun Fact: Danielle plays and writes music and is a member of the UMass Marching Band. She is involved in student programming through House Council and is among the top 1 percent of student leaders as a member of National Residence Hall Honorary.

Previous Contributor: Seth Pouliot

University of Miami

Author: Sana Khan

Hometown: Lauderhill, FL

Major: Biochemistry/Mathematics

Fun Fact: Sana has a black belt in tae kwon do!

Previous Contributor: Shawn Wines

University of Michigan

Author: Michael Hondorp

Fun Fact: Michael is currently pursuing a role on the Broadway stage.

University of Minnesota

Author: Alison Henderson

Previous Contributor: Amy Palmer

University of Mississippi

Author: Janna Jones

Hometown: Booneville, Miss.

Major: Print Journalism

Fun Fact: Janna graduated high school with exactly 50 people?and that was a BIG class for New Site High!

Previous Contributor: Ricki Renick

University of Missouri

Author: Jason Rosenbaum

Hometown: Chicago, Ill.

Major: Journalism

Fun Fact: When not writing, Jason enjoys running around Stankowski Field in his trademark Nike headband and going through the arduous grind of pledgeship for his future fraternity, Alpha Epsilon Pi.

University of Montana

Author: Samantha Steven

Hometown: N/A

Fun Fact: Previous Author: Shanda Aguirre, with additional contributions from Amanda Peterson.

Previous Contributor: Shanda Aguirre

University of Mount Union

Author: Stephanie Monsanty
Hometown: Doylestown, OH
Major: English Literature & History
Fun Fact: Steph marched with the Capital Regiment drum and bugle corps in 2009.Steph won College Prowler's 2010 Summer Contributing Author scholarship.

University of Nebraska

Author: Mandi Pflasterer
Hometown: Grand Island, NE
Major: Animal Science
Fun Fact: Mandi and her mom are trying to run a race in all 50 states.

Previous Contributor: Aaron Eske

University of New Hampshire

Author: Kate Dube
Hometown: Manchester, NH
Major: Chemistry
Fun Fact: Kate has practiced karate for eight years and earned her second degree black belt.

Previous Contributor: Jeff Lewis

University of North Carolina

Author: Kellie Oviosun
Hometown: Greensboro, NC
Major: Spanish
Fun Fact: Kellie intends to travel to a different state every year until she's seen all 50.

Previous Contributor: Adrianna Hopkins

University of North Carolina - Greensboro

Author: Brook Taylor
Major: English
Fun Fact: Brook wouldn't feel right without thanking Starbucks for its white chocolate mochas, which fueled the writing of this guide.

University of Notre Dame

Author: Alex Barker
Hometown: Unknown

Previous Contributor: Anikka Ayala

University of Oklahoma

Author: Peter Jones
Hometown: Castle Rock, CO
Major: International and Area Studies/Spanish
Fun Fact: Peter went to high school in Costa Rica for two years.

Previous Contributor: Andrea Chadderdon

University of Oregon

Author: Emily Ebel
Hometown: Estacada, OR
Major: Biology
Fun Fact: Emily is growing a vegetable garden on her dorm room windowsill.

Previous Contributor: Jesse Thomas

University of Pennsylvania

Author: Perry Petra-Wong
Hometown: Pasadena, Calif.
Major: Philosophy, Politics, and Economics
Fun Fact: Perry is a huge live music fan.

Previous Contributor: Jennifer Klein

University of Pittsburgh

Author: Courtney Vock
Hometown: Pittsburgh, PA
Major: Creative Non-Fiction Writing
Fun Fact: Courtney dares you to challenge her to a "Friends" quote/trivia-off.

Previous Contributors: Jamie Cruttenden, Tim Williams

University of Puget Sound

Author: Elayna Zammarelli
Hometown: Eugene, OR
Major: Business/Communications
Fun Fact: Elayna plays violin in the Puget Sound Symphony Orchestra and has been playing for 10 years.

Previous Contributor: Russell Knight

University of Rhode Island

Author: Anthony aRusso

Hometown: Johnston, RI

Major: Journalism

Fun Fact: Anthony's last name begins with a lowercase letter??weird huh?

Previous Contributor: Jessica Pritz

University of Richmond

Author: Laura DiLibero

Hometown: Loveland, OH

Major: Rhetoric & Communication Studies

Fun Fact: Laura has a Yorkshire Terrier named Chanel No. 5.

Previous Contributor: Peter Hansen

University of Rochester

Author: Dave Levy

Hometown: Randolph, NJ

Major: History and International Relations

Fun Fact: Dave writes with his left hand, but does everything else righty.

Previous Contributor: Kerri Linden

University of San Diego

Author: Jessica Ford

Hometown: San Diego, Calif.

Major: Business

Fun Fact: Jessica lived in Europe for seven years.

Previous Contributor: James Leonard

University of San Francisco

Author: Ishtar Schneider

Hometown: Albuquerque, NM

Major: Communication Studies/Public Relations minor

Fun Fact: Ishtar has three loves in life: dancing, figure skating, and shopping. She is also half Chinese, but you would never know it!

Previous Contributor: Sara Allshouse

University of South Carolina

Author: Gregory Goetz

Hometown: Fort Mitchell, KY

Major: Media Arts/Entrepreneurial Business

Fun Fact: Gregory recently qualified for the Boston Marathon.

Previous Contributor: Jessica Foster

University of South Dakota

Author: Kerry Hacecky

Major: Journalism/Public Relations/English minor

Fun Fact: At USD, Kerry has been active at the school newspaper, The Volante; the National Society of Collegiate Scholars; the TV station (KYOT); and in the University admissions office.

University of South Florida

Author: Michael Trimm

Hometown: Newberry, FL

Major: Computer Science (Minor: Music Academic Studies)

Fun Fact: +Tenor Sax Player in Herd of Thunder+Brother of Kappa Kappa Psi+Future youth pastor

Previous Contributor: Whitney Meers

University of Southern California

Author: BJ Grip

Hometown: Colorado Springs, CO

Major: Theater

Fun Fact: BJ has been to more than 15 different countries, including England, Italy, and Australia.

Previous Contributors: Alex Valhouli, David Magidoff

University of St Thomas - Texas

Author: Anna Fata

Hometown: Houston, TX

Major: Communication

Fun Fact: After graduation, Anna plans to become a broadcast journalist. At the University of St. Thomas, she serves as a senator for the Student Government Association, and an editor for the University newspaper, The Summa. She also works in the UST PR department as a student writer.

University of Tampa

Author: Arturo Uzcategui

Hometown: Valencia, Venezuela

Major: Communications

Fun Fact: Worked on Radio Stations in both Venezuela and United States.Can speak 3 different languages: Spanish, English and Portuguese.

University of Tennessee

Author: Kristen Lewis

Hometown: Litchfield, NH

Major: Anthropology

Fun Fact: Kristen has a titanium rod in her leg because during summer 2008, she managed to break her right tibia and fibula while walking across a creek in Montana.

Previous Contributor: Jacob Williams

University of Tennessee at Chattanooga

Author: Chelsea Crouse/Kelcie Sharp

Hometown: Jackson, Tenn./Memphis, Tenn.

Major: Communications/English Writing

Fun Fact: Chelsea's dream job is to be a correspondent for Country Music Television. Kelcie likes to go bowling.

University of Texas

Author: Tony Griffin

Hometown: Houston, TX

Major: Marketing

Fun Fact: Tony would be perfect if he just had a little more humility.

Previous Contributor: Erin Hall

University of Texas - El Paso

Author: Kristopher Rivera

Hometown: Clint, TX

Major: Multimedia Journalism

Fun Fact: I grew up in a small town.I want to make a career in music.

University of the District of Columbia

Author: Jasmine Grant

Hometown: Miami

Major: Urban Studies

Fun Fact: Jasmine loves DC and Maryland.

University of the Incarnate Word

Author: Paola Cardenas

Hometown: El Paso, TX

Major: Bilingual Communications

Fun Fact: Graduated high school in 3 years

University of Utah

Author: Brian Washburn

Hometown: Salt Lake City, UT

Major: Marketing/Finance

Fun Fact: I love the Outdoors and living in Utah. Studying at the University of Utah has let me pursue my two passions: business and snowmobiling.

Previous Contributor: Jared Whitley

University of Vermont

Author: Jason Bushey

Hometown: Burlington, VT

Major: English

Fun Fact: Jason once ran into (literally) the entire Green Bay Packer football team ... in Philly. Also, he got an A+ in bowling last semester.

Previous Contributors: Kevyn Lenfest, Alyssa Vine

University of Virginia

Author: Haley Bryant

Hometown: London, UK

Major: Media Studies

Fun Fact: Haley's iTunes library houses more than 8,000 songs.

Previous Contributor: Miriam Nicklin

University of Washington

Author: Emily Sugiyama

Hometown: Seattle, WA

Major: English/Women's Studies

Fun Fact: There's a strong likelihood that Emily will be teaching ESL in Korea next year.

Previous Contributor: Katie Shaw

University of Western Ontario

Author: Lauren A. Moore

Hometown: Vancouver, BC, Canada

Major: BA in English Literature with a minor in Health Sciences

Fun Fact: I'm a self-professed nerd with passions for pop culture, Starbucks, and sarcasm.

University of Wisconsin

Author: Marie Puissant

Hometown: Green Bay, Wis.

Major: Marketing and English

Fun Fact: Marie is allergic to cashews and pistachios but no other nuts.

Previous Contributor: Nicole Rosario

University of Wisconsin - Stout

Author: Jeffrey Keenan

Fun Fact: From the day Jeffrey moved into the dorms his freshman year at Stout, he was employed by Stout Adventures, where he learned about, gained experience in, and discovered his passion for outdoor recreation.

UNLV

Author: Meryl Manaog

Hometown: Las Vegas, NV

Major: Marketing/Film minor

Fun Fact: Meryl aspires to one day work for the Sundance Film Festival.

Previous Contributors: Marek Biernacinski, Melissa Rothermel

Urbana University

Author: Jessica Friermood

Hometown: Mount Victory

Major: English and AYA Education with an emphasis in Language Arts.

Fun Fact: I love to play the tenor and bari sax, I raise sheep, and out of school, I work at Kroger back home.

Ursinus College

Author: Bart Brooks

Fun Fact: If he's learned nothing else in life, Bart has learned that putting more of himself into a project only means that the reward is far greater when it is finished.

Valparaiso University

Author: Amber Will

Hometown: Schofield, WI

Major: Political Science and History

Fun Fact: I am a die hard Packers fan... but I still love Brett Favre!

Previous Contributor: Matthew A. Stevens

Vanderbilt University

Author: Christopher McDonald

Previous Contributor: Matthew Woolsey

Vassar College

Author: Sam Murray

Hometown: Bend, IN

Major: Philosophy/Economics

Fun Fact: Sam once got slimed on a Nickelodeon TV show as a kid.

Previous Contributors: Rachel Falcone, Emily Goldsmith

Villanova University

Author: Margaret Rigas

Hometown: Lancaster, PA

Major: History

Fun Fact: Margaret's favorite team is the New England Patriots. Go Pats!

Previous Contributor: Sean L. Wright

Virginia Commonwealth University

Author: Carrie Lefler

Major: Communications

Fun Fact: Good, bad, or otherwise, Carrie is glad she chose VCU, and if she had to do it all over again, she would make the same decision.

Virginia Tech

Author: Heather Priestley

Hometown: Toano, VA

Major: Wildlife Science

Previous Contributor: Elisabeth Grant

Wagner College

Author: Alex Videll

Hometown: Laurel, Md.

Major: English, minor in Anthropology, pre-med program

Fun Fact: Alex is involved in the Wagner chapter of Habitat for Humanity. She is also one of the assistant editors for the literary magazine on campus. She just got back from a trip to Kenya. In her spare time, she goes exploring in the city, aimlessly driving around Staten Island, and going on ridiculous adventures with her best friend.

Wake Forest University

Author: Will Geiger

Hometown: Brielle, NJ

Major: History

Fun Fact: I wrote my undergraduate thesis on Cherokee Indians and enjoy watching romantic comedies. I am the co-founder of a college admissions advice blog called Admissions360.net.

Previous Contributors: Aubrey V., Aaron Mass

Warren Wilson College

Author: Michelle Metzler

Hometown: Columbia, SC

Major: History

Fun Fact: Michelle's two rat friends, Beebo and Rat, helped her write this guide.

Previous Contributor: Roxy Todd

Washington & Jefferson College

Author: Dylan Jesse

Major: English/Philosophy

Fun Fact: Dylan would like to extend his deepest thanks to caffeine—without you, none of this would have been possible. And to his bed, he says he's sorry he hasn't seen as much of you recently as he would like.

Washington & Lee University

Author: Zachary John Barbieri

Hometown: Wayne, NJ

Major: Accounting and Philosophy

Fun Fact: Zachary is the first person in his immediate family to attend college.

Previous Contributor: Jeremiah McWilliams

Washington University in St. Louis

Author: Ben Shanken

Previous Contributor: Dan Carlin

Wayne State University

Author: Kirsten Freitel

Hometown: Marshall, Mich.

Major: Pharmacy

Fun Fact: Kirsten likes to do archery, but her girl side loves to shop for shoes.

Wellesley College

Author: Jean Kim

Hometown: Chicago, IL

Major: English

Fun Fact: Jean has every Simon and Garfunkel song on her iTunes.

Previous Contributor: Genevieve Brennan

Wesleyan University

Author: Rachel Carpman

Hometown: Ann Arbor, Mich.

Major: English

Fun Fact: Rachel collects hedgehog figurines.

Previous Contributor: John Cusick

West Point Military Academy

Author: Ryan Peckyno

Hometown: Bradford, Pa.

Fun Fact: Besides giving him the skills to further his education and make a difference, Ryan says that the Academy redefined hard work for him.

West Virginia University

Author: Jessica Murphy

Hometown: Parkersburg, WV

Major: English

Fun Fact: Jessica loves researching and writing essays about science, animal behavior, civil rights, literature, and philosophy.

Previous Contributor: Matthew Bretzius

Western Illinois University

Author: Victoria Boateng
Hometown: Chicago, Illinois
Major: Communications
Fun Fact: Victoria is a musician who plays the bongos. She is also a songwriter who writes songs from R&B and gospel.

Western Kentucky University

Author: Alyssa Stephens

Wheaton College - Illinois

Author: Debbie Knubley
Hometown: St. Louis, MO
Major: English Lit with Writing Concentration
Fun Fact: "The important thing is that in every way, whether from false motives or true, Christ is preached. And because of this I rejoice."Philippians 1:18

Previous Contributor: Steve Dziedzic

Wheaton College - Massachusetts

Author: Mandi DeGroff
Hometown: Glastonbury, CT
Major: Political Science/Communications
Fun Fact: Mandi dances and is part of Wheaton's first cheerleading team.

Previous Contributor: Jessica Takach

Whitman College

Author: Sara Rasmussen
Hometown: Salem, Ore.
Major: Politics
Fun Fact: Sara plays the accordion.

Previous Contributor: Carly Sanders

Wilkes University

Author: Nicole Frail
Hometown: Wilkes-Barre, PA
Major: Communications
Fun Fact: As an attempt to get out of her comfort zone, Nicole will be studying in Italy this summer!

Previous Contributor: Donna Talarico

Willamette University

Author: Christine Riippi
Major: Art History/Mathematics minor
Fun Fact: Christine is a prime example of the Bearcat All-Star, but even with the abundance of activities to choose from, her favorite thing to do at Willamette was to sit by the Mill Stream with a good cup of coffee and watch the ducks.

Williams College

Author: Semira Menghes
Hometown: Atlanta, GA
Major: American Studies - Arts in Context
Fun Fact: At times, Semira has purple hair, purple eyes, and if she could??purple skin.

Previous Contributor: Alexandra Grashkina

Worcester Polytechnic Institute

Author: Kaitlyn Kelley
Hometown: Cottonwood, Utah
Major: Aerospace Engineering
Fun Fact: Kaitlyn went skydiving in the summer of 2008.

Xavier University

Author: Michelle Rosmarin
Hometown: Columbus, Ohio
Major: English
Fun Fact: If she had the money, Michelle would take college classes for the rest of her life.

Previous Contributor: David Gilmore

Yale University

Author: Rachel Glodo
Hometown: Winter Park, FL
Major: Music
Fun Fact: I am a sophomore in Calhoun residential college ("Go Houn!"). I love music, the Russian language, coffee, and shoes. I was in the IB (international baccalaureate) program in high school and intend to pursue musicology (focus on Russian music history) in graduate school.Current classes:-Russian (level 4)-Music history (Romantic era)-Infinity (philosophy of math)-Music theory-Sacred Harp (traditional American music)Activities at Yale:-Yale Glee Club-Living Water a cappella-Yale Students for Christ-Yale School of Music opera-voice lessons-Reformed University Fellowship-hair, wig, and makeup artist for shows (Amadeus, Cherry Orchard, Chorus Line, etc.)-Yale host for PreFrosh

Previous Contributor: Melissa Doscher

Youngstown State University

Author: Kayla Boye

Hometown: Howland, OH

Major: Professional Writing and Editing

Fun Fact: YSU Activities: University Scholars, University Theater, Dance Ensemble, Student Literary Arts Association, & the YSU Writing Center.

Notes

Notes

Notes